RICHARD & DEBORAH SZABO
428 7th Avenue North
Buhl, ID 83316

TRAVEL GUIDE USA

READER'S DIGEST
TRAVEL GUIDE USA

Reader's Digest®

The Reader's Digest Association, Inc.
Pleasantville, New York • Montreal

Travel Guide USA

STAFF

PROJECT EDITOR: Paula Pines

SENIOR ART EDITOR: Henrietta Stern

RESEARCH EDITORS: Susan H. Biederman, Barbara Guarino Lester

EDITORIAL ASSISTANT: Jeff Akellian

CONTRIBUTORS

EDITOR: Jill Maynard

ART ASSOCIATE: Ed Jacobus

WRITERS: Thomas Barr, Tania Bissell, Mary Lyn Maiscott,
Honey Naylor, Margaret Perry, Marianne Wait, Carol Weeg

RESEARCH ASSOCIATES: Pamela Kladzyk, Carol F. Mascolo, Joan Walsh

PICTURE EDITOR: Sybille Millard

MAP/TEXT COORDINATOR: David J. Fleischmann

COPY EDITOR: Nancy Ramsey

INDEXER: Sydney Wolfe Cohen

MAPS: GeoSystems, an R.R. Donnelley & Sons Company

READER'S DIGEST GENERAL BOOKS

EDITOR IN CHIEF: John A. Pope, Jr.

MANAGING EDITOR: Jane Polley

EXECUTIVE EDITOR: Susan J. Wernert

ART DIRECTOR: David Trooper

GROUP EDITORS: Will Bradbury, Sally French, Norman B. Mack, Kaari Ward

GROUP ART EDITORS: Evelyn Bauer, Robert M. Grant, Joel Musler

CHIEF OF RESEARCH: Laurel A. Gilbride

COPY CHIEF: Edward W. Atkinson

PICTURE EDITOR: Richard Pasqual

RIGHTS AND PERMISSIONS: Pat Colomban

HEAD LIBRARIAN: Jo Manning

Library of Congress Cataloging in Publication Data
Travel guide USA.
    p.   cm.
Includes index.
ISBN 0-89577-564-6
    1. United States—Guidebooks. I. Reader's Digest Association.
E158.T755 1994
917.304'929—dc20   93-5857

Photo on pages 2–3: A countryside view from the scenic Blue Ridge Parkway in Virginia

Contents

About This Book

TRAVEL GUIDE USA combines clear, detailed road maps and fact-filled site descriptions in a way that makes every corner of this vast and varied land of ours instantly accessible to the traveler. Practical and easy to use, it is an ideal vacation planner and on-the-road traveling companion.

The Guide to America's Highlights on pages 8–9 features a master map of the United States. This serves as a graphic directory to the 198 in-depth maps contained in the book, each created especially for TRAVEL GUIDE USA utilizing state-of-the-art computer technology and updated to the time of publication. The maps are divided into three color-coded regions — Western, Central, and Eastern — and are numbered in rows, from west to east, within each section of the country. Each region has a corresponding section in the book, opening with a two-page table-of-contents map that shows the page maps appearing in that chapter.

Accompanying each map are capsule descriptions of selected attractions, number-keyed to their precise location on the map. The 5,000-plus sites — illustrated with more than 150 color photographs — are widely diversified to appeal to the tastes and inclinations of virtually any traveler. For an even greater choice of places to visit, other points of interest are labeled directly on the maps.

All information in this book has been carefully researched to ensure accuracy. Admission charges are indicated in the site descriptions; hours may vary according to the season, however, so it is prudent to confirm the exact schedules at the sites you intend to visit. To facilitate pre-trip planning, contact information for state tourism offices, major city convention and visitors bureaus, and national parks appears in the back of the book. A U.S. interstate and major highway map, a city-to-city mileage chart, and a comprehensive index are also provided for easy reference.

As you turn the pages of TRAVEL GUIDE USA, prepare to explore the best of America — the magnificent natural splendors, the stunning man-made spectacles, the places that recall our proud past or offer glimpses of a wondrous future. If it's historic, scenic, inspiring, or beautiful; if it's a bustling cityscape or a serene landscape; if it's fascinating, breathtaking, or just plain fun — it's in this book.

— THE EDITORS

Symbols and Features

Passenger ferry
Auto ferry
Interchanges
Ski area
Campground
Inset area
Scenic route
State park without camping
Military or government areas
Mountain peak
National park
Mileage between points
Pass
State park with camping
National or state forest
Trail
Other park areas
Point of interest
Indian reservation
TRAVEL GUIDE USA site
Dam

Locator Maps

Preceding each page map is a locator map, which indicates where the area shown in detail on the page lies within the surrounding section of the country.

Abbreviations

A.F.B.	Air Force Base	R.S.P.	Resort State Park
I.R.	Indian Reservation	S.B.	State Beach
MIL. RES.	Military Reservation	S.F.	State Forest
N.B.P.	National Battlefield Park	S.H.M.	State Historical Monument
N.F.	National Forest	S.H.P.	State Historical Park
N.H.S.	National Historic Site	S.H.S.	State Historic Site
N.H.P.	National Historical Park	S.N.A.	State Natural Area
N.M.P.	National Military Park	S.P.	State Park
N.M.	National Monument	S.R.A.	State Recreation Area
N.P.	National Park	S.R.S.	State Recreation Site
N.R.A.	National Recreation Area	S.R.	State Reserve
N.W.R.	National Wildlife Refuge	S.U.A.	State Unique Area
N.A.S.	Naval Air Station	S.V.R.A.	State Vehicular Recreation Area

ROADS

Limited access-free
Limited access-toll
Divided highway
Primary route
Secondary route
Other road
Unpaved road
Scenic route
TRAVEL GUIDE USA special route
Under construction
Interstate route
U.S. route
Mexican federal route
Canadian autoroute
Trans-Canada route
State or province route
Other route
Mileage between points
Interchanges
Service areas
Tunnel
Pass
Closed in winter

TOWNS AND CITIES

0 - 2,500 .... Germann ○
2,500 - 5,000 .... Wickenburg ○
5,000 -25,000 .... Florence ◎
25,000 - 100,000 .... **Chandler** ◎
100,000 - 500,000 ....**Glendale** ◉
Over 500,00 .... **Phoenix** ◉
State capital .... ✪
National capital .... ✪

City tints ....

Urban areas ....

SITES

Inset area ....
TRAVEL GUIDE USA point of interest ....
Port of entry.................................
Mountain peak .... Mt. Graham +
10,713
Campground................................. ▲
State park (with camping)..................... Roper Lake S.P. ▲▲
State park (without camping)................. Roper Lake S.P. ▲
Ski area ....
Point of interest............................. SUNSET CRATER NATL. MON. ■
Dam...

OTHER MAP FEATURES

Auto ferry
Passenger ferry
Trail
International boundary
State boundary
Time zone boundary
Continental Divide
Perennial drainage
Intermittent drainage
Intracoastal waterway
Water ....
National park ....
National or state forest ....
Other park areas ....
Indian reservation ....
Military or government areas ....
Glacier ....
Swamp ....

Guide to America's Highlights

The color-coded map of the United States shown to the right serves as a table of contents for this book, which contains 56 Area Maps, 100 Zoom-In Maps, and 42 Specialty Maps.

Area Maps

A grid divides the contiguous states into Area Maps, which are of equal scale and, with few exceptions, of equal size. The number that appears on each Area Map shows the page on which information about that section begins. (The Area Maps for Alaska and Hawaii use separate scales and are not placed within a grid.)

Zoom-In Maps

Within most of the Area Maps are insets with page numbers indicated on them. These Zoom-In Maps focus on sections that contain a density of attractions.

Specialty Maps

In cases where there are especially fascinating places to explore, Specialty Maps appear with their own page numbers within the Area Maps. For a complete listing of Specialty Maps by page number and geographical location, see the opposite page.

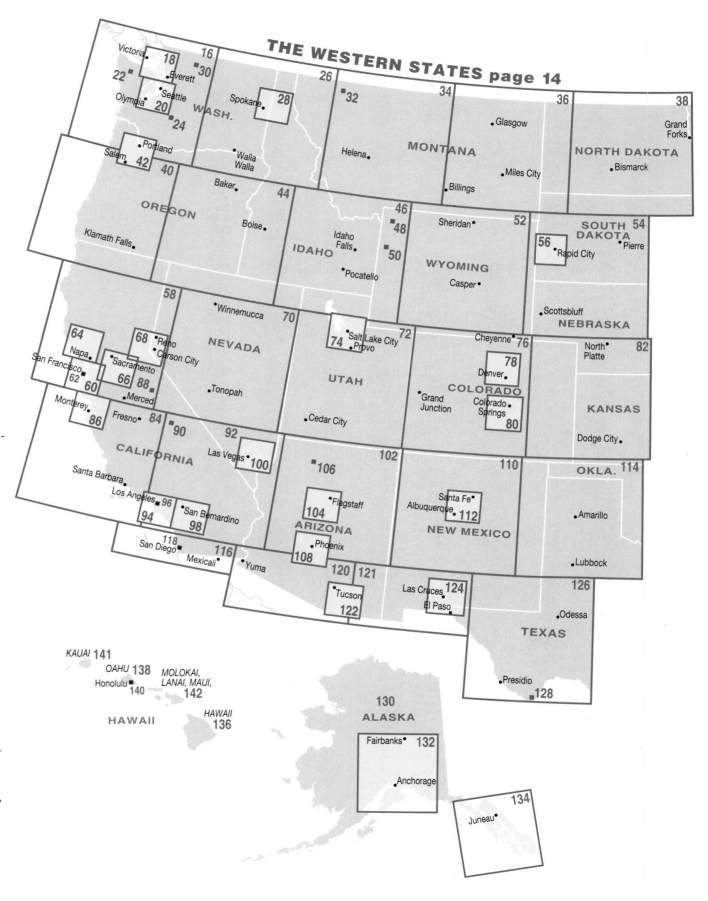

THE WESTERN STATES page 14

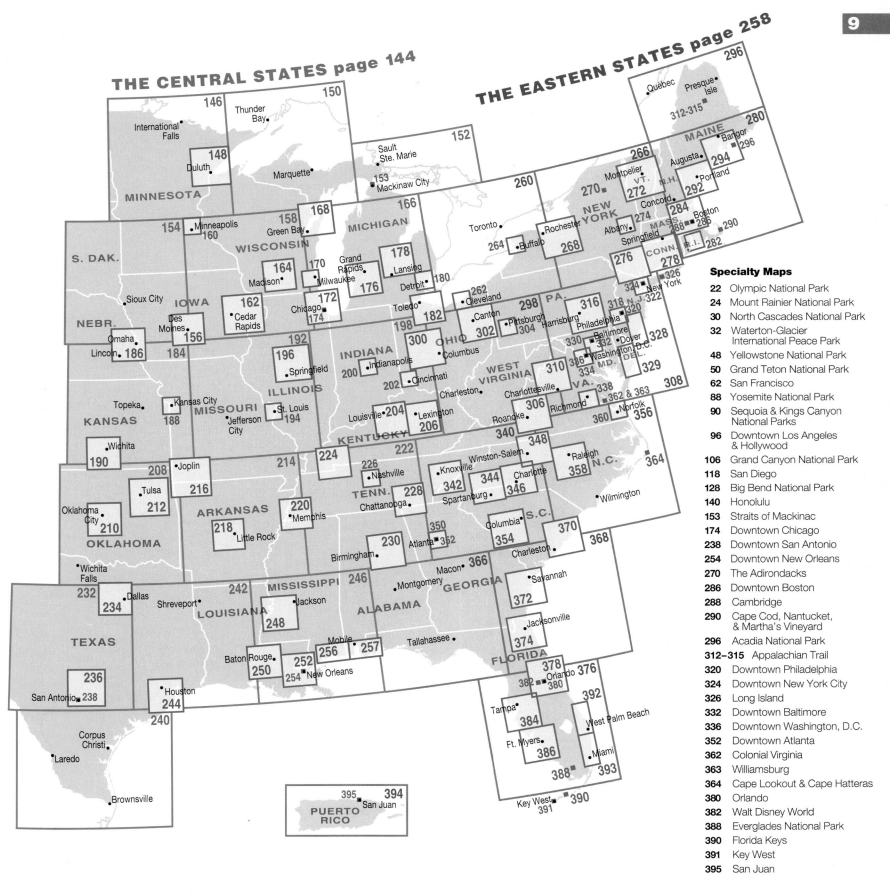

THE CENTRAL STATES page 144

THE EASTERN STATES page 258

Specialty Maps

22 Olympic National Park
24 Mount Rainier National Park
30 North Cascades National Park
32 Waterton-Glacier International Peace Park
48 Yellowstone National Park
50 Grand Teton National Park
62 San Francisco
88 Yosemite National Park
90 Sequoia & Kings Canyon National Parks
96 Downtown Los Angeles & Hollywood
106 Grand Canyon National Park
118 San Diego
128 Big Bend National Park
140 Honolulu
153 Straits of Mackinac
174 Downtown Chicago
238 Downtown San Antonio
254 Downtown New Orleans
270 The Adirondacks
286 Downtown Boston
288 Cambridge
290 Cape Cod, Nantucket, & Martha's Vineyard
296 Acadia National Park
312–315 Appalachian Trail
320 Downtown Philadelphia
324 Downtown New York City
326 Long Island
332 Downtown Baltimore
336 Downtown Washington, D.C.
352 Downtown Atlanta
362 Colonial Virginia
363 Williamsburg
364 Cape Lookout & Cape Hatteras
380 Orlando
382 Walt Disney World
388 Everglades National Park
390 Florida Keys
391 Key West
395 San Juan

U.S. Road Map

The vast network of roads shown on the map to the right includes the Interstate Highway System, designated by signs in the shape of a shield, along with other major U.S. and state highways that serve as connecting links.

Created in 1956, the Interstate system has expanded to some 42,700 miles today, connecting most major U.S. cities with populations of more than 50,000. Americans drive about 1.3 billion miles on these roads each day, according to the Federal Highway Administration. In general the route number is odd if the road runs north–south (I-5 from Seattle to San Diego), while even-numbered routes run east–west (I-90 from Boston to Seattle). The higher-numbered routes are found in the North and East, with lower-numbered routes located in the South and West.

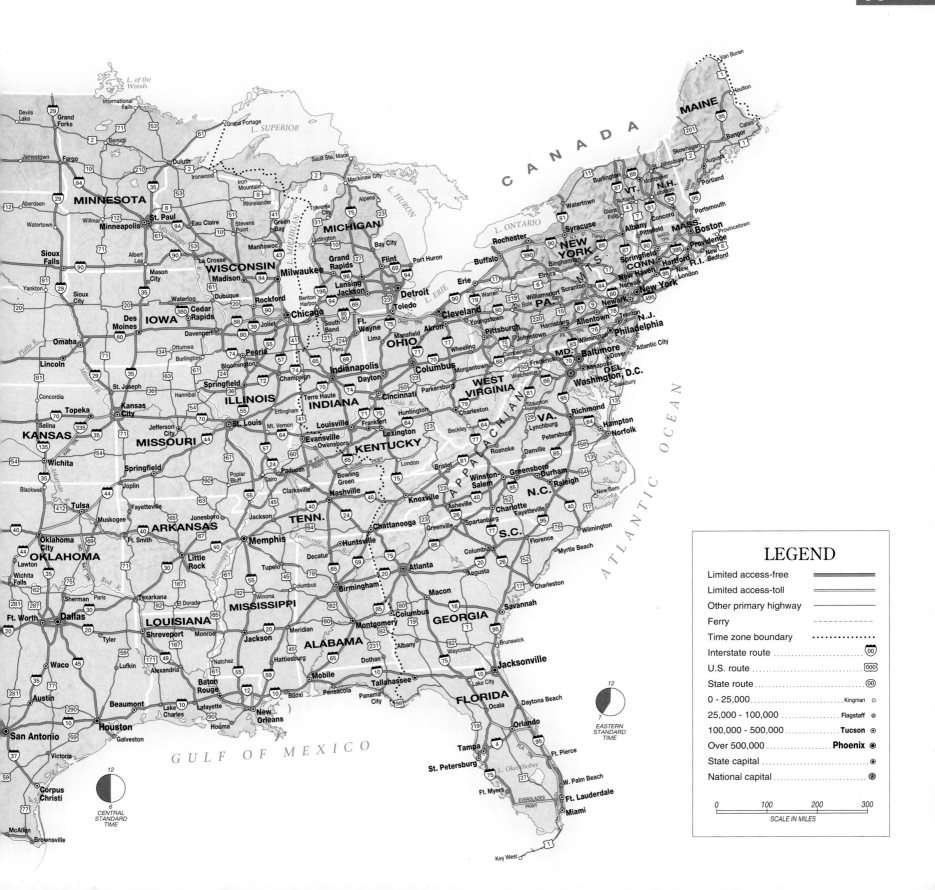

Mileage Chart

The distances given between cities in the chart to the right are the number of miles you would drive via easy-to-follow major routes. When traveling on the road, leave plenty of time to reach your destination — fatigue is a major cause of accidents in long-distance driving. Remember, too, that all passengers should use safety restraints; infants and young children should ride in safety seats. Drive defensively and maintain ample distance behind the car ahead, particularly in adverse weather conditions, when it takes more time to brake. To save on gas, choose the proper grade for your automobile — usually unleaded regular. Check that your tires are inflated to the manufacturer's recommended pressure; use air conditioning sparingly; and avoid overloading the car with heavy items or stowing cargo on roof racks. Staying within the speed limit of 55 m.p.h. also helps to conserve fuel — as well as the environment.

	Albuquerque, N. Mex.	Atlanta, Ga.	Bangor, Maine	Billings, Mont.	Boston, Mass.	Charlotte, N.C.	Chicago, Ill.	Cleveland, Ohio	Dallas, Tex.	Denver, Colo.	Detroit, Mich.	Kansas City, Mo.	Los Angeles, Calif.
Albuquerque, N. Mex.		1409	2490	992	2236	1665	1353	1577	665	444	1547	795	806
Atlanta, Ga.	1409		1331	1831	1044	238	717	725	791	1403	730	800	2258
Bangor, Maine	2490	1331		2498	238	1093	1243	883	2050	2244	942	1676	3273
Billings, Mont.	992	1831	2498		2254	2025	1264	1601	1353	555	1532	1077	1236
Boston, Mass.	2236	1044	238	2254		864	990	659	1781	1985	722	1441	3044
Charlotte, N.C.	1665	238	1093	2025	864		772	520	1031	1575	675	972	2479
Chicago, Ill.	1353	717	1243	1264	990	772		346	936	1013	282	530	2041
Cleveland, Ohio	1577	725	883	1601	659	520	346		1208	1347	172	806	2375
Dallas, Tex.	665	791	2050	1353	1781	1031	936	1208		797	1218	518	1446
Denver, Colo.	444	1403	2244	555	1985	1575	1013	1347	797		1283	606	1030
Detroit, Mich.	1547	730	942	1532	722	675	282	172	1218	1283		752	2311
Kansas City, Mo.	795	800	1676	1077	1441	972	530	806	518	606	752		1628
Los Angeles, Calif.	806	2258	3273	1236	3044	2479	2041	2375	1446	1030	2311	1628	
Memphis, Tenn.	1034	382	1584	1527	1330	630	539	742	466	1069	752	450	1840
Miami, Fla.	1951	665	1756	2516	1527	729	1350	1248	1370	2081	1395	1462	2744
Minneapolis, Minn.	1250	1130	1661	838	1432	1188	409	760	999	924	679	442	1932
Nashville, Tenn.	1238	242	1367	1613	1096	413	473	530	681	1161	541	558	2055
New Orleans, La.	1175	472	1793	1863	1529	713	935	1055	510	1307	1067	819	1943
New York, N.Y.	2014	868	448	2051	204	630	796	466	1587	1798	622	1255	2820
Orlando, Fla.	1934	440	1552	2333	1323	524	1161	1044	1144	1847	1179	1244	2535
Phoenix, Ariz.	468	1825	2957	1202	2687	2109	1750	2028	1025	787	1998	1246	374
Portland, Oreg.	1355	2708	3368	889	3139	2821	2118	2449	2142	1257	2386	1848	971
Rapid City, S. Dak.	817	1511	2166	358	1913	1693	913	1254	1080	404	1191	710	1394
St. Louis, Mo.	1050	575	1429	1340	1200	720	288	559	634	861	548	252	1857
Salt Lake City, Utah	607	1923	2643	556	2390	2025	1411	1745	1267	538	1668	1122	691
San Antonio, Tex.	818	999	2323	1503	2094	1240	1226	1481	271	960	1491	795	1356
San Francisco, Calif.	1109	2588	3375	1241	3141	2774	2151	2482	1830	1255	2399	1861	387
Seattle, Wash.	1454	2653	3309	813	3056	2839	2060	2414	2119	1329	2351	1902	1150
Tampa, Fla.	1951	456	1608	2350	1379	581	1177	1101	1161	1863	1196	1261	2552
Washington, D.C.	1871	635	688	1963	460	397	703	372	1307	1679	525	1077	2697

	Memphis, Tenn.	Miami, Fla.	Minneapolis, Minn.	Nashville, Tenn.	New Orleans, La.	New York, N.Y.	Orlando, Fla.	Phoenix, Ariz.	Portland, Oreg.	Rapid City, S. Dak.	St. Louis, Mo.	Salt Lake City, Utah	San Antonio, Tex.	San Francisco, Calif.	Seattle, Wash.	Tampa, Fla.	Washington, D.C.
Albuquerque, N. Mex.	1034	1951	1250	1238	1175	2014	1934	468	1355	817	1050	607	818	1109	1454	1951	1871
Atlanta, Ga.	382	665	1130	242	472	868	440	1825	2708	1511	575	1923	999	2588	2653	456	635
Bangor, Maine	1584	1756	1661	1367	1793	448	1552	2957	3368	2166	1429	2643	2323	3375	3309	1608	688
Billings, Mont.	1527	2516	838	1613	1863	2051	2333	1202	889	358	1340	556	1503	1241	813	2350	1963
Boston, Mass.	1330	1527	1432	1096	1529	204	1323	2687	3139	1913	1200	2390	2094	3141	3056	1379	460
Charlotte, N.C.	630	729	1188	413	713	630	524	2109	2821	1693	720	2025	1240	2774	2839	581	397
Chicago, Ill.	539	1350	409	473	935	796	1161	1750	2118	913	288	1411	1226	2151	2060	1177	703
Cleveland, Ohio	742	1248	760	530	1055	466	1044	2028	2449	1254	559	1745	1481	2482	2414	1101	372
Dallas, Tex.	466	1370	999	681	510	1587	1144	1025	2142	1080	634	1267	271	1830	2119	1161	1307
Denver, Colo.	1069	2081	924	1161	1307	1798	1847	787	1257	404	861	538	960	1255	1329	1863	1679
Detroit, Mich.	752	1395	679	541	1067	622	1179	1998	2386	1191	548	1668	1491	2399	2351	1196	525
Kansas City, Mo.	450	1462	442	558	819	1255	1244	1246	1848	710	252	1122	795	1861	1902	1261	1077
Los Angeles, Calif.	1840	2744	1932	2055	1943	2820	2535	374	971	1394	1857	691	1356	387	1150	2552	2697
Memphis, Tenn.		1007	941	215	397	1092	900	1476	2313	1169	293	1573	739	2143	2419	917	856
Miami, Fla.	1007		1761	903	876	1342	233	2391	3306	2181	1218	2593	1403	3130	3363	289	1060
Minneapolis, Minn.	941	1761		858	1337	1211	1577	1684	1727	580	621	1322	1257	2034	1655	1594	1118
Nashville, Tenn.	215	903	858		539	904	685	1676	2407	1255	337	1681	954	2358	2461	702	656
New Orleans, La.	397	876	1337	539		1330	650	1525	2530	1560	689	1777	557	2301	2665	667	1089
New York, N.Y.	1092	1342	1211	904	1330		1089	2482	2921	1719	982	2196	1860	2927	2901	1145	236
Orlando, Fla.	900	233	1577	685	650	1089		2165	3092	1955	992	2367	1178	2919	3146	81	855
Phoenix, Ariz.	1476	2391	1684	1676	1525	2482	2165		1293	1160	1501	650	986	757	1520	2182	2322
Portland, Oreg.	2313	3306	1727	2407	2530	2921	3092	1293		1268	2100	753	2098	636	173	3109	2861
Rapid City, S. Dak.	1169	2181	580	1255	1560	1719	1955	1160	1268		962	746	1230	1454	1160	1971	1605
St. Louis, Mo.	293	1218	621	337	689	982	992	1501	2100	962		1375	916	2110	2154	1009	831
Salt Lake City, Utah	1573	2593	1322	1681	1777	2196	2367	650	753	746	1375		1425	749	852	2384	2108
San Antonio, Tex.	739	1403	1257	954	557	1860	1178	986	2098	1230	916	1425		1740	2278	1194	1635
San Francisco, Calif.	2143	3130	2034	2358	2301	2927	2919	757	636	1454	2110	749	1740		811	2936	2859
Seattle, Wash.	2419	3363	1655	2461	2665	2901	3146	1520	173	1160	2154	852	2278	811		3163	2765
Tampa, Fla.	917	289	1594	702	667	1145	81	2182	3109	1971	1009	2384	1194	2936	3163		912
Washington, D.C.	856	1060	1118	656	1089	236	855	2322	2861	1605	831	2108	1635	2859	2765	912	

The Western States

A land of scenic splendor, the West boasts the grandeur of the Rockies, stands of soaring sequoias, and beaches that form a sandy fringe along the sparkling Pacific. It is home to Yellowstone, Yosemite, Grand Canyon, and other national parks of equally enduring beauty. Here are sites that span centuries past: the mysterious Mesa Verde cliff dwellings; the Spanish missions along the West Coast and in the Southwest. Today's travelers find ample reminders of the intrepid pioneers who settled the region—in traces of the Oregon Trail, in the ghost towns that were boomtowns in gold-rush days, in the solitary remnants of forts that protected settlers on the open plains. With campgrounds and cowtowns, Indian museums and historic villages, and marvels from Mount Rushmore to the Golden Gate Bridge, the West is, indeed, a panorama of America's proud past and vibrant present.

Morning light captures the graceful flight of Canada geese high above Grand Teton National Park.

1. Neah Bay

Neah Bay is home to the **Makah Cultural and Research Center,** one of the finest museums of Native American culture in the United States. Its extensive collection encompasses more than 55,000 archeological items from a nearby Makah Indian village that was buried and preserved by mud slides about five centuries ago. **Cape Flattery,** the northwesternmost point in the lower 48 states, is a 7-mile drive from town and an additional half-mile hike from the parking area. Other area attractions include **Koitlah Point** and **Hobuck Beach,** which offer rugged coastal scenery, excellent birding, and whale watching. *Admission charged for museum.*

2. Humptulips Salmon Hatchery

1704 Kirkpatrick Rd., Humptulips. Visitors can observe various species of young salmon raised in large outdoor tanks near the banks of the Humptulips River, where they are released upon reaching the proper age for ocean migration.

3. Ocean City State Park

Swimming and surf fishing in the Pacific are popular activities in this seaside park, along with digging for succulent razor clams in season. Clamming information and permits are available at local stores.

4. Leadbetter Point State Park and Natural Area

Sand dunes, salt marsh, and seasonal clamming beaches provide a way station for more than 200 species of migratory birds, including such rarities as gyrfalcons and snowy owls. Visitors may even catch a glimpse of seals sunning themselves on the ocean side of the point.

5. Fort Clatsop National Memorial

A reconstructed 50-foot-square log stockade with two rows of cabins marks the site of the 1805–06 winter camp of explorers Lewis and Clark. Informative exhibits on the expedition are offered at the visitor center, and in summer costumed staff members reenact the routines of daily life at the fort. *Admission charged.*

6. Cape Meares State Park and National Wildlife Refuge

A 233-acre state park and a lighthouse built in 1890 sit atop Cape Meares, a 217-foot-high bluff whose sheer cliffs drop vertically to the sea. The Octopus Tree — a Sitka spruce famed for its enormous candelabra branching — marks a good vantage point for lovely views of the rugged coast and the Pacific Ocean.

7. Cowlitz County Historical Museum

405 Allen St., Kelso. This well-organized museum chronicles the life and times of Pacific Northwest inhabitants, from Indians and pioneers to subsequent loggers and settlers, in a series of entertaining artifact exhibits and tableaux.

8. Silver Lake

The excellent trout and bass fishing draws scores of anglers to these waters, and boats can be rented for day trips to several islands on the lake. Hiking trails and camping and picnicking facilities are nearby at **Seaquest State Park.**

9. Mount St. Helens National Volcanic Monument

The volcanic eruption that blew out the northern face of Mt. St. Helens in 1980 is graphically depicted at the visitor center on **Silver Lake,** which offers a walk-through model of a volcano and a simulated magma chamber. A seismograph constantly monitors the real mountain's activity. The actual devastation wreaked by the volcano can best be viewed from two lookout points on the mountain above Spirit Lake. The visitor center at **Coldwater Ridge** offers the best vantage point from the west side of the mountain, and from the overlook at **Windy Ridge,** on the east side of the mountain, the inside of the crater is clearly visible.

10. Hood River Vineyards

4693 Westwood Dr., Hood River. This small, family-run winery sits atop a hill overlooking the picturesque orchards of the Hood River Valley and the Columbia River Gorge. The vineyard produces about a dozen different types of wine and offers wine tastings and tours, in which all stages of the winemaking process are explained by a vintner.

11. Panorama Point Park

This aptly named spot is the ideal vantage point from which to admire the orchards of the **Hood River Valley** in springtime bloom, with snowcapped Mt. Hood rising majestically in the distance.

12. Timberline Lodge

A winding scenic drive up **Mount Hood** leads to this national historic landmark. Built in the 1930's as a WPA project, the impressive wood-and-stone ski lodge was painstakingly constructed from local granite and other materials. Today the lodge attracts skiers to the surrounding slopes.

13. Fort Dalles Museum

15th and Garrison Sts., The Dalles. Once the surgeon's quarters of Fort Dalles, a mid-1800's army post on the Oregon Trail, the present-day museum displays a varied collection of 19th- and early–20th-century frontier memorabilia, including Indian artifacts, military hardware, and pioneer tools and furnishings. *Admission charged*

14. The Dalles Dam

A train ride and guided tour of the 1½-mile-long Dalles Dam give visitors a good overview of the huge powerhouse and navigation locks, with fish ladders to assist migrating salmon, steelhead trout, and other varieties of fish. The visitor center offers informative exhibits on history, ecology, and technology.

15. Maryhill Museum of Art

Off Rte. 14, Maryhill. An imposing mansion set high on a remote spot overlooking the Columbia River houses a fascinating cache of "Rodin's Rodins" — bronzes, plasters, and drawings executed by the sculptor as preliminary studies for later works. The centerpiece of the collection is a plaster cast of a reduced version of *The Thinker.* Near the museum, visitors are often surprised to discover a partial replica of Stonehenge in concrete. *Admission charged.*

16. Fort Simcoe State Park

Fort Simcoe first served as a military fort in the mid-19th century and then as headquarters for the Yakima Indian Agency until 1923. The present-day complex includes five original and several reconstructed military buildings, as well as a small museum. In the adjoining 200-acre state park, there are hiking trails, picnic areas, and a playground for children.

17. Olmstead Place State Park

Once a 19th-century working farm, today this 218-acre historical park tracks the Olmstead family's progression from a humble four-room log cabin to a later, more elegantly appointed farmhouse. Attractions include a granary, wagon shed, and dairy barn. Visitors who follow a half-mile trail along the Altapes Creek will come to the one-room **Seaton Schoolhouse,** a log cabin built more than 100 years ago.

18. Ginkgo Petrified Forest State Park

Named for the ginkgo tree, which had disappeared from North America until its recent reintroduction, this 7,400-acre state park also contains hundreds of varieties of other fossilized trees. A number of noteworthy Indian petroglyphs found in the area are on display. In addition to hiking trails and a visitor center with interpretive exhibits, the park offers good opportunities for fishing on the majestic Columbia River.

19. Cle Elum Historical Museum

221 East First St., Cle Elum. The evolution of the telephone is chronicled in this museum, whose eclectic collection ranges from an 1894 crank model to a 1920's dial phone. The town's former switchboard, with an impressive 1,200 terminals, is also on display. Other exhibits relate to Cle Elum's history as a coal-mining center.

20. Alpine Lakes Wilderness

In the heart of the rugged Cascade Range, deep blue lakes set in a glacier-cut landscape grace this highlands area above Snoqualmie Pass.

21. Leavenworth

Chamber of Commerce, 894 Rte. 2. Bounded by the mountains of the Cascade Range, this quaint village is known for its Bavarian architecture and Old World charm. It is a popular stop for hikers, fishermen, and other outdoor enthusiasts.

22. Chelan County Historical Museum and Pioneer Village

600 Cottage Ave., Cashmere. This combination museum and pioneer village traces the lives of area inhabitants as far back as 9,000 years. The museum, with its imaginative displays of Indian and pioneer artifacts, serves as an introduction to the 21 authentically furnished buildings of the re-created village — among them a blacksmith shop, general store, hotel, and saloon.

VANCOUVER ISLAND

PACIFIC RIM NATIONAL PARK

BRITISH COLUMBIA
WASHINGTON

Strait of Georgia
Strait of Juan de Fuca

CANADA
UNITED STATES

Vancouver
N. Vancouver
Burnaby
Richmond
Delta
Surrey
Langley
White Rock
Port Moody
Port Coquitlam
Maple Ridge
Ft. Langley
Mission
Abbotsford
Chilliwack
Hope

Parksville
Port Alberni
Nanaimo
Ladysmith
Duncan
Sidney
Saanich
Colwood
Victoria
Oak Bay
Sooke
Neah Bay

Ferndale
Bellingham
Anacortes
Sedro Woolley
Burlington
Mount Vernon
Oak Harbor
Coupeville
Port Townsend
Port Angeles
Sequim
Forks
La Push

OLYMPIC MOUNTAINS
OLYMPIC NATIONAL PARK
OLYMPIC NATIONAL FOREST
Mt. Olympus 7,965

Everett
Marysville
Lynnwood
Edmonds
Bothell
Kirkland
Redmond
Bellevue
Seattle
Mercer Island
Renton
Bremerton
Sea-Tac
Federal Way
Kent
Auburn
Sumner
Enumclaw
Tacoma
University Place
Puyallup
Parkland
Spanaway
Olympia
Tumwater
Lacey

MT. BAKER - SNOQUALMIE NATIONAL FOREST
NORTH CASCADES NATIONAL PARK
ROSS LAKE NATIONAL REC. AREA
Mt. Baker 10,778
OKANOGAN NATIONAL FOREST
Lake Chelan
Chelan
WENATCHEE NATIONAL FOREST
Leavenworth
Cashmere
Wenatchee
East Wenatchee
Ellensburg
Yakima
Union Gap
Selah
Toppenish
Sunnyside
Grandview

CASCADE RANGE

Aberdeen
Hoquiam
Ocean City
Westport
Raymond
Centralia
Chehalis

MT. RAINIER NATIONAL PARK
Mt. Rainier 14,410

MT. ST. HELENS NATIONAL VOLCANIC MONUMENT
Mt. St. Helens
Mt. Adams 12,307

GIFFORD PINCHOT NATIONAL FOREST

YAKIMA INDIAN RESERVATION

PACIFIC OCEAN

Longview
Kelso
Astoria
Warrenton
Seaside
Cannon Beach

COAST RANGES

Vancouver
Portland
Hillsboro
Beaverton
Tigard
Gresham
Lake Oswego
West Linn
Oregon City
Camas
Washougal

The Dalles
Hood River
Goldendale
MT. HOOD NATIONAL FOREST
Mt. Hood 11,235

HORSE HEAVEN HILLS

WASH.
ORE.

Columbia River

MAP PG. 19
MAP PG. 23
MAP PG. 21
MAP PG. 25
MAP PG. 31
MAP PG. 43
MAP PG. 27
MAP PG. 41
MAP PG. 45

0 10 20 30 40 50
SCALE IN MILES

1. Sidney

Saanich Peninsula Travel Infocentre, 10392 Patricia Bay Hwy. Near the northern end of the Saanich Peninsula, the town is convenient to year-round golf, quiet countryside, and Victoria International Airport. Visitors can take a day trip on a seaplane, stopping at lakes and beaches for a picnic lunch and swim, or charter a boat to try the excellent salmon fishing off the Gulf Islands.

2. Butchart Gardens

800 Benvenuto Ave., Victoria. Set on 50 acres of the Butchart family estate, these eight theme gardens are ranked among the most beautiful in the world. Some flowers are in bloom year-round, and exotic plants are always on exhibit in the Show Greenhouse. On summer evenings the grounds are illuminated, and firework displays are staged on Saturday nights. *Admission charged.*

3. Victoria

Visitor Information Center, 812 Wharf St. This picturesque city is noted for its **Royal British Columbia Museum** as well as for galleries and museums that feature Eskimo and American Indian arts and crafts. Visitors can shop for British china and linens or sample a traditional English tea. Across from the landmark Empress Hotel, ferries depart for Port Angeles and sightseeing vessels offer tours of the harbor and the Gorge Waterway. *Admission charged for some attractions.*

4. Port Angeles

Chamber of Commerce, 121 East Rutherford Ave. This bustling fishing port has ferry service to Victoria, British Columbia. The observation tower at **City Pier** provides a good view of ferries, freighters, and pleasure boats crossing the Strait of Juan de Fuca. There is a marine laboratory on the pier, and the **Clallum County Historical Museum** is a short walk away. The city also serves as an entry point to Olympic National Park. *Admission charged for some attractions.*

Accessible from the mainland by ferry, the serene setting of the wooded San Juan Islands beckons to visitors.

5. Dungeness

Chamber of Commerce, 1192 East Washington St. This town's famous namesake — the succulent Dungeness crab — can be gathered on the public beach at low tide from September through April. **Dungeness National Wildlife Refuge,** which stretches for about 6 miles along the Strait of Juan de Fuca, encompasses a bay, beaches, and tidal flats that provide protection for an abundant variety of wildlife. *Admission charged.*

6. Olympic Game Farm

383 Ward Rd., Sequim. Animals from Olympic Game Farm have made guest appearances on commercials, TV shows, and in features by such well-known studios as Walt Disney. Glancing out a car window, visitors can see the free-roaming celebrities — including bison, zebras, and elk — going about their off-camera routines. The bears contained behind fencing are apt to audition for a handout. *Admission charged.*

7. Port Townsend

Chamber of Commerce, 2437 East Sims Way. The gateway to Puget Sound, Port Townsend enjoyed boom times as a maritime center in the late 19th century. That era is evoked today in the Victorian homes and buildings that grace the town. On historic Water Street, visitors can sample seafood in waterfront cafes, or browse in antiques shops and art galleries.

8. Port Gamble

The architecture of this Pacific logging-company town is strikingly reminiscent of its founders' native New England. The town mill is said to be one of the oldest continuously operating sawmills in the United States.

9. Boeing Everett Tour Center

U.S. 5 exit 189, near Everett. Boeing 747's and 767's are assembled in this 11-story structure covering 62 acres — by volume one of the biggest in the world. The guided tour includes an introductory film and a balcony view of actual construction work on the planes, followed by a close-up look at the mammoth finished products. Expansion of the present facility to accommodate construction of 777's is due to be completed sometime in the mid-1990's.

10. Coupeville

Chamber of Commerce, 5 South Main St. Founded in 1853, Coupeville is among the first towns that were settled in the state of Washington. Front Street, which sweeps around Penn Cove, is lined with shops and restaurants housed in restored 19th-century buildings. Original blockhouses and churches are also open to the public.

11. Deception Pass

The strong, swift current of Puget Sound rushes through this narrow channel between Fidalgo and Whidbey islands, connected by Deception Pass Bridge.

A 2,477-acre state park spanning both islands offers camping, hiking, swimming, and fishing. Rosario Beach is an excellent spot to watch the surf.

12. San Juan Islands

This tranquil wooded archipelago near the Strait of Juan de Fuca was once the site of a border dispute between the United States and Great Britain, commemorated at **San Juan Island National Historical Park.** In Friday Harbor, the **Whale Museum** houses displays about whales, dolphins, and porpoises. *Admission charged at museum.*

13. Moran State Park

From Mt. Constitution in Moran State Park, there is a spectacular 360-degree view of the San Juan and Gulf islands, Vancouver Island, Bellingham, the snowcapped Olympics, and Mt. Baker.

14. Chuckanut Drive

The northern end of this scenic drive hugs forested cliffs, providing dazzling views of the San Juan Islands across the Bellingham, Chuckanut, and Samish bays.

15. Hovander Homestead Park

5299 Neilsen Rd., Ferndale. The 60-acre park includes a Victorian-era farmhouse, barnyard animals, and antique farm equipment. A half-mile trail leads to the **Tennant Lake Natural History Interpretive Center,** which features a fragrance garden. *Admission charged.*

Map Labels

STRAIT OF GEORGIA
To Alaska

CASCADE
RANGE

MOUNTAIN STATE FOREST
SLIDE

Lawrence
Deming
Van Zandt
VAN ZANDT STATE FOREST
Acme
Wickersham
Lyman
Hamilton

543 · Ferndale · SMITH RD · Laurel
SLATER RD
LUMMI IND. RES.
Marietta
BELLINGHAM INTL. AIRPORT
539
5
Hannegan Rd
542
Nooksack R.
Middle Fork
South Fork

Bellingham
WHATCOM MUSEUM
W. WASHINGTON UNIV.
FAIRHAVEN HISTORIC DISTRICT
Geneva
Sudden Valley
Lake Whatcom
Bellingham Bay
9

MT BAKER-SNOQUALMIE NATIONAL FOREST
South Twin 6,93 2

Long Harbour
Mayne
Village Bay
Mayne Island
Winter Cove P.P.
Port Washington
Otter Bay
Saturna
Cabbage Island P.P.
Saturna Island
Patos Island S.P.
Sucia Island S.P.
Matia Island S.P.
Clark Island S.P.
13

Mount Maxwell P.P.
N. Pender Island
Beaumont P.P.
S. Pender Island
Prior Centennial P.P.
Bedwell Harbour
Fulford Harbour
Ruckle P.P.
Princess Margaret P.P.
Saltspring Island

Eastsound
Waldron Island
Waldron
Rosario
MORAN S.P.
Doe Bay
Olga
Urban
14
Lummi Island
Lummi Island
Chuckanut Bay
LARRABEE S.P.
11
Lake Samish
Samish
Blanchard
Bow
BOW HILL
Edison
Samish Bay
Alger
Bald Mtn. 4,550
South Twin 6,93 2

Swartz Bay
McDonald P.P.
Isle-de-Lis P.P.
Stuart Island S.P.
West Sound
Deer Harbor
Orcas Island
Doe Island S.P.
Sinclair Island

Sidney
1
VICTORIA INTL. AIRPORT
Saanichton
Sidney Spit P.P.
Sidney Island
Stuart Island
Roche Harbor
Orcas
Shaw Island
Port Stanley
Blakely Island
Cypress Island
Guemes Island
Saddlebag Island S.P.
Samish Bay
Bayview
Allen
Sedro Woolley
COOK RD
Lyman
Hamilton
12

COLE BAY I.R.
S. SAANICH I.R.
E. SAANICH I.R.
Keating
Brentwood Bay
John Dean P.P.
BRITISH CAMP
SAN JUAN ISLAND N.H.P.
BEAVERTON VALLEY RD
Friday Harbor
Turn Island S.P.
Lopez
Spencer Spit S.P.
Decatur Island
James Island S.P.
Anacortes
20
Padilla Bay
Fidalgo Island
Summit Park
Bayview S.P.
WILSON RD
BEST RD
Burlington
Clear Lake
SKAGIT HWY
Skagit River

2
17A
17
Cordova Bay
D'Arcy Island P.P.
W. SIDE RD
San Juan Island
American Camp
Richardson
Otis
Lopez Island
Rosario Strait
SWINOMISH IND. RES.
Snee Oosh
La Conner
SKAGIT CO. HIST. MUSEUM
536
538
Mount Vernon
5
Big Lake
Big Lake

Vancouver I.
View Royal
Saanich
UNIV. OF VICTORIA
1
14
Esquimalt
Colwood
FT. RODD HILL N.H.P.
GOVERNMENT HOUSE
ROYAL BRITISH COLUMBIA MUSEUM
3
Victoria
Oak Bay
Discovery Island P.P.
HARO STRAIT
BRITISH COLUMBIA
WASHINGTON
DECEPTION PASS S.P.
11
WHIDBEY ISLAND N.A.S.
Dewey
Hope Island S.P.
534
McMurray
Lake Cavanaugh
9

Joseph Whidbey S.P.
Oak Harbor
WHIDBEY ISLAND N.A.S.
Conway
FIR ISLAND RD
Fir Island
Skagit Bay
532
Stanwood
530
Bryant
North Fork
Arlington

STRAIT OF JUAN DE FUCA
CANADA
UNITED STATES
Summer only
San de Fuca
Fort Ebey S.P.
Coupeville
10
20
Utsalady
Camano Island
Camano
300TH ST
531
Warm Beach
Wenberg S.P.
Lakewood
Smokey Point
JORDAN RD
BURN RD

DUNGENESS N.W.R.
4
Port Angeles
FAIRCHILD INTL. AIRPORT
5
Dungeness
6
PROTECTION ISLAND N.W.R.
7
Port Townsend
Fort Worden S.P.
WHIDBEY ISLAND N.A.S
Fort Casey S.P.
Keystone
Admiralty Inlet
Camano Island S.P.
Saratoga Passage
Port Susan
Mabana
MARINE DR
TULALIP IND. RES.
Tulalip Bay
67TH AV
9
Marysville
92
528
204

PIONEER MEM. MUSEUM VISITOR CENTER
101
OLYMPIC HWY
Agnew
Carlsborg
Sequim
WARD RD
Mt. Pleasant 2,368
Sequim Bay S.P.
Gardiner
Blyn
18
Old Fort Townsend S.P.
Fort Flagler S.P.
Indian Island
20
Greenbank
Langley
Whidbey Island
Saratoga
Possession Sound
Bay View
525
Everett
EVERETT PUB. MARKET
9
Lake Stevens
Lake Stevens
SNOHOMISH CO. MUSEUM
Machias
2

Mt. Angeles 6,454
OLYMPIC NATIONAL PARK
HURRICANE RIDGE
Blue Mtn. 6,007
Obstruction Peak 6,450
BUCKHORN WILDERNESS
Tyler Peak 6,364
Mt. Zion 4,273
101
19
Port Hadlock
Chimacum
Irondale
Nordland
116
Mystery Bay S.P.
South Whidbey S.P.
Marrowstone Island
Anderson Lake S.P.
Discovery Bay
Uncas
Center
Port Ludlow
Freeland
Clinton
Mukilteo S.P.
Mukilteo
Maxwelton
Glendale
9
529
Snohomish
Snohomish River
Pilchuck
2

Elwha R.
OLYMPIC MOUNTAINS
Gray Wolf River
Dungeness River
Mt. Townsend 6,280
OLYMPIC NATIONAL FOREST
Leland
104
Shine
Shine Tidelands S.P.
Port Gamble
PORT GAMBLE IND. RES.
3
Paradise Bay
Hansville
8
PUGET SOUND
To Seattle
10
SNOHOMISH CO. AIRPORT (PAINE FIELD)
99
35TH AV
527
Mill Creek
Martha Lake
Lynnwood
Edmonds
96
Cathcart
522

0   5   10   15
SCALE IN MILES

1. Mount Walker

Many of Washington's premier peaks are visible from this mountain in the Olympics: the cones of Mt. Baker and Mt. Rainier, as well as many of the other summits of the Cascade Range. A gravel road climbs 2,800 feet to the top of Mt. Walker, one of the few area peaks accessible by car.

2. Hood Canal Drive

U.S. 101 follows the shoreline of Hood Canal, which is actually a natural channel of Puget Sound. Beach views make this a beautiful drive, which is enhanced by roadside rhododendrons in late spring and bright maple trees in autumn.

3. Simpson Timber Company

Third and Franklin Sts., Shelton. The logging community of Shelton bills itself as the Christmas Tree Capital of the World. This company offers summer tours on Fridays of the seed orchard, where cones that bear the seeds are produced, and the plantation, where trees are grown.

4. Olympia

Chamber of Commerce, 1000 Plum St. The immense masonry dome of the state capitol is a striking feature of the city skyline. Tours of the building are available. A few blocks away, the **State Capital Museum** has exhibits related to Washington's history. Other points of interest include the **Olympia Brewery, Priest Point Park,** the public market, and the waterfront.

5. Tolmie State Park

An unusual array of activities is offered here: snorkeling and scuba diving on submerged wooden barges; fishing for flounder and ling cod; digging for clams; and hiking through forests of fir, alder, and maple trees.

6. Pioneer Farm Museum

7716 Ohop Valley Rd., Eatonville. This living-history museum, with a one-room schoolhouse, trading post, and fully furnished pioneer cabin, is particularly intriguing to children. The museum also has a picnic area. *Admission charged.*

7. Mud Mountain Dam

This dam is a federal flood-control project. Cliffs that were formed when the original river eroded the volcanic bedrock now rise more than 200 feet above the narrow river channel. The area, surrounded by forests, offers a hiking trail and picnic area.

8. Manfred Vierthaler Winery

17136 Rte. 410E, Sumner. Since this charming winery uses the traditional techniques of German vintners, it's perhaps not surprising that the main building resembles a Bavarian chalet. Visitors can sample wines made from both California and local grapes in a tasting room that overlooks the Sumner Puyallup River Valley.

9. Puyallup

Chamber of Commerce, 322 Second St. SW. In the 1800's, an area resident named Ezra Meeker made a fortune cultivating beer hops and built an ornate mansion in the town. The **Meeker Mansion,** with its original furnishings, is now a national historic site. Located in the south end of the downtown area is the **Western Washington Fairgrounds,** where a large county fair, complete with grandstand shows and tasty desserts, begins the first Friday after Labor Day and runs for 17 days. *Admission charged.*

10. Tacoma

Convention and Visitors Bureau, 906 Broadway. This industrial and shipping center holds many attractions for visitors. **Fireman's Park** boasts a 105-foot totem pole created by Alaskan Indians. The **Washington State Historical Society Museum** displays the art and artifacts of Native Americans, Eskimos, and pioneers. **Point Defiance Park** offers both recreation and education. Besides its zoo, aquarium, and rose garden, the 698-acre park contains a logging museum and a reconstruction of **Fort Nisqually,** built by the British in 1833. A steam train offers transportation to various sites. *Admission charged for some attractions.*

11. Bremerton Naval Memorial

The former Navy destroyer U.S.S. *Turner Joy* serves as a memorial both to members of the navy and to the civilians who help build naval ships. The 418-foot destroyer is moored at **Bremerton,** home of the Puget Sound Naval Shipyard. Visitors to Bremerton's waterfront, easily reached by ferry from Seattle, can tour the combat ship and watch presentations related to its history. *Admission charged.*

12. Seattle

Convention and Visitors Bureau, 1815 Seventh Ave. Its water-dominated topography makes Seattle one of the most beautiful cities in the nation. From the observation deck of the **Space Needle,** a futuristic-looking city landmark, there are clear-day views of Puget Sound, Lake Washington, the Olympics, and the Cascades, including Mt. Rainier. The **Pioneer Square Historic District** preserves turn-of-the-century architecture; one highlight is the glass and cast-iron pergola at Pioneer Park. The **Pike Place Farmer's Market,** founded in 1907, presents a cornucopia of fresh produce, fish, and other foods. The original arcade has mushroomed into several levels of shops and restaurants. Near the market stands the **Seattle Art Museum,** with exceptional collections of Northwest Coast Indian works and of African art. The **Burke Museum** at the University of Washington is one of the major natural history museums in the Pacific Northwest. At Boeing Field, the **Museum of Flight** offers an exceptional exhibit on the history of aviation, including airplanes dating back to the Wright brothers. *Admission charged for some attractions.*

13. Snoqualmie Falls

These spectacular falls plunge 268 feet into the Snoqualmie River. An observation platform stands above the river, connected by trail to the base of the waterfall. Behind this cascade is an electric generating station, built into the rock in 1898. Farther down the river, visitors can kayak and fish for steelhead trout.

The Museum of Flight in Seattle displays aviation memorabilia, including airplanes that recall the daring days of early aviation.

OLYMPIC NATIONAL PARK

1. Ozette Lake
The lake offers excellent swimming, boating, and fishing. At its northern end there are two 3-mile-long boardwalk trails through old-growth forests leading to an ocean beach, the site of ancient American Indian petroglyphs.

2. Bogachiel State Park
Hiking trails meander through both the small rain forest and the more typical northwestern forest in this valley, which is home to plentiful deer, elk, and other wildlife. In the fall, anglers stand a good chance of catching steelhead trout in the Bogachiel River. The river has a camp-ground right on its banks.

3. The Ocean Strip
Some of the country's wildest, most undeveloped beachfront is located here

Luxuriant moss and big-leaf maple intertwine in the silence of the Hoh Rain Forest.

along U.S. 101 from **Ruby Beach** south to Kalaloch. Area beaches contain tide pools filled with marine life, and trees bent low by the wind. Offshore sea stacks — remnants of headlands — provide a home for gulls and other seabirds. Many of the beaches are good for clam digging at low tide; driftwood and smooth stones also turn up in the foamy surf.

4. Kalaloch
Kalaloch boasts a dramatically placed campground, which is poised on a bluff 50 feet above an ocean beach frequented by gulls, cormorants, and oyster catchers. A ranger station provides information on clamming and surf fishing.

5. Queets Valley Rain Forest
Here a rough road leads along 14 miles of dense rain forest skirting the Queets River. This remote section of Olympic National Park receives about 145 inches of precipitation annually, and the resulting luxuriant growth includes Sitka spruces, hemlocks hung with club moss, red alders, and licorice ferns. A 3-mile hiking trail sometimes yields glimpses of the huge but furtive Roosevelt elk, for whose preservation the park was originally founded. Today Olympic National Park boasts the largest remaining herd in the world, with as many as 5,000 of the handsome, white-rumped animals.

6. Lake Quinault
Lush rain forest encircles this 4-mile-long lake. A forest station on the south shore has a nature trail and information about boating and fishing.

7. Mount Olympus
The grand Mt. Olympus rises nearly 8,000 feet above the Olympic Peninsula. Seven

glaciers with ice to a depth of 900 feet partially cover its slopes, which receive nearly 200 inches of snow each year.

8. Hoh Rain Forest
The Hoh River Road follows the river for 19 miles to a visitor center, where trails head off into the dense, moist, quiet realm of the rain forest. On one trail, named the Hall of Mosses, the moss enveloping the trees has formed a dramatic canopy over the course of the path.

9. Obstruction Point
Accessible via a 9-mile narrow dirt road on Hurricane Ridge, Obstruction Point amply rewards visitors with the most spectacular views of Mt. Olympus.

10. Hurricane Ridge
A 17-mile road twists through unspoiled woodland up a mountain to Hurricane Ridge, famed for its many deer and its sweeping vistas of the Olympic Mountains. Along the way, **Lookout Rock** provides excellent views of the Strait of Juan de Fuca and, on clear days, Mt. Baker. The road ends at a lodge, where visitors can get information on hiking and nature walks through the wildflowers of nearby **Big Meadow**.

11. Sol Duc Hot Springs
These springs are located on the banks of the Soleduck River, where salmon swim

Flett violets grace subalpine regions.

Along the Ocean Strip, offshore sea stacks shelter gulls and other seabirds.

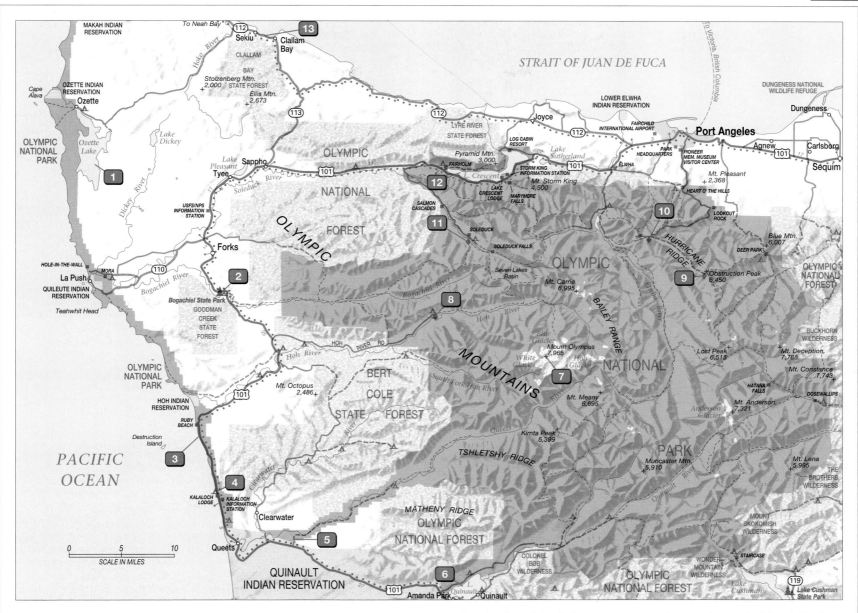

upstream to spawn from August to October. At **Salmon Cascades** the fish fairly fling themselves from one shallow pool to another to reach the headwaters, where they themselves were spawned. A 7-mile hiking trail originating at the springs leads to **Seven Lakes Basin,** a valley dotted with sparkling ponds.

12. Lake Crescent

Reflecting beautiful wooded slopes in its glistening blue water, this 11-mile glacier-formed lake offers outdoor enthusiasts superb boating and fishing. A short trail through a lovely forested area leads to the 90-foot-high **Marymere Falls.**

13. Scenic Coast Drive

This dramatic stretch of Washington State Highway 112 hugs the north shore of the Olympic Peninsula from Clallam Bay to Neah Bay. The roadway alternately meanders along at beach level and climbs to towering overlooks; the higher elevations allow for sweeping northern vistas of the Strait of Juan de Fuca and Vancouver Island. Visitors should also be on the lookout for bald eagles, which are frequently sighted in the surrounding forest, where they make their nests.

Admission charged for national park.

A black-tail buck and doe exchange tentative greetings on Hurricane Ridge.

MOUNT RAINIER NATIONAL PARK

1. Sunshine Point
Located near the Nisqually entrance, Sunshine Point is the only campground within the park that is open to visitors year-round.

2. Kautz Creek Mud Flow
This is the site of a 1947 mudflow that buried the park road under 20 feet of mud and debris. Today a roadside exhibit explains the flow's devastation and the processes by which the forest is currently renewing itself.

3. Longmire
Open year-round, this area of the park includes a visitor center and the **Trail of the Shadows.** The circular half-mile nature walk through forest and meadow passes mineral springs and an original pioneer cabin.

4. Wonderland Trail
The 93-mile trail, linked at several points to park roads, encircles the mountain. Depending on the trail segment, hikers will encounter terrain ranging from meadows and forests to ridges; some steep climbs even approach glaciers.

5. Cougar Rock
One of three major campgrounds in the park, Cougar Rock is easily accessible from the Nisqually entrance. Nearby are **Christine Falls** and a scenic overlook at **Ricksecker Point.**

6. Inspiration Point
A plaque inscribed in part: "There stood the mountain, wholly unveiled, awful in bulk and majesty" — words attributed to American naturalist John Muir — pays tribute to Mt. Rainier from this breath-taking lookout point.

7. Paradise
Overlooking the Paradise River Valley, this is the most popular area on Mt. Rainier. Hiking trails — from beginning to advanced — lead through subalpine meadowland or up to the mountain summit; particularly recommended is the **Nisqually Vista Trail.** The party led by mountaineer Jim Whittaker trained on these slopes for their 1963 ascent of Mt. Everest; exhibits at the visitor center include the gear used by that group for that historic climb.

Mist-shrouded Reflection Lake is one of many scenic delights on Stevens Canyon Road.

8. Stevens Canyon Road
One of the most scenic drives in the Northwest, the route originates at Inspiration Point on the Nisqually–Paradise Road and ends north of Ohanapecosh. Along the way are the glistening Reflection and Louise lakes. The road scales canyon walls, yielding vistas of lava formations, mountain peaks, and glacier-etched valleys.

9. Box Canyon
Spanning this narrow gorge is a bridge from which visitors can look down to the churning water of the Muddy Fork of the Cowlitz River 180 feet below.

10. Ohanapecosh
Several splendid trails are located in this area surrounded by old-growth forests. A 3-mile loop, originating from the campground at Ohanapecosh River Bridge, wends through dense forest to the spectacular **Silver Falls,** made especially voluminous in spring by snowmelt. A lovely shorter trail leads to the **Grove of the Patriarchs,** filled with western red cedars and huge Douglas firs. A more challenging trail ascends to **Shriner Peak,** where elk can often be glimpsed; the panoramic view from here includes Mts. Rainier, Adams, St. Helens, and Hood.

11. Mount Rainier
A dormant volcano towering 14,410 feet (almost 3 miles) above sea level, Mt. Rainier is one of the outstanding scenic wonders of the Pacific Northwest. Its perpetually snowcapped summit is ringed with 26 glaciers, giving way farther down the slopes to subalpine meadowland that bursts into brilliant bloom in summer.

12. Emmons Glacier
More than 1 mile wide by 4½ miles long, Emmons Glacier is the largest glacier in

Summertime fun on Paradise Glacier, circa 1926: Tin trousers smooth the way for a merry band of "nature coasters."

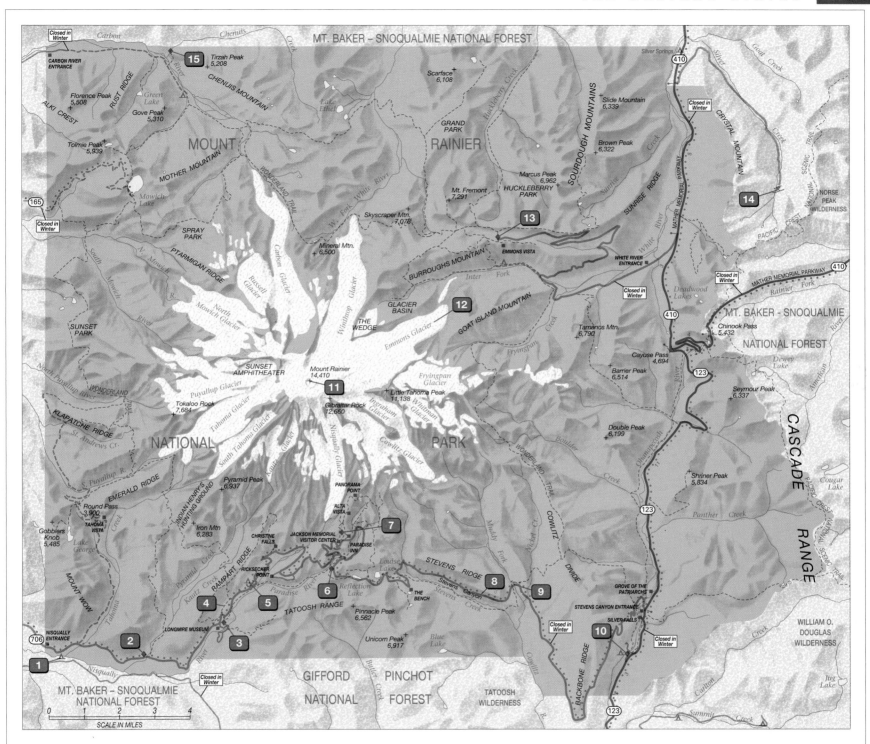

MT. BAKER – SNOQUALMIE NATIONAL FOREST

Closed in Winter

Carbon River

Chenuis Creek

Silver Springs

15 Tirzah Peak
5,208

CHENUIS MOUNTAIN

Scarface
6,108

Slide Mountain
6,339

CRYSTAL MOUNTAIN

CARBON RIVER ENTRANCE

Florence Peak
5,508

Green Lake

RUST RIDGE

Lake Ethel

GRAND PARK

SOURDOUGH MOUNTAINS

Brown Peak
6,322

NORSE PEAK WILDERNESS

Gove Peak
5,310

ALKI CREST

MOUNT

RAINIER

14

Tolmie Peak
5,939

MOTHER MOUNTAIN

Marcus Peak
6,962

HUCKLEBERRY PARK

PACIFIC CREST NATIONAL SCENIC TRAIL

Mowich Lake

Skyscraper Mtn.
7,078

Mt. Fremont
7,291

13

EMMONS VISTA

SUNRISE RIDGE

Closed in Winter

SPRAY PARK

PTARMIGAN RIDGE

Mineral Mtn.
6,500

BURROUGHS MOUNTAIN

WHITE RIVER ENTRANCE

MT. BAKER – SNOQUALMIE

SUNSET PARK

Russell Glacier

Carbon Glacier

North Mowich Glacier

Winthrop Glacier

THE WEDGE

GLACIER BASIN

12

GOAT ISLAND MOUNTAIN

Deadwood Lakes

Closed in Winter

Chinook Pass
5,432

NATIONAL FOREST

Dewey Lake

WONDERLAND TRAIL

Emmons Glacier

Tamanos Mtn.
6,790

Cayuse Pass
4,694

SUNSET AMPHITHEATER

Mount Rainier
14,410

Fryingpan Glacier

Barrier Peak
6,514

Seymour Peak
6,337

KLAPATCHE RIDGE

Puyallup Glacier

11

Little Tahoma Peak
11,138

Whitman Glacier

CASCADE

Tokaloo Rock
7,684

Gibraltar Rock
12,660

Ingraham Glacier

Double Peak
6,199

NATIONAL

Tahoma Glacier

South Tahoma Glacier

Cowlitz Glacier

PARK

WONDERLAND TRAIL

Boulder Creek

RANGE

EMERALD RIDGE

Nisqually Glacier

Shriner Peak
5,834

Cougar Lake

St. Andrews Cr.

Pyramid Peak
6,937

PANORAMA POINT

ALTA VISTA

Panther Creek

Round Pass
3,900

TAHOMA VISTA

INDIAN HENRY'S HUNTING GROUND

Iron Mtn
6,283

7

Gobblers Knob
5,485

Lake George

CHRISTINE FALLS

JACKSON MEMORIAL VISITOR CENTER

PARADISE INN

Louise Lake

STEVENS RIDGE

GROVE OF THE PATRIARCHS

MOUNT WOW

RAMPART RIDGE

RICKSECKER POINT

6

Reflection Lake

STEVENS RIDGE

8

Stevens Canyon

DIVIDE

9

STEVENS CANYON ENTRANCE

4

5

Paradise River

THE BENCH

Stevens Creek

SILVER FALLS

2

3

TATOOSH RANGE

Pinnacle Peak
6,562

Closed in Winter

10

WILLIAM O. DOUGLAS WILDERNESS

NISQUALLY ENTRANCE

LONGMIRE MUSEUM

Unicorn Peak
6,917

Blue Lake

Closed in Winter

1

Nisqually

Closed in Winter

GIFFORD PINCHOT

Backbone Ridge

TATOOSH WILDERNESS

Jug Lake

MT. BAKER – SNOQUALMIE NATIONAL FOREST

0 1 2 3 4
SCALE IN MILES

NATIONAL FOREST

Summit Creek

---

the lower 48 states. It is best viewed from the visitor center at Sunrise.

13. Sunrise

The highest point — 6,400 feet — that can be reached by car on Mt. Rainier, this area affords superb views of the entire mountain and of Emmons Glacier in particular. Good hiking trails originate from here, and a visitor center offers exhibits and provides park information.

14. Crystal Mountain Ski Area

For dazzling views of Mt. Rainier and its glaciers, visitors can take a chair-lift ride to the summit of Crystal Mountain. At nearby **Silver Springs,** camping and picnicking facilities are available.

15. Chenuis Falls

These picturesque "falls" are in fact a series of water slides flowing across colorful rock layers.

Admission charged for national park.

1. Grand Coulee Dam

As one of the world's largest concrete dams — twice as high as Niagara Falls and 5,223 feet long — Grand Coulee draws hundreds of thousands of visitors each year. A visitor center offers guided tours.

2. Sun Lakes State Park and Dry Falls

The 4,000-acre state park's main attraction is Dry Falls, whose 3½-mile-wide lava walls are estimated to have created a 400-foot falls during the last ice age — one of the greatest waterfalls in geological history. The area's geology is explained at an interpretive center and can be explored on hiking and equestrian trails.

3. Adam East Museum

122 West Third St., Moses Lake. Local collector Adam East spent a lifetime scouring the Columbia River area for treasures related to the history of the land and the inhabitants. His legacy, housed in this museum, includes an impressive array of Indian artifacts, fossils, and rocks.

4. Palouse Falls State Park and Palouse River Canyon

The Palouse Falls plunge 198 feet into a horseshoe-shaped basin, where the waters of the Palouse River surge through an 8-mile canyon to converge with the Snake River. The state park offers hiking trails, campsites, and picnic areas.

5. Whitman Mission National Historic Site

Markers indicate the site where the mission, headed by Marcus and Narcissa Whitman, a husband-and-wife missionary team, once offered aid to westward-bound wagon trains on the Oregon Trail. The couple ministered less successfully to the local Cayuse Indians who, after losing half their population in a measles epidemic, slaughtered the Whitmans and 11 mission guests. A plaque marks their gravesite, and the history of the mission is recounted at the visitor center. *Admission charged.*

6. Doll and Toy Museum

Rte. 395, Hermiston. Among 2,000-odd antique dolls, many from the 1850's, is the first doll patented in America. Doll accessories dating back to the Civil War and other vintage toys round out the museum's collection. *Admission charged.*

7. Pendleton Woolen Mills

1307 SE Court Place, Pendleton. The mills began making Indian blankets in 1909, and the company has since become famous for its woolen fabrics. On a factory tour visitors can see the wool for the blankets being carded, spun, and woven on various machines.

8. McKay Creek National Wildlife Refuge

The 1,800-acre refuge provides a year-round sanctuary for migratory birds. Its reservoir creates a huge lake in spring and early summer, attracting boaters, fishermen, and water-skiers.

9. Wallowa Lake

This sapphire-colored, crescent-shaped lake draws scores of fishing and boating enthusiasts to its waters. Campsites and other recreational facilities are available in the surrounding state park. The lake sits in the foothills of the **Wallowa Mountains,** whose jagged cliffs and snowcapped peaks shelter more than 60 glacier-carved lakes. The **Eagle Cap Wilderness** is a popular area with hikers and horseback riders.

10. Hat Point Overlook

A 24-mile drive on a gravel road leads to this scenic lookout in the **Hells Canyon National Recreation Area.** From the summit there are unparalleled views of Hells Canyon, the deepest gorge in North America; the Snake River, more than a mile below; and the craggy peaks of the Seven Devils Mountains.

11. Heaven's Gate

In the **Seven Devils Mountains,** Heaven's Gate offers dramatic views of Hells Canyon on the Snake River. From a nearby Forest Service lookout, visitors can also see partial views of Oregon, Idaho, Washington, and Montana.

12. Grangeville

This farming town serves as the gateway to **Camas Prairie,** where the Nez Perces traditionally gathered to dig camas roots.

13. Clearwater Battlefield

This steep canyon is the site of a clash between the U.S. Army and the Nez Perce Indians, which resulted in the Nez Perces' decision to leave their homeland.

14. Selway-Bitterroot Wilderness

At more than 1 million acres, this second-largest wilderness area in the United States straddles the Idaho-Montana border. The wild and scenic **Selway River** is the major attraction here. Moose, elk, and mountain goats roam freely in the back country, where opportunities for hiking and horseback riding are superb. The **Lewis and Clark Highway** is a nearby point of interest.

15. Dworshak Dam and Fish Hatchery

Built on the Clearwater River, one of the nation's highest dams rises near the world's largest hatchery for steelhead trout. Both the dam and hatchery have observation areas for visitors.

16. Spalding Visitor Center, Nez Perce National Historical Park

The visitor center, which also serves as park headquarters, features exhibits on the Nez Perce culture and early area missionary activity. The park itself is spread over 24 historic sites, mainly located in the Nez Perce Reservation.

17. Lewiston

Chamber of Commerce, 2207 East Main St. Lewiston is the departure point for a driving tour of the **Nez Perce Homeland.** Just outside of town, the route passes two rock formations — Coyote's Fishnet, and Ant and Yellowjacket — that played an important part in Nez Perce mythology. The town is also the starting point for boat trips along the Snake River to Hells Canyon, as well as the entrance point to **Hells Gate State Park.** The park offers swimming, hiking, horseback riding, and camping. Excursion boats to Hells Canyon may also be boarded here. *Fee charged for boat ride.*

18. Route 95 Scenic Drive

The 300-plus-mile route from New Meadows to Bonners Ferry is one of the nation's most scenic drives. Skirting the Salmon River north from Riggins for 30 miles, the route passes meadows, canyons, and abandoned mines; Camas Prairie, the

Clearwater River, and rich wheatlands. Coeur d'Alene and Pend Oreille lakes flank the northern end of the drive.

19. Shattuck Arboretum

This tranquil wooded area with specimens of incense cedar, giant sequoia, and Canadian hemlock has been augmented by a new 63-acre arboretum on the campus of the **University of Idaho at Moscow.**

20. St. Maries

St. Maries is the starting point for canoe trips along the **St. Joe River** to the ghost town of **St. Joe,** and beyond to **St. Joe National Forest.** Within the forest, **Hobo Cedar Grove** shelters a 240-acre virgin stand of large western red cedars up to 8 feet in diameter.

21. Wallace

Chamber of Commerce, 509 Bank St. The **Wallace District Mining Museum** has interesting exhibits of actual mine workings. Tools, equipment, and rock samples from the area — which still produces much of the nation's newly mined silver — are also on display. In the town of Wallace, whose turn-of-the-century buildings are remarkably preserved, a trolley transports visitors to the outskirts of town, where an abandoned mine shaft can be toured. *Admission charged for some attractions.*

22. Hot Springs

At this celebrated health resort on the **Flathead Indian Reservation,** mineral springs flow at a constant year-round temperature of 120° F. Visitors can test the waters with a dip in the springs or try a hot mud bath.

23. Priest Lake State Park

Nestled in dense forest, Priest Lake is in fact two lakes — Upper Priest and Priest — connected by a thoroughfare. Some of the finest trout fishing in the country is done in these waters, against the dramatic backdrop of the Selkirk Mountains.

24. Crawford State Park and Gardner Cave

A sinkhole serves as the entrance to the 2,000-foot-long cavern, whose glistening stone formations can be viewed on a guided tour. The cave's most outstanding feature is a speleothem — a floor-to-ceiling calcite column formed by the union of a stalactite and a stalagmite.

MAP PG. 17

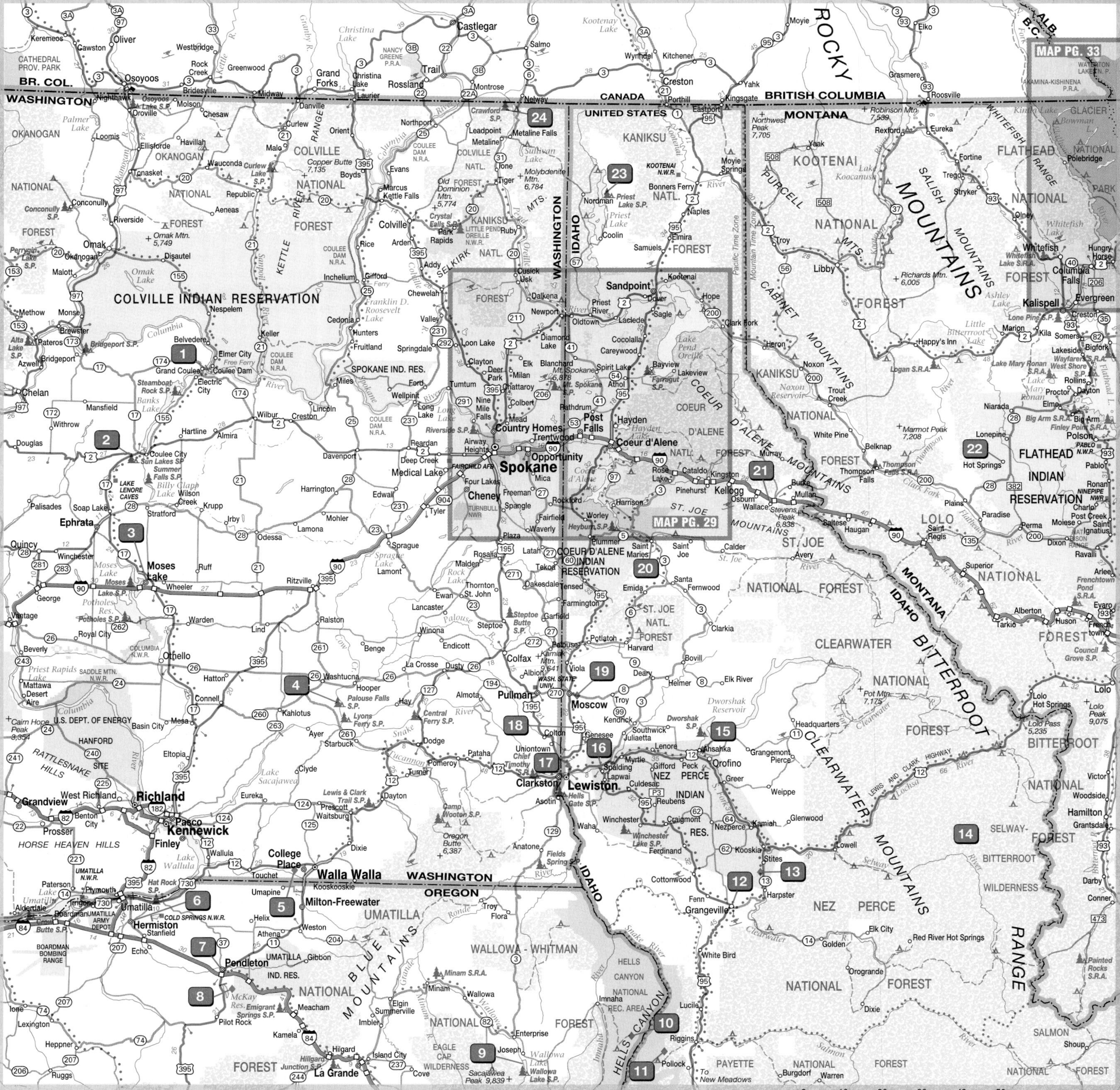

MAP PG. 35

WASHINGTON

BR. COL.

BRITISH COLUMBIA

CANADA

UNITED STATES

ROCKY

MONTANA

IDAHO

WASHINGTON

OREGON

IDAHO

MONTANA

GLACIER NATIONAL PARK

KOOTENAI NATIONAL FOREST

FLATHEAD NATIONAL FOREST

SALISH MOUNTAINS

PURCELL MOUNTAINS

CABINET MOUNTAINS

KANIKSU NATIONAL FOREST

COEUR D'ALENE MOUNTAINS

ST. JOE NATIONAL FOREST

CLEARWATER NATIONAL FOREST

BITTERROOT

LOLO NATIONAL FOREST

SELWAY BITTERROOT WILDERNESS

NEZ PERCE NATIONAL FOREST

PAYETTE NATIONAL FOREST

SALMON NATIONAL FOREST

COLVILLE INDIAN RESERVATION

SPOKANE IND. RES.

COEUR D'ALENE INDIAN RESERVATION

NEZ PERCE INDIAN RES.

FLATHEAD INDIAN RESERVATION

COLVILLE NATIONAL FOREST

KANIKSU NATL. FOREST

OKANOGAN NATIONAL FOREST

BLUE MOUNTAINS

WALLOWA - WHITMAN NATIONAL FOREST

UMATILLA NATIONAL FOREST

HELLS CANYON NATIONAL REC. AREA

HORSE HEAVEN HILLS

RATTLESNAKE HILLS

HANFORD SITE

U.S. DEPT. OF ENERGY

BOARDMAN BOMBING RANGE

Spokane

Coeur d'Alene

Post Falls

Sandpoint

Kalispell

Whitefish

Columbia Falls

Bonners Ferry

Libby

Troy

Lewiston

Clarkston

Pullman

Moscow

Richland

Kennewick

Pasco

Walla Walla

Pendleton

La Grande

Milton-Freewater

Moses Lake

Ephrata

Omak

Okanogan

Chelan

Brewster

Grand Coulee

Coulee Dam

Colville

Kettle Falls

Republic

Osoyoos

Oliver

Castlegar

Trail

Rossland

Grand Forks

Creston

Orofino

Grangeville

Kamiah

Kooskia

Lapwai

Craigmont

Cottonwood

White Bird

Riggins

Joseph

Enterprise

MAP PG. 45

MAP PG. 47

0 10 20 30 40 50
SCALE IN MILES

1. John A. Finch Arboretum

Sunset and Woodland Blvds., Spokane. This 65-acre arboretum is made up of areas named to reflect their main attractions. More than 75 varieties of fragrant lilacs blossom in the spring in Lilac Lane. The Corey Rhododendron Glen, with secluded trails along Garden Springs Creek, blooms with azaleas as well as rhododendrons. The Touch and See nature trail has 850 feet of walkway with signs in Braille. Most of the trees and shrubs, which number over 2,000 and represent some 600 species, are labeled. They provide a lovely setting for summer picnicking.

2. Mount Spokane State Park

Hiking trails and ski runs lace the slopes of Mt. Spokane, the core of Washington's largest state park. The mountain's crest — 5,878 feet up — provides a breathtaking vista of lake-dotted mountains in the eastern part of the state as well as in the neighboring state of Idaho.

Old Mission State Park

3. Albeni Falls Dam

A self-guided tour gives visitors a look at the workings of this dam, which has a picnic area and a great view of the Pend Oreille River and surroundings. Campsites are located at Albeni Cove, on the dam's south end.

4. Spirit Lake

This appealing little town shares the name of its lake, which rests like a jewel in a mountain setting at 2,440 feet. Spirit Lake, whose name was derived from an Indian legend, was once part of a gigantic Ice Age lake called Clearwater.

5. Silverwood Theme Park

North 26225 Rte. 95, Athol. Silverwood's Victorian Village re-creates a turn-of-the-century mining community, complete with saloon and train depot. The park's Norton Aero Museum and the Curtiss Aeroplane Factory house antique aircraft, and there are biplanes and gliders that participate in shows and take passengers. For rides of a different sort, the Country Carnival section boasts a roller coaster, white-water flume, Ferris wheel, bumper boats, and ponies. *Admission charged.*

6. Farragut State Park

Located at the southern end of Lake Pend Oreille, this park is popular for swimming, boating, and fishing. Trails wind through forests, sometimes providing glimpses of white-tailed deer. Mountain goats live on the cliffs opposite Eagle Marina, and birds such as red-tailed hawks and bald eagles fly overhead. A museum has exhibits on the wildlife and history of the area, including the naval station that once occupied this site. *Admission charged.*

7. Lake Pend Oreille

Trout and landlocked salmon swim in this huge, clear lake set amid craggy mountains. It is accessible by a boat trip up the Pend Oreille River from the town of Priest River. The river itself is known for its trout and as a prime flyway for migrating ducks and geese. Priest River Park offers campsites.

8. Coeur d'Alene

Convention and Visitors Bureau, 202 Sherman Ave. This is timber country, as evidenced by **Coeur d'Alene National Forest.** Visitors may tour the **U. S. Forest Service Nursery,** which nurtures up to 38 million trees a year for a reforestation program. The **Museum of North Idaho** exhibits photographs of early loggers and other locals; it also features a pioneer kitchen, blacksmith shop, and logging equipment. Even in the city, outdoor beauty abounds: The forested slopes of Tubbs Hill lead down to the promenade at **Coeur d'Alene Lake,** which offers water-sport facilities. The lake itself extends some 30 miles south of the town, with sandy beaches, marinas, resorts, and launching ramps. Anglers try these waters for cutthroat trout and kokanee salmon.

9. Old Mission State Park

Constructed in the mid-1800's by members of the Coeur d'Alene Indian tribe, the Catholic mission is Idaho's oldest standing building. Now restored, it retains some of its elaborate features, such as the wooden altar painted to resemble marble. This lovely park also preserves the parish house and part of the original cemetery. The visitor center displays Jesuit missionary memorabilia and Indian handiwork. A trail guide explains the former way of life in this community, once a farming village for the Coeur d'Alene Indians. *Admission charged.*

A bobcat on the Coeur d'Alene River

10. Heyburn State Park

Wooded hills roll throughout this park, which is situated along the shores of Chatcolet Lake. A turnout on Rte. 5, about 2 miles inside the park, provides a good view of the St. Joe River flowing between Chatcolet and Round lakes. The lakes attract numerous boating, fishing, and bird-watching enthusiasts. Hiking trails lead visitors to marvelous views, and camping facilities are available.

Beargrass abloom on Scotchman's Peak, overlooking Lake Pend Oreille.

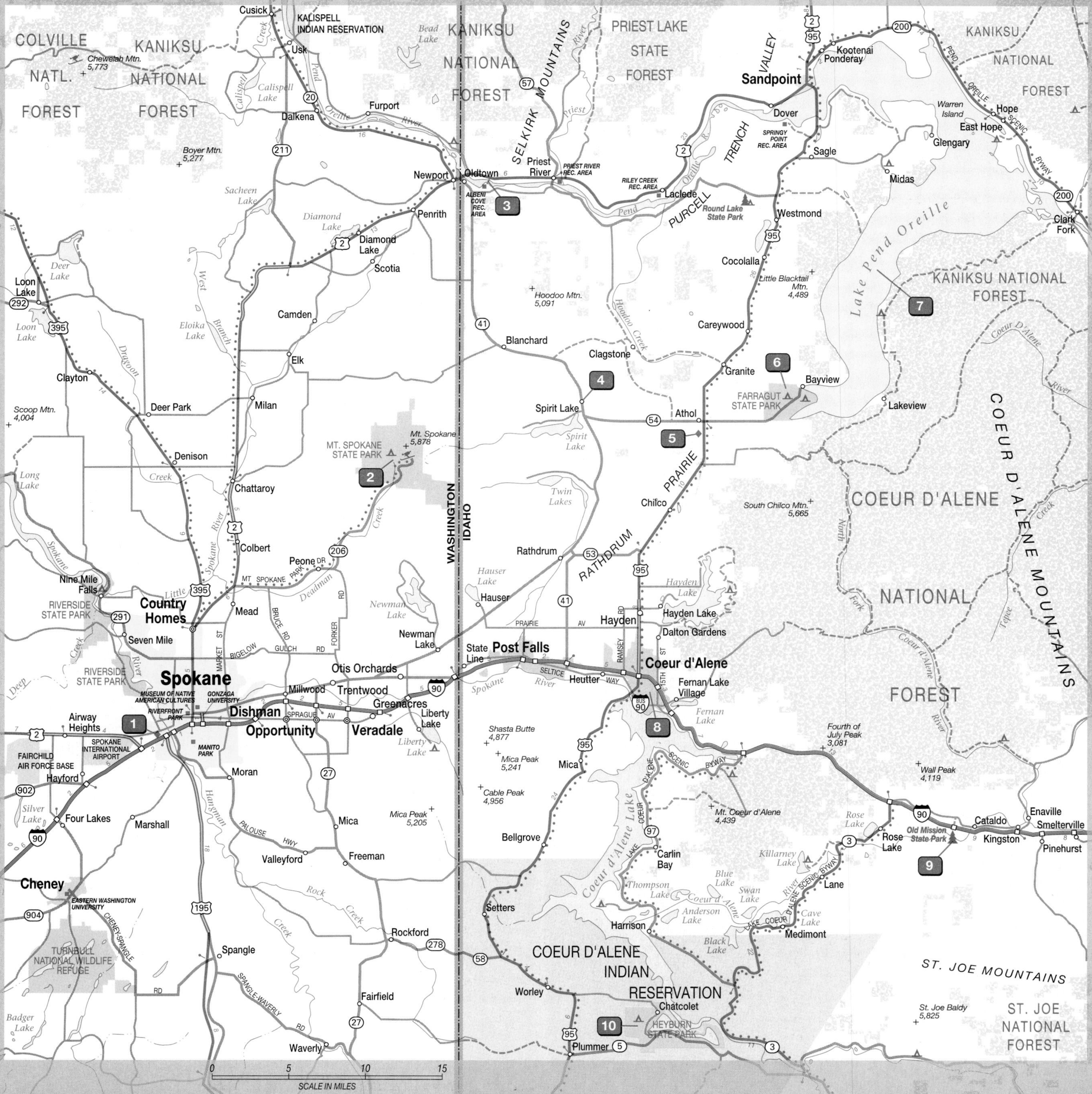

COLVILLE
KANIKSU
NATL.
NATIONAL
FOREST
FOREST

Chewelah Mtn.
5,773

Boyer Mtn.
5,277

Cusick
KALISPELL
INDIAN RESERVATION
Usk
Dalkena
Furport

Bead
Lake
KANIKSU
NATIONAL
FOREST
SELKIRK MOUNTAINS
PRIEST LAKE
STATE
FOREST

Sandpoint
Kootenai
Ponderay
Dover
Sagle

Warren Island
Hope
East Hope
Glengary
Midas

KANIKSU
NATIONAL
FOREST

Clark
Fork

Loon
Lake
292

Loon
Lake
395

Deer
Lake

Scoop Mtn.
4,004

Clayton

Deer Park

Milan

Denison

Chattaroy

Colbert

Peone

Mead

Country
Homes

Seven Mile

Nine Mile
Falls

RIVERSIDE
STATE PARK

291

Spokane

MUSEUM OF NATIVE
AMERICAN CULTURES
GONZAGA
UNIVERSITY
RIVERFRONT
PARK
MANITO
PARK

Airway
Heights
1
SPOKANE
INTERNATIONAL
AIRPORT

Dishman
Opportunity

Millwood
Trentwood
Greenacres
Veradale
Liberty
Lake

FAIRCHILD
AIR FORCE BASE
Hayford
902
Silver
Lake
Four Lakes
90

Marshall

Cheney
904
EASTERN WASHINGTON
UNIVERSITY

TURNBULL
NATIONAL
WILDLIFE
REFUGE

Badger
Lake

Spangle

Fairfield

Waverly

Rockford
278

58

Worley

COEUR D'ALENE
INDIAN
RESERVATION

Chatcolet
HEYBURN
STATE PARK
10
Plummer
95
5

211

Dalkena

Diamond
Lake

Scotia

Camden

Elk

Sacheen
Lake

Newport
Oldtown
2
Penrith
Diamond
Lake

Blanchard

Clagstone

Spirit Lake

Chilco

Rathdrum
53
41

Hauser
Lake
Hauser

Newman
Lake

State
Line
Post Falls

Otis Orchards

SPRAGUE AV

Mica

Mica Peak
5,205

Mica Peak
5,241

Cable Peak
4,956

Shasta Butte
4,877

Bellgrove

Setters

Harrison

Medimont

Priest
River
Laclede
Westmond

Cocolalla

Little Blacktail
Mtn.
4,489

Careywood

Granite
6
Bayview

Athol
54
5
FARRAGUT
STATE PARK

Lakeview

KANIKSU NATIONAL
FOREST
7

Lake Pend Oreille

COEUR D'ALENE MOUNTAINS

COEUR D'ALENE

NATIONAL

FOREST

Hayden
Hayden Lake
Dalton Gardens

Hayden
Lake

Coeur d'Alene
8
Heutter
Fernan Lake
Village
Fernan
Lake

Fourth of
July Peak
3,081

Wall Peak
4,119

Cataldo
90
9
Old Mission
State Park
Kingston
Enaville
Smelterville
Pinehurst

Rose
Lake
Rose Lake
Lane

Mt. Coeur d'Alene
4,439

Carlin
Bay
Thompson
Lake
Blue
Lake
Swan
Lake
Killarney
Lake
Cave
Lake
Black
Lake
Anderson
Lake

Coeur d'Alene Lake

ST. JOE MOUNTAINS

St. Joe Baldy
5,825

ST. JOE
NATIONAL
FOREST

Hoodoo Mtn.
5,091

South Chilco Mtn.
5,665

MT. SPOKANE
STATE PARK
Mt. Spokane
5,878
2

Twin
Lakes

Spirit
Lake

Liberty
Lake

Moran

Valleyford

Freeman

Spangle

PRIEST RIVER
REC. AREA
RILEY CREEK
REC. AREA
Round Lake
State Park

PURCELL
TRENCH
VALLEY

SPRINGY
POINT
REC. AREA

ALBENI
COVE
REC. AREA
3

PRAIRIE
RATHDRUM

WASHINGTON
IDAHO

200

95

2

57

20

16

41

SCALE IN MILES
0   5   10   15

NORTH CASCADES NATIONAL PARK

1. Mount Shuksan

Even in this mountainous park, 9,131-foot-high Mt. Shuksan dominates the landscape with its rocky, uneven slopes and immense glaciers. The Indian word *Shuksan,* appropriately enough, translates as "steep and precipitous."

2. Baker Lake

Boating, waterskiing, and fishing are the chief activities at Baker Lake, which lies below Mt. Baker. Camping and hiking are also available.

3. Rockport State Park

Hikers can follow a nature trail that encircles a stand of Douglas fir trees more than 300 years old. The park is also a favorite with campers.

4. Skagit and Cascade Rivers Area

Camping and hiking are popular around these rivers. Anglers fish the Skagit for steelhead and rainbow trout. Winter float trips may provide sightings of bald eagles from a 1,500-acre sanctuary in the area.

5. Glacier Peak Wilderness

This pristine region south of the park thrills hikers with its alpine meadows, ice blue lakes, and grand mountains with massive glaciers, including the 10,541-foot-high Glacier Peak.

6. Lake Chelan

This body of water fills a glacier-carved gorge, at times to a depth of almost 1,500 feet. Fifty-five miles long, it extends to the town of **Chelan,** south of the recreation area that shares its name. From Chelan a passenger boat cruises up the lake, past mountains and wilderness, taking 4 hours to reach Stehekin. The ferry can also be boarded at Fields Point, farther north, for a 3-hour ride. *Fee charged for ferry.*

7. Stehekin

Many outdoor enthusiasts — backpackers, day hikers, and horseback riders — begin their wilderness treks from this quiet, isolated village. Camping and lodging are available here.

8. Rainbow Falls

A bus from Stehekin takes visitors to these dramatic 312-foot falls. The name is apt, as sunlight hitting the copious spray often forms a glistening rainbow.

9. Horseshoe Basin

Once overrun with prospectors, the park area now has several abandoned mining centers, including this one. A challenging 6-hour round-trip trail past cliffs and waterfalls leads to the entrance of the **Black Warrior Mine,** which may be explored by flashlight.

10. Pacific Crest National Scenic Trail

A small part of this trail, which stretches all the way from Mexico to Canada, traverses the park. It crosses the North Cascades Highway at Rainy Pass, which has a picnic area.

11. Washington Pass Overlook

A rest area here offers picnic facilities and information, and a short loop trail leads to the 5,477-foot-high overlook. The splendor of the North Cascades — and especially of

On an alpine trail, a lone hiker treks through the pristine Glacier Peak Wilderness.

Liberty Bell Mountain — unfolds dramatically from this vantage point.

12. Whistler Basin Overlook

In spring, waterfalls cascade from 8,000-foot-high Whistler Mountain into the lovely alpine meadows of Whistler Basin. The falls and meadowland can be seen from this turnout at milepost 160 on the main highway.

13. Slate Peak Lookout

From Harts Pass, a steep, gravelly road wends its way up 2 miles to the lookout point, with a stunning view of Mt. Baker and Glacier Peak.

14. Canyon Creek

Here a trail leads to a bridge with views of Canyon and Granite creeks, an old barn, and a cabin once used by miners. Nearly

Douglas fir cones, like the ones above, produced this virgin stand of old-growth forest, left, in Rockport State Park.

A snowshoe hare at the Skagit River

2 miles farther along is Rowley's Chasm, a fissure penetrating 200 feet into the face of a rocky hill.

15. Ross Lake

A recreation area bisecting the park takes its name from this 12,000-acre reservoir created by a dam on the Skagit River. Many boat-access campgrounds surround the lake. A turnout on Highway 20 provides an excellent view of Ross Lake and Ross Dam.

16. Diablo Lake

Formed by a dam, this glacier-fed lake is a stunning aqua blue color. It offers choice trout fishing as well as boating. Nearby are a campground and the head of Thunder Creek Trail, which leads through a forested valley to connect with the Pacific Crest Trail.

17. Gorge Dam and Gorge Creek Falls

The sparkling lake created by Gorge Dam is fed by nearby Gorge Creek, which cascades 242 feet in a dramatic waterfall.

18. Newhalem Visitor Center

The largest of the park visitor centers offers exhibits, programs, films, and information. Other visitor centers are located at Sedro Woolley, Chelan, Glacier, Stehekin, and Marblemount.

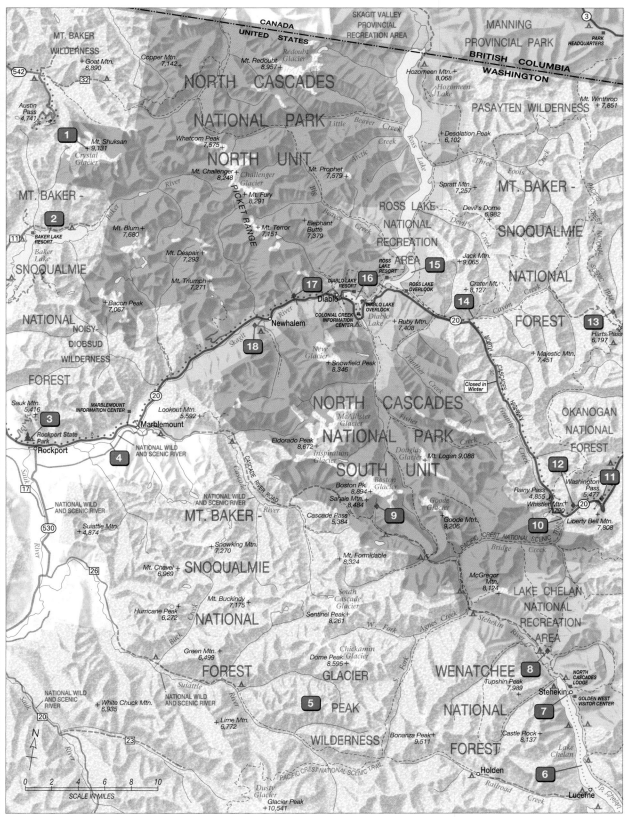

CANADA

MONTANA
★ Helena
● Butte

IDAHO

WYO.

WATERTON-GLACIER INTERNATIONAL PEACE PARK

1. Akamina Parkway
Waterton's scenic 10-mile Akamina Parkway takes visitors along the historic Cameron Valley, where stops may include the lovely **Cameron Lake;** a picnic area at Cameron Creek; and Oil City, the site of one of the first producing oil wells in Canada. At **Cameron Falls,** water cascades over the oldest exposed bedrock in the Canadian Rockies.

2. Red Rock Parkway
This narrow road provides access to a campground, trails, and several lookouts with breathtaking views of **Mount Blakiston,** the highest mountain in Waterton Lakes National Park. After traversing hilly prairies and a valley, the road ends at **Red Rock Canyon.**

3. Bison Paddock
In this paddock lives a small herd of bison, kept to represent the many such herds that once thundered through the region. A self-guided auto route allows drivers and passengers the opportunity to observe the animals in close proximity.

4. Waterton Lakes National Park
This Canadian national park has been united with the adjoining Glacier National Park in the United States to form the Waterton-Glacier International Peace Park. Waterton shares the glacier-carved Upper Waterton Valley and vast expanse of the Rocky Mountains with its southern neighbor, as well as similar indigenous plants and animals.

5. Chief Mountain International Highway
This scenic highway, traveling through aspen stands and lodgepole pine forests, is the main route between Waterton and Glacier parks. It provides excellent views of the rocky Chief Mountain and the lofty Mt. Cleveland.

6. St. Mary Visitor Center
Located at the eastern entrance to the park, this visitor center offers explanatory exhibits and information on the plants and wildlife found in the area. Campgrounds are available nearby.

A profusion of multicolored wildflowers complements the cool beauty of St. Mary Lake.

7. St. Mary Lake
Ten miles long and up to a mile wide, this magnificent glacier-rimmed lake is a frequently photographed site in Glacier National Park. Photos may be taken from **Wild Goose Island Overlook,** which lies about 10 miles below Logan Pass. The lake's small, rocky Wild Goose Island was named for a pair of geese that nested there for many years.

8. Grinnell Formation
Here a small turnout gives visitors an opportunity to take a close look at this colorful red mudstone formation and to view the more distant Reynolds and Heavy Runner mountains rising splendidly from a forest of Engelmann spruce and lodgepole pine.

9. Garden Wall
Created eons ago by glaciers pressing in on each side, this dramatic knifelike ridge rises majestically alongside the Going-to-the-Sun Road.

10. Logan Pass
Here Going-to-the-Sun Road crosses the Continental Divide. (Water that falls on the west side of the divide flows to the Pacific; water on the east flows toward Hudson Bay or the Gulf of Mexico.) Along the road, the wildflower meadows present a summertime palette of brilliant colors. From the visitor center, a 1½-mile-long elevated boardwalk through the Hanging Gardens takes hikers to an overlook with a breathtaking view of Hidden Lake.

11. Avalanche Campground
Campers should heed the park's warnings concerning bears that wander through this area, and hikers in the backcountry should make noise, such as rattling rocks in a can. The campground and a short interpretive trail, the **Trail-of-the-Cedars,** which borders Avalanche Creek, are in one of the most beautiful parts of the park. Ice melt from Sperry Glacier flows into the creek, whose shade of green depends on the amount of powdered rock in the ice.

Park visitors may sight an occasional mountain goat from Flathead River Drive.

12. Lake McDonald
At 10 miles long, 1½ miles wide, and 440 feet deep, this magnificent lake is the largest in Glacier National Park. Its crystalline water reflects the surrounding mountain peaks and allows viewing of the colorful boulders at the bottom of its basin. The fishing is excellent here for Mackinaw and other lake trout.

Logan Pass marks the spot where Going-to-the-Sun Road crosses the Continental Divide.

A glacier lily adds beauty to the roadside.

13. Going-to-the-Sun Road

An extraordinary feat of engineering, this famous 50-mile highway traverses Glacier National Park. The spectacular drive follows St. Mary Lake on the east and Lake McDonald on the west, passing along the way through forests, wetlands, plains, and mountains. Five miles in from the eastern entrance is a parking turnoff that offers a view of **Triple Divide Peak.**

14. Apgar

The tiny community of Apgar provides both a visitor center and a splendid view of Lake McDonald. A detour off Going-to-the-Sun Road loops through the village. Camping facilities are available nearby.

15. Hungry Horse Dam and Reservoir

At 3,565 feet above sea level, Hungry Horse Dam ranks as one of the world's highest dams. It spans the south fork of the Flathead River, helping to control flooding on the Columbia farther downstream. Visitors may tour the mammoth power plant where, at peak capacity, 80 tons of water per second drive four massive generator turbines. The highway across the top of the dam leads to the 115-mile gravel road that encircles the reservoir, which is part of the **Flathead National Forest.** There are awesome views of the surrounding mountains and access to campgrounds. Swimming, fishing, boating, and waterskiing are permitted in the reservoir.

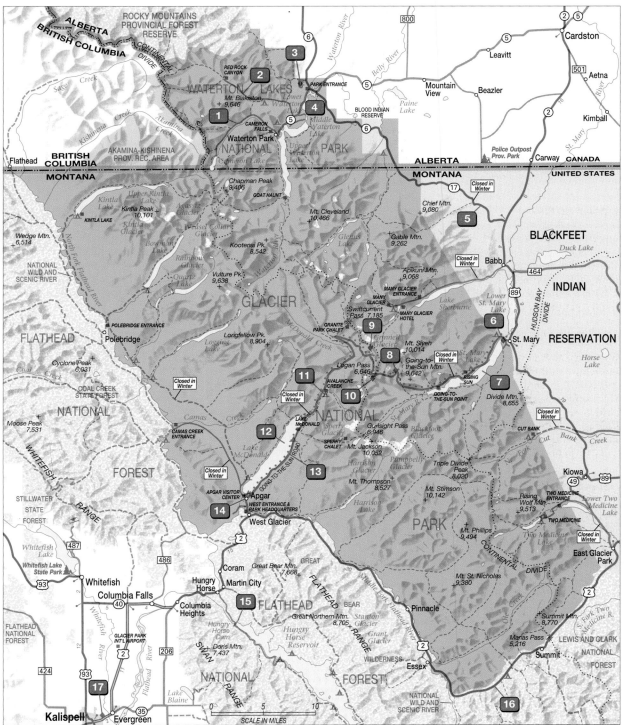

16. Flathead River Drive

Highway 2 follows the Middle Fork of the Flathead River through rugged mountains and coniferous forests, with the wild river rushing below. From some of the overlooks along the way, visitors may glimpse mountain goats traversing the crags.

17. Conrad Mansion

Fourth St. East, Kalispell. Visitors can tour this opulent home, featuring original furnishings, built by town founder Charles Conrad in 1895. *Admission charged.*

Admission charged for international park.

1. Museum of the Plains Indian and the Bob Scriver Museum of Montana Wildlife and Hall of Bronze

Junction U.S. 2 and 89, Browning. One museum pays tribute to the Northern Plains Indians with costume and artifact displays of early tribes, and art and craftwork exhibits of contemporary tribes. The other celebrates both Montana's abundant wildlife and the Old West. *Admission charged at wildlife museum.*

2. Flathead Lake

The largest freshwater lake west of the Mississippi holds great rewards for anglers — cutthroat and Dolly Varden trout and kokanee salmon among them. A road along the east shore wends its way through evergreens and orchards.

3. Ninepipe National Wildlife Refuge

Thousands of migrating ducks and geese stop here in the spring and fall. Both this and the nearby **Pablo National Wildlife Refuge** are superimposed on irrigation-water reservoirs. A county road traverses the Ninepipe Reservoir's dike, which provides the most scenic view of the lake, with the Mission Range forming the picturesque backdrop.

4. National Bison Range

Consisting of native grassland that lies amid valley ranches, this refuge protects a large herd of bison, along with elk, pronghorn antelope, mule deer, bighorn sheep, and mountain goats. Golden eagles and other birds soar overhead. Two self-guiding auto tours of different lengths give a good area orientation.

5. Aerial Fire Depot Smokejumper Center

Many smokejumpers are stationed at this U.S. Forest Service facility. Visitors to the center can see training sites, aircraft, special equipment, and displays that explain their firefighting techniques.

6. Historical Museum at Fort Missoula

Building 322, Fort Missoula. This museum preserves and interprets the history of Missoula County and western Montana, with exhibits including the remains of a late–19th-century fort, a depot, church, and schoolhouse.

7. Grant-Kohrs Ranch National Historic Site

Trapper-turned-cattle-raiser Johnny Grant built this ranch in the 1860's and sold it to Conrad Kohrs in 1866. Although only 1,498 of the original 25,000 acres remain, the fine house, with original furnishings, is open for touring, as well as the bunkhouse and barns. *Admission charged.*

8. Deer Lodge

Chamber of Commerce, 1171 Main St. The **Towe Ford Museum** holds one of the world's largest collections of antique Ford automobiles — about 110 models made between 1903 and 1970. Along with an antique toy museum, it is housed in the **Old Montana Prison,** an imposing structure in use as a prison from 1871 to 1979. *Admission charged.*

9. Butte

Chamber of Commerce, 2950 Harrison Ave. A copper-mining town, Butte retains many buildings from its heyday (about 1880 to 1920) in the commercial uptown district and on the residential west side. Visitors can tour the **Copper King Mansion** and the **World Museum of Mining,** which features a mining-camp replica. The **Neversweat and Washoe Railroad** offers summer locomotive tours of the old mining district. Van tours depart for **Our Lady of the Rockies,** a 90-foot statue atop the east ridge of the Continental Divide. *Fee charged for some activities.*

10. Nevada City and Virginia City

The 1860's are evoked by these two restored frontier mining towns, connected by a narrow-gauge railway line. Among their attractions are Victorian hotels, a music hall, a railroad museum, shops, and sod-roofed miners' cabins. *Admission charged for some attractions.*

11. Lewis and Clark Caverns State Park

A guided tour of the corridors and chambers of the limestone caverns reveals an astounding assortment of stalactites, stalagmites, and other formations of various shapes and colors. Outside, self-guiding trails take hikers through the foothills of the Tobacco Root Mountains. *Admission charged.*

12. Museum of the Rockies

600 West Kagy Blvd., Bozeman. Part of **Montana State University,** this museum preserves much of the history of the region, from dinosaur fossils to Indian craftwork, Western art, photographic portraits, and even a 100-year-old homestead. *Admission charged.*

13. Chief Plenty Coups State Park

The park and a museum pay homage to Chief Plenty Coups, leader of the Crow Indians, who deeded 190 acres of his own land to the federal government "to be enjoyed by everyone without discrimination." *Admission charged.*

14. Elkhorn

Silver, gold, and lead created a boomtown here about the turn of the century, but present-day Elkhorn is nearly a ghost town, with rusting mining equipment and abandoned shafts attesting to former times. From town, visitors can take hiking trails into the beautiful **Deerlodge National Forest.**

15. Helena

Chamber of Commerce, 201 East Lyndale St. Helena's historic district reflects the boom years of the late 19th century, when the surrounding hills yielded gold and other precious minerals. Here many ornate office buildings and mansions harking back to that era still stand. The **Norwest Bank Helena Museum of Gold** contains a collection of gold nuggets from Montana, Alaska, and California.

16. McDonald Pass

A scenic drive among wooded mountains leads to the 6,320-foot-high McDonald Pass, whose summit is part of the Continental Divide. From here, the sweeping view encompasses the Helena Valley and magnificent mountains. This is also the site of **Frontier Town,** a complex built in the 1940's that contains a fort, jail, bank, and other structures. *Admission charged at Frontier Town.*

17. Gates of the Mountains

Cruise boats ply the waters of the Missouri River through this dramatic canyon in Helena National Forest. Mountain goats may be spotted on the limestone cliffs, and bighorn sheep near the river's edge. The cruise includes a stop at the **Meriwether Campground,** where the Lewis party made camp. *Fee charged for cruise.*

18. Helena National Forest

Major attractions within this lush national forest include **Rogers Pass,** which crosses the Continental Divide; the **Continental Divide National Scenic Trail;** and **Deep Creek Canyon,** which offers glimpses of moose, elk, and eagles.

19. Missouri River Recreation Road

This drive follows the Missouri River and Prickly Pear Creek for 33 miles over hills covered with ponderosa pine. Along the way are campgrounds and fishing spots.

20. Ulm Pishkun State Monument

Pishkun is a Blackfoot Indian word meaning "buffalo jump," and indeed herds of bison were once stampeded over this cliff — a primitive hunting technique used by American Indians. Interpretive signs explain both the history of this method and the daily life of prairie dogs, which have a town near the picnic area here. *Donation encouraged.*

21. Freezout Lake Wildlife Management Area

Snow geese, whistling swans, and other migrating waterfowl find refuge on this 12,000-acre preserve, where their population can swell to half a million in spring and fall.

22. C. M. Russell Museum and Studio

400 13th St., Great Falls. The museum houses paintings and other artwork of the Cowboy Artist. Charles Russell's log-cabin studio, built in 1903, still holds his easel, brushes, and Western artifacts that appear in his works. The Russell house is also on the grounds. *Admission charged.*

23. Giant Springs Heritage State Park and Fish Hatchery

True to its name, Giant Springs discharges 134,000 gallons of water per minute into the Missouri River. Visitors can enjoy the springs from a viewing area and see nearby Rainbow Falls from two scenic overlooks. Also in the park are hiking trails, picnic facilities, and a fish hatchery. *Fee charged for some activities.*

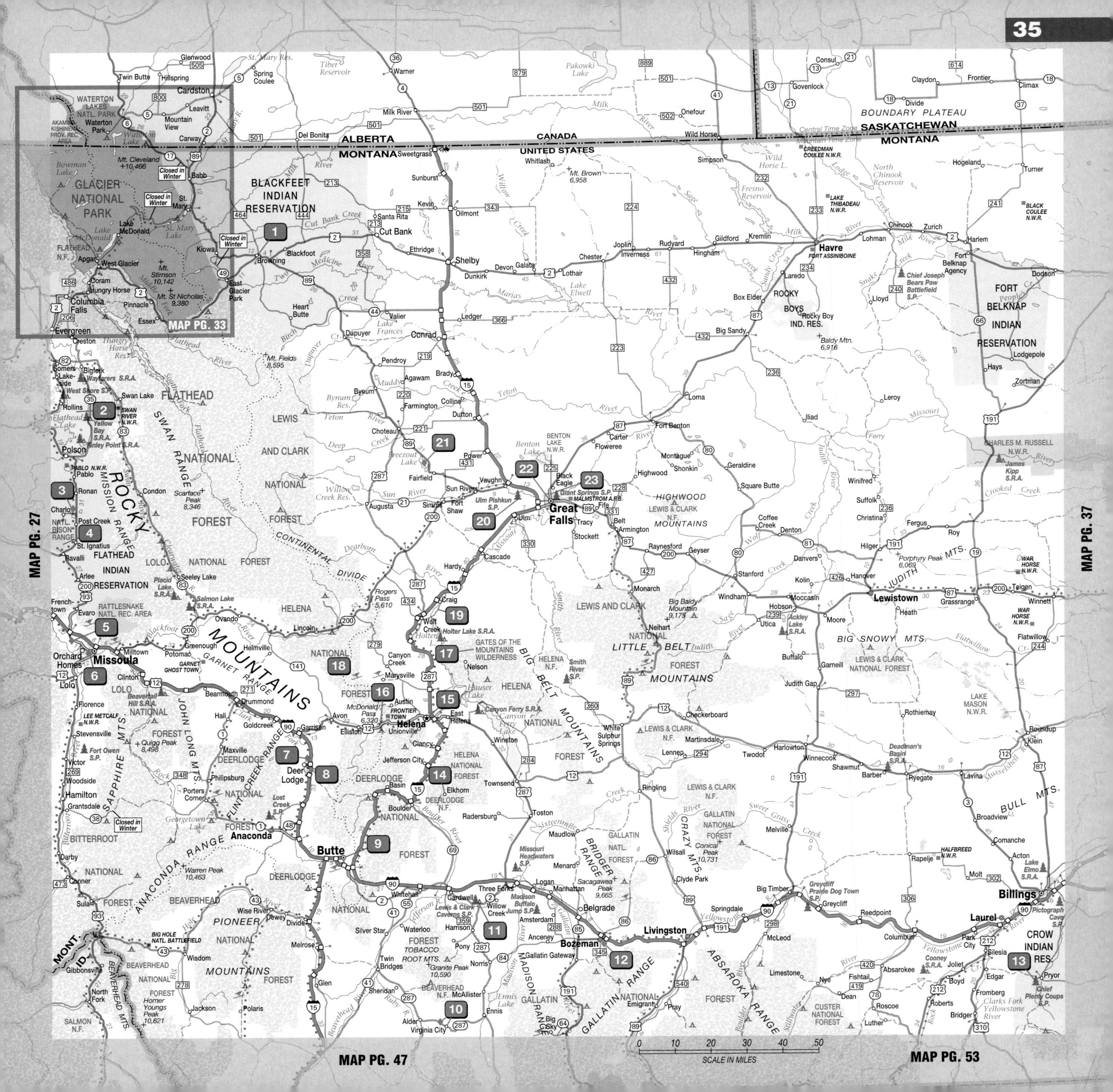

MAP PG. 33

MAP PG. 27

MAP PG. 37

MAP PG. 47

MAP PG. 53

ALBERTA
MONTANA
CANADA
UNITED STATES
SASKATCHEWAN
MONTANA
BOUNDARY PLATEAU
Central Time Zone

WATERTON LAKES NATL. PARK
AKAMINA KISHINENA PROV. REC. AREA
Waterton Park
Mt. Cleveland +10,466
Closed in Winter

GLACIER NATIONAL PARK
Bowman Lake
Lake McDonald
St. Mary Lake
Closed in Winter
St. Mary
Mt. Stimson 10,142
Mt. St. Nicholas 9,380

Twin Butte Hillspring Glenwood St. Mary Res. Tiber Reservoir Pakowki Lake Consul Claydon Frontier Climax
Cardston Leavitt Spring Coulee Warner Milk River Whitlash Simpson Govenlock Divide
Waterton Mountain View Del Bonita Sweetgrass Onefour Wild Horse Creedman Coulee N.W.R. Hogeland Turner
Carway Sunburst Mt. Brown 6,958 Wild Horse L. North Chinook Reservoir

BLACKFEET INDIAN RESERVATION
Browning Blackfoot Kiowa Cut Bank Santa Rita Kevin Oilmont Joplin Rudyard Gildford Kremlin Chinook Zurich Harlem
East Glacier Park Heart Butte Ethridge Shelby Devon Galata Chester Inverness Hingham Havre FORT ASSINIBOINE Lohman Laredo
Dunkirk Lothair Box Elder ROCKY BOYS IND. RES. Lloyd Dodson
Valier Conrad Ledger Loma Chief Joseph Bears Paw Battlefield S.P. Hays Zortman
Dupuyer Pendroy Brady Big Sandy FORT BELKNAP INDIAN RESERVATION Lodgepole

FLATHEAD
Somers Lakeside Bigfork Swan Lake SWAN RIVER N.W.R. Yellow Bay S.R.A. Finley Point S.R.A.
Rollins Polson PABLO N.W.R. Pablo Ronan NATL. BISON RANGE St. Ignatius Ravalli Arlee
FLATHEAD INDIAN RESERVATION
ROCKY MOUNTAINS MISSION RANGE SWAN RANGE
Mt. Fields 8,595
Bynum Res. Choteau Fairfield Power Vaughn Sun River Great Falls
Agawam Farmington Collins Dutton Benton Lake N.W.R. Black Eagle MALMSTROM A.R.B. Fife Highwood
Bynum Simms Fort Shaw Ulm Pishkun S.P. Giant Springs S.P. Square Butte HIGHWOOD MTS.
Augusta Ulm Tracy Stockett Belt Armington Geraldine Shonkin Montague Coffee Creek

LEWIS AND CLARK NATIONAL FOREST
CONTINENTAL DIVIDE
HELENA Frenchtown Evaro RATTLESNAKE NATL. REC. AREA Ovando Lincoln Rogers Pass 5,610
Missoula Orchard Homes Lolo Clinton GARNET RANGE GARNET GHOST TOWN Helmville Canyon Creek Marysville Nelson
Florence Stevensville LEE METCALF N.W.R. Bearmouth Drummond Avon Austin Helena East Helena
Victor Fort Owen S.P. Hall Goldcreek Garrison Elliston Unionville Winston Canyon Ferry S.R.A.
Hamilton Quigg Peak 8,498 Maxville Philipsburg Deer Lodge Clancy Jefferson City Townsend White Sulphur Springs
Grantsdale DEERLODGE Porters Corner Anaconda Boulder Radersburg Ringling Martinsdale Harlowton
BITTERROOT FLINT CREEK RANGE Warren Peak 10,463 Butte Elkhorn Toston Maudlow Twodot Winnecook Shawmut
ANACONDA RANGE Lost Creek S.P. Boulder Melville Barber Ryegate Lavina

BEAVERHEAD NATIONAL FOREST PIONEER MOUNTAINS TOBACCO ROOT MTS. Granite Peak 10,590
Conner Sula Darby Wise River Dewey Divide Silver Star Harrison Pony Norris GALLATIN RANGE BRIDGER RANGE
BIG HOLE NATL. BATTLEFIELD Wisdom Melrose Twin Bridges Lewis & Clark Caverns S.P. Willow Creek Three Forks Logan Manhattan Belgrade Bozeman Livingston
Gibbonsville North Fork Jackson Polaris Glen Sheridan Alder Ennis Gallatin Gateway Amsterdam Anceney Springdale Big Timber Greycliff
Homer Youngs Peak 10,621 Wisdom Virginia City McAllister Ennis Lake Sacagawea Peak 9,665 Conical Peak 10,731 Reedpoint Columbus Laurel Billings

CROW INDIAN RES. Pryor Edgar Fromberg Bridger Roberts Luther Nye Fishtail Absarokee Joliet Silesia Pictograph Cave S.P. Chief Plenty Coups S.P.
ABSAROKA RANGE CUSTER NATIONAL FOREST Emigrant Pray McLeod Limestone Dean Roscoe Boyd Edgar

CHARLES M. RUSSELL N.W.R. James Kipp S.R.A. Lewistown Grassrange Winnett Teigen WAR HORSE N.W.R. BIG SNOWY MTS. Flatwillow LAKE MASON N.W.R. Roundup Klein
Windham Stanford Moccasin Hobson Utica Ackley Lake S.R.A. Moore Heath Buffalo Garneill Judith Gap Checkerboard Martinsdale Lennep Two Dot

SCALE IN MILES
0 10 20 30 40 50

1. Fort Peck Dam and Fossil Museum

Nearly 4 miles long and 250 feet high, Fort Peck Dam is one of the biggest earth-fill dams in the world. More than 400 fossils excavated during construction are on display at the museum in the dam's powerhouse, including the horn core of a 63-million-year-old dinosaur.

2. Billings

Chamber of Commerce, 815 South 27th St. The fanciful **Oscar's Dreamland** has acres of restored tractors, steam engines, threshing machines, 19th-century hearses, and a 1906 Best steam truck that could pull 60 tons. Visitors can ride on a restored railroad or stroll down a main street straight out of pioneer days. At the **Peter Yegen, Jr., Yellowstone County Museum,** an 1893 log cabin houses an intriguing collection of military uniforms, fossils, peace pipes, and branding irons — all serving to illustrate local history from prehistoric times to the pioneer era. In **Pictograph Cave State Historic Park,** nearly 30,000 weapons, bones, and projectiles left behind by ancient hunter tribes have been unearthed in three caves. Colored pictures of animals, weapons, tepees, and warriors cover the sandstone walls of the largest cave. *Admission charged for some attractions.*

3. Pompeys Pillar

When William Clark passed this imposing sandstone butte during his expedition, he carved his name and the date — July 25, 1806 — alongside pre-existing Indian carvings of animals. For years a landmark for westward travelers, today the butte is a national historic landmark with interpretive markers and a walking trail. *Admission charged.*

4. Little Bighorn Battlefield National Monument

White marble markers dot the hills above the Little Bighorn River where Custer and his men died in their doomed encounter with Chief Crazy Horse and the Sioux and Cheyenne nations in 1876. Battle sites are connected by an excellent auto route that makes a loop around the battlefield. At the visitor center dioramas and a scale model of the battle show what is known of the still-debated events. *Admission charged.*

5. East and West Rosebud Recreation Areas

The fishing is excellent here, and so are the views of the bluffs on the northern banks of the Yellowstone River at both of these recreation areas. East Rosebud also offers camping facilities, and West Rosebud has a playground and picnic area.

6. Range Riders Museum and Memorial Hall

Main St., Miles City. This outstanding museum of Old West memorabilia convincingly re-creates the town's 1880's Main Street, with a trading post, hotel, jail, and shops. A fine collection that includes buggies, fossils, Indian artifacts, guns, and photographs of pioneers shows how the plains were settled. *Admission charged.*

7. Frontier Gateway Museum

Belle Prairie Rd., Glendive. This appealingly eclectic museum presents local history with a re-created street that includes a general store and a drugstore. Fossils, saddlebags, and war bonnets share space with replicas of 16th- and 17th-century European suits of armor. Outside, a firehouse and a 1938 fire engine, a log cabin, and one-room schoolhouse round out the exhibit. *Admission charged.*

8. Makoshika State Park

The Sioux word *makoshika* means "hell cooled over," an apt description of this expanse of twisted badlands and high prairie. A 9-mile self-guiding drive leads to dramatic views of gulches, hogback ridges, spires, steep-walled valleys, and table-topped buttes carved by the relentless elements. Turkey vultures and hawks circle the sky, and mule deer find shelter in stands of juniper and pine. *Admission charged.*

9. Medicine Rocks State Park

From a prehistoric riverbed, strange sandstone formations carved by rain and wind rise up to 80 feet above the prairie. Mesas, arches, columns, and caves here have yielded mammal fossils 50 million years old and signs of human life dating back more than 11,000 years. The park offers campgrounds, a 6-mile guided nature trail, and a steep path down to the badlands. *Admission charged.*

10. Cave Hills

Weirdly eroded badlands meet the magnificent wooded Black Hills to the south in this remote section of **Custer National Forest.** A somewhat bumpy drive is amply rewarded by the rugged beauty of these hills, dotted with the small caves that give the area its name. *Admission charged.*

11. Reva Gap

The scenic red-rock cliffs of Reva Gap and Slim Buttes, which stretch for 30 miles into the horizon, were the site of a famous Indian battle in 1876.

12. White Butte

Jutting abruptly from the flat prairie, White Butte is the highest point in North Dakota, rising to an altitude of more than 3,500 feet above sea level.

13. Little Missouri National Grassland

Red bricklike scoriae cover a burning vein of lignite 30 feet underground that has belched smoke and steam for more than a century. Junipers near the burning coal vein grow tall and straight, their normally shrubby shape distorted by the fumes. *Admission charged.*

14. Sully Creek State Recreation Area

Dramatic landforms created by runoff from the rising Rocky Mountains some 60 million years ago have been sculpted by rain and wind to reveal beautiful multicolored layers in this 80-acre park. There are camping and picnicking areas among the cottonwoods and sagebrush, and facilities for hiking, fishing, and horseback riding. *Admission charged.*

15. Château de Mores State Historic Site

Old Hwy. 10, Medora. An elegant 26-room château is all that remains of the dream of the marquis de Mores, a Parisian who in 1883 built a short-lived cattle empire and the boomtown of Medora. The home's well-preserved original furnishings, from buffalo-skin robes and bear traps to French watercolors, illustrate the marquis's aristocratic way of life in the Wild West. *Admission charged.*

16. Edward A. Patterson Recreation Area

Man-made Patterson Lake is an inviting spot for swimming or fishing, with almost 1,200 acres of water banked by graceful reeds. Visitors can also enjoy the area's nature trails, playgrounds, and camping facilities. *Admission charged.*

17. Joachim Regional Museum

1226 Sims St., Dickinson. Colorful exhibits of folk costumes, photographs, tools, and household items recall the various ethnic groups that settled this region, and Indian artifacts illustrate the native way of life these pioneers encountered.

18. Killdeer Mountains

The 51-mile "Lost Bridge Road" winds to the top of the Killdeer Mountains, with observation points along the way for spectacular views of the badlands, a look at Lake Sakakawea with its towering dam, and, from the peak, a sweeping panorama of the vast prairie below.

19. Theodore Roosevelt National Park

Scenic drives through this spectacular park, which is divided into three separate units, feature multicolored badlands, immense valleys and tableland, riverbanks lined with cottonwoods, and sagebrush-covered meadows. Trails offer glimpses of the park's abundant wildlife, including bison, coyotes, prairie dogs, and golden eagles. A cabin from one of Theodore Roosevelt's two ranches in the area is now located next to the Medora visitor center, which interprets the park's geology and natural history. *Admission charged.*

20. Fort Union Trading Post

Rte. 1804, west of Williston. A thriving trade in beaver pelts and buffalo hides made Fort Union one of the biggest and most luxurious of the Western outposts in the mid-1800's. Today excavated remains and reconstructed buildings let visitors sense its spirited past, guided by staff members dressed as trappers and traders.

21. Writing Rock State Historic Site

Mystery shrouds the origin of the circles, lines, and dots that are carved in this 5-foot-high granite boulder, which Plains Indians believed could foretell the future. Today the rock, and another smaller one, remain a cryptic testament to the distant past. *Admission charged.*

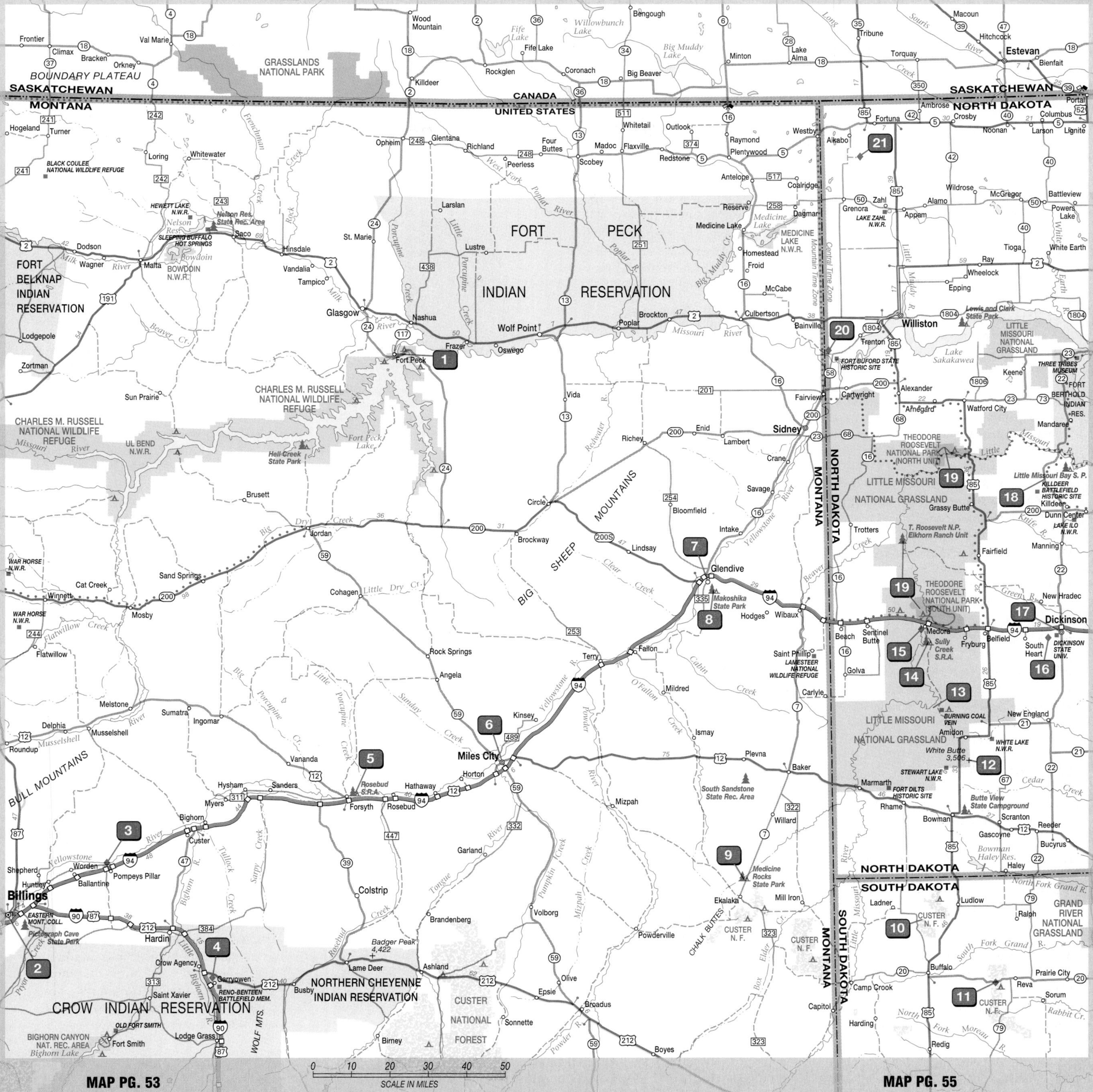

MAP PG. 35
MAP PG. 39
MAP PG. 53
MAP PG. 55

SASKATCHEWAN
MONTANA
BOUNDARY PLATEAU
CANADA
UNITED STATES
SASKATCHEWAN
NORTH DAKOTA

Frontier
Climax
Bracken
Orkney
Val Marie
Wood Mountain
Fife Lake
Willowbunch Lake
Bengough
Macoun
Hitchcock
Estevan
Bienfait
Portal

GRASSLANDS NATIONAL PARK
Big Muddy Lake
Tribune
Torquay
Ambrose
Fortuna
Crosby
Columbus
Lignite
Larson
Noonan

Hogeland
Turner
BLACK COULEE NATIONAL WILDLIFE REFUGE
Whitewater
Loring
Opheim
Glentana
Richland
Four Buttes
Madoc
Flaxville
Scobey
Redstone
Raymond
Plentywood
Westby
Alkabo
Wildrose
McGregor
Battleview
Powers Lake

FORT BELKNAP INDIAN RESERVATION
Lodgepole
Zortman
Dodson
Wagner
Malta
Saco
Hinsdale
St. Marie
Larslan
Lustre
Reserve
Antelope
Coalridge
Medicine Lake
LAKE ZAHL N.W.R.
Grenora
Zahl
Alamo
Appam
Tioga
Ray
White Earth

FORT PECK INDIAN RESERVATION
Peerless
Homestead
Froid
McCabe
MEDICINE LAKE N.W.R.
Dagmar
Wheelock
Epping
Williston
LEWIS AND CLARK STATE PARK

Glasgow
Nashua
Wolf Point
Brockton
Poplar
Culbertson
Bainville
Trenton
FORT BUFORD STATE HISTORIC SITE
Lake Sakakawea
Keene
THREE TRIBES MUSEUM
FORT BERTHOLD INDIAN RES.

CHARLES M. RUSSELL NATIONAL WILDLIFE REFUGE
Frazer
Fort Peck
Oswego
Fort Peck Lake
Vida
Fairview
Cartwright
Alexander
Arnegard
Watford City
Mandaree

Sun Prairie
Brusett
Hell Creek State Park
Richey
Enid
Lambert
Sidney
Crane
Savage
THEODORE ROOSEVELT NATIONAL PARK (NORTH UNIT)
LITTLE MISSOURI NATIONAL GRASSLAND
Little Missouri Bay S.P.
KILLDEER BATTLEFIELD HISTORIC SITE
Killdeer
Dunn Center
LAKE ILO N.W.R.

Cat Creek
Sand Springs
Circle
Bloomfield
Intake
Glendive
Trotters
Fairfield
Manning
New Hradec

Winnett
Mosby
Cohagen
Jordan
Brockway
Lindsay
Makoshika State Park
Hodges
Wibaux
Beach
Sentinel Butte
Medora
Belfield
Dickinson
DICKINSON STATE UNIV.

WAR HORSE N.W.R.
Flatwillow
Melstone
Delphia
Flatwillow
Sumatra
Ingomar
Rock Springs
Terry
Fallon
Mildred
SAINT PHILIP
LAMESTEER NATIONAL WILDLIFE REFUGE
Golva
Fryburg
Sully Creek S.R.A.
South Heart

Roundup
Musselshell
BULL MOUNTAINS
Vananda
Angela
Ismay
Carlyle
BURNING COAL VEIN
Amidon
New England
WHITE LAKE N.W.R.
LITTLE MISSOURI NATIONAL GRASSLAND
White Butte 3,506

Shepherd
Huntley
Billings
EASTERN MONT. COLL.
Pictograph Cave State Park
Worden
Ballantine
Pompeys Pillar
Hysham
Sanders
Myers
Bighorn
Custer
Forsyth
Rosebud
Miles City
Kinsey
Horton
Hathaway
Baker
Plevna
Mizpah
STEWART LAKE N.W.R.
Marmarth
FORT DILTS HISTORIC SITE
Rhame
Butte View State Campground
Scranton
Reeder
Bucyrus
Gascoyne
Bowman

Garland
Colstrip
Garryowen
Lame Deer
Brandenberg
Powderville
Willard
Mill Iron
Ekalaka
Medicine Rocks State Park
CUSTER N.F.
Bowman Haley Res.
Haley

CROW INDIAN RESERVATION
Saint Xavier
OLD FORT SMITH
Fort Smith
BIGHORN CANYON NAT. REC. AREA
Bighorn Lake
Lodge Grass
WOLF MTS.
Crow Agency
RENO-BENTEEN BATTLEFIELD MEM.
Busby
NORTHERN CHEYENNE INDIAN RESERVATION
Birney
Ashland
Epsie
Olive
Sonnette
Broadus
Boyes
CUSTER NATIONAL FOREST
CUSTER N.F.
NORTH DAKOTA
SOUTH DAKOTA
Ladner
Ludlow
Ralph
GRAND RIVER NATIONAL GRASSLAND
Buffalo
Camp Crook
Harding
Capitol
Reva
Sorum
Prairie City
Redig
CUSTER N.F.

Missouri River
Milk River
Yellowstone River
Powder River
Tongue River
Musselshell River
Big Dry Creek
Little Missouri River
Knife R.
Cedar Creek
Grand R.

CENTRAL TIME ZONE
MOUNTAIN TIME ZONE

SCALE IN MILES
0 10 20 30 40 50

1. Lake Ilo National Wildlife Refuge

Water birds flock to Lake Ilo, an oasis on the semiarid plains. A park provides ducks, hawks, and eagles for visitors to view, and recreational activities such as fishing, boating, hiking, and picnicking.

2. Little Missouri Bay State Park

Contrary to its diminutive name, this park consists of a vast badlands wilderness. Trails offer dramatic vistas of the eroded landscape and the Little Missouri River. This is great country for horseback riding, and guided horseback tours are available. The park also has a primitive campground and a horse corral.

3. Fort Berthold Indian Reservation

The **Three Affiliated Tribes Museum** tells the story of the occupants of this reservation — the Mandan, Hidatsa, and Arikara tribes. **Four Bears Recreation Area,** whose entrance is next to the museum, features Lake Sakakawea's **Four Bears Memorial Bridge.**

4. Makoti Threshers Museum

Main St., Makoti. This museum, housed in six buildings, displays antique threshers, tractors, and engines, including a 110-horsepower, 14-foot-high steam traction engine. During the October threshing show, vintage tractors and trucks are paraded down Main Street. *Admission charged at show.*

5. Fort Stevenson State Park

Located on a peninsula in Lake Sakakawea, this park provides a play-land for both adults and children, with camping, fishing, boating, winter sports, hiking, and even a prairie-dog town. The former fort now rests below the man-made lake. *Admission charged.*

6. Garrison Dam and Garrison Dam National Fish Hatchery

Highway 200 gives an impressive overview of the gigantic Garrison Dam, which not only generates electricity but also controls Missouri River flooding. Tours are offered in the summer. At the Garrison Dam National Fish Hatchery, the visitor center conducts a guided tour in which visitors may observe the breeding of trout, salmon, walleyes, and northern pike.

7. Knife River Indian Villages

Centuries ago, the Hidatsa and Mandan Indians began farming this prairie land next to the Missouri River. Today visitors can take a guided tour to three village sites. Bison bone fragments, pottery remnants, and trade beads can be seen. In the summer, demonstrations of tribal activities are presented.

8. Cross Ranch Nature Preserve

This park protects native prairie and floodplain forest, as well as over 100 archeological sites, dating back as far as 6000 B.C. Mule deer, songbirds, bison, and other wildlife make their home on these 6,000 acres.

9. Bismarck

Convention and Visitors Bureau, 523 North Fourth St. **Camp Hancock State Historic Site** marks the location of a former military camp for crews building the Northern Pacific Railroad. A log structure that was once headquarters for the camp is now an interpretive museum. The **North Dakota Heritage Center** has excellent exhibits that chronicle the history of the state. **Sertoma Riverside Park,** on the banks of the Missouri River, offers tennis courts, playgrounds, hiking trails, and a zoo that shelters such animals as pygmy goats, African porcupines, and wallabies. *Admission charged for zoo.*

10. Fort Abraham Lincoln State Park

This fort was Custer's final post before the fateful battle at the Little Bighorn. The Custer House, main commissary, and central barracks have been reconstructed and may be toured, as can a museum and a Mandan village that preceded the fort. *Admission charged.*

11. Petrified Wood Park

500 Main Ave., Lemmon. Petrified materials take a number of intriguing forms in this park: a castle made partially of stone tree trunks, and a circular museum built of petrified logs and grass. Various fossils of animal and marine life can also be seen.

12. Klein Museum

1820 West Grand Crossing, Mobridge. This museum commemorates the days of homesteading. A life-size image of a trapper stands in his shack, a wood-burning stove nearby. In addition to other rooms, such as a dentist's and a doctor's offices, the museum features vintage vehicles and machinery and both pioneer and Indian artifacts. *Admission charged.*

A Mandan Indian girl is portrayed in "Mint, A Pretty Girl," by George Catlin.

13. Fort Sisseton State Park

On shaded, grassy grounds stand the remains of the 19th-century fort — 15 brick-and-fieldstone buildings, including the hospital, bakery, library-schoolhouse, and stable. The North Barracks houses the visitor center. The park has picnic grounds and primitive camping facilities. *Admission charged.*

14. Clausen Springs Recreation Complex

While known for its excellent fishing, this recreation area also offers visitors seasonal boating, camping, and hiking.

15. Jamestown

Promotion and Tourism Center, 212 Third Ave. NE. Near the Jamestown Dam **Lakeside Marina,** cliffs and small coves line the shores of the lake. Picnickers can choose between an island opposite the marina or a stand of ash trees and Russian olives. Five miles from the marina, **Frontier Village** boasts a firehouse, sheriff's office, and other reconstructed buildings of the Old West. Buffalo roam the surrounding fields.

16. Arrowwood National Wildlife Refuge

Marshes, ravines, and grasslands act as a haven for birds and other wildlife. White pelicans, Canada geese, and many duck species congregate in the James River Valley. White-tailed deer, minks, and prairie dogs live along the refuge's auto route. Activities enjoyed here include canoeing, ice fishing, cross-country skiing, berry picking, and picnicking.

17. Fort Totten State Historical Site

Arranged around a parade field, the 16 original buildings of this well-preserved fort include the commanding officer's house and the soldiers' quarters. Nearby, self-guided auto and walking tours in **Sullys Hill National Game Preserve** let the visitor see buffalo, elk, deer, prairie dogs, wild turkeys, and waterfowl. Sullys Hill boasts two scenic overlooks.

18. Grand Forks

Convention and Visitors Bureau, 202 North Third St. The **Grand Forks County Historical Society** includes a museum, a furnished log cabin, and a restored post office and schoolhouse. Grand Forks lies on the Red River, where the **Dakota Queen Riverboat** offers a variety of cruises. *Admission charged.*

19. Pembina State Historic Site

Off U.S. 29, Pembina. The Pembina State Museum has exhibits on both Ft. Pembina, which was North Dakota's first white settlement, and the military Ft. Daer. Also on the grounds are a park and picnic area.

20. International Peace Garden

This wooded garden, ensconced in the Turtle Mountains' foothills, celebrates the peaceable coexistence of the United States and Canada. Scenic drives wind through both countries, with a floral clock marking the beginning of the U.S. route. Reflecting pools and fountains add to the elegance of the formal gardens at the nations' common border. *Admission charged.*

21. Geographical Center Pioneer Village Museum

Rte. 2 East, Rugby. This site, the geographical center of North America, has a pioneer museum displaying many frontier artifacts. Pioneer Village features authentic frontier homes, offices, stores, and other structures. *Admission charged.*

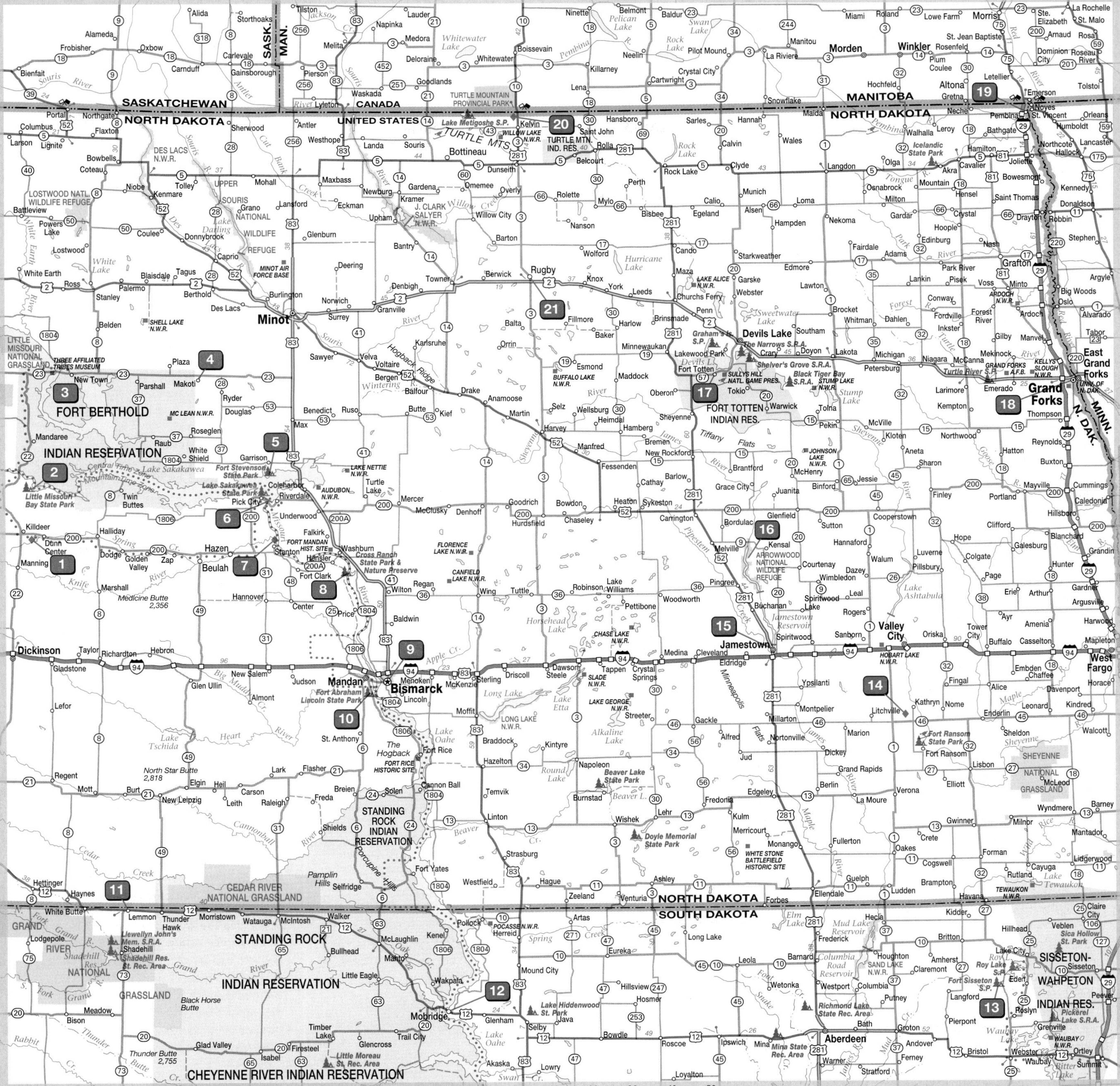

SASKATCHEWAN
MANITOBA
NORTH DAKOTA
SOUTH DAKOTA
CANADA
UNITED STATES

MAP PG. 37
MAP PG. 147
MAP PG. 55
MAP PG. 155

TURTLE MTS.
TURTLE MOUNTAIN PROVINCIAL PARK
TURTLE MTN. IND. RES.

DES LACS N.W.R.
LOSTWOOD NATL. WILDLIFE REFUGE
UPPER SOURIS NATIONAL WILDLIFE REFUGE
J. CLARK SALYER N.W.R.
MINOT AIR FORCE BASE
LITTLE MISSOURI NATIONAL GRASSLAND
THREE AFFILIATED TRIBES MUSEUM
SHELL LAKE N.W.R.
FORT BERTHOLD INDIAN RESERVATION
MC LEAN N.W.R.
LAKE NETTIE N.W.R.
FORT STEVENSON STATE PARK
Lake Sakakawea
Lake Sakakawea State Park
AUDUBON N.W.R.
TURTLE LAKE
Little Missouri Bay State Park
Central Flyway Mountain Time Zone

LAKE ALICE N.W.R.
Devils Lake
Graham's Is. S.P.
The Narrows S.R.A.
Shelver's Grove S.R.A.
Black Tiger Bay S.R.A.
SULLYS HILL NATL. GAME PRES.
STUMP LAKE N.W.R.
BUFFALO LAKE N.W.R.
FORT TOTTEN INDIAN RES.
Sweetwater Lake
Hurricane Lake
JOHNSON LAKE N.W.R.
GRAND FORKS A.F.B.
KELLYS SLOUGH N.W.R.
TURTLE RIVER S.P.
ARDOCH N.W.R.
ICELANDIC STATE PARK

FORT MANDAN HIST. SITE
CROSS RANCH STATE PARK & NATURE PRESERVE
FLORENCE LAKE N.W.R.
CANFIELD LAKE N.W.R.
FORT CLARK
ARROWWOOD NATIONAL WILDLIFE REFUGE
Jamestown Reservoir
Lake Ashtabula
HOBART LAKE N.W.R.
Fort Ransom State Park
SHEYENNE NATIONAL GRASSLAND
McLeod

FORT ABRAHAM LINCOLN STATE PARK
The Hogback
FORT RICE HISTORIC SITE
Lake Oahe
Lake Tschida
North Star Butte 2,818
Medicine Butte 2,356
SLADE N.W.R.
LAKE GEORGE N.W.R.
LONG LAKE N.W.R.
Long Lake
Lake Etta
Alkaline Lake
Horsehead Lake
CHASE LAKE N.W.R.
Lake Williams
Beaver Lake State Park
Doyle Memorial State Park
WHITE STONE BATTLEFIELD HISTORIC SITE

STANDING ROCK INDIAN RESERVATION
CEDAR RIVER NATIONAL GRASSLAND
Pamplin Hills
Porcupine Hills
GRAND RIVER NATIONAL GRASSLAND
Llewellyn John's Mem. S.R.A.
Shadehill Res.
Shadehill Res. St. Rec. Area
Black Horse Butte
North Star Butte 2,755
Thunder Butte 2,755
Little Moreau St. Rec. Area
CHEYENNE RIVER INDIAN RESERVATION

Lake Hiddenwood St. Park
Richmond Lake State Rec. Area
Mina State Rec. Area
SAND LAKE N.W.R.
MUD LAKE N.W.R.
Columbia Road Reservoir
Roy Lake S.P.
Fort Sisseton S.P.
Sica Hollow St. Park
SISSETON-WAHPETON INDIAN RES.
Pickerel Lake S.R.A.
Waubay N.W.R.
Bitter Lake

0 10 20 30 40 50
SCALE IN MILES

1. Depoe Bay

From an arched bridge, visitors can watch the fishing boats enter and leave the picturesque harbor. Whales also appear most of the year. Local restaurants feature tasty chowders.

2. Oregon Coast Aquarium

2820 SE Ferry Slip Rd., Newport. The facility ingeniously traces the progress of a raindrop from the Coast Range forests upland through waterways and estuaries and out into the Pacific Ocean. Both indoor and outdoor exhibits focus on marine life found along the Oregon coast. Authentically replicated habitats — tidal pools, beaches, coastal caves — shelter denizens such as sea otters, seals, and a giant octopus. *Admission charged.*

3. Horner Museum

26th and Washington Sts., Corvallis. Located in Gill Coliseum on the **Oregon State University** campus, the Horner Museum displays a splendid collection of Northwest history, natural science, and cross-cultural exhibits.

4. Linn County Historical Museum and Moyer House

101 Park Ave., Brownsville. The museum, housed in a turn-of-the-century depot with six railroad cars and a caboose, has a collection of railroad memorabilia. Local history is recalled by a prairie schooner that brought settlers to Brownsville and replicas of a 19th-century barbershop, millinery salon, general store, and bank. The nearby **Moyer House,** built in 1881, can be toured on request.

5. Sea Lion Caves

Hundreds of sea lions make their year-round abode here. An elevator descends 208 feet to an observation window that looks out on the area, which also attracts pigeon guillemots in the spring and summer. The visitor center is a favorite spot of visitors hoping to see whales. *Admission charged.*

6. Shore Acres State Park

This park features formal gardens in an area overlooking the shoreline, which can be observed from a glass-enclosed shelter that shields visitors from the spray of the surf. Nearby attractions include **Sunset Bay State Park,** which provides water sports and campsites on a sheltered bay, and **Cape Arago State Park,** a jagged headland surrounded by coves. *Admission charged at Shore Acres.*

7. World Wildlife Safari

Safari Rd., Winston. Animals and birds roam freely on this 600-acre preserve. Visitors can drive through both the Asian and African sections to see such magnificent creatures as cheetahs, Bengal tigers, yaks, emus, hippos, antelopes, lions, zebras, and rhinos. The Safari Village caters to children, with educational programs, a petting zoo, and elephant rides. *Admission charged.*

8. Port Orford

In season, the waters of this commercial fishing village teem with salmon and steelhead trout. Vendors sell fresh fish near the harbor.

9. Gold Beach

This is the starting point for boat trips up the **Rogue River.** Jet-boat trips journey about 35 miles to **Agness** or 52 miles through white-water rapids. Anglers will find plentiful steelhead trout and both chinook and coho salmon in the river.

10. Samuel H. Boardman State Park

This park is actually a conjunction of a series of parks along the coast. **Lone Ranch** has a picnic site on grassy hills with a view of the offshore Twin Rocks. The trails at **Cape Ferrelo** and **House Rock points** lead to spectacular ocean vistas. At **Whaleshead Cove,** picnic areas lie near the shore and among groves of gnarled trees. A trail at **Natural Bridge Cove** leads to a rock arch created by the pounding surf.

11. Redwood National Park

This park preserves 39,000 acres of ancient coast redwood forest, found only along California's northern coast. These magnificent trees have bare trunks for about their first 100 feet, so that the feathery foliage lets in splinters of light from high above. Alongside the forests, ocean waves pound against the wild, rocky beaches. Harbor seals and, in late fall and spring, gray whales are sometimes seen.

12. Oregon Caves National Monument

Marble formations have developed within the labyrinthine cavern, and they are subtly lit for tours. The cave is in the middle of a large, old-growth forest laced with hiking trails. *Fee charged for tour.*

13. Josephine County Kerbyville Museum

24195 Redwood Hwy., Kerby. In the mid-1800's, towns like Kerbyville (now Kerby) grew quickly after gold was discovered. This museum evokes that time with heirlooms and artifacts — quilts, clothing, farm equipment — and restored buildings such as a one-room schoolhouse and a Victorian home.

14. Hellgate Canyon and Indian Mary Park

These contrasting sites are located on the Rogue River. The sheer cliffs of the canyon provide only a narrow passageway for the river and its white-water rafters. At the park the river becomes wide and calm — excellent for swimmers and anglers. Here picnic grounds and campsites nestle among pines, firs, and exotic plants.

15. Jacksonville National Historic Landmark

During Jacksonville's gold-induced heyday in the latter part of the 19th century, the town's residents built many wonderful buildings that are now landmarked. Among the refurbished structures are a hotel, bank, saloon, railroad depot, dry-goods store, and courthouse, which today is a museum with fine old photographs and historical displays. A music festival draws 40,000 people here every summer.

16. Lithia Park

Set in a canyon at the foot of Mt. Ashland, the park includes a Japanese garden, a formal rose garden, duck ponds, various kinds of trees and shrubs, and naturally carbonated water available from a drinking fountain. The town of **Ashland** has gained renown for hosting the annual Oregon Shakespeare Festival.

17. Siskiyou County Museum

910 South Main St., Yreka. Housed in a reconstruction of an 1854 ranch hotel, the museum displays begin chronologically with prehistoric fossils and move on to Indian artifacts and pioneer mementos — tools, firearms, and horse-drawn vehicles, as well as replicas of stores from the era.

18. Lava Beds National Monument

Volcanic activity created this strange landscape of lava rocks and caves. Cave Loop Road, beginning at the visitor center, provides access to many of the caves, which are filled with dripstones and iciclelike formations of lava. There is excellent bird watching in the **Tule Lake National Wildlife Refuge,** where falcons and bald eagles congregate on the cliffs. *Admission charged.*

19. Crater Lake National Park

Surrounded by steep mountain slopes softened by evergreen trees, Crater Lake startles the eye with its remarkable blue color. The deepest lake in the nation, it fills the caldera of an extinct volcano. This beautiful park offers skiing, fishing, camping, and hiking. *Admission charged.*

20. Diamond Lake

Covering an area of 3,000 acres, this high-country, crystal-clear lake draws many campers as well as boating and fishing enthusiasts. Some of the hiking and horseback-riding trails have splendid views of the Cascade Range.

21. Lava Butte Viewpoint and Lava River Cave

Several major Cascade peaks can be viewed from the top of Lava Butte, a small cinder cone. An interpretive trail leads around the butte's crater. Lava River Cave, formed by a volcanic eruption, is more than a mile long. Visitors can view its walls glazed with lava. *Admission charged.*

22. Century Drive

This 100-mile route travels past mountain meadows, lustrous lakes, tumbling streams, snow-topped peaks, and lovely pine woodlands. Such wildlife as mule deer and golden eagles can often be seen.

23. The High Desert Museum

59800 South Highway 97, Bend. This museum celebrates the natural and cultural history of the region with indoor and outdoor exhibits. Twenty acres of nature trails lead through desert shrub and ponderosa pine to a weather station, a birds-of-prey demonstration, and an otter pond. *Admission charged.*

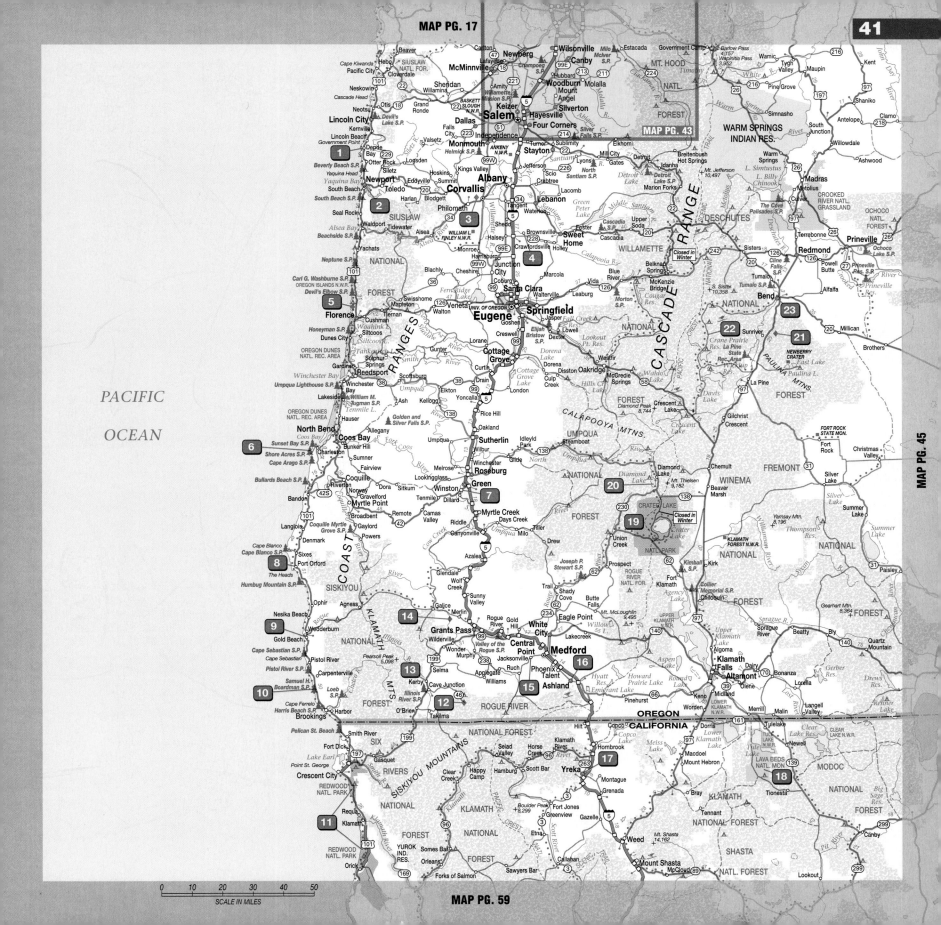

1. Tualatin River Valley

With its temperate climate and fertile soil, the Tualatin River Valley is the base of Oregon's vineyards and wineries, which offer tours and tastings.

2. Willamette River Valley

Lying between the Coast Range and the rugged Cascades, this wide valley of rolling farmland and timberland is noted for its bountiful crops of raspberries, blackberries, and loganberries. Among several area parks, **Champoeg State Park** is especially popular for fishing and bicycling. *Admission charged at park.*

3. Salem

Convention and Visitors Bureau, 1313 Mill St. SE. The state capital's downtown area is dominated by the handsome white-marble **Capitol,** crowned with a golden statue of a pioneer. Several buildings dating from the mid-1800's, including a working woolen mill museum, can be seen in **Mission Mill Village.** The village is near the campus of **Willamette University,** the oldest university west of the Mississippi. Not far from town, the **Enchanted Forest** theme park is stocked with storybook characters, a gingerbread house, and children's rides. *Admission charged for some attractions.*

4. Old Aurora Colony Museum

Liberty and Second Sts., Aurora. The museum is a treasure trove of clothing, furniture, tools, and photographs documenting the short-lived Aurora Colony, a communal religious society founded by German settlers in 1856. *Admission charged.*

5. Willamette Falls

Fishermen still catch salmon at the base of this 41-foot-high falls, which has been harnessed for hydroelectric power and made navigable by a series of locks. The falls can best be seen from an observation area in **Oregon City.**

6. McLoughlin House

713 Center St., Oregon City. This beautifully refurbished mansion, built by a Hudson's Bay fur baron, is now a national historic site. *Admission charged.*

7. Portland

Visitors Assn., 26 SW Salmon St. The indisputable highlight of the city is **Washington Park,** which features the International Rose Test Garden, with more than 400 varieties of roses; the Hoyt Arboretum; the Japanese Gardens; and an excellent zoo. The **Oregon Museum of Science and Industry** and the ornate **Pittock Mansion** are other notable sights. *Admission charged for some attractions.*

8. Fort Vancouver National Historic Site

1501 East Evergreen Blvd., Vancouver. Dating from 1825, Fort Vancouver was the administrative headquarters as well as a major fur-trading post of the Hudson's Bay Company through the mid-19th century. The present-day reconstruction includes seven buildings, several of which have been furnished as they appeared in 1845. Artifacts excavated from the site are on display in the visitor center.

9. Oxbow Park

The park is a favorite departure point for leisurely boat rides down the **Sandy River,** past tree-lined banks, canyons, waterfalls, and bubbling springs of crystal-clear water. *Admission charged.*

10. Columbia River Gorge Scenic Highway

The mighty Columbia River is nowhere more spectacular than where it flows through the towering 75-mile-long Columbia River Gorge. From **Troutdale** to **Dodson,** this highway follows its course past dramatic ravines, scenic overlooks, parks, picnic areas, and campgrounds.

11. Crown Point State Park

Atop a bluff off the scenic highway, the park contains the **Vista House,** an ornate Tudor-style structure, and has excellent views of the Columbia River Gorge.

12. Multnomah Falls

Plunging 620 feet into the Columbia River Gorge, Multnomah Falls is the second-highest year-round falls in the United States. **Latourell** and **Wahkeena falls** are the other major waterfalls in the area.

13. Beacon Rock State Park

The 850-foot-high rock was formed from the core of an ancient volcano. A hiking trail leads to its peak and magnificent views of the Columbia River Gorge.

14. Bonneville Lock and Dam

This hydroelectric giant is a favorite stopping point off the Columbia River

Majestic Multnomah Falls

Gorge Scenic Highway. Visitors can watch salmon and steelhead trout navigating upstream via fish ladders, observe boats being raised and lowered in the locks, and view the workings of the mammoth powerhouse generators.

15. Cascade Locks Visitor Center

Four miles east of the Bonneville Lock and Dam, this visitor center houses the only stern-wheeler museum in the Pacific Northwest, filled with memorabilia from the days when paddle-wheel steamboats carried freight and passengers up and down the mighty Columbia. Visitors may also board a paddle-wheel riverboat for a ride through the Columbia River Gorge. *Fee charged for boat ride.*

16. Wind River Road

The scenic road runs northwest from the Columbia River Gorge for 14 miles along the Wind River, at one point crossing the river on a bridge suspended 285 feet above the chasm. From the highway, an access road leads on to **Goose Lake** and a number of lookout points.

A view of Mt. Hood from Washington Park's International Rose Test Garden, Portland

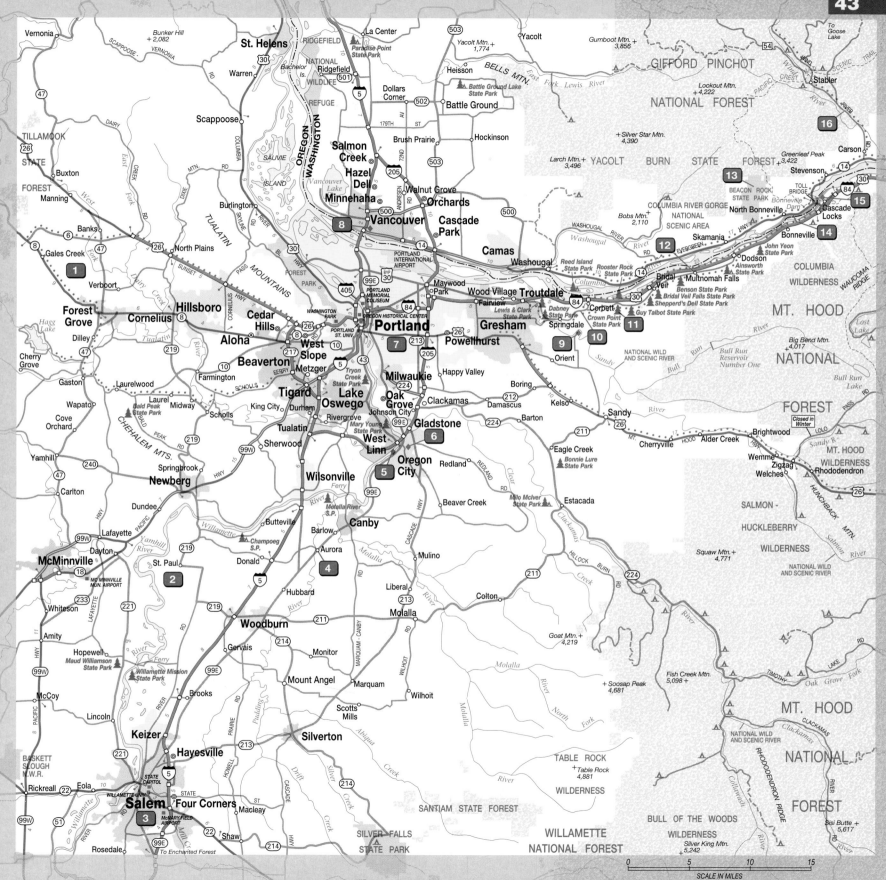

1. Payette Lake

An elevation of 5,200 feet guarantees this delightful horseshoe-shaped lake a comfortable climate in summer, when many visitors come to enjoy the water.

2. Farewell Bend State Park

Pioneer families that had traveled along the Snake River caught their last glimpse of the river at this bend. Today the state park is an ideal spot for picnicking, mineral hunting, swimming, and fishing. The visitor center features exhibits on the history of the Oregon Trail.

3. Oregon Trail Regional Museum

Campbell and Grove Sts., Baker City. The museum has an outstanding collection of gemstones, minerals, petrified wood, and seashells. Of particular interest are a half-ton cluster of Arkansas crystals and a black-light room, as well as items from the area's history of mining, lumbering, and farming. *Donation encouraged.*

4. Elkhorn Scenic Drive

Old mining towns are among the highlights of this 106-mile driving tour. The self-guided journey follows Rte. 7 from **Baker City** to **Sumpter** along the Powder River, and then continues west to several mining towns, including an optional side trip to the town of **Bourne.**

5. Sumpter Valley Railroad Restoration

Railroad Park on Dredge Loop Rd., Sumpter. Visitors can travel back to the prosperous lumber and mining days of turn-of-the-century Oregon aboard this restored narrow-gauge railway. An authentic wood-burning Heisler locomotive pulls the open-air cars through beautiful countryside once dotted with gold mines. *Admission charged.*

6. Kam Wah Chung & Co. Museum

NW Canton St., John Day. This former trading post bought by two young Chinese immigrants in 1887 served local Chinese laborers as a combination general store, doctor's office, temple, and gambling den. Traditional herbal remedies and decorated shrines share space with bootleg-whiskey bottles and gold-mining pans, illustrating the meeting of two cultures in the Old West. *Admission charged.*

7. John Day Fossil Beds National Monument

Fossils of saber-toothed cats and other prehistoric mammals are preserved in the area's volcanic rock and sediment, and the visitor center has many examples on display. Hiking trails lead into the badlands, where fossils are still being excavated.

8. Glass Butte Recreational Rockhound Area

This 6,400-foot mountain sparkles with outcrops of obsidian — lava dense with silica that has cooled to black volcanic glass. Indians used the brittle rock for axes and weapon points, but today it is used to make jewelry. Rock hounds can pick up samples from the rutted road or dig them out with picks and hammers.

9. Malheur National Wildlife Refuge

Depending on the season, a drive through this 183,000-acre wetlands preserve may offer glimpses of pintail ducks, tundra swans, mallards, songbirds, great horned owls, or bald eagles. Two large shallow lakes and a system of ponds, ditches, and canals also support a population of beavers and muskrats, while mule deer roam the marshes and desert uplands.

10. Steens Mountain

Dramatic summer storms often appear unannounced on the peaks of this massive fault block, at over 9,000 feet the highest land in southeast Oregon. A drive along the crest from Frenchglen provides sweeping views of the barren **Alvord Desert** below.

11. Hart Mountain National Antelope Refuge

Pronghorn antelope roam this immense volcanic ridge that rises more than 8,000 feet above sea level. The 275,000-acre refuge is also home to such wildlife as California bighorn sheep, mule deer, and many bird species.

12. Abert Rim

Stretching for some 30 miles and climbing to more than 2,000 feet, this ridge is considered to be one of the largest earth faults in the world. From Rte. 395 there are good views of the rim and of Lake Abert, a large body of salt water located at the base of the fault.

13. Modoc National Wildlife Refuge

Ducks, geese, whistling swans, herons, and egrets populate this 6,000-acre desert refuge of lakes, ponds, and marshes. Blue-gray sandhill cranes can be spotted in spring and summer, while coyotes, minks, and muskrats are in residence year-round.

14. Tuscarora

Only a few weathered buildings remain from Tuscarora's boomtown days that followed the big gold strike of 1867. On Main Street the town museum displays photographs and other 19th-century memorabilia, along with minerals and ore samples that once graced the town saloon.

15. Jarbidge Wilderness

Eight mountain peaks climb more than 10,000 feet in this remote area, offering glorious views of alpine scenery and Wild Horse Reservoir.

16. Bruneau Dunes State Park

Two mountainous sand dunes, one of them 470 feet high, pose a striking contrast to the small lakes at their base. Climbing the dunes is a popular, although strenuous, activity. There are nature walks, picnic areas, campsites, and fishing for bass and bluegill in the lakes. *Admission charged.*

17. Silver City

Some 68 weathered buildings are all that remain of the boomtown created when rich veins of silver were found here in 1863. Remnants of the town's boisterous past include Deadman's Alley, where gunfights settled disagreements; the former drugstore with its old-time potions; and a museum housed in the old school. Visitors can tour historic cemeteries in the area and pan for gold in Jordan Creek.

18. Snake River Birds of Prey Area

More than 700 pairs of birds of prey nest annually in this nearly half-million-acre protected habitat along the Snake River. From mid-March through June visitors with binoculars can spot courting and nesting golden eagles and prairie falcons, as well as migrating bald eagles, peregrine falcons, and ospreys. The **World Center for Birds of Prey,** the largest raptor breeding and research center in the world, attracts thousands of visitors annually.

19. Lake Lowell Sector of Deer Flat National Wildlife Refuge

From September to April this 9,000-acre lake is alive with wintering ducks, geese, and other waterfowl. At various times of year, the refuge is also home to bald eagles, prairie falcons, red-tailed hawks, and more than 190 other species of birds. The lake attracts anglers year-round, and boaters in the summer.

20. Lake Owyhee State Park

A cruise along the 52-mile length of this narrow reservoir provides spectacular views of the rocky gorge through which it runs. Anglers enjoy the lake's excellent stock of largemouth and smallmouth bass, catfish, perch, and crappie.

21. Boise

Convention and Visitors Bureau, 168 North Ninth St. Idaho's capital and largest city preserves its pioneer past at the **Idaho State Historical Museum** in **Julia Davis Park.** The park also features a pioneer village and a zoo, and during the summer the 1890's-style **Boise Tour Train** leaves from here for a lively tour of the town. Other attractions include the turn-of-the-century **Old Boise National Historic District** and the domed **Capitol.**

22. Warm Springs

Comfortable year-round swimming is provided for visitors in a pool fed by a natural hot spring. Nearby are inviting facilities for picnicking and camping. *Admission charged.*

23. Idaho City

The discovery of gold here in 1862 led to a boomtown of more than 6,000 residents within a year. As much as $250 million in gold was mined locally during Idaho City's heyday, but by World War II all that was left was the legend. Today reminders of the town's riotous past include the brick courthouse and forbidding jailhouse.

24. Boise National Forest

Visitors to this vast national forest can see a segment of the historic **Oregon Trail** as it descends from the rimrock near the ranger station to the flatlands below. Both hunting and fishing are permitted here, as well as in the **Sawtooth Wilderness Area** located nearby.

SCALE IN MILES
0 10 20 30 40 50

1. Leesburg Town Site

Located high above the Salmon Valley, this old mining town established by former Confederate soldiers still has some 15 original log structures. Along the 33-mile drive from Salmon to Leesburg, visitors will encounter some especially beautiful mountain scenery.

2. Grandview Canyon

These dramatic canyon walls, rising 700 feet, are best viewed from **Borah Peak,** at 12,662 feet Idaho's highest peak. To the south, the **Mackay Reservoir** provides a welcome desert oasis, with its inviting picnic grounds and splendid views of the surrounding mountains.

3. Custer

Custer was a mining town at the turn of the century. Today remnants of the town still stand, and what were once a schoolhouse and a saloon now serve as a mining museum. On the way to the nearby ghost town of **Bonanza,** visitors will pass the **Yankee Fork Gold Dredge,** which was used to extract the last of the area's retrievable gold in the 1950's. Former workers give tours of the gold dredge and explain its operation. *Fee charged for tour.*

4. Stanley

Chamber of Commerce, Rte. 21. Once a gold-mining camp and now a ranching center, Stanley is a rustic town with log buildings and unpaved streets. It is the departure point for expeditions both to **Sawtooth Lake** in **Sawtooth National Forest** and to the **Sawtooth National Recreation Area.** White-water float trips down the challenging **Salmon River** also originate from here.

5. Sun Valley

A popular vacation spot, the valley is surrounded by the Sawtooth National Forest and the Challis National Forest. Many resorts have year-round sports facilities, but the area has been developed carefully to protect its natural beauty.

6. Ketchum

Chamber of Commerce, 411 North Main St. Surrounded by the gracious peaks of the Smoky, Boulder, and Pioneer mountains, this former mining town fell on hard times with the crash of the silver market in 1893. It is now part of an area that offers year-round recreational activities, including golf, tennis, horseback riding, and some of the finest skiing in the country.

7. Craters of the Moon National Monument

These black basaltic lava fields have the aspect of a lunar landscape. The 83-square-mile terrain consists of cinder cones rising to 800 feet, spatter cones, fissure vents, lava tubes, and molds of trees once encased in molten lava. The visitor center gives a good area orientation, and a 7-mile auto loop passes the major points of interest. *Admission charged.*

8. Lava Beds

This site is one example of the many lava beds scattered throughout the Snake River Plain. One notable formation called **Big Southern Butte** is the remainder of a volcano that predates the Craters of the Moon eruptions.

9. Mammoth Cave

Visitors who take a self-guided tour of the mile-long lava tube are especially struck by the oddly configured, multicolored walls of the cave. *Admission charged.*

10. Shoshone Falls

Called the Niagara of the West, this awe-inspiring cascade plunging 210 feet into the Snake River is actually 52 feet higher than Niagara's Horseshoe Falls. The park area offers excellent overlooks and facilities for swimming, boating, hiking, and picnicking. *Admission charged.*

11. Silent City of Rocks

Covering a 25-square-mile area, these huge granite megaliths have such evocative names as Squaw and Papoose, King on the Throne, and Devil's Bedstead. Some bear graffiti inscribed by California-bound pioneers in the mid-1800's.

12. Golden Spike National Historic Site

On May 10, 1869, executives from the Union Pacific and Central Pacific met here to drive ceremonial golden spikes into the tie that completed the nation's first trans-continental railroad. Replicas of the two companies' locomotive engines stand facing each other in the same spot as did the originals, and a self-guided auto route runs along 9 miles of the original track. Films and exhibits related to the historic event are offered at the visitor center. *Admission charged.*

13. Fort Bridger State Historic Site

At the former trading post and military fort, stables used by the Pony Express and a general store stocked with goods and fashions from the 1880's are on display. The junior officers' quarters as well as the commanding officer's residence have been faithfully restored with period furnishings. *Admission charged.*

14. Fossil Butte National Monument

At this 8,198-acre monument, fossils of 22 species of fish are exhibited in the visitor center, along with rare fossils of a stingray, a crocodile skull, a boa constrictor, and a prehistoric bird. Hikers can follow an interpretive trail to a historic quarry area, and a driving route traverses open-range country, where mule deer, pronghorn antelopes, and moose can sometimes be sighted from the road.

15. Periodic Spring

Located in **Bridger-Teton National Forest,** the spring gushes at precise 18-minute intervals from an opening in the wall of Swift Creek Canyon, feeding a streambed 400 feet below. At 7,100 feet above sea level, Periodic Spring can be reached by a hiking trail through dramatic mountain terrain. Camping and picnicking facilities are located nearby.

16. Idaho's World Famous Hot Pools

430 East Main St., Lava Hot Springs. It is estimated that these springs have flowed at a constant 110° F for a period of some 50 million years. The springs feed hot mineral pools and two large swimming pools, which are surrounded by parks and tennis courts. Located nearby are golf courses and the **Portneuf River,** which attracts anglers year-round.

17. Pocatello

Chamber of Commerce, 427 North Main St. Before the coming of the railroad, the Shoshone Indians inhabited the land on which the town of Pocatello now stands.

The **Bannock County Historical Museum** provides excellent documentation of that era through photographs, railroad memorabilia, Shoshone artifacts, and examples of Victorian-era women's fashion. **Ross Park** offers an excellent zoo. Nearby is the historic **Old Fort Hall,** a full-scale replica of a fur-trading post established in 1834, which was a well-known landmark on the Oregon Trail. *Admission charged for some attractions.*

18. Idaho Falls

Chamber of Commerce, 505 Lindsay Blvd. Combining natural cascades with a 1,500-foot-wide man-made dam, the magnificent **Idaho Falls of the Snake River** are bounded both by the cityscape of Idaho Falls and the greenery of its numerous parks. Among them, **Tautphaus Park** has boating and fishing facilities, picnic areas, a children's amusement park, and zoo. The **Bonneville Museum** chronicles the evolution of Idaho Falls with artifacts, photographs, and displays ranging from gold panning and potato harvesting to ranching and nuclear energy. *Admission charged for some attractions.*

19. U.S. Sheep Experiment Station

Visitors who take the interesting tour provided by this research facility have the opportunity to observe various breeds of sheep and, depending on the time of year, watch the birthing of lambs or the process of sheepshearing.

20. Spencer Opal Mines

Company headquarters in town will rent visitors the necessary equipment to dig for opals in these mines, which are open seasonally. *Fee charged.*

21. Madison River Canyon Earthquake Area

In a 1959 earthquake, a landslide piled up 400 feet of debris against the northern wall of Madison River Canyon, forming what is now called Earthquake Lake. Several overlooks give a view of the quake's aftermath, and the visitor center, which is built on the landslide area itself, provides exhibits related to the phenomenon.

22. Gallatin Petrified Forest

In this 40-square-mile section of **Gallatin National Forest** are examples of more than 100 species of ancient trees and shrubs, buried millions of years ago by volcanic ash.

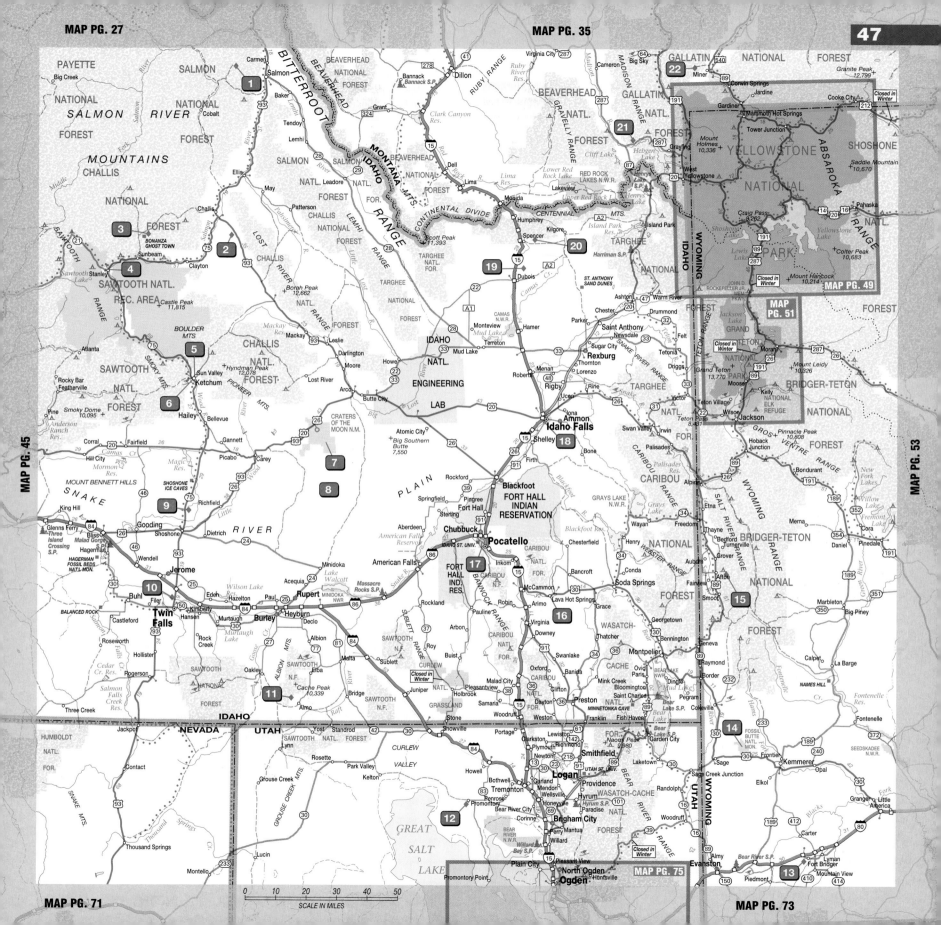

YELLOWSTONE NATIONAL PARK

1. Mammoth Hot Springs
Here subterranean hot water seeps to the surface through limestone, leaving deposits that form unusual, oddly beautiful travertine terraces, some with shallow pools of water delicately colored by algae. Minerva and Opal terraces are particularly enchanting. More fantastic thermal formations can be viewed from **Upper Terrace Loop Drive,** where gnarled pine trees — some more than 500 years old — are surrounded by ever-rising layers of travertine.

2. Obsidian Cliff
Indians once chipped the prized obsidian (a black glass created by molten lava) from this cliff to use for trading and to make tools and arrowheads.

3. Virginia Cascade Drive
This scenic loop road affords a great view of the waterfall called the Virginia Cascade. A popular picnic area surrounded by meadow is a short drive from the falls. Elk and other wildlife are often spotted here, especially in early morning and late afternoon.

4. Fountain Paint Pot Trail
This boardwalk in the Lower Geyser Basin passes all sorts of bubbling, hissing, sulfurous phenomena, including the "paint pots" made when steam and sulfuric acid changed rock into clay colored by minerals.

5. Grand Prismatic Spring
Located in the Midway Geyser Basin, this is the park's largest hot spring, with a diameter of nearly 370 feet. The deep blue center gives way to orange, green, yellow, and red colors created by algae at the periphery.

6. Old Faithful
The most popular attraction in Yellowstone is Old Faithful. When it erupts, after some spurts and splashes, a steaming fountain of water surges over 100 feet into the air. The eruptions, each lasting between 1½ and 5 minutes, take place on average every 76 minutes; a sign in the visitor center gives the next likely time. Also in the Upper Geyser Basin are the graceful Riverside Geyser; the long-spouting Grotto Geyser;

Mammoth Hot Springs' travertine terraces

and the stunning Morning Glory Pool, a body of water resembling the flower.

7. Lewis and Shoshone Lakes
A canoe or rowboat trip from Lewis to Shoshone takes about three hours and can be combined with fishing and camping. Boaters should be mindful of sudden winds and the extremely cold water.

8. West Thumb
In West Thumb, on the shore of Yellowstone Lake, visitors can stroll down a

geyser-basin boardwalk. Nearby **Grant Village** has a visitor center featuring exhibits on Yellowstone's attractions and the aftermath of its devastating forest fires in 1988.

9. Yellowstone Lake
These sparkling blue waters, fed by snow melt, occupy part of a caldera formed 600,000 years ago. Yellowstone — 20 miles long and 14 miles wide, with a shoreline of 110 miles — is the largest high-elevation lake in North America. Pelicans, cormorants, and other water birds nest in its islands. An excellent viewing spot for Yellowstone Lake is at an overlook on **Lake Butte,** about 9 miles west of Sylvan Pass.

10. Fishing Bridge
Contrary to its name, this bridge, which spans the Yellowstone River, can no longer be used for fishing. During the summer, however, it's a great place to watch spawning trout. The Fishing Bridge Museum has displays about birdlife found in the park.

11. Hayden Valley
This former glacial lake bed is now home to such large waterfowl as trumpeter swans and Canada geese and mammals such as bison and moose, which should always be viewed from a distance. In June and July spawning cutthroat trout jumping in the LeHardy Rapids are sometimes visible.

Nineteenth-century artist Thomas Moran (above) was acclaimed for his paintings of Yellowstone National Park. "The Grand Canyon of the Yellowstone" (right), considered to be his masterwork, was purchased by Congress and displayed for many years in the lobby of the U.S. Senate.

A trumpeter swan takes wing.

12. Upper Falls and Lower Falls

These two famous waterfalls are located about a mile south of Artist Point. The bottle-green water of the Yellowstone River cascades 109 feet at the Upper Falls, and plummets 308 feet at the Lower Falls. Trails that originate from Uncle Tom's Parking Area, off Artist Point Road, lead to good viewing points.

13. Artist, Inspiration, and Lookout Points

These points provide sensational views of the upper Grand Canyon of the Yellowstone River. Here the canyon's volcanic rock, resplendent in its multicolored hues, is 24 miles long and reaches a depth of 1,200 feet. Ospreys can be sighted flying between the towering walls.

14. Canyon Village

The village offers lodging and other services for visitors, including a visitor center, which explains the park's geology through exhibits. There is a nearby campground that borders the Grand Canyon of the Yellowstone River, one of the park's most popular attractions.

15. Mount Washburn

In summer, a hike through forests and meadows to the top of this mountain—a 3-mile trip—brings spectacular rewards: a panorama of the entire park and possible glimpses of bighorn sheep. Parking areas at **Dunraven Pass** offer picnic facilities set amid broad-topped whitebark pines and spire-shaped subalpine fir, which thrive at the 8,850-foot elevation. Hiking trails are also accessible here.

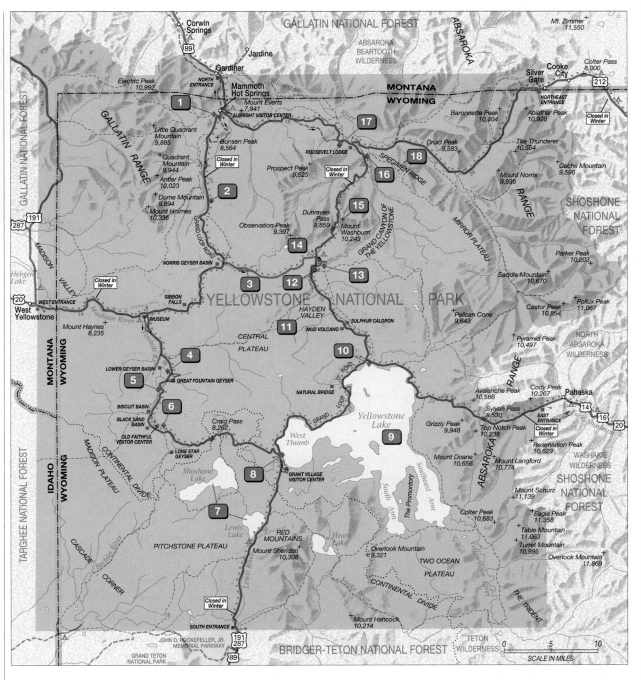

16. Tower Fall

Just south of Tower Junction, the shimmering waterfall, which descends 132 feet, is appropriately named for the striking, pillar-like volcanic-rock formations on the adjacent canyon walls. The falls are best observed from a viewing platform at the end of the path leading from the parking lot.

17. Petrified Tree

This is the park's only stone tree standing close to the road, on a well-marked side road about 18 miles east of Mammoth. There were once three petrified trees at this spot, but after thoughtless souvenir-seekers carried off the other two specimens piece by piece, a protective fence was placed around the remaining, now solitary, tree.

18. Specimen Ridge

This ridge holds a forest of petrified trees, which were killed and buried by periodic volcanic activity. The trees' organic tissue was so exactly replaced by dissolved minerals that many of them are still identifiable. Visitors can view these specimens with binoculars or by hiking to the site.

Admission charged for national park.

Herds of migrating elk seeking winter sanctuary may be observed at close range in the National Elk Refuge.

GRAND TETON NATIONAL PARK

1. Highway 89

This excellent highway follows the geological transition zone between Grand Teton National Park and Yellowstone Park. Various Park Service turnouts interpret the geology, history, and other aspects of the area. From the **Snake River Overlook,** the serpentine river offers a dramatic contrast to solid, jagged Grand Teton. The highway is open to the southern boundary of Yellowstone Park in the winter, allowing visitors access to a veritable winter wonderland.

2. Jackson Lake

Fed by melting snow, Jackson Lake — by far the largest lake in the park — mirrors mountain images on its shimmering surface. This is a very popular spot for all forms of water recreation. Various types of cruises, including some heading off to islands in the lake, are available here.

3. Colter Bay

Colter Bay's visitor center includes the Indian Arts Museum, which exhibits such crafts as masks and pipes. The village also offers horseback-riding trips, boat rentals, and campgrounds. More unusual lodging options include tentlike cabins made of canvas and logs, as well as log cabins that date back to early settlements. *Fee charged.*

4. Signal Mountain

Periodic turnouts on the drive up this mountain provide magnificent views along the way, capped by the panorama seen from the summit. Here visitors can look down on the Snake River Valley and out onto the Teton Range, which rises with startling abruptness from the valley floor.

5. The Potholes

These depressions in the ground were formed when isolated blocks of glacial ice melted; today the area is home to roaming bison. Some potholes, now water-filled, are found near **Jackson Hole.**

6. Snake River

A variety of guided float trips, ranging from 5 to 25 miles, are available on this challenging scenic river, whose waters eventually flow into the Columbia River.

7. Teton Park Road

During good weather, this is an alternative route to Highway 89. The road hugs the base of the towering mountains and crosses Cottonwood Creek, where moose often congregate. In summer and fall the fields are ablaze with wildflowers.

8. Cascade Canyon Trail

A boat ride on Jenny Lake leads to the trailhead. Though an easy walk, the trail — some 18 miles round-trip — takes a full day. It passes waterfalls such as the lovely **Hidden Falls** and wonderful views, including that of Jackson Hole from **Inspiration Point.** In summer wildflowers such as columbine and Indian paintbrush are in radiant bloom. Rainwear is a good idea in this part of the park, which is subject to sudden showers. *Fee charged for boat ride.*

9. Teton Canyon Campground

Nestled along Teton Creek, this small campground lies at the foot of mountain cliffs. Trails range from the moderately challenging Alaska Basin Trail to the Devil's Stair, for more experienced hikers. The area is home to deer, elk, and moose, and in midsummer wildflowers attract hundreds of hummingbirds. *Fee charged.*

10. Cathedral Group

Teewinot Mountain, Grand Teton, and Mt. Owen together form the Cathedral Group, their three peaks rising majestically like church spires. For the best views — including the group's remarkable reflection in **String Lake** — visitors may take the scenic drive at Jenny Lake, which originates at North Jenny Lake Junction.

11. Chapel of the Transfiguration

Built in 1925, this log chapel has a perfectly placed window above its altar, framing the magnificent peak of Grand Teton.

12. Menor's Ferry

A self-guiding trail tells the history of Menor's Ferry, which transported pioneers across the Snake River. Rides are sometimes given in a replica of the ferryboat.

13. Moose Village Visitor Center

The visitor center here provides park information, as well as exhibits about the park's natural history and geology.

River rafters test the winding waters of the Snake River below the towering Grand Teton.

14. Aerial Tram to Rendezvous Mountain

At Teton Village, visitors can embark on an aerial tram ride up to a 10,450-foot pinnacle on Rendezvous Mountain. The view from this crest includes the Teton Range and the Jackson Hole basin. The tram is also a convenient way to approach the scenic high-elevation hiking trails that are found in the southern Teton Range.

15. Teton Pass

At 8,431 feet, the top of this pass presents a wonderful view of the surrounding snow-topped peaks. In summer the slopes are studded with colorful flowers. Turnouts on the road provide access to hiking trails.

16. Jackson

As a supply center for local ranchers, Jackson maintains an old-fashioned Western look with its boardwalks, but also offers fine art galleries and craft shops for visitors.

17. National Elk Refuge

This refuge provides a wintering ground for thousands of migrating elk. While being transported in horse-drawn sleighs, visitors can observe these animals at close range. *Fee charged for sleigh ride.*

18. Gros Ventre Slide

In 1925, 50 million cubic yards of earth, rocks, and trees sealed off Lower Slide Lake, forming a natural dam. The Gros Ventre Slide is a result of floodwaters that barreled over the dam two years later.

Admission charged for national park.

A black bear cub greets the new day.

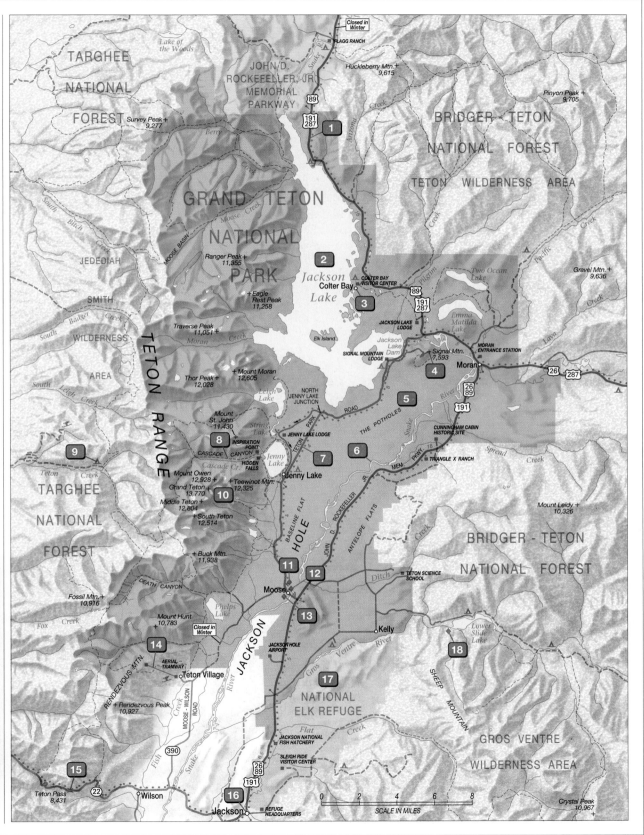

1. Devils Tower National Monument

Devils Tower, a once-active volcano, was designated the country's first national monument in 1906. A trail skirts the base of the imposing 865-foot tower, and the surrounding park offers hiking, cross-country skiing, and birdwatching. *Admission charged.*

2. Jim Gatchell Memorial Museum

100 Fort St., Buffalo. The museum houses a huge collection of Sioux, Cheyenne, and Crow artifacts amassed by a pioneer druggist named Jim Gatchell. More than 5,000 items are exhibited here, including war bonnets, shell casings believed to be from the Battle of the Little Bighorn, and beaded rifle scabbards. *Admission charged.*

3. Fort Phil Kearny State Historic Site

Once an important stronghold on the Bozeman Trail, Fort Phil Kearny was abandoned in 1868 and later destroyed by fire. Visitors can learn about the fort, the trail, and reservation and frontier life through displays at the site. *Admission charged.*

4. Bradford Brinton Memorial

239 Brinton Rd., Big Horn. The Quarter Circle A Ranch, built in 1892 and bought by Bradford Brinton in 1923, exemplifies the spreads of the wealthy cattle ranchers of that time. The 20 rooms of the ranch-style house still have their original furnishings, and visitors may also view Brinton's impressive collection of Western art. Antique wagons and buggies are displayed on the grounds. *Donation suggested.*

5. Bighorn National Forest

Situated high in the mountains, this national forest has open valleys and wide meadows, making the plentiful wildlife easy to view. Adjacent to the forest are the **Medicine Lodge State Archaeological Site,** with outstanding examples of petroglyphs and pictographs, and the **Medicine Wheel National Historic Landmark,** a mysterious circle of boulders.

6. Bighorn Canyon National Recreation Area

The Yellowtail Dam created 71-mile-long **Bighorn Lake,** most of which lies in a spectacular canyon. In this area visitors can enjoy both the natural beauty and activities such as swimming, boating, and fishing.

7. Beartooth Highway

This beautiful section of U.S. 212 provides stunning mountain scenery and views, climbing from 5,000 feet at Red Lodge to 10,942 feet at Beartooth Pass on its way to Yellowstone National Park.

8. Shoshone National Forest

Within this forest lies the **Absaroka Wilderness Area** — a rugged, vast region that ranges in elevation from 4,600 to 13,140 feet and adjoins the Shoshone River canyon. The summit of **Dead Indian Hill** offers a breathtaking view of this area and the deep, jagged **Clarks Fork** canyon.

9. Cody

Chamber of Commerce, 836 Sheridan Ave. This town holds a significant reminder of its namesake. The **Buffalo Bill Historical Center** consists of four museums containing memorabilia related to Bill Cody, vintage firearms, Western art, and Indian artifacts. Another attraction, **Trail Town,** contains historic buildings and gravesites.

10. Hot Springs State Park

220 Park St., Thermopolis. The world's largest mineral hot springs yield millions of gallons of water at 134° F daily. Their mineral deposits have resulted in dramatic terraces, which can be viewed from a scenic walkway. Some of the water is channeled into bathhouses and lovely outdoor pools.

11. Boysen State Park

Boysen Reservoir is the centerpiece of this park. Surrounded by sagebrush hills, rocky desert plains, and red sandstone cliffs, the lake provides water sports and fishing.

12. Museum of Northern Arapaho History

St. Stephens Mission, St. Stephens. Housed in an old mission building on the Wind River Reservation, this new museum exhibits artifacts and photographs relating to the Northern Arapaho Indians, many of whom still live on the reservation.

13. Sinks Canyon State Park

Here the Popo Agie River "sinks" into a cave and then reappears a half-mile down

the valley. The canyon's slopes support two different ecosystems — one with evergreens and the other with juniper and sagebrush. The river contains trout, and the hillsides are home to bighorn sheep, beavers, moose, and various other wildlife.

14. South Pass City State Historic Site

South Pass City had a few years of glory after gold was discovered in 1867, only to decline quickly when the mines didn't live up to their promise. Today many buildings from that time have been rebuilt, and remnants of mining equipment still remain.

15. Sweetwater County Historical Museum

80 West Flaming Gorge Way, Green River. The courthouse holds a museum that depicts the evolution of the Sweetwater County area. Exhibits include a palm-leaf fossil, a dinosaur footprint, Sioux craftwork, farm implements, and artifacts of the many Chinese immigrants who mined coal.

16. Snowy Range Pass

Snowy Range Highway climbs from sagebrush flats up to the 10,847-foot Snowy Range Pass. Along the way are forests with lustrous alpine lakes. At the pass is the **Libby Flats Observation Point.**

17. Laramie

Chamber of Commerce, 800 South Third St. Of special interest here are the **University of Wyoming Geological Museum,** whose extensive fossil collection includes a complete Apatosaurus (formerly Brontosaurus) skeleton, and the excellent **Laramie Plains Museum,** a Victorian mansion filled with regional artifacts. In **Wyoming Territorial Park,** a prison that once held Butch Cassidy has now been turned into a museum. *Admission charged for some attractions.*

18. Oregon Trail Ruts– Register Cliff State Historic Sites

So many pioneer wagons traveled the Oregon Trail that their iron-rimmed wheels left ruts up to 6 feet deep in a sandstone ridge here, near the North Platte River. Carvings made by some of the settlers can still be seen in nearby Register Cliff.

19. Fort Laramie National Historic Site

Several buildings of this 19th-century fort have been restored — among them the officers' quarters, cavalry barracks, guardhouse, and post traders' store. Staff mem-

bers in period costume reenact the daily activities of the soldiers and civilians who inhabited the fort in the 1870's.

20. Guernsey State Park

Planned around Guernsey Reservoir, this park features limestone cliffs, grassy hills, and the lake itself, with a sandy beach for swimming. A 4-mile drive along the shore provides panoramic vistas and access to campgrounds. Wildlife is abundant, and a museum offers exhibits related to the region. *Admission charged.*

21. Wyoming Pioneer Memorial Museum

400 West Center St., Douglas. This museum holds a plethora of Western objects, such as Winchesters, arrowheads, tomahawks, swords, branding irons, saddlebags, carriages, furniture, and glassware.

22. Casper

Convention and Visitors Bureau, 500 North Center St. Visitors to the **Nicolaysen Art Museum and Discovery Center** can view rotating exhibits that range from the historical to the contemporary; the interactive educational displays are especially appealing to children. On the banks of the North Platte River stands historic **Fort Caspar.** The reconstructed 1862 fort includes officers' and enlisted men's quarters, a stable, mess hall, commissary, and telegraph office. Art, including several paintings by William Henry Jackson, and artifacts relating to the social and natural history of central Wyoming are among the displays in the interpretive center.

23. Independence Rock State Historic Site

Visitors can follow an interpretive trail to Independence Rock, a huge granite mound rising to 136 feet, which served as a landmark to wagon-train travelers on the Oregon Trail. Here they rested and drank from the Sweetwater River. Thousands may have carved their names and other messages on the rock. Today, hundreds of the inscriptions are still visible.

24. Hell's Half Acre

Here wind and water have carved out a 320-acre chasm studded with clay-and-shale spires and other odd shapes. From a restaurant on the rim, visitors can view the formations, as well as the multicolored canyon walls. The more adventurous can take trails down into these miniature badlands.

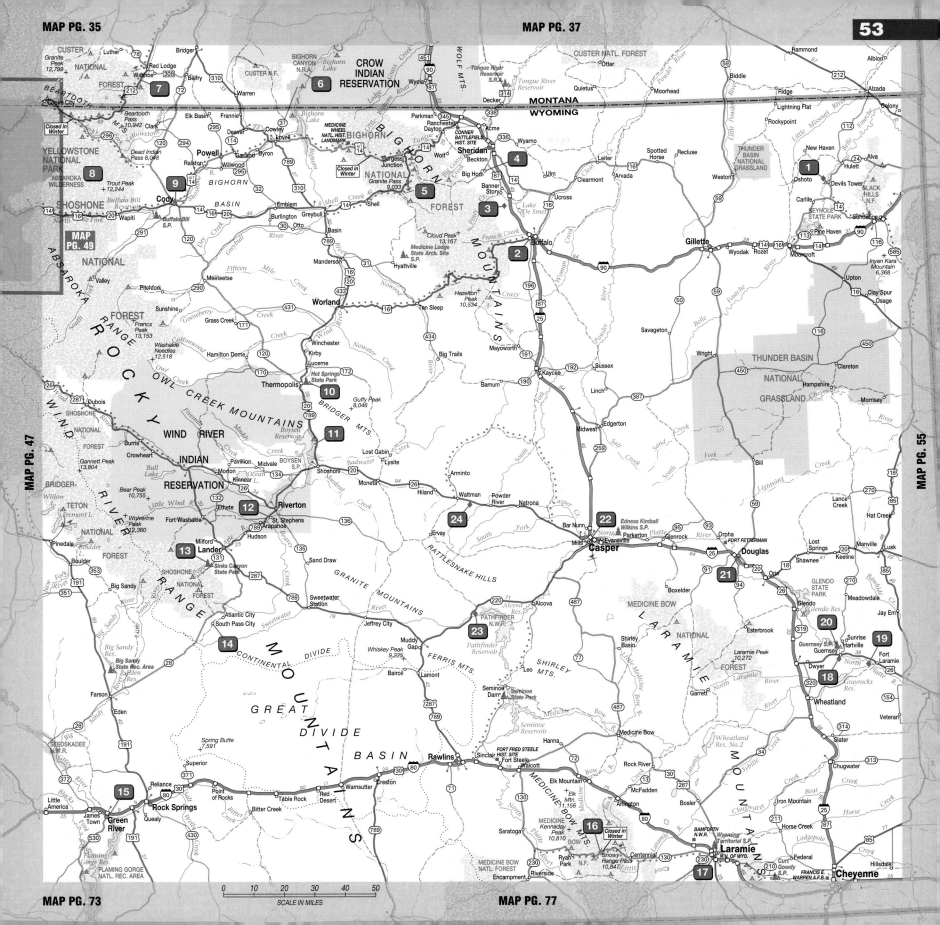

1. Old West Museum

Off Rte. 90, west of Chamberlain. A potpourri of cowboy, American Indian, and pioneer artifacts — among them rifles, bear traps, beads, and tractors — fill six entire buildings in this museum complex. Also on the grounds, Old Time Main Street re-creates a bygone era with replicas of 19th-century shops and offices. *Admission charged.*

2. Cultural Heritage Center

900 Governors Dr., Pierre. Beginning with early American Indian cultures and continuing through World War II, this museum captures the history of South Dakota. Exhibits include the 1743 lead plate left by the La Ve'rendrye brothers, who claimed the area for France; a life-size diorama of a Sioux campsite and teepee; and a splendid wooden carving of a galloping horse.

3. Pioneer Auto Show and Antique Town

503 East 55th St., Murdo. This sprawling complex encompasses more than 30 buildings, including a train station, blacksmith's shop, bank, and barbershop. Two highlights of the antique automobile collection are an early motor home and a 1909 Auburn. *Admission charged.*

4. Badlands Petrified Gardens

Millions of years ago trees sank into the bed of the inland sea that once covered western South Dakota. The trees eventually turned to stone, and these gardens display an extensive collection of their remnants. A museum contains other rare examples of petrified wood, as well as minerals and fossils. *Admission charged.*

5. Prairie Homestead Historic Site

The Homestead Act of 1862 allowed Ed and Alice Brown to stake a claim in the Badlands in 1909. Like other Great Plains settlers they built a dugout house, topped by sod walls and fronted with logs, into a hillside. The two-room dwelling remains, giving present-day visitors a sense of the lives of these "sodbusters." *Admission charged.*

6. Badlands National Park

Wind and water have created a fantastic landscape of spires, mesas, cliffs, ridges, gorges, and fossil-filled canyons, which can be viewed from many overlooks along the **Scenic Loop Road.** A visitor center offers guided walks and information about where wildlife such as bighorn sheep, pronghorns, buffalo, and golden eagles are likely to be sighted. *Admission charged.*

7. Wounded Knee

Here at Wounded Knee Creek, cavalrymen slaughtered at least 200 Sioux. Today the **Big Foot Massacre Monument,** named for the Indian group's chief, rises as a memorial on the stark plain.

8. Museum of the Fur Trade

U.S. 20, east of Chadron. Appropriately located on the site of the old Bordeaux Trading Post, this museum reveals the lives led by people involved in the fur trade during America's formative years. Trade goods, weapons, and pelts are among the exhibits on display. *Admission charged.*

9. Toadstool Park

Erosion has carved strange shapes out of the clay and rock in these badlands, which are full of fossils. There are well-marked trails through the park, where visitors may spot pronghorns, jackrabbits, and even an occasional rattlesnake.

10. Fort Robinson State Park

Nebraska's largest state park, set in the appealing Pine Ridge region, holds diverse attractions. Several original and restored buildings of the fort are on view, and a museum housed in the former headquarters displays frontier artifacts. Visitors can take stagecoach and horseback rides or hike along the many trails. *Admission charged.*

11. Agate Fossil Beds National Monument

Beasts now extinct once ranged freely in this area. Two hills preserve a wealth of their fossilized remains, many of which are exposed under Plexiglas. Visitors can also see the present-day wildlife — including pronghorns, coyotes, and mule deer — that roam through the bright wildflowers of the open prairie.

12. Scotts Bluff National Monument

Compared by one settler to a castle or fort, this imposing bluff served as an important landmark. The promontory, rising 800 feet above the North Platte River valley, indicated the location of Mitchells Pass, a corridor through the rocky area. Some wagon-trail ruts are still visible. Both a road and a challenging trail lead to the bluff's summit and spectacular vistas. *Admission charged.*

13. North Platte Valley Museum

10th and J Sts., Gering. The museum complex includes an authentic sod house, a log house, and an Union Pacific caboose. In the main building, replicas ranging from a printing shop to a country kitchen re-create life in 19th-century Nebraska.

14. Wildcat Hills Game Refuge and Recreation Area

Bobcats share this refuge with elk, deer, buffalo, and wild turkeys. The adjacent recreation area contains canyons laced with trails leading to stone shelters. Picnic tables are located in the largest shelter, which commands an imposing view of Scotts Bluff. *Admission charged.*

15. Seybolt Park

This park features two landmarks on the Oregon Trail: **Courthouse Rock** and **Jail Rock.** At least one pioneer thought the taller, 400-foot clay formation resembled a courthouse, and proximity caused the other rock to be named for a jail. These monoliths mark the beginning of a ridge that gradually widens into the Wildcat Hills.

16. Ash Hollow State Historical Park

Freshwater springs have drawn many visitors to this canyon, from prehistoric mammals to Plains Indians to pioneers taking the Overland Trail. The park's visitor center offers information about the site, which in addition to the springs features a rock shelter, a covered wagon, and wagon-train tracks. *Admission charged.*

17. Sand Hills

Without Nebraska's native grasses, which help to keep the sand in place, these hills could not prevail against the strong winds. At 20,000 square miles the largest dune area in North America, the sandy ridges, knolls, and hills serve as a home to wild animals and a grazing ground for cattle.

18. Bessey Arboretum and Scott Lookout Tower

In the early 1900's, botanist Charles Bessey persuaded the federal government to bring trees to the prairie. Bessey Arboretum shows the surprising variety of plants that now grow in the surrounding **Nebraska National Forest.** A road that passes the arboretum continues up a bluff to the Scott Lookout Tower, with its panoramic view of the rolling countryside.

19. Fort Hartsuff State Historical Park

Construction of this military post on the North Loup River was begun in 1874, in response to attacks on white settlers and Pawnees by the Teton Sioux. Constructed mainly of mortar, the barracks, officers' quarters, and several other restored fort buildings still stand today. Living-history demonstrations sometimes take place in the park. *Admission charged.*

20. Valentine National Wildlife Refuge

In spring and fall thousands of migrating ducks and other waterfowl take refuge in this preserve's lakes and marshes. The Hackberry Lake headquarters provides information on these birds and other wildlife in the area, including white-tailed deer, coyotes, and badgers. Fishing is permitted in several of the lakes.

21. Fort Niobrara National Wildlife Refuge

Longhorn cattle, pronghorns, bison, and elk graze in this 19,122-acre refuge. Prairie dogs, deer, and blue herons are examples of other area wildlife that visitors can glimpse on an auto route or from foot trails. One especially pretty path, leading past the tumbling **Fort Falls,** ends at the Niobrara River. A mile-long detour off Rte. 12 leads to the State Fish Hatchery in nearby Valentine, which can also be toured.

22. Sandhills Museum

U.S. 20, west of Valentine. This idiosyncratic museum houses one man's collection of Americana and antique cars. The latter include such rare makes as Patterson and Rattler. Indian artifacts, vintage firearms, farming equipment, and other items document aspects of the Sandhills region's history. *Admission charged.*

23. Buechel Memorial Lakota Museum

350 South Oak St., St. Francis. The Jesuit missionary Eugene Buechel spent much of his life among the Dakota Sioux. This small museum maintains his collection of tribal robes, headdresses, bows and arrows, and other Sioux artifacts.

MONT. / S. DAK.
WYO.

CHEYENNE RIVER INDIAN RESERVATION

BLACK HILLS NATL. FOR.

BLACK HILLS NATIONAL FOREST

Rapid City

Spearfish
Deadwood
Lead
Sturgis
Belle Fourche

Geographical Center of the U.S.

Castle Rock Butte 3,775

MT. RUSHMORE NATL. MEM.
Harney Peak 7,242
CRAZY HORSE MONUMENT
JEWEL CAVE NATL. MON.
WIND CAVE N.P.
Custer S.P.
Hot Springs

BADLANDS NATL. PARK
BADLANDS NATL. PARK

PINE RIDGE INDIAN RESERVATION

BUFFALO GAP NATL. GRASSLAND

Pierre
Fort Pierre
FORT PIERRE NATL. GRASSLAND
Lake Sharpe
Lake Oahe

CROW CREEK IND. RES.
LOWER BRULE IND. RES.
Fort Thompson
Chamberlain

ROSEBUD INDIAN RESERVATION
SIOUX INDIAN MUSEUM
Rosebud
Mission

Valentine
VALENTINE N.W.R.
FT. NIOGRARA N.W.R.
SAMUEL R. McKELVIE NATL. FOR.
NEBRASKA NATL. FOR.

Chadron
Chadron S.P.
FT. ROBINSON
Fort Robinson
NEBRASKA NATL. FOR.
OGLALA NATL. GRASSLAND

Alliance

Scottsbluff
Gering
CHIMNEY ROCK N.H.S.
SCOTTS BLUFF
WILDCAT HILLS
NORTH PLATTE N.W.R.

SAND HILLS
CRESCENT LAKE N.W.R.
SURVEY VALLEY

Big Hill 4,144
Giant Hill 3,400

Broken Bow

LAKE McCONAUGHY
LAKE C.W. McCONAUGHY S.R.A.
BLUEWATER BATTLEFIELD

Mountain Time Zone / Central Time Zone

MAP PG. 57

WYOMING / S. DAK.
NEBRASKA
SOUTH DAKOTA / NEBRASKA

0 10 20 30 40 50
SCALE IN MILES

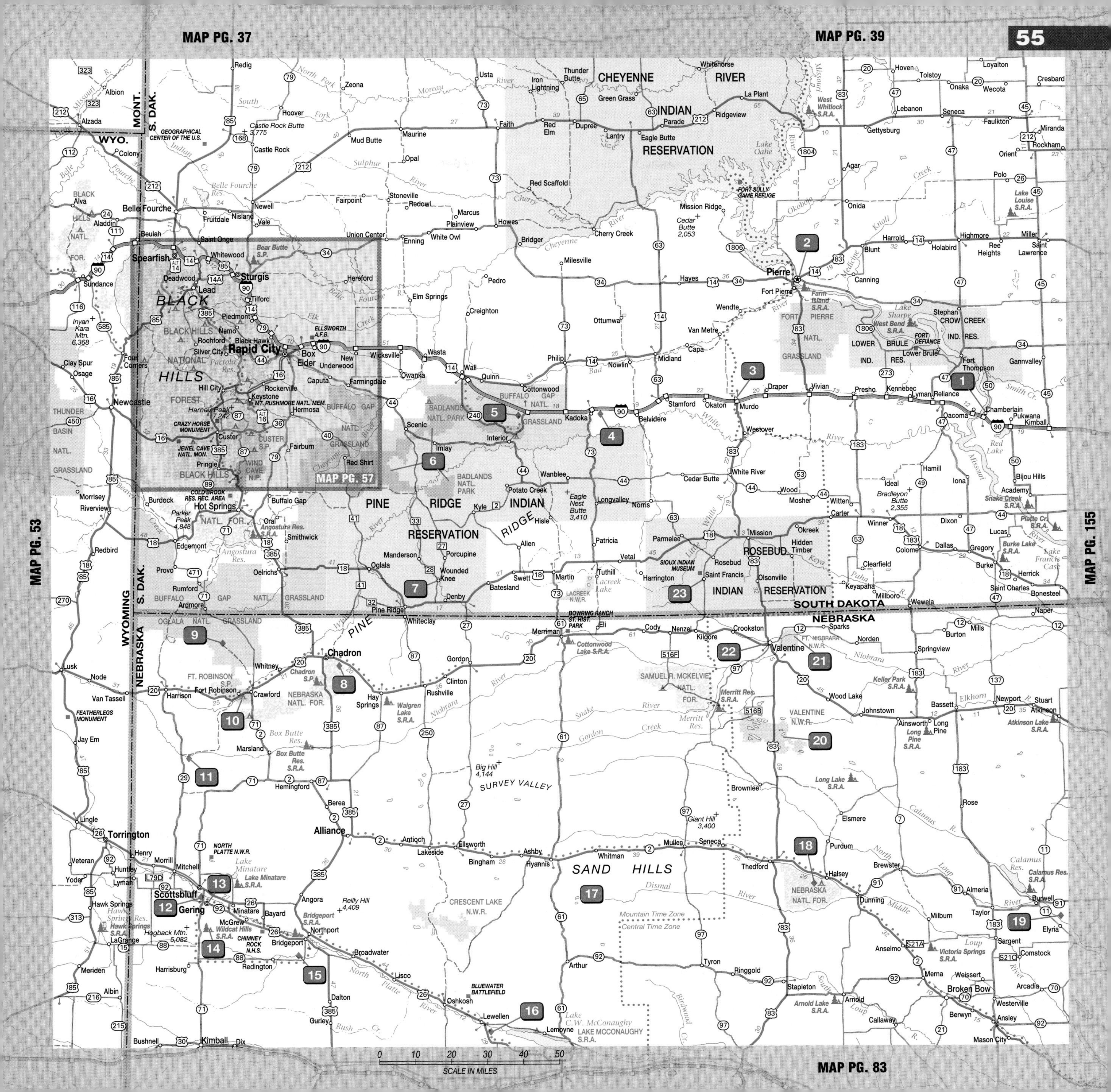

1. D. C. Booth Historic Fish Hatchery

423 Hatchery Circle, Spearfish. The Black Hills, full of streams and lakes, were devoid of trout until the D. C. Booth Hatchery was authorized by Congress in 1896. Trout were imported, and Booth built the fish hatchery in 1899 near Spearfish Canyon; today it is a multimillion-dollar business. The National Fish Culture Hall of Fame and a small museum, now in the original building, present Booth's work through photographs and other displays. Anglers also have the opportunity to test their luck in the tumbling trout-filled waters.

2. Roughlock Falls

The sylvan beauty of this 30-foot natural treasure is almost completely concealed by the cool, green shade of aspen trees. Visitors can best enjoy the view from a path that leads down along the side of the falls.

3. Terry Peak

The roadway to the summit of this 7,064-foot pinnacle winds through stands of spruce, oaks, elms, birches, and cottonwoods, varieties that give way to the state tree — the ponderosa pine — toward the top. A chair lift carries visitors to within a few hundred feet of the summit. For hardy souls, a steep trail continues on to the crest. From a fire lookout the breathtaking view sweeps over Inyan Kara Mountain, Harney Peak, Bear Butte, and beyond.

4. Homestake Gold Mine

215 West Main St., Lead. Gold was discovered in 1876 in a mountain near the town of Lead, and throughout the years the extraction of the mineral created a huge canyon called Open Cut. Gold ore is still mined here today, both in the canyon and underground. The mine is reached by vertical shafts that descend to hundreds of miles of tunnels. The subsequent process of converting the ore into gold bars is explained at the visitor center, and guided tours, offered seasonally, take visitors through the topside areas of the mine. *Fee charged for tour.*

5. Deadwood

Chamber of Commerce, 735 Main St. In 1875 gold was discovered in remote Deadwood Gulch, and the gold rush that ensued brought some 25,000 prospectors and entrepreneurs to the scene. Guided tours are offered at **Broken Boot Gold Mine,** and visitors can supplement their mining knowledge by touring the **Black Hills Mining Museum.** Today, in the town where Wild Bill Hickok, Calamity Jane, and preacher Henry Smith are buried, the **Adams Memorial Museum** and the **Ghosts of Deadwood Gulch Wax Museum** recount the past. Colorful reenactments of local history are also staged here during the summer. *Admission charged for some attractions.*

6. Bear Butte State Park

This cone-shaped mountain soars some 1,500 feet above the grassy slopes where buffalo graze. The mountain is sacred to the Sioux, who still make pilgrimages to the summit, and to the Cheyennes; it is known to geologists as a laccolith — an intrusion of molten rock that occurred millions of years ago. The park campground offers a lake, and hiking trails lead to the mountaintop. *Admission charged.*

7. Black Hills Petrified Forest

The petrified trunks of cypress and palm trees scattered along the top of Piedmont Butte create a scene of eerie wonder. Visitors can take a guided tour through the forest and see a short film in the theater that explains the geological history of the Black Hills. A museum displays hundreds of examples of petrified wood, which illustrate the gradual process by which forest is converted into stone. *Admission charged.*

8. Sioux Indian and Minnilusa Pioneer Museums

515 West Blvd., Rapid City. The two museums, sharing one building, are located in Halley Park. On display at the Sioux Indian Museum are the modern arts and crafts, as well as the ancient artifacts, of various North American tribes. The history of the early trappers, fur traders, and gold prospectors, who came into this great wilderness more than a hundred years ago, is interpreted through displays of tools, photographs, artifacts, and other memorabilia at the Minnilusa Pioneer Museum.

9. Pactola Lake

Set in a high mountain landscape, this jewel-like lake is almost entirely encircled by thick growths of pines, oaks, and white birches. A break in the woodlands, opening like a window onto another world, reveals a luxuriant meadowland stretching eastward from the lake.

10. Black Hills National Forest

More than a million acres of grandeur make up this heavily forested mountainous region. The many lakes, streams, sparkling waterfalls, and deep canyons add to the splendor of this natural treasure.

11. Sheridan Lake

The lake spreads out through dense pine woods, its uneven coastline well hidden from the nearby highway. Visitors come to enjoy the excellent fishing and boating, as well as the several campsites along the lake's southern shore.

12. Mount Rushmore National Memorial

Gutzon Borglum began the monumental task of carving four U. S. presidents on the southeast face of Mt. Rushmore in 1927; the work was completed by his son in 1941. The patriots — Washington, Jefferson, Lincoln, and Theodore Roosevelt — were chosen for their extraordinary contributions to the nation. The sculptor's studio, below the visitor center, contains a model of the work, several work-in-progress photographs, and an assortment of sculptors' tools.

13. Crazy Horse Memorial

Avenue of the Chiefs, Crazy Horse. From a viewing veranda, visitors can watch this work-in-progress, which ultimately will take shape as a giant mountain carving of the legendary Sioux chief in the Black Hills. The memorial complex also includes one of the region's foremost Native American museums. *Admission charged.*

14. Jewel Cave National Monument

Discovered in the early 1900's, this underground wonderland is located in Hell's Canyon, an area of hills, ravines, and meadows carpeted with wildflowers. The cave is one of the longest in the country, extending for almost 100 miles through brilliantly colorful crystal-filled passages. Several guided tours are offered, and the visitor center displays various types of crystal formations. *Fee charged for tour.*

15. Needles Highway

This spectacular roadway, a ribbon of hairpin turns and narrow tunnels, takes the traveler on a 14-mile journey through a rugged landscape of jagged peaks and towering pinnacles of granite carved and shaped by thousands of years of erosion.

16. Center Lake

The charm of this crystal-clear mountain lake is enhanced by the sheltering stands of ponderosa pine that almost completely conceal it from view. A 3-mile trail follows a creek from the lake through rough undergrowth, offering good opportunities for hiking and fishing.

17. Custer State Park

More than 1,400 head of bison, along with elk, deer, bighorn sheep, pronghorn antelope, and other indigenous species, can often be glimpsed by visitors on the **Wildlife Loop Road,** a picturesque 18-mile scenic drive through the rolling prairie. Many of the lakes and streams in the park provide excellent fishing and swimming. *Admission charged.*

Bison and calves at Custer State Park

18. Wind Cave National Park

Visitors can take a guided tour of the cave, in which air currents whisk through 66 miles of underground passages formed in rock once covered by an ancient, shallow sea. Above the hidden cavern, the grasslands abound with bison, elk, and other prairie wildlife. The park also includes acres of ponderosa pine and a scattering of deciduous woodland. *Fee charged for tour.*

19. Buffalo Gap National Grassland

This great prairie, which through eons had become acclimated to the rigors of the area's weather, was almost destroyed during the 1930's by drought and other factors. Pasturing is now strictly limited, and through the efforts of the U. S. Forest Service, the grassland is slowly being brought back to its natural condition.

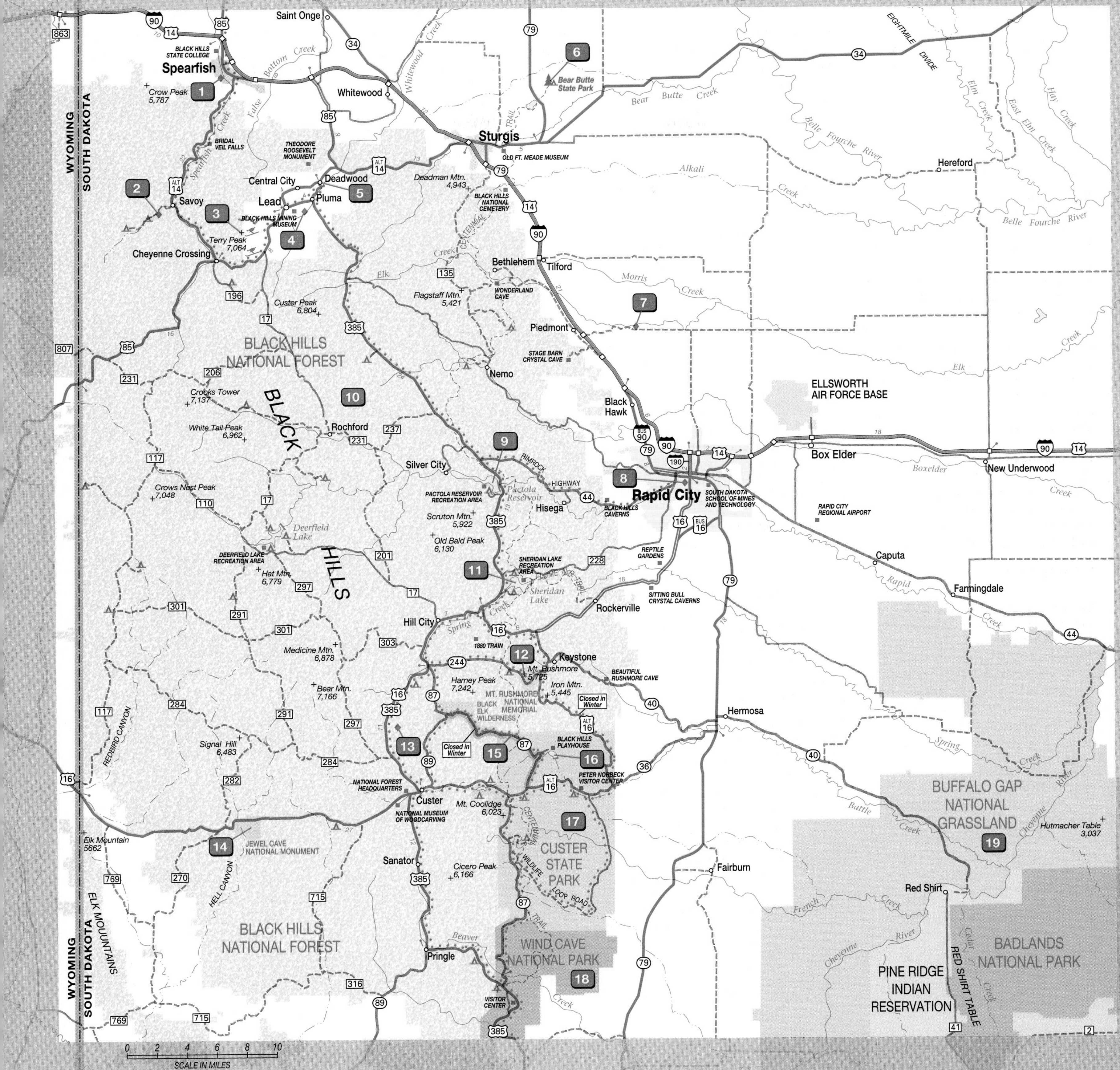

WYOMING
SOUTH DAKOTA

Spearfish

BLACK HILLS STATE COLLEGE

Saint Onge

Crow Peak
5,787

1

BRIDAL VEIL FALLS

2

Savoy

3

Central City

Lead

BLACK HILLS MINING MUSEUM

4

Terry Peak
7,064

Cheyenne Crossing

THEODORE ROOSEVELT MONUMENT

Deadwood

Pluma

5

Whitewood

Deadman Mtn.
4,943

BLACK HILLS NATIONAL CEMETERY

Sturgis

OLD FT. MEADE MUSEUM

6

Bear Butte State Park

Hereford

196

17

Custer Peak
6,804

385

135

Flagstaff Mtn.
5,421

WONDERLAND CAVE

Bethlehem

Tilford

7

Belle Fourche River

Belle Fourche River

BLACK HILLS NATIONAL FOREST

206

Crooks Tower
7,137

10

231

Rochford

237

231

White Tail Peak
6,962

BLACK

Nemo

Piedmont

STAGE BARN CRYSTAL CAVE

Black Hawk

ELLSWORTH AIR FORCE BASE

117

Crows Nest Peak
7,048

110

17

Silver City

9

RIMROCK

HIGHWAY

PACTOLA RESERVOIR RECREATION AREA

Pactola Reservoir

HILLS

Deerfield Lake

DEERFIELD LAKE RECREATION AREA

Hat Mtn.
6,779

297

201

Scruton Mtn.
5,922

385

Hisega

44

BLACK HILLS CAVERNS

Rapid City

SOUTH DAKOTA SCHOOL OF MINES AND TECHNOLOGY

Box Elder

New Underwood

Boxelder Creek

RAPID CITY REGIONAL AIRPORT

301

291

301

Old Bald Peak
6,130

11

SHERIDAN LAKE RECREATION AREA

Sheridan Lake

228

REPTILE GARDENS

16

Caputa

303

17

Hill City

16

SITTING BULL CRYSTAL CAVERNS

Rockerville

79

Rapid Creek

Farmingdale

Medicine Mtn.
6,878

244

1880 TRAIN

12

Keystone

Mt. Rushmore
5,725

BEAUTIFUL RUSHMORE CAVE

Iron Mtn.
5,445

Closed in Winter

40

Hermosa

44

Bear Mtn.
7,166

16

385

87

Harney Peak
7,242

BLACK ELK WILDERNESS

MT. RUSHMORE NATIONAL MEMORIAL

ALT 16

117

284

291

297

Signal Hill
6,483

282

89

13

Closed in Winter

15

87

BLACK HILLS PLAYHOUSE

16

PETER NORBECK VISITOR CENTER

36

40

BUFFALO GAP NATIONAL GRASSLAND

Hutmacher Table
3,037

19

Elk Mountain
5662

14

JEWEL CAVE NATIONAL MONUMENT

NATIONAL FOREST HEADQUARTERS

Custer

NATIONAL MUSEUM OF WOODCARVING

Mt. Coolidge
6,023

17

CUSTER STATE PARK

Fairburn

Red Shirt

270

769

715

385

Sanator

Cicero Peak
6,166

BLACK HILLS NATIONAL FOREST

Pringle

316

89

385

WILDLIFE LOOP ROAD

87

WIND CAVE NATIONAL PARK

18

VISITOR CENTER

79

PINE RIDGE INDIAN RESERVATION

BADLANDS NATIONAL PARK

41

WYOMING
SOUTH DAKOTA

ELK MOUNTAINS

HELL CANYON

REDBIRD CANYON

RED SHIRT TABLE

0 2 4 6 8 10
SCALE IN MILES

1. Eureka

Chamber of Commerce, 2112 Broadway. Founded in 1850 during the gold rush, Eureka is now the largest city in northwestern California. The city's early days are preserved in **Old Town Eureka,** where Victorian commercial and residential buildings still remain, along with a gazebo, fountain, and trolley. The awe-inspiring **Carson Mansion,** built in 1885 for lumber baron William Carson, is one of the most photographed homes in the nation. The history of Eureka as a logging and shipping town is chronicled in the **Clarke Memorial Museum.** The remains of a fort where Ulysses S. Grant was stationed in 1854 still stand in **Fort Humboldt State Historic Park.** *Fee charged for trolley.*

2. Weaverville Joss House State Historic Park

419 Main St., Weaverville. A surprising touch of Asia occurs here. A Taoist temple, built in 1874 by Chinese gold miners, has been in continuous use since its construction. On display are tapestries, carvings, and other fine art works. *Admission charged.*

3. French Gulch

Unlike many of the nation's old mining towns, French Gulch still bustles with activity. The charming village, however, looks much as it did more than 100 years ago, with a church, general store, and hotel.

4. Castle Crags State Park

The park is named for its jagged mountain peaks that rise regally from a base of dense evergreen forests to an elevation of about 6,000 feet. Activities in the park include camping, swimming, hiking, and trout fishing. *Admission charged.*

5. Whiskeytown-Shasta-Trinity National Recreation Area

Boaters and anglers can gaze on evergreen-covered hills and pine-forested slopes while sporting on the lakes. Picnicking and camping facilities are also available.

6. Shasta Dam and Lake

A huge dam has created both Lake Shasta and one of California's largest power plants. The visitor center's observation theater looks out on the dam's spillway, which is three times as high as Niagara Falls. The lake is the core of a very popular recreation area, offering marinas and hiking trails, as well as fishing and camping sites.

7. Shasta State Historic Park

This park maintains the ruins of Shasta City, a boomtown during California's gold-rush era. The county courthouse, which still has its original jail cells, now serves as a museum. *Admission charged.*

8. William B. Ide Adobe State Historic Park

21659 Adobe Rd., Red Bluff. Built in the 1850's, an adobe home overlooking the Sacramento River now stands as a memorial to William B. Ide, a leader in the 1846 revolt against Mexico by California settlers. The house, with period furnishings, is open to the public. The grounds include a refreshing picnic grove, and the river abounds in trout and salmon. *Admission charged.*

9. Lassen Volcanic National Park

Prehistoric volcanic activity formed this park, where glacial lakes and snow-fed streams mix with thermal phenomena such as mud pots and fumaroles. A road curves up **Lassen Peak,** a quiescent volcano, to a parking lot from which a rugged trail, with many splendid views, climbs to the mountain's summit. The park also offers skiing, boating, fishing, and camping.

10. Bidwell Mansion State Historic Park

525 Esplanade, Chico. The handsome estate centers on the 19th-century, 26-room mansion that once belonged to John Bidwell, a farmer, statesman, and humanitarian. Visitors can stroll the grounds through stands of oaks and sycamores and cross the Chico Creek footbridge. *Admission charged.*

11. Colusa-Sacramento River State Recreation Area

Outdoor enthusiasts enjoy this 63-acre park for its dense forest, sandy swimming beach, and a stretch of river that rewards anglers with king salmon, sturgeon, and steelhead trout. *Admission charged.*

12. Feather Falls Scenic Area

These 15,000 acres are named for the 640-foot waterfall that descends into a rugged valley in the Sierra foothills. A 4-mile trail leads visitors to a viewing platform overlooking the falls. Two miles away, **Bald Rock Dome,** formed 140 million years ago, rises majestically. Swimming and canoeing are popular at the **Middle Feather River.**

13. Pyramid Lake

The blue of this lake is set off by the desert that surrounds it. Along the shoreline, tufa (a porous rock) has formed various intriguing formations. A tufa island in the middle of the lake, reminiscent of a pyramid, inspired the lake's name. On the island of Anaho, white pelicans find sanctuary.

14. Fort Churchill State Historic Park

Rte. 95A, south of Silver Springs. The ruins of Nevada's first military post stand in the desert near the Carson River. Named for an army inspector general, the white adobe compound was built after an Indian uprising in 1860. Nine years later the post was abandoned, and now only crumbling buildings remain — among them a barracks and officers' quarters, hospital, and guard house.

15. Empire Mine State Historic Park

10791 East Empire St., Grass Valley. Extremely productive in its day, the Empire Gold Mine closed in 1956. Today visitors can walk a short distance into the mine tunnel, see explanatory exhibits at the park's visitor center, and tour the residence and formal gardens of the mine's former owner. *Admission charged.*

16. Marshall Gold Discovery State Historic Park

Rte. 49, Coloma. The park commemorates James Marshall's 1848 discovery of gold at Sutter's Mill, marking the beginning of the gold rush. It contains a replica of the mill, a river in which visitors can still pan for gold, a museum devoted to the area's history, and the old town of Coloma. *Admission charged.*

17. Angels Camp

This town began as a mining camp, and many 19th-century structures remain, such as a dry-goods store, hospital, footbridge, and hotel. It was at the **Angels Hotel** that Mark Twain reportedly heard the story that prompted him to write the "The Celebrated Jumping Frog of Calaveras County."

18. Columbia State Historic Park

Columbia exploded onto the Mother Lode scene when gold was discovered here in 1850. In an 8-block area stand dozens of original or re-created structures, including a church, firehouse, and theater. Visitors can observe a blacksmith at work, enjoy toe-tapping music in a historic saloon, pan for gold, and even take a ride on a Wells Fargo stagecoach. *Fee charged for stagecoach ride.*

19. Jamestown

This picturesque gold-mining town numbers two hotels among its carefully restored buildings. It also preserves the yards of the Sierra Railway Depot — complete with early cars and steam engines — in a complex called **Railtown 1897,** which offers excursions through the Mother Lode country.

20. Sonora

Sonora boasts wonderful historic buildings, such as the *Union Democrat* newspaper office and the red-frame Episcopal church. It also sponsors an annual rodeo, held in May, that attracts many visitors.

21. Rim of the World Vista Point

The scenic outlook's name hardly seems an exaggeration to visitors, who can gaze from this point across a seemingly endless expanse of mountains and canyons, and down 1,700 feet to the Tuolumne River.

22. Bear Valley

Surrounded by hills, Bear Valley affords phenomenal views of the rocky slopes of Hell's Hollow, Lake McClure, and the Merced River.

23. Mariposa Museum and History Center

5119 Jessie St., Mariposa. The center's exhibits illustrate aspects of everyday life during the gold-fever days of the mid-1800's, such as touching passages from a young miner's letters to a Massachusetts friend. *Donation suggested.*

24. Hornitos

A narrow, tortuous road leads to Hornitos, once one of the nation's most colorful mining towns. Some of the buildings that still face the earthen square include a Wells Fargo office, a saloon, and a jail.

25. Caswell Memorial State Park

Huge valley oaks, which once graced this entire region, are protected here. Swimming holes dot the Stanislaus River, where bluegill, bass, salmon, and other fish abound. The shady park lends itself well to picnicking and camping. *Admission charged.*

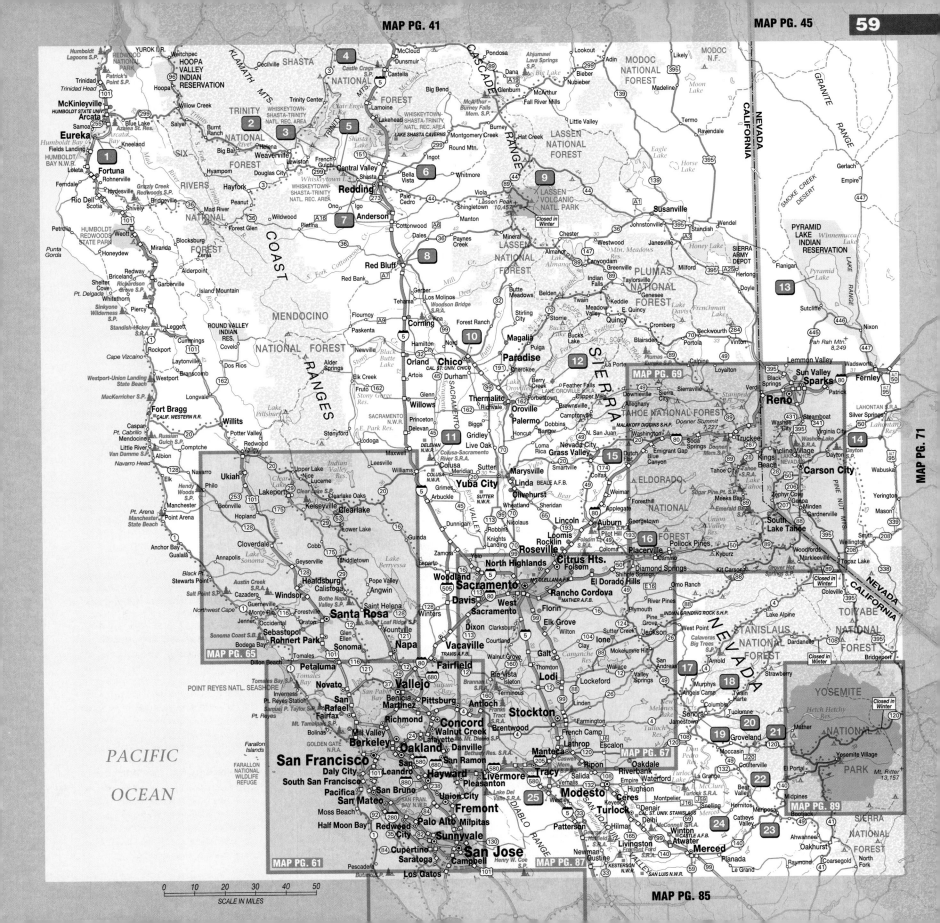

CALIFORNIA

NEVADA

Sacramento ★

Stockton ●

San Francisco

● San Jose

1. Tomales Bay State Park

Information on the flora and fauna of the park is available at the ranger's office near the entrance. Beaches offer chilly swimming and clamming for littlenecks; two hiking trails take visitors through the coastal landscape. *Admission charged.*

2. Point Reyes National Seashore

One hundred miles of coastline along a peninsula and several designated wilderness areas comprise this seashore preserve. **Earthquake Trail** leads along the San Andreas Fault to a spot where a rift in the earth occurred in 1906. At the peninsula's tip, Point Reyes Lighthouse stands near **Drake's Beach,** said to be the area where Sir Francis Drake stopped to repair his ship.

3. Mission San Rafael Arcangel

1102 Fifth Ave., San Rafael. Built in 1817, the mission started as a hospital. So successful was it in treating American Indians that it soon earned full mission status. The rebuilt structure contains replicas of the original star windows and bells.

4. Mount Tamalpais

Hiking and riding trails wind through the woodlands of this mountain, which rises 2,571 feet above the beaches at its base. Located near San Francisco, the landmark offers an almost limitless view from its peak.

5. Muir Woods National Monument

In 1908, this awesome 559-acre redwood forest was established as a national monument in tribute to John Muir, the famed conservationist who devoted his life to the protection of America's natural wonders.

6. San Francisco Bay and Delta Hydraulic Model

2100 Bridgeway, Sausalito. Set in a 2-acre building, this huge hydraulic model reproduces the tidal action of local waters. Recorded information is provided by telephones set at intervals around the model, and a video presentation is given at the visitor center.

7. Alcatraz

Named for its many pelicans (*alcatraces* in Spanish), this rocky bit of land in San Francisco Bay was home to a federal prison, nicknamed The Rock, from 1934 to 1963. It now attracts visitors who come by ferry for a glimpse of its unhappy past and a superb view of the Bay. *Admission charged.*

8. Acres of Orchids

1450 El Camino Real, South San Francisco. A brilliant explosion of color as far as the eye can see greets visitors to one of the world's largest orchid growers and hybridizers. Thousands of flowers are on display, and guided tours are available.

9. Pacifica

Chamber of Commerce, 220 Paloma Ave. Several communities along the coastal mountains make up this area, which has two popular historic sites: **Sweeney Ridge,** the peak from which Gaspar de Portolá first saw San Francisco Bay in 1769; and **Sanchez Adobe,** the restored two-story home of Francisco Sanchez, the Presidio's first commander.

10. Half Moon Bay

Chamber of Commerce, 225 South Cabrillo Hwy. The town is known for its flower markets, pumpkin farms, and lush forests. Fishing fleets and pleasure craft dock at **Pillar Point Harbor,** whose waterfront features restaurants and handicraft shops. Markers in Pilarcitos Cemetery testify to the ethnic diversity of Half Moon Bay's early settlers.

11. Filoli House and Gardens

8300 Cañada Rd., Woodside. Built in 1915 by William B. Bourn, one of San Francisco's most prominent citizens, the impressive mansion was featured on the popular television series *Dynasty.* Visitors may tour both the house and the unusually beautiful gardens that surround it. *Admission charged.*

12. Stanford University

Visitors to this Palo Alto campus may tour the **Memorial Church,** built in 1903 in memory of the university's founder, Leland Stanford; and **Hoover Tower,** a research institute founded by President Hoover. The nearby **Barbie Hall of Fame** boasts an impressive collection that includes 16,000 of the ever-popular dolls and their accessories.

13. Pescadero

At **Coastways Ranch,** visitors are invited to pick their own pumpkins, blackberries,

and kiwi fruit. The only spot on the California mainland where elephant seals can be seen at close range, the **Año Nuevo State Reserve** offers guided tours of the rookery. *Admission charged.*

14. Villa Montalvo

15400 Montalvo Rd., Saratoga. Built as a summer home in 1912 by Senator James D. Phelan, the estate is now a cultural center offering concerts, plays, lectures, guided tours, and facilities for artists in residence. The extensive grounds encompass formal gardens, an open-air amphitheater, an arboretum, and several hiking trails. *Fee charged for tour.*

15. San Jose

Visitors and Convention Bureau, 333 West San Carlos St. Founded in 1777, the city was the first capital of California. Sights of interest include the **Winchester Mystery House,** built by Sarah Winchester, widow of the firearms manufacturer. Advised by a medium that she would be safe from the spirits of those killed by the Winchester rifle as long as she kept her house under construction, she employed a battalion of carpenters 24 hours a day for 38 years at a cost of more than $5,500,000. The result is a mansion with 160 rooms, 40 stairways (many with 13 steps, leading nowhere), blind chimneys, trapdoors, and secret passageways. Among other city attractions are **Rosicrucian Park,** featuring a planetarium and an Egyptian museum; **Alum Rock Park,** nicknamed "Little Yosemite"; and the **San Jose Historical Museum,** with original and reconstructed buildings of early San Jose. *Admission charged for some attractions.*

16. Great America

Great America Pkwy., Santa Clara. Here visitors can enjoy many attractions, including five roller coasters, a rafting ride, a delightful double-deck carousel, a midway, and several kinds of variety shows. Restaurants and shops are scattered throughout the grounds. *Admission charged.*

17. Mission San Jose

43300 Mission Blvd., Fremont. Only recently reconstructed after having been destroyed in an 1868 earthquake, this 1797 mission was known for its many American Indian converts, and for an orchestra made up of American Indian musicians. The church contains two original statues and the original baptismal font. A small museum houses other mission artifacts.

18. Mount Diablo

Protected as a state park, the mountain attracts many visitors to its summit for magnificent views of the surrounding mountains, valleys, and coastal waters.

19. Oakland

Convention and Visitors Bureau, 1000 Broadway. Situated across the Bay from San Francisco, the city is known for its historical sites, including the **Oakland Museum,** which features science, history, and art exhibits; the **Jack London Waterfront,** with various locales frequented by the author; **Joaquin Miller Park,** scene of outdoor summer musicals; and the **Northern California Center for Afro-American History and Life,** which highlights African-American contributions to California's history.

20. University of California, Berkeley

The campus offers a number of attractions, including the **Lawrence Hall of Science;** the **Phoebe Apperson Hearst Museum of Anthropology;** the **Sather Tower,** modeled after the clock tower in Venice's Piazza San Marco; the **Botanical Garden;** and the **University Art Museum.** *Admission charged for some attractions.*

21. Martinez

Chamber of Commerce, 620 Las Juntas St. Named for a commander of the Spanish Presidio at San Francisco, this small town was home to naturalist and author John Muir, who was responsible for the creation of Yosemite as a national park. Both the 1882 Muir House and the two-story Martinez Adobe have been preserved as part of the **John Muir National Historic Site.** *Admission charged.*

22. Marine World Africa USA

Marine World Pkwy., Vallejo. In this combination wildlife park and oceanarium the animals, accompanied by their trainers, wander freely throughout the grounds. Gentle sea lions interact with visitors; dolphins and killer whales perform lively shows; and tropical sharks can be viewed in a tunneled aquarium. *Admission charged.*

23. Western Railway Museum

5848 State Hwy. 12, between Fairfield and Rio Vista. Antique trolleys, railroad cars, and a boat-shaped tram car are on display at this outdoor museum. Visitors can also ride a mile-long rail line and picnic beside a shady pond. *Admission charged.*

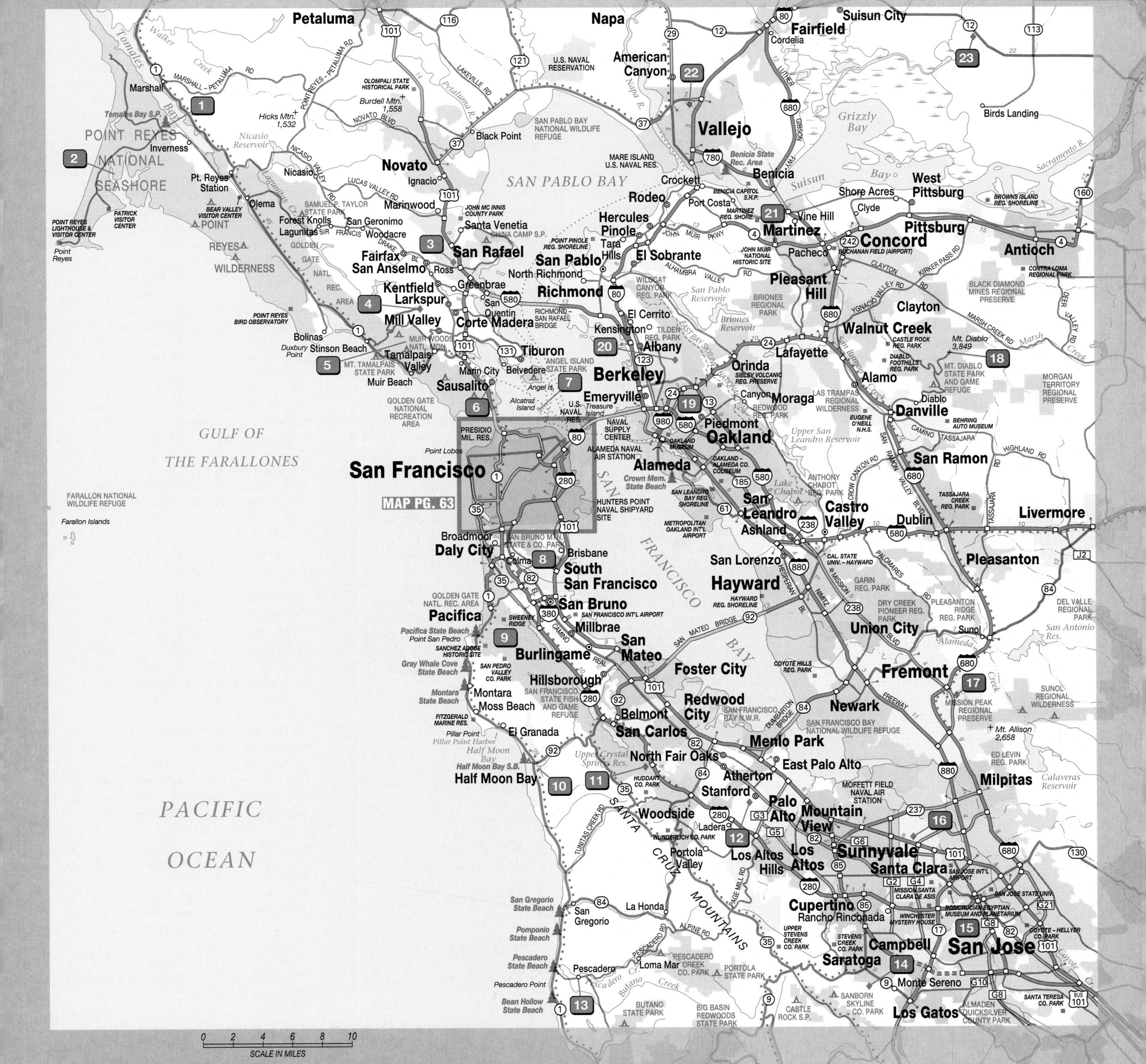

Petaluma

Napa

Suisun City

Fairfield
Cordelia

American Canyon

Birds Landing

Marshall

1

Walker Creek

MARSHALL - PETALUMA RD

U.S. NAVAL RESERVATION

22

23

Tomales Bay S.P.

Hicks Mtn. 1,532

Burdell Mtn. 1,558

OLOMPALI STATE HISTORICAL PARK

Black Point

Vallejo

Grizzly Bay

2

POINT REYES NATIONAL SEASHORE

Inverness

Nicasio Reservoir

SAN PABLO BAY NATIONAL WILDLIFE REFUGE

MARE ISLAND U.S. NAVAL RES.

Benicia State Rec. Area

Shore Acres

West Pittsburg

BROWNS ISLAND REG. SHORELINE

Pt. Reyes Station

Nicasio

Novato

Ignacio

SAN PABLO BAY

Crockett

Benicia

Suisun Bay

Benicia Capitol S.H.P.

Pittsburg

Point Reyes

REYES WILDERNESS

Olema

Marinwood

Rodeo

Port Costa

Clyde

Pacheco

Point Reyes Lighthouse & Visitor Center

Forest Knolls Woodacre

Santa Venetia

Hercules

Martinez Reg. Shore.

Vine Hill

Antioch

CHINA CAMP S.P.

Pinole

21

Concord

242

Lagunitas

San Geronimo

Fairfax

3

San Rafael

San Pablo

Tara Hills

Martinez

Buchanan Field (AIRPORT)

CONTRA LOMA REGIONAL PARK

Point Reyes Bird Observatory

4

Kentfield Larkspur

Greenbrae

North Richmond

El Sobrante

Pleasant Hill

Clayton

BLACK DIAMOND MINES REGIONAL PRESERVE

Point Reyes

Bolinas

5

Mill Valley

Corte Madera

Richmond

El Cerrito

Walnut Creek

Mt. Diablo 3,849

Stinson Beach

Tiburon

20

Kensington

Albany

Orinda

Lafayette

Alamo

DIABLO STATE PARK

Muir Beach

Sausalito

7

Berkeley

19

Piedmont

Danville

18

6

San Francisco

8

Oakland

Alameda

San Leandro

Castro Valley

Dublin

Livermore

MAP PG. 63

Broadmoor Daly City

Colma

Brisbane

South San Francisco

Hayward

Pleasanton

Pacifica

San Bruno

Millbrae

San Mateo

Union City

Fremont

17

Half Moon Bay

9

Burlingame

Hillsborough

Foster City

Newark

10 **11**

Belmont

San Carlos

Redwood City

Milpitas

Menlo Park

East Palo Alto

Atherton

Stanford

Palo Alto

Mountain View

16

Woodside

12

Los Altos Hills

Los Altos

Sunnyvale

Santa Clara

San Jose

Portola Valley

Cupertino

Rancho Rinconada

17

15

La Honda

San Gregorio

Campbell

Saratoga

14

PACIFIC OCEAN

Pescadero

Monte Sereno

13

Los Gatos

SAN FRANCISCO

1. Forty-Nine-Mile Drive
This scenic drive, marked by blue and white seagull signs, passes San Francisco's major attractions, including Chinatown, Nob Hill, Fisherman's Wharf, Golden Gate Park, Mission Dolores, Golden Gate Bridge, and Telegraph Hill.

2. Golden Gate Bridge
Soaring over the entrance to San Francisco Bay, this reddish orange bridge, more than 3 miles long, is often called the world's most beautiful. Completed in 1937, the bridge was designed with a delicacy that belies its exceptional strength. *Toll charged.*

3. The Presidio
In 1776 the Spanish established a fort on what was then barren terrain. Now landscaped, it was used as a U. S. Army base from 1846 until recently. Today visitors come to enjoy its historic trails and sweeping views of the Pacific. Also popular are the **Presidio Army Museum** and **Fort Point National Historic Site,** a restored fort under the Golden Gate Bridge.

4. National Maritime Museum
890 Beach St. Located at the foot of Polk Street, the museum traces the history of California's shipping industry. The sizable collection includes ship models, paintings, photographs, and other maritime memorabilia. Several restored vessels, moored at Hyde Street Pier, are open to visitors. *Admission charged.*

5. Ghirardelli Square
The square's 19th-century factory buildings, once the home of the Ghirardelli Chocolate Company, have been transformed into an unusual shopping mall, with boutiques, restaurants, cafes, and art galleries.

6. The Cannery
2801 Leavenworth St. Built in 1906 as a fruit cannery, the brick structure and its courtyard are now home to a collection of specialty shops, boutiques, restaurants, craft centers, and street performers. Its proximity to Fisherman's Wharf makes it an especially popular spot with tourists.

7. Fisherman's Wharf
At the end of the 19th century, when hundreds of fishing vessels docked here, this wharf became a busy commercial fishing center. Today boats still come to the wharf with their daily catch. Visitors throng the colorful waterfront, home to seafood restaurants, cafes, shops, and fast-food stalls offering shrimp and crab.

8. Coit Tower
Lombard St. on Telegraph Hill. Built to commemorate Lillie Coit and the city's firefighters, the monument includes murals, in the style of Mexican artist Diego Rivera, which were painted by government-commissioned artists in the 1930's. An elevator ride to the top provides visitors with glorious views of the Bay and Golden Gate Bridge. *Fee charged for elevator.*

9. Embarcadero
Along this famous waterfront boulevard stands the historic **Ferry Building,** once known as the gateway to San Francisco, where thousands of visitors arrived by both rail and ferry. The **Embarcadero Center,** a pedestrian complex of plazas, high rises, modern sculptures, and fountains, extends from Clay to Sacramento streets.

10. Chinatown
The oldest Chinese settlement outside of Asia dates from the mid-1800's and features pagodas, a ceremonial gateway, shops, restaurants, and teahouses. The community was rebuilt after the 1906 earthquake. The Chinese Culture Center offers several exhibits as well as guided tours of the area. *Fee charged for tours.*

11. Old U.S. Mint
Fifth and Mission Sts. This brick-and-stone Classical Revival building, dating from 1874, is now a museum containing rare coins and medals. Visitors can view the steel vault, with its gold bars and coins, and strike a souvenir medal on an 1869 coin press.

12. Wells Fargo Bank History Museum
420 Montgomery St. The story of the famous Wells Fargo Bank is told in exhibits of the gold-rush days that include gold nuggets, paintings, and "wanted" posters. Here is the Concord stagecoach, which during the 1850's carried 15 passengers per trip on the 18-day trek from St. Joseph, Missouri, to Sacramento, where passengers then traveled by boat to San Francisco. Close to the museum, the **Transamerica Pyramid** — considered by many to be the most spectacular high rise in the U.S. since its completion in 1972 — soars to an impressive height of 853 feet.

13. Grace Cathedral
1051 Taylor St. This towering Gothic-style cathedral, located in posh Nob Hill, is the seat of the Episcopalian church in the San Francisco Bay area. It features an eye-catching rose window and gilded bronze doors that are replicas of Ghiberti's Doors of Paradise in Florence.

From Coit Tower, sightseers delight in sweeping views of downtown San Francisco, the Bay, Alcatraz, and the Golden Gate Bridge.

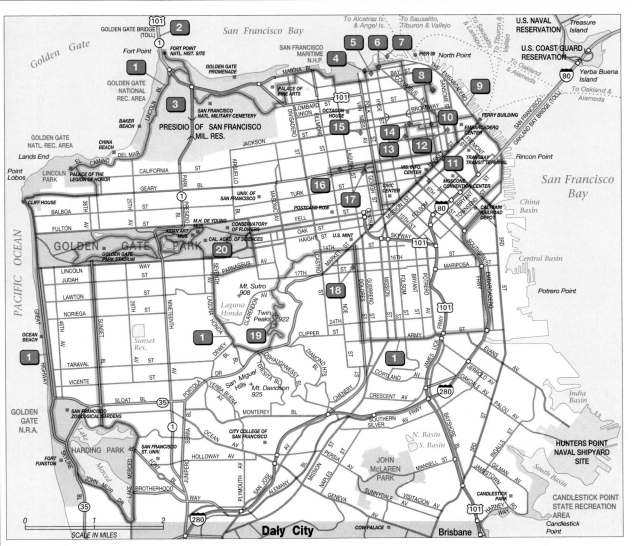

A cable car bound for Hyde Street Pier

14. San Francisco Cable Car Museum

1201 Mason St. Several of the cars that have carried passengers up the impossibly steep San Francisco hills since 1873 are on display here, as are vintage photographs and the cable mechanism that operates the system. For a modern-day experience, visitors can take the cable car from Hyde Street to Powell Street, which is considered to be a very scenic route. Lombard Street, known for its winding curves, and Filbert — at an angle of 31.5 degrees the steepest street in the city — are encountered along the way.

15. Haas-Lilienthal House

2007 Franklin St. This lovely Queen Anne–style domicile, which miraculously survived the great earthquake and fire of 1906, is the city's only fully furnished Victorian home open to the public. Tours of the house are given by docents from the Foundation for San Francisco's Architectural Heritage. *Admission charged.*

16. Japan Center

This popular modern complex, designed by the architect of the World Trade Center in New York, draws many visitors to its Japanese restaurants, art galleries, and shops. At its center is the Peace Plaza, an area of Japanese gardens and reflecting pools, where traditional festivals are held. The Peace Pagoda, a five-tiered structure towering over the plaza, was a goodwill gift from Japan to the people of San Francisco.

17. St. Mary's Cathedral

1111 Gough St. This magnificent cathedral boasts seating for 2,400 and a glittering cascade above the altar containing 7,000 aluminum triangular prisms. The noteworthy dome is composed of four stained-glass windows representing the four elements of air, fire, water, and earth.

18. Mission Dolores

16th and Dolores Sts. Established in 1776 by the Franciscans, this church marks the beginning of San Francisco. The whitewashed adobe brick structure is the oldest original church building in the state, as well as the city's oldest extant building. Early settlers are buried in an adjacent cemetery. A nearby 1916 basilica towers over the little mission. *Donation encouraged.*

19. Twin Peaks

These famous landmarks, rising 922 feet above the city, provide outstanding views of San Francisco and the Bay. A scenic drive leads to the summit, where visitors come to witness spectacular sunsets.

20. Golden Gate Park

Extending eastward from the Pacific Coast the 1,017-acre park, developed in the late 1800's by the botanist John McLaren, is considered to be one of the most beautiful parks in the world. On its grounds are an arboretum, waterfalls, lakes, many gardens, and several fine museums. Its Conservatory of Flowers includes a large collection of orchids. Sports fans enjoy the tennis courts, soccer fields, and golf course. Weekly band concerts are given on Sundays.

A Victorian home on Telegraph Hill

1. Montgomery Woods State Reserve

Their massive trunks fringed by ferns, giant redwoods soar to the sky in this peaceful forest. Starting at a picnic area near a creek, a steep trail leads to a clearing encircled by the reserve's biggest trees, which are up to 15 feet in diameter. The road to the reserve is narrow and winding, but offers fine views of verdant farmland and rolling hills.

2. Lake Mendocino

Created by the Coyote Dam, this beautiful lake surrounded by rolling hills offers great opportunities for fishing, boating, sailing, swimming, and jet skiing. On land there are hiking trails and picnicking and camping among forests of oak and conifer. At the adjacent wildlife habitat, visitors may spot black-tail deer, gray fox, and wild turkey.

3. Ukiah

Chamber of Commerce, 495-E East Perkins St. This agricultural center is home to the **Grace Hudson Museum,** with many fine paintings by Hudson of the Pomo Indians. Tours of Hudson's 1911 Craftsman house reveal the bohemian lifestyle she shared with her ethnologist husband. Nearby wineries include **Dunnewood Vineyards, Parducci Wine Cellars,** and **Fetzer Vineyards,** all of which offer free wine tastings.

4. Clear Lake State Park

An appealing mix of recreational opportunities and nature programs makes this state park a popular destination. Swimming, boating, fishing, and waterskiing take place on Clear Lake, with picnic tables on the shore. The informative visitor center features an aquarium, nature films, and wildlife dioramas; nature and hiking trails lead visitors through the park. *Admission charged.*

5. Fort Ross State Historic Park

This outpost along scenic Rte. 1 was built by the Russians in 1812 to enable them to take part in the profitable sea otter trade. Many of the fort's buildings have been reconstructed, including the Russian Orthodox chapel, a barracks, and two blockhouses. The elegant house of the first commander has been restored and furnished in period style. *Admission charged.*

6. Sonoma Coast State Beach

Miles of sandy beaches, dunes, and rocky headlands offer good hiking, beachcombing, picnicking, and camping. Harbor seals gather where the Russian River meets the ocean near Jenner, while the **Pacific Coast Highway** (Rte. 1) beckons iron-nerved drivers to traverse California's jagged coast. *Admission charged at beach.*

7. Armstrong Redwoods State Reserve

This 700-acre reserve contains some spectacular examples of the Coast Redwood — the tallest of the redwood trees — from the 310-foot-tall Parson Jones Tree to the Armstrong Tree, 308 feet tall and more than 14 feet across. **Korbel Champagne Cellars** in nearby Guerneville provides a pictorial history of wine making in Sonoma County. *Admission charged.*

8. Healdsburg

Chamber of Commerce, 217 Healdsburg Ave. Healdsburg is surrounded by wineries, but for state-of-the-art wine making, **Clos du Bois** and **Piper Sonoma Cellars** are not to be missed. The **Healdsburg Museum** boasts an unusually fine collection of artifacts from Pomo Indian basketry to vintage guns. **Warm Springs Dam/Lake Sonoma** features a fish hatchery as well as good fishing, swimming, boating, and hiking.

9. Santa Rosa

Convention and Visitors Bureau, 10 Fourth St. The county seat of Sonoma County, Santa Rosa was home to the great horticulturalist Luther Burbank for about 50 years. Some of his pioneering work in developing plant hybrids is demonstrated at the **Luther Burbank Home and Gardens,** along with memorabilia from his life. The **Sonoma County Museum** focuses on regional history and art, while **Snoopy's Gallery** is devoted to Charles Schulz's original drawings of the Peanuts gang. *Admission charged for some attractions.*

10. Petaluma

Chamber of Commerce, 215 Howard St. Elegant Victorian houses line the streets of this dairy-farming center. Local history is the theme of the **Petaluma Adobe State Historic Park,** a restored adobe ranch house built in the mid-1800's. The **Petaluma Historical Library and Museum** features one of the state's only free-standing glass domes, and the **Great Petaluma Mill** contains shops and restaurants in a restored grain mill. The **California Cooperative Creamery** and the **Marin French Cheese Company** have exhibits on cheese making. *Admission charged for some attractions.*

11. Sonoma

Sonoma Visitors Bureau, 453 East First St. Sonoma County's numerous award-winning wineries include **Sebastiani Vineyards, Glen Ellen Winery,** and **Buena Vista Winery,** the oldest premium winery in California. Many wineries offer tours and free wine tastings. **Sonoma State Historic Park** features the **Mission San Francisco Solano,** the last Franciscan mission built in California, and **Lachryma Montis,** an opulent Victorian Gothic house built by Gen. Mariano Vallejo. **Jack London State Historic Park** in nearby Glen Ellen contains memorabilia from the author's life and work, as well as his grave. **Sonoma Depot Park Museum** re-creates an 1880 train depot, complete with railroad items and scenes of local history. A steam train at **Train Town** offers a 20-minute ride through a small-scale replica of an old mining town, which includes a stop at a petting zoo with miniature animals. *Admission charged for some attractions.*

12. Napa

Chamber of Commerce, 1556 First St. The town of Napa, with its lovely Victorian homes typical of the area, is the gateway to the famous wine-producing valley. Roads are lined with the neat rows of vineyards that belong to the area's hundreds of wineries; most offer tours and, for a small fee, wine tastings. The **Silverado Trail** leads to such wine producers as **Clos du Val, Stag's Leap Wine Cellars,** and **Rutherford Hill Winery,** which has the largest man-made wine-aging facility in the country.

13. Yountville

State-of-the-art **Domaine Chandon,** owned by the renowned French champagne and cognac producers Moët-Hennessy, is located here. Visitors can view the classic French method of making champagne and, for a fee, sample flutes of the sparkling wine. At **Vintage 1870,** 23 acres of gourmet stores, restaurants, and fashionable shops are housed in a former winery, livery stable, and distillery built in 1870.

14. Oakville

At **Robert Mondavi,** a tour of the winery's gracious mission-style building ends with a free sample of the finished product. Concerts are held on Saturday evenings in the summer, with wine and cheese served at intermission. *Admission charged at concerts.*

15. Rutherford

Notable area wineries include **Inglenook – Napa Valley,** which features an 1887 neo-Gothic cellar house with vaulted ceilings, as well as wines from the same period. Both **Beaulieu Vineyard,** which dates to the turn of the century, and **Franciscan Vineyards** offer tours and wine tastings.

16. St. Helena

Chamber of Commerce, 1080 Main St. The **Silverado Museum** houses a fascinating collection of Robert Louis Stevenson's manuscripts and memorabilia, including first editions and old photographs. North of town, the **Bale Grist Mill State Historic Park** features a well-preserved redwood flour mill built in 1846 and driven by a 36-foot water wheel. Area wine makers include **Beringer Vineyards,** with underground cellars dug in the late 1800's; **Christian Brothers Greystone Cellars;** and **Charles Krug Winery,** the oldest producer in the Napa Valley, dating from 1861. Other local wineries are **Heitz Wine Cellars, Spring Mountain Winery, Freemark Abbey Winery,** and **Louis Martini Winery.** All offer tours and wine tastings. *Admission charged for some attractions.*

17. Calistoga

Chamber of Commerce, 1458 Lincoln Ave. The **Sharpsteen Museum** and **Sam Brannan Cottage** display Calistoga's history as a mineral springs resort. Visitors can still enjoy mudbaths and a mineral-water whirlpool at **Dr. Wilkinson's Hot Springs.** Just north of town, **Old Faithful Geyser of California,** fed by a boiling underground river that flows over a bed of molten lava, shoots a 60-foot jet of steam skyward about every 40 minutes. In **Robert Louis Stevenson State Park,** a monument on **Mount St. Helena** marks the place where the author honeymooned and was inspired to write *The Silverado Squatters.* The volcano's eruption over 3 million years ago created the **Petrified Forest,** giant uprooted redwoods coated with volcanic ash and silica. **Sterling Vineyards** opens its estate for daily visits and wine tastings. *Admission charged for some attractions.*

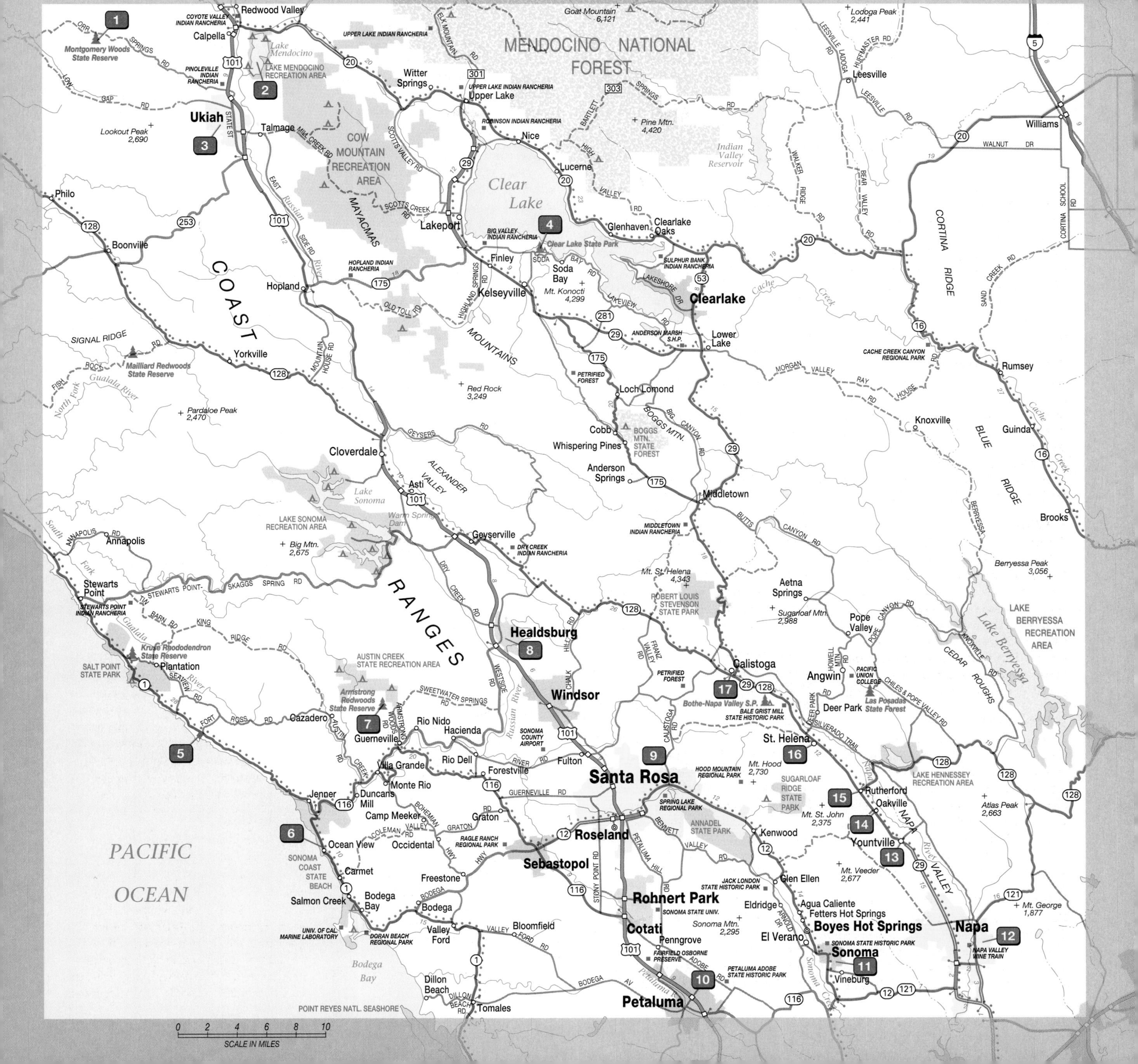

Redwood Valley
COYOTE VALLEY INDIAN RANCHERIA
Calpella
Lake Mendocino
LAKE MENDOCINO RECREATION AREA
UPPER LAKE INDIAN RANCHERIA
Goat Mountain 6,121
Lodoga Peak 2,441
MENDOCINO NATIONAL FOREST
Leesville
Witter Springs
Upper Lake
ROBINSON INDIAN RANCHERIA
Pine Mtn. 4,420
Indian Valley Reservoir
Williams

ORR SPRINGS RD
PINOLEVILLE INDIAN RANCHERIA
Ukiah
Talmage
MILL CREEK RD
COW MOUNTAIN RECREATION AREA
SCOTTS VALLEY RD
Nice
HIGH VALLEY RD
Lucerne
Clearlake Oaks
CORTINA RIDGE
WALNUT DR
CORTINA SCHOOL RD

Lookout Peak 2,690
STATE ST
EAST Russian River
Scotts Creek
MAYACMAS
Lakeport
BIG VALLEY INDIAN RANCHERIA
Clear Lake
Glenhaven
Clearlake Oaks
SAND CREEK RD
BEAR VALLEY RD

Philo
Boonville
SIDE RD
Hopland
HOPLAND INDIAN RANCHERIA
Finley
SODA BAY
Soda Bay
Mt. Konocti 4,299
SULPHUR BANK INDIAN RANCHERIA
Clearlake
Cache Creek
Rumsey

COAST
Yorkville
MOUNTAIN HOUSE RD
OLD TOLL RD
MOUNTAINS
HIGHLAND SPRINGS RD
Kelseyville
ANDERSON MARSH S.H.P.
Lower Lake
CACHE CREEK CANYON REGIONAL PARK
MORGAN VALLEY RD
RAY RD
HOUSE RD
Knoxville
BLUE RIDGE
Guinda

SIGNAL RIDGE
ROCK RD
MAILLIARD REDWOODS STATE RESERVE
Gualala River
FISH RD
North Fork
Pardaloe Peak 2,470
GEYSERS RD
Red Rock 3,249
PETRIFIED FOREST
Loch Lomond
BIG CANYON RD
BOGGS MTN. STATE FOREST
Cobb
Whispering Pines
Anderson Springs
Brooks

Cloverdale
ALEXANDER VALLEY
Lake Sonoma
Asti
LAKE SONOMA RECREATION AREA
WARM SPRINGS DAM
Middletown
MIDDLETOWN INDIAN RANCHERIA
BUTTS CANYON RD
BERRYESSA
Berryessa Peak 3,056

ANNAPOLIS RD
Annapolis
SKAGGS SPRING RD
Big Mtn. 2,675
DRY CREEK
DRY CREEK INDIAN RANCHERIA
Geyserville
Mt. St. Helena 4,343
ROBERT LOUIS STEVENSON STATE PARK
Aetna Springs
Sugarloaf Mtn. 2,988
Pope Valley
CHILES & POPE VALLEY RD
LAKE BERRYESSA RECREATION AREA

Stewarts Point
STEWARTS POINT INDIAN RANCHERIA
TIN BARN RD
KING RIDGE RD
KRUSE RHODODENDRON STATE RESERVE
SALT POINT STATE PARK
Plantation
SEAVIEW RD
FORT ROSS RD
Gualala River
South Fork
AUSTIN CREEK STATE RECREATION AREA
SWEETWATER SPRINGS RD
WESTSIDE RD
Healdsburg
CHALK HILL RD
FRANZ VALLEY RD
Calistoga
PETRIFIED FOREST
BOTHE-NAPA VALLEY S.P.
BALE GRIST MILL STATE HISTORIC PARK
St. Helena
Angwin
PACIFIC UNION COLLEGE
Deer Park
LAS POSADAS STATE FOREST
HOWELL MTN RD
CEDAR ROUGHS
KNOXVILLE RD

RANGES
Windsor
ARMSTRONG REDWOODS STATE RESERVE
Rio Nido
Hacienda
SONOMA COUNTY AIRPORT
Fulton
Santa Rosa
Mt. Hood 2,730
HOOD MOUNTAIN REGIONAL PARK
SUGARLOAF RIDGE STATE PARK
Mt. St. John 2,375
Rutherford
Oakville
Yountville
Atlas Peak 2,663

Cazadero
Guerneville
Villa Grande
Rio Dell
Forestville
Russian River
GUERNEVILLE RD
Roseland
SPRING LAKE REGIONAL PARK
ANNADEL STATE PARK
Kenwood
SILVERADO TRAIL
NAPA VALLEY
Mt. Veeder 2,677
NAPA River
LAKE HENNESSEY RECREATION AREA

Jenner
Duncans Mill
Monte Rio
Camp Meeker
Graton
Occidental
Sebastopol
BOHEMIAN HWY
COLEMAN VALLEY RD
RAGLE RANCH REGIONAL PARK
BENNETT VALLEY RD
Glen Ellen
JACK LONDON STATE HISTORIC PARK
Mt. Veeder
Glen Ellen
Eldridge
Agua Caliente
Fetters Hot Springs
Boyes Hot Springs
Mt. George 1,877

PACIFIC OCEAN

SONOMA COAST STATE BEACH
Ocean View
Carmet
Salmon Creek
Bodega Bay
Freestone
BODEGA HWY
STONY POINT RD
PETALUMA HILL RD
Rohnert Park
SONOMA STATE UNIV.
Sonoma Mtn. 2,295
El Verano
SONOMA STATE HISTORIC PARK
Sonoma
NAPA VALLEY WINE TRAIN
Napa

UNIV. OF CAL. MARINE LABORATORY
DORAN BEACH REGIONAL PARK
Bodega Bay
Bodega
Valley Ford
Bloomfield
Cotati
Penngrove
FAIRFIELD OSBORNE PRESERVE
Vineburg
ARNOLD DR

Dillon Beach
DILLON BEACH RD
Tomales
BODEGA AV
PETALUMA ADOBE STATE HISTORIC PARK
Petaluma
Bodega Bay
POINT REYES NATL. SEASHORE

SCALE IN MILES
0 2 4 6 8 10

1. University of California at Davis

The 5,100-acre university campus is located in the farming community of Davis. Sights of interest include an arboretum, student farms, and conservation projects. The university's art galleries and libraries are also open to the public.

2. Sacramento

Convention and Visitors Bureau, 1421 K St. The city's early gold-rush days are recalled in the restored buildings of the **Old Sacra-**mento Historic District. Of special note is the **Hastings Building,** once the western terminus of the legendary Pony Express. Exhibits at **Sutter's Fort State Historic Park** include carpenter and blacksmith shops dating to the 1840's, while the **California State Railroad Museum** displays 21 locomotives and cars in mint condition. *Admission charged for some attractions.*

3. Folsom Lake State Recreation Area

In 1895 the Folsom Powerhouse sent electricity 22 miles to Sacramento, an unprecedented distance. Today visitors can tour the powerhouse as well as swim, water-ski, or fish for trout and catfish in the 18,000-acre man-made lake. Onshore attractions include 80 miles of hiking and horseback-riding trails, picnic and camping sites, and wetlands that are home to beavers and muskrats. *Admission charged.*

A Great Northern Railway mail car (above) is among the many models of vintage railroad cars and locomotives (left) on display at the California State Railroad Museum in Sacramento.

4. Drytown

The town's history is well preserved in its interesting old buildings, from a butcher-shop to an old schoolhouse to the ironic remains of some 26 saloons that did a land-slide business during Drytown's gold-mining heyday.

5. Amador City

The charming old buildings of Amador City include the former headquarters of the Key-stone mine, which is now an inn outfitted in gold-rush style.

6. Sutter Creek

Charming shops with second-story porches, neat flower beds, and tree-lined streets give this well-preserved town a picturesque air. Eureka Street is the site of **Knight's Foundry,** the only water-powered foundry in the country, built in 1873.

7. Jackson

Chamber of Commerce, 125 Peek St. This appealing old town of narrow, hilly streets is the site of the now-defunct **Kennedy Mine,** once the deepest gold mine in the country. **Kennedy Tailing Wheels Park** contains four enormous tailing wheels, an innovative method for discarding mining wastes in the early part of the century. The large-scale working models that are on view at the **Amador County Museum** show the mine and the wheels in full operation.

8. Volcano

Named for its location in a bowl-shaped valley, Volcano features original buildings from its days as one of the richest towns on the Mother Lode. Daffodil Hill, which promises a burst of color in spring, was first planted with bulbs brought by homesick Dutch settlers.

9. Chaw' Se Indian Grinding Rock State Historic Park

Pine Grove–Volcano Rd., Pine Grove. The highlight of the 40-acre park is a limestone outcropping measuring 173 by 82 feet, covered with hundreds of petroglyphs and more than a thousand mortar holes, each called a *chaw' se.* The local Northern Sierra Miwok Indians used these holes to crush acorns and other nuts, seeds, and berries. Adjacent to the grinding rock is a recon-struction of the former Miwok village, com-plete with bark houses, a ceremonial roundhouse, and even a football field. A museum offers tours of the structures and informative exhibits. *Admission charged.*

10. San Andreas

Founded in 1848 by Mexican gold miners and decimated by several fires, the town's historic buildings bear witness to its colorful past. There are cafes where miners ate, a brewery, saloons with names like Gooney's and the Courthouse Saloon, the brick classical revival Calaveras County Courthouse, elaborate Queen Anne–style houses of citizens who prospered, and an undertaker's parlor.

11. Micke Grove Park and Zoo

Micke Grove Rd., Lodi. This inviting 259-acre park and golf course contains a bit of everything: a zoo that harbors rare snow leopards and bald eagles; a Japanese gar-den; a museum of farming equipment; and an amusement park. The **San Joaquin County Historical Museum** illustrates the county's heritage with farming and ranch-ing displays and an original blacksmith shop. *Admission charged.*

12. Stockton

Convention and Visitors Bureau, 46 West Fremont St. This lively inland shipping port was once a gateway to gold-rush country. The area's history is exhibited at the **Haggin Museum,** which highlights Indian bas-ketry, historic firefighting equipment, early tractors, and a re-created turn-of-the-century town. The fine collection of 19th-century French and American paintings includes examples of the Barbizon and Hudson River schools. *Donation encouraged.*

13. Brannan Island and Franks Tract State Recreation Areas

The 1,000 miles of rivers, levees, and marshes that surround Brannan Island add up to outstanding year-round opportunities for swimming, boating, fishing, and camp-ing. Franks Tract, which lies 5 miles south-east of the island and is accessible only by water, offers excellent fishing for striped bass, sturgeon, and catfish, as well as water-fowl hunting.

14. Antioch

The Black Diamond Mines Regional Preserve, south of Antioch, offers weekend educational programs that include a visit to nearby **Rose Hill Cemetery.** Here the many grave markers attest to the rugged lives of the coal miners who founded Anti-och in the 1860's. Forty miles of trails wind through the surrounding woodland and grassland areas, a refuge for deer, skunk, and an occasional mountain lion.

SCALE IN MILES

1. Forty-Niner Gold Route

Named for the famous 1849 gold-rush participants, Rte. 49 winds through the Sierra Nevada foothills, passing mining towns such as **Downieville** and **El Dorado,** where many images of the bygone era still remain.

2. Tahoe National Forest

This forest contains the historic **Overland Emigrant Trail,** which took settlers heading to California through the rugged Sierra Nevada country. To cover the entire trail, stopping at its many historic sites, requires two full days of combined driving and hiking. Points of interest along the way include **Stampede Dam,** where the immigrants forded a river; **Bear Valley,** about which a pioneer wrote, "We camped near this rivulet of the lonely mountain vale, under some tall pines"; and the **Donner Memorial State Park,** which commemorates the sad fate of the Donner party, stranded here by heavy snow. Today the park, with a lake encircled by evergreens, delights boaters, anglers, and nature lovers. Also in the forest, located near Sierra City, the **Kentucky Mine Museum** features exhibits on early mining,

starlight concerts, and other programs. *Admission charged for some attractions.*

3. Reno

Convention and Visitors Authority, 4590 South Virginia St. Although best known for its gambling establishments, this Western resort town boasts several museums and other attractions. The **Nevada Museum of Art** features regional art from the Great Basin states of Nevada, California, Utah, and Idaho. Located on the **University of Nevada, Reno** campus, the **Nevada Historical Society** exhibits frontier, mining, and American Indian artifacts, including some exquisite Washo Indian basketwork. Also on campus is the **Fleischmann Planetarium,** featuring star shows and nature films. Not far from the university, the **Wilbur D. May Museum** contains many eccentric collections, including more than 80 mounted animal heads. The **Mackay School of Mines** displays minerals, fossils, and early mining artifacts. *Admission charged for some attractions.*

4. Virginia City Historic District

The Comstock Lode, a rich mountain vein of gold and silver, turned Virginia City into the world's wealthiest boomtown. Saloons and stores from that era still line the boardwalks. Among the other 19th-century buildings are an opera house, a school, and a mansion known as The Castle, which still has its original furnishings. The Virginia & Truckee Railroad once carried supplies into the area; today there are guided tours of the

railroad. The Chollar Mine and a mining museum elaborate further on The Way It Was, as the museum is called.

5. Dayton

Swinging-door saloons and old-fashioned country stores lend charm to this former mining town and Pony Express station. Brought back to life when the Marilyn Monroe–Clark Gable movie *The Misfits* was filmed here in 1960, the village now features a frontier museum. **Dayton State Park,** on its eastern edge, offers mining exhibits, campsites, a picnic area, and a nature trail.

6. Carson City

Convention and Visitors Bureau, 1900 South Carson St. Nestled in the foothills of the Sierra Nevada, the picturesque state capital contains handsome 19th-century homes and public buildings. One standout is the **Bowers Mansion,** a palatial residence built by two mine owners who pooled their fortunes when they married; its landscaped grounds include a picnic area. The old U.S. Mint now houses the **Nevada State Museum,** which exhibits an early coin press and 19th-century gold and silver coins. *Admission charged at mansion.*

7. Lake Tahoe Nevada State Park

This park centers on the crystalline Lake Tahoe, set high amid snowcapped mountains. **Sand Harbor** beaches and picnic sites highlight the shorefront area. Leading from the lake, trails of various lengths take hikers to flowered meadows, aspen groves, and sublime vistas. In the backcountry are primitive campsites. *Admission charged.*

8. Ponderosa Ranch

Rte. 28, Incline Village. Visitors who can remember the *Bonanza* television series will particularly enjoy touring the Cartwright ranch house, which is set in the wooded Sierra Nevada mountains. The surrounding park contains an abundance of diversions, including a museum of Western memorabilia, a collection of antique cars and other vehicles, a frontier town, and an animal farm. Visitors can hike or take hayrides through the backcountry in the summer. *Admission charged.*

9. Lake Tahoe

One of the most beautiful lakes in the world, Lake Tahoe is also one of the highest (6,225 feet) and deepest (1,645 feet) in all of North America. The 72-mile drive around its rim reveals its loveliness, enhanced by the sur-

rounding snow-topped mountains and, in season, yellow *wyethia,* known locally as Mule Ears. **Mount Rose Highway** offers a wonderful vista from an overlook at the northern end of the lake. One of the lake's most famous locales is **Emerald Bay,** in which green Fannette Island rests like a jewel. The visitor center located on Rte. 89 can provide information on nature activities.

10. Cave Rock

Fishing enthusiasts congregate to catch Mackinaw and rainbow trout at Cave Rock, a granite formation that protrudes into Lake Tahoe. A tunnel takes drivers through this enormous rock; south of the tunnel, a turnout leads to spectacular views of the lake and its environs.

11. Genoa

The state's oldest saloon, decorated with electrified gas and kerosene chandeliers, joins with other attractions to make this a delightful town. The community's roots are evident at the **Mormon Station State Historic Park,** the site of the 1851 log-cabin trading post that eventually grew into present-day Genoa. The **Genoa Courthouse Museum** maintains an 1860's courtroom and jail and also displays Washo Indian artifacts and a blacksmith's shop.

12. Carson Pass

Kit Carson and John Fremont discovered this pass through the Sierra Nevada mountains in 1843. Those who later made use of it included thousands of gold prospectors. Rte. 88, which now traverses the pass, has several overlook turnouts.

13. Bridal Veil Falls

The sound of Bridal Veil Falls teases drivers well before they are within viewing range of the cascade, but upon reaching the turnout at the base of the falls, the reward is a spectacular view. Plunging down the side of a pine-forested mountain, the waterfall enters the South Fork of the American River.

14. Placerville

Chamber of Commerce, 542 Main St. This is a picture-book town, complete with apple orchards, Victorian houses, cascades of roses, and quaint old stores. Once a depot and outfitting spot for gold seekers heading to Coloma, Placerville still contains several points of nostalgic interest, such as **City Hall, Justice Court, the Gold Bug Mine** in Bedford Park, and the museum at the **El Dorado County Fairgrounds.**

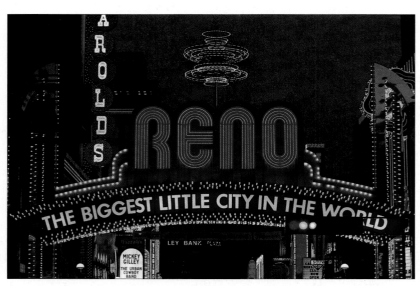

An exuberant, neon-lit greeting welcomes visitors to one of Nevada's best-known cities.

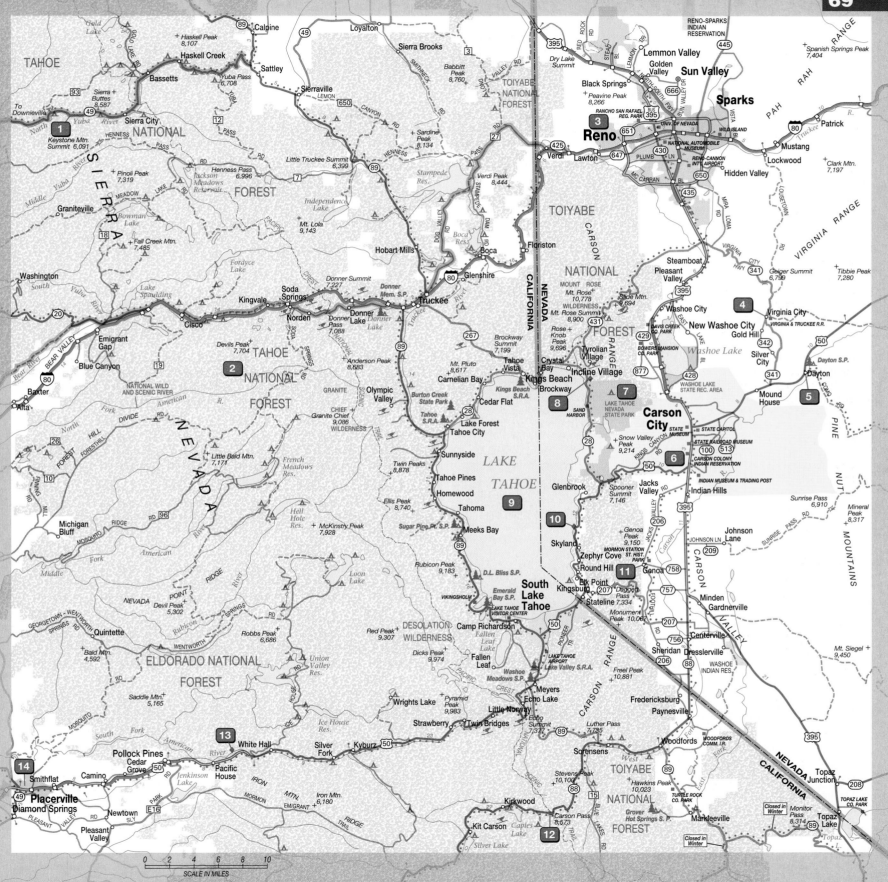

TAHOE

To Downieville

NATIONAL

SIERRA

NEVADA

FOREST

ELDORADO NATIONAL

FOREST

1. Ruby Mountain Scenic Area

Many hikers and campers are drawn to the pristine wilderness of this glacier-carved canyon country, where waterfalls plummet some 2,000 feet down the walls of the U-shaped chasms.

2. Northeastern Nevada Museum

1515 Idaho St., Elko. This museum illustrates the many aspects of this region, with exhibits related to mining, ranching, railroading, and the Basques, who once herded sheep in the area. Shoshone Indian baskets, pioneer period rooms, and antique vehicles are other museum highlights.

3. Humboldt Museum

Jungo Rd. and Maple Ave., Winnemucca. Housed partially in a former church, this delightful little museum has a particular focus on American Indian, pioneer, cowboy, and mining memorabilia. In a second building, antique vehicles and Indian carvings are featured.

4. Unionville

Silver miners settled Unionville in 1861, but when production slackened 20 years later, the population dwindled, until finally few were left. The town, which winds down into a canyon, still holds charm for visitors today, who can picnic in a shady park and view the old walls along the main street.

5. Rye Patch State Recreation Area

This inviting spot includes picnic areas, swimming beaches, and campgrounds. The 11,000-acre Rye Patch Reservoir, a welcome oasis amid the desert terrain, is fed by the Humboldt River. Archeological digs have revealed that humans visited the riverbanks as early as 8,000 years ago, and even camels and elephants once dwelt on its shores. *Admission charged.*

6. Giant Tufa Formations

Here miles of oddly shaped porous limestone deposits stretch along an ancient seabed. Formed underwater some 10,000 years ago, these curious configurations — many rising more than 10 feet — were shaped over time into their present forms by the action of wind and other weather.

7. Pershing County Courthouse

Central Ave., Lovelock. Built in 1919, the courthouse has a grand rotunda and a round courtroom, which is open to visitors when court is not in session. A public swimming pool, picnic tables, and shade trees enhance the surrounding grounds.

8. Stillwater National Wildlife Refuge

Thousands of waterfowl stop for food and rest in this vast, marshy refuge — ducks, shorebirds, and tundra swans, which remain here during the winter. A 26-mile loop road has several spots for visitors to park and watch. The Indian Lakes yield catfish, bullheads, and crappies.

9. Bodie State Historic Park

Bodie's present appearance — deserted streets with dilapidated old buildings — belies its notorious reputation during the gold rush as a wild and wicked town. Still, the existing remnants, aided by a little imagination, can evoke that past. One of three 19th-century structures in the park that are open to the public, the Miners' Union Hall contains numerous artifacts that recall Bodie's heyday. *Admission charged.*

10. Mono Lake Basin

Dramatic limestone towers and knobs protrude from the surface of Mono Lake; tufa formations are also visible when the water is low. The lake's salty waters buoy swimmers at Navy Beach. At dusk, a phenomenon called alpenglow illuminates the mountains in pink and gold.

11. Ancient Bristlecone Pine Forest

Twisted, sun-bleached bristlecone pines grow on the slopes of the White Mountains. Among these ancient trees are Methuselah, which is 4,700 years old, and Old Patriarch, the world's largest of the species. The road to the forest presents a chance to gaze at the sheer white face of the Sierra Nevada, and the forest offers trails and picnic sites.

12. Berlin-Ichthyosaur State Park

Relics of two different kinds coexist in this park. The ghost town of Berlin, once populated by miners, contains the weathered remains of a mill, boardinghouse, worker's cabin, and other buildings. Two miles away, a shelter protects the fossils of several ichthyosaurs, gigantic prehistoric reptiles that once swam in a warm inland sea.

13. Kingston Canyon

A road passing meadows and an old mining camp leads to this canyon. Here forested mountains rim Groves Lake, a man-made reservoir. The canyon, renowned for its beauty, is particularly lovely in autumn.

14. Austin

Another silver boomtown, Austin retains many nostalgic landmarks, including **Gridley's** grocery store, the **Lander County Court,** and the **International Hotel.** Built as a summer residence on the side of a mountain, **Stokes Castle** is a replica of a three-story Roman tower.

15. Hickison Petroglyph Recreation Site

Near the campground and picnic area are Indian rock carvings that include hoof-shaped symbols, possibly created as a form of magic connected with deer hunting.

16. Eureka

Chamber of Commerce, Monroe and Bateman Sts. This mining town has proven more stable than most and remains today an interesting place. The carefully restored courthouse offers a guide map to the many well-preserved buildings, such as the **Opera House** and the **Sentinel Newspaper Museum,** which houses an old press and other printing-related exhibits.

17. Ely

Chamber of Commerce, 636 Aultman St. The **White Pine Public Museum,** with exhibits on mining and minerals, reflects the town's former status as a copper-industry center. The **Nevada Northern Railway Museum** preserves the railroad station from that time and sponsors exciting excursions on several vintage trains. A highway, the **Ely Scenic Drive,** leads into the high mountain ranges and semiarid valleys of the surrounding countryside. *Admission charged at railway museum.*

18. Ward Charcoal Ovens State Historical Monument

The Ward Charcoal Ovens, which at 30 feet high look like colossal stone beehives, were built in the desert in 1876 to produce charcoal as fuel for Ward's ore smelters.

19. Great Basin National Park

This young national park is part of Nevada's huge low-lying Great Basin. The mountains of the **South Snake Range** host a dazzling diversity of plant and animal life as they climb from desert flats to alpine heights. Among the park's natural treasures are groves of ancient bristlecone pines and the state's only glacier. A tour of the **Lehman Caves** reveals many fantastic, richly colored mineral formations, including rippling drapery and rare pallets (discs with streamers). **Wheeler Peak** rises over 13,000 feet from the flat plateau country. A road that scales most of the mountain stops at a picnic area; here a challenging trail ascends to the summit, and an easy, mile-long path leads to an alpine lake. The area named for the peak affords good horseback riding, hiking, and camping. *Admission charged.*

20. Pioche

Chamber of Commerce, 60 Main St. Soon after silver miners founded this still-thriving community, Pioche became infamous for its lawless residents, many of whom were laid to rest in the cemetery's **Boot Hill.** Reminders of that turbulent time include the photographic collection in the **Lincoln County Museum,** and the still-standing **Masonic Hall, Thompson's Opera House,** and **Million Dollar Courthouse.**

21. Cathedral Gorge State Park

Here erosion has sculpted the buff-colored clay cliffs into spectacular fluted spires and domes, reminiscent of a cathedral. The park also has walking trails and picnic sites.

22. Pahranagat National Wildlife Refuge

This refuge is a paradise for birders, with such denizens and visitors as bald eagles, sandhill cranes, orioles, meadowlarks, blackbirds, cormorants, and great blue herons. Anglers catch white crappie, black bullheads, and carp in the waters, some of which can be traveled in motorless boats.

23. Crystal Spring

Flowering yerba mansa and shady cottonwoods border this lovely pond. In its green waters swim small, tropical-looking fish called desert striped dace.

24. Lunar Crater Volcanic Field

Deriving its name from its resemblance to a moonscape, the area was created by volcanic activity long ago. Lunar Crater measures nearly four-fifths of a mile across and 430 feet deep. It shares this desolate, fascinating land with a smaller crater, cinder cones, a basalt plateau, and alkali mud flats.

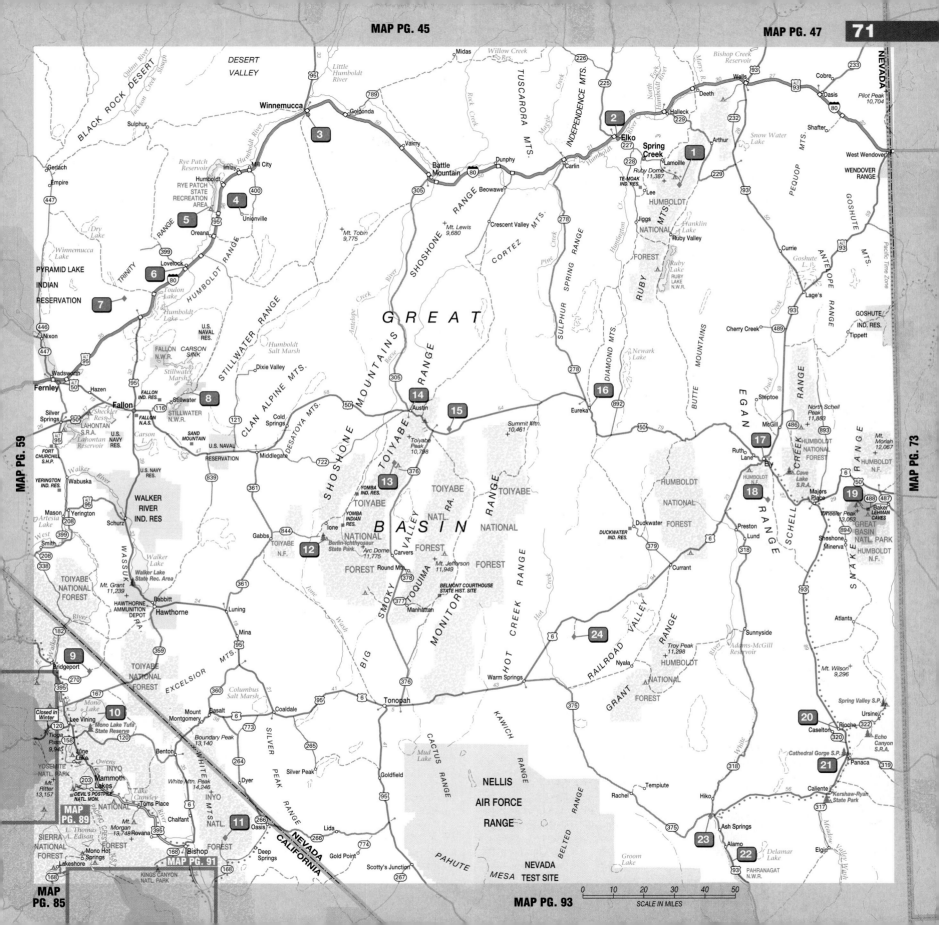

MAP PG. 59

MAP PG. 73

DESERT
VALLEY

BLACK ROCK DESERT

Midas
Willow Creek Res.
Bishop Creek Reservoir
Wells
Cobre
233

Gerlach
Sulphur
Winnemucca
Golconda
TUSCARORA MTS.
INDEPENDENCE MTS.
226
225
Deeth
Halleck
Oasis
Pilot Peak 10,704

Empire
Rye Patch Reservoir
Imlay
Mill City
Battle Mountain
Dunphy
Carlin
Elko
Spring Creek
Arthur
Snow Water Lake
West Wendover

447
Humboldt
RYE PATCH STATE RECREATION AREA
Unionville
Beowawe
Crescent Valley
Lee
Jiggs
Franklin Lake
Currie
WENDOVER RANGE

Dry Lake
Oreana
Mt. Tobin 9,775
Mt. Lewis 9,680
Ruby Valley
RUBY LAKE N.W.R.
Lage's
GOSHUTE MTS.
GOSHUTE IND. RES.
Tippett

Winnemucca Lake
Lovelock
Cherry Creek
489

PYRAMID LAKE INDIAN RESERVATION

Nixon
Wadsworth
Fernley
Hazen
Fallon
Stillwater
GREAT
Eureka
Newark Lake
McGill
North Schell Peak 11,883
Mt. Moriah 12,067

Silver Springs
LAHONTAN S.R.A.
SAND MOUNTAIN
Cold Springs
Middlegate
Austin
BASIN
Ruth
Ely
Cave Lake S.R.A.
Baker
LEHMAN CAVES
Wheeler Peak 13,063

FORT CHURCHILL S.H.P.
YERINGTON IND. RES.
Wabuska
Gabbs
Ione
Berlin-Ichthyosaur State Park
Carvers
Round Mtn.
Mt. Jefferson 11,949
Duckwater
Preston
Lund
Shoshone
Minerva
GREAT BASIN NATL. PARK

WALKER RIVER IND. RES.

Mason
Yerington
Schurz
Hawthorne
Babbitt
Luning
Manhattan
BELMONT COURTHOUSE STATE HIST. SITE
Currant
Sunnyside
Atlanta

Walker Lake
Mt. Grant 11,239
HAWTHORNE AMMUNITION DEPOT
Mina
Warm Springs
Nyala
Troy Peak 11,298
Mt. Wilson 9,296

Bridgeport
Mono Lake
Lee Vining
Basalt
Coaldale
Tonopah
Rachel
Hiko
Ursine
Pioche
Caselton
Cathedral Gorge S.P.
Panaca

Mammoth Lakes
White Mtn. Peak 14,246
Silver Peak
Goldfield
NELLIS AIR FORCE RANGE
Tempiute
Ash Springs
Alamo
Caliente
Elgin

NEVADA
CALIFORNIA

Bishop
Oasis
Lida
Gold Point
Scotty's Junction
PAHUTE MESA
NEVADA TEST SITE
Groom Lake
PAHRANAGAT N.W.R.
Delamar Lake

SCALE IN MILES
0　10　20　30　40　50

1. Bonneville Speedway Museum

1000 Wendover Blvd., Wendover. Record-breaking racing cars from the nearby **Bonneville Salt Flats** are often on display in this eclectic museum, along with classic cars in mint condition, Pima Indian baskets, and a gun collection. *Admission charged.*

2. Little Sahara Recreation Area

Named for its vast sand dunes, this 60,000-acre park is, in part, a magnet for dune buggies and dirt bikes. The Jericho and White Sands campgrounds and the Rockwell Natural Area offer more tranquil settings for enjoying the view of the distant mountains. *Admission charged.*

3. Territorial Statehouse State Park

50 West Capitol Ave., Fillmore. The Utah Territorial Legislature met in this red sandstone structure, commissioned by Brigham Young, before the state capital was moved to Salt Lake City. Today the building is a remarkable museum of 19th-century furniture, clothing, weapons, and Paiute Indian artifacts. *Admission charged.*

4. Fremont Indian State Park

Evidence of the Fremont Indians, who once inhabited the area, extends from the petroglyphs along the Show Me Rock Art Trail to the wealth of artifacts on display in the visitor center. Clear Creek offers good fishing, and overlook trails provide fascinating views of the land. *Admission charged.*

5. Daughters of the Utah Pioneers Museum — Old County Courthouse

95 East Center St., Beaver. Begun in 1877, this brick structure houses a museum dedicated to the county's Mormon pioneers. More than 100 buildings in the town of Beaver are listed in the National Register of Historic Places. *Donation encouraged.*

6. Frisco

Located at the foot of the San Francisco Mountains, this former boomtown rewarded prospectors' sweat with millions of dollars' worth of silver and gold from the Silver Horn Mine. A ghost town by the 1920's, Frisco recalls its mining past with rusting machinery, boarded-up mine entrances, charcoal kilns, and weathered buildings.

7. Iron Mission State Historical Monument

585 North Main St., Cedar City. The monument commemorates the start of Cedar City's iron industry, while **Iron Mission State Park** features early modes of transportation. Its fine collection of horse-drawn vehicles features a stagecoach, riddled with bullet holes, from Butch Cassidy's territory. *Admission charged at park.*

8. Zion National Park

Zion's outstanding scenery includes petrified sand dunes, red sandstone monoliths that soar above narrow box canyons, and vertical rock faces in brilliant colors that loom over a narrow valley. Visitors can tour the vast park on the winding **Zion–Mount Carmel Highway,** or travel on foot or horseback to such natural wonders as the **Great White Throne,** a giant flat-top cliff face, and the **Emerald Pools,** set between two waterfalls. *Admission charged.*

9. Cedar Breaks National Monument

This 3-mile-long natural amphitheater with multicolored cliffs cuts deep into the side of the Markagunt Plateau. From overlooks along a 5-mile scenic drive there are stirring views of the cliffs and of the ancient bristlecone pines that have lived for thousands of years atop the plateau. *Admission charged.*

10. Bryce Canyon National Park

The canyon is an 18-mile-long series of natural amphitheaters eroded into the edge of the Paunsaugunt Plateau. From its rim there are dramatic views of multicolored arches, spires, windows, and weirdly eroded pinnacles called hoodoos because of their ghostly appearance at twilight. Steep hiking trails wind from stands of ponderosa pine at the rim to pinion pine on the valley floor. *Admission charged.*

11. Capitol Reef National Park

The white-domed peaks that give the park its name dominate this harsh desert landscape, which in its time has sheltered prospectors, cowboys, Mormon farmers, and moonshiners. A 25-mile round-trip scenic drive leads into canyons, while hiking trails pass by panoramas of Capitol Reef's multicolored ridge line. Located near the visitor center is an orchard planted by Mormons in the 19th century, where visitors can pick fruit. *Admission charged.*

12. Natural Bridges National Monument

These three natural bridges display varying stages of the erosion process: Owachomo has been worn thin for nearly 10 million years; Sipapu, one of the longest natural bridges in the world, is barely affected by its stream; and Kachina is still being gouged by floodwaters. A 9-mile loop road provides views of the bridges, as do almost 6 miles of hiking trails. *Admission charged.*

13. Valley of the Gods

In this expanse, soft red sandstone and clay have eroded into mysterious shapes. The nearby Mexican Hat rock looks like an inverted sombrero set against a backdrop of colorful rocks that appear wrinkled.

14. Edge of the Cedars State Park

Rte. 191, Blanding. This excavated ruin of an Anasazi Indian pueblo contains both dwellings and round, depressed kivas used for religious ceremonies. An adjoining museum illustrates the ancient inhabitants' way of life, with displays of pottery, jewelry, and stone tools, as well as video shows. *Admission charged.*

15. Canyonlands National Park

Overlooks and scenic flights offer grand panoramas of this rugged wilderness, which features canyons, flat-topped mesas, and colorful arches and spires. The **Great Gallery** in Horseshoe Canyon attracts visitors with its ghostly prehistoric pictographs, while the **Colorado River** draws river runners with its hair-raising stretches of raging waves. *Admission charged.*

16. Dead Horse Point State Park

Legend has it that cowboys left a pack of wild mustangs corralled on this cliff high above the Colorado River, where the animals died of thirst. Visitors can get a look at the river 2,000 feet below from observation points, or hike the self-guiding trails through the park's pinion pines, junipers, wildflowers, and cactus. *Admission charged.*

17. Canyonlands by Night

1861 North Hwy. 191, Moab. Every evening from May through October, passengers can cruise up the **Colorado River** for a spectacular light-and-sound show. As music sets the mood and lights throw dancing shadows on the steep canyon walls, narrators relate Indian legends and the history and geology of the area. *Admission charged.*

18. Arches National Park

Wind and water have worn away the ancient sandstone in this 73,000-acre park, creating some 1,500 magnificent arches, as well as spires, fins, and balanced boulders. Visitors can hike to the arches, including the mammoth **Landscape Arch,** a 306-foot-long span that appears to defy the laws of engineering, and **Delicate Arch,** a graceful pink stone arch that stands at the rim of a natural amphitheater. *Admission charged.*

19. Sego Canyon Indian Rock Art

Early area inhabitants — from the Archaic people to the Ute Indians — carved petroglyphs and painted pictographs on these sandstone canyon walls. The abstract designs and images of desert wildlife are an enduring window into the lives of these farmers and hunters.

20. San Rafael Reef and San Rafael Swell

An 80-mile-long fold in the earth's crust, San Rafael Swell is edged on its eastern face with the San Rafael Reef, a sawtooth ridge that juts 1,200 feet above the desert. From observation points along Rte. 70 there are stunning panoramas of the area's narrow canyons, mesas, and pinnacles.

21. Goblin Valley State Park

Thousands of red sandstone monoliths have eroded into spooky shapes that resemble demons, animals, and people, making Goblin Valley a particularly popular park to visit with children. Hiking trails wind past spires, balanced rocks, and the goblins with "eyes" that seem to see all. *Admission charged.*

22. Dinosaur National Monument

Excavations on this quarry face have revealed 14 species of dinosaurs, including some nearly complete skeletons. At nearby **Cub Creek,** visitors can view prehistoric petroglyphs of animals, humans, and geometric designs. *Admission charged.*

23. Flaming Gorge National Recreation Area

The 91-mile Flaming Gorge Reservoir is popular with anglers, boaters, water-skiers, and river runners. Hiking trails offer occasional glimpses of the rare golden eagles that soar above the red cliffs.

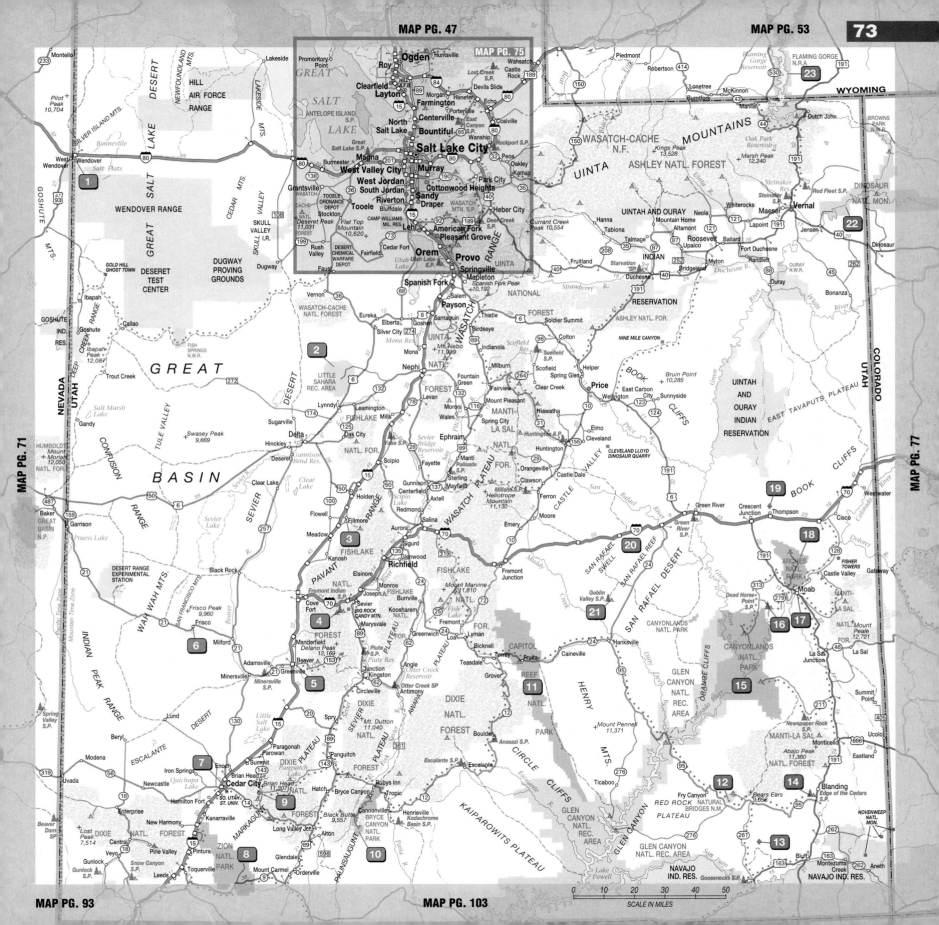

1. Ogden

Convention and Visitors Bureau, 2501 Wall Ave. Evidence of Ogden's prosperous early railroad days can be seen in its Mediterranean-style **Union Station** depot — displaying vintage cars, model railroads, and a gunsmith's shop — and in the restored shops of the **25th Street Historic District.** East of town, anglers try for rainbow trout in the twisting **Ogden River,** crowded by the steep walls of Ogden Canyon. **Pineview Reservoir,** set in Ogden Valley, offers excellent swimming, fishing, and boating. *Admission charged for some attractions.*

2. Lagoon Amusement Park, Lagoon Beach, and Pioneer Village

Lagoon Dr., Farmington. This appealing century-old amusement park has everything from a merry-go-round with hand-carved animals to an 85-foot-high double-loop roller coaster called the Fire Dragon. A lazy river winds through the water park, which features nine water slides. Pioneer Village recalls 19th-century life with 45 authentic period buildings, a restored Pony Express station, and staged shoot-out scenes. *Admission charged.*

3. Skyline Drive

This unpaved 17-mile drive, accessible from Rte. 15 out of Farmington or Bountiful, winds along the foothills of the Wasatch Mountains, with spectacular views of **Great Salt Lake** and the Weber River Valley.

4. Salt Lake City

Convention and Visitors Bureau, 180 SW Temple. Founded by Brigham Young in 1847, Salt Lake City's proud Mormon heritage is everywhere in sight. At the heart of the city, **Temple Square** is dominated by the monumental Temple crowned by six Gothic spires. On Sunday mornings and Thursday nights, the acoustically superb **Tabernacle** rings with the voices of the renowned choir. The spacious and lavish **Beehive House** was the official residence of Brigham Young and one of his 27 wives; others lived next door with their children in the **Lion House.** City attractions also include **Capitol Hill,** with the historic state capitol and Council Hall, and **Pioneer Memorial Museum,** featuring a comprehensive art collection. *Admission charged for some attractions.*

5. University of Utah

The 1,500-acre campus boasts the **Utah Museum of Natural History,** with dinosaur and present-day wildlife exhibits; relics from early area cultures; a simulated mine; and more than 6,000 mineral and gemstone samples. Ancient Egyptian, Italian Renaissance, and Asian art are featured at the **Utah Museum of Fine Arts.** Highlights of the **State Arboretum of Utah** include the world's largest Russian olive tree and the exotic Red Butte Gardens, which are filled with orchids, tropical plants, succulents, and cacti. *Admission charged at fine arts museum.*

6. Fort Douglas Military Museum

32 Potter St., Fort Douglas. Hundreds of photographs and artifacts — from cannonballs to canteens — trace the history of Ft. Douglas and other military bases in Utah from Mormon days through the recent Operation Desert Storm. Outdoor exhibits include artillery, tanks, and ambulances; the post cemetery contains graves of German POW's who were interned here during the first and second world wars.

Brigham Young with Mormon pioneers

The world-renowned Mormon Tabernacle Choir raises its voice in song.

7. Pioneer Trail State Park

This popular attraction marks the end of the arduous 1,300-mile journey that brought the first Mormons to Utah. At **Old Deseret,** a living-history museum, the daily life of the early area settlers is reenacted against a backdrop of buildings — including Brigham Young's farmhouse — from the mid-1800's. *Admission charged.*

8. Bingham Canyon Mine

At the visitor center on the rim of this copper mine, a massive pit 2½ miles wide and a half mile deep, visitors can watch blasting, drilling, and loading with electric shovels that lift 61 tons of ore at a time.

9. Provo

Utah County Travel Council, 51 South University Ave. In town, the **McCurdy Historical Doll Museum** uses historical settings as backdrops for its collection of some 4,000 dolls. At **Brigham Young University,** visitors can attend events at the fine arts center, see shows at the planetarium, and tour both the Monte L. Bean Life Science Museum and the Museum of Peoples and Cultures. *Admission charged for some attractions.*

10. Alpine Scenic Loop

The winding 19-mile Alpine Scenic Loop leads to **Sundance,** a ski resort and arts community surrounded by an extensive network of hiking and biking trails. A few miles farther, **Timpanogos Cave National Monument** offers guided tours of its three caverns, which are adorned with stalactites, stalagmites, and flowstone formations. At **Cascade Springs,** raised boardwalks allow for a close look at the crystal-clear cascading springs and pools. The best way to see nearby **Bridal Veil Falls** is from a glass-bottomed tram, which makes a hair-raisingly steep ascent to the top of **Cascade Mountain** and over the falls. *Admission charged for some attractions.*

11. Wasatch Mountain State Park

The park offers a lovely, mountainous golf course, hiking and horseback-riding trails, pastoral picnic sites, and breathtaking views. In the winter it is a haven for cross-country skiers and snowmobilers. Good trout fishing and boating are nearby at **Deer Creek State Park.** *Admission charged.*

12. Park City Ski Area

Convention and Visitors Bureau, 1910 Prospector Ave. This legendary silver-mining boomtown is today Utah's largest ski resort. The 82 trails that line the eastern slope of the Wasatch Range can be reached by gondola or by triple- or double-chair lifts. For nonskiers, ice skating and sleigh riding are available, as well as gondola rides to the Summit House, which houses a popular restaurant. *Admission charged.*

13. Rockport State Park

Rockport Reservoir, created by the Wanship Dam, is an inviting spot for swimming, fishing, boating, sailboarding, and water skiing, with pleasant picnic sites on shore. In winter, the park attracts ice fishermen and cross-country skiers. *Admission charged.*

14. Devil's Slide

Two steep limestone outcrops, projecting 40 feet above the mountainside, run parallel to each other for about 800 feet, forming a giant chute. From a roadside turnout there are memorable views of this colossal slide.

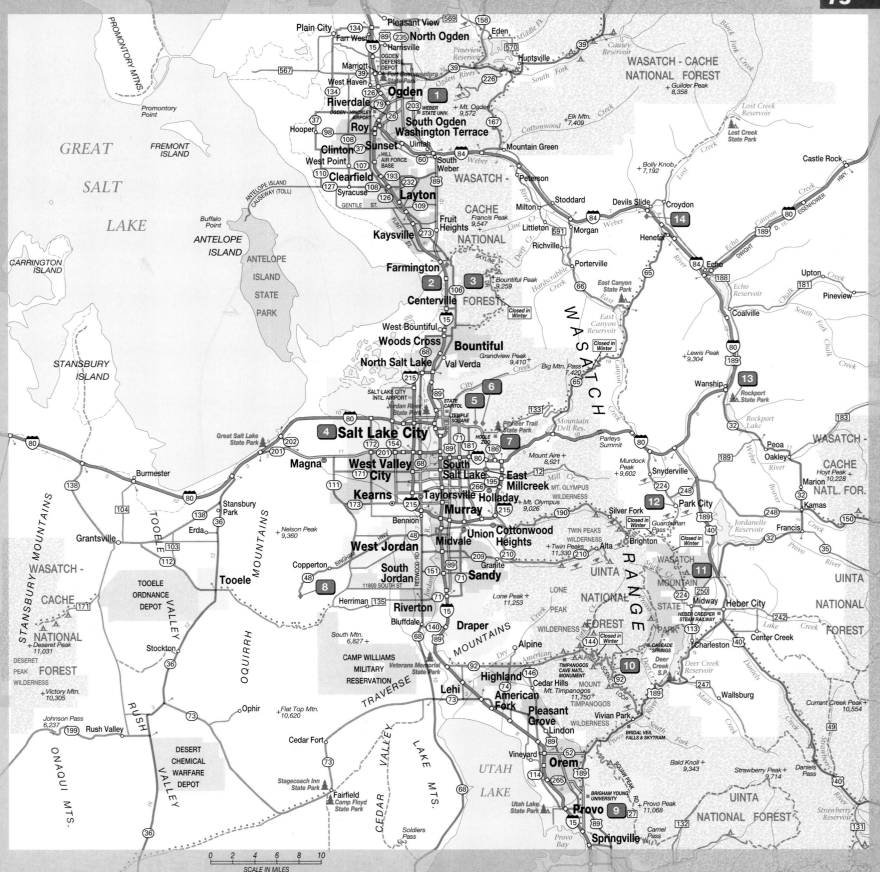

1. Grand Encampment Museum

817 Barnett Ave., Encampment. A guided tour of this reconstructed ghost town takes visitors back to its turn-of-the-century boom-town days of copper mining. Weather-beaten buildings house an 1870's stage-coach station, saloon, general store with a brass cash register, and a two-story out-house for use in deep snow.

2. Pole Mountain Division, Medicine Bow National Forest

Ancient crystalline rock and pink-streaked granite loom over the Happy Jack Road. A turn onto the Vedauwoo Road leads to the **Vedauwoo Picnic and Campground,** where these pink boulders — many bigger than a house — balance over picnic sites. Fishing, camping, and hiking are among the recreational activities available here.

3. Cheyenne

Convention and Visitors Bureau, 309 West Lincoln Way. The Wild West of cowboys, Indians, miners, and desperadoes comes to life in Cheyenne's colorful museums. The **Wyoming State Museum** displays branding irons, American Indian beadwork, and guns owned by Buffalo Bill Cody. The **Cheyenne Frontier Days Old West Museum** focuses on horse-drawn coaches, including an ambulance and a hearse. The

delightful, solar-heated **Cheyenne Botanic Gardens** in Lions Park draws many visitors. *Admission charged for some attractions.*

4. Comanche Crossing Historical Society Museum

Rte. 36, Strasburg. A homesteader's cottage, a railroad depot, and a one-room schoolhouse, all furnished in period style, invite visitors to travel back to the 19th century in this appealing museum. Visitors can also see an old-fashioned beauty parlor and barbershop, and view old farm vehicles and fire trucks in an annex.

5. Vail

Tourism and Convention Bureau, 100 East Meadow Dr. The history of this famous skiing town is preserved through films and old photographs at the **Colorado Ski Museum and Ski Hall of Fame.** Today the town is a year-round planned pedestrian community, with a gondola lift that takes skiers and hikers to high-elevation trails. Also popular with hikers are the trails of the **Vail Nature Center,** along the banks of Gore Creek. *Admission charged for some attractions.*

6. Leadville

Chamber of Commerce, 809 Harrison Ave. Leadville's silver-rush boom days live on in its 19th-century homes and present-day museums. At the Healy House, a late-1800's boardinghouse for schoolteachers, costumed guides enact the role of Victorian boarders. In sober contrast is the shack where Baby Doe Tabor froze to death at the entrance to the mine she wouldn't abandon.

7. Aspen

Chamber Resort Assn., 328 East Hyman Ave. Founded by silver prospectors, Aspen today

is a glamorous international ski resort in winter and home to the Aspen Music Festival in summer. Summer or winter, a ride on the ski lifts provides beautiful vistas of the town and valley below. South of town, visitors can tour 13 original buildings in the restored ghost town of **Ashcroft.**

8. Glenwood Canyon

Inside this 17-mile canyon, **Hanging Lake** draws picnickers, campers, and hikers. From the lake there are spectacular views of **Hanging Lake Falls** as the water plunges over the cliff. **Hot Springs Pool** in nearby Glenwood Springs, with a comfortable year-round temperature of 90° F, is one of the world's largest mineral pools. *Admission charged for some attractions.*

9. Museum of Western Colorado

248 South Fourth St., Grand Junction. The focus here is on local history and geology, through exhibits of American Indian artifacts, early settlers' tools, and minerals. The museum's nearby Dinosaur Valley branch concentrates on prehistoric times, with fossil and dinosaur displays. At the museum's Cross Orchards Historic Site, tour guides relate the history of the local orchards. *Admission charged for some attractions.*

10. Colorado National Monument

Orange, red, and yellow sandstone monoliths, some as tall as 500 feet, dominate this 20,400-acre park. The 23-mile **Rim Rock Drive** offers breathtaking views of the pinnacles, and hiking trails descend the canyon walls, where bighorn sheep, mountain lions, and golden eagles make their home. *Admission charged.*

11. Ute Indian Museum

17253 Chipeta Dr., Montrose. Situated on the grounds of the former residence of the great Ute chief Ouray, the museum commemorates the heritage of the Ute Indians. Items on display include buckskin artifacts, baskets, musical instruments, weapons, and photographs. *Admission charged.*

12. Black Canyon of the Gunnison National Monument

American Indians and pioneers alike believed that anyone who entered this canyon would never come out alive. The 8-mile-long **South Rim Drive,** a continuation of Rte. 347, overlooks the deep, narrow gorge, whose walls are barely touched by sunlight. *Admission charged.*

13. Telluride

Chamber Resort Assn., 666 West Colorado Ave. Butch Cassidy robbed his first bank in Telluride, which is now a national historic landmark district and a popular resort. The surrounding mountains provide excellent skiing, fishing, hiking, and thermal currents for hang gliding. Music, dance, and film festivals also draw visitors.

14. Lowry Pueblo Ruins

A national historic landmark, this ancient pueblo dwelling was built by Anasazi Indians in about the 11th century A.D. Once a farming community of some 100 people, the present-day ruins of more than 40 rooms and 8 kivas, or ceremonial chambers, are all that remain of their way of life.

15. Mesa Verde National Park

The surrounding mountains provide a dramatic setting for the park's Indian cliff dwellings, painstakingly built by the Anasazi in about A.D. 1200 and mysteriously abandoned only a century later. Visitors can tour the remarkable ruins and see Anasazi artifacts at the **Chapin Mesa Museum.** *Admission charged at park.*

16. Durango

The **Durango & Silverton Narrow Gauge Railroad** once transported gold and silver, but today it carries passengers on a cliff-hanging 90-mile round-trip ride between Durango and the old mining town of Silverton. The steam locomotive pulls passenger cars — some dating to the 1880's — through canyons and along cliffside ledges, with excellent views of the mountains and the wild Animas River. *Admission charged.*

17. Fort Garland State Museum

Rte. 159, Fort Garland. Frontiersman Kit Carson once commanded this post, established in 1858 to protect settlers from the Ute Indians. In the restored barracks are dioramas of a meeting between Carson and the Utes, an army pack train, and a stage holdup. *Admission charged.*

18. Great Sand Dunes National Monument

Up to 700 feet high, these massive dunes are the tallest in North America. The 55-square-mile dune field is a magnet for sand skiers, hikers, and backpackers, as well as nighttime visitors with flashlights who hope to spot the park's giant sand-treader camel crickets. *Admission charged.*

A cliff-hanging ride aboard the Durango & Silverton Narrow Gauge Railroad

MAP PG. 53

WYOMING
COLORADO
UTAH
COLORADO
WYO.
NEB.
MEDICINE BOW
NATL. FOREST
Bridger Peak 11,004
Closed in Winter
Riverside
Encampment
Albany
Keystone
Foxpark
Woods Landing
HUTTON LAKE N.W.R.
Tie Siding
MEDICINE BOW N.F.
FRANCIS E. WARREN A.F.B.
Curt Gowdy S.P.
Cheyenne
Orchard Valley
Buford
Harriman
Hillsdale
Burns
Egbert
Carpenter
Bushnell
Pine Bluffs
Panorama Point 5,424
Baggs
Dixon
Savery
Slater
SIERRA MADRE
Mountain Home
Sparks
Hiawatha
Powder Wash
BROWNS PARK NATIONAL WILDLIFE REFUGE
Columbine
Hahns Peak
Steamboat Lake State Rec. Area
Pearl Lake S.P.
Mount Zirkel 12,180
PARK RANGE
Cowdrey
Walden
Walden Res.
Glendevey
MEDICINE BOW MTS.
LARAMIE MTS.
Virginia Dale
ROOSEVELT
Red Feather Lakes
NATL. FOR.
Livermore
Rustic
Picnic Rock State Park
Wellington
Nunn
Carr
Hereford
Grover
PAWNEE NATIONAL GRASSLAND
Keota
Pierce
Purcell
Briggsdale
Buckingham
Raymer
Great Divide
ELKHEAD MTS.
ROUTT NATIONAL FOREST
Clark
NORTH PARK
COLORADO STATE FOR.
ARAPAHO N.W.R.
Coalmont
DINOSAUR NATIONAL MONUMENT
Greystone
Sunbeam
Maybell
Lay
Craig
Hayden
Milner
Steamboat Springs
ROCKY
Rand
ROUTT NATL. FOREST
Yampa
Elk Springs
Hamilton
Pagoda
Blue Mountain
Dinosaur
Massadona
DANFORTH HILLS
Oak Creek
Phippsburg
Stagecoach St. Rec. Area
ARAPAHO NATIONAL FOREST
MAP PG. 79
Gould
Closed in Winter
ROCKY MOUNTAIN NATL. PARK
Glen Haven
Masonville
Drake
Boyd Lake S.R.A.
Bellvue
Lory S.P.
Poudre Park
Ft. Collins
Ault
Timnath
Windsor
Eaton
Galeton
Lucerne
Greeley
Cornish
Barnesville
Gill
Kersey
Jackson Lake St. Rec. Area
Weldona
Goodrich
Orchard
Masters
Wiggins
Estes Park
Loveland
Johnstown
Milliken
Evans
La Salle
Grand Lake
Longs Peak 14,255
Berthoud
Allenspark
Lyons
Mead
Barbour Ponds S.R.A.
Platteville
Gilcrest
Longmont
Lake Granby
Niwot
Ione
Fort Lupton
Keenesburg
Roggen
Prospect Valley
Hoyt
Bonanza
Rangely
Meeker
Cathedral Bluffs
Buford
WHITE RIVER NATIONAL FOREST
Sheep Mtn. 12,246
Toponas
Hot Sulphur Springs
Kremmling
Parshall
Williams Fork Res.
Granby
Tabernash
Fraser
Winter Park
Berthoud Pass 11,315
Ward
Boulder
Nederland
Eldora
Louisville
Lafayette
Dacono
Hudson
Brighton
Broomfield
Pinecliffe
Rollinsville
East Portal
Central City
Westminster
Thornton
Arvada
ROCKY MOUNTAIN ARSENAL
Wheat Ridge
Golden
Aurora
Denver
Watkins
Bennett
Strasburg
Byers
Deer Trail
Radium
McCoy
Bond
Burns
State Bridge
GORE RANGE
ARAPAHO NATIONAL FOREST
WILLIAMS FORK MTS.
Dumont
Empire
Georgetown
Idaho Springs
Loveland Pass 11,992
Lakewood
Evergreen
Mount Evans 14,264
Littleton
Englewood
Chatfield S.R.A.
Parker
Conifer
Agate
ROAN PLATEAU
TAVAPUTS PLATEAU
EAST
Rio Blanco
Rifle Gap St. Rec. Area
Rifle Falls State Park
Harvey Gap St. Rec. Area
THE FLAT TOPS
NAVAL OIL SHALE RESERVE
Rifle
Silt
New Castle
Gypsum
Eagle
Wolcott
Edwards
Avon
Minturn
Vail
Silverthorne
Frisco
Dillon
Keystone
Dillon Res.
Copper Mtn.
Breckenridge
Blue River
Roan Cliffs
Grand Valley
Glenwood Springs
Cardiff
Carbondale
Sylvan Lake State Park
WHITE RIVER NATIONAL FOREST
Gilman
Redcliff
Climax
Hoosier Pass 11,541
Alma
Como
Jefferson
Grant
Shawnee
Bailey
Pine
Roxborough S.P.
Foxton
Louviers
Sedalia
Franktown
Elizabeth
Castle Rock
Castlewood Canyon S.P.
Kiowa
Elbert
BOOK CLIFFS
Battlement Mesa
De Beque
Highline State Rec. Area
Island Acres State Recreation Area
Mack
Loma
Fruita
Westwater
Grand Junction
COLORADO NATL. MON.
Clifton
Fruitvale
Palisade
Cameo
Molina
Collbran
Mesa
Vega State Recreation Area
GRAND MESA
Grand Mesa
GRAND MESA NATIONAL FOREST
Skyway
Basalt
Snowmass
Meredith
Tennessee Pass 10,424
Snowmass Village
Woody Creek
Aspen
Redstone
Marble
MAROON BELLS
ELK MTS.
SAWATCH
Independence Pass 12,095
ASHCROFT GHOST TOWN
Castle Peak 14,265
Closed in Winter
Mount Elbert 14,433
Leadville
Twin Lakes
Granite
Mount Harvard 14,414
Fairplay
SOUTH PARK
TARRYALL MTS.
Tarryall
Deckers
PIKE NATIONAL FOREST
RAMPART RANGE
Larkspur
Palmer Lake
Monument
U.S. AIR FORCE ACADEMY
Black Forest
Peyton
Calhan
Matheson
Simla
Ramah
Big Sandy Cr.
Horse Creek
Glade Park
Orchard Mesa
Whitewater
GRAND MESA N.F.
Paonia State Recreation Area
Somerset
Bowie
Paonia
Hotchkiss
Cedaredge
Orchard City
Lazear
Crawford
Crawford St. Rec. Area
BLACK CANYON OF THE GUNNISON NATIONAL MON.
Maher
Mount Gunnison 12,719
Crested Butte
Taylor Park Res.
GUNNISON NATIONAL FOREST
WEST ELK MTS.
RUBY RANGE
Tincup
Almont
Pitkin
Ohio
Gunnison
Parlin
Blue Mesa Reservoir
Monarch Pass 11,312
SAN ISABEL NATL. FOREST
Nathrop
St. Elmo
Mount Antero 14,269
Buena Vista
Garfield
Maysville
Salida
Poncha Springs
Howard
Coaldale
Cotopaxi
MOUNTAINS
Hartsel
Antero Res.
Garo
Spinney Mtn. St. Rec. Area
Eleven-Mile St. Rec. Area
Lake George
Florissant
FLORISSANT FOSSIL BEDS NATL. MON.
Woodland Park
Divide
Crystola
Cascade
Manitou Springs
Pikes Peak 14,110
Colorado Springs
PETERSON A.F.B.
Falcon
Ellicott
Yoder
Rush
Security
Fountain
FORT CARSON MILITARY RESERVATION
Cripple Creek
Victor
Guffey
Parkdale
ROYAL GORGE
Canon City
Penrose
Portland
Florence
Texas Creek
Pueblo West
PUEBLO STATE REC. AREA
Pueblo
Devine
Avondale
PUEBLO ORDNANCE DEPOT
Boone
Olney Springs
Fowler
Hillside
Wetmore
Greenwood
Westcliffe
Silver Cliff
WET MOUNTAINS
Beulah
Rosita
MAP PG. 81
Gateway
UNCOMPAHGRE NATIONAL FOREST
UNCOMPAHGRE PLATEAU
Delta
Switzer Lake State Rec. Area
Olathe
Montrose
Cimarron
Sapinero
CURECANTI NATIONAL RECREATION AREA
Doyleville
Sargents
COCHETOPA HILLS
Bonanza
Villa Grove
MANTI-LA SAL NATIONAL FOREST
Paradox
Uravan
Bedrock
Vancorum
Naturita
Nucla
Redvale
Norwood
Colona
Ridgway State Recreation Area
Ridgway
Powderhorn
UNCOMPAHGRE NATIONAL FOREST
GUNNISON NATIONAL FOREST
Mineral Hot Springs
Saguache
SANGRE DE CRISTO MTS.
SAN LUIS VALLEY
Slick Rock
Placerville
Sawpit
Telluride
Uncompahgre Peak 14,309
Ouray
Camp Bird
Pandora
Ophir
Gladstone
Silverton
Mount Wilson 14,246
Lake City
San Luis Peak 14,014
LA GARITA MOUNTAINS
CONTINENTAL DIVIDE
RIO GRANDE NATIONAL FOREST
Creede
Wagon Wheel Gap
La Garita
Crestone
Crestone Peak 14,294
Moffat
SAN ISABEL NATIONAL FOREST
Colorado City
Rye
Cedarwood
GREAT SAND DUNES NATL. MONUMENT
Gardner
Farisita
Red Wing
North LaVeta Pass 9,413
Walsenburg
Lathrop St. Park
Cucharas Res.
COMANCHE NATIONAL GRASSLAND
Egnar
Dove Creek
Cahone
Pleasant View
Yellow Jacket
McPhee Res.
Lewis
Arriola
Dunton
Rico
Stoner
SAN JUAN MOUNTAINS
SAN JUAN NATIONAL FOREST
Rio Grande Res.
Mt. Eolus 14,084
Spar City
South Fork
Del Norte
Center
Hooper
Mosca
San Luis Lake
Monte Vista
Alamosa
Blanca Peak 14,345
Blanca
La Veta
Aguilar
Ludlow
Thatcher
Tyrone
PORT CARSON MILITARY RESERVATION
Model
Hoehne
Delhi
Pryor
HOVENWEEP NATIONAL MONUMENT
Dolores
Mancos St. Rec. Area
LA PLATA MTS.
Rockwood
Hermosa
Vallecito
Vallecito Res.
Wolf Creek Pass 10,850
Summitville
MONTE VISTA N.W.R.
Waverly
ALAMOSA N.W.R.
Fort Garland
CULEBRA RANGE
Cuchara
SAN ISABEL NATIONAL FOREST
Gulnare
Monument Park
Boncarbo
El Moro
Cortez
Mancos
Mayday
Durango
Hesperus
YUCCA HOUSE NATIONAL MONUMENT (no visitors)
MESA VERDE NATL. PARK
Towaoc
Mesa Verde
UTE MOUNTAIN IND. RES.
SOUTHERN UTE INDIAN RESERVATION
Bayfield
Gem Village
Pagosa Springs
Chimney Rock
Montezuma Peak 13,150
Platoro
Platoro Res.
La Jara Res.
Capulin
La Jara
Estrella
Sanford
Manassa
San Acacio
San Luis
Nutria
SCALE IN MILES
0 10 20 30 40 50

MAP PG. 73

MAP PG. 83

MAP PG. 111

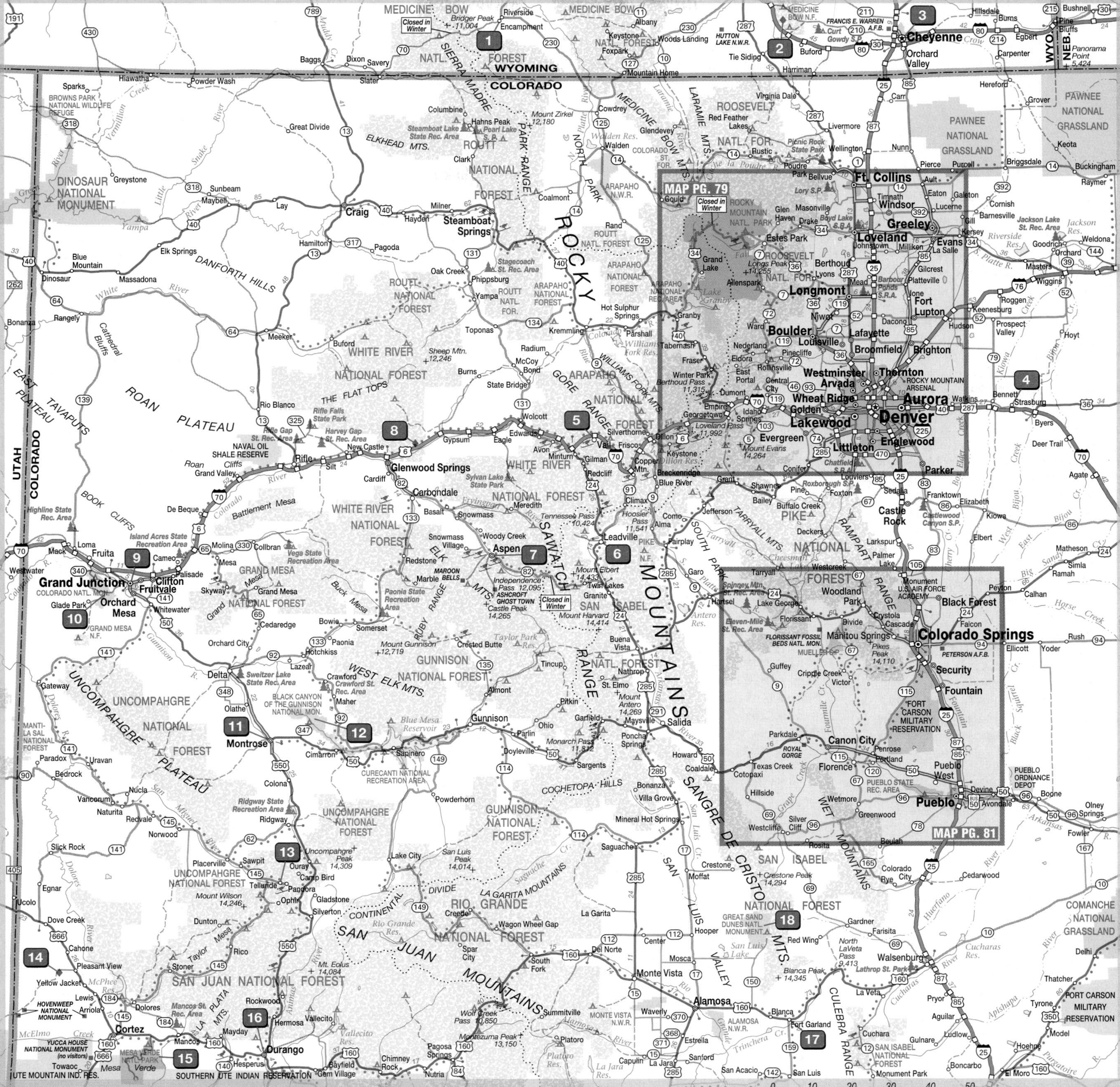

1. Centennial Village

1475 A St., Greeley. This museum village opened in 1976 in commemoration of Colorado's 100th and the nation's 200th anniversary. Visitors can tour adobe buildings, a Swedish-American farmhouse, a firehouse, and other structures. Authentic 1860's–1920's furnishings include tea-leaf china, parlor pianos, and pump organs.

2. Lory State Park

This 2,500-acre former cattle ranch offers activities ranging from camping and hiking to rock climbing and horseback riding at elevations of 5,000 to 7,000 feet. Sagebrush, sandstone ridges, and ponderosa pine forests can be explored along more than 25 miles of trails. Rock climbers and hikers alike delight in reaching the peak of 6,789-foot Arthur's Rock. *Admission charged.*

3. Estes Park

This year-round resort surrounded by lakes and snowcapped peaks features the historic **Stanley Hotel,** the Big Thompson River, Estes Park Riverwalk, Lake Estes, and spectacular views along the Continental Divide from the **Prospect Mountain Aerial Tramway.** As gateway to Rocky Mountain National Park, the village also serves as the site of the **Rocky Mountain National Park Visitor Center.** The center highlights more than 400 square miles of park attractions and recreational opportunities with relief maps, films, and other information. *Admission charged for some attractions.*

4. Bear Lake Road

Some of Colorado's most magnificent scenery lines this 9-mile route — past Moraine Park, Glacier Creek, and stands of Colorado blue spruce — to scenic Bear Lake. A trail leads around the lake, where deer, elk, and other wildlife can be spotted.

5. Moraine Park

This area is named for a long, forested ridge, called a lateral moraine, that rises from the valley floor. A museum gives information on park topography and wildlife.

6. Trail Ridge Road

The nation's highest continuously paved highway climbs to 12,183 feet, crosses the Continental Divide, and enters the heart of Rocky Mountain National Park's spectacular scenery. Unique treeless tundra walks, marmots, birds, and beaver dams are seen along with vistas of mountain glaciation. The route is closed in the winter.

7. Milner Pass

A park sign near the 10,758-foot summit explains the meaning of the Continental Divide: Water west of the Divide flows into the Pacific Ocean, while water to the east flows into the Atlantic or the Gulf of Mexico.

8. Grand Lake

Colorado's largest natural lake offers a variety of water sports and the world's highest yacht club. Reddish peaks of the Never Summer Range are seen en route to **Never Summer Ranch,** a National Park Service museum featuring buildings maintained as a 1920's dude ranch.

9. Arapaho National Recreation Area

The enlarged and renamed Shadow Mountain Recreation Area covers 36,000 acres and five lakes in a glacier-carved valley situated near the Colorado River's headwaters, Rocky Mountain National Park, and the Indian Peaks Wilderness. Boating, fishing, interpretive programs, and wilderness hikes are popular summer activities here.

10. Brainard Lake Recreation Area

Three miles west of the community of Ward, this recreation area gives access to the **Indian Peaks Wilderness,** where Sawtooth, Arapaho, and Longs peaks provide a dramatic skyline.

11. Loveland Pass

Twenty-one miles of magnificent alpine scenery frame the road en route to the 11,992-foot Loveland Pass. When the route is closed because of snow, the **Eisenhower Memorial Tunnel,** 1,500 feet below, provides drivers with an alternative way across the Continental Divide.

12. Georgetown

Here the **Georgetown–Silver Plume National Historic Landmark District** features more than 200 Victorian buildings. Restored Hamill House has converted gaslights and an outhouse topped with a cupola, while the Hotel de Paris, now a

A Colorado Stegosaurus finds a new home at Denver's Museum of Natural History.

museum, features former guest rooms with marble sinks and carved headboards. The **Georgetown Loop Railroad** travels 6 miles round-trip through breathtaking mountain scenery. *Admission charged.*

13. Central City–Blackhawk National Historic District

In the 1870's, when precious metals worth about $500 million were mined here, some called Central City "the richest square mile on earth." Visitors can pan for gold, take mountain train rides, and view some of Colorado's finest 19th-century commercial buildings, including a restored opera house. *Admission charged.*

14. Golden Gate Canyon State Park

Deer, elk, and eagles are among the wildlife that may be seen from the park's 16 trails through 60 miles of forested valleys and mountains. **Panorama Point,** near the access road, provides sweeping views along the Continental Divide. *Admission charged.*

15. Hiwan Homestead Museum

4208 South Timbervale Dr., Evergreen. This 17-room log lodge with twin octagonal towers and a chapel is on the National Register of Historic Places. The restored rooms appear as they were furnished between 1915 and 1930. Visitors will also see local memorabilia and a large doll collection.

16. Coors Brewing Company

Thirteenth and Ford Sts., Golden. At the world's single largest brewery, visitors can observe the brewing and malting processes, as well as sample the finished product.

17. Denver

Convention and Visitors Bureau, 225 West Colfax Ave. Attractions of the "Mile-High City" include the **Molly Brown House Museum,** the former home of the "unsinkable" heroine of the Broadway musical and movie. Covered with a million reflecting tiles, the 10-story **Denver Art Museum** houses one of the finest American Indian art collections in the world. At the **U.S. Mint,** visitors can observe the money-making process. The flavor of Denver's past has been preserved on picturesque **Larimer Square,** with its restored shops, restaurants, arcades, and gaslights. **City Park** is the home of the **Denver Zoo,** which has been rated among the top 10 zoos in the nation. Also located in the park, the **Museum of Natural History** features dinosaurs that once inhabited the area and 90 dioramas of regional plant and animal life. The **Colorado History Museum** documents the heritage of the state with displays of Anasazi pottery, mining equipment, and other interpretive exhibits. *Admission charged for some attractions.*

18. Longmont Museum

375 Kimbark St., Longmont. The region's history is recalled through exhibits ranging from prospectors' pans, beaver traps, and Indian grinding stones to a reconstructed one-room schoolhouse and a stagecoach. *Admission charged.*

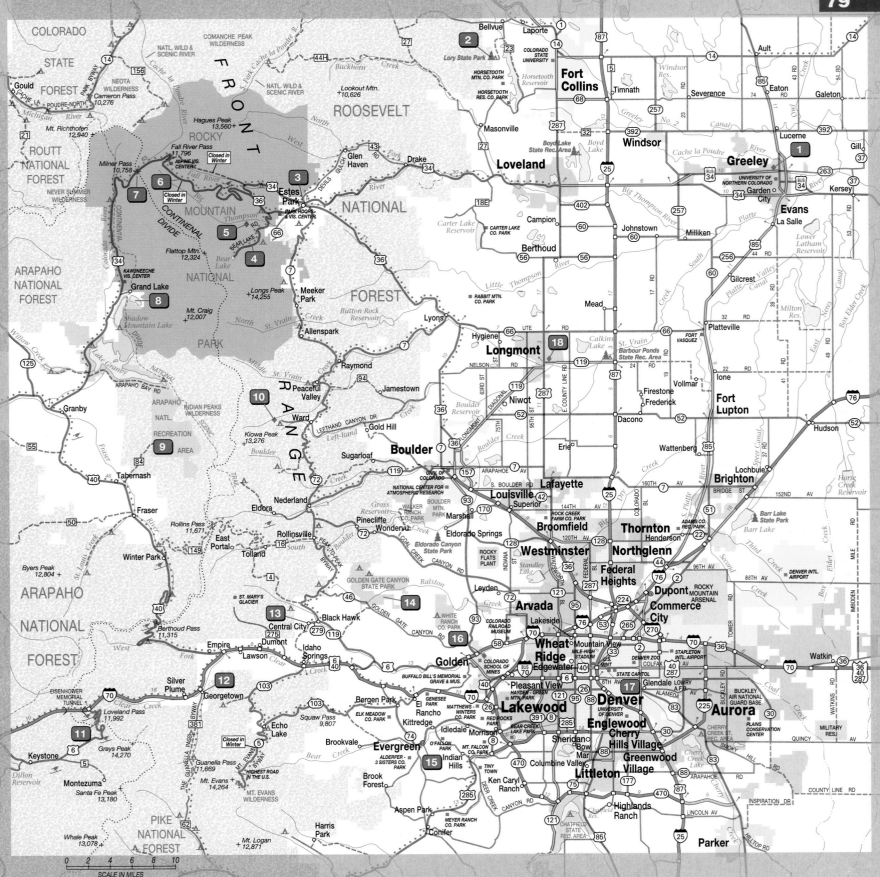

1. Florissant Fossil Beds National Monument

Set in a hilly region punctuated with pine, aspen, spruce, and wildflowers, this 6,000-acre site contains insect, fish, foliage, bird, butterfly, and other fossils of the Oligocene period. More than 140 species of plants, 1,100 species of insects, and several species of fish and birds have been identified here. Discovered in 1874 and now maintained by the National Park Service, the site has 12 miles of hiking trails. *Admission charged.*

2. United States Air Force Academy

The nation's youngest service academy, founded in 1954, is Colorado's top man-made attraction. In a spectacular setting north of Colorado Springs, it is spread out over an 18,000-acre prairie at an elevation of 7,900 feet, with the Rocky Mountains forming a dramatic backdrop. Maps for a self-guided driving tour are available at the gatehouses; the grounds and most buildings are open to the public. A visitor center houses informative exhibits. A nature trail leads to the **Cadet Chapel,** with its soaring aluminum spires and 4,334-pipe organ. Other attractions include **Falcon Stadium,** the **American Legion Memorial Tower,** the **Thunderbird Airmanship Overlook,** and the **planetarium.**

3. Cave of the Winds

About 70 million years ago, an inland sea surged into cracks created by the formation of the Rocky Mountains, eventually fashioning the series of underground caverns now called Cave of the Winds. The grandeur of the caverns, which were discovered in the 1880's by two children, has inspired such names as the Temple of Silence, Oriental Garden, and Canopy Hall. There are guided tours through 21 well-lit chambers. The nearby **Manitou Cliff Dwelling Museum** has exhibits on the architecture and artifacts of the Anasazi Indians, who lived here more than 800 years ago. On a self-guided tour visitors can see a three-story dwelling, numerous rooms, and displays of Anasazi artwork. During the summer there are performances of Native American dance. *Admission charged.*

4. Garden of the Gods Park

Once a winter campground for the Ute Indians, this 1,300-acre park is now a haven for rock climbers, hikers, and horseback riders. The park's spectacular red-and-white sandstone monoliths were deposited between 100 million and 300 million years ago. The colossal rocks, some of which soar to a height of 300 feet, include the famed **Balanced Rock,** the Kissing Camels, and the Three Graces. There are magnificent views of Pikes Peak, as well as guided nature walks and a visitor center. The park was named in the 19th century, when an enterprising visitor pronounced the locale ideal for a beer garden, and his companion replied that the setting was more suggestive of a "garden of the gods."

5. Colorado Springs

Convention and Visitors Bureau, 104 South Cascade Ave. Spread over a mesa at the base of Pikes Peak, Colorado Springs was founded in 1871 as a health resort. Home to the American Numismatic Association and the U. S. Olympic Committee, with its **Olympic Training Center,** the city also boasts the **ProRodeo Hall of Fame and Museum of the American Cowboy,** the **Pioneers Museum,** and the **Fine Arts Center.** The Wild West comes alive in **Pikes Peak Ghost Town,** with its saloon, general store, and evocative buildings. *Admission charged for some attractions.*

6. Cheyenne Mountain Zoo

4250 Cheyenne Mountain Zoo Rd., Colorado Springs. The only mountainside zoo in the nation is located here, in a striking 70-acre setting of ponderosa pine, spruce, and stark granite. It's home to more than 500 animals, including monkeys, elephants, rhinos, tigers, and a herd of giraffes. There is also a carousel and a picnic area. From the zoo, a mountain road spirals upward to **Shrine of the Sun.** After American humorist Will Rogers' death in a 1935 plane crash, his good friend Spencer Penrose honored his memory by dedicating this 100-foot stone tower, which offers awe-inspiring views of Colorado Springs, Pikes Peak, and the Great Plains. *Admission charged.*

7. Miramont Castle Museum

9 Capitol Hill Ave., Manitou Springs. Replete with crenellated turrets and 32 rooms on display, this fanciful "castle" draws more than 35,000 visitors annually. Built in 1895 and incorporating nine different architectural styles, it has four stories, walls 2 feet thick, and 14,000 square feet of space. Among its attractions are a gold-ceilinged drawing room, a 400-square-foot bedroom, a chapel, and a museum featuring miniature replicas of turn-of-the-century buildings. A tearoom provides not only food but breathtaking views of the mountains. Built by a wealthy French priest, the castle has been, in various incarnations, a sanatorium and an apartment house. *Admission charged.*

8. Pikes Peak

Soaring to 14,110 feet, America's most famous peak is named for Zebulon Pike, who encountered the astounding mountain in 1806. Dr. Edwin James became the first white man to reach the summit, in 1820; the first woman was Julia Archibald Holmes, who reached the top in 1858. The mountain was the inspiration for "America the Beautiful," penned in 1893 by Katharine Lee Bates. The **Manitou and Pikes Peak Railway,** the nation's highest railroad, and **Pikes Peak Highway,** 19 miles long, wind through lush mountain scenery on the way to the summit. Atop the peak the Summit House has an information center. Popular annual events are the Pikes Peak Marathon and the Pikes Peak Auto Hill Climb, called the Race to the Clouds. *Fee charged for railroad and toll for highway.*

9. Cripple Creek

Chamber of Commerce, 337 Bennett Ave. Settled just over a century ago, Cripple Creek was a gold-producing boomtown at the turn of the century, mining some $25 million in gold in a single year. Visitors can learn the colorful history of this mining town at the **Cripple Creek District Museum** or take the **Cripple Creek–Victor Narrow Gauge Railroad** for a rollicking tour of Wild West ghost towns and old gold mines. Guided tours of the **Mollie Kathleen Mine** descend 1,000 feet into the mountain. *Admission charged.*

10. Victor

Like Cripple Creek, Victor was once a rip-roaring mining town; workers even struck gold here while constructing the foundation for a new hotel. Nowadays only vestiges remain of some of the more than 400 mines that were in operation, and the local population has shrunk from thousands down to a few hundred souls. In 1899 a fire destroyed the original wooden structures, and the present brick buildings — including a hotel, a school, and a railway station — date from around the turn of the century. Newscaster Lowell Thomas was born in Victor, and the **Lowell Thomas Museum** has memorabilia pertinent both to his life and to the town itself. Early streets were surfaced with a low-grade ore, giving rise to the town's boast of "streets paved with gold!"

11. Red Canyon Park

This rugged region near Cañon City takes its name from its sunburned sandstone formations and small canyons. The park features a natural amphitheater sculpted over time by wind and weather, hiking trails, and picnic facilities. Excavations in this area have uncovered the fossils of five prehistoric dinosaurs.

12. Royal Gorge

In a 360-acre section of **Royal Gorge Park,** the stunning focal point is this steep canyon of sun-splashed red granite, which was carved out over a period of some 3 million years by the rushing waters of the Arkansas River. The river lies more than 1,000 dizzying feet below **Royal Gorge Bridge,** the world's highest suspension bridge, constructed in 1929. There are breathtaking views from the bridge, an aerial tramway that crosses the canyon, and what is reputed to be the world's steepest incline railway, which takes sightseers to the bottom of the gorge. Numerous scenic overlooks are scattered throughout the park, as well as shops, restaurants, an entertainment gazebo, and a children's playground with a miniature train. *Admission charged.*

13. City Park

In the heart of Pueblo's enchanting City Park is the **Pueblo Zoo,** with its penguins, antelope, zebras, prairie dogs, camels, deer, and even a herd of bison. In the popular "backyard" petting zoo, roosters and goats skitter about, and penned sheep, donkeys, and pigs wait to be petted. The park's other attractions include a pool, free tennis courts, and children's rides. The **Greenway,** a 36-mile network of trails, connects City Park to other parks, including the nearby **Nature Center,** the Greenway's main access point. Nestled in a canyon lush with cottonwood, the center showcases the region's animal and plant life, and at the Raptor Center wounded birds of prey are lovingly rehabilitated. *Admission charged for some attractions.*

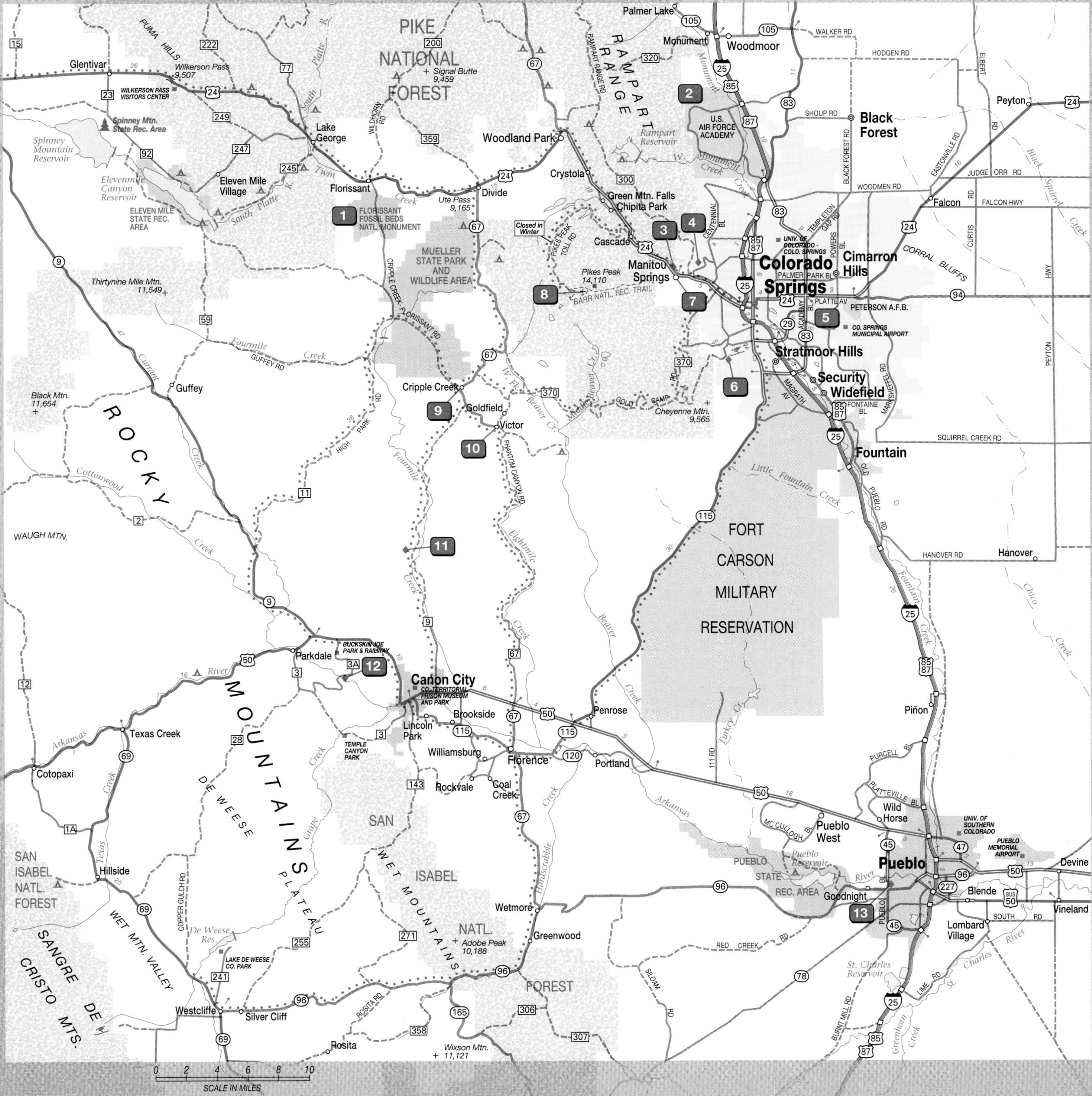

PIKE NATIONAL FOREST

RAMPART RANGE

Palmer Lake
Monument
Woodmoor
WALKER RD
HODGEN RD

15
Glentivar
222
PUMA HILLS
Wilkerson Pass
9,507
200
Signal Butte
9,459
105
105
ELBERT RD

23
WILKERSON PASS VISITORS CENTER
26
24
77
67
RAMPART RANGE RD
320
U.S. AIR FORCE ACADEMY
25
85
83
SHOUP RD
Black Forest
Peyton
24

249
Spinney Mtn. State Rec. Area
Lake George
359
Rampart Reservoir
87

Spinney Mountain Reservoir
92
247
245
Woodland Park
300
Monument Creek
WOODMEN RD
83
Black Forest
Falcon
FALCON HWY

Eleven Mile Village
Florissant
24
Crystola
Green Mtn. Falls
Chipita Park
Ute Pass 9,165
87
85
UNIV. OF COLORADO - COLO. SPRINGS
Powers Bl
Cimarron Hills
CORRAL BLUFFS

Elevenmile Canyon Reservoir
1
FLORISSANT FOSSIL BEDS NATL. MONUMENT
Divide
Cascade
3
4
Colorado Springs
Palmer Park Bl
94

ELEVEN MILE STATE REC. AREA
South Platte
67
Closed in Winter
PIKES PEAK TOLL RD
Manitou Springs
25
24
PETERSON A.F.B.

9
MUELLER STATE PARK AND WILDLIFE AREA
8
Pikes Peak 14,110
BARR NATL. REC. TRAIL
7
29
5
CO. SPRINGS MUNICIPAL AIRPORT

Thirtynine Mile Mtn. 11,549
59
CRIPPLE CREEK - FLORISSANT RD
Stratmoor Hills
Security Widefield

FOURMILE
GUFFEY RD
Creek
67
370
6
FONTAINE BL

Black Mtn. 11,654
Guffey
Cripple Creek
9
W. Fk. Beaver Cr.
Cheyenne Mtn. 9,565
GOLD CAMP RD
Fountain

ROCKY
Goldfield
10
Victor
PHANTOM CANYON RD
115

2
11
Eightmile
FORT CARSON MILITARY RESERVATION
HANOVER RD
Hanover

Cottonwood Creek
Current Creek
HIGH PARK RD
9
67
Beaver
SQUIRREL CREEK RD

WAUGH MTN.
Fourmile
Little Fountain Creek
85
87

MOUNTAINS
Parkdale
BUCKSKIN JOE PARK & RAILWAY
3A
12
Cañon City
CO. TERRITORIAL PRISON MUSEUM AND PARK
25

50
Texas Creek
River
9
Brookside
Penrose
Piñon

12
28
DE WEESE
3
Lincoln Park
67
50
4
Arkansas
PURCELL BL

Cotopaxi
69
Arkansas
TEMPLE CANYON PARK
115
Williamsburg
Florence
120
Portland
50
18
PLATTEVILLE BL

1A
Hillside
143
Rockvale
Coal Creek
67
5
UNIV. OF SOUTHERN COLORADO

SAN ISABEL NATL. FOREST
25
SAN ISABEL NATL. FOREST
Thirteen mile creek
MC CULLOGH
Pueblo West
Wild Horse
PUEBLO MEMORIAL AIRPORT

WET MTN. VALLEY
De Weese Res.
LAKE DE WEESE CO. PARK
255
271
Wetmore
Adobe Peak 10,188
Greenwood
96
Pueblo Reservoir
45
Pueblo
227
47
Devine

SANGRE DE CRISTO MTS.
241
69
Westcliffe
Silver Cliff
96
165
358
306
307
Rosita
Wixson Mtn. 11,121
SILOAM RD
RED CREEK RD
78
St. Charles Reservoir
Goodnight
13
Lombard Village
BUS 50
Blende
Vineland

0 2 4 6 8 10
SCALE IN MILES

1. Overland Trail Museum

Rte. 6, south of Sterling. Regional artifacts, from prehistoric mammoth bones to branding irons, and outbuildings such as a furnished one-room schoolhouse, a church, a blacksmith shop, and a country store are featured at this museum.

2. Fort Sidney Museum and Commander's Home

Sixth and Jackson Sts., Sidney. The museum houses memorabilia from the former fort and exhibits commemorating conflicts from the Spanish-American War to the Persian Gulf War. The Commander's Home, built in 1871 and listed on the National Register of Historic Places, displays relics from civilian frontier and farming days, including late Victorian fashion and antique furniture.

3. North Platte

Convention and Visitors Bureau, 502 South Dewey. The **Lincoln County Historical Museum** displays a reconstructed frontier town complete with an army headquarters, schoolhouse, depot, Pony Express building, and a pioneer home. Nearby **Buffalo Bill Ranch State Historical Park** holds Scout's Rest, the house built by William Cody (alias "Buffalo Bill") in 1887 during the height of his Wild West show. Outside of town, the lush, rolling **Sand Hills,** at more than 12 million acres, comprise the largest grassland area in the nation. *Admission charged at park.*

4. Chevyland U.S.A.

Exit 257 off Rte. 80, Elm Creek. Here visitors will encounter one of the best Chevrolet collections in the United States, kept polished and in running order, with models dating from 1914 to 1975. *Admission charged.*

5. The Frank House

George Washington Frank, a wealthy New York entrepreneur who helped finance the construction of the Kearney canal, built this mansion in 1889. One of the first domiciles in the town to have electricity and steam heat, this three-story home, located on the present-day West Campus of the **University of Nebraska at Kearney,** soon became the talk of the town. *Admission charged.*

6. Fort Kearny State Historical Park

Dating from 1848, this original fort was the first one built by the U.S. War Department near the Oregon Trail to protect westward-bound emigrants and workers on the Union Pacific Railroad. Troops were stationed here from the 1840's until the fort was abandoned in 1871. *Admission charged.*

7. Harold Warp Pioneer Village Foundation

Junction Rtes. 6 and 10, Minden. This 20-acre village contains more than 50,000 artifacts dating back to 1830, including 300 antique cars, a steam-powered carousel, a Pony Express relay station, antique farm machinery, and replicas of seven furnished rooms. *Admission charged.*

8. Last Indian Raid Museum

258 South Penn Ave., Oberlin. The museum commemorates a raid staged by Northern Cheyenne Indians who were hoping to reclaim their native land after having been forcibly removed to Oklahoma. In addition to relics from the battle, there are displays depicting pioneer and town life at the turn of the century. *Admission charged.*

9. High Plains Museum

1717 Cherry St., Goodland. Highlights of this museum's eclectic collection include prehistoric artifacts from the region, a life-size automated replica of America's first patented helicopter (invented in Goodland in 1910), and dioramas of Sherman County history.

10. Fort Wallace Memorial Museum

Rte. 40, Wallace. The army post that once stood here protected travelers on the Smoky Hill Trail and Overland Trail Dispatch from attack by the Plains Indians in the late 1800's. While all that remains of the actual fort today is the cemetery, visitors can find imaginative displays of old military and cowboy gear, as well as local artifacts from the Indian Wars, at the museum.

11. Fick Fossil and History Museum

700 West Third St., Oakley. The museum exhibits prehistoric fossils found in Kansas, such as 11,000 specimens of sharks' teeth and a 15-foot, 80-million-year-old fossilized fish. Also on display are an array of artifacts covering the state's later history, including an old printing press, farm wagon, sod house, and railroad depot.

12. Monument Rocks

These 60-foot-tall monoliths, sculpted over time by wind and water erosion, are vestiges of what were once ancient sea chalk beds. Used as guideposts for military parties and early wagon trains during the 1800's, they are now a national landmark. The site of the first white settlement in Kansas, a 17th-century pueblo called **El Quartelejo,** is found in nearby **Scott State Park.** Visitors to the park can also enjoy swimming, canoeing, hiking, and camping. *Admission charged at park.*

13. Nicodemus

Named for the first slave to buy his freedom in the United States, this town was established in 1877 by blacks from Kentucky. Nicodemus is now designated a historic landmark, as the only all-black pioneer town west of the Mississippi.

14. Kirwin National Wildlife Refuge

Wildlife abounds in this woodland and grassland preserve, where bird-watchers delight in the migration of birds from the eastern and western United States. Some of the more magnificent birds that visit the refuge seasonally include the white pelican, the sandhill crane, and the bald eagle.

15. Historic Fort Hays

1472 Rte. 183 Alt., Hays. Built in 1867, the fort was a 45-building complex established to protect local settlers. The four buildings that remain today give visitors excellent insight into the period through displays and information on noted figures who have been associated with the fort — Wild Bill Hickok, Buffalo Bill Cody, Gen. George Armstrong Custer, among others.

16. Cathedral of the Plains

900 Cathedral Ave., Victoria. Twin spires that tower 141 feet are among the most awe-inspiring aspects of this magnificent Roman Catholic church, built out of local Kansas limestone by Volga Germans in 1911. The church's Romanesque interior features stained-glass windows, wood carvings, and hand-carved stone.

17. Kansas Barbed Wire Museum

120 West First, La Crosse. This unusual museum displays more than 500 varieties of barbed wire, which proved to be a sure-fire method of protecting livestock and crops across the Old West. The **Post Rock Museum,** just down the street, exhibits tools and a quarry to demonstrate the process by which limestone was collected and cut to size for farm fence posts, water troughs, and building material.

18. Fort Larned National Historic Site

This fort was a major guardian of the Santa Fe Trail from 1859 to 1878, and 8 of its original 10 structures remain open to the public. What was formerly a barrack has been turned into a visitor center and museum, with exhibits that include a life-size model of a 10th Cavalry soldier and numerous military artifacts. *Admission charged.*

19. Dodge City

The past of Dodge City is brought to life on **Front Street,** a reconstruction of the town's main street in the 1870's, with a blacksmith shop, a general store, and several saloons. Nine miles west of the city there are still traces — remarkably discernible despite years of erosion — of the old **Santa Fe Trail,** the major commercial route in the mid-1800's, which stretched from Independence, Missouri, all the way to Santa Fe. *Admission charged at Front Street.*

20. Finney Game Refuge

Located on the south bank of the Arkansas River, the refuge was created in 1912. Visitors can sometimes arrange for guided tours to view the bison that roam its 3,800 acres today.

21. Bent's Old Fort National Historic Site

35110 Rte. 194 East, La Junta. A replica of what was in olden times one of the most important trading posts in the area, Bent's Old Fort is located on the Santa Fe Trail. Staff guides dressed as Indians, Mexicans, and trappers demonstrate frontier activity during the fort's heyday, from 1833 to 1849. *Admission charged.*

22. Kit Carson Museum

Rte. 40, Kit Carson. Housed in a 1904 Union Pacific Depot, this museum is dedicated to the history of the town of Kit Carson, which became a quiet farming and livestock center after the rowdier saloon town of Kit Carson burned down. The museum boasts inventive displays of 19th-century rooms, doll collections, costumed mannequins, and old-time farm tools.

SAND HILLS

BUFFALO BILL RANCH S.H.P.

ASH HOLLOW S.H.P.

PAWNEE NATIONAL GRASSLAND

NEBRASKA
COLORADO

PEETZ TABLE

CHAMPION MILL S.H.P.

NEBRASKA
KANSAS

BEECHER ISLAND BATTLEGROUND

COLORADO
KANSAS

Mt. Sunflower 4,039

COMANCHE NATL. GRASSLAND

FORT CARSON MILITARY RES.

CIMARRON NATIONAL GRASSLAND

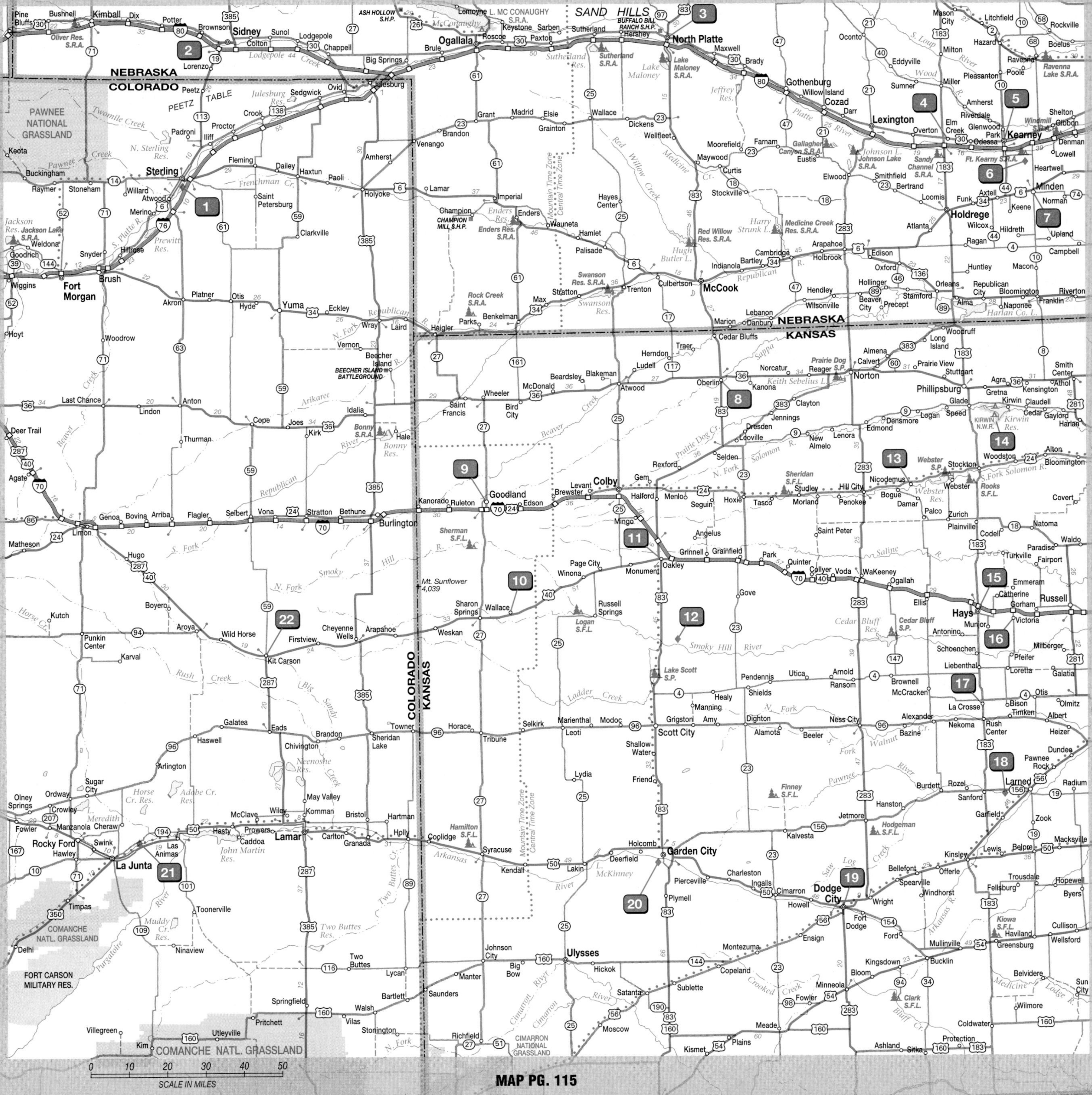

Mountain Time Zone / Central Time Zone

0 10 20 30 40 50
SCALE IN MILES

1. Fresno

Convention and Visitors Bureau, 808 M St. Set in an important agricultural area, the city and its environs hold diverse attractions, including the **Metropolitan Museum of Art, History and Science;** the **Fresno Art Museum;** and the **Discovery Center,** with hands-on science exhibits. **Roeding Park** features a zoo, children's rides, and picnic areas set amid a striking variety of trees and shrubs, while **Woodward Park** offers a Japanese garden, bird sanctuary, and children's fishing ponds. *Admission charged.*

2. R. C. Baker Memorial Museum

297 West Elm Ave., Coalinga. The discovery of oil and coal produced the town of Coalinga, whose history is recounted at this museum through an array of objects ranging from oil-field equipment to a large fossil and mineral collection.

3. Mission San Miguel Archangel

801 Mission St., San Miguel. Still an active parish, this church is the best preserved of the early California missions. A museum devoted to the Franciscan monastic order displays habits, books, and artwork.

4. Jade Cove

Beachcombing may yield a special reward here: pieces of Pacific blue jade, thought to be unique to this area, and other shades of nephrite jade. Another popular activity is whale-watching on the promontory, from which sea otters can also be seen.

5. Hearst San Simeon State Historical Monument

750 Hearst Castle Rd., San Simeon. In the 1920's William Randolph Hearst, the enormously wealthy owner of a media conglomerate, built himself a grand-scale pleasure palace: a 100-room castle surrounded by ornate guest houses, exquisite gardens, imported statues, and indoor and outdoor swimming pools. The unique estate is now open to the public, with reservations recommended. *Admission charged.*

6. Morro Bay

Drivers on Rte. 1 are often surprised by the sight of **Morro Rock,** a conical formation jutting 578 feet out of the sea at Morro Bay. Called the Gibraltar of the Pacific, the monolith is a natural preserve for peregrine falcons and other nesting seabirds.

7. Montaña de Oro State Park

Pebble-strewn beaches, glorious spring flowers, tide pools teeming with life, migrating whales and monarch butterflies, coastal sage and live oak are all attributes of this 7,979-acre park. With picnic and camping areas and a network of trails, this oceanside plateau lives up to its name, "mountain of gold."

An elephant seal in the Channel Islands

8. San Luis Obispo

Chamber of Commerce, 1039 Chorro St. The **San Luis Obispo County Historical Museum** documents the region's history with photographs, a re-created period parlor, a mail wagon, and other displays. Along with its restored adobe church and Spanish paintings, the **Mission San Luis Obispo de Tolosa** has a museum with many American Indian artifacts and the church's original altar. The mission sometimes hosts the town's Mozart Festival, held in August.

9. Pismo Beach

Chamber of Commerce, 581 Dolliver St. This area boasts about 20 miles of seashore, allowing for swimming, surfing, fishing, and diving. The **Nipomo Dunes,** 8 miles long, provide an excellent vantage point for birdwatching. Water sports also take place at the **Lopez Lake Recreation Area.** *Admission charged at recreation area.*

10. La Purisima Mission State Historic Park

2295 Purisima Rd., Lompoc. The buildings of La Purisima Mission were lost first to an earthquake and then to neglect, but 10 of the early–19th-century structures have been rebuilt. The park contains exhibits on the mission's secular activities, such as making candles, crushing olives, and processing cowhide. The locale offers a bonus to visitors in the summer, when the Lompoc Valley blazes with bright flowers, which are grown commercially. *Admission charged.*

11. Solvang

Visitors Bureau, 1593 Mission Dr. Windmills and half-timbered structures attest to this town's Danish heritage. Numerous shops sell Danish knickknacks and other products. The gold adobe **Mission Santa Ines** — the 19th of the 21 Spanish missions in California — offers a striking visual contrast, with its red-tiled roof and arched colonnade. *Admission charged at mission.*

12. Nojoqui Falls Park

A 2-mile side road through farmlands and stands of oak trees leads to this county park. Its main attraction is **Nojoqui Falls,** a ribbonlike waterfall that descends among hanging shrubs between rocky cliffs.

13. Santa Barbara

Visitor Information Center, 1 Santa Barbara St. A scenic drive marked with blue signs shows off the harbor, beaches, and hills of Santa Barbara, with a detour into downtown. Two special features are the **County Courthouse,** known for its magnificent Spanish Revival architecture, and the beautiful **Mission Santa Barbara.** The latter has the facade of a Greek temple and an arcade of Roman arches. Ancient bells toll in the twin towers of the 1786 sandstone church. *Admission charged at mission.*

14. Ojai

Chamber of Commerce, 338 East Ojai Ave. Filled with groves of oranges and avocados, the Ojai Valley has long attracted artists and sightseers with its pastoral beauty. The town has a historical society and museum, and a Spanish-style shopping arcade that features the work of local artists.

15. Ventura

Visitor and Convention Bureau, 89-C South California St. Nestled between the ocean and rolling hills, this town was named for the **Mission San Buenaventura,** now represented by the restored church and a museum. Other sites of interest are the **Olivas Adobe** and the **Ortega Adobe,** restored 19th-century homes; the **Albinger Archaeological Museum,** with Chumash Indian artifacts; and the **Ventura County Museum of History and Art,** whose displays include outdoor agricultural exhibits. *Admission charged for some attractions.*

16. Channel Islands National Park

Of the eight Channel Islands, the most accessible are **Anacapa** and **Santa Barbara,** reached by boats departing from a dock adjacent to the park's visitor center in Ventura. These pristine islands sustain sea lions, seals, and many seabirds; out in the ocean, dolphins and whales can often be spotted by visitors. *Fee charged for boat ride.*

17. Leo Carrillo State Beach

Headlands protruding into the sea form a series of coves that give this part of the shore its dramatic look. Often used as a setting for movies, the public beach is but one of many along the coast in this area. *Fee charged for parking.*

18. Six Flags Magic Mountain

Thrill seekers can ride any of seven world-class roller coasters or shoot the rapids in a raft. Others can enjoy tamer rides, musical and animal shows, and the strolling Looney Tunes characters. Younger children especially enjoy Bugs Bunny World and the petting zoo. *Admission charged.*

19. Fort Tejon State Historic Park

4200 Fort Tejon Rd., Lebec. The 1st U.S. Dragoons were stationed here to guard the frontier in the latter half of the 19th century. Their barracks, officers' residence, and orderlies' quarters still stand, and a museum gives further detail about the daily lives of the troops and of the region's other inhabitants. *Admission charged.*

20. Kern County Museum

3801 Chester Ave., Bakersfield. A log cabin, one-room schoolhouse, ranch house with cook wagon, and turn-of-the-century homes furnished in period style are among the museum's 60 buildings that recall Kern County's pioneer days. Native American artifacts, photographs, and dioramas provide historical insight. *Admission charged.*

21. Tule Elk State Reserve

Between 20 and 50 tule elk live on this grassland, a tiny fraction of the number that once roamed freely in the area. From a shady picnic area, visitors can watch these animals, some with enormous racks of antlers, grazing or wallowing in a water hole. *Fee charged for parking.*

MAP PG. 61

MAP PG. 87

MAP PG. 91

MAP PG. 93

MAP PG. 95

MAP PG. 117

PACIFIC

OCEAN

1. Big Basin Redwoods State Park

This 19,000-acre park protects stands of lofty redwoods, some 300 feet high. Visitors can take in the grandeur of these trees while hiking or riding horses on the extensive trails. A nature lodge contains exhibits on the park's plant and animal life, and picnic sites and campground facilities are available. *Admission charged.*

2. Santa Cruz

Conference and Visitors Center, 701 Front St. Among all the ocean towns in California, Santa Cruz has the only seaside amusement park along its boardwalk. Another city attraction, the **Long Marine Laboratory and Aquarium,** features a unique tidepool aquarium. The lovely redwood forests surrounding the town can be seen at **Henry Cowell Redwoods State Park,** or from the **Roaring Camp & Big Trees Narrow-Gauge Railroad,** where passengers are carried through the forests by 19th-century steam locomotives. **West Cliff Drive,** a famous scenic route that skirts the shoreline, leads to **Natural Bridges State Beach,** with its sandstone arches. *Admission charged for some attractions.*

3. Elkhorn Slough Reserve

At various times of year hundreds of birds, including egrets, cormorants, and loons, find refuge in the salt marshes and tidal flats of this 1,500-acre sanctuary. A network of hiking trails provides a good opportunity to observe the birds' seasonal comings and goings; a footpath leads to a heron rookery that is open to the public Wednesday through Sunday. *Admission charged.*

4. Castroville

For good reason, Castroville has nicknamed itself the Artichoke Center of the World. Roadside stands heaped with artichokes abound, and every September the town holds an artichoke festival during which a young woman is crowned Artichoke Queen (a title first held by Marilyn Monroe). In nearby **Gilroy** — which likes to be billed as the Garlic Capital of the World — an annual garlic festival is held each July, when visitors can sample garlic-based foods of all kinds, including garlic ice cream.

5. San Juan Bautista

Chamber of Commerce, 1402-A Third St. With its many well-preserved 19th-century buildings, this hilltop town maintains a quaint, early-California flavor. The **San Juan Bautista State Historic Park** features a charming plaza with aged adobe structures, the most famous of which is the **Mission San Juan Bautista.** A highlight of the mission's chapel is a brightly hued altar wall, painted by a Boston seaman. Several period rooms, including a music room, reveal further glimpses of mission life. *Admission charged at park.*

6. Salinas

Chamber of Commerce, 119 East Alisal St. Set amid rich agricultural land, Salinas has carefully preserved several of its old residences. The one-story **Boronda Adobe,** constructed in the 1840's by José Eusebio Boronda for his large family, still holds many period furnishings and artifacts. Another landmark, the redwood-frame **Harvey-Baker House,** was built by the town's first mayor in 1868. Salinas's most famous son, the Nobel Prize–winning writer John Steinbeck, was born in a turreted Victorian home that today is a restaurant called the **Steinbeck House.** Also in town, the **Steinbeck Library** pays tribute to the author's distinguished literary career.

7. Monterey

Chamber of Commerce, 380 Alvarado St. The heritage of this charming seaside town is evident in the old adobe structures preserved in **Monterey State Historic Park. Fisherman's Wharf** is a colorful pier offering shops, restaurants, fish stores, and fishing charter-boat expeditions. Nearby, the old cannery buildings of **Cannery Row,** immortalized by John Steinbeck, now house boutiques and art galleries. Another highlight of the town is the **Monterey Bay Aquarium,** which features sea otters, sharks, and a three-story kelp forest. *Admission charged for some attractions.*

8. Pacific Grove

Chamber of Commerce, Central and Forest Aves. The trees here look as though they might flutter away when thousands of migrating monarch butterflies collect on them each winter. For those who miss this annual event, the **Pacific Grove Museum of Nat-** ural History has a video that documents the phenomenon. The town's **Ocean View Boulevard** presents a pleasant dilemma—whether to look at the magnificent coast on one side or at the Victorian mansions on the other. People often stop at **Lovers Point** to swim or have a picnic.

9. Seventeen-Mile Drive

This beautiful drive follows in part the coastline of the Monterey Peninsula, passing pines, scrub oaks, wind-bent cypresses, ice plants, glittering beaches, and craggy cliffs. **Cypress Point Lookout** and the **Seal and Bird Rocks lookouts** provide excellent vantage points from which visitors can observe sea lions and both leopard and harbor seals. *Admission charged.*

Monarch butterflies alight in Pacific Grove.

10. Carmel-by-the-Sea

Once an active art colony, the village of Carmel still retains a cozy yet elegant atmosphere. Sights of interest here include the 1920's **Tor House** and **Hawk Tower,** constructed by the poet Robinson Jeffers out of local Santa Lucia granite and embellished with stones brought from all over the world. Visitors can also tour the **Mission San Carlos Borromeo del Río Carmelo,** whose ornate church, with its star-shaped window and Moorish-style tower, stands on a quadrangle where Father Junípero Serra's room and an early kitchen are re-created. Inviting shops and art galleries line **Ocean Avenue,** which ends at a lovely public beach. *Donation encouraged at mission.*

11. Point Lobos State Reserve

The rare Monterey cypresses clinging to the rocks have almost come to symbolize Point Lobos, along with the colonies of sea lions that make their home here. Hikers can follow trails to the cypress stand, as well as to lovely meadows, surf-pounded rocks, and good observation sites for viewing otters, seals, and migrating whales, along with the sea lions. *Admission charged.*

12. Point Sur Lightstation

Once a beacon to sailors, Point Sur Lightstation now serves as a landmark to drivers on the Pacific Coast Highway (Rte. 1). The structure was built in 1889, at the site of numerous shipwrecks. Several miles up the highway from the lightstation, **Bixby Creek Bridge** arches 285 feet over a canyon.

13. Pfeiffer Big Sur State Park

Located in Big Sur country, this park fairly bursts with natural wonders, including redwood forests, waterfalls, sea caves, lagoons, and gorges. Wildlife, including boar, is plentiful. The summit of **Mount Manuel,** reached by trail, provides a lovely coastal vista. From the spectacular **Pacific Coast Highway,** which curves and dips alongside the ocean, drivers can see the famous attributes of Big Sur — foamy surf, rugged cliffs, rocky headlands, and tree-capped mountains. *Admission charged.*

14. Mission Nuestra Señora de la Soledad

36641 Fort Romie Rd., Soledad. The mission's original church was built in 1791 but collapsed in a flood 40 years later. Remaining wall fragments now share the site with a chapel and a small museum dedicated to the 13th Spanish mission in California. Just south of the town of Soledad stands the historic **Los Coches Adobe,** a 19th-century house that has variously served as a stagecoach depot and a post office.

15. Pinnacles National Monument

The pinnacles are formed of volcanic rock, with craggy red spires creating deep canyons. These stone formations contain open areas with 35 miles of trails, ranging from cave trails (spelunkers should take flashlights) to more difficult wilderness treks. Only experienced rock climbers should attempt to scale the pinnacles' sheer cliffs. A visitor center provides maps and information, and there are picnic facilities as well as a campground situated among fragrant digger pines. *Admission charged.*

PACIFIC
OCEAN

PACIFIC

MONTEREY
BAY

HENRY W. COE
STATE PARK

DIABLO

RANGE

SANTA

CLARA

VALLEY

San Jose

Morgan Hill

Gilroy

Hollister

GABILAN

RANGE

SALINAS

Salinas

SIERRA

DE

SALINAS

VALLEY

Soledad

Greenfield

King City

LOS PADRES

NATIONAL

FOREST

SANTA LUCIA RANGE

Big Sur

Santa Cruz

Watsonville

Castroville

Marina

Monterey

Pacific
Grove

Carmel-by-the-Sea

Carmel Valley

Gonzales

PINNACLES
NATIONAL
MONUMENT

SCALE IN MILES
0 2 4 6 8 10

YOSEMITE NATIONAL PARK

1. Tuolumne Grove
Located within this lovely grove of mature giant sequoias is a 70-foot-tall dead tree. The victim of an ancient fire, this sequoia contains the only drive-through tree tunnel in the park.

2. Valley View
While exiting Yosemite Valley on Northside Drive heading west, visitors may wish to pull off the road to enjoy Valley View. Also known as the Gates of the Valley, this vista offers breathtaking panoramas of Yosemite's granite summits. From this point, Bridalveil Meadow, the Merced River, and Bridalveil Fall are visible as well.

A porcupine adult and the next generation

3. Ribbon Fall
Here water plummets more than 1,600 feet in one uninterrupted descent, making this the park's highest single waterfall. Ribbon Fall is also one of the first falls in the park to dry up in the summer.

4. El Capitan
The nearly vertical El Capitan, looming over the western end of Yosemite Valley, is the largest granite monolith in the world. Soaring 3,604 feet above the Merced River, this massive rock is truly captivating.

5. Yosemite Falls
The highest falls in North America, this awe-inspiring cascade is 15 times the height of Niagara. The Upper Fall plunges 1,430 feet, followed by the Middle Fall's drop of 675 feet, and finally by the Lower Fall's 320-foot cascade. A short trail leads to a bridge at the base of the falls, where the view changes from a thundering torrent in spring to a trickle in late summer to an ice cone in winter.

6. Yosemite Village
The park headquarters and visitor center are located in Yosemite Village. Here visitors can get information, maps, and permits as well as see natural and human history exhibits. The **Indian Cultural Museum** next door re-creates the life of the area's Miwok and Paiute Indians with demonstrations of beadwork, basket-weaving, and traditional games. The **Indian Village of the Ahwahnee** is a re-created Miwok-Paiute village.

7. Half Dome
Half Dome guards the eastern end of the valley, its enormous rounded bulk of granite rising nearly a mile above the valley floor. On its west side is a sheer 2,000-foot cliff.

8. Nevada Fall
The first major fall where the Merced River leaves the High Sierra, Nevada Fall drops 594 feet. Visitors can hike to the fall from Happy Isles.

9. Vernal Fall
Framed by the deep green of ferns, water plunges 317 feet down Vernal Fall even in the summer, when other falls dry up. A mile-long paved hiking trail leads from Happy Isles to a bridge near the base of the fall; from there it's a steep ¾-mile climb to the top.

10. Happy Isles Nature Center
At Happy Isles the white water of the Merced River branches into several channels. This is the trailhead for hikes to Vernal and Nevada falls and Half Dome and Tuolumne Meadows. From May through September the nature center features ecology and natural history exhibits as well as children's programs.

11. Glacier Point
From the rim of the Yosemite Valley, Glacier Point offers unsurpassed

Park proponent and naturalist John Muir

panoramas of the valley more than 3,000 feet below, as well as of Nevada, Vernal, and Yosemite falls, and Half Dome, Mt. Watkins, and other peaks. To reach the point, visitors can either make a steep but easy 5-mile hike or drive 30 miles from Yosemite Village.

12. Yosemite Valley
This grassy corridor, 7 miles long and up to a mile wide, is dominated at one end by El Capitan and at the other by Half Dome. In between, waterfalls course over the cliffs, and stands of dogwoods, incense cedars, black oaks, and firs line the banks of the Merced River, which runs through the valley. There are spectacular views of the valley, which is probably the world's best-known example of a glacier-carved canyon, from **Tunnel View.** For a closer look, there are free shuttle-bus rides, bicycles for rent, a stable, and both guided and self-guided walking tours.

13. Bridalveil Fall
This mist-enshrouded cataract falls 620 feet to a pool that is often crowned by a rainbow. Unlike many other falls in Yosemite, Bridalveil Fall never dries up.

14. Badger Pass Ski Area
Downhill skiing for all levels, snow-shoeing, and trailheads for fine cross-country ski trails make this area a popular winter attraction.

15. Pioneer Yosemite History Center
Nineteenth-century life at Yosemite is effectively re-created at this museum with furnished pioneer cabins and wagons. In summer a living-history program includes stagecoach rides.

16. Mariposa Grove
A short uphill walk through this impressive grove of more than 500 mature giant sequoias leads to the 2,700-year-old

Hikers are dwarfed by the scale of Yosemite Falls, the highest falls in North America.

El Capitan, Yosemite's towering monolith

Grizzly Giant, the oldest known sequoia. With a base diameter of nearly 31 feet, the colossus climbs more than 200 feet into the sky. In 1881 a tunnel was cut through the base of the **Wawona Tunnel Tree** and, until it fell in 1969, cars could drive through it. In summer visitors can take one-hour tram rides around the grove. *Fee charged for tram.*

17. Tenaya Lake

American Indians called this beautiful blue lake *Pywiack,* or "lake of the shining rocks," because of the glacially polished domes and cliffs surrounding it.

18. Tuolumne River

A wonderful place to enjoy a peaceful walk, the banks of the Tuolumne River offer not only tranquility but also a very popular spot for catching rainbow trout. The river leads into the Hetch Hetchy Reservoir, which supplies water for the city of San Francisco, so swimming and boating are prohibited.

19. Tuolumne Meadows

The largest of the Sierra's subalpine meadows, this grassy expanse framed by granite cliffs and domes is a popular point of departure for hikers and backpackers. There are naturalist-guided hikes as well as guided horseback rides along trails where black bears and deer may be spotted. In the summer a visitor center provides information and maps.

Admission charged for national park.

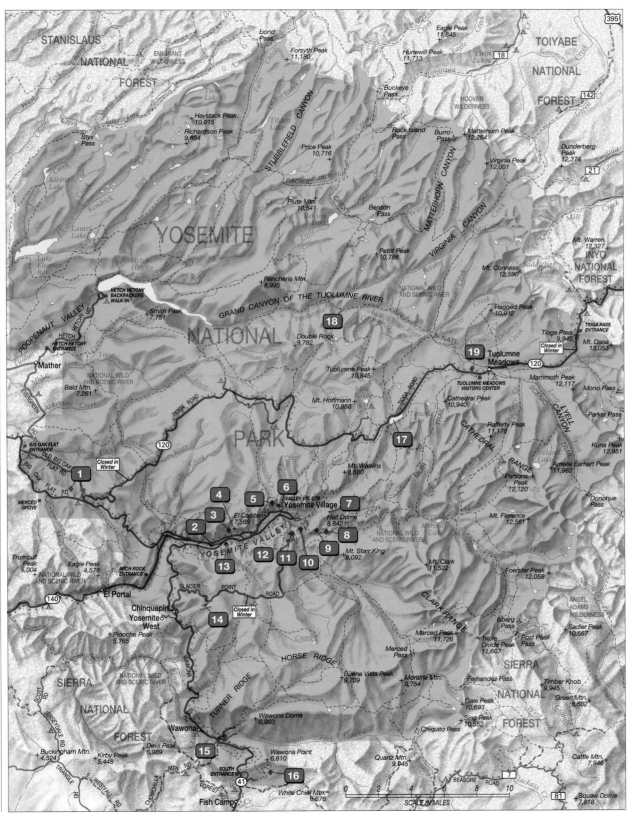

SEQUOIA & KINGS CANYON NATIONAL PARKS

1. Zumwalt Meadow

A footpath leads to bucolic Zumwalt Meadow, a wide grassland abloom with delicate wildflowers in summer. To the east, Grand Sentinel Viewpoint offers fine views of striking **Grand Sentinel,** an 8,504-foot-tall monolith. An easy 8-mile round-trip trail, leaving from Road's End, leads to **Mist Falls.**

2. Kings Canyon

The deepest canyon in North America, rugged Kings Canyon has granite walls that drop more than 8,000 feet from the peak of Spanish Mountain to the Kings River. From **Canyon Viewpoint,** a mile east of Cedar Grove Village, there are breathtaking views of the backcountry of **Kings Canyon National Park.**

3. Cedar Grove

Named for its forest of incense cedars, Cedar Grove is the trailhead for hundreds of miles of spectacular horseback and hiking trails. A ranger station here has maps of the park and trail guides.

4. Hume Lake

Just outside Kings Canyon National Park, this small, pretty reservoir was built by loggers at the turn of the century. Today it offers fine swimming, fishing, boating, camping, and wonderful views of the distant mountains.

5. Grant Grove Visitor Center

The center has exhibits and a slide show of the area's natural history. There are naturalist-guided snowshoe walks on winter weekends, and during the summer months there are daily walks.

6. Grant Grove

This stand of giant sequoias can be traversed by a number of quiet trails. A short trail leads to the **General Grant Tree;** at 267 feet tall and 107 feet around, it is the third-largest tree in the world and the second-largest in the park. It was proclaimed the nation's Christmas tree by President Calvin Coolidge and is honored every year by celebrators, who place a large wreath at its base and gather for special Yuletide services. Visitors can also see the stump of a giant sequoia, which was cut for the 1876 Philadelphia Exhibition. Near the grove, a steep, narrow road leads to a fine overview of the park from **Panoramic Point.**

7. Big Stump Basin

A 1-mile loop trail circles around Big Stump Basin, the site of logging operations before the park was created. Visitors can now see encouraging evidence of the trees' regeneration.

8. Redwood Mountain Grove

The largest grove of giant sequoias in the world, Redwood Mountain Grove can be viewed from highway turnouts or explored on foot or horseback. Stands of trees along the 4- to 10-mile-long trails range from the newly sprouted to the majestic **Hart Tree,** one of the largest of the sequoias.

9. Generals Highway

The 46-mile scenic drive along the Generals Highway, between Ash Mountain and Grant Grove, offers breathtaking views of vast canyons, unusual rock formations, giant sequoias, and the vast Sierra skyline. From **Lost Grove,** a hiking trail leads to **Muir Grove,** an exceptionally beautiful stand of sequoias.

10. Lodgepole Visitor Center

From this visitor center, which has excellent exhibits about the park, the 3½-mile round-trip **Tokopah Falls Trail** runs along the Marble Fork of the Kaweah River to a beautiful cascade.

11. Giant Forest

Sequoia National Park is the home of the ancient giant sequoias, among the largest living things on earth. Hiking trails wind through Giant Forest, where churchlike silence envelops majestic rows of colossal trees. Naturalist John Muir explored and named this forest, where four of the world's five largest trees stand. At 275 feet in height and 103 feet in circumference, the **General Sherman Tree** is the grandest of them all.

12. The Trail for All People

This ⅔-mile paved trail circles **Round Meadow,** a beautiful open area bounded by sequoias on one side and ablaze with summer wildflowers on the other.

13. Crystal Cave

Guided tours are offered of this marble cavern encrusted with stalactites and stalagmites. *Admission charged.*

14. Auto Log

Earth has been piled to form a ramp up to this fallen sequoia, enabling cars to drive onto the 21-foot-diameter tree.

15. Moro Rock

A strenuous ¼-mile climb up steep steps leads to the top of Moro Rock, a treeless granite dome 6,725 feet above sea level.

The reward is a panoramic view of the Kaweah River and the Central Valley below, as well as across the High Sierra.

16. The Parker Group

A stunning stand of sequoias known for their beauty, the Parker Group is one of the park's most photographed sites.

17. Tunnel Log

The giant sequoia, with a diameter of 21 feet, fell across the road in 1937. Today visitors can drive through a tunnel 17 feet wide by 8 feet high, which was cut through the massive tree.

18. Crescent Meadow Road

This 3-mile dead-end road through the southwest portion of Giant Forest gives excellent access to its main sights, which

The monumental General Sherman Tree is among the largest living trees on earth.

include Moro Rock, Crescent Meadow, Tharp's Log, the Parker Group, Tunnel Log, and Auto Log.

19. Crescent Meadow

The meadow has lovely midsummer wildflowers and is the starting point of a half-mile walk to **Tharp's Log.** This fallen sequoia, hollowed naturally by fire and rot, has a cabin built at its end that once served as the home of a local rancher named Hale Tharp.

20. Congress Trail

Originating from the Sherman Tree, the 2-mile Congress Trail leads through the heart of Giant Forest, passing by sequoia stands known as the **House** and **Senate Groups.**

21. Mineral King

From Rte. 198 near Three Rivers, a winding 25-mile road, open only in the summer, leads to this beautiful high valley. Here visitors will find horseback riding, campgrounds, a ranger station, and, for serious hikers, excellent trails leading to alpine lakes, meadows, and lofty Sierra mountain peaks.

22. Mount Whitney

At 14,494 feet, Mt. Whitney is the highest point in the contiguous United States. There are no roads on the mountain, but climbers can follow wilderness hiking trails to the windswept peak, from which there are unsurpassed views of the Owens Valley and the High Sierra.

Admission charged for national parks.

The pileated woodpecker is a colorful example of the parks' wildlife.

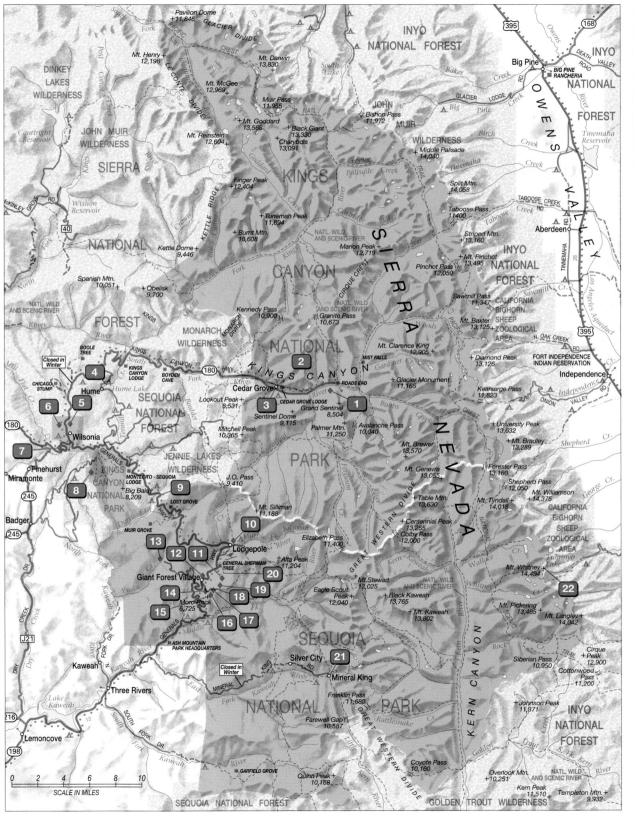

1. Rhyolite

All that is left of this once-prosperous gold-mining town, which was known for its brightly lit streets and its own stock exchange, is the Spanish-style railroad depot and the walls and foundations of its formerly flourishing business center.

2. Death Valley National Monument

Highlights of this awesome wilderness include **Badwater,** named for its mineral-laden pool, which at 282 feet below sea level is the lowest point in America; the **Devil's Golf Course,** a forbidding expanse of jagged spikes of salt crystals, some as high as 2 feet; and the ever-popular **Dantes View,** the 5,000-foot peak that overlooks the entire valley. **Scotty's Castle,** an elegant 25-room dwelling of redwood, stucco, and tile, was begun in 1922 by a Chicago entrepreneur as a desert retreat and today is open to visitors. *Admission charged.*

3. Red Rock Canyon State Park

Brilliantly carpeted in spring with wildflowers, this colorful canyon has been eroded by wind and water into strange formations such as the columned **White House Cliffs.** The park provides hiking trails and campgrounds. *Admission charged.*

4. Edwards Air Force Base

America's premier flight test and aeronautical research facility — and the runway on which space shuttles often land — is set in Antelope Valley, which is carpeted in spring by resplendent orange California poppies. Visitors can see test aircraft and hangars, as well as tour the NASA Ames – Dryden Flight Research Facility.

5. Newhall

After some sizable oil strikes, the Standard Oil Company of California was founded in this extensive rocky wilderness. Sights of interest include the **Vasquez Rocks County Park,** named for a bandit who supposedly hid treasure here; the **William S. Hart County Park and Museum,** the estate of America's first star of Western movies; and **Placerita Canyon State Park,** where one Francisco Lopez found gold while digging in his onion patch.

6. Roy Rogers – Dale Evans Museum

15650 Seneca Rd., Victorville. Extensive memorabilia document the careers of these world-renowned performers, including mounted displays of their famous horses, Trigger and Buttermilk. *Admission charged.*

7. Barstow

Chamber of Commerce, 408 East Fredericks. The **California Desert Information Center** displays examples of the local flora and fauna, including a sidewinder rattler and a 6,000-pound meteor. At the **Mojave River Valley Museum,** the history and geology of the region are depicted by displays ranging from space stations to prehistoric stone tools to 15-million-year-old fossils found at the **Calico Early Man Archeology Site.** Guided tours of the site are available.

8. Calico Ghost Town

In the mid-19th century, silver was found here, and the town that quickly sprang up was named for the landscape's brightly colored rocks. Today visitors come to explore a silver mine, catch a ride on an ore train, and camp at the edge of the Mojave Desert. *Admission charged.*

9. Camp Pendleton

Once the site of the early 19th-century Rancho Santa Margarita y Las Flores, this marine base, established in 1942, has preserved several of the original adobe buildings. Two such buildings make up the **Chapel and Bunkhouse Museum,** whose restored rooms depict the everyday life of the original ranch.

10. Mission San Luis Rey de Francia

The mission dates from 1798, but the present church was built in 1815 in Spanish-Moorish style, featuring quiet arcades, cloister gardens, a bell tower, and an American Indian cemetery. *Admission charged.*

11. Anza-Borrego Desert State Park

More than a half million acres of desert make up this park, where only the most adaptable species of plants and animals survive. In **Bow Willow Canyon,** traces of the ancient Kumeyaay Indians are found in petroglyphs and pictographs. In **Borrego Palm Canyon,** a nature trail follows a rocky stream to a grove of waving fan palms. At **Agua Caliente Hot Spring,** visitors can enjoy a swim in a mineral-water pool. *Admission charged for some attractions.*

12. Shields Date Gardens

80-225 Rte. 111, Indio. Sampling date-based confections is encouraged at this family-owned farm in the Coachella Valley. Nearby **Jensen's Date and Citrus Gardens** offers information about the valley's date and citrus industry and displays a citrus tree that produces nine varieties of fruit.

13. Salton Sea State Recreation Area

In 1905 the Salton Sea, a huge freshwater lake, was formed in what had been a desert expanse. Today this tremendously popular water-sports area offers excellent fishing, boating, swimming, and camping.

14. Joshua Tree National Monument

Two deserts make up this great national preserve: the northern **High Mojave,** where the Joshua tree grows, and the southern low **Colorado River Desert.** The **Oasis of Mara,** once inhabited by American Indians and later by prospectors, is today the site of a visitor center. Points of interest at Joshua Tree include **Hidden Valley,** thought to be a cattle rustler's hideout, and **Lost Horse Mine,** a historic gold-mining site. Overlooking this great expanse at an elevation of 5,185 feet is **Keys View.** *Admission charged.*

15. Blythe Intaglios

This mysterious series of enormous intaglios, depicting both humans and animals, was carved in the rocky landscape perhaps thousands of years ago and discovered in 1932. There is speculation that the engravings, one of which is 171 feet high, are based on creation mythology.

16. Colorado River Indian Tribes Museum

Mohave Rd. and Second Ave., Parker. The museum explores the histories, lifestyles, and artistic achievements of the Hopi, Mohave, Chemehuevi, and Navajo tribes, which share the Colorado River Indian Reservation.

17. Lake Havasu City

Convention and Visitors Bureau, 1930 Mesquite Ave. A major attraction in this modern planned city is the **London Bridge,** built in 1825 and carried here stone by stone in 1968 from its home across London's Thames River. It now stretches across the waters to the lake's largest island. An English Tudor village adorns the city end of the bridge. The island, a popular resort, offers boating, swimming, and other outdoor recreational activities.

18. Oatman

Chamber of Commerce, 140 Main St. Once a mining town, Oatman now attracts tourists who come to explore its shops and cafes and to feed the wild burros whose ancestors were abandoned by the departing prospectors. Several movies, including *How the West Was Won,* have been filmed here, with the colorful town and the encircling mountains as a backdrop.

19. Providence Mountains State Recreation Area

From the visitor center at **Mitchell Caverns** a remarkable view of this majestic countryside extends in all directions. The caverns, with their intricately carved limestone formations, can be seen on guided tours. *Admission charged.*

20. Cottonwood Cove

This part of the **Lake Mead National Recreation Area,** created by Davis Dam on the Colorado River, is a popular destination for fishermen, boaters, campers, swimmers, and hikers.

21. Mohave Museum of History and Art

400 West Beale St., Kingman. The museum traces the history of the Mohave and Hualapai Indian tribes, along with that of the nearby Hoover Dam. *Admission charged.*

22. Joshua Tree Forest

Here visitors are presented with the enchanting spectacle of hundreds of Joshua trees, all with their thorny arms reaching heavenward. It is said they were given their name by the Mormons, who were reminded by the curiously formed trees of Joshua in prayer. In spring the trees produce lovely cream-colored blossoms, adding to the magic of the landscape.

23. Charleston Peak

This towering snow-covered peak soars skyward in the **Toiyabe National Forest,** offering skiing far above the surrounding desert landscape. A hiking trail leads to **Cathedral Rock,** a promontory that provides a striking view of the canyon below.

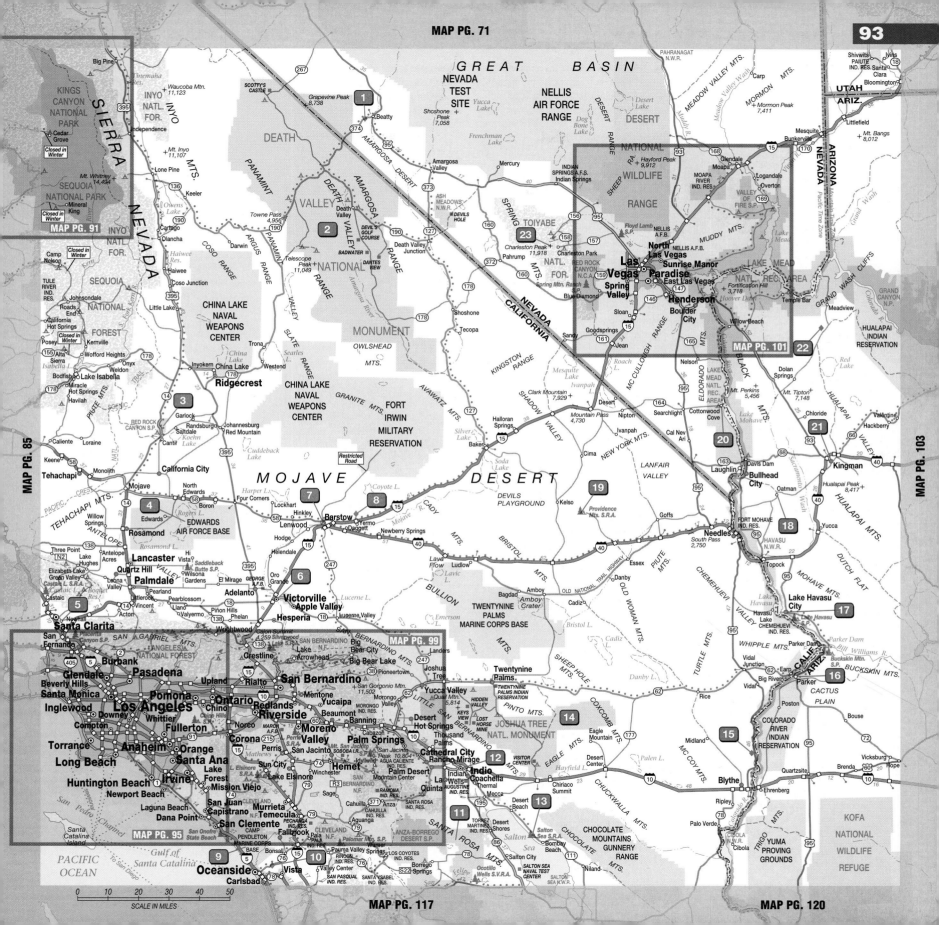

1. Ronald Reagan Presidential Library and Center for Public Affairs

40 Presidential Dr., Simi Valley. The Spanish mission–style library houses more than 50 million official documents and personal papers of the nation's 40th president. A section of the Berlin Wall is also displayed, as well as a life-size replica of the Oval Office. *Admission charged.*

2. San Fernando

Chamber of Commerce, 519 South Brand Blvd. The fabled **San Fernando Valley** is nestled in the mountains northwest of Los Angeles. Dating from 1797, the **Mission San Fernando Rey de España** was the 17th in the chain founded by the Franciscans along the Camino Real. The convent, graced with 19 arches, is said to be the state's largest free-standing adobe structure. It features collections of furnishings and artifacts, a 35-bell carillon, and an archival center exhibiting religious relics and church documents. *Admission charged.*

3. J. Paul Getty Museum

17985 Pacific Coast Hwy., Malibu. This replica of a first-century Roman villa was built to house the billionaire tycoon's burgeoning art collection. Exhibits include one of the country's most impressive collections of Greek and Roman antiquities; decorative arts, including pieces made for European royalty; and Western artwork from the 13th to the 19th century, including Old Master paintings and drawings. *Parking reservations must be made in advance.*

4. Will Rogers State Historic Park

14253 Sunset Blvd., Pacific Palisades. The rustic 31-room home of cowboy-humorist-philosopher Will Rogers sits in this 186-acre park, which also offers splendid views of the Pacific Ocean and polo matches on the weekends. *Admission charged.*

5. Santa Monica

Convention and Visitors Bureau, 2219 Main St. With the Pacific Ocean as a magnificent backdrop, **Palisades Park** is popular with strollers, joggers, and people watchers, as is the nearby **3rd Street Promenade.** The **Santa Monica Pier** is lined with arcades and cafes, and its grand carousel has a turn-of-the-century Wurlitzer organ.

6. Venice

Back in 1904 it was the dream of tobacco heir Abbott Kinney to re-create Venice, Italy; now only three canals remain from the ambitious venture. The **Venice Boardwalk** is a popular venue for rollerskaters and dog walkers, while bodybuilders take to the adjacent beach. There is a lot of boat-related activity south of Venice in **Marina del Rey,** whose 6,000-slip marina is the world's largest man-made boat harbor.

7. Wayfarers Chapel

5755 Palos Verdes Dr. S., Rancho Palos Verdes. Designed by Lloyd Wright, son of Frank Lloyd Wright, the Wayfarers Chapel is a glass-and-wood structure nestled in lush gardens with awe-inspiring views of the Pacific. Exhibits trace the history of the church, which is based on the writings of 18th-century philosopher and theologian Emanuel Swedenborg.

8. Santa Catalina Island

Chamber of Commerce and Visitors Bureau, Green Pleasure Pier. In 1919 this 22-mile-long, 8-mile-wide isle was bought by chewing gum tycoon and baseball club owner William Wrigley, Jr., whose Chicago Cubs came here for spring training. The popular resort's only town is **Avalon,** where palms line the main street and yachts bob in a half-moon harbor. There is tram service from Avalon to the **Wrigley Memorial and Botanical Garden,** a 38-acre park with almost 400 plant species native to the island. Glass-bottom boat rides are popular, as are tours of the **Avalon Ballroom and Casino,** an Art Deco masterpiece that at the peak of its popularity drew 6,000 Big Band aficionados a night from the mainland. *Admission charged for some attractions.*

9. Queen Mary

Pier J, Long Beach. In her heyday the largest passenger ship afloat, the Queen Mary is now permanently berthed in Long Beach Harbor. Visitors can explore two decks of the Art Deco ship — with shops, restaurants, and beautiful views of Long Beach and Shoreline Bay — or take a more extensive guided tour of this veritable floating palace. *Fee charged for tour and parking.*

10. Huntington Beach

Convention and Visitors Bureau, 2100 Main St. **Huntington Pier** is a fine vantage point from which to view the lively beach scene; a surfing competition held annually in September draws world-class surfers from all over the globe.

11. Newport Beach

Chamber of Commerce, 1470 Jamboree Rd. Once a commercial shipping center, Newport Beach is the playground of the well-heeled yacht and country-club set. Boats by the thousands are docked in **Newport Harbor,** and there's even more activity here during the annual Flight of the Snowbirds Regatta, held in June. Reachable by ferry, **Balboa Island** is known for its Victorian-style **Balboa Pavilion,** which features harbor cruises and a sport-fishing fleet, as well as whale-watching excursions.

12. Laguna Beach

Chamber of Commerce, 357 Glenneyre St. Laguna Beach is still very much in the mood of the sixties. Shops cater to those of an artistic nature, and **Main Beach** has a slew of art galleries, where styles range from the sublime to the silly. Laguna is known the world over for its Pageant of the Masters, in which hundreds of local volunteers stand stock-still in detailed stage sets that duplicate famous paintings. *Admission charged for pageant.*

13. Mission San Juan Capistrano

Camino Capistrano and Ortega Hwy., Capistrano. The seventh of California's chain of 21 Franciscan missions was dedicated by Father Junipero Serra in 1776. The crumbled, vine-covered ruins of a great stone cruciform church are surrounded by gardens and graceful fountains. This is the place to which the swallows return, unfailingly, on March 19. *Admission charged.*

14. Santa Ana

Chamber of Commerce, 801 Civic Center Dr. The revitalized downtown area of Santa Ana is a charming blend of the old and the new, featuring the Spanish-style **Fiesta Marketplace;** the **Bowers Museum,** showcasing artworks of the Americas, Africa, and the Pacific Rim; and the **Santa Ana Zoo at Prentice Park,** with picnic areas and playgrounds. *Admission charged at zoo.*

15. Crystal Cathedral

12141 Lewis St., Garden Grove. The aptly named cathedral, founded by television evangelist Robert Schuller, contains 10,000 panes of glass. The impressive translucent structure, shaped like a giant four-pointed star, was designed by noted architect Philip Johnson, and guided tours are conducted.

16. Disneyland

1313 Harbor Blvd., Anaheim. It's just home to Mickey and Goofy, but for the rest of the world this 76-acre amusement park — with seven theme areas ranging from turn-of-the-century Main Street U.S.A. to futuristic Tomorrowland — defines enchantment for the entire family. *Admission charged.*

17. Buena Park

Convention and Visitors Bureau, 6280 Manchester Blvd. **Knott's Berry Farm,** a 150-acre theme park, features more than 100 rides, a ghost town, and a river wilderness park. The nearby **Movieland Wax Museum** waxes eloquent on the subject of movie stars, with Judy Garland, Marilyn Monroe, and Clint Eastwood among the 270 lifelike stars who are showcased in realistic movie sets. *Admission charged.*

18. Richard Nixon Library and Birthplace

18001 Yorba Linda Blvd., Yorba Linda. A documentary film on the life of the former chief executive, displays highlighting various political campaigns, and gifts from world leaders are among the center's permanent exhibits. *Admission charged.*

19. Prado Regional Park

Among the excellent facilities in the 2,000-acre park are an equestrian center and riding trails, a 60-acre lake for fishing and boating, a golf course, picnic areas, and campsites. *Admission charged.*

20. Adobe de Palomares

419 East Arrow Hwy., Pomona. The virtual prototype for suburban ranch-style houses was built in 1854 by the wealthy Don Ygnacio de Palomares. The restored one-story casa has seven rooms done in period furnishings, which are open to the public on Sunday or by appointment.

21. Los Angeles State and County Arboretum

301 North Baldwin Ave., Arcadia. Peacocks strut in this 127-acre arboretum, which showcases flora from around the globe. Lush with jungles and waterfalls, the gardens have served as a set for movies such as *The African Queen. Admission charged.*

SCALE IN MILES
0 2 4 6 8 10

DOWNTOWN LOS ANGELES & HOLLYWOOD

1. Mulholland Drive

The scenic drive meanders along the crest of the Santa Monica Mountains from the Hollywood Hills almost to the Pacific Ocean, offering unsurpassed vistas of the city and the San Fernando Valley.

2. Universal Studios

100 Universal City Plaza, Universal City. The 7-hour tour of this television and movie studio, the largest in the world, offers an entertaining behind-the-scenes look at the movie business. Enthusiastic guides escort visitors on trams to live shows based on *Star Trek* and *Miami Vice*, the parting of the Red Sea, a meeting with a 30-foot-tall version of King Kong, and a visit to E.T.'s home planet. There are terrifying simulations of an avalanche and an 8.3 earthquake, an attack by the *Jaws* killer shark, and other special effects. The Lucille Ball exhibition features film clips, personal memorabilia, and a re-creation of the original *I Love Lucy* set. *Admission charged.*

3. Hollywood Sign

Its 50-foot-high letters visible for miles, the famous sign is located 1 mile east of Hollywood and Vine, on the side of Mt. Lee in the Hollywood Hills.

4. Forest Lawn Memorial–Park, Hollywood Hills

6300 Forest Lawn Dr. Just west of Griffith Park, the final resting place of Hollywood luminaries such as Buster Keaton, Liberace, and Bette Davis is done in a Revolutionary War theme, complete with full-scale replicas of the Liberty Bell and Boston's Old North Church.

5. Griffith Park

This vast, mountainous park contains the renowned **Los Angeles Zoo.** The 2,000 geographically grouped animals include white tigers and, displayed in a nocturnal environment, koala bears. From the **Griffith Observatory** there are spectacular views of the city below and, at night, of the stars above through one of the world's largest telescopes. The Planetarium has daily shows and nighttime laser concerts. *Admission charged for some attractions.*

6. Hollyhock House

4808 Hollywood Blvd., Barnksdall Park. Completed in 1921, this was the first of a number of houses designed by Frank Lloyd Wright in the Los Angeles area. Visitors can tour the Mayan-style home that Wright termed California *romanza,* now restored and furnished with originals and reproductions of his furniture. *Admission charged.*

7. Hollywood Bowl

2301 North Highland Ave. A tradition since 1922, this world-famous amphitheater presents evening concerts from July to mid-September that now range from pop to jazz to classical. *Admission charged.*

8. Hollywood Boulevard

Attractions along this famous boulevard include **Mann's Chinese Theater,** where handprints, footprints, and signatures of stars decorate the courtyard; the **Hollywood Walk of Fame,** with nearly 2,000 pink stars, each framing the name of an entertainment legend, embedded in the sidewalks; and the **Hollywood Wax Museum,** displaying more than 170 lifelike statues of movie stars and presidents. *Admission charged at museum.*

9. Sunset Boulevard

The Strip is fun to drive or walk for all its glamour and glitz — from huge billboards hawking the latest records and movies to chic celebrity restaurants.

10. Greystone Park

905 Loma Vista Dr., Beverly Hills. With its panoramic views of the Pacific, the elegant Tudor-style Greystone Mansion was completed in 1928. The estate's lovely landscaped grounds, where walkways wind past formal gardens, fountains, and ponds covered with water lilies and hibiscus blossoms, are open to the public.

11. University of California at Los Angeles

The university's parklike campus invites visitors to stroll on their own, or take part in a weekday guided walking tour. Sights of particular interest are the **Franklin D. Murphy Sculpture Garden,** with works by Henry Moore, Maillol, and other artists; the **Wight Art Gallery,** with its fine art and architectural collection; and the **Mildred E. Mathias Botanical Garden.**

12. Rodeo Drive

Window shopping and people watching are a delight along this Beverly Hills thoroughfare of designer shops and boutiques, which cater to an exclusive clientele.

13. Farmers Market

Third St. and Fairfax Ave. The bustling market offers occasional movie star sightings, along with fresh produce and outdoor dining at dozens of open-air food stalls.

14. Hancock Park

5801 Wilshire Blvd. This lively park is the site of the world-famous **La Brea Tar Pits,** watched over by several life-size fiberglass mammoths. The **George C. Page Museum of La Brea Discoveries** displays the remarkable remains of Ice Age mammoths, sloths, saber-tooth cats, and a 9,000-year-old woman, all recovered from their sticky graves in the asphalt pools. More than 100 tons of bones have been removed so far, and visitors can watch the ongoing excavations from a special viewing station. The **Los Angeles County Museum of Art** is the largest museum complex in Los Angeles, housing an outstanding collection of paintings, costumes, and decorative arts from prehistory to the present. Along with works by Picasso, Rembrandt, Dürer, and Winslow Homer, the museum features one of the world's finest collections of Indian, Tibetan, and Nepalese art. *Admission charged at art museum.*

15. Hollywood Memorial Park Cemetery

6000 Santa Monica Blvd. Here lie the remains of many early movie stars and directors, including Cecil B. DeMille and Douglas Fairbanks, Sr. Annual memorial services are also held here for Rudolph Valentino on August 23 and Tyrone Power on November 15.

16. Paramount Film and Television Studios

5555 Melrose Ave. Visitors can take a 2-hour walking tour of the giant entertainment company's production studios and possibly attend the tapings of talk shows and situation comedies. *Admission charged.*

17. Exposition Park

Figueroa St. and Exposition Blvd. The site of two Olympics, this beautiful park boasts a 7-acre sunken rose garden, with 16,000 bushes of almost 200 varieties, and three fine museums. The **Natural History Museum of Los Angeles County** displays a collection of prehistoric fossils, cut gems, and California gold; other exhibits pertain to pre-Columbian culture and California history from early Indian life to the founding of the movie industry. The **California Afro-American Museum** documents the contributions made to education, arts, politics, and sports by African-Americans; films, plays, and dance performances are presented here as well. Highlights of the enormous **California Museum of Science and Industry** include an earthquake simulator, the Aerospace Hall, and an IMAX Theater with a five-story-high screen. *Admission charged for some attractions.*

18. Museum of Contemporary Art

250 South Grand Ave. The seven-level museum houses an excellent collection of modern art dating from 1940 to the present.

19. Bradbury Building

304 South Broadway. Built in 1893, the Victorian-style Bradbury Building is the only office building in Los Angeles that is a national historic landmark. Soaring five stories, its skylit grand atrium contains French wrought-iron grillwork, rose-colored wood paneling, ornate open-cage elevators, Belgian marble, and Mexican tile.

20. Little Tokyo

With its annual parades, festivals, and other events, Little Tokyo remains the cultural center of the now largely dispersed Japanese community. The neighborhood also serves as a culinary magnet to visitors, featuring dozens of sushi bars, tempura restaurants, and even an eatery with an all-eel menu.

21. El Pueblo de Los Angeles Historic Monument

Visitor Center, 622 North Main St. The birthplace of Los Angeles is marked by these restored 19th-century buildings, at the heart of which is **Olvera Street,** the site of an active Mexican marketplace. Of particular interest here are the **Sepulveda House,** furnished in the style of the 1880's; the simple **Avila Adobe,** thought to be the city's oldest remaining building; and the **Old Plaza Firehouse,** with its displays of

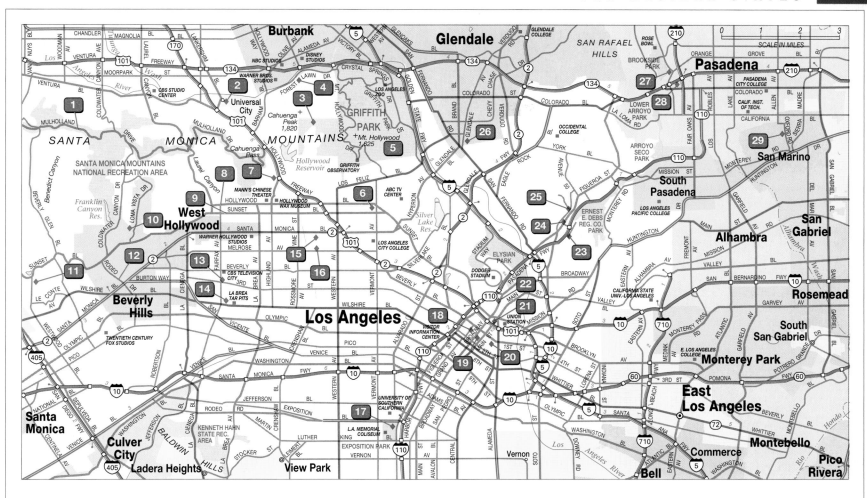

19th-century firefighting equipment. **Nuestra Señora La Reina de Los Angeles,** built around 1820, is still an active Catholic church. Buildings seen on guided tours include the Masonic Hall, the Merced Theatre, the Pico House hotel, and the Garnier Block — all elaborate examples of the city's late–19th-century architectural style.

22. Chinatown

Here visitors flock to the excellent Chinese restaurants and small shops that line the Street of the Golden Palace.

23. Heritage Square

3800 Homer St. This reconstructed square contains elegant Victorian homes, a church, a depot, and a carriage barn — all built between 1865 and 1914, and moved here from other parts of the city. Among the buildings, the **Hale House,** with its arresting colors, ornate details, and period furnishings, best typifies the architectural style of the time. *Admission charged.*

24. El Alisal

200 East Ave. 43. Built out of boulders by Charles Lummis between 1898 and 1910, the craftsmanship of the building reflects Southwestern influences from Native American to Mission. *Donation encouraged.*

25. Southwest Museum

234 Museum Dr. This huge Mission Revival building houses an excellent collection of Native American art and artifacts. Exhibits range from displays on the Navajo Indians to the Eskimos, and from prehistory to the present, including a remarkable basketry collection and an 18-foot-high Cheyenne teepee. *Admission charged.*

26. Forest Lawn Memorial–Park, Glendale

1712 South Glendale Ave. In this legendary cemetery, grave markers of the rich and famous run the gamut from simple plaques to an elaborate Roman temple. The 300-acre park contains reproductions of old European churches, a replica of Leonardo da Vinci's *The Last Supper* in stained glass, and two of the largest paintings in the world.

27. Gamble House

4 Westmoreland Pl., Pasadena. The Japanese-inspired two-story "bungalow," built in 1908, is an outstanding example of the American Arts and Crafts movement. It showcases the work of architects Charles and Henry Greene, who also handcrafted everything in the house, from air vents to switch plates to the jewellike stained-glass windows. *Admission charged.*

28. Norton Simon Museum

411 West Colorado Blvd., Pasadena. This modern building houses one of the finest art collections in the world. The museum is especially rich in major paintings by Rembrandt, Degas, Goya, and Picasso, and Rodin sculptures are displayed throughout the premises. A strong Impressionist and post-Impressionist collection includes works by van Gogh, Matisse, Cezanne, Monet, and Renoir. Dating back to 100 B.C., an Asian sculpture collection complements the museum's extraordinary wealth of Early Renaissance, Baroque, and Rococo art, representing such masters as Raphael and Rubens. *Admission charged.*

29. Huntington Library, Art Collections, and Botanical Gardens

1151 Oxford Rd., San Marino. Built in 1910 as railroad tycoon Henry E. Huntington's home, the complex today is a preeminent cultural center. The outstanding library's 4 million items include a Gutenberg Bible, first editions of Shakespeare, and a set of Audubon's *Birds of America*. The main gallery features 18th- and 19th-century British and French art, including Gainsborough's *Blue Boy*. The magnificent 105-acre garden encompasses a cactus garden, a traditional Japanese garden, and more than 2,000 varieties of camellias and roses. *Donation encouraged.*

1. Silverwood Lake State Recreation Area

The charm of this sparkling lake, set at the desert's edge, is enhanced by the cool, green encircling mountains. The park has many picnic areas around the lake's shoreline and several miles of hiking trails. Visitors often see bears at nearby **Miller Canyon.** *Admission charged.*

2. Glen Helen Regional Park

Wild grapes and watercress thrive in this lovely valley nestled in the midst of the mountains. Sparkling blue lakes add color to the groves of sycamore and ash trees, and tumbling streams meander through the glen. A log walkway following a self-guided ecology trail leads visitors through a pristine marshland. *Admission charged.*

3. Rim of the World Highway

Following the crest of the San Bernardino range, this scenic drive reaches a height of more than 7,000 feet as it skirts **Arrowhead, Big Bear,** and **Gregory lakes.**

4. San Bernardino

Convention and Visitors Bureau, 440 West Court St. Surrounded by the majestic **San Bernardino National Forest,** this great scenic countryside, thought to have been inhabited by American Indians periodically during the past 4,000 years, is today a popular recreational area. **Heritage House,** a museum that depicts life in San Bernardino during the 1890's, contains a vast array of artifacts and memorabilia related to that period. The origin of the **Arrowhead,** an enormous rock formation covering more than 7 acres, is not known, but one theory is that a cloudburst hit the mountain's peak and cascaded downward, carving the sides of the formation into an arrowhead shape. *Admission charged at museum.*

5. Riverside

Visitors and Convention Center, 3443 Orange St. Established in 1870, the city is the center of the California navel orange industry, its reputation evidenced by the **Parent Washington Navel Orange Tree,** grown from a cutting brought from Brazil in 1875. The city's 1912 post office is used as the home of the **Riverside Municipal Museum,** which has exhibits of local history and early Indian days, along with artifacts from the colorful time of the Spanish explorations. The nearby Queen Anne–style **Heritage House,** run by the museum, has been restored to bring back a sample of the city's elegant Victorian days. The **March Air Force Base,** America's oldest western military installation, is known for its museum's displays of some 40 antique aircraft.

Citrus label, Riverside Municipal Museum

6. Redlands

Chamber of Commerce, 1 East Redlands Blvd. Named for the remarkable color of its soil, this onetime agricultural center has preserved many of its handsome Victorian dwellings, including the 1897 **Kimberly Crest House,** a splendid French-style mansion surrounded by Italian gardens and citrus groves. Nearby are the **San Bernardino County Museum,** featuring an unusual collection of mammals and birds, and the **Lincoln Memorial Shrine,** which houses an impressive collection of Lincoln materials. The restored **San Bernardino Asistencia,** dating back to 1819, depicts the lives of converts and priests during the early 19th century. Free concerts are held during the summertime in the **Redlands Bowl,** often called the Little Hollywood Bowl. *Admission charged for some attractions.*

7. Yucaipa

Chamber of Commerce, 33733 Yucaipa Blvd. In this town, whose name means "marshy place," stands the 1842 **Yucaipa Adobe,** thought to be the county's oldest dwelling, which has been restored and furnished with period antiques. An interesting collection of fossils, shells, minerals, and early artifacts from the area are on display at the **Mousley Museum of Natural History.** A picnic park is provided for the public on the grounds of **Los Ríos Apple Ranch,** a complex of orchards, packing houses, and cider mills.

8. Oak Glen

Twenty-five different varieties of apple are grown in this mile-high orchard region, known for the delicacy of its fragrance in April, when the apple trees, lilacs, and spring bulbs present their glorious annual display. An animal park and picnic grounds attract visitors, who also congregate for the colorful fall Harvest Festival.

9. Desert Hot Springs

Chamber of Commerce and Visitors Bureau, 13560 Palm Dr. A wide assortment of motels and resorts have sprung up here since subterranean hot springs were first discovered in the area. Use of the natural mineral pools, whose temperatures vary from 95° F to 170° F, is offered to visitors for a fee. The intriguing remains of several adobe structures give evidence of an earlier settlement in the arid landscape.

10. Palm Springs

Convention and Visitors Bureau, 69-930 Rte. 111, Rancho Mirage. The natural splendor of this palm-filled desert plateau, set at the foot of towering **San Jacinto Peak,** was once the home of the Cahuilla Indians. Today it is a resort that draws celebrities and those who pursue the pleasures of golf, tennis, and other outdoor activities. Visitors can take an aerial tramway to the mountaintop for a panoramic view of the landscape. The **Village Green Heritage Center,** filled with colorful memorabilia, documents Palm Springs' early days. The **Desert Museum,** featuring Western-style art, includes exhibits of the wonders of the desert. At the **Moorten Botanical Garden** more than 3,000 varieties of plants are on display, along with an array of Indian artifacts. A mountain stream wanders through stands of sycamore, mesquite, and palms in the **Indian Canyons,** where ancient Indian relics and pictographs can be seen. In nearby **Palm Desert,** a 6-mile trail winds through the **Living Desert,** where local wildlife can be seen. Children especially enjoy the **Dinosaur Gardens,** a zoological park and botanical garden located in Cabazon, with its replicas of prehistoric creatures. *Admission charged.*

11. Palm Canyon

A gentle mountain stream flows through this refreshingly cool canyon, which is named for the 3,000 native palms that thrive along the water's edge. Spectacular views of the encircling mountains and surrounding countryside can be seen from the canyon floor. *Admission charged.*

12. Idyllwild County Park

Spreading upward along the slopes of the San Jacinto Mountains, the park overlooks forested valleys, rocky peaks, and the quaint village of Idyllwild. Hikers can follow the **Deer Springs Trail** up the mountain to an elevation of more than 10,000 feet.

13. San Jacinto

Chamber of Commerce, 180 East Main St. The **San Jacinto Valley Museum** exhibits early Californian and American Indian artifacts, as well as memorabilia related to the history of the valley (such as the 1937 arrival of a Soviet plane, which was one of the first to fly over the North Pole). The annual Ramona Pageant, an Indian love story set in early California, is staged outside of nearby Hemet; the **Ramona Bowl Museum** gives the history of the event. Also nearby are several prehistoric Indian petroglyph sites and the **Maze Stone County Park,** named for a mysterious mazelike pattern on one of its huge granite boulders.

14. Orange Empire Railway Museum

2201 South A St., Perris. The museum's collection of more than 150 pieces of railroad equipment draws railroad buffs from far and wide. Rides on some of the old cars are available. *Fee charged for rides.*

15. Lake Elsinore State Recreation Area

This jewel of a lake, with its palm-fringed sandy beach, is especially suited to family vacations. It offers excellent fishing, swimming, boating, tree-shaded campgrounds, and a playground. *Admission charged.*

16. Mission San Antonio de Pala

Pala Mission Rd., Pala. Built in 1816 on the Pala Indian Reservation, the simple white church with a red tile roof is remarkable for its handsomely decorated interior. Pala Indians still make up a large part of its congregation. There is a cemetery garden whose bell tower rings regularly, and a museum containing Indian and mission artifacts. *Admission charged at museum.*

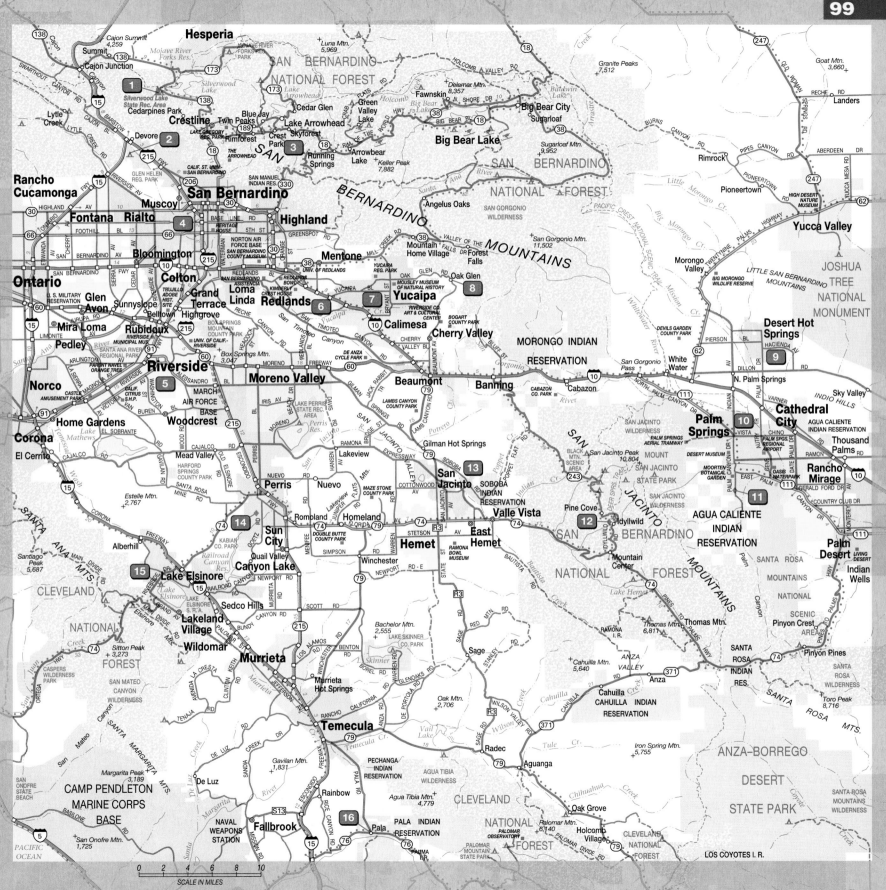

1. Desert National Wildlife Range

Among the creatures to be found in this preserve, where wildlife roams freely, is the desert bighorn sheep. The visitor center provides information on all the animals and where they can best be seen.

2. Red Rock Canyon National Conservation Area

A series of trails lead into the canyons of this variegated sandstone landscape — among them one to **Lost Creek,** which erupts seasonally into a waterfall, and another to **Pine Creek Canyon,** where the remains of a historic homestead still stand. A 13-mile scenic drive through the area offers spectacular views. Picnic areas are provided at Red Spring and Willow Spring.

3. Imperial Palace Auto Collection

3535 Las Vegas Blvd. South, Las Vegas. More than 200 antique, classic, and unusual automobiles make up this collection, one of the world's largest. Special attractions include cars that belonged to Mussolini, Eisenhower, and Hitler. *Admission charged.*

4. Guinness World of Records Museum

2780 Las Vegas Blvd. South, Las Vegas. Lifelike exhibits from the famous Guinness book are guaranteed to amuse as well as amaze; the museum also has displays on space, the entertainment world, the animal kingdom, and sports. *Admission charged.*

5. Southern Nevada Zoological Park

1775 North Rancho Dr., Las Vegas. Home to exotic birds, monkeys and apes, a cougar, and a Bengal tiger, the park also has a breeding program for endangered species and a petting zoo. *Admission charged.*

6. Lorenzi Park

The **Nevada State Museum and Historical Society,** located in the park, recounts the area's history with displays ranging from Indian artifacts to a slot machine. The **Las Vegas Art Museum** has changing exhibits of local and international artists.

7. North Las Vegas

Chamber of Commerce, 1023 East Lake Mead Blvd. The city is the gateway to the **Nellis Air Force Base,** home of the Thunderbirds, a precision flying team. Visitors flock here every October for the 3-day Fairshow, featuring the Nevada Championship Hot Air Balloon Races.

8. Las Vegas Natural History Museum

900 Las Vegas Blvd. North, Las Vegas. The museum's collection of wildlife specimens from around the world contains mounted sharks and predatory birds among its popular displays. *Admission charged.*

9. Ripley's Believe It or Not!

202 East Fremont St., Las Vegas. Thousands of exhibits, ranging from the bizarre to the unbelievable, include some of the world's most unusual and mysterious phenomena, both natural and man-made. Lifelike wax figures illustrate amazing human feats, such as a model of a man who remained on a bed of nails for 18 years. *Admission charged.*

10. Old Las Vegas Mormon Fort State Historic Park

908 Las Vegas Blvd. North, Las Vegas. Established in 1855 by Mormon missionaries to provide a safe way station between the Great Salt Lake and San Bernardino, this is the oldest original building in Nevada and the site of the first Anglo settlement in the Las Vegas Valley. The fort was later expanded into a ranch, out of which grew the modern-day city of Las Vegas. Guided tours of the fort are available, and archeological digs are under way to bring to light new remnants of the city's history.

11. Wet 'n Wild

2601 Las Vegas Blvd. South, Las Vegas. Visitors throng this aquatic park, a complex with water slides, white-water rafting rides, pools with 4-foot waves, a children's area, and picnic grounds. *Admission charged.*

12. The Strip

Sometimes called the most dazzling street in the world, Las Vegas Boulevard, the hub of the Strip, is lined with glittering casinos, show palaces for superstar entertainers and glamorous chorus lines, and extravagantly luxurious hotels. Millions of visitors are attracted here each year to gamble, to enjoy a variety of shows, and to marvel at the astounding theme decor of the leading hotels — from a Polynesian wonderland featuring an erupting volcano to the Land of Oz, complete with a Yellow Brick Road.

13. University of Nevada, Las Vegas

The architectural highlight of the campus is a Claes Oldenburg sculpture of an enormous flashlight, interpreted to represent a beacon of knowledge. The university's **Museum of Natural History** interprets Southwestern Indian culture from prehistoric times to the present. Other displays include the geology, history, and archeology of the area, live animals, fossils, and various traveling exhibits.

A piano at the Liberace Museum

14. Liberace Museum

1775 East Tropicana Ave., Las Vegas. Celebrating the world-famous Mr. Showmanship, the museum attests to the opulence of Liberace's lifestyle. Included are galleries that feature the entertainer's matchless collection of jewels and costumes, his priceless antiques, and his fabulous array of antique cars and pianos. The museum's library contains an array of memorabilia detailing the life of one of the world's most flamboyant entertainers. *Admission charged.*

15. Henderson

Chamber of Commerce, 1830 South Boulder Hwy. The city is the home of the **Clark County Heritage Museum,** which traces human life in the area from 10,000 years ago to the 1950's. On display at the museum's Heritage Street are a restored California bungalow, a mining town cottage, a 1931 train depot, and several other structures. Also in town, **Ethel M. Chocolates** offers a self-guided tour of the chocolate-making process. *Admission charged at museum.*

16. Boulder City

Chamber of Commerce, 1497 Nevada Hwy. Dating from the 1930's, when the Hoover Dam was constructed, the city is a planned suburbanlike community with well-manicured lawns, flower-filled gardens, and lovely homes. It is known for its beautiful golf course and its no-gambling law, the only area in Nevada with such a statute.

17. Hoover Dam

Completed in 1935, this enormous structure is 660 feet thick at the bottom, 45 feet thick at the top, and stretches more than 1,200 feet across the Colorado River, providing water and electricity for both agricultural and domestic use. Tours of the dam take visitors inside the great structure, where the throbbing sounds of the enormous turbines can be heard. *Fee charged for tour.*

18. Lake Mead National Recreation Area

Stretching 140 miles along the Colorado River, the expansive recreation area encompasses Lake Mead, one of the world's largest man-made lakes, and Lake Mohave. Wide bays, sandy coves, and steep-walled canyons entice visitors to explore the area by boat. The lakes provide a striking visual contrast to the surrounding desert, as well as good swimming and fishing. *Fee charged for boat cruises.*

19. Valley of Fire State Park

This enormous park, set in a valley of fiery red sandstone rocks that have been carved into spectacular domes, towers, arches, and other remarkable shapes by millions of years of erosion, contains many examples of ancient Indian petroglyphs. Visitors can follow interpretive trails to many of the more spectacular sites, including **Fire Canyon,** a massive hollow made of dazzling multicolored sandstone.

20. Lost City Museum

721 South Rte. 169, Overton. The museum is noted for having one of the largest collections of early Pueblo Indian artifacts in the country. Other historical exhibits range from the Desert Culture of 10,000 years ago to the more recent arrival of Mormon farmers in 1865. *Admission charged.*

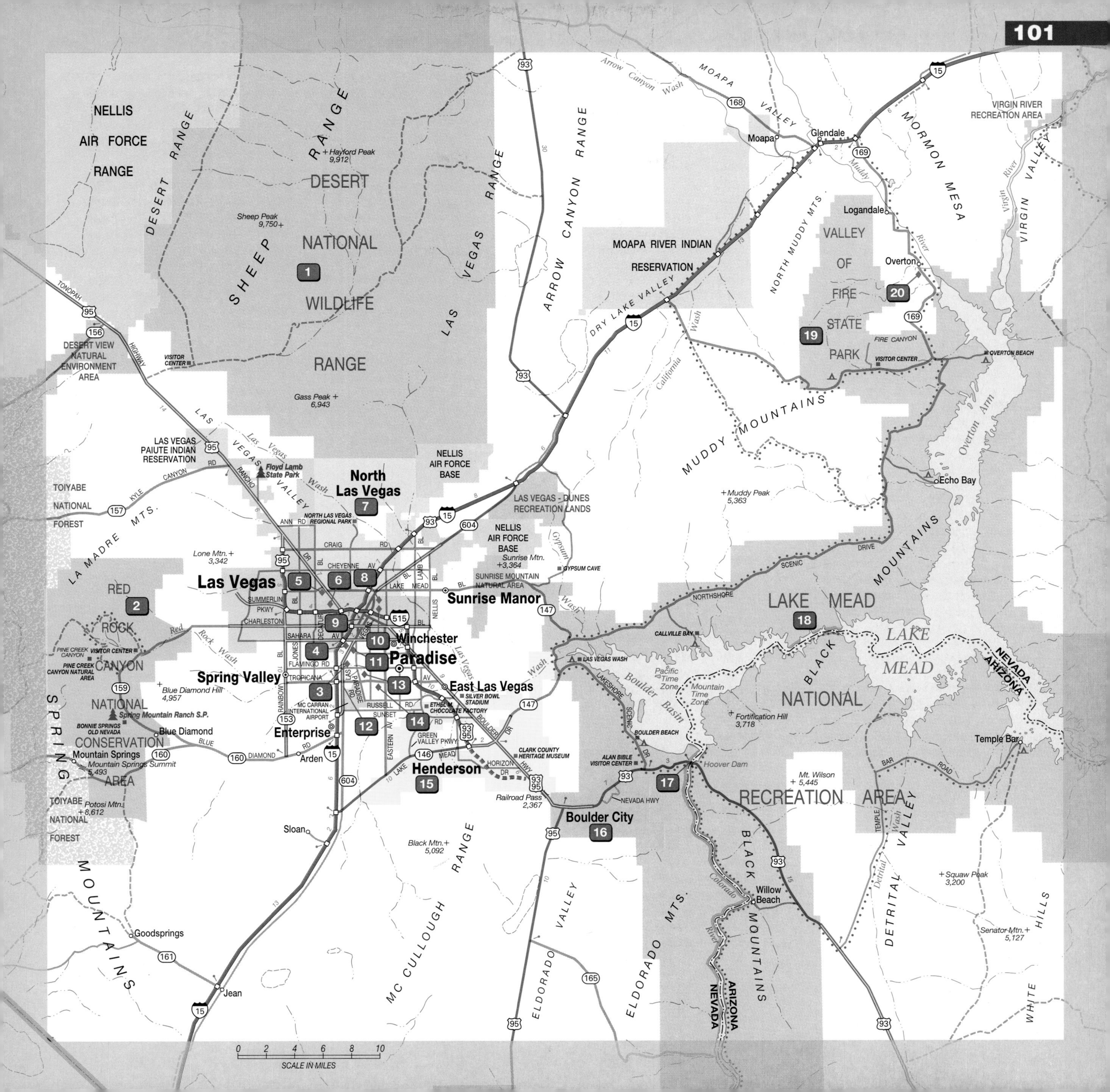

NELLIS AIR FORCE RANGE

DESERT RANGE

SHEEP RANGE

+ Hayford Peak 9,912

Sheep Peak 9,750+

DESERT NATIONAL WILDLIFE RANGE

[1]

LAS VEGAS RANGE

ARROW CANYON RANGE

MOAPA VALLEY

Arrow Canyon Wash

MOAPA MTS.

168

15

VIRGIN RIVER RECREATION AREA

Moapa

Glendale

169

MORMON MESA

NORTH MUDDY MTS.

Logandale

VALLEY OF FIRE STATE PARK

Overton

[20]

169

FIRE CANYON

[19]

VISITOR CENTER

OVERTON BEACH

Virgin River

VIRGIN VALLEY

NEVADA ARIZONA

TONOPAH

95

156

DESERT VIEW NATURAL ENVIRONMENT AREA

VISITOR CENTER

Gass Peak + 6,943

93

MOAPA RIVER INDIAN RESERVATION

Dry Lake Valley

15

California Wash

Overton Arm

Echo Bay

LAS VEGAS PAIUTE INDIAN RESERVATION

95

KYLE CANYON

TOIYABE NATIONAL FOREST

157

LA MADRE MTS.

14

RANCHO

LAS VEGAS VALLEY

Floyd Lamb State Park

North Las Vegas

[7]

NELLIS AIR FORCE BASE

LAS VEGAS - DUNES RECREATION LANDS

+ Muddy Peak 5,363

MUDDY MOUNTAINS

SCENIC

DRIVE

LAKE MEAD

[18]

Lone Mtn.+ 3,342

NORTH LAS VEGAS REGIONAL PARK

ANN RD

CRAIG RD

93 15

604

CHEYENNE AV

Sunrise Mtn. +3,364

GYPSUM CAVE

Gypsum Wash

NORTHSHORE

LAKE MEAD

RED ROCK

[2]

95

Las Vegas

[5] [6] [8]

SUMMERLIN PKWY

CHARLESTON

NELLIS AIR FORCE BASE

SUNRISE MOUNTAIN NATURAL AREA

Sunrise Manor

147

CALLVILLE BAY

LAS VEGAS WASH

LAKE MEAD NATIONAL RECREATION AREA

PINE CREEK CANYON

VISITOR CENTER

PINE CREEK CANYON NATURAL AREA

[9]

SAHARA AV

[4]

FLAMINGO RD

[10] Winchester

[11] Paradise

East Las Vegas

SILVER BOWL STADIUM

ETHEL M CHOCOLATE FACTORY

Pacific Time Zone

Mountain Time Zone

Boulder Basin

+ Fortification Hill 3,718

159

Blue Diamond Hill 4,957

SPRING VALLEY

Spring Valley

TROPICANA

[3]

MC CARRAN INTERNATIONAL AIRPORT

[13]

RUSSELL RD

[12]

[14]

GREEN VALLEY PKWY

147

LAKESHORE

BOULDER BEACH

NEVADA ARIZONA

BONNIE SPRINGS OLD NEVADA

Spring Mountain Ranch S.P.

CONSERVATION AREA

Blue Diamond

BLUE DIAMOND

160

Enterprise

Arden

15

MEAD

146

CLARK COUNTY HERITAGE MUSEUM

ALAN BIBLE VISITOR CENTER

Temple Bar

BAR ROAD

TEMPLE BAR WASH

Mountain Springs

Mountain Springs Summit 5,493

160

604

Henderson

[15]

Railroad Pass 2,367

HORIZON DR

93 95

Hoover Dam

[17]

Mt. Wilson + 5,445

BLACK MOUNTAINS

Potosi Mtn. + 8,612

TOIYABE NATIONAL FOREST

Sloan

Black Mtn.+ 5,092

MC CULLOUGH RANGE

Boulder City

[16]

NEVADA HWY

95

93

ELDORADO MTS.

Willow Beach

Colorado River

DETRITAL VALLEY

+ Squaw Peak 3,200

SPRING MOUNTAINS

Goodsprings

161

Jean

15

ELDORADO VALLEY

165

ARIZONA NEVADA

93

+ Senator Mtn.+ 5,127

WHITE HILLS

0 2 4 6 8 10

SCALE IN MILES

1. Grand Canyon Caverns
Almost a mile of trails winds through these caverns, whose chambers maintain a year-round temperature of 56° F. Guides take visitors by elevator down into the caverns, which are located 210 feet below ground. *Admission charged.*

2. Historic Jacob Hamblin Home
Santa Clara Blvd., Santa Clara. The 1862 sandstone dwelling of Mormon missionary Jacob Hamblin has been restored and is open to visitors. Nearby is **Snow Canyon State Park,** famous for its lava caves, stratified sandstone cliffs, and petroglyphs. *Admission charged at park.*

3. Pipe Spring National Monument
In the 1860's the Mormons established a cattle ranch at this bountiful source of fresh water. The ranch flourished, and soon a cheese-making operation became an important adjunct. Today the site commemorates Western pioneer life. The restored castle and several outbuildings are open to visitors, who can watch staff demonstrations of ranching activities and cheese-making techniques. *Admission charged.*

4. Glen Canyon National Recreation Area/Lake Powell
Formed by the huge Glen Canyon Dam, the lake stretches for nearly 200 miles through a rocky sandstone landscape, providing a pleasure-filled recreation area of fishing, boating, swimming, and camping.

5. Rainbow Bridge National Monument
This natural sandstone span rises above Bridge Canyon, whose water source is Lake Powell. The enormous monument is reachable by cruise boat from Lake Powell or by a two-day hike.

6. Navajo National Monument
Here visitors can see the most famous of the sandstone cliff dwellings built by the Kayenta Anasazi in the 13th century. **Keet Seel** (Broken Pottery), reachable by horse-back or an 8-mile hike, is so fragile that guided tours are limited to 20 persons a day. **Betatakin** (Ledge House) can be reached by a 2½-mile hike or viewed from a lookout across the canyon.

7. Goosenecks State Park
Set at the top of a tall mesa, the park overlooks the San Juan River's four gooseneck bends, for which it is named. The arid desert climate limits the wildlife mostly to lizards, skunks, and jackrabbits, all of which manage to survive among the prickly pears and Indian ricegrasses.

8. Monument Valley Navajo Tribal Park
Massive red sandstone buttes, towering walls, and sharp cliffs, interspersed with sand flats and dunes, fill this amazing landscape of the Navajo Indians. The crafts of the Navajos are on display at the visitor center. *Admission charged.*

9. Canyon de Chelly National Monument
This landscape of sheer sandstone cliffs containing hundreds of prehistoric Indian villages is home to the Navajos, many of whom live in hogans and raise crops on the canyon floor. Tours of Canyon de Chelly are offered by guides; the drive along the canyon's rim also provides excellent views of the pueblo ruins. *Fee charged for tour.*

10. Hopi Cultural Center
Rte. 264, Second Mesa. A museum recounts the history of the Hopis through displays of their costumes, jewelry, pottery, and baskets. At a cooperative guild, visitors can watch skillful craftsmen fashioning art works. Two ancient Hopi villages, **Oraibi** and **Walpi,** built on high desert mesas some 1,500 years ago by ancestors of this agricultural tribe, are located nearby. *Admission charged at museum.*

11. Hubbell Trading Post National Historic Site
Rte. 264, Ganado. Established in 1878 by John Lorenzo Hubbell, the post was for many years the social and commercial center of the surrounding communities. It is the oldest Native American trading post still in operation on the Navajo Reservation. Tours of the Hubbell home are available.

12. Window Rock
Set in a red sandstone rock landscape, the once quiet town is now the bustling capital of the Navajo nation, whose history and culture is documented at the **Navajo Tribal Museum.** At the nearby **Navajo Arts and Crafts Enterprise** a wide assortment of hand-crafted silver jewelry, intricate carvings, colorful paintings, and handsome hand-woven rugs is exhibited. The tribe's elected governing body, the Navajo Tribal Council, is housed in a building set in the midst of enormous rock formations, one of which forms the large, windowlike, 47-foot-wide opening that gave the town its name.

13. Petrified Forest National Park
About 225 million years ago a forest was buried by flood waters and silt, and eventually the trees turned into brilliantly colored stone in the midst of a valley of sandstone buttes. A museum illustrates the area's history and geology with fascinating specimens of petrified wood. Other park highlights include ruins of a pueblo built of petrified wood and Blue Mesa, where rainbow-hued logs rest on red sandstone pedestals. *Admission charged.*

14. Casa Malpais Museum
Rte. 60, Springerville. Once a ceremonial center for the Mogollon tribe, **Casa Malpais,** just north of town, is an important archeological site. There visitors can take a guided tour or follow self-guided interpretive trails, and study the ancient tribe's activities at the museum. *Fee charged for tour.*

15. Fort Apache Indian Reservation
Extensive forestlands along the White River constitute the landscape of the reservation, home of the White Mountain Apache tribe, whose headquarters is located in the town of Whiteriver. At nearby **Fort Apache,** built in 1870 to quell a local uprising, the log building that served as headquarters for the fort's general has been restored and is now used as a shop for the arts and crafts produced by the resident tribes.

16. Show Low
Chamber of Commerce, 951 West Deuce of Clubs. Show Low was named for a local card game that many years ago settled the ownership of the land. Today the spectacular landscape surrounding the town, filled with lakes created by several nearby dams, is a major fishing and boating area.

17. Barringer Meteor Crater
This 570-foot-deep cavity, created by a meteor nearly 50,000 years ago, served as the training ground for the Apollo astronauts. A museum presents informative exhibits relating to the site and to the study of earth and space sciences. *Admission charged.*

18. Mogollon Rim
The wide shoulders of the road, which rises to 7,600 feet as it winds up to the top of the rim, allows drivers to stop along the way and marvel at the grandeur of the view. Here is found part of the world's largest contiguous stand of ponderosa pine. This landscape was the setting for many of the Western novels written by Zane Grey.

19. Tonto Natural Bridge State Park
In this state park the world's largest natural travertine bridge rises to a height of 183 feet over a 400-foot-long tunnel that measures 150 feet at its widest point — theoretically wide enough to allow a helicopter to fly through. *Admission charged.*

20. Roosevelt Dam
This was the world's largest masonry dam at the time of its dedication by Theodore Roosevelt in 1911. **Roosevelt Lake,** formed by the dam, is a popular spot for fishing, boating, and waterskiing.

21. Tonto National Monument
The story of the Salado Indians is detailed at the monument's visitor center, where woven textiles, artfully decorated pottery, and other artifacts of their ancient culture are displayed. A short nature trail leads to the ruins of the Salados' cave dwellings.

22. Apache Trail
This 78-mile trail runs along a series of sparkling sapphire-blue lakes and wanders through stretches of impressive sandstone buttes, patches of desert, and canyon valleys, as it meanders around the Superstition Mountains. Visitors can explore a gold mine at **Goldfield Ghost Town,** enjoy a cruise on **Canyon Lake,** and pause for chili and a taste of prickly pear ice cream at **Tortilla Flat,** an old stagecoach stop. *Admission charged for some attractions.*

23. Boyce Thompson Southwestern Arboretum
Rte. 60, near Superior. More than 2,000 species of hot-climate plants can be seen here, along with indigenous wildlife. The plants range from yuccas and saguaros to shade-loving herb and aloe plants, which thrive under olive, pomegranate, and Chinese pistachio trees. *Admission charged.*

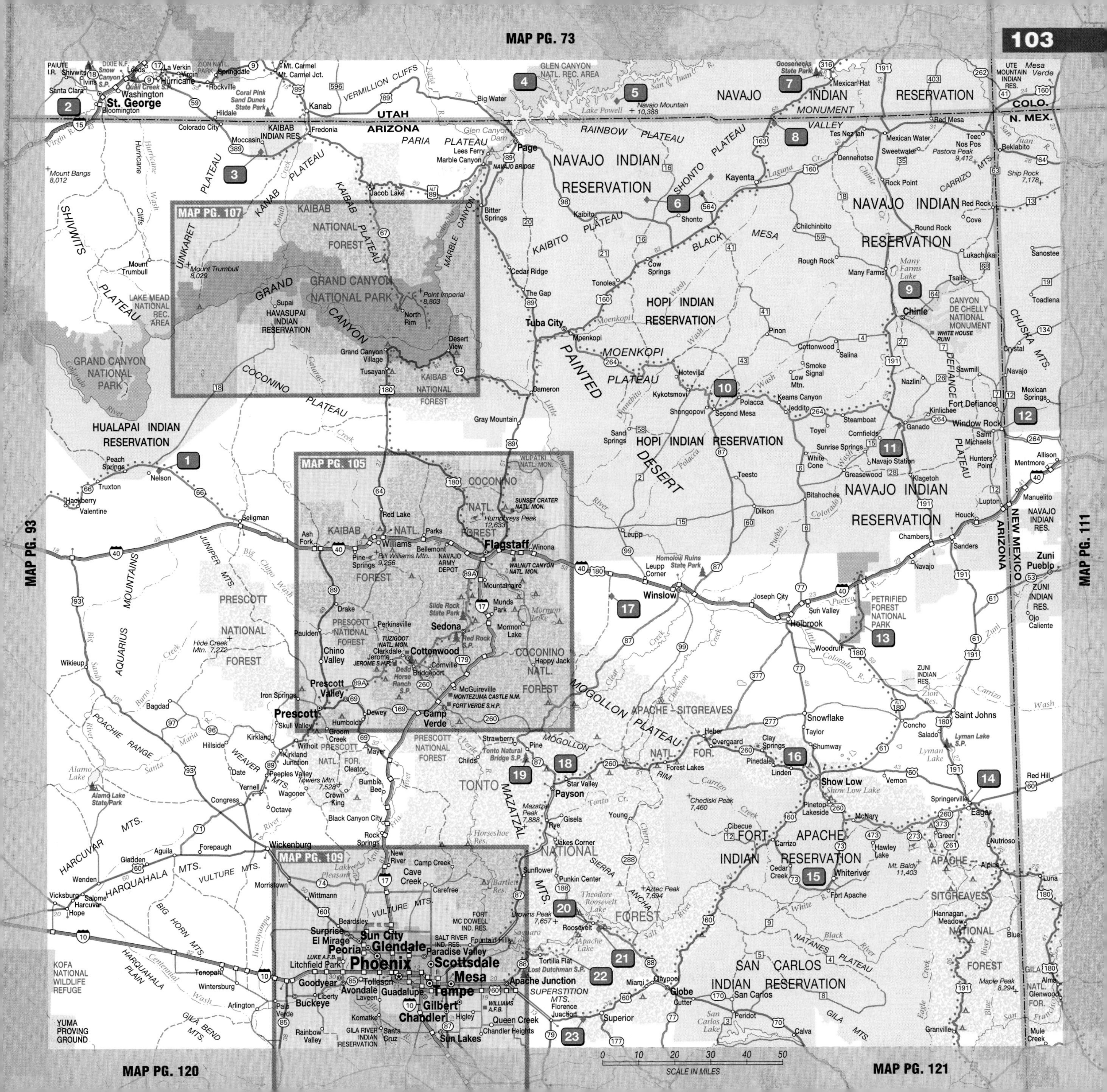

MAP PG. 93

MAP PG. 111

MAP PG. 107

MAP PG. 105

MAP PG. 109

UTAH
ARIZONA

ARIZONA
N. MEX.

COLO.
N. MEX.

NAVAJO INDIAN RESERVATION

HOPI INDIAN RESERVATION

HUALAPAI INDIAN RESERVATION

GRAND CANYON NATIONAL PARK

HAVASUPAI INDIAN RESERVATION

KAIBAB NATIONAL FOREST

PRESCOTT NATIONAL FOREST

COCONINO NATIONAL FOREST

TONTO NATIONAL FOREST

APACHE – SITGREAVES NATIONAL FOREST

FORT APACHE INDIAN RESERVATION

SAN CARLOS INDIAN RESERVATION

ZUNI INDIAN RES.

St. George
Washington
Bloomington
Santa Clara
Hurricane
Leeds
La Verkin
Springdale
Rockville
Hildale
Colorado City
Moccasin
Fredonia
Kanab
Mt. Carmel
Mt. Carmel Jct.
Big Water
Page
Lees Ferry
Marble Canyon
Jacob Lake
Bitter Springs
Cedar Ridge
The Gap
Tuba City
Moenkopi
Cameron
Gray Mountain
Kayenta
Mexican Hat
Red Mesa
Mexican Water
Sweetwater
Dennehotso
Rock Point
Round Rock
Red Rock
Cove
Ship Rock
Lukachukai
Tsaile
Chinle
Sawmill
Navajo
Window Rock
Fort Defiance
St. Michaels
Ganado
Steamboat
Cornfields
Greasewood
Klagetoh
Houck
Lupton
Sanders
Chambers
Navajo
Holbrook
Winslow
Joseph City
Sun Valley
Woodruff
Snowflake
Taylor
Show Low
Pinetop-Lakeside
McNary
Springerville
Eager
Greer
Nutrioso
Alpine
Luna

Peach Springs
Nelson
Truxton
Hackberry
Valentine
Wikieup
Bagdad
Seligman
Ash Fork
Williams
Parks
Flagstaff
Winona
Sedona
Cottonwood
Clarkdale
Jerome
Chino Valley
Paulden
Prescott
Prescott Valley
Dewey
Mayer
Humboldt
Skull Valley
Kirkland
Yarnell
Congress
Wickenburg
Wittmann
Morristown
Surprise
El Mirage
Peoria
Sun City
Glendale
Phoenix
Scottsdale
Paradise Valley
Mesa
Tempe
Gilbert
Chandler
Gilbert
Guadalupe
Goodyear
Avondale
Buckeye
Tolleson
Cave Creek
Carefree
New River
Black Canyon City
Rock Springs
Payson
Pine
Strawberry
Star Valley
Globe
Miami
San Carlos
Superior
Florence Junction
Queen Creek
Apache Junction
Sun Lakes

SCALE IN MILES
0 10 20 30 40 50

KOFA NATIONAL WILDLIFE REFUGE

YUMA PROVING GROUND

GRAND CANYON NATIONAL PARK

1. Kaibab National Forest

The forest's southern section offers scenic driving along the 22 miles that parallel Rte. 40 between Williams and Bellemont; this is a section of historic Rte. 66. Visitors can hike and horseback ride along Kendrick Mountain Trail, or camp and fish in the area. The road passes **Garland Prairie Vista,** a favorite of photographers that reaches its highest point near Parks.

2. Grand Canyon Railway

518 East Bill Williams Ave., Williams. An all-day nostalgic 65-mile ride takes passengers through wide-open plains, canyons, and ponderosa pine forests to the Grand Canyon's South Rim, arriving at the historic **Grand Canyon Depot.** The **Grand Canyon Railway Museum,** located in the old Fray Marcos Hotel in Williams, features railroad artifacts and mining, ranching, and logging exhibits. *Fee charged for train ride.*

3. Grand Canyon Deer Farm

100 Deer Farm Rd., Williams. A great place to bring children, this storybook red barn with white trim is home for a menagerie of more than 200 monkeys, llamas, miniature donkeys, deer, and other animals, many of which can be fed and petted. *Admission charged.*

4. Humphreys Peak

At 12,633 feet, Humphreys Peak is Arizona's tallest mountain. The extinct volcano is part of the San Francisco Peaks, named in the 1600's by Spanish explorers.

5. Sunset Crater Volcano National Monument

The 1,000-foot-high cinder cone is the product of an eruption in A.D. 1065, and is named for the sunset-colored mineral deposits around its summit. A 1-mile loop trail circles lava beds, which are near the visitor center. *Admission charged.*

6. Wupatki National Monument

The ruins of more than 2,000 structures built by 12th-century Sinagua Indian farmers are preserved here today. Most impressive are a 100-room, four-story pueblo, an oval ball court, and a large stone amphitheater. Visitor center exhibits explain the Sinagua culture. Sightseeing is by self-guiding trails and roads.

7. Flagstaff

Chamber of Commerce, 101 West Santa Fe Ave. Diverse attractions include the **Arizona Historical Society Pioneer Museum,** with its period rooms and changing exhibits on local history, and the **Lowell Observatory,** featuring guided tours and telescope viewing. In **Riordan State Historic Park,** a 40-room log mansion with Tiffany windows has 1900's furnishings, and is an excellent example of craftsman-style architecture. Visitors to the **Museum of Northern Arizona** can see displays on earth sciences, fine arts, and contemporary American Indian cultures, or browse in an Indian arts and crafts center and bookstore. Special shows and presentations by Native American artists are held in the summer. *Admission charged for some attractions.*

8. Walnut Canyon National Monument

Cliffside ruins in a 400-foot-high canyon wall can be entered from a steep self-guiding trail, or seen from a distance on an easier path. The ruins are the remains of Sinagua Indian dwellings used until about A.D. 1250. Deer, elk, and other wildlife inhabit the area. *Admission charged.*

9. Slide Rock State Park

Situated in Oak Creek Canyon, this park is aptly named for its natural sandstone waterslide. Rainbow trout fishing and hiking are popular pastimes. The spectacular canyon, with its languid creek, lush vegetation, and magnificent 2,500-foot-high bluffs, is a premier scenic drive. *Admission charged.*

10. Sedona

Chamber of Commerce, Forest Rd. and Rte. 89A. This resort center is known for its beautiful homes, fine art galleries, and the **Chapel of the Holy Cross,** which stands near two pinnacles of uniquely colored sandstone. The **Tlaquepaque area** incorporates Old Mexico's architectural forms in 4 acres of gardens, courtyards, fountains, shops, and art galleries.

11. Tuzigoot National Monument

This ridgetop town, 120 feet above the Verde Valley, flourished between A.D. 1125 and 1400. The stone-and-adobe pueblo was built by Sinagua Indians and contained about 90 rooms, many of which can still be seen. Extensive artifacts are exhibited at the visitor center. *Admission charged.*

12. Verde River Canyon Excursion Train

300 North Broadway, Clarkdale. The railroad, which once linked Jerome and Prescott, offers visitors the only access to the scenic Verde Canyon's towering crimson cliffs, river, and prehistoric Indian ruins. *Fee charged.*

13. Jerome

Chamber of Commerce, 50 Main St. Amid shops and art galleries, historic buildings stacked precariously on a mountainside hint at Jerome's rowdy past as a boom-and-bust copper-mining town. **Jerome State Historic Park,** a former copper baron's estate, traces its history with mining equipment, models, and historical photographs. *Admission charged at park.*

14. Phippen Museum of Western Art

4701 Rte. 89, Prescott. Bronzes, paintings, and sketches by Western artists are featured at this museum. Special tribute is paid to Western artist George Phippen, one of the founders of the Cowboy Artists of America organization. *Admission charged.*

15. Prescott

Chamber of Commerce, 117 West Goodwin St. The colorful past of Arizona's territorial capital, established in 1864, is reflected in the **Courthouse Plaza,** stately Victorian architecture, and illustrious **Whiskey Row.** At the **Sharlot Hall Museum,** visitors can tour the first Territorial Governor's Mansion, explorer John C. Frémont's home, and the ornate Bashford House.

16. Montezuma Castle National Monument

The "castle" is in reality a communal limestone cliff dwelling built by Sinagua Indian farmers in about A.D. 1150. Visitor center displays include their sophisticated textiles and ingeniously fashioned tools and jewelry. **Montezuma Well,** located 11 miles upstream from the dwelling, is a limestone spring; around its rim are the ruins of two large pueblos. The well, which produces more than a million gallons of water a day, was used by the Sinaguas to irrigate their fields until drought, soil depletion, and overcrowding forced them to abandon the land in about A.D. 1400. *Admission charged.*

17. Fort Verde State Historic Park

East Lane St., Camp Verde. In the early 1870's, pioneers began to settle on land in the Verde Valley that had served as the traditional hunting grounds of the Yavapai-Apache Indians. A conflict ensued between the two groups, which led to the establishment of the fort. Visitors to the park today can see four of the former military post's original buildings that are still standing. *Admission charged.*

The Museum of Northern Arizona in Flagstaff displays many superb examples of Native American art and craftwork, as typified by the parrot effigy vessel below and the Tularosa black-on-white pitcher at right.

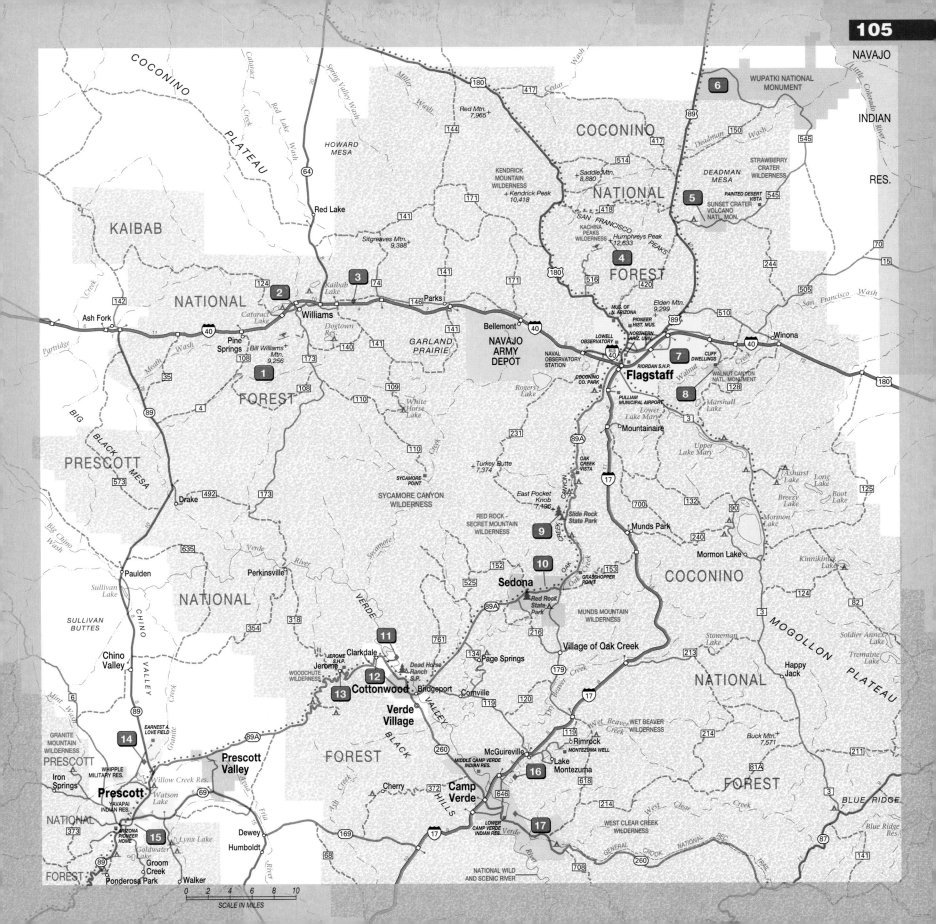

GRAND CANYON NATIONAL PARK

1. Marble Canyon

From a boat or raft on the Colorado River, visitors can look up in awe at this narrow canyon's redwall limestone cliffs. The **Navajo Bridge,** made of thin steel, crosses 467 feet above the river. North of the bridge, **Lees Ferry,** the departure point for most river trips, marks the start of Marble Canyon, and is also the official beginning of Grand Canyon. Marble Canyon ends where the Colorado and Little Colorado rivers meet.

2. Kaibab Plateau–North Rim Parkway

This scenic byway, open in season, is the only paved road into Grand Canyon's North Rim. The 44 miles of magnificent forests, mountain meadows, and tiny lakes are rich in history and wildlife, as well as recreational opportunities.

3. Point Imperial

A 3-mile spur road north of Cape Royal leads to the highest viewpoint on the North Rim, at 8,803 feet above sea level. Offering the best view across the canyon, it also provides views of Marble Canyon, the **Colorado River, Mount Hayden,** the **Vermilion Cliffs,** and **Navajo Mountain.** Grand Canyon geology is explained on bus tours from Grand Canyon Lodge to Point Imperial and Cape Royal, and in ranger programs at the point.

4. Scenic Drive to Cape Royal

This 23-mile drive leads to some of the highest and widest parts of the canyon. Amid the woodland of Walhalla Plateau, lies **Vista Encantadora,** which boasts a view of the multicolored Painted Desert. Anasazi Indians farmed a nearby area from A.D. 700 to 1175, and ruins from their settlement still exist at **Walhalla Glades.** From Cape Royal, the Colorado River can

be seen more than a mile below, along with the distant South Rim, the huge ridge called **Wotan's Throne,** and **Vishnu Temple,** a white-crowned butte.

5. Bright Angel Point

Panoramic views from this mile-long promontory encompass nearby **Deva, Brahma,** and **Zoroaster temples,** the **South Rim,** distant **San Francisco Peaks,** sprawling **Coconino Plateau,** and Arizona's tallest mountain, **Humphreys Peak.** The vista is so dazzling that in 1934 it was illustrated on a U.S. postage stamp. Nearby facilities include accommodations at Grand Canyon Lodge, plus a National Park Service Information Station that arranges seasonal exhibits and campfire talks.

6. North Kaibab Trail

Here hikers descend 3,041 feet to Roaring Springs on the only maintained trail into the canyon from the North Rim. Allow a full day for the rugged 9-mile round-trip trek. Options include continuing on to the Colorado River and overnighting at Bright Angel or Cottonwood Campground.

7. South Kaibab Trail

The rugged 7-mile trail from South Rim's Yaki Point descends 4,800 feet to the Colorado River. Trekkers should not attempt to hike to the river and back in one day nor, because of a lack of shade and drinking water, should summer hikes be undertaken without adequate preparation.

8. Phantom Ranch

This rustic lodge, situated by a rushing stream at the base of the 1,500-foot walls of the Inner Gorge, lies in a wooded area on the canyon floor and can be reached only by mule, hiking, or river rafting. The resort's name comes from an Indian myth that tells of the first human being (the "phantom"), who arose here from the underworld and liked the setting enough to send for his tribe.

9. Kaibab Suspension Bridge

Mules brought down the steel sections that form this bridge, completed in 1928. The 440-foot-long structure hangs about 60 feet above the rushing water.

10. Yavapai Point and Museum

Located on the South Entrance Road, Yavapai Point looks out on the rock formations

named Vishnu and Zoroaster temples. Ten miles away, but still well within sight, is the **North Rim.** The museum provides geological history exhibits, lectures by park naturalists, and a videotape presentation. Binoculars, set on significant canyon features, are available.

11. Bright Angel Trail

Visitors can take this 18-mile round-trip path to the river by mule or by foot. Remarkable views make the steep climb back up to the rim well worth the effort. Highlights include **Tonto Platform,** the spectacular **Inner Gorge,** and a crossing of Kaibab Suspension Bridge. At **Indian Garden** ranger station, weary travelers will find a welcome oasis, with campsites and a shaded picnic area.

A mule caravan plies a canyon trail.

12. West Rim Drive

This 8-mile drive from Grand Canyon Village to Hermits Rest features eight major viewpoints. Buses take visitors to the main overlooks during the summer, when the drive, west of Grand Canyon Village, is closed to cars. At **Maricopa Point,** travelers can see an old mine and the **Vishnu Schist** — black rock that is 2 billion years old. **Hopi, Mohave,** and **Pima points** provide sweeping vistas that include the Kaibab National Forest, the Colorado River, the Granite Gorge, and Mts. Trumball and Logan.

13. Hermits Rest

This building at the end of West Rim Drive is made of stone taken from the canyon. Here hikers can relax in front of one of the

largest fireplaces in the world. The spacious porch, perched at an elevation of 6,300 feet, provides visitors with a beautiful view of the **Hindu Amphitheater,** a dramatic chasm that was sliced through the rock by Crystal Creek. Across the canyon, **Point Sublime** presents another feast for the eyes.

14. Visitor Information Center

Located in Grand Canyon Village, the center includes an exhibit hall that interprets Grand Canyon's culture and natural history. Park maps, brochures, and books can be obtained at the bookstore, and rangers are available to answer questions and help plan sightseeing.

15. Grand Canyon Village

Located at the South Rim, the village offers, in addition to a visitor center, facilities such as lodges, cabins, a campground, and a picnic area. Many sites here are listed on the National Register of Historic Landmarks, including **Hopi House, Kolb Studio,** and **El Tovar Hotel,** which is open for tours and overnight stays. The Grand Canyon Railway, a restored 1901 steam train, stops here at the 1910 **Grand Canyon Depot.**

16. East Rim Drive

This 23-mile drive, from Grand Canyon Village to the entrance gate at Desert View, features striking views of **Grand Canyon, Painted Desert,** and **San Francisco Peaks** from **Grandview, Yaki, Yavapai, Moran, Lipan** and **Navajo points.** The grandeur visible from **Mather Point** is the first glimpse of the canyon for many visitors.

17. Grandview Point

Located on the South Rim, this site was once a mining village. Today it is one of the most popular lookouts in the park, where visitors can gaze upon a spectacular view of the Colorado River, dwarfed by purple-streaked red rocks. Also visible are the Vermilion Cliffs and, 100 miles in the distance, Navajo Mountain.

18. Moran Point

This overlook, situated along the East Rim Drive, was named for artist Thomas Moran, who explored the canyon with John Wesley Powell in 1873. Moran's paintings of the canyon memorialize its grandeur, but visitors here can see the real thing: the beautiful rock shapes and strata,

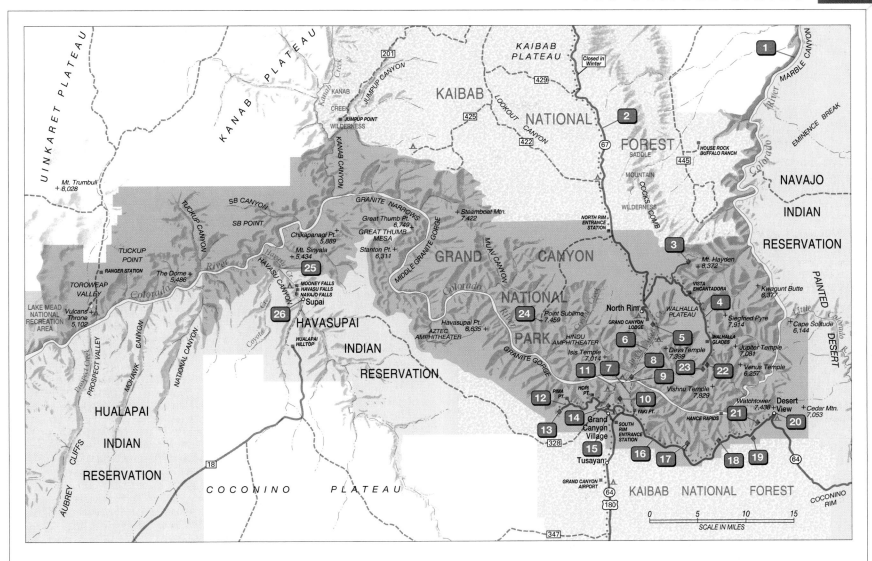

the powerful river, and the dangerous white-water **Hance Rapids.**

19. Tusayan Ruin and Museum

Visitors can tour a prehistoric pueblo built around A.D. 1200 by Anasazi Indians, who hunted, farmed, and gathered wild plants in the area. The adjacent Tusayan Museum contains artifacts from the ruins and exhibits on the American Southwest.

20. Desert View

On the eastern end of East Rim Drive, this lookout affords a view to the north as well as to the west, including the Painted Desert, with its breathtaking colors. Visitors can climb the **Watchtower**—a 67-foot-high replica of an early Indian structure—to reach the highest point on the South Rim and to look through

powerful telescopes in the windowed observatory. The Watchtower also features a sand painting by Hopi artist Fred Kabotie. Close by, **Navajo Point** offers yet another astounding view.

21. Lipan Point

Lipan Point, situated along the East Rim Drive and considered by some to provide the best of all canyon views, offers travelers a glimpse of the widest part of the "big ditch," as locals call it. Here the Colorado River curves in a broad, serpentine sweep. Also within view are the Kaibab Plateau's southerly slant and the North Rim's high, color-ribboned wall.

22. Angel's Window

Several hundred feet below the North Rim, a narrow limestone spur juts out over the

canyon. Wind and water have carved out a large hole in the stone, forming a window. A trail leads down from Cape Royal to this point, where the Painted Desert is still within view from across the chasm.

23. Cape Royal Trail

From Cape Royal's parking lot, visitors can enjoy an easy half-hour walk that offers views of Grand Canyon, Angel's Window, and the Colorado River. Markers along the trail interpret the area's natural history.

24. Point Sublime

In 1880 explorer Clarence E. Dutton pronounced the view from here "the most sublime of earthly spectacles." What Dutton saw is just as exhilarating today: the Inner Gorge at its narrowest opening between the North and South rims.

25. Havasu Creek

On its way to the Colorado River, this creek creates three spectacular waterfalls. **Navajo Falls** lies about 1½ miles below Supai village. Another mile below, the wide **Havasu Falls** makes its red-rock descent onto travertine terraces. One mile farther, **Mooney Falls** takes a 196-foot plunge over a bluff.

26. Supai

The Havasupai Reservation lies in **Havasu Canyon,** a 4- to 5-hour drive from Grand Canyon Village, and an 8-mile hike or horseback ride down a precipitous trail, which becomes Supai village's main street. The turquoise-colored Havasu Creek turns this area into a lovely oasis.

Admission charged for national park.

1. Wildlife World Zoo

16501 West Northern Ave., Glendale. This zoo specializes in breeding and raising rare and endangered species. Among the birds are South American black curassows and Australasian Lowry parrots (which nibble apples held by visitors). Other animals include a white tiger and the rare oryx. The petting area delights children of all ages. *Admission charged.*

2. Pioneer Arizona Living History Museum

3901 West Pioneer Rd., Phoenix. This 300-acre museum is home to rare Colonial Spanish horses. The state's pioneer days are re-created by costumed guides and artisans demonstrating activities of the period in restored buildings, including a schoolhouse, a stagecoach station, and even an 1870 opera house that stages old-fashioned melodramas. *Admission charged.*

3. Rawhide

23023 North Scottsdale Rd., Scottsdale. This replica of an 1880's town recalls the Old West. The many buildings include a general store, marshal's office, and steakhouse. A museum houses such frontier relics as Belle Starr's buffalo-horn table and Geronimo's moccasins. Actors stage shootouts and often involve visitors in impromptu performances. Stagecoach, burro, and even camel rides are available. *Fee charged for rides.*

4. Fleischer Museum

The Perimeter Center, 17207 North Perimeter Dr., Scottsdale. This is the only museum dedicated to the California school of American Impressionism. Many of the artists represented here painted such splendid natural wonders as the Grand Canyon, the High Sierras, and Point Lobos.

5. Taliesin West

13201 North 108 St., Scottsdale. In the late 1930's, architect Frank Lloyd Wright designed a winter home and studio to fit in with the desert landscape. Set beneath the McDowell Mountains, the long, low buildings, made of native stone and redwood, now house Wright's foundation and architecture school. *Admission charged.*

6. Fountain Hills

This residential desert community boasts the world's highest fountain. Its water jets up to 560 feet from a lagoon for 15 minutes at a time, on the hour from 10 A.M. to 9 P.M.

7. Lost Dutchman State Park

Set in the Superstition Mountains, the legendary site of the Lost Dutchman gold mine is now a 300-acre park featuring hiking trails, a campground, and access to a nearby wilderness area. *Admission charged.*

8. Champlin Fighter Museum

4636 Fighter Aces Dr., Mesa. This museum contains more than 30 planes from World War I to the Vietnam War, including the English Sopwith Camel and the American P-47 Thunderbolt. Also on display are memorabilia of flying aces such as Joe Foss and Baron von Richthofen. *Admission charged.*

9. McCormick Railroad Park

7301 East Indian Bend Rd., Scottsdale. Miniature trains carry passengers through this 30-acre park, part of which is a lovely arboretum. Full-size vintage railway cars rest permanently near the turn-of-the-century stations that are now stores catering to train buffs. *Fee charged for train ride.*

10. Scottsdale Center for the Arts and Downtown Shopping District

Located in the Scottsdale Mall, the Center for the Arts features both classic and contemporary art and hosts concerts, films, and festivals. The exciting downtown area also offers first-rate shopping in an open-air venue; a trolley goes to many of the stores, restaurants, and galleries.

11. Mesa Southwest Museum

53 North Macdonald, Mesa. Various elements of the region's background come together in this museum, with such displays as dinosaur models, Apache artifacts, Spanish armor, glistening minerals, and a 1920's local street scene. Visitors can even pan for gold in a small stream. *Admission charged.*

12. Mormon Temple Visitor's Center

525 East Main St., Mesa. A 10-foot reproduction of Thorvaldsen's statue of Christ dominates this center, which is also decorated with murals. Although the temple itself, one of the nation's largest, is closed to the general public, its lovely gardens are open to visitors; tours are available.

13. Arizona State University

The **Nelson Fine Arts Center** is one of the highlights of the university campus. The award-winning lavender stucco building houses the University Art Museum, whose excellent collection is particularly strong in American arts and crafts. Another architectural marvel on the campus is Frank Lloyd Wright's circular **Grady Gammage Memorial Auditorium.**

14. Big Surf

1500 North McClintock Rd., Tempe. At this huge man-made lagoon, breakers created by a wave machine crash onto the beach as palm trees sway above. Inland ocean-lovers can swim, body surf, raft, and zip down the long water slide. *Admission charged.*

15. Old Town Tempe

Mill Ave., Tempe. The shops and saloons of yesteryear are reflected on Mill Avenue in this historic part of Tempe. The tree-lined street still offers goods and refreshments to visitors walking past the Victorian lampposts on the red-brick sidewalks.

16. Papago Park

Besides its lakes and trails, this vast city park holds many attractions. The **Desert Botanical Garden** grows plants from deserts worldwide, and the **Phoenix Zoo** features animals from tropical lands. The new **Arizona Historical Society/Marley Center Museum** concentrates on state history with hands-on and multimedia exhibits. *Admission charged for some attractions.*

Kachina dolls at the Heard Museum

17. Arizona Biltmore

24th St. and Missouri, Phoenix. Frank Lloyd Wright helped design this "Jewel of the Desert," a sculpted-block hotel recently redone in its original 1929 colors. Lush palm trees and cacti accent the specially patterned exterior walls; inside, the lobby glows with a stained-glass mosaic.

18. Heard Museum of Native Cultures and Art

22 East Monte Vista Rd., Phoenix. The museum's art and artifacts, including an extraordinary collection of kachina dolls, illustrates the cultures of American Indians who have inhabited the Southwest from prehistoric to current times. Not far away, the **Phoenix Art Museum** features art of the American West, along with Asian and European works. *Admission charged.*

19. Heritage Square

Seventh and Monroe Sts., Phoenix. Beautiful Victorian houses, some containing museums and shops, grace this historic city block. A shuttle service brings visitors to the **Arizona State Capital Museum,** which also recalls earlier days with its original legislative chambers and a replica of the 1912 governor's office. Moving into the present, the **Arizona Museum of Science and Technology** offers dynamic exhibits and a young people's discovery area. *Admission charged at science museum.*

20. Mystery Castle

800 East Mineral Rd., Phoenix. It took 18 years for Boyce Luther Gulley to build this quirky 18-room "castle" out of stone and sand for his daughter. The unique domicile has Southwestern furnishings, fireplaces, parapets, a cantilever stairway, and a chapel. *Admission charged.*

21. South Mountain Park

A huge city oasis, this former Indian hunting ground today offers miles of hiking and horseback-riding trails, mountains, petroglyphs, and a natural bridge and tunnel; an excellent panorama of Phoenix can be seen from **Dobbins Lookout.**

22. Gila River Arts and Crafts Center

Replicas of Hohokam dwellings coexist with more recent artifacts in this park, located on the **Gila River Indian Reservation.** The museum contains artifacts dating from 2000 B.C., such as jewelry, tools, and pottery. Tours are available.

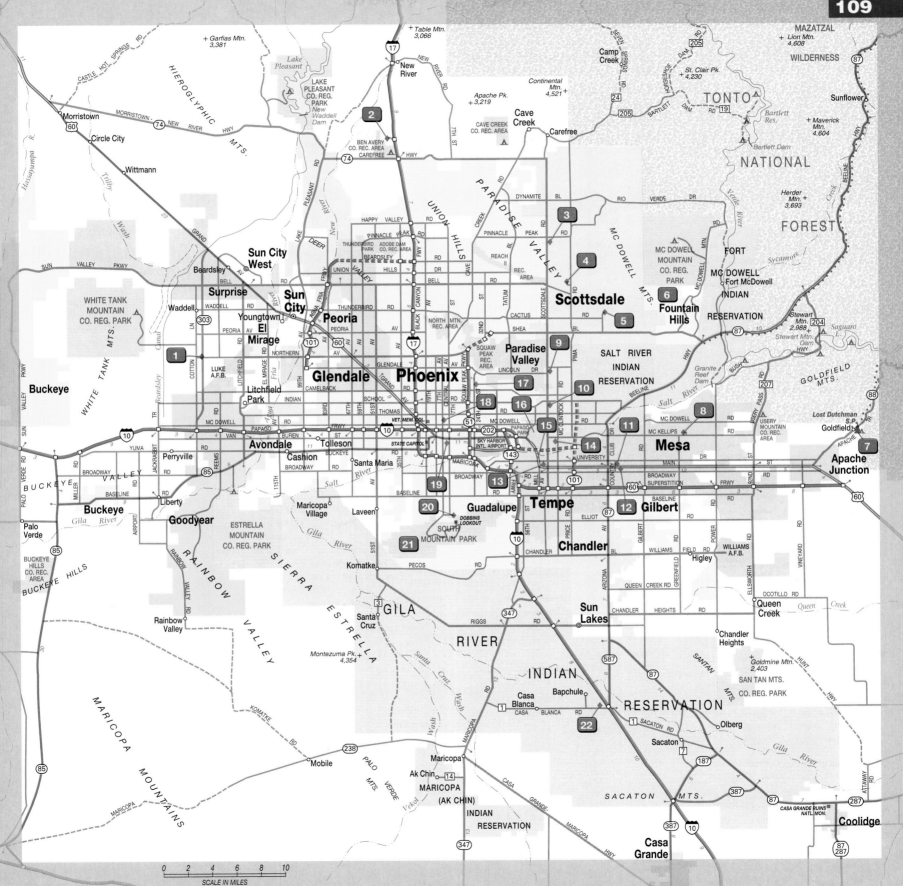

1. Shiprock

This imposing monolith was once the molten core of a volcano. It rises 1,700 feet above the Navajo plains, resembles a sailing ship, and stands as a symbol of the Four Corners area, where New Mexico, Colorado, Utah, and Arizona meet.

2. Aztec Ruins National Monument

Although Aztecs were mistakenly credited with its construction, this structure was actually built in the 1100's by local Anasazi Indians. A 500-room, three-story building and restored kiva are seen on the self-guiding trail. *Admission charged.*

3. Salmon Ruin

The large Anasazi Indian ruin dates back to between A.D. 1088 and 1095. The adjacent **Heritage Park** features Navajo hogans and Ute and Apache teepees. *Admission charged at park.*

4. Chaco Culture National Historical Park

Twenty-nine miles of rough road lead to ruins of a culture that flourished between A.D. 950 and 1150. The spectacular **Pueblo Bonito Ruins** cover more than 2 acres, with approximately 600 rooms and 40 kivas. The site includes seven other major towns, a visitor center, and a nearby campground. *Admission charged.*

5. Zuni Reservation

This reservation includes New Mexico's largest pueblo. To the north, **Red Rock State Park** is known for its outstanding museum of American Indian artifacts. **El Morro National Monument,** east of the reservation, contains petroglyphs of Anasazi, Spanish, and Anglo origin. *Admission charged for some attractions.*

6. El Malpais National Monument and National Conservation Area

The area's 376,000 acres — complete with lava beds, splatter cones, miles of lava tubes, and Anasazi ruins — can be explored by foot, bicycle, horseback, or car.

Short trails, on private land, ascend 100 feet to **Bandera Crater and Ice Caves,** located near the Continental Divide. *Admission charged for some attractions.*

7. Acoma Pueblo

One of the nation's oldest communities has sat atop its magnificent mesa since at least A.D. 1150. Visitors are bused to the village, where residents make and sell traditionally decorated pottery. Guided walking tours feature a 1600's chapel, sweeping desert views, and ancient homes. *Admission charged.*

8. National Radio Astronomy Observatory

Off Rte. 52, west of Socorro. Twenty-seven huge dish-shaped antennae collect and analyze cosmic radio waves at this observatory. The visitor center contains displays that explain radio astronomy, as well as the observatory's remarkable telescope.

9. Gila Cliff Dwellings National Monument

Ruins of dwellings built by Mogollon Indians between A.D. 1270 and 1300 are housed in five natural caves high on a cliff face. A 1-mile interpretive trail leads up a canyon to the dwellings.

10. Bosque del Apache National Wildlife Refuge

Along a 15-mile auto-tour loop visitors may spot bald eagles, endangered greater sandhill cranes, and the rare whooping crane. Great blue herons, deer, and coyotes are common; during the winter thousands of ducks and geese are in residence as well. *Admission charged.*

11. San Miguel Mission Socorro

403 El Camino Real NW, Socorro. Red-tiled spires and twin bell towers make this one of the Southwest's most beautiful churches. An original mission wall from 1598 is part of the present adobe structure, which was built between 1615 and 1626. Inside the church are antique statues and hand-carved ceiling beams.

12. Isleta Pueblo

The pueblo, established early in the 13th century, was flourishing when Spanish explorers arrived. An adobe mission church, restored in 1710, has a beautiful altar and sanctuary. At the town plaza, visitors can also see pottery fired and bread baked in outdoor ovens.

13. Salinas Pueblo Missions National Monument

The monument includes Abó, Gran Quivira, and Quarai pueblos. While all were once large villages, today each site consists of mainly unexcavated pueblo mounds surrounding huge mission churches. Self-guiding trails lead to remains of pueblos, kivas, and chapels.

14. Three Rivers Petroglyphs

More than 15,000 Mogollon Indian petroglyphs dating from between A.D. 900 and 1400 are spread over 50 acres. Also located on the site are the remains of an excavated Mogollon village.

15. Lincoln State Monument

Period buildings and relics recall the 1878 Lincoln County War and its famous participant, Billy the Kid — including the bullet holes he left in the wall of the former courthouse. *Admission charged.*

16. Roswell Museum and Art Center

100 West 11th St., Roswell. Southwestern art, culture, and history are highlighted here in eclectic collections of pottery, kachina dolls, and the work of painters Peter Hurd and Georgia O'Keeffe.

17. Rock Lake Trout Rearing Station

River Rd., Santa Rosa. More than 33 million walleyed pike and 305,000 rainbow trout are raised here annually. **Santa Rosa Lake State Park** offers camping, boating, fishing, bird-watching, and hikes through high desert forest and cacti. The visitor center, overlooking the dam, chronicles more than 250 archeological sites. *Admission charged at park.*

18. Fort Union National Monument

Stone fortifications and crumbling walls set the stage for a walking tour of the post and depot. Visitor center exhibits chronicle the fort's ever-changing role in westward expansion — as an 1800's Santa Fe Trail station, Civil War fortification, and major participant in American Indian campaigns. *Admission charged.*

19. Chimayo

Here **El Santuario de Chimayó,** called the Lourdes of North America, is a popular stop on the **High Road to Taos.** Other sights on the route are the Spanish Colonial pueblo architecture at **Las Trampas** church and the lofty **Truchas Peaks.**

20. Mission San Francisco de Asis

St. Francis Plaza, Ranchos de Taos. The lovely mission, built by Franciscans in the early 1800's, is a favorite of artists and photographers. It contains antique ornamental screens behind the altar made by the folk artist Molleno. "The Shadow of the Cross," a painting that actually glows in the dark, is located across the street.

21. Martinez Hacienda

Ranchitos Rd., south of Taos. This fortresslike adobe structure is one of the few restored Spanish Colonial haciendas offering a vivid glimpse into the everyday life of the colonials. *Admission charged.*

22. Taos

Chamber of Commerce, 229 Paseo del Pueblo Sur. The town of Taos was founded on **Taos Plaza,** which is still the center of activity for the many artists and craftspeople who now populate the area. The nearby **Kit Carson Home and Museum** features art, a gun room, and memorabilia pertaining to the famous scout. The **Ernest Blumenschein Home,** built in 1780, contains a collection of works by local artists.

23. Taos Pueblo

Located in the pueblo are two major adobe structures, five stories tall and separated by the Rio Pueblo; the buildings may have been inhabited continuously for more than 1,000 years. Handcrafted jewelry, mica-flecked pottery, and leather goods are featured in local shops. The nearby **Millicent Rogers Museum** has a fine collection of Hispanic and Native American art. *Admission charged.*

24. Red River

Chamber of Commerce, Town Hall, Main St. Set in an alpine valley at an 8,750-foot elevation, this village offers visitors year-round outdoor recreation. Activities include winter skiing, spring and autumn hikes, summer wildflower and wildlife observation, and pack trips to a high mountain lake for trout fishing.

25. Capulin Volcano National Monument

When this dormant volcano erupted about 10,000 years ago, it created a perfectly symmetrical cinder cone. On clear days visitors can drive up a spiraling road to the 1,400-foot rim of the caldera and see four states. *Admission charged.*

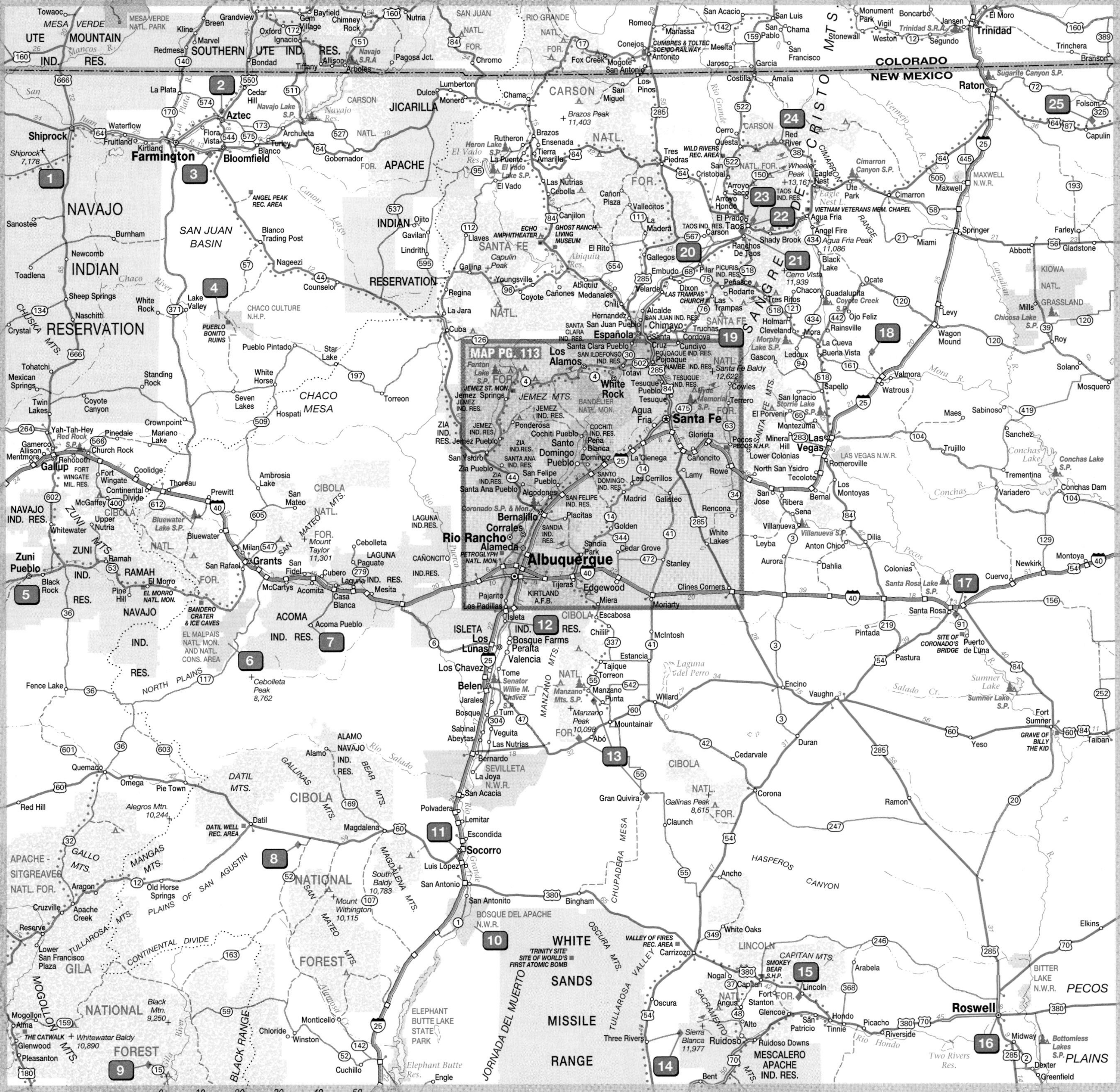

MAP PG. 103

MAP PG. 115

MAP PG. 113

COLORADO
NEW MEXICO

UTE MOUNTAIN IND. RES.

MESA VERDE NATL. PARK

SOUTHERN UTE IND. RES.

JICARILLA APACHE INDIAN RESERVATION

CARSON NATL. FOR.

NAVAJO INDIAN RESERVATION

SAN JUAN BASIN

CHACO MESA

CIBOLA NATL. FOR.

Shiprock

Farmington

Bloomfield

Aztec

Gallup

Grants

Albuquerque

Rio Rancho
Corrales
Bernalillo
Alameda

Santa Fe

Los Alamos
White Rock

Española

Taos

Red River

Raton

Trinidad

Las Vegas

Santa Rosa

Socorro

Belen
Los Lunas

Roswell

Ruidoso

ZUNI IND. RES.

ACOMA IND. RES.

LAGUNA IND. RES.

ISLETA IND. RES.

SEVILLETA N.W.R.

BOSQUE DEL APACHE N.W.R.

WHITE SANDS MISSILE RANGE

'TRINITY SITE' SITE OF WORLD'S FIRST ATOMIC BOMB

MESCALERO APACHE IND. RES.

LINCOLN NATL. FOR.

CIBOLA NATL. FOR.

GILA NATIONAL FOREST

APACHE - SITGREAVES NATL. FOR.

DATIL MTS.

MANZANO MTS.

SANGRE DE CRISTO MTS

PECOS

BITTER LAKE N.W.R.

KIOWA NATL. GRASSLAND

SCALE IN MILES
0 10 20 30 40 50

COLORADO
Taos
Santa Fe
Albuquerque
NEW MEXICO

1. National Atomic Museum

Kirtland Air Force Base, Wyoming Blvd., Albuquerque. Rockets, missiles, and a B-52 are displayed outside the museum. Inside, exhibits trace the history of the atomic age and associated technologies, including waste cleanup and nuclear medicine. Weapons technology and the development of the hydrogen bomb are also examined. A theater shows documentary films such as one about the Manhattan Project called *10 Seconds That Shook the World.*

2. Ernie Pyle Branch Library

900 Girard Blvd. SE, Albuquerque. The former home of the famous World War II correspondent has a modest collection of photographs and letters pertaining to his journalistic career.

3. Old Town Albuquerque

On the site of the original 1706 settlement, Old Town is redolent of Albuquerque's Spanish colonial past, with its pleasant tree-shaded plaza and winding alleyways. The focal point of the area's plaza is the 18th-century **Church of San Felipe de Neri,** which has been enlarged from a simple adobe chapel. Some of the adobe buildings of the early Spanish settlers remain; the first two-story adobe building in Old Town was the **Sister Blandina Convent**. The district is dotted with charming craft shops and restaurants, many of them in historic buildings. Additional points of interest include the nearby **Albuquerque Museum,** which focuses on the city's rich Spanish heritage, and the **New Mexico Museum of Natural History,** which displays life-size dinosaurs, an Ice Age cave, and a volcano. *Admission charged at natural history museum.*

4. Indian Pueblo Cultural Center

2401 12th St. NW, Albuquerque. Seeking to promote understanding of native culture and heritage, New Mexico's 19 Indian pueblos jointly operate this facility. The history, artwork, and crafts of the Pueblo Indians are examined in a museum, and traditional dance performances take place on weekends. *Admission charged at museum.*

5. University of New Mexico

The handsomely landscaped Albuquerque campus of New Mexico's largest university includes the vast **Zimmerman Library,** whose reading room was designed to resemble the interior of a pueblo church. At the **Maxwell Museum of Anthropology,** the Southwest is showcased in exhibits of early Indian culture. The **Museum of Geology and Meteoritics** displays 200 meteorites from around the world, as well as samples of animals, plants, and minerals from ancient times.

6. Sandia Peak

From a garden of cacti at its base, the 2.7-mile **Sandia Peak Aerial Tramway** — one of the world's longest — rises 3,800 feet over steep canyons and verdant forests. During the winter the tram operates as a ski lift. The ride provides soul-stirring views from the 10,676-foot peak, where visitors can survey some 11,000 square miles. Part of the **Cibola National Forest,** Sandia Peak is also a great place for hiking and hang gliding. *Fee charged for tram.*

7. Coronado State Park and Monument

This area consists of a campsite on the banks of the Rio Grande, used in the 16th century by explorer Francisco Vásquez de Coronado, and an excavation site that dates from about A.D. 1300. Excavations of a Kuaua pueblo revealed a kiva whose walls were covered with murals, some of which are displayed in the park museum. Visitors can tour the partially restored 1,200-room village. *Admission charged.*

8. Santo Domingo Pueblo

A major event of this large pueblo is its annual Corn Dance, held each August, in which some 500 participants celebrate the sacred rain and fertility rite. Other festivals take place at Christmas and Easter. The pueblo is also noted for jewelry making.

9. Cochiti Dam and Cochiti Pueblo

Waters of the Santa Fe River and Rio Grande are harnessed by the 5-mile-long Cochiti Dam. A visitor center exhibits contemporary and ancient pottery crafted by the Cochiti Indians. The two distinctive water towers of the Cochiti pueblo are painted to resemble the ceremonial drums for which the Cochitis are famous.

10. Jemez State Monument

This monument pays tribute to the Jemez people and preserves the ruins of a 17th-century mission church they built at the site of the Giusewa pueblo. The church also served as a fortress, but despite walls several feet thick it was gutted during a rebellion. The pueblo's history is traced in a museum, and there are self-guided trails on the grounds. *Admission charged.*

11. Bradbury Science Museum

15th St. and Central Ave., Los Alamos. Among the high-tech exhibits here are World War II atomic bomb casings, which indicate the size of the bombs dropped on Hiroshima and Nagasaki. Documents include a 1939 letter from Albert Einstein to Franklin Roosevelt urging U.S. nuclear weapons development. A nearby cabin is home to the **Los Alamos County Historical Museum,** whose exhibits trace the early history of the Manhattan Project.

12. Bandelier National Monument

Named for 19th-century anthropologist A. F. A. Bandelier, this 50-square-mile park, set among spectacular mountains, mesas, and canyons, was the home of the Anasazi Indians from A.D. 1200 to 1500. Hiking trails wind along the base of the canyon walls, where the Anasazis created their dwellings and fashioned pictographs and petroglyphs out of soft volcanic rock. Information is available at the visitor center in **Frijoles Canyon.** Hikers who persevere along rugged trails will be rewarded with magnificent mesa-top vistas, waterfalls, and views of sheer-walled canyons. *Admission charged.*

13. San Ildefonso Pueblo

Situated in a valley beside the Rio Grande, with lavender mountains hovering in the distance, this pueblo was the home of world-famous artisan Maria Martinez, who fashioned exotic black matte pottery. The pueblo is also well known for other finely crafted pottery and artworks. *Fee charged for taking photographs.*

14. Santuario de Guadalupe

100 Guadalupe St., Santa Fe. This adobe cruciform church and museum dating from the late 18th century is the oldest shrine in the country dedicated to Our Lady of Guadalupe. The impressive altar painting depicts the 16th-century appearance of the Virgin in what is now Mexico City. The museum features a permanent collection and showcases changing exhibits.

15. Santa Fe Plaza

Santa Fe's centerpiece is this charming plaza, which is laced with flagstone walks and shaded by arching trees. The **Palace of the Governors,** on the north side of the plaza, is the oldest continuously occupied public building in America. Today it houses a museum of Southwestern history. **La Fonda Hotel,** on the southeastern corner, was one of the famed Harvey hotels. Across from La Fonda, the **Museum of Fine Arts** exhibits regional art. Nearby is the Romanesque **St. Francis Cathedral,** which was begun in 1869. A plaque on the plaza designates the end of the **Santa Fe Trail.** *Admission charged for some attractions.*

16. Loretto Chapel

211 Old Santa Fe Trail, Santa Fe. This Gothic chapel located on the Santa Fe Trail was built for the Sisters of Loretto. Legend has it that a mysterious itinerant carpenter built the 33-step **Miraculous Staircase** leading to the choir loft. Constructed without nails or any visible support, it spirals up 22 feet and makes two 360-degree turns. *Admission charged.*

17. Canyon Road

Once an Indian trail, Canyon Road is now home to many Santa Fe artists. A walking tour of about 3 miles along ancient streets leads past the **Cristo Rey Church,** reputed to be the largest adobe structure in America, with exquisite stone altar screens and walls several feet thick.

18. Museum of International Folk Art

706 Camino Lejo, Santa Fe. Housing the world's largest collection of folk art, the museum displays ceramics, textiles, jewelry, toys, and furnishings. Next door, the **Wheelwright Museum of the American Indian** contains a working trading post as well as exhibits illustrating the history of the Navajo Indians and other tribes. *Admission charged at folk art museum.*

19. Pecos National Historical Park

Some 600 years ago this site was home to 2,000 Pecos Indians, who built dwellings here four and five stories high. A trail winds through the pueblo ruins, and visitors can descend on wooden ladders to explore kivas. The ruins of an 18th-century Spanish mission can also be seen. The visitor center displays artifacts and shows a film depicting the tribe's history. *Admission charged.*

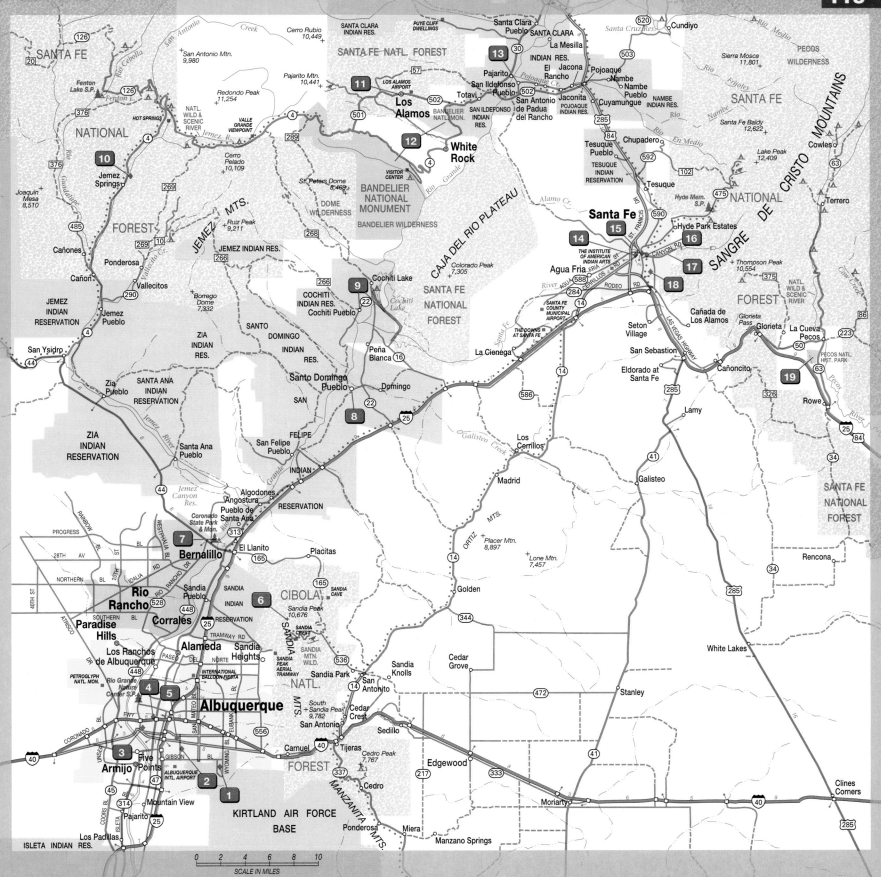

SANTA FE

126

San Antonio Creek

Cerro Rubio
10,449

SANTA CLARA
INDIAN RES.

PUYE CLIFF
DWELLINGS

Santa Clara
Pueblo

SANTA CLARA

La Mesilla

520

Santa Cruz Res.

Cundiyo

Rio Medio

20

Fenton
Lake S.P.

126

Fenton L.

376

NATIONAL

376

10

Jemez
Springs

Joaquin
Mesa
8,510

485

FOREST

269

Cañones

269

10

Ponderosa

Cañon

290

JEMEZ
INDIAN
RESERVATION

Jemez
Pueblo

San Antonio Mtn.
9,980

SANTA FE NATL. FOREST

Pajarito Mtn.
10,441

11

LOS ALAMOS
AIRPORT

Los
Alamos

Redondo Peak
11,254

Cerro
Pelado
10,109

HOT SPRINGS

VALLE
GRANDE
VIEWPOINT

NATL.
WILD &
SCENIC
RIVER

Jemez R.

4

289

JEMEZ MTS.

Ruiz Peak
9,211

DOME
WILDERNESS

268

266

JEMEZ INDIAN RES.

269

Vallecitos

Borrego
Dome
7,332

266

9

501

57

12

502

White
Rock

4

St. Peters Dome
8,463

BANDELIER
NATIONAL
MONUMENT

BANDELIER WILDERNESS

VISITOR
CENTER

Rio Grande

Santa Clara
Pueblo

13

30

INDIAN RES.

Pajarito

San Ildefonso
Pueblo

Totavi

502

SAN ILDEFONSO
INDIAN
RES.

El
Rancho

San Antonio
de Padua
del Rancho

503

Pojoaque Cr.

Pojoaque

Nambe

Nambe
Pueblo

Jaconita

Jacona

Cuyamungue

POJOAQUE
INDIAN RES.

285

Sierra Mosca
11,801

SANTA FE

Rio Frijoles

NAMBE
INDIAN RES.

84

Chupadero

Tesuque
Pueblo

592

102

TESUQUE
INDIAN
RESERVATION

Tesuque

Rio En Medio

Santa Fe Baldy
12,622

Lake Peak
12,409

475

Hyde Mem.
S.P.

590

NATIONAL

Cowles

63

Terrero

DE

CRISTO

MOUNTAINS

SANGRE

CAJA DEL RIO PLATEAU

Colorado Peak
7,305

SANTA FE

NATIONAL

FOREST

Santa Fe

15

Agua Fria

14

Hyde Park Estates

16

17

18

Thompson Peak
10,554

375

FOREST

SANGRE

86

NATL.
WILD &
SCENIC
RIVER

Cow Creek

Cochiti Lake

22

COCHITI
INDIAN RES.
Cochiti Pueblo

Cochiti
Lake

SANTO

DOMINGO

INDIAN

RES.

Peña
Blanca

16

Santa Fe River

588

284

SANTA FE
COUNTY
MUNICIPAL
AIRPORT

THE INSTITUTE
OF AMERICAN
INDIAN ARTS

CERRILLOS RD

RODEO RD

THE DOWNS
AT SANTA FE

14

Seton
Village

La Cienega

San Sebastian

Cañada de
Los Alamos

Glorieta
Pass

Cañoncito

Glorieta

La Cueva
Pecos

223

PECOS NATL.
HIST. PARK

50

63

19

Rowe

25

84

SAN

FELIPE

San Felipe
Pueblo

Santo Domingo
Pueblo

22

Domingo

8

25

586

Eldorado at
Santa Fe

285

Lamy

Galisteo Creek

Los
Cerrillos

Galisteo

41

SANTA FE

NATIONAL

FOREST

34

Rencona

ZIA
PUEBLO

Zia
Pueblo

SANTA ANA
INDIAN
RESERVATION

Santa Ana
Pueblo

ZIA

INDIAN

RESERVATION

Jemez River

44

INDIAN

Algodones

Angostura

Pueblo de
Santa Ana

Coronado
State Park
& Mon.

313

RESERVATION

Madrid

ORTIZ

Placer Mtn.
8,897

MTS.

Lone Mtn.
7,457

14

Golden

344

White Lakes

San Ysidro

Jemez
Canyon
Res.

7

El Llanito

Placitas

165

165

SANDIA
CAVE

Cedar
Grove

Stanley

44

7

Bernalillo

Rio
Rancho

528

Corrales

Alameda

Los Ranchos
de Albuquerque

PROGRESS

RAINBOW BL

WESTPHALIA BL

28TH AV

NORTHERN BL

20TH ST

IDALIA

RIO RANCHO DR

SOUTHERN BL

Paradise
Hills

40TH ST

ATRISCO DR

448

PETROGLYPH
NATL. MON.

Rio Grande
Nature
Center S.P.

PASEO DEL NORTE

SANDIA
Pueblo

SANDIA

INDIAN

RESERVATION

Sandia
Heights

CIBOLA

Sandia Peak
10,676

SANDIA CREST

S A N D I A

SANDIA
PEAK
AERIAL
TRAMWAY

Sandia
Knolls

San Antonito

Cedar
Grove

472

Stanley

Alameda

4

5

Albuquerque

CORONADO BL

COORS BL

UNSER BL

40

3

Armijo

Five
Points

45

314

47

Mountain View

Pajarito

25

ISLETA INDIAN RES.

Los Padillas

GIBSON

556

2

1

ALBUQUERQUE
INTL. AIRPORT

SAN MATEO BL

WYOMING BL

EUBANK BL

MENAUL BL

KIRTLAND AIR FORCE

BASE

International
Balloon Fiesta

TRAMWAY RD

6

SANDIA

MTN.

NATL.

Sandia Park

Cedar
Crest

536

South
Sandia Peak
9,782

San Antonio

Carnuel

Tijeras

40

Cedro Peak
7,767

FOREST

337

Cedro

Sedillo

Edgewood

333

217

Moriarty

MANZANITA MTS.

MANZANO MTS.

Ponderosa

Miera

Manzano Springs

41

Clines
Corners

40

285

0   2   4   6   8   10
SCALE IN MILES

1. Alabaster Caverns State Park

Tours are available of this sectioned, 2,300-foot-long gypsum cave, which was hollowed by underground streams over the course of 200 million years. The park's **Cedar Canyon** offers hiking trails and a swimming pool. *Fee charged for tour.*

2. Lake Meade State Park

Adjacent to rolling pastures and fields of wheat, Lake Meade is surrounded by a shady glen of cottonwood, towering elms, and berry bushes. While hiking or picnicking near the wooded areas, birdwatchers can spot native woodpeckers, owls, and Mississippi kites. *Admission charged.*

3. No Man's Land Historical Museum

Sewell St., Goodwell. The museum's name makes reference to the fact that during the era of slavery, no state would claim the land that is today's Oklahoma Panhandle. Here the area's history comes alive with displays about the age of mastodons and mammoths as well as about the devastating Dust Bowl of the 1930's.

4. Cimarron National Grassland

Established to protect native flora and fauna and to restore eroded land, this area contains more than 100,000 acres of grasses, cottonwood trees, and flowers. Here nature and technology coexist, for cattle, antlered mammals, and fowl live among windmills, oil rigs, and gas wells.

5. Black Mesa and Black Mesa State Park

Located in the Oklahoma Panhandle, the lava-topped mesa rises to an elevation of almost 5,000 feet, the highest point in the state. Huge, odd-shaped rock formations, the result of erosion, are the most prominent features in the park.

6. Ute Lake State Park

One of the largest and most popular lakes in New Mexico, Ute attracts visitors from neighboring states to fish for walleye, crap-

pie, bass, and channel catfish. The narrow lake also offers recreational opportunities to scuba divers, sailboarders, and waterskiers. *Admission charged.*

7. Tucumcari Historical Museum

416 South Adams St., Tucumcari. Visitors will find a wide range of memorabilia here, from 12,000-year-old Indian artifacts to pioneers' ranching implements. The town's roots as a railroad construction camp called Six Shooter Siding are recalled by an old sheriff's office. *Admission charged.*

8. National Cowgirl Hall of Fame and Western Heritage Center

515 Avenue B, Hereford. The Hall of Fame pays tribute to female rodeo stars and pioneers, as well as to contemporary women artists, writers, and humanitarians. The Heritage Center includes an intriguing Western art collection. *Admission charged.*

9. Panhandle–Plains Historical Museum

2401 Fourth Ave., Canyon. From dinosaur skeletons to reconstructed buildings, exhibits at this impressive museum — one of the largest in the state — celebrate the Panhandle's past. Other displays include a full-size 1925 oil drilling rig and a retrospective on fashion over the course of a century. Also in the vicinity, **Palo Duro Canyon State Park** is known as the Grand Canyon of Texas. During the summer, the musical drama *Texas* is performed nightly in the park's Pioneer Amphitheatre. *Admission charged for some attractions.*

10. Amarillo

Convention and Visitors Bureau, 1000 South Polk St. Attractions at the **Don Harrington Discovery Center** include an intriguing exhibit of a black hole, a planetarium, and a giant bubble-maker. The **Helium Monument** is said to contain the only aboveground time capsules in the world, which are slated to be opened in the next millennium. Also in this complex is the sweet-smelling **Amarillo Garden Center.** The city's **Wonderland Amusement Park** offers rides and other family entertainment. Just outside Amarillo is **Cadillac Ranch,** which has a collection of the manufacturer's cars buried nose down. *Admission charged for some attractions.*

11. Cal Farley's Boys Ranch

Rte. 385, Boys Ranch. This 10,000-acre ranch was founded in 1939 as a refuge for

troubled youths; today it benefits nearly 400 students. An abandoned town's old courthouse, once home to the ranch's first students, is now a museum with displays of pioneer and cowboy memorabilia. Student-led tours are available.

12. Lake Meredith National Recreation Area

Man-made Lake Meredith is a 21,600-acre haven for boating, swimming, and waterskiing. For anglers, the lake is stocked with walleye, bass, channel and blue catfish, perch, and crappie.

13. Alibates Flint Quarries National Monument

These shallow quarries, a rich mottle of rainbow-colored flint, were mined as long as 12,000 years ago by Indians to construct arrowheads and other weapons for hunting mammoth and buffalo. Visitors can take seasonal guided tours originating from **Bates Canyon** on Lake Meredith.

14. Carson County Square House Museum

Fifth St., Panhandle. A square wooden frame house — the oldest house in town — serves as the museum's main building. A nearby dugout is more indicative of the typical dwelling for many of this area's pioneers, who struggled against shortages of wood and water. Other displays include a railroad caboose, wildlife dioramas, and paintings by Native American artists.

15. Pioneer West Museum

204 North Madden St., Shamrock. This museum, which was once a hotel, houses memorabilia from Shamrock's pioneer past. While touring the 28 restored rooms, visitors will find displays of Plains Indian artifacts, old weapons, and cowboy gear.

16. Black Kettle Museum

Rtes. 283 and 47, Cheyenne. Black Kettle, a Cheyenne Indian chief, died defending his people against Custer's troops in 1868. The museum features artifacts from the battle as well as from the period; the battle site itself is 2 miles away on Rte. 47A. Nearby, the 31,000-acre **Black Kettle National Grassland** preserves a variety of native grasses.

17. Washita National Wildlife Refuge

Wild turkey, deer, and quail roam free through the serene wooded terrain of the northern end of Foss Lake. During the win-

Ride 'em, Cowboy: A decal bears greetings from Amarillo.

ter months, Canada geese and sandhill cranes find sanctuary within the refuge.

18. Foss Lake

This 8,800-acre reservoir draws scores of boating, fishing, and waterskiing enthusiasts. A sandy beach at the lake's northern end is ideal for swimming.

19. Old Town Museum

Rte. 66 and Pioneer Rd., Elk City. Elk City's homesteading and ranching roots are recalled at this museum through exhibits ranging from an antique wagon and one-room schoolhouse to old rodeo photographs. Several restored Victorian rooms, including a doctor's office, shed further light on the period. *Admission charged.*

20. Quartz Mountain Resort Park

Named after the towering red granite peaks of the Quartz Mountains, the park provides facilities that include campsites and picnic grounds, tennis courts and golf courses. **Lake Altus-Lugert,** nestled between the mountains, is popular for water sports. A park nature center displays plants, wildlife, and historical memorabilia.

21. Lubbock

Convention and Visitors Bureau, 14th St. and Ave. K. Attractions in town include **Buddy Holly's Statue,** which salutes Lubbock's famous native son. The **National Ranching Heritage Center** evokes the era of the cowboy through exhibits of more than 30 historic structures as well as related paraphernalia. An unexpected find, the **Llano Estacado Winery** proves that the Lone Star State can produce medal-winning wines. Archeological digs have unearthed relics that are more than 11,000 years old at the **Lubbock Lake Landmark,** which features an interpretive center and tours of the site. *Admission charged at landmark.*

MAP PG. 111

MAP PG. 209

SCALE IN MILES
0 10 20 30 40 50

1. Tijuana

International Visitor Information Center, 11 Horton Plaza, San Diego. Claiming to be the foreign city most visited by Americans, Tijuana, chaotic and colorful, is an easy day trip from San Diego. The **Tijuana Cultural Center** houses a museum and concert hall; **Mexitlán** is a unique history and entertainment park, where a variety of wares from throughout the country are sold. The **Fronton Palacio** is home to jai alai; dog racing and bullfighting are also popular events. The city has discos, nightclubs, simple sidewalk cafés, and fine restaurants that serve world-class cuisine. The nearby town of **Tecate** produces the popular beer. In July, the town has its annual Expo Tecate, which features food, games, and shows.

2. Del Mar

Known for its remarkably beautiful beaches, this little village attracts visitors who enjoy the ocean view and the many galleries, shops, and restaurants at the well-shaded plaza. The **Del Mar Thoroughbred Club,** organized in the 1930's by several Hollywood stars, is especially popular with celebrities and other well-heeled patrons who come to the track to bet on their favorite horses. *Admission charged.*

3. Encinitas

Visitor Center, 345-H First St. Nicknamed the Flower Capital of the World, Encinitas is home to the **Quail Botanical Gardens.** Here thousands of varieties of plants and flowers can be seen, including exotic tropical plants, the largest hibiscus collection on the West Coast, and the greatest number of bamboo species in the United States — all of which grow on sunny hillsides overlooking the ocean. A hike through the **San Elijo Lagoon Ecological Reserve** may reward birdwatchers with sightings of great blue herons, cinnamon teal, and sandpipers.

4. Carlsbad

Convention and Visitors Bureau, 400 Carlsbad Village Dr. Also known as the Village by the Sea, Carlsbad retains all the attractiveness of a European village, with its charming little shops, antiques galleries, old-world architecture, a well-known spa, and superb hotels and restaurants. The **Alt Karlsbad** building houses an interesting museum that traces the history of the town with charming memorabilia; the highlight among its exhibits is the mineral-water well that made Carlsbad famous. The well, which fell into disuse after the Depression, was rediscovered by the museum's founders and restored to a depth of 40 feet.

5. Antique Gas and Steam Engine Museum

2040 North Santa Fe Ave., Vista. Set amid 40 acres of pretty farmland, this agricultural museum exhibits antique farming implements and old-time engines; special shows are featured each October and June. *Admission charged at shows.*

6. Escondido

Convention and Visitors Bureau, 720 North Broadway. In the **Lawrence Welk Museum,** housed in the theater lobby of a resort community that bears the famed bandleader's name, there is a wealth of Welk memorabilia. Attractions of the **Escondido Heritage Walk** include an 1888 Santa Fe railroad depot and a blacksmith's shop. At the **San Diego Wild Animal Park,** visitors can see more than 2,400 animals. *Admission charged for some attractions.*

7. San Pasqual Battlefield State Historic Park

Rte. 78, east of Escondido. Interpretive displays and a short filmstrip in the museum of this 50-acre park relate the story of the Battle of San Pasqual, fought in 1846 between Mexican and American forces. The engagement took the lives of 22 Americans and left another 16 wounded. The park is laced with nature walks and hiking trails, and there are also picnic facilities.

8. Mission Santa Ysabel

Rte. 79, near Santa Ysabel. An ancient American Indian burial ground, a museum, and church walls decorated with murals are among the sights awaiting visitors at Mission Santa Ysabel. The mission has been ministering to the spiritual needs of three Native American reservations since its founding in 1818. *Donation encouraged.*

9. Mount Laguna Recreation Area

The Sunrise Highway winds upward through the chaparral-carpeted Laguna Mountains to the 8,600-acre **Cleveland National Forest.** From the information center here, a footpath strewn with pine needles leads a short distance to the **Mount Laguna Observatory,** which yields lovely vistas of the surrounding mountains. To the north, the campground area is situated in a lush setting. Local lore can be soaked up in the tiny town of **Mount Laguna,** which offers visitors a general store, a few restaurants, and limited overnight facilities.

Colorful crafts across the Mexican border

10. Julian

Chamber of Commerce, 2133 Main St. Noted today for apple growing, the rustic mountain retreat of Julian was once a thriving gold-boom town in the 1870's. Antique shops and homey restaurants line its wooden sidewalks; historic photographs and artifacts can be seen at the **Julian Pioneer Museum.** The pretty **Julian Hotel** is the oldest operating hotel in Southern California. Guided tours of the abandoned **Eagle and High Peak Mines** are replete with tall tales and antique autos. *Admission charged for some attractions.*

11. Cuyamaca Rancho State Park

Cuyamaca Peak, which reaches an elevation of 6,515 feet, is a prominent feature of this 25,000-acre park, where lush stands of oak and conifer are home to a variety of birds. Gray foxes, coyotes, and other wildlife inhabit the park's chaparral-covered slopes and meadows, and horseback-riding and hiking trails lead visitors alongside a river to lookouts with magnificent vistas. The nearby lake is well stocked with trout, and the park provides camping and picnicking facilities. *Admission charged.*

12. San Diego Railroad Museum

916 Sheridan Rd., Campo. Rides in restored cars of the San Diego and Arizona Railway are a popular attraction of the museum. Some 85 examples of antique "iron horses" and other rolling stock can be seen at this

Ranunculus flower fields bloom near Encinitas, known as the Flower Capital of the World.

main facility of the Pacific Southwest Railway. *Fee charged for rides.*

13. Desert View Tower

Rte. 8, near Jacumba. This five-story stone tower was erected in 1922 to commemorate the pioneers who first settled the area. On a clear day, the tower affords visitors sweeping views of the **Coyote Mountains.** A museum located on the grounds features exhibits that include Western paintings and American Indian artifacts. Also in the area are shallow caves with animal carvings incised on boulders and an outdoor rock garden to explore. *Admission charged.*

14. Ocotillo Wells
State Vehicular Recreation Area

During World War II, General Patton's troops trained here to prepare for action in the deserts of North Africa. The 14,000-acre site is now the domain of dune buggy and cycle buffs. With names like Devil's Slide and Blow Sand Hill, the dunes and buttes make for exciting rides. Facilities are few, but there is a camping area; supplies are available in nearby **Ocotillo Wells.**

15. Salton Sea
National Wildlife Refuge

This wildlife preserve, located in the Imperial Valley, is the southernmost refuge of the Pacific Flyway. Thousands of migrating birds nest here during the winter; black-necked stilts, green-winged teal, and white pelicans are among the species that have been spotted. Boat-fishing is permitted in certain sections of the 380-square-mile

Salton Sea; there is also an observation tower and walking and hiking trails that lead visitors through the surrounding area.

16. Calipatria

The largest irrigation system in the Western Hemisphere can be seen on a drive through this rural area. Other sights include the **U.S. Fish and Wildlife Refuge,** where the viewing is best in the early morning and evening hours. Rock hounds should head for the **Cargo Muchacho** and **Chocolate mountains.**

17. Imperial

Chamber of Commerce, 101 East Fourth St. With some 4,600 acres of natural playground, Imperial County has much to offer enthusiasts of the great outdoors. Golfing, rock hunting, rafting, water-skiing, and off-roading on daunting dunes are but a few of the many activities available here. The **Imperial County Historical Society,** located at **Imperial Valley College,** displays photographs, artifacts, and farm machinery from the area.

18. El Centro

Visitors Bureau, 1100 Main St. El Centro will appeal to aficionados both of antiques and history. It's home to **Alford's Antique Car Museum,** which has a fine display of vintage automobiles, and to **Ryerson's,** a concrete manufacturer whose lobby displays artifacts, antique stoves, and wool spinners. The **Imperial Valley College Barker Museum of Prehistory** casts an eye on the more distant past.

A great horned owl tests its wings at the San Diego Wild Animal Park in Escondido.

19. Mexicali

Calzada Independencia 1199, Centro Civico. Shopping is a major draw for the capital of northern Baja California. Handmade jewelry, rugs, and pottery are among the items sold here. The city has excellent Chinese restaurants, and food fairs take place in June, September, and November. The **Mexicali Zoo** is in the center of town. It's best to visit the city beginning in September, as summers are extremely hot.

20. Imperial Sand Dunes

California's largest mass of sand dunes stretches for more than 40 miles over the

Imperial Valley. With dunes rising more than 300 feet above the desert floor, the ever-shifting sands created a natural obstacle for early explorers. In 1915 the first Plank Road was laid, an engineering marvel that provided motorists with a jarring ride across the treacherous desert. Ruins of the long-abandoned roadway may be seen at the west end of **Gray's Well Road;** a monument and interpretative display are about 3 miles west of the Sand Hills interchange. Scorchingly hot in the summer, the area draws tens of thousands of off-road vehicle buffs between October and May.

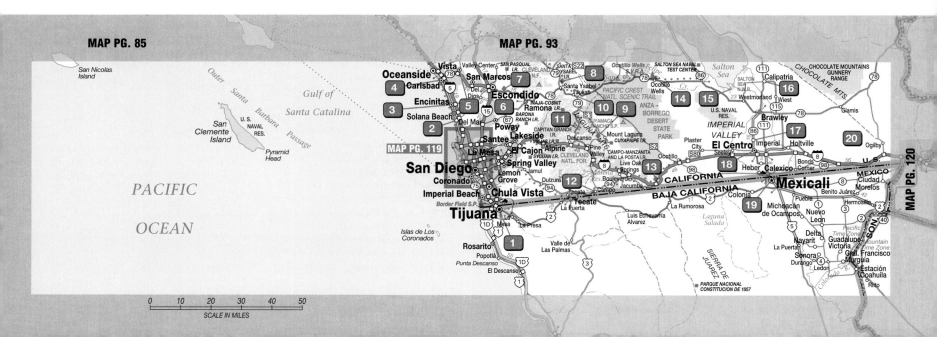

SAN DIEGO

1. 59-Mile Scenic Drive

This round-trip route, which is well marked by yellow-and-blue signs of seagulls, traverses the San Diego area, passing Point Loma, Shelter Island, Old Town, and many more of the city's highlights. It reaches the top of **Soledad Mountain,** from which visitors have a wonderful view.

2. Cabrillo National Monument

Named in honor of Juan Rodríguez Cabrillo, the Portuguese explorer who landed here in 1542, the great windswept headland at the entrance to San Diego Bay is a popular gathering spot for whale watchers, who come in late December to see the annual migration of the giant mammals from arctic waters to southern climes. Views of this event are also excellent from **Sunset Cliffs Park,** which is located farther up the coast. The **Old Point Loma Lighthouse,** now replaced by a modern structure, has been restored and is open to visitors. *Admission charged for some attractions.*

3. Shelter Island

A man-made strip of land just offshore in the harbor, the island is known for its marinas, its world-class resorts and motels, and its restaurants and shops. It is also the center of yacht building in the city. Along the waterfront, which is fringed with soaring palm trees, fishermen launch their crafts and visitors enjoy the grassy picnic areas.

4. Harbor Island

The high-rise buildings on this peninsula, which was created by tons of rocks and soil dredged from the harbor, overlook the water and the area's many shops and restaurants. Gardens and pathways, interspersed with several picnic areas, border the shore. **Tom Ham's Lighthouse,** a neighborhood restaurant, assists the harbor traffic with its handsome Coast Guard–approved beacon.

5. Maritime Museum Association

1306 North Harbor Dr., San Diego. Three ships make up the museum: the *Star of India,* a bark built on the Isle of Man in 1863; the steam yacht *Medea;* and the *Berkeley,* an 1898 ferry, which contains exhibits of various nautical artifacts. All three have been restored and are open to visitors, who may also enjoy the many fish markets and restaurants that line the waterfront here. Whale-watching cruises depart from these docks. *Admission charged.*

6. Gaslamp Quarter

This beautifully restored area of handsome commercial Victorian buildings, now designated a national historic district, was the center of town at the turn of the century. Today its tree-lined streets are bustling again with attractive shops, art galleries, and restaurants. Visitors can take a walking tour of the quarter beginning at a 19th-century restored saltbox known as the **William Heath Davis House.** *Fee charged for tour.*

Koala bears at the San Diego Zoo

7. Coronado

Located on a peninsula that extends into San Diego Harbor, Coronado boasts wide boulevards and fine Victorian mansions. The area is best known for the luxurious **Hotel del Coronado** — affectionately called The Del — which opened in 1888. The 691-room structure, with its ornate gingerbread trim and numerous domes, has housed royalty and celebrities from around the world. It is now designated a national historic landmark.

8. San Diego Aerospace Museum and International Aerospace Hall of Fame

2001 Pan American Plaza, Balboa Park. Located in an unusual round structure, which is outlined by blue neon light after dark, this outstanding museum features displays about the history of aviation and space. Its large collection of aircraft includes some 65 vintage planes and 700 scale models — from a replica of the Wright Flyer, biplanes, and flying boats to supersonic jets and a former spy plane that holds the world speed record. Pioneers in the field are honored in the Hall of Fame. *Admission charged.*

9. Balboa Park Visitor Center

1549 El Prado, Balboa Park. Located in the House of Hospitality, the center surrounds a charming Spanish patio and fountain. The garden, bright with flowers and shaded by eucalyptus trees, is often chosen by couples as the setting for their weddings.

10. Casa de Balboa

1649 El Prado, Balboa Park. Two notable museums are housed in this historic building: the **San Diego Hall of Champions,** whose large collection of photographs and paintings honors famous athletes, and the **Museum of Photographic Art,** which features the works of many well-known photographers and explains the history of this art form. The nearby **Organ Pavilion** contains the magnificent Spreckels Organ, a 5,000-pipe instrument. Concerts are occasionally given in the pavilion on Sunday afternoons. *Admission charged.*

11. Reuben H. Fleet Space Theater and Science Center

1875 El Prado, Balboa Park. Exceptionally beautiful films on nature and space exploration are shown daily at the theater. Displays at the Science Center include demonstrations of several basic scientific principles, which most children find fascinating. *Admission charged.*

12. San Diego Natural History Museum

1788 El Prado, Balboa Park. Known for its unusually large collection of indigenous flora and fauna from Southern California and Baja California, the museum also features dinosaur exhibits, which are especially enjoyed by children. The museum displays a variety of gemstones and crystals, and offers activities that include lectures and nature hikes. *Admission charged.*

13. Timken Museum of Art

1500 El Prado, Balboa Park. Works by the Old Masters, 18th- and 19th-century American art, and a fine collection of Russian icons are displayed at this private gallery. Guided tours of the museum are offered.

14. San Diego Zoo

2920 Zoo Dr., Balboa Park. This extraordinary collection of nearly 4,000 animals, including rare Przewalski's horses from Mongolia, koala bears, tigers, and painted storks, is showcased among teeming tropical gardens. The 100-acre zoo displays many of the animals in bar-free, moated enclosures and features exhibits in which the animals' natural habitats are painstakingly re-created. Open-sided buses, traveling sidewalks, and an aerial tram allow visitors easy transport around this world-famous park. *Admission charged.*

15. San Diego Museum of Art

1450 El Prado, Balboa Park. Paintings by many Old Masters, as well as Southern California's largest collection of contemporary works by California artists, are displayed in this outstanding museum. The changing exhibits often feature selections from a broad range of internationally acclaimed artists. Visitors may also walk through the museum's sculpture garden, which includes works by Henry Moore and Alexander Calder. *Admission charged.*

16. Museum of Man

1350 El Prado, Balboa Park. Known for one of the country's most extensive collections of anthropological and archeological articles, this museum, which expanded out of a 1915 exposition entitled the Story of Man, has holdings of some 70,000 objects, including many fine examples of the basketry and pottery of Southern California. Other exhibits emphasize the cultures of the Southwest, Mexico, and South America, where the museum sponsors ongoing research expeditions. *Admission charged.*

17. Old Town

Life in San Diego originally centered on a mission and a fortress on Presidio Hill. Soldiers began farming the lands below, forming a settlement called Old Town. Now restored, the old plaza area is once again full of activity, with shops and restaurants proliferating in many of the refurbished original buildings. In the vicinity, the **Junípero Serra Museum** recounts Old Town's history. *Admission charged.*

18. Mission Bay

Visitor Center, 2688 East Mission Bay Dr.
Called San Diego's center for sports, fitness, and other outdoor activities, Mission Bay offers miles of bayside beaches and many oceanside trails. Brochures and sightseeing suggestions are available at the visitor center. The area is home to **Sea World,** the largest park in the world devoted to marine life, where the famous killer whale Shamu can be seen. The park also features shows in which a variety of aquatic animals perform. **Sea World Drive,** a 5-mile route popular with joggers, winds through gardens and picnic grounds along the water. *Admission charged at Sea World.*

19. La Jolla

Set on tree-covered hills rising above the curving ocean coastline, this well-known area of luxurious homes, elegant hotels and resorts, and superior surfing beaches is frequented by some of the world's greatest celebrities. **Ellen Browning Scripps Park,** filled with great stands of palm trees, wraps around a cove, offering magnificent views of the Pacific. On a nearby hillside, the **Scripps Institute of Oceanography** has an aquarium featuring many kinds of saltwater fish and an exhibit that explains the action of the tides. An outdoor tidal pool contains marine life found in local waters. *Admission charged at institute.*

20. Torrey Pines State Reserve and State Beach

Named for the rare pine tree that grows only here and on Santa Rosa Island, the reserve attracts visitors who come to enjoy the sandy beach and the many trails that wind upward to rocky bluffs overlooking the sea. Dolphins are often seen in these waters, and from December through March, gray whales can be spotted too. *Fee charged for parking.*

21. Mission Basilica San Diego de Alcala

10818 San Diego Mission Rd., San Diego.
Services are still held at this mission, established in 1769. Its inner sanctuary of gardens and shrines is enclosed by tall white walls. The simple decor of the church interior and the friars' rooms provide a dramatic contrast to the elaborate religious vestments that are displayed in the little mission museum. The garden's wishing well, according to legend, brings answers to one's prayers. *Donation encouraged.*

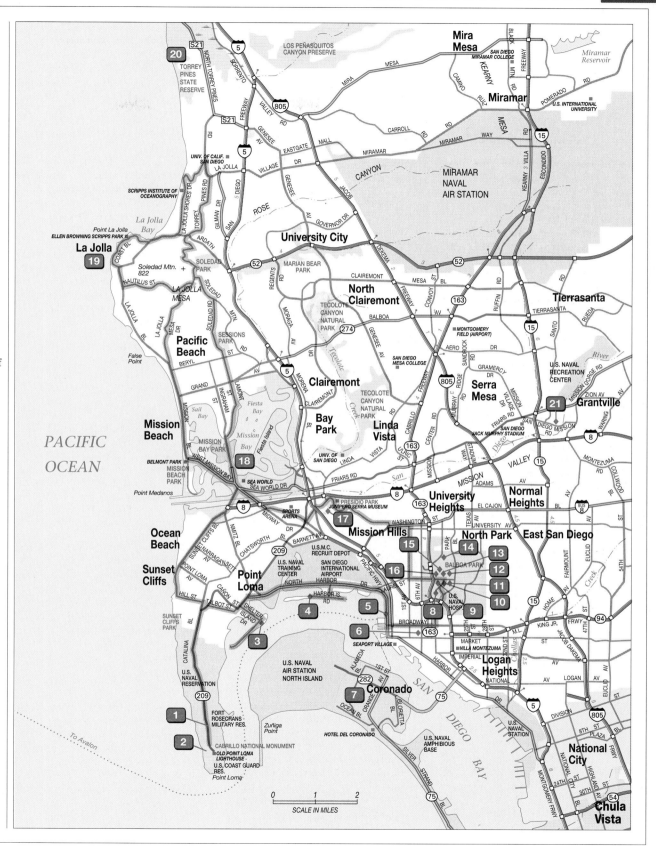

1. Quechan Reservation

Pioneers sought refuge in **Fort Yuma,** now the headquarters of the Quechan Indians. Each March the Quechans host an intertribal powwow. The area's oldest settlement also has a charming Spanish mission. *Admission charged.*

2. Yuma

Chamber of Commerce, 377 South Main St. Here boat tours and train rides along the Colorado River are popular excursions; desert trails beckon hikers and horseback riders. The **Arizona Historical Society Century House Museum and Gardens** evokes turn-of-the-century Yuma, while the **Yuma Quartermaster Depot** is one of Arizona's oldest structures. **Yuma Territorial Prison State Historic Park** was built by convicts between 1876 and 1909; a reconstruction of the mess hall today houses a museum. *Admission charged for some attractions.*

3. Painted Rock Petroglyph Campground

These huge black boulders were a landmark for pioneers traveling the Mormon Battalion Trail in the 1840's. Petroglyphs on the rocks dating back 1,000 years can be seen from a walkway; picnic areas and campsites are available.

4. Casa Grande Valley Historical Society Museum

110 West Florence Blvd., Casa Grande. Exhibits set in an old stone building that was once a church bring to life the colorful history of the region. *Admission charged.*

5. Picacho Peak State Park

The largest Civil War battle fought in Arizona is commemorated in this 3,440-acre park. A scenic drive winds around the base of **Picacho Peak,** a steep, 2-mile hiking trail leads to the top, and there are picnic sites and campgrounds within the park. *Admission charged.*

6. Biosphere 2

The Biosphere 2 project was inaugurated in 1991, when an eight-member crew and some 3,800 species of animals, insects, and plants were sealed within a 3-acre domed enclosure. It is a miniature world of seven ecosystems. Tour programs allow visitors to observe the biosphere and interact with the crew members through state-of-the-art video technology. *Admission charged.*

7. Kitt Peak National Observatory

Set at 6,882 feet in the **Quinlan Mountains,** this facility has the world's largest solar telescope, as well as the world's largest collection of optical telescopes. There is a visitor center and museum.

8. Tohono O'odham Nation Reservation

The Tohono O'odham farm, raise cattle, and make handsome baskets on this 3-million-acre reservation. Adobe villages are sprinkled throughout the area. The town of **Sells** is the tribal headquarters. Visitors are welcome at the Feast of St.

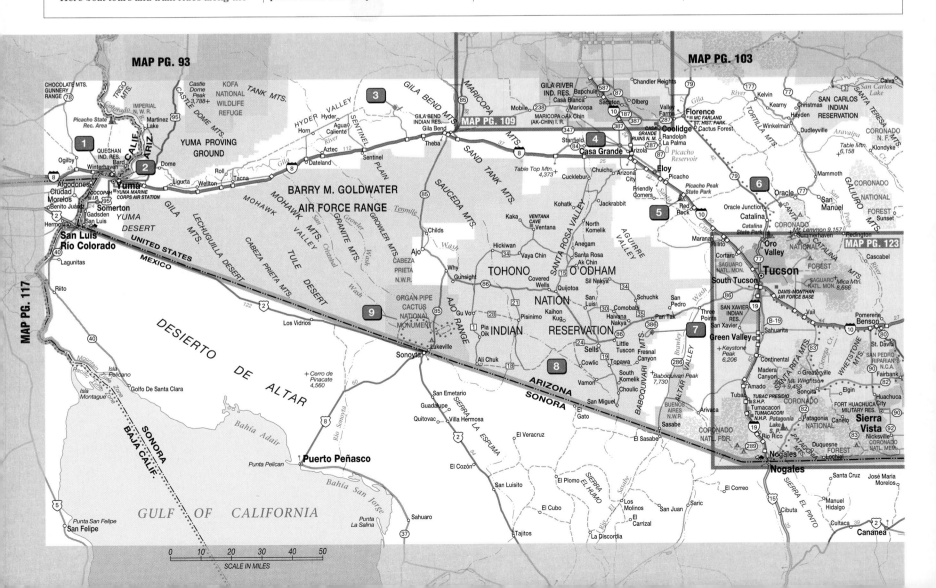

Francis in October, and at the All-Indian Rodeo and Fair, held each February. Near Santa Rosa is the **Children's Shrine,** where according to legend children were once sacrificed to stop a great flood. At the **Ventana Cave,** excavations have revealed evidence of human life 10,000 years ago; two of the caverns are open for tours.

9. Organ Pipe Cactus National Monument

This 330,000-acre Sonoran Desert site is named for a cactus whose slender stems stretch up to 20 feet. Nearly 30 species of cactus grow in this unspoiled desert, which in spring and summer is dotted with wildflowers. The 21-mile **Ajo Mountain Drive** and the 53-mile **Puerto Blanco Drive** are both scenic roads through the site. *Admission charged.*

10. Museum of the Southwest

1500 North Circle I Rd., Willcox. Southwestern artifacts are exhibited in this information center and museum. The nearby **Rex Allen Arizona Cowboy Museum** honors the town's native son with a showcase of his memorabilia. *Admission charged at cowboy museum.*

11. Pearce

Once the site of the richest gold mine in southern Arizona, Pearce was abandoned in the 1930's. Some buildings remain, and remnants of the mine can also be seen.

12. Chiricahua National Monument

A scenic 6-mile drive through canyon country leads up to **Massai Point,** where a building contains displays explaining the natural creation of the **Chiricahua Mountains.** Named for the Chiricahua

Apaches, the mountains rise to heights of more than 7,000 feet. There are hiking trails and picnic and camping facilities.

13. Silver City Museum

312 West Broadway, Silver City. This 1881 Victorian house was the home of prospector H. B. Ailman, who struck it rich in the 1870's. The rooms display articles including period furnishings, musical instruments, and photographs.

14. Kingston

In this gateway to **Gila National Forest,** the old bank houses local memorabilia. Visitors can hunt for fossils and crystals in the woods of the once-thriving boomtown.

15. Rock Hound State Park

This 250-acre park has special appeal for those who love to search the earth for

semiprecious stones. Visitors provide their own equipment and are permitted to take away 20 pounds per visit. A visitor center exhibits the minerals that can be found. *Admission charged.*

16. Sunspot Highway

This 15-mile scenic stretch of Rte. 6563 winds along the front rim of the breathtaking **Sacramento Mountains,** where black bears, mule deer, elk, eagles, and spotted owls dwell. From roadway lookouts visitors can see the **White Sands National Monument;** on a clear day the space shuttle landing port is also visible. The mountains offer many recreational opportunities, including hiking and camping. The **Sacramento Peak Solar Observatory,** at the end of the road, is open to the public for self-guided tours. *Admission charged for some attractions.*

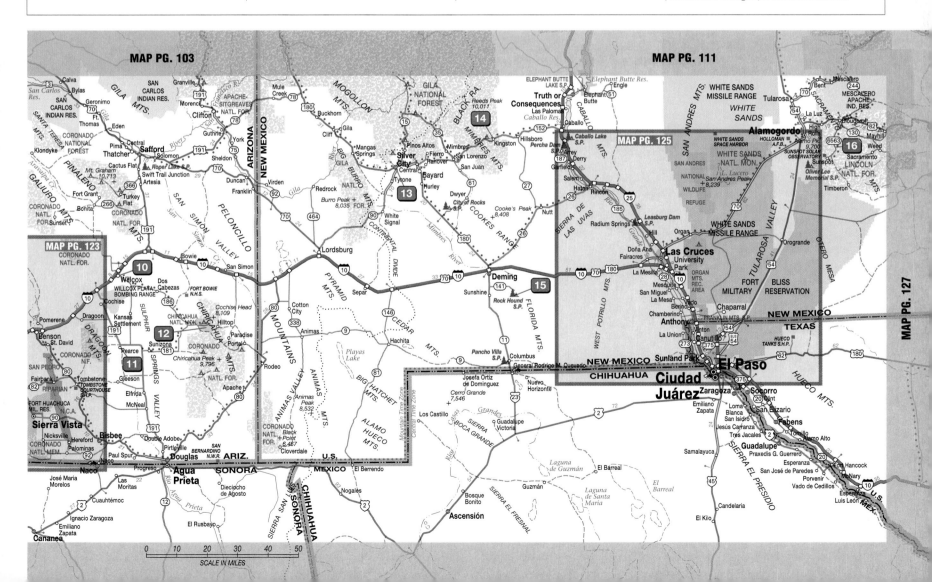

1. Nogales

Chamber of Commerce, Kino Park. Just across the border from the Mexican Nogales, this city is the home of the **Pimería Alta Historical Society Museum,** which depicts the history of southern Arizona and northern Sonora. Guided tours of both sides of the border are offered. Nogales, Mexico, is a colorful and popular market town, where visitors can find many kinds of native crafts.

2. Tumacacori National Historical Park

Off Rte. 19, Tumacacori. Construction of the mission church here was begun in the early 1800's, although the mission's history in the area dates as far back as 1691. A nearby museum features dioramas and paintings that depict both the cultures of ancient Indian tribes and early mission life. *Admission charged.*

3. Tubac

Established in the 1750's as a garrison to protect local missions from Apache attacks, the village of Tubac is now a flourishing art center, with many shops and studios. In **Tubac Presidio State Historic Park,** visitors can see the foundation and lower walls of the commandant's quarters, along with the **Old Tubac School,** dating back to 1885. Next door is **El Presidio de Tubac Archaeological Park,** which includes the ruins of many of the town's original buildings. *Admission charged at state park.*

4. Titan Missile Museum

Off Duval Mine Rd., Green Valley. During the Cold War, these projectiles and their launching complexes were kept loaded and ready to be fired at a moment's notice; they were deactivated starting in 1982. All the complexes were destroyed except this one, which is maintained as a museum. Guided tours include visits into the underground silo, which can also be observed from ground level. Reservations are suggested. *Admission charged.*

5. Mission San Xavier del Bac

1950 West San Xavier Rd., south of Tucson. Built in the desert in the late 1700's in a curious blend of Spanish, Moorish, and Mexican baroque styles, the handsomely towered and domed mission serves the Tohono O'odham Indians today.

6. Old Tucson Studios

201 South Kinney Rd., Tucson. This replica of an Old West town was built in 1939 for the film *Arizona.* Since then it has been used as the background for many movies and TV films. Visitors can ride in a stagecoach, take a brief trip on a narrow-gauge railroad, and see daily performances that may include gunfights, stunt shows, and a musical revue. *Admission charged.*

7. Arizona-Sonora Desert Museum

2021 North Kinney Rd., Tucson. Hundreds of species of desert plants and animals are presented here in real or unusually realistic man-made habitats, including a zoo, a botanical garden, an enormous aviary, and a cave. *Admission charged.*

8. Saguaro National Monument, West

Towering saguaros punctuate the peaks and rolling hills of this section of the monument. An unpaved 6-mile loop drive leads around one of the thickest saguaro stands in the country, and there are 15 miles of hiking trails. *Admission charged.*

9. John C. Frémont House

151 South Granada Ave., Tucson. This restored adobe home was the official residence of John C. Frémont, territorial governor during the late 1800's.

10. Tucson Museum of Art

140 North Main Ave., Tucson. Located in **El Presidio Historic District,** this museum features collections of pre-Columbian, Western, and contemporary American art. On the grounds, **La Casa Cordova,** a restored adobe structure dating from 1850, houses the **Mexican Heritage Museum.** *Admission charged.*

11. Arizona Historical Society Museum

949 East Second St., Tucson. Exhibits that include a stagecoach, an ox cart, rooms with period furnishings, and 19th-century mining equipment trace Arizona's history from Spanish colonial days to the present.

12. University of Arizona

Visitors to the Tucson campus can tour the **Arizona State Museum,** with its collection of Southwest Indian artifacts; the **Museum of Art,** which exhibits Renaissance, baroque, and contemporary works; the **Flandrau Science Center and Planetarium;** and the **John P. Schaefer Center for Creative Photography,** whose archives contain memorabilia of famous photographers.

Cactus in bloom at the Desert Museum

13. Fort Lowell

Craycroft and Ft. Lowell Rds., Tucson. Built a century ago as protection for Tucson during the Apache wars, today the fort is a museum surrounded by a park. Hiking and bicycling trails lead into the desert landscape of the **Sabino Canyon Recreation Area,** which also offers visitors shuttle-bus service but is otherwise closed to vehicles. *Fee charged for bus.*

14. Pima Air Museum

6000 East Valencia Rd., Tucson. The history of American aviation is recorded in this collection of some 180 aircraft, ranging from a replica of the 1903 Wright Flyer to the latest aircraft designs. *Admission charged.*

15. Saguaro National Monument, East

An 8-mile scenic drive winds through a forest of older saguaros. One of the largest saguaros in the world — more than 52 feet tall, with 56 arms — can be seen on a 12-mile hike. Trails ascend the nearby Rincon Mountains. *Admission charged.*

16. Colossal Cave

Extending for several miles under the **Rincon Mountains,** this great cavern was formed millions of years ago by the ocean that once covered the surrounding desert. On a guided tour, visitors can see the cave's beautifully colored rooms encrusted with crystal; the site served at various times as an Indian refuge and a hideout for bandits. *Fee charged for tour.*

17. Amerind Foundation

Off Dragoon Rd., Dragoon. Dedicated to the study of the American Indian, this foundation, housed in a Spanish Colonial building in a rocky canyon, exhibits artifacts from its archeological digs, dance costumes, and the crafts of various tribes. Next door an art gallery displays paintings by both Western and Native American artists. *Admission charged.*

18. Tombstone

Visitor Center, 345 East Allen St. Prospector Ed Schieffelin arrived here in 1877 in search of silver, and the town of Tombstone was born. The scene of the shoot-out at the O.K. Corral between the Clanton and McLowry brothers on one side and the Earp brothers and "Doc" Holliday on the other, the town has been designated a national historic landmark.

19. Ramsey Canyon Preserve

Bird lovers flock to this preserve to see many kinds of birds, including 14 species of hummingbirds. An unusually large variety of butterflies can also be spotted here. Reservations are required.

20. Coronado National Memorial

This 4,800-acre mountainous park commemorates Francisco Vásquez de Coronado, who explored the Southwest from 1540 to 1542 in search of the legendary Seven Cities of Gold. Visitors can follow hiking trails to **Coronado Peak,** which offers a panoramic view of the dramatic countryside.

21. Bisbee

Chamber of Commerce, Naco Rd. and O.K. St. An active mining center until 1975, Bisbee features the **Mule Pass Tunnel,** a 1,400-foot road cut through a mountainside; the **Bisbee Mining and Historical Museum,** which displays pioneer artifacts and mining equipment; the **Copper Queen Hotel,** a 1902 building still in operation; and the **Bisbee Restoration Association Museum,** which recounts the history of the town. Guided tours take visitors past the **Lavender Pit,** an open-pit mine, and down into the **Queen Mine.** *Admission charged for some attractions.*

1. Fort Selden State Monument

Off Rte. 25, north of Las Cruces. Only the walls remain today of this fort on the Rio Grande, which was built in 1865 to protect the settlers from Apache attacks. The history of the fort, where black troops known as Buffalo Soldiers were stationed, is told at the visitor center. Gen. Douglas MacArthur lived at the fort as a child from 1884 to 1886. *Admission charged.*

2. Leasburg Dam State Park

Extending along the Rio Grande, the park offers swimming at a sandy beach, picnicking in the shade by the water, and fishing below the dam. A short trail winds up to the top of a bluff overlooking the river as it flows through the desert on its way to the dam. *Admission charged.*

3. El Camino Real

Conquistadors, Spanish colonists, early traders, and the U.S. military all followed this great royal road, which ran from Santa Fe to Mexico City until the 1880's. Today highway markers indicate the ancient roadway; many are in the Las Cruces area along routes 25 and 10. Near Radium Springs, a remnant of the road can be seen etched in the landscape; directions to the site are available at Ft. Selden.

4. La Mesilla

With many of its early adobe buildings surrounding the plaza, this charming historic town once harbored the outlaw Billy the Kid, who was sentenced to death here. The **Gadsden Museum,** named for the purchase that made much of the nearby area part of the United States, features the original jail cell that held the Kid during his trial. *Admission charged.*

5. New Mexico State University

Located in Las Cruces, the campus features the **New Mexico State University Museum,** which offers exhibits, lectures, and films. The Las Cruces Symphony presents concerts at the music center. Astronomy buffs come to the **Clyde Tombaugh Observatory,** which is open to visitors one night a month, and golfers enjoy the university's excellent 18-hole course. *Admission charged for some attractions.*

6. Aguirre Spring Recreation Site

Set in the Organ Mountains, whose rocky landscape has been eroded to form organ pipe–like shapes, the area offers scenic hiking trails, horseback riding, campsites, and picnic areas. *Admission charged.*

7. White Sands Missile Range

Here in 1945, at what is called **Trinity Site,** the first atomic bomb was exploded. Preserved as a national historic landmark, the site is open to the public twice a year. In 1982, the Space Shuttle Columbia made a historic landing at the missile range.

8. Ranger Peak Aerial Tramway

Rising skyward 2,000 feet, the glass-enclosed cable car rises slowly to the top of the Rocky Mountains. From the summit visitors can enjoy the unbelievably beautiful view of Mexico and the United States, with the Rio Grande flowing between them.

9. University of Texas at El Paso

Founded in 1914, the university is known for its **Sun Bowl Stadium,** which seats 52,000, and for its **Centennial Museum,** which focuses on the natural and cultural history of the Southwest and Mexico.

10. El Paso Museum of Art

1211 Montana Ave., El Paso. Located in an elegant mansion, the museum features the collection of Samuel H. Kress, which traces the works of the European masters from the 1300's to the 1800's. The American collection contains a Gilbert Stuart portrait of George Washington and Frederic Remington's *Sign of Friendship.* The museum also has many changing exhibits and special shows.

11. Ciudad Juárez

Known for its great array of shops, this vibrant city annually attracts thousands of visitors from the United States, who walk across the bridge from El Paso. Exhibits at the **Museum of Art,** located in the center of the shopping district, range from pre-Columbian to contemporary. The city also boasts a **Museum of Archeology** in Chamizal Park, which features excellent replicas of pre-Columbian sculpture. *Admission charged at art museum.*

12. Magoffin Home State Historic Site

1120 Magoffin Ave., El Paso. Built in 1875, the handsome sunbaked adobe mansion has a Greek Revival style typical of the late 19th century. Six rooms of the restored home are decorated with their original furnishings, which include a bed with a 13-foot canopy and an intricately carved 1870's Knabe piano. *Admission charged.*

13. Tigua Reservation

The Tigua Indians, an ancient tribe said to date back as far as 1500 B.C., have a cultural center at their reservation, where they perform tribal dances and present exhibits that tell of their history and display their many crafts. Also located on the reservation is the **Ysleta Mission.** Dating from 1682, this well-preserved mission is the oldest in Texas; crops are still grown on the surrounding land. *Admission charged at dance performances.*

14. Fort Bliss

Rte. 54, El Paso. The reconstructed fort, a series of adobe structures, recounts the history of the stronghold from its 1848 founding to the present. The **Fort Bliss Museum** depicts the early life of the fort. Historical dioramas are featured at the **U.S. Army Air Defense Artillery Museum.** The history of the army from the time of the Revolution until today is presented at the U.S. Army **Museum of the Noncommissioned Officer,** while the **3rd Cavalry Museum** explores the Regiment of the Mounted Rifleman.

A modern marker recalls a historic route.

15. Hueco Tanks State Historical Park

Natural depressions in this rocky landscape serve as reservoirs, catching rainwater that in former times saved the lives of many travelers who had crossed the deserts while heading west. Many of the California-bound goldrushers inscribed their names on the rocks, alongside the Indian pictographs that were created there hundreds of years earlier.

16. Oliver Lee Memorial State Park

Mountain climbers, photographers, and students of history come to this scenic landscape, whose 2,000-foot bluffs contrast vividly with the extensive groves of cottonwoods. Once an Apache-held area and the site of several battles, the park today offers campgrounds, hiking trails, and tours of a restored ranch house. *Admission charged.*

17. Lincoln National Forest

This great expanse of forestland, known as the birthplace of Smokey Bear, extends through more than 1 million acres of the **Sacramento, Capitan,** and **Guadalupe mountains.** With landscapes that range from desertlike terrain to 11,000-foot subalpine peaks, its vegetation varies from cacti to evergreens. The forest has many trails, including one to **Mill Ridge,** popular with hang gliders; **Railroad Trestle Trail,** with its view of the historic cloud-climbing railroad route; and **Cathey Vista Trail,** which reaches an elevation of 9,500 feet. Camping, picnicking, fishing, hunting, and various winter sports are available throughout the forest.

18. Space Center

Off Rte. 70, Alamogordo. Set in a somewhat desolate, moonlike landscape, the center houses the International Space Hall of Fame. Displays include space capsules, rockets, and lunar vehicles. Visitors can inspect the inside of a space station and purchase dried food typical of that eaten by the astronauts in space. An Omnimax theater offers startlingly beautiful films. *Admission charged.*

19. White Sands National Monument

Formed by gypsum carried down by rains and snows from the surrounding mountains, this vast, brilliantly white area of sand dunes is shaped by the winds. The wraithlike drifts that sometimes can be seen are said to be Spanish maidens searching for their lost lovers. Hiking and driving trails wind through the national monument, whose geology is explained at the visitor center. Picnic areas are also provided. *Admission charged.*

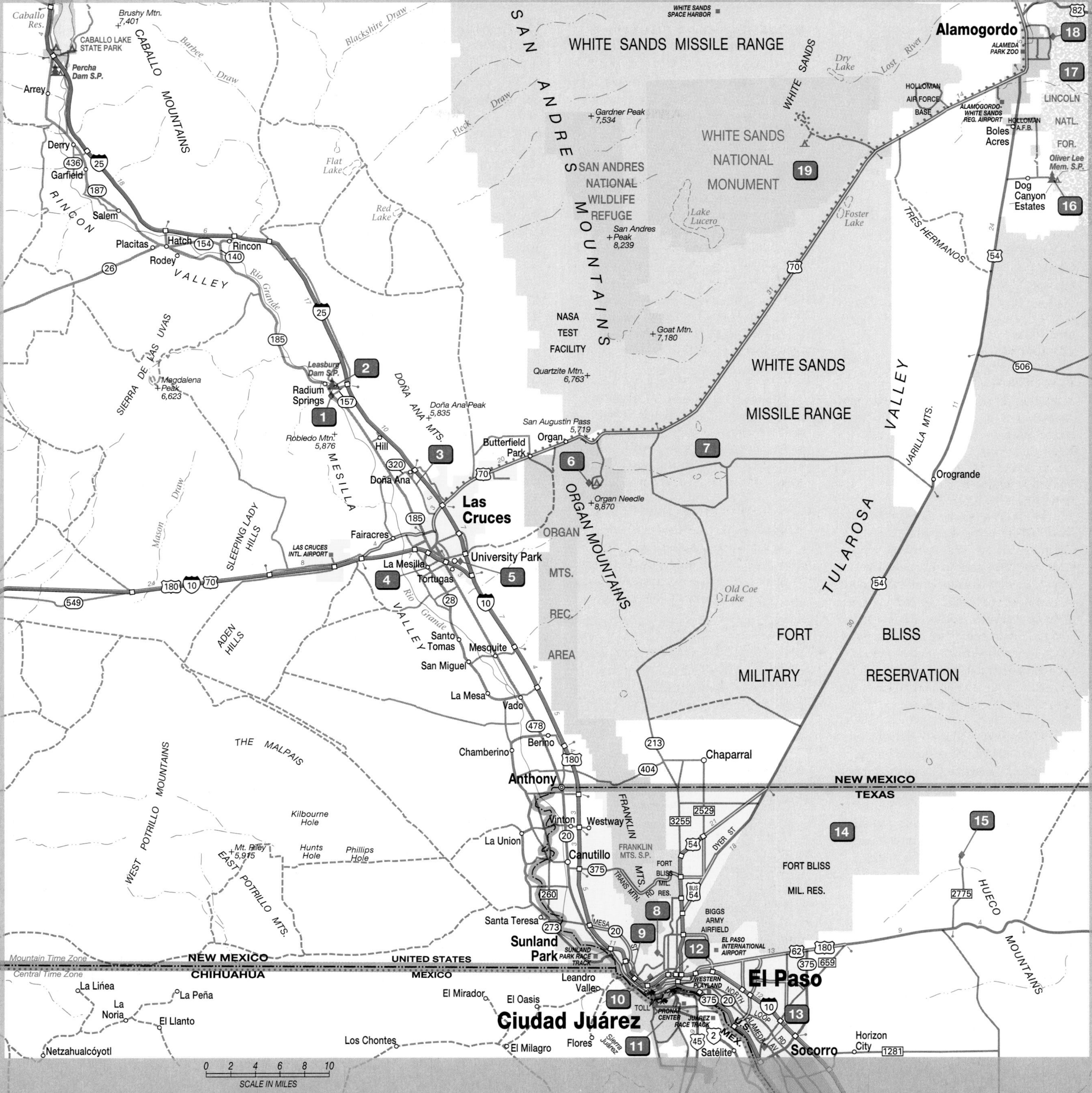

Caballo
Res.

Brushy Mtn.
7,401

Blackshire Draw

WHITE SANDS
SPACE HARBOR

WHITE SANDS MISSILE RANGE

Alamogordo

82

18

17

CABALLO LAKE
STATE PARK

Barbee   Draw

ALAMEDA
PARK ZOO

Percha
Dam S.P.

Arrey

Derry

25

436

Garfield

187

18

Salem

Placitas

Hatch   154

Rincon

140

Rodey

26

Draw

Fleck

Flat
Lake

Red Lake

CABALLO   MOUNTAINS

RINCON

VALLEY

Rio Grande

SIERRA DE LAS UVAS

Magdalena
Peak
6,623

Radium
Springs

185

25

Leasburg
Dam S.P.

2

157

1

SAN   ANDRES

Gardner Peak
7,534

Dry
Lake

Lost   River

HOLLOMAN
AIR FORCE
BASE

ALAMOGORDO-
WHITE SANDS
REG. AIRPORT

HOLLOMAN
A.F.B.

Boles
Acres

LINCOLN

NATL.

FOR.

Oliver Lee
Mem. S.P.

Dog
Canyon
Estates

16

WHITE   SANDS

WHITE
SANDS
NATIONAL
MONUMENT

SAN ANDRES
NATIONAL
WILDLIFE
REFUGE

San Andres
Peak
8,239

Lake
Lucero

Foster
Lake

19

54

506

TRES HERMANOS

MOUNTAINS

NASA
TEST
FACILITY

Goat Mtn.
7,180

Quartzite Mtn.
6,763

WHITE SANDS

MISSILE RANGE

70

31

TULAROSA   VALLEY

JARILLA MTS.

Robledo Mtn.
5,876

Hill

320

Doña Ana

MESILLA

DOÑA ANA MTS.

Doña Ana Peak
5,835

3

10

Butterfield
Park

70

Organ

San Augustin Pass
5,719

6

Organ Needle
8,870

7

Orogrande

Las
Cruces

185

Fairacres

La Mesilla

Tortugas

28

University Park

5

ORGAN   MOUNTAINS

ORGAN

MTS.

REC.

AREA

Old Coe
Lake

54

SLEEPING LADY HILLS

LAS CRUCES
INTL. AIRPORT

8

4

549

180 10 70

VALLEY

Rio Grande

Santo
Tomas

Mesquite

San Miguel

24

FORT   BLISS

MILITARY   RESERVATION

30

ADEN
HILLS

THE   MALPAIS

Kilbourne
Hole

Mt. Riley
5,915

Hunts
Hole

Phillips
Hole

La Mesa

Vado

478

Berino

Chamberino

213

Chaparral

180

404

NEW MEXICO

TEXAS

WEST POTRILLO MOUNTAINS

EAST POTRILLO   MTS.

Anthony

Vinton

20

Westway

3255

2529

FRANKLIN

FORT
BLISS
MIL. RES.

54

DYER ST.

14

15

La Union

Canutillo

375

FRANKLIN
MTS. S.P.

TRANS MTN. RD.

BUS.
54

FORT BLISS

MIL. RES.

2775

HUECO

260

BIGGS
ARMY
AIRFIELD

Santa Teresa

273

MESA

20

8

9

12

EL PASO
INTERNATIONAL
AIRPORT

Mountain Time Zone

Central Time Zone

NEW MEXICO

UNITED STATES

Sunland
Park

SUNLAND
PARK RACE
TRACK

Leandro
Valley

WESTERN
PLAYLAND

El Paso

375 20

62 180

375 659

HUECO

MOUNTAINS

9

CHIHUAHUA

MEXICO

La Línea

La
Noria

La Peña

El Llanto

El Mirador

El Oasis

Ciudad Juárez

Los Chontes

El Milagro

Netzahualcóyotl

El Llanto

PRONAF
CENTER

JUAREZ
RACE TRACK

10

Flores

11

Satélite

45

2

MEX

LOOP

ALAMEDA AVE.

NORTH

TOLL

Socorro

13

Horizon
City

1281

0 2 4 6 8 10
SCALE IN MILES

1. Sierra Blanca

Dramatic views of Sierra Blanca, also called White Mountain, greet the eye from virtually any spot in this town, where the last rails of the nation's second transcontinental railroad were laid. The town is home to the only adobe courthouse still in use in the state.

2. Guadalupe Mountains National Park

Amid these mountains — a haven for hikers and the site of a spectacular 250-million-year-old fossilized reef — rises **Guadalupe Peak,** at 8,751 feet the highest point in Texas.

3. Carlsbad Caverns National Park

These caverns include the world's largest natural underground chamber: the size of 14 football fields, with a ceiling so high that the U.S. Capitol could fit neatly inside. Self-guided tours pass spectacular stone formations. At dusk in the summer, the curious can see thousands of bats at the cavern's entrance. The expansive view from the park's visitor center extends for 100 miles. *Admission charged.*

4. Carlsbad

Convention and Visitors Bureau, 302 South Canal St. The **Carlsbad Museum and Art Center** relates local history through exhibits that include mammoth bones, Pueblo pottery, meteorite remains, and pioneer and Apache relics. Visitors can ride a narrow-gauge train or paddle wheeler, each named for a particular president, at **Presidents Park.** The **Living Desert State Park** is home to an array of indigenous plants and animals from the **Chihuahuan Desert.** The **Million Dollar Museum** features a collection of early Americana, including exquisite antique dolls and doll houses. **Sitting Bull Falls** in **Lincoln National Forest** provides a refreshing contrast to the surrounding desert plains. *Admission charged for some attractions.*

5. Confederate Air Force Flying Museum

Lea County Airport, Hobbs. A dozen World War II planes are housed here in a classic hangar. The aircraft are kept in working order by a group of airplane enthusiasts called the Confederate Air Force, whose motto is "Keep 'em Flying."

6. Pecos

Chamber of Commerce, 111 South Cedar St. In frontier days, law in these parts meant every man for himself. The **West of the Pecos Museum,** set in and around a 19th-century hotel, tells the story of the Old West. In the hotel's saloon, markers indicate where two outlaws were shot dead by a local cowboy. At nearby **Maxie Park,** cacti and flowers bloom, while buffalo, longhorn, and mountain goats roam free. *Admission charged at museum.*

7. Monahans Sandhills State Park

Undulating dunes rise to heights of 70 feet in this 3,840-acre park. Many dunes are stabilized by vegetation, but others are constantly reshaped by incessant winds. An interpretive center explains local natural history. *Admission charged.*

8. Odessa

Chamber of Commerce, 400 West Fourth St. At the **Presidential Museum** visitors can browse through memorabilia of each chief executive, as well as a collection of dolls dressed in reproductions of the Inaugural gowns worn by the First Ladies. Nearby **Water Wonderland** has a 30-mile-per-hour water-toboggan ride and a beach. At the **Odessa Meteor Crater,** the outline made by a 1,000-ton iron meteorite 20,000 years ago is still discernible. *Admission charged for some attractions.*

9. Midland

Convention and Visitors Bureau, 109 North Main St. Once a water stop for the railroad, Midland is so named because it lies halfway between El Paso and Ft. Worth. The history and technology of the oil industry are depicted at the **Permian Basin Petroleum Museum,** while the nearby **Museum of the Southwest** is home to Southwestern art and American Indian artifacts. *Admission charged at petroleum museum.*

10. Big Spring

Convention and Visitors Bureau, 215 West Third St. The once-abundant water source for which this town was named made it a popular stop for travelers. Local history is recalled at the **Heritage Museum,** whose artifacts include long-horned cattle horns. **Scenic Mountain** in the **Big Spring State Recreation Area** offers fine views of the town and the surrounding plains. *Admission charged for some attractions.*

11. Snyder

Chamber of Commerce, 2302 Avenue R. Snyder was once nicknamed Robbers' Roost for the many outlaws who set up buffalo-hide huts around the trading post here. The **Scurry County Museum** features displays on local history from ancient times to the oil boom.

12. Ozona

Chamber of Commerce, 1110 Avenue E. The largest unincorporated town in the nation, Ozona was once claimed by locals to have more millionaires per capita than any other city in the country. At the **Fort Lancaster State Historical Park,** now a stabilized ruin, the history of the garrison is detailed with photographs and maps.

13. Seminole Canyon State Historical Park

This landscape of rock formations and colorful pictographs, painted some 8,000 years ago, can be seen by guided hikes from the visitor center to the canyon floor. Near the park, a high bridge offers a stunning view of **Pecos River Canyon,** where Indian caves are visible in the canyon walls. *Admission charged.*

14. Judge Roy Bean Visitor Center

Loop 25 and Torres Ave., Langtry. Armed with a law book and a pair of six-shooters, Roy Bean handed down judgments in his combination courthouse-saloon, now restored and open to the public. Lucky criminals were fined only a round of drinks for the jury. The visitor center provides information on the judge's life and times.

15. Fort Stockton

Chamber of Commerce, 222 West Dickinson Blvd. This area was once a watering hole for stagecoaches and wagon trains. In 1858 a cavalry post was built here, and some of the original **Old Fort Stockton** remains, including adobe officers' quarters, a guardhouse, and a cemetery.

16. Great Marathon Basin

Amateur rock hounds and geologists alike will find a treasure trove of varied rocks and minerals here, including a striking series of jagged formations known as **Hell's Half Acre.** Hunters, fishermen, and nature photographers flock to nearby **Black Gap Wildlife Management Area,** the largest such preserve in the state.

17. Alpine

Chamber of Commerce, 106 North Third St. The gateway to **Big Bend National Park,** Alpine is also the seat of the state's largest county. The **Museum of the Big Bend** recalls local history through displays that include a bullet-ridden stagecoach. At the 4,000-acre **Woodward Ranch,** visitors can go rock hunting for more than 70 varieties of cutting stones. *Donation encouraged at museum.*

18. Fort Davis

One of the best-preserved forts in the entire Southwest is contained in the **Fort Davis National Historic Site.** At the mouth of **Hospital Canyon,** the military outpost was a vital link in the area's strategic defense. In the summer, daily life in the fort is re-created by costumed staff members. Seventeen miles northwest of town, atop **Mount Locke,** sits the **McDonald Observatory,** home to one of the world's most powerful telescopes. *Admission charged for some attractions.*

19. Marfa

Chamber of Commerce, 207 North Highland St. Perched at an elevation of 4,688 feet and surrounded by mountains, Marfa boasts the highest golf course in the state and is known as one of the best spots in the country for sailplanes. In this region, the mysterious Marfa Ghost Lights can be seen toward the horizon.

20. Shafter

Picturesque ruins mark the site of a once-rowdy silver-mining boomtown of the 1880's. The area was known as the richest acre in Texas, producing $60 million in silver. The road through town provides dramatic views of the **Chinati Mountains.**

21. Fort Leaton State Historic Site

River Rd., southeast of Presidio. Here border trader Benjamin Leaton established a fortified trading post to outfit travelers. A fine example of native adobe construction and once the largest such structure in the state, the fort — now partially restored — is a reminder of the rugged frontier. *Admission charged.*

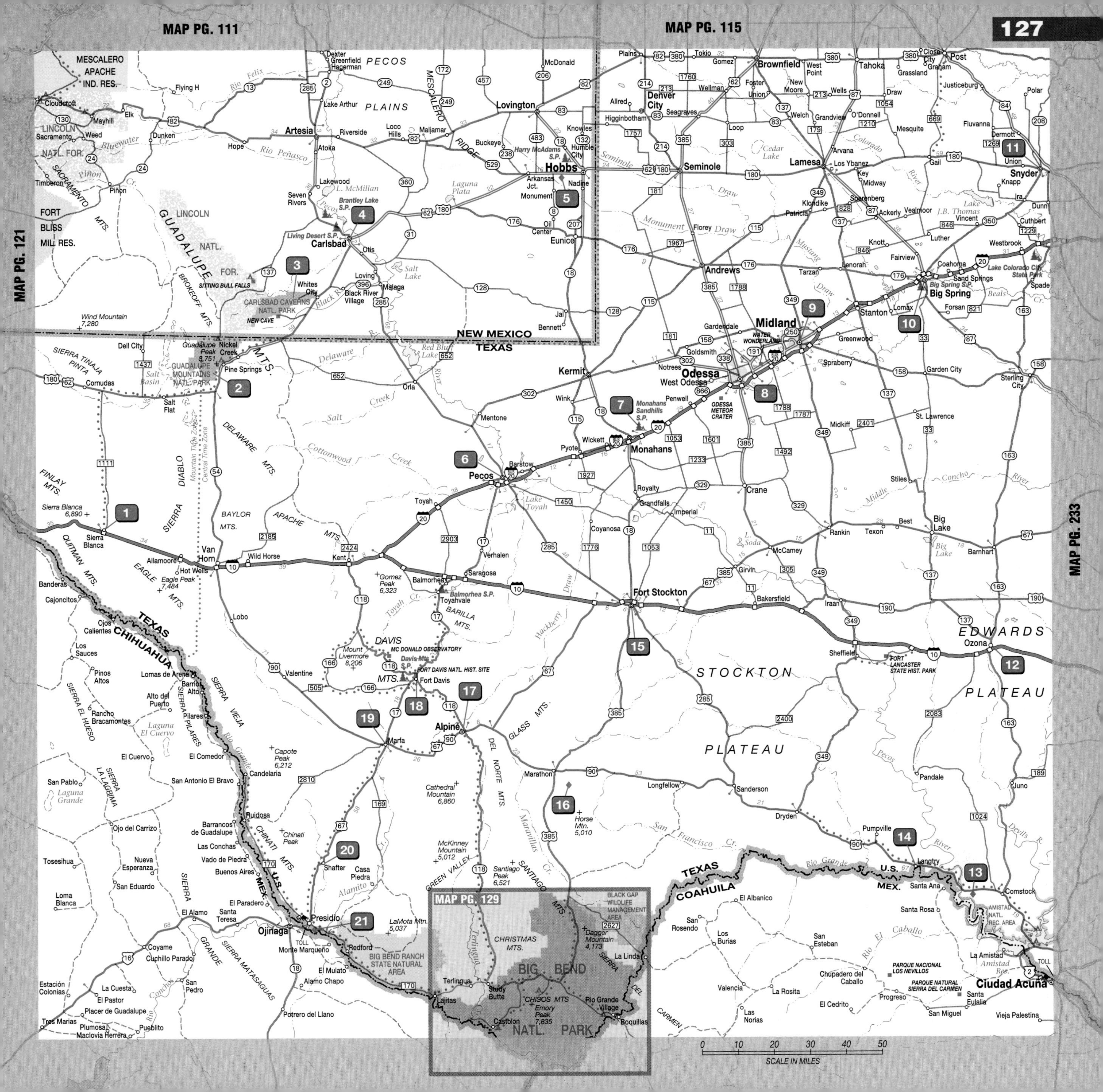

MAP PG. 121

MAP PG. 233

MAP PG. 129

MESCALERO APACHE IND. RES.

PECOS PLAINS

MESCALERO RIDGE

LINCOLN NATL. FOR.
SACRAMENTO MTS.
GUADALUPE NATL. FOR.

FORT BLISS MIL. RES.

NEW MEXICO
TEXAS

Cloudcroft, Mayhill, Elk, Weed, Dunken, Piñon, Timberon, Flying H, Hope, Artesia, Atoka, Lake Arthur, Riverside, Loco Hills, Maljamar, Buckeye, Knowles, Humble City, Hobbs, Eunice, Jal, Bennett

Dexter, Greenfield, Hagerman, McDonald, Lovington, Denver City, Seagraves, Seminole, Lamesa, Brownfield, Tahoka, Post, Snyder

Carlsbad, Living Desert S.P., Lakewood, L. McMillan, Brantley Lake S.P., Seven Rivers, Whites City, Loving, Malaga, Black River Village, Carlsbad Caverns Natl. Park, New Cave, Sitting Bull Falls

Guadalupe Peak 8,751, Nickel Creek, Pine Springs, Guadalupe Mountains Natl. Park, Dell City, Cornudas, Salt Flat, Salt Basin

SIERRA TINAJA PINTA, SIERRA DIABLO, DELAWARE MTS., APACHE MTS., BAYLOR MTS.

FINLAY MTS., Sierra Blanca 6,890, Van Horn, Allamoore, Hot Wells, Wild Horse, Kent, Verhalen, Saragosa, Balmorhea, Toyahvale, Balmorhea S.P., BARILLA MTS.

QUITMAN MTS., EAGLE MTS., Eagle Peak 7,484, Banderas, Cajoncitos, Lobo, Valentine, DAVIS MTS., Mount Livermore 8,206, MC Donald Observatory, Davis Mts. S.P., Fort Davis Natl. Hist. Site, Fort Davis, Marfa, Alpine

TEXAS / CHIHUAHUA, RIO GRANDE, SIERRA VIEJA, SIERRA PILARES, CHINATI MTS., Chinati Peak, Capote Peak 6,212, Candelaria, Ruidosa, Shafter, Casa Piedra, Presidio, Ojinaga, Redford, Lajitas, Terlingua

Kermit, Wink, Mentone, Pyote, Wickett, Monahans, Monahans Sandhills S.P., Barstow, Pecos, Toyah, Pecos, Coyanosa, Royalty, Grandfalls, Imperial, Girvin, Fort Stockton, Bakersfield, Iraan

Odessa, West Odessa, Odessa Meteor Crater, Midland, Water Wonderland, Gardendale, Goldsmith, Notrees, Penwell, Andrews, Tarzan, Stanton, Big Spring, Big Spring S.P., Coahoma, Forsan, Lomax, Lenorah, Knott, Luther, Fairview, Westbrook, Lake Colorado City State Park

STOCKTON PLATEAU, EDWARDS PLATEAU, Ozona, Sheffield, Fort Lancaster State Hist. Park, Crane, McCamey, Rankin, Texon, Big Lake, Barnhart, Mertzon, Garden City, Sterling City, St. Lawrence, Midkiff, Stiles, Best

GLASS MTS., DEL NORTE MTS., SANTIAGO MTS., Cathedral Mountain 6,860, McKinney Mountain 5,012, Santiago Peak 6,521, Marathon, Longfellow, Sanderson, Dryden, Pumpville, Langtry, Comstock, Del Rio

Ciudad Acuña, Amistad Natl. Rec. Area, Parque Nacional Los Novillos, Parque Natural Sierra del Carmen

BIG BEND NATL. PARK, CHISOS MTS., Emory Peak 7,835, Study Butte, Castolon, Rio Grande Village, Boquillas, LaMota Mtn. 5,037, Dagger Mountain 4,173, Black Gap Wildlife Management Area, Big Bend Ranch State Natural Area, CHRISTMAS MTS.

TEXAS / COAHUILA, TEXAS / MEX., RIO GRANDE

SCALE IN MILES
0 10 20 30 40 50

BIG BEND NATIONAL PARK

1. Persimmon Gap
Rte. 385 leads from Persimmon Gap, the north entrance to the park, down to Panther Junction. The road follows a trail once used by Comanche Indians, army expeditions, settlers, and miners. A detour along the way is the **Dagger Flat Auto Trail,** particularly colorful in spring when giant dagger yuccas bloom.

2. Lajitas
This resort community on the famous **El Camino del Rio Scenic Drive** to Presidio was a crossing for Indians, Mexicans, and Anglos. A hacienda-style museum with a 4-acre garden has exhibits on natural history and archeology. National park concessionaires offer Rio Grande raft trips. Visitors will also find a working trading post.

3. Terlingua
Between the 1890's and 1946, millions of dollars' worth of quicksilver was mined in this reborn ghost town. Some former company stores and offices now house businesses, and adobe homes have been restored as private residences.

4. Luna's Jacal
This stabilized ruin is all that remains of a jacal, or house, built by a Mexican farmer near the **Comanche War Trail.** Typical of the area's earliest buildings, a huge flat boulder forms one wall of the 5½-foot-high sandstone and limestone structure.

5. Santa Elena
Visitors can access this Mexican ranching village (which is not a port of entry) by a rowboat operated as a ferry. The town has adobe buildings, churches, a plaza used for dances and fiestas, and restaurants.

6. Castolon Historic District
The park's oldest adobe structure, **Alvino House,** is located here along with the barracks, canteen, and officers' quarters from the **Camp Santa Elena** cavalry post, which protected the border during the Mexican Revolution. Nearby, the **Rancho Estelle** ruins include an adobe and a large house with a petrified wood fireplace.

7. Ross Maxwell Scenic Drive
A half to a full day is needed for this 31-mile drive from **Santa Elena Junction** to **Santa Elena Canyon.** Striking 1,500-foot canyon walls, sweeping mountain vistas, and shear rocky peaks share the landscape with an abandoned army post, ranches, and adobe ruins dating back to the early 1900's. A scenic high point toward the drive's end, **Santa Elena Canyon Overlook** has views of the awesome canyon walls and the Rio Grande. At the end of the drive is the start of the **Santa Elena Canyon Trail,** which follows the river's edge into the canyon.

8. Sam Nail Ranch
A short trail leads to stands of willow and pecan trees, which are good bird-watching spots, and to the remains of windmills and a ranch house. Along the Ross Maxwell Scenic Drive are prime examples of lava dikes, the result of molten rock forced to the surface through underground cracks.

9. The Window
All rain and melting snow from the Chisos Basin drains through this V-shaped opening. The Window can be seen from a short trail off the Ross Maxwell Scenic Drive and is most photogenic at sunset. A more difficult path leads through desert and canyon to the Window itself, where hikers will be rewarded with views framed by the pines and oaks of **Casa Grande.**

10. The Basin
Visitors can hike the 1½-mile **Chisos Basin Loop Trail** to wonderful views of the park's highest point, 7,835-foot **Emory Peak.** Roadside attractions near Chisos Basin include **Pulliam Bluff,** which resembles a man's face, and the castlelike Casa Grande mountain. The Basin also features a visitor center and the only restaurant and lodging in the park.

11. Panther Pass
The 5,679-foot-high pass is named for resident mountain lions, which are seldom encountered or seen. Nearby **Lost Mine Trail** is a moderately strenuous self-guiding nature hike to one of the park's best viewpoints. For less ambitious hikers, the first mile of the trail leads to the scenic **Juniper Canyon Overlook.**

12. Panther Path
This nature trail near the visitor center highlights the plants visitors will see on trips through Big Bend National Park.

13. Panther Junction Visitor Center
Much of Big Bend National Park's 801,163 acres of desert, river, and mountain is wild and remote country. Bird-watchers delight in the park's many species, which are more numerous than in any other national park. The visitor center has exhibits, including the bones of an ancient pterodactyl found in the park; nature programs; camping and hiking information; and safety tips for avoiding flash floods, mountain lions, and rattlesnakes.

14. Dugout Wells
Accessible by unpaved road, this former ranch and schoolhouse is a favorite spot for picnicking and wildlife-watching. The main road to the Rio Grande Village has striking views of the **Elephant Tusk** and **Chilicotal mountains** and the rock formations of Mexico's Sierra del Carmen.

15. Rio Grande Overlook
A 50-yard trail from the main road rewards visitors with outstanding views of the Rio Grande floodplain, Sierra del Carmen, and Boquillas village. Springtime heightens the beauty of the landscape with the added color of Big Bend bluebonnets.

16. Boquillas Canyon Overlook
Accessible by a paved road, this overlook provides an exceptionally lovely view of the rugged canyon below.

17. Boquillas
Travelers cross the river by ferry and rent burros or truck taxis for the 1-mile ride into this 25-family Mexican village. Boquillas has no electricity but offers a craft shop, cantina, guides, and horse rentals to the **Sierra del Carmen.**

Above left, a ranger leads the way into Santa Elena Canyon; above right, hikers on the Chisos Basin Loop Trail head toward Casa Grande.

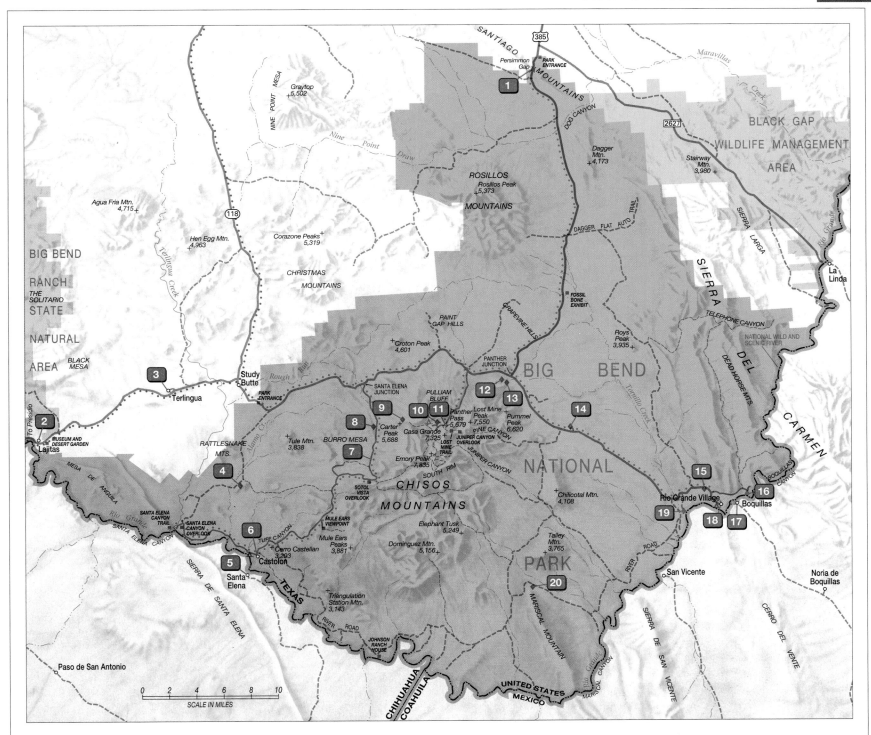

18. Rio Grande Village

In addition to camping and bird-watching, the village offers an easy ¾-mile loop trail. Starting from a thickly vegetated flood-plain, it ascends a ridge with outstanding vistas of the river and Sierra del Carmen.

19. Hot Springs

Intriguing remnants remain of this 1909 settlement and resort, including a limestone hotel, post office, and cemetery. Today the springs, which are accessible to visitors by a rough road, still flow at a constant temperature of 105° F and fill the foundation of the former bathhouse.

20. Mariscal Mine

Along the 51-mile River Road, which requires a high-clearance vehicle, visitors can explore adobe, stone, and concrete buildings at the early 1900's Mariscal mercury mine, and see Big Bend's largest adobe ruin at **Johnson Ranch House.**

Admission charged for national park.

1. Pribilof Islands

A 1,500-mile round-trip from Anchorage, these tiny islands are breeding and nesting grounds for Northern fur seals and some 210 species of birds. Visitors can see both at close range: Seals by the thousands fill the beaches and birds nest in easily visible cliffs. **St. Paul** and **St. George islands** offer limited services for visitors.

2. Aniakchak National Monument and Preserve

At 6 miles across, Aniakchak is one of the world's largest calderas. Situated in largely untamed country with inclement weather, the least taxing means of visiting is by a floatplane landing on the caldera's **Surprise Lake.** Camping is permitted throughout the area.

3. Kodiak Island

Convention and Visitors Bureau, 100 Marine Way. Alaska's largest island features the **Baranov Museum,** which exhibits Russian samovars, Easter eggs, and native artifacts, and **Fort Abercrombie**

An Inupiat Eskimo girl in Kotzebue

State Historic Park and campground, where World War II bunkers and gun pits still remain. Spanning two islands, the **Kodiak National Wildlife Refuge** is a preserve for the Kodiak brown bear. Access is by plane from Anchorage or by ferry from Seward or Homer. *Donation encouraged for museum.*

4. Katmai National Park and Preserve

A 1912 volcanic eruption created spectacular ash gorges in the **Valley of Ten Thousand Smokes.** Wildlife — including moose, grizzly bears, and eagles — combine with terrific fishing and scenic splendor to attract summer hikers, campers, fishermen, and other outdoor enthusiasts to the park. No road leads into Katmai; arrivals and departures are by air from Anchorage, with a plane change required. Transportation within the park is by tour bus or plane.

5. Wood-Tikchik State Park

Twelve lakes provide a magnificent setting for canoeing, wilderness hiking, salmon fishing, and other recreational activities in the park's 1.4 million acres.

6. Bethel

Accessible via bush plane, this rustic trading center serves more than 50 native villages. **Yugtarvik Regional Museum** showcases Eskimo artifacts and sells local crafts. Just outside town, area streams reward anglers with Arctic grayling, Dolly Varden trout, and salmon.

7. Yukon Delta National Wildlife Refuge

While reindeer and musk-oxen herds can be seen at the refuge, the main attraction for many visitors is the nearby Eskimo village of **Mekoryuk.** Craftsmen and weavers produce masks, as well as hats, sweaters, mittens, and scarves knitted from the wool of musk-oxen. Accommodations are limited and primitive.

8. Nome

Convention and Visitors Bureau, Front St. Visitors can relive Nome's colorful gold-rush history at the **Carrie M. McLain Memorial Museum,** or by touring gold fields, panning for gold, and watching dogsled demonstrations. Situated on the **Bering Sea,** 165 miles from Siberia, Nome also offers charter flights for two-, three-, or four-night tours of Russian cities

and wilderness areas; reservations for these excursions are required in advance.

9. Kotzebue

Located 26 miles above the Arctic Circle, Alaska's second-largest Eskimo community is the home of the **Museum of the Arctic,** which features Eskimo dances, jade carving, and information on nearby **Cape Krusenstern National Monument,** the site of 5,000-year-old archaeological ruins.

10. Kobuk Valley National Park

Among the surprising features of this park, which is north of the Arctic Circle, are its 30 square miles of sand dunes — some 100 feet high — that are characteristic of the African Sahara. The park also preserves the Arctic's most important archaeological discoveries, which indicate some 12,500 years of human habitation. Backpacking, camping, canoeing, and wildlife observation can be enjoyed along four large rivers that meander through the pristine wilderness.

11. Gates of the Arctic National Park and Preserve

Lying north of the Arctic Circle, the park is accessible by plane to **Bettles** village. At more than 8 million acres, this ultimate wilderness area encompasses towering mountains, tundra, lakes, rivers, and valleys, and is home to throngs of birds, lemmings, caribou, and grizzly bears. Visitors can explore the park by boating, hiking, or mountain climbing.

12. Barrow

Situated 1,300 miles south of the North Pole, Alaska's largest Eskimo community is also the northernmost settlement in the United States. From May through August visitors can take advantage of 82 days of perpetual sunlight to observe the native lifestyle and to shop for Eskimo clothing, dolls, and masks.

13. Arctic National Wildlife Refuge

This spectacular wilderness area encompasses thousands of lakes and ponds, vast expanses of tundra, and bountiful wildlife, including one of the greatest porcupine caribou herds in the world, numbering about 180,000. Among the recreational opportunities here are camping, hiking, and river runs. The refuge is accessible by a variety of airlines; from the air, intriguing geometric patterns are visible, etched in the landscape by permafrost.

14. Fort Yukon

In this Athapaskan Indian village and former Hudson's Bay Company outpost, some buildings date back to the 19th century. Visitors can ride dogsleds, experience a subsistence lifestyle, see local cultural exhibits at the **Dinjii Zhuu Enjit Museum,** and even receive a certificate for crossing the Arctic Circle.

15. Eagle

During the Klondike gold rush, Eagle was the military, communications, and transportation headquarters for interior Alaska. Visitors today can see many buildings much as they were in the early 1900's, including the first courthouse, a church, and an army mule barn with a name plate for each animal.

16. Dawson City

Visitor Reception Center, Front and King Sts. The heart of the Klondike gold rush, Dawson City relives its history with tours of diggings and dredges, cancan dances at the reconstructed **Palace Grand Theatre,** gold-rush exhibits at the **Dawson City Museum,** and prose and poetry readings at **Jack London's** and **Robert Service's cabins.** Alaska Highway travelers can reach this Yukon Territory town from Whitehorse on the Klondike Highway or by the Taylor Highway from Tetlin Junction. *Admission charged for some attractions.*

17. Whitehorse

Chamber of Commerce, 101–302 Steele St. Visitors to the capital of the Yukon Territory enjoy its museums, historical tours, and natural sites relating to the Klondike gold rush, including the **Yukon River** and **Miles Canyon.** A restored paddle wheeler, the **S.S. Klondike,** and a 1900 log church are among the other sights in town. Nearby **Kluane National Park** includes magnificent glaciers and Canada's highest mountain. *Admission charged for some attractions.*

18. Aleutian Islands

The Aleutian chain extends for more than 1,000 miles off the Alaskan mainland. The majority of the beautiful windswept isles are wildlife refuges for grizzly bears, sea otters, caribou, wolverines, and some 185 species of birds. Remnants of World War II military installations remain on several others. There is airline service between Anchorage and the islands.

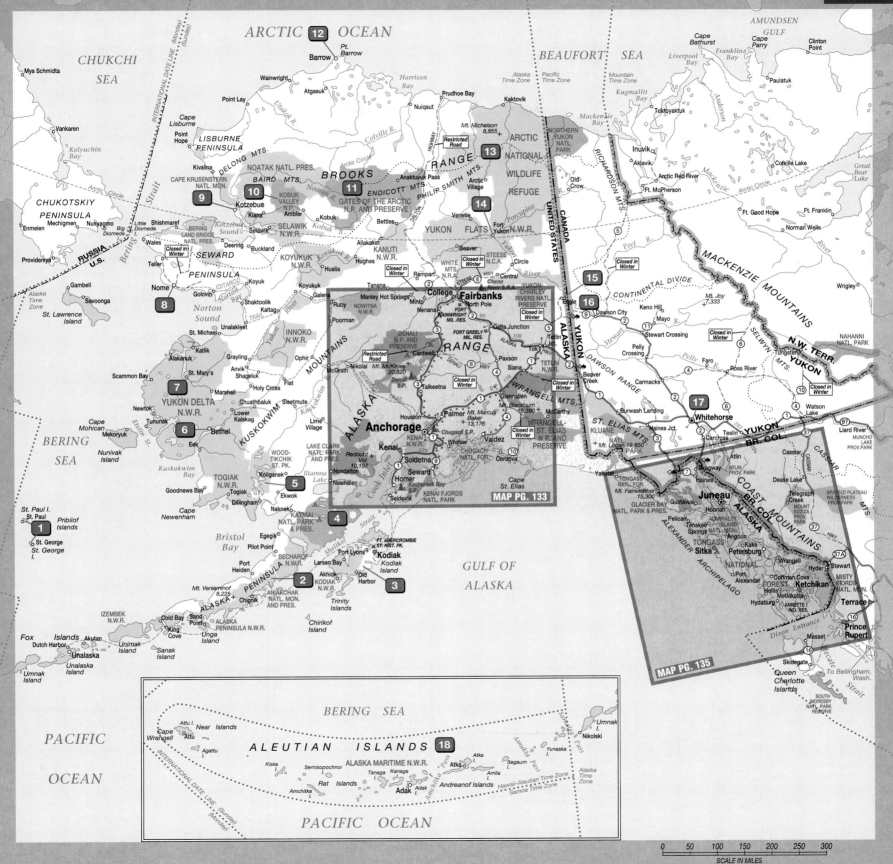

ARCTIC **12** OCEAN

CHUKCHI SEA

AMUNDSEN GULF

BEAUFORT SEA

Mys Schmidta

Cape Bathurst
Cape Parry
Franklin Bay
Liverpool Bay
Clinton Point

Vankaren

Kolyuchin Bay

CHUKOTSKIY PENINSULA

Wainwright
Atqasuk
Pt. Barrow
Barrow

Harrison Bay

Prudhoe Bay
Nuiqsut
Kaktovik

Kugmallit Bay
Paulatuk

Tuktoyaktuk

Mackenzie Bay

Point Lay

LISBURNE PENINSULA

Cape Lisburne

Point Hope

DELONG MTS.

NOATAK NATL. PRES.

BAIRD MTS.

10

CAPE KRUSENSTERN NATL. MON.

9

Kotzebue

Kivalina

Kiana

Shishmaref

Little Diomede
Big Diomede

Wales

SEWARD PENINSULA

Teller

Nome

8

RUSSIA
U.S.

Providenlya

Enmelen

Mechigmen

Nunyamo

Gambell

Savoonga

St. Lawrence Island

Norton Sound

Golovin

Koyuk

Unalakleet

St. Michael

INNOKO N.W.R.

Alakanuk

Scammon Bay

St. Mary's

Newtok

Chuathbaluk

7

YUKON DELTA N.W.R.

6

Bethel

Eek

Cape Mohican

Nunivak Island

Mekoryuk

BERING SEA

St. Paul I.
St. Paul

1

Pribilof Islands

St. George
St. George I.

Fox Islands

Dutch Harbor

Unalaska

Umnak Island

Unalaska Island

Umnak Island

PACIFIC OCEAN

BROOKS

Anaktuvuk Pass

ENDICOTT MTS.

GATES OF THE ARCTIC N.P. AND PRESERVE

RANGE

PHILIP SMITH MTS.

ARCTIC NAT'L. WILDLIFE REFUGE

NORTHERN YUKON NATL. PARK

Old Crow

Inuvik

Aklavik

Arctic Red River

Ft. McPherson

Colville Lake

Great Bear Lake

MACKENZIE MTS.

Ft. Good Hope

Ft. Franklin

Norman Wells

Wrigley

13

Mt. Michelson 8,855

Arctic Village

14

Venetie

Fort Yukon N.W.R.

YUKON FLATS

Beaver

15

CONTINENTAL DIVIDE

Mt. Joy 7,333

N.W. TERR.

NAHANNI NATL. PARK

RICHARDSON MTS.

CANADA
UNITED STATES

Eagle

16

Dawson City

Keno Hill
Mayo

SELWYN MTS.

YUKON

Tungsten

Ross River

Faro

Carmacks

Pelly Crossing
Stewart Crossing

DAWSON RANGE

PELLY

MACKENZIE MOUNTAINS

Whitehorse

17

Teslin

YUKON
BR. COL.

Watson Lake

Liard River

MUNCHO LAKE PROV. PARK

CASSIAR

Cassiar

Dease Lake

Telegraph Creek

SPATSIZI PLATEAU WILDERNESS PROV. PARK

Atlin

Skagway

Haines

Juneau

GLACIER BAY NATL. PARK & PRES.

Gustavus

Hoonah

Sitka

TONGASS NATL. FOREST

Angoon

Kake

Petersburg

Wrangell

Hyder

Stewart

COAST MOUNTAINS

Terrace

Prince Rupert

Ketchikan

Metlakatla
Hydaburg

MISTY FIORDS NATL. MON.

Masset

Queen Charlotte Islands

SKidegate

To Bellingham, Wash.

MAP PG. 135

MAP PG. 133

Fairbanks

Anchorage

SCALE IN MILES

0 50 100 150 200 250 300

BERING SEA

ALEUTIAN ISLANDS **18**

ALASKA MARITIME N.W.R.

PACIFIC OCEAN

1. Lake Clark National Park and Preserve

Often described as the Alaskan Alps, this park contains huge glaciers, two active volcanos, and unexplored valleys. During the summer, millions of sockeye salmon come to spawn in the clear blue waters of 50-mile-long **Lake Clark.**

2. Ninilchik

This Kenai Peninsula village of 750 people was founded by Russian fur traders in the early 1800's. Visitors can tour an original village of fishermen's log dwellings and an onion-domed Russian Orthodox Church, or enjoy good sport fishing and excellent low-tide beachcombing.

3. Homer

Visitor Information Center, 3735 Homer Spit Rd. Spectacular scenery, picturesque buildings, and a mild, sunny climate make this former coal-mining camp a popular weekend retreat. Along with excellent halibut fishing, recreational opportunities include camping at Homer Spit on **Kachemak Bay** and boat excursions to **Halibut Cove** and **Seldovia.** *Admission charged for some attractions.*

4. Kachemak Bay State Park

This undeveloped park is accessible only by boat or floatplane. It features some of the world's highest tides, as well as inner tidal areas that are ideal for fishing, kayaking, and walks along the beach. Other attractions include hiking trails, coastal campsites, bird rookeries, and wildlife ranging from giant starfish to sea otters, porpoises, and occasional whales.

5. Kenai Fjords National Park

The 650,000-acre park encompasses soaring mountains, deep fjords, and the **Harding Icefield,** which covers 700 square miles and 32 named glaciers. Bald eagles, harbor seals, sea lions, whales, and porpoises add excitement to boat trips along the park's coast and to the **Alaska Maritime National Wildlife Refuge.**

6. Kenai National Wildlife Refuge

Rivers teeming with salmon, more than 1,000 lakes, Dall sheep, mountain goats, trumpeter swans, and thousands of moose make this a popular spot for hikers, fishermen, canoeists, and wildlife observers. Designated canoe routes, 200 miles of hiking trails, and chartered floatplanes provide access to remote areas.

7. Portage Glacier

Whether seen from the visitor center or by tour boat, Portage Glacier is one of Alaska's most visited sites. Visitors may also spot beaver, Dall sheep, moose, and other wildlife in the area's varied landscape of mountains, lakes, woodlands, and inlets. *Fee charged for boat ride.*

8. Crow Creek Mine

Mining operations were begun here in 1898 and continue today on a recreational basis, with equipment available to visitors for gold panning in the creek. The mine's original equipment and buildings are listed on the National Register of Historic Places. *Admission charged.*

9. Girdwood

At **Alyeska Village** visitors can ride a 1½-mile chair lift 2,000 feet to the summit of **Mount Alyeska,** with its sweeping views of **Turnagain Arm,** the Kenai Peninsula, and eight glaciers. Alaska's largest resort and ski area also features a jade workshop and a 22-ton jade boulder.

10. Chugach State Park

Park mountain ranges, alpine meadows, lakes, and tidal flats extend from sea level to 8,000 feet. They support Dall sheep, brown and black bears, wolves, and moose. Nearby **Anchorage Coastal Wildlife Refuge** attracts trumpeter swans, bald eagles, mink, and muskrats.

11. Eklutna

The town offers camping in a scenic mountain setting at **Eklutna Lake Recreation Area,** the onion-domed **St. Nicholas Russian Orthodox Church,** and an **Athabascan cemetery** with colorful spirit houses.

12. Anchorage

Convention and Visitors Bureau, 1600 A St. Alaska's largest city features the **Alaska Public Lands Information Center,** where visitors can use a computer trip planner, and watch the summer salmon runs at **Ship Creek.**

Great stops for children include the experimental science museum at the **Imaginarium;** the **Alaska Zoo,** with polar bears, musk-oxen, and seals; and the **Anchorage Museum of History and Art,** which fills a city block with exhibits and includes a children's section. A trail at **Earthquake Park** leads through the crumpled landscape to the shore of **Cook Inlet,** past foundations of homes that were destroyed in the 1964 earthquake. *Admission charged for some attractions.*

13. Independence Mine State Historic Park

The rewards to those who brave the difficult access to this park are many. In the summer months visitors may tour historic buildings and go berry picking, fishing, hiking, or wildflower viewing. Never short of snow, the park is also a wonderland for winter sports buffs. Wildlife is plentiful and includes moose, bears, lynx, occasional caribou, and numerous birds.

14. Denali State Park

A tour of the park provides visitors with views of wildlife, including Dall sheep, grizzlies, and moose, as well as of snowcapped **Mount McKinley.**

15. Denali National Park and Preserve

At an elevation of 20,320 feet, **Mount McKinley** is North America's tallest mountain and the centerpiece of this 6-million-acre park. About 37 animal species and some 140 kinds of birds live here. Visitors can camp, hike, mountain climb, or see the varied wildlife on free bus tours. *Admission charged.*

16. Nenana

Located at the confluence of the **Nenana** and **Tanana rivers,** this town of fewer than 700 people is a major rail and barge terminus. The Tanana River ice breakup is a major gambling event, and the River Daze rafting competition also attracts large numbers of participants.

17. Fairbanks

Convention and Visitors Bureau, 550 First Ave. Alaska's heritage is interpreted at **Alaskaland,** with gold-rush cabins, an Athabascan village, and other exhibits. At the **University of Alaska Museum,** visitors can see a bison from the Ice Age, a Russian blockhouse, mounted polar and grizzly bears, and seals. Cruises on the

stern-wheeler *Discovery* offer a glimpse into the lifestyles of trappers, fishermen, and traders. *Fee charged for cruise.*

18. Pedro Creek Monument

Felix Pedro, who made the area's first gold discovery in 1902, is immortalized beside the creek, which is open for recreational gold panning. Nearby **Cleary Summit,** at 2,233 feet, offers sweeping views of the **Tanana Valley, Alaska Range,** and the **Cleary Hill Mine.**

19. North Pole

Visitor Information Center, 2550 Mistletoe Dr. Here is where **Santa Claus House,** a gaily decorated toy and gift shop (and a thriving commercial enterprise), celebrates Christmas all year long. The town's name refers to its severe, long winters.

20. Tanacross

Time-honored traditions live on in this old Athabascan Indian village, which includes **St. Timothy's Mission** and an Indian graveyard with spirit houses. In winter, when temperatures sometimes plunge to minus 70° F, dog teams are still vital modes of transportation.

21. Tok

Visitor Information Center, Main St. This small community is a major service center for Alaska Highway travelers, campers, hunters, and fishermen. From Tok to Anchorage, **State Highway 1** is a premier scenic drive with outstanding views of lakes, mountains, and streams.

22. Wrangell–St. Elias National Park and Preserve

America's largest national park covers more than 12 million acres and includes a great number of glaciers and mountain peaks more than 16,000 feet high. Among the scenic highlights are a glacier larger than Rhode Island and 14,163-foot **Mount Wrangell,** an active volcano.

23. Valdez

Convention and Visitors Bureau, 200 Chenega St. This is the southern terminus of the **Trans-Alaska Pipeline,** on **Prince William Sound.** Visitors can tour the pipeline facilities, stop at **Worthington Glacier,** and view waterfalls in **Keystone Canyon.** Summer cruises to magnificent **Columbia Glacier** may include the sighting of whales, porpoises, and seals. *Admission charged for some attractions.*

1. Glacier Bay National Park and Preserve

The bay has 16 glaciers, which create huge chunks of ice. Boats travel out to the "snouts," or ice cliffs, and park naturalists are on hand to explain the glaciers' formation and movement. This 3.3-million-acre park also contains a moss-laden rain forest and an abundance of wildlife such as harbor seals, black bears, and whales.

2. Alaska Chilkat Bald Eagle Preserve

Drivers heading north on Haines Highway can often see, around milepost 19, magnificent bald eagles from this nearby preserve. The refuge attracts as many as 3,500 of the birds, many of which come to feed on the late run of spawned salmon from October to January.

3. Skagway

Convention and Visitors Bureau, City Hall. As part of the **Klondike Gold Rush National Historical Park,** Skagway preserves boardwalks, stores, and other structures from its days as a setting-off point for gold seekers. The **Trail of '98 Museum** holds artifacts from that exciting time, and the **Chilkoot Trail,** a strenuous 33-mile trek, follows an old prospectors' route. An easier way to see this gold-rush country is to take a ride on the narrow-gauge **White Pass & Yukon Railroad.** *Admission charged for some attractions.*

4. Haines

Convention and Visitors Center, Second Ave. and Willard St. Situated on a peninsula, this seaside town has a military background. **Fort William H. Seward,** founded in 1903, maintains its handsome white buildings and 9-acre parade ground. Today its recreation hall hosts Chilkat Indian dances, and the former hospital is a Tlingit crafts workshop. The downtown **Sheldon Museum and Cultural Center** holds an interesting family collection of Indian and gold-rush artifacts. *Admission charged at museum.*

5. Mendenhall Glacier Recreation Area

The focal point of this area is the tremendous **Mendenhall Glacier,** formed about 3,000 years ago. The glacier has gradually been receding, allowing visitors to witness various stages of forest growth on the newly exposed land, as well as to see the many animals that now live in the older woods. A visitor center explains the phenomenon, and trails access various sites.

6. Juneau

Visitor Information Center, Third and Seward Sts. The **Davis Log Cabin** provides maps of the downtown area of this cosmopolitan port, whose sights include the **State Capitol Building,** flanked by a life-size statue of a bronze bear, and the **St. Nicholas Russian Orthodox Church,** with its golden dome. Among the city's museums are the **House of Wickersham,** filled with a pioneer judge's memorabilia; the **Juneau-Douglas City Museum,** with gold-mining exhibits; and the **Alaska State Museum.** Guided excursions into the rain forest outside Juneau are available. *Admission charged for some attractions.*

7. Admiralty Island National Monument

Alaskan brown bears are the main residents of this island, accessible by ferry and floatplane from Juneau. Bald eagles also live here, along with deer, sea lions, and river otters. The Tlingit Indian village of **Angoon** offers boat rentals, modest accommodations, and guide services.

8. Sitka

Visitor Bureau, 330 Harbor Dr. This island community retains its dual Russian and Tlingit Indian heritage. **Sitka National Historical Park** preserves both the site of a Tlingit fort and the **Russian Bishop's House,** built in 1842. The reconstructed **St. Michael's Russian Orthodox Cathedral** holds the original church's icons and chalices. The **Sheldon Jackson Museum** displays the artifacts of Tlingit and other Indian societies, including spectacular tribal masks. *Admission charged for some attractions.*

9. Petersburg

Visitor Center, First and Fram Sts. The neat Scandinavian-style homes attest to this town's Norwegian heritage, which is celebrated at a May festival. Fishing is a mainstay of the economy; the harbor supports Alaska's largest halibut fleet. The **Clausen Museum** focuses on the history and process of fishing. In the downtown area stand three pioneer churches — Catholic, Lutheran, and Presbyterian. *Admission charged at museum.*

10. Wrangell

Chamber of Commerce, Front St. and Outer Dr. This town, surrounded by woods, has a very appealing simplicity. The **Wrangell City Museum** illustrates its history with Indian and pioneer artifacts. **Chief Shakes Island,** reached by footbridge, contains a re-created tribal house and splendid totem poles. **Petroglyph Beach** contains large stones etched with designs by mysterious ancient artisans. *Admission charged for some attractions.*

11. Prince of Wales Island

The country's third-largest island, Prince of Wales has more than 2,000 square miles of unspoiled wilderness and nearly 1,000 miles of coastline. The waters here abound in salmon and halibut, making this a fishing enthusiast's dream.

12. Saxman Native Village

Twenty-seven totem poles, some more than 100 years old, decorate this Tlingit Indian village. The extraordinary collection includes many works retrieved from various graveyards and other sites. The village also boasts a large cedar tribal house and a carver's shed, where artisans create totem poles and masks.

13. Ketchikan

Visitor Bureau, 131-FA Front St. The visitor bureau distributes maps for walking tours of the city's historic downtown area. The crafts of the Tlingits, Haidas, and Tsimshians are on display at the **Tongass Historical Museum.** The **Totem Heritage Center** and the **Totem Bight State Historical Park** feature magnificent examples of symbolic carvings; the park also displays a replica of a 19th-century community house. The salmon industry is important here, as visitors can observe by touring the **Deer Mountain Hatchery.** *Admission charged for some attractions.*

14. Misty Fiords National Monument

Abundant precipitation has created an evergreen rain forest next to granite cliffs that rise to 3,000 feet. Below the cliffs, blue-green fjords make dents in the coastline. This rugged paradise is a 2.3-million-acre section of **Tongass National Forest.** Sitka black-tailed deer, bears, mountain goats, and bald eagles populate the woodlands, while salmon, whales, and porpoises swim in the coastal waters.

15. Highway 16 to Prince George

Heading through the British Columbia interior, this route passes the town of **Hazelton,** home to eight Indian villages and the peaceful **Lakes District.** Prince George, a large, centrally located city, provides a rest stop for travelers.

16. Prince Rupert

Information Center, 100 First Ave. E. The **Museum of Northern British Columbia** offers boat tours of this fishing town's harbor as well as a Metlakatla Indian village. In the museum itself there is an excellent collection of regional Indian artifacts. *Donation encouraged.*

17. Queen Charlotte Islands

Chamber of Commerce, 93 Bayview Dr. Ferry service is available to this archipelago, which is so isolated that unique subspecies, such as the world's largest black bear, have evolved here. **Graham Island,** the most developed island of the group, features **Naikoon Provincial Park,** a wilderness area that encompasses forestland, lakes, and beaches.

Totem pole, Sitka National Historical Park

PACIFIC

OCEAN

Yakutat
Bay

Ocean
Cape

Yakutat
Situk
TONGASS
NATL.
FOREST

ST. ELIAS MTS.

Crescent Mtn.
4,770

RUSSELL FIORD
WILDERNESS

Novatak Glacier

Dry Bay

Alsek R.

Grand
Plateau
Glacier

Mt. Root
12,850

Mt. Fairweather
15,300

Cape
Fairweather

Mt. Crillon
12,700

Mt. La Perouse
10,728

Lituya Bay

Brady
Icefield

Icy Point
Palma Bay

Cape Spencer

ALEXANDER

ARCHIPELAGO

St. Elias Mts.

Mt. Turner
8,500

GLACIER BAY
NATIONAL
PARK
AND PRESERVE

Glacier
Bay

1

CHILKAT RANGE

ENDICOTT RIVER
WILDERNESS

Gustavus

Chilkat Pass
3,493

Klukwan

2

Haines

4

Chilkat S.P.

Mt. Foster
7,127

White Pass
2,915

3

KLONDIKE GOLD
RUSH N.H.P.
Skagway

COAST

Taku
Arm

Atlin

Surprise
L.

Teresa
L.

ATLIN
PROVINCIAL
PARK

Paradise Peak
7,215

Mt. Barham
6,868

Mt. Snowdon
6,987

Simpson Peak
7,130

CASSIAR

Cassiar

HIGHWAY

Boya
Lake P.P.

MOUNTAINS

Pyramid Mtn.
7,030

Mt. Poletica
7,620

Mt. Nesselrode
8,105

Point
Bridget S.P.

5

Devils Paw
8,584
Taku
Glacier

Tulsequah

Mt. Ogden
7,484

Mt. Lester Jones
7,016

Heart Peaks
6,602

Kawdy Mtn.
6,364

STIKINE

PLATEAU

Mt. Rath
6,234

Dome Mtn.
6,660

Dease
Lake
Dease
Lake

CONTINENTAL DIVIDE

Cry
Lake

BRITISH COLUMBIA

ALASKA

MOUNTAINS

Cross Sound

Elfin
Cove

Hoonah

TONGASS

CHICHAGOF
ISLAND

Yakobi
Island

WEST CHICHAGOF
YAKOBI
WILDERNESS

Pelican

Tenakee
Springs

Herbert
Graves I.

Salisbury
Sound

Kruzof
Island

Shelikof Bay

Cape
Edgecumbe

Funter

Douglas I.

Juneau

6

Hawk
Inlet

Icy Strait

Inside

Chatham

Passage

Stephens

Tracy Arm

7

ADMIRALTY
ISLAND
NATIONAL
MONUMENT

Angoon

ADMIRALTY

ISLAND

Pybus
Bay

Marine
Highway

Seymour

Port
Houghton

Strait

Frederick

Sound

Kake

Kupreanof

Petersburg

TRACY ARM-
FORDS TERROR
WILDERNESS

Endicott Arm

Baird
Glacier

Devils Thumb
9,077

Sheppard Peak
8,250

Mt. Ratz
10,290

Kates Needle
10,023

Mt. Hickman
9,740

Mt. Gordon
7,700

Telegraph
Creek

Kaketsa Mtn.
6,233

STIKINE
RIVER PROV.
REC. AREA

Iskut

Edziza Peak
9,143

MT.
EDZIZA
PROV.
PARK

Kinaskan
Lake

Kinaskan
Lake P.P.

Cold
Fish
L.

SPATSIZI PLATEAU
WILDERNESS
PROVINCIAL
PARK

Mt. Will
8,250

SKEENA

MTS.

Mt. Gunanoot
7,478

OLD SITKA
S.H.P.

Sitka
SITKA N.H.P.

8

BARANOF
ISLAND

Sitka
Sound

Baranof
Bay

NATIONAL

KUIU
ISLAND

KUPREANOF
ISLAND

9

Mitkof
Island

SOUTH BARANOF
WILDERNESS

Whale Bay

Tebenkof
Bay

TEBENKOF BAY
WILDERNESS

Point
Baker

Kuiu
Strait

Sumner

Port
Alexander

Mt. Calder
3,370

Whale
Pass

Zarembo
Island

10

Wrangell

Wrangell
Island

Blake
Channel

Etolin
Island

Stikine

Mt. Whipple
5,745

Mt. Talbot
4,461

STIKINE
LECONTE
WILDERNESS

Mt. John Jay
7,499

Kshwan Mtn.
7,500

Mt. Pounder
7,600

Mt. Knipple
8,400

Delta Peak
7,640

Meziadin
Lake P.P.

CASSIAR
HIGHWAY

Bell
R.

Bowser
L.

Cape Ommaney

Christian Sound

Cape Decision

CORONATION ISLAND
WILDERNESS

Coronation I.

Warren
I.

Helm Point

Iphigenia Bay

Heceta
I.

Shakan
Bay

Cape
Pole

Kosciusko
I.

Coffman
Cove

Edna
Bay

11

Thorne
Bay

FOREST

Whale
Pass

Clarence

Meyers
Chuck

Cleveland
Peninsula

Bell Island
Hot Springs

MISTY
FIORDS
NATIONAL
MONUMENT

Stewart

Hyder

Cambria
Icefield

37A

Meziadin
Jct.

Meziadin
L.

37

Restricted
Road

Alice Arm

Klawock

Noyes I.

Cape Addington

Baker I.

Craig

Cape Bartolome

PRINCE
OF
WALES
ISLAND

Waterfall
Hydaburg

Kasaan

Hollis

Ketchikan
Gateway

REVILLAGIGEDO
ISLAND

Saxman

TOTEM
BIGHT S.H.P.
Ward Cove
Ketchikan

13

Mountain Point

Camp
Point

CAN.
U.S.

Observatory
Inlet

Kincolith

Greenville

Suemez I.
Meares Pass

Cape Lookout

Sukkwan
I.

Dall
I.

Long
I.

12

Gravina
I.

Annette I.
Metlakatla
ANNETTE I.
IND. RES.

Duke I.

Cape Fox

Nakat

Portland
Inlet

Pearse
I.

15

Port
Simpson

16

37

ALASKA
MARITIME N.W.R.
WILDERNESS
Forrester I.

Cape Augustine

Cape
Muzon

SOUTH PRINCE
OF WALES
WILDERNESS

Cape
Chacon

Dundas
Island

Alaska Time Zone
Pacific Time Zone

Dixon   *Entrance*

Langara
Island

Cape Knox

Pivot Mtn.
1,922

Virago
Sound

McIntyre
Bay

Masset

NAIKOON
PROV.
PARK

Rose
Point

Hooper Pt.

Stephens
Island

Porcher I.

Oona
River

Port
Edward

**Prince
Rupert**

16

Skeena River

GITNADOIX
RIVER PROV.
REC. AREA

Hecate

Strait

17

QUEEN
CHARLOTTE
ISLANDS

GRAHAM
ISLAND

16

To Skidegate

Goschen
I.

Kitkatla

Pitt
I.

McCauley I.

To Port Hardy, B.C.
& Bellingham, Wash.

0 10 20 30 40 50 60 70 80
SCALE IN MILES

HAWAII ISLAND

1. Mookini Heiau

Built in A.D. 480, this temple complex is almost as large as a football field. It contains a scalloped altar, which can be decorated only with the 'ie'ie flower. Still considered sacred, the heiau was the site of birth rituals for King Kamehameha.

2. Lapakahi State Historical Park

Set in a protected cove, an ancient fishing village has been restored here. The park offers exhibits on fishing, crops, games, and other aspects of early island life.

3. The Laurance Rockefeller Collection of Asian and Pacific Art

1 Mauna Kea Beach Dr., Kohala Coast. The **Mauna Kea Beach Hotel** houses more than 1,600 art works — assembled by Laurance Rockefeller, founder of the resort — representing both Asian and

Pacific countries. The highlights of this comprehensive collection include a seventh-century Indian Buddha, 18th-century Japanese wooden horses, and 19th-century Hawaiian quilts.

4. Hapuna Beach State Recreation Area

Gleaming white sands draw snorkelers, scuba divers, and swimmers to this park. Rocks jutting into the ocean define the park borders; just north is a cove with tidal pools that are the right size for children.

5. Puukohola Heiau National Historic Site

King Kamehameha I rebuilt this ancient temple, dedicated it to the god of war, and sacrificed his main rival here as a prelude to conquering the Hawaiian Islands. Nearby is the smaller **Mailekini Heiau,** reputed to have been built in celebration of peace between the Big Island and Maui.

6. Kamuela Museum

Rtes. 19 and 250, west of Waimea. This idiosyncratic museum holds one family's private collection of objects from around the world, including items from Hawaii. The exhibits range from antique poi pounders and fishhooks fashioned from bone to temple idols and palace furnishings. Of special interest are a Kamikaze gun and an 1843 Bible written in English and Hawaiian. *Admission charged.*

7. Parker Ranch Visitor Center

Rte. 19, Waimea. Here a museum relates the history of the Parker Ranch, the largest individually owned cattle ranch in the United States. Founded in 1847 by a Massachusetts sailor who married King Kamehameha's granddaughter, the spread now comprises 225,000 acres. Two Parker family homes, one rustic and the other luxurious, can also be viewed by the public. *Admission charged.*

8. Waipio Valley

A black-sand beach is only one of the attractions of this breathtakingly beautiful jungle valley. Waterfalls cascade down cliffs as high as 2,000 feet, and numerous streams beckon swimmers. Fruit trees and white naupaka flowers share the same rich soil with the taro cultivated for poi by the area's few residents. The entry to the valley can be traveled on foot or by shuttle bus through a tour company, which can also arrange for horseback riding. *Fee charged for some activities.*

9. Mauna Kea

Perched atop Hawaii's tallest mountain is one of the world's leading centers for astronomical research, where many countries have built telescopes in domed white observatories. A four-wheel-drive vehicle is needed to reach the summit, but several outfits offer tours beginning at the visitor center, located at the 9,200-foot level. *Fee charged for tours.*

10. Akaka Falls State Park

The highlight of the park is the spectacular Akaka Falls, which descends 420 feet, surrounded by moss-covered cliffs and profuse tropical vegetation, to a delicate pond at the base of the cascade. The scene is even more breathtaking when rainbows form in the mist. The site can be reached by a paved path that also leads on to **Kahuna Falls.**

11. Hawaii Tropical Botanical Garden

Birds vie with flowers in creating the explosion of color in this nature preserve, located in a rain forest on craggy **Onomea Bay.** More than 1,800 botanical species grow here — ginger, bromeliads, heliconias, and palms among them. A three-tiered waterfall and streams complement the flowers' beauty. Koi, valued by fish collectors, swim in the lily lake. *Admission charged.*

12. Hilo

Hawaii Visitors Bureau, 250 Keawe St. This pretty town set on a bay features the Japanese-style **Liliuokalani Gardens,** the large-leafed trees of **Banyan Drive,** and the lovely **Rainbow Falls.** The **Lyman House Memorial Museum** displays Hawaiian artifacts, and early-morning visitors to the **Suisan Fish Market** can see the wares of returning fishermen. Hawaii is nicknamed the Orchid Island, and most of the flowers are grown in Hilo. *Admission charged at museum.*

Red torch ginger thrives on the Big Island.

13. Mauna Loa Macadamia Nut Corporation

Macadamia Rd., south of Hilo. Here visitors can take a self-guided tour through the inner workings of a company that produces a food product synonomous with Hawaii. Both the orchard and mill are open to the public, where there is ample opportunity to sample the world-renowned macadamia nuts.

14. Kapoho

In 1960 a volcanic eruption destroyed the village of Kapoho, sparing only a lighthouse, some metal roofs that now poke through the black lava, and a few gravestones. It also left behind a 6-foot-high, lava-rock wall. Near this former village are fish ponds, where visitors are offered the unusual opportunity of swimming with sea turtles in the geothermally heated water.

Steam clouds billow as lava enters the sea in Hawaii Volcanoes National Park.

15. Hawaii Volcanoes National Park

The park contains the active volcanoes **Kilauea** and **Mauna Loa,** the latter being the largest in the world, as well as remnants of old volcanic activity. From the visitor center, **Crater Rim Drive** leads to such sites as the **Thurston Lava Tube,** a tunnel created by hardened lava, and **Halemaumau Crater,** a steaming crater within the **Kilauea Caldera.** Off Mauna Loa Road lies **Kipuka Puaulu,** a native old-growth forest surrounded by lava. The **Chain of Craters Road** passes gigantic pit craters and a black sand beach on its way down to the coast. *Admission charged.*

16. Punaluu

This picturesque village boasts a coconut grove and an ebony beach. The stunning black sands border rough waters, which are home to many sea turtles. Nearby are fish ponds and the ruins of a heiau. Picnic and camping facilities are available in the adjacent beach park.

17. Ka Lae

A narrow, bumpy road leads to Ka Lae, the southernmost tip of the United States. Ka Lae is famous for its **Green Sand Beach,** made of olivine crystals formed when hot lava hit the cool sea.

18. Puuhonua o Honaunau National Historical Park

Puuhonua o Honaunau was one of many sanctuaries for those who broke ancient religious taboos punishable by death unless the lawbreaker could reach an official place of refuge. This sanctuary, the last such site to be preserved, was separated from the palace grounds by the massive Great Wall. Today this park holds the restored refuge and the palm-shaded grounds, with artisans on hand to demonstrate traditional crafts. *Admission charged.*

19. Kealakekua Bay

Snorkelers can swim with brightly hued fish in this marine preserve, which can also by seen by glassbottom boat or by scuba diving off the rocky coast. On the northwest side of the bay, the **Captain Cook Monument** pays tribute to the British navigator, who died here. Nearby are the temple ruins of **Hikiau Heiau.**

20. Mauna Loa Royal Kona Coffee Mill and Museum

160 Napoopoo Rd., near Captain Cook. The state of Hawaii contains the only commercial coffee orchards in the United States outside Puerto Rico. The history of the coffee industry on the Big Island is recorded in the museum's photography gallery, which chronicles 150 years of growing and harvesting the world-famous Kona coffee beans. Visitors can also sample the delicious coffee.

21. Kailua-Kona

Hawaii Visitors Bureau, 75-5719W Alii Dr. Nestled between a mountain and the ocean, this lovely coastal town contains many points of historic interest. Visitors can take a guided tour of the **Hulihee Palace,** a royal summer residence built in 1838. Across the street from it stands the black-stone **Mokuaikaua Church,** said to be Hawaii's first Christian place of worship. On the grounds of the **King Kamehameha Kana Beach Resort** lies an area where the king once resided; thatched huts from **Ahuena Heiau,** his final royal residence, have been re-created. *Fee charged for palace tour.*

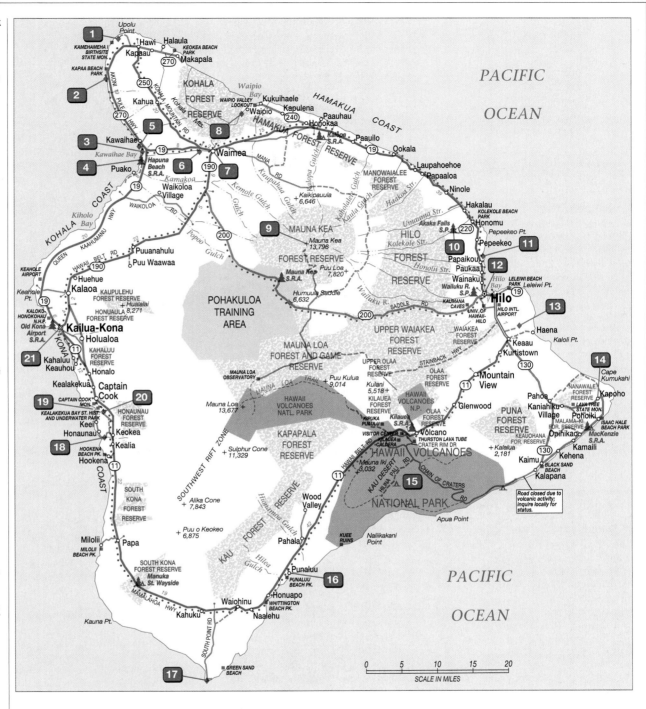

OAHU ISLAND

1. Mokuleia Field

Weekly polo matches take place in this charming seaside setting. Here spectators can enjoy one of society's favorite sports, particularly during the official playing season from March to August, when local teams compete with other local — as well as national and international — players. *Admission charged.*

2. Haleiwa

Although this old plantation town has gone through many incarnations — a seaside vacation spot for city dwellers, a gathering place for hippies, and an inspiring oasis for artists — its architectural style has remained virtually the same since the 1920's. Handsome wooden structures, both old and new, house boutiques, restaurants, and art galleries. During an annual August festival, Japanese residents traditionally float paper lanterns down the lovely Anahulu River.

3. Dole Pineapple Plantation

64-1550 Kamehameha Hwy., Wahiawa. Popular since its opening in 1951, this major tourist attraction celebrates one of Hawaii's most famous exports. Visitors can take a self-guided tour to study different varieties of the fruit — such as Saigon Red and Philippine Green — on display in the pineapple variety garden. Samples may be purchased on the plantation.

4. Waimea Falls Park

In this lush green valley, visitors can walk the lovely garden trails, with their labeled plants from around the world, or ride a tram to the 45-foot falls to watch daring cliff divers. The 1,800-acre site also harbors many animals (including the endangered Hawaiian nene, a goose), the remnants of an ancient village, and picnic areas. *Admission charged.*

5. Puu o Mahuka Heiau

These ancient temple ruins provide a glimpse of Hawaii's pre-Christian past. Called a heiau, the rectangular stone platform was made for worship and sacrifice. With one wall measuring 520 feet, this is one of the largest structures in Oahu. The site also offers extraordinary views of the island.

6. Sunset Beach

In the summer, this beach draws many swimmers and puka-shell collectors. In the winter, when the surf is rough, it becomes, along with the **Banzai Pipeline,** the festive site of the Triple Crown Hawaiian Pro Surfing Championships.

7. The Mill at Kahuku

56-565 Kamehameha Hwy., Kahuku. A defunct turn-of-the-century sugar mill is now open to the public as a cleverly renovated shopping center. Attesting to the work that once took place here, huge gears and a cane grabber, which was used to lift sugarcane from the locomotives that hauled it, are on display. Other pieces of machinery now serve as sculptures in a small, fragrant garden. Guided tours are available. *Fee charged for tour.*

8. Polynesian Cultural Center

55-370 Kamehameha Hwy., Laie. This astounding 42-acre complex holds re-creations of seven ancient South Pacific villages. Islanders demonstrate traditional skills and crafts from such locales as Fiji and Tahiti. Outrigger canoes provide visitors with transportation throughout the center. Dinnertime entertainment features a spectacular canoe show, complete with dancers representing each Polynesian island. *Admission charged.*

9. Sacred Falls State Park

A 2-mile trail follows a stream through thick vegetation into the valley that contains the Sacred Falls. Although the waterfall is 80 feet high, it's nearly dwarfed by the valley walls rising more than 1,000 feet above it. The water forms a pool at the cascade's base, where weary hikers can swim in an idyllic setting. The valley is subject to flash floods, and the park closes at any sign of rain.

10. Kualoa Ranch

49-560 Kamehameha Hwy., Kaaawa. On this working cattle ranch, visitors can take trail rides in the beautiful **Kaaawa Valley**

A snorkeler at Hanauma Bay Nature Park is escorted by friendly, multicolored reef fish.

or enjoy a more comprehensive activities package that includes horseback riding, dune-buggy rides, and snorkeling. Just across the highway is **Kualoa Regional Park,** with a wonderful beach for camping, picnicking, and taking in the sweeping view of the bay and mountains. *Fee charged for ranch activities.*

11. Mokolii Island

Topped by a smattering of palm trees and frequently surrounded by octopuses, Mokolii has been nicknamed Chinaman's Hat because of its cone shape. Rising 206 feet above the water off Kualoa Beach, it can be seen from Kamehameha Highway; for the more adventurous, the island can be reached at low tide by wading out on the reef.

12. Senator Fong's Plantation and Gardens

47-285 Pulama Rd., Kahaluu. Hiram Fong, who served in the U.S. Senate for many years, now runs this 725-acre estate, which comprises both a working plantation and impressive botanic gardens. A 45-minute narrated tram tour familiarizes visitors with some of Hawaii's exotic plant life, including fruit and nut trees and flowering vines. Classes in the art of lei-making are also offered. *Admission charged.*

13. U.S.S. Arizona Memorial

Offshore at Pearl Harbor, a simple, white monument spans the hull of the battleship U.S.S. *Arizona,* which sank during the 1941 Japanese attack. Visitors begin their tour onshore by viewing a short documentary film about the event, and then are transported by navy boat out to the memorial, which contains a wall engraved with the names of those who lost their lives on board the ship.

14. Byodo-In Temple

47-200 Kahekili Hwy., Kaneohe. This architectural jewel lies in the **Valley of the Temples,** surrounded by steep, deeply grooved green mountains. Its graceful lines reveal a strong Japanese influence, and indeed, the building is a replica of a 900-year-old Buddhist temple. Visitors can ring the 3-ton brass bell and stroll in the tranquil garden, which contains a large pond stocked with colorful carp. *Admission charged.*

15. Kailua Beach

Windsurfing is the main sport in Kailua Bay's turquoise waters, and there are several places in town that rent the necessary equipment. The ocean here is also fine for swimming; picnic facilities are provided along the lovely beach.

16. Sea Life Park

Makapuu Point, Waimanalo. Whales and dolphins frolic and cavort to the delight of visitors at this oceanside park, home of the world's only known "wholphin," the offspring of members of the two species.

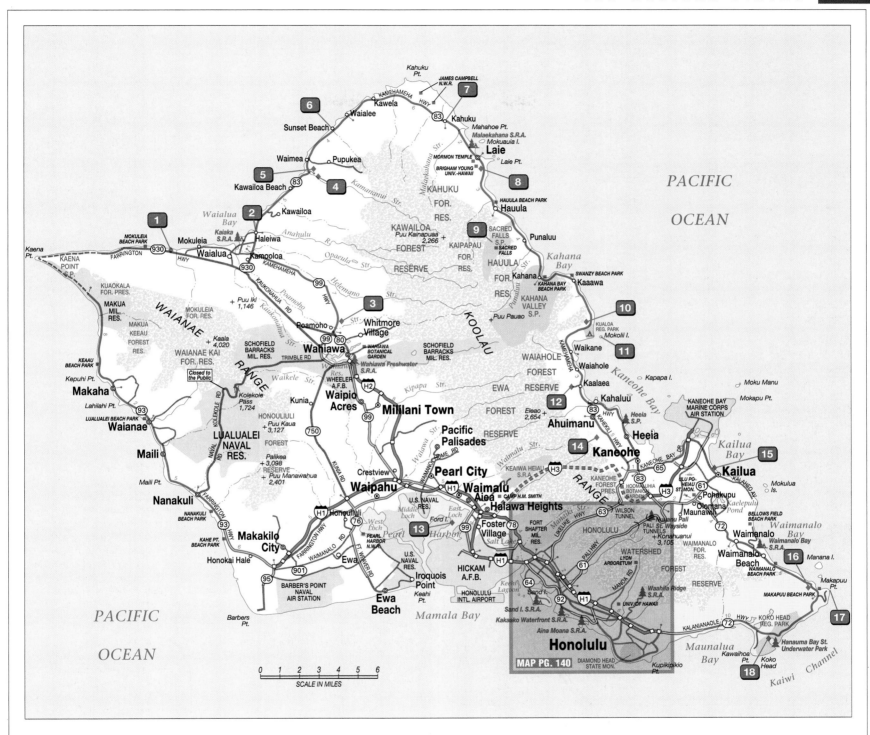

PACIFIC OCEAN

PACIFIC OCEAN

0 1 2 3 4 5 6
SCALE IN MILES

MAP PG. 140

The huge Hawaiian Reef Tank contains fascinating specimens of Hawaiian marine life, including sharks and stingrays. Also popular is a large replica of the state's shorelines, which illustrates and explains the Hawaiian coast. *Admission charged.*

17. Makapuu Point
From this headland the entire windward coast of Oahu is visible in all its splendor: the Koolau Mountains, the bay, the ocean, and Rabbit and Turtle islands, among others. A lighthouse with one of the world's largest lenses stands guard at the end of this massive, lava-rock point.

18. Hanauma Bay Nature Park
An overlook with a picnic and parking area gives a preview of this park — a palm-shaded crescent beach on a bay created by the remains of a volcanic crater. At the beach, which is a steep descent from the overlook on foot or by trolley, snorkelers enjoy encounters with reef fish in the calm water. As use of the park is restricted, visitors should call ahead for information.

HAWAII

OAHU

Honolulu

PACIFIC OCEAN

HONOLULU

1. Nuuanu Pali State Wayside

A terrace at 1,000 feet provides magnificent views of Nuuanu Valley's hills and the bays of the windward coast. King Kamehameha conquered Oahu by driving his opponents over the edge of these cliffs, although visitors may feel that the powerful trade winds did most of the work.

2. Manoa Falls

An easy hike from the end of Manoa Road leads through a forest of mixed exotic and indigenous plant life to Manoa Falls, just minutes from the bustle of Honolulu. The waterfall plunges 200 feet into a pool and often has a dazzling rainbow near its top.

3. Queen Emma Summer Palace

2913 Pali Hwy. Once the summer home of King Kamehameha and Queen Emma, this Colonial mansion now houses a fine collection of period furniture and memorabilia. On display are feather fans, quilts, silverware, koa cabinets, and the cradle of Prince Albert, the heir to the throne who died at age four. *Admission charged.*

4. Bernice P. Bishop Museum

1525 Bernice St. Hawaii's heritage is celebrated in this renowned collection of Hawaiian and Polynesian artifacts and natural history exhibits. Stunning royal feather cloaks, frightening god images, an authentic grass house, and a mounted 55-foot sperm whale are displayed in rooms trimmed with gleaming koa wood. A narrated show at the planetarium explains the tropical sky. *Admission charged.*

5. Foster Botanic Garden

50 North Vineyard Blvd. Orchids, pineapple bushes, vanilla plants, and thousands of other species of tropical vegetation line the walkways through this lovely 20-acre garden. Next door, the **Kwan Yin Temple** provides a tranquil

setting in which to enjoy the surrounding beauty. *Admission charged at garden.*

6. National Memorial Cemetery of the Pacific

2177 Puowaina Dr. This extinct volcano, called **Punchbowl Crater,** holds the remains of American soldiers, as well as the grave of World War II correspondent Ernie Pyle. An impressive monument commemorates the men and women missing in war. From the volcano's rim, there are spectacular views of the island.

7. The Contemporary Museum

2411 Makiki Heights Dr. This excellent collection of contemporary art is rivaled only by its spectacular location. Perched on the side of **Tantalus,** this former estate, with its beautiful sculpture gardens, offers fine views of Diamond Head. Along the 7-mile **Tantalus–Round Top Drive** there are also breathtaking views of the famous crater, as well as of the city and harbor, the Waianae Range, and Koko Head. *Admission charged.*

8. Honolulu Academy of Arts

900 South Beretania St. Asian art dominates this splendid collection, which also includes traditional and contemporary Western works, set in tranquil courtyards with tiled fountains. *Donation encouraged.*

9. Hawaii State Capitol

415 South Beretania St. The capitol's architecture clearly symbolizes the island state itself, with columns shaped like palm trees, chambers that look like volcanic cinder cones, an open-air central court, and reflecting pools that encircle the building. Guided tours take in statues of Queen Liliuokalani and of Father Damien, who ministered to victims of leprosy.

10. Dole Cannery

650 Iwilei Rd. A water tower shaped like a giant pineapple marks the entrance to this cannery, where guided tours illustrate the canning process, followed by samples of Dole's products. Exhibits and films in the visitor center illustrate the history of the pineapple industry. *Admission charged.*

11. Chinatown

A colorful mix of somewhat tattered herb shops and noodle factories along with gentrified stretches of art galleries, Chinatown offers acupuncture offices, lei shops, aromatic Chinese and Thai restaurants,

and, at the open-air **Oahu Market,** displays of exotic produce and fresh fish.

12. Hawaii Maritime Center

Pier 7, Honolulu Harbor. A museum in a century-old four-masted ship, a 60-foot replica of a double-hulled canoe, and artifacts from Hawaii's early whaling days examine the islands' dependence on the sea. At the nearby **Hawaii Children's Museum,** kids can pilot a submarine and explore the deck of a 19th-century ship. From the observation deck of the 10-story **Aloha Tower,** there are spectacular views of the city and harbor. *Admission charged for some attractions.*

13. Iolani Palace

King and Richards Sts. On guided tours of the only royal palace in the United States, visitors can see the thrones of King Kalakaua and the last monarch, Queen Liliuokalani, deposed in 1893. The Royal Hawaiian Band performs most Fridays on the palace grounds; reservations are required. *Admission charged.*

14. Kawaiahao Church

957 Punchbowl St. Built in 1842 from hand-cut coral stone, this church was the site of weddings, funerals, and coronations of the islands' royalty. The mausoleum of King Lunalilo is located in the churchyard.

15. Mission Houses Museum

553 South King St. The first American missionaries to the islands lived in these three historic buildings, including a frame house shipped from Boston and reassembled here in 1820. A reproduction of the old printing press the missionaries used to record the Hawaiian language for the first time is exhibited, and once a month costumed guides show how the missionaries lived and worked. *Admission charged.*

16. Ala Moana Park

A protective reef makes this one of the most popular beaches in greater Honolulu. Tourists and residents alike sun and frolic on the long sandy beach and swim in the calm lagoon. Shade and palm trees invite picnicking and ball playing. On the Waikiki

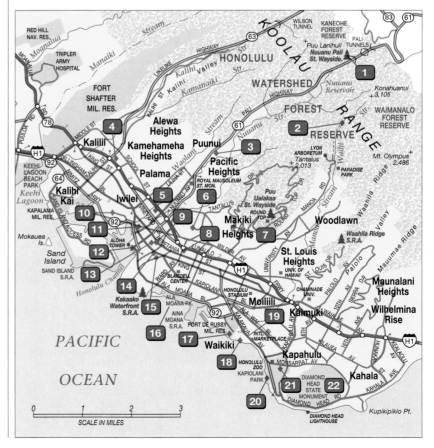

side, a peninsula named **Magic Island** offers similar delights.

17. U.S. Army Museum

Battery Randolph, Kalia Rd. World War II weaponry and memorabilia are the focus of this army museum, housed in a building with walls in some places more than 20 feet thick. Other displays illustrate military history from ancient Hawaiian battles to the Vietnam War.

18. Waikiki Beach

This world-famous 2½-mile stretch of beach lined with luxury hotels is the ideal place to stroll, sun, swim, or watch the daredevil surfers. Visitors can try the sport for themselves, rent catamarans or outrigger canoes, or enjoy a sunset cruise.

19. Kalakaua Avenue

Majestic palm trees tower over the glamorous shops that line this fashionable beachside thoroughfare. At the open-air **International Marketplace,** island artisans demonstrate their crafts. **King's Village,** around the corner on Kaiulani Avenue, is a shopping mall with costumed salespeople and a colorful Changing of the Guard Ceremony every night.

20. Waikiki Aquarium

2777 Kalakaua Ave. Giant clams, mesmerizing sharks, and more than 300 other species of marine life found in the South Pacific make their home in this small but surprisingly well-stocked aquarium. *Admission charged.*

21. Waikiki Shell

This amphitheater in **Kapiolani Park** presents fine performances of Hawaiian, classical, and popular music against the dramatic backdrop of moonlit Diamond Head. Visitors can bring a picnic and sit on the grass. Nearby, the colorful **Kodak Hula Show** has been entertaining enthusiastic audiences for more than 50 years. *Admission charged.*

22. Diamond Head State Monument

This famous crater was named by sailors who thought crystals in the rock were diamonds. Visitors can drive inside the extinct volcano or hike to the top for a grand view of Waikiki Beach from 760 feet up. A little farther along on Diamond Head Road is the **Diamond Head Lighthouse,** one of the oldest in the Pacific.

KAUAI ISLAND

1. Kilauea Lighthouse

From Kilauea Point visitors can watch the emerald ocean crashing against the bottom of the cliffs and try to sight sea turtles, dolphins, monk seals, and humpback whales. The **Kilauea Point National Wildlife Refuge,** marked by the lighthouse, is a sanctuary for nesting shearwaters and red-footed boobies, among other seabirds. Located nearby, the **Hanalei Valley Lookout** offers sweeping views of taro fields as well as of the **Hanalei National Wildlife Refuge** for endangered birds. *Admission charged for some attractions.*

2. Caves of Haena

The **Maniniholo Dry Cave,** perched high on a cliff in **Haena County Park,** was used for religious rites in ancient times. Today visitors can explore its spooky depths. The nearby **Waikapalae and Waikanaloa Wet Caves** contain pools of eerie green water.

3. Kee Beach and Kalalau Trail

Kee Beach is the only beach in the area where visitors can safely swim, scuba dive, and snorkel. From here, the views of the rugged Na Pali coast are spectacular. Affording a closer look, the 11-mile Kalalau Trail to Kalalau Valley follows the coastline, with branch trails leading off to waterfalls, sea caves, beaches, and verdant valleys. It's no surprise that the area has been used as the setting for several feature films, including *South Pacific, Raiders of the Lost Ark,* and *The Thornbirds.*

4. Kokee State Park

Set at an elevation of nearly 4,000 feet, this wilderness area enjoys cool temperatures that allow pine trees and ferns to grow along with passion fruit. Here visitors can enjoy miles of scenic hiking trails, occasional sightings of rare birds, and good trout fishing in the summertime. A

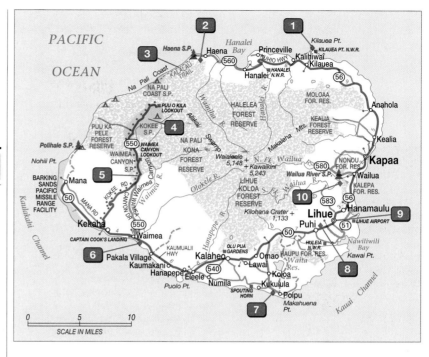

magnificent scenic drive leads to **Kalalau** and **Puu o Kila lookouts,** with lovely views of Waimea Canyon, Kalalau Valley, and the Pacific Ocean.

5. Waimea Canyon State Park

Called the Grand Canyon of the Pacific, Waimea Canyon is a 10-mile-long, 2-mile-wide, 3,600-foot-deep rift of multicolored cliffs and green mountains leading to the sea. **Waimea Canyon** and **Puu Hinahina lookouts** provide sweeping views of the surrounding area.

6. Russian Fort Elizabeth

Rte. 50, Waimea. These fort ruins are all that remain of Imperialist Russia's unsuccessful attempts to gain a toehold in the Hawaiian islands. At the nearby **Hanapepe Valley and Canyon Lookout,** visitors can enjoy spectacular views of the verdant valley, canyon, and the winding Hanapepe River.

7. Kiahuna Plantation Resort

2253 Poipu Rd., near Koloa. Visitors can view hundreds of varieties of plants, including orchids, hibiscus, and African aloes, which are set among lava-rock pools on the lovely grounds of the resort.

8. Kilohana

Rte. 50, Lihue. This former sugar plantation home now boasts agricultural exhi-

bits, horse-and-carriage rides, an open-air restaurant, and intriguing boutiques that sell everything from Hawaiian artifacts to paintings to Japanese antiques. At nearby **Grove Farm Homestead Museum,** a working farm and living history museum, visitors can learn about 19th-century life on one of the island's oldest sugar plantations. Reservations are required. *Admission charged at museum.*

9. Kauai Museum

4428 Rice St., Lihue. This informative collection gives a good overview of the island, with displays that range from Hawaiian quilts to the work of local artists to dioramas of area geology. There are bowls made from calabash gourds and native woods, displays that tell the story of Kauai and Niihau, and a 30-minute film that gives an aerial view of Kauai. *Admission charged.*

10. Fern Grotto

Off Rte. 56, Wailua. From Wailua Marina a leisurely 3-mile boat trip — to the accompaniment of Hawaiian songs played by the boat's musicians — motors to the grotto past craggy mountains, steep cliffs, and flowering trees. At the grotto, lush fishtail ferns cover the walls, and an 80-foot waterfall cascades over the cave's overhang. *Fee charged for boat ride.*

KAUAI · HAWAII
OAHU ★ Honolulu
MOLOKAI · · MAUI
LANAI · Lahaina

HAWAII
(The Big Island)

PACIFIC OCEAN

MOLOKAI, LANAI, & MAUI ISLANDS

1. Molokai Ranch Wildlife Park

This 1,500-acre reserve shelters oryxes, elands, ostriches, Barbary sheep, axis deer, the greater kudu, and other rare and endangered species. Guided passenger vans take camera-laden visitors through the veldlike landscape, where animals often approach the vehicles. Reservations are required. *Admission charged.*

2. Maunaloa

This tiny isolated town, once a plantation settlement, today has an assortment of shops that visitors will find appealing; some are run by the former laborers who worked the surrounding pineapple fields.

3. Kapuaiwa Grove

Planted for Prince Lot, who later became King Kamehameha V, this is one of the last royal coconut groves in all of the Hawaiian islands. **Church Row,** across the street, consists of plain 19th-century churches built by early missionaries.

4. Kaunakakai

Although this is the island's biggest city, what it mostly offers is atmosphere. Its few restaurants, wooden general stores, and the local landmark Kanemitsu Bakery resemble the set of a Wild West movie. Fishing boats can be chartered at the Kaunakakai Wharf.

5. Kalaupapa

Victims of Hansen's Disease (leprosy) were exiled in the 19th century to this difficult-to-reach peninsula, where they were tended by Father Damien, a Catholic priest who himself eventually succumbed to the disease in 1889. Today only a few patients remain in this virtually deserted village. Guided tours are offered of the settlement — reachable by air, mule, or foot — that include St. Philomena's

church, a cemetery, and an abandoned hospital, among other historic buildings.

6. Halawa Valley Overlook

From this overlook, there are dramatic views of beautiful Halawa Valley and the ruins of Molokai's oldest settlement. Trails lead to 250-foot **Moaula Falls,** which attracts swimmers to the refreshing pool at its base, and to 500-foot **Hipuapua Falls.**

7. Iliiliopae Heiau

Built in the 16th century, this is the largest outdoor shrine in all of Hawaii. Human sacrifices were once carried out here to appease the ancient gods. Today people leave more gentle offerings of stones wrapped in ti leaves at what is still considered a very sacred site.

8. St. Joseph's Church

In addition to his work at Kalaupapa, Father Damien was also the pastor to the rest of the island. St. Joseph's, built in 1876, has a life-size statue of the selfless priest. The construction of **Our Lady of Sorrows,** a church nearby, is also attributed to Father Damien.

9. Garden of the Gods

In the early morning and late afternoon, these weirdly shaped rocks appear to change color. Placed in what seems to be a purposeful pattern, the mysterious stones make an unforgettable sight, with the glistening Pacific in the background.

10. Kaiolohia Bay

A World War II ship lies rusting in the waters here, a victim of the choppy seas and unpredictable winds that cause many ships to founder on the reef. Nicknamed Shipwreck Beach, this is a good spot for fishing. In the distance, Molokai and Maui provide a breathtaking backdrop.

11. Keomuku Village

Located along a 12-mile coastal drive accessible only by four-wheel-drive vehicles, this was the last inhabited coastal village on the island. Once a sugar mill settlement, it became a ranching village after the sugar company failed in 1901. Visitors can see the only remaining structure in the settlement — a church built in 1903 — which has been restored.

12. Lanaihale

The 9-mile **Munro Trail,** for serious hikers or those with four-wheel-drive vehicles, winds through a forest of pine, eucalyptus,

and ironwood to Lanaihale, at 3,370 feet the highest point on the island. From this vantage point there are stunning views of most of the Hawaiian islands.

13. Hulopoe Beach

One of the best beaches in the state, this white-sand crescent attracts swimmers, bodysurfers, snorkelers, scuba divers, and picnickers. The bay is in a marine conservation district, and schools of dolphin sometimes swim by. From a nearby road there are striking views of **Puupehe,** a towering offshore monolith.

14. Lahaina

Visitors Bureau, 250 Alamaha St. The capital of Hawaii in the early 19th century, this well-preserved coastal town later became an important whaling center. A museum in a replica of a ship, the **Brig Carthaginian** documents that period with films and displays about whaling. Several renovated buildings in the **Historic District** can be toured, including the **Baldwin Home,** which was built by a missionary in 1834 and is now refurbished in period style. Restaurants, art galleries, and shops line the bustling waterfront, and the shade of the gigantic banyan tree next to the **Court House** is a perfect spot for people watching. Boat tours offer trips to the coral reefs, as well as seasonal whale watching. The **Lahaina Kaanapali & Pacific Railroad** features a 12-mile round-trip ride aboard antique cars pulled by steam engines. *Admission charged for some attractions.*

15. Iao Valley State Park

Thanks to frequent rain, lush tropical vegetation covers this beautiful park. Wild apple, mango, and guava trees grow in abundance, inviting hikers to sample their fruits. The majestic **Iao Needle,** a moss-covered rock that towers 1,200 feet above the valley, is often veiled in mist.

16. Wailuku

The **Historic District** of this appealing, hilly town is centered around High, Vineyard, and Market streets. Points of interest include the Art Deco–style **Iao Theater,** which dates back to 1927. **Kaahumanu Church,** a classic New England–style structure built in 1876, has services partly in Hawaiian each Sunday. **Hale Hoikeike,** built as the home of missionaries in the mid-19th century, now houses a collection of Hawaiian artifacts,

missionary furniture, and early weaponry. *Admission charged for some attractions.*

17. Alexander & Baldwin Sugar Museum

3957 Hansen Rd., Puunene. Located in a restored mill superintendent's house, this fascinating museum illustrates the history of the sugar industry and of plantation life in Hawaii. A working model of a sugarcane crushing machine, artifacts, and historical photographs detail how the company of Alexander & Baldwin grew to prominence in the sugarcane industry. The displays also document how the arrival of immigrant field workers contributed to Maui's complex ethnic mix. *Admission charged.*

18. Hookipa Beach

This beach has long been famous as a surfing spot, and since the late 1970's some of the best windsurfers in the world have also honed their skills here, where the waves can get as high as 15 feet. There are picnic sites that make fine viewing areas for this exciting sport.

19. Hui Noeau Visual Arts Center

2841 Baldwin Ave., Makawao. Located in a historic Mediterranean-style building, the arts center welcomes visitors to its exhibits, lectures, and classes that range from lei making to Chinese calligraphy. From its vantage point on the side of Haleakala volcano, the center has a stunning view of the island. The village of **Makawao** is home to cowboys who work on the neighboring ranches; an annual rodeo is held here on the Fourth of July.

20. Kaumahina State Wayside

Shaded by palm and eucalyptus trees, this grassy area is ideal for a picnic. From an overlook, there's a panoramic view of the Keanae Peninsula and the Pacific.

21. Keanae Arboretum

Hana Hwy., Keanae. The winding trail through this arboretum passes stands of breadfruit, papaya, and bamboo trees, as well as flowers and plants native to the islands. **Keanae Valley Wailua Lookout** affords fine views of taro fields and dikes, with the ocean in the background and Haleakala volcano in the distance.

22. Waianapanapa State Park

With its oceanside location, this park is an inviting spot to swim, picnic, hike, pick fruit, and camp. Visitors can see a heiau, an ancient burial site, and one of the few black sand beaches located on Maui.

23. Hana

Sights of interest in this isolated, sleepy community include the recently restored **Wananalua Church,** which was built in 1838 from coral blocks. Picnic sites at **Hana Bay Beach Park** overlook fishing boats at anchor. The famous **Hasegawa's General Store,** rebuilt after a 1990 fire, is a local institution, having served village residents and Hana Highway travelers faithfully for some 70 years. About a mile west of town, the peaceful **Helani Gardens** exhibit tropical and subtropical plant species gathered worldwide, along with the handwritten quotations and aphorisms of founder Howard Cooper. *Admission charged for some attractions.*

24. Oheo Gulch

The bumpy, winding trip from Hana is rewarded by a swim in the refreshing pools of Oheo Gulch, part of the Kipahulu section of Haleakala National Park. Called the Seven Sacred Pools, these volcanic waterholes actually number about 30. One mile farther on, the grave of aviator Charles Lindbergh can be found next to the **Hoomau Congregational Church.**

25. Haleakala National Park

At park headquarters, visitors can get camping permits and information about **Mount Haleakala,** a dormant volcano 3,000 feet deep and 21 miles in circumference. From the **House of the Sun Visitor Center,** at 9,800 feet, there are awe-inspiring views of the crater's barren, moonlike interior. In the morning, rangers give hourly talks about the volcano. The interior of the crater, tinged with multicolored lava ash, can also be viewed from several vantage points along **Haleakala Crater Road.** From **Leleiwi Overlook,** visitors may see themselves reflected in the clouds below if the weather conditions permit. From **Kalahaku Overlook,** 9,325 feet above sea level, the rare silversword plant can be viewed, its stalks covered with hundreds of delicate purple and yellow flowers when in bloom. From **Puu Ulaula Overlook,** the highest point on the island, there is a breathtaking panorama of the volcano and the other islands in the distance. Here the temperature can be 30 degrees cooler than on the coast. Rangers give regularly scheduled talks in the glass-enclosed lookout. For a closer look into the center of the crater, hikers can follow the **Halemauu Trail,** beginning at the visitor center, or take the **Sliding Sands Trail.** *Admission charged.*

26. Kula Botanical Gardens

Rte. 377, Kula. Rare koa trees, orchids, protea, and other tropical plants and flowers grow in their natural setting in this lovely mountainside garden. Streams crisscross the grounds, where shaded benches and picnic areas beckon visitors to enjoy the scenery. *Admission charged.*

27. Tedeschi Vineyards and Winery

Rte. 37, Ulupalakua. Hawaii's only homegrown wines and champagnes are produced in this fine winery, which also makes Maui Blanc, a dry pineapple wine. Visitors can tour the grounds and sample the wines in a tasting room that formerly served as a jail.

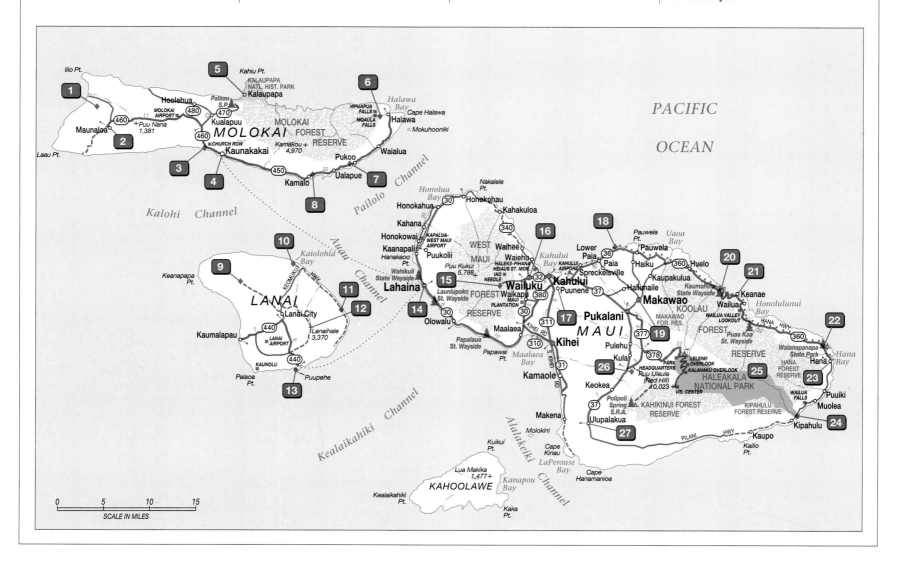

The Central States

From sod houses to stately mansions, wheat-filled fields to watery bayous, all of our nation's diversity can be found in America's midsection. The wonders of a varied landscape are revealed in the sparkling lakes and northern woodlands of Minnesota, the grassy plains of Nebraska, the rolling hills of Missouri, the rugged mountains and peaceful pasturelands of Arkansas. This is the land that gave us Mark Twain's enchanting tales of *Life on the Mississippi* and Laura Ingalls Wilder's beloved story of her *Little House on the Prairie;* whose broad horizons symbolize the optimism of the American spirit. Here are sites that echo the distant voices of the Indians who first inhabited the land and the pioneers who later pushed westward; that portray a Texas rancher's giant spread and a small Michigan fishing village; that reflect our heritage in the stirring Alamo and the simple cabin where Abraham Lincoln was born. For sheer awe there are nature's spectacles, like the water-sculpted stone fantasies in Wisconsin at The Dells, and modern man-made wonders such as Chicago's stylish buildings that scrape the sky— dazzling both mind and eye.

The dynamic Chicago skyline rises up from America's heartland.

1. Agassiz National Wildlife Refuge

This refuge, spanning 61,500 acres of forest, marshland, and water, is home to 49 species of mammals and more than 277 species of birds. The only national wildlife refuge in the lower 48 states to have a resident wolf pack, it is also the best place in Minnesota to spot a wild moose.

2. Polk County Museum

Rte. 2 East, Crookston. This superb museum consists of several buildings that recall early America, including a one-room schoolhouse and a pioneer log cabin. The main building contains several carefully restored rooms, such as a doctor's office, barbershop, and general store. *Donation encouraged.*

3. Moorhead

Chamber of Commerce, 725 Center Ave. A major agricultural center, Moorhead offers several attractions. The **Comstock Historic House** is the restored 11-room Victorian home of Solomon Comstock, politician and founder of local Moorhead State University. The **Plains Art Museum** displays colorful examples of Indian art and clothing, and paintings by American impressionists. The **Heritage Hjemkomst Interpretive Center** features a full-scale replica of an ancient 77-foot Viking ship. *Admission charged for some attractions.*

4. Tamarac National Wildlife Refuge

Receding glaciers left lakes, swamps, and bogs in more than a third of these 43,000 acres, where wetlands provide a nesting place for native bird species and migrating flocks. The landscape includes areas of conifers, hardwoods, and prairie grass where deer, black bears, and an occasional moose can be observed.

5. Bemidji

Chamber of Commerce, 300 Bemidji Ave. Named as a home of the legendary Paul Bunyan, Bemidji offers the **Bunyan House Information Center,** which has humorous displays of the lumberjack's tools and artifacts. The **Bemidji Arts Center** exhibits the works of talented local artists. At **Bemidji State Park,** visitors can hike on nature trails through a beautiful virgin red pine and sugar maple forest, and enjoy a pleasant lakeside beach. *Admission charged for some attractions.*

6. Cass Lake

This lake is surrounded by the scenic nesting grounds of one of the densest populations of bald eagles in the mainland United States. The nearby three-story headquarters of the **Chippewa National Forest** is one of the world's largest log buildings.

7. Grand Rapids

Convention and Visitors Bureau, 1 NW Third St. This former logging town recalls the past with the 105-acre **Forest History Center.** Re-created buildings such as a 1900 logging camp depict lumberjack life, and a wooded trail introduces visitors to indigenous trees. Grand Rapids is the hometown of actress Judy Garland, and the **Central School Heritage and Arts Center,** located in a restored 19th-century schoolhouse, has the world's largest collection of Garland memorabilia, including childhood family portraits and mementos from *The Wizard of Oz.* Boating, camping, fishing, and picnicking are popular at **Pokegama Lake Recreation Area,** which contains a concrete dam dating from 1903. *Admission charged for some attractions.*

8. Brainerd

Chamber of Commerce, Sixth and Washington Sts. Associated with the fictional character of Paul Bunyan, this town features the **Paul Bunyan Arboretum,** which, reversing the legend, grows trees rather than fells them. A 26-foot statue of the character presides over the **Paul Bunyan Amusement Center.** An impressive re-creation of an 1870's mining town, **Lumbertown U.S.A.** comes complete with a riverboat, a train replica, and nearly 30 new and restored buildings evoking town life in pioneer days. Exhibits at the **Crow Wing County Historical Society Museum** relate to local Indian tribes, the fur and logging industries, and life in rural 19th-century Minnesota. *Admission charged for some attractions.*

9. Tipsinah Mounds Park

Located on the southern shore of serene **Pomme de Terre Lake,** this park is a living bastion of history. Within its borders are the traces of 40 Indian mounds, dating from A.D. 1000 to 1600, as well as numerous prehistoric bone and stone tools.

10. Runestone Museum

206 Broadway, Alexandria. The museum's most intriguing display is a 3-foot-high stone covered with runic inscriptions, leading to speculation that the Vikings explored the area in 1362. The adjacent **Fort Alexandria Agricultural Museum** depicts pioneer life with agricultural machinery and Indian artifact exhibits. *Admission charged.*

11. Sinclair Lewis Boyhood Home

810 Sinclair Lewis Ave., Sauk Centre. Sinclair Lewis, the first American to win a Nobel Prize in Literature, spent most of his youth in this house and based his novel *Main Street* on that very street in the town. The house includes Lewis family memorabilia, the author's bedroom, and the office of his father, a doctor. *Admission charged.*

12. Charles A. Lindbergh House

1200 Lindbergh Dr. South, Little Falls. This restored farmhouse was the boyhood home of Charles Lindbergh who, in 1927, became the first pilot to fly solo nonstop from New York to Paris. *Admission charged.*

13. St. Cloud

Convention and Visitors Bureau, Sixth Ave. South. Central Minnesota's past is documented at the **Stearns County Heritage Center,** where displays include a two-story replica of a granite quarry. The **College of St. Benedict** in St. Joseph boasts a $5 million library, and its **Benedicta Arts Center** offers art exhibits, plays, films, and concerts. There is a Benedictine abbey in nearby Collegeville, and the order also founded **St. John's University** there in 1857. *Admission charged for some attractions.*

14. Elk River

Chamber of Commerce, 729 Main St. In 1867, Elk River's Oliver Kelley founded the famous Grange, a farmers' organization that grew to more than a million members. Built by Kelley in the 1870's, the **Oliver H. Kelley Farm** now operates as a living-history farm. The nearby **Sherburne National Wildlife Refuge** offers year-round recreational activities, including hiking, skiing, and canoeing. *Admission charged at farm.*

15. St. Croix Falls

A small farming and tourist community, St. Croix Falls includes several natural areas.

Crex Meadows Wildlife Area is a 30,000-acre state-preserved prairie-wetlands habitat. **St. Croix National Scenic Riverway** is a 200-mile river, twisting through pine and hardwood forests and high rocky bluffs. **Interstate State Park,** the oldest in Wisconsin, offers all kinds of water activities, hiking, nature walks, and skiing trails.

16. Hayward

Chamber of Commerce, Rte. 63 and Main St. At **Historyland,** visitors can tour a logging camp and museums that feature Indian artifacts. The **National Freshwater Fishing Hall of Fame** includes a 143-foot-long, 4½-story building shaped like a muskie, with an observation deck in its mouth. World records and trophies are featured among the exhibits. *Admission charged.*

17. Soudan Underground Mine State Park

The main attraction here is the state's first and deepest iron mine, which operated for 80 years until 1962. Visitors are sent down almost 2,400 feet to the mine's lowest level, where a tour and a train ride through hand-dug tunnels are offered. The 1,300-acre park also has a visitor center, which features educational displays explaining local geology and mining. *Admission charged.*

18. Ely

Chamber of Commerce, 1600 East Sheridan St. The town's **Voyageur Visitor Center** commemorates the era of Indians, fur traders, and loggers through audiovisual presentations and artifacts such as a large birchbark freight canoe. In the **Boundary Waters Canoe Area Wilderness** visitors can enjoy some of the best canoeing waterways in the country.

19. Voyageurs National Park

This magnificent 219,000-acre park is dotted with streams, marshes, and more than 30 lakes. Among the wildlife of this watery terrain are black bears, beavers, white-tailed deer, moose, bald eagles, and many species of waterfowl and fish.

20. International Falls

Convention and Visitors Bureau, 200 Fourth St. A small paper-manufacturing community on the Canadian border, this town is a port of entry to Ontario. The region's early history is commemorated at the **Grand Mound Center,** which exhibits mounds built by the Laurel Indians about 200 B.C., as well as artifacts from later Indian tribes.

MAP PG. 39

MAP PG. 151

SCALE IN MILES
0 10 20 30 40 50

1. Hibbing

Chamber of Commerce, 211 East Howard St. This mining town was moved 2 miles to its present location because the **Hull-Rust-Mahoning Mine,** the largest open-pit iron mine in the world, threatened to undercut it. From an observation platform at the mile-wide and 3-mile-long pit that has been mined since 1895, there are spectacular views of the earth-moving equipment far below. The **Paulucci Space Theatre** uses computerized special effects and a large curved screen in presentations on space exploration, astronomy, and the environment. *Admission charged at theater.*

2. Minnesota Museum of Mining

Memorial Park Dr., Chisholm. This vast museum highlights the treacherous life of early miners and the scope of mining operations here today. Exhibits include a replica of a cramped turn-of-the-century mine drift, complete with vintage picks, water pumps, and rescue stretchers. Enormous pieces of heavy mining machinery dot the grounds, including an ore truck's tire weighing nearly 3 tons. Nearby **Ironworld U.S.A.** is a 15-acre park, whose interpretive center offers informative programs about the area's mining industry. Rides on an excursion train take visitors along the Glen open-pit iron mine. *Admission charged.*

3. Mountain Iron

Chamber of Commerce, 8878 Main St. The city of Mountain Iron is literally built on iron from the Mesabi Range. The **Mountain Iron Mine Viewpoint** overlooks the original mine, started in 1890. In the distance, visitors can see the enormous **Minntac Plant,** the largest taconite mining and processing operation in the world. A 1910 Baldwin locomotive, used to haul natural ore in the Mountain Iron pit, now serves as a reminder of the town's mining past.

4. Virginia

Chamber of Commerce, 1 Vermilion Dr. This mining town and recreational area is the site of several mines, where bus tours offer a look at the process of iron-ore mining. **Mineview in the Sky** is an observation platform that looks down 600 feet into the open pit of the 3-mile-long Rouchleau Mine Group. The **Virginia Heritage Museum,** which occupies a log house from the early 1900's, exhibits Swedish Bibles, wedding dresses, tools, and other artifacts that reflect the town's ethnic variety.

5. U.S. Hockey Hall of Fame

801 Hat Trick Ave., Eveleth. This entertaining collection of hockey memorabilia, along with photos and a slide show, explains the game of hockey and commemorates some of its notable players. *Admission charged.*

6. Eli Wirtanen Finnish Farmstead

Off Rte. 4, north of Duluth. The life of the area's Finnish homesteaders is detailed in this cluster of buildings, which includes a square-hewed log house, outhouse, horse barn, root cellar, and a traditional Finnish smoke sauna. Most of these were built by homesteader Eli Wirtanen himself.

7. Seasons of Yesteryear Pioneer Museum

7778 Pine Rd., Meadowlands. Pioneer history comes alive at this museum, with authentically furnished buildings from the period, an extensive collection of artifacts, and demonstrations of traditional crafts.

8. Moose Lake State Park

Located near the town of Moose Lake, activities in this state park center on **Echo Lake,** which offers good fishing for bass, pike, and panfish. Hiking trails edge the lake and traverse stands of aspen, maple, and birch. *Admission charged.*

9. Jay Cooke State Park

Some 50 miles of trails through this lovely park wind along the deep gorge cut by the rushing **St. Louis River** — past a swinging bridge, jagged rock formations, and islands in the river, and into hardwood forests. From **Oldenburg Point** there are striking views of the river valley. Fishing, hiking, cross-country skiing, and snowmobiling are all popular here. *Admission charged.*

10. Pattison State Park

Big Manitou Falls, the highest in the state, cascades 165 feet in this park. Visitors can also view 30-foot **Little Manitou Falls** and a variety of bird habitats sheltering waterfowl, falcons, barred owls, and songbirds. The park's year-round recreational activities

Split Rock Lighthouse on Lake Superior

include swimming, hiking, skating, and cross-country skiing. *Admission charged.*

11. Superior

Tourist Information Center, 305 Harbor View Pkwy. The **Fairlawn Mansion and Museum,** a 42-room lakeside Victorian mansion built in 1890, has marble fireplaces, decorative silver, stained glass, and exhibits on Lake Superior Indians and early shipping. The **Old Fire House and Police Museum** displays vintage vehicles and other artifacts. From **Barker's Island** boats depart on narrated cruises of the harbor and the lake. At the dock is the **S.S. Meteor,** the last remaining whaleback freighter and now a maritime museum. *Admission charged for some attractions.*

12. Duluth

Convention and Visitors Bureau, 100 Lake Place Dr. The **Aerial Lift Bridge,** which joins the mainland to Minnesota Point and can be raised 138 feet in less than a minute, is a symbol of this international port city. Nearby **Canal Park Marine Museum** explores the lake's maritime history. From **Skyline Parkway Drive,** a 27-mile-long road atop the city's bluffs, there are spectacular views of the lake and harbor and, at **Hawk Ridge Nature Preserve,** frequent sightings of soaring hawks. Scenic **North Shore Drive** winds past magnificent lake scenery from Duluth to Canada. Visitors can tour the mansion and formal gardens of **Glensheen,** a 39-room lakeside estate built

about 1908. The **St. Louis County Heritage and Arts Center** is a former depot that now houses museums devoted to early life in Duluth, natural history, and the area's railroading past. The University of Minnesota's **Tweed Museum of Art** features paintings from the 16th through 20th centuries. *Admission charged for some attractions.*

13. Lake County Historical Depot Museum

Waterfront Dr. and Salt Ave., Two Harbors. Set in the 1907 depot of the Duluth, Missabe & Iron Range Railroad Company, this museum chronicles the area's railroading history. On display are the first locomotive used in the area and a 1941 Mallet locomotive, one of the most powerful steam engines in the world. *Admission charged.*

14. Gooseberry Falls State Park

As it courses through this 1,600-acre park, the **Gooseberry River** has five waterfalls, two of them more than 30 feet high. Anglers try for trout in the river, and at its mouth rock hounds search for Lake Superior agates. From the 15 miles of trails that loop through hardwood forests to overlooks above the lake, some of the park's white-tailed deer, black bears, and other wildlife can be seen. *Admission charged.*

15. Split Rock Lighthouse State Park

The beacon of this octagonal lighthouse, built in 1910 atop a rugged 100-foot-high cliff, flashed a warning to iron-ore carriers whose compasses were thrown off by the area's metallic rocks. Today the restored lighthouse is open to guided tours. The park's hiking and cross-country skiing trails lead to scenic overlooks and to the shoreline of Lake Superior. *Admission charged.*

16. Tettegouche State Park

Some of the most spectacular scenery in the state can be found in this park. Walking paths lead to **Shovel Point,** its 170-foot cliffs formed over eons by glaciers and wave action on ancient volcanic flows. The **Baptism River** boasts the highest waterfall in Minnesota. Visitors will also find a mile of shoreline on Lake Superior, four inland lakes, a hardwood forest, and the remains of a logging camp. Nearby **Palisade Head,** a bluff with a 350-foot drop to the lake's north shore, presents a beautiful view of the **Sawtooth Mountains** as well as a challenge to rock climbers. *Admission charged.*

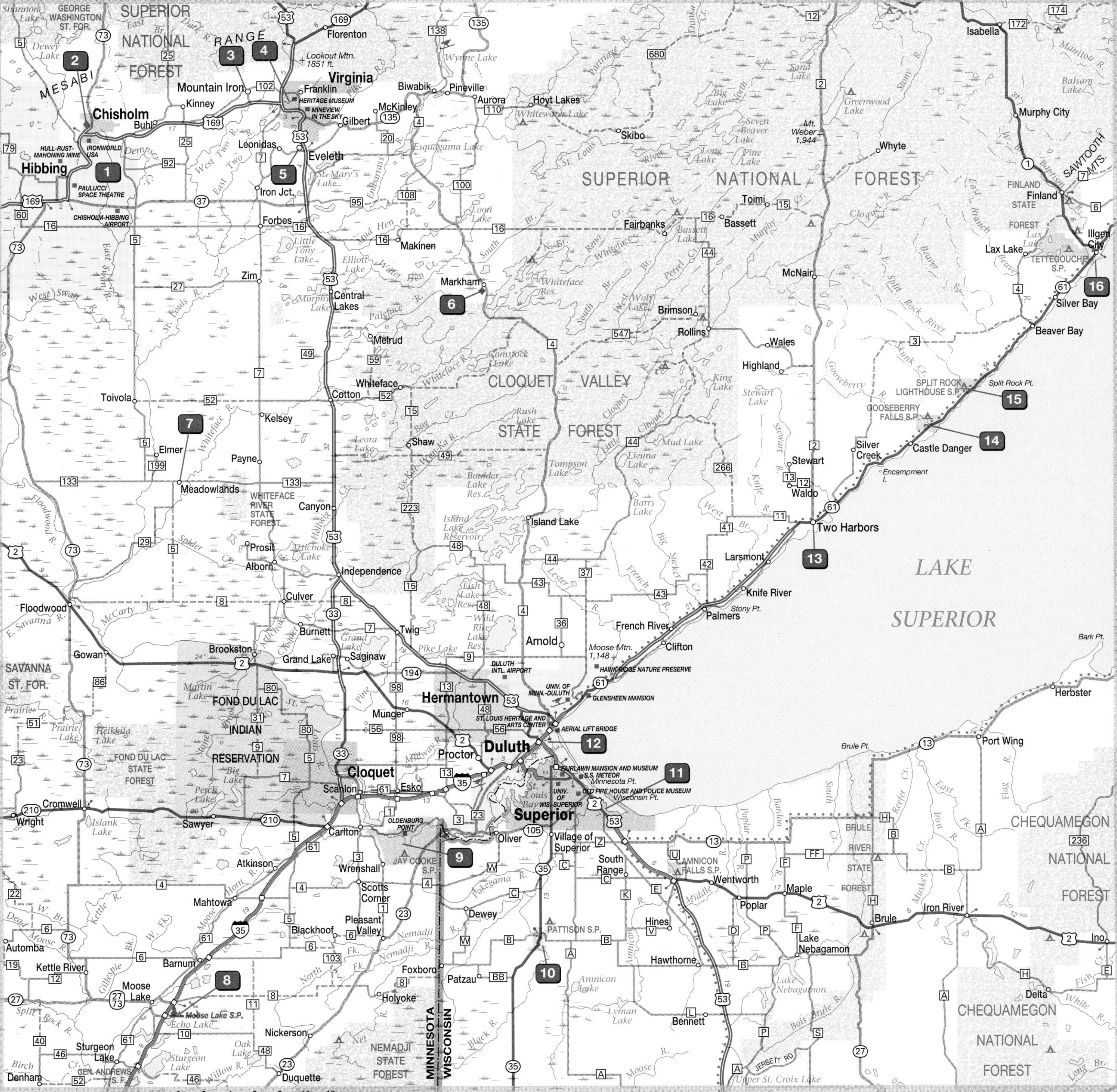

SUPERIOR NATIONAL FOREST

MESABI RANGE

GEORGE WASHINGTON ST. FOR.

Shannon Lake
Dewey Lake
Florenton
Lookout Mtn. 1851 ft.
Wynne Lake
Isabella
Manitou R.
Balsam Lake
Murphy City

Mountain Iron
Kinney
Franklin
HERITAGE MUSEUM
MINEVIEW IN THE SKY
Virginia
Biwabik
Pineville
Aurora
Hoyt Lakes
Whitewater Lake
Big Lake
Greenwood Lake
Sand Lake
Whyte

Chisholm
Buhl
Gilbert
McKinley
Skibo
Seven Beaver Lake
Long Lake
Pine Lake
Mt. Weber 1,944

Hibbing
HULL-RUST-MAHONING MINE USA
IRONWORLD USA
Leonidas
Eveleth
St. Mary's Lake
SUPERIOR NATIONAL FOREST
Finland
FINLAND STATE FOREST
Illgen City
Lax Lake
TETTEGOUCHE S.P.

PAULUCCI SPACE THEATRE
Iron Jct.
Esquagama Lake
Loon Lake
Fairbanks
Bassett Lake
Bassett
Toimi
Murphy
McNair
Silver Bay

CHISHOLM-HIBBING AIRPORT
Forbes
Makinen
Whiteface Res.
Renn
Brimson
Beaver Bay

Zim
Markham
Central Lakes
Whiteface Lake
West Wolf Lake
Rollins
Wales
Highland
Stewart Lake
SPLIT ROCK LIGHTHOUSE S.P.
Split Rock Pt.

Toivola
Melrud
Comstock Lake
CLOQUET VALLEY
King Lake
GOOSEBERRY FALLS S.P.
Encampment I.

Kelsey
Whiteface
Cotton
Rush Lake
STATE FOREST
Stewart
Silver Creek
Castle Danger

Elmer
Payne
Shaw
Leora Lake
Tompson Lake
Lieuna Lake
Waldo
Mud Lake

Meadowlands
WHITEFACE RIVER STATE FOREST
Bonuka Lake Res.
Barrs Lake
Two Harbors

Canyon
Island Lake
Island Lake Reservoir
Larsmont

Prosit
Alborn
Independence
Fish Lake Res.
Knife River
Palmers
Stony Pt.

Floodwood
Culver
Wild Rice Lake Res.
Arnold
Clifton
Moose Mtn. 1,148
HAWK RIDGE NATURE PRESERVE
Bark Pt.

Gowan
Burnett
Twig
Pike Lake
DULUTH INTL. AIRPORT
UNIV. OF MINN-DULUTH
GLENSHEEN MANSION

SAVANNA ST. FOR.
Brookston
Grand Lake
Saginaw
Hermantown
ST. LOUIS HERITAGE AND ARTS CENTER
Herbster

Martin Lake
FOND DU LAC
Munger
AERIAL LIFT BRIDGE
Duluth

Prairie Lake
Heikkila Lake
INDIAN RESERVATION
Proctor
FAIRLAWN MANSION AND MUSEUM
S.S. METEOR
Minnesota Pt.

FOND DU LAC STATE FOREST
Big Lake
Cloquet
Scanlon
Esko
OLD FIRE HOUSE AND POLICE MUSEUM
Wisconsin Pt.
Port Wing
Brule Pt.

Cromwell
Wright
Island Lake
Sawyer
Carlton
OLDENBURG POINT
Superior
UNIV. OF WIS-SUPERIOR
St. Louis Bay
BRULE RIVER STATE FOREST

Atkinson
Wrenshall
JAY COOKE S.P.
Oliver
Village of Superior
South Range
AMNICON FALLS S.P.
Wentworth
CHEQUAMEGON NATIONAL FOREST

Automba
Mahtowa
Scotts Corner
Dewey
Maple
Poplar
Iron River

Kettle River
Blackhoof
Pleasant Valley
PATTISON S.P.
Hines
Lake Nebagamon
Ino

Moose Lake
Barnum
Foxboro
Patzau
Hawthorne
Bennett
Delta

Sturgeon Lake
MOOSE LAKE S.P.
Echo Lake
Nickerson
Holyoke
NEMADJI STATE FOREST
Lyman Lake
CHEQUAMEGON NATIONAL FOREST

Denham
GEN. ANDREWS S.F.
Duquette
MINNESOTA / WISCONSIN
Upper St. Croix Lake

LAKE SUPERIOR

SCALE IN MILES
0 2 4 6 8 10 12

1. Isle Royale National Park

This 45-mile-long wilderness island, reachable by ferry, is the largest in Lake Superior. The park is populated by wolves, moose, fox, beavers, and other mammals, as well as by nesting loons and bald eagles. More than 160 miles of hiking trails lead to lakes that offer excellent fishing for trout, pike, perch, and walleyes. *Fee charged for ferry.*

2. Thunder Bay

Convention and Visitors Bureau, 520 Leith St. Tours and crafts demonstrations at 19th-century **Fort William** recall the fur-trading history of this port town. **Thunder Bay Art Gallery's** fine collection focuses on Canadian native art from pottery to quilts. Guided tours of the **Thunder Bay Amethyst Mine** show how amethyst is mined and cleaned; local amethyst factories display the finished product. At **Kakabeka Falls Provincial Park,** water takes a spectacular 128-foot plunge to the river below. *Admission charged for some attractions.*

3. Grand Portage National Monument

A monument marks the site of the "great carrying place," where 18th-century fur traders carried goods and pelts over an 8½-mile trail into the Canadian wilderness. The intrepid can still try the rugged route for themselves today. At the foot of the trail, a partially reconstructed trading post includes a fully equipped kitchen, a Great Hall with period furnishings, and birchbark canoes. *Admission charged.*

4. Grand Marais

Chamber of Commerce, 15 North Broadway. This quaint harborside town is surrounded by outstanding recreational opportunities. The **Gunflint Trail,** a 58-mile-long road to Saganaga Lake on the Canadian border, traverses the 3-million-acre **Superior National Forest,** with its glacial lakes and hiking trails. To the west, the **Boundary Waters Canoe Area Wilderness** offers excellent fishing and canoeing. *Admission charged at wilderness area.*

5. Apostle Islands National Lakeshore

Twelve spectacular miles of mainland shoreline and 21 islands with sandstone cliffs and sandy beaches add up to a multitude of outdoor activities. Good fishing, swimming, boat tours of the islands, and primitive campsites are available. Hiking trails lead to 19th-century lighthouses, an abandoned brownstone quarry, and an old commercial fishing camp.

6. Bayfield

Chamber of Commerce, 42 South Broad St. This tiny town of Victorian mansions contains 50 buildings listed on the National Register of Historic Places. Visitors to the **Cooperage Museum,** the state's only working barrel factory, can watch barrels being assembled around an open hearth just as they were in the 19th century. The Apostle Islands National Lakeshore Visitor Center provides information about the 21 islands. *Admission charged at museum.*

7. Madeline Island

Chamber of Commerce, Main St. The largest of the Apostle Islands features the **Madeline Island Historical Museum,** whose exhibits include a 19th-century fur-company building and a glass-sided hearse on runners. The old **Indian Cemetery** contains Ojibwa and pioneer graves. **Big Bay State Park** offers year-round recreation. *Admission charged for some attractions.*

8. Calumet

Chamber of Commerce, 1197 Calumet Ave. Calumet's mining history is examined at **Coppertown U.S.A.,** where displays include mining equipment and a grim doctor's office containing artificial legs and hands. The **Calumet and Hecla Industrial District** features a mining company blacksmith shop, roundhouse, and boiler house. The **Keeweenaw National Historical Park** tells the story of America's first copper-mining boom. *Admission charged.*

9. Fort Wilkins Historic Complex and State Park

The bakery, mess hall, stores, and other log buildings of this 1844 fort are furnished in period style, and costumed guides demonstrate 19th-century fort activities. The state park provides good fishing, boating, and camping. The oldest light station on the lake, **Copper Harbor Lighthouse** is now refurbished as a combination museum and early 1900's residence. *Admission charged.*

10. Marquette

Chamber of Commerce, 501 South Front St. The **Marquette County Historical Society Museum** exhibits this bustling town's past as a lumber, mining, shipping, and railroad center. The **Marquette Maritime Museum** displays boats related to the town's nautical history, old photographs, and diving gear. **Presque Isle Park** is an inviting spot to picnic, swim, and stroll along nature trails. At the nearby **Ore Dock,** visitors can watch ore being loaded onto the massive freighters that travel the Great Lakes. There are tours of **Northern Michigan University,** the location of an Olympic Education Center. *Admission charged for some attractions.*

Loons at Isle Royale National Park

11. Pictured Rocks National Lakeshore

This magnificent 40-mile-long strip along Lake Superior's shoreline is composed of multicolored sandstone cliffs eroded into arches and caves, followed by a 12-mile stretch of sand beaches and the **Grand Sable Banks,** topped by sand dunes. Swimming, fishing, and camping are among the activities here; boating is permitted on inland lakes, and cruises take place on Lake Superior. *Fee charged for cruises.*

12. Seney National Wildlife Refuge

This 95,000-acre preserve provides a habitat for bald eagles, loons, trumpeter swans, otters, and beavers. Fishing is permitted, and there are hiking trails and a wildlife drive. *Admission charged.*

13. Big Springs

More than 10,000 gallons of water per minute gush from underground fissures into this startlingly clear green spring in **Palms Book State Park.** Visitors can view its translucent depths from observation rafts. *Admission charged.*

14. Fayette Historic State Park

In the mid-19th century, Fayette was a booming iron-smelting town. Today a blast furnace, beehive-shaped charcoal kiln, opera house, hotel, and numerous houses stand in silent witness to the ghost town's bygone prosperity. *Admission charged.*

15. Iron Mountain

Chamber of Commerce, 600 South Stephenson Ave. Once an important mining center, Iron Mountain now recalls the past at the **Menominee Range Historical Foundation Museum,** with exhibits that include a trading post stocked with whiskey and bear grease. The **Cornish Pumping Engine and Mining Museum** features a huge steam-driven pumping engine built in 1889, antique mining equipment, and a World War II glider display. *Admission charged.*

16. Iron County Museum

Museum Rd., Caspian. The engine house and headframe of the old Caspian Mine dominate this museum devoted to the area's mining history. The **Monigal Miniature Logging Camp** features some 2,000 hand-carved items and re-creations of a two-story loghouse, logging camp cookhouse, and Chicago Northwest railroad depot. *Admission charged.*

17. Lumberjack Special and Camp Five Museum Complex

Rtes. 8 and 32, Laona. A ride aboard the steam-powered "Lumberjack Special" to the Camp Five complex is a journey back to the area's 19th-century logging days, along with a logging museum, bird refuge, animal barn, and nature center. *Admission charged.*

18. Rhinelander

Chamber of Commerce, 135 South Stevens St. Surrounded by hundreds of lakes and trout streams, Rhinelander today is a thriving resort area. The **Logging Museum,** however, conjures up a different sort of town, with exhibits of a reproduced sawmill, cook house, bunkhouse, and the last narrow-gauge locomotive to work the area.

19. Minocqua

Chamber of Commerce, Rte. 51 and Front St. This popular resort town is virtually surrounded by 2,000-acre **Lake Minocqua.** Some 3,200 other area lakes offer excellent freshwater fishing and clear water for diving. **Wildwood,** a 20-acre wildlife park, features timber wolves, bobcats, and other native animals. *Admission charged at park.*

Lake Superior Region Map

LAKE SUPERIOR

ISLE ROYALE NATIONAL PARK

PUKASKWA NATIONAL PARK

KEWEENAW PENINSULA

MICHIGAN

QUETICO PROV. PARK

SUPERIOR NATL. FOR.

CHEQUAMEGON NATIONAL FOREST

HIAWATHA NATL. FOREST

NICOLET NATL. FOR.

Major cities and towns:
- Thunder Bay
- Nipigon
- Red Rock
- Marathon
- Manitouwadge
- Houghton
- Hancock
- Marquette
- Ishpeming
- Negaunee
- Munising
- Ashland
- Ironwood
- Escanaba
- Iron Mountain
- Kingsford
- Rhinelander
- Manistique
- Gladstone

Boxed map reference numbers: 1, 2, 3, 4, 5, 6, 7, 8, 9, 10, 11, 12, 13, 14, 15, 16, 17, 18, 19

CANADA / UNITED STATES
ONTARIO / MICHIGAN
MINN. / WIS.
WIS. / MICH.
MINN. / MICH.
ONT. / MINN.
CAN. / U.S.

Central Time Zone / Eastern Time Zone

SCALE IN MILES — 0 10 20 30 40 50

MAP PG. 147

MAP PG. 149

MAP PG. 152

MAP PG. 159

MAP PG. 167

MAP PG. 169

1. Newberry

Chamber of Commerce, Rtes. 28 and 123. A popular site for tobogganing, cross-country skiing, and other winter activities, the town of Newberry is also home to the **Luce County Historical Museum.** Housed in a restored Queen Anne structure that was once a sheriff's residence and jail, the museum contains regional history exhibits.

2. Tahquamenon Falls State Park

Longfellow's fictional Hiawatha built his canoe on the banks of the **Tahquamenon River,** which flows through this lush 36,000-acre park. There are walkways and observation decks from which visitors can see the spectacular rushing waters of the Upper and Lower falls. *Admission charged.*

3. Whitefish Point

This treacherous stretch of Lake Superior's waters is known as the "Graveyard of the Great Lakes." Wooden schooners and steamers are among the vessels that lie in its depths, making wreck-diving a popular pursuit in the **Whitefish Point Underwater Preserve.** At the tip of the point, the **Great Lakes Shipwreck Museum** traces the waters' eerie history from the wreck of the *Invincible* in 1816 to that of the *Edmund Fitzgerald* in 1975. *Admission charged at museum.*

4. Sault Sainte Marie

Chamber of Commerce, 2581 I-75 Business Spur. A visitor center at the **Soo Locks** explains the workings of one of the world's largest lock systems; viewing decks are in an adjacent park, and tours are offered by boat and by train. At the 21-story **Tower of History** is an observation deck, a museum, and a slide show on regional history. The **Museum Ship Valley Camp and Great Lakes Maritime Museum,** in a 550-foot freighter, features exhibits that examine the maritime history of the area. *Admission charged for some attractions.*

5. St. Joseph Island

The island is a year-round 140,000-acre oasis for outdoor enthusiasts. Visitors flock here in the spring for the annual Maple Syrup Festival. At the **St. Joseph Island Museum Village,** more than 4,000 items are displayed in a six-building complex. The **Fort St. Joseph National Historical Site** commemorates an 18th-century fort. *Admission charged at museum.*

6. Drummond Island

Noted for hunting, boating, fishing, and birding, Drummond Island also attracts photographers with a lavish display of wildflowers in spring and fall. Rock hounds find fossils of coral and shellfish in the area's limestone, in addition to prized pudding stones made of red jasper, dark bluish gray chert, and white quartz. The **Drummond Island Historical Museum** contains artifacts from Ft. Drummond, which was the last British stronghold in the United States.

7. Old Presque Isle Lighthouse and Museum

5295 Grand Lake Rd., Presque Isle. In service in the mid-19th century, when Presque Isle was a busy port, the Old Lighthouse has walls 4 feet thick and a spiral staircase leading to a catwalk with a stirring view of Lake Huron. The adjacent museum, once the caretaker's cottage, is filled with intriguing exhibits. *Admission charged.*

8. Cheboygan

Chamber of Commerce, 124 North Main St. Surrounded by three large inland lakes,

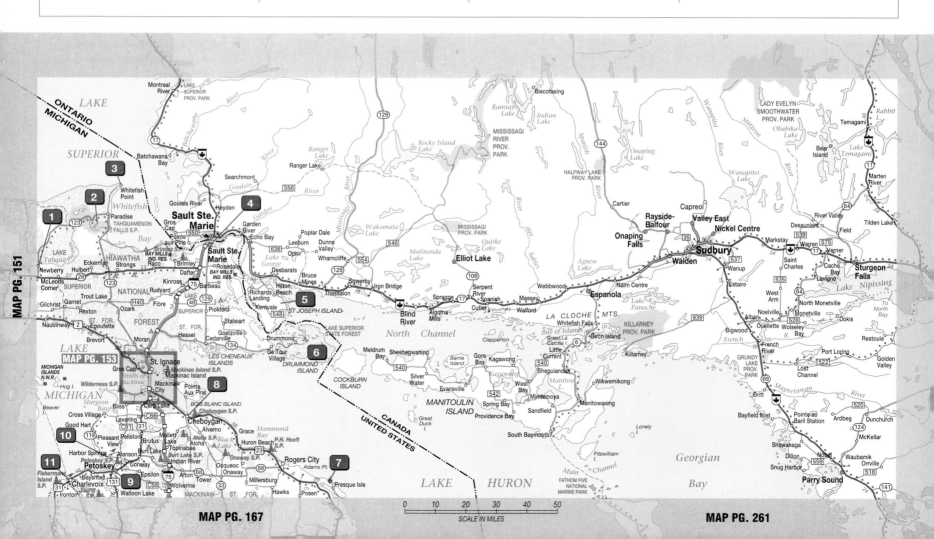

Cheboygan is a popular place for swimming, boating, and fishing. It's the only place in Michigan where sturgeon spearing is legal in winter. Golfers enjoy the 18-hole championship golf course, while hunters head for the 715,000-acre **Mackinaw State Forest.** The U.S. Coast Guard Cutter **Mackinaw,** moored in the Cheboygan River, is one of the world's largest icebreakers. *Admission charged for some attractions.*

9. Petoskey

Convention and Visitors Bureau, 401 East Mitchell St. Settled in the 1870's, Petoskey is a fishing and sailing community. Its downtown **Gaslight District** is a charming shopping center; many shops purvey the popular Petoskey stones, a kind of fossilized coral. Rock collectors search for the stones on the long sandy beach at **Petoskey State Park.** This was the home of Civil War historian Bruce Catton and a summer retreat of Ernest Hemingway; memorabilia pertaining to both writers can be seen in the **Little Traverse Historical Society Museum.** Hemingway's cottage is south of town on **Walloon Lake.** Adjoining Petoskey is **Bay View,** a summer resort with an abundance of handsome Victorian homes. *Admission charged for some attractions.*

10. Harbor Springs

With its splendid summer climate and scenery, Harbor Springs has attracted an array of prestigious seasonal residents, including the Fords, the Gambles, and the Upjohns. The **Andrew J. Blackbird Museum** contains exhibits about the Ottawa Indians. The **Tunnel of Trees** is a spectacular scenic drive between Harbor Springs and Cross Village. **Deer Park** is a year-round area for viewing and feeding deer.

11. Charlevoix

Chamber of Commerce, 408 Bridge St. The town of Charlevoix rides on a raft of land between Lake Michigan and Lake Charlevoix. Abounding with lakes and streams, this area is ideal for fishing. **Lake Michigan Beach,** one of Charlevoix's three beaches, is especially popular with seekers of Petoskey stones. Secluded **Beaver Island,** accessible by plane and by boat, is a peaceful retreat in which to fish or just relax. In spring, when the meadows are painted with colorful wildflowers, the road between Petoskey and Charlevoix is among Michigan's most scenic drives. *Fee charged for plane and boat rides.*

STRAITS OF MACKINAC

1. Hiawatha National Forest

Named for Longfellow's famous "The Song of Hiawatha," the shoreline of this 892,600-acre forest is washed by Lakes Michigan, Huron, and Superior. In addition to glorious scenery, the area offers boating, fishing, swimming, camping, and all manner of outdoor pursuits.

2. Father Marquette National Memorial Park and Museum

Located in **Straits State Park,** a bronze plaque within a small modern structure commemorates the missionary-explorer's accomplishments, while an adjoining museum interprets Marquette's mission and the early history of the Upper Great Lakes area. *Fee charged for parking.*

3. St. Ignace

Chamber of Commerce, 11 South State St. The town of St. Ignace was founded more than 300 years ago by Father Marquette. A century-old monument in **Marquette Mission Park** marks the spot believed to be his grave. In a 150-year-old church is the **Museum of Ojibwa Culture,** which traces the history and culture of the first inhabitants of the Upper Great Lakes. The park and museum are both located on the site of the 17th-century Huron village and Jesuit mission. *Admission charged at museum.*

4. Mackinac Island

Chamber of Commerce, Main St. About 80 percent of this little island is protected by the **Mackinac Island State Park,** whose primary attraction for visitors is **Fort Mackinac.** Perched on a bluff, with a commanding view of the town and the harbor, the 18th-century fort consists of 14 restored structures. Regularly scheduled presentations at the fort include military band concerts, rifle and cannon firings, and the re-enactment of a court-martial. Other historic structures located nearby include the

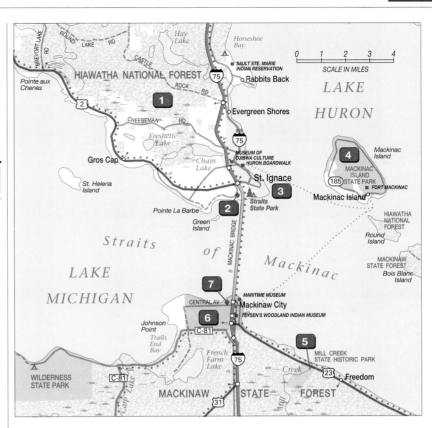

Biddle House, said to be the oldest house on the island; the **Mission Church;** the **Benjamin Blacksmith Shop;** the 1838 **Indian Dormitory;** and the **Beaumont Memorial,** whose exhibits relate to the work of a noted 19th-century army surgeon. Mackinac Island was the Great Lakes headquarters for John Jacob Astor's American Fur Trading Company; the company agent lived in the **Stuart House,** which now contains exhibits describing the fur trade. The famous 317-room **Grand Hotel,** built in 1887, and the 1895 **Round Island Lighthouse** are other notable landmarks. *Admission charged for some attractions.*

5. Mill Creek State Historic Park

Part of **Mackinac State Historic Parks,** this site includes a restored water-powered sawmill, where guides prepare lumber for cutting, and nature trails. A visitor center offers exhibits, and in summer, visitors can observe archeological excavations of an old sawmill that began operating on the island in 1780. *Admission charged.*

6. Mackinaw City

Tourist Bureau, 708 South Huron. The 5-mile-long **Mackinac Bridge,** spanning the Straits of Mackinac and connecting the Upper and Lower peninsulas, is one of the longest suspension bridges in the world. At the **Mackinac Bridge Museum** there are informative exhibits about the bridge's impressive engineering. A popular Labor Day event, the Mackinac Bridge Walk attracts some 40,000 participants. Prehistoric Indian artifacts and relics dating back to 10,000 B.C. are exhibited at **Teysen's Woodland Indian Museum,** along with other displays related to sailing and the state's lumbering era. *Admission charged for some attractions.*

7. Colonial Michilimackinac State Historic Park

The focal point of this park is a reconstruction of **Fort St. Philippe de Michilimackinac,** an outpost originally built by the French in 1715 and later occupied by the English. Among the site's re-created structures are a church, a barracks, and a blacksmith's shop. Numerous exhibits interpret the history of the fort, and costumed guides demonstrate cannon-firing and other facets of military life during that era. Visitors can also view archeological excavations in the summer. *Admission charged.*

1. Papineau Trading Post

Fifth and Main Sts., Geddes. The log cabin trading post, built in 1857 and later moved to its present site, displays various necessities for 19th-century fur trapping. The nearby **Fort Randall Dam** harnesses a portion of the Missouri River; at the dam's base, the **Fort Randall Historic Site** commemorates a 19th-century military outpost.

2. Mitchell

Chamber of Commerce, 604 North Main St. Saluting the region's all-important crop, Mitchell's best-known attraction is the fabulously gaudy **Corn Palace.** The huge structure, replete with domes, towers, and turrets, is gussied up with splashy murals made of corn, grains, and grasses. Several 19th-century structures dot the grounds of the **Friends of the Middle Border Museum,** while inside are displays pertaining to the state's pioneer days. **Lake Mitchell** draws scores of fishing, boating, and swimming enthusiasts. At the **Mitchell Prehistoric Indian Village,** visitors can browse museum exhibits and tour an archeological dig site, where a 1,000-year-old Indian village is being researched. *Admission charged for some attractions.*

3. Laura Ingalls Wilder Memorial Society

105 Olivet Ave., De Smet. De Smet is the small prairie town that Mrs. Wilder wrote about in six of her beloved *Little House on the Prairie* books, which in turn were the inspiration for the popular television series. The Surveyors' House is one of 16 sites and structures that appeared in the books, and next door is the headquarters for the society, which provides maps and guided tours. *Admission charged.*

4. Watertown

Convention and Visitors Bureau, 26 South Broadway. A 25-mile scenic drive laces around pretty **Lake Kampeska,** which offers ample opportunity for water sports and abounds with picnic, camp, and trailer sites. The **Kampeska Heritage Museum** offers local history exhibits. The 1883 **Mellette House,** built by South Dakota's first state governor, contains original furnishings and heirlooms. More than 400 birds and animals representing 100 different species can be seen at the **Bramble Park Zoo,** which also has a playground, picnic area, and summertime band concerts. *Admission charged for some attractions.*

5. Brookings

Chamber of Commerce, 2308 Sixth St. Brookings is home to **South Dakota State University,** whose campus features the **McCrory Gardens,** an idyllic 70-acre site lush with flowers, plants, and trees. The **State Agricultural Heritage Museum** and the **South Dakota Art Museum** are other points of interest in the town. *Admission charged for some attractions.*

6. Madison

Chamber of Commerce, 315 South Egan Ave. A 19th-century town is replicated in **Prairie Village,** while on the campus of **Dakota State University,** furnishings and memorabilia pertaining to homesteading days are found at the **Smith-Zimmermann State Museum.** In **Lake Herman State Park,** the **Herman Luce Cabin,** made of hewn oak logs, brings the pioneer era back to life. *Admission charged for some attractions.*

7. Pipestone National Monument

According to an ancient Sioux legend, the Great Spirit created the first peace pipe from the soft stone found in the quarries here. A sacred place for the Sioux people, the 283-acre park includes a visitor center, where exhibits explain the significance of the site. A self-guided nature trail loops around the quarry and leads past tumbling waterfalls. *Admission charged.*

8. Sioux Falls

Chamber of Commerce, 200 North Phillips Ave. The two sites that constitute the **Siouxland Heritage Museums** are the Pettigrew Home and Museum and the Old Courthouse Museum. The former is a Queen Anne house furnished in period style; the latter, a stone structure containing regional exhibits. **Sherman Park** is home to the Great Plains Zoo and Delbridge Museum of Natural History, and the USS South Dakota Battleship Memorial, a full-size concrete outline of the World War II vessel that houses a museum. *Admission charged for some attractions.*

9. Nobles County Pioneer Village

407 12th St., Worthington. A Lutheran church, a blacksmith's shop, and a firehouse are among the more than 40 structures in this re-created pioneer village. Exhibits include antique buggies and sleighs, vintage railroad cars, and old-time farming equipment. *Admission charged.*

10. Jeffers Petroglyphs

Virgin prairies surround Minnesota's largest cache of Indian rock carvings — some 2,000 curious figures etched in reddish-pink quartzite. The carvings include stick figures, animals, and weapons; some date from around 3000 B.C., while others are as recent as the mid-18th century.

11. Granite Falls

Chamber of Commerce, 155 Seventh Ave. Formerly the home of a beloved community leader, the **Olof Swensson Farm Museum** is a 22-room brick farmhouse whose 17-acre site includes a barn and family cemetery. Life in the 1800's is memorialized in the **Yellow Medicine County Museum.** Canoeing, camping, and horseback riding are among the activities in the **Upper Sioux Agency State Park.** *Admission charged for some attractions.*

12. Kandiyohi County Historical Society Center

610 NE Rte. 71, Willmar. Local history is colorfully depicted in this museum. Exhibits include a steam locomotive, a partially restored 1893 house with a pump organ and stained-glass windows, a furnished schoolhouse, old cars, and antique implements of various trades and professions.

13. Le Sueur

Chamber of Commerce, 500 North Main St. Dating from 1859, the **W. W. Mayo House,** with its period furnishings and displays of medical instruments, was the home of one of the founders of the Mayo Clinic. The Green Giant Canning Company was founded in Le Sueur, and the history of the vegetable-canning industry is traced in the **Le Sueur Museum.** In nearby Ottawa township, the **Little Stone Church** has 19th-century pews and fixtures, and the **Geldner Saw Mill,** about 15 miles south, is the region's oldest standing sawmill. *Admission charged for some attractions.*

14. Mankato

Convention and Visitors Bureau, 220 East Main St. The **Blue Earth County Histori-**cal Museum contains a research library and displays on early county history. The **Hubbard House,** a Victorian mansion whose elegant appointments include Tiffany lampshades and silk wall coverings, is also open to the public. The nearby 1,145-acre **Minneopa State Park** offers fishing, camping, and hiking, as well as 45-foot twin waterfalls and an 1860's stone windmill. *Admission charged for some attractions.*

15. Algona

Chamber of Commerce, 117 East Call St. A nostalgic drugstore museum, **Pharmacists Mutual Insurance Company** displays antique apothecaries and an 1890's soda fountain. A turn-of-the-century post office, schoolroom, and kitchen are exhibited at the **Kossuth County Historical Museum.** There is a Frisbee golf course in the **Ambrose A. Call State Park,** while water sports are popular at **Smith Lake Park.**

16. Fort Dodge

Chamber of Commerce, 1406 Central Ave. The outdoor **Fort Museum and Frontier Village,** which includes a one-room schoolhouse, jail, printing office, and church, is a replica of a fort built here in 1862. Nearby **Dolliver Memorial State Park** features water activities and ancient Indian mounds. *Admission charged.*

17. Sioux City

Sergeant Floyd Welcome Center, Hamilton Blvd. The **Sioux City Public Museum** offers exhibits relating to pioneer days and natural history. Completed in 1918, the **Woodbury County Courthouse** is the nation's largest structure built in the Prairie School style. The 1,090-acre **Stone State Park** is laced with nature trails, and overlooks provide views of three states. *Admission charged for some attractions.*

18. John G. Neihardt Center

Elm and Washington Sts., Bancroft. Nebraska's Poet Laureate in Perpetuity is memorialized in this center, which contains interpretive exhibits and a research library with first editions. Of special interest is the Sioux Prayer Garden. *Admission charged.*

19. Neligh Mills Historic Site

N St. and Wylie Dr., Neligh. Beginning in 1874, flour for worldwide markets was produced in this little town. Visitors can tour the mill, which contains its original equipment, and learn about the 19th-century flour-milling process. *Admission charged.*

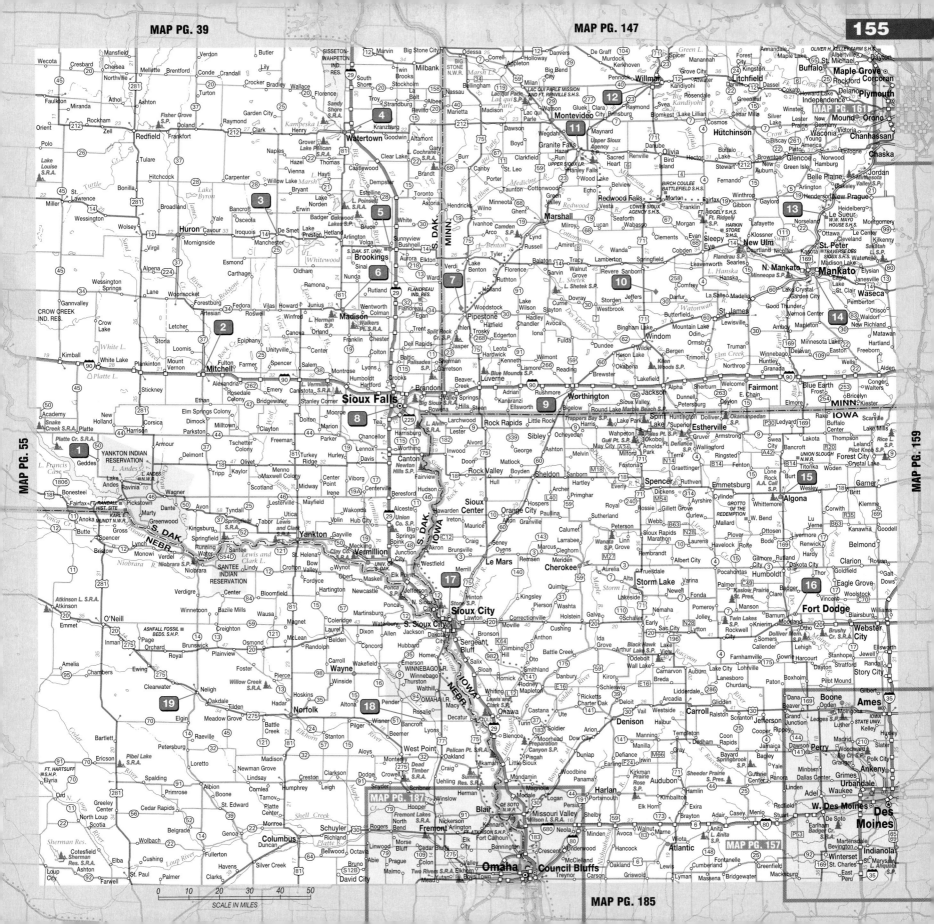

1. Boone

Chamber of Commerce, 806 Seventh St. Tours of the **Mamie Doud Eisenhower Birthplace** reveal a restored one-story frame house, furnished with many items from the Doud and Eisenhower families and augmented by a library and museum. The **Boone & Scenic Valley Railroad** offers a 15-mile round-trip journey in 1920's cars pulled by a steam or diesel engine. In the **Iowa Railroad Museum** exhibits illustrate railroad history. *Admission charged.*

2. Ames

Convention and Visitors Bureau, 125 South Third St. One of the country's oldest land-grant universities, **Iowa State University** is the focal point of this handsome town. The university's **Farm House** has been restored to its 1860's appearance and decorated with period furnishings. Nine Grant Wood murals, considered to be among his finest, decorate the **Parks Library.** Trails through the nearby **Iowa Arboretum** lead past 340 acres of gardens, trees, ravines, streams, and scenic overlooks.

3. Big Creek State Park

The park's 866-acre lake beckons to swimmers as well as to anglers trying for crappie, largemouth bass, walleye, and channel catfish. From hiking trails, visitors may glimpse deer and pheasants.

4. Living History Farms

Hickman Rd. and Rte. 80, Urbandale. At this intriguing complex of farms and settlements, visitors can relive Iowa's history. An Iowa Indian settlement from 1700 contains early bark shelters and gardens. A pioneer farm with oxen, a turn-of-the-century farm with work horses, and modern displays illustrate the evolution of farming. A church, newspaper office, and various shops reveal how life was lived in the 1875 town of Walnut Hill. *Admission charged.*

5. Hoyt Sherman Place

1501 Woodland Ave., Des Moines. Built in 1877 by Hoyt Sherman, a local businessman

and brother of Gen. William Tecumseh Sherman, the stately home now contains an art gallery. Of particular interest are the 19th-century paintings, the glass and silver collections, and the antique furniture.

6. Botanical Center

909 East River Dr., Des Moines. More than 1,500 species of plants gathered worldwide are displayed here, along with a succession of seasonal shows. *Admission charged.*

7. Heritage Village

East 30th St. and University Ave., Des Moines. This cluster of 19th-century buildings set on the state fairgrounds includes an exposition hall with antique farm machinery, an authentically furnished country school, and replicas of a pharmacy, church, and general store. *Admission charged.*

Country cooking at Living History Farms

8. Iowa State Capitol

East Ninth St. and Grand Ave., Des Moines. The central dome of this imposing Greek Revival building set on a hill is covered in 23-karat gold leaf, making it a beacon for the entire city. The sumptuous interior features carved woodwork, marble, mosaics, paintings, statues, and flag exhibits.

9. State of Iowa Historical Building

600 East Locust, Des Moines. This cultural center chronicles Iowa's history with displays that include a stuffed bison and

moose, a coal mine replica, a walk-through Indian wickiup, and a Conestoga wagon.

10. Polk County Heritage Gallery

First and Walnut Sts., Des Moines. Rotating exhibits of art and local history are showcased in the classic beaux-arts lobby of this former post office. The gallery features the building's original fixtures, including gas lamps and brass writing desks.

11. Salisbury House

4025 Tonawanda Dr., Des Moines. The 42-room Tudor mansion — a replica of King's House in Salisbury, England — contains authentic 15th-, 16th-, and 17th-century furnishings, stained-glass windows, massive fireplaces, and oriental rugs. A collection of paintings, sculpture, tapestries, and rare books is also featured. *Admission charged.*

12. Science Center of Iowa

4500 Grand Ave., Des Moines. Exhibits and demonstrations of physical and natural sciences, computers, and daily planetarium shows draw visitors to this informative science museum. *Admission charged.*

13. Des Moines Art Center

4700 Grand Ave., Des Moines. Designed by Eliel Saarinen, with wings by I. M. Pei and Richard Meier, this striking contemporary building houses a fine collection of 19th- and 20th-century paintings and sculpture. *Admission charged.*

14. Winterset

Chamber of Commerce, 122 North First Ave. The **Madison County Museum and Historical Complex** displays antique toys, musical instruments, quilts, farm equipment, fossils, and an 1850's schoolhouse. One of the county's six covered bridges, the 1870 **Cutler-Donahoe Bridge,** is located in Winterset's city park. The partially restored **John Wayne Birthplace Site,** where the actor was born in 1907, is also in town. *Admission charged for some attractions.*

15. Pammel State Park

Iowa's only highway tunnel — a channel dug through an unusual limestone ridge — is located in this peaceful 280-acre state park. Popular activities here include primitive camping and fishing in Middle River, which also has inviting picnic sites on its banks. From hiking and snowmobile trails visitors occasionally can spot wild turkeys, deer, coyotes, and hawks.

16. National Balloon Museum

North Jefferson St., Indianola. The spacious museum — big enough to accommodate an inflated balloon — is an offshoot of the annual national hot-air balloon competition held in July in Indianola. Fabric samples, gas cylinders, a World War II training basket, and old photos trace the 200-year-old history of this colorful sport.

17. Pella

Chamber of Commerce, 518 Franklin St. Windmills and colorful tulip gardens reflect this charming town's Dutch heritage. The **Pella Historical Village Museum** chronicles local history with 21 restored buildings that include a pioneer log cabin, the **Wyatt Earp Boyhood Home,** and a museum devoted to the town's founders. The **Scholte House,** the town's oldest permanent dwelling, is furnished in period style, with a garden of 25,000 tulips or annuals. The **Klokkenspel** at Franklin Place is a 147-bell carillon decorated with figurines from Pella's past. Nearby **Lake Red Rock,** the state's biggest lake, offers excellent fishing, boating, and swimming. Hiking and biking trails wind through its 50,000 acres of rocky bluffs and sandy shores. *Admission charged for some attractions.*

18. Trainland U.S.A.

Rte. 117, Colfax. In this amazing museum, Lionel trains travel cross-country through authentically detailed dioramas of the frontier, steam, and diesel eras. Miniature scenes range from an Old West gunfight to a three-ring circus, and there are a number of displays that visitors can activate, including a ski lift in Colorado and a missile launch crane at the Florida Space Center. The fine craftsmanship of this exhibit is not to be missed. *Admission charged.*

19. Marshalltown

Chamber of Commerce, 709 South Center St. This picturesque town, with its courthouse, parks, and many churches, supports several worthwhile art and history museums. The excellent collection at the **Fisher Community Center** art gallery features paintings by Degas, Monet, and Cassatt, contemporary works of art, and sculptures. The **Susie Sower Historical House,** authentically furnished in Victorian style, is also open to the public. Visitors to the **Marshall County Historical Museum** can view fossil crinoids, Indian stone weaponry, and artifacts that illustrate local history.

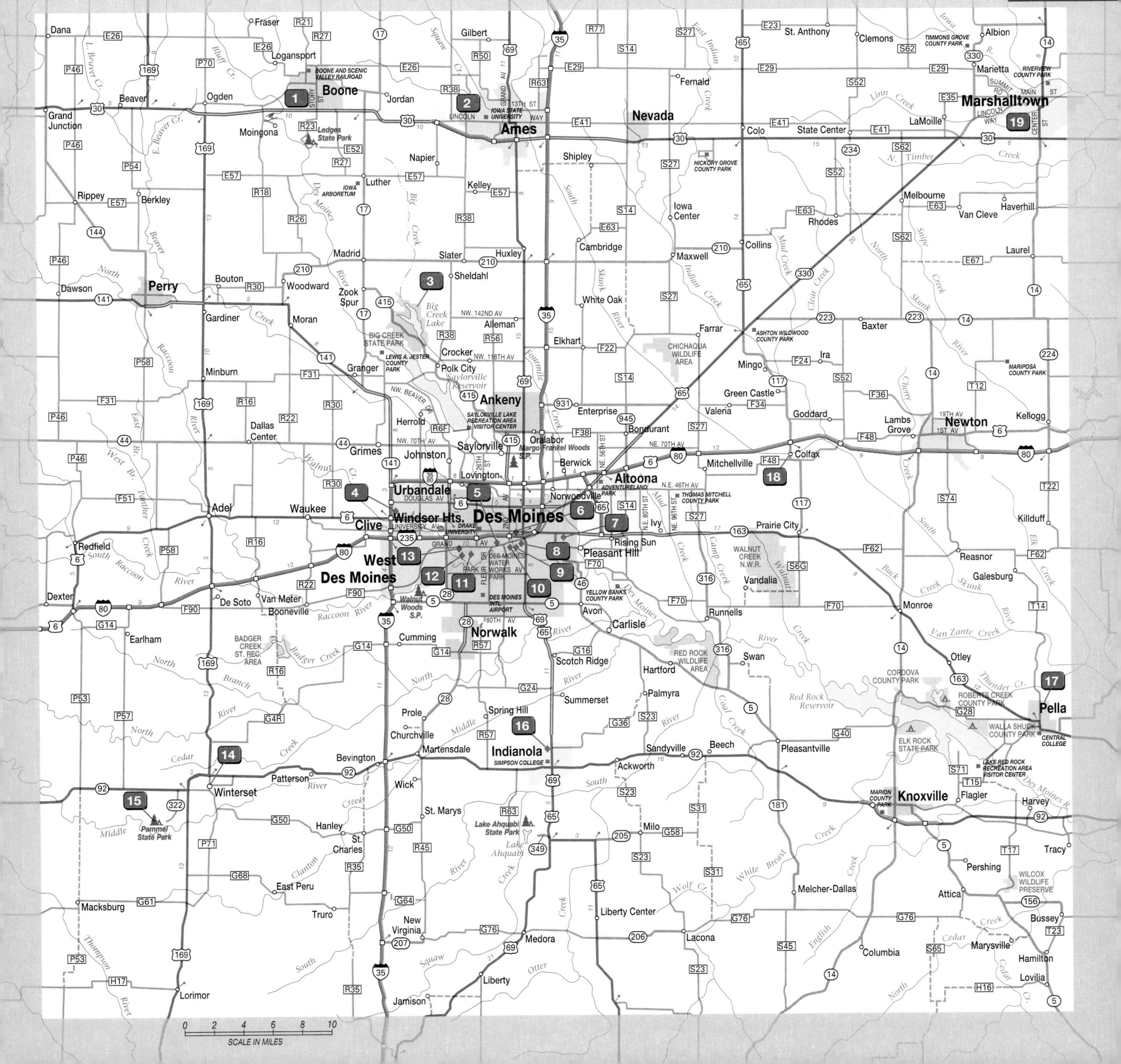

Dana
Fraser
R21
R27
Gilbert
E23
St. Anthony
Clemons
TIMMONS GROVE COUNTY PARK
Albion
Iowa R.
14

E26
Logansport
R50
65
S14
S27
E23
330
Marietta
RIVERVIEW COUNTY PARK
MAIN ST

169
P70
E26
BOONE AND SCENIC VALLEY RAILROAD
1 Boone
Jordan
2
13TH ST
E41
Nevada
Fernald
E29
S52
E35
Marshalltown
8

Grand Junction
30
Beaver
Ogden
Moingona
LINCOLN
IOWA STATE UNIVERSITY
Ames
Colo
E41
State Center
E41
LaMoille
LINCOLN WAY
19
CENTER ST

P46
E52
R23
Ledges State Park
30
234
30

P54
E57
Napier
Shipley
S27
HICKORY GROVE COUNTY PARK
S62
N. Timber
Melbourne
E63
Van Cleve
Haverhill

Rippey
E57
Berkley
R18
Luther
IOWA ARBORETUM
E57
Kelley
E57
Iowa Center
E63
S14
Rhodes
E63
Laurel
14

144
R26
Madrid
R38
Slater
Huxley
210
Cambridge
Maxwell
Collins
S62
Snipe
E67
14

P46
Dawson
141
Perry
Bouton
R30
Woodward
210
Zook Spur
415
Sheldahl
3
White Oak
S27
Farrar
223
Baxter
223
Cherry
224

Gardiner
Moran
BIG CREEK LAKE
NW. 142ND AV
Alleman
35
Elkhart
F22
CHICHAQUA WILDLIFE AREA
ASHTON WILDWOOD COUNTY PARK
F24
Ira
S52
F36
14
MARIPOSA COUNTY PARK

P58
Minburn
141
Granger
BIG CREEK STATE PARK
LEWIS A. JESTER COUNTY PARK
Crocker
NW. 118TH AV
Polk City
F22
Mingo
117
Green Castle
F34
Goddard
F36
14

P46
F31
Dallas Center
R22
R30
169
R16
Herrold
SAYLORVILLE RESERVOIR
Ankeny
Enterprise
931
945
Bondurant
S27
Valeria
Lambs Grove
Newton
Kellogg

44
Grimes
141
Johnston
Saylorville
415
Oralabor
F38
NE. 70TH AV
80
Mitchellville
F48
Colfax
T22
6
80

F51
Adel
Waukee
6
4
5 Urbandale
DOUGLAS AV
Lovington
Berwick
Altoona
ADVENTURELAND PARK
THOMAS MITCHELL COUNTY PARK
117
S74

Redfield
R16
Clive
Windsor Hts.
Des Moines
Norwoodville
6
65
S14
Ivy
S27
Prairie City
F62
Reasnor
F62

6
80
235
DRAKE UNIVERSITY
7
Rising Sun
163
Galesburg

Dexter
80
F90
De Soto
Van Meter Booneville
R22
F90
13
West Des Moines
PARK
DES MOINES WATER WORKS PARK
8
Pleasant Hill
F70
316
Vandalia
Monroe
T14

6
G14
Cumming
12
11
10
DES MOINES INTL. AIRPORT
9
YELLOW BANKS COUNTY PARK
F70
Runnells
Swan
163
Otley

Earlham
169
R16
G14
Norwalk
89
65
Avon
Carlisle
G16
RED ROCK WILDLIFE AREA
316
RED ROCK RESERVOIR
CORDOVA COUNTY PARK
ROBERTS CREEK COUNTY PARK
17 Pella

BADGER CREEK ST. REC. AREA
WALNUT WOODS S.P.
80TH AV
28
Scotch Ridge
Hartford
Coal Creek
Van Zante Creek
WALLA SHUCK COUNTY PARK
CENTRAL COLLEGE

P53
P57
G14
Prole
28
Spring Hill
G24
Summerset
Palmyra
5
ELK ROCK STATE PARK
G40
S71
LAKE RED ROCK RECREATION AREA VISITOR CENTER

14
14
Bevington
R57
Churchville
16
Martensdale
G36
S23
Sandyville
Beech
Pleasantville
MARION COUNTY PARK
Knoxville
T15
Flagler
Harvey

92
15
PAMMEL STATE PARK
Patterson
92
Wick
Indianola
SIMPSON COLLEGE
69
Ackworth
92
181
5
92

Winterset
322
Hanley
St. Charles
G50
R45
St. Marys
R63
LAKE AHQUABI STATE PARK
205
Milo
G58
S23
S31
Pershing
T17
Tracy

Macksburg
G61
G68
East Peru
G50
G64
Truro
New Virginia
207
Medora
206
Lacona
S45
Columbia
S65
Bussey
156

P53
H17
Lorimor
R35
Jamison
Liberty
35
69
Liberty Center
G76
G76
Melcher-Dallas
G76
Attica
WILCOX WILDLIFE PRESERVE
Marysville
Hamilton
H16
Lovilia
T23
5

SCALE IN MILES
0 2 4 6 8 10

1. Wausau

Convention and Visitors Bureau, 300 Third St. Beautiful wildlife art, from prints by John James Audubon to exquisite porcelain birds, is on display at the **Leigh Yawkey Woodson Art Museum.** Exhibits at the **Marathon County Historical Society Museum,** once the house of an early lumberman, trace the history of the region's lumber industry. At **Rib Mountain State Park,** an observation tower located near the summit — one of the highest points in the state — provides a magnificent view of the **Wisconsin River Valley**.

2. Paul Bunyan Logging Camp

Carson Park Dr., Eau Claire. A statue of the mythical folk hero watches over the entrance to this logging camp, built in 1934 as a replica of an 1890's logging camp. Next to the camp, the **Chippewa Valley Museum** examines the history of the area, with Indian artifacts and exhibits on pioneer life. *Admission charged.*

3. Crystal Cave

Fascinating formations of flowstone, stalactites, and stalagmites dip, swirl, and ripple throughout the 33 rooms of this 17,000-year-old cavern. Some resemble a cascading waterfall, others stark white cake frosting. The chambers at the deepest level were carved by whirlpools of an ancient glacial river. *Admission charged.*

4. Julius C. Wilkie Steamboat Center

Levee Park, Winona. This full-scale sternwheeler replica recalls the glorious heyday of the riverboat. Visitors can tour the pilot house and Grand Salon and, on the lower deck, a museum with exhibits that include models, Currier and Ives prints, and Robert Fulton's original papers. *Admission charged.*

5. Mayo Clinic

200 First St. SW, Rochester. In the late 1800's Dr. William Mayo and his two sons, Dr. Will and Dr. Charlie, set up a family practice that was to become the world-famous clinic; it now boasts nearly 1,000 physicians, surgeons, and medical scientists, as well as a reputation for personalized care. Visitors can tour the facility, including the Plummer Building, which houses the **Rochester Carillon,** the two sons' last offices, and exhibits on the history of medical practice. Tour buses take visitors on to **Mayowood,** the country mansion where Dr. Charlie lived. *Admission charged at Mayowood.*

6. Austin

Convention and Visitors Bureau, 300 North Main St. The early days of southern Minnesota come alive at the **Mower County Historical Center,** a complex of historic buildings that includes a general store and Civil War recruiting station, and museums with exhibits ranging from Indian artifacts and pioneer relics to old-time firefighting equipment and a steam locomotive. At the **J. C. Hormel Nature Center,** ponds, prairies, forests, and floodplains shelter a variety of birds and animals, some of which are on display at the interpretive center.

7. Spillville

Chamber of Commerce, 102 East Water St. In picturesque Riverside Park stands the **Dvorak Memorial,** a tribute to the famous composer, who spent the summer in this predominantly Czech village while finishing work on his *New World* symphony. He and his family stayed at the modest building that now houses the **Bily Clocks Museum,** which displays an amazing collection of large, elaborately carved clocks — some musical and many with moving figures. *Admission charged at museum.*

8. Decorah

Chamber of Commerce, 102 East Water St. Located in town, the **Vesterheim Norwegian-American Museum** is one of the oldest and largest immigrant museums in the nation. Displays focus on 19th-century folk culture in Norway and life in the New World, with furnishings, costumes, handicrafts, a ship's gallery, and a mill. Just east of Decorah, the restored **Jacobson Farmstead,** settled in 1850 by a Norwegian family, is open for tours. *Admission charged.*

9. Effigy Mounds National Monument

Nearly 200 Indian burial mounds, some dating as far back as 500 B.C., have been constructed atop dramatic 400-foot-high bluffs overlooking the Mississippi River. Visitors can take a walking tour of the area conducted by park rangers, who offer possible interpretations of the significance of the mounds. *Admission charged.*

10. Villa Louis

521 North Villa Louis Rd., Prairie du Chien. This Italianate mansion, built by the wife of a fur trader after his death, is said to be one of the most authentically furnished Victorian homes in America. It overlooks the site of a War of 1812 battlefield. Visitors can take a tour of the house led by costumed guides and stop in the nearby **Astor Fur Trade Museum.** *Admission charged.*

11. Stonefield

This re-created turn-of-the-century hamlet was once part of the estate of Nelson Dewey, Wisconsin's first governor and a large-scale farmer. His lavish two-story Victorian home, across the highway in **Nelson Dewey State Park,** is open for tours. In Stonefield, visitors can ride a horse-drawn carriage, stroll through quaint shops, watch brooms being made at the broom factory, or stop in at the cheese factory. The adjacent **State Farm Museum** depicts Wisconsin's agricultural history. *Admission charged.*

12. Bishop Hill State Historic Site

South Bishop Hill St., Bishop Hill. In 1846, a group of religious dissenters led by Erik Jansson emigrated from Sweden and formed a communal colony on this site. Today the Bishop Hill Museum documents colony life through exhibits and folk art, while the Colony Church and Steeple Building reflect the community's original architecture. *Donation encouraged.*

13. Rockford

Convention and Visitors Bureau, 211 North Main St. Time is of the essence at the **Time Museum,** where thousands of devices mark its passing — from water clocks and hourglasses to one of the earliest pendulum clocks. At the riverfront **Sinnissippi Gardens Greenhouse and Lagoon,** visitors can stroll through sunken gardens and an aviary. Other attractions in the state's second-largest city include the **Tinker Swiss Cottage,** a Swiss chalet replica brimming with treasures from around the world; the **Midway Village Rockford Museum Center,** featuring a turn-of-the-century blacksmith shop, jail and bank; and the **Burpee Museum of Natural History,** with Indian artifacts and wildlife exhibits. *Admission charged for some attractions.*

14. Union

Chamber of Commerce, 2115 State St. Here the **Illinois Railway Museum** is a train-lovers' delight, with the country's oldest diesel locomotive still in operation, a 1910 Pullman observation car, and vintage Chicago elevated cars; visitors can ride the rails on trains departing from an authentic depot. Old-time treasures at the **Antique Village Museum and Wildwest Town** include toys, military items, and an extensive collection of antique phonographs and records, while artifacts at the **McHenry County Historical Museum** trace local history from the 1830's. *Admission charged.*

15. Old World Wisconsin

Within **Kettle Moraine State Forest, South Unit,** lies this unique outdoor museum, which pays tribute to Wisconsin's early settlers. Dozens of structures, built by turn-of-the-century pioneers and immigrants from various ethnic groups, have been gathered from across the state and reconstructed to form a series of working farms and a country village. Costumed interpreters demonstrate plowing, baking, and other daily activities. *Admission charged.*

16. Fond du Lac

Convention and Visitors Bureau, 19 West Scott St. A hidden room, secret passageways, and an underground tunnel add to the fascination of the 1856 **Octagon House.** Originally built as an Indian fortress, it was later used as a shelter in the Underground Railroad. **Lakeside Park** offers canoeing, boating, picnicking, and a petting zoo. The town's European roots are evident in the **Episcopal Cathedral of St. Paul the Apostle,** a Gothic church with life-size German wood carvings of the Apostles and a cloister garden. At the **Galloway House and Village,** visitors can tour a restored 30-room Victorian mansion and take a stroll through a pioneer settlement. *Admission charged for some attractions.*

17. Kettle Moraine State Forest, North Unit

Evidence of the massive glaciers that moved through this forest includes moraines (rippling mounds of earth and stones deposited by retreating glaciers) and kettles (steep-sided hollows left by chunks of ice imbedded in the earth). The area is part of the Ice Age National Scientific Reserve, and information is provided at the **Ice Age Visitor Center.** *Admission charged.*

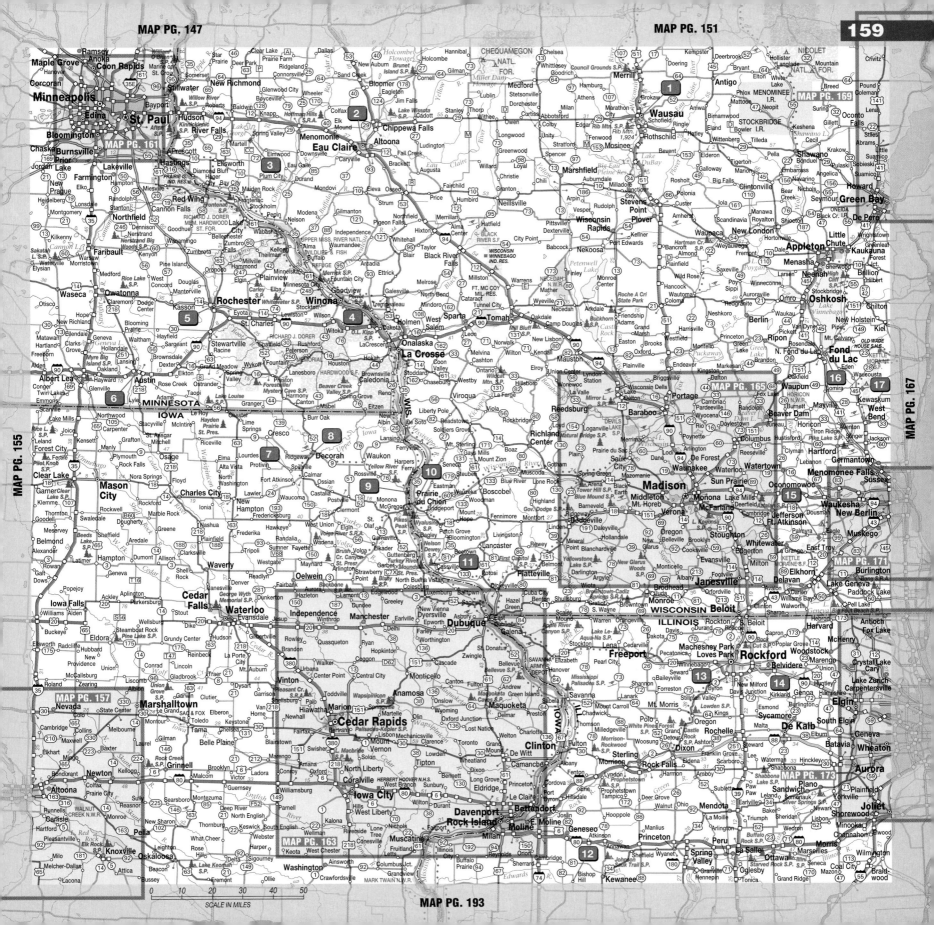

1. Eloise Butler Wildflower Garden and Bird Sanctuary

Theodore Wirth Pkwy. and Glenwood Ave., Minneapolis. Prairie, forest, and bog sustain colorful flowers and a variety of birds within this U-shaped valley sanctuary.

2. Minneapolis Grain Exchange

400 South Fourth St., Minneapolis. A film explains the workings of the grain exchange, which can be observed in its daily operation from the visitors balcony. Displays show the history of grain marketing.

3. Minneapolis Planetarium

300 Nicollet Mall, Minneapolis. Located in the public library, the 40-foot planetarium dome duplicates the night sky. Programs include "tours" of the stars and planets, as well as multi-image presentations on topics relating to astronomy and space exploration. Rock concerts with laser shows are presented regularly. *Admission charged.*

4. Our Lady of Lourdes Church

1 Lourdes Pl., Minneapolis. Built in 1857, this Catholic church is Minneapolis's oldest church in continuous use.

5. James Ford Bell Museum of Natural History

17th Ave. SE and University Ave., Minneapolis. Dioramas in this museum depict Minnesota animals in various settings. In the Touch and See Room, both children and adults can handle objects including antlers and a dinosaur bone. *Admission charged.*

6. Gibbs Farm Museum

2097 West Larpenteur Ave., Falcon Heights. This 7-acre farmstead features a restored 19th-century home, schoolhouse, and barn, and demonstrations of quilting and bee-keeping. *Admission charged.*

7. Como Zoo and Como Park Conservatory

Midway Pkwy. and Kaufman Dr., St. Paul. Although it holds other attractions, Como Park is particularly known for its zoo and conservatory. The zoo houses large cats, primates, a performing sea lion, and other animals. The conservatory features sunken gardens and seasonal flower shows. *Admission charged at conservatory.*

8. Alexander Ramsey House

265 South Exchange St., St. Paul. Built in 1872, this French Second Empire mansion was the home of Minnesota's first territorial governor after he left office. Adorned with black walnut woodwork and crystal chandeliers, the house still contains its original furnishings. Tours are conducted by guides in period costume. *Admission charged.*

9. State Capitol

75 Constitution Ave., St. Paul. One of the world's largest unsupported marble domes caps this impressive building. Adding to the grandeur are the gilded chariot sculpture at the base of the dome and the glass and brass star (symbolizing Minnesota as the North Star State) that forms part of the first floor. Guided tours are available.

10. The Science Museum of Minnesota

30 East 10th St., St. Paul. Archeology, biology, paleontology, ecology, and technology all come together in this exciting museum. Children enjoy the many hands-on exhibits. The **Great American History Theatre** stages historical plays, and the Omnitheater shows films on a colossal overhead screen. *Admission charged.*

11. Indian Mounds Park

Located in the Dayton's Bluff section of St. Paul, overlooking the Mississippi River, this park preserves six prehistoric burial mounds. It also offers picnic facilities, a ball field, and tennis courts.

12. The Landmark Center

75 West Fifth St., St. Paul. The former federal courthouse, built in 1902, has become a center for the arts. The pink granite towered structure shelters a skylit indoor courtyard, a branch of the **Minnesota Museum of Art** dedicated to 19th- and 20th-century American art, and the **Schubert Club Musical Instrument Museum,** with its wonderful keyboard collection. Free tours of the facility are available.

13. St. Paul City Hall and Court House

15 West Kellogg Blvd., St. Paul. An Art Deco interior lends elegance to this 20-story building. Its Memorial Hall, finished in dark blue marble, provides a fitting setting for the statue "Indian God of Peace." Made of white Mexican onyx, the astounding sculpture stands three stories high and weighs an impressive 60 tons.

14. James J. Hill House

240 Summit Ave., St. Paul. Railroad magnate James J. Hill built this red sandstone mansion toward the end of the 19th century. The 32-room house contains hand-carved woodwork, cut-glass chandeliers, tiled fireplaces, and an art gallery featuring Minnesota artists. Guided tours cover four floors of the home. *Admission charged.*

15. Mendota

The town boasts two notable homes. The **Henry H. Sibley House,** built in 1835, once belonged to Minnesota's first governor. The stone residence still contains some original furnishings. Next door is the 1837 **Jean B. Faribault House,** constructed by a fur trader, which serves today as a museum housing Indian artifacts. *Admission charged.*

16. Fort Snelling State Park

Off Rte. 5, St. Paul. Located where the Minnesota and Mississippi rivers meet, the 3,000-acre park offers swimming, fishing, boating, hiking, and picnicking. In the restored **Fort Snelling,** soldiers still march through the stone stronghold much as they did in the 1820's. Visitors can watch them drill, and other costumed guides help to recreate the era as well. *Admission charged.*

17. Minnesota Air Guard Museum

In a corner of the **Minneapolis-St. Paul International Airport** stand aircraft, dating back to the 1930's, and other displays that illustrate the history of the state's air guard.

18. Minnehaha Falls

Located in **Minnehaha Regional Park** just above the Mississippi River, this cascade helped to inspire Longfellow's poem *The Song of Hiawatha.* The **John H. Stevens House,** the first house in the state built on the west bank of the river, has been relocated here. The park also contains statues of the Indians Hiawatha and Minnehaha.

19. American Swedish Institute

2600 Park Ave., Minneapolis. This institute is housed in a French château–style mansion decorated with elaborate woodwork and stained glass, containing porcelain tile stoves. The institute displays the art and artifacts of Swedish immigrants who settled the region in great numbers, and it hosts changing exhibits by contemporary Swedish artists. *Admission charged.*

20. Minneapolis Institute of Arts

2400 Third Ave. S., Minneapolis. The 85,000 objects in this excellent museum cover a remarkable range of cultures and centuries. Examples include a 2,000-year-old mummy, ancient Greek pottery, 18th-century Italian furniture, diverse American photographs, French Impressionist paintings, and intriguing African masks.

21. Walker Art Center/ Minneapolis Sculpture Garden

725 Vineland Pl., Minneapolis. In addition to exhibiting an important collection of 20th-century art, the Walker Art Center hosts concerts, films, and other events. Outside the museum lies the nation's largest urban sculpture garden, which includes a whimsical giant spoon and a footbridge that leads visitors to the downtown area. *Admission charged.*

22. Minnesota Transportation Museum

West 42nd St. and Queen Ave. S., Minneapolis. Besides viewing displays of old-time transportation, visitors have the opportunity to experience the travel of yesteryear in electric streetcars, dating from the late-19th century, which offer rides along a reconstructed 1-mile line. *Fee charged for ride.*

23. Bloomington

Chamber of Commerce, 9633 Lyndale Ave. South. Surprisingly set in an urban area, the huge **Minnesota Valley National Wildlife Refuge** teems with plants and animals. Hiking trails wind through oak savanna and wetlands, where visitors may see mallards or blue-winged teal. Located on the campus of **Normandale Community College,** the **Japanese Gardens** form a serene oasis of trees, bridges, a waterfall, and a lagoon.

24. Minnesota Zoo

13000 Zoo Blvd., Apple Valley. More than 2,000 animals, including many endangered species, live in this 485-acre zoological park traversed by six trail systems. A monorail offers a bird's-eye view of timber wolves, caribou, and Asian wild horses in close-to-natural habitats, while colorful birds and gibbons share the lush Tropics Trail area with a rare Southeast Asian sun bear, the smallest bear species. *Admission charged.*

Diamond Lake

Dayton

Anoka

Andover

Ham Lake

Coon Rapids

Champlin

Blaine

Lino Lakes

Circle Pines

Lexington

Centerville

Hugo

Maple Grove

Osseo

Brooklyn Park

Spring Lake Park

Mounds View

Shoreview

North Oaks

Bald Eagle

Mahtomedi

Stillwater

Plymouth

Crystal

Brooklyn Center

Fridley

New Brighton

Arden Hills

Vadnais Heights

Dellwood

Birchwood Village

Willernie

Pine Springs

New Hope

Robbinsdale

Columbia Hts.

St. Anthony

Roseville

Little Canada

Maplewood

North St. Paul

White Bear Lake

Minnetonka

Golden Valley

Lauderdale

Falcon Heights

Oakdale

Lake Elmo

Deephaven

Woodland

Wayzata

St. Louis Park

Minneapolis

St. Paul

Landfall

Hopkins

Edina

Richfield

Mendota Heights

West St. Paul

South St. Paul

Woodbury

Eden Prairie

Bloomington

Mendota

Lilydale

Sunfish Lake

Newport

St. Paul Park

Cottage Grove

Shakopee

Savage

Burnsville

Eagan

Inver Grove Heights

Apple Valley

Rosemount

Hastings

Prior Lake

Coates

Nininger

SCALE IN MILES
0 1 2 3 4 5

1. Galena

Convention and Visitors Bureau, 101 Bouthillier St. The highlight of this river town is the **Ulysses S. Grant Home State Historic Site,** filled with family furnishings and memorabilia. Exhibits on Grant and the Civil War can also be seen at the **Galena-Jo Daviess County History Museum.** *Admission charged.*

2. Dubuque

Convention and Visitors Bureau, 770 Town Clock Plaza. Located in Iowa's oldest city, the **Old Shot Tower** produced ammunition for the Civil War. The **Dubuque Museum of Art** now occupies the former courthouse. **River Adventure,** a museum complex, recalls the city's river history. **Eagle Point Park** and **Crystal Lake Cave** offer outdoor fun, including riverboat cruises. *Admission charged for some attractions.*

3. Basilica of St. Francis Xavier

104 Third St. SW, Dyersville. Spires soaring 212 feet top this monumental Catholic church. The awesome Gothic structure, completed in 1889, contains an ornate, hand-painted sanctuary ceiling.

4. Stone City

Stately 19th-century stone houses reflect this town's history as a limestone quarrying center. The community was also the site of an art colony founded by Grant Wood, the painter of "American Gothic." Each June, crowds gather for the colorful Grant Wood Art Festival. *Admission charged at festival.*

5. Cedar Rapids

Convention and Visitors Bureau, 119 First Ave. SE. In **Czech Village,** buildings still stand from the original Czech neighborhood that once flourished in this industrial city. The **Cedar Rapids Museum of Art** spotlights the work of Grant Wood and other regional artists. The marble **Iowa Masonic Library** contains one of the most complete Masonic collections in the nation. The **Indian Creek Nature Center,** a combination nature preserve and museum, is set in a remodeled dairy barn. *Admission charged for some attractions.*

6. Amana Colonies

Convention and Visitors Bureau, Rtes. 151 and 220. In 1855 a Lutheran sect settled this group of seven villages and started several industries. Today visitors are welcome at a number of the colonies' shops and other buildings, such as the **Museum of Amana History,** which features structures and artifacts from the 1860's. *Admission charged for some attractions.*

7. Lake Macbride State Park

The huge lake offers swimming, boating, and fishing, with picnic areas and campsites nearby. Visitors to **Raptor Center,** south of the park, can observe the recovery of injured birds of prey prior to their release.

8. Iowa City

Convention and Visitors Bureau, 325 East Washington St. Visitors to Iowa's former state capital can tour the **Old Capitol,** a handsome Greek Revival building from the mid-1800's, now part of the **University of Iowa** campus. **Plum Grove,** the restored home of Iowa's first territorial governor, is also open to the public.

9. Herbert Hoover National Historic Site

Parkside Dr. and Main St., West Branch. Several restored buildings associated with Hoover's life stand on this 186-acre site, most notably the small cottage where he was born and the Quaker meetinghouse where he worshiped. The **Herbert Hoover Presidential Library Museum** contains mementos of his distinguished public career. *Admission charged.*

10. Kalona Historical Village

Rte. 22 and Ninth St., Kalona. This village celebrates the history of Kalona and of the Mennonites who populate the region. The **Wahl Museum** displays fine antique glassware. Other attractions include a restored 1879 railroad depot, a working windmill, and the **Iowa Mennonite Museum and Archives.** *Admission charged.*

11. Muscatine

Convention and Visitors Bureau, 319 East Second St. Visitors to this town, which was once home to Mark Twain, can enjoy a sweeping view of the Mississippi River Valley from the **Mark Twain Overlook.** The **Muscatine Art Center,** housed in an Edwardian mansion, has a fascinating collection of paintings, drawings, prints, and maps portraying the mighty river.

12. Wildcat Den State Park

The wildcats are gone, but the natural beauty of this park remains, with jewelweed and other blossoming plants lining the trails. Pine Creek follows the valley floor to a 19th-century gristmill and an old bridge.

13. Davenport

Set on bluffs along the Mississippi River, Davenport is one of the Quad Cities, along with Bettendorf, Rock Island, and Moline. Local attractions include the **Davenport Museum of Art** and the **Putnam Museum of History and Natural Science.** *Admission charged at Putnam museum.*

14. Black Hawk State Historic Site

1510 46th Ave., Rock Island. These 208 wooded acres were once home to the Sauk and Mesquakie Indians, who are commemorated at the **Hauberg Indian Museum.**

15. Rock Island

At the **Arsenal Museum,** military firearms are on display. The 1833 **Colonel Davenport House** is the island's oldest building. A replica of 1816 **Fort Armstrong** stands on the nearby bluffs. Civil War prisoners are buried in the **Confederate Cemetery.** *Admission charged at house.*

16. Buffalo Bill Museum

200 North River Dr., Le Claire. In the town where Buffalo Bill Cody was born, this museum features Cody memorabilia and other artifacts from his era. *Admission charged.*

17. Buffalo Bill Cody Homestead

Rte. 33, Princeton. The 1847 house where Cody lived for three years as a child has been preserved and decorated with period furnishings. Buffalo and longhorn cattle roam the grounds.

18. Walnut Grove Pioneer Village

18817 290th St., Long Grove. Vintage local buildings that have been moved to this 3-acre site include a rural Catholic church, blacksmith shop, schoolhouse, general store, saloon, and frontier home.

19. Maquoketa

Chamber of Commerce, 112 North Main St. At the **Maquoketa Caves State Park,** spelunkers can explore a network of caverns. The **Jackson County Historical Museum** features replicas of 19th-century buildings, such as a general store and blacksmith shop. **Costello's Old Mill Gallery** is a restored 1867 stone mill with a waterwheel. *Admission charged at museum.*

20. Eden Valley Wildlife Refuge

This lovely area of woods and meadows shelters wildflowers, birds, and other wildlife. Visitors can follow a 1-mile interpretive trail beginning at the nature center.

"The Birthplace of Herbert Hoover," painted by Grant Wood in 1931

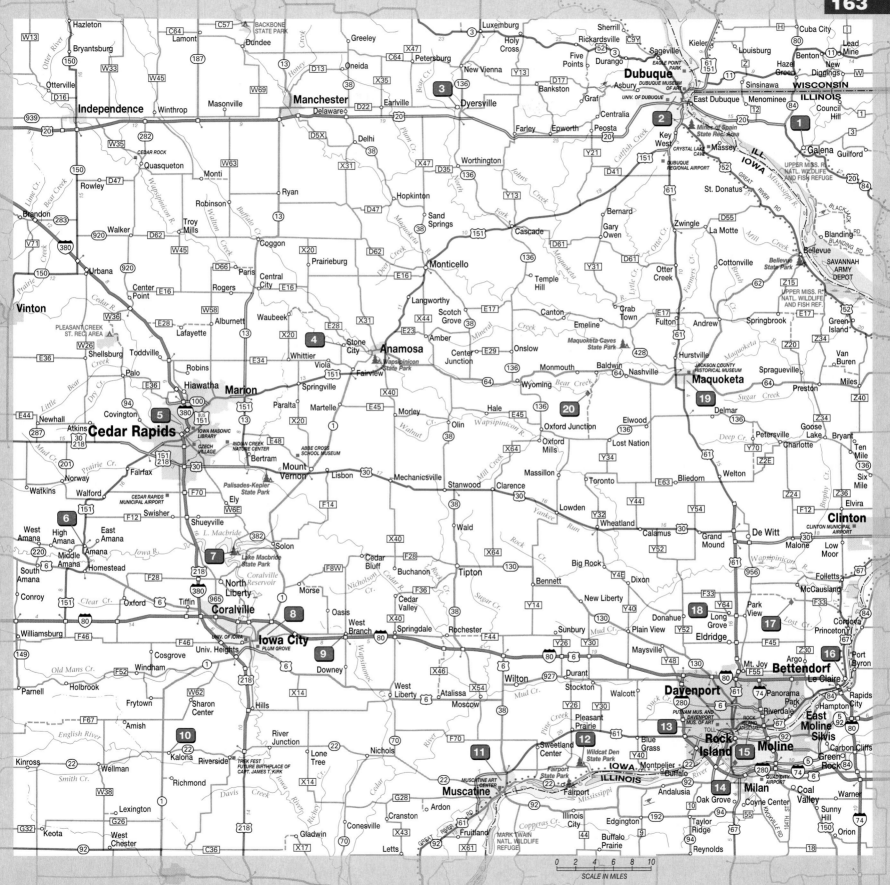

1. Portage

Chamber of Commerce, 301 West Wisconsin St. Known by locals as the "point where the north begins," Portage lies between the Fox and Wisconsin rivers. A canal linking the two rivers is visible from the **Old Indian Agency House,** which has period furnishings. Artifacts and documents from Ft. Winnebago are displayed in the restored **Surgeon's Quarters.** *Admission charged.*

2. The Dells

Some 15 miles of spectacular narrow chasms with bizarre sandstone formations line the Wisconsin River's deep blue waters. These premier natural attractions, which were formed by thousands of years of erosion, can be toured on boat excursions from Wisconsin Dells. *Fee charged for cruises.*

3. Wisconsin Dells

Convention and Visitors Bureau, 701 Superior St. Wisconsin's number-one travel destination is a recreational paradise for children and adults alike. At the **H. H. Bennett Studio** visitors can see equipment and early photographs of the pioneer photographer whose work attracted the first vacationers to the area. The **Dells Country Historical Society** displays a letter from Abraham Lincoln commending one of the town founders, Gen. Joseph Bailey, for his Civil War service. Large collections of clothing, artifacts, and weapons are featured at the **Winnebago Indian Museum.** Full-size statues illustrate nursery rhymes at **Storybook Gardens** and the life of Christ at **Biblical Gardens.** *Admission charged for some attractions.*

4. International Crane Foundation

E-11376 Shady Lane Rd., Baraboo. Cranes and their chicks are on exhibit here. Guided tours include video presentations, and trails lead past a prairie with groves of oak and cherry trees. *Admission charged.*

5. Mid-Continent Railway Museum

Walnut St., North Freedom. From a restored 1894 depot, visitors depart for a 9-mile ride on an early 1900's train pulled by authentic steam locomotives. Displays include a gas-electric car, wooden water tower, and railroad equipment. *Admission charged.*

6. Circus World Museum

426 Water St., Baraboo. The former winter quarters of the Ringling Brothers Circus, this museum — encompassing 50 acres — now features the world's largest collection of circus wagons, a steam calliope, and other circus memorabilia. Highlights for visitors include live circus performances, magic shows, and a parade through the grounds. *Admission charged.*

7. Devils Lake State Park

One of Wisconsin's most beautiful parks contains spring-fed Devils Lake, where quartzite cliffs rise 500 feet above the water. Part of the Ice Age National Scientific Reserve, the park offers sandy swimming beaches, hiking and skiing trails, and Indian mounds. A nature center gives information on local glaciation. *Admission charged.*

8. Wollersheim Winery

7876 Rte. 188, Prairie du Sac. This picturesque old vineyard, on the National Register of Historic Places, was founded by the father of California viticulture, Count Agoston Haraszthy. Guided tours of the vineyard and cellars are offered, as well as free wine tastings. *Fee charged for tour.*

9. Taliesin Fellowship Buildings

Rte. 23, Spring Green. Taliesin was the home of architect Frank Lloyd Wright, whose designs were influenced by surrounding landscapes. Fellowship buildings designed and built by Wright include the 1901 **Hillside Home School,** with galleries, studio, and a theater. They house his architecture school and can be toured in the summer. *Admission charged.*

10. The House on the Rock

Rte. 23, Spring Green. Artist Alexander Jordan built his home into and atop a chimney-shaped rock. Its 14 rooms contain waterfalls, pools, and trees growing through floors and ceilings. Also included in the 30-acre complex is a re-created 19th-century street, collections of dolls, ship models, and armor, and one of the world's largest carousels. *Admission charged.*

11. Pendarvis

114 Shake Rag St., Mineral Point. Six limestone and log cottages, built around 1840 by Cornish lead miners, contain antiques, mining tools, and equipment. Trails lead to old mine shafts. Visitors can find traditional crafts for sale in historic buildings at **Shake Rag Under the Hill.** *Admission charged.*

12. Little Norway

3576 Rte. JG North, Blue Mounds. The centerpiece of this restored 1856 homestead is a replica of a 12th-century Norwegian church, intricately hand-carved in Norway and reassembled in this scenic valley. Other original log buildings with unique adornments contain outstanding collections of Norwegian antiques and pioneer arts and crafts. *Admission charged.*

13. Cave of the Mounds

Off Rtes. 18 and 151, Blue Mounds. Visitors can take a guided tour of this limestone cave, known for its colorful onyx and many diverse formations spread throughout 18 rooms on two levels. This national natural landmark, discovered in 1939, includes picnic areas and gardens. *Admission charged.*

14. New Glarus

Chamber of Commerce, Sixth Ave. and Railroad St. **Swiss Historical Village** exhibits Swiss trades and skills with replicas of a log church, cabin, cheese factory, and other buildings furnished with appropriate tools and artifacts. The mountain-style **Chalet of the Golden Fleece** contains Swiss stamp, coin, wood-carving, and doll collections. *Admission charged.*

15. Henry Vilas Zoo and Park

702 South Randall Ave., Madison. Known for its successful breeding in captivity of orangutans, Siberian tigers, penguins, camels, and endangered spectacled bears, this zoo is a family favorite. Nearby, the **University of Wisconsin Arboretum** showcases restored ecosystems indigenous to the state.

16. Forest Products Laboratory

Gifford Pinchot Dr., Madison. This federally funded research laboratory conducts studies on the properties, methods of processing, and uses of wood. A 10-minute slide show introduces visitors to the facility and its research, and guided tours are available.

17. University of Wisconsin at Madison

Many consider this to be one of the most beautiful campuses in the Midwest. Along **Observatory** and **Willow drives** there are outstanding views of Madison and Lake Mendota's shoreline parks. Visitors can enjoy the 56 bells of **Carillon Tower** and observe the celestial sky through a telescope at the **Washburn Observatory.** More than 14,000 paintings, sculpture, and other art from 2300 B.C. to the present are on display at the **Elvehjem Museum of Art.** A nearby architectural gem, the **First Unitarian Society Meeting House** is a classic example of Frank Lloyd Wright's Prairie School of architecture.

18. Wisconsin State Capitol

Capitol Square, Madison. The magnificent Classic Revival building provides sweeping city views from an observation deck, and tours of the Rotunda, Supreme Court, and Governor's Conference Rooms are available. Nearby, the **State Historical Museum** interprets regional Indian culture, the history of the fur-trading industry, and various aspects of pioneer life.

19. Aztalan State Park

Ruins of a 12th-century Indian village are preserved at one of Wisconsin's largest and most important archeological sites. The biggest structure is a platform mound, believed to have been used as a ceremonial structure or residence for high officials.

20. Fort Atkinson

Chamber of Commerce, 89 North Main St. **Hoard Historical Museum and Dairy Shrine** interprets local Indian history, the Black Hawk War, and the development of state and national dairy industries with artifact collections and building replicas. The nearby **Panther Intaglio Effigy,** one of the two surviving intaglios in the world, is in the form of a mythical beast that was excavated in the ground.

21. Milton House Museum

18 South Janesville St., Milton. Built in 1844, this hexagonal stagecoach inn and Underground Railroad station still contains Civil War artifacts, the original guest book, and a tunnel that sheltered slaves. A buggy shed, blacksmith shop, and 1837 log cabin are also on the grounds. *Admission charged.*

22. Lincoln Tallman Restorations

440 North Jackson St., Janesville. This opulent Italianate mansion, built in 1857, has 26 rooms of period furnishings and decorative arts. A former horse barn houses a visitor center. *Admission charged.*

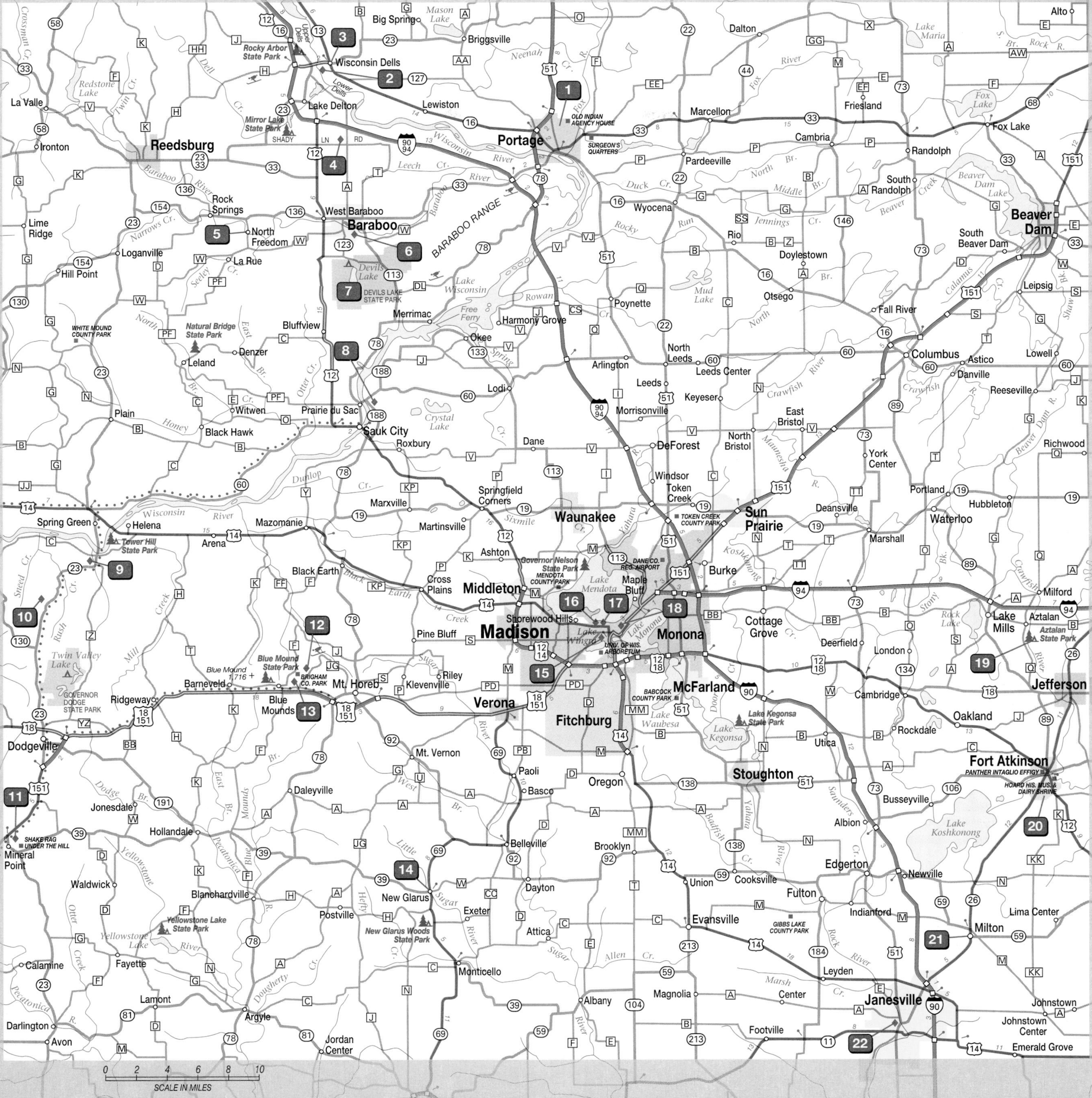

Alto

Lake Maria

Dalton

X

E

GG

N. Br. Rock R.

AW

58

K

HH

J

Rocky Arbor State Park

Big Spring

B

G

Mason Lake

A

O

Neenah

Cr.

F

Marcellon

33

Friesland

M

EF

73

Fox Lake

12 16

13

3

Wisconsin Dells

23

Briggsville

51

44

Fox

E

68

33

La Valle

V

F

Redstone Lake

H

2 127

Lewiston

14

16

Wisconsin River

Portage

Old Indian Agency House

Cambria

15

33

EE

P

Friesland

Fox Lake

151

33

Ironton

58

Twin Cr.

Mirror Lake State Park

Lake Delton

SHADY LN RD

Surgeon's Quarters

33

Pardeeville

Duck Cr.

22

Wyocena

16

North Br.

Middle Br.

South Randolph

Randolph

Beaver

A

Beaver Dam Lake

Beaver Dam

Reedsburg

23 33

12

4

90 94

78

Rocky

Run

Q

G

Doylestown

South Beaver Dam

E

33

Lime Ridge

23

Baraboo River

Rock Springs

136

West Baraboo

Baraboo

BARABOO RANGE

Rio

SS

Jennings Cr.

146

Fall River

73

Leipsig

151

S

Loganville

154

North Freedom

W

123

6

78

Devils Lake

V

51

Otsego

Columbus

Astico

Lowell

60

Hill Point

154

La Rue

PF

7

DEVILS LAKE STATE PARK

113

Lake Wisconsin

Poynette

Q

Mud Lake

C

Danville

Reeseville

Richwood

130

White Mound County Park

Natural Bridge State Park

Bluffview

Merrimac

Free Ferry

Rowan

22

North Leeds

Leeds Center

60

60

89

York Center

Portland

19

Hubbleton

19

G

North

PF

Denzer

C

78

133

Okee

Arlington

Leeds

51

Keyeser

Crawfish River

73

Deansville

Waterloo

Plain

Leland

Witwen

PF

12

188

Lodi

60

Dane

113

DeForest

Windsor

Morrisonville

North Bristol

East Bristol

V

89

Marshall

O

Q

Honey Cr.

Black Hawk

Prairie du Sac

188

Crystal Lake

Roxbury

Sauk City

60

Dunlop Cr.

78

Springfield Corners

19

Sixmile Cr.

Token Creek

Token Creek County Park

151

Sun Prairie

19

T

Milford

94

14

Spring Green

Helena

Wisconsin River

Mazomanie

Marxville

Martinsville

12

Ashton

Waunakee

113

Dane Co. Reg. Airport

Burke

94

Lake Mills

Aztalan

Aztalan State Park

Tower Hill State Park

9

23

Arena

14

15

KP

Black Earth

Cross Plains

Governor Nelson State Park

Mendota County Park

Lake Mendota

Maple Bluff

16

17

18

BB

73

Cottage Grove

Deerfield

London

Rock Lake

19

Jefferson

10

130

Twin Valley Lake

Governor Dodge State Park

12

Pine Bluff

Middleton

14

Shorewood Hills

Madison

Lake Wingra

Univ. of Wis. Arboretum

Monona

Babcock County Park

134

Cambridge

Oakland

J

89

26

Blue Mound State Park

Blue Mound 1,716

Barneveld

Brigham Co. Park

Mt. Horeb

Riley

Klevenville

15

Lake Monona

McFarland

90

MM

Lake Waubesa

Rockdale

Utica

Ridgeway

YZ

18 151

13

18 151

Verona

18 151

Fitchburg

Lake Kegonsa State Park

Lake Kegonsa

B

Fort Atkinson

Panther Intaglio Effigy

Hoard His. Mus. & Dairy Shrine

Dodgeville

11

151

Dodge Br.

191

Mt. Vernon

92

69

PB

Oregon

138

Stoughton

51

73

Busseyville

106

20

Jonesdale

Hollandale

JG

Paoli

Basco

A

D

Albion

Lake Koshkonong

Edgerton

N

KK

Mineral Point

Shake Rag Under the Hill

39

Yellowstone River

Blue Mounds

Daleyville

Belleville

MM

138

Union

Cooksville

14

Fulton

Indianford

59

Lima Center

Waldwick

Yellowstone Lake State Park

Blanchardville

Postville

JG

92

Brooklyn

92

213

14

184

Milton

21

59

Calamine

Fayette

78

New Glarus

New Glarus Woods State Park

Exeter

Attica

Evansville

Gibbs Lake County Park

Leyden

E

26

Lamont

81

Argyle

Jordan Center

69

Monticello

Albany

104

Magnolia

Center

59

Janesville

90

Johnstown

Darlington

Avon

M

78

81

69

Footville

213

11

22

14

Emerald Grove

Johnstown Center

A

0 2 4 6 8 10

SCALE IN MILES

1. Leland

Chamber of Commerce, 105 Philip St. While only vestiges of Fishtown's angling past remain, the **Leelanau Historical Museum** recalls the history of the former fishing settlement with exhibits that include artifacts and pictures. Among the attractions at **Leelanau State Park,** located on the Leelanau Peninsula, is the **Grand Traverse Lighthouse,** one of the oldest lighthouses on the Great Lakes. *Admission charged.*

2. Sleeping Bear Dunes National Lakeshore

The 7.6-mile **Pierce Stocking Scenic Drive** crosses the spectacular Sleeping Bear Dunes, overlooks North Manitou and South Manitou islands, and passes picnic areas and hiking trails. **Sleeping Bear Point Maritime Museum,** in a restored Coast Guard station, concentrates on U.S. Life Saving Service history.

3. Ludington

Convention and Visitors Bureau, 5827 West Rte. 10. At **White Pine Village** an 1849 courthouse on its original site is the centerpiece for an extensive reconstruction of a 19th-century town. Collections of Indian and marine artifacts, tools, and Victorian furnishings are displayed at the **Rose Hawley Museum.** *Admission charged at village.*

4. Two Rivers

Visitors can see gear used by commercial fishermen, artifacts retrieved from sunken ships, and an 1886 lighthouse at **Rogers Street Fishing Village Museum;** solar energy systems and a nuclear reactor simulated at **Point Beach Energy Center;** and dunes and woods that are lovely for hiking at **Point Beach State Forest** on Lake Michigan. *Admission charged at museum.*

5. Manitowoc

Visitor Bureau, 1515 Memorial Dr. Manitowoc's shipbuilding history dates to the 19th century, when it was known as Clipper City, and extends to the construction of submarines and warships during World War II.

Its diverse attractions range from **Lincoln Park and Municipal Zoo** to the **Manitowoc Maritime Museum,** which has numerous models, artifacts, a two-story facade of the streets of a 19th-century harbor town, and a World War II submarine. The **Rahr-West Museum,** in an 1891 Victorian mansion, displays 19th-century art, prehistoric Indian artifacts, Chinese ivories, and Boehm porcelains. At **Pinecrest Historical Village,** 23 relocated and restored buildings depict life in a 1900's law office, sawmill, and a train depot with an 1887 locomotive. *Admission charged for some attractions.*

1950 Bullet Nose, Studebaker Museum

6. Old Wade House and Wesley W. Jung Carriage Museum

West 7747 Plank Rd., Greenbush. Costumed guides conduct tours of an 1851 stagecoach inn whose taproom and ballroom contain many original furnishings. In the adjacent Jung museum is one of America's finest carriage collections, with more than 100 wagons, coaches, ladies' phaetons, and sleighs from 1879 to 1910. *Admission charged.*

7. Sheboygan

Convention and Visitors Bureau, 631 New York Ave. Sightseeing includes scenic drives along the Lake Michigan shoreline; the **Sheboygan County Museum,** a handsome 1852 brick home and restored barn; the **John Michael Kohler Arts Center,** housed in an 1882 Italianate villa, with five art galleries; **Waelderhaus,** a reproduction of Kohler's family chalet in the Austrian Alps with original furnishings; and **Indian Mound Park,** with a dozen burial mounds in a rare variety of animal and abstract shapes. *Admission charged at museum.*

8. Whitehall

Chamber of Commerce, 124 West Hanson St. Area artifacts, ship models, and Lake Michigan sand dunes can be seen at the **White**

River Light Station Museum, housed in an 1875 lighthouse. The **world's largest weather vane** — 4,300 pounds and 48 feet high — is located north of town. *Admission charged at museum.*

9. Michigan City

Convention and Visitors Bureau, 1503 South Meer Rd. At Washington Park's **Old Lighthouse Museum,** built in 1858, implements, shipbuilding tools, and displays interpret the history of this commercial port, fishery, and 1900's resort community. The 38-room **Barker Mansion,** featuring hand-carved woodwork, marble fireplaces, Tiffany glass, and a Victorian sunken garden, is open to the public. *Admission charged.*

10. South Bend

Convention and Visitors Bureau, 401 East Colfax Ave. The **Northern Indiana Historical Society Museum,** located in an 1855 former county courthouse, depicts northern Indiana history through costumes, antique toys, and doll collections. The University of Notre Dame's **Snite Museum of Art** displays more than 18,000 artworks representing all periods, with work by Chagall, Rodin, and Boucher. The **Studebaker National Museum** illustrates America's evolution into an industrial nation, along with exhibits of carriages, wagons, and cars produced by the Studebaker Company from the 1800's to 1963. *Admission charged at Studebaker museum.*

11. Sauder Farm and Craft Village

Rte. 2, near Archbold. Situated in a once-impenetrable forest bog, the Sauder Farm and Craft Village complex features costumed guides and working craftsmen in shops and homes, most of which were built by settlers in the 19th century. A museum exhibits household items, machinery, quilts, and tools. *Admission charged.*

12. Honolulu House

107 North Kalamazoo, Marshall. Built in 1860 by a former U.S. consul to Hawaii, and patterned after Honolulu's executive mansion, this exotic sandstone home with board and batten siding features a spiral staircase leading to an observation tower, a large veranda, tropical murals, 15-foot ceilings, and 1860's furnishings. *Admission charged.*

13. Jackson

Convention and Visitors Bureau, 6007 Ann Arbor Rd. **Cascade Falls** features 15 man-made waterfalls and six fountains; the

Michigan Space Center displays the original Apollo 9 command module, Mercury and Gemini spacecraft, moon rocks, and a lunar rover. The **Ella Sharp Museum** displays a Victorian farmhouse, art galleries, and historic exhibits. *Admission charged.*

14. Ann Arbor

Convention and Visitors Bureau, 211 East Huron St. Ann Arbor is home to the **University of Michigan,** more than 100 research and technology firms, and major scientific and cultural attractions. The university sprawls over 2,600 acres, encompassing portions of downtown. Its main attractions include one of the world's largest carillons, in the **Burton Memorial Tower;** nature trails through the 250-acre **Matthaei Botanical Gardens** and the 125-acre **Nichols Arboretum;** and the **Phoenix Memorial Laboratory,** which houses a 2-million-watt nuclear reactor. The university's **Kelsey Museum of Archaeology** exhibits artifacts from ancient Rome and the Near East; the **Museum of Art** contains excellent collections of Western art from the Middle Ages to the present; and the **Ruthven Exhibit Museum** features natural history. At the **Ann Arbor Hands-On Museum** visitors can participate in science and art exhibits, and then see an unusual example of Greek Revival architecture at the **Kempf House.** The **National Center for the Study of Frank Lloyd Wright** has the nation's largest collection of the famed architect's decorative designs. *Admission charged for some attractions.*

15. Huron City Museums

7930 Huron City Rd., Port Austin. Visitors can tour eight preserved buildings from the 1850–1890 Victorian era, such as a log cabin, carriage house, church, U.S. Life Saving Service station, general store, and inn. Each contains appropriate period furnishings, including fine pottery and a desk made from a grand piano. *Admission charged.*

16. Alpena

Chamber of Commerce, 133 Johnson St. Visitors can hike on nature trails at **Island Park,** view reproductions of extinct animals at the **Dinosaur Gardens Prehistorical Zoo,** and browse science, history, and industrial exhibits at the **Jesse Besser Museum and Planetarium.** Experienced divers descend to shipwrecks at **Thunder Bay Underwater Preserve.** *Admission charged for some attractions.*

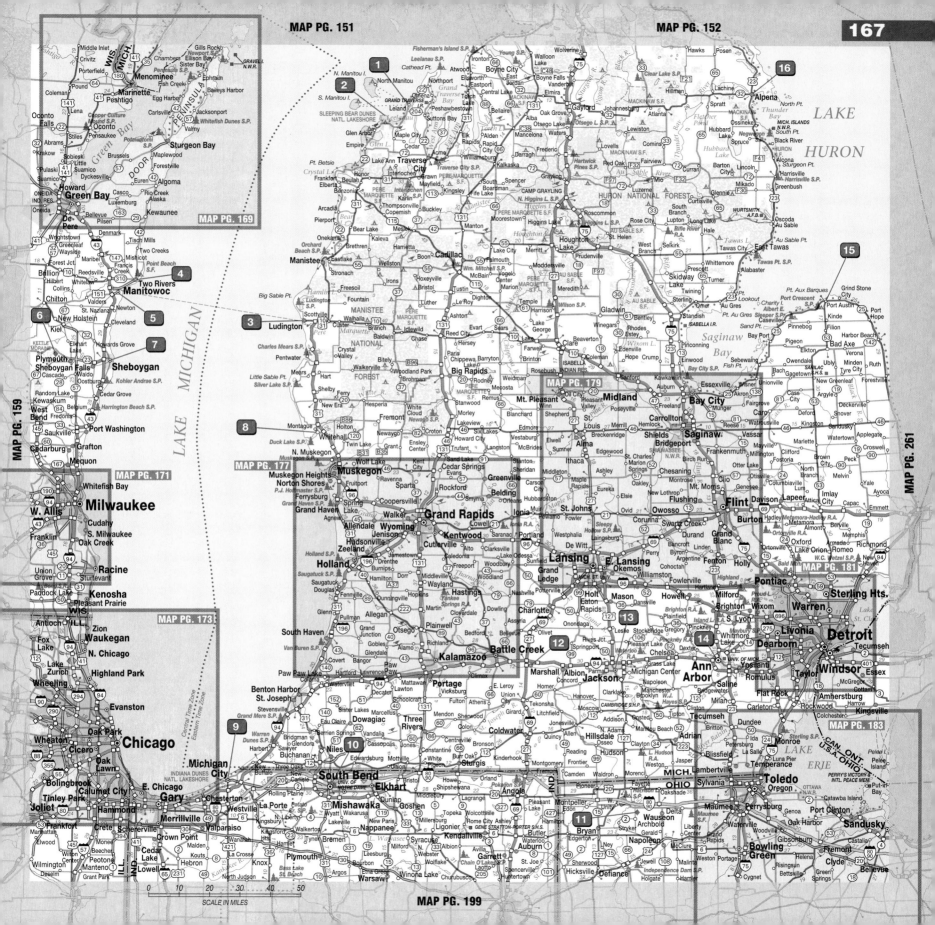

1. The Crivitz Area Museum

South St., Crivitz. The history and heritage of the Crivitz area is depicted with exhibits about Indians, pioneers, early resorts, lumbering, and railroading.

2. Marinette County Historical Museum

Rte. 41, Stephenson Island. Along with excellent exhibits on local Indians, visitors can see the area's logging history interpreted in photographs, dioramas of logging camps, wood carvings, and several scale models of Great Lakes schooners used to transport lumber. *Admission charged.*

3. Peshtigo

America's greatest forest fire occurred here on the same October night in 1871 as the Great Chicago Fire. The **Peshtigo Fire Museum** contains documents and artifacts from the blaze, and some 350 unidentified victims are buried in a mass grave at **Peshtigo Fire Cemetery.**

4. Oconto

Visitor Information Center, 110 Brazeau Ave. At the **Beyer Home Museum** visitors can step into a Victorian house with 1880's furnishings, and see antique cars, logging displays, and Civil War artifacts. Examples of 4,500-year-old Indian copper implements are also displayed here as well as at **Copper Culture Mound State Park.** *Admission charged at museum.*

5. Oneida Nation Museum

E and EE Rds., De Pere. A full-scale reconstruction of an Oneida longhouse serves as the centerpiece in this museum, which traces the history of the Oneida Indian Nation from New York to Wisconsin. *Admission charged.*

6. National Railroad Museum

2285 South Broadway, Green Bay. Seventy-five pieces of rolling stock include General Eisenhower's World War II staff train and Winston Churchill's private car. Also displayed are one of the smallest engines and one of the largest steam locomotives in America. Admission includes a ride on an 1890's coach. *Admission charged.*

7. Green Bay Packer Hall of Fame

855 Lombardi Ave., Green Bay. Here the history of the National Football League's only team owned by a city is recounted from 1919 to the present. Participatory activities, Vince Lombardi memorabilia, the Super Bowl I trophy, and films and videos of the Packers' games and highlights are featured. *Admission charged.*

8. Neville Public Museum

210 Museum Pl., Green Bay. Six galleries of art history and science displays are housed in the Neville Public Museum, including a silver monstrance from the 1686 Green Bay mission and an exhibit that traces the history — from the Ice Age through the mid-20th century — of northeast Wisconsin.

9. Bay Beach Wildlife Sanctuary

1660 East Shore Dr., Green Bay. The 700-acre park is a great place for children. Attractions include nature trails, a nature education center, and children's fishing lagoons. A 60-year-old family amusement park across the street has wading pools, playgrounds, a midway, and miniature train rides. *Fee charged for rides.*

10. Heritage Hill State Park

2640 South Webster Ave., Green Bay. At this 48-acre living-history museum, northeast Wisconsin's development is interpreted by guides in period dress reenacting pioneers' daily lives and various occupations. Twenty-five historic buildings, furnished with 10,000 artifacts, were relocated here from the Green Bay region.

11. Kewaunee County Museum

Vliet and Dodge Sts., Kewaunee. Antiques, artifacts, and memorabilia are exhibited in a jail, sheriff's office, and home that were in use from 1876 to 1969. Displays include a life-size wood carving of Father Marquette with Indians and a basswood carving of Custer's Last Stand. *Admission charged.*

12. Sturgeon Bay

Chamber of Commerce, 1015 Green Bay Rd. This major shipbuilding center, home to many artists and craftsmen, includes 100 historic buildings in two National Historic Districts. Indian pioneer relics, period rooms, and firefighting equipment are displayed at the **Door County Museum.** The

Packer coach Vince Lombardi, 1967

Door County Maritime Museum has the world's first shipping container, historic boats from 1900, a Great Lakes pilothouse, and artifacts from shipwrecks. Changing exhibits at the **Miller Art Center** concentrate on Midwestern artists.

13. Potawatomi State Park

In this 12,000-acre park with 2½ miles of shoreline, a 75-foot observation tower atop a limestone bluff offers panoramic views of Green Bay and Sturgeon Bay. Camping, hiking, fishing, canoeing, and cross-country and downhill skiing are all popular activities here. *Admission charged.*

14. The Farm

Rte. 57, north of Sturgeon Bay. Breeding is scheduled so that there are always plenty of young animals on hand to pet and feed. The changing menagerie may include calves, chicks, kids, kittens, lambs, piglets, puppies, and rabbits as well as cows, donkeys, and horses. Reconstructed homestead buildings contain antique farm tools and equipment. *Admission charged.*

15. Egg Harbor

Points of interest here include the **Chief Oshkosh Indian Museum,** dedicated to the last chief of the Menominee Indians, featuring war bonnets, stone implements, and a buffalo robe painted by Sacajawea. **Cupola House,** on the National Register of Historic Homes, has antiques, unique collectibles, and Amish quilts.

16. Peninsula State Park

The 3,763-acre park draws over 1 million visitors annually to its 9 miles of waterfront, 18-hole golf course, four campgrounds, sandy beaches, caves, cliffs, observation tower, and the historic **Eagle Bluff Lighthouse,** built in 1868 and furnished with antiques. *Admission charged.*

17. Baileys Harbor

Carnivorous pitcher plants and 27 native Wisconsin orchids can be seen at **Ridges Sanctuary,** where nature has formed ridges and swales containing rare plant communities in a boreal-type climate. **Björklunden Chapel** is a magnificent example of artistry in hand carving, with an ornate baptismal font, pulpit, altar, and murals. *Admission charged at chapel.*

18. Cana Island Lighthouse

The lighthouse is operated by the Coast Guard. Although the tower and buildings are not open to the public, the grounds are open and are maintained much as they were in the 19th century. It remains a photographer's favorite and can be visited by wading or walking a stone causeway to the island.

19. Newport State Park

This 2,400-acre semi-wilderness along 11 miles of Lake Michigan's shore is an exquisite setting for hiking, swimming, backpacking, and cross-country skiing. Deer, coyotes, and many birds are seen along shorelines. Access is by 28 miles of trails. Vehicles, including snowmobiles, are prohibited. *Admission charged.*

20. Door County Maritime Museum

Wisconsin Bay Dr., Gills Rock. At this sister museum to the one in Sturgeon Bay, visitors can board a fishing tug and see an old ice sled, carved ship models, and artifacts recovered from local sunken ships.

21. Washington Island Farm Museum

Jackson Harbor Rd., Washington Island. Agricultural history is interpreted through tours and demonstrations of farm chores and crafts. The 3-acre site contains horse-drawn machinery, hand tools, and exhibits in original and reconstructed buildings.

22. Rock Island State Park

Once the estate of inventor Chester Thordarson, this remote 912-acre park is accessible only by ferry, which docks near **Viking Hall.** Built with massive stones, the hall displays Icelandic carved furniture and Indian artifacts. **Potawatomi Lighthouse,** a half-hour hike from the dock, is the oldest on Lake Michigan. Island travel is limited to walking and hiking. *Fee charged for ferry.*

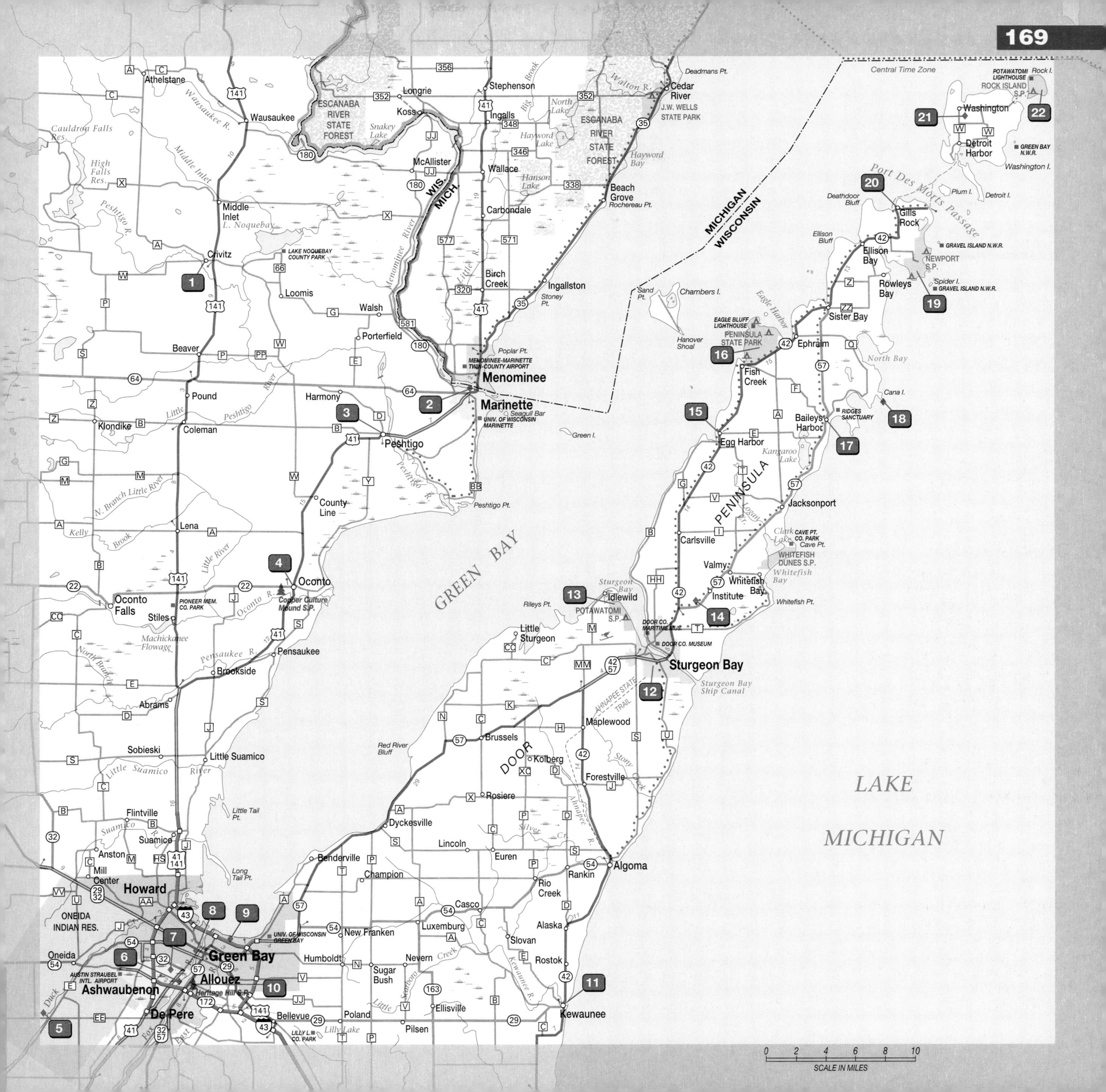

Central Time Zone
MICHIGAN
WISCONSIN
WIS.
MICH.
GREEN BAY
LAKE
MICHIGAN
DOOR
PENINSULA
Athelstane
Wausaukee
Middle Inlet
Crivitz
Loomis
Walsh
Porterfield
Beaver
Pound
Harmony
Klondike
Coleman
Peshtigo
Lena
County Line
Oconto
Oconto Falls
Stiles
Pensaukee
Brookside
Abrams
Sobieski
Little Suamico
Flintville
Suamico
Anston
Mill Center
Howard
ONEIDA INDIAN RES.
Oneida
Green Bay
Allouez
Ashwaubenon
De Pere
Bellevue
Humboldt
New Franken
Sugar Bush
Nevern
Ellisville
Poland
Pilsen
Benderville
Champion
Luxemburg
Casco
Slovan
Rostok
Alaska
Kewaunee
Algoma
Rankin
Rio Creek
Euren
Lincoln
Dyckesville
Rosiere
Kolberg
Brussels
Forestville
Maplewood
Sturgeon Bay
Sturgeon Bay Ship Canal
Little Sturgeon
Idlewild
POTAWATOMI S.P.
DOOR CO. MARITIME MUS.
DOOR CO. MUSEUM
Institute
Whitefish Bay
Whitefish Pt.
WHITEFISH DUNES S.P.
Valmy
Carlsville
Jacksonport
Egg Harbor
Baileys Harbor
RIDGES SANCTUARY
Kangaroo Lake
Fish Creek
PENINSULA STATE PARK
EAGLE BLUFF LIGHTHOUSE
Ephraim
Sister Bay
Rowleys Bay
Ellison Bay
Gills Rock
NEWPORT S.P.
Port Des Morts Passage
Washington
Detroit Harbor
Washington I.
ROCK ISLAND S.P.
POTAWATOMI LIGHTHOUSE
Rock I.
GREEN BAY N.W.R.
GRAVEL ISLAND N.W.R.
Spider I.
Plum I.
Detroit I.
Deathdoor Bluff
Ellison Bluff
North Bay
Cana I.
Chambers I.
Hanover Shoal
Sand Pt.
Green I.
Rileys Pt.
Red River Bluff
Little Tail Pt.
Long Tail Pt.
Peshtigo Pt.
Seagull Bar
Poplar Pt.
Marinette
Menominee
MENOMINEE-MARINETTE TWIN-COUNTY AIRPORT
UNIV. OF WISCONSIN MARINETTE
Ingallston
Stoney Pt.
Birch Creek
Carbondale
Wallace
McAllister
Koss
Longrie
Stephenson
Ingalls
Cedar River
Deadmans Pt.
J.W. WELLS STATE PARK
Beach Grove
Rochereau Pt.
Hayword Bay
ESCANABA RIVER STATE FOREST
Snakey Lake
Hayword Lake
Hanson Lake
North Lake
Walton R.
Cauldron Falls Res.
High Falls Res.
LAKE NOQUEBAY COUNTY PARK
L. Noquebay
PIONEER MEM. CO. PARK
Copper Culture Mound S.P.
Machickanee Flowage
AUSTIN STRAUBEL INTL. AIRPORT
UNIV. OF WISCONSIN GREEN BAY
Heritage Hill S.P.
LILLY L. CO. PARK
Lilly Lake
AHNAPEE STATE TRAIL
CAVE PT. CO. PARK
Cave Pt.
Clark Lake
SCALE IN MILES
0 2 4 6 8 10

1. The Annunciation Greek Orthodox Church

9400 West Congress St., Wauwatosa. Created in 1961 by Frank Lloyd Wright, who called it his Little Jewel, this saucer-shaped church, the last of the Wisconsin architect's major projects, supports a beautiful blue dome. Greek Orthodox symbols are incorporated into the overall design. Guided tours are available. *Fee charged for tours.*

2. Lowell Damon House

2107 North 76th St., Wauwatosa. Famous as Wauwatosa's oldest house, this excellent example of classic colonial architecture contains beautiful 19th-century furnishings. Guided tours are offered.

3. Caves Museum

4251 West State St., Milwaukee. In the mid-19th century, the Miller Brewing Company excavated caves in the bluffs along the Milwaukee River to use as cool storage areas in which to age beer. Today guided tours take visitors through the caves, which now contain a collection of artifacts from the early beer-brewing days.

4. Pabst Mansion

2000 West Wisconsin Ave., Milwaukee. The magnificent 37-room mansion of Milwaukee's famous beer baron, with its ornately decorated facade and stepped gables, dates from 1893. The mansion is furnished in elegant 19th-century style, featuring a sumptuous interior of hand-carved woodwork, stained-glass windows, intricate wrought-iron work, and carved panels from a 17th-century Bavarian castle. Guided tours are offered here, as well as tours of the nearby **Pabst Brewing Company.** *Admission charged at mansion.*

5. Marquette University

Outstanding sights on the Milwaukee campus include the **Saint Joan of Arc Chapel,** a 15th-century French structure, which offers tours; the **Haggerty Museum of Art,** with displays of paintings, sculpture, and decorative arts from medieval times to the present; and the 48-bell **Marquette Hall Carillon,** one of the largest bell towers in the United States.

6. Milwaukee Public Museum

800 West Wells St., Milwaukee. Walk-through exhibits of old Milwaukee are featured in this museum, which also includes dinosaurs, Indian artifacts, and a rain forest display. The Wizard Wing, a hands-on children's area, tells of both natural and human history. *Admission charged.*

7. Villa Terrace Decorative Arts Museum

2220 North Terrace Ave., Milwaukee. This 1923 mansion, built in Italian Renaissance style, is now a museum featuring 17th- and 18th-century decorative arts and furniture. Reservations are required in advance for guided tours. *Admission charged.*

8. Charles Allis Art Museum

1801 North Prospect Ave., Milwaukee. The personal art collection of Charles Allis, including paintings, furniture, and decorative arts from around the world, is displayed in his 1909 Tudor-style mansion. Although 18th- and 19th-century art is the focal point of the museum, some pieces date as far back as 500 B.C. *Admission charged.*

9. Milwaukee Art Museum

750 North Lincoln Memorial Dr., Milwaukee. American and European art of the 19th and 20th centuries is included in the permanent collection of this museum, which is located in the handsome lakefront **War Memorial Center,** one of Eero Saarinen's creations. Changing exhibits, lectures, and tours are also offered. *Admission charged.*

10. Grain Exchange Room

225 East Michigan St., Milwaukee. Two carved heads representing the bull and bear of trading glare at each other over the entrance to this elaborate Victorian structure, dating from 1879. The grain room, a nostalgic reminder of Milwaukee's wheat-trading days, is said to be the place where pit trading was first developed.

11. Milwaukee City Hall

200 East Wells St., Milwaukee. Built in 1895 in Flemish Renaissance style, the building is famous for the elaborately carved woodwork and stenciled ceilings in the Common Council Chamber. It also has a handsome belltower and an eight-story atrium surrounded by intricate wrought-iron balconies.

12. Allen-Bradley Clock Tower

1201 South Second St., Milwaukee. This famous timepiece is said to be the world's largest four-faced clock, with each face almost twice the size of London's Big Ben. In clear weather it can be seen from many miles and often is used as a landmark by ships navigating the sometimes treacherous waters of Lake Michigan.

13. St. Josaphat's Basilica

601 West Lincoln St., Milwaukee. Built in 1901 by Polish parishioners, who used the remnants of the old Chicago main post office, this remarkable building contains an unusual collection of relics, wood carvings, and stained glass. Its huge dome is patterned after St. Peter's in Rome, and in 1929 it was designated a basilica.

14. Mitchell Park Conservatory

524 South Layton Blvd., Milwaukee. Three enormous glass domes, encompassing three climates — for arid, tropical, and seasonal plants — provide spectacular year-round displays. Visitors can see habitats with birds, reptiles, fish, and amphibians in the arid and tropical domes. Picnic areas are provided. *Admission charged.*

15. Milwaukee County Zoo

10001 West Bluemound Rd., Milwaukee. An unusual feature of this world-renowned, 3,000-animal zoo is an exhibit in which predators and their prey, who are actually housed in separate areas, appear to be peacefully coexisting in the same environment. A miniature train and a zoomobile carry passengers through the extensive wooded grounds. *Admission charged.*

16. Trimborn Farm Park

8881 West Grange Ave., Greendale. Named for the Prussian immigrant who ran lime kilns here from 1847 to 1900, when the local limestone quarries were in operation, the park today contains a Greek Revival farmhouse, a granary, two barns, and kilns.

17. Waukesha

Information Bureau, N14 W23777 Stone Ridge Dr. A historic courthouse serves as the **Waukesha County Historical Museum,** whose exhibits include Indian and pioneer artifacts. The **Chandler House,** a mansion dating from the early 1870's, contains Victorian furniture, mechanical musical instruments, and antique dolls and toys. The house is open by appointment only. *Admission charged at mansion.*

18. Kettle Moraine Scenic Steam Train

Off Rte. 83, North Lake. An 8-mile round-trip train ride, starting at an 1890's railroad depot, takes visitors through two moraine cuts, farmlands, and over a 125-foot timber tressel 30 feet above the Oconomowoc River. *Fee charged for ride.*

19. East Troy Electric Railroad Museum

2002 Church St., East Troy. In tribute to the electrical system that once was the connecting link between Milwaukee and its various suburban areas, the museum displays many different styles of electric railway cars and rail equipment. A 10-mile round-trip train ride from the museum is also available to visitors. *Admission charged.*

20. Burlington

Chamber of Commerce, 140 East Chestnut St. The **Burlington Historical Museum,** with exhibits of artifacts from pioneer days to the present, tells the story of the town from 1835 onward. The **Spinning Top Exploratory Museum,** which features more than 1,000 tops, gyroscopes, and yo-yos, invites visitors to play with some of the items. *Admission charged.*

21. Charles A. Wustum Museum of Fine Arts

2519 Northwestern Ave., Racine. Bordered by a park and formal gardens, the museum contains paintings, sculpture, and crafts of local and national artists. The permanent collection is a commentary on the days of the Great Depression.

22. Racine Zoological Park

2131 North Main St., Racine. The zoo, which overlooks Lake Michigan, has a large collection of unusual animals, including the handsome blue-eyed white tiger. A swimming beach and picnic areas are provided.

23. SC Johnson Wax Administration Building

14th and Franklin Sts., Racine. The strikingly beautiful Cherokee red brick building designed by Wisconsin-born Frank Lloyd Wright is complemented by the space-age design of the multiscreen **Golden Rondelle Theatre.** Tours of the Johnson Wax headquarters leave from the theater. Also located in town is **Wingspread,** the former home of the H. F. Johnson family, designed by Wright. The house, now a conference center, offers tours by appointment only.

1. Fox River Trolley Museum

Rte. 31, South Elgin. The museum's collection includes antique railway cars and equipment. Visitors may take a 3-mile ride along the Fox River on an intercity trolley from 1900. *Admission charged.*

2. Moraine Hills State Park

Set in a rocky area left by a receding glacier, the park, with its three small lakes, offers fishing, hiking trails, and picnic grounds. Visitors can follow a boardwalk to the nearby **Volo Bog State Natural Area,** a quaking bog of spongy vegetation. Also found here are pitcher plants, bulrushes, orchids, and many kinds of wildlife.

3. Libertyville

Founded in 1836, the town is known for the **David Adler Cultural Center,** where art exhibits and occasional concerts are held in the architect's 1917 home. Other attractions include the **Lambs Farm,** with a petting zoo, animal nursery, and country shops, and the **Cuneo Museum and Gardens,** a 1914 mansion with an art collection, formal gardens, fountains, and a conservatory.

4. Illinois Beach State Park

Stretching for more than 7 beautiful sandy miles along Lake Michigan, the park offers an array of recreational opportunities — bicycling, camping, fishing, boating, and other water sports. An observation tower at the magnificent **North Point Marina** offers a spectacular view of the lake.

5. Highland Park

Chamber of Commerce, 600 Central Ave. Settled in 1834, this Chicago suburb is the scene of the annual Ravinia Festival, summer home of the renowned Chicago Symphony Orchestra. *Admission charged.*

6. The Chicago Botanic Garden

Lake Cook Road, Glencoe. With 300 acres of lakes, streams, and woodlands, the garden contains sections for roses, fruits and vegetables, perennials, and herbs. The Education Center includes greenhouses and a floral arts museum. Trams offer rides through the grounds. *Admission charged.*

7. Baha'i House of Worship

112 Linden Ave., Wilmette. Overlooking Lake Michigan, the beautiful nine-sided building, enhanced by gardens and fountains, is the spiritual center of the Baha'i religion in North America. A visitor center offers exhibits and slide shows.

8. Evanston

Chamber of Commerce, 807 Davis St. The city is home to **Northwestern University,** whose attractions include the **Dearborn Observatory,** open to visitors during the summer by reservation, and the lovely **Shakespeare Garden.** Other points of interest in town are the **Frances E. Willard Home/National Woman's Christian Temperance Union,** now restored and open to visitors, and the famous **Grosse Point Lighthouse,** built after a tragic shipwreck on Lake Michigan. *Admission charged at lighthouse.*

9. Lincoln Park

Chicago's largest city park features the **Lincoln Park Conservatory,** with several greenhouses, as well as rock and formal gardens, and the **Lincoln Park Zoological Gardens,** known for its gorilla exhibit. The nearby **Chicago Academy of Sciences** focuses on the natural history of the Chicago area. *Admission charged at academy.*

10. Oak Park

Visitor Center, 158 North Forest Ave. Considered to be the birthplace of the Prairie style of American architecture, the suburb is famous for its many homes designed by Frank Lloyd Wright. **Unity Temple,** Wright's first all-concrete structure, and his home and studio are also located here. Guided tours are available.

11. Brookfield Zoo

31st St. and First Ave., Brookfield. Trams provide seasonal transportation through the zoo, which features some 2,000 animals in realistic habitats, a dolphin demonstration, and three rain forests. *Admission charged.*

12. Lizzardo Museum of Lapidary Art

220 Cottage Hill Ave., Elmhurst. Chinese jade and other stone carvings, agate cameo bowls, minerals, gemstones, and meteorites are among the highlights of this impressive collection. *Admission charged.*

13. Wheaton

Chamber of Commerce, 331 West Wesley St. Known primarily as a religious center, with 39 churches and many religious publishing organizations, Wheaton is the site of the **Billy Graham Center Museum,** which is dedicated to the history of American evangelism. Other sites include the **Du Page County Heritage Gallery,** containing archives on football hero Red Grange, and the **Du Page County Historical Museum,** which focuses on local history. **Cantigny,** the former estate of Robert R. McCormick of the Chicago *Tribune,* offers tours. *Parking fee charged at Cantigny.*

14. Naper Settlement Museum Village

201 West Porter Ave., Naperville. A 12-acre living-history museum with some 25 structures, this settlement re-creates pioneer and Victorian life in northern Illinois. Visitors can tour public buildings, a print shop, a blacksmith shop, post office, windmill, and four homes. The **Martin-Mitchell Mansion,** dating from 1883, displays period furnishings. Costumed guides interpret the life-style of the times. *Admission charged.*

15. Fermi National Accelerator Laboratory

Kirk Rd. and Pine St., Batavia. The world's highest-energy particle accelerator shares its 6,800-acre grounds with a herd of buffalo. The visitor center offers information and a 25-minute film. Self-guided laboratory tours are available daily; guided tours are given by appointment.

16. Joliet

Visitor Bureau, 81 North Chicago St. Settled in the early 1800's on the banks of the Des Plaines River, the town is a former center of shipping and industry. The **Rialto Square Theatre,** a 1920's movie palace famous for its ornate lobby modeled after the Hall of Mirrors in Versailles, is today a popular entertainment venue. Among the elegant restored Victorian residences featured in **Historic Districts,** visitors can tour the 44-room **Jacob Henry Mansion.**

17. Lockport

Chamber of Commerce, 132 East Ninth St. Four of the original five locks remain in this river town, which was built in the 1830's as headquarters for the Illinois and Michigan Canal. The **Illinois and Michigan Canal Museum,** located in an 1837 office building, displays artifacts from the construction of the canal. The **Pioneer Settlement,** a restoration of a 19th-century village, and the **Gaylord Building,** an early warehouse that now serves as a visitor center, provide further insight into life here in the early 1800's.

18. Pullman Historic District

This planned community, created in the 1880's for employees of the Pullman Palace Car Company, was outfitted with all kinds of facilities and services. The houses ranged from humble to elegant; the more skilled the worker, the finer the home. Today most of the original buildings are still standing and the neighborhood is thriving. Guided tours are available.

19. Illinois Institute of Technology

Most of the institute's buildings were designed by Mies van der Rohe, who completed his first structure here in 1943. Typical of Mies' style, the box-shaped design is evident on the campus, which boasts **Crown Hall,** considered to be one of the architect's finest achievements.

20. University of Chicago

Founded in 1892, the university offers several points of interest for visitors to the campus. The **Oriental Institute** focuses on the history, art, and archeology of the Near East from prehistoric times to the time of Christ. The **Rockefeller Memorial Chapel** commemorates the university's founder. Buildings of architectural note include **Bond Chapel,** a Gothic-style structure on the quadrangle, and **Robie House,** one of Frank Lloyd Wright's masterpieces. Guided tours are available.

21. Museum of Science and Industry

57th St. and Lake Shore Dr., Chicago. This museum is one of Chicago's most popular attractions, with more than 2,000 intriguing exhibits that include a submarine, the Apollo 8 capsule, a replica of a coal mine, an enormous walk-through human heart, a miniature circus with 22,000 hand-carved pieces, and a hands-on section for toddlers. *Admission charged.*

22. Indiana Dunes National Lakeshore

These geologically fascinating dunes along Lake Michigan's southern shore — whose flora ranges from tundra plants to western cacti — offer a swimming beach, hiking trails, picnic areas, and a magnificent view of the lake. *Fee charged at beach.*

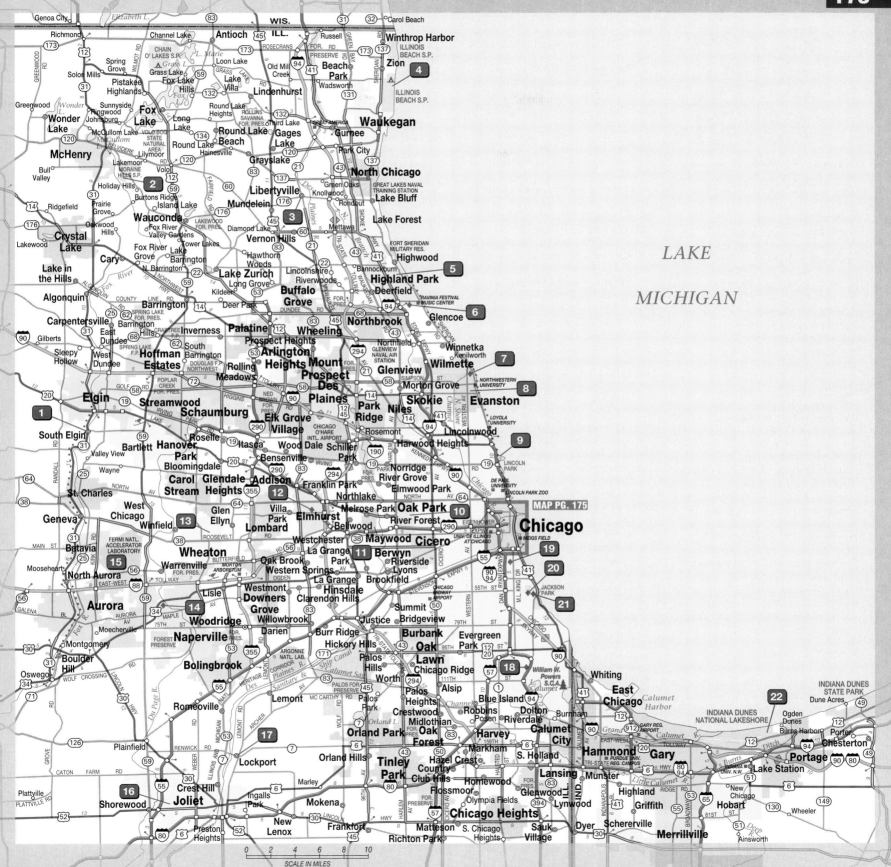

SCALE IN MILES

DOWNTOWN CHICAGO

1. Navy Pier
600 East Grand Ave. Extending for almost a mile into Lake Michigan, this pier, a former navy training grounds and barracks, contains parks, auditoriums, picnic areas, and boat-docking facilities.

2. Magnificent Mile
Magnificent indeed is this section of Michigan Avenue, with a wide selection of elegant shops. **Water Tower Place,** a mall and atrium, is named for the fortresslike tower that survived the Great Chicago Fire of 1871. Here too is the **John Hancock Center,** an office structure offering a dazzling view from its top. **Oak Street Beach** is a popular swimming and recreation area.

3. River North
Once a neighborhood of warehouses and other commercial buildings, the area is now an artists' colony akin to New York's SoHo, with intriguing shops, boutiques, restaurants, and more than 80 art galleries displaying mostly contemporary works.

4. Terra Museum of American Art
666 North Michigan Ave. With Ambassador Daniel Terra's private art collection as its nucleus, this museum features 18th-, 19th-, and 20th-century paintings by American artists. *Admission charged.*

5. Museum of Contemporary Art
237 East Ontario St. Somewhat hampered by space constrictions, the museum currently rotates its extensive collection of some 4,000 works, most of which date from the 1940's to the present. In 1995 the museum plans to move to expanded facilities located at the current site of the Chicago Armory. *Admission charged.*

6. Tribune Tower
435 North Michigan Ave. Notable for its architecture, the home of Chicago's largest newspaper is a handsome 36-story skyscraper built in 1925 in neo-Gothic style.

7. Wrigley Building
400 North Michigan Ave. Another architectural landmark, the Wrigley Building is dominated by a square tower topped by a four-faced clock.

8. Merchandise Mart
Wacker Dr. between Wells and Orleans Sts. Tours are offered of this massive building, said to be the world's largest commercial structure, with more than 900 showrooms displaying all kinds of furnishings. For an excellent overview of the entire city, visitors often board the elevated train here for a trip around the **Loop**. *Fee charged for tour.*

9. State of Illinois Center
100 West Randolph St. The center has an innovative exterior of curving plain and mirrored glass and colored panels. Its lovely atrium, rising 17 stories to a sky-lit dome, is adorned with a spectacular circular floor and exposed elevators. Adding to the outdoors scene is the striking black-and-white Jean Dubuffet sculpture "Monument to a Standing Beast."

10. Civic Opera House
20 North Wacker Dr. Housed in a 45-story Art Deco building, the huge 3,600-seat auditorium is the epitome of elegance, with marble pillars, crystal chandeliers, and a sweeping staircase. Also located in the building is the 900-seat **Civic Theatre**.

11. Daley Center
Randolph and Clark Sts. Named for the former mayor, the building houses county and city courts. The plaza, dominated by a Picasso sculpture, contains an eternal flame

A 1912 triptych window by Frank Lloyd Wright and an 1898 elevator grille medallion by Louis H. Sullivan, at the Art Institute of Chicago

in memory of Americans who died in the Korean and Vietnam wars. From the plaza the lovely spire of the nearby **Chicago Temple** can be seen.

12. Marshall Field's
111 North State St. Renowned as one of the greatest stores in the world and a landmark for more than a century, this venerable Chicago emporium features an exceptional Tiffany dome and a Crystal Palace ice cream parlor.

13. Chicago Cultural Center
78 East Washington St. Famous for its mosaics, marble walls, curving stairways, and Tiffany domes, the center offers art exhibits, concerts, and other performances. With extensive collections of old TV and radio broadcast tapes, the **Museum of Broadcast Communications** has facilities for study and gives weekly broadcasts from a reconstructed radio studio.

14. Carson Pirie Scott
1 South State St. Another outstanding store, Carson Pirie Scott features so-called Chicago windows — a large fixed pane flanked by two small, double-hung windows — and an especially handsome entranceway enhanced by lavish ornamentation and grillwork by Louis S. Sullivan. The nearby 1890 **Reliance Building,** considered to be a forerunner of 20th-century skyscrapers, has a glass and terracotta facade.

15. The Rookery
209 South La Salle. This impressive redstone and iron and steel-framed skyscraper, built in 1886, is known for its unusually fine lobby, which was redesigned in 1905 by Frank Lloyd Wright.

16. Sears Tower
233 South Wacker Dr. The views from the observation deck on the 103rd floor of this 110-story structure, the tallest in the world, extend in clear weather for 37 miles. A Calder mobile enhances the lobby.

17. Chicago Mercantile Exchange
30 South Wacker Dr. The visitor center of this financial center, commonly called the Merc, overlooks the unbelievably frenetic trading floor, the site of major national and international business transactions.

18. Union Station
A masterpiece of railroad depot architecture, Union Station has a 10-story dome over the waiting room, soaring pillars, and gilded sculpture.

19. Jane Addams' Hull House Museum
800 South Halsted St. Located on the campus of the **University of Illinois,** the 1856 Hull Mansion and the 1905 Residents' Dining Hall are all that remain of the complex founded in 1889 by social workers Jane Addams and Ellen Gates Starr. Today a museum, the two buildings depict the history of Hull House and the city's Near West Side with a variety of exhibits.

20. Chicago Main Post Office
433 West Van Buren St. This is the world's largest postal facility under one roof and is remarkable for its extensive use of automated equipment. Advance reservations are required for tours of the building.

21. Chicago Board of Trade
141 West Jackson Blvd. A large gilded statue of Ceres, the Roman goddess of agriculture, adorns the top of this 1930 Art Deco structure. The 44-story building is the world's largest commodity trading center. Viewing galleries overlook the trading floor.

22. Monadnock Building
53 West Jackson Blvd. Dating from the early 1890's, this remarkable structure, whose walls at the base are 6 feet thick to support the all-masonry construction, is the tallest such building in the world.

23. Orchestra Hall
220 South Michigan Ave. Home of the world-famous Chicago Symphony Orchestra, this 1904 hall, whose acoustics are exceptionally fine, is also the scene of various other musical events. Tours are available by reservation.

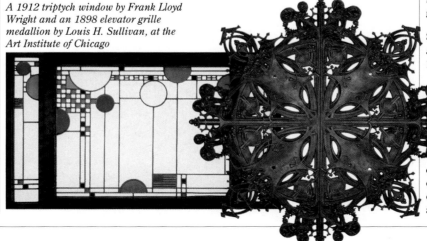

24. The Art Institute of Chicago

Michigan Ave. and Adams St. The institute is known throughout the world for its collection of American and European paintings and sculpture as well as decorative arts from virtually every country, and its beautiful stained-glass windows by Marc Chagall. The entrance to the handsome Italian Renaissance–style palazzo, which dates from 1893, is flanked by lions.

25. Auditorium Theatre

55 East Congress Pkwy. This stunning hall is acclaimed for its elegant design and near-perfect acoustics. The theater is located in the **Roosevelt University** building, which has a splendid library worth exploring.

26. Grant Park

Extending through downtown Chicago, the park is filled with flowers all summer. The elaborately carved pink marble **Buckingham Fountain,** whose waters rise to 135 feet, presents colorful displays from spring to late fall. Summer concerts are given in the James C. Petrillo Band Shell.

27. Field Museum of Natural History

Lake Shore Dr. and Roosevelt Rd. One of the world's great natural history museums, its exhibits present animals, gems, and many facets of world cultures, from ancient Egyptian to Native American. The Place For Wonder, a special section for children, features shells, mounted animals, and toys from around the world. *Admission charged.*

28. John G. Shedd Aquarium

1200 South Lake Shore Dr. Some 6,000 examples of aquatic life are exhibited in realistic habitats. Once a day divers enter the Coral Reef to feed the fish. Two beluga whales and several dolphins are showcased in the remarkably naturalistic Oceanarium. *Admission charged.*

29. Adler Planetarium

1300 South Lake Shore Dr. Its entrance marked by a Henry Moore sundial, the planetarium presents sky shows in two theaters, various exhibits, and special weekend shows for children. *Admission charged.*

30. Prairie Avenue Historic District

This once-affluent residential enclave offers guided tours of the 1836 **Clarke House,** the oldest house in the city, and the **Glessner House,** a 35-room mansion built in 1886. *Fee charged for tours.*

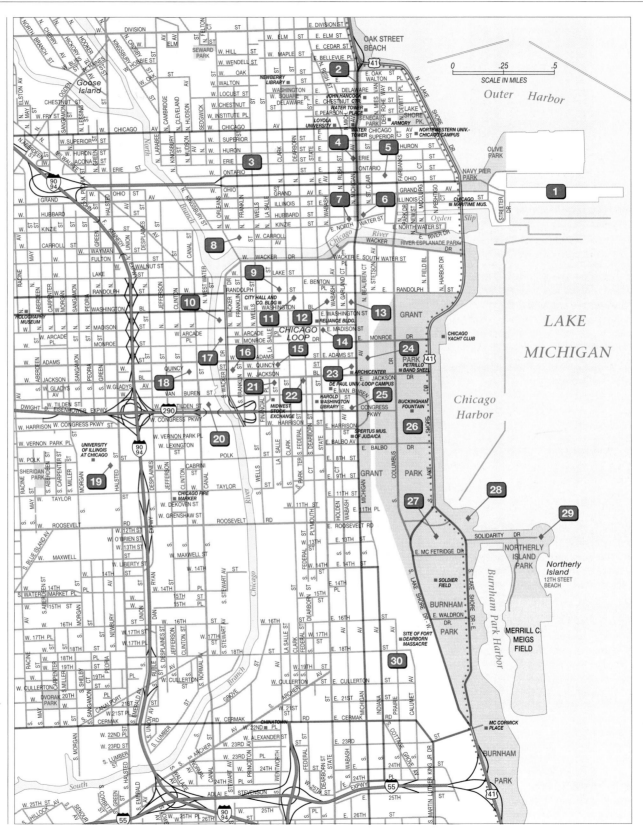

1. Muskegon

Visitor Bureau, 349 West Webster Ave. Paintings by Degas, Whistler, Rembrandt, and Hopper are among the works exhibited in the **Muskegon Museum of Art.** At the **Hackley and Hume Historic Site** are ornate 1888 Queen Anne mansions, with carved woodwork, tiled fireplaces, stenciled walls, and stained-glass windows. Guided tours are conducted of the **U.S.S. Silversides,** a World War II submarine. At the **Muskegon County Museum,** the lumber industry and the fur trade are examined, and the fishing is good in **Muskegon Lake.** *Admission charged for some attractions.*

2. E. Genevieve Gillette Sand Dune Visitor Center

6585 Lake Harbor Rd., Muskegon. Sheltered in a most impressive dune system, the center is a departure point for trails leading into the dunes; it also offers lectures, guided tours, and special audiovisual programs.

3. Grand Haven

Visitor Bureau, 1 South Harbor Dr. The **Tri-Cities Historical Museum** features Victorian period rooms and regional exhibits. Water, lights, and music are synchronized in the **Musical Fountain.** Picnic sites, beachfront camping, and water sports are available at **Grand Haven State Park.** *Admission charged for some attractions.*

4. Holland

Chamber of Commerce, 272 East 8th St. **Windmill Island,** whose centerpiece is a 200-year-old windmill, is a tiny Dutch village. The **Netherlands Museum** has exhibits pertaining to local and Dutch lore, while vintage vehicles are displayed in the **Poll Museum of Transportation.** Visitors can observe the workings of the **Wooden Shoe Factory** on a guided tour, and in **Dutch Village** a 19th-century ambience pervades the architecture, windmills, and canals. At the **DeKlomp Wooden Shoe and Delftware Factory** visitors can watch artisans craft shoes and paint delftware. *Admission charged for some attractions.*

5. Blandford Nature Center

1715 Hillburn Ave. NW, Grand Rapids. A wildlife care center and self-guided nature trails attract visitors to this 143-acre site, where tours are conducted. There is also an interpretive center. *Fee charged for tour.*

6. John Ball Zoological Garden

1300 West Fulton St., Grand Rapids. Some 500 animals can be seen here in the zoological garden, a herpetarium (reptile house), an aquarium, a children's zoo, and a South American panorama. *Admission charged.*

7. Gerald R. Ford Museum

303 Pearl St. NW, Grand Rapids. The life and times of the nation's 38th president — a Grand Rapids resident — are showcased here. So is a model of the White House and a replica of the Oval Office. Exhibits include historic documents and bicentennial gifts from heads of state. *Admission charged.*

A Holland artisan handcrafts wooden shoes.

8. Fish Ladder

Sixth St. Dam, Grand Rapids. During spawning season, salmon can be seen leaping the rapids along this unusual series of steps, designed by a local artist.

9. La Grande Vitesse ("The Calder")

Calder Plaza, Grand Rapids. Its official name is La Grande Vitesse (the Grand Rapid), but it's known to locals as The Calder — a 42-ton bright red stabile by artist Alexander Calder. A county building

adjacent to the sculpture is adorned with a 127-foot abstract painting, also by Calder.

10. The Grand Rapids Art Museum

155 Division Ave. N., Grand Rapids. Housed in the city's first federal building, the museum's permanent collection includes German Expressionist and 19th- and 20th-century American paintings. A children's gallery provides hands-on exhibits and special programs. *Admission charged.*

11. Public Museum of Grand Rapids

54 Jefferson St. SE, Grand Rapids. Among this museum's eclectic collection is the charming Gaslight Village, replete with a horsedrawn streetcar, reminiscent of late 19th-century Grand Rapids. Other displays pertain to the local history of furniture manufacturing and the Native American community. The **Roger B. Chaffee Planetarium** provides programs on astronomy, meteorology, and space science in a 50-foot dome theater. *Admission charged.*

12. Heritage Hill Historic District

There are some 1,300 buildings in this historic district — Grand Rapid's most fashionable residential area in the 1890's — that represent more than 60 different architectural styles. The Heritage Hill Association provides information for self-guided tours.

13. Ada Covered Bridge

7507 Thornapple River Dr., Ada. Charmingly evocative of another era, this is one of the few extant covered bridges in Michigan. The footbridge, constructed in 1867, spans the Thornapple River.

14. Fallasburg Covered Bridge

Off Rte. 21, Lowell. The Fallasburg Covered Bridge, next to **Fallasburg Park,** has been in continuous service since its construction in 1871; the nearby **Whites Covered Bridge** in Keene Township dates from 1869. Both are open to vehicular traffic.

15. Charlton Park Village

2545 South Charlton Park Rd., east of Hastings. This 300-acre park offers a restored turn-of-the-century village, water sports, museums, nature trails, and hands-on educational programs. *Admission charged.*

16. Gilmore–C.C.C.A. Museum

6865 Hickory Rd., Hickory Corners. Antique automobile buffs will love this 90-acre garden of cars. The collection includes an 1899 Locomobile, a 1984 Pontiac Fiero Indy

Breakfast favorite from Battle Creek

Pace Car, and an impressive array of Rolls-Royces, Packards, Cadillacs, and Fords. *Admission charged.*

17. Battle Creek

Convention and Visitors Bureau, 34 West Jackson St. Cheetahs, zebras, and red pandas are among the animals at the **Binder Park Zoo.** Dinosaur bones and a dugout canoe are some of the hands-on displays in the **Kingman Museum of Natural History,** at the **Leila Arboretum.** The **Kimball House Museum,** a Queen Anne house with period furnishings, has exhibits pertaining to the black abolitionist Sojourner Truth, who is buried in **Oak Hill Cemetery.** *Admission charged for some attractions.*

18. Augusta

Swans, ducks, and geese grace the ponds and lakes of the **W. K. Kellogg Bird Sanctuary** of **Michigan State University.** Water sports, hiking, biking, and campgrounds are available at the **Fort Custer Recreation Area.** *Admission charged.*

19. Kalamazoo

Convention and Visitors Bureau, 128 North Kalamazoo Mall. World War II aircraft are on display at the **Kalamazoo Aviation History Museum.** A 19th-century pioneer homestead, eight nature trails, and a prairie are featured at the **Kalamazoo Nature Center.** The **Kalamazoo Public Museum** has hands-on exhibits related to history and technology, as well as a planetarium. German Expressionist and 20th-century American art are showcased in the **Kalamazoo Institute of Arts.** *Admission charged for some attractions.*

1. Center for Cultural and Natural History

124 Rowe Hall, Central Michigan University, Mt. Pleasant. A veritable time machine, this university museum examines natural and cultural history through interpretive displays. Exhibits range from the skeletal remains of a mastodon to a trapper's cabin.

2. Michigan Masonic Home

1200 Wright Ave., Alma. Guided tours are conducted through this vast complex, which was erected by the Masonic Grand Lodge as a retirement community for members of the Masonic family.

3. Midland

Convention and Visitors Bureau, 300 Rodd St. **Dow Gardens** is a lavishly landscaped 60-acre site, graced with waterfalls, laced with streams, and planted with an exquisite array of annuals and perennials. Adjacent to the gardens, the history of Michigan is spotlighted in exhibits at the **Midland Center for the Arts.** This cultural and entertainment complex also features concerts, plays, and lectures. Some 14 miles of trails loop through the **Chippewa Nature Center,** whose many attractions include a homestead farm complex, a reconstructed log cabin, and a natural history museum. *Admission charged for some attractions.*

4. Historical Museum of Bay County

321 Washington Ave., Bay City. American Indian and pioneer artifacts are on display in this handsome structure that was once the Michigan National Guard Armory. Among the exhibits are costumes, maps, and a chronological history of Bay County.

5. Castle Museum of Saginaw County History

500 Federal Ave., Saginaw. The history of Saginaw County is traced in exhibits housed in a former post office. Designed along the lines of a French château, the Romanesque building is replete with towers and turrets. *Admission charged.*

6. Saginaw Art Museum

1126 North Michigan Ave., Saginaw. The Ring Mansion is home to this site's collection of Oriental and contemporary artwork. There are formal gardens with sculptures, a children's gallery, and art classes and films.

7. Japanese Cultural Center

527 Ezra Rust Dr., Saginaw. A cooperative effort between Saginaw and her sister city, Tokushima, Japan, resulted in the creation of these lovely Japanese gardens. Tours of the gardens are available, as are tours of the **Japanese Tea House,** where visitors can enjoy an informal tea. Tea ceremonies are presented regularly by Japanese hosts and hostesses in traditional garb. *Admission charged at tea house.*

8. Shiawassee National Wildlife Refuge

During migration seasons thousands of geese and ducks, attracted by the extensive wetlands and river systems, arrive in this refuge. In addition to bird-watching, visitors can enjoy miles of hiking trails and explore the remnants of early lumber and coal-mining operations.

9. Frankenmuth

Convention and Visitors Bureau, 635 South Main St. Lt. Commander Roger Chaffee, who lost his life when the *Apollo 1* capsule caught fire, is among the Michigan astronauts and war heroes to whom the **Michigan's Own Inc. Military and Space Museum** pays tribute. Local history is the focus of the **Frankenmuth Historical Museum.** Brewing is a large industry in the city, and brewery tours are another popular activity among visitors here. *Admission charged for some attractions.*

10. Crossroads Village and Huckleberry Railroad

G-6140 Bray Rd., Flint. Costumed docents portray the "inhabitants" in this re-creation of a 19th-century village, where an old-time steam locomotive takes visitors on an 8-mile excursion. Sightseers will find among the 28 restored buildings a general store, railroad depot, and sawmill. The village is brightly adorned with Christmas lights in December. *Admission charged.*

11. Flint Cultural Center

1231 East Kearsley St., Flint. This complex contains the **Flint Institute of Arts,** whose permanent collection includes Renaissance art and 19th- and 20th-century paintings; the

Robert T. Longway Planetarium, which boasts a 60-foot dome theater; and the **Sloan Museum,** where displays of vintage automobiles remind visitors that General Motors started in Flint. *Admission charged for some attractions.*

12. Whaley Historical House

624 East Kearsley St., Flint. This 1885 mansion was the home of banker Robert Whaley, who financed the early manufacturing of carriages. *Admission charged.*

13. For-Mar Nature Preserve and Arboretum

5360 East Potter Rd., Burton. Trails wind through this 380-acre park, which features an interpretive center with nature exhibits.

14. Holly

Chamber of Commerce, 102 Civic Dr. In **Historic Battle Alley,** a restored Victorian street, specialty shops have replaced the taverns in which Carry Nation conducted her famous 1908 crusade against alcohol. Nearby, hunting and fishing are excellent in the **Holly Recreation Area.** *Admission charged at recreation area.*

15. Seven Lakes State Park

Graced with six lakes and miles of shoreline, this lovely park has trails for hikers, cross-country skiers, and snowmobilers, as well as excellent fishing, hunting, and boating. There are also facilities for softball, volleyball, picnics, and camping. Nearby, the **Seven Lakes Vineyard** offers free wine tastings and guided tours by appointment. *Admission charged.*

16. Curwood Castle

224 Curwood Castle Dr., Owosso. Novelist and conservationist James Oliver Curwood built this replica of a Norman château in 1922. **Comstock Cabin,** adjacent to the castle, is the oldest house in Owosso.

17. State Capitol

1 Capitol Ave., Lansing. Designed along the lines of the U.S. Capitol in Washington, D.C., this home to the state legislature, dedicated in 1879, has been recently restored. It features Victorian-era decorative paintings throughout and a glass floor in the rotunda. Guided tours are available.

18. Impression 5 Science Museum

200 Museum Dr., Lansing. More than 200 interactive exhibits are featured in this innovative museum, where people of all ages can become better acquainted with

physics, chemistry, biology, electronics, and computing. In the nearby **R.E. Olds Transportation Museum,** classic vehicles produced in Lansing are on view, including the Reo, Star, Durant, and the first Oldsmobile, built in 1897. *Admission charged.*

19. Potter Park Zoo

1301 South Pennsylvania Ave., Lansing. There are canoes for rent, camel and pony rides, and 400 animals to see in this zoo, located on the banks of the Red Cedar River. *Admission charged.*

20. Michigan State University

Attractions on this East Lansing campus include more than 4,000 works of art, from prehistoric to contemporary, which make up the permanent collection of the **Kresge Art Museum.** The **Beal Botanical Garden** showcases more than 5,000 species of plants, while the **Gardens of Michigan State University** feature five gardens on 7 acres. The sky's the limit at the **Abrams Planetarium,** which hosts sky shows and lectures and has astronomical displays. Cultural and natural history are the highlights at the **MSU Museum.** *Admission charged for planetarium shows.*

21. Carl G. Fenner Arboretum

2020 East Mt. Hope Ave., Lansing. Five miles of easy hiking trails wind through 120 acres of fields, forests, and ponds, with trailside exhibits that include an herb garden and a log cabin replica. A nature center offers seasonal displays, and educational tours are available. *Fee charged for tours.*

22. Michigan Women's Historical Center and Hall of Fame

213 West Main St., Lansing. Honoring the history and achievements of Michigan women, the center is housed in a building listed on the State Register of Historic Sites. *Admission charged.*

23. Michigan Historical Museum

717 West Allegan St., Lansing. The state's history is highlighted in the exhibits and educational programs of this museum, which is a part of the **Michigan Library and Historical Center Complex.**

24. Woldumar Nature Center

5539 Lansing Rd., Lansing. Hiking and cross-country skiing trails, nature walks, and an interpretive center are some of the attractions in this 188-acre wildlife preserve. *Admission charged.*

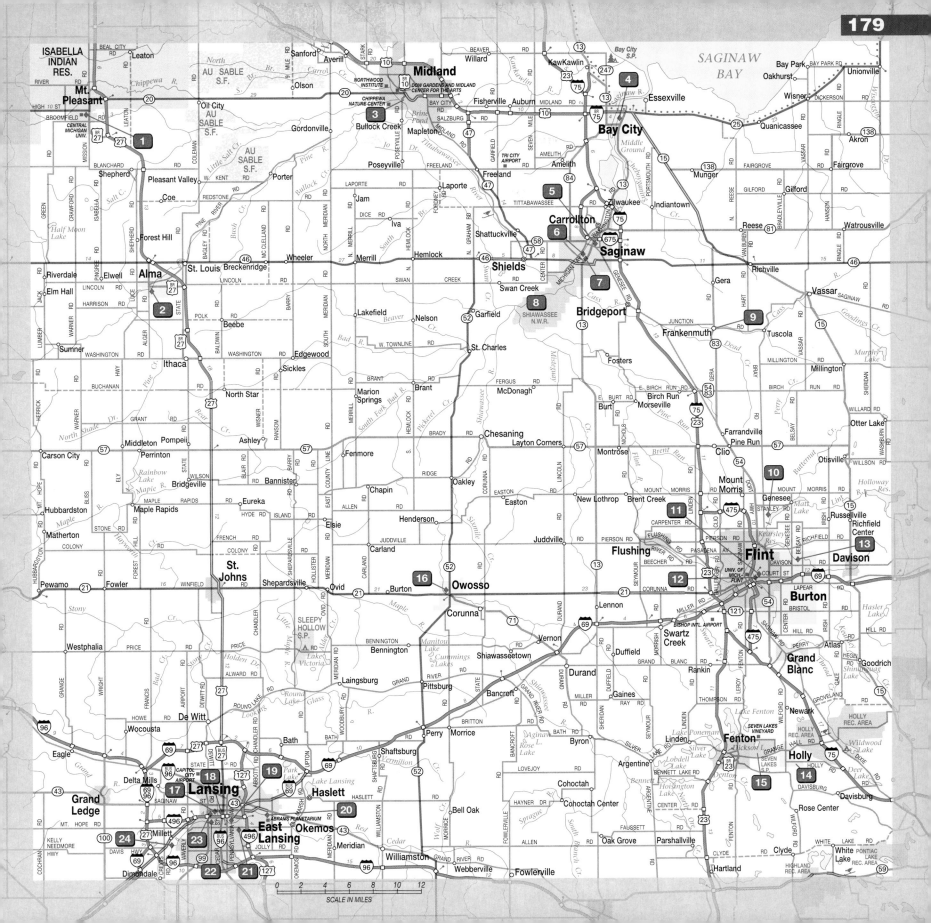

1. Meadow Brook Hall

Completed in 1929 for Alfred and Matilda Dodge Wilson, Meadow Brook Hall is now a cultural and conference center for **Oakland University** in Rochester. Among the features of the castlelike, 100-room building are an imposing Great Hall, 24 fireplaces, a solarium, magnificent works of art, handsomely carved ceilings, a ballroom resplendent with gargoyles, and formal gardens. *Admission charged.*

2. Troy Museum and Historical Village

60 West Wattles Rd., Troy. Situated around a picturesque village green are several 19th-century structures, including a log cabin, a blacksmith shop, a general store, and a Greek Revival farmhouse. A replica of a Dutch Colonial tavern houses a museum with displays featuring memorabilia related to local history.

3. Cranbrook Educational Community

1221 Woodward Ave., Bloomfield Hills. Spread over 315 acres, Cranbrook was the former estate of George Booth, publisher of the *Detroit Evening News.* Now an educational and cultural complex, its facilities include **Cranbrook House and Gardens,** a Tudor-style house built in 1908 and set in 40 acres of gardens; the 150-student **Cranbrook Academy of Art and Museum;** the **Cranbrook Institute of Science,** an extensive natural history museum with hands-on exhibits, a planetarium, and a nature center; and the noted **Cranbrook Schools.** *Admission charged.*

4. Detroit Zoo

8450 West Ten Mile Rd., Royal Oak. More than 1,200 animals inhabit this 122-acre zoo, grouped by continent in surroundings that realistically depict their natural habitats. *Admission charged.*

5. Dearborn

Chamber of Commerce, 15544 Michigan Ave. The 254-acre **Henry Ford Museum and Greenfield Village** is one of the nation's largest indoor-outdoor museums. Among the treasures in its vast collection are the chair Abraham Lincoln was sitting in when he was assassinated, George Washington's travel chest, and Henry Ford's first car. Adjacent to the museum is the 81-acre Greenfield Village, a 19th-century small town replete with a traditional village green and tree-lined streets. Its historic structures, all moved here from elsewhere around the country, include Henry Ford's birthplace, the Ohio home and cycle shop of the Wright brothers, and Thomas Edison's Menlo Park laboratory. The **Henry Ford Estate,** set on 72 beautifully landscaped acres on the banks of the River Rouge, cost $2 million to build and is connected by a 300-foot tunnel to a six-level powerhouse. *Admission charged.*

6. Detroit Historical Museum

5401 Woodward Ave., Detroit. Visitors can stroll through three historical periods in the Streets of Old Detroit exhibit and see costume displays that relate to the city's past at the Booth-Wilkinson Costume Gallery. *Donation encouraged.*

7. Motown Museum

2648 West Grand Blvd., Detroit. The history of the Motown Sound is traced in this museum, which was the home of Berry Gordy, Jr., the founder of the famed record company. *Admission charged.*

8. Fisher Building

3011 West Grand Blvd., Detroit. Albert Kahn, architect to Detroit's automotive industrialists, built this award-winning commercial building in 1928. Today it houses the Fisher Theater, art galleries, and shops.

9. International Institute

111 East Kirby Ave., Detroit. Visitors can see costumes, jewelry, and other cultural exhibits from 50 countries spanning five continents in the Hall of Nations.

10. Museum of African American History

Warren Ave. and Bush St., Detroit. Historical documents, exhibits, artworks, and educational and cultural programs trace the history and achievements of African-Americans. *Admission charged.*

11. Detroit Institute of Arts

5200 Woodward Ave., Detroit. One of the nation's largest museums of fine arts, the institute has a collection of more than 55,000 works of art and houses more than 100 galleries. Among the exhibits are major works by Picasso, van Gogh, and Rembrandt, along with those of leading American artists, and the William Randolph Hearst armor collection. An entire room is devoted to a 27-panel mural by Diego Rivera, which depicts Detroit's automotive industry. *Admission charged.*

12. Eastern Farmer's Market

2934 Russell St., Detroit. This century-old, 10-acre market is home to the world's largest bedding flower market and includes produce, fish, and meat-packing houses. Gourmands will delight in the market's many restaurants and the nut, exotic spice, coffee, and cheese specialty shops.

13. Historic Trinity Lutheran Church

1345 Gratiot Ave., Detroit. This Tudor Gothic church, dedicated in 1931, is constructed of varicolored granite and Indiana limestone; it has a slate roof and floor and oak woodwork. Visitors will especially enjoy its fine statuary and stained-glass windows.

14. Trappers Alley

508 Monroe Ave., Detroit. In the center of bustling **Greektown** stand five century-old buildings, which once served in Detroit's fur-tannery industry. Now enclosed under one roof, they comprise a festive marketplace where visitors will find a number of shops and eateries.

15. Renaissance Center

Jefferson Ave. at Beaubien, Detroit. The "Ren Cen" — a multipurpose complex including atriums, gardens, walkways, and even an indoor lake — stands as a symbol of the revival that is taking place in downtown Detroit. Visitors can board the **Detroit People Mover** for a 13-stop trip around the central loop via an automated monorail. *Fee charged for monorail.*

16. Civic Center

1 Washington Blvd., Detroit. The 75-acre center has as its centerpiece the busy **Philip A. Hart Plaza.** Also located in the complex are the **Veterans' Memorial Building,** whose lobby showcases works of battlefront artists, the $30-million, computer-controlled **Dodge Fountain,** and the sprawling 2.4-million-square-foot **Cobo Conference/Exhibition Center,** one of the world's largest facilities of its kind.

17. Windsor

Convention and Visitors Bureau, 333 Riverside Dr. The works of 19th- and 20th-century Canadian artists are showcased in the **Art Gallery of Windsor.** Dedicated to the history of Windsor, the **François Baby House** features changing exhibits from the 18th century to the present. Illuminated at night with dazzling lights, the **Coventry Gardens and Peace Fountain** features a floating fountain 75 feet high and spectacular special effects. In 1906 Edward Chandler Walker built **Willistead Manor,** a handsome 36-room Tudor-style mansion with carved paneling and Carrara marble fireplaces. Set on 15 landscaped acres, today the mansion is open for tours. *Admission charged at mansion.*

18. Belle Isle

There are myriad attractions in this 985-acre city island park, set in the Detroit River. The **Anna Scripps Whitcomb Conservatory** boasts an exquisite orchid collection, as well as palms, ferns, and year-round flower shows. Opened in 1904, the **Belle Isle Aquarium** is one of the oldest freshwater aquariums in the nation. The **Belle Isle Nature Center** has trails that focus on the area's plants and animals. In the 13-acre **Belle Isle Zoo** the animals roam free, and at the **Dossin Great Lakes Museum** vessels that have plied the waters of the Great Lakes are displayed. *Admission charged.*

19. Fisher Mansion

383 Lenox Ave., Detroit. Built in 1927 for Fisher Body Works founder Lawrence Fisher, the opulent Italianate mansion contains stone and marble work, hand-carved paneling of imported woods, parquet floors, and stained glass. *Admission charged.*

20. Pewabic Pottery

10125 East Jefferson Ave., Detroit. A combination gallery, studio, and museum are housed in this Tudor Revival building, which was built as a studio for Mary Chase Perry Stratton, the noted ceramist who founded Pewabic Pottery.

21. Edsel and Eleanor Ford House

1100 Lake Shore Rd., Grosse Pointe Shores. Evocative of the Cotswolds in England, this estate, with 87 acres of landscaped grounds on the banks of Lake St. Clair, was built for Henry Ford's only son. The mansion features 18th-century French antiques, Art Deco rooms, and Old Master and Impressionist paintings. *Admission charged.*

WHITE LAKE RD
Lotus Lake
Waterford
Lake Angelus
THE PALACE
Macomb

PONTIAC LAKE REC. AREA
Pontiac Lake
Lake Angelus
Rochester
Milton

Drayton Plains
Clintonville
Auburn Hills
Yates
Disco
Chesterfield
Waldenburg

OAKLAND-PONTIAC AIRPORT
Pontiac
PONTIAC SILVERDOME
Rochester Hills
ROCHESTER-UTICA RECREATION AREA

Huron Heights
Oxbow
Union Lake
PROUD LAKE RECREATION AREA
Keego Harbor
Sylvan Lake
Utica
Mount Clemens
SELFRIDGE AIR NATIONAL GUARD BASE
Sand Point
Anchor Bay

Commerce
West Acres
Orchard Lake
Bloomfield Hills
Sterling Heights
METRO BEACH METROPARK

Wolverine Lake
Walled Lake
Troy
Huron Point

Wixom
Walled Lake
Birmingham
Clawson
Fraser
Huron Point

Bingham Farms
Beverly Hills
Franklin
Royal Oak
Madison Heights
Roseville

Farmington Hills
Lathrup Village
Berkley
Warren
Center Line
St. Clair Shores

Novi
Farmington
Southfield
Huntington Woods
Oak Park
Hazel Park
Eastpointe
Gaukler Point

Northville
MAYBURY S.P.
Pleasant Ridge
Ferndale
Harper Woods
Grosse Pointe Woods
Grosse Pointe Shores

STATE FAIR GROUNDS
UNIV. OF DETROIT
Highland Park
Grosse Pointe Farms
UNITED STATES / CANADA

Livonia
Hamtramck
Grosse Pointe

Plymouth
Detroit
DETROIT CITY AIRPORT
Grosse Pointe Park
MICHIGAN / ONTARIO

Dearborn Heights
Garden City
Dearborn
TIGER STADIUM
Windmill Point
PECHE ISLAND PROVINCIAL PARK
BELLE ISLE PARK
DOSSIN GREAT LAKES MUSEUM

Westland
HENRY FORD ESTATE
HENRY FORD MUSEUM AND GREENFIELD VILLAGE
St. Clair Beach

Inkster
Wayne
Windsor
WILLISTEAD MANOR
Tecumseh
Puce
Emeryville

Romulus
Taylor
Allen Park
OJIBWAY PROVINCIAL PARK
WINDSOR INTL. AIRPORT
Oldcastle
Maidstone

DETROIT METRO. WAYNE COUNTY AIRPORT
Lincoln Park
La Salle
Oliver

Belleville
Belleville Lake
Southgate
Wyandotte
Fighting Island
River Canard
Delisle's Corners
Paquette Corners
Essex

WILLOW RUN AIRPORT
Riverview
Grosse Ile
Mc Gregor
North Ridge

New Boston
Woodhaven
Trenton
LOWER HURON METROPARK
WILLOW METROPARK

LAKE ST. CLAIR

0 1 2 3 4 5
SCALE IN MILES

1. Toledo Firefighters Museum

918 Sylvania Ave., Toledo. Located in a former fire station, this museum tells the history of the Toledo Fire Division. Thousands of items are displayed, including photographs, uniforms, and the city's first fire pumper. A safety and learning center educates visitors in fire prevention and safety.

2. Toledo Botanical Garden

5403 Elmer Dr., Toledo. This 60-acre site abounds with roses, herbs, wildflowers, and azaleas and includes shade and pioneer gardens. There are also art and glassblowing studios and a pioneer homestead.

3. Maumee

Chamber of Commerce, 222 Conant St. On the banks of the Maumee River, the quaint **Wolcott House Museum Complex** depicts life in the mid-1800's with six historic buildings: a Greek Revival–style home, log house, railroad depot, saltbox-style farmhouse, a church, and the elegant Wolcott house. The **Ohio Baseball Hall of Fame** honors Ohioans including Cy Young, the record-holding pitcher, and Moses Fleetwood Walker, the first black major leaguer. *Admission charged.*

4. Fort Meigs

29100 West River Rd., Perrysburg. Situated above the quick-flowing waters of the scenic Maumee River, this authentically restored fort is one of the largest military reconstructions in the United States. The museum features exhibits on the War of 1812, during which the original fort was constructed, and explains the fort's design. On weekends, the military life of the era is re-enacted by interpreters. *Admission charged.*

5. The Toledo Zoo

2700 Broadway, Toledo. Among the zoo's 2,000 animals are hippos, which can even be seen underwater in the hippoquarium. Further attractions include a simulated African savanna, where leopards, giraffes, and other wildlife roam free, and an award-winning Diversity of Life exhibit. *Admission charged.*

6. S.S. Willis B. Boyer Museum Ship

26 Main St., Toledo. At this nautical museum, visitors can explore the carefully restored S.S. *Willis B. Boyer,* which ruled as the king of the Great Lakes Freighters for 69 years. Photographs, artifacts, and other memorabilia pay tribute to seafaring life. *Admission charged.*

7. Toledo Museum of Art

2445 Monroe St., Toledo. This splendid art museum displays one of the world's finest collections of glass. Other treasures include artworks from ancient Rome, Greece, and Egypt; works by European and American masters; a medieval cloister; and a room from a French château.

8. Maumee Bay State Park

The park's many wetlands and marshes make bird-watching and fishing popular activities here. These 1,860 acres also include two swimming beaches, hiking and biking trails, facilities for camping and picnicking, a golf course, and a nature center with interpretive displays.

9. Monroe

Chamber of Commerce, 22 West Second St. Monroe's French heritage comes alive at the **Navarre Anderson Trading Post and Country Store,** which exhibits colonial furnishings, trade goods, and period merchandise. The trading post, built by French trappers in 1789, is one of the oldest standing structures in Michigan. The **Monroe County Historical Museum** houses a large collection of regional pioneer, military, and American Indian artifacts.

10. Crane Creek State Park

Perfect for bird-watching, the park's marshes and wetlands are inhabited by many wood ducks and herons; it is also a resting place for hundreds of species of migratory birds. Nature trails, scenic roads, and an information center devoted to migration help visitors enjoy the surrounding wildlife. Lake Erie provides opportunities for ice fishing, boating, and swimming.

11. Magee Marsh Wildlife Area

Spanning 1,821 acres, this marshland contains a great variety of water and game mammals and more than 300 species of birds. A visitor center displays mounted birds and decoys. Among the area's many opportunities for outdoor recreation are a bird trail and a beach.

12. South Bass Island

Chamber of Commerce, Delaware and Toledo Aves. Conveniently reached by ferry, this island is great for black bass and wall-eye fishing and, in winter, ice fishing. In the tourist village of **Put-in-Bay** is **Perry's Victory and International Peace Memorial,** a park commemorating Commodore Perry's victory over the British in the 1813 Battle of Lake Erie. The memorial is an impressive 352-foot granite column, and the visitor center has interpretive exhibits.

13. Kelleys Island

Chamber of Commerce, West Lakeshore Dr. On the island's south shore is **Inscription Rock,** a limestone petroglyph carved by American Indians in the 1600's. **Kelleys Island State Park** offers water activities, picnicking, camping, and **Glacial Grooves,** where visitors can see some of the finest examples of glacial grooving in the world. *Admission charged at park.*

Findlay glass, Hancock Historical Museum

14. Marblehead Peninsula and Lighthouse

At the end of this scenic peninsula stands the picturesque, lime-white Marblehead Lighthouse, the oldest continuously used lighthouse on the Great Lakes. Visitors can climb 87 spiral steps to the top of the 100-foot building, where its powerful beam is visible for 10 miles. Nearby **Lakeside,** established in 1873 as a Christian camp, is now a vibrant Chautauqua resort.

15. Follett House Museum

404 Wayne St., Sandusky. This lovely Greek Revival mansion is filled with antiques, such as rare china, glassware, jewelry, dolls and dollhouses, and early housekeeping inventions. History displays include early local maps and artifacts from the Civil War and the Johnson's Island Prison.

16. Milan

Chamber of Commerce, 9 East Church St. Here the **Thomas Edison Birthplace Museum,** where the inventor spent his first seven years, displays family furnishings and many of his creations, including a 1901 mimeograph machine and a talking doll. The nearby seven-building **Milan Historical Museum** includes a country store and blacksmith shop; the main building displays collections of glass, costumes, and antique dolls. The town's **Mitchell-Turner House** is one of the most exquisitely adorned Greek Revival houses in the country. *Admission charged at Edison museum.*

17. The Firelands Museum

4 Case Ave., Norwalk. This museum, which is named for the 500,000 acres given to Connecticut residents whose land was burned by the British during the Revolutionary War, displays early maps, surveyor's equipment, and documents relating to the settlement of the area. Other exhibits include period furnishings, pioneer farm implements, and an impressive display of antique firearms. *Admission charged.*

18. Seneca Caverns

Created by unknown geologic forces, this unusual crack in the earth is one of Ohio's largest caverns, with eight rooms on seven levels. **Old Mist'ry River** flows through the lowest level. *Admission charged.*

19. Rutherford B. Hayes Presidential Center

1337 Hayes Ave., Fremont. The 25-acre estate includes a stately Victorian mansion, once home to the 19th president of the United States. The site became the nation's first presidential library and museum and today contains over 75,000 books and an equal number of photographs, as well as memorabilia from Hayes's military and political careers. *Admission charged.*

20. Findlay

Convention and Visitors Bureau, 123 East Main Cross St. The **Hancock Historical Museum** holds one of the largest and most distinctive Findlay glass collections in the country, as well as Victorian memorabilia, a genuine log house, and interpretive displays on gas-boom industries. The **Mazza Collection Gallery,** located at the **University of Findlay,** specializes in illustrations for children's books and includes the work of such award-winning illustrators as Maurice Sendak and Ezra Jack Keats.

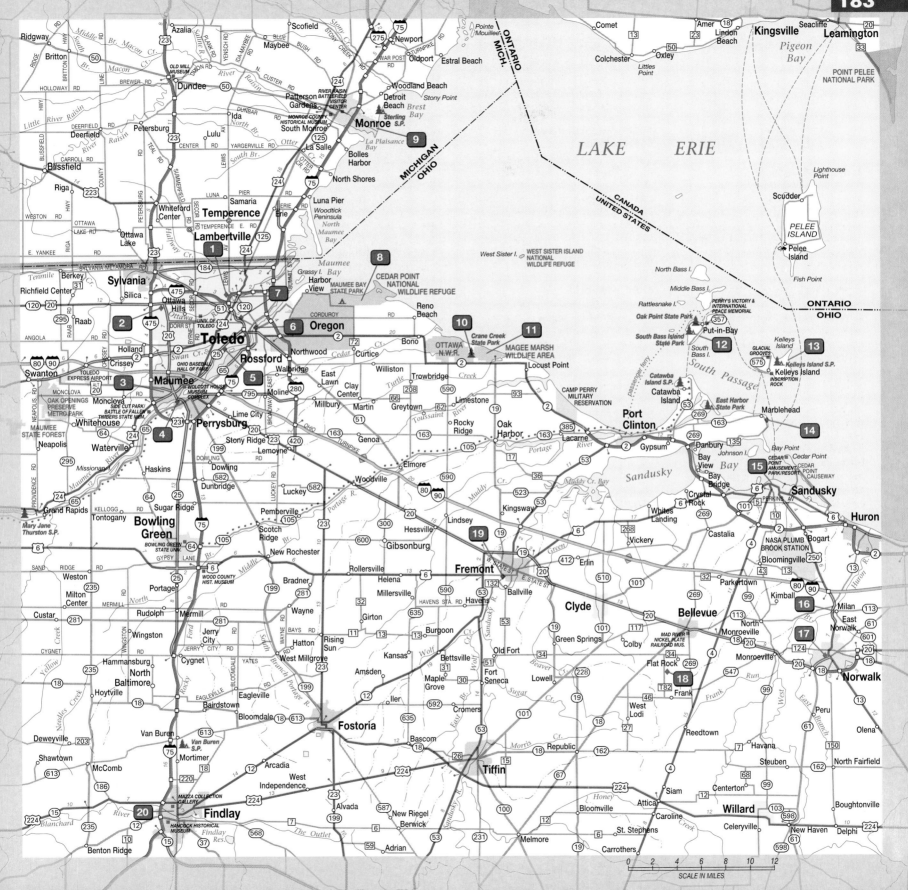

1. Stuhr Museum of the Prairie Pioneer

Rtes. 281 and 34, Grand Island. This 200-acre museum, on an island in a man-made lake, features artifacts that include 200 antique tractors and automobiles. **Railroad Town,** a re-creation of a prairie community, has more than 60 relocated buildings, including the cottage where Henry Fonda was born. *Admission charged.*

2. Willa Cather Historical Center

338 North Webster St., Red Cloud. The small house in which the author lived from ages 10 to 16, and which she described in her books, contains letters, first editions, and family memorabilia. Passages from her works are narrated as rooms are toured. Other buildings described in her books are included in the center. *Admission charged.*

3. Pawnee Indian Village Museum State Historic Site

Rte. 266, Republic. A two-family dwelling with 2,000 square feet of floor space contains ashes from the last fire and corn and weapons lying where they were abandoned, probably in the 1830s. Twenty-two other lodge sites can also be seen.

4. Hollenberg Pony Express Station Museum

Rte. 243, Hanover. This is the only unaltered Pony Express station still standing at its original location. Visitors can see the loft where riders slept, and displays tell the stories of both the Pony Express and the Oregon–California trails.

5. Homestead National Monument

Rte. 4, Beatrice. The 160-acre park sits on one of the first land claims filed under the Homestead Act of 1862. Facilities include a 2½-mile trail through forest and prairie, an 1867 cabin with furnishings from the bygone era, and a visitor center with exhibits recounting the homestead movement.

6. Indian Cave State Park

Scenic drives, horseback and hiking trails, and catfish and carp fishing are among the attractions at this 3,000-acre park on the banks of the Missouri River. Sites of interest include a cave with Indian rock carvings, historic graveyards, and reconstructed buildings, in which living-history demonstrations take place. *Admission charged.*

7. International Forest of Friendship

The forest was a bicentennial gift to the United States from an organization of women pilots. It includes trees from all 50 states and more than 35 countries, a statue of Amelia Earhart, and plaques honoring contributors to aviation's advancement. Earhart's birthplace in nearby **Atchison** can also be toured. *Admission charged at Earhart birthplace.*

8. St. Joseph

Chamber of Commerce, 3003 Frederick Ave. The **Jesse James Home** contains original furnishings, personal memorabilia, and the hole left in the wall from the bullet that killed the outlaw. **St. Joseph Museum,** housed in an 1879 Gothic Revival mansion, features a Jesse James room and American Indian arts and crafts. The **Pony Express National Memorial** displays hands-on exhibits, as well as an 80-foot diorama of the Pony Express Trail. The **Patee House Museum** was the Pony Express headquarters and features railway equipment, Civil War artifacts, and Victorian furnishings. *Admission charged.*

9. Watkins Woolen Mill State Historic Site

26600 Park Rd. N., Lawson. The three-story mill is said to be the nation's only 19th-century textile factory with its original machinery still intact. The complex includes an 1850 Greek Revival home with original furnishings, an 1856 school, and an 1871 church. **Jesse James' Birthplace and Museum** is located nearby.

10. Battle of Lexington State Historic Site

The historic site encompasses many antebellum homes and Union Army entrenchments. A major 1861 Civil War battle site surrounds a Greek Revival home peppered with bullet scars, which visitors can see on a guided tour. *Fee charged for tour.*

11. Agricultural Hall of Fame and National Center

126th St., Bonner Springs. The 172-acre complex features a large collection of agricultural equipment, Harry Truman's plow, and a rural parlor, sewing room, kitchen, and general store. *Admission charged.*

12. Fort Leavenworth

Rte. 73, Leavenworth. A monument honors the famous Buffalo Soldiers, the African-American cavalrymen once stationed here, who helped to settle the West. Also on the grounds are a military prison and a museum that chronicles frontier life.

13. Topeka

Convention and Visitors Bureau, 120 SE Sixth St. Points of interest include the French Renaissance Revival–style state capitol, adorned with elaborate grill- and plasterwork, whose interior contains John Steuart Curry's mural of an apocalyptic John Brown. The **Kansas Museum of History** offers displays on prehistoric Indians, railroads, and Bleeding Kansas. **Historic Ward-Meade Park** features an 1874 Victorian mansion with period furnishings and a turn-of-the-century town square. The **Combat Air Museum** displays aircraft from World War I through the Vietnam War. *Admission charged for some attractions.*

14. Beecher Bible and Rifle Church

Rte. 18, Wabaunsee. Built in 1859 and still used, this church served anti-slavery congregationalists. Henry Ward Beecher gave abolitionists $625 to buy rifles and sent each a Bible; the nearby **Wabaunsee County Museum** displays one of the original rifles as well as an original Bible.

15. Fort Riley

Rte. 70, Junction City. Visitors can tour the fort's 1850's limestone buildings, Kansas' **First Territorial Capitol,** and explore the **U.S. Cavalry Museum,** with paintings by Frederic Remington, uniforms, weapons, and saddles. Named for General Custer, who once served here, the **Custer House** contains 1880's furnishings.

16. Abilene

Chamber of Commerce, 201 NW Second St. Several attractions celebrate Abilene's colorful past as a Chisholm Trail railhead and boyhood home of Dwight D. Eisenhower, World War II general and president. The **Eisenhower Center** complex includes his presidential library and family tomb, boyhood home with original furnishings, and a museum of military and presidential mementos. The **Hall of Generals Wax Museum** depicts some of Ike's World War II colleagues. **Old Abilene Town** features original and reconstructed buildings from the cattle-drive era, and the **Dickinson County Historical Museum** gives more information on local history. *Admission charged for some attractions.*

17. Mushroom Rock State Park

Wind and water have eroded the mass of sandstone that once covered the area, leaving dramatic spheres of harder rock perched, like mushrooms, atop pedestals. The awesome shapes soar up to 25 feet, with 15-foot-wide tops.

18. Maxwell Wildlife Refuge

From an observation tower visitors may see some of the 200 bison, 50 elk, and numerous birds that inhabit the 2,254-acre refuge.

19. Council Grove

Chamber of Commerce, 313 West Main St. Several historic buildings are preserved on the Santa Fe Trail, which runs through town, including the 1857 **Last Chance Store,** the 1867 brick **Seth Hays Home,** and an 1860's jail. **Kaw Mission,** established as an 1851 school, is now a history museum. *Admission charged at Hays home.*

20. Flint Hills National Wildlife Refuge

Situated on a reservoir amid agricultural fields, the 18,500-acre refuge attracts wintering bald eagles and as many as 100,000 ducks and geese during spring and fall. Visitors can hike, camp, and hunt and fish in season. Portions are closed to the public during autumn migrations.

21. Fort Scott National Historic Site

Old Fort Blvd., Fort Scott. Twenty original and reconstructed buildings feature 33 rooms with period furnishings, reflecting life at the fort from 1842 to 1853. A museum relates the fort's history. *Admission charged.*

22. Harry S. Truman Birthplace State Historic Site

1009 Truman Ave., Lamar. Guided tours are conducted at the former president's modest frame home, which was built about 1881 and contains period furnishings.

23. Carry Nation Home

211 West Fowler Ave., Medicine Lodge. A shrine to the famed temperance crusader, the seven-room home contains original furnishings and her personal effects, including the hatchet and brickbats she once used to destroy saloons. *Admission charged.*

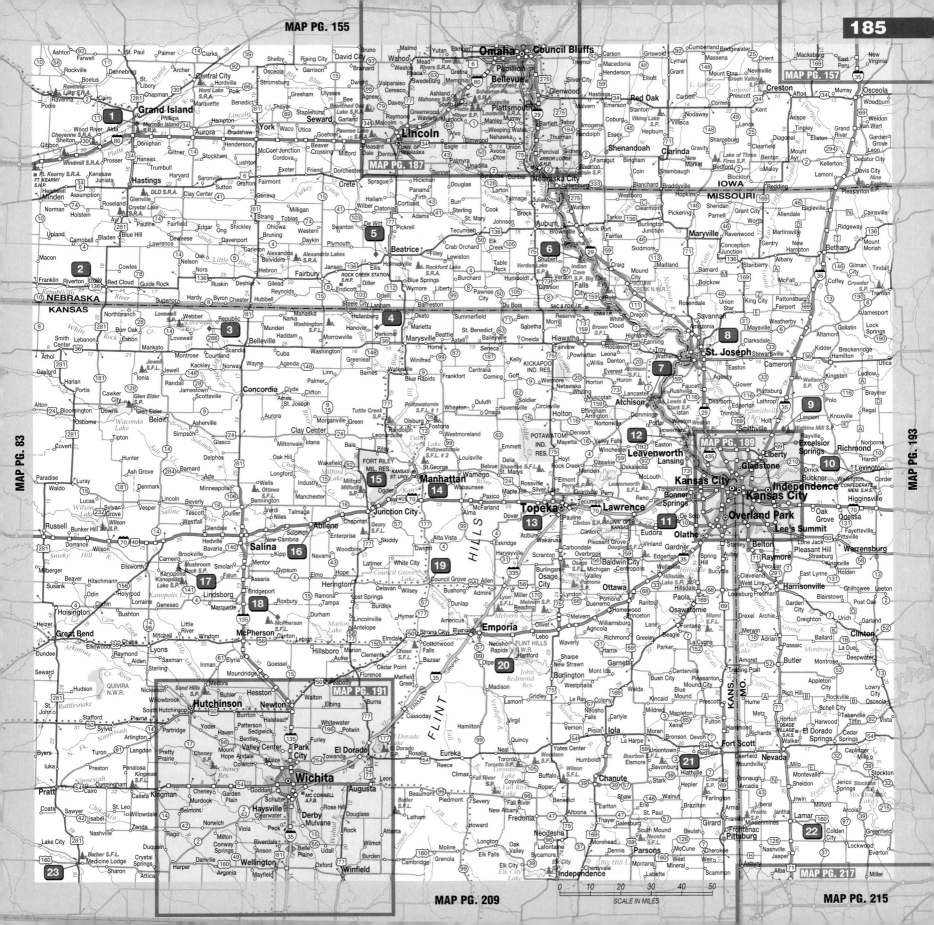

1. Lewis E. May Museum

1643 North Nye Ave., Fremont. This 25-room Classical Revival home displays carved oak and mahogany paneling, art glass windows, and unique tilework. As headquarters for the Dodge County Historical Society, it offers changing exhibits of photography, antiques, and decorative arts. *Admission charged.*

2. Harrison County Historical Museum

Rte. 30, Missouri Valley. Ten buildings, including an 1853 log house and an 1868 school, display such curiosities as a 1540 Spanish pike, 100-year-old light bulbs, an early X-ray machine, a New Testament written in Cherokee, and a 12-pound buffalo gun. *Admission charged.*

3. De Soto National Wildlife Refuge and Visitor Center

Visitors can take auto tours of the refuge, which surrounds De Soto Lake, to see thousands of ducks and geese in spring and fall. A visitor center houses wildlife exhibits, as well as merchandise and artifacts recovered from the steamboat *Bertrand,* which sank here in 1865. *Admission charged.*

4. Fort Atkinson State Historical Park

Off Rte. 75, Ft. Calhoun. The first military post west of the Missouri River was established in 1820 both to protect American fur trading interests and to forge Indian alliances. Restoration of the fort is in progress, with several rooms now open to the public. The visitor center exhibits artifacts excavated from the site. *Admission charged.*

5. The Winter Quarters and Mormon Pioneer Cemetery

3215 State St., North Omaha. From 1846 to 1848, approximately 3,500 Mormons camped here while Brigham Young searched for an appropriate western destination. More than 600 Mormons died from disease and are buried in a hillside cemetery overlooking the Missouri River, where a monument commemorates their ordeal.

6. Fort Omaha and the General Crook House Museum

30th and Fort Sts., Omaha. Crook, a Civil War general, commanded the Department of the Platte from his Italianate quarters, designed for entertaining presidents and other dignitaries at the fort. Now a museum, the house features period furnishings and a Victorian garden. *Admission charged.*

7. Great Plains Black Museum

2213 Lake St., Omaha. The history of African-American settlers in the Great Plains — including women, soldiers, and cowboys — is well documented in this museum. *Admission charged.*

8. Joslyn Art Museum

2200 Dodge St., Omaha. The striking Art Deco building, featuring pink marble walls with eight exterior bas-relief panels, has works by George Catlin, Frederic Remington, and other 19th- and 20th-century European and American artists. There is also a sculpture garden. *Admission charged.*

9. Union Pacific Museum

1416 Dodge St., Omaha. The history of the railroad and its role in western expansion is interpreted here through railway artifacts, train models, a traffic control board, and 19th-century paintings. Exhibits also include western outlaw memorabilia and firearms, and a cutaway model of President Lincoln's funeral car.

10. Boys Town

13628 Flanagan Blvd., Boys Town. In the **Hall of History,** visitors can follow the story of Boys Town, which was founded in 1917 by Father Edward J. Flanagan and later immortalized in motion pictures. The beloved priest's personal memorabilia is displayed in the **Father Flanagan Home.**

11. Gerald R. Ford Birth Site and Gardens

32nd St. and Woolworth Ave., Omaha. A model of the former president's home is set in a park, which features exhibits and a rose garden dedicated to Betty Ford.

12. Western Heritage Museum

801 South Tenth St., Omaha. Housed in a 1931 Art Deco railroad station, the museum traces Omaha's development from 1880 to 1954. Exhibits include a fully outfitted Conestoga wagon, a restored streetcar, Civil War records, and documents signed by presidents from Washington to Cleveland. *Admission charged.*

Indoor rainforest at the Henry Doorly Zoo

13. Henry Doorly Zoo

3701 South Tenth St., Omaha. Visitors can see more than 5,000 animals, many of them rare, in habitats that include the world's largest indoor rain forest, an aquarium, an aviary, a white tiger courtyard, and a penguin pool. Steam train rides are available in summer. *Admission charged.*

14. Fontenelle Forest Nature Center

1111 Bellevue Blvd. N., Bellevue. Seventeen miles of trails through 1,300 acres of forest, lake, prairie, and Missouri River marshes lead to a prehistoric Indian site. Visitors may also sight white-tailed deer, red foxes, and 200 species of birds. *Admission charged.*

15. Council Bluffs

Chamber of Commerce, 119 South Main St. The **Historic General Dodge House,** built in 1869 by Grenville Dodge, a Civil War general and chief construction engineer for the Union Pacific Railroad, radiates opulence with a Louis XVI Revival–style parlor, marble fireplaces, and a ballroom. Another Victorian antiquity, the **Historic Squirrel Cage Jail** has rotating cells and was called the Lazy Susan Jail. *Admission charged.*

16. Forney Lake Wildlife Management Area

During seasonal migrations, great blue herons, bald eagles, ducks, and more than 100,000 geese flock to this 800-acre shallow marsh in the Missouri flood plain.

17. Waubonsie State Park

Glacial sediment deposited by wind has created a spectacular landscape that supports yucca and other dry-land plants, colorful spring wildflowers, and brilliant fall foliage. Visitors can enjoy the beauty from hiking trails, campgrounds, and picnic areas.

18. Nebraska City

Chamber of Commerce, 806 First Ave. **Arbor Lodge State Historical Park** encompasses a 65-acre arboretum with more than 260 varieties of trees and shrubs. Also in the park is the residence of Arbor Day founder J. Sterling Morton, a 52-room Neocolonial mansion with original furnishings. Located nearby, **John Brown's Cave** was operated by the abolitionist as an Underground Railway station. *Admission charged.*

19. William Jennings Bryan House

4900 Sumner St., Lincoln. The brilliant orator — and unsuccessful presidential nominee — combined Queen Anne and Classic Revival elements in his brick and stone home, completed in 1903. Inside are some of the original furnishings and numerous family mementos.

20. Museum of Nebraska History

131 Centennial Mall N., Lincoln. Nebraska history from prehistoric times to the recent past is illustrated with exhibits on European immigration and the Homestead Act, bone tools, and American Indian costumes. Period settings include an 1800's Pawnee earth lodge, a Victorian parlor, a sod house interior, and a walk-through general store.

21. University of Nebraska

At the **State Museum,** campus visitors can view fossils of prehistoric animals who once roamed the Great Plains, and there's a fine 20th-century art collection at the **Sheldon Memorial Art Gallery.** Hundreds of paintings, drawings, and sculptures, including works by Charles M. Russell and Frederic Remington, are on exhibit in the **Great Plains Art Collection.**

22. Nebraska State Capital

1445 K St., Lincoln. This impressive 400-foot limestone building features exterior bas-relief sculptures, capped by a 32-foot bronze statue. Interior mosaic murals, tapestries, and inlaid woodworks depict Nebraska's Indian and pioneer heritage. The nearby **Lincoln Monument** was designed by Daniel Chester French, who created the statue at the Lincoln Memorial.

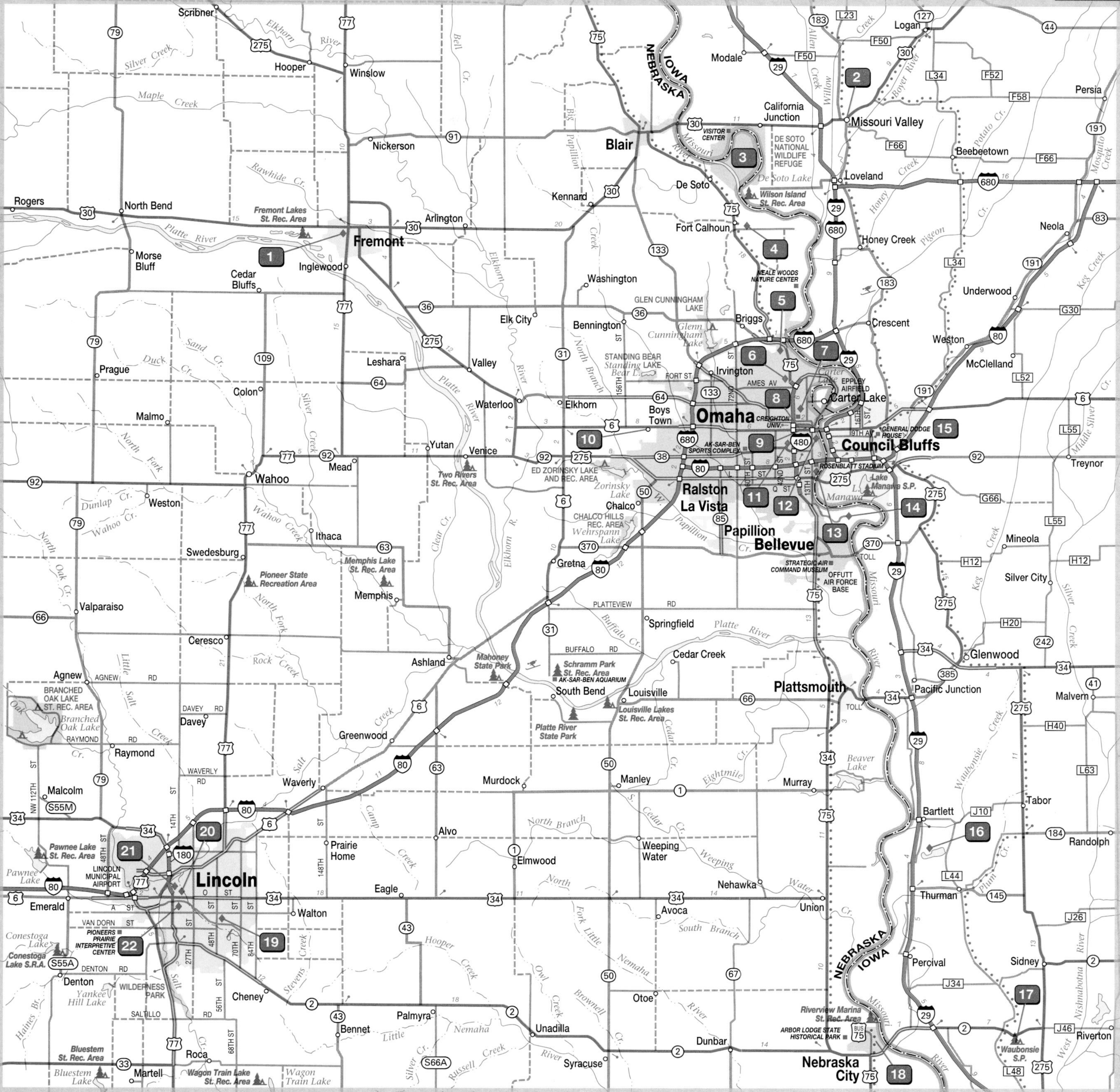

Scribner
Hooper
Winslow
Silver Creek
Maple Creek
Elkhorn River
Bell Cr.
Big Papillion Cr.
Nickerson
Blair
IOWA
NEBRASKA
Modale
California Junction
Missouri Valley
Logan
Persia
Beebeetown
Loveland
Honey Creek
Neola
Underwood
Weston
McClelland
Crescent
VISITOR CENTER
DE SOTO NATIONAL WILDLIFE REFUGE
De Soto Lake
De Soto
Wilson Island St. Rec. Area
Fort Calhoun
NEALE WOODS NATURE CENTER
Kennard
Rogers
North Bend
Fremont Lakes St. Rec. Area
Platte River
Fremont
Arlington
Inglewood
Morse Bluff
Cedar Bluffs
Rawhide Cr.
Washington
GLEN CUNNINGHAM LAKE
Glenn Cunningham Lake
Bennington
Elk City
Briggs
Irvington
STANDING BEAR LAKE
Standing Bear L.
FORT ST
AMES AV
EPPLEY AIRFIELD
Carter Lake
Omaha
CREIGHTON UNIV.
GENERAL DODGE HOUSE
Council Bluffs
9TH AV
ROSENBLATT STADIUM
Lake Manawa S.P.
Manawa
Treynor
Boys Town
Elkhorn
Valley
Leshara
Waterloo
Prague
Colon
Malmo
Sand Cr.
Duck Cr.
North Fork
Yutan
Venice
Mead
Two Rivers St. Rec. Area
AK-SAR-BEN SPORTS COMPLEX
ED ZORINSKY LAKE AND REC. AREA
Zorinsky Lake
Ralston
La Vista
Chalco
CHALCO HILLS REC. AREA
Wehrspann Lake
Papillion
Bellevue
STRATEGIC AIR COMMAND MUSEUM
OFFUTT AIR FORCE BASE
Wahoo
Weston
Dunlap Cr.
Wahoo Cr.
Wahoo Creek
Ithaca
Swedesburg
Memphis Lake St. Rec. Area
Memphis
Pioneer State Recreation Area
Gretna
Clear Cr.
Elkhorn R.
Mineola
Silver City
Glenwood
PLATTEVIEW RD
Springfield
Buffalo Cr.
BUFFALO RD
Valparaiso
Ceresco
Ashland
Mahoney State Park
Schramm Park St. Rec. Area
AK-SAR-BEN AQUARIUM
Cedar Creek
Plattsmouth
Pacific Junction
Malvern
Agnew
AGNEW RD
BRANCHED OAK LAKE ST. REC. AREA
Branched Oak Lake
RAYMOND RD
Raymond
DAVEY RD
Davey
Rock Creek
Little Salt Creek
South Bend
Louisville
Louisville Lakes St. Rec. Area
Platte River State Park
Greenwood
Waverly
WAVERLY RD
Malcolm
Murdock
Manley
Eightmile Cr.
Murray
Beaver Lake
Bartlett
Tabor
Randolph
Alvo
Prairie Home
Camp Creek
North Branch
Weeping Water
Elmwood
Pawnee Lake St. Rec. Area
Pawnee Lake
LINCOLN MUNICIPAL AIRPORT
Lincoln
Emerald
VAN DORN
PIONEERS PRAIRIE INTERPRETIVE CENTER
Walton
Eagle
Nehawka
Union
Avoca
Thurman
Conestoga Lake
Conestoga Lake S.R.A.
DENTON RD
Denton
WILDERNESS PARK
Yankee Hill Lake
Haines Br.
SALTILLO RD
Cheney
Hooper Creek
Stevens Creek
North Fork Little Nemaha
South Branch
Percival
Sidney
Palmyra
Bennet
Unadilla
Otoe
Owl Creek
Brownell Cr.
Nemaha River
Little Nemaha
Riverview Marina St. Rec. Area
ARBOR LODGE STATE HISTORICAL PARK
Nebraska City
Dunbar
Syracuse
Waubonsie S.P.
Riverton
West Nishnabotna River
Roca
Martell
Bluestem St. Rec. Area
Bluestem Lake
Wagon Train Lake St. Rec. Area
Wagon Train Lake
Russell Creek
Silver Cr.
SCALE IN MILES
0 2 4 6 8 10

1. Mahaffie Farmstead and Stagecoach Stop Historic Site

1100 Kansas City Rd., Olathe. Visitors can tour this beautiful two-story stone house with period furnishings. Built in 1865, it served as a stagecoach stop on the Santa Fe Trail. *Admission charged.*

2. Adam Legler Barn Museum

14907 West 87th St. Pkwy., Lenexa. Built in 1864, this splendid stone barn stood on the Santa Fe Trail and was visited by William C. Quantrill and Jesse James en route to raiding Lawrence in the 1860's. Historic artifacts are displayed in the barn; a restored railroad caboose and depot with late 1800's exhibits are on the grounds.

3. Old Shawnee Town

57th and Cody Sts., Shawnee. Guided tours take visitors through this artful re-creation of a typical turn-of-the-century American town. *Fee charged for tour.*

4. Grinter House

1420 South 78th St., Kansas City. This 1857 two-story brick home with Greek Revival elements sits atop a bluff overlooking the Kansas River. Period furnishings are seen on guided tours.

5. Community Nature Center Nature Trail

7250 State Ave., Kansas City. The state's largest bur oak tree — 110 feet high with a circumference of more than 17 feet — is just one of the many varieties of flora and fauna in this wildlife preserve located on the campus of **Kansas Community College.**

6. Historic Huron Indian Cemetery

Seventh and Ann Sts., Kansas City. This cemetery was established by Wyandot Indians in 1843. Although there were at least 400 burials here between 1844 and 1855, most are in unmarked graves, as there are only about 40 headstones.

7. Arabia Steamboat Museum

400 Grand Ave., Kansas City. The museum displays more than 200 tons of artifacts recovered from the sidewheeler *Arabia,* which sank in the Missouri River in 1856. A cargo of china, jewelry, and hardware is exhibited in a re-created general store. A full-scale deck replica features a 28-foot working paddle wheel, original engines, and boilers. *Admission charged.*

8. Kansas City Museum

3218 Gladstone Blvd., Kansas City. Native American artifacts, a natural history hall, and a planetarium are among the exhibits housed in the magnificent former estate of a lumber baron. *Admission charged.*

9. Liberty Memorial Museum

100 West 26th St., Kansas City. This unique museum , which specializes in the World War I period, exhibits a full-scale replica of a battle trench. Weapons, memorabilia, and uniforms are also on display, as well as one of the world's largest collections of war posters. The 217-foot-high World War I memorial tower yields a sweeping view of Kansas City. *Admission charged.*

10. Union Cemetery

227 East 28th St., Kansas City. The cemetery contains the graves of more than 1,000 Civil War soldiers. Artist George Caleb Bingham and Pony Express cofounder Alexander Majors are also buried here.

11. Thomas Hart Benton Home and Studio State Historic Site

3616 Belleview, Kansas City. Built in 1903, the home contains the personal effects of painter Thomas Hart Benton, known for his large murals and realistic works depicting regional history and rural life. The artist's tools and equipment are displayed in the carriage house studio. *Admission charged.*

12. Shawnee Indian Mission

3403 West 53rd St., Fairway. Founded in the 1830's as an Indian mission and school, Shawnee Mission became the region's most influential religious outpost. In 1855 the first territorial legislature met here to enact the Bogus Laws in an attempt to keep slavery in the territory. Today the superintendent's house, boys' school and chapel, and girls' school and dormitory comprise one of the state's oldest building complexes. Period furnishings, items made by students, and an 1845 United States map are displayed.

13. Nelson-Atkins Museum of Art

4525 Oak St., Kansas City. This museum is considered one of the nation's most comprehensive art showcases, and has achieved an international reputation for its Oriental collection. The Classical Revival building is decorated with sculptured panels depicting the settlement of the Midwest. Also on the grounds is the **Henry Moore Sculpture Garden,** which features the largest collection of the eminent sculptor's work outside of Great Britain. *Admission charged.*

14. John Wornall House Museum

146 West 61st Terrace, Kansas City. The restored home of one of the area's earliest settlers was used as a hospital during the Civil War, and is considered Kansas City's finest example of Greek Revival architecture. Originally part of a 500-acre farm, it contains period furnishings, examples of 1800's textiles, glass, silver, and ironware, and an herb garden. *Admission charged.*

15. Alexander Majors House

8201 State Line Rd., Kansas City. The home of Pony Express cofounder Majors was also headquarters for two freighting ventures. Built in 1856, the restored Greek Revival home is furnished with period pieces. Barn and smokehouse replicas sit on their original sites. A variety of 1800's vehicles, including a Conestoga wagon, are displayed. *Admission charged.*

16. Kansas City Zoo

6700 Zoo Dr., Kansas City. Many animals can be seen here in their native habitats. The 180-acre complex includes an African veld, a free-flight aviary, a sea lion pool, an ape house, and a waterfowl exhibit. A children's zoo and pony, camel, and train rides are also featured. *Admission charged.*

17. Harry S. Truman Farm Home

12301 Blue Ridge Blvd., Grandview. From 1906 to 1917, Truman operated his family's 600-acre farm and lived in this late–19th-century frame house. The home contains family belongings and period furnishings. *Donation encouraged.*

18. Missouri Town 1855

8010 East Park Rd., Lee's Summit. More than 30 buildings dating from 1820 to 1860 have been relocated to create a typical pre–Civil War southern farmstead. They include a Greek Revival house, slave quarters, barns, and an 1844 cruciform church. Furnishings are period items, and there are collections of farm equipment and land-grant documents. Costumed staff demonstrate 1800's crafts. *Admission charged.*

19. World Headquarters Complex of the Reorganized Church of Jesus Christ of Latter-day Saints

1001 West Walnut St., Independence. The 1860 church features an auditorium, where daily organ recitals are held in summer; a temple, with a 300-foot spiral roof; and a museum displaying church artifacts.

20. Marshal's Home, Jail, and Museum

217 North Main St., Independence. This restored Civil War–era compound was stormed by Quantrill's Raiders and once held Frank James as a prisoner. Today it contains 1870's furnishings and historical exhibits. *Admission charged.*

21. Harry S. Truman National Historic Site

223 North Main St., Independence. Truman's home from 1919 until his death in 1972 also served as the summer White House during his presidency. The house is an excellent example of late 1800's Victorian architecture and contains family heirlooms and original furnishings. Nearby is the **Harry S. Truman Library and Museum,** which features a reproduction of the Oval Office and contains a courtyard where the Trumans are buried. The **Harry S. Truman Courtroom and Office Museum,** in the Jackson County Courthouse, includes the restored courtroom where he began his political career. *Admission charged.*

22. Liberty

Chamber of Commerce, 9 South Leonard St. The **Jesse James Bank Museum,** the scene of the James gang's first robbery, contains an original 1858 safe, James memorabilia, and handwritten ledgers. **Clay County Historical Museum** is housed in an 1865 drugstore, with exhibits of patent medicines and 1800's furnishings. Joseph Smith, founder of the Mormon church, was incarcerated in the old stone jail reconstructed in the **Liberty Jail Visitor's Center,** which also contains Mormon artifacts. *Admission charged at bank museum.*

23. Fort Osage

Fort Osage Rd., Sibley. As the first outpost built after the Louisiana Purchase, the 1808 fort grew into a thriving enterprise. Five blockhouses, officers' quarters, barracks, and a fur-trading facility have been reconstructed and furnished with early 1800's items. Fort artifacts are exhibited at the visitor center. *Admission charged.*

Platte City
Kearney
Crystal Lakes
Excelsior Springs
Mosby
Prathersville
Ferrelview
Farley
KANSAS CITY INTERNATIONAL AIRPORT
Weatherby Lake
Lake Waukomis
Platte Woods
Houston Lake
Waldron
Parkville
Northmoor
Riverside
North Kansas City
Gladstone
Oakview
Oakwood Park
Oakwood
Oakwood Manor
Oaks
Pleasant Valley
Glenaire
Claycomo
Liberty
Missouri City
WORLDS OF FUN AND OCEANS OF FUN
Birmingham
Avondale
Randolph
Sugar Creek
Atherton
Sibley
Buckner
Kansas City
MISSOURI
KANSAS
Wyandotte County Park
Wyandotte County L.
Lake Quivira
Quivira Lake
Edwardsville
Kansas City
Kansas City Downtown Airport
Kemper Arena
Crown Center
KANSAS TPK
Shawnee
Merriam
Countryside
Roeland Park
Mission Park
Fairway
Westwood Hills
Westwood
Mission Hills
Univ. Mo. K.C.
Independence
NATL FRONTIER TRAILS CENTER
U.S. GOVT. LAKE CITY RESERVATION
Lake City
Blue Springs
Grain Valley
H.S. Truman Sports Complex
Starlight Theatre
Swope Park
Raytown
Prairie Village
NCAA VISITORS CENTER
Leawood
Overland Park
Lenexa
Olathe
Blue River Parkway
Grandview
Lee's Summit
Lake Lotawana
Lake Tapawingo
Lake Jacomo
Longview Lake
Unity Village
Jim Bridger Nature Tract
Lakewood Lakes
Little Blue Trace County Park
James A. Reed Wildlife Area
Lone Jack Wildlife Area
Blue and Grey County Reserve
Shawnee Mission Park
Shawnee Mission Lake
Cooley Lake State Wildlife Area
Mill Creek

SCALE IN MILES
0   2   4   6

1. Lake Afton Public Observatory

25000 39th St. S., Wichita. From the moon's strange landscape to Jupiter and distant galaxies, the observatory's 16-inch telescope brings the wonders of the night sky into focus for all to see. Exhibits explore the satellites and computers astronomers rely on, and star-gazers can make their own telescope and play astronomical computer games. *Admission charged.*

2. Cheney State Park

The 9,500-acre lake here is popular with fishing, windsurfing, and sailing enthusiasts, as well as spectators who come to watch the frequent regattas. A beautiful wooded nature trail winds through the surrounding park. *Admission charged.*

3. Reno County Museum

100 South Walnut St., Hutchinson. Pioneer exhibits trace the county's early history with artifacts such as clothing, furniture, and farm equipment. A hands-on gallery for children includes large-scale models of a tractor, train, post office, and grocery store.

4. Kansas Cosmosphere and Space Center

1100 North Plum St., Hutchinson. Out-of-this-world displays pay tribute to man's exploration of space. The **Hall of Space** features actual spacecraft, moon rocks, and the world's largest display of space suits. The center also includes an Omnimax theater and a planetarium with impressive special effects. *Admission charged.*

5. Dillon Nature Center

3002 30th Ave. E., Hutchinson. Home to hundreds of species of songbirds, waterfowl, and other native animals, the center offers tranquil nature trails through woods and prairies, and an arboretum with several hundred species of trees, shrubs, wildflowers, and native grasses.

6. Sand Hills State Park

Hiking trails in this aptly named park wind through 1,123 acres of dunes, prairies, wet-lands, and woodlands. Dune Trail, nearly a mile long, wanders up and down several sand hills to the top of one 40-foot swell. *Admission charged.*

7. Kansas Learning Center for Health

505 Main St., Halstead. Hands-on exhibits explore the wonders of the human body in this museum. A transparent talking model and other interactive displays show how the heart and five senses work, and how a baby is born. *Admission charged.*

8. Warkentin House

211 East First St., Newton. This Victorian mansion, complete with original furnishings, was built in 1886 by a Russian immigrant, who helped fellow Russian Mennonites to resettle in Kansas. The turkey red wheat they introduced here revolutionized the agricultural industry in the state, which is today a leading producer of wheat. A carriage house and gazebo are also on view. *Admission charged.*

9. Kauffman Museum

27th and Main Sts., North Newton. The natural history of the plains and the arrival of the Mennonites are explored through displays ranging from a living prairie reconstruction to Cheyenne Indian artifacts and Mennonite clothing, furnishings, and religious items. Also on the grounds are a log cabin, frame farmhouse, barn, and windmill. *Admission charged.*

The Old Cowtown Museum in Wichita

10. The Peabody Historical Museum

106 East Division St., Peabody. This former railroad town was named after the vice president of the Santa Fe Railway, as was the museum. The 1874 building once housed the first free public library in the state, and now contains a pioneer kitchen, old photographs, a miniature doll house, and other local antiquities.

11. El Dorado State Park and Wildlife Area

Horseback-riding and hiking trails wind through the gentle hills, wooded valleys, and open prairies of Kansas's largest state park. The 8,000-acre **El Dorado Lake** is a perfect spot for boating, swimming, and fishing. Camping and picnicking sites are available. *Admission charged.*

12. Kansas Oil Museum

383 East Central Ave., El Dorado. The colorful oil history of the area is seen at the museum, which includes a re-created oilfield with authentic equipment. Also on the grounds is another museum run by the Butler County Historical Society, which captures the region's ranching and agricultural past, from the days of the Wichita Indians to the frenzy of the state's largest oil boom.

13. Wichita-Sedgwick County Historical Museum

204 South Main St., Wichita. Housed in a massive 1892 Romanesque building that used to be the city hall, this museum recalls Wichita life in Victorian times. Local history is explored through Indian artifacts, a costume collection, and period rooms including a 1910 drug store and a turn-of-the-century cottage. *Admission charged.*

14. Wichita Art Museum

619 Stackman Dr., Wichita. Works by renowned artists such as Winslow Homer, Mary Cassatt, and Edward Hopper grace this museum focusing on American art from the 1700's to the present. Of special interest are the Charles M. Russell western art collection and the outdoor sculptures.

15. Sedgwick County Zoo and Botanical Garden

5555 Zoo Blvd., Wichita. Rhinos, Bengal tigers, and rare baby chimps roam within natural barriers in this first-rate zoo, dedicated to presenting animals in realistic environments. Nature lovers can hear the call of the wild in the walk-through jungle, pampas, and outback exhibits. A reptile house features an alligator swamp and a barrier-free exhibit of boas. *Admission charged.*

16. Botanica, The Wichita Gardens

701 North Amidon St., Wichita. Flowers are the focus in these fragrant display gardens. Annuals show their colors while other blooms form rings around a flowing fountain. Also featured are a rockery with cascading pools, a woodland nature walk, and a horticultural library. *Admission charged.*

17. Old Cowtown Museum

1871 Sim Park Dr., Wichita. This re-created town recalls the early days of Wichita, when cattle were brought from Texas for shipment east. More than 30 restored 19th-century buildings include the first residence in Wichita, a one-room schoolhouse, and a blacksmith shop. *Admission charged.*

18. Indian Center Museum of the Mid-America All-Indian Center

650 North Seneca, Wichita. Here visitors find a special focus on the historic and contemporary artwork of the Plains Indians, including the impressive 44-foot Keeper of the Plains sculpture. *Admission charged.*

19. Mulvane Historical Museum

300 West Main St., Mulvane. Exhibits on the history of this rail town are housed in a 1910 brick depot, including hundreds of photographs and instruments belonging to the town's first doctor. On the grounds is a reconstruction of the 1885 city jail, built with the original stones and wooden doors carved with prisoners' initials.

20. Bartlett Arboretum

301 North Line, Belle Plaine. Serene walkways meander through 20 acres of flowers, ornamental trees, and shrubs from all over the world in this lovely garden complete with a picturesque lagoon. Each spring, thousands of tulips burst into bloom; come fall, the chrysanthemums steal the show. *Admission charged.*

21. Cherokee Strip Land Rush Museum

South Summit St. Rd., Arkansas City. Here the Cherokee Strip Land Rush of 1893 — the largest land rush in history — is documented with artifacts and memorabilia, including an original Run Claim Flag given to run registrants. At the nearby **Chaplin Nature Center,** walking trails wind through 200 acres of woodlands, prairies, and wetlands. *Admission charged at museum.*

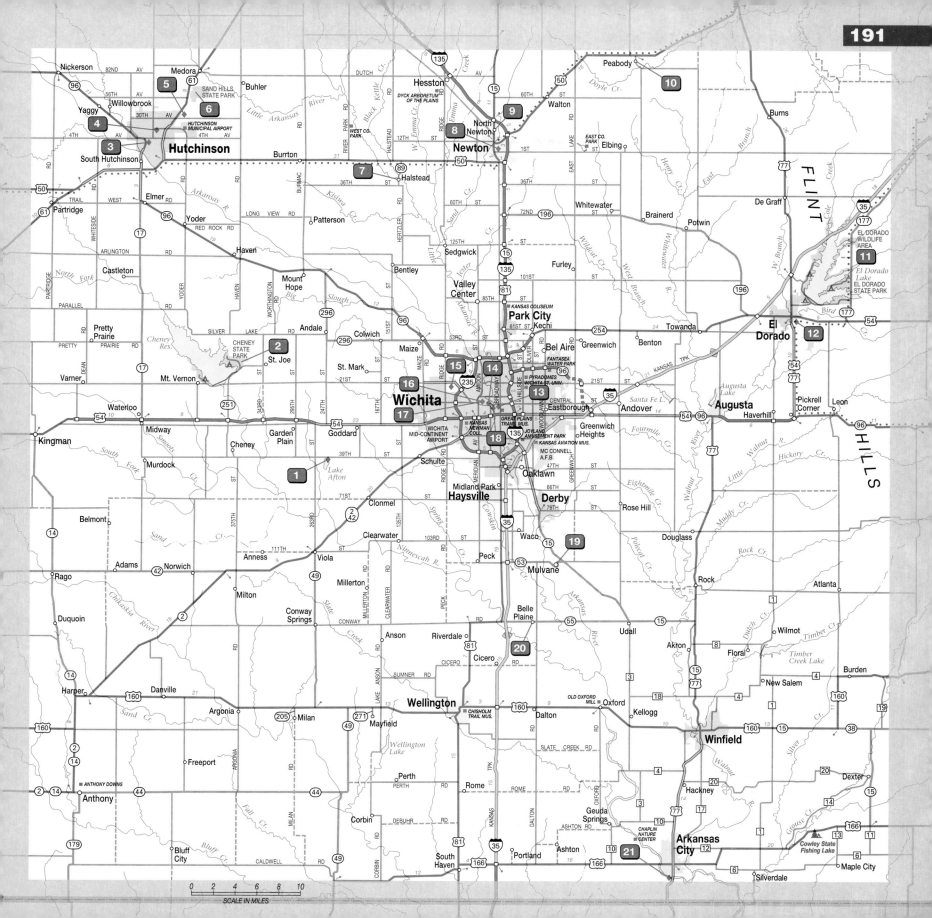

1. Wayne County Historical Museum

Rte. 2, Corydon. Filled with some 80,000 items, the museum has a replica of a typical main street in 19th-century Wayne County. Included are a general store, courtroom, dentist's office, jail, and a bank that Jesse James robbed. *Admission charged.*

2. Historic Bentonsport

Dating from 1839, this town on the Des Moines River was named for Senator Thomas Hart Benton, a strong advocate of pioneers. When a dam and locks were constructed, the little river town flourished, only to be bypassed by the railroads in 1870. Today visitors come to see the unspoiled hamlet and visit the various buildings that survive from that bygone era.

3. Nauvoo Restoration

Young and North Main Sts., Nauvoo. In 1839, when Joseph Smith, founder of the Mormon church, and his followers were driven from Missouri, they settled in a bend on the Mississippi River. They named their new home *Nauvoo,* meaning "beautiful place." After Smith was murdered, they went on to Utah, led by Brigham Young. Many of the buildings from their abandoned city are still open. The visitor center offers pamphlets and a film about the town.

4. Galesburg

Visitors Bureau, 154 East Simmons St. The historic district of this city contains the **Carl Sandburg State Historic Site,** a complex that includes the restored cottage where the poet was born and a visitor center. Also in the historic district is **Old Main,** an 1857 brick structure that was the scene of the fifth Lincoln-Douglas debate.

5. Dickson Mounds Museum

Off Rtes. 97 and 78, near Lewiston. This on-site archeological museum reveals the culture of the prehistoric Indians whose villages flourished here on the Illinois River. Displays at the museum include pottery, weapons, tools, and ornaments.

6. Quincy

Chamber of Commerce, 314 Maine St. The 1835 **Governor John Wood Mansion,** home of Qunicy's first settler, is a splendid example of Greek Revival architecture and has been restored to its 19th-century appearance. The visitor center next door houses the **Historical Society of Quincy and Adams County.** In the main square, **Washington Park** was the setting of the sixth Lincoln-Douglas debate. *Admission charged at mansion.*

7. Mark Twain Boyhood Home and Museum

208 Hill St., Hannibal. The white clapboard boyhood home of Mark Twain is now restored and serves as the centerpiece of a complex dedicated to the beloved author. An adjacent museum displays photographs, manuscripts, and the robes worn by Twain when he was given an honorary degree at Oxford University. *Admission charged.*

8. Mark Twain Birthplace and Museum State Historic Site

Off Rte. 107, Florida. The simple two-room cabin where Mark Twain was born in 1835 is now located in the museum, whose collection includes memorabilia harking back to the author's life as a steamboat pilot. A picnic area is provided for visitors, and swimming is permitted in nearby Mark Twain Lake. *Admission charged.*

9. Arrow Rock State Historic Site

Dating from 1829, the town of Arrow Rock was once a flourishing port, but it became a drowsy village when the railroads passed it by. Today several of the restored buildings, including the 1837 brick home of frontier painter George Caleb Bingham, may be toured. A visitor center displays interpretive exhibits spanning prehistoric times to the present. *Fee charged for tours.*

10. Harry S. Truman Dam and Reservoir

The visitor center at Kaysinger Bluff, which overlooks the dam, contains artifacts depicting some 30,000 years of Ozark history. The reservoir and the beautifully wooded **Harry S. Truman State Park** offer vacationers fine facilities for water sports and camping.

11. Lake of the Ozarks State Park

The park affords miles of trails, camping facilities, and all kinds of water sports, as well as the brilliantly colored **Ozark Caverns,** which can be toured. At nearby **Ha Ha**

Tonka State Park, the ruins of a once-magnificent 60-room castle can be visited. *Fee charged for cavern tours.*

12. Winston Churchill Memorial and Library

Seventh St. and Westminster Ave., Fulton. As a memorial to Sir Winston Churchill, who gave his historic Iron Curtain address here at **Westminster College** in 1946, a 17th-century London church destroyed by bombs in 1940 has been faithfully reconstructed on the campus. The library and museum depict the life of the wartime British prime minister. *Admission charged.*

13. Historic Daniel Boone Home

1868 Hwy. F, Defiance. After many years in Tennessee, the famous pioneer settled in St. Louis at the encouragement of the Spanish government. Here he and his son Nathan built a handsome home, in which Daniel lived during his last years. The restored house, with many of Boone's belongings, is now open to visitors. *Admission charged.*

14. Dillard Mill State Historic Site

Off Rte. 49, Dillard. This storybook barn-red mill on Huzzah Creek, constructed between 1904 and 1908, continued to grind grain for local farmers until the 1950's. Visitors can tour the site, as well as enjoy the picnic areas and hiking trails in the surrounding woodlands. *Admission charged.*

15. Ste. Genevieve

Settled in the 1730's by French Canadians, the little river town has retained its unique flavor and preserved many of its unusual structures. The **Bolduc House,** considered to be the most authentically restored French Colonial house in America, and several other buildings are open to visitors. *Admission charged.*

16. Fort de Chartres State Historic Site

Rte. 155, Prairie du Rocher. The 1753 fort, a reminder of the French occupation of the American heartland, was surrendered to the British in 1765. Severely damaged by the flood waters of the Mississippi, it has been partially restored and its guardhouse and chapel reconstructed. Local artifacts are displayed at the **Peithmann Museum.**

17. Cape Girardeau

Convention and Visitors Bureau, 601 North Kings Hwy. Near the cape is the site of the **Trail of Tears State Park,** a popular recre-

ation area named for the forced migration of the Cherokees from the Southeast to western reservations. Also popular is the **Capaha Rose Display Garden,** with some 75 varieties of roses. The **Glenn House,** built in 1883, features local 19th-century memorabilia. *Admission charged.*

18. Crab Orchard National Wildlife Refuge

This 43,000-acre refuge is a favorite stopping place for migrating waterfowl, and a wintering habitat for the Canada goose. Here too are the nesting grounds for bald eagles and many kinds of songbirds. An observation tower offers excellent views of a feeding area, and in the surrounding lakes and woodlands visitors can enjoy water sports and camping. *Admission charged.*

19. Mount Vernon

Chamber of Commerce, 200 Potomac Blvd. The **Mitchell Museum,** a colonnaded building set on the estate of the late John R. and Eleanor Mitchell, displays their extensive collection of art. In nearby McLeansboro, the ornate 1884 home of a banker is now occupied by the **McCoy Memorial Library** and the **Hamilton County Historical Society Museum.** The mansion contains many original furnishings, which reflect the lavish style of the era. *Donation encouraged at historical society museum.*

20. William Jennings Bryan Museum

408 South Broadway, Salem. The 1852 Greek Revival residence, birthplace of the famous orator and three-time presidential nominee, contains a collection of memorabilia and a recording of the well-known Cross of Gold speech.

21. Ingram's Pioneer Log Cabin Village

Off Rte. 37, Kinmundy. Built between 1818 and 1860, the village includes authentically furnished homes, shops, a general store, and an inn where stagecoach travelers paid 6 cents a night for a bed likely to be shared with a stranger. *Admission charged.*

22. Vandalia Statehouse State Historic Site

315 West Gallatin St., Vandalia. The statehouse was put up hurriedly in 1836, in an unsuccessful attempt to halt plans to move the state capital to Springfield. Both Lincoln and Douglas served in the legislature here. Today the brick Greek Revival structure has been restored and is open to visitors.

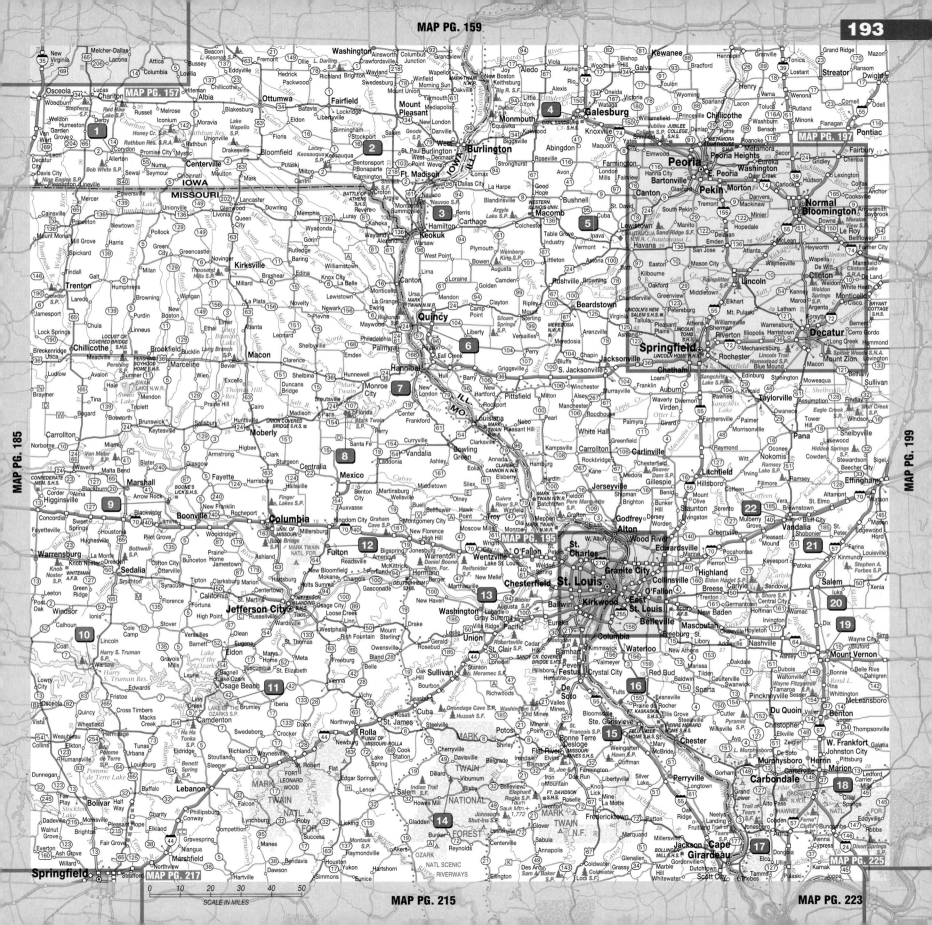

MAP PG. 157

MAP PG. 197

MAP PG. 185

MAP PG. 199

MAP PG. 195

MAP PG. 217

MAP PG. 225

1. Jefferson Barracks County Park

10000 South Broadway, St. Louis. Built in 1826 to protect frontier settlers, this vital fort served successively as an infantry school, supply depot, arsenal, and army hospital over the next 120 years. Today the restored civilian laborers' house, ordnance buildings, and the old stable exhibit photos and dioramas that depict the history of this post manned by soldiers such as Grant, Lee, Sherman, and Zachary Taylor.

2. Grant's Farm

10501 Gravois Rd., St. Louis. Once owned by Ulysses S. Grant, the country's 18th president, this 281-acre farm maintains an 1856 log cabin, a trophy room, a Clydesdale horse barn, and horse-drawn carriages and sleighs. Buffalo, deer, zebra, and elk roam in a game preserve. Visitors can feed small animals, see bird and animal shows, and tour the grounds by a miniature trackless train; reservations are required.

3. Museum of Transportation

3015 Barrett Station Rd., St. Louis. Two centuries of transportation, from horse-drawn wagons to airplanes, are represented in this comprehensive collection. There are antique buses and trucks, mule-drawn streetcars, vintage automobiles, railroad cars, and the largest collection of locomotives in the world. *Admission charged.*

4. Florissant

Chamber of Commerce, 1060 Rue Ste. Catherine. Area history is preserved in the buildings of this city. **Taille de Noyer** originated in 1790 as a three-room trading post; by 1820, it had expanded to become a 22-room antebellum mansion. **John B. Myers House and Barn,** built in 1870, is a fine old Victorian structure that now houses antique and crafts shops, and **Old St. Ferdinand's Shrine** dates from the early 1800's.

5. Cathedral of St. Louis

Lindell Blvd. and Newstead Ave., St. Louis. Started in 1907, this superb example of Romanesque and Byzantine architecture is lav-ishly decorated with marble, art treasures, and a large collection of mosaic art that illustrates 19th-century church history in Missouri. Guided tours are by appointment.

6. Forest Park

The site of the Louisiana Purchase Exposition in 1904, this 1,200-acre park today encompasses several museums and a zoo. Visitors step into the future at the **St. Louis Science Center,** with a multi-image dome theater, exhibits on alien research and "virtual reality," and a close-up look at biotechnology. The **Missouri Historical Society** focuses on the city's early days, with exhibits on Lewis and Clark, 19th-century firefighting equipment, a display on the 1904 World's Fair, and memorabilia from Charles Lindbergh. The **Saint Louis Art Museum** ranks among the nation's top 10 art museums, with collections ranging from the ancient to the contemporary; the pre-Columbian and German Expressionist collections are among the best in the world. The **St. Louis Zoological Park** features more than 3,400 animals in simulated natural habitats, from Big Cat Country, with its lions and tigers, to the Cheetah Survival Center, where cubs are bred, to the walk-through Bird House.

7. Missouri Botanical Garden

4344 Shaw Blvd., St. Louis. Some 79 acres, combining woodland and flower gardens, greenhouses and historic buildings, make this a uniquely beautiful botanic garden. Visitors can tour botanist Henry Shaw's 1849 country estate furnished in period style, follow the fragrances at the scented garden for the blind, see tropical plants in the world's first geodesic dome greenhouse, and visit houses of succulents and camellias. The traditional Japanese garden is graced by waterfalls, footbridges, and a teahouse. *Admission charged.*

8. Anheuser-Busch Brewery

12th and Lynch Sts., St. Louis. A tour of this famous brewery shows state-of-the-art brewing equipment housed in a national historic landmark building dating from 1891. Visitors can see the Clydesdale horses, watch the brewing process, and sample each beer that Anheuser-Busch makes.

9. Cahokia

Chamber of Commerce, 901 Falling Springs Rd. Founded in 1699 by French missionaries, Cahokia is the oldest town in Illinois. The 1799 **Church of the Holy Family,** now restored, was built in the typical French vertical-log style. A cemetery with graves dating from that period sits in its shadow. The **Cahokia Courthouse,** built around 1737 and thought to be the oldest house in the state, later served as a territorial courthouse and jail. Inside, a museum depicts the lifestyle of the early missionaries.

10. St. Louis Cardinals Hall of Fame Museum

100 Stadium Plaza, St. Louis. This museum brings St. Louis sports history to life. There are films of the St. Louis Cardinals dating from 1926, Stan Musial trophies, and tours of Busch Stadium. Across the street, the **National Bowling Hall of Fame and Museum** boasts the only 1936 vintage bowling pin car and other exhibits that trace the history of the sport. Visitors can bowl a few frames in an old-time alley with hand-set pins. *Admission charged.*

11. Jefferson National Expansion Memorial

11 North Fourth St., St. Louis. The spectacular **Gateway Arch** soars 630 feet above St. Louis, a dynamic symbol of the city's role as Gateway to the West. Designed by Eero Saarinen, the stainless-steel arch was built without an inner frame or skeleton. Capsule rides to the observation deck at its top provide stunning views of the Mississippi River and the city. The **Museum of Westward Expansion,** at its base, has exhibits on the construction of the arch, striking landscape murals, and artifacts from the pioneers who passed through the area. Guided tours of the **Old Courthouse** reveal living-history galleries and restored courtrooms that detail the city's frontier days. The nearby **Old Cathedral** (Basilica of St. Louis the King), on the site of the first church built in St. Louis in 1770, contains the original church bell and the tomb of the city's first bishop. *Admission charged for some attractions.*

12. St. Louis Union Station

1820 Market St., St. Louis. When it opened in 1894, this fortresslike train station was the largest in the world. Today it has been reincarnated as a festive marketplace, with railroad memorabilia, a 1-acre lake, luxury hotel, and dozens of restaurants and shops in a relaxed, inviting atmosphere.

13. Eads Bridge

East end of Washington St., St. Louis. An engineering marvel when it opened in 1874, Eads Bridge was the first bridge to use can-tilevered arches, the first to make extensive use of steel, and the first to span 1,500 feet. A few blocks to the south, a World War II minesweeper, the **U.S.S. Inaugural #242,** awarded two battle stars for heroic service, now houses a naval museum. Restored compartments and equipment give visitors an accurate picture of wartime life on the ship. Riverboat cruises on the Mississippi depart from the next dock south. A few blocks north, **Laclede's Landing** was the first settlement in St. Louis and today is a popular 9-square-block shopping area teeming with boutiques, restaurants, and nightclubs in restored 19th-century buildings. *Admission charged for some attractions.*

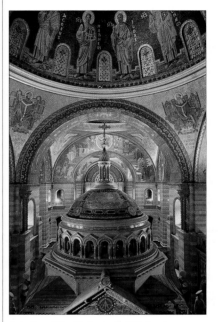

Interior of the Cathedral of St. Louis

14. Cahokia Mounds State Historic Site

30 Ramey St., East St. Louis. The largest prehistoric Indian city north of central Mexico, Cahokia was once a thriving trading and farming community with a population numbering tens of thousands. Sixty of the city's original mounds, some of which were used for ceremonial purposes, have been preserved. Monks Mound — the largest Indian mound in the New World — rises to 100 feet and covers 14 acres. Visitors can also see a reconstructed circular sun calendar. An interpretive center features artifacts and exhibits that provide further insight on this ancient culture, which had vanished mysteriously by 1500.

1. Chautauqua National Wildlife Refuge

Great flocks of waterfowl and other migrating birds stop at this 4,500-acre refuge for rest and refreshment on their annual journeys. Fishing and boating are permitted on **Lake Chautauqua.** Campgrounds are available at nearby **Sand Ridge State Forest** and also at the **Spring Lake Conservation Area,** a habitat for deer, mink, foxes, muskrats, and beavers.

2. Wildlife Prairie Park

3826 North Taylor Rd., Peoria. More than 2,000 acres shelter animals once native to Illinois in their natural surroundings, including cougars, bears, bobcats, and wolves. Also featured is a pioneer homestead and working farm from the late 1800's, hiking trails, and a small-scale railroad that circles the park. *Admission charged.*

3. Peoria

Convention and Visitors Bureau, 403 NE Jefferson St. The **Lakeview Museum of Arts and Sciences** features changing exhibits, areas for children, and a planetarium. Outdoor activities are popular at **Glen Oak Park,** which has a fishing lagoon and a zoo, whose inhabitants range from lions to reptiles and birds. Also in the park is the **George L. Luthy Memorial Botanical Garden,** with herb and rose gardens and a tropical rain forest conservatory. The 1837 **John C. Flanagan Residence** and the 1868 **Pettengill-Morron House,** restored and furnished with Victorian pieces, attract many visitors, as does the **West Bluff Historic District.** This residential neighborhood includes a Frank Lloyd Wright house, which he designed for the Francis W. Little family in his famous Prairie style. *Admission charged for some attractions.*

4. Metamora Courthouse State Historic District

113 East Partridge St., Metamora. This handsome 1845 brick Greek Revival building, one of two remaining of the Eighth Judicial Circuit courthouses used by Abra-

ham Lincoln, contains a small museum of pioneer articles on the ground floor. The second-floor courtroom has been authentically restored. Guided tours are available.

5. Illinois State University

Visitors to the Normal, Illinois, campus can see the university's unusual collection of family photographs and memorabilia in the **Adlai E. Stevenson Memorial Room** as well as changing contemporary art exhibits at the **University Galleries.**

6. Bloomington

Convention and Visitors Bureau, 210 South East St. Highlights of the **Miller Park Zoo** include its Sumatran tigers and tropical rain forest, where free-flying birds mingle with the colorful plants. The zoo also has natural settings for seals, big cats, and other wild creatures. Swimming, boating, and fishing are permitted in **Miller Park.** The **David Davis Mansion,** known as Clover Lawn, was built for the U. S. Supreme Court justice in 1872. Now restored, the elegant 20-room Victorian home contains many of its original furnishings. At **Illinois Wesleyan University,** visitors can tour the **Evelyn Chapel,** whose Moravian-style exterior, highly skilled interior woodwork, and excellent acoustics have received architectural and interior design awards. Also on campus, the **Sheean Library** contains the Indian pottery collection of Maj. John Wesley Powell, an early explorer of the Colorado River and the Grand Canyon. *Admission charged at zoo.*

7. DeWitt County Museum

219 East Woodlawn, Clinton. The headquarters of this museum, the **Homestead,** is a handsome 1867 Victorian mansion where Clinton H. Moore, law partner of Abraham Lincoln, once lived. Exhibits include a carriage collection, a farm and railroad museum, outstanding period furnishings, and an antique doll collection. *Admission charged.*

8. Weldon Springs State Park

The area features a spring-fed lake, where fishing and boating are popular activities, and nearby campsites. Visitors can obtain a map and guide that describe the varied plant and animal life to be found along the 2-mile nature trail.

9. Decatur

Convention and Visitors Bureau, 202 East North St. The **Macon County Museum**

Complex depicts the history of this area, with replicas of buildings that feature Macon County's first courthouse, where Lincoln practiced law, and a collection of artifacts dating from 1829 to the early 20th century. The **James Millikin Homestead** is the elegant 1876 mansion of the founder of Millikin University, and is adjacent to **Millikin Place,** a group of houses started in 1909 that includes one home designed by Frank Lloyd Wright.

10. Lincoln

Tourism Bureau, 303 South Kickapoo. This historic town, which was christened with watermelon juice by Abraham Lincoln in 1833, is the seat of Logan County. Chief among its attractions is the re-created **Postville Courthouse,** where Lincoln practiced law. He also served at the **Mount Pulaski Courthouse,** a handsomely restored Greek Revival building, which was one of the Eighth Circuit courthouses. At **Lincoln College,** established in 1865, the **Museum of Presidents** contains a large collection of Lincoln memorabilia.

11. Lincoln Memorial Garden and Nature Center

2301 East Lake Dr., Springfield. Located on the south side of Lake Springfield, this beautiful garden was created in the 1930's by landscape architect Jens Jensen, who used only trees, shrubs, and flowering plants native to the states where Lincoln lived. Five miles of trails wind through the grounds. The nature center contains educational and hands-on exhibits.

12. Springfield

Convention and Visitors Bureau, 109 North Seventh St. Memorable sites in this city include the **Lincoln Depot,** where the president-to-be gave his farewell address as he left for Washington; the **Old State Capitol State Historic Site,** where Lincoln debated Stephen A. Douglas on the issue of slavery; and the handsome clapboard **Lincoln Home National Historic Site.** At **Oak Ridge Cemetery,** Lincoln's gravesite is marked by the **Lincoln Tomb State Historic Site.** The marble memorial contains a series of statues commemorating various periods in Lincoln's life. Mary Todd Lincoln and three of their sons are also buried here. The **Executive Mansion,** home of Illinois governors since 1855, and the nearby **Vachel Lindsay Home** are both restored, as is the **Dana-Thomas House,** designed by Frank Lloyd Wright in his Prairie style.

The **Illinois State Museum** depicts the history of the state and showcases the works of 19th- and 20th-century Illinois artists.

13. Lincoln's New Salem State Historic Site

Off Rte. 97, Petersburg. The site of the village where Lincoln lived for six years has been authentically re-created, with replicas of its original gristmill and sawmill, several shops, a blacksmith's shop, a tavern, and a number of log houses. Costumed guides relate the history of the village.

14. Petersburg

Chamber of Commerce, 125 South Seventh St. Dating from 1836, when it was surveyed by Abraham Lincoln, this historic town is the Menard County seat. The **Menard County Courthouse,** a handsome 1897 granite and sandstone structure, displays on its second floor a reproduced collection of Lincoln documents relating to his law practice. The Victorian **Edgar Lee Masters Home,** where the poet spent his boyhood, has now been restored and contains family photographs and other artifacts. The **Menard County Museum,** another striking example of Victorian architecture, is located nearby. Masters's gravesite can be found in the **Oakland Cemetery,** along with that of Ann Rutledge, who was said to be Lincoln's first love.

Statue at Lincoln's New Salem Historic Site

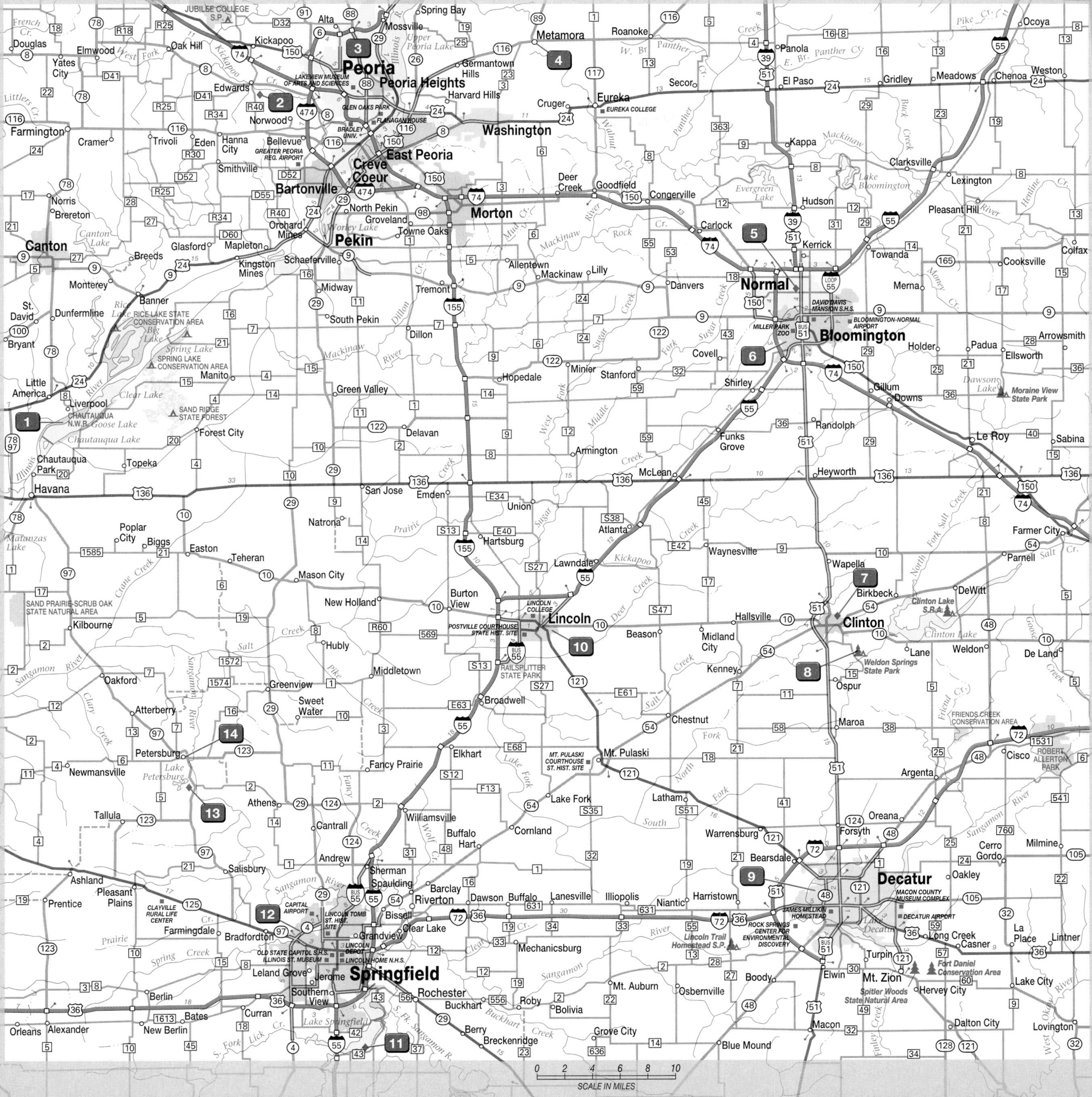
Peoria
Peoria Heights
East Peoria
Creve Coeur
Bartonville
Pekin
Morton
Washington
Canton
Normal
Bloomington
Lincoln
Clinton
Decatur
Springfield
Havana
Jubilee College S.P.
Kickapoo
Oak Hill
Elmwood
Yates City
Douglas
Farmington
Cramer
Trivoli
Eden
Hanna City
Edwards
Norwood
Bellevue
Greater Peoria Reg. Airport
Smithville
Lakeview Museum of Arts and Sciences
Glen Oaks Park
Flanagan House
Bradley Univ.
Alta
Mossville
Spring Bay
Upper Peoria Lake
Germantown Hills
Harvard Hills
Metamora
Roanoke
Eureka
Eureka College
Cruger
Secor
Panola
El Paso
Gridley
Meadows
Chenoa
Weston
Ocoya
Kappa
Hudson
Carlock
Kerrick
Towanda
Lake Bloomington
Evergreen Lake
Clarksville
Lexington
Pleasant Hill
Cooksville
Colfax
Merna
Congerville
Goodfield
Deer Creek
North Pekin
Groveland
Towne Oaks
Orchard Mines
Norris
Brereton
Canton Lake
Glasford
Mapleton
Breeds
Kingston Mines
Schaeferville
Monterey
Banner
St. David
Dunfermline
Bryant
Rice Lake State Conservation Area
Spring Lake Conservation Area
Manito
Little America
Liverpool
Chautauqua N.W.R.
Goose Lake
Chautauqua Lake
Sand Ridge State Forest
Forest City
Chautauqua Park
Topeka
Midway
South Pekin
Tremont
Allentown
Mackinaw
Lilly
Danvers
Dillon
Hopedale
Minier
Stanford
Covell
Shirley
David Davis Mansion S.H.S.
Miller Park Zoo
Bloomington-Normal Airport
Holder
Padua
Arrowsmith
Ellsworth
Gillum
Downs
Moraine View State Park
Dawson Lake
Green Valley
Delavan
Armington
Funks Grove
Randolph
Le Roy
Sabina
Heyworth
McLean
San Jose
Emden
Union
Atlanta
Natrona
Hartsburg
Lawndale
Waynesville
Wapella
Farmer City
Parnell
DeWitt
Birkbeck
Clinton Lake S.R.A.
Weldon
De Land
Lane
Weldon Springs State Park
Ospur
Poplar City
Biggs
Easton
Teheran
Mason City
Matanzas Lake
Sand Prairie-Scrub Oak State Natural Area
Kilbourne
New Holland
Burton View
Lincoln College
Postville Courthouse State Hist. Site
Railsplitter State Park
Beason
Hallsville
Midland City
Kenney
Hubly
Middletown
Oakford
Greenview
Sweet Water
Atterberry
Broadwell
Chestnut
Maroa
Friends Creek Conservation Area
Cisco
Robert Allerton Park
Argenta
Petersburg
Newmansville
Lake Petersburg
Tallula
Athens
Fancy Prairie
Elkhart
Mt. Pulaski Courthouse St. Hist. Site
Mt. Pulaski
Lake Fork
Latham
Cantrall
Williamsville
Buffalo Hart
Cornland
Warrensburg
Oreana
Forsyth
Cerro Gordo
Milmine
Oakley
Bearsdale
Andrew
Salisbury
Ashland
Prentice
Pleasant Plains
Clayville Rural Life Center
Farmingdale
Bradfordton
Capital Airport
Lincoln Tomb St. Hist. Site
Sherman
Spaulding
Barclay
Riverton
Bissell
Dawson
Buffalo
Lanesville
Illiopolis
Niantic
Harristown
James Millikin Homestead
Rock Springs Center for Environmental Discovery
Macon County Museum Complex
Decatur Airport
Lincoln Trail Homestead S.P.
Long Creek
Casner
La Place
Lintner
Clear Lake
Grandview
Lincoln Depot
Old State Capitol S.H.S.
Illinois St. Museum
Lincoln Home N.H.S.
Leland Grove
Jerome
Southern View
Mechanicsburg
Mt. Auburn
Osbernville
Boody
Turpin
Fort Daniel Conservation Area
Mt. Zion
Elwin
Spitler Woods State Natural Area
Hervey City
Lake City
Berlin
Bates
Curran
New Berlin
Orleans
Alexander
Lake Springfield
Rochester
Buckhart
Roby
Bolivia
Berry
Breckenridge
Grove City
Blue Mound
Macon
Dalton City
Lovington
Sangamon River
Illinois River
Mackinaw River
Salt Creek
Kickapoo Creek
SCALE IN MILES
0
2
4
6
8
10

1. Lincoln Log Cabin State Historic Site

South Fourth St. Rd., south of Charleston. The faithfully reconstructed two-room cabin where Abraham Lincoln's father and stepmother lived during the 1840's is maintained today as a working farm, with a staff performing farm chores in period dress.

2. Rockome Gardens

Off Rte. 133W, near Arcola. Arches, fences, and other fanciful rock formations are the highlights here, along with beautiful flower gardens. A re-created frontier town with a blacksmith shop, general store, bakery, and crafts shop adds an old-time atmosphere. *Admission charged.*

3. Champaign/Urbana

Convention and Visitors Bureau, 40 East University Ave., Champaign. Sites of exceptional interest here include the **University of Illinois,** dating from 1867, whose main library contains one of the largest scholarly collections in the country. Also on campus, the **Morrow Plots,** where land is cultivated for agricultural experimentation, and the **Krannert Art Museum** are both worth a look. In town, the **Champaign County Historical Museum,** housed in a turn-of-the-century mansion on a street with many other period homes, and the **William M. Staerkel Planetarium** welcome visitors. Nearby is **Lake of the Woods,** a county park with nature trails, all kinds of water sports, a botanical garden, and a museum. *Admission charged for some attractions.*

4. Terre Haute

Convention and Visitors Bureau, 643 Wabash Ave. The emphasis is on American art at the **Sheldon Swope Art Museum,** with paintings by Thomas Hart Benton, Grant Wood, and Edward Hopper. At the **Eugene V. Debs Home,** memorabilia from the union and the Socialist Party leader are on view. A restored 1850's cottage can be seen at the **Paul Dresser Birthplace** (author of the state song, "On the Banks of the Wabash"). Picturesque **Dobbs Park**

has a 25-acre nature preserve, butterfly and hummingbird garden, and fishing lake.

5. Tippecanoe Battlefield Memorial Park

Off Rte. 43, Battle Ground. On November 7, 1811, a battle between Tecumseh's Indian tribesmen and William Henry Harrison's forces took place after discussions failed to settle a territorial dispute. Harrison's forces were victorious, and some 30 years later, Harrison was elected president with the slogan "Tippecanoe and Tyler too" (John Tyler was his running mate). The scenic park that commemorates the battle has hiking trails, a nature center, and a small museum. *Admission charged.*

6. Elwood Haynes Museum

1915 South Webster St., Kokomo. Located in the home of Elwood Haynes, who invented one of the first gasoline-powered cars, the museum displays three Haynes automobiles and other historic memorabilia.

7. Fort Wayne

Convention and Visitors Bureau, 1021 South Calhoun St. The town features **Historic Fort Wayne,** with reconstructed blockhouses and other structures based on the original early 19th-century frontier outpost. The **Allen County-Fort Wayne Historical Society Museum** recounts local history from early Indian times to the present. Nearby, the **Lincoln Museum** contains literature, paintings, and other items related to Abraham Lincoln. *Admission charged for some attractions.*

8. Amishville

844 East 900 S., Geneva. An authentic farmhouse, barn, and smokehouse, restored and open to visitors, depict the Amish way of life. Buggies are still seen along these roads, and rides are offered to visitors. Guides lead tours of the farmhouse, which contains original furnishings. *Admission charged.*

9. Muncie

Convention and Visitors Bureau, 425 North High St. The **Ball Glass Museum,** at the Ball Corporation's Muncie headquarters, displays a large collection of rare glass preserving jars of various shapes and sizes, an assortment that traces the preserving of food from the early 1800's to the present. The **Minnetrista Cultural Center,** surrounded by extensive landscaped grounds, offers displays utilizing computers, ani-

mated mannequins, and walk-through exhibits pertaining to art, history, and science. Concerts and other festivals are held here during the summer. *Admission charged at cultural center.*

10. Levi Coffin House

Rte. 27, Fountain City. This Federal-style redbrick home of Levi and Catharine Coffin, who were Quakers, once served as a major link in the Underground Railroad. Coffin is said to have helped so many slaves escape to Canada that his home was called Grand Central Station. Today the house, furnished in 19th-century style, is open to visitors. *Admission charged.*

11. Huddleston Farmhouse Inn Museum

Rte. 40, west of Cambridge City. The 1840 farmhouse was built by John Huddleston as a family home. Travelers on the National Road were welcome here; they could feed their horses, cook their food, and find a relatively comfortable and safe place to sleep. This area and one floor of the family's quarters have been restored and are open to visitors. *Donation encouraged.*

12. Bluespring Caverns Park

These limestone caves contain more than 20 miles of passageways and what is said to be the country's longest navigable underground stream — the eerie habitat of eyeless Northern cave fish and blind crawfish. Boat tours of the caverns are available. *Fee charged for boat tour.*

13. Vincennes Mile of History

Second St., Vincennes. Along the historic mile are **Grouseland,** the stately 1804 mansion of the first governor of the Indiana Territory, and the **Capitol,** built in 1805; both are restored and open to visitors. The **George Rogers Clark National Historical Park** commemorates Clark's victory over the British. Also on the route is the 1826 **Basilica of St. Francis Xavier.** *Admission charged for some attractions.*

14. Historic New Harmony

Visitor Center, North and Arthur Sts. In 1814 a religious group led by George Rapp founded a settlement here called Harmonie, which became a thriving town of some 150 buildings. Later sold to another utopian leader, the town eventually became known as New Harmony. Today guided tours are conducted through its handsomely restored buildings. *Fee charged for tour.*

15. Old Shawneetown

Dating from the early 1800's, Shawneetown served as a gateway to the nearby prairies. After suffering several major floods, the town was moved in 1937 to higher ground. Two of the original buildings in the old town, abandoned and left to deteriorate, have been restored and are open to visitors. *Admission charged.*

16. John James Audubon State Park and Museum

With miles of trails through a nature preserve, a lake for swimming and boating, and a golf course, the popular park is highlighted by the John James Audubon Museum, which contains an impressive collection of original Audubon paintings and prints and a wide assortment of family memorabilia. A nature center offers exhibits on Audubon birds. *Admission charged.*

17. Corydon Capitol State Historic Site

202 East Walnut St., Corydon. Two outstanding buildings are part of the site: the first state capitol, built in 1816 of local blue limestone, and Gov. William Hendrick's Federal-style home and headquarters, which is located nearby. Both have been restored and furnished in period style, and are open to visitors. *Donation encouraged.*

18. Big Bone Lick State Park

Prehistoric mammals once roamed this ice-age marshland, which became the creatures' graveyard. A museum displays models of the animals and local artifacts. Interpretive trails reveal the geological and ecological history of the park; camping, swimming, and fishing are other activities available. *Admission charged at museum.*

19. U. S. Grant Birthplace

1591 Rte. 232, Point Pleasant. The 18th president of the United States was born in a simple clapboard cottage here in 1822. Visitors can tour the home, which is restored and furnished with Grant family memorabilia and period pieces. *Admission charged.*

20. Fort Ancient State Memorial

Walls, mounds, and gateways are among the prehistoric earthworks built by the Hopewell Indians between 100 B.C. and A.D. 500, on a site overlooking the Little Miami River. In A.D. 900 the area was occupied by the Fort Ancient Indians, who lived by farming and fishing. A museum displays related artifacts. *Fee charged for parking.*

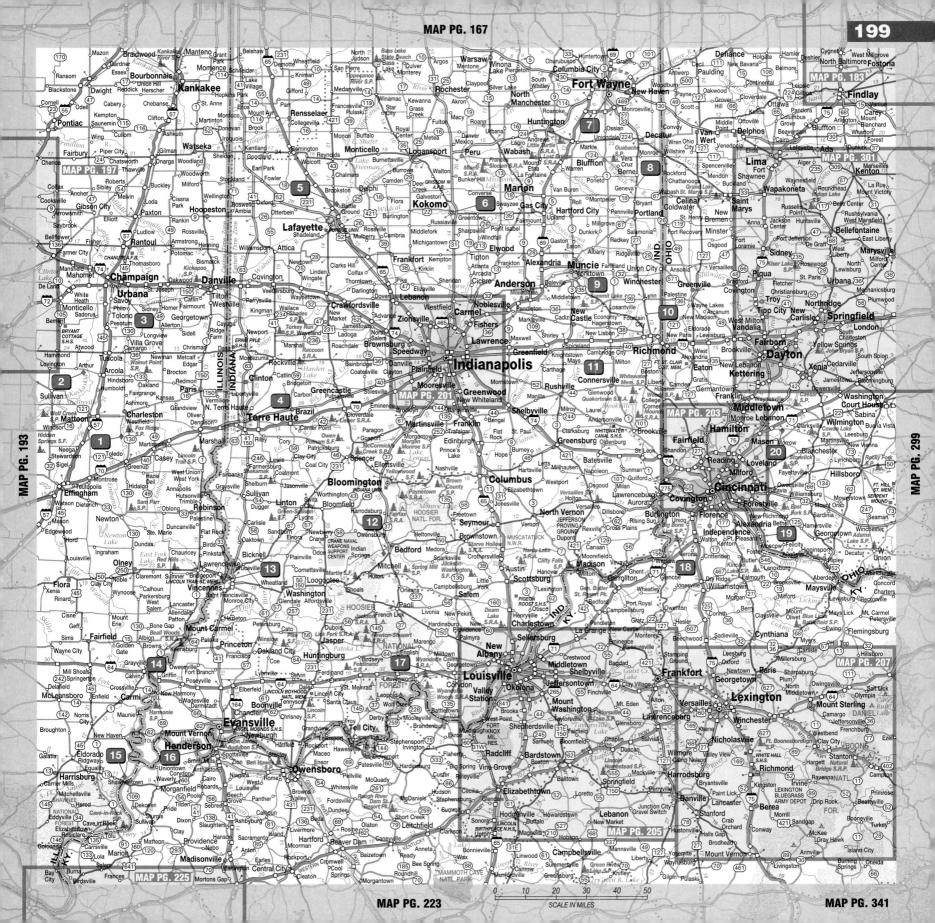

MAP PG. 197

MAP PG. 193

MAP PG. 201

MAP PG. 203

MAP PG. 299

MAP PG. 207

MAP PG. 205

SCALE IN MILES
0 10 20 30 40 50

1. Conner Prairie

13400 Allisonville Rd., Fishers. The lifestyle of local pioneers in 1836 is depicted in this frontier village of some 36 restored buildings, including the opulent Federal-style mansion of fur trader William Conner. Authentically costumed townspeople celebrate a wedding, hold a town meeting, demonstrate smithing and weaving, and even preserve a hog. The museum presents films and exhibits. *Admission charged.*

2. Patrick Henry Sullivan Museum

225 West Hawthorne St., Zionsville. Created to commemorate the first white settler in Boone County, this museum depicts the lives of the county's early settlers with historical exhibits and memorabilia.

3. Eagle Creek Park

With 3,800 acres of unspoiled woodland and a 1,300-acre reservoir, this park provides excellent opportunities for swimming, fishing, sailing, canoeing, golfing, and picnicking. From hiking and cross-country ski trails, visitors may glimpse some of the park's wild deer. *Admission charged.*

4. Indianapolis Motor Speedway and Hall of Fame Museum

4790 West 16th St., Indianapolis. Visitors can take a bus tour around the 2½-mile oval of this famous speedway, where in May state-of-the-art race cars line up for the thrilling 500-mile race. Some 30 winning cars dating from 1911 are on display at the Hall of Fame Museum, along with antique and classic cars. *Admission charged.*

5. Indianapolis Museum of Art

1200 West 38th St., Indianapolis. This remarkable collection of art, furniture, and decorative arts ranges from pre-Columbian artifacts to Robert Indiana's pop sculpture, LOVE. Set within a 152-acre botanical garden, the museum's five pavilions display medieval and Renaissance paintings; 20th-century textiles; Oriental, African and South Pacific art; a sculpture court; and fine English silver housed in a French château.

6. Crown Hill Cemetery

3402 Boulevard Pl., Indianapolis. In this vast cemetery lie the graves of such notables as President Benjamin Harrison, poet James Whitcomb Riley, and the infamous John Dillinger.

7. Indiana State Fairgrounds

East 38th St., Indianapolis. At **Hook's Historic Drug Store and Pharmacy Museum,** a restored 19th-century drugstore, visitors can sample an old-fashioned ice cream soda and examine antique medical and dental equipment. In August a state fair features agricultural exhibits, horse racing, and celebrity entertainment. *Admission charged at fair.*

8. The Children's Museum

3000 North Meridian St., Indianapolis. This large five-story museum has exhibits that range from natural sciences to foreign cultures. Visitors can excavate at an archeological dig, pet a skunk, see a 30-foot-high water clock, take a three-dimensional space trip, and tour an Egyptian tomb complete with real mummies. *Admission charged.*

9. War Memorial Plaza

431 North Meridian St., Indianapolis. The massive limestone Indiana World War Memorial in the center of this five-block plaza honors the state's citizens who died in the two world wars and the Korean and Vietnam wars. The Shrine Room bathes a 17- by 30-foot American flag in light refracted through stained-glass windows; the Military Museum depicts Hoosier soldiers in conflicts dating to the Battle of Tippecanoe.

10. President Benjamin Harrison Memorial Home

1230 North Delaware St., Indianapolis. The home of the country's 23rd president from 1875 until his death in 1901, this restored Victorian mansion has guided tours of 10 of its rooms. Original furnishings, including a unique chair made from cattlehorns and bobcat fur, and family and political memorabilia are on view. The surrounding **Old Northside** neighborhood displays many grand Victorian homes. *Admission charged.*

11. James Whitcomb Riley Home

528 Lockerbie St., Indianapolis. Located in the **Historic Lockerbie Square District,** a neighborhood of restored 19th-century homes, this exquisitely preserved Victorian dwelling was home to the well-known Hoosier poet James Whitcomb Riley from 1893 to 1916. The residence features period furnishings and decorative arts, which include Riley's favorite easy chair and Tiffany silver. *Admission charged.*

12. Indiana State Museum

202 North Alabama St., Indianapolis. Natural and cultural history displays featured in this museum include a 450-million-year-old fossil, 200-year-old forests, and a giant Foucault pendulum that demonstrates the earth's rotation. Freetown Village is a living-history exhibit of the lives of free blacks in the state in 1870, while the Indiana Museum of Sports highlights famous Hoosier athletes and the enduring popularity of the state high school basketball tournament.

13. City Market

222 East Market St., Indianapolis. Built in 1886, this downtown historical landmark houses a mixture of restaurants, boutiques, and food stands in a picturesque brick and stone building.

Madam Walker built a cosmetics empire.

14. Soldiers' and Sailors' Monument

Monument Circle, Indianapolis.. This 284-foot-high Beaux Arts obelisk was dedicated in 1902 to commemorate the bravery of Indiana's soldiers and sailors who served in the Civil War. An observation tower gives a panoramic view of the city.

15. Union Station

39 West Jackson Pl., Indianapolis. This historic railroad station has been renovated into a very popular marketplace with more than 90 shops and boutiques, restaurants, and nightclubs.

16. Indiana Convention Center and Hoosier Dome

100 South Capitol Ave., Indianapolis. This massive convention center features the 60,500-seat Hoosier Dome, home of the Indianapolis Colts football team and one of the few air-supported dome stadiums in the country. On guided tours of the Hoosier Dome visitors see the VIP suites and the locker rooms. The **National Track & Field Hall of Fame Museum** displays vintage track equipment, and memorabilia of Jim Thorpe, Jesse Owens, and Bruce Jenner. *Admission charged.*

17. Eiteljorg Museum of American Indian and Western Art

500 West Washington St., Indianapolis. One of the finest collections of American Indian and Western art is on display in this adobe-style museum. There are bronzes by cowboy artist Frederic Remington, paintings by Georgia O'Keeffe, and Indian clothing and crafts from all over the United States and Canada. *Admission charged.*

18. Indianapolis Zoo

1200 West Washington St., Indianapolis. This spectacular zoo includes one of the world's largest enclosed whale and dolphin pavilions, the biggest aquarium in the state, an "encounters area" with domesticated animals, and exhibits of rare birds and endangered plantlife. At Living Deserts of the World, birds fly free and lizards and other animals roam at will through a desert conservatory. *Admission charged.*

19. Madame Walker Urban Life Center

617 Indiana Ave., Indianapolis. In tribute to Madam C. J. Walker — entrepreneur, philanthropist, and social activist — the center is a cultural showcase for the city's black community. Dance, jazz, and film programs are presented amid the splendid African and Egyptian decor of the **Walker Theatre.** *Admission charged at theater.*

20. Scottish Rite Cathedral

650 North Meridian St., Indianapolis. This beautiful Gothic Tudor-style cathedral is crowned with a 54-bell carillon. Inside, Russian white oak beams and elaborate wood carvings provide a stunning backdrop for the cathedral's two organs with 7,000 pipes.

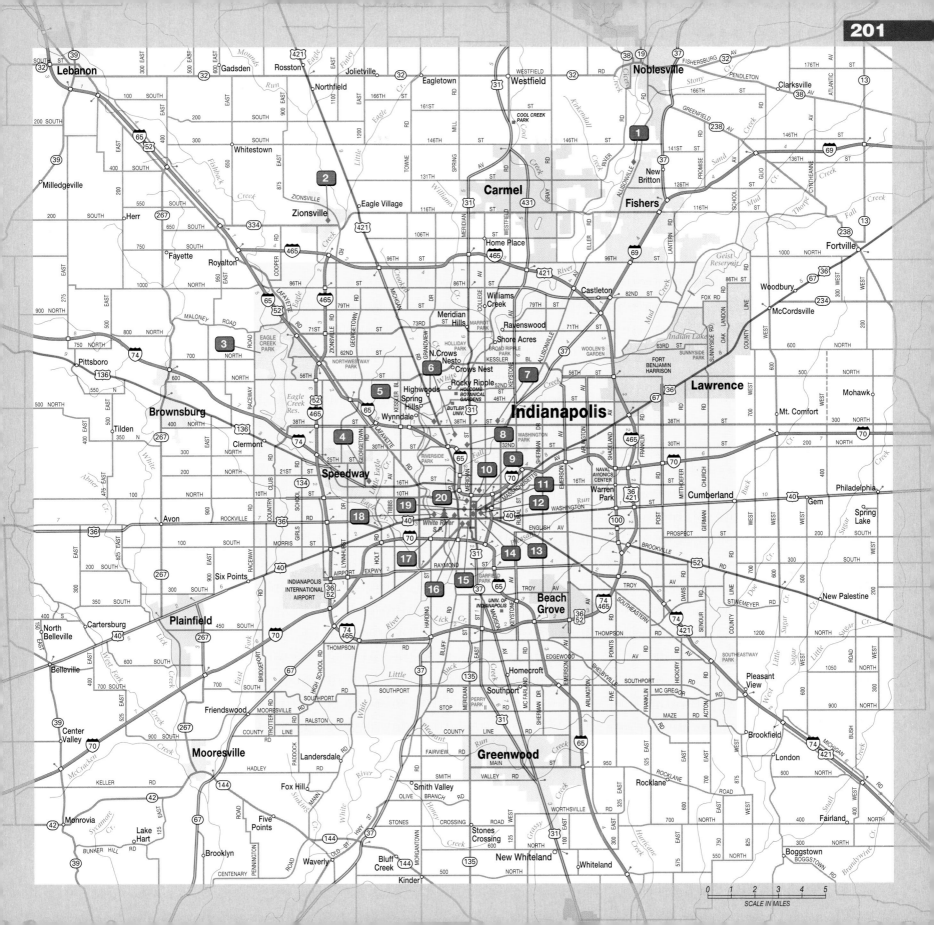

1. Hamilton

Chamber of Commerce, 201 Dayton St. A walking tour of **German Village** covers a 9-block area of this 19th-century industrial center that includes its early schools, courts, and businesses. Of particular interest are the **Butler County Historical Museum,** housed in an Italianate mansion, with period furnishings and antique clothing and toys, and the **Lane-Hooven House,** a restored Gothic Revival octagonal home. **Rossville** features historical buildings dating from 1830 to 1920 on the west side of the Great Miami River. *Admission charged at museum.*

2. Lebanon

Chamber of Commerce, 46 East Mulberry St. The **Warren County Historical Society Museum** displays an extensive collection of Shaker furniture from a nearby 19th-century Shaker community, as well as prehistoric Indian artifacts, a pioneer cabin, and a village green. The **Golden Lamb Inn,** whose guests since its opening in 1803 have included 10 American presidents, also boasts an extensive collection of Shaker furniture. The **Glendower State Memorial,** a stately Greek Revival mansion completed in 1840, exhibits period furnishings from the area. *Admission charged for some attractions.*

3. Kings Island

6300 Kings Island Dr., Mason. This sprawling amusement park is divided into theme areas that range from a historical river town of the 1800's to a white-knuckle trip down Rushing River at Waterworks. Visitors can take a hair-raising ride on one of the biggest roller coasters in the country, see an ice show, meet Fred Flintstone and other Hanna-Barbera characters, or glide on a monorail over a 100-acre enclosure of snow leopards, giraffes, and other exotic animals. *Admission charged.*

4. Sharon Woods Village

11450 Lebanon Pike, Sharonville. Guided tours of this village accurately convey a sense of the area's small-town life before 1880. Reconstructed buildings include a two-story double-pen log house from 1804, a Greek Revival farmhouse built in the 1840's, and an 1870's railroad station, all authentically furnished. *Admission charged.*

5. Meier's Wine Cellars

6955 Plainfield Pike, Silverton. In operation for more than 100 years, Ohio's oldest and largest winery lets visitors watch the winemaking process and sample its award-winning sherries, wines, and champagnes.

6. Stowe House

2950 Gilbert Ave., Cincinnati. Harriet Beecher Stowe, who would one day pen the influential *Uncle Tom's Cabin,* honed her writing skills as a young woman in this gabled house. The Greek Revival home has been restored and decorated with original furniture and Stowe family portraits.

7. Eden Park

This lovely city park is the site of the **Krohn Conservatory,** with plants and flowers ranging from desert specimens to a tropical rain forest. The nearby **Cincinnati Art Museum** offers more than a hundred galleries of paintings, sculpture, costumes, musical instruments, and decorative arts spanning 5,000 years, including the popular Rookwood pottery made in Cincinnati in the 19th century. *Admission charged at museum.*

8. Taft Museum

316 Pike St., Cincinnati. Housed in the 1820 Federal-style former home of Charles Phelps Taft, this small museum presents a remarkable collection of artworks. There are portraits by Rembrandt and Sargent, landscapes by Turner, Chinese porcelains, Limoges enamels from the French Renaissance, and American furniture from the early 1800's. *Admission charged.*

9. John A. Roebling Suspension Bridge

Designed by John A. Roebling, and later a model for the Brooklyn Bridge, this 1,056-foot span was the longest in the world at the time of its completion in 1867.

10. Covington Landing

Madison Ave., Covington. This enormous commercial and entertainment complex floating on the Ohio River offers an exciting array of restaurants, shops, music, theater, and beautiful views of the Cincinnati skyline. From here, there are riverboat cruises for sightseeing, dining, or dancing.

11. The Cathedral Basilica of the Assumption

1130 Madison Ave., Covington. Gargoyles guard this majestic house of worship modeled after Notre Dame in Paris. Its Gothic interior is decorated with mural-size paintings by Frank Duveneck, mosaics from Venice, and one of the largest handmade, stained-glass windows in the world.

12. The American Museum of Brewing History and Arts

Rte. 75 and Buttermilk Pike, Fort Mitchell. Located at the **Oldenberg Brewery,** this museum contains one of the largest collections of brewing memorabilia in the world, including 12,500 beer cans and 23,000 bottles. Guided tours take visitors to the microbrewery, where they may sample the finished product. A restaurant and a seasonal outdoor beer garden help to make this a very popular attraction. *Admission charged.*

13. Carroll Chimes Bell Tower

Philadelphia St., Covington. Featuring 21 animated figures, the tower's 43-bell carillon plays hourly concerts. When the enchanting music stops, mechanical puppets act out the story of the Pied Piper of Hamelin on the balcony of the 100-foot tower. Surrounding the tower is **MainStrasse Village,** a restored 19th-century German neighborhood with quaint shops and restaurants.

14. Riverfront Stadium

201 East Pete Rose Way, Cincinnati. No visit to the self-proclaimed baseball capital of the world is complete without a visit to this 60,000-seat stadium, where baseball fans can enjoy watching the Cincinnati Reds, and football fans can cheer on the Cincinnati Bengals. *Admission charged.*

15. Fountain Square Plaza

Fifth and Vine Sts., Cincinnati. Performances at the bandstand pavilion draw lunchtime crowds to this lively plaza, built around the 1871 Tyler Davidson Fountain. From the square, horse-drawn carriages leave for tours of the downtown area. The second-level Skywalk system winds around the square, connecting hotels, shops, restaurants, and businesses for 20 blocks. *Fee charged for carriage ride.*

16. Museum Center at Union Terminal

1301 Western Ave., Cincinnati. Since its completion in 1933, the Art Deco terminal has been famous for its imposing rotunda, mosaic murals, terrazzo floors, and marble walls. Today it's the dynamic home of museums and entertainment venues that traverse time from the Pleistocene era to the high-tech future. At the **Cincinnati Museum of Natural History,** visitors can see mounted saber-toothed tigers set in a glacier habitat or explore a Kentucky limestone cavern inhabited by live bats. The **Cincinnati Historical Society Museum and Library** has hands-on exhibits about the city's waterfront past, while at the **Robert D. Lindner Family Omnimax Theater** films are projected onto a 260-degree domed screen that is five stories high and 72 feet wide. *Admission charged for some attractions.*

17. John Hauck House Museum

812 Dayton St., Cincinnati. Owned in the late 19th century by a wealthy German brewer, this Italianate mansion, located on what was called Millionaires' Row, offers a look at the lifestyle of the period's very rich, complete with its ornate furnishings and antique children's toys. *Admission charged.*

18. William Howard Taft National Historic Site

2038 Auburn Ave., Cincinnati. The birthplace and boyhood home of the country's 27th president, this handsome Italianate house has been partially restored and decorated with ornate period furnishings and Taft family portraits and memorabilia. Exhibits on the second floor chronicle the illustrious career of this brilliant man, who became president and chief justice of the Supreme Court.

19. Cincinnati Zoo and Botanical Garden

3400 Vine St., Cincinnati. More than 6,000 animals reside in their natural habitats in this zoo, including rare white Bengal tigers in a jungle, lowland gorilla families in a tropical garden, fierce Komodo dragons, and the many endangered species that the zoo is renowned for breeding. The botanical garden also features natural habitat areas and has more than 2,000 kinds of plants. *Admission charged.*

20. Mount Airy Forest and Arboretum

More than 1,400 reforested acres include native hardwoods, conifers, and grasslands. Hiking trails invite visitors to explore the area, and picnic sites offer welcome rest areas. The arboretum has a colorful variety of flower gardens.

SCALE IN MILES
0 1 2 3 4 5

1. Howard Steamboat Museum

1101 East Market St., Jeffersonville. Depicting the history of the riverboat, the museum is housed in a Victorian mansion built by Edmunds Howard. The Howard family operated one of the country's largest steamboat-building companies. The mansion reflects this, with staircases and chandeliers modeled after those designed for the great stern-wheelers. *Admission charged.*

2. Culbertson Mansion

914 East Main St., New Albany. Entrepreneur William S. Culbertson built this elegant residence in 1869. Part of the Mansion Row Historic District, the house's opulent interior includes a hand-painted ceiling, marble fireplaces, and period furnishings.

3. Museum of History and Science

727 West Main St., Louisville. Highlights of this exciting museum include many hands-on educational exhibits, a fossil-laden cave, an Egyptian mummy's tomb, the Apollo 13 capsule, and a four-story-high movie screen. *Admission charged.*

4. The Filson Club

1310 South Third St., Louisville. This historical society maintains a museum dedicated to Kentucky, located in the Beaux-Arts **Ferguson Mansion.** The club's impressive collection includes Civil War documents, Shaker manuscripts, a Rocky Mountain ram horn from the Lewis and Clark expedition, and a tree stump inscribed by Daniel Boone. *Admission charged.*

5. J. B. Speed Art Museum

2035 South Third St., Louisville. Kentucky's oldest and largest museum features the works of Rubens, Rembrandt, Monet, and Picasso. The collection is housed in one of the finest neoclassical buildings in the South, which also contains sculpture, tapestries, and furniture. *Admission charged.*

6. Churchill Downs

700 Central Ave., Louisville. Home of the famous Kentucky Derby, Churchill Downs is open to visitors year-round. Besides its grandstand, track, and paddock area, the Downs contains the **Derby Museum,** which shows simulated races as well as exhibits on the derby and the Thoroughbred horse. *Admission charged.*

7. Louisville Zoo

1100 Trevilian Way, Louisville. More than 1,600 birds and mammals live here in settings that are arranged by geographic area. At the **Meta Zoo Education Center,** visitors can view small creatures close up and learn about animals through their skeletons, skins, and feathers. A miniature train and a tram provide transportation to the various sections, and there are picnic areas. *Admission charged.*

8. Farmington

3033 Bardstown Rd., Louisville. Built in 1810 from a design by Thomas Jefferson, this Federal-style house has twin octagonal rooms, a hidden stairway, and fanlights over the doors. *Admission charged.*

9. Cave Hill Cemetery

701 Baxter Ave., Louisville. Among the graves here are those of Colonel Harland Sanders (of Kentucky Fried Chicken fame) and explorer George Rogers Clark. This cemetery is also a botanical garden, with rare trees, shrubs, and other plants, as well as ducks, swans, and geese.

10. Locust Grove

561 Blankenbaker La., Louisville. George Rogers Clark, a Revolutionary War general and founder of Louisville, lived in this handsome mansion after he retired. Surrounded by plantation outbuildings, the Georgian brick house boasts original walnut paneling and period furnishings. *Admission charged.*

11. Zachary Taylor National Cemetery

4701 Brownsboro Rd., Louisville. The twelfth president and his wife are interred here in a limestone mausoleum; a huge statue of Taylor is nearby. The cemetery also contains the gravesites of more than 50 other members of the Taylor family.

12. Frankfort

Tourist and Convention Commission, 100 Capitol Ave. Seventy Ionic columns adorn the monumental **State Capitol,** while the flower-bedecked Floral Clock keeps time on the capitol grounds. Next door is the Beaux-Arts **Governor's Mansion,** and across the river lies the **Frankfort Cemetery,** where Daniel Boone is buried. The fighting spirit of Kentucky is honored at the **Kentucky Military History Museum.** Other noteworthy sights include the **Old State Capitol,** which houses the **Kentucky History Museum,** the **Old Governor's Mansion,** and the **Liberty Hall Historic Site.** *Admission charged for some attractions.*

13. Buckley Wildlife Sanctuary

1305 Germany Rd., Frankfort. Operated by the National Audubon Society, this forested preserve contains nature trails, a nature center, and a "bird blind," with one-way windows that allow visitors to observe birds at a feeding station. *Admission charged.*

14. Old Fort Harrod State Park

Rtes. 127 and 68, Harrodsburg. The centerpiece of this park is a reconstruction of **Fort Harrod,** built in 1775 by the first settlers west of the Allegheny Mountains. It contains blockhouses and cabins with authentic furnishings. Also on the grounds are a pioneer cemetery, the cabin in which Abraham Lincoln's parents were married, and the **Mansion Museum.** Dedicated to Kentucky's divided allegiance during the Civil War, it displays both Union and Confederate memorabilia. *Admission charged.*

15. Perryville Battlefield State Historic Site

1825 Mackville Rd., Perryville. On this site Union forces took control of Kentucky in one of the bloodiest battles of the Civil War. The Confederate headquarters building still stands, as does the cemetery where soldiers were buried. A museum displays battle artifacts and dioramas depicting the conflict. *Admission charged at museum.*

16. Lincoln Homestead State Park

5079 Lincoln Park Rd., Springfield. Located on land settled by the Lincoln family, the park contains three buildings related to Abraham Lincoln's parents: the original childhood home of Nancy Hanks; a replica of the log cabin Thomas Lincoln lived in as a boy; and a replica of the blacksmith and carpenter shop where Thomas learned his trade. *Admission charged.*

17. Bardstown

Tourist Commission, 107 East Stephen Foster Ave. This historic town holds many landmarks, including the **Old Talbott Tavern,** a onetime stagecoach stop built in 1797, and **St. Joseph Cathedral,** completed in 1819. **My Old Kentucky Home State Park** preserves the Federal-style house said to have inspired Stephen Foster's famous song. Located in Spalding Hall are the **Museum of Whiskey History,** which documents Bardstown's role as the center of Kentucky's bourbon industry, and the **Bardstown Historical Museum.** *Admission charged for some attractions.*

18. Bernheim Forest

This beautiful nature preserve has a landscaped arboretum with a nature center, museum, and fishing and waterfowl ponds, as well as a wilderness area crisscrossed by hiking trails.

19. Fort Knox Military Reservation

Off Rte. 31W, Fort Knox. Within this famous post stands the **U.S. Bullion Depository.** Constructed of steel, granite, and concrete, the depository protects the largest part of the nation's gold reserve; it may be viewed only from the outside. Also on the grounds is the **Patton Museum of Cavalry and Armor,** displaying memorabilia related to Gen. George S. Patton, Jr., as well as weaponry, military artifacts, and a portion of the Berlin Wall.

20. Otter Creek Park

Set on the Ohio River, this wooded park offers many activities including swimming, fishing, boating, hiking, and camping. A nature center features exhibits of local plant and animal life.

21. Schmidt's Coca-Cola Museum

1201 North Dixie, Elizabethtown. Located at the Schmidt family's Coca-Cola bottling plant, this museum houses an astounding collection of items related to the famous soft drink, including such advertising memorabilia as logo-inscribed trays, clocks, and ashtrays, as well as a charming 1893 soda fountain. *Admission charged.*

22. Lincoln Birthplace National Historic Site

Rte. 61, Hodgenville. A granite monument shelters the one-room cabin where Abraham Lincoln was born. The house was part of Sinking Springs Farm, and the spring still flows in the park, which also has trails and picnic areas. In nearby **Knob Creek** there is a replica of the cabin to which the Lincoln family next moved. Also in the vicinity is the **Lincoln Museum,** where wax figures portray scenes from the Great Emancipator's life. *Admission charged for some attractions.*

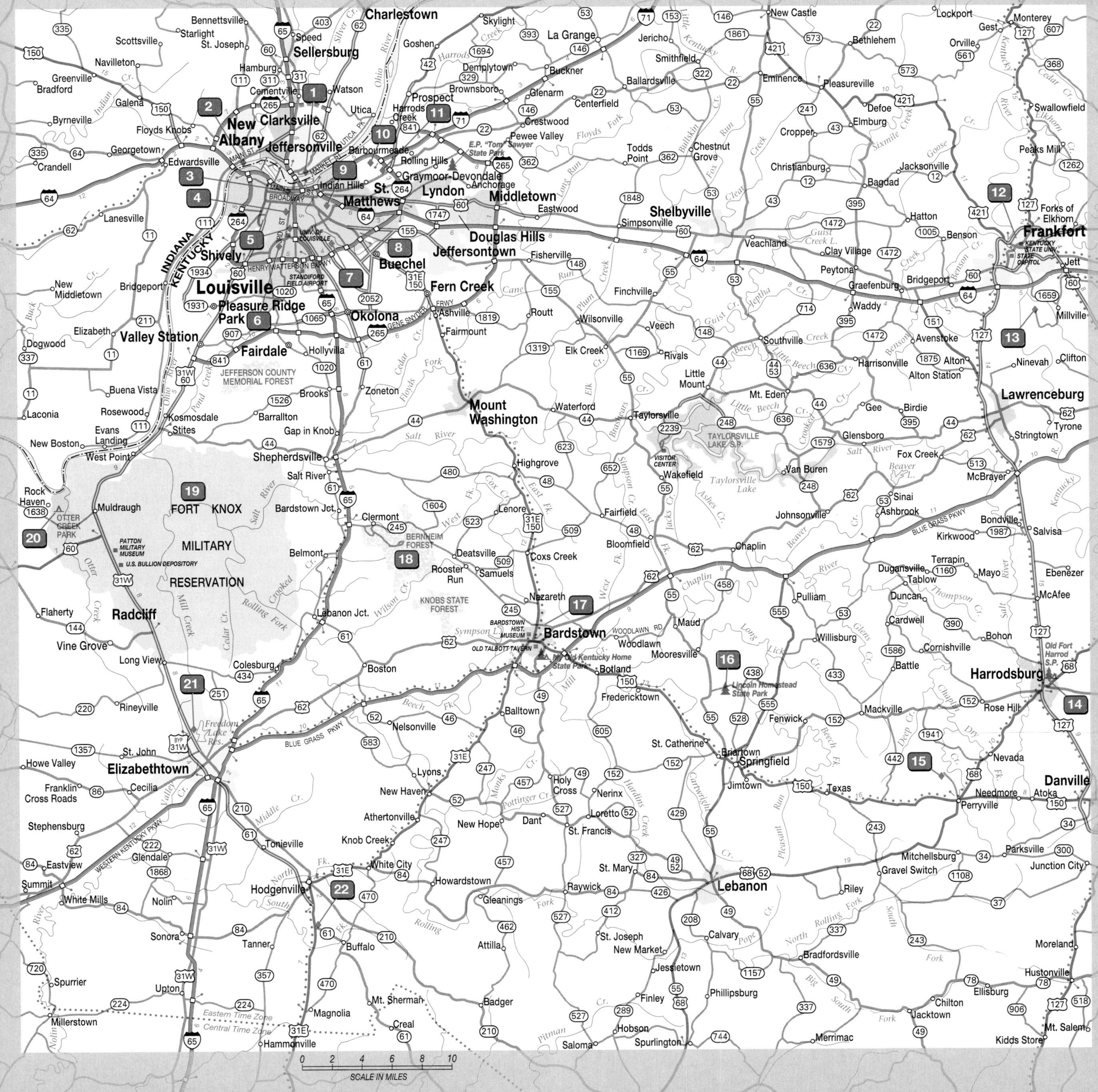
Charlestown
Bennettsville
Starlight
St. Joseph
Scottsville
Speed
Sellersburg
Goshen
Skylight
La Grange
Jericho
Smithfield
New Castle
Lockport
Gest
Monterey
Navilleton
Hamburg
Greenville
Bradford
Cementville
Watson
Demplytown
Brownsboro
Buckner
Ballardsville
Eminence
Bethlehem
Orville
Pleasureville
Galena
Prospect
Utica
Glenarm
Centerfield
Defoe
Swallowfield
Byrneville
New Albany
Clarksville
Jeffersonville
Harrods Creek
Crestwood
Elmburg
Floyds Knobs
Georgetown
Edwardsville
Crandell
Barbourmeade
Pewee Valley
E.P. "Tom" Sawyer State Park
Todds Point
Chestnut Grove
Cropper
Peaks Mill
Rolling Hills
Graymoor-Devondale
Anchorage
Christianburg
Jacksonville
Indian Hills
St. Matthews
Lyndon
Middletown
Bagdad
Broadway
Eastwood
Shelbyville
Hatton
Forks of Elkhorn
Frankfort
Kentucky State Univ.
State Capitol
Lanesville
Simpsonville
Benson
Veachland
Clay Village
Jett
Indiana
Kentucky
Univ. of Louisville
Douglas Hills
Jeffersontown
Shively
Buechel
Henry Watterson Expwy
Fisherville
Peytona
Louisville
Standiford Field Airport
Fern Creek
Graefenburg
Bridgeport
New Middletown
Bridgeport
Finchville
Waddy
Millville
Pleasure Ridge Park
Okolona
Gene Snyder Frwy
Ashville
Routt
Wilsonville
Veech
Southville
Elizabeth
Valley Station
Fairmount
Avenstoke
Dogwood
Fairdale
Hollyvilla
Elk Creek
Rivals
Harrisonville
Alton
Ninevah
Clifton
Jefferson County Memorial Forest
Little Mount
Alton Station
Buena Vista
Zoneton
Brooks
Mount Washington
Mt. Eden
Lawrenceburg
Laconia
Rosewood
Kosmosdale
Barrallton
Waterford
Taylorsville
Gee
Birdie
Tyrone
Evans Landing
Stites
Gap in Knob
Taylorsville Lake S.P.
Glensboro
Stringtown
New Boston
West Point
Shepherdsville
Highgrove
Visitor Center
Fox Creek
McBrayer
Rock Haven
Salt River
Wakefield
Van Buren
Muldraugh
Fort Knox
Military Reservation
Bardstown Jct.
Lenore
Sinai
Ashbrook
Otter Creek Park
Clermont
Fairfield
Johnsonville
Bondville
Patton Military Museum
U.S. Bullion Depository
Bernheim Forest
Kirkwood
Salvisa
Belmont
Deatsville
Coxs Creek
Bloomfield
Chaplin
Blue Grass Pkwy
Terrapin
Rooster Run
Samuels
Dugansville
Tablow
Mayo
Ebenezer
Flaherty
Radcliff
Knobs State Forest
Nazareth
Pulliam
Duncan
McAfee
Lebanon Jct.
Bardstown Hist. Museum
Bardstown
Woodlawn Rd
Maud
Cardwell
Bohon
Vine Grove
Old Talbott Tavern
Woodlawn
Mooresville
Willisburg
Cornishville
Old Fort Harrod S.P.
Long View
My Old Kentucky Home State Park
Colesburg
Boston
Botland
Battle
Harrodsburg
Fredericktown
Lincoln Homestead State Park
Rineyville
Balltown
Freedom Lake Res.
Fenwick
Mackville
Rose Hill
Nelsonville
St. Catherine
Howe Valley
St. John
Elizabethtown
Bardstown
Lyons
Holy Cross
Springfield
Nevada
Franklin Cross Roads
Cecilia
New Haven
Nerinx
Jimtown
Texas
Needmore
Atoka
Danville
Perryville
Stephensburg
Athertonville
New Hope
Dant
Loretto
St. Francis
Western Kentucky Pkwy
Glendale
Tonieville
Knob Creek
Eastview
White City
St. Mary
Mitchellsburg
Parksville
Junction City
Gravel Switch
Summit
Hodgenville
Howardstown
Raywick
Lebanon
Riley
White Mills
Nolin
Gleanings
Sonora
Tanner
Buffalo
Attilla
St. Joseph
Calvary
Moreland
New Market
Bradfordsville
Spurrier
Jessietown
Hustonville
Upton
Mt. Sherman
Badger
Phillipsburg
Ellisburg
Chilton
Millerstown
Magnolia
Finley
Jacktown
Eastern Time Zone
Central Time Zone
Creal
Hobson
Saloma
Spurlington
Merrimac
Kidds Store
Mt. Salem
Hammonville
0 2 4 6 8 10
SCALE IN MILES

1. Berea

Tourism Commission, 201 North Broadway. Nestled in the foothills of the Cumberland Mountains, Berea is best known as a crafts center. At **Churchill Weavers,** a handweaving company, visitors can observe the making of baby blankets and couch throws, which are also on display in the gift shop. Exhibits and regional artifacts from spinning wheels to musical instruments are on view at the **Berea College Appalachian Museum.** *Admission charged.*

2. Renfro Valley

Visitor Center, Rte. 25. The traditional music of the Kentucky hills reverberates throughout this colorful valley. An entertainment center, which started out 50 years ago as a country barn, today offers country, bluegrass, and gospel music shows. A museum interprets the state's musical heritage, and a shopping village provides visitors with a chance to buy such local crafts as handloomed rugs and elaborate wood carvings. *Admission charged at music shows.*

3. William Whitley House State Shrine

625 Whitley Rd., Stanford. A Revolutionary War hero, Whitley constructed this fortress-like brick dwelling in 1792. With its walls nearly 2 feet thick and a secret staircase, the house was constructed to provide protection from Indian attacks. On his property Whitley built one of Kentucky's first horse-racing tracks. *Admission charged.*

4. Danville

Tourist Commission, 134 South Second St. In a log courthouse in Danville in 1792, settlers decided that their territory should become a state. A replica of that structure and other early buildings now make up the **Constitution Square State Historic Site.** Also in town is the **McDowell House, Apothecary, and Gardens,** the former residence of pioneer surgeon Dr. Ephraim McDowell. The house and shop contain period furnishings and medical instruments. *Admission charged at house.*

5. Shaker Village of Pleasant Hill

3500 Lexington Rd., Pleasant Hill. This 19th-century Shaker village features 33 restored buildings on 2,700 acres. Costumed interpreters make the community come alive again with demonstrations of woodworking and other skills. The Centre Family Dwelling contains Shaker furniture and artifacts. *Admission charged.*

6. Versailles

Chamber of Commerce, 183 South Main St. In this town lived Jack Jouett, who rode 40 miles to warn Thomas Jefferson of the British plan to arrest him. Jouett's house, built around 1797, is open to the public. Visitors to Versailles can also ride in vintage trains, starting at the **Bluegrass Railroad Museum.** *Fee charged for train rides.*

Kentucky's bluegrass horse country

7. Headley-Whitney Museum

4435 Old Frankfort Pike, Lexington. Bibelots, seashells, and Asian porcelains are among the eclectic items featured in this unusual museum. *Admission charged.*

8. Ward Hall

U.S. 460, Georgetown. This imposing Greek Revival mansion, with massive columns at the entrance, was once under consideration for the state capitol. Completed in 1853, the house contains period furnishings, lovely fresco ceilings, and a chambered-nautilus stairway. *Admission charged.*

9. Duncan Tavern

323 High St., Paris. Daniel Boone and other famous frontiersmen frequented this three-story limestone tavern. The building and an adjoining house have both been faithfully restored to their original appearance and filled with elegant furnishings that predate 1820. *Admission charged.*

10. Kentucky Horse Park

4089 Iron Works Pike, Lexington. Located in bluegrass country, this large park celebrates horses, including Kentucky's famous Thoroughbreds. Highlights include the **International Museum of the Horse, the Man O' War Monument,** the **Hall of Champions** stable, and the **Parade of Breeds.** Visitors can ride horses and also observe the workings of a horse farm. The resort campground offers swimming and other activities. *Admission charged.*

11. Lexington Cemetery

833 West Main St., Lexington. Among the eminent Americans buried here are Henry Clay, John Hunt Morgan, and suffragist Laura Clay (daughter of Cassius M. Clay). Hundreds of Confederate and Union veterans are also laid side by side in this beautifully landscaped cemetery, with its sunken gardens and lily ponds.

12. Transylvania University

Located in Lexington, the oldest university west of the Allegheny Mountains educated Jefferson Davis, Cassius M. Clay, and other U.S. officials, including two vice presidents. The Greek Revival administration building served as a hospital during the Civil War; today a medical museum is on the campus.

13. Ashland

120 Sycamore Rd., Lexington. This gracious estate set on 20 acres of wooded grassland was the home of statesman Henry Clay from 1811 to the year of his death in 1852. Clay's chess table, travel trunk, and other family possessions are on display throughout the mansion. *Admission charged.*

14. Hunt-Morgan House

201 North Mill St., Lexington. Built about 1811 for millionaire John Wesley Hunt and later occupied by Confederate General John Hunt Morgan, this Federal-style home has lovely architectural details, including a fanlight doorway and a cantilevered staircase. *Admission charged.*

15. Mary Todd Lincoln House

578 West Main St., Lexington. This brick Georgian-style structure was the girlhood home of Mary Todd, who married Abraham Lincoln. The house features period furnishings and personal effects of the Todd and Lincoln families. *Admission charged.*

16. Waveland State Historic Site

225 Higbee Mill Rd., Lexington. Built in 1847, this Greek Revival mansion contains authentic furnishings and vividly conveys life in an antebellum plantation home. The estate also includes outbuildings such as slave quarters, an icehouse, and a smokehouse. *Admission charged.*

17. White Hall State Historic House

500 White Hall Shrine Rd., White Hall. White Hall was the birthplace and home of Cassius M. Clay, an abolitionist, ambassador, and college founder. The original house was Georgian, but Clay added an Italianate section that now predominates. The three-story mansion holds some of Clay's original furnishings, law books, and other memorabilia. *Admission charged.*

18. Fort Boonesborough State Park

A replica of the original Fort Boonesborough, which was built by Daniel Boone and other pioneers, stands a half mile from the Kentucky River in this state park. Cabins hold period furnishings, and costumed artisans demonstrate the crafts of the day. Swimmers can enjoy the sandy river beach; other activities include fishing, boating, picnicking, camping, and hiking. *Admission charged at fort.*

19. Daniel Boone National Forest

Among the many natural highlights of this vast national forest are **Cave Run Lake, Clifty Wilderness Area, Red River Gorge, Zilpo Road Scenic Byway,** and **Sheltowee Trace National Recreation Trail.** The forest's rugged mountains harbor waterfalls, caves, cliffs, old and new timber, diverse wildlife, and flowering plants.

20. Natural Bridge State Resort Park

Located within Daniel Boone National Forest, this park is named for the **Kentucky Natural Bridge,** a sandstone phenomenon that measures 85 feet wide at its base and 30 feet wide at its top. Visitors can reach the bridge either by trail or skylift, which also gives an expansive view of the eastern part of the state. Other park attractions include old saltpeter mines, a balanced rock, and a cave. A huge lake provides good fishing and boating, and campsites are available.

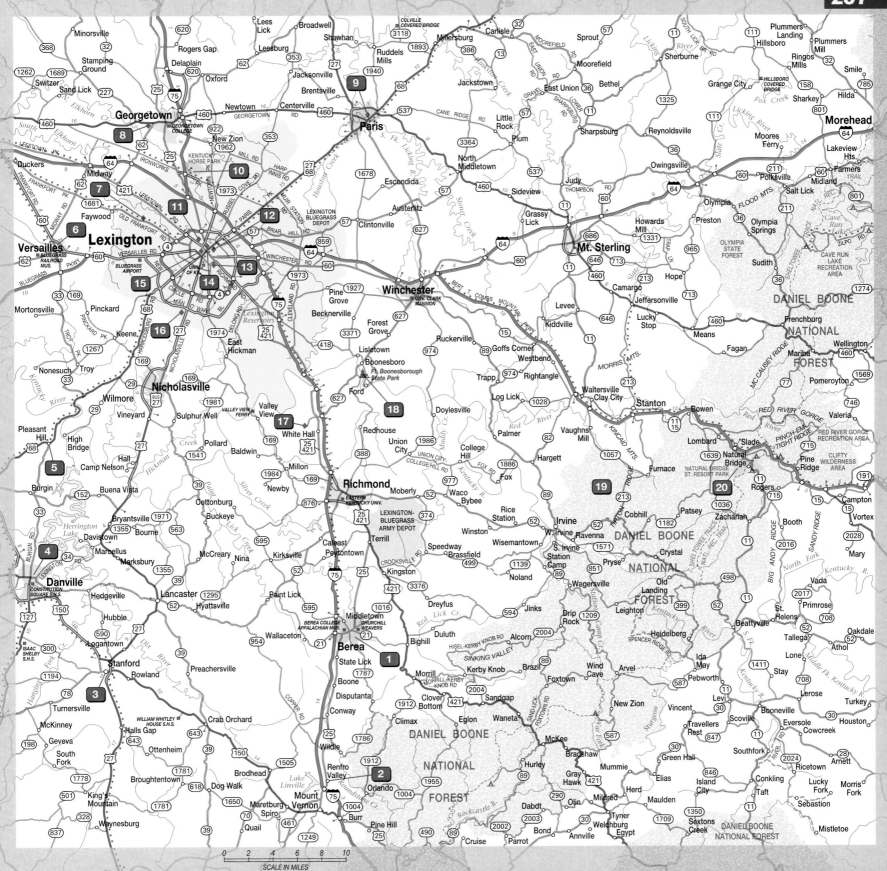

SCALE IN MILES

1. Bartlesville

Chamber of Commerce, 201 SW Keeler St. The city's notable architecture includes the 19-story, copper and glass **Price Tower,** designed by Frank Lloyd Wright, and the elaborate Japanese-style house called **Shin 'en Kan,** by Bruce Goff. The **Frank Phillips Home,** with ornate baths and imported woodwork, was built in 1909 by the founder of Phillips Petroleum. Visitors can learn about the oil industry at **Phillips Exhibit Hall** and view the **Nellie Johnstone Number One,** a reproduction of Oklahoma's first commercial gusher. *Admission charged for some attractions.*

2. Pioneer Woman Statue and Museum

701 Monument Rd., Ponca City. This 17-foot bronze sculpture of a bonneted female and her young son pays homage to the women who helped to settle the nation. The adjacent museum has exhibits relating to the era of westward expansion, and the nearby **Marland Mansion,** fashioned after a Florentine palazzo, is a 55-room extravaganza. *Admission charged for some attractions.*

3. Pawnee Bill Ranch

Rte. 64, Pawnee. After joining Buffalo Bill's Wild West Show as an interpreter for the Pawnee Indians, Gordon William Lillie became known as Pawnee Bill. His rambling ranch house is lavishly decorated, and other structures on the 483-acre site include a log cabin, blacksmith shop, and large barn.

4. Cherokee Strip Museum

2617 West First St., Perry. Exhibits at this museum recall the legendary 1893 land run and depict the rugged lifestyle of the homesteaders. Displays include a one-room schoolhouse, a sorghum mill, and an antique threshing machine.

5. Great Salt Plains State Park

Bird-watchers, hikers, hunters, and water-sports enthusiasts will find much to occupy them in, on, and around the vast Great Salt Plains Lake.

6. Sod House Museum

Rte. 8, near Cleo Springs. Featured here is Oklahoma's only extant "soddie," which was made in 1894. Typical of the primitive, make-do dwellings of the homesteaders, it was constructed with sod blocks of buffalo grass. The two-room house is furnished in turn-of-the-century style and preserved within a frame structure.

7. Red Rock Canyon State Park

A steep road leads to the floor of this canyon, named for its sun-burnished walls. There are campsites, picnic areas, a swimming pool, stream, and pond.

8. Wichita Mountains Wildlife Refuge

Fishing, camping, picnicking, 12 lakes, and 15 miles of hiking trails are all here in this vast wildlife refuge, which also includes a prairie-dog town and a scenic overlook from towering Mt. Scott.

9. Fort Sill

Rte. 277, Fort Sill. Now an army training center, the fort was established in 1869 by Lt. Gen. Philip Sheridan to protect American Indians; later it was used to aid settlers. Great historic leaders who came to this site, however, occasionally met with an unkind fate: Gen. William Tecumseh Sherman was almost killed by a band of Kiowa Indians, and Geronimo — who was incarcerated at the fort as a prisoner of war — died here and is buried in the Apache cemetery.

10. Wichita Falls

Convention and Visitors Bureau, Eighth St. and Lamar Ave. The 54-foot tiered falls north of town were constructed to replace those that were destroyed by a flood. The **Wichita Falls Museum and Art Center** features works of American artists, regional exhibits, and a planetarium. The **Kell House Museum,** built by a town founder in 1909, contains ornate woodwork and period furnishings, while the **Wichita Falls Area Fire and Police Museum** displays vintage vehicles along with Victorian firefighting and police memorabilia. *Admission charged for some attractions.*

11. Chisholm Trail Historical Museum

Junction Rtes. 81 and 70, Waurika. The trail is named for the trader Jesse Chisholm, who first opened the way for the fabled route along which great herds of cattle from Texas reached the railways in Kansas.

The museum features a slide show and exhibits that range from branding irons to a stained-glass map of the trail.

12. Fort Richardson State Historical Park

Off Rte. 199, Jacksboro. The history of this restored fort, originally constructed during the Indian wars, is traced at a museum in the post hospital. Other restorations include a powder magazine, bakery, and barracks. *Admission charged.*

13. Leonard Park

1000 West California St., Gainesville. The park features the **Frank Buck Zoo,** with some 200 animals, including ostriches, llamas, monkeys, peacocks, flamingos, and an elephant. The first jail in the area and a Civil War monument are also in the park.

14. Lake Texoma

Sprawled across the Texas-Oklahoma border, this large lake, surrounded by recreation areas, two state parks, and two wildlife refuges, features a variety of water sports, tennis courts, horseback riding, and a golf course. *Fee charged for some activities.*

15. Sam Rayburn House and Fort Inglish

Rte. 82, Bonham. In 1916 Sam Rayburn, Speaker of the U. S. House of Representatives for 17 years, built this house, which now holds a collection of memorabilia pertaining to his life. Nearby Ft. Inglish is a replica of an 1837 fort and stockade.

16. Beavers Bend State Park

In a wooded mountain setting, visitors can trek a 26-mile trail, ride horses, water-ski, swim, fish, camp, and examine the exhibits in the **Forest Heritage Center.** *Fee charged for some activities.*

17. Heavener Runestone State Park

On a huge upright stone slab is carved an inscription of Norse runes, or alphabet characters, dated between A.D. 600 and 900, leading some to believe that Norseman had reached the New World long before Columbus. There are also picnic sites, a visitor center, and a nature trail.

18. Fort Smith National Historic Site

Visitor Center, Roger Ave., Fort Smith. This 75-acre park, home to the 1817 fort, contains the restored courtroom of Isaac Parker, the "Hanging Judge," and a reproduc-

tion of the grim gallows on which 79 prisoners died. The **Old Fort Museum** contains regional artifacts and a 1920's pharmacy complete with a vintage soda fountain. *Admission charged.*

19. Sequoyah's Home Site

Off Rte. 101, near Sallisaw. On the grounds of these 10 wooded acres is a log cabin constructed in 1829 by a Cherokee named Sequoyah, for whom the giant sequoia tree is named. Among his achievements was the invention of the Cherokee alphabet. Sequoyah's one-room cabin, containing many of his personal belongings, is now located within a stone structure, where visitors can learn more about the life of this extraordinary man.

20. Spiro Mounds State Park

Spiro Mounds Rd., Spiro. The park features Spiro Indian mounds, which were erected for religious rites between the 7th and the 15th centuries. An on-site interpretive center gives further information about this ancient culture.

21. Robbers Cave State Park

Named for a cave where outlaws once hid, the park offers water sports and camping amid its 8,500 forested acres.

22. Seminole Nation Museum

524 South Wewoka Ave., Wewoka. Exhibits here include Seminole artifacts and displays interpreting the nation's tragic Trail of Tears forced march from Florida.

23. Pauls Valley

Chamber of Commerce, 112 East Paul St. Prehistoric Indian artifacts and pioneer exhibits are housed in the **Washita Valley Museum.** To the northwest lies Erin Springs, where visitors can tour the 1879 **Murray-Lindsay Mansion.**

24. Turner Falls Park

Oklahoma's most spectacular falls cascade 77 feet into a pool, which is a popular swimming spot. Hiking trails, picnic areas, campsites, and several caves are all within the 720-acre park. *Admission charged.*

25. Chickasaw National Recreation Area

Aficionados of the great outdoors flock to this 10,000-acre recreation area, which offers water sports, hiking trails, picnic areas, campgrounds, and natural history exhibits in the **Travertine Nature Center.**

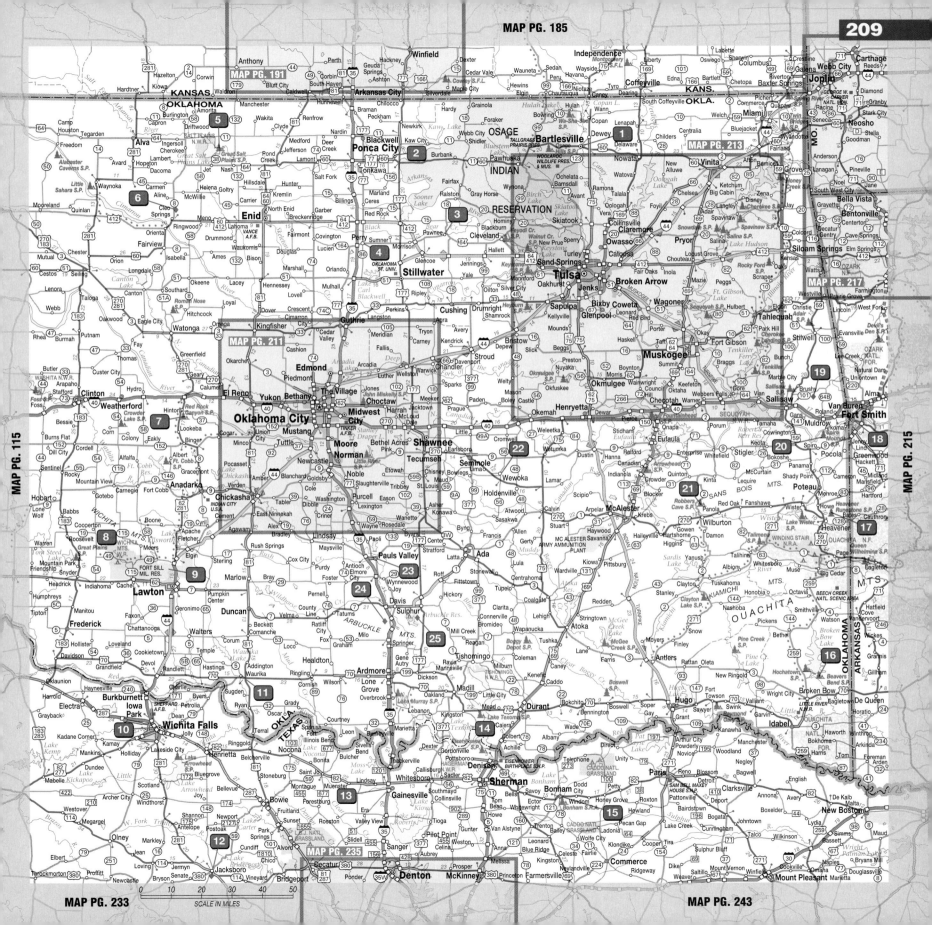

1. Chisholm Trail Museum

605 Zellers Ave., Kingfisher. This museum's collection includes items ranging from a log cabin and a chuck wagon to a Sioux ceremonial dress and a game bag that once belonged to Sitting Bull. The late Victorian–style **Governor Seay Mansion,** built in 1892, is located across the street.

2. Fort Reno

Off Sunset Dr., El Reno. Established during the Indian uprisings of the 1870's, the fort played a major role in the settlement of the territory. A few of the original buildings remain; soldiers and civilians alike were laid to rest in the post cemetery, as well as POW's from World War II.

3. Oklahoma National Stockyards

2500 Exchange Ave., Oklahoma City. Auctions for cattle, hogs, and sheep are held in this vast stockyard, one of the world's largest livestock markets.

4. Overholser Mansion

405 NW 15th St., Oklahoma City. Built by Henry Overholser, a pioneer entrepreneur who was called the Father of Oklahoma City, this 1903 Victorian mansion features original French and Oriental furnishings and a period doll collection.

5. Will Rogers Garden Exhibition Building and Horticultural Gardens

3400 NW 36th St., Oklahoma City. Seasonal flower shows with such varieties as orchids, mums, and roses are held in the exhibition building. The surrounding landscape boasts an arboretum, peony garden, and an azalea trail, along with four conservatories featuring cacti, succulents, and tropical plants.

6. Martin Park Nature Center

5000 West Memorial Rd., Oklahoma City. Nature trails lace through this 140-acre site, graced with creeks, prairies, and woodlands. A nature museum has displays pertaining to the wildlife that inhabits the center. Reservations are required for a guided tour. *Fee charged for tour.*

7. Oklahoma City Art Museum

3113 Pershing Blvd., Oklahoma City. There are more than 5,000 artworks in this museum's collection, with an emphasis on historical graphics and 20th-century American art. *Admission charged.*

8. National Cowboy Hall of Fame and Western Heritage Center

1700 NE 63rd St., Oklahoma City. In addition to housing three halls of fame, this site celebrates the Old West with displays of Western art and historic artifacts, as well as a depiction of an old-time street featuring a stagecoach depot, saloon, gold mine, and jail. *Admission charged.*

Hibiscus at the Myriad Botanical Gardens

9. Kirkpatrick Center

NE 52nd St. and Martin Luther King Ave., Oklahoma City. Tranquil Japanese gardens and an Oklahoma artists gallery are among the numerous attractions contained in this vast cultural complex. Other points of interest include the **Oklahoma Air Space Museum;** the **Red Earth Indian Center;** the **Kirkpatrick Planetarium;** the **Navy Gallery;** the **International Photography Hall of Fame and Museum;** and the **Omniplex Science Museum.** The nearby 180-acre **Oklahoma City Zoo** is home to some 2,000 animals, such as elephants, gorillas, and other primates; other facilities include a petting zoo, walk-through aviary, children's playground, and tram. A highlight here is the Aquaticus, which features a shark tank, dolphin and sea lion shows, and displays of marine life. *Admission charged.*

10. Oklahoma State Firefighters Museum

2716 NE 50th St., Oklahoma City. This museum's collection includes a replica of Oklahoma's first firehouse, built in 1869, and 18th-century firefighting equipment used by Ben Franklin, George Washington, and Paul Revere. *Admission charged.*

11. The 45th Infantry Division Museum

2145 NE 36th St., Oklahoma City. The state's military history — from Coronado's visit in 1541 through the Revolutionary and Civil wars, and up to the present — are examined in this museum. In addition to antique weaponry, several items taken from Hitler's apartment are on display, including copies of *Mein Kampf.*

12. State Capitol

2300 Lincoln Blvd., Oklahoma City. The state legislature convenes in this impressive neoclassical building, whose rotunda features a collection of portraits of distinguished Oklahomans. Also located in the capitol complex is the **State Museum of History,** where exhibits range from prehistoric displays to pioneer artifacts.

13. Harn Homestead Museum

313 NE 16th St., Oklahoma City. Homesteaded after the 1889 land run, this 10-acre site includes a two-story frame house built in 1904, a working farm and windmill, a three-story stone-and-cedar barn, an 1897 one-room schoolhouse, and shady picnic sites. *Admission charged.*

14. Oklahoma Heritage Center

201 NW 14th St., Oklahoma City. Located in a stately mansion that dates from 1917, this museum displays Meissen china, antique canes, American and European furnishings, and personal items belonging to a former owner, Robert Hefner, who was at various times a mayor, an oilman, and a state supreme court justice. *Admission charged.*

15. Myriad Botanical Gardens

Reno Ave. and Robinson St., Oklahoma City. The centerpiece of a revitalized business district, these botanical gardens comprise 17 acres that surround a beautiful sunken lake. Of special note is the **Crystal Bridge Tropical Conservatory,** which showcases exotic flowers and plants from around the world. *Admission charged.*

16. Norman

Chamber of Commerce, 115 East Gray St. Home to the 20,000-student **University of Oklahoma,** Norman also boasts two notable museums: the **Norman and Cleveland County Historical Museum** and the **Oklahoma Museum of Natural History.** The former, housed in a Queen Anne–style home replete with gables and a turret, depicts the affluent lifestyle of an early Oklahoma family; the latter contains a collection of some 5 million fossils, artifacts, and Greek and Roman antiquities.

17. Little River State Park

Set among rolling hills shaded by oak trees, 6,000-acre **Thunderbird Lake** is a popular place for water activities such as fishing, swimming, boating, sailboarding, and waterskiing. The surrounding park has a playground and facilities for hiking, archery, horseback riding, and camping. *Fee charged for some activities.*

18. Shawnee

Chamber of Commerce, 128 North Broadway. On the grounds of **St. Gregory College,** the **Mabee-Gerrer Museum of Art** has displays of contemporary European and American art, as well as artifacts from ancient civilizations. Feathery American Indian headdresses and intricate beadwork are among the items on view in the **Potawatomi Indian Museum.** The **Santa Fe Depot Museum** contains artifacts pertinent to the history of the county.

19. Museum of Pioneer History

719 Manvel Ave., Chandler. A doctor's office, the kitchen of a pioneer, a replica of a general store, and an old-fashioned printing press are among the displays in this museum that evoke the early days of the territories.

20. Guthrie

Chamber of Commerce, 202 West Harrison Ave. Once the state capital and an integral part of the 1889 Oklahoma land run, Guthrie features many historic buildings. The **State Capital Publishing Museum** originally housed the state's first newspaper, the *State Capital,* founded in 1889. The **Scottish Rite Masonic Temple,** considered to be the world's largest Masonic temple, is a multimillion-dollar Classic Revival structure with 149 stained-glass windows, gold doorknobs, and many other deluxe details. Funded by Andrew Carnegie, the **Carnegie Library** is the state's oldest existing library. Early pioneer days are portrayed at the adjacent **Oklahoma Territorial Museum,** where the focus is on the 1889 land run and the subsequent development of this "instant city." *Admission charged at temple.*

Oklahoma City Area Map

Kingfisher • Cimarron City • Cedar Valley • Guthrie • Meridian • Tryon • Agra • Carney • Chandler • Warwick • Midlothian

Cashion • Navina • Seward • Fallis • Bellow Cr.

OKLAHOMA TERRITORIAL MUS. • STATE CAPITAL PUBLISHING MUS. • SCOTTISH RITE MASONIC TEMPLE

Okarche • Waterloo • WATERLOO RD • LAZY E ARENA

Edmond • Arcadia • Luther • Wellston

Piedmont • Richland • EDMOND HIST. MUS. • ENTERPRISE SQUARE, USA

Calumet • DARLINGTON GAME BIRD HATCHERY

The Village • Nichols Hills • Jones

El Reno • CANADIAN COUNTY HISTORICAL MUSEUM • FOREMAN DR • SUNSET DR

Warr Acres • Yukon • Bethany • Woodlawn Park • Lake Overholser

Oklahoma City • Spencer • Forest Park • John Miskelly S.P. • Jacktown • McLoud • Meeker

Midwest City • Choctaw • Nicoma Park • Harrah • Meeker Lake • Aydelotte

Mustang • Del City • Smith Village • Valley Brook • TINKER AIR FORCE BASE • Dale • Shawnee

WILL ROGERS WORLD AIRPORT • MABEE-GERRER MUSEUM OF ART

Union City • Minco • Tuttle • Moore • Stanley Draper Lake • Shawnee Res. • Bethel Acres • POTAWATOMI INDIAN TRIBAL MUSEUM • SANTA FE DEPOT MUS.

Pocasset • Newcastle • LITTLE RIVER ST. PARK • Pink • Tecumseh

Norman • Hall Park • CLEVELAND CO. HIST. MUSEUM • UNIV. OF OKLAHOMA • OKLAHOMA MUS. OF NATURAL HISTORY • Lake Thunderbird • Brooksville

Amber • Blanchard • Goldsby • Noble • ROSE ROCK MUSEUM • Etowah • Macomb • Chisney

Verden • Chickasha • Middleberg • Cole • Washington • Slaughterville • Tribbey • Romulus

CHICKASHA ANTIQUE AUTO MUSEUM • GRADY COUNTY HIST. MUSEUM • Tabler • Dibble • Woody Chapel • Lexington • Purcell • Eason • Trousdale • Pearson

Norge • Criner • Payne • Wayne • Rosedale • Wanette • Asher

East Ninnekah • Alex • Bradley • Agawam

SCALE IN MILES 0 2 4 6 8 10

1. Eastern Trails Museum

215 West Illinois Ave., Vinita. Oklahoma history is explored at this museum through exhibits of American Indian and pioneer artifacts, items related to both world wars, and other regional memorabilia.

2. Pensacola Dam

Junction of Rtes. 82 and 28, Langley. In addition to its primary function as a source of electric power, the 43,500-acre **Grand Lake O' the Cherokees** (called Grand Lake) created by the Pensacola Dam is a popular resort area and an excellent spot for many kinds of water sports. Tours of the power plant are available.

3. Claremore

Chamber of Commerce, 419 West Will Rogers Blvd. A statue of the rope-twirling humorist stands outside the **Will Rogers Memorial,** where the entertainer's colorful life is depicted in dioramas, film clips, newsreels, and various memorabilia. The **Lynn Riggs Memorial** at **Rogers State College** pays tribute to the author of *Green Grow the Lilacs,* which became the hit Broadway musical *Oklahoma!* At the nearby **J. M. Davis Gun Museum** is an extensive collection of firearms dating from the 1300's to the Vietnam War era. *Admission charged at Will Rogers Memorial.*

4. Will Rogers Birthplace

Off Rte. 169, Oologah. Rogers was fond of saying that he was born in a log cabin, and the truth of that statement is confirmed here. Abounding with personal mementos, the house where the cowboy humorist-actor was born in 1879 may be toured by visitors.

5. Woolaroc Ranch and Museum

Rte. 123, near Bartlesville. Bison and longhorns graze the grounds of this 3,500-acre site, once the property of Phillips Petroleum founder, Frank Phillips. There are several ponds; a wildlife preserve; Phillips' roomy lodge, where he entertained heads of state and movie stars; nature trails; and a museum filled with a Southwestern art collection and items of American Indian and pioneer lore. *Admission charged.*

6. Pawhuska

Chamber of Commerce, 114 West Main St. Visitors to the **Osage County Historical Museum** will find an eclectic collection that features a chuck wagon and Western paraphernalia; American Indian and pioneer artifacts; displays pertaining to the oil industry; and documents relating to the first Boy Scout troop in America, organized here in 1909. The **Osage Tribal Museum** houses an assortment of displays reflecting the culture of the Osage nation, including ribbons, beads, treaties, paintings, dance regalia, and a trading post.

7. Drummond Home

305 North Price St., Hominy. Frederick Drummond, a successful local trader and rancher, built this three-story Victorian mansion in 1905. The sandstone house, done up with balconies, dormers, and a square central tower, contains most of its original furnishings.

8. Thomas Gilcrease Museum

1400 Gilcrease Museum Rd., Tulsa. The museum's founder, Thomas Gilcrease, was part Creek Indian. Gilcrease amassed a fortune and collected works by Winslow Homer, Whistler, Sargent, Audubon, Remington, Russell, and Catlin — all of which are among the nearly 300,000 paintings, rare books, artifacts, and documents displayed here today. *Admission charged.*

9. Tulsa Zoological Park

5701 East 36th St., Tulsa. Occupying 70 acres of **Mohawk Park** and home to some 250 animal species, this zoo includes a simulated African savanna, where buffalos, zebras, giraffes, and antelopes roam; the Chimpanzee Connection, with monkeys in both indoor and outdoor environments; and sea lion habitats, where visitors can watch the aquatic mammals feed. The 800-acre **Oxley Nature Center** and the **Robert J. LaFortune North American Living Museum** are other attractions in the park. *Admission charged for some attractions.*

10. Fenster Museum of Jewish Art

1223 East 17th Pl., Tulsa. Located in the **B'nai Emunah Synagogue,** this museum has the Southwest's most extensive collection of Judaica, including a 19th-century Polish Torah crown and other artifacts, some of which date back more than 4,000 years.

11. Philbrook Museum of Art

2727 South Rockford Rd., Tulsa. Set in an opulent Italian Renaissance–style villa surrounded by 23 acres of formal and informal gardens, this museum has a permanent collection of American, European, Oriental, African, and American Indian art. Lectures, films, and traveling exhibits are regularly scheduled. *Admission charged.*

12. Woodward Park and Tulsa Garden Center

21st St. and Peoria Ave., Tulsa. Gardens of azaleas, roses, irises, and fragrant herbs, as well as an arboretum and conservatory, are spread across this park's 40 wooded acres. At the Tulsa Garden Center, part of which is housed in a 1919 mansion, visitors can enjoy flower shows and seasonal events.

13. Oral Roberts University

7777 South Lewis Ave., Tulsa. From atop a 200-foot prayer tower there is a sweeping view of the campus, with its diamond-shaped library, sports center, symphony hall, and chapel. A film entitled "Journey Through the Bible" can be seen in the Healing Outreach Visitor Center.

14. Creek Council House Museum

106 West Sixth St., Okmulgee. Erected in 1878, this handsomely restored house served as the capitol for the Creek Indians, who formed a government patterned after that of the United States. At this site, where their supreme court and legislature once convened, visitors today can see displays linked to Creek history and culture.

15. Five Civilized Tribes Museum

Agency Hill on Honor Heights Dr., Muskogee. The name of the museum makes reference to the Cherokee, Chickasaw, Choctaw, Creek, and Seminole tribes, labeled by the U.S. government as the Five Civilized Tribes. With costume and artifact exhibits, an art gallery, and a library, this complex examines their varied histories and cultures. *Admission charged.*

16. Greenleaf State Park

The focal point of this lovely state park is its 930-acre lake, which provides visitors with a fine beach, boat rentals, and excellent fishing. The hiking trail that makes a loop around the lake affords magnificent vistas. A swimming pool, children's playground, and campsites are among other park facilities.

17. Tenkiller Ferry Lake

This crystal-clear, 12,900-acre lake has bluffs, coves, and woods along its shoreline, where fishing camps, boat docks, and 14 recreation areas offer beaches, bathhouses, playgrounds, and picnicking and camping facilities. *Admission charged.*

18. Murrell Home and Nature Trail

Off Rte. 82, Park Hill. In 1845 George Murrell, a longtime friend of the Cherokees, built this fine home with high ceilings, a fireplace in each room, and period furnishings. Here too is a ¾-mile wheelchair-accessible nature trail, which offers special features for the blind. *Admission charged.*

19. Cherokee Heritage Center

Willis Rd., Tahlequah. Attractions in this center include the **Cherokee National Museum,** which illustrates the history of the tribe. There are also re-creations of two villages — one from the 17th century and another from the 19th — where Cherokees demonstrate traditional crafts, and an amphitheater, where their tragic forced march in 1838–39, known as the Trail of Tears, is dramatized. *Admission charged.*

20. Fort Gibson Military Park

110 East Ash Ave., Fort Gibson. The standing fort in this 55-acre park is part reconstruction and part restoration of a military outpost established in 1824. Within the stockade are barracks, guardhouses, and blockhouses. The nearby **Fort Gibson National Cemetery,** dating back to 1868, is one of the 13 original national cemeteries.

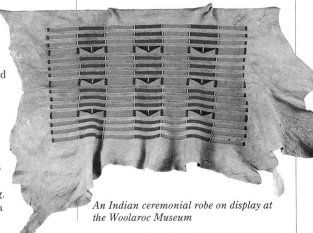

An Indian ceremonial robe on display at the Woolaroc Museum

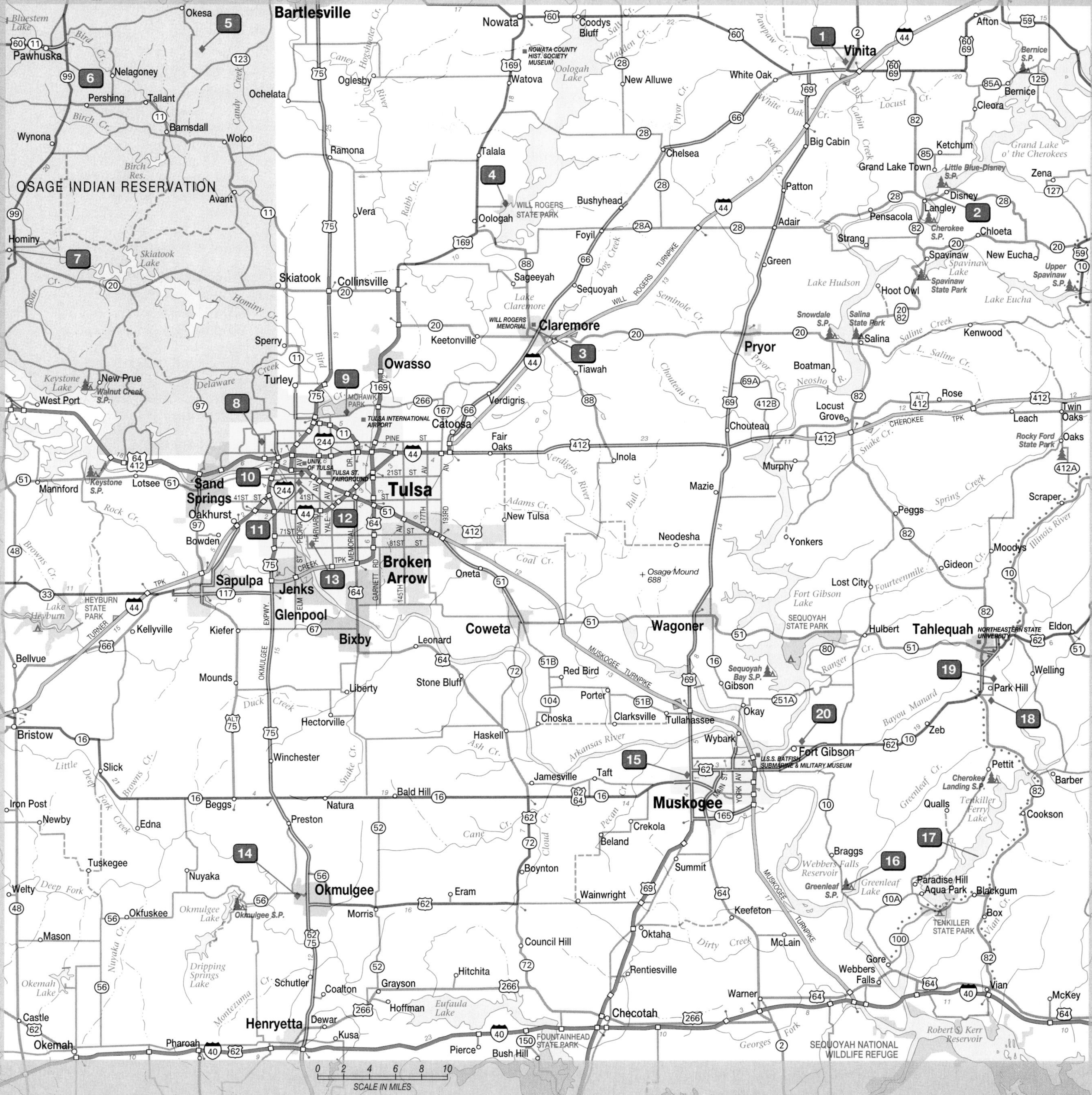

Bluestem Lake
Okesa
5
Bartlesville
Nowata
Coodys Bluff
60
2
44
Afton
59
15
60
11
Pawhuska
NOWATA COUNTY HIST. SOCIETY MUSEUM
60
69
1
Vinita
60
69
Bernice S.P.
125
99
6
Nelagoney
123
Oglesby
75
Watova
169
New Alluwe
28
White Oak
69
Big Cabin
85A
Bernice
Pershing
Tallant
Ochelata
Caney
Hogshooter Cr.
Salt Cr.
Madden Cr.
22
66
Cleora
82
Ketchum
85
11
Barnsdall
Wolco
Ramona
Vera
Talala
Chelsea
28
Patton
Grand Lake Town
Grand Lake o' the Cherokees
Zena
127
Wynona
Birch Cr.
Birch Res.
75
Ologah Lake
Pryor Cr.
66
28
Disney
Little Blue-Disney S.P.
OSAGE INDIAN RESERVATION
Avant
11
4
Bushyhead
44
Adair
Langley
2
28
99
Hominy
Skiatook Lake
169
Oologah
WILL ROGERS STATE PARK
Foyil
28A
Green
Pensacola
82
Cherokee S.P.
Chloeta
20
Hominy Cr.
Skiatook
Collinsville
20
88
Sageeyah
66
WILL ROGERS TURNPIKE
Strang
Spavinaw
New Eucha
Upper Spavinaw S.P.
20
59
10
Briar Cr.
7
20
Sequoyah
Seminole Cr.
Lake Hudson
Spavinaw Lake
Spavinaw State Park
Lake Eucha
Sperry
Lake Claremore
WILL ROGERS MEMORIAL
Claremore
20
Hoot Owl
Snowdale S.P.
Salina State Park
Kenwood
West Port
Keystone Lake
New Prue
Walnut Creek S.P.
11
Turley
Owasso
9
169
Keetonville
20
44
3
Tiawah
Pryor
Boatman
Salina
L. Saline Cr.
Saline Creek
8
97
Delaware Creek
75
266
167
66
Verdigris
88
69A
Neosho R.
Rose
ALT 412
412
Twin Oaks
51
Mannford
Keystone S.P.
Lotsee
51
Sand Springs
10
TULSA INTERNATIONAL AIRPORT
MOHAWK PARK
Catoosa
Chouteau Cr.
69
412B
Locust Grove
82
12
CHEROKEE TPK
Leach
412
412A
64
412
244
11
PINE ST
266
Fair Oaks
412
23
Inola
Chouteau
Oaks
Rocky Ford State Park
UNIV OF TULSA
TULSA ST FAIRGROUND
21ST ST
44
Tulsa
Verdigris River
Scraper
48
Oakhurst
10
244
Sand Springs
Bowden
97
11
12
51
Mazie
Murphy
Peggs
Moodys
Illinois River
Browns Cr.
11
71ST
PEORIA AV
HARVARD
YALE
MEMORIAL
177TH
64
Broken Arrow
412
New Tulsa
Neodesha
Yonkers
82
Gideon
10
33
Lake Heyburn
HEYBURN STATE PARK
44
TURNER TPK
117
Sapulpa
Jenks
13
64
GARNETT RD
81ST ST
145TH
Oneta
51
Coal Cr.
Adams Cr.
Osage Mound 688
Fort Gibson Lake
Lost City
Fourteenmile Cr.
Tahlequah
NORTHEASTERN STATE UNIVERSITY
62
Eldon
51
Kellyville
Kiefer
66
Glenpool
67
Bixby
Leonard
64
Mounds
Liberty
Stone Bluff
72
51B
Red Bird
Porter
16
Muskogee Turnpike
Coweta
Wagoner
51
SEQUOYAH STATE PARK
Sequoyah Bay S.P.
Gibson
251A
Hulbert
19
Park Hill
Welling
18
Bellvue
OKMULGEE EXPWY
75
ALT 75
Hectorville
Haskell
104
Choska
51B
Clarksville
Tullahassee
Okay
Okmulgee Turnpike
20
Zeb
62
10
Pettit
82
Barber
Bristow
16
Slick
Winchester
Jamesville
Taft
62
64
Wybark
165
Fort Gibson
U.S.S. BATFISH SUBMARINE & MILITARY MUSEUM
10
Qualls
Cherokee Landing S.P.
Tenkiller Ferry Lake
Cookson
Iron Post
Newby
Edna
Beggs
Bald Hill
Natura
16
Cane Cr.
Pecan Cr.
62
64
15
Muskogee
Braggs
17
Little Deep Fork Cr.
21
Preston
52
72
Crekola
Beland
Webbers Falls Reservoir
Greenleaf S.P.
Qualls
Tuskegee
14
Nuyaka
56
Morris
Boynton
Wainwright
69
Summit
64
Keefeton
Greenleaf Lake
16
Paradise Hill Aqua Park
Blackgum
Welty
Deep Fork
48
Okfuskee
Okmulgee Lake
Okmulgee S.P.
56
Okmulgee
Eram
75
Council Hill
Oktaha
McLain
Muskogee Turnpike
10A
Box
Mason
62
75
52
Hitchita
72
Rentiesville
TENKILLER STATE PARK
100
Gore
Okemah Lake
Schutler
Coalton
Grayson
266
Hoffman
Eufaula Lake
Warner
64
Webbers Falls
64
Vian
40
McKey
Castle
62
Okemah
Pharoah
40
62
Dewar
Henryetta
Kusa
23
Pierce
Bush Hill
40
150
FOUNTAINHEAD STATE PARK
Checotah
266
10
2
Robert S. Kerr Reservoir
SEQUOYAH NATIONAL WILDLIFE REFUGE
64
10

0 2 4 6 8 10
SCALE IN MILES

1. Prairie Grove Battlefield State Park

Rte. 62 East, Prairie Grove. This 130-acre park commemorates the Civil War battle on December 7, 1862, in which 2,500 troops were killed, wounded, or declared missing. The conflict is recalled with a monument, artifacts, audiovisual and living-history presentations, and guided tours of a re-created wartime village.

2. Van Buren Historic District

Chamber of Commerce, Van Buren Frisco Depot, 813 Main St. A 10-block restoration at the site of an 1800's steamboat landing and stagecoach stop includes shops; the Albert Pike Schoolhouse, where the poet, writer, and Civil War general taught in 1883; and the Italian villa–style Crawford County Courthouse, which is still in use.

3. Old Washington Historic State Park

Rte. 4, Washington. In this 1820's village are reconstructions of a blacksmith's shop where Jim Bowie's famous knife was made and a tavern reportedly visited by both Sam Houston and Davy Crockett. Other sites include the Confederate State Capitol and Greek Revival and Victorian homes. Not far from here is **Hope,** the hometown of President Clinton. *Admission charged at park.*

4. Texarkana

Chamber of Commerce, 819 State Line Ave. Built with money won in a poker game in 1885, the **Ace of Clubs House** is a 22-sided Victorian home furnished in a variety of decors. At the **Texarkana Historical Museum,** housed in an 1879 building listed on the National Register of Historic Places, the area's development especially as an agricultural and timber center is examined. **Atlanta State Park** offers excellent fishing, waterskiing, and bird watching at **Lake Wright Patman.** *Admission charged.*

5. Arkansas Oil and Brine Museum

Rte. 7, Smackover. Giant antique derricks, a working oil well, and other exhibits chroni-cle the history and impact of the petroleum and brine industry on this area, which was the site of a 1920's oil boom.

6. Camden

Chamber of Commerce, 141 Jackson St. SW. Here the **McCollum-Chidester House Museum,** a stagecoach stop built in 1847, was occupied by both Confederate and Union forces; bullet holes are visible in the upstairs walls. The nearby **Reader Railroad,** the nation's oldest all-steam standard-gauge railroad, offers 1½-hour trips through the countryside. *Admission charged.*

7. Winterville Mounds State Park

Rte. 1, near Greenville. Ancient artifacts, jewelry, pottery, and 13 mounds built as far back as 2,000 years ago by Mississippi-area inhabitants are found at this 40-acre site. *Admission charged.*

8. Arkansas Post National Memorial

Rte. 169, near Gillett. Founded in 1686 at the confluence of the White, Arkansas, and Mississippi rivers, this post was the lower Mississippi Valley's first permanent European settlement and the first capital of the Arkansas Territory. The memorial features interpretive trails and a replica of a 1783 Spanish fort.

9. Stuttgart Agricultural Museum

921 East Fourth St., Stuttgart. Dubbed the Rice and Duck Capital of the World, the town of Stuttgart was founded by German immigrants. The museum contains collections of rice-farming machinery, guns, and decoy and mounted ducks. A re-created village includes a doctor's office, a toy store, a post office, and a jail.

10. Helena

Chamber of Commerce, 111 Hickory Hill Dr. Mark Twain wrote, "Helena occupies one of the prettiest situations on the Mississippi." In the Civil War the town was an important Union supply depot and the scene of a Confederate defeat on July 4, 1863. The **Confederate Cemetery** contains a monument and about 100 graves. **Phillips County Museum** displays Indian and military artifacts, including the bullet that killed the South's Gen. Thomas Hindman. Guided tours are offered of the town's antebellum, Victorian, and Edwardian homes; **Estevan Hall,** built in 1826, is one of Arkansas's oldest abodes. *Fee charged for tours.*

11. Delta Blues Museum

114 Delta Ave., Clarksdale. The Mississippi Delta was the birthplace of the Delta blues and home to prominent musicians, including W. C. Handy, Muddy Waters, and John Lee Hooker. The museum features recordings, musical instruments, videotapes, books, and memorabilia.

12. Greenwood

Chamber of Commerce, 402 Rte. 82 Bypass. The **Cottonlandia Museum** spotlights the history of the Mississippi Delta from 10,000 B.C. to the present. At **Florewood River Plantation,** costumed guides conduct tours and perform period tasks in 25 authentically furnished buildings on a re-created 1850's cotton plantation. *Admission charged.*

13. Historic Old Grenada

Chamber of Commerce, 701 Sunset Dr. A self-guided tour takes visitors to a plantation, Confederate cemetery, and 27 homes and sites from Mississippi's antebellum past. Many recreational activities are available at **Grenada Lake,** including boating, camping, fishing, interpretive programs, swimming, and waterskiing.

14. Oxford

Chamber of Commerce, 399 West Jackson Ave. **Rowan Oak,** the Greek Revival home of writer William Faulkner, contains original furnishings, memorabilia, and the outline of the Pulitzer Prize–winning novel *A Fable,* which Faulkner sketched on his office walls. Exhibits at the **University Museums,** located on the campus of the **University of Mississippi,** range from Greek and Roman antiquities to Southern folk art.

15. Arkansas State University Museum

Aggie and Caraway Rds., Jonesboro. This university museum focuses on natural and regional history, with displays of ancient effigy pots, arrowheads, prehistoric mastodon and llama bones, and a reconstructed town. Other collections include decorative glass and U.S. military memorabilia.

16. Reelfoot Lake State Resort Park

This 14-mile-long lake — an excellent spot to fish for crappie and largemouth bass — was created by earthquakes in 1811–12. In the spring and summer, boat excursions take visitors through expanses of waterlilies and giant cypress and, come December, bus tours feature the area's wildlife, which includes wintering ducks and bald eagles. *Fee charged for boat cruise and bus tour.*

17. Hunter-Dawson State Historic Site

101 New Dawson Rd., New Madrid. This two-story home with white clapboard siding, green shutters, and long rear porches was built in 1859–60. Surrounded by giant oak and gum trees, it is a blend of Italianate and Greek Revival styles, typical of antebellum Missouri. The rooms contain many of their original Rococo Revival and Eastlake furnishings. *Admission charged.*

18. Mingo National Wildlife Refuge

Some 21,676 acres of marshland and bottomland hardwood forest constitute this wildlife refuge, which is a rich feeding ground for waterfowl migrating along the Mississippi Flyway. Visitors can observe these seasonal birds by car, on hiking or horseback-riding trails, by canoe, or on a mile-long boardwalk. *Admission charged.*

19. Ozark Folk Center State Park

Rte. 382, Mountain View. This 50-building complex, where craftsmen demonstrate traditional skills such as wood carving and weaving, keeps alive the heritage of the Ozarks. Folk music and dance performances are held in a 1,000-seat auditorium nightly except Sunday. *Admission charged.*

20. Blanchard Springs Caverns

The caverns can be explored on the easy half-mile Dripstone Trail; other spectacular calcite formations can be seen on a longer trail with 700 steps. The recreation area boasts a spring producing 7,000 gallons of water per minute. *Admission charged.*

21. Wolf House

Rte. 5, Norfork. Built about 1825, this two-story log structure served as a county courthouse, post office, residence, and trading post. Inside the house, visitors will find pioneer artifacts, early medical instruments, a pre–Civil War kitchen, and a re-created courtroom. *Admission charged.*

22. Laura Ingalls Wilder–Rose Wilder Lane House and Museum

Rte. A, near Mansfield. Guided tours are conducted at the home of the author of *Little House on the Prairie.* The museum next door displays editions of her books, original manuscripts, and family belongings that include those of her daughter Rose, who was also an author. *Admission charged.*

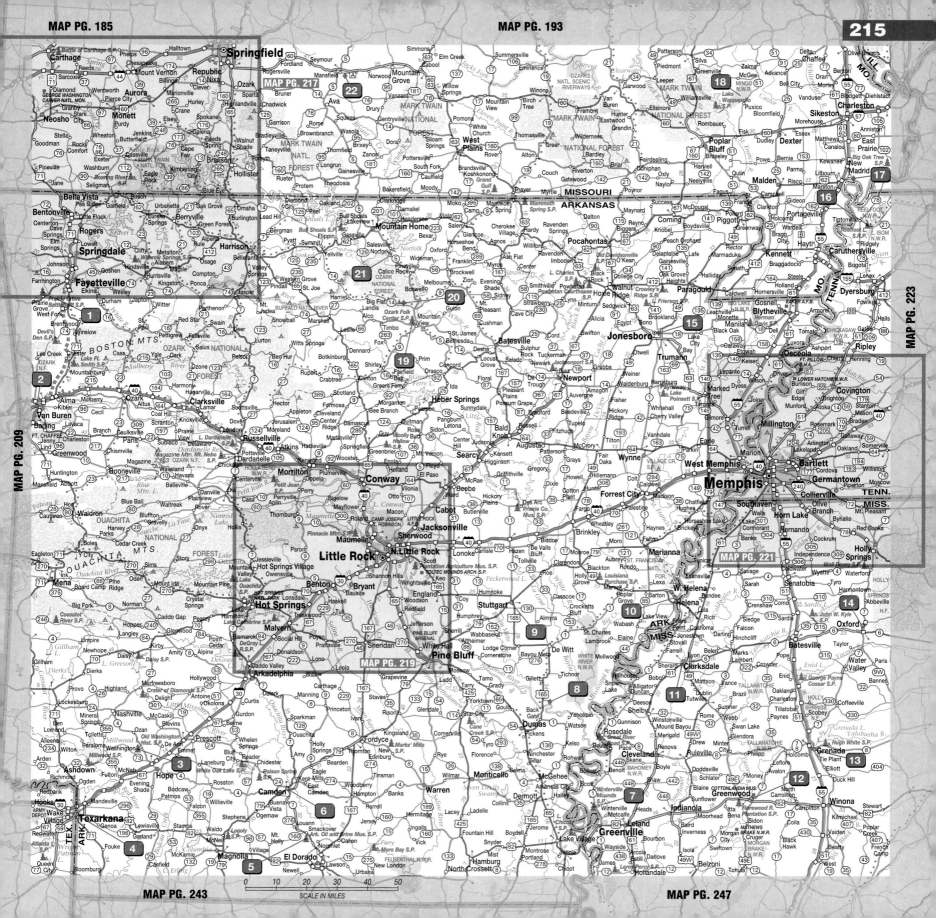

1. Joplin

Convention and Visitors Bureau, 303 East Third St. Although named for a minister, Joplin was a rowdy mining camp in the 1870's. From 1890 to 1940 some 50 to 80 percent of the country's zinc and lead was produced in this area. The history of the local mining industry is recalled at the **Tri-State Mineral Museum** in Schifferdecker Park. The **Dorothea B. Hoover Historical Museum** emphasizes the Victorian era with displays of period furnishings, cut glass, antique toys, and even a small circus. The work of Thomas Hart Benton, an American painter who died in 1975, is exhibited in the **Municipal Building,** while exquisite furniture and artwork dating from the 13th century are on display at the **Post Memorial Art Reference Library,** whose interior resembles a 16th-century English hall.

2. George Washington Carver National Monument

Off Rte. V, Diamond. Born a slave, Carver later became an eminent teacher, humanitarian, agronomist, and botanist who perfected 400 by-products from peanuts and sweet potatoes. This national monument encompasses Carver's boyhood home and a museum with audiovisual presentations explaining his work. A trail leads visitors past his birthplace, his foster family's restored 1881 house, and a cemetery, and continues on to the springs and forest where he played as a youth. *Admission charged.*

3. Neosho National Fish Hatchery

520 East Park St., Neosho. This is one of the nation's oldest federal fish hatcheries still in operation, producing more than 300,000 rainbow trout fingerlings per year. The site's water comes from four springs, together supplying about 1,400 gallons per minute. Picnic facilities are available.

4. Fayetteville

Chamber of Commerce, 123 West Mountain St. This resort city in the Ozark Mountains is home to the **Arkansas Air Museum,** which features a variety of antique aircraft

and engines. The **University Museum** on the Fayetteville campus of the **University of Arkansas** exhibits quartz crystals and pressed glass, along with zoological, anthropological, and prehistoric artifacts. The 1853 Greek Revival **Headquarters House,** containing period furnishings and Civil War relics, served at various times as a Confederate and a Union command post.

5. Shiloh Museum

118 West Johnson Ave., Springdale. This highly rated museum traces the region's agricultural heritage and exhibits a large collection of American Indian artifacts. Occupying an entire block of the **Shiloh Historic District,** the facility encompasses six buildings — four of them relocated to this site — including a 19th-century log cabin, doctor's office, residence, and store.

6. Withrow Springs State Park

Hiking trails lead through 786 acres of scenic wilderness in this state park, whose attractions include a 100-foot cave with an inaccessible underground stream and a 150-foot bluff overlooking the War Eagle River. Camping and canoeing are popular here, and there's fine fishing for perch, catfish, bream, and bass. *Admission charged.*

7. Rogers Historical Museum

322 South Second St., Rogers. Partially housed in the 1895 brick Hawkins House, replete with Victorian furnishings, this museum features exhibits on local history. The Key Wing contains turn-of-the-century building-front replicas of a bank, barber shop, and general store. The Attic offers hands-on displays for children.

8. Pea Ridge National Military Park

Rte. 62, Garfield. On a marked 7-mile auto route or a 10-mile hiking trail, visitors can retrace a Civil War battle that took place here in March 1862, which was decisive in winning Missouri for the Union. Situated in the park's 4,278 acres of rugged bluffs and valleys is the **Elkhorn Tavern,** a strategic location in the conflict. *Admission charged.*

9. Roaring River State Park

This 3,400-acre wilderness park features Roaring River Spring, which surges into trout hatchery ponds, a river stocked with trout, hiking trails, and naturalist programs. The **Sugar Camp Road Scenic Drive** through nearby **Mark Twain National Forest** passes by limestone outcroppings, oak-canopied corridors, and a log cabin.

10. Eureka Springs

Chamber of Commerce, 81 Kingshighway. Perched on a mountainside, Eureka Springs has been a renowned resort and health spa since the 1800's. Mt. Oberammergau's Great Passion Play, staged throughout the summer in a 4,100-seat amphitheater, has generated a **Bible Museum, Sacred Arts Center,** a **New Holy Land** re-creation, and a Christ of the Ozarks statue seven stories tall. **Eureka Springs Historic District** encompasses the downtown area and many Victorian homes, including **Rosalie House,** a flamboyant blend of Queen Anne and Carpenter Gothic architectures. Other attractions include **Hammond Museum of Bells,** with more than 1,000 antique bells; the instruments and toy animations of the **Miles Musical Museum;** the **Castle and Museum at Inspiration Point,** an unusual rock home in a magnificent natural setting; and **Eureka Springs Historical Museum,** situated in an 1889 stone house. *Admission charged for some attractions.*

11. Berryville

Tourist Information Center, Rte. 62E. The **Saunders Memorial Museum** maintains one of the nation's largest private gun collections, including firearms owned by Jesse James, Wild Bill Hickok, and Billy the Kid. **Carroll County Heritage Center,** in an 1880 courthouse, exhibits an early funeral parlor, moonshine still, clocks, and miniature trains. *Admission charged.*

12. Parker-Hickman Farmstead

Off Rte. 7, near Jasper. Listed on the National Register of Historic Places, this farm is one of the oldest in the region and chronicles 150 years of Ozark history. A hand-hewn red-cedar log residence, built about 1840, exhibits such skillful workmanship as a curved cornice and a tongue-and-groove flooring. Trails link the farm to other local historic sites. *Admission charged.*

13. Mystic Caverns

Situated in one of the most scenic sections of the Ozarks in Arkansas, these caverns can be explored by guided tour. Highlights include a 35-foot formation that resembles a pipe organ and a spectacular eight-story crystal dome. **Dogpatch USA** is located nearby. *Fee charged for tour.*

14. Ralph Foster Museum

College of the Ozarks, Point Lookout. This eclectic museum displays some 750,000 items, including President Grant's rolltop

desk, Tom Mix's saddle, Doc Holliday's suit, and Bat Masterson's gold-handled sword-cane. There are also collections of Kewpie dolls, coins, firearms, and American Indian artifacts. *Admission charged.*

15. Silver Dollar City

Off Rte. 76, west of Branson. This combination pioneer settlement and old-time theme park is the largest attraction in the Ozarks. More than 100 artisans demonstrate a variety of crafts, while musicians perform on fiddles, dulcimers, and other traditional instruments. Beneath the park, one of Missouri's deepest caverns, **Marvel Cave,** has an entrance room as big as the Astrodome and, 505 feet below the surface, a 70-foot waterfall. *Admission charged.*

16. Shepherd of the Hills Homestead and Outdoor Theater

Rte. 76, Branson. This was the setting for Harold Bell Wright's *Shepherd of the Hills,* written at Inspiration Point. Attractions include the main character's cabin, with its original furnishings; Inspiration Tower; and an operating gristmill and sawmill. Visitors can also watch craftsmen at work and view nightly summer reenactments of the story in an amphitheater. South on Rte. 76, a host of theaters offer country music and comedy shows. *Admission charged.*

17. Wilson's Creek National Battlefield

Rtes. ZZ and 182, Republic. At this site films and lighted maps interpret the first major Civil War battle fought west of the Mississippi River. Self-guiding auto routes and trails lead to **Bloody Hill** and **Ray House,** used as a Confederate field hospital during the engagement.

18. Springfield

Convention and Visitors Bureau, 3315 East Battlefield Rd. The city's natural and historic attractions include Buena Vista's **Exotic Animal Paradise,** where approximately 3,000 wild animals and rare birds can be seen along a 9-mile drive; the **History Museum,** located in a restored 1892 Queen Anne–style mansion with hand-carved woodwork, period furnishings, and 19th-century china; **Springfield National Cemetery,** one of the few containing the remains of both Confederate and Union soldiers; and **Fantastic Caverns,** among Missouri's largest caves and once the site of a speakeasy and a country music theater. *Admission charged for some attractions.*

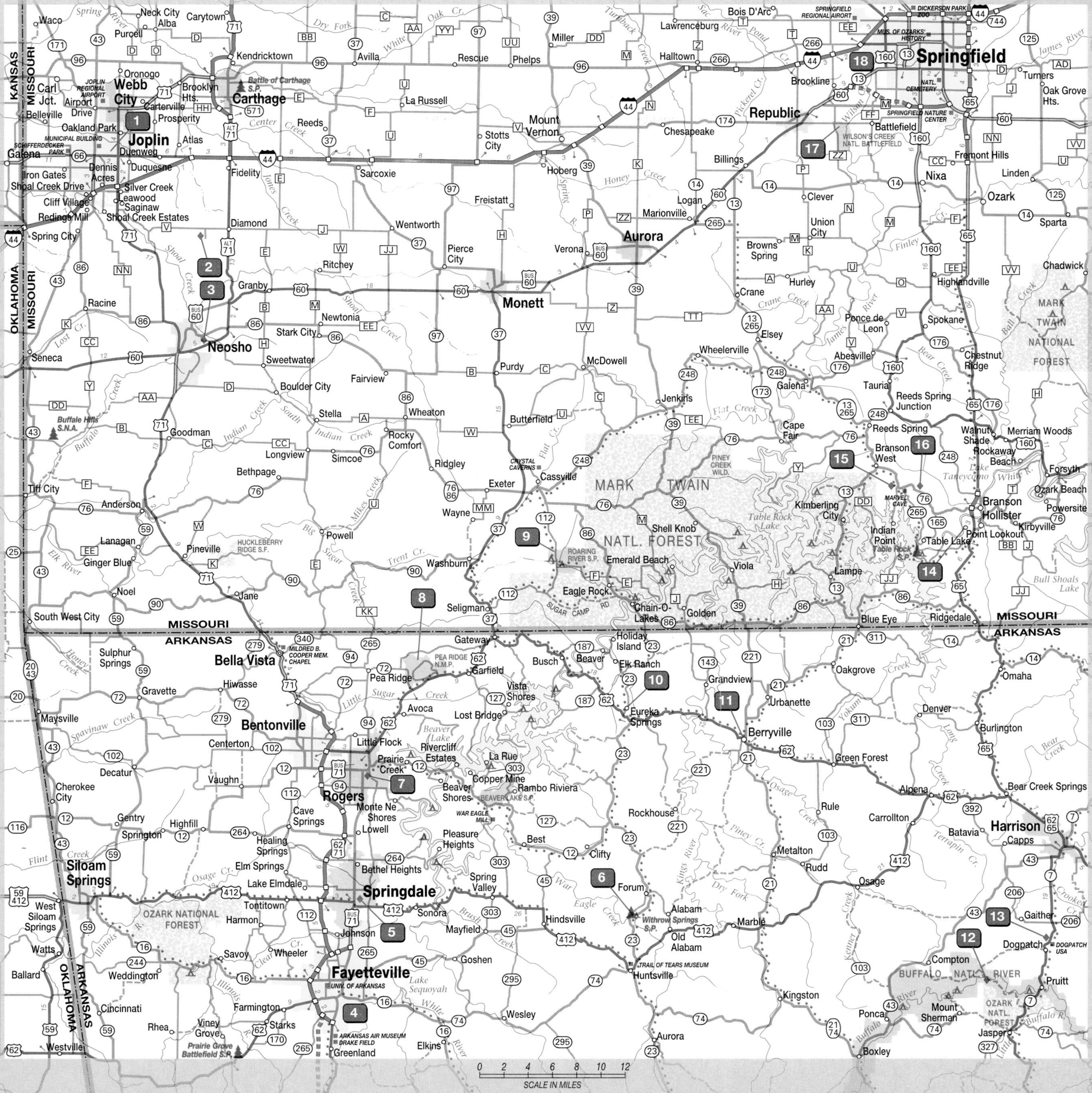

KANSAS
MISSOURI
OKLAHOMA
MISSOURI
ARKANSAS
OKLAHOMA
ARKANSAS
Waco
Neck City
Alba
Carytown
Purcell
Kendricktown
Avilla
Rescue
Phelps
Miller
Lawrenceburg
Bois D'Arc
Halltown
Brookline
Springfield
SPRINGFIELD REGIONAL AIRPORT
DICKERSON PARK ZOO
MUS. OF OZARKS' HISTORY
NATL. CEMETERY
SPRINGFIELD NATURE CENTER
Turners
Oak Grove Hts.
Oronogo
Carl Jct.
Webb City
JOPLIN REGIONAL AIRPORT
Airport Drive
Belleville
Carterville
Prosperity
Brooklyn Hts.
Battle of Carthage S.P.
Carthage
La Russell
Reeds
Mount Vernon
Stotts City
Republic
Chesapeake
Battlefield
WILSON'S CREEK NATL. BATTLEFIELD
Oakland Park
MUNICIPAL BUILDING
SCHIFFERDECKER PARK
Galena
Joplin
Atlas
Duenweg
Duquesne
Dennis Acres
Iron Gates
Shoal Creek Drive
Silver Creek
Leawood
Saginaw
Cliff Village
Redings Mill
Shoal Creek Estates
Spring City
Fidelity
Sarcoxie
Hoberg
Billings
Fremont Hills
Nixa
Linden
Ozark
Clever
Logan
Marionville
Freistatt
Diamond
Wentworth
Union City
Sparta
Aurora
Verona
Browns Spring
Pierce City
Ritchey
Granby
Monett
Racine
Newtonia
Stark City
Neosho
Seneca
Sweetwater
Crane
Hurley
Highlandville
Chadwick
MARK TWAIN NATIONAL FOREST
Spokane
Ponce de Leon
Elsey
Wheelerville
McDowell
Purdy
Boulder City
Fairview
Abesville
Chestnut Ridge
Galena
Tauria
Reeds Spring Junction
Jenkins
Buffalo Hills S.N.A.
Stella
Wheaton
Goodman
Rocky Comfort
Butterfield
Cape Fair
Reeds Spring
Walnut Shade
Merriam Woods
Rockaway Beach
Forsyth
Branson West
Longview
Simcoe
Bethpage
Ridgley
CRYSTAL CAVERNS
Cassville
PINEY CREEK WILD.
MARK TWAIN NATL. FOREST
Tiff City
Exeter
Wayne
Anderson
Kimberling City
Table Rock Lake
MARVEL CAVE
Branson
Hollister
Ozark Beach
Powersite
Kirbyville
Indian Point
Table Rock S.P.
Point Lookout
Table Lake
Shell Knob
Lanagan
Powell
Pineville
HUCKLEBERRY RIDGE S.F.
ROARING RIVER S.P.
Emerald Beach
Ginger Blue
Washburn
Viola
Lampe
Eagle Rock
SUGAR CAMP RD
Chain-O-Lakes
Golden
Bull Shoals Lake
Noel
Jane
Seligman
Blue Eye
Ridgedale
South West City
MISSOURI
ARKANSAS
Gateway
Holiday Island
MILDRED B. COOPER MEM. CHAPEL
Bella Vista
Sulphur Springs
PEA RIDGE N.M.P.
Garfield
Beaver
Busch
Elk Ranch
Grandview
Oakgrove
Omaha
Pea Ridge
Gravette
Hiwasse
Vista Shores
Eureka Springs
Urbanette
Avoca
Lost Bridge
Denver
Burlington
Maysville
Bentonville
Centerton
Little Flock
Beaver Lake
Rivercliff Estates
Berryville
Prairie Creek
La Rue
Green Forest
Decatur
Vaughn
Copper Mine
Rambo Riviera
Cherokee City
Rogers
Beaver Shores
BEAVER LAKE S.P.
Alpena
Bear Creek Springs
WAR EAGLE MILL
Rockhouse
Rule
Gentry
Cave Springs
Monte Ne Shores
Carrollton
Batavia
Harrison
Springtown
Highfill
Lowell
Capps
Healing Springs
Pleasure Heights
Best
Clifty
Metalton
Rudd
Siloam Springs
Elm Springs
Bethel Heights
Lake Elmdale
Springdale
Spring Valley
Forum
Osage
West Siloam Springs
OZARK NATIONAL FOREST
Tontitown
Sonora
Alabam
Withrow Springs S.P.
Marble
Gaither
Harmon
Mayfield
Hindsville
Dogpatch
DOGPATCH USA
Watts
Johnson
Old Alabam
Savoy
Wheeler
Goshen
TRAIL OF TEARS MUSEUM
Huntsville
Compton
Ballard
Weddington
Fayetteville
UNIV. OF ARKANSAS
Lake Sequoyah
BUFFALO NATL. RIVER
Pruitt
Kingston
Cincinnati
Farmington
Wesley
Ponca
Mount Sherman
OZARK NATL. FOREST
Rhea
Viney Grove
Starks
ARKANSAS AIR MUSEUM
DRAKE FIELD
Aurora
Jasper
Westville
Prairie Grove Battlefield S.P.
Elkins
Greenland
Boxley
0 2 4 6 8 10 12
SCALE IN MILES

1. Holla Bend National Wildlife Refuge

An island wilderness on the Arkansas River, this 6,367-acre sanctuary offers fishing and an opportunity to observe a variety of wildlife, including deer, raccoon, turkey, opossum, wildcat, heron, egret, and tern. It is also the northernmost terrain for alligators. Winter usually brings bald eagles, snow geese, Canada geese, and ducks. An 8-mile, self-guiding, all-weather road leads through the refuge. *Admission charged.*

2. Petit Jean State Park

At an elevation of 1,100 feet, Petit Jean Mountain is the centerpiece of this beautiful park, the oldest in Arkansas. Trails across the area's 3,500 acres lead to waterfalls, caves, unusual rock formations, a natural bridge, and American Indian pictographs. The nearby **Museum of Automobiles** displays a rare 1920's Arkansas-built Climber, Mae West's pink-and-pearl 1937 Packard, a 1914 Cretors Popcorn Wagon, and other antique cars. *Admission charged at museum.*

3. Hot Springs National Park

Situated in the picturesque Ouachita Mountains, these forested 4,800 acres are partly surrounded by the city of Hot Springs. About 800,000 gallons of thermal water flow daily from 47 park springs to a reservoir, where a portion is cooled from 143° F to 90° F and distributed with uncooled water to bathhouses. The park has three bathhouses, two open-air hot springs, plus a thermal cascade. **Fordyce Bathhouse Visitor Center** features an 8,000-piece stained-glass skylight and interpretive exhibits; park rangers are on hand to explain the region's geology and history. Ten miles of mountain roads, soaring to 1,400 feet, as well as walking and horseback-riding trails lead to scenic vistas and campgrounds.

4. Hot Springs

Visitor Center, 134 Convention Blvd. The spring water at this health-and-pleasure resort, popular since the 1840's, attracts visitors all year long. Other attractions include

Hot Springs Mountain Observation Tower, where a glass-enclosed elevator rises 1,256 feet above sea level to spectacular views of the Ouachita Mountains. The **Mid-America Museum** boasts a 35,000-gallon freshwater aquarium, laser theater, and participatory exhibits about energy, perception, sound, and gravity. Visitors can also launch a hot-air balloon and create mountains and rivers in a land model. Located nearby, the **Josephine Tussaud Wax Museum** depicts more than 100 historic figures, from the explorer de Soto to modern-day astronauts. *Admission charged.*

5. Benton

Chamber of Commerce, 607 North Market St. The **Gann Museum** is housed in a former doctor's office built by patients who could not afford to pay for services. It is the only known building made of bauxite and is on the National Register of Historic Places. Exhibits include Niloak pottery, Indian artifacts, pioneer tools, and war memorabilia. **Kentucky Missionary Baptist Church,** in use since 1824, is the oldest Baptist church in Arkansas. *Admission charged at museum.*

6. Jenkins' Ferry State Park

Rte. 46, north of Leola. In April 1864, Gen. Frederick Steele's retreat to Little Rock was halted here temporarily by the flooding Saline River. While the general waited for his Union Army engineers to bridge the stream, he attacked pursuing Confederates. The site offers exhibits that commemorate the springtime battle in which between 800 and 1,000 Confederate and 700 Union troops fell. Swimming, fishing, and picnicking facilities are available in the park.

7. Jefferson County Historical Museum

201 East Fourth St., Pine Bluff. Located in the **Union Station** train depot, which is listed on the National Register of Historic Places, the museum traces Pine Bluff and Jefferson County history from the time of Spanish and French explorers to the present. Extensive displays include Quapaw Indian relics, tools, Victorian clothing, and cotton-farming implements.

8. Toltec Mounds Archeological State Park

Rte. 386, southeast of North Little Rock. These mounds were probably built about A.D. 700–900, not by Mexican Toltecs, as was once believed, but by American Indi-

ans. The mounds were an important religious and ceremonial center and an integral part of one of the largest and most complex prehistoric Indian settlements in the Lower Mississippi Valley. Several mounds can be viewed on guided tours or from paved trails through the 145-acre park. Two mounds — at 49 feet high and 41 feet high — are the tallest in Arkansas. The visitor center has artifacts, history exhibits, and an archeological laboratory. *Fee charged for tour.*

9. Villa Marre

1321 South Scott St., Little Rock. Located in the historic Quapaw Quarter, this restored brick Italianate mansion is notable for its fine furnishings and intricate parquet floors, elaborate wall treatments, richly decorated stenciled ceilings, and an ornate hand-carved fireplace. *Admission charged.*

10. Arkansas Museum of Science and History

Ninth and Commerce Sts., Little Rock. The museum is housed in an 1842 arsenal set in **MacArthur Park** (named after Gen. Douglas MacArthur, who was born here). Exhibits focus on Arkansas pioneers, local Indian cultures, geology, and prehistoric fossils. *Admission charged.*

11. Decorative Arts Museum

Seventh and Rock Sts., Little Rock. Pulitzer Prize–winning poet John Gould Fletcher spent his childhood in this restored Greek Revival mansion, which was constructed in 1840. The flamboyant builder, Albert Pike, was a lawyer, soldier, poet, mystic, and Masonic leader. The house has been converted into a museum with galleries that display artifacts and textiles, including early Roman glassware, Oriental works, and contemporary American crafts.

12. The Old Mill

Fairway Ave. and Lakeshore Dr., North Little Rock. Located in a scenic city park, this gristmill and waterwheel appeared in the opening scene of *Gone With the Wind.* Two stones in the road to the mill were originally laid by Jefferson Davis.

13. The Old State House

300 West Markham St., Little Rock. This is one of the finest examples of Greek Revival architecture to be found in the South, as well as one of Arkansas's most historically significant buildings. Completed in 1836, the year that Arkansas was granted statehood, it is now an elegant museum fur-

nished to illustrate evolving decorative tastes. On view are two galleries with changing art and history exhibits, a gas-burning chandelier, the gowns worn by governors' wives, Victorian-era decorative arts, state legislature and supreme court chambers, and a Civil War cannon.

14. Arkansas Territorial Restoration

Third and Scott Sts., Little Rock. Occupying an entire block, the restored 19th-century buildings include the 1820's log **Hinderliter Grog Shop,** the city's oldest building. **Brownlee House,** from the 1840's, has hand-carved doors and mantels and an old-time well. **Woodruff House** was built by the founder of the *Arkansas Gazette,* the oldest newspaper west of the Mississippi, and outlines a state chronology with the use of newspaper headlines from territorial days up to the beginning of the Civil War. Guided tours are available. *Admission charged.*

15. Arkansas State Capitol

Capitol Ave and Martin Luther King Dr., Little Rock. Arkansas's capitol is an exact replica — although four times smaller — of the U.S. Capitol. On guided tours visitors can see the 2-ton central chandelier and front doors made of brass by Tiffany and Company, plus state history and changing cultural exhibitions. A garden on the south lawn has 150 varieties of roses.

16. Pinnacle Mountain State Park

Dome-shaped Pinnacle Mountain, at an elevation of 1,011 feet, is surrounded by forested lowlands in this 1,800-acre park. Its summit affords scenic views of the area and of 9,000-acre **Lake Maumelle,** which offers good boating and fishing. Known for its abundant plant and animal life, natural history exhibits, and interpretive programs, the park attracts wildflower lovers and birdwatchers, who might spot migrating ospreys, herons, bald eagles, and white pelicans. Marked hiking trails range from handicapped-accessible to advanced.

17. Cadron Settlement Park

Off Rte. 319, west of Conway. Established in the 1770's as a Spanish trading post, the settlement eventually added a grist mill, tannery, and general store. Hiking trails past hills and 100-foot-high bluffs follow old stagecoach and military roads to a reconstructed blockhouse, perched on its original hilltop site overlooking a bend in the Arkansas River. There are also picnic sites and a self-guided nature path.

Holla Bend N.W.R.
Gibson Lake
Pullen Pond
Petit Jean River
Petit Jean State Park
MUSEUM OF AUTOMOBILES
Morrilton
Plumerville
Menifee
Conway
UNIV. OF CENTRAL ARKANSAS
Holland
Naylor
El Paso
Antioch
Pontoon
Ada
Oppelo
Vilonia
Ward
Austin
Cabot
Birta
Casa
Adona
Perry
Houston
Hamlet
Saltillo
Otto
Perryville
Bigelow
Fourche
Gold Creek
Magness
Fourche Junction
Nimrod
Aplin
Pleasant Valley
Mayflower
Macon
LITTLE ROCK A.F.B.
Parnell
Jacksonville
Hollis
Thornburg
Wye
Little Italy
Monnie Springs
CAMP
Cato
Gravel Ridge
Sherwood
South Bend
Furlow
OUACHITA NATIONAL FOREST
FLATSIDE NATL. WILDERNESS
Williams Junction
Roland
Lake Maumelle
JOSEPH T. ROBINSON
Maumelle
North Little Rock
Natural Steps
PINNACLE MOUNTAIN STATE PARK
Pinnacle
Cammack Village
Paron
Ferndale
Shady Grove
Little Rock
Kerr
Galloway
Lake Norrell
UNIV. OF ARKANSAS AT LITTLE ROCK
ADAMS FIELD AIRPORT
Scott
PLANTATION AGRICULTURE MUSEUM S.P.
Blakely
Jessieville
Lake De Soto
Lake Cortez
Hot Springs Village
Lake Lago
Avilla
Congo
Salem
Sweet Home
Higgins
Blue Springs
Mountain Valley
Lake Coronado
Lake Pineda
Owensville
Crows
KENTUCKY MISSIONARY BAPTIST CHURCH
Hurricane Lake
Shannon Hills
Wrightsville
Keo
England
Hot Springs Reservoir
Fountain Lake
Benton
GANN MUSEUM
Alexander
Vimy Ridge
East End
HOT SPRINGS NATL. PARK
MID-AMERICA MUSEUM
HOT SPRINGS MOUNTAIN OBSERVATION TOWER
FORDYCE BATHHOUSE VISITOR CENTER
Morning Star
Lonsdale
Nance
Bauxite
BAUXITE MUSEUM
Sardis
Woodson
Redfield
Wright
Tucker
JOSEPHINE TUSSAUD WAX MUSEUM
MEMORIAL FIELD AIRPORT
Hot Springs
Magnet Cove
Glen Rose
Traskwood
Tull
Ico
Ferda
Lake Catherine
Jones Mill
Butterfield
Haskell
Hensley
Sherrill
Lake Hamilton
LAKE CATHERINE S.P.
Rockport
Malvern
Gifford
Belfast
Jefferson
PINE BLUFF
Pastoria
De Roche
Oak Grove
Perla
Redfield
Social Hill
Antioch
Central
Sheridan
Hardin
White Hall
UNIV. OF ARKANSAS AT PINE BLUFF
DEGRAY LAKE RESORT S.P.
Caney
Midway
Donaldson
Friendship
Rolla
Lono
Brush Creek
Prattsville
Cross Roads
Sulphur Springs
Pine Bluff
De Gray Lake
Caddo Valley
Leola
Cox Creek Lake

SCALE IN MILES
0 2 4 6 8 10

1. Hatchie National Wildlife Refuge

Migrating and wintering waterfowl find this watery landscape — an area often flooded by the Hatchie River — a welcome resting and feeding ground. Mallards, wood ducks, red-shouldered hawks, barred owls, and wild turkeys flourish in the refuge, which also serves as a breeding ground for many species of songbirds.

2. Alex Haley State Historic Site and Museum

200 South Church St., Henning. The restored childhood home of novelist Alex Haley, where he lived with his grandparents, is open to visitors. Displays include memorabilia, family portraits, and many of the original furnishings. *Admission charged.*

3. Fort Pillow State Historic Area

Rte. 207, west of Henning. The remains of this Civil War fort, named for a Confederate general, is situated on Chickasaw Bluff overlooking the Mississippi. Camping grounds, picnic areas, and woodland trails are available, and displays at an interpretive center recall the fierce battle that occurred here on April 12, 1864.

4. Hampson Museum State Park

Rte. 61 and Lake Dr., Wilson. Artifacts of a group of Indians who lived some thousand years ago in the area of Nodena, the family plantation of Dr. J. K. Hampson, are shown at the museum. Of special interest is a display of painted pottery, now known as Nodena Red and White.

5. Mud Island

A pedestrian bridge and a monorail lead from downtown Memphis to this island park, where the **Mississippi River Museum** displays reproductions of riverboats, models of bridges, and Indian artifacts. The **River Walk,** a quarter-mile-long model of the Mississippi from Cairo, Illinois, to New Orleans, duplicates every turn and sandbar of the famous waterway. The park also features the famous World War II B-17 bomber

Memphis Belle, shops, restaurants, and an amphitheater. *Admission charged.*

6. The Danny Thomas ALSAC Pavilion

332 North Lauderdale, Memphis. Located on the grounds of the St. Jude Children's Research Hospital, this golden-domed pavilion was fashioned after the Dome of the Rock in Jerusalem. Displays on the history of the hospital as well as Thomas's career are located here, near the tomb of the great philanthropist and entertainer.

7. The Center for Southern Folklore

152 Beale St., Memphis. The center presents exhibits of local culture, photographs, memorabilia, and films. Walking tours of **Historic Beale Street** begin here, leading to the area called the Home of the Blues, where famous musicians such as W. C. Handy, who wrote "Memphis Blues" and "Beale Street Blues," held forth. *Admission charged for some attractions.*

8. Chucalissa Museum

1987 Indian Village Dr., Memphis. This reconstruction of a prehistoric Indian village includes thatched-roof huts bordering a village square and a platform mound with a large house that presumably belonged to the chief. A museum contains artifacts found on the site. Picnic areas and campgrounds are provided in **T. O. Fuller State Park.** *Admission charged at museum.*

9. Graceland

3734 Elvis Presley Blvd., Memphis. Guided tours of the elaborate mansion of the King of Rock and Roll include his pool, TV and music rooms, trophy room, and his magnificent show costume collection. At the museums across the street, Presley's private jets and collection of cars are on display. The tour ends in the garden, where his tomb is located. *Admission charged.*

10. Victorian Village Historic District

The charm of this historic area is especially apparent in three restored mansions located on Adams Street. Dating to about 1836, the **Magevney House** is considered to be the oldest residence in Memphis. The **Mallory-Neely House,** a 25-room Italian villa, dates back to 1852. The French Victorian **Woodruff-Fontaine House** offers a view of the city skyline from its tower room. *Admission charged for some attractions.*

11. Overton Park

Located in the park, the **Memphis Zoo and Aquarium** provides natural settings for more than 400 species. Children can pet animals in the Animal Contact Area and enjoy children's rides. The **Memphis Brooks Museum of Art** has an outstanding collection of early European and 20th-century American paintings, decorative arts, and sculpture. *Admission charged.*

12. Memphis Pink Palace Museum and Planetarium

3050 Central Ave., Memphis. Built in 1920 as the home of Clarence Saunders, founder of the Piggly Wiggly self-service grocery stores, the pink marble mansion serves as the educational division of the adjacent museum. Exhibits at the museum feature the history of the Memphis area and include displays about pioneer life, the Civil War, medical history, and indigenous insect and animal life. Planetarium shows are given on weekends. *Admission charged.*

13. The Dixon Gallery and Gardens

4339 Park Ave., Memphis. In a beautifully landscaped setting of gardens and woodlands, the former home of Margaret and Hugo Dixon serves today as a museum with unusually fine paintings by American and French Impressionists, works by important English artists of the 18th century, and a collection of handsome 18th-century German porcelain. *Admission charged.*

14. Memphis Botanic Garden and Goldsmith Civic Garden Center

750 Cherry Rd., Memphis. Many kinds of flowering plants, a Japanese garden and pavilion along a lake, and dogwood and azalea trails entice visitors to the garden. The center has a large reference library and features exotic plant displays and occasional horticultural shows. *Admission charged.*

15. Memorial Park

5668 Poplar Ave., Memphis. The main feature of this memorial cemetery is the **Crystal Shrine Grotto,** a spectacular natural rock and quartz crystal cave. Here during the 1930's Dionicio Rodriguez carved several relief sculptures portraying various events in the life of Christ.

16. Lichterman Nature Center

5992 Quince Rd., Memphis. Attractions here include a greenhouse where native wildflowers grow and a hospital for injured wild animals, as well as an environmental and

educational facility. Picnic areas and hiking trails are available. *Admission charged.*

17. Arkabutla Lake Recreation Area

This large lake was formed in 1942 when the Coldwater River was dammed. Fishermen come to try their luck in its well-stocked waters, and vacationers enjoy swimming, hiking, picnicking, and camping in this 40,000-acre federally protected area.

18. Holly Springs

Chamber of Commerce, 154 South Memphis St. This historic town is noted for its many handsome private mansions and churches. The wooden **Saint Joseph's Catholic Church,** built in 1840, is marked by an unusual bell tower. **Montrose,** an 1858 mansion known for its spiral stairway and handsomely decorated ceilings, is open to visitors by appointment. The **Kate Freeman Clark Art Gallery** is devoted entirely to the works of the Holly Springs artist, for whom the gallery is named. Local history is featured at the **Marshall County Historical Museum,** which displays antique quilts, household objects, dolls, Civil War relics, and Indian artifacts. Many of the handsome wrought-iron fences in the **Hillcrest Cemetery,** where a number of Confederate soldiers are buried, were made in Holly Springs before the Civil War. *Admission charged for some attractions.*

Composer/bandmaster W.C. Handy, c.1910

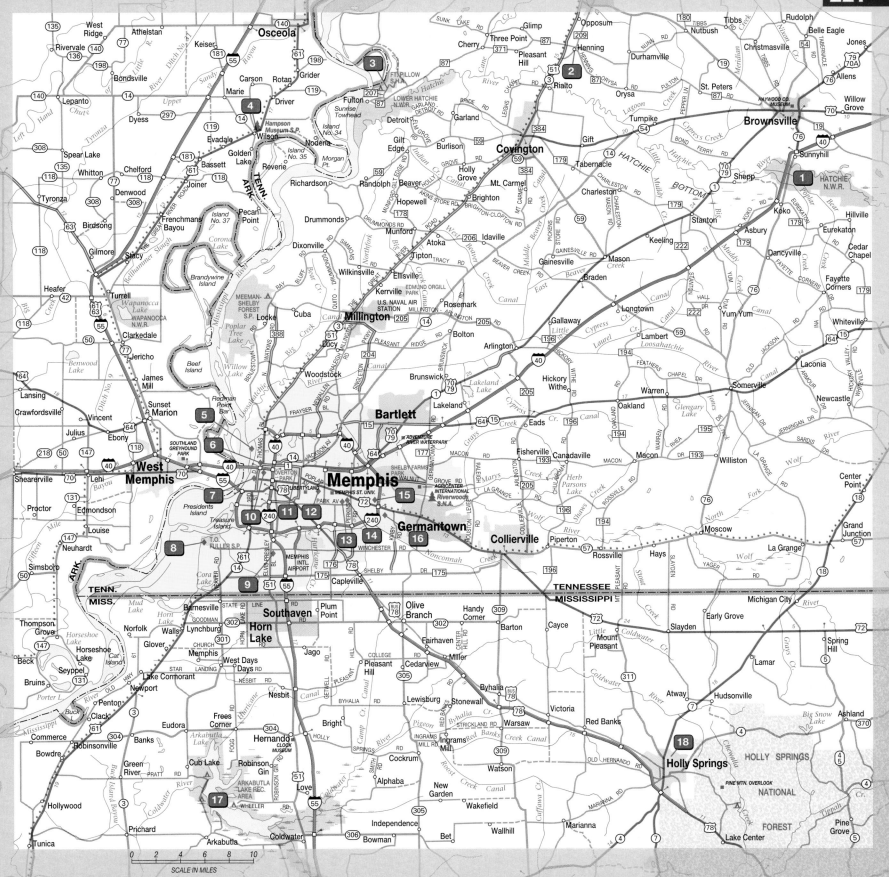

SCALE IN MILES
0 2 4 6 8 10

1. Davy Crockett Cabin

Rte. 45W, Rutherford. The reconstructed structure, made with hand-hewn logs from the home of the famous frontiersman, is now a museum featuring 19th-century pioneer artifacts. On the grounds is the grave of Crockett's mother. The cabin is open daily from late May to Labor Day, or by appointment. *Admission charged.*

2. Casey Jones Home and Railroad Museum

Rte. 45 Bypass and Rte. 40, Jackson. The white clapboard house, home of the famous train engineer, contains railroad memorabilia. A replica of the fateful engine in which Casey was killed stands beside the house, along with a historic coach car that contains model trains depicting 100 years of rail history in America. *Admission charged.*

3. Pinson Mounds State Archaeological Area

460 Ozier Rd., Pinson. Well-marked trails traverse the site, which includes 13 Middle Woodland Indian mounds and a circular earthen embankment dating back some 2,000 years. A building designed to resemble a mound serves as an office and museum containing Indian artifacts.

4. Shiloh National Military Park

Rte. 22, Shiloh. One of the Civil War's bloodiest battles was fought around Shiloh Church, resulting in more than 23,746 casualties. The visitor center contains uniforms, firearms, and other artifacts found on the battlefield. *Admission charged.*

5. Florence

Chamber of Commerce, 104S Pine St. One of the town's important sites is the **Wilson Dam,** whose powerhouse lobby and lockmaster's control building welcome visitors. Rising over the dam is the **Renaissance Tower,** which provides a spectacular view from the observation deck. **Pope's Tavern Museum** has Civil War exhibits, while the **Indian Mound and Museum** examines pre-Columbian Indian tribes. The **W. C.**

Handy Home and Museum is the birthplace of the famous Father of the Blues. *Admission charged for some attractions.*

6. Ivy Green

300 West North Commons, Tuscumbia. Helen Keller was born in this white clapboard cottage in 1880. It is maintained today as a shrine to this incredible woman and to her teacher, Anne Sullivan. The house contains family mementos and an alarm clock, typewriter, and books in braille. The pump where Keller learned her first word, *water,* is located outside the main house. *Admission charged.*

7. Dismals Canyon

Perhaps named for the dim light that filters through the groves of trees and into the rocky canyon, the park is filled with colorful vegetation. A mile-long trail follows a stream and winds under several natural bridges. Camping, picnicking, and canoeing are available. *Admission charged.*

8. Natchez Trace Parkway

The 450-mile path from Natchez to Nashville was used by American Indians and then by Mississippi boatmen, who sold their boats along with their cargoes and then walked home along the trail. The scenic route today parallels the old trail and passes several historic sites. Information is available at the visitor center in **Tupelo.**

9. Columbus

Convention and Visitors Bureau, 402 Second Ave. N. The picturesque town, dating from 1816, features more than 100 pre–Civil War buildings still intact; several mansions are open to the public year-round. **Friendship Cemetery,** where many Civil War victims are buried, was named in 1866 after several widows decorated both Confederate and Union graves. Nearby **Waverley Plantation,** built in 1852, is known for its unusual architecture, which includes curving stairways, a rotunda, and an octagonal cupola. *Admission charged.*

10. Tuscaloosa

Convention and Visitors Bureau, 600 South Lurleen Wallace Blvd. Once the state capital, the city is home to the **University of Alabama** and is known for its many well-preserved Greek Revival mansions, including the 1822 **Mildred Warner House,** which contains an important art collection, and the 1835 **Battle-Friedman House.** The national headquarters of the **Gulf**

States Paper Corporation has an impressive art collection that is open to the public.

11. Huntsville

Tourist Information Center, Von Braun Civic Center, 700 Monroe St. The **Huntsville Depot Transportation Museum** was used as an infirmary and confinement area during the Civil War. Commemorating Alabama's statehood is the museum village at **Constitution Hall Village.** The **Burritt Museum and Park** features local history, and at the **Space and Rocket Center** visitors ride in a simulated space shuttle. *Admission charged for some attractions.*

12. Jack Daniel Distillery

Rte. 55, Lynchburg. The original office of this famous distillery serves as a museum, depicting the early days of whiskey making. Visitors can take a guided tour of the entire plant, including the grain silos, fermenting vats, stills, and warehouses.

13. President James K. Polk Ancestral Home

301 West Seventh St., Columbia. The brick Federal-style house, built by Polk's father in 1816, was home to the 11th president for 6 years during the early days of his career. Personal memorabilia, including pieces of White House china and crystal, are among the items on view. *Admission charged.*

14. Loretta Lynn's Ranch

Rte. 40W, Hurricane Mills. Costumes, gold records, a replica of a coal mine, and other mementos of the country singer's career are displayed in her plantation home and a museum housed in a restored 100-year-old gristmill. Swimming, camping, and fishing are also available. *Admission charged.*

15. Jefferson Davis Historic Site

Rte. 68, Fairview. A 351-foot obelisk built in the 1920's commemorates the birthplace of the Confederacy's only president. Visitors are carried by elevator to the top for a panoramic view of the landscape below. *Admission charged.*

16. Mammoth Cave National Park

The longest cave system in the world, this amazing network of underground passageways extends over 330 miles. Easy tours to the best dripstone formations as well as challenging Wild Cave tours are available; reservations are required. Above ground, the park offers 52,000 acres for camping, fishing, and canoeing. *Admission charged.*

17. Castalian Springs

Chamber of Commerce, 118 West Main St. This area of mineral springs was once occupied by Indian tribes. **Wynnewood,** the largest log stagecoach inn in Tennessee, was built in 1828. Nearby stands **Cragfont,** home of Gen. James Winchester, one of the founders of Memphis. Both buildings are open to visitors. *Admission charged.*

18. Old Mulkey Meeting House State Historic Site

Rte. 1446, Tompkinsville. John Mulkey, leader of the Mill Creek Baptist Congregation, built this simple log meeting house in 1804 and preached more than 10,000 sermons here. Shaded picnic areas are located in the surrounding grounds.

19. Mill Springs Gristmill

Rte. 1275, near Monticello. A gristmill has been operating here since the early 1800's. The present structure, dating from 1877, still runs on power from 13 nearby springs and on weekends grinds cornmeal, which is sold at local shops.

20. Historic Rugby

Rte. 52, Rugby. This handsome Victorian colony was founded in 1880 by Thomas Hughes, author of *Tom Brown's School Days,* as a model community where English boys could learn useful trades. The experiment never succeeded, but many of the original buildings still stand. Guided tours are available. *Admission charged.*

21. Joe L. Evins Appalachian Center for Crafts

Scenic Hwy. 56, Smithville. A division of Tennessee Tech University, the center offers courses in woodworking, ceramics, and weaving. The work of students, faculty, and local artists is sold at a nearby shop.

22. New Echota State Historic Site

Rte. 225, near Calhoun. This reconstructed town, built by the Cherokees in the early 1800's, today stands in silent testimony to their forced departure on the 1838 Trail of Tears march. *Admission charged.*

23. Rome

Convention and Visitors Bureau, 402 Civic Center Hill. The 1871 **Old Town Clock** sits atop a water tower on one of Rome's seven hills. A replica of the famous **Romulus and Remus statue,** donated in 1929 by Rome, Italy, graces the city hall. Cherokee history is portrayed at the **Chieftains Museum.**

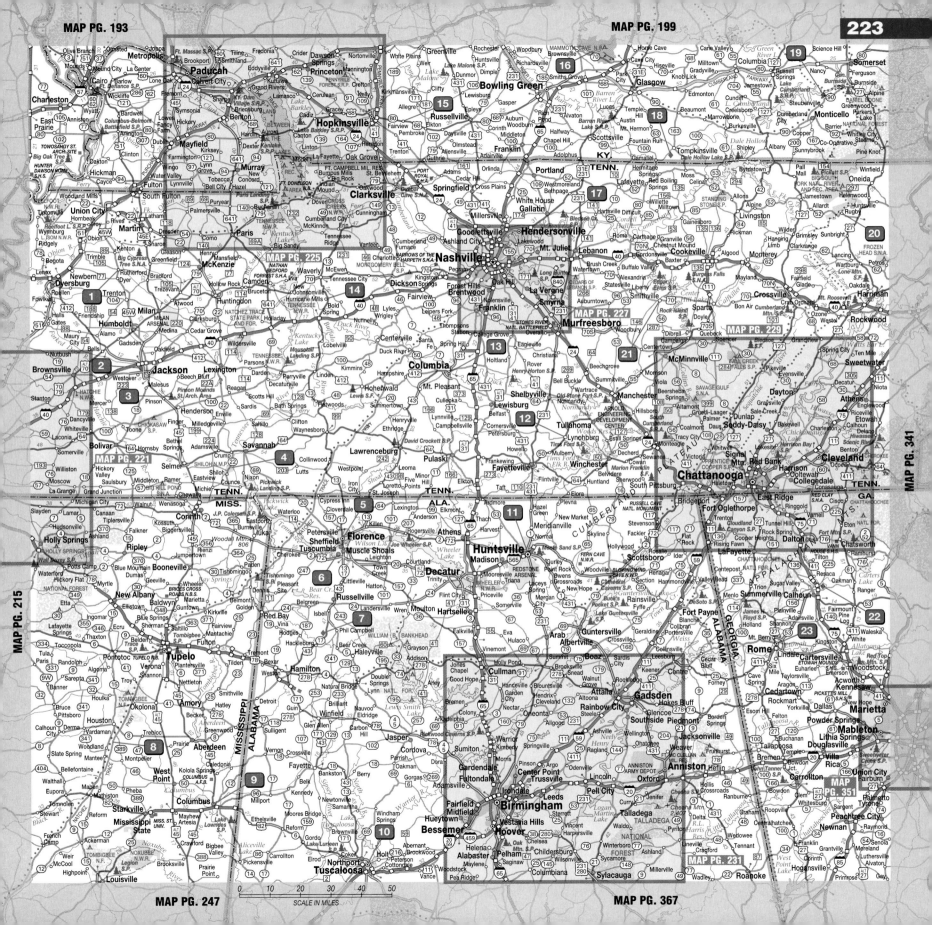

SCALE IN MILES

1. Paducah

Tourist and Convention Commission, 417 South Fourth St. The **Whitehaven Welcome Center,** an imposing columned mansion, contains furnishings from the early 20th century and memorabilia of Vice President Alben W. Barkley. The 1852 Greek Revival **Alben W. Barkley Museum** and the 1905 brick **Market House Museum** portray the town's history with regional artifacts. At the **Museum of the American Quilter's Society,** visitors can view award-winning contemporary quilts or take part in classes and workshops. *Admission charged.*

2. Wooldridge Monuments

Maplewood Cemetery, Lochridge St., Mayfield. Surrounding the tomb of Henry G. Wooldridge, a breeder of horses, are 18 life-size marble and sandstone figures of his family. Represented are his mother, his seven brothers and sisters, and two nieces, as well as the breeder himself riding Fop, his favorite horse.

3. National Scouting Museum of the Boy Scouts of America

North 16th and Calloway Sts., Murray. Situated on the campus of **Murray State University,** the museum holds more than

Wild turkeys roam Land Between the Lakes.

50 paintings by Norman Rockwell that depict scouting; there's also a large collection of Boy Scout memorabilia. Also on the college campus, the **Wrather West Kentucky Museum** has exhibits related to western Kentucky's social and economic development and a gun collection consisting of more than 40 different kinds of firearms, most of them antiques. *Admission charged at scouting museum.*

4. Kenlake State Resort Park

Rte. 94E, near Murray. With both indoor and outdoor tennis courts, a golf course, rental cottages, and tent and trailer sites, this is one of the state's most popular resorts. Along the 4-mile shoreline are bathhouses, sandy beaches, and a marina with boat rentals. A wooded campground and picnic area overlook the lake. *Fee charged for some activities.*

5. Paris Landing State Park

Rte. 79E, Buchanan. On the shores of Kentucky Lake, this park features an 18-hole golf course, tennis courts, a beach, an Olympic-size swimming pool, and well-equipped campgrounds. Pontoon, fishing, and ski boats can be rented at the marina. *Fee charged for some activities.*

6. Tennessee National Wildlife Refuge

A resting and feeding area for waterfowl, this refuge on Kentucky Lake is divided into three separate units. An array of wildlife can be seen throughout the area, especially at the **Big Sandy Unit,** where a 10-mile marked auto route winds past the habitats of deer, bobcats, raccoons, beavers, and American bald eagles.

7. Fort Donelson National Battlefield

Rte. 79, Dover. An important Civil War battle was fought here in 1862, with Ulysses S. Grant leading the Union forces. It was the first major victory for the North, and convinced President Lincoln to promote Grant to a major general.

8. Cross Creeks National Wildlife Refuge

Extending for some 11 miles along both banks of the Cumberland River, this refuge of marsh and woodland provides an ideal habitat for waterfowl, bald eagles, songbirds, deer, and other wildlife. In winter thousands of ducks and Canada geese can be spotted from the refuge's many roads and hiking trails.

9. Hopkinsville

Chamber of Commerce, 1209 South Virginia St. **Round Table Literary Park,** located on the campus of **Hopkinsville Community College,** is well known for its replica of a 5th-century B.C. Greek amphitheater and a 22,000-pound copy of King Arthur's Round Table. The town also boasts the **Pennyroyal Area Museum,** which has displays on tobacco, railroading, and the Civil War. *Admission charged at museum.*

Museum of the American Quilter's Society

10. Pennyrile Forest State Resort Park

Rte. 109S, near Dawson Springs. Named for the pennyroyal, a fragrant blue wildflower that grows on hillsides, this secluded park looks upon a small lake and offers a wide variety of recreation, including swimming, hiking, camping, and boating. The **Pennyrile Lodge,** built of local stone, is beautifully landscaped with flowering shrubs and trees. *Fee charged for some activities.*

11. Adsmore House Museum

304 North Jefferson St., Princeton. Located in the restored former home of the Smith-Garrett family, this 1850's mansion, with a Corinthian portico added in the early 1900's, features changing decor to re-create events such as an authentic Victorian Christmas and a 1907 wedding. *Admission charged.*

12. Rose Hill

Rte. 730, Eddyville. This Federal-style mansion with views of Lake Barkley was built in the 1830's by Robert Livingston Cobb, grandfather of the well-known humorist Irvin S. Cobb. In his book, *Exit Laughing,* Irvin Cobb tells the story of his ancestors' journey from Vermont to the

original site of Eddyville, on the banks of the Cumberland River, which later became the site of the Barkley Dam. Before the opening of the dam in 1963, the town was transported to its present location. The restored home serves today as the **Lyon County Museum,** where exhibits include a pictorial history of the old Eddyville. *Admission charged.*

13. Kentucky Dam Village State Resort Park

Rte. 641, near Gilbertsville. The 206-foot-tall Kentucky Dam was completed in 1944, creating **Kentucky Lake.** The lake — now some 184 miles long — is the centerpiece of a huge recreation area whose facilities include rental cottages, sandy beaches, a golf course, tennis courts, and campgrounds. Visitors will find houseboats and fishing boats for rent at the park's marina. *Fee charged for some activities.*

14. Land Between the Lakes

Golden Pond Visitor Center, 100 Van Morgan Dr., Golden Pond. This federal recreation area covers a peninsula some 40 miles long and 8 miles wide, which extends into the waters of Lake Barkley and Kentucky Lake. With more than 200 miles of hiking and backpacking trails and 300-plus miles of backcountry roads, the area draws vacationers who come to enjoy the outdoors, try the excellent fishing, and watch for wildlife. The visitor center, which has a theater and planetarium, provides a splendid overview of the area. In the 5,000-acre **Environmental Education Area,** the **Woodlands Nature Center** has displays of live animals and audiovisual shows. **Silo Overlook,** a high point in the forest, provides a full view of Lake Barkley. The **Homeplace-1850,** a living-history farm run by a staff dressed in period costumes, features 16 reconstructed log buildings brought from nearby locations and presentations on 19th-century farm life in the western Kentucky–Tennessee area.

15. Lake Barkley State Resort Park

Rte. 68W, Cadiz. Spread along the eastern shore of Lake Barkley, this extensive recreation park is home to a wide variety of water sports, as well as tennis courts, an 18-hole golf course, and miles of hiking trails. Other visitor facilities include rental cottages, a campground, and the beautiful lakeside **Barkley Lodge,** notable for its design by architect Edward Durell Stone. *Fee charged for some activities.*

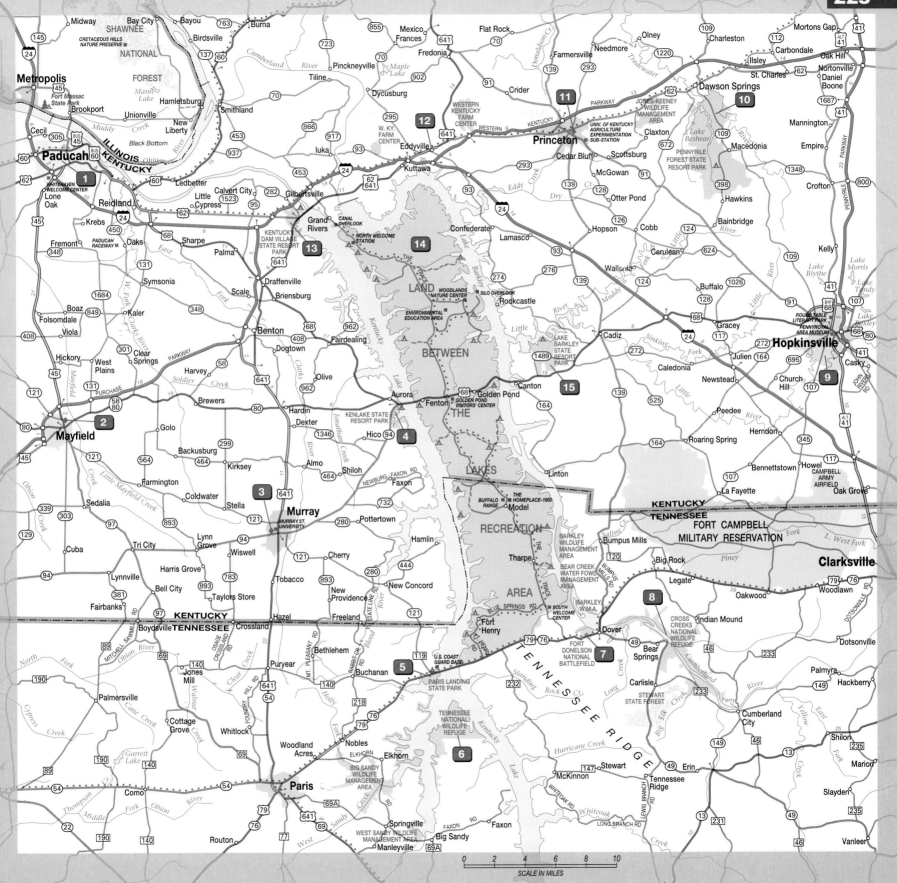

1. Twitty City

#1 Music Village Blvd., Hendersonville. The home of country music star Conway Twitty is the centerpiece of this 8-acre entertainment complex. A museum features displays and videos of the singer's life and career. *Admission charged.*

2. House of Cash

700 Johnny Cash Pkwy., Hendersonville. The career of legendary country singer Johnny Cash is documented with exhibits that include music awards and personal belongings. Other displays — many with handwritten descriptions by Cash — include fine Remington bronzes, pre–Civil War weapons, and guitars. *Admission charged.*

3. The Hermitage

4580 Rachel's La., Hermitage. This stately white-columned mansion was the home of Andrew Jackson, the nation's seventh president, from 1819 until his death in 1845. The family's furnishings and portraits decorate the house, and on the estate are 13 other structures, including log cabins and a formal garden, where, in the shade of hickory trees, lies the tomb of Jackson and his beloved wife, Rachel. *Admission charged.*

4. Opryland USA

Exit 11 off Briley Pkwy., Nashville. The legendary Grand Ole Opry radio show is the jewel of this entertainment complex, where weekend broadcasts of country music stars are performed before a live audience. At the Opryland musical theme park, 12 productions cover the spectrum from gospel to country to Broadway. The park's rides feature a roller coaster with audiovisual effects; three museums display memorabilia from country music's past. *Admission charged for some attractions.*

5. Fort Nashborough

170 First Ave. N., Nashville. This reproduction of a 1779 log fort stands on the bluffs overlooking the Cumberland River. Self-guiding tours within the stockade lead to five cabins with period furnishings and memorabilia recalling the rugged lives of the first area settlers. *Admission charged.*

6. Tennessee State Museum

505 Deaderick St., Nashville. Centered on an operating gristmill, this museum chronicles the history of Tennessee from prehistoric times to the 20th century, with an extensive Civil War display, Davy Crockett's rifle, Daniel Boone's pocketknife, and Andrew Jackson's inaugural top hat.

7. Tennessee State Capitol

Charlotte and Sixth Aves., Nashville. Built between 1845 and 1859 on the highest hill in the city, this fine example of Greek Revival architecture gleams with locally quarried limestone. The grounds contain statues of Andrew Jackson and other Tennessee heroes, as well as the graves of former president James K. Polk and his wife.

8. Fisk University

One of the country's most prestigious black colleges since its founding in 1866, Fisk University is located in a National Historic District. Notable sights on campus include **Jubilee Hall,** an 1876 Victorian Gothic structure, and the **Carl Van Vechten Gallery of Fine Arts,** which holds the Alfred Stieglitz Collection of Modern Art. *Admission charged at art gallery.*

9. Parthenon

Centennial Park, Nashville. This full-scale replica of the ancient Athenian temple was built for the Tennessee Centennial Exposition of 1897. Today the building houses 19th- and 20th-century American art, as well as replicas of the Elgin Marbles and a 42-foot-tall statue of the Greek goddess Athena. *Admission charged.*

10. Upper Room Chapel and Museum

1908 Grand Ave., Nashville. A woodcarving of Leonardo da Vinci's *Last Supper,* thought to be the largest of its kind in the world, adorns a wall in this Georgian-style chapel draped with fine tapestries. A garden and museum are also on the premises.

11. Belle Meade Plantation

5025 Harding Rd., Nashville. In the 19th century, the 5,300-acre Belle Meade plantation was the finest Thoroughbred horse farm in the nation. A tour of the antebellum mansion, with its equestrian trophies and original Victorian and Empire antiques, recalls its glorious past. On the grounds, a rambling Victorian carriage house and stable showcase an extensive collection of horse-drawn vehicles. *Admission charged.*

12. Cheekwood-Tennessee Botanical Gardens and Museum of Art

1200 Forrest Park Dr., Nashville. Featured at the museum is a fine collection of 19th- and 20th-century American art and decorative art, housed in a Georgian-style mansion surrounded by 55 landscaped acres. There are trails past a Japanese garden, wildflowers, and vibrant displays of roses, herbs, and irises, while the banks of quiet streams offer inviting spots for picnics. Greenhouses maintain orchids and camellias, among other exotic plants. *Admission charged.*

13. Belmont Mansion

1900 Belmont Blvd., Nashville. Located on the campus of **Belmont University,** this opulent Italian villa–style summer home was built in 1850 for Adelicia Acklen, then one of the wealthiest women in the country. An artificial lake stocked with alligators is gone, but a vaulted-ceiling ballroom, ornate chandeliers, an extensive art collection, and marble statuary attest to Mrs. Acklen's flamboyant lifestyle. *Admission charged.*

14. Country Music Hall of Fame

4 Music Square East, Music Row, Nashville. Dedicated to country music singers, the museum features costumes, records, musical instruments, and films. Mementos of the stars include Elvis Presley's "solid gold" Cadillac, and a tour of RCA's Studio B reveals what goes on behind the scenes during a recording session. *Admission charged.*

15. Cumberland Science Museum

800 Ridley Blvd., Nashville. Astronomy, natural history, world cultures, and the physical sciences are all examined in this museum. Special programs and exhibits include the Van de Graaf generator; a fully stocked late–19th-century country store; hands-on displays for children; and weekly planetarium shows. *Admission charged.*

16. Historic Travellers Rest

636 Farrell Pkwy., Nashville. Built in 1799 by John Overton, the first state supreme court justice, the home contains historic furnishings, letters, and the judge's reconstructed offices. *Admission charged.*

17. Franklin

Chamber of Commerce, 109 Second Ave. S. Ornate Victorian and antebellum homes grace Franklin's downtown area, which has been designated a National Historic District. Civil War buffs like to retrace the Battle of Franklin, a brutal skirmish that resulted in more than 8,000 casualties. The **Carter House,** a command post of the Union troops, today houses a Confederate museum with guns, maps, uniforms, and Civil War relics. The elegant **Carnton Plantation,** noted for its fine Thoroughbreds, served as a makeshift hospital during the battle. Inside, bloodstains are still visible on the floors, and the cemetery on the grounds contains more than 1,400 Confederate graves. *Admission charged.*

18. Smyrna

Chamber of Commerce, 315 South Lowry St. This town was the home of Sam Davis, a 21-year-old Confederate scout who chose death by hanging rather than inform on a friend. The memory of his loyalty lives on in the **Sam Davis Home,** a simple Greek Revival building with many original furnishings. In September, the skies above Smyrna are abuzz with the 2-day Tennessee Aviation Days Charity Air Show — one of the largest aviation shows in the country — with aerial presentations and displays of antique aircraft. *Admission charged.*

19. Stones River National Battlefield

Old Nashville Hwy., Murfreesboro. The 351-acre park was the site of one of the bloodiest campaigns in the Civil War, with more than 23,000 casualties. Among the points of interest are the 1863 **Hazen Brigade Monument,** one of the oldest Civil War memorials still intact, and the **Stones River National Cemetery,** the final resting place for more than 6,000 Union soldiers. There are hiking trails and a 5-mile auto route through the battleground, with living-history demonstrations in summer.

20. Murfreesboro

Chamber of Commerce, 302 South Front St. The state capital from 1819 to 1826, Murfreesboro today features **Cannonsburgh,** a village of some 20 historic buildings that re-create rural life in the South in the 19th and early 20th centuries. The **Oaklands Historic House Museum** is an Italianate plantation home, built over a period of 40 years, where visitors can learn about the lifestyle of a wealthy antebellum planter family. The home is also the site where Union forces were forced to surrender the town. *Admission charged.*

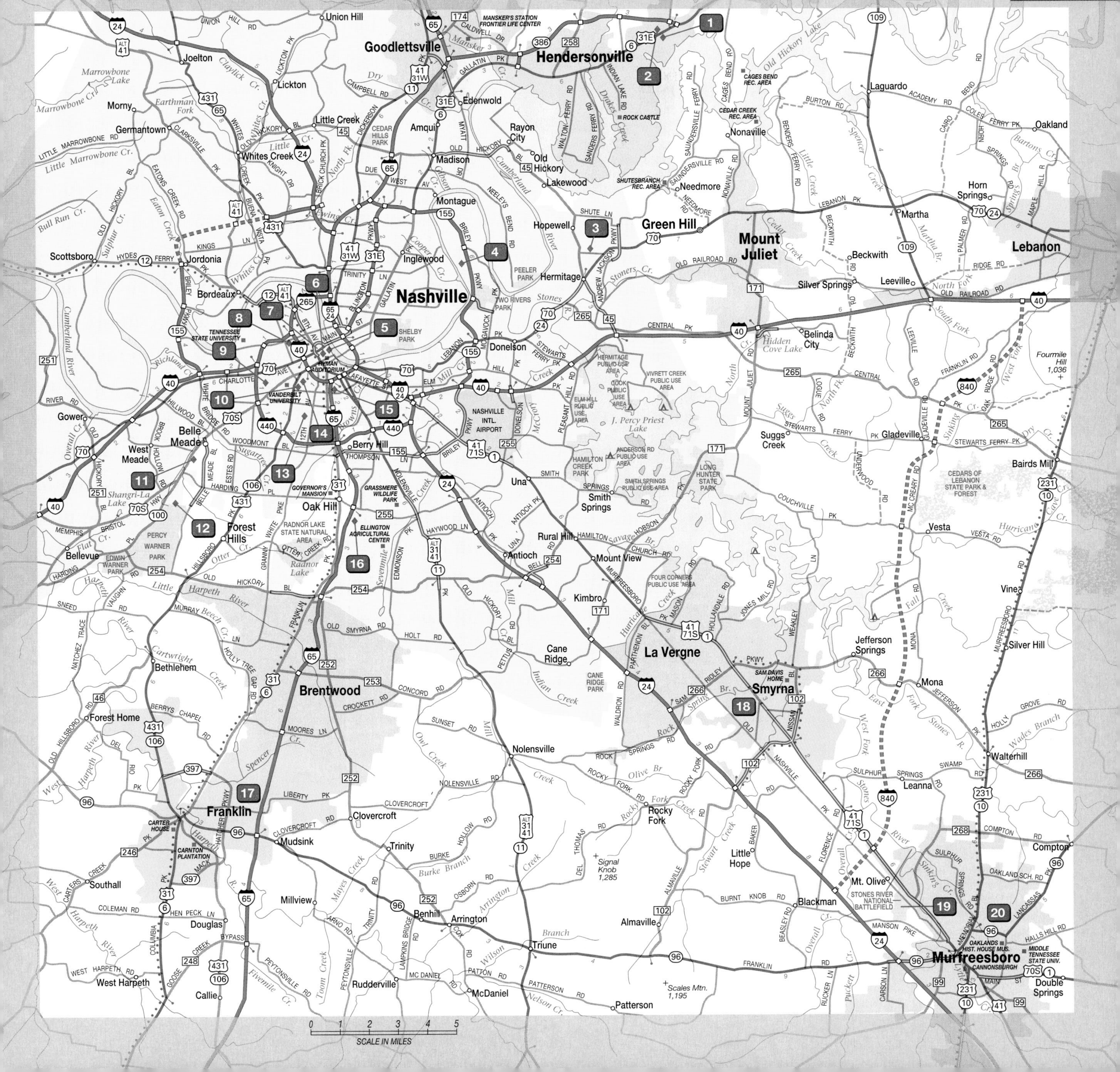

Union Hill
Joelton
Marrowbone Lake
Lickton
Goodlettsville
Mansker's Station Frontier Life Center
Hendersonville
Cages Bend Rec. Area
Old Hickory Lake
Morny
Earthman Fork
Germantown
Little Creek
Edenwold
Amqui
Cedar Hills Park
Rayon City
Old Hickory
Rock Castle
Cedar Creek Rec. Area
Nonaville
Laguardo
Oakland
Whites Creek
Madison
Lakewood
Shutesbranch Rec. Area
Needmore
Horn Springs
Montague
Martha
Hopewell
Green Hill
Mount Juliet
Lebanon
Scottsboro
Jordonia
Inglewood
Beckwith
Hermitage
Peeler Park
Leeville
Silver Springs
Bordeaux
Nashville
Two Rivers Park
Shelby Park
Tennessee State University
Belinda City
Hidden Cove Lake
Donelson
Fourmile Hill 1,036
Ryman Auditorium
Hermitage Public Use Area
Vivrett Creek Public Use Area
Cook Public Use Area
Vanderbilt University
Elm Hill Public Use Area
J. Percy Priest Lake
Gower
Belle Meade
Nashville Intl. Airport
Berry Hill
Suggs Creek
Gladeville
West Meade
Anderson Rd Public Use Area
Hamilton Creek Park
Bairds Mill
Cedars of Lebanon State Park & Forest
Una
Smith Springs
Smith Springs Public Use Area
Long Hunter State Park
Shangri-La Lake
Governor's Mansion
Grassmere Wildlife Park
Oak Hill
Percy Warner Park
Forest Hills
Radnor Lake State Natural Area
Ellington Agricultural Center
Radnor Lake
Vesta
Bellevue
Edwin Warner Park
Rural Hill
Antioch
Mount View
Four Corners Public Use Area
Kimbro
Vine
Bethlehem
Cane Ridge
Cane Ridge Park
La Vergne
Jefferson Springs
Silver Hill
Brentwood
Sam Davis Home
Smyrna
Mona
Forest Home
Nolensville
Walterhill
Leanna
Franklin
Carter House
Carnton Plantation
Clovercroft
Mudsink
Trinity
Rocky Fork
Signal Knob 1,285
Little Hope
Compton
Southall
Millview
Benhill
Arrington
Mt. Olive
Stones River National Battlefield
Blackman
Douglas
Almaville
Triune
Oaklands Hist. House Mus.
Middle Tennessee State Univ.
Murfreesboro
Cannonsburgh
West Harpeth
Callie
Rudderville
McDaniel
Patterson
Scales Mtn. 1,195
Double Springs
Cumberland River
Harpeth River
Stones River
0 1 2 3 4 5
SCALE IN MILES

1. McMinn County Living Heritage Museum

522 West Madison Ave., Athens. An eclectic collection of regional artifacts from 1830 to the 1930's is housed in this museum. The exhibits include a large collection of quilts, antique toys and books, 17th-century African trade beads, and Cherokee Indian artifacts. *Admission charged.*

2. Rhea County Courthouse and Museum

301 North Market St., Dayton. Before a crowded courtroom in 1925, Clarence Darrow and William Jennings Bryan debated Darwin's theory of evolution versus creationism in the famous Scopes "Monkey Trial." The courtroom has been restored to its original appearance, and a museum gives further information on the event.

3. Cumberland Caverns

Off Rte. 8, near McMinnville. Dramatic sculptural formations encrust these mysterious caves; in one, a flowstone named Moby Dick, which is thousands of years old, rises from a pool, while a curtainlike stalactite descends from the ceiling. The massive Volcano Room contains rock balconies and a cut-lead crystal chandelier. The huge Hall of the Mountain King, 600 feet across and 140 feet high, is one of the largest caves in the eastern United States. The tour includes a sound-and-light show. *Admission charged.*

4. Russell Cave National Monument

Off County Rd. 75, near Bridgeport. About 9,000 years ago, nomadic Americans settled in this ballroom-size cave among limestone cliffs and used it regularly until roughly A.D. 500. Hiking trails traverse the park's 310 acres, and the visitor center displays artifacts belonging to the cave dwellers.

5. Tennessee Aquarium

1 Broad St., Chattanooga. This unique aquarium, which focuses on freshwater animals and marine life, explores the underwater world of rivers, from the Tennessee to the Amazon. In simulated habitats, otters frolic in a mountain stream, alligators lurk in black swamp water, and 50-pound catfish patrol the river depths. *Admission charged.*

6. Chattanooga Choo-Choo/ Terminal Station

1400 Market St., Chattanooga. This splendid Beaux Arts terminus, completed in 1909, today accommodates a shopping complex and unique hotel, where a number of guest rooms are Victorian sleeping cars. Visitors can ride an antique trolley, stroll through shops, relax beside formal fountains and gardens, and see an enormous model railroad and a miniature of the city as it appeared at the turn of the century. *Admission charged for some attractions.*

7. Ruby Falls–Lookout Mountain Caverns

Off Rte. 24, Chattanooga. Tours descend more than 1,100 feet underground for a look at spectacular Ruby Falls, a sheer 145-foot drop. In surrounding caves, onyx formations and multicolored stalactites and stalagmites dazzle the eye. From Lookout Mountain Tower, there's a lovely view of Chattanooga and the Tennessee River. *Admission charged.*

8. Lookout Mountain Incline Railway

3917 St. Elmo Ave., Chattanooga. This mile-long incline up Lookout Mountain is one of the steepest railways in the world, with a gradient of up to 72.7 percent. Visitors can enjoy a breathtaking view of the rolling **Tennessee Valley** on the ride up, and from an observation deck at the summit, the **Smoky Mountains** are visible far in the distance. *Admission charged.*

9. Rock City Gardens

Off Rte. 157, Lookout Mountain. The 4,000-foot-long **Enchanted Trail** winds through tunnels and over a swinging bridge, past 14 mountaintop acres of rare lichen-covered sandstone formations. From observation points along the way there are spectacular panoramas of seven states, and at the trail's end are **Fairyland Caverns** and **Mother Goose Village,** home to three-dimensional fairytale scenes. *Admission charged.*

10. Chickamauga and Chattanooga National Military Park

Rte. 27 in Georgia or off Rte. 24 in Tennessee. This military park — the first in the country — was established in 1890 to commemorate the intense Civil War battle for Chattanooga, which resulted in 34,000 casualties in just two days of fighting. The visitor center on Rte. 27 displays the **Fuller Gun Museum,** with antique and rare firearms and a lifelike multimedia presentation of the fighting in which the room vibrates during some battle scenes. A 7-mile auto tour of the battlefield is marked by arrows, and in summer there are guided tours, walks, and cannon-firing demonstrations. **Point Park** on Lookout Mountain has a smaller visitor center that features a majestic overview of the area, and staff members interpret the events that transpired here. During the battle for the mountain, the nearby **Cravens House** bore the brunt of the fierce exchanges. It was rebuilt after the war and is now open for tours. Throughout Chattanooga there are smaller sites related to the battle, such as **Signal Point Military Park** on **Signal Mountain,** which once was inhabited by American Indians and today offers superb views of the countryside. *Admission charged for some attractions.*

A river habitat at the Tennessee Aquarium

11. Confederama

3742 Tennessee Ave., Chattanooga. A re-creation of the Battle of Chattanooga is displayed here in miniature, complete with narration, 5,000 model soldiers, smoking cannons, and flashing lights. Dioramas illustrate a meeting between explorer Hernando de Soto and American Indians in 1540, the final battle of the Revolutionary War, and the fighting of the Battle of Chickamauga. *Admission charged.*

12. Houston Museum of Decorative Arts

201 High St., Chattanooga. Porcelain, textiles, and furniture from the 18th century to the early 20th century are featured here. Also on display are antique music boxes, shaving mugs, pitchers, lamps, and dolls.

13. Hunter Museum of Art

10 Bluff View, Chattanooga. Covering nearly 300 years of American art, this noted collection features works by Thomas Hart Benton, Mary Cassatt, Andrew Wyeth, and John Singer Sargent. The museum is housed in a classical mansion with a contemporary wing; from the rooftop sculpture garden there's a beautiful view of the Tennessee River. *Admission charged.*

14. Tennessee Valley Railroad and Museum

4119 Cromwell Rd., Chattanooga. This 6-mile round-trip ride aboard a steam-powered passenger train is an excursion into railroading's colorful past. Rides depart seven times a day from a turn-of-the-century station, traveling over bridges and through an antebellum tunnel. At the end of the line, visitors can tour the museum and see a fine collection of Pullman cars, steam and diesel engines, mail cars, and an elegant private car. *Admission charged.*

15. Red Clay State Historic Park

Off Blue Springs Rd., south of Cleveland. Red Clay was the last eastern capital of the Cherokee nation, from 1832 to 1838, when the tribe was forced to relocate to Oklahoma. This harrowing journey, known as the Trail of Tears, eventually claimed more than 4,000 lives. At the interpretive center, replicas of a council house and a Cherokee homestead depict daily life. A nearby natural spring that served as the Cherokee's water source still produces some 313,000 gallons per day.

16. Chief Vann House

Junction Rtes. 52A and 225, Spring Place. Called the showplace of the Cherokee nation when it was built in 1805, this three-story brick Federal-style home was constructed by Chief James Vann, who helped establish the now-defunct Moravian Mission to educate young Cherokees. The interior features period furnishings and especially fine woodwork handcarved by Moravian artisans. *Admission charged.*

17. Fort Mountain

An observation tower at the summit of this 2,854-foot-high mountain provides captivating views of the countryside. Nearby, the ruins of a mysterious stone wall, possibly the creation of prehistoric American Indians, snake for some 855 feet. **Fort Mountain State Park** offers fishing, boating, swimming, picnic sites, and hiking trails.

Spencer
McMinnville
Dark Hollow Rd
Irving College
Northcutts Cove Rd
Rocky River
Welchland Rd
Rocky River Rd
Old State Hwy. 111
Bledsoe S.F.
Fall Creek Falls St. Park
Piney Cr.
Cane Creek
Mount Crest
Cold Spring
Pikeville
Upper East Valley Rd
Melvine
Grandview
Spring City
Watts Bar Lake
Pleasant Hill
Ten Mile
Hurricane Ridge
Erie
Pennine
Peakland
Watts Bar Dam
Sewee
Tranquility
Mt. Verd Rd
Shut-in Gap Rd
Summer City Rd
Central Time Zone
Eastern Time Zone
Soak Cr.
Piney Creek
Pine Creek Rd
Liberty Hill Rd
Summer City
Morgan Springs
New Harmony
Cumberland Springs
Evensville
Smyrna Ln
Whites Flat Rd
Black Valley Rd
Old Washington
Decatur
Dayton
William Jennings Bryan College
Cottonwood Fy Rd
Morgantown
Ogden Rd
Smartt Mtn. 2,142
Brockdell Rd
Dill
Lee
Brockdell
Lusk
College
Plateau
Griffith Rd
Jakes Mtn. 2,204
Big Brush Creek
Dry Creek
Collins
Beersheba Springs
Savage Gulf S.N.A. (South Cumberland S.R.A.)
Altamont
Cumberland Heights
Big Cr.
Elk River
Barkertown
Tatesville
Gruetli Laager
Palmer
Daus Mountain Rd
Coalmont
Cumberland
Sanders Crossing
Visitor Center
Tracy City
White City
Grundy Lakes S.P.
Grundy Forest S.N.A.
South Cumberland State Recreation Areas
Griffith Creek
Mount Olive
Foster Falls Small Wild Area
Little Gizzard Cr. Small Wild Area
South Cumberland S.R.A.
Battle Creek
Sweden Creek
Victoria
Sequatchie
Jordan Rd
Sequatchie R.
Whitwell
Powells Crossroads
Cagle
Savage Cr.
Little Brush Cr.
Fredonia Rd
Paillo
Mount Airy
Dunlap
Lower East Valley Rd
Sequatchie Valley
Walden Ridge
Hendon
Hendon Rd
Braytop
McGill Creek
Leggett Rd
Roaring Creek
Rock Creek
Jones Gap Rd
Henson Gap Rd
Bakewell
Sale Creek
Graysville
Soddy Creek
Poe Rd
Cain Creek
Chickamauga Creek
Ridge
Lone Oak
Fairmount
Walden
Signal Mountain
Signal Point Reservation
Mullens Cr.
Prentice Cooper State Forest
Nickajack Lake
Raccoon Mtn. Caverns
Raccoon Mtn.
Soddy-Daisy
Shady Grove
Lakesite
Middle Valley
Chester Frost Co. Park
Harrison Bay State Park
Red Bank
Booker T. Washington State Park
Harrison
Volunteer Ordnance Works
Chattanooga
Ridgeside
Lovell Field Airport
East Ridge
Ooltewah
Collegedale
Apison
McDonald
Blue Springs
Ooltewah-Georgetown Pk
Georgetown
Hopewell
Birchwood
Chickamauga Lake
Hiwassee Wildlife Refuge
Tennessee River
Hiwassee River
Cottonport Rd
Big Spring
Lamontville Rd
Price Cr.
No Pone Ridge
McMinn Ridge
Rogers Creek
Hillsview-Sanford Rd
Riceville-Decatur Rd
Spring Creek
Riceville
Athens
Mouse Cr.
Cedar Springs Rd
Valley
Piney Grove Rd
Calhoun
Oostanaula Creek
Claxton Rd
Charleston
Delano Rd
Chestuee Creek
Candies Cr.
S. Mouse Cr.
Fairview
Tasso
Cleveland
Benton Station
Benton
Dentville Rd
Oswald Rd
Ocoee
Parksville
Lake Ocoee
Old Federal Rd
Baker Cr. Rd
Oldfort
Sand Mtn.
Cherokee National Forest
South Mill Creek
Candies Creek
Blue Springs Rd
Conasauga
Tennessee
Georgia
Alabama
Kimball
Jasper
Ebenezer
South Pittsburg
Orme
Orme Rd
New Hope
Haletown
Whiteside
Bridgeport
Mount Carmel
Bryant
Ferry
Tennessee River
New Home
Wildwood
Point Park and Lookout Mtn.
Lookout Mt.
Rossville
Lakeview
Ft. Oglethorpe
Flintstone
Chickamauga and Chattanooga N.M.P.
Chickamauga Battlefield
Missionary Ridge
New England
Hinkles
Wallaceville
Chickamauga
High Point
Trenton
Floral Crest
Higdon
Fabius
Cloudland Canyon S.P.
Lookout Mountain
Lookout Creek
Cooper Heights
West Chickamauga Creek
Rock Spring
Kensington
Davis Crossroads
La Fayette
Noble
Catlett
Little
Rising Fawn
Flat Rock
Graysville
Indian Springs
Ringgold
Cherokee Valley Rd
Catoosa Co. Rd
Red Clay
Cohutta
Keith
Varnell
Tunnel Hill
Waring
Rocky Face
Dalton
Mount Vernon
Chattahoochee National Forest
Mill Creek
Coahulla Creek
Lower Beaverdale Rd
Beaverdale
Sumac
Sumac Cr.
Tennga Rd
Tennga
Cisco
West Cow Pen Rd
Cohutta Wilderness Area
Mill Creek Rd
Crandall
Grassy Mtn. 3,682
Eton
Camp Rd
Chattahoochee National Forest
Dawnville
Holly Cr.
Ft. Mountain 2,854
Fort Mountain State Park
Chatsworth
Spring Place
Rock Cr.
Scale in Miles
0 2 4 6 8 10 12

1. Noccalula Falls Park

1500 Noccalula Rd., Gadsden. This 250-acre park encompasses multicolored botanical gardens, pioneer homesteads, a covered bridge, and a beautiful 90-foot falls watched over by a statue of the tragic Cherokee princess for whom it is named. The park is also the starting point for **Lookout Mountain Parkway,** a scenic route across the Appalachian foothills that leads all the way to Chattanooga. *Admission charged at park.*

2. Horton Mill Covered Bridge

Rte. 75, near Oneonta. Suspended 70 feet above Calvert Prong, this 220-foot-long bridge is the country's highest covered bridge above water.

3. Ave Maria Grotto

1600 St. Bernard Dr. SE, Cullman. More than 150 miniatures of famous buildings and shrines cover a terraced hillside, the lifework of Brother Joseph Zoettl, who lived in the adjacent abbey. There are replicas of the Parthenon, the Hanging Gardens of Babylon, the city of Jerusalem, and St. Peter's Basilica, built from materials such as cold cream jars, marbles, limestone, and seashells. *Admission charged.*

4. Clarkson Covered Bridge

Off Rte. 278, west of Cullman. With a span of 290 feet, this truss-style covered bridge is the largest in Alabama. Nearby are a working gristmill, a pioneer dogtrot cabin, hiking trails, and a picnic area.

5. Rickwood Caverns State Park

The massive limestone stalactites and stalagmites that cover this mysterious cave date back some 260 million years. A path that winds through the Miracle Mile of underground chambers travels 175 feet below ground; at the lowest level blind fish swim the eerie waters of an underground lake. *Admission charged.*

6. Bessemer

Chamber of Commerce, 321 North 18th St. The town's former railway station, built in 1916, now serves as the **Hall of History.** The museum chronicles Bessemer's past with prehistoric fossils, Civil War memorabilia, and displays on the town's important role in the steel industry. Listed on the National Register of Historic Places, the **Bessemer Historic Pioneer Homes** date from 1818 and are all furnished in period style — the **Sadler House** being an especially fine example of a dogtrot home. *Admission charged for some attractions.*

7. Tannehill Historical State Park

Off Rte. 59, near Bessemer. The 1,600-acre densely wooded park contains the partially reconstructed **Tannehill Furnaces,** major iron producers for the South in the Civil War. A nearby museum examines Alabama's important iron- and steel-making industries, and a re-created 19th-century village features a working gristmill, blacksmith's shop, farm buildings, and crafts demonstrations. *Admission charged.*

8. Oak Mountain State Park

Recreational opportunities abound in these rugged 10,000 wooded acres set in a scenic Appalachian valley, including tennis, golf, a bicycle motocross race track, and more than 30 miles of mountain trails. Three lakes offer fishing, swimming, and boating. A drive along twisting mountain roads, followed by a half-mile walk, is rewarded by a look at beautiful **Peavine Falls and Gorge.** *Admission charged.*

9. Vulcan

Off U.S. 31, Birmingham. A 55-foot-high statue of Vulcan, the ancient god of metallurgy, stands atop **Red Mountain** in tribute to the state's iron industry. Made from native Alabama iron for the 1904 Louisiana Purchase Exposition in St. Louis, the statue is one of the largest iron figures ever cast. For views of the city, a glass-enclosed elevator in **Vulcan Park** rises to an observation deck. *Admission charged at park.*

10. Arlington

331 Cotton Ave. SW, Birmingham. This lovely Greek Revival home is the only antebellum house that remains in Birmingham. Fine period furnishings and decorative arts reflect the gracious lifestyle of its 19th-century inhabitants. *Admission charged.*

11. Birmingham Museum of Art

2000 Eighth Ave. N., Birmingham. This museum's works of art include Renaissance drawings and paintings, bronzes by Remington, contemporary Chinese paintings, Alabama textiles and furnishings, an outdoor contemporary sculpture garden, and the largest 18th-century Wedgwood ceramic collection to be found outside of England.

12. Southern Museum of Flight

4343 73rd St. N., Birmingham. Exhibits include a replica of a 1910 Curtiss Pusher, a 1966 F-4 Phantom fighter, and a display about the flying school opened here in 1910 by the Wright brothers. *Admission charged.*

13. Sloss Furnaces National Historic Landmark

20 32nd St., Birmingham. In operation from 1882 to 1971, this massive ironworks plant is now open for tours. Visitors can walk through a boiler room, ovens, and casting areas, guided by retired blast-furnace workers who offer colorful first-hand accounts.

14. Discovery 2000

1421 22nd St. S., Birmingham. A walkway carved into a mountain provides a unique look at 150 million years of geology as it passes layers of fossil deposits, ash, shale and sandstone, and seams of iron ore. Exhibit areas offer a place to see, touch, and better understand the world of the arts, science, and technology. *Admission charged.*

15. Birmingham Botanical Gardens

2612 Lane Park Rd., Birmingham. The 67-acre gardens encompass trees, shrubs, specialized flower gardens, hundreds of species of birds, fine sculptures, and a rare plant conservatory that is the largest of its kind in the Southeast.

16. Kymulga Gristmill

Rtes. 175 and 180, Kymulga. One of the oldest water-powered gristmills in Alabama, this 3½-story structure built in 1864 still operates on Saturdays, when visitors can watch one of its five massive sets of stones grind corn. *Admission charged.*

17. De Soto Caverns

Rte. 76, Childersburg. Visited by Hernando de Soto in 1540, these vast caverns are the birthplace of the Creek Indian Nation, as well as a 2,000-year-old burial site of the Coopena Indians. Artifacts from the caves' later reincarnations as a Confederate gunpowder mining center and a Prohibition speakeasy are displayed. The Kymulga Room, a 12-story-high cave hung with sheets of golden onyx, features sound-and-light performances. *Admission charged.*

18. Sylacauga

Chamber of Commerce, 17 West Fort Williams St. White marble excavated here has been used in the U.S. Supreme Court and many other notable buildings. Area artifacts from the 19th century are the focus of the **Isabel Anderson Comer Museum.**

19. Talladega

Chamber of Commerce, 210 East St. S. The city's historic areas include the **Silk Stocking District,** with turn-of-the-century and antebellum houses, and **Talladega Square,** constructed in 1834. The Greek Revival **Talladega County Courthouse** has been in continuous use since its completion in 1836, making it the oldest such building in the state.

20. Talladega Super Speedway

3366 Speedway Blvd., near Talladega. One of the world's fastest speedways, the track is used as a test facility and sponsors two race weekends a year. Tours are available daily except for days of racing and testing. The **International Motorsports Hall of Fame** has a $12 million collection of record-breaking and other special cars dating from 1902. *Admission charged.*

21. Cheaha State Park

Surrounded by the **Talladega National Forest,** the park occupies some 2,700 wooded acres on **Cheaha Mountain,** at 2,407 feet the highest point in the state. At the summit, visitors can swim and fish in a lake, hike in pine-scented woods, and climb a stone tower for superb views.

22. Anniston

Chamber of Commerce, 1330 Quintard Ave. City attractions include the 1888 **Church of St. Michael and All Angels,** a romantic Romanesque building with a 12-foot Carrara marble altar and exquisite stained-glass windows. The **Anniston Museum of Natural History** displays 600 bird specimens, a 30-foot prehistoric Pteranodon, more than 100 African animals, and geological exhibits. *Admission charged at museum.*

23. Women's Army Corps Museum

Building 1077, Fort McClellan. The last training center of the Women's Army Corps, created during World War II and closed in 1978, is located here. Uniforms, re-created rooms, photos, and films document the proud history of the WAC's, as well as other women in the army from the Revolutionary War up to the present.

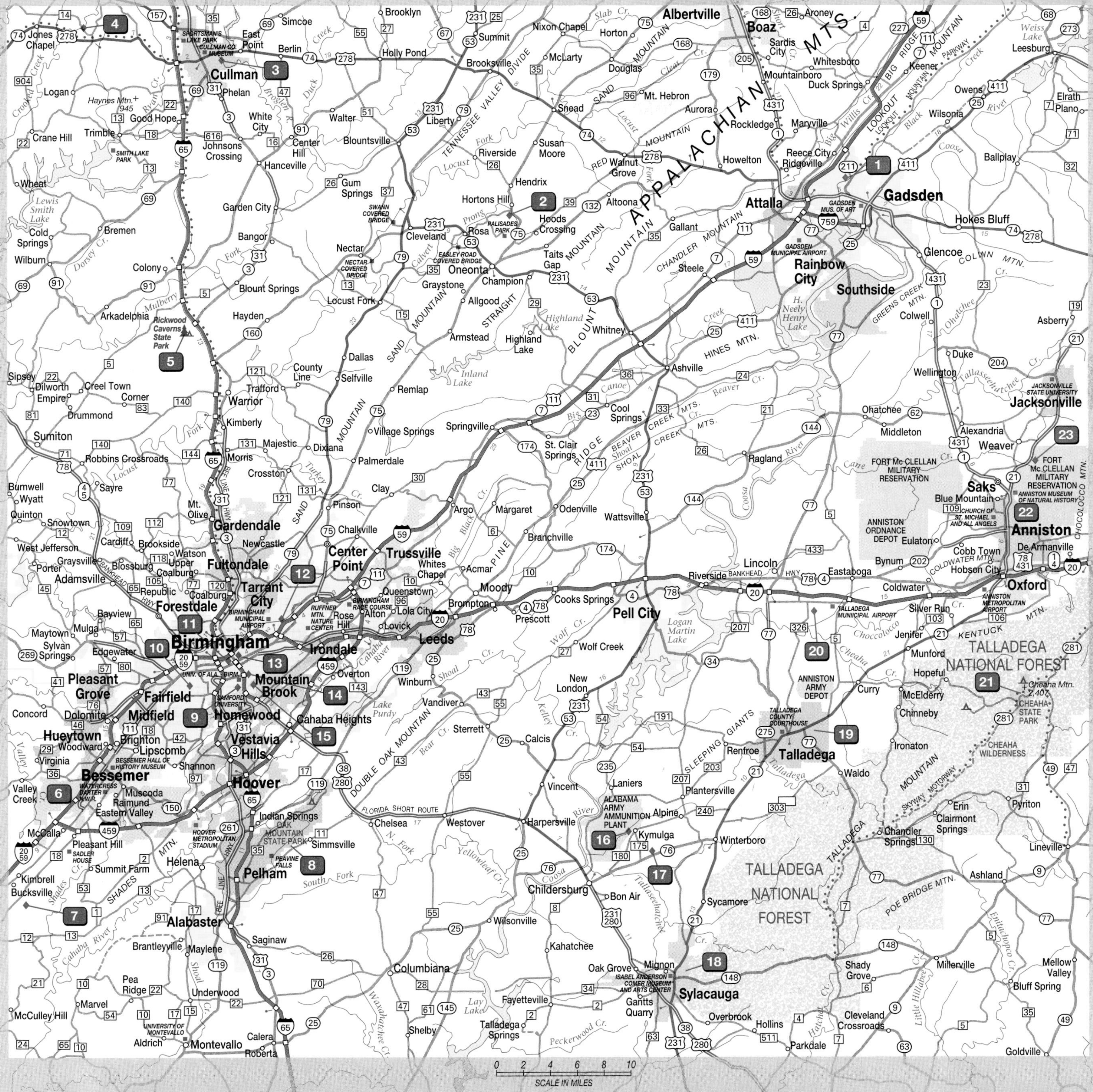

Cullman
Albertville
Boaz
Gadsden
Attalla
Rainbow City
Southside
Jacksonville
Anniston
Oxford
Birmingham
Bessemer
Hoover
Pelham
Alabaster
Sylacauga
Talladega
Pell City
Leeds
Trussville
Center Point
Tarrant City
Fultondale
Forestdale
Gardendale
Irondale
Mountain Brook
Homewood
Vestavia Hills
Fairfield
Midfield
Hueytown
Pleasant Grove
Oneonta
Childersburg
Montevallo
Columbiana
Warrior
Blountsville
Ashville
Springville
Moody
Helena
Calera
Saks
Weaver
Leesburg
APPALACHIAN MTS.
TALLADEGA NATIONAL FOREST
Cheaha Mtn. 2,407
CHEAHA STATE PARK
CHEAHA WILDERNESS
Logan Martin Lake
Lay Lake
Inland Lake
Highland Lake
H. Neely Henry Lake
Lewis Smith Lake
FORT McCLELLAN MILITARY RESERVATION
ANNISTON ORDNANCE DEPOT
ANNISTON ARMY DEPOT
ALABAMA ARMY AMMUNITION PLANT
Rickwood Caverns State Park
OAK MOUNTAIN STATE PARK
0 2 4 6 8 10
SCALE IN MILES

1. Sweetwater

Convention and Visitors Bureau, 810 East Broadway. Founded in 1877, this town preserves many old buildings in its historic district. The **Pioneer Museum,** once a judge's frontier house, contains American Indian artifacts, schoolroom and courtroom replicas, and an exhibit on female pilots who trained nearby during World War II.

2. Abilene

Convention and Visitors Bureau, 325 Hickory St. The **Abilene Zoological Gardens** draws comparisons between animals of the Texas plains and those of the African veld, a similar habitat. The **Buffalo Gap Historic Village** features buildings such as a railroad depot and blacksmith shop, while the **Dyess Air Force Base** displays several decades' worth of military aircraft. *Admission charged for some attractions.*

3. Douglas MacArthur Academy of Freedom

1320 Austin Ave., Brownwood. Located on the campus of **Howard Payne University,** this site contains a replica of Independence Hall and an exhibit about the signing of the Magna Carta. The **MacArthur Gallery** holds memorabilia of the famous general.

4. Fort Concho National Historic Landmark and Museum

213 East Ave. D., San Angelo. Established in 1867, this fort consists of more than 20 restored stone structures. On guided tours, visitors see the barracks, mess hall, and headquarters, which offers exhibits on the fort and the U.S. Army's role in the area during the Indian Wars. *Admission charged.*

5. Caverns of Sonora

Off Rte. 10W, near Sonora. Various tours reveal the wonders of this subterranean realm, whose crystals and other formations are world-famous. *Admission charged.*

6. Del Rio

Chamber of Commerce, 1915 Ave. F. The **San Felipe Springs** have made this town

an oasis. Located nearby, the **Amistad National Recreation Area** features a colossal lake ideal for boating and other water sports. In town are the **Whitehead Memorial Museum,** whose frontier buildings include a replica of Judge Roy Bean's saloon, the **Jersey Lily;** and the 19th-century **Courthouse Square Area.** Across the border lies **Ciudad Acuña,** a picturesque Mexican city whose good shopping attracts visitors. *Admission charged at museum.*

7. Uvalde

Chamber of Commerce, 300 East Main St. This town honors its most famous son, John Nance Garner — who served as vice president under Franklin Roosevelt — at the **Garner Memorial Museum.** The 1891 **Grand Opera House,** once owned by Garner, has been restored and is now used as a theater. *Admission charged at museum.*

8. Bandera

Convention and Visitors Bureau, 1206 Cypress St. Dude ranches, two-stepping, and an annual rodeo lend legitimacy to the claim that Bandera is the Cowboy Capital of the World. In a wooded canyon northwest of town, **Lost Maples State Natural Area** is a refuge for a variety of wildlife; hiking trails, picnic facilities, and campsites are available. *Admission charged.*

9. Kerrville

Convention and Visitors Bureau, 1700 Sidney Baker St. This town boasts the **Cowboy Artists of America Museum,** a striking building with art works that focus on Western themes. Housed in a turreted mansion, the **Hill Country Museum** features local-history displays. **Kerrville-Schreiner State Park,** on the Guadalupe River, offers a variety of outdoor activities.

10. Enchanted Rock State Natural Area

This colossal pink dome of granite can sometimes be heard creaking and groaning in the night — the result of cooling after a day's heat. As a geological phenomenon more than a billion years old, the rock is the focal point of this park, which also contains interesting plant life, a creek, camping facilities, and hiking trails. *Admission charged.*

11. Longhorn Cavern State Park

In this huge cavern, visitors can tour the Hall of Marble and marvel at the calcite crystals. Outside are picnic sites and hiking trails. *Fee charged for tour.*

12. Buchanan Dam

Chamber of Commerce, Rte. 29. Dams along the Colorado River have created seven lakes known as the **Highland Lakes Chain. Lake Buchanan,** the largest and northernmost, offers boating, fishing, camping, picnicking, and swimming. **Inks Lake State Park** also provides an array of recreational activities. *Admission charged at park.*

13. Fort Hood

Rte. 190, west of Killeen. This military post contains two museums. One celebrates the 1st Cavalry Division, which went from horseback to tanks in the course of several wars; the other pays tribute to the 2nd Armored Division and the III Corps. The Army Corps of Engineers runs nearby **Belton Lake,** whose many parks provide good opportunities for fishing, waterskiing, sailing, swimming, and camping.

14. Lake Whitney State Park

Boating, fishing, swimming, and camping are popular in this park on Lake Whitney, which extends for 45 miles along the Brazos River. Armadillos, deer, and other wildlife live in the park's grasslands and hardwood forests. *Admission charged.*

15. Waco

Tourist Information Center, Rte. 35 and University Park Dr., Ft. Fisher Park. After the suspension bridge across the Brazos River

Texas Ranger Hall of Fame and Museum

opened in 1870, Waco became a thriving commercial center. Today only pedestrians may use the bridge, which connects the lovely parks on both sides. Other historic structures in the city include residences from the mid-1800's and the Southwest's first skyscraper. The **Texas Ranger Hall of Fame and Museum** honors the legendary police force founded by Stephen Austin. *Admission charged at museum.*

16. Bastrop

Chamber of Commerce, 1009 Main St. Bastrop's historic sites include the 1883 county courthouse; the adjacent **Old Bastrop County Jail;** several Greek Revival residences; and the **Opera House,** constructed in 1889 and now home to a theater group. **Bastrop State Park,** set in a pine forest, has a swimming pool, lake, golf course, and facilities for picnicking and camping. *Admission charged for some attractions..*

17. Round Top

In the middle of this charming town lies **Henkel Square,** whose relocated and restored buildings, which date from 1820 to 1870, include homes, a school, and a church. The **Winedale Historical Center,** an 1831 farmstead, also contains restored 19th-century buildings. The **International Festival-Institute at Round Top** presents classical music performances and exhibits of decorative arts. *Admission charged for some attractions.*

18. La Grange

Chamber of Commerce, 129 North Main St. History is reflected in many of this town's attractions — from the 1800's county courthouse and jail to the **Fayette Heritage Museum and Archives,** where exhibits include artifacts, photographs, and documents related to Fayette County. At **Monument Hill** and **Kreische Brewery State Historical Parks,** one park honors Texans who died in encounters with Mexicans, and the other is an old-time brewery.

19. Gonzales

Chamber of Commerce, 414 St. Lawrence St. The **Gonzales Memorial Museum** houses the cannon that fired the first shot of the Texas Revolution, while the **Gonzales County Jail Museum** preserves an 1887 brick jailhouse. Restored 19th-century buildings, including a log cabin and church, are featured at the **Gonzales Pioneer Village Living History Center.** *Admission charged at center.*

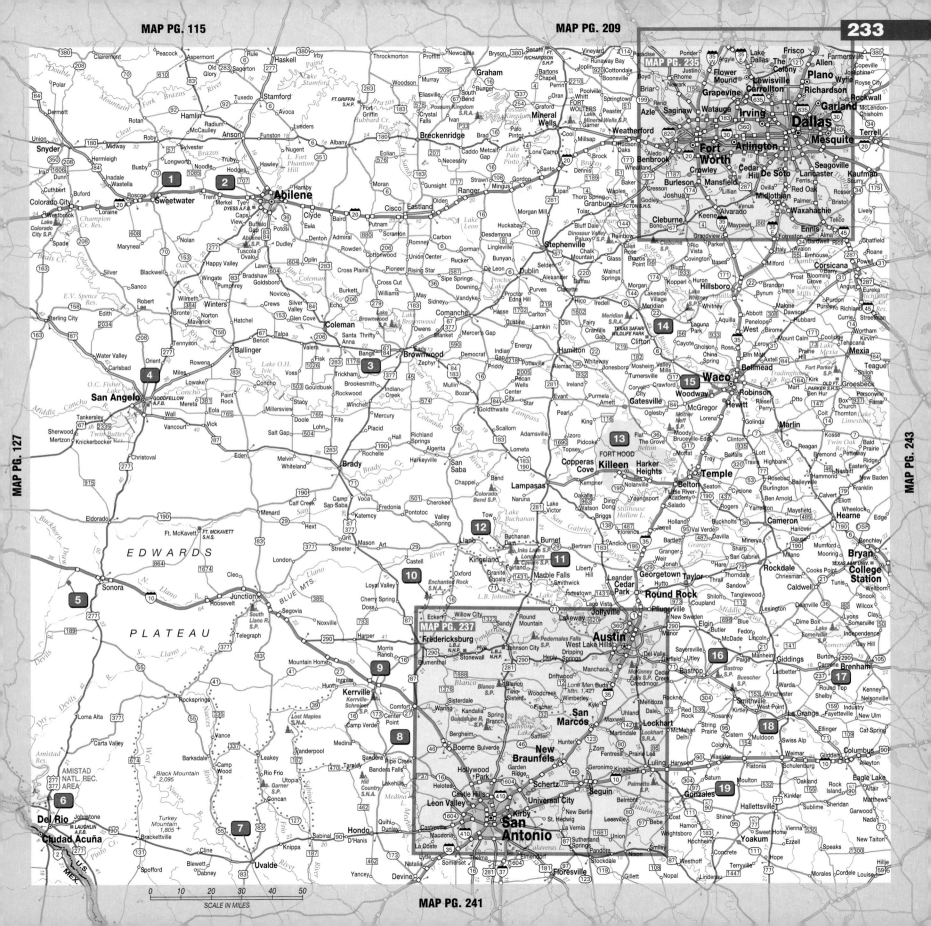

MAP PG. 235

MAP PG. 237

Snyder

Sweetwater

Abilene

Del Rio

Ciudad Acuña

San Angelo

Brady

Uvalde

San Antonio

Kerrville

Fredericksburg

Austin

San Marcos

New Braunfels

Round Rock

Killeen

Temple

Waco

Corsicana

Dallas

Fort Worth

Arlington

Plano

Garland

Mesquite

Bryan

College Station

EDWARDS PLATEAU

0   10   20   30   40   50
SCALE IN MILES

1. McKinney

Chamber of Commerce, 1801 West Louisiana. Situated near an artificial lake, McKinney has two intriguing museums. An oilman's hunting trophies — mounted animals from Texas and around the world — are presented at the **Bolin Wildlife Exhibit.** The **Heard Natural Science Museum and Wildlife Sanctuary** exhibits fossils, seashells, and gemstones, and has a preserve for native plants and animals.

2. Denton

Convention and Visitors Bureau, 414 Parkway. The **Denton County Courthouse-on-the-Square,** an impressive structure, houses a history museum with collections of 19th-century dolls, pressed blue glass, and Indian pottery. **Texas Woman's University** features one of the country's few research collections on women and the **Little Chapel-in-the-Woods,** with all artwork done by students.

3. Fort Worth Nature Center and Refuge

9601 Fossil Ridge Rd., Fort Worth. Buffaloes, bobcats, white-tailed deer, and migrating birds are among the wildlife that can be observed from trails and a boardwalk that protrudes into the marshland.

4. Fort Worth Museum of Science and History

1501 Montgomery St., Fort Worth. Exhibits here examine geology, medicine, computer technology, Texas history, and the history of humankind. The Noble Planetarium and the Omni Theater feature special shows. *Admission charged.*

5. Fort Worth Cultural District

Located within blocks of one another are three internationally known art museums. The **Amon Carter Museum** boasts an excellent collection of American, and particularly Western, art. The **Kimbell Art Museum** displays works that span centuries and cultures, including masterpieces by Rembrandt, Cezanne, and El Greco. The

Modern Art Museum of Fort Worth is devoted to 20th-century paintings, sculptures, and drawings.

6. Stockyards National Historic District

Exchange Ave. and North Main St., Fort Worth. Though still active in cattle sales, the famous stockyards are today better known as a tourist attraction and historic site. The **Cowtown Coliseum** and **Livestock Exchange Building** are still in use, but a cattle-pen complex has become a huge honky-tonk, and both old and new stores sell Western gear. Rodeos, mock gunfights, and other shows keep the Old West alive.

7. The Cattleman's Museum

1301 West Seventh St., Fort Worth. The cattle industry is examined and explained at this museum through photographs, films, videos, dioramas, and artifacts including saddles and branding irons.

8. Fort Worth Water Gardens

Commerce and 15th Sts., Fort Worth. Adding splendor to its downtown locale, the park features enormous concrete terraces, over which flow 19,000 gallons of water per minute before forming a pool. The park is also a green oasis; amid its plants and trees, other pools and fountains sparkle in the sun or the night lights.

9. Sid Richardson Collection of Western Art

309 Main St., Fort Worth. The collection features 52 paintings by Western artists Frederic Remington and Charles M. Russell, all acquisitions of oilman Richardson.

10. Forest Park

Forest Park Blvd., Fort Worth. This park and its neighbor, **Trinity,** offer many diversions, such as a swimming pool, casting pool, duck pond, and miniature train. These attractions can be seen on the scenic drive through both parks, along the Clear Fork of the Trinity River. Within Forest Park lie the seven restored pioneer homes and working gristmill of **Log Cabin Village.** Demonstrations of candle-dipping, spinning, and other activities take place regularly in the cabins. *Admission charged at village.*

11. Fort Worth Zoological Park

Colonial Pkwy., Fort Worth. More than 4,000 animals live in this beautifully landscaped zoo. Habitats include a huge aquarium with one of the largest freshwater tanks in the country, an award-winning herpetarium, a

free-flight aviary, and a frontier Texas village featuring longhorn steers and other native animals. *Admission charged.*

12. Fort Worth Botanic Gardens

3220 Botanic Garden Blvd., Fort Worth. Trees, shrubs, and flowers from around the world thrive in this beautiful, 110-acre setting. The **Conservatory** shelters tropical plants, growing near waterfalls and ponds. The tranquil **Japanese Garden** has a pagoda, moon-viewing deck, and traditional arrangements of plants, stones, and water. *Admission charged for some attractions.*

13. Cleburne

Chamber of Commerce, 1511 West Henderson. The forests and springs of the **Cleburne State Park** draw deer, quail, and other wildlife, and a large lake provides good boating, fishing, and swimming. Cleburne's history is chronicled in the **Layland Museum,** which displays American Indian pottery and artifacts, along with Civil War and frontier exhibits. *Admission charged at recreation area.*

14. Six Flags Over Texas

2201 Road to Six Flags, Arlington. The amusements here include shows and numerous rides — from the tame Silver Star Carousel to the heart-stopping Shock Wave roller coaster. There's also a narrow-gauge railway, which takes visitors through the park. *Admission charged.*

15. The Sixth Floor

411 Elm Street, Dallas. The former Texas School Book Depository, from which John F. Kennedy was allegedly shot, now has an exhibit dedicated to President Kennedy on the sixth floor. Displays document the early 1960's, the assassination, and the investigation that followed. From the window, visitors can see **Dealey Plaza,** where the president was shot, and the motorcade route. *Admission charged.*

16. Dallas Theater Center

3636 Turtle Creek Blvd., Dallas. Mainstage performances take place at the **Arts District Theater** and the **Kalita Humphreys Theater** — the latter designed by Frank Lloyd Wright — while a performance space called In the Basement is dedicated to works of an experimental nature.

17. Meadows Museum

6101 Bishop Blvd., Dallas. Located in the Meadows School of the Arts at **Southern**

Methodist University, this small museum boasts a sculpture garden and an excellent collection of paintings by Picasso, Goya, and other Spanish masters.

18. Biblical Arts Center

7500 Park Lane, Dallas. This center holds religious art and artifacts from around the world. Representing numerous denominations, the collection includes a replica of Christ's tomb and "Miracle at Pentecost," a colossal mural. *Admission charged for some exhibits.*

19. Dallas Museum of Art

1717 North Harwood St., Dallas. With works ranging from pre-Columbian to modern, this fascinating museum has something to suit everyone's taste. The Wendy and Emery Reves Collection features rooms that replicate the Reves's Mediterranean villa, complete with French furnishings. *Admission charged for some exhibits.*

20. Fair Park

An impressive collection of Art Deco buildings constructed for the 1936 Texas Centennial grace this Dallas park, which is home to the **Cotton Bowl Stadium,** the state fair, and a number of museums. The imposing **Hall of State,** with its 12-foot gold medallion, houses **A Shrine to Texas History.** The **Science Place** and **The Science Place Planetarium** have entertaining and educational exhibits; the **Age of Steam Railroad Museum** displays steam locomotives and passenger cars; and the **Dallas Museum of Natural History** examines the plant and animal life of Texas. The **Dallas Aquarium** features more than 375 species of aquatic animals. *Admission charged for some attractions.*

21. Dallas County Historical Plaza

Three historical sites occupy the plaza: the 1841 log cabin of Dallas founder John Neely Bryan; the gargoyle-topped Romanesque courthouse, built from sandstone in 1890 and nicknamed Old Red; and the **John F. Kennedy Memorial,** a simple monument that honors America's 35th president.

22. Dallas Zoo

621 East Clarendon Dr., Dallas. Visitors can take a monorail or follow a nature trail in the Wilds of Africa, where animals can be observed in naturalistic habitats. Especially popular with children are the Reptile Discovery Center and the seasonal petting zoo. *Admission charged.*

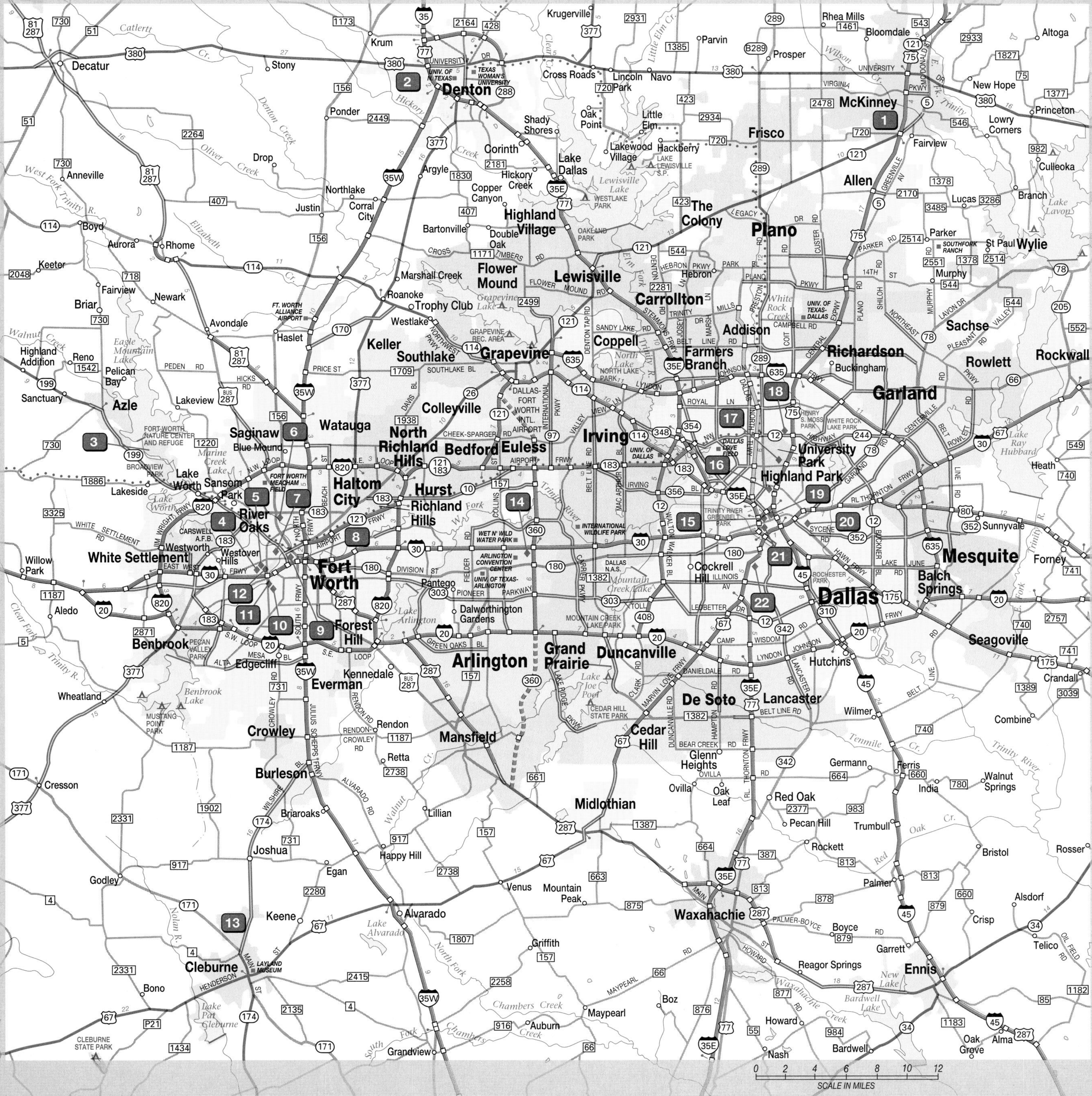

Decatur
Stony
Krum
Denton
Krugerville
Cross Roads
Lincoln Park
Navo
Parvin
Prosper
Rhea Mills
Bloomdale
Altoga
McKinney
New Hope
Princeton
Lowry Corners
Fairview
Ponder
Shady Shores
Oak Point
Little Elm
Lakewood Village
Hackberry
Frisco
Drop
Corinth
Lake Dallas
Argyle
Hickory Creek
Anneville
Northlake
Copper Canyon
Allen
Lucas
Branch
Culleoka
Justin
Corral City
Highland Village
The Colony
Boyd
Aurora
Rhome
Bartonville
Double Oak
Plano
Parker
St Paul
Wylie
Keeter
Flower Mound
Lewisville
Carrollton
Murphy
Fairview
Newark
Marshall Creek
Roanoke
Briar
Trophy Club
Sachse
Avondale
Westlake
Addison
Haslet
Keller
Coppell
Farmers Branch
Richardson
Highland Addition
Reno
Southlake
Grapevine
Rowlett
Rockwall
Pelican Bay
Sanctuary
Buckingham
Azle
Lakeview
Colleyville
Garland
Saginaw
Watauga
North Richland Hills
Bedford
Euless
Irving
Blue Mound
University Park
Heath
Lake Worth
Sansom Park
Lakeside
Haltom City
Hurst
Highland Park
Richland Hills
River Oaks
Sunnyvale
Westworth
Westover Hills
White Settlement
Willow Park
Fort Worth
Mesquite
Forney
Cockrell Hill
Pantego
Balch Springs
Dallas
Aledo
Dalworthington Gardens
Forest Hill
Benbrook
Edgecliff
Arlington
Grand Prairie
Duncanville
Seagoville
Hutchins
Kennedale
Everman
Crandall
Wheatland
Crowley
Rendon
De Soto
Lancaster
Wilmer
Combine
Cedar Hill
Mansfield
Retta
Glenn Heights
Burleson
Ferris
India
Walnut Springs
Cresson
Ovilla
Oak Leaf
Red Oak
Pecan Hill
Midlothian
Briaroaks
Lillian
Trumbull
Joshua
Happy Hill
Rockett
Bristol
Rosser
Egan
Godley
Venus
Mountain Peak
Palmer
Alsdorf
Crisp
Keene
Alvarado
Waxahachie
Boyce
Telico
Cleburne
Griffith
Garrett
Reagor Springs
Ennis
Bono
Maypearl
Boz
Howard
Auburn
Bardwell
Oak Grove
Alma
Nash
Grandview
Cleburne State Park
0 2 4 6 8 10 12
SCALE IN MILES

1. Fredericksburg

Chamber of Commerce, 106 North Adams St. The town was first settled by German farmers in 1846, and the **Pioneer Museum Complex** recalls that past with displays of antique furniture and five restored buildings. The **Admiral Nimitz Museum State Historical Park,** located in the former Nimitz Hotel, traces the impressive career of Adm. Chester Nimitz, a native of Fredericksburg who commanded the U.S. Navy during World War II. *Admission charged.*

2. Lyndon B. Johnson State Historical Park

Rte. 290, west of Johnson City. The park's visitor center exhibits presidential gifts and a pioneer log cabin and offers displays on the Johnson family and on local history. The **Sauer-Beckmann Homestead** is an operating living-history farm, where costumed interpreters perform turn-of-the-century chores such as tending farm animals, gardening, and cooking. On the nature trail, which is more than a mile long, visitors pass enclosures of Texas longhorns.

3. Lyndon B. Johnson National Historical Park

Off Rte. 290, Johnson City. This park is dedicated to the 36th president and consists of two units. Located in the Johnson City Unit are **Johnson's Boyhood Home,** restored to its early 1920's appearance, and the **Johnson Settlement,** a re-created ranch once owned by the president's grandfather. At the ranch unit, visitors pass by the **Ranch House,** once known as the Texas White House. Nearby are the **Johnson Birthplace,** a reconstructed farmhouse where the president was born; the **Junction School,** where he studied as a boy; and the **Johnson Family Cemetery,** which is the site of his grave. Buses for the ranch unit leave from the Lyndon B. Johnson State Historical Park.

4. Sea World of Texas

10500 Sea World Dr., San Antonio. A 250-acre park dedicated to marine life, Sea World of Texas offers more than 25 shows, attractions, and exhibits. Highlights include a Shamu the Killer Whale show, a large coral reef aquarium, a penguin habitat, and a re-created tropical paradise for children. *Admission charged.*

5. San Antonio Missions National Historical Park

2202 Roosevelt Ave., San Antonio. These missions, built by Spain during the 1700's in an effort to retain power in America and convert the native inhabitants, are among the oldest structures in the country. The churches were constructed from thick stone, and each complex spans several acres. San José, known as the Queen of the Missions, is the loveliest of the group and features a baroque rose window.

6. Brackenridge Park

3500 North Saint Mary's St., San Antonio. This 344-acre verdant park includes a golf course, riding stables, paddle boats, the **San Antonio Zoo,** and the **Japanese Tea Garden.** The **Witte Museum** focuses on the history and natural science of the state and features many participatory exhibits. The adjacent **Pioneer Hall** is devoted to the story of early Texas, with displays covering the lives of the original Texas Rangers, pioneers, and a Texas trail driver. For fine views of the park, visitors can take the skyride or miniature train. *Admission charged for some attractions.*

7. Fort Sam Houston

Off Rte. 35, San Antonio. Near the main gate of this large fort — named after the first governor of Texas — is a limestone quadrangle, which has been designated a National Historic Landmark. Located within the complex, the **U.S. Army Medical Museum** traces the history of this army department from the Civil War up to the present with uniforms, photographs, equipment, and other memorabilia. At the **Sam Houston Museum,** visitors can relive the history of the fort with the help of artifacts and other exhibits.

8. McNay Art Museum

6000 North New Braunfels Ave., San Antonio. A popular San Antonio attraction, this museum is housed in a quaint, Spanish Colonial–style mansion, the grounds of which contain an elegant courtyard. The museum's fine collection includes examples of post-Impressionist, Expressionist, European, and American art.

9. Natural Bridge Caverns

Off Rte. 35, north of San Antonio. Below a 60-foot bridge of limestone lies an enormous cave system, formed more than 140 million years ago. On a guided tour visitors view the cavern's large rooms, which have odd and colorful calcite formations — one resembling a hanging chandelier and another a high watchtower. *Fee charged for tour.*

10. Seguin

Chamber of Commerce, 427 North Austin St. This historic town is known for its concrete buildings, the most famous being the 19th-century Greek Revival home in **Sebastopol State Historical Park.** The **Campbell-Hoermann Cabin** was constructed in the dogtrot style favored by pioneers. **Max Starcke Park,** on the Guadalupe River, offers a scenic drive, picnic areas with barbecue pits, and sports facilities. *Admission charged for some attractions.*

11. New Braunfels

Chamber of Commerce, 390 South Seguin Ave. Fine landscapes and Victorian homes give New Braunfels an Old World flavor. The **Gruene Historical District** has many well-preserved buildings, including Texas's oldest dance hall. More than 75 original woodworks are exhibited at the **Museum of Texas Handmade Furniture.** The **Sophienburg Museum** displays handmade furniture, needlework, re-created stores, and a miniature of a German castle. *Admission charged for some attractions.*

12. Canyon Lake

This 8,231-acre lake, whose crystal-clear blue waters are nestled among steep green hills, is bordered by six parks. Outdoor enthusiasts will find excellent opportunities here for fishing, boating, swimming, scuba diving, and waterskiing. Campsites and picnicking facilities are also available. *Fee charged for some activities.*

13. Pioneer Town

Off Rte. 12, Wimberley. This replica of an 1880's town includes an opera house, saloon, general store, and even a house made from soda bottles. Visitors can take a mile-long scenic ride on an old-fashioned steam train. Two museums exhibit Western art, including reproductions of bronzes by artist Frederic Remington.

14. San Marcos

Convention and Visitors Bureau, 202 C.M. Allen Pkwy. The **Belvin Street National Historic District** preserves a lovely residential part of town, where ancient oaks tower above rows of private Victorian homes. The **Charles S. Cock House Museum** is the oldest stone house in San Marcos. For modern-day fun, visitors head to **Aquarena Springs,** an amusement park featuring a 45-minute water show and one of the only glass-bottom boat rides in Texas. *Admission charged for some attractions.*

15. Zilker Park

2201 Barton Springs Rd., Austin. The beautiful landscaping featured at this 360-acre park is especially apparent at **Zilker Botanical Garden,** where azaleas, roses, and an Oriental garden thrive. The **Austin Nature Center** is located nearby, offering displays on dinosaurs as well as indigenous plants and animals. Other attractions at the park include a miniature train ride and Barton Springs, which is popular as a local swimming spot.

16. Governor's Mansion

1010 Colorado St., Austin. This mansion was built in the 1850's as a residence for the state governor. Today, after having been carefully restored to its original state, the home represents an excellent example of Greek Revival architecture. The brick structure has 30-foot-tall columns made of cyprus and pine; historical furnishings and artwork decorate the rooms.

17. State Capitol

11th St. and Congress Ave., Austin. Taller than the U.S. Capitol and considered by many to be quite as grand, this Renaissance Revival–style structure dating from 1888 features a large painted metal dome, statuary, and paintings. Leading away from the capitol is **Congress Avenue,** a historic street with the time-traveling juxtaposition of skyscrapers and 19th-century buildings.

18. University of Texas at Austin

UTA is the cornerstone of the University of Texas system. Its **Lyndon B. Johnson Library and Museum** traces the former president's life and career and displays political memorabilia. Also on campus is the **Harry Ransom Humanities Research Center,** which exhibits more than 300 paintings, ancient sculptures, and a rare Gutenberg Bible. It also contains the **Flawn Academic Center,** where a splendid collection of rare books is housed.

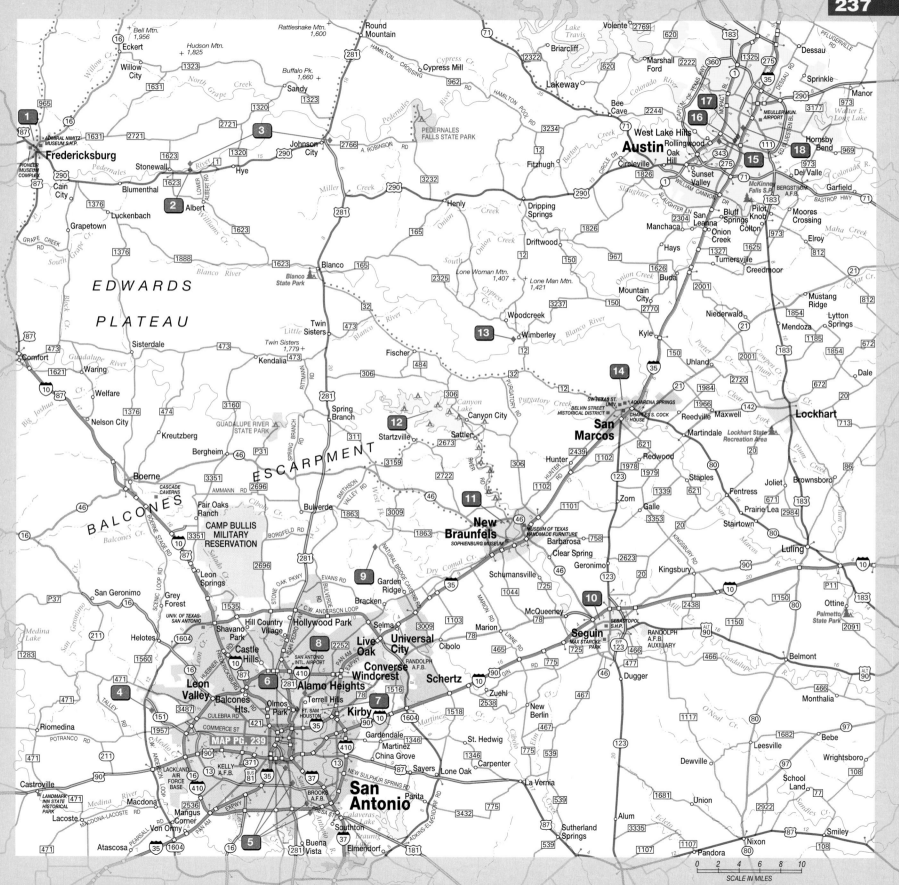

Bell Mtn.
1,956
Eckert
Hudson Mtn.
1,825
Rattlesnake Mtn.
1,600
Round Mountain
Volente
Dessau
PFLUGERVILLE RD
Briarcliff
Willow City
Buffalo Pk.
1,660
Sandy
Marshall Ford
Lake Travis
Sprinkle
Lakeway
Manor
Bee Cave
Cypress Mill
Cypress Mill
HAMILTON CROSSING
HAMILTON POOL RD
West Lake Hills
MEULLERMUN. AIRPORT
Fredericksburg
ADMIRAL NIMITZ MUSEUM S.H.P.
PIONEER MUSEUM COMPLEX
Johnson City
A. ROBINSON RD
PEDERNALES FALLS STATE PARK
Austin
Rollingwood
Oak Hill
Hornsby Bend
Del Valle
Garfield
Stonewall
Hye
Circleville
Sunset Valley
McKINNEY FALLS S.P.
BERGSTROM A.F.B.
BASTROP HWY
Cain City
Blumenthal
Fitzhugh
Manchaca
San Leanna
Bluff Springs
Colton
Moores Crossing
Elroy
Luckenbach
Henly
Dripping Springs
Hays
Onion Creek
Pilot Knob
Grapetown
Driftwood
Mountain City
Buda
Mustang Ridge
Lytton Springs
Blanco
Blanco State Park
Woodcreek
Niederwald
Mendoza
EDWARDS PLATEAU
Lone Woman Mtn.
1,407
Lone Man Mtn.
1,421
Wimberley
Kyle
Dale
Sisterdale
Twin Sisters
Fischer
Uhland
Twin Sisters
1,779
Kendalia
Comfort
Waring
Reedville
Maxwell
Lockhart
Welfare
Nelson City
Kreutzberg
Canyon Lake
Canyon City
San Marcos
SW TEXAS ST. UNIV.
BELVIN STREET HISTORICAL DISTRICT
AQUARENA SPRINGS
CHARLES S. COCK HOUSE
Martindale
Lockhart State Recreation Area
Bergheim
Spring Branch
Startzville
Sattler
Hunter
Redwood
Staples
Joliet
Brownsboro
Boerne
CASCADE CAVERNS
GUADALUPE RIVER STATE PARK
Zorn
Fentress
ESCARPMENT
BALCONES
Fair Oaks Ranch
CAMP BULLIS MILITARY RESERVATION
Bulverde
New Braunfels
SOPHIENBURG MUSEUM
MUSEUM OF TEXAS HANDMADE FURNITURE
Galle
Prairie Lea
Stairtown
Barbarosa
Clear Spring
Geronimo
Kingsbury
Luling
San Geronimo
Grey Forest
Leon Springs
Schumansville
Kingsbury
Helotes
UNIV. OF TEXAS-SAN ANTONIO
Shavano Park
Hill Country Village
Hollywood Park
Garden Ridge
McQueeney
Seguin
MAX STARCKE PARK
SEBASTOPOL S.H.P.
Medina Lake
Bracken
Marion
RANDOLPH A.F.B. AUXILIARY
Castle Hills
SAN ANTONIO INTL. AIRPORT
Live Oak
Selma
Universal City
Cibolo
Ottine
PALMETTO STATE PARK
Leon Valley
Balcones Hts.
RANDOLPH A.F.B.
Converse
Windcrest
Schertz
Belmont
Monthalia
Riomedina
Olmos Park
Alamo Heights
Terrell Hills
FT. SAM HOUSTON
Kirby
Zuehl
New Berlin
Dugger
San Geronimo
MAP PG. 239
KELLY A.F.B.
Gardendale
Martinez
China Grove
St. Hedwig
Leesville
Bebe
Castroville
LANDMARK INN STATE HISTORICAL PARK
LACKLAND AIR FORCE BASE
BROOKS A.F.B.
San Antonio
Sayers
Lone Oak
Carpenter
La Vernia
Wrightsboro
School Land
Lacoste
Macdona
Mangus Corner
Von Ormy
Southton
Elmendorf
Panita
Sutherland Springs
Union
Atascosa
Buena Vista
Dewville
Alum
Nixon
Smiley
Pandora

SCALE IN MILES
0 2 4 6 8 10

DOWNTOWN SAN ANTONIO

1. San Antonio Museum of Art

200 West Jones Ave. Housed in the former Lone Star Brewing Company buildings — replete with Romanesque towers and turrets — the museum features pre-Columbian sculpture and pottery, Spanish Colonial art, and Latin American folk art. Other exhibits include European and American works from the 18th century to the present. *Admission charged.*

2. Plaza Theatre of Wax/ Ripley's Believe It Or Not!

301 Alamo Plaza. Here visitors can gaze at some 225 wax likenesses of heroes, Hollywood stars, and horror figures. The extent of life's strangeness is also on view, with more than 500 truly unbelievable oddities that were collected from around the world. *Admission charged.*

3. The Alamo

Alamo Plaza. Known as the cradle of Texas liberty, the Alamo was originally built by Franciscans as a part of the Mission San Antonio de Valero. After the 1740's a chapel was added, and about 50 years later the compound became a fort. In February 1836, during the Texas Revolution, more than 4,000 Mexican troops led by Gen. Santa Anna laid siege to the site, which was defended by some 188 men. The Texan forces, including Davy Crockett and James Bowie, refused to surrender and fought to their deaths. Six weeks later revenge was had at San Jacinto, where the Mexicans were routed by the Texans, who rallied around the cry of "Remember the Alamo!"

4. Menger Hotel

204 Alamo Plaza. Washington may not have slept here, but Robert E. Lee, Theodore Roosevelt, and William Jennings Bryan did. Visitors to this local landmark may still sidle up to the bar where Roosevelt

once sought recruits for his army of Rough Riders during the Spanish-American War.

5. San Fernando Cathedral

115 Main Plaza. This fine example of French Gothic architecture, completed in 1873, was added on to a 1738 Spanish Baroque church, which is one of the oldest cathedral sanctuaries in the country. Remains of the defenders of the Alamo, rescued from funeral pyres, are said to be buried in the site's foundations.

6. Spanish Governor's Palace

105 Plaza de Armas. Built from the remnants of a Spanish fort into a military commander's residence, the palace is the only remaining example of a Spanish Colonial home in Texas. The original keystone, dated 1749, bears the Hapsburg coat of arms. Ten rooms, including a family chapel and a kitchen with an open stone brazier, are furnished with beautiful Spanish Colonial antiques. *Admission charged.*

7. Market Square

514 West Commerce St.. This large and lively Mexican marketplace has been in operation for more than a century. Fresh-picked fruits and vegetables can be found at

the **Farmers' Market,** and savvy shoppers can haggle for a good deal on folk art, pottery, blankets, and more at **El Mercado.**

8. José Antonio Navarro State Historic Site

228 South Laredo St. This former home of a prominent rancher and statesman features three restored adobe and limestone buildings — a residence, a law office, and a kitchen — built in a mixture of architectural styles and furnished with simple period antiques to re-create how they appeared in the mid-19th century. Occasional demonstrations of adobe making are also presented here. *Admission charged.*

9. Plaza de Armas

100 Plaza de Armas. Once a drilling ground for Spanish troops and then a marketplace, the plaza is now home to **City Hall,** which was built in 1891 in Second Empire and Renaissance Revival styles and later modernized. Watching over the plaza is a statue of Moses Austin, an American pioneer often referred to as the Father of Texas.

10. Hertzberg Circus and Museum

210 Market St. More than 20,000 items compose this entertaining collection

The siege of the Alamo proved to be the turning point of the Texas Revolution.

of circus memorabilia, including Tom Thumb's small carriage, a miniature circus, autographed pictures, and a variety of items once belonging to P. T. Barnum. For research buffs, there's also an extensive library. *Admission charged.*

11. La Villita

La Villita, meaning "little town," is a 250-year-old Spanish settlement nestled on a quiet block in the center of downtown. It was here that Mexican General Cos was said to have surrendered San Antonio to Texas revolutionaries. Today the streets are lined with studios where artists demonstrate their crafts. At the unique, open-air **Arneson River Theater,** spectators sit on grassy seats on one side of the Paseo del Rio while performances take place on the other. Music, theater, and Mexican folk dances are presented in the summer. *Admission charged at theater.*

12. Henry B. Gonzalez Convention Center

200 East Market St. The San Antonio River flows right through this ultra-modern center. Passengers aboard the quaint boat-taxis that tour the downtown area will have a dramatic view of the giant mural created on the exterior wall of the center by Mexican artist Juan O'Gorman. *Fee charged for boat-taxi ride.*

13. Paseo del Rio

Off Rte. 35. Often called the River Walk, this charming walkway follows the San Antonio River through the heart of the downtown district. The landscaped area contains arched bridges, subtropical plants, and lovely trees. Here cobblestone paths meander past delightful cafes, shops, restaurants, and the Mediterranean-style buildings lining the riverbanks.

14. HemisFair Park

This sprawling esplanade was built for the San Antonio World's Fair in 1968, the year of the city's 250th anniversary. Located in the park are several government buildings, museums, restaurants, fountains, pools, waterfalls, and landscaped walking trails.

15. Institute of Mexican Cultures

600 HemisFair Park. Four galleries present changing contemporary art exhibits from Mexico as well as South America. Mexican crafts and archeological exhibits are also on display here.

16. Tower of the Americas

600 HemisFair Park. Soaring above all of San Antonio, the tower offers grand views reaching some 100 miles in each direction from its 579-foot-high observation deck. It is crowned by a revolving restaurant and surrounded at its base by a picturesque park overflowing with pools, waterfalls, and fountains. *Admission charged.*

17. Institute of Texan Cultures

801 South Bowie. Exhibits and demonstrations at this exceptional museum illustrate the lives of people from the many ethnic groups that helped settle the Lone Star state. Displays examine varied aspects of early Texas culture, from Mexican cooking to tales of the pioneer trail. Artifacts include clothing, textile handiwork, and musical instruments. Tours are available.

18. King William Historic District

A stroll down tree-lined King William Street, the heart of this stylish residential district, takes visitors back to a gentler age, complete with handsome Victorian houses and Germanic architecture. The lovely 1876 Second Empire **Steves Homestead,** which is filled with period antiques, features elaborate interior and exterior wood trims. *Donation encouraged at the homestead.*

19. Buckhorn Hall of Horns

600 Lone Star Blvd. During the 1880's, hunters brought animal trophies from around the world to the **Buckhorn Saloon** in exchange for a cold brew. Today a collection of mounted horns awaits visitors to this museum, which is located in the **Lone Star Brewery.** Also here are the **Hall of Texas History Wax Museum** and the **O. Henry House,** home of the renowned short-story writer. *Admission charged.*

20. Yturri-Edmunds Home and Mill

257 Yellowstone. This restored structure is one of the few remaining adobe-block farmhouses that once lined the San Antonio River in the 1840's. Corn-grinding demonstrations are occasionally held in the gristmill. *Admission charged.*

21. Mission Concepción

807 Mission Rd. Established in 1731, this is one of the nation's oldest unrestored stone missions, with traces of its original frescoes remaining. Still in use, it is one of four missions located within the **San Antonio Missions National Historical Park.**

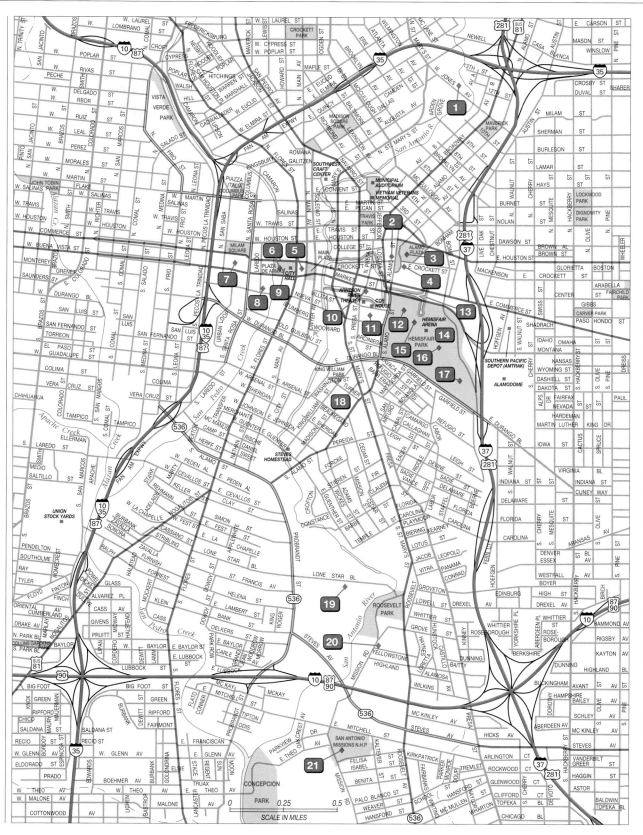

1. Eagle Pass

Chamber of Commerce, 400 Garrison Ave. At **Fort Duncan Park,** a museum in the old headquarters has regional artifacts and exhibits on past occupants. Nearby **Piedras Negras, Mexico,** has popular restaurants, a central market, and arts-and-crafts shops.

2. Laredo

Convention and Visitors Bureau, 2310 San Bernardo Ave. Housed in what once was the capitol, the **Museum of the Republic of the Rio Grande** examines this short-lived government. The **Laredo Children's Museum** is in the former chapel and guardhouse of Ft. McIntosh. Across the Rio Grande, visitors will find shops and restaurants in **Nuevo Laredo, Mexico.** *Admission charged at children's museum.*

3. McAllen

Chamber of Commerce, 10 North Broadway. The **McAllen International Museum** exhibits paintings, folk art, and more. Nearby **Reynosa, Mexico,** offers bargain shopping and, on occasion, bullfights. *Admission charged for some attractions.*

4. Santa Ana National Wildlife Refuge

Some 12 miles of interconnected trails lead through this refuge, which is considered by bird-watchers to be one of the finest. Wildcats and more than 370 species of birds, many of which cannot be seen elsewhere in the country, have been sighted in this habitat's subtropical forest.

5. Harlingen

Chamber of Commerce, 311 East Tyler St. The **Rio Grande Valley Museum** traces this valley's history, and the **Marine Military Academy** displays the original mold for the U.S. Marine Corps War Memorial, which immortalized the flag raising at Iwo Jima. World War II aircraft, taking to the sky in an October air show, are preserved at the **American Airpower Heritage Museum/Confederate Air Force.** *Admission charged for some attractions.*

6. Brownsville

Convention and Visitors Bureau, 650 Rte. 802. This city was the site of the first battle in the Mexican War and of the last land engagement in the Civil War. The **Gladys Porter Zoo** breeds endangered species and has wonderful animal displays. Nearby **Matamoros, Mexico,** boasts a historic fort and cathedral, in addition to a lively market. *Admission charged for some attractions.*

7. South Padre Island

Convention and Visitors Bureau, 600 Padre Blvd. Sunbathers and swimmers enjoy the many white beaches here. The resort area is also an artists' haven and home to **Sea Turtle, Inc.,** which offers shows that allow visitors a firsthand look at the marine reptiles.

8. Laguna Atascosa National Wildlife Refuge

This 45,000-acre refuge is the southernmost waterfowl preserve in the country. From well-marked hiking trails and driving routes, visitors may spot various rare and endangered species, such as ocelots and peregrines. *Admission charged.*

9. Padre Island National Seashore

Nearly 70 miles of sandy beach and dunes make up this undeveloped seashore, part of 113-mile-long Padre Island. **Malaquite Beach,** toward the northern end, has good swimming; remote stretches farther south, reached on foot or by four-wheel-drive vehicles, boast fishing, swimming, beachcombing, and bird-watching. *Admission charged.*

10. King Ranch

Rte. 141, Kingsville. Bus tours travel a 12-mile road past stables, an auction area, dam, and ranch headquarters on this 825,000-acre cattle ranch. *Fee charged for tour.*

11. Corpus Christi

Convention and Visitors Bureau, 1201 North Shoreline Blvd. **Sidbury House** is the city's only remaining example of high-Victorian architecture. The **Art Museum of South Texas** displays contemporary American artworks, while the **Museum of Oriental Cultures** has an excellent collection of Asian art and Japanese dolls. The **Corpus Christi Museum of Science and History** has exhibits on natural history, archeology, and marine science. The **Texas State Aquarium** explores the life of marine plants and animals indigenous to the gulf. The **Corpus Christi Seawall,** a concrete barrier with stairs leading to the water, was de-

signed by the sculptor of Mt. Rushmore. *Admission charged for some attractions.*

12. Welder Wildlife Foundation Refuge

This 7,800-acre private wildlife refuge shelters about 55 species of mammals, 55 species of amphibians and reptiles, and more than 400 species of birds. Tours and research facilities are available.

13. Rockport

Chamber of Commerce, 404 Broadway. This resort town has several art galleries. The area's historic gem is the **Fulton Mansion State Historical Park,** a 30-room mansion built in the 1870's. The **Connie Hagar Wildlife Sanctuary** is a favorite of bird-watchers, and the **Copano Bay Causeway State Fishing Pier** is popular with anglers. *Admission charged for some attractions.*

14. Aransas National Wildlife Refuge

The 55,000-acre refuge is the winter home of the whooping crane, nearly extinct at one time. Mounted telescopes on the observation tower allow visitors to spot the cranes. From hiking trails and paved roads, javelinas, alligators, and more than 380 species of migratory birds may also be seen.

15. Goose Island State Park

Besides offering fishing, camping, swimming, and boating, this park is home to one of the country's three biggest live oaks — some 35 feet in circumference and more than 1,000 years old. *Admission charged.*

16. Goliad

Chamber of Commerce, 205 South Market St. **Fannin Battleground State Historical Park** contains a monument to the 1836 Battle of Coleto Creek, in which Texan forces surrendered to the Mexicans. On tours of the grounds, visitors can see the chapel where the soldiers were imprisoned, as well as the **Presidio La Bahia,** the site of their execution. **Goliad State Historical Park** features a reconstructed mission, where a museum depicts the lives of local Indians and missionaries. *Admission charged for some attractions.*

17. Victoria

Convention and Visitors Bureau, 700 Main Center. Built in 1876, the **McNamara House Museum** is a fine example of Victoria's many historic homes. **Memorial Square** contains the graves of pioneers and Texas Revolution soldiers.

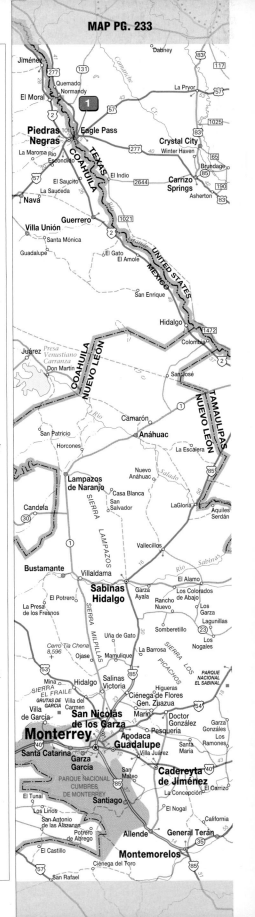

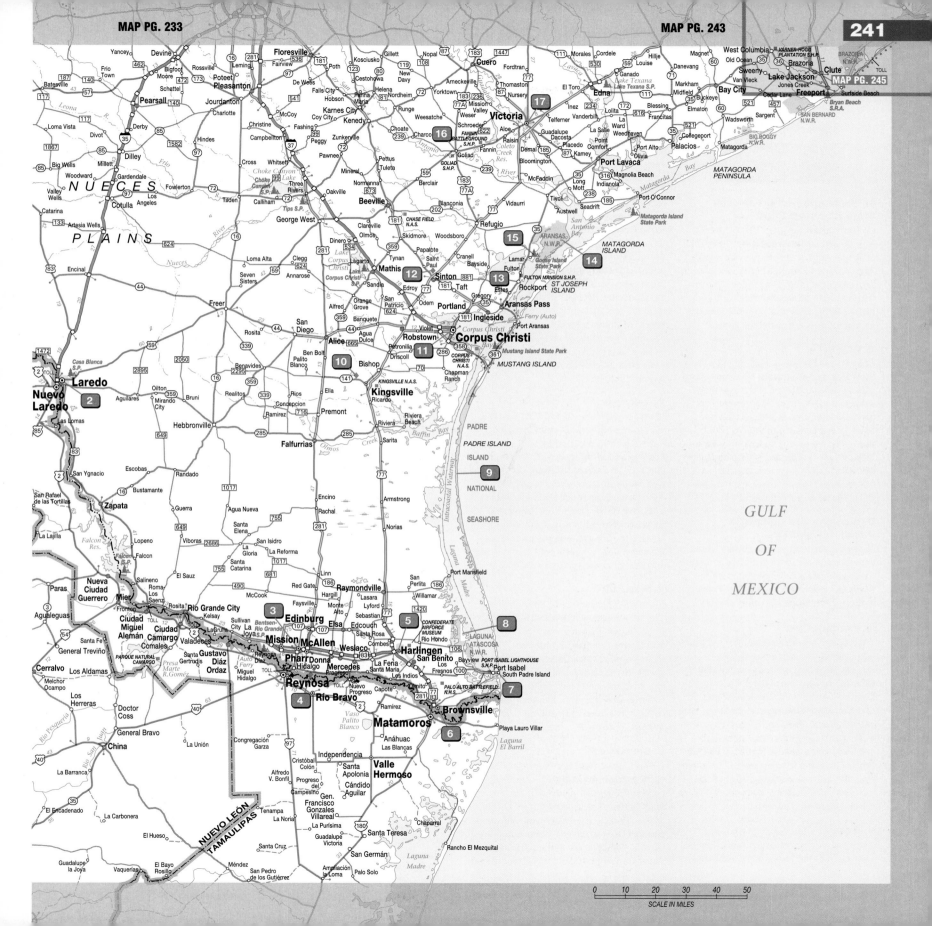

1. Washington-on-the-Brazos State Historical Park

Off Rte. 105, Washington. This quiet town was the first and last capital of the Republic of Texas, and visitors can tour the restored **Anson Jones Home,** where the republic's final president lived. The modern **Star of the Republic Museum** relates that era's history with audiovisual presentations and exhibits. *Admission charged at home.*

2. Huntsville

Chamber of Commerce, 1327 11th St. The **Sam Houston Memorial Museum Complex** includes the home of the legendary soldier and statesman. The museum displays Houston's dueling pistols, his law office, and artifacts from the Texas Revolution, while the nearby **Oakwood Cemetery** contains his grave. The **Texas Prison Museum** exhibits a prison cell, weapons, and an electric chair. *Admission charged at prison museum.*

3. Alabama and Coushatta Indian Reservation

Visitors to the reservation can watch craft demonstrations and tribal dances and sample traditional food. Reservations are required for ranger-led tours of **Big Thicket National Preserve.** *Fee charged for tour.*

4. Nacogdoches

Chamber of Commerce, 1801 North St. One of the oldest towns in Texas, Nacogdoches's rich history begins with **Indian Mound,** the remains of pyramidlike formations built by the Caddo Indians. The 1779 **Old Stone Fort Museum** showcases excavated Indian artifacts and Texan relics. Early Texan and Victorian items furnish the 1830 **Adolphus Sterne House,** while **Millard's Crossing** encompasses 14 buildings from the 19th century, including a chapel, log cabin, and Victorian mansion. *Admission charged for some attractions.*

5. Rusk

Chamber of Commerce, 415 South Main St. Leaving from the **Texas State Railroad**

State Historical Park, restored steam-powered trains make a 50-mile round trip from Rusk to the town of Palestine. Near both towns' depots lies the **Rusk-Palestine State Park,** and in Rusk there is a 100-acre forest offering fishing, hiking, and camping. *Admission charged for some attractions.*

6. Tyler

Chamber of Commerce, 407 North Broadway. Known as the Rose Capital of America, the town is home to the **Tyler Municipal Rose Garden Center,** abloom with more than 38,000 fragrant rosebushes from May through October, and the **Tyler Rose Museum.** The **Carnegie History Center** exhibits county and Civil War artifacts, while the **Goodman Museum** features antique furniture and vintage photos. **Brookshires World of Wildlife and Country Store** combines a menagerie of more than 250 animals from around the world with a full-size early grocery store. *Admission charged for some attractions.*

7. Jefferson

Chamber of Commerce, 116 West Austin St. This town's **Historic District** includes many Greek Revival homes, such as the **Freeman Plantation** and the **Captain's Castle.** The **Jefferson Historical Society and Museum** features European and American paintings and Caddo Indian artifacts. Across the street from the elegant **Excelsior House,** still in operation as a hotel, is the luxurious **Jay Gould Private Railroad Car,** complete with carved wood and stained glass. *Admission charged.*

8. Marshall

Chamber of Commerce, 213 West Austin St. The town's history is detailed, from the Caddo Indians to the present, at the **Harrison County Historical Museum.** The **Starr Family State Historical Park** has a grand 1870 Italianate house furnished in turn-of-the-century style, and the **Franks Antique Doll Museum** has an impressive collection of some 1,600 antique dolls. *Admission charged.*

9. Shreveport

Visitor Center, 405 Clyde Fort Pkwy. The **R. W. Norton Art Gallery** features a fine collection of works by Frederic Remington and Charles Russell, as well as by European artists. Visitors to the **Barnwell Garden and Art Center** can enjoy both artwork and plant-life exhibits, and at the **American Rose Center** pretty walkways lead through

60 gardens, each of which is individually designed. *Admission charged at rose center.*

10. Germantown Colony Museum

Off Germantown Rd., Minden. German settlers established a communal colony here in 1835. Today visitors can tour the original log cabins and replicas of a smokehouse and blacksmith shop. *Admission charged.*

11. Monroe

Convention and Visitors Bureau, 1333 State Farm Dr. At the **Louisiana Purchase Gardens and Zoo,** visitors can see primates and rare African and Asian animals. The **Emy-Lou Biedenharn Foundation** contains the **Bible Museum,** which holds priceless bibles, including a 1550 Danish Martin Luther Bible. The **Biedenharn Home,** built by the first bottler of Coca-Cola, displays memorabilia of the soft-drink company. *Admission charged at zoo.*

12. Mansfield State Commemorative Area

Off Rte. 175, Mansfield. In April 1864 this farmland was the site of the last major Confederate victory in the Civil War. Visitors can take a self-guided walking tour of the battlefield and view military artifacts in the museum. *Admission charged.*

13. Los Adaes State Commemorative Area

Rte. 485, near Robeline. A Spanish mission and fort, Los Adaes was the capital of Spanish Texas until 1773. The visitor center displays excavated weapons, eating utensils, and other artifacts from both Mexican soldiers and American Indians.

14. Natchitoches

Tourist Commission, 781 Front St. The oldest city in Louisiana, Natchitoches maintains its past in the **Historic District,** which is the setting for well-preserved colonial, antebellum, and Victorian houses. The **Fort St. Jean Baptiste State Commemorative Area** is a reconstruction of a French trading post and fort built in 1732. At the **National Fish Hatchery,** alligators, fish, and turtles occupy a 20-tank aquarium. *Admission charged at fort.*

15. Melrose Plantation

Rte. 493, Melrose. The former home of a freedwoman, this plantation today is a complex of eight structures — some simple, some grand. At the turn of the century, Melrose was a haven for artists and writers. *Admission charged.*

16. Bayou Folk Museum

Rte. 495, Cloutierville. Housed in the restored home of writer Kate Chopin, this site features an original edition of *Bayou Folk,* a collection of her short stories, and 19th-century furniture crafted by local artisans. On the grounds are a blacksmith shop and a rural doctor's office with antique medical instruments. *Admission charged.*

17. Kent House

3601 Bayou Rapides Rd., Alexandria. Built in 1800, this restored Creole-style plantation house contains fine examples of Empire, Federal, and Sheraton furnishings dating as far back as 1796. Outside the home are herb and vegetable gardens, a slave cabin, milkhouse, kitchen, barn, and blacksmith shop. *Admission charged.*

18. Fort Polk Military Museum

917 South Carolina Ave., Ft. Polk. The fort was established just before World War II and has served as a base for 12 U.S. Army divisions, training such notable commanders as Eisenhower, Patton, and Bradley. The museum displays weapons and uniforms, and a small park contains tanks, helicopters, and field artillery.

19. Lake Charles

Convention and Visitors Bureau, 1211 North Lakeshore Dr. A 300-year-old oak tree stands on the grounds of the **Imperial Calcasieu Museum,** whose exhibits include a turn-of-the-century parlor, pharmacy, and barbershop, as well as a collection of Audubon prints in the library. The **Creole Nature Trail,** which can be driven or walked, offers diverse views of shrimp boats, wildlife refuges, and oil platforms. *Admission charged at museum.*

20. Beaumont

Chamber of Commerce, 450 Bowie St. This area was once an oil boomtown, and the **Spindletop/Gladys City Boomtown Museum** pays tribute to those days. A smokehouse and tannery are on the grounds of the **John J. French Historic House Museum,** and the 1906 **McFaddin-Ward House** contains fine furnishings, silver, and porcelain. The **Fire Museum of Texas** exhibits old-time fire trucks and firefighting equipment. The **Edison Plaza Museum** has examples of Thomas Edison's inventions, and the **Art Museum of Southeast Texas** features local, ethnic, and folk art. *Admission charged for some attractions.*

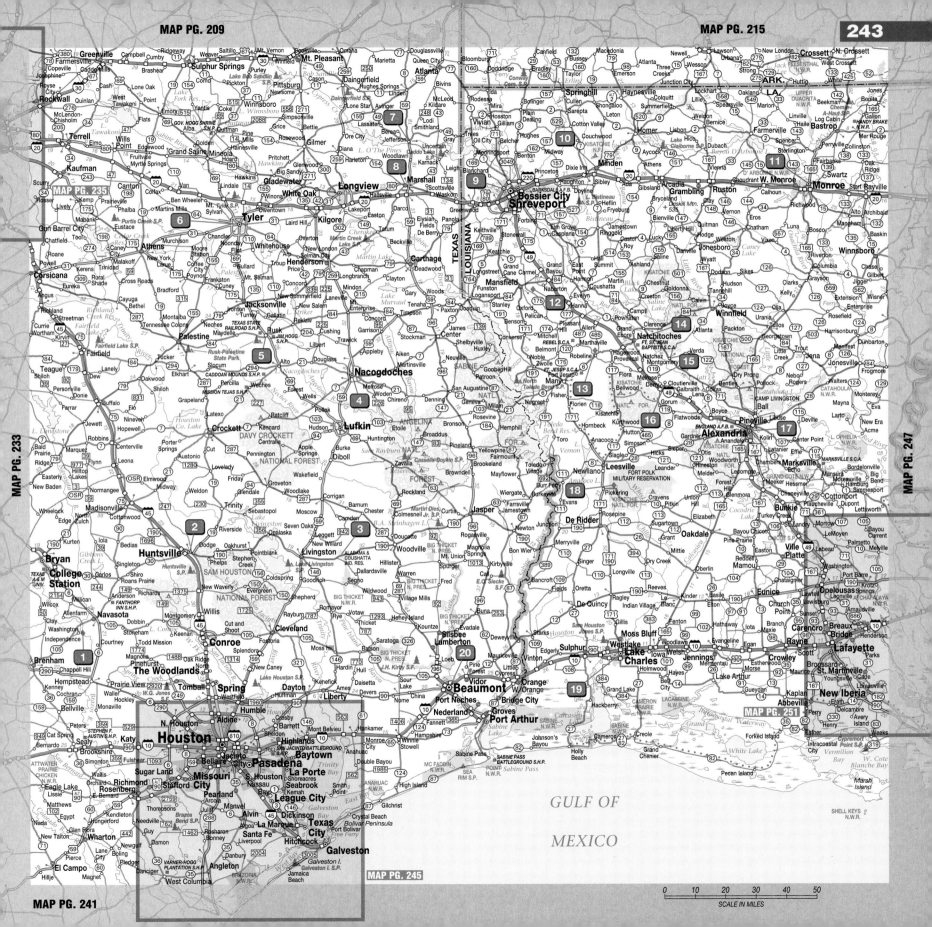

1. Varner-Hogg State Historical Park

1702 North 17th St., West Columbia. Begun in the 1820's by one of Stephen F. Austin's colonists, the plantation here was later owned by James S. Hogg, a governor of Texas. When oil was discovered, the Hogg family's considerable fortune was established. Today, the house contains early American and antebellum furniture, prints, and family memorabilia. *Admission charged.*

2. Brazos Bend State Park

Small lakes dot this nearly 5,000-acre park, which offers an observation tower for viewing the wildlife — from migratory birds to alligators. Visitors can camp, fish, picnic, and hike. *Admission charged.*

3. George Ranch Historical Park

10215 Rte. 762, Richmond. In this 470-acre park, a working farmstead re-creates life in the 1820's and costumed interpreters demonstrate 1880's ranching techniques. The park also contains a restored 1890 mansion and a 1930 ranch. *Admission charged.*

4. Fort Bend Museum Complex

500 Houston St., Richmond. This historical complex with homes and reproduced buildings contains the 1830's **Long-Smith Cottage** and the 1883 Greek Revival **John M. Moore Home**, both with some original furnishings. Displays in the **Fort Bend Museum** explain the region's historical events from 1822 to the 1930's, including the founding of Ft. Bend by Stephen F. Austin's colonists. *Admission charged.*

5. Astrodome

8400 Kirby Dr., Houston. Guided tours of this famous home of the Houston Oilers and Astros include visits to superboxes and press areas. Across the freeway is **AstroWorld,** with the latest amusement park rides, elaborate live shows, and an Enchanted Kingdom for children. Adjacent to AstroWorld, **WaterWorld** offers surfing in a wave pool, inner tubing down rapids, and speed slides. *Admission charged.*

6. Houston Zoological Gardens

1513 North MacGregor, Houston. A selection of animals — gorillas, big cats, rare albino reptiles, and marine species — are displayed in simulated natural habitats, allowing visitors close-up views. The nearby **Houston Museum of Natural Science** features a 70-foot dinosaur skeleton, exhibits on the area's oil history, outstanding mineral and gem collections, and a planetarium. *Admission charged.*

7. Museum of Fine Arts

1001 Bissonnet Ave., Houston. The exterior of this museum, a blend of neoclassical and modern design, mirrors the wide range of holdings within, such as pre-Columbian art, American Indian pottery, paintings by early European masters, 19th- and 20th-century decorative arts, and a large Frederic Remington display. There is also a first-rate sculpture garden designed by Isamu Noguchi. *Admission charged.*

Roseate spoonbills on Galveston Island

8. The Menil Collection

1515 Sul Ross St., Houston. This fine assemblage of art and antiquities ranges from rare Paleolithic artifacts to surrealist paintings. There are also Byzantine and medieval artworks, tribal art from Africa and the Pacific, European paintings from the 1500's through the 1800's, and contemporary paintings and sculptures. The nearby **Rothko Chapel** houses paintings by the abstract expressionist Mark Rothko.

9. Bayou Bend

1 Westcott St., Houston. The philanthropist Ima Hogg once lived in this antebellum mansion, where today her comprehensive collection of American paintings, furniture, and decorative arts from the 17th to the 19th centuries are displayed. Tours of the gardens and 28-room house reveal the "old things with a history" that were Miss Ima's passion, including Federal silver fashioned by Paul Revere and furniture crafted by Duncan Phyfe. *Admission charged.*

10. Heritage Society at Sam Houston Park

1100 Bagby St., Houston. In the shadow of Houston's skyscrapers, the city's past comes to life in the form of a frontier cabin, a Texas plantation house, an 1850 Greek Revival house, and a reconstruction of the city's first commercial building, all painstakingly restored and decorated in period style. Guided tours are available. The Museum of Texas History examines state history from the time of the Spanish explorers. *Fee charged for tour.*

11. Port of Houston Turning Basin

Gate 8, Port Area, Houston. Bird's-eye views of this busy port at the head of the 50-mile Houston Ship Channel can be seen from an observation platform atop Wharf 9, while 90-minute boat tours allow passengers a closer look at the Turning Basin and more than 40 wharves. In the summertime, reservations should be made at least two months in advance for the boat tours.

12. San Jacinto Battleground State Historical Park

Rte. 134, near La Porte. A 570-foot limestone tower topped by a 220-ton Texas lone star marks the site where, in 1836, Sam Houston and a ragtag band of men won independence for Texas and avenged the Alamo. Exhibits in the **Museum of History** at the tower's base depict the brief but bloody battle, and from an observation deck, there's a splendid view of Houston's skyline. At berth in the nearby waters is the 573-foot-long **U.S.S. Texas,** the only remaining battleship that served in both world wars. *Admission charged at ship.*

13. NASA Lyndon B. Johnson Space Center

NASA Rd. 1, Houston. The Johnson Space Center's role as the command post of the country's manned spaceflight program is evident throughout the grounds of this campuslike complex. Visitors can take a guided 1-hour tram tour that includes **Rocket Park, Mission Control Center,** and astronaut training facilities, and view early spacecraft and space suits along with films and demonstrations at **Space Center Houston.** *Admission charged.*

14. Galveston Island State Park

The 32 miles of sandy public beach on Galveston Island are ideal for swimming, surf and jetty fishing, and year-round boating. The park's 2,000 acres encompass camping and picnic sites, hiking and nature trails, and observation towers for birdwatching. **Stewart Beach Park** is a popular city beach with a nearby water slide and bumper boat rides. *Admission charged for some attractions.*

15. Center for Transportation and Commerce

123 Rosenberg St., Galveston. It is forever 1932 in the waiting room of this railroad museum, where 30 life-size sculptures of travelers wait to board dozens of vintage trains on the station's tracks. In other areas of this former Santa Fe terminal, there are depictions, complete with light-and-sound shows, of the city's history; a replica of an 1875 depot; and a miniature of the Port of Galveston. *Admission charged.*

16. Texas Seaport Museum

Pier 21, 22nd St., Galveston. The city's history as a 19th-century port is chronicled at this museum. Exhibits include a computer that enables visitors to search for ancestors who immigrated through this landing and a display that tells of the 1877 sailing ship *Elissa.* Visitors can also tour a 150-foot-long square-rigged iron bark, which carried cargoes worldwide until the late 1960's. From a nearby wharf, a three-deck paddlewheel boat departs on 2-hour sightseeing cruises of Galveston Harbor. *Admission charged.*

17. The Bishop's Palace

1402 Broadway, Galveston. Completed in 1893 at a cost of $250,000, this magnificent stone residence features an interior bedecked with intricately hand-carved wood, jeweled-glass windows, and period furnishings imported from Europe. Located nearby, the **Ashton Villa** is a restored 1859 Italianate mansion with many of its original furnishings. *Admission charged.*

18. Strand Historic District

More than 50 historic buildings in this former commercial district in Galveston— known as the Wall Street of the Southwest in the second half of the 19th century — have been restored and interspersed with lively restaurants, shops, and galleries. A visitor center provides information on self-guided tours.

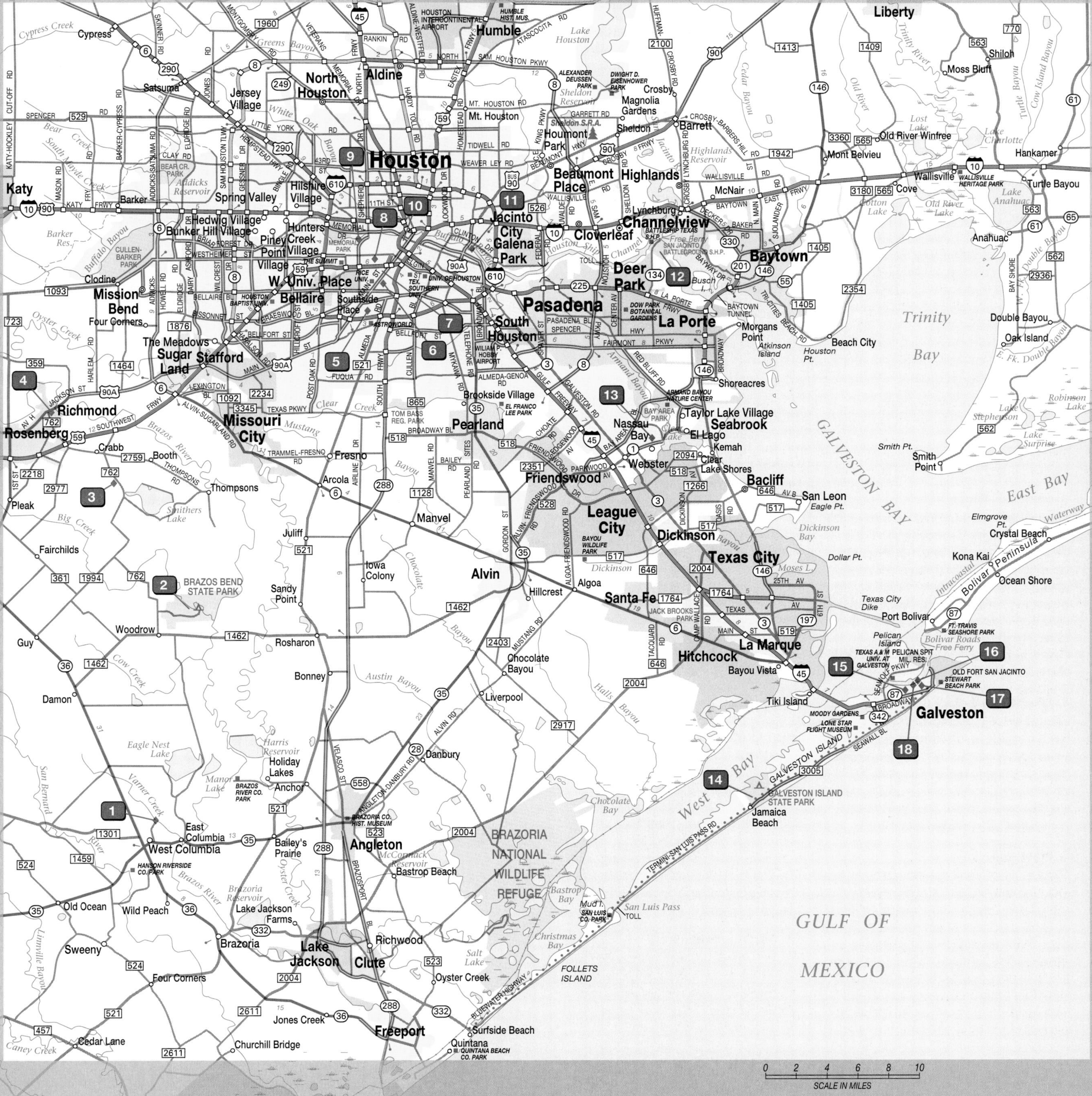
Houston
North Houston
Aldine
Humble
Mt. Houston
Jersey Village
Cypress
Satsuma
Katy
Barker
Spring Valley
Hilshire Village
Hedwig Village
Bunker Hill Village
Hunters Creek Village
Piney Point Village
W. Univ. Place
Bellaire
Southside Place
Mission Bend
Four Corners
The Meadows
Sugar Land
Stafford
Richmond
Rosenberg
Missouri City
Fresno
Arcola
Crabb
Booth
Thompsons
Pleak
Fairchilds
Guy
Damon
Woodrow
Sandy Point
Rosharon
Bonney
Juliff
Iowa Colony
Manvel
Alvin
Hillcrest
Pearland
Brookside Village
South Houston
Pasadena
Jacinto City
Galena Park
Cloverleaf
Channelview
Highlands
Beaumont Place
Houmont Park
Sheldon
Crosby
Barrett
Magnolia Gardens
Deer Park
La Porte
Baytown
McNair
Lynchburg
Shoreacres
Morgans Point
Taylor Lake Village
Seabrook
El Lago
Kemah
Nassau Bay
Webster
Clear Lake Shores
Bacliff
San Leon
Friendswood
League City
Dickinson
Texas City
Santa Fe
Algoa
La Marque
Hitchcock
Bayou Vista
Tiki Island
Galveston
Port Bolivar
Crystal Beach
Kona Kai
Ocean Shore
Jamaica Beach
Liberty
Shiloh
Moss Bluff
Old River Winfree
Mont Belvieu
Cove
Wallisville
Hankamer
Turtle Bayou
Anahuac
Double Bayou
Oak Island
Beach City
Smith Point
Chocolate Bayou
Liverpool
Danbury
Holiday Lakes
Anchor
Angleton
Bailey's Prairie
East Columbia
West Columbia
Old Ocean
Wild Peach
Sweeny
Brazoria
Lake Jackson Farms
Lake Jackson
Clute
Richwood
Oyster Creek
Freeport
Jones Creek
Four Corners
Cedar Lane
Churchill Bridge
Surfside Beach
Quintana
Bastrop Beach
BRAZOS BEND STATE PARK
BRAZORIA NATIONAL WILDLIFE REFUGE
GALVESTON ISLAND STATE PARK
Trinity Bay
GALVESTON BAY
East Bay
West Bay
GULF OF MEXICO
FOLLETTS ISLAND
SCALE IN MILES
0 2 4 6 8 10
1 2 3 4 5 6 7 8 9 10 11 12 13 14 15 16 17 18

1. Casey Jones Railroad Museum State Park

Off Rte. 55, Vaughan. This museum is located close to where the ill-fated Cannonball Express, with the courageous Casey Jones at the controls, rammed a freight train in 1900. The collision took the famous engineer "to the Promised Land," as the ballad tells it. The museum features the bell from Casey's engine. *Admission charged.*

2. Roosevelt State Park

Several miles of excellent hiking trails wind through a dense forest and end at a picturesque lake, where anglers can try their luck. The park also offers camping, swimming, and tennis. *Admission charged.*

3. Choctaw Museum

Rte. 16, west of Philadelphia. Located on the reservation of the Mississippi Band of Choctaw Indians, this museum interprets the tribe's customs, beliefs, and culture through displays that include costumes and handicrafts. In August the annual weeklong Neshoba County Fair is held on the campgrounds off Rte. 21. This event features religious and political speeches, cow shows, and harness races.

4. Okatibbee Lake

Created in 1968 by a flood-control dam, this is a popular recreation area, with five swimming beaches, boat launches, a marina, campgrounds, and picnic areas. The environs are home to many animals, including alligators, beavers, deer, bald eagles, herons, and other wading birds.

5. Meridian

This turn-of-the-century town has many late-Victorian and Art Deco structures, including a restored opera house and an old-time carousel — a national landmark that visitors can still ride for a quarter. The **Jimmie Rodgers Museum** has displays honoring the Father of Country Music, and an annual festival in tribute to the musician is held each May. Another well-known Meridian site is the **Merrehope Mansion,** a hand-

some 20-room home, now restored and open to the public. *Admission charged.*

6. Alamuchee-Bellamy Covered Bridge

Livingston University, Livingston. Built in 1861 to span a nearby river, this historical structure, now restored, was moved to the campus of **Livingston University** in 1969. One of the few remaining covered bridges in the area, it spans 88 feet and features hand-hewn heartwood timbers joined with large wooden pegs. An example of fine craftsmanship, the bridge has weathered the years quite well, thanks to a strong frame of lattice-type construction.

7. Moundville Archaeological Park

Rte. 69, Moundville. Twenty mounds built by Mississippian Indians from the 11th through the 15th centuries remain virtually intact today, having been left undisturbed for some 500 years. A museum and a reconstructed village help to explain this ancient culture. *Admission charged.*

8. Greensboro

This picturesque 19th-century town, which escaped the Civil War unscathed, contains more than 150 outstanding examples of Victorian buildings, many with ornately carved wooden trim. **Magnolia Grove,** a handsome 1840's Greek Revival home in the historic district, was the boyhood home of Admiral Richmond Pearson Hobson, a naval hero in the Spanish-American War. *Admission charged.*

9. Demopolis

Chamber of Commerce, 213 North Walnut St. Two exquisite antebellum mansions highlight this city. **Gaineswood,** sometimes called America's most elegant plantation, was built in the 1840's and 1850's by a wealthy cotton grower, who furnished it with the furniture, tapestries, wallpapers, and other objects he collected as he traveled around the world. **Bluff Hall,** named for its location on a cliff overlooking the Tombigbee River, has a handsome columned portico marking its entrance and combines Federal and Greek Revival styles. *Admission charged.*

10. Clarkco State Park

Popular with vacationers, this wooded park and its 65-acre lake offer a 5-mile nature trail, swimming, boat rentals, tennis courts, camping and picnicking facilities, and a visitor center. *Admission charged.*

11. Coffeeville Lock and Dam

Off Rte. 84, Coffeeville. Built on the Tombigbee River in 1960, this system helps ships travel from the Gulf of Mexico to as far north as Pittsburgh. A parking area above the dam allows visitors to watch the intricate system operate as ships pass through the locks.

12. Claude D. Kelley State Park

Deer, wild turkeys, and other wildlife can often be seen from the trails of this 960-acre park. Towering pines guard a small lake into which a fishing pier juts, and in summer, the waters of the Little River provide good swimming. Picnicking, camping, and boating are other popular activities here. *Admission charged.*

13. Palestinian Gardens

Rte. 98, north of Lucedale. The Rev. W. Harvell Jackson, believing that a knowledge of the geography of the Middle East was important to an understanding of the Bible, spent 10 years creating a scale model of Palestine as it was during the life of Jesus. Encompassing 15 wooded acres, the gardens contain white concrete and plaster buildings grouped into cities and ponds that represent the Dead Sea and the Mediterranean. Guided tours are conducted of the site, which is open to visitors from March through December.

14. Lauren Rogers Museum of Art

Fifth Ave. at Seventh St., Laurel. Located in a handsome Georgian Revival building, this museum contains 19th- and 20th-century paintings, a collection of Georgian silver, and an assortment of baskets woven by artisans ranging from North American Indians to Pacific Islanders.

15. Hattiesburg

This charming turn-of-the-century city, with a historic neighborhood, old courthouse, and many splendid Victorian homes, is the site of the **University of Southern Mississippi,** where the **McCain Graduate Library** houses the Lena Y. deGrummond Collection of Children's Literature — an extensive compilation of original manuscripts and illustrations for children's books. The **American Rose Society Gardens,** also on the campus, is in glorious bloom from spring to mid-December.

16. DeSoto National Forest

This great pine forest includes a wildlife refuge, extensive footpaths, and 11 recre-

ation areas, where visitors can enjoy camping, hiking, fishing, swimming, and canoeing along Black Creek, a 33-mile stream running through the forest. The **W. W. Ashe Nursery,** near Brooklyn, is one of the largest tree nurseries in the country, producing millions of tree seedlings for the reforestation programs of 11 southeastern states.

17. Zemurray Gardens

Rte. 40, Loranger. Azaleas, redbuds, and camelias flower in early spring around Mirror Lake, which was created by a dam on a stream that runs through the area. Several pieces of European statuary accent the pathway through the grounds, which are open to the public from about mid-March to mid-April; exact dates vary according to when the gardens are actually in bloom. *Admission charged.*

18. Percy Quin State Park

Shaded by stands of oaks and pines, this park stretches along the shores of **Lake Tangipahoa.** Boating, fishing, swimming, miniature golf, and picnicking are popular here. One of the many hiking trails passes a beaver dam, where the occupants can sometimes be observed.

19. McComb

Chamber of Commerce, 202 Third St. This city, a busy commercial center landscaped with azaleas and dogwoods, has many antique shops in the **Ice House,** an eye-catching structure built in the 1890's to store ice for railroad cars and private homes. There is also an annual Lighted Azalea Festival which, while dependent upon when the flowers bloom, is usually held sometime in late March. Outside of town, **Bogue Chitto Water Park,** with lovely woodlands and a float trail along the Bogue Chitto River, offers canoeing, a picnic grove, and well-equipped campgrounds.

20. Rosemont Plantation

Rte. 24, east of Woodville. This Federal Cottage–style manor house, built in 1810 by Jefferson Davis's father, was the boyhood home of the Confederate president. Shaded by magnolias and live oaks, the plantation grounds have been bordered by split-rail fences. Many of the rosebushes for which the plantation was named continue to bloom today. The area also contains a number of handsome antebellum homes, historic churches, and a striking courthouse. *Admission charged at plantation.*

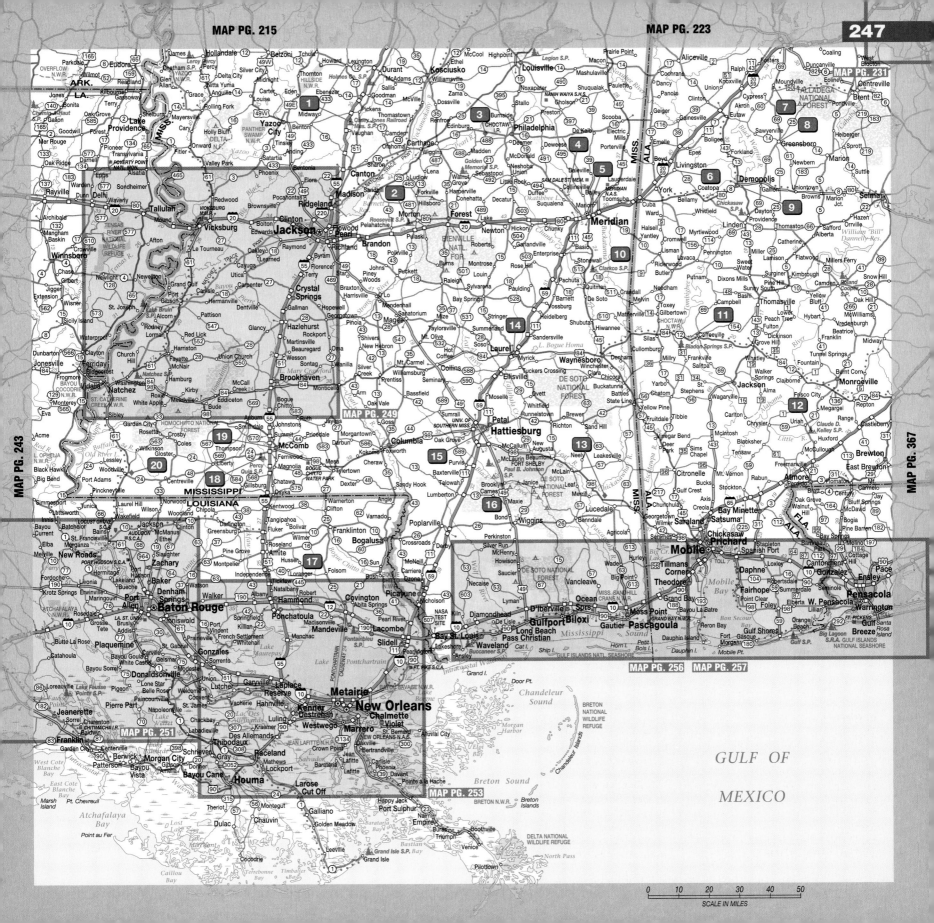

1. Natchez

Convention and Visitors Bureau, 422 Main St. With more than 500 spectacular antebellum mansions and other buildings, this city epitomizes the elegance of the Old South. Many restored homes are open to visitors, including **Stanton Hall,** a large white-columned structure with Italian marble mantelpieces. **Longwood** is a red-brick octagonal building never completed because of the Civil War. **Dunleith,** surrounded by 26 columns, is furnished with outstanding antiques. **Melrose,** a highlight of the **Natchez National Historical Park,** contains an excellent collection of furniture and is one of the best examples of Greek Revival architecture in the South. **Magnolia Hall** is known for its collections of costumes and antiques. These and many other sites can be visited on the various tours of the city. *Admission charged for some attractions.*

2. Natchez Trace

This ancient pathway, originally an American Indian trail leading north from Natchez into Tennessee, was used by early flatboat men who sailed their cargoes downriver to Natchez and New Orleans, sold everything — including their boats — and trekked home on the trace. Today, the Natchez Trace Parkway, commemorating the ancient footpath, runs more than 400 miles from Natchez to Nashville. Several of the historic sites along the route, such as **Mount Locust,** a 1780's inn north of Natchez, and **Emerald Mound,** an enormous ancient American Indian mound built for ceremonial activities, have been carefully restored and are open to visitors.

3. Port Gibson

Chamber of Commerce, Rte. 61. Dating from 1803, the historic town on Bayou Pierre was a successful trading center with many handsome homes and churches, including **Oak Square Plantation,** a striking 1850's mansion. During the Civil War the town was spared by General Grant, who is reputed to have said it was too beautiful to burn. Self-guiding tour maps are available in the visi-

tor center. About 12 miles west of the town are the ruins of **Windsor,** believed to have been the largest plantation home ever built in Mississippi. All that remains of the mansion today are 23 Corinthian columns, stark reminders of the handsome gallery they once supported. *Admission charged at Oak Square Plantation.*

4. Grand Gulf Military Monument Park

Off Rte. 61, north of Port Gibson. This park commemorates Grand Gulf, once a thriving river port, and the Civil War battle that virtually destroyed the city. Artifacts from the war are on view in the museum, and a boardwalk leads to a lake and observation tower. *Admission charged.*

5. Waterways Experiment Station

Halls Ferry Rd., Vicksburg. This research laboratory of the U. S. Army Corps of Engineers has more than 50 scale models of various U.S. waterways, which are used in the study of flood control. Conducted tours are available.

6. Biedenharn Candy Company Museum

1107 Washington St., Vicksburg. Coca-Cola was first bottled here in 1894 by a candy dealer named Joseph A. Biedenharn, who then had it shipped to vendors outside the city. The restored Biedenharn shop houses a collection of advertisements and other memorabilia that describe the history of the now-world-famous drink from the 1890's to the present. *Admission charged.*

7. Old Court House Museum

1008 Cherry St., Vicksburg. Surrounded by columns, this striking Greek Revival courthouse survived the Siege of Vicksburg and is today home to a museum that features Civil War memorabilia, Jefferson Davis belongings, and American Indian relics. *Admission charged.*

8. Toys and Soldiers Museum

1100 Cherry St., Vicksburg. In addition to collections of dolls and model trains, the museum has a miniature circus and displays more than 30,000 authentically costumed toy soldiers. *Admission charged.*

9. Vicksburg National Military Park

Visitor Center, 3201 Clay St., Vicksburg. In this park, the story of the disastrous Siege of Vicksburg is told along a 16-mile drive — maps are available in the visitor center —

with markers identifying the principal sites. The **U.S.S. Cairo Museum,** also in the park, holds the recovered and reconstructed ship, which was the first ever sunk by electrically detonated mines. *Admission charged at museum.*

10. McRaven

1444 Harrison St., Vicksburg. This beautiful antebellum town house, known for its skillfully designed carvings and plaster work, contains an outstanding collection of Civil War memorabilia. The **Duff Green Mansion** is a four-story Venetian-style house built in 1856, which at different times was used by Union and Confederate forces as a hospital during the Civil War. These mansions and other historic buildings are included in tours of the city. *Admission charged.*

11. Mississippi Petrified Forest

Off Rte. 49, Flora. The logs in this fossilized forest were carried here as driftwood some 36 million years ago. A self-guiding trail leads through the strange landscape, and the visitor center's museum contains dioramas and displays of fossils and minerals. The area also has provisions for camping and picnicking. *Admission charged.*

12. Smith Robertson Museum

528 Bloom St., Jackson. Housed in the city's first public school for black children, the museum depicts the history and culture of African-American Mississippians with its extensive collection of photographs, documents, paintings, books, and crafts. *Admission charged.*

13. Mynelle Gardens

4736 Clinton Blvd., Jackson. Thousands of flowering trees and shrubs, several reflecting pools, and Oriental landscapes enhance the beauty of the grounds surrounding **Westbrook House,** a turn-of-the-century mansion. This is the site each April of an art exhibit featuring the works of Mississippi residents. *Admission charged.*

14. Mississippi Museum of Art

201 East Pascagoula St., Jackson. While known for its extensive collection of works by 19th- and 20th-century American and European artists, the Mississippi Museum of Art also focuses on local artists. Other highlights are a hands-on gallery for children and a research library. Guided tours are available. *Admission charged.*

One of the more than 18,000 gravesites in the national cemetery at Vicksburg

15. Governor's Mansion

300 East Capitol St., Jackson. This grand mansion, a white-painted brick structure, was built in 1842 and has served as home to Mississippi's governors ever since. Nearby, the Old Capitol, now the **State Historical Museum,** has exhibits on Mississippi history. Around the corner, the **Mississippi Museum of Natural Science** features an aquarium, dioramas, and other displays.

16. Eudora Welty Library

300 North State St., Jackson. Named for Jackson's famous native novelist, this library, the largest public one in the state, was opened in 1986. In its Writers' Room, artifacts and memorabilia of several well-known Mississippi writers are on display.

17. Mississippi Agriculture and Forestry Museum

1150 Lakeland Dr., Jackson. The history of the cotton and lumber industries in Mississippi is told with dramatic displays of loggers and cotton workers in action. At the **Forrtenberry-Parkman Farm** restoration across the road, workers don 1920's costumes on holidays and for special events to explain farm life in the South during the early 20th century. *Admission charged.*

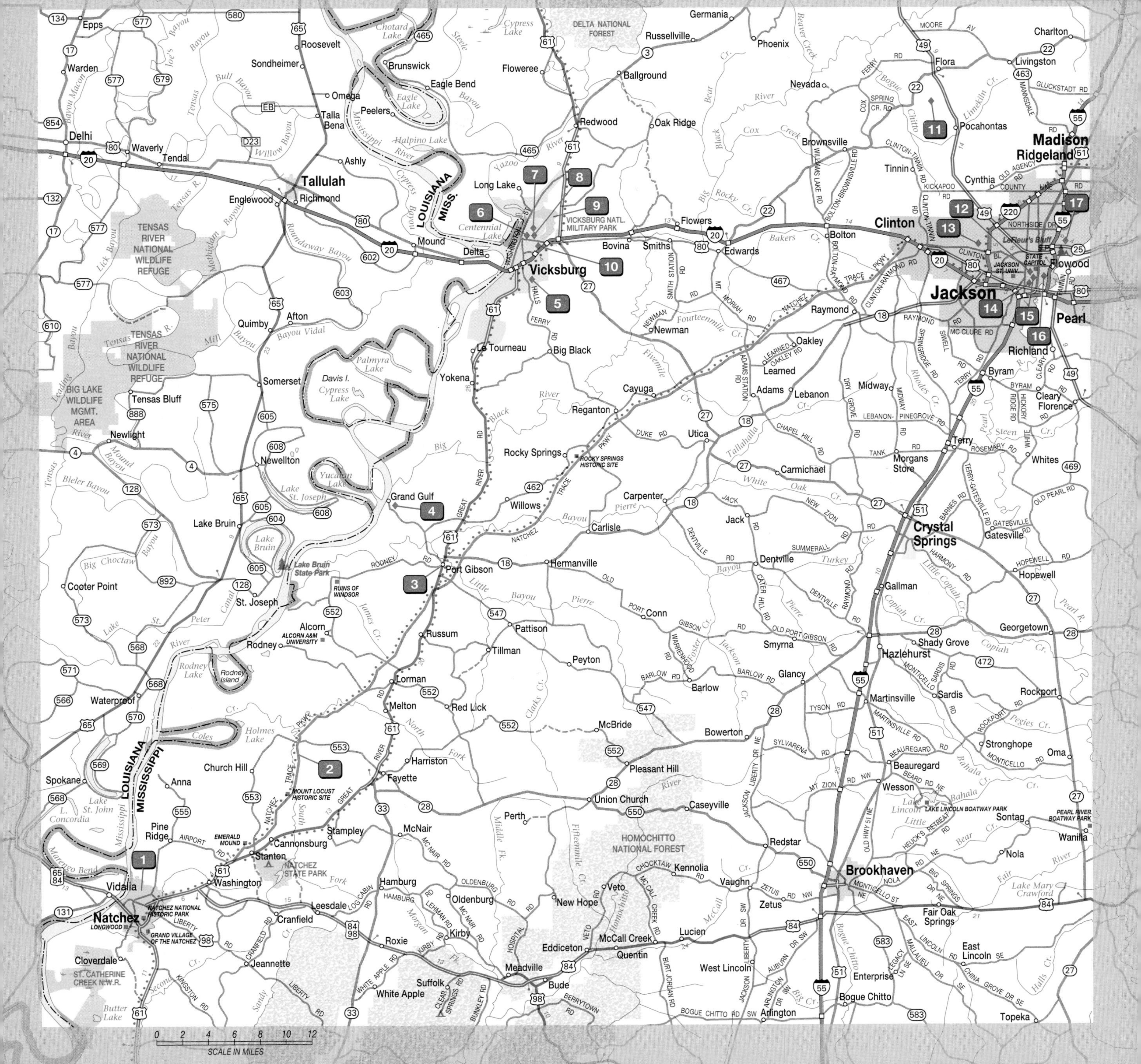

Epps
134
577
Warden
17
579
577
854
Delhi
Waverly
Tendal
80
20
132
Tallulah
Englewood
Richmond
80
Mound
Delta
602
20
603
Quimby
Afton
65
Somerset
605
Tensas Bluff
888
575
Newlight
128
Big Lake Wildlife Mgmt. Area
Bieler Bayou
4
Mound Bayou
608
Newellton
608
Lake St. Joseph
Yucatan Lake
Lake Bruin
Davis I. Cypress Lake
Palmyra Lake
Grand Gulf
4
Yokena
Le Tourneau
Big Black
Lake Bruin State Park
605
604
573
St. Joseph
128
Ruins of Windsor
552
Port Gibson
18
3
Rodney
Alcorn A&M University
Rodney Lake
Rodney Island
568
571
569
Waterproof
Spokane
565
Anna
566
570
Pine Ridge
Church Hill
553
2
Mount Locust Historic Site
Vidalia
131
65 84
13
Natchez
Longwood
Washington
Natchez National Historic Park
Grand Village of the Natchez
Cloverdale
St. Catherine Creek N.W.R.
Emerald Mound
Stanton
Natchez State Park
Cannonsburg
Leesdale
Cranfield
98
Jeannette
Roxie
White Apple
Suffolk
13
84 98
Meadville
Bude

Roosevelt
Sondheimer
Brunswick
Eagle Bend
580
65
465
Omega
Peelers
Talla Bena
Ashly
Chotard Lake
Eagle Lake
Halpino Lake
Willow Bayou
Centennial Lake
Long Lake
6
7
8
9
465
61
Redwood
Oak Ridge
Floweree
Ballground
Germania
Russellville
Phoenix
3
Nevada
Brownsville
Vicksburg Natl. Military Park
Flowers
13
Bolton
Smiths
Bovina
Edwards
80
467
Raymond
18
Newman
Fourteenmile Cr.
Cayuga
Reganton
27
Utica
Adams
Learned
Oakley
Carmichael
Rocky Springs
Rocky Springs Historic Site
462
Willows
Carpenter
Jack
Carlisle
Hermanville
18
Dentville
547
Pattison
Russum
Smyrna
Tillman
Peyton
Lorman
Melton
552
Red Lick
McBride
547
Glancy
Barlow
Harriston
Fayette
Pleasant Hill
28
Union Church
550
Caseyville
McNair
Hamburg
Oldenburg
New Hope
Veto
Kennolia
Homochitto National Forest
Perth
McCall Creek
Lucien
Eddiceton
Quentin
West Lincoln
84
Bogue Chitto

Madison
Ridgeland
51
55
Flora
Livingston
22
Charlton
463
Pocahontas
11
Tinnin
Cynthia
12
13
Clinton
17
Jackson
14
15
Pearl
16
Richland
Byram
Florence
Cleary
Whites
469
Terry
51
Crystal Springs
Gatesville
Georgetown
27
28
Hazlehurst
Shady Grove
Gallman
Martinsville
Sardis
Rockport
Beauregard
Wesson
Stronghope
Oma
Lake Lincoln Boatway Park
Pearl River Boatway Park
Sontag
Wanilla
Brookhaven
Redstar
Nola
Fair Oak Springs
East Lincoln
Enterprise
Topeka
84
55
583

SCALE IN MILES
0 2 4 6 8 10 12

1. Washington

The antebellum houses in and toward the outskirts of this quaint steamboat town include the three-story brick-and-wood **Arlington**; the **Hinckley House,** a cypress abode dating from about 1800 and filled with family heirlooms and antiques; **Camellia Cove,** a two-story 1825 home that's also a bed-and-breakfast; and the **Nicholson House of History,** which, besides being built by the first mayor of Washington, was converted into a hospital by Confederate troops during the Civil War. *Admission charged.*

2. Jim Bowie Museum

Rtes. 49 and 190, Opelousas. This small museum is located in the town where Jim Bowie spent his boyhood. Memorabilia pertaining to the frontiersman and hero in the Texas Revolution are exhibited.

3. Acadian Village

West Broussard Rd., Lafayette. A replica of a 19th-century Acadian village, this tranquil 10-acre site is replete with a man-made bayou and authentic structures, including homes, a blacksmith shop, chapel, and general store. During the holiday season in December, the whole village is aglow with Christmas lights. *Admission charged.*

4. Lafayette Natural History Museum and Planetarium

637 Girard Park Dr., Lafayette. In addition to exhibits on Louisianan and Cajun cultures, this facility explores natural history, offering many special programs, and includes a planetarium. The museum also features a nature center in **Acadiana Park.** *Admission charged at museum.*

5. Vermilionville

1600 Surrey St., Lafayette. Quite different from Acadian Village, 23-acre Vermilionville is a living-history museum, both indoors and out, where French-speaking Cajuns and Creoles create traditional crafts, tell wonderful stories, and perform plays and dances. *Admission charged.*

6. Longfellow-Evangeline State Commemorative Area

1200 North Main St., St. Martinville. Luxuriant with trees and plants, this 157-acre park near the Bayou Teche is a fine place for boating and picnicking; there are also quaint Acadian structures to explore and a visitor center. *Admission charged.*

7. St. Martinville

Chamber of Commerce, 201 South Main St. Longfellow based his poem *Evangeline* on the Acadians who settled here in the 18th century after being exiled from Nova Scotia. According to legend, the lovers in the poem last met beneath the branches of the enormous **Evangeline Oak** on the bank of the Bayou Teche, where today a gazebo overlooks the water. Nearby is **St. Martin de Tours,** the mother church of the Acadians. In the 1700's, St. Martinville was called Petit Paris because of the large number of French aristocrats who found refuge here.

8. Shadows-on-the-Teche

317 East Main St., New Iberia. One of the South's most famous antebellum homes, the Shadows is a stately pink-brick mansion with white columns, 16 rooms, and a 2 ½-acre garden of azaleas, magnolias, and crape myrtles. *Admission charged.*

9. Life Oak Gardens

5505 Rip Van Winkle Rd., Jefferson Island. This onetime winter home of 19th-century American actor Joseph Jefferson is an exquisite three-story Victorian house with Moorish accents set among 20 acres of splendid gardens. Boat tours on Lake Peigneur, located nearby, are included with admission. *Admission charged.*

10. Avery Island

This is one of several southern Louisiana "islands" that are actually salt domes. It was here in the 1800's that E. A. McIlhenny concocted Tabasco sauce, and his descendants still produce the red-hot seasoning (free tours of the factory are available). The 250-acre **Jungle Gardens,** noted for its camelias and azaleas, include a sanctuary for herons and egrets and a Chinese garden with an imported Buddha dating from A.D. 1000. *Admission charged at gardens.*

11. Chitimacha Reservation

The Chitimacha Indians lived here long before the Europeans arrived, and the tribe's history and culture are examined in an interpretive center. Two craft shops sell traditional handiwork, including jewelry, beads, pipes, and various tribal weapons.

12. Oaklawn Manor

Irish Bend Rd., off Rte. 182, Franklin. One of several mansions in the pretty town of Franklin, the 1837 Oaklawn Manor is an antiques-filled Greek Revival house situated in the shade of picturesque, moss-draped, live oak trees. *Admission charged.*

13. Madewood Plantation House

Rte. 308, south of Napoleonville. Rolling lawns surround a carefully preserved 21-room Greek Revival mansion and historic outbuildings. Today a bed-and-breakfast, the house is furnished with antiques and offers tours. *Admission charged.*

Antebellum splendor: Shadows-on-the-Teche

14. Houmas House

Rte. 942, Burnside. Set back from a levee, this columned Greek Revival mansion is noted for a graceful spiral staircase. Its main house dates from about 1840 and is connected by carriageway to an 18th-century cottage. Several movies have been filmed here, and guides in period costume conduct tours. *Admission charged.*

15. Nottoway

Rte. 1, north of White Castle. This magnificent Greek Revival–Italianate mansion, which is among the largest plantation homes in the South, contains a total of 53,000 square feet, 64 rooms, 22 columns, and 200 windows. Guided tours are conducted, and overnight accommodations are available. *Admission charged.*

16. Rural Life Museum

Rte. 10 and Essen Ln., Burden Research Plantation, Baton Rouge. A re-creation of a 19th-century working plantation, this 5-acre outdoor museum features many restored structures, including a kitchen, an overseer's house, slave cabins, a sugar mill, and a gristmill, in addition to cultural exhibits and a barn complex. *Admission charged.*

17. The U.S.S. Kidd DD-661/ Nautical Historic Center

305 South River Rd., Baton Rouge. This complex includes the World War II destroyer U.S.S. *Kidd* and a museum with model ships and a P-40 Flying Tiger fighter plane. *Admission charged.*

18. Louisiana Arts and Sciences Center Riverside Museum

100 South River Rd., Baton Rouge. This museum's collection includes a vintage steam engine, a children's learning center, and an informative hands-on science gallery. *Admission charged.*

19. Louisiana State Capitol

State Capitol Dr., Baton Rouge. This is the nation's tallest state capitol, with an observation deck offering expansive views of the Mississippi River. In 1935 former governor Huey Long was assassinated here and now lies buried in the gardens. The capitol complex includes the Greek Revival **Governor's Mansion** and the **Pentagon Barracks,** built around 1823, which housed Louisiana State University when the school first moved to Baton Rouge.

20. Port Hudson State Commemorative Area

Rte. 61, Port Hudson. Infamous for its role in the Civil War as the site of a bloody, 48-day siege in which the Union gained control of the Mississippi River, the area is now a peaceful 650-acre park with hiking trails. *Admission charged.*

21. Audubon State Commemorative Area

Rte. 965, east of St. Francisville. Ornithologist and artist John James Audubon created many of his *Birds of America* paintings while working as a tutor here in the **Oakley Plantation,** a 19th-century West Indies–style house set in a 100-acre park adjacent to a formal garden. *Admission charged.*

22. St. Francisville

The charming town of St. Francisville boasts a number of historic homes. In a lush 28-acre setting, **Rosedown Plantation and Gardens,** built around 1835, is one of the finest and contains many original furnishings. **Greenwood Plantation** is a 1984 re-creation of a lavish 1830's Greek Revival mansion that was destroyed by a fire in 1960. *Admission charged.*

SCALE IN MILES
0 2 4 6 8 10

1. Houma

Tourist Commission, 1701 Saint Charles St. This little town south of New Orleans is the departure point for a variety of swamp tours, charter fishing trips, and air tours of the wetlands. Houma also boasts the 18-room Victorian and Queen Anne **Southdown Plantation/Terrebonne Museum,** where displays include antique furnishings, Boehm porcelain birds, and a re-creation of the Washington office of U.S. senator and town native Allen J. Ellender. An 80-mile circular drive to the Gulf of Mexico via Rtes. 56, 57, and 315 begins and ends just south of Houma. The way is lined with shrimp boats, which, at the start of the spring fishing season, are colorfully decorated for the blessing of the fleet.

2. Thibodaux

The **Wetlands Acadian Culture Center,** a unit of the Jean Lafitte National Historical Park, examines the history and culture of the Acadians, or Cajuns, in this region. South of Thibodaux, the **Laurel Valley Village** is the remnant of a once-flourishing

Bald cypresses in Swamp Lake, Barataria

turn-of-the-century sugar-cane plantation. The more than 50 buildings include an 1845 sugar mill, blacksmith shop, general store, schoolhouse, and boarding houses.

3. Oak Alley Plantation

3645 Rte. 18, Vacherie. The plantation is particularly noted for the 28 spreading oak trees that arch over the grounds and for the fact that the TV movie *The Long Hot Summer* was partially filmed here. Cottages provide bed-and-breakfast accommodations, and tours are conducted of the Greek Revival main house. *Admission charged.*

4. San Francisco

Rte. 44, west of Reserve. Novelist Frances Parkinson Keyes based her novel *Steamboat Gothic* on this house, which does indeed resemble a steamboat run aground. The picturesque 17-room home is noted for its exquisite ceiling frescoes and elaborate millwork. *Admission charged.*

5. Destrehan Plantation

9999 River Rd., Destrehan. This West Indies–style house, with its hipped roof and dormer windows, was built in 1787 by a freedman. Today it's reputed to be the oldest documented plantation house in the Lower Mississippi Valley. The two *garçonnières,* or bachelors' quarters, and the Greek Revival flourishes were added in the early 19th century. *Admission charged.*

6. Kenner

Tourist Information Center, Rte. 10 and Loyola Ave. **New Orleans International Airport,** also known as Moisant Field, is located here. Sights of interest include **Rivertown,** a historic district with a pedestrian mall, museums, and restored homes. Within the area are the **Louisiana Toy Train Museum,** which has thousands of antique and modern toy trains, and the fascinating **Louisiana Wildlife and Fisheries Museum/Aquarium,** with a 15,000-gallon freshwater tank and exhibits on wildlife indigenous to southern Louisiana. *Admission charged for some attractions.*

7. Lake Pontchartrain Causeway

The world's longest overwater causeway spans the vast Lake Pontchartrain, linking its northern and southern shores. There are stretches along the 24-mile-long elevated route where not a trace of land can be seen. In late July afternoons, hundreds of purple martins flock to the bridge to jockey for a

place to pass the night in the shelter of the underpinnings. *Toll charged for bridge.*

8. Fairview-Riverside State Park

At the entrance to this 99-acre park is the **Otis House,** a 19th-century summer home. The park itself is on the shores of the **Tchefuncta River,** where visitors can boat, camp, and fish. *Admission charged.*

9. Fontainebleau State Park

North of New Orleans, this 2,700-acre site lies on the banks of Lake Pontchartrain, a fine place for swimming, boating, camping, and picnicking. The park is part of an estate; on it, the brick ruins of an old sugar mill can be found. *Admission charged.*

10. Longue Vue House and Gardens

7 Bamboo Rd., New Orleans. Eight acres of magnificently manicured lawns and gardens provide the setting for this stately Greek Revival mansion, which was once home to the heiress to the Sears fortune. The house is decorated with a handsome collection of 18th- and 19th-century antiques. *Admission charged.*

11. City Park

Spanish moss dangles from ancient gnarled oaks in this splendid 1,500-acre urban oasis, home to the **New Orleans Museum of Art,** whose treasures include Fabergé Easter eggs and paintings by Degas. Botanical gardens and lagoons are also found in the park, along with golf, tennis, and fishing. *Admission charged for some attractions.*

12. Louisiana Superdome

Sugar Bowl Dr., New Orleans. This is one of the world's largest indoor sports arena, and guided tours of the site disclose mind-boggling statistics. The huge facility is home to the New Orleans Saints; it also hosts the annual Sugar Bowl football game, circuses, major concerts, and other events. *Admission charged.*

13. Louisiana Nature and Science Center

Nature Center Dr., Joe Brown Memorial Park, New Orleans. The 86 acres of this nature preserve are composed of bottomland forest and wetlands, where a planetarium, hands-on museum, and greenhouse have been built. Naturalists conduct informative nature hikes and bird-watching classes along the center's three trails,

affording visitors an excellent opportunity to experience a taste of the outlying swamplands while remaining in a relatively urban locale. *Admission charged.*

14. Jean Lafitte National Historical Park, Chalmette Unit

8606 West St. Bernard Hwy., Chalmette. In 1815 Andrew Jackson and his ragtag army defeated the British on the green fields here in what was the final battle of the last war between the British and the Americans. Audiovisual displays are shown in the visitor center, and both self-guided and guided tours examine the encounter.

15. Isleño Center

Rte. 46, Toca. Descendants of the Canary Islanders who settled here more than 200 years ago live and work in this area as trappers and fishermen. Their cultural heritage is interpreted in this center.

16. Garden District

Accessible via the St. Charles Streetcar, this posh residential district is virtually carpeted with grand mansions. Among the area's notable structures, which may be viewed from the outside, are the **Toby-Westfeldt House,** dating from 1838 and said to be the oldest house in the district; the impressive **Bradish-Johnson House,** built in 1872; and the huge Italianate **Colonel Short Villa,** built in 1859 and surrounded by a cast-iron cornstalk fence.

17. Audubon Park and Zoological Gardens

Majestic live oaks in shawls of Spanish moss make this one of the country's prettiest urban parks. Its 380 acres include a golf course, tennis courts, and jogging and biking trails. There's also a wonderful zoo — home to some 1,500 animals — where some of the naturalistic habitats are linked by wooden walkways. Other features include a petting zoo and animal rides. *Admission charged at zoo.*

18. Jean Lafitte National Historical Park and Preserve, Barataria Unit

7400 Rte. 45, Marrero. Louisiana's fabled swamps and animals — alligators, snakes, and splendid birds such as the ibis and egret — can be seen from walkways through dense hardwood forest or in the bayous from canoes, which are available for rent. For information from the experts, visitors can take canoe tours led by rangers.

MISSISSIPPI
LOUISIANA

Picayune
Nicholson

Walker
Satsuma Livingston Holden Albany Baptist
Magnolia
Tickfaw
Natalbany
Woodhaven
SOUTHEASTERN LOUISIANA UNIV.
Hammond
Ponchatoula
Robert
Goodbee
Covington
Abita Springs
Waldheim
St. Benedict
ST. JOSEPH'S ABBEY
Talisheek
St. Tammany
Hickory
Pearl River
Afton

Springville
Pumpkin Center
Springfield
Wadesboro
Lees Landing
Madisonville
Houltonville
Chinchuba
Mandeville
Lacombe
Oaklawn
Slidell
North Shore
Eden Isle

Frost
Killian
Bayou Barbary
Port Manchac
Manchac (Akers)
MADISONVILLE LIGHTHOUSE
FONTAINEBLEAU STATE PARK
Bonfouca

Port Vincent
Verdun
Maurepas
Whitehall
Denson
Galva
MANCHAC WILDLIFE MANAGEMENT AREA

French Settlement
Head of Island
Brignac
St. Amant
Brittany Acy
Sorrento

Lake Maurepas

Lake Pontchartrain

Goose Point
Point aux Herbes
FT. PIKE ST. COMM. AREA
Lake St. Catherine

BAYOU SAVAGE N.W.R.

Alligator Point

Lake Borgne

Frenier
Central
Grand Point
Welcome
Gramercy Garyville
Reserve Laplace
Kenner
LAKEFRONT AIRPORT
SOUTHERN UNIV AT NEW ORLEANS
NASA MICHOUD ASSEMBLY FACILITY

Hymel Convent
Lutcher Wallace Edgard
Tigerville Lucy
Mt. Airy
Paulina
Vacherie
Montz
Taft
Norco
New Sarpy
New Orleans Int'l Airport (Moisant Field)
Metairie
CITY PARK
UNIV. OF NEW ORLEANS
New Orleans
Chalmette
Meraux

St. James Lagan
Lower Vacherie
Hahnville
Destrehan
Luling
St. Rose
Ama
River Ridge
Harahan
Jefferson
Bridge City
TULANE UNIV.
Arabi
MAP PG. 255
Violet

Chackbay
Choctaw
Des Allemands
Paradis
Boutte
Waggaman
Avondale
Westwego
Harvey
Gretna
Marrero
Terrytown
English Turn
Braithwaite
Poydras
Caernarvon
St. Bernard S.P.
Reggio
Alluvial City (Ysclosky)

Laurel Grove
Kraemer
Mimosa Park
Estelle
Belle Chasse
NAVAL AIR STATION (CALLENDER FIELD)
Scarsdale
Dalcour

Thibodaux
NICHOLLS STATE UNIV.
Lafourche
Schriever
St. Charles
Raceland
JEAN LAFITTE N.H.P. AND PRES. (BARATARIA UNIT)
Oakville
Crown Point
Wills Point
Jesuit Bend
Belair
Bertrandville
Delacroix

Magnolia Gray
Mathews
Gheens
Clotilda
SALVADOR WILDLIFE MANAGEMENT AREA
Lake Salvador
Barataria
Jean Lafitte
Naomi
Alliance
Carlisle

Ellsworth
Allemand
Oakshire
Central Manor
Savoie-Bayou Blue
Lockport
Jay
Lafitte
The Pen
Ironton
Myrtle Grove
Harlem
Phoenix

Bayou Cane
Humphreys
Hollywood
Southdown
SOUTHDOWN PLANTATION
Houma
Presque Isle
Bourg
Ludevine
Larose
Cut Off
GRAND BOIS PARISH PARK
Lake Judge Perez
Davant
Pointe a la Hache
West Pointe a la Hache
Bohemia
BOHEMIA WILDLIFE MANAGEMENT AREA
Diamond
Mandalay
Crozier
Ashland
Klondyke

BOGUE CHITTO N.W.R.
PEARL RIVER WILDLIFE MGMT. AREA
STATE NATURAL AND SCENIC RIVER
NASA COMPUTER CENTER

1 2 3 4 5 6 7 8 9 10 11 12 13 14 15 16 17 18

0 2 4 6 8 10
SCALE IN MILES

DOWNTOWN NEW ORLEANS

1. City Cemeteries

New Orleans is famed for its cemeteries, with their above-ground tombs and statuary. Guided tours are available of the city's oldest existing cemetery, St. Louis Cemetery No. 1. *Fee charged for tour.*

2. Musée Conti Wax Museum

917 Conti St. Scores of lifelike wax figures of persons as diverse as Andrew Jackson, Napoleon, and Louis Armstrong — who together represent nearly 300 years of New Orleans history — are displayed in period settings in this museum. *Admission charged.*

3. Hermann-Grima House

820 St. Louis St. This lovely 1831 house museum is especially noted for its old-fashioned kitchen and its Creole cooking demonstrations. Guided tours are conducted. *Admission charged.*

4. Historic New Orleans Collection

533 Royal St. This complex holds historic documents pertaining to virtually every structure in the French Quarter. Serious researchers study in the library, and docents guide visitors through the buildings. *Fee charged for tours.*

5. Preservation Hall

726 Saint Peter St. Located a half block off world-famous Bourbon Street, this cramped locale is filled with the sounds of traditional New Orleans jazz. It serves neither food nor drink — just the soul-searching music. *Admission charged.*

6. St. Louis Cathedral

Chartres St., on Jackson Sq. Rebuilt in 1851, this is one of the oldest cathedrals in the nation; guided tours are available except during services. In **Pirate's Alley,** sidewalk artists often paint and display their work on the fence around **St. Anthony's Garden,**

a green park behind the church. William Faulkner penned his first novel, *Soldiers' Pay,* at 624 Pirate's Alley, and Tennessee Williams wrote his play *A Streetcar Named Desire* in a nearby house located on St. Peter Street.

7. New Orleans Historic Voodoo Museum

724 Dumaine St. This museum exhibits a variety of items associated with the practice of voodoo, including charms, potions, and dolls. *Admission charged.*

8. Bourbon Street

Stretching from Canal Street to Esplanade Avenue, bawdy Bourbon is home to music clubs, bars, peep shows, sidewalk tap dancers, and all sorts of revelers. Below St. Ann Street, the street becomes more residential and the atmosphere more sedate.

9. Gallier House

1118–32 Royal St. Among the lovely features seen on guided tours of this handsome home, built in 1857, are exquisite period furnishings and a truly regal formal drawing room. *Admission charged.*

10. Beauregard-Keyes House

1113 Chartres St. A 19th-century Greek Revival raised cottage, this house museum was briefly the residence of Confederate General P.G.T. Beauregard and then, many years later, that of novelist Frances Parkinson Keyes. Costumed guides conduct tours. *Admission charged.*

11. Ursuline Convent

1114 Chartres St. Completed in the 1750's for the French order of nuns who came to the city in the 1720's, this convent was a large building at that time and is one of the oldest colonial-built structures in the Lower Mississippi Valley. It contains the archives of the archdiocese of New Orleans and can be visited by permission only.

12. Pontalba Apartments

Saint Peter and Saint Ann Sts., on Jackson Sq. One of the country's oldest apartment houses, the Pontalbas are twin buildings with exquisite cast-iron galleries. The **1850 House,** decorated in period style, is a good example of the lifestyle of many early Creoles. *Admission charged at house.*

13. The Presbytère

Chartres St., on Jackson Sq. This structure was originally built to provide housing for priests of the church but probably was never used for that purpose. Today it maintains permanent exhibits on the history and culture of the state and showcases changing exhibits. *Admission charged.*

14. The Cabildo

Chartres St., on Jackson Sq. In 1988 a fire caused serious damage here, but the museum is being reconstructed and due to reopen by early 1994. The original building, dating from about 1795, was the seat of the governing council, or Cabildo, under Spanish rule; here the transfer papers for the 1803 Louisiana Purchase were signed. The

site also houses historical regional memorabilia and, along with the Presbytère, flanks the cathedral. *Admission charged.*

15. Pharmacy Museum

514 Chartres St. The country's first licensed pharmacist opened his office here in 1823, and the museum displays an interesting selection of vintage medical and pharmaceutical paraphernalia. *Admission charged.*

16. Jean Lafitte National Historical Park, French Quarter Unit

419 Decatur St. Local lore is examined in the visitor center here, and park rangers conduct free walking tours of the French Quarter and Garden District.

17. Jackson Square

The **French Quarter** is the original colony founded by French Creoles in 1718. Later ceded to Spain, it became a U.S. possession in 1803. Now a historic and residential district, the Quarter is also a world-class party place. The streets are lined with quaint buildings that hold homes, shops, hotels, jazz joints, and several fine Cajun and Creole restaurants. The hub is Jackson Square where, surrounded by historic buildings and a vaudevillian cast of street entertainers, artists paint and display their wares.

18. Washington Artillery Park

Between Jackson Sq. and the Moon Walk. Here, a raised walkway winds among fountains and gardens. It's also a good place to take photos of Jackson Square and the river.

Few celebrations on earth can measure up to the pomp and merriment found in New Orleans during the annual Mardi Gras.

19. Moon Walk

Decatur St., behind Jackson Sq. Locals love to sit near the Mississippi River on this wooden promenade, named after former mayor Moon Landrieu, and listen to the waters lapping on the nearby shore.

20. French Market

Decatur St., between Saint Ann and Saint Philip Sts. On the site of a longtime trading post, this market has celebrated its 200th anniversary. Shops nestle among its colonnades, and bands — Dixieland, Cajun, blues, and jazz — play in outdoor cafes. *Admission for some attractions.*

21. Old U.S. Mint

400 Esplanade Ave. This imposing structure began operating as a federal mint in the first half of the 19th century; during the Civil War, it produced Confederate currency. Today the mint is no longer active but is maintained as part of the Louisiana State Museum. Its highlights include the **Jazz Exhibition,** which examines the city's musical heritage, and the **Carnival Exhibition,** with memorabilia from the annual Mardi Gras bashes. *Admission charged.*

22. Riverfront Streetcar Line

The Ladies in Red, as these cars are called, transport passengers along the Mississippi, making stops between Esplanade Avenue and the Robin Street Wharf. The St. Charles Streetcar Line, which boards on Canal Street, is the oldest streetcar line in the city. *Admission charged.*

23. Blaine Kern's Mardi Gras World

233 Newton St.. Accessible via the Canal Street Ferry are warehouses chockful of fanciful props and artisans busily preparing carnival floats for the next Mardi Gras. If the ferry whets an appetite for further cruising, several riverboats make excursions, including one from the aquarium to the zoo. *Admission charged for some attractions.*

24. Aquarium of the Americas

On the Mississippi River, between Canal and Bienville Sts. Located in **Woldenburg Riverfront Park,** this aquarium teems with sea animals indigenous to both tropical and subtropical waters. *Admission charged.*

25. Old Custom House

Decatur and Canal Sts. On the second floor of this large structure is the Great Marble Hall, where business is conducted amid the palatial Greek Revival flourishes.

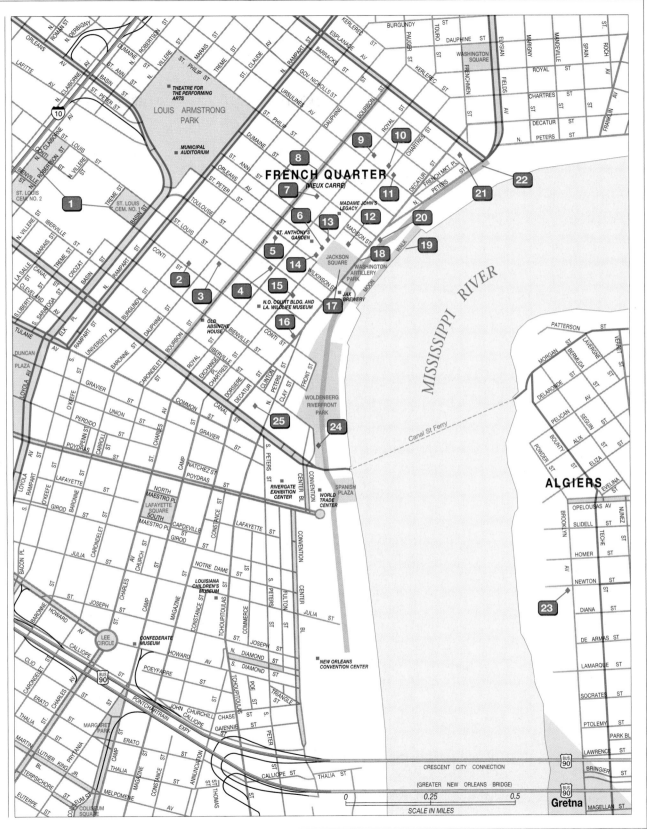

1. Pass Christian

Chamber of Commerce, Rte. 90 and Small Craft Harbor. Just offshore this popular resort is one of the largest oyster reefs in the world. The **Scenic Drive,** running parallel to the beach, passes lovely antebellum homes with semitropical gardens.

2. Gulfport

Chamber of Commerce, 1401 20th Ave. This resort town features **Historic Grass Lawn,** a lovely plantation home on the Gulf, with spacious galleries and furnishings from the early 1800's. The **John C. Stennis Space Center** is one of NASA's largest field installations; the visitor center features films and exhibits, including a 90-foot Space Tower. *Admission charged at Grass Lawn.*

3. Ship Island

Accessible by ferry from Biloxi and Gulfport, this island was settled by the French in the 1700's and served as a British camp in 1814. On **West Ship Island** visitors can tour **Fort Massachusetts,** built during the Civil War. It features a guardroom and one of the only remaining 15-inch Rodman cannons in the country. *Fee charged for ferry.*

4. Beauvoir

2244 Beach Blvd., Biloxi. Jefferson Davis, the president of the Confederate states, spent the last 12 years of his life in this Greek Revival house. Visitors can see the library where he wrote two books on the Confederacy and rooms decorated with tapestries, lace, and fine Mallard furniture. A museum exhibits Confederate memorabilia, while the grounds include lovely pavilions and a military cemetery used by the army. *Admission charged.*

5. Biloxi

Visitor Center, 710 Beach Blvd. Built in 1847, the 65-foot **Biloxi Lighthouse** is a prominent landmark of Mississippi's second-largest city. Exhibits at the **Maritime and Seafood Industry Museum** include ancient tools and fishing equipment. **Gulf Marine State Park** is a popular spot for fishing, while at the **J. L. Scott Marine Education Center,** a 42,000-gallon tank holds a wide array of sea creatures. *Admission charged for some attractions.*

6. Ocean Springs

Chamber of Commerce, 1000 Washington Ave. This art community centers on native artist Walter Anderson, whose works — among those of other artists — are on display at **Shearwater Pottery, Anderson's Cottage,** the **Walter Anderson Museum of Art,** and the 3,000-square-foot **Community Center.** Exhibits include paintings, thrown and glazed pottery, and murals, some of which were painted by the artist in the 1950's for only one dollar but are worth considerably more today. *Admission charged at museum.*

7. Gulf Islands National Seashore, Mississippi District

Headquarters, off Rte. 90, Ocean Springs. This area includes part of the mainland coast and four offshore islands. Dunes, beaches, and marshes dot the shores. Films and exhibits at the headquarters examine the flora and fauna of the region, and nature trails follow the winding bayou.

8. Pascagoula

Chamber of Commerce, 825 Denny Ave. This renowned shipbuilding center on the Pascagoula River is the site of the **Old Spanish Fort,** the oldest-standing structure in the Mississippi Valley. An adja-

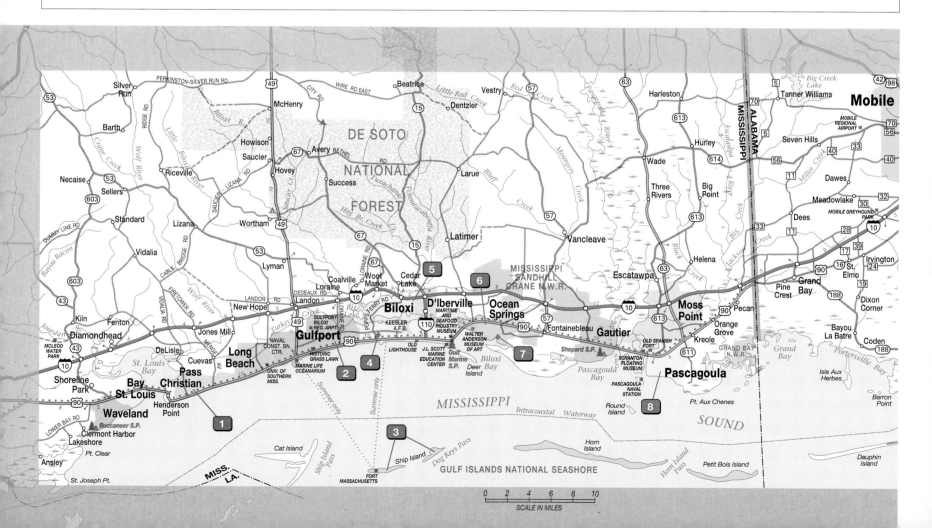

cent museum displays American Indian and historical relics. The **Scranton Floating Museum,** located in a retired shrimp boat, has marine and nautical exhibits, and the 20,000-acre **Mississippi Sandhill Crane National Wildlife Refuge** shelters endangered cranes. *Admission charged at fort.*

9. Historic Blakeley State Park

Off Rte. 225, near Mobile. Here visitors can picnic along the Tensaw River, fish in Beaver Pond, and view mounds built by an Indian civilization more than 4,000 years ago. There are also preserved rifle pits, makeshift fortifications, and redoubts from a Civil War battle. *Admission charged.*

10. Mobile

Ft. Conde Welcome Center, 150 South Royal St. Among the city's many gracious antebellum homes are the **Richards-DAR House,** an Italianate town house with laced ironwork, and **Oakleigh,** a Greek Revival home. Reconstructed **Fort Conde** displays

military artifacts, and the adjacent **Conde-Charlotte Museum House** is furnished with antiques. The **U.S.S. Alabama Battleship Memorial Park** features a 35,000-ton World War II warship. First-rate museums include the **Fine Arts Museum of the South** and the **Museum of the City of Mobile.** Each year Mardi Gras is celebrated with numerous balls and parades. *Admission charged for some attractions.*

11. Bellingrath Gardens and Home

12401 Bellingrath Gardens Rd., south of Theodore. Set on 65 acres, these exquisite gardens offer such seasonal attractions as a vast rose garden from April to December, one of the world's largest outdoor displays of chrysanthemums in autumn, a quarter of a million azaleas in spring, and weeping cherry trees, in a garden complete with a teahouse, stream, and lake. The home contains fine antique furnishings, china, crystal, and the world's largest public display of Boehm porcelain. *Admission charged.*

12. Fort Gaines Historic Site

Bienville Blvd., Dauphin Island. Completed in the 1850's, the fort fell prey to Admiral Farragut's Union forces in the 1864 Battle of Mobile Bay. Today its cannons, kitchen, and blacksmith shop can be seen; a museum displays the anchor from Farragut's flagship. A ferry connects this site with Ft. Morgan. *Admission charged.*

13. Fort Morgan Historic Site

51 Rte. 180, Mobile Pt. This star-shaped brick fort, built in the early 1800's, was also captured in the Battle of Mobile Bay after a 14-day siege. Visitors can see gun batteries, bakeries, officers' quarters, and the furnace where soldiers heated cannonballs. A museum traces the fort's history and displays military relics. *Admission charged.*

14. Gulf State Park

Set on more than 6,000 acres of Pleasure Island, the park features white sand beaches, freshwater lakes, and excellent

fishing. Water sports and camping facilities are available, and trails lead through pine woods, where alligators can be spotted. *Admission charged for some attractions.*

15. Pensacola

Convention and Visitors Bureau, 1401 East Gregory St. **Historic Pensacola Village** is an amalgam of 18th- and 19th-century buildings clustered around the **Seville Square District.** The **Pensacola Historical Museum** displays local American Indian, Civil War, and shipping memorabilia; the **Museum of Commerce** allows visitors to tour re-created streets and shops; and the Creole-style **Charles Lavalle House** is one of the oldest sites in town. The Naval Air Station compound includes the **National Museum of Naval Aviation,** with more than 100 full-size craft, and **Fort Barrancas,** dating back to the 1800's. **Fort Pickens,** built in the early 1800's, has an impressive display of guns. *Admission charged for some attractions.*

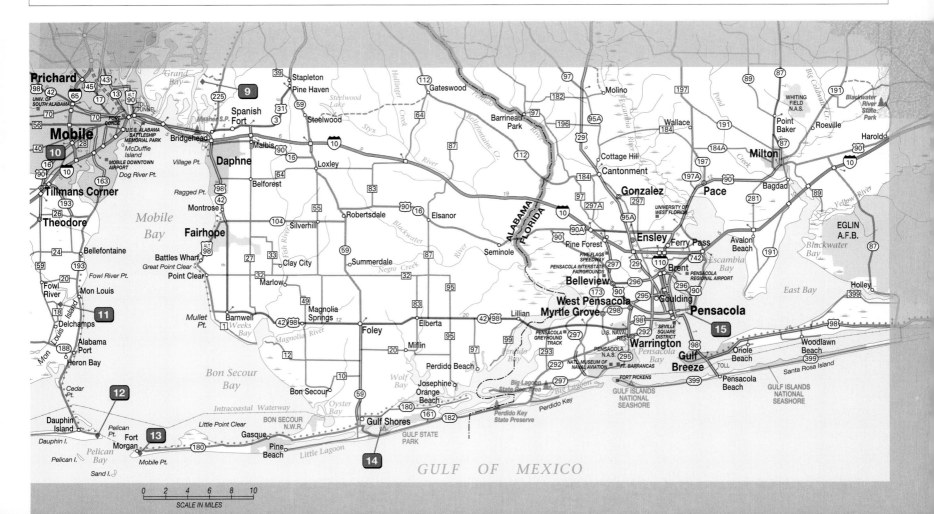

The Eastern States

The very emblems of our nation are present in the birthplace of the United States, from the Liberty Bell in Philadelphia to the Statue of Liberty in New York Harbor. The past is apparent, too, in the string of landmarks along Boston's Freedom Trail and the dramatic dignity of the Lincoln Memorial in Washington, D.C. This is also the section of our country where lavish summer mansions of yesteryear grace Rhode Island's shore; where timeless Amish farms spread their green carpets across Pennsylvania's southeastern corner; where grand plantation homes recall the antebellum South. And the land itself offers unending beauty: the Appalachian Trail, beckoning hikers from Maine to Georgia; the Everglades, Florida's unique river of grass; the Great Smokies — rolling mountains named for their gentle haze — ranging along the Tennessee–North Carolina border. Here, in the eastern region, natural wonders combine with historic treasures in a remarkable array.

The rugged beauty of the eastern seaboard is characterized by Nauset Beach on Cape Cod, Massachusetts.

WIS.

MICHIGAN

ILLINOIS

INDIANA

KENTUCKY

TENNESSEE

MISS.

ALABAMA

LA.

Québec

Presque Isle

MAINE

312-315   296

280   Bangor   294   296

Augusta   292   Portland

Montpelier   Concord

NEW YORK   270   272   284   Boston   288 286

274   VT.   N.H.   290

Albany   MASS.   278   282

Springfield   276   R.I.   CONN.

Toronto   264   260   266   326   324   New York

Rochester   262   308   PA.   316   318 322   320

Buffalo   268   Cleveland   Harrisburg   Philadelphia   N.J.

298   Canton   302   304   330   328

300   Pittsburgh   Baltimore   332   Dover   DEL.

Columbus   OHIO   WEST VIRGINIA   310   336   Washington, D.C.   334   329

Charleston   Charlottesville   VA.   362 & 363

306   Richmond   338   Norfolk

Roanoke   356   360

340   348   Raleigh   364

Winston-Salem   342   344   358   N.C.

Knoxville   346   Charlotte

Spartanburg   350   Columbia   370

352   Atlanta   354   S.C.

368   Charleston

366   Macon   Wilmington

Montgomery   GEORGIA   372   Savannah

374   Jacksonville

Tallahassee   FLORIDA   378   Orlando

376   382   380

Tampa   392

384   West Palm Beach

386   393

Ft. Myers   Miami

388

San Juan   395   391   390

PUERTO RICO   Key West

394

1. Museum of Arts and History

1115 Sixth St., Port Huron. Exhibits include articles from Thomas Edison's boyhood home, the reconstructed pilothouse of a Great Lakes freighter, and skeletal remains of a wooly mammoth. The nearby **Historic Huron Lightship** is the last of such vessels still anchored in Lake Huron. *Admission charged at lightship.*

2. Great Lakes Historical Society Museum

480 Main St., Vermilion. At this museum overlooking Lake Erie, models of sailing ships and lake freighters, paintings and photographs, a pilothouse, and a replica of the 1877 Vermilion lighthouse all help tell the story of navigating the waters of the Great Lakes. *Admission charged.*

3. Kirtland

Chamber of Commerce, 7547 Mentor Ave. The **Kirtland Temple,** an 1836 stone structure overlooking the city, is the first permanent temple built by Mormons. With 20 miles of walking trails, the **Holden Arboretum** is a sight to behold in spring, when some of the 7,000 varieties of plants are in bloom. *Admission charged at arboretum.*

4. Lawnfield

8095 Mentor Ave., Mentor. This 30-room Victorian home built in 1832 was the residence of James A. Garfield, the 20th president of the United States. His campaign office is next door. *Admission charged.*

5. Fairport Harbor Marine Museum

129 Second St., Fairport Harbor. A large collection of Great Lakes maritime memorabilia is contained in this museum, which is located in the keeper's dwelling of the 1871 **Fairport Lighthouse.** *Admission charged.*

6. Great Lakes Marine and U.S. Coast Guard Memorial Museum

1071-73 Walnut Blvd., Ashtabula. Set in an 1898 lighthouse attendant's home with harbor views and a picnic area, this museum displays paintings, photos, and ship models, along with early navigational equipment. *Donation encouraged.*

7. Conneaut Historical Railway Museum

342 Depot St., Conneaut. Housed in an old New York Central Railroad depot, the museum features a unique collection of railroad memorabilia, including an 1857 railroad pass signed by Abraham Lincoln. *Donation encouraged.*

8. Erie

Chamber of Commerce, 1006 State St. The city is home to the **U.S.S. Niagara,** a ship under the command of Lt. Oliver Hazzard Perry in the War of 1812. The **Erie Historical Museum and Planetarium** features regional history and changing art exhibits. Beaches, lagoons, and woodland trails are found in **Presque Isle State Park,** set on a peninsula in Lake Erie. *Admission charged for some attractions.*

9. Fort Le Boeuf Museum

123 South High St., Waterford. In 1753 George Washington was sent to this fort, occupied by the French, to request their withdrawal. Their refusal led to the French and Indian War from 1754 to 1763, the history of which is chronicled in the museum.

10. Meadville

Tourist Assn., 211 Chestnut St. In 1893 the zipper was first manufactured in this city, although it was not produced commercially until the early 1920's. The **Baldwin-Reynolds House Museum** features exhibits on local history. In nearby New Richmond, the stone walls are all that remain of the **John Brown Tannery,** which the abolitionist ran from 1825 to 1835. *Admission charged at museum.*

11. Drake Well Museum

Off Rte. 8, near Titusville. This museum commemorates the world's first commercially drilled oil well in 1859, which triggered a Pennsylvania oil rush. The history of the industry is detailed with early equipment and photos. *Admission charged.*

12. Jamestown

Chamber of Commerce, 101 West Fifth St. The hometown of Lucille Ball, who is honored by a festival each May, features local history exhibits at the **Fenton Historical Center,** set in an elaborate mansion. The **Roger Tory Peterson Institute of Natural History,** named for the man who devised the bird identification system, is a nature center with educational programs. *Admission charged for some attractions.*

13. Griffis Sculpture Park

Rte. 219, Ashford Hollow. Hiking trails wind through this park, where some 200 sculptures, from royalty to a giraffe, adorn the landscape. *Donation encouraged.*

14. Allegany State Park

Partly located on the Allegany Indian Reservation, this huge, 64,000-acre state park has facilities for many outdoor activities. The reservation is also home to the **Seneca-Iroquois National Museum,** which depicts the history and culture of the Seneca Nation. *Admission charged.*

15. Bradford

Chamber of Commerce, 10 Main St. The **Penn-Brad Oil Museum** contains antique tools and wooden drilling equipment dating from 1875, the year oil was discovered here. The **Crook Farm,** with its restored farmhouse, barn, and other buildings, re-creates life in this region in the mid-1800's. *Admission charged at museum.*

16. Rock City Park

Rte. 16, Olean. A trail in this park begins where Indians once lit signal fires and climbs through narrow crevasses and up a stone stairway, built long ago by the tribe, to a pinnacle with inspiring views. During spring and early summer, mountain laurel and other plants bloom on the hillsides. *Admission charged.*

17. Pennsylvania Lumber Museum

Rte. 6, near Coudersport. A reconstructed lumber camp and sawmill are among the exhibits portraying the history of the logging industry. The musem also maintains a visitor center, nature trails, and picnic areas. *Admission charged.*

18. Letchworth State Park

Extending for 17 miles along the Genesee River, which cascades through steep canyons and over three waterfalls, this park offers swimming, hunting, fishing, camping, picnicking, and hiking. The **Pioneer and Indian Museum** reviews the history of the area. *Admission charged.*

19. Genesee Country Museum

1410 Flint Hill Rd., Mumford. More than 50 buildings, brought together from the surrounding region, make up this re-created 19th-century village, where period crafts are demonstrated daily. *Admission charged.*

20. Holland Land Office Museum

131 West Main St., Batavia. Pioneer and Indian artifacts are displayed in the original 1815 office building of the Holland Land Company, whose holdings of some 3 million acres sold so rapidly that the expression "doing a land office business" resulted.

21. Victorian Doll Museum and Chili Doll Hospital

4332 Buffalo Rd., North Chili. Using her childhood dolls as the starting point, Linda Greenfield assembled more than 2,000 dolls dating from the 1840's to the present. The museum, which features a puppet theater and circus, is located in a quaint, turn-of-the-century structure, as is the doll hospital. *Admission charged.*

22. Iroquois National Wildlife Refuge

More than 10,000 acres of marshland and meadow offer sanctuary to a variety of waterfowl, which include Canada geese, mallards, blue-winged teal, and great blue herons. Hiking, canoeing, and fishing are also available.

23. Toronto

Convention and Visitors Assn., 207 Queens Quay W. Points of interest here include the **Art Gallery of Ontario,** with changing exhibits that cover the past seven centuries; the restored War of 1812 **Fort York;** the **Royal Ontario Museum,** featuring an excellent collection of ancient art and artifacts; the **Marine Museum of Upper Canada,** depicting the country's waterways; **Huronia Historical Parks,** portraying early local history; **Casa Loma,** a 1912 medieval-style castle; the impressive **McMichael Canadian Art Collection;** and the re-created 19th-century **Black Creek Pioneer Village.** *Admission charged.*

24. Hamilton

Tourism and Convention Services, 1 James St. S. This harborside city is home to several outstanding sites, including the **Battlefield House and Monument,** which commemorates the War of 1812; the **Art Gallery of Hamilton,** containing international works; **Dundurn Castle,** a restored 1850's mansion; and the **Royal Botanical Gardens,** with formal plantings, parklands, and wildlife sanctuaries. *Admission charged.*

1. Gardenville Horticultural Park

16711 Pearl Rd., Strongsville. This delightful park is composed of 30 informal English cottage–style gardens containing rare and unusual plants from around the world, as well as a 10-acre arboretum and two peaceful ponds. *Admission charged.*

2. Trolleyville U.S.A.

7100 Columbia Rd., Olmsted Township. Via a nostalgic 3-mile trolley ride, this unique museum takes railroad buffs back to the days before the closing of Cleveland's electric trolley system in 1954. Displays that include streetcars, a restored depot, rare photos, and other rail memorabilia further evoke that bygone era. *Admission charged.*

3. NASA-Lewis Visitor Center

2100 Brookpark Rd., Cleveland. Located in one of NASA's research facilities, the visitor center presents lectures and out-of-this-world displays on space exploration, including exhibits on the space shuttle, an Apollo capsule, space stations, and Skylab 3. Outside, visitors are greeted by scale models of the Centaur and Agena rockets.

4. Lake Erie Nature and Science Center

28728 Wolf Rd., Bay Village. Animals, a marine tank, and a planetarium are the highlights at this educational facility, along with an outdoor wildlife display, teaching garden, and a deer run. Nature hikes and bird walks are offered seasonally.

5. Oldest Stone House Museum

14710 Lake Ave., Lakewood. This 1838 sandstone dwelling, the town's oldest stone house, has been restored and turned into a museum. Spinning wheels, a four-harness loom, clothing, books, toys, roped beds, and homespun sheets afford visitors a firsthand look at the lives of local pioneers. Tours are conducted by costumed guides.

6. Cleveland Metroparks Zoo

3900 Brookside Park Dr., Cleveland. The zoo features more than 4,000 animals, including 600 animals and 7,000 plants in a unique 2-acre simulated rain forest, complete with man-made thunderstorms. A re-created African plain is another highlight, as well as a comprehensive exhibit of birds from all over the world. Moats separate visitors from such mighty predators as lions, tigers, and bears. *Admission charged.*

7. Great Lakes Brewing Co.

2516 Market St., Cleveland. Beer connoisseurs will enjoy this popular brewery and brew pub, built in the 1860's. The fresh seasonal brews on tap are all made strictly from the four ingredients that were stipulated in the Bavarian Purity Law of 1516 — barley, hops, yeast, and water. Guided tours of the brewery are available.

8. Tower City Center

50 Public Square, Cleveland. The focal point of this urban complex is **Terminal Tower,** a local landmark completed in 1930 in Beaux Arts style. An observation deck on the 42nd floor provides sweeping views of the city. The tower also overlooks the sprawling 10-acre **Public Square,** dominated by the **Soldiers and Sailors Monument,** which is dedicated to local men who served in the Civil War. Also in the square is the **Old Stone Church,** an 1855 Romanesque Revival structure.

9. U.S.S. Cod

1089 North Marginal Dr., Cleveland. Visitors climb through hatchways to board this vintage World War II submarine, left in nearly the same condition as it was in wartime, when it sank some 30,000 tons of enemy vessels. Navy veterans conduct seasonal tours. *Admission charged.*

10. The Temple Museum of Religious Art

1855 Amsel Rd., Cleveland. Here visitors will find one of the most comprehensive collections of Judaic art, including an assortment of antique Torah hangings from the 17th century, ceremonial artifacts, and ancient pottery from the Holy Land.

11. Cleveland Museum of Natural History

1 Wade Oval, Cleveland. Lucy, one of the oldest and most complete fossils of a human skeleton, is a star attraction at this museum, where natural history is explored through exhibits of dinosaurs, mammals, birds, gems, and early human habitats, as well as a planetarium. *Admission charged.*

12. Rockefeller Park Greenhouse

750 East 88th St., Cleveland. Indoor showhouses in this plant-lover's paradise feature a water garden, tropical plants, and beautiful seasonal flowers. An array of gardens cover the grounds, including a Japanese and a Peace garden, as well as a "talking" garden with taped narration for the blind.

A roundel displayed at the Temple Museum

13. Western Reserve Historical Society

10825 East Blvd., Cleveland. This museum complex offers an informative journey through time, with decorative arts from 1620 to the present displayed in 20 period rooms, an extensive costume collection, and exhibits that interpret the history of industrialization. Also featured here is the fascinating **Frederick C. Crawford Auto-Aviation Collection,** with more than 200 rare cars and planes, including the first plane used to transport the U.S. mail. *Admission charged.*

14. Garden Center of Greater Cleveland

11030 East Blvd., Cleveland. Changing indoor plant exhibits and a horticultural library are among the main attractions here, along with a beautiful landscape of gardens that contain roses, herbs, wildflowers, and perennials. Flower shows and lectures are regularly scheduled events. *Fee charged for lectures and tours.*

15. Our Lady of Lourdes Shrine

21281 Chardon Rd., Euclid. Built into a hillside, this unusual grotto in the midst of serene woods is a replica of the Lourdes shrine in France. The Stations of the Cross line a winding path.

16. Lake View Cemetery

12316 Euclid Ave., Cleveland. The founder of this cemetery as well as of the Western Union Telegraph Co. is honored in the **Jeptha Wade Memorial Chapel.** Its sumptuous interior was designed by Louis Comfort Tiffany and features a stained-glass window and mosaic murals. The **Garfield Monument,** an impressive 180-foot-high Romanesque tower, pays tribute to the nation's 20th president, who is buried on the grounds, along with John D. Rockefeller and other notables.

17. Shaker Historical Museum

16740 South Park Blvd, Shaker Heights. Shaker furniture, clothing, photographs, boxes, and farm tools fill this quaint museum, which is located on what was once the grounds of the North Union Shaker Community, established in 1822. There are also exhibits that depict the history of Shaker Heights, one of the earliest "garden city" suburbs in the country.

18. Dittrick Museum of Medical History

11000 Euclid Ave., Cleveland. Visitors to this museum will come away with a new appreciation of modern health professionals upon discovering more about the evolution of medical practices through the ages. A wide assortment of objects, from X-rays to reflex hammers, depict the history of medicine, dentistry, pharmacy, and nursing. Replicas of doctors' offices from 1880 and 1930 provide further insight.

19. Cleveland Museum of Art

11150 East Blvd., Cleveland. Considered to be one of the finest general art museums in the United States, the collection features outstanding works of art that represent nearly every culture and historical period. The Asian and medieval European displays are especially commendable. *Admission charged for some exhibits.*

20. Dunham Tavern Museum

6709 Euclid Ave., Cleveland. This former stagecoach stop was built in 1824 and for many years served as the hub of social and political life in the area. Now restored and operating as a museum, it contains period furnishings and a variety of Shaker items. *Admission charged.*

LAKE ERIE

Mentor-on-the-Lake

Mentor

Eastlake

Willoughby

Timberlake
Lakeline

Willowick

Waite Hill

Wickliffe

Willoughby
Hills

Euclid

Kirtland

Moss Point

Richmond
Heights

Highland
Heights

Mayfield

Bratenahl

Cleveland

South Euclid

Gates Mills

East
Cleveland

Mayfield
Heights

Burke Lakefront Airport

Cleveland
Hts.

Lyndhurst

Hunting Valley

University
Heights

Cleveland Stadium

Edgewater Park

The Flats

Cleveland State Univ.

Case Western Reserve Univ.

Pepper Pike

Lakewood

John Carroll University

Shaker
Heights

Beachwood

Avon Lake

Bay Village

Westlake

Rocky River

Woodmere

Warrensville
Heights

Orange

Moreland Hills

Chagrin Falls

Fairview
Park

Linndale

Brooklyn

Newburgh
Heights

North Randall

Chagrin Falls Park

Avon

Brooklyn
Heights

Cuyahoga
Heights

Maple
Heights

Bentleyville

North
Ridgeville

North Olmsted

Parma

Garfield
Heights

Bedford

Bedford
Heights

Solon

Brook Park

Middleburg
Heights

Parma
Heights

Seven
Hills

Independence

Valley View

Oakwood

Olmsted
Falls

Berea

Eaton Estates

North Eaton

Columbia Station

Columbia Hills Corners

Columbia Center

Capel

North
Royalton

Broadview
Heights

Sagamore
Hills

Glenwillow

Reminderville

Sea World of Ohio

Twinsburg

Northfield

Macedonia

Strongsville

Northfield
Center

Brecksville

Western
Reserve
Estates

Aurora

Aurora Pond

Brunswick

Boston Heights

Hudson

Streetsboro

Tinkers Creek State Park

SCALE IN MILES
0 1 2 3 4 5

1. Niagara Apothecary

5 Queen St., Niagara-on-the-Lake. The handsome black walnut cabinets, arched doors, and intricate moldings of this 1866 pharmacy have been charmingly restored. Rows of gleaming apothecary bottles and odd Victorian remedies fill the shelves.

2. Niagara Historical Society Museum

43 Castlereagh St., Niagara-on-the-Lake. This museum boasts a superb collection of 18th-century pioneer artifacts and early military uniforms, including several from the War of 1812. *Admission charged.*

3. Fort George National Historic Site

Niagara Pkwy., Niagara-on-the-Lake. This British post was seized by Americans during the War of 1812, only to be recaptured later. Today the reconstructed fort contains large ramparts, officers' quarters, barracks, and a kitchen. *Admission charged.*

4. Fort Niagara State Park

Off Rte. 18F, Youngstown. In 1726 the French built a stone structure called the Castle inside the wooden stockade of Old Fort Niagara. The building still stands, along with the original magazine, redoubts, and storehouse. *Admission charged.*

5. Niagara Power Project Visitor Center

5777 Lewiston Rd., Lewiston. Working models and other exhibits describe the hydroelectric operation of the Niagara Power Project. A glass-enclosed observation building looks out to the Niagara River Gorge, and the center contains a Thomas Hart Benton mural depicting Father Louis Hennepin's first sighting of Niagara Falls.

6. Native American Center for the Living Arts

25 Rainbow Blvd. S., Niagara Falls. Shaped like a turtle and overlooking the falls, this unusual museum explores the artistic heritage of various American Indian cultures. *Admission charged.*

7. Tivoli Miniature World

5930 Victoria Ave., Niagara Falls. Landmarks from all over the world have been re-created in miniature at this unique park, where a train takes visitors to such sites as the Acropolis and the Great Pyramids. *Admission charged.*

8. Lundy's Lane Historical Museum

5810 Ferry St., Niagara Falls. In an 1874 cut-stone building, this museum covers the settlement of Niagara Falls and the War of 1812. Displays of antique toys, a pioneer kitchen, and a Victorian parlor evoke earlier times. *Admission charged.*

9. Welland Canal Viewing Complex

1932 Canal Rd., St. Catharines. From an elevated platform, visitors can watch ships from more than 50 countries pass through Welland Canal, part of a passageway designed to circumvent Niagara Falls. The viewing center is at the third in a series of eight locks and houses **St. Catharines Museum,** which, in addition to a working model of the lock, features transportation, manufacturing, and military exhibits. *Admission charged at museum.*

10. Niagara Falls Art Gallery

8058 Oakwood Dr., Niagara Falls. This gallery features the work of Canadian artist William Kurelek, most notably his impressive 160-panel painting called *The Passion of Christ.* Other Canadian artists, including Niagara Falls youths, are represented here, along with U.S. and European painters and sculptors. *Donation encouraged.*

11. Niagara Falls

The breathtaking beauty of these famous waterfalls can be viewed from **Niagara Reservation State Park,** where visitors can enjoy the splendid sight from **Goat Island,** which separates the American and Canadian falls, or from the **Prospect Point Observation Tower.** The boat *Maid of the Mist* departs from both sides of the falls and transports visitors to a thrilling, up-close view of the falls. The **Schoellkopf Geological Museum** offers informative exhibits on Niagara Falls. *Admission charged.*

12. Minolta Tower Centre

6732 Oakes Dr., Niagara Falls. This 325-foot-high tower provides a magnificent view of the falls from observation decks and dining rooms. *Admission charged.*

13. Buffalo and Erie County Historical Society Museum

25 Nottingham Ct., Buffalo. Housed in the only remaining public building from the 1901 Pan-American Exposition, this site displays period rooms and shops as well as exhibits on the history and ethnic heritages of western New York. *Admission charged.*

14. Buffalo Zoological Gardens

Parkside and Jewett Aves., Buffalo. From anacondas to zebras, the amazing diversity of animals is revealed in this 23-acre park. Many of the species here live in their natural habitats, and children can ride camels and ponies. *Admission charged.*

15. Buffalo Museum of Science

1020 Humboldt Pkwy., Buffalo. Insects, dinosaurs, spaceships, and endangered species are all displayed in this museum, along with many other exhibits representing the wide range of topics of concern to natural scientists. *Admission charged.*

16. Albright-Knox Art Gallery

1285 Elmwood Ave., Buffalo. Part neoclassical, part ultramodern, this structure houses an art collection that spans many centuries. Particularly notable are the modern American and European works, including paintings by Willem de Kooning and Jackson Pollock and sculptures by Henry Moore and George Segal. *Admission charged.*

17. Theodore Roosevelt Inaugural National Historic Site

641 Delaware Ave., Buffalo. After President McKinley was killed, Theodore Roosevelt took the oath of office in the library of this brick mansion. Furnished with original and period pieces, the house now holds exhibits on the assassination and swearing-in. *Admission charged.*

18. City Hall Observation Deck

65 Niagara Sq., Buffalo. On the 28th floor of City Hall, a splendid Art Deco building, is an observation deck that commands a panoramic view of Buffalo. This important industrial city holds many other examples of outstanding architecture, including the **Frank Lloyd Wright Residences,** the skyscraping **Guaranty Building,** which was codesigned by Louis Sullivan, and the Victorian structures in the historic preservation district of **Allentown.** Visitors also enjoy touring **QRS Music Rolls,** a company that manufactures player-piano rolls. *Fee charged for tour.*

19. Buffalo & Erie County Naval and Servicemen's Park

One Naval Park Cove, Buffalo. Visitors to this large inland naval park can board a guided missile cruiser, destroyer, and submarine. Also on view are aircraft and military artifacts. Adjacent to the park are boats that offer summer cruises on the Niagara River and Lake Erie. *Admission charged.*

20. Tifft Nature Preserve

1200 Fuhrmann Blvd., Buffalo. Set on the shores of Lake Erie, this nature preserve in an urban setting provides a resting place for a multitude of migratory birds. Visitors can observe them from hiking trails and from viewing blinds in a cattail marsh. Other attractions include a garden of wildflowers and Lake Kirsty, where fishing is permitted.

21. Buffalo and Erie County Botanical Gardens

2655 South Park Ave., Buffalo. Twelve greenhouses here compose a Victorian conservatory with palm trees, ferns, cacti, orchids, and other tropical and subtropical plants. Seasonal shows include a colorful chrysanthemum celebration.

22. Elbert Hubbard– Roycroft Museum

363 Oakwood Ave., East Aurora. Elbert Hubbard, a leader of the Arts and Crafts movement, founded the Roycroft, or "craft of kings," community, which was dedicated to excellence in craftsmanship. Inside a bungalow built by a Roycrofter are examples of the artisans' many fine works, including furniture, copperware, and leather goods. *Admission charged.*

23. Millard Fillmore Museum

24 Shearer Ave., East Aurora. The 1825 frame cottage where President Fillmore lived as a young man has been restored and contains the family's furnishings and memorabilia. Outside is a period rose and herb garden. *Donations requested.*

24. Niagara County Historical Society

215 Niagara St., Lockport. The five buildings that make up this center contain artifacts from pioneers, American Indians, and the military. The site also exhibits both farming and firefighting equipment from the 19th century. A nearby brick house, built in 1860, has a room designed especially for children.

Hall of Famer Joe DiMaggio in 1941

1. Kingston
Tourist Information Office, 209 Ontario St. Located in the Thousand Islands region, the port city of Kingston has numerous points of interest, including its 19th-century limestone **City Hall,** the **International Hockey Hall of Fame and Museum,** the **Marine Museum of the Great Lakes, Fort Henry,** and the Italianate **Bellevue House National Historic Site.** *Admission charged for some attractions.*

2. Thousand Islands
More than 1,500 islands punctuate both Canadian and American waters. Their numerous parks include the extensive **St. Lawrence Islands National Park,** with headquarters at Mallorytown Landing on the mainland. Popular sites include **Boldt Castle** on Heart Island and the **Antique Boat Museum** in Clayton. Boat tours of the archipelago depart from several points on both sides of the river. *Admission charged for some attractions.*

3. Lorenzo State Historic Site
Ledyard Ave., Cazenovia. In 1807 Dutchman John Lincklaen built a Federal-style mansion on a hill overlooking Lake Cazenovia. Today the brick house contains the family's furnishings and is open to the public. On the grounds are formal gardens and a carriage house with old horse-drawn vehicles.

4. Corning
Chamber of Commerce, 42 East Market St. The **Corning Glass Center** is composed of the **Museum of Glass,** the **Hall of Science and Industry,** and the **Steuben Factory,** where visitors can see molten glass transformed into crystal. Other interesting museums are the **Rockwell Museum,** with an impressive collection of Western art and early Steuben glass, and the 1796 **Benjamin Patterson Inn Museum,** with antique furnishings. *Admission charged.*

5. Elmira
Chamber of Commerce, 215 East Church St. Mark Twain spent many summers in this town, and his octagonal study remains on the **Elmira College** campus. The **Chemung County Historical Society** features memorabilia of the author, who is buried at the **Woodlawn Cemetery.** The **Arnot Art Museum** displays European and American works, and the city's **National Soaring Museum** examines motorless flight. *Admission charged for some attractions.*

6. Williamsport
Chamber of Commerce, 848 West Fourth St. The **Peter J. McGovern Little League Baseball Museum** chronicles the development of the children's league, which started in this town. Additional local history is on view at the **Lycoming County Historical Museum,** which features an extraordinary collection of toy trains. *Admission charged.*

7. Scranton
Chamber of Commerce, 222 Mulberry St. Coal mining is the theme of the **Pennsylvania Anthracite Heritage Museum,** as well as of the **Lackawanna Coal Mine Tour.** The city is also home to the restored 19th-century **Scranton Historic Iron Furnaces** and the **Steamtown National Historic Site,** where visitors can see old steam locomotives on display. *Admission charged for some attractions.*

8. Binghamton
Chamber of Commerce, 49 Court St. The **Roberson Museum and Science Center** maintains a turn-of-the-century mansion and a planetarium, along with exhibits that cover regional art, history, and science. Other attractions include the **Ross Park Zoo** and **The Forum,** where a display honors Rod Sterling, creator of the popular television series *The Twilight Zone.* *Admission charged at museum.*

9. Wayne County Historical Society Museum
810 Main St., Honesdale. The key roles played by various industries in Wayne County's early days are examined here. This museum also holds Indian, pioneer, and military artifacts. *Admission charged.*

10. Hanford Mills Museum
Rtes. 10 and 12, East Meredith. This 19th-century complex — eight buildings clustered around a pond — pays tribute to the power of water. A waterwheel drives a sawmill, gristmill, and woodworking facility. There are also 25 antique milling machines. *Admission charged.*

11. Cooperstown
Chamber of Commerce, 31 Chestnut St. This town is the site of the **National Baseball Hall of Fame and Museum,** where displays celebrate the sport and its notable players. The **Fenimore House** features both folk art and James Fenimore Cooper memorabilia, and the **Farmers' Museum** is a re-creation of a settlement from the early 1800's. *Admission charged.*

12. Olana
Rte. 9G, Hudson. Atop Church Hill sits this fantastic Persian-influenced villa built by landscape painter Frederic Edwin Church in the early 1870's. Exotic furnishings and masterly paintings fill the 16-room castle, which offers inspiring views of the Hudson River. *Admission charged.*

13. Martin Van Buren National Historic Site
Rte. 9H, Kinderhook. This modified Federal-style house served as the retirement home of the eighth U.S. president. The mansion contains period furniture and some of Van Buren's possessions. *Admission charged.*

14. Hancock Shaker Village
Off Rte. 20, Hancock. Founded in the early 19th century by the Shakers, this restored village, complete with a working historic farm, reveals much about the members' everyday life. *Admission charged.*

15. Stockbridge
Chamber of Commerce, Main St. The **Norman Rockwell Museum at Stockbridge** holds many works by the artist, who once lived in this quaint town. Visitors can tour **Chesterwood,** the estate of sculptor Daniel Chester French, and **Naumkeag,** an elaborate cottage designed by Stanford White. In nearby **Lenox** are **The Mount,** writer Edith Wharton's white mansion, and **Tanglewood,** known for its beautiful grounds and concerts. *Admission charged.*

16. Deerfield
The **Historic Deerfield** section of town preserves many early structures, including 13 Colonial and Federal-style homes open to visitors. **Memorial Hall Museum** features period rooms. *Admission charged.*

17. Amherst
Chamber of Commerce, 11 Spring St. The tree-lined common in this pretty town adjoins **Amherst College.** The college's **Robert Frost Library** has a collection of the well-known poet's work as well as manuscripts from the hand of Emily Dickinson. At the **Emily Dickinson Homestead** some of the rooms are open for tours. *Admission charged at homestead.*

18. Williamstown
Tourist Information Center, Rtes. 2 and 7. This charming town centers on **Williams College,** whose campus features an excellent museum of art. Williamstown is also the site of the **Sterling and Francine Clark Art Institute,** whose collection of French Impressionism, as well as other works, is world-renowned.

19. Bennington Museum
West Main St., Bennington. This museum specializes in regional art and history. Highlights include paintings by Grandma Moses and the actual schoolhouse she attended, Bennington pottery, American glass and furniture, military items, and a 1925 luxury touring car. *Admission charged.*

20. Hildene
Rte. 7A, Manchester. This was the summer estate of Robert Todd Lincoln, son of Abraham Lincoln. The Georgian Revival mansion holds many of the original furnishings, including a 1908 pipe organ and a stovepipe hat belonging to the president. Nearby, scenic **Equinox Sky Line Drive** traverses some 5 miles to the top of Mt. Equinox. *Admission charged.*

21. Saint-Gaudens National Historic Site
Off Rte. 12A, Cornish. The estate of Augustus Saint-Gaudens, the famous sculptor, includes his white brick home, studios, formal gardens, and artworks. Nearby is the **Cornish-Windsor Covered Bridge,** which spans the upper Connecticut River. *Admission charged at estate.*

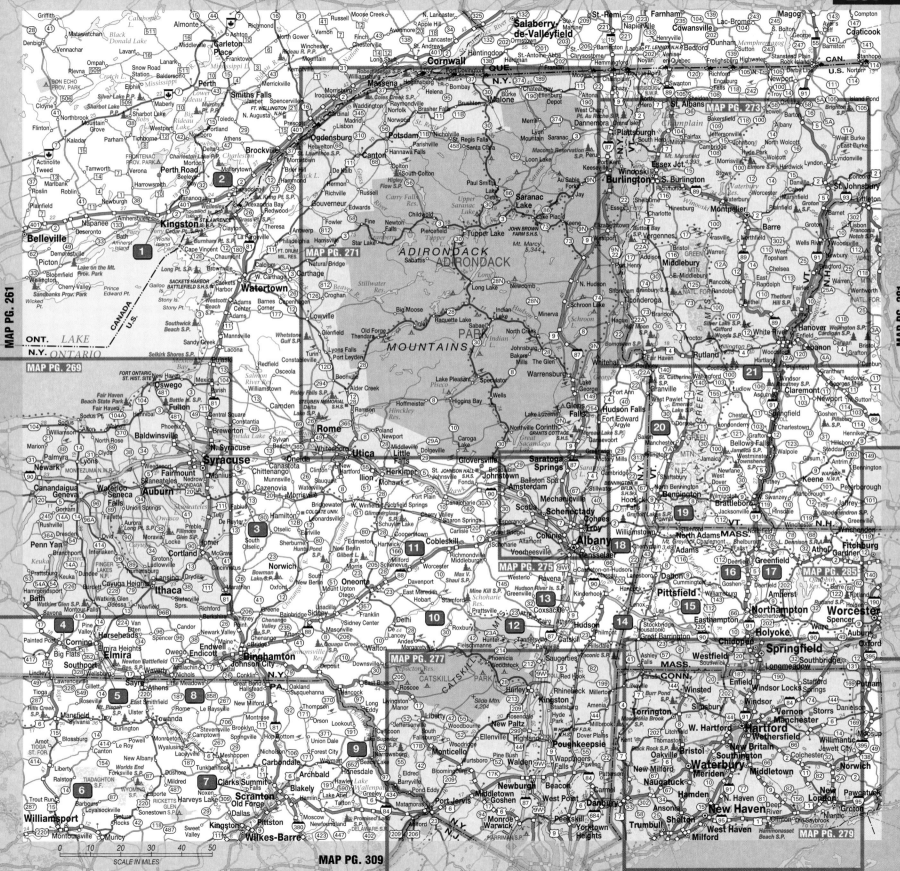

MAP PG. 261
MAP PG. 269
MAP PG. 271
MAP PG. 273
MAP PG. 281
MAP PG. 275
MAP PG. 277
MAP PG. 285
MAP PG. 279

SCALE IN MILES
0   10   20   30   40   50

1. Susan B. Anthony House

17 Madison St., Rochester. Built before the Civil War, this three-story brick house contains family heirlooms, original furnishings, photos, and memorabilia of the famed crusader for women's suffrage, abolition, and temperance. *Admission charged.*

2. Rochester Museum and Science Center

657 East Ave., Rochester. Regional history, natural science, technology, and Seneca Iroquois life are the focus of this museum. The **Strasenburgh Planetarium** offers shows under a 65-foot dome. *Admission charged.*

3. International Museum of Photography

900 East Ave., Rochester. Built in 1905 by George Eastman, who made photography available to the masses, this 50-room Georgian mansion holds one of the world's largest collections of photographic art and technology, with 600,000 prints and negatives, 12,000 films, 3 million movie stills, and 20,000 cameras. Changing exhibits and two theaters interpret more than 150 years of photography. *Admission charged.*

4. The Strong Museum

1 Manhattan Sq., Rochester. More than 500,000 items reflect everyday American life since 1820. They include Victorian furniture, 20,000 antique dolls, decorative glass, ceramics, silver, engravings, and 80 miniature rooms. There is also a hands-on learning center for children. *Admission charged.*

5. Palmyra

Visitor Center, Rte. 21. The birthplace of Mormonism includes the restored 1826 **Joseph Smith Home,** the sacred grove where he had his first vision, and the **E. B. Grandin Print Shop,** printer of the first *Book of Mormon.* **Hill Cumorah,** where Smith is said to have received the golden plates from the angel Moroni, is home to the visitor center and paintings that depict the beginnings of the Church of Jesus Christ of Latter-day Saints. A summer

pageant with 7 stages and a 600-member cast interprets scriptures. Nearby **Alling Coverlet Museum** has one of the nation's largest collections of 19th-century coverlets.

6. Canandaigua

Chamber of Commerce, 3210 Eastern Blvd. **Granger Homestead,** the estate of Gideon Granger, postmaster general under presidents Jefferson and Madison, features an 1816 Federal-style mansion with elegant woodwork and original furnishings. The **Carriage Museum** displays more than 50 antique coaches, cutters, surreys, sleighs, and hearses. The 50-acre **Sonnenburg Gardens,** with an arboretum and nine theme gardens ranging from colonial to Japanese to Italian, represents Gilded Age extravagance. *Admission charged.*

7. Cumming Nature Center

Gulick Rd., South Bristol. This National Environmental Study Area covers 900 acres of wooded hills and marshland. Theme trails lead to a reconstructed 1790 homestead, beaver pond, and Iroquois Indian exhibits. The visitor center offers films and displays. *Admission charged.*

8. Hammondsport

Housed in a 100-year-old building filled with antique equipment and various mementos, the **Wine and Grape Museum of Greyton H. Taylor** traces the brandy, champagne, and wine production processes. Displays at the **Curtiss Museum** include historic aircraft, military artifacts, and exhibits on the career of aviation pioneer Glenn H. Curtiss. *Admission charged.*

9. Watkins Glen State Park

Caverns, grottoes, and 19 waterfalls and cataracts within a deep serpentine canyon combine to make this 1,000-acre park one of the East's most impressive natural wonders. **Timespell,** a sound, light, and laser show, interprets the gorge's geologic and human history. *Admission charged.*

10. Cornell University

Outstanding attractions on this beautiful Ithaca campus include spectacular **Cascadilla Gorge;** 3,000 acres of natural areas, trails, gardens, streams, and a lake at **Cornell Plantations; Sapsucker Woods,** home to **Cornell Laboratory of Ornithology** and 4 miles of trails through bird habitats; and **Herbert F. Johnson Museum of Art,** known for its contemporary art collection and fifth-floor views of the magnificent

countryside. The nearby **Taughannock Falls State Park** features the 215-foot **Taughannock Falls,** trails, and camping. *Admission charged at park.*

11. The 1890 House Museum

37 Tompkins St., Cortland. This 1890 Victorian home contains 30 rooms featuring parquet floors, period furnishings, and a conservatory with a stained-glass ceiling. Nearby in **Fillmore Glen State Park** stands a replica of the cabin where President Millard Fillmore was born. *Admission charged at museum.*

12. Rose Hill Mansion

Rte. 96A, Geneva. According to local Indian lore, the 11 Finger Lakes were originally formed when the Creator placed his hand on this beautiful land. The mansion, near the shore of Seneca Lake, is a National Register landmark and one of the nation's finest Greek Revival structures. The 1839 house has 21 rooms with Empire-style furnishings, and on the grounds are a boxwood garden and carriage house. *Admission charged.*

13. Waterloo

In 1830 Joseph Smith organized the Church of Jesus Christ of Latter-day Saints at the **Peter Whitmer Farm.** The **Waterloo Memorial Day Museum,** in a 20-room mansion with ornate ironwork, exhibits Civil War and Memorial Day mementos. *Admission charged at museum.*

14. Seneca Falls

Chamber of Commerce, Rtes. 5 and 20W. The first women's rights convention, planned by early feminist leader Elizabeth Cady Stanton, was held here in 1848. **Women's Rights National Historical Park,** encompassing several city blocks, includes Stanton's home and exhibits on the history of the movement. The **National Women's Hall of Fame** honors the achievements of women in art, athletics, business, education, government, humanities, philanthropy, and science. Exhibits at the **Seneca Falls Historical Society Museum,** which is housed in a 23-room Victorian Queen Anne–style mansion, include 1800's decorative and fine arts. *Admission charged at museum.*

15. Cayuga Museum

203 Genesee St., Auburn. In this Greek Revival mansion the work of Theodore W. Case, developer of the motion picture soundtrack, is explored. His photographic

and recording equipment are displayed, as well as historic films, 1800's furnishings, and hands-on exhibits. Nearby **Schweinfurth Memorial Art Center** shows classical and contemporary fine art and folk art. *Admission charged at art center.*

16. William H. Seward House

33 South St., Auburn. This three-story home, built in 1816, contains mementos of Seward, who served as Lincoln's secretary of state and was a key player in the purchase of Alaska. *Admission charged.*

17. Harriet Tubman House

180 South St., Auburn. Born a slave, Tubman managed to escape and later rescue more than 300 others from bondage. Today, her home is open for tours and contains original furnishings and memorabilia.

18. Emerson Park

East Lake Rd., Owasco. Park attractions include a theater, a 1912 Edwardian garden pavilion, children's rides, and a museum dedicated to agriculture. The **Owasco Teyetasta/Iroquois Museum** traces the regional Owasco and Iroquois cultures from 7500 B.C. to the present. *Admission charged.*

19. Everson Museum of Art

401 Harrison St., Syracuse. As home to the Syracuse China Center for the Study of American Ceramics, this museum features one of the most extensive ceramic collections in the nation. Visitors can also see a collection of American and Oriental artworks spanning some 200 years.

20. Erie Canal Museum

318 Erie Blvd. East, Syracuse. This 1850 museum, housed in a national historical landmark, is the only existing Erie Canal weigh station. Visitors can board a canal boat replica, tour the weighmaster's office, and enjoy participatory exhibits.

21. Beaver Lake Nature Center

East Mud Lake Rd., Baldwinsville. In addition to a 238-acre lake, this center has 600 acres of wetlands, meadows, and forests in which visitors can hike, ski, and canoe.

22. Oswego

Chamber of Commerce, 156 West Second St. Guides in period uniforms re-create military life in the 1860's at **Fort Ontario State Historic Site.** The **Richardson-Bates House Museum** is an Italian villa–style home with 1890's furnishings. *Admission charged.*

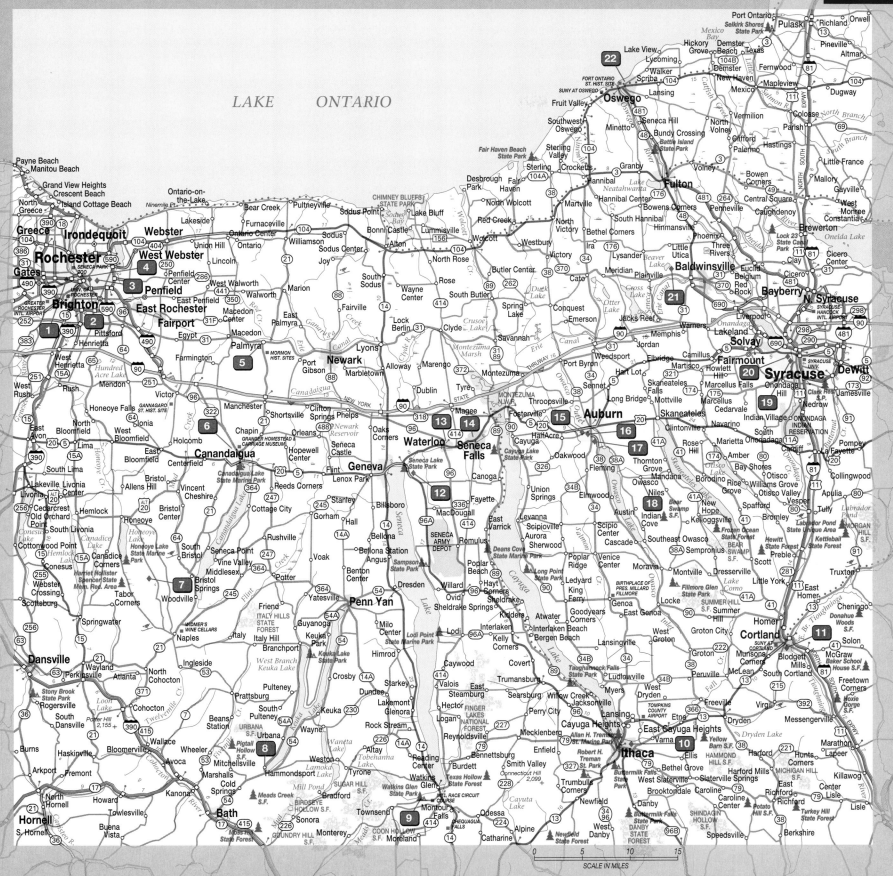

LAKE ONTARIO

SCALE IN MILES
0   5   10   15

THE ADIRONDACKS

1. Frederic Remington Art Museum

303 Washington St., Ogdensburg. This museum, housed in an 1810 mansion, contains the largest single collection of works by Frederic Remington, who, with great talent, captured the beauty, hardships, and personalities of the Old West. Included in the display are some 70 oil paintings, 17 bronzes, 140 watercolors, and many pen-and-ink sketches. Among other exhibits at the museum are personal belongings of the artist and a reconstruction of his last studio. *Admission charged.*

2. Massena

Chamber of Commerce, Main St. The **St. Lawrence Seaway,** a joint U.S.-Canadian project linking the Great Lakes to the Atlantic Ocean, extends for 2,342 miles. Two of the 15 locks that make the passage possible are the **Eisenhower** and **Snell locks,** of which the former contains viewing decks for watching ships and vehicular tunnel traffic. The **Moses-Saunders Power Dam** has computerized exhibits on the production and usage of electricity, as well as a terrain map of the power project. The 4,100-acre **Robert Moses State Park** offers lock overlooks, swimming, fishing, and boating. Another point of interest here is the **Massena Museum,** where displays of local artifacts can be seen. *Admission charged for some attractions.*

3. High Falls Park

Off Rte. 11, Chateaugay. As they lead to a 120-foot-high waterfall, the nature trails in this park have signs that identify the trees and plants along the way. Also among the woods here are picnic areas, campgrounds, and a playground. *Admission charged.*

4. Six Nations Indian Museum

Back Pond Rd., Onchiota. The history and culture of the Iroquois Indians from pre-Columbian to contemporary times are interpreted at this museum through indoor and outdoor exhibits, artifacts, and recent handiwork, including elaborately beaded belts, baskets, drums, clothing, and jewelry. *Admission charged.*

5. Saranac Lake

Chamber of Commerce, 30 Main St. Attractions here include the **Robert Louis Stevenson Memorial Cottage,** where the writer lived in 1887–88 and conceived *The Master of Ballantrae;* a Winter Carnival, held the second week in February, featuring ice sculptures and fireworks; and the **St. Regis Canoe Area,** where various lakes and ponds are linked together by the Raquette and Saranac rivers. *Admission charged for some attractions.*

6. Cranberry Lake

This lake, which can be viewed from several long and gentle trails following its shores, is the largest body of water in the relatively unexplored northwestern corner of Adirondack Park. A short hike to a lookout on **Bear Mountain** leads to sweeping views of the lake and unspoiled surrounding countryside. Swimming, canoeing, camping, and boat rentals are available nearby. *Fee charged for some activities.*

7. Lake Placid

Visitors Bureau, Olympic Ctr. This resort village was the site of the 1932 and 1980 Winter Olympics. Visitors can take boat rides on the peaceful, romantic lake around which the quaint town has grown. The **Lake Placid/North Elba Historical Society Museum,** in a former train depot, chronicles 200 years of local history with presentations of Olympic memorabilia, primitive farm implements, and sports equipment. **John Brown Farm State Historic Site** contains furniture that once belonged to the abolitionist, who, along with two sons and 10 followers, is buried nearby. *Admission charged at museum.*

8. High Falls Gorge

Rte. 86, Wilmington. Observable from trails and bridges, glaciation and river erosion have created a spectacular deep ravine with waterfalls and rapids at the foot of Whiteface Mountain. By taking **Whiteface Mountain Memorial Highway** to the 4,867-foot-high summit, visitors obtain views that extend for miles — Montreal's Mt. Royal, the St. Lawrence River, Lake Champlain, Lake Placid, and the Green Mountains of Vermont. *Admission charged.*

9. Adirondack Center Museum and Colonial Garden

Rte. 9, Elizabethtown. Facilities and displays here range from art galleries, nature trails, picnic areas, and a formal garden to restored carriages, a mining exhibit, a doll collection, and a sound-and-light show interpreting the history of the Champlain Valley. *Admission charged at museum.*

10. Raquette Lake

Visitors can take a guided tour of **Sagamore Historic Adirondack Great Camp,** a rustic, yet luxurious, summer retreat exemplifying the typical Great Camps of the 1800's that catered to the vacationing wealthy. **Eighth Lake Public Campsite** extends from Seventh Lake to Eighth Lake and offers swimming, fishing, and spaces for more than 100 campers. *Admission charged.*

11. Adirondack Museum

Rte. 28N/30, Blue Mountain Lake. Regional history and art are explored at this outstanding museum, where visitors can spend days investigating indoor and outdoor displays that include more than 20 buildings filled with fascinating exhibits on logging, transportation, boating, mining, schooling, and rustic furniture. *Admission charged.*

12. North Creek

Chamber of Commerce, Main St. As an Adirondack sporting capital, this town provides access to cross-country and downhill skiing, as well as white-water rafting. Visitors can ride a gondola to the top of the 2,100-foot vertical drop found at the state's second largest ski area, **Gore Mountain,** and, 800 feet below the summit, walk through an open-pit mine on the tours at **Gore Mountain Garnet Mine.** *Admission charged for some attractions.*

13. Natural Stone Bridge and Caves

Off Rte. 87, Pottersville. In the area, marked nature trails lead to a gorge with waterfalls, underground waterways, trout fishing, several caves, and interesting rock formations. *Admission charged.*

14. Lake George

Chamber of Commerce, Rte. 9. Travelers can explore the 32-mile-long lake with 365 islands on narrated cruises; see the countryside from **Prospect Mountain Veteran's Memorial Highway,** which climbs to the peak's 2,030-foot summit; and visit historic sites that figured prominently in colonial wars. The **Fort William Henry Museum,** reconstructed from the original fort plans, recalls the 1755 fortification's history with artifacts, cannon firings, and other demonstrations. **Lake George Battlefield Park,** the site of a 1755 French and Indian War battle, contains the ruins of **Fort George** and a monument to American Indians. *Admission charged for some attractions.*

15. Glens Falls

Chamber of Commerce, 136 Warren St. The **Hyde Collection,** displayed in a Florentine Renaissance mansion, contains some of the best and most expressive work by 15th-to-20th-century European and American artists — such luminaries as Rembrandt, Van Dyke, Rubens, El Greco, Picasso, Matisse, Homer, and Whistler. **Chapman Historical Museum** offers changing regional exhibits in an 1868 Second Empire house. *Admission charged.*

A view from the peak of Whiteface Mountain, with shimmering Lake Placid in the distance

16. Munson-Williams-Proctor Institute

310 Genesee St., Utica. Here, a sculpture grove separates an 1850's Italianate mansion from an art museum, where the collection is primarily composed of 19th- and 20th-century American and European works, representing such modern notables as Picasso, Pollock, and Calder. **Fountain Elms,** a restored 1850 mansion, displays Victorian-era watches, dolls, silver, and glassware.

17. Oriskany Battlefield State Historic Site

Off Rte. 69, Oriskany. A granite shaft marks the site of an August 6, 1777, engagement in which an American force was ambushed by British troops. Guided tours interpret the battle, which was one of the bloodiest in the Revolutionary War.

18. Rome

Chamber of Commerce, 200 Liberty Plaza. **Fort Stanwix National Monument** features costumed interpreters as well as numerous artifacts discovered at the fortification, which was used during the French and Indian War and the Revolutionary War. The **Tomb of the Unknown Soldier of the American Revolution** was designed by Lorimer Rich, who also planned Arlington National Cemetery's Tomb of the Unknown Soldier. Visitors to the **Erie Canal Village** can take horse-drawn packet boat rides along a restored section of the canal, beside which stands a reconstructed Victorian-era community. *Admission charged for some attractions.*

19. Steuben Memorial State Historic Site

Star Hill Rd., Steuben. Gen. Friedrich Wilhelm von Steuben was the Continental Army drillmaster who turned ragtag rebel volunteers into a disciplined, effective fighting unit. In gratitude, the state of New York granted him 16,000 acres of land after the war. A replica of his cabin contains panels depicting his life.

20. Constable Hall

John St., Constableville. Built in 1819, this Georgian mansion listed on the National Register of Historic Places is known for its plantation veranda and double-bowed front joined by a portico. It includes original furnishings, seven generations' worth of family belongings, and restored formal gardens. *Admission charged.*

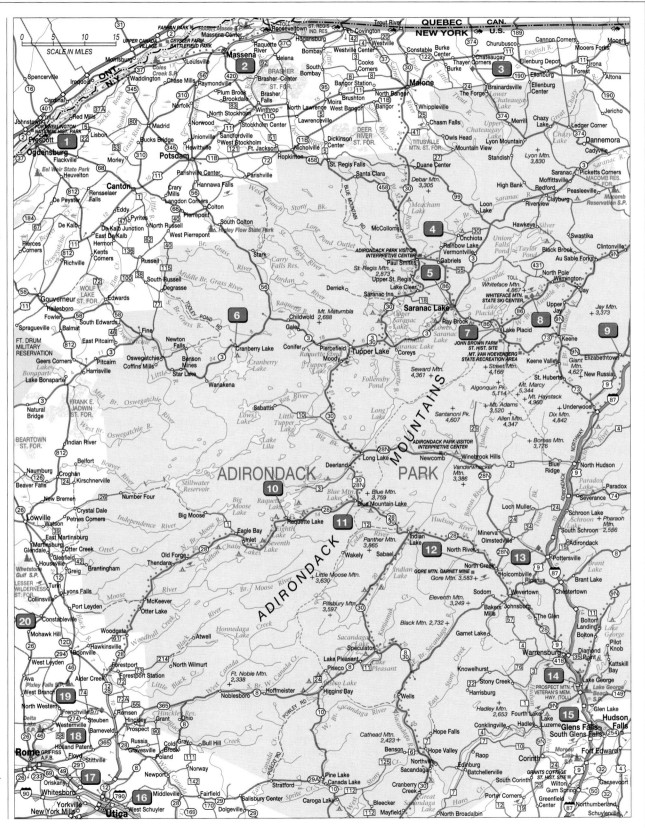

1. Kent-Delord House Museum

17 Cumberland Ave., Plattsburgh. This 1797 Federal-style home on the banks of Lake Champlain was commandeered by the British in 1814. Today it contains period furnishings, a fine collection of portrait paintings, and artifacts from the War of 1812. *Admission charged.*

2. Ausable Chasm

Off Rte. 87, Ausable Chasm. This plunging gorge was carved more than 500 million years ago by the Ausable River. The resultant sandstone cliffs and stupendous rock formations can be viewed from dizzying walkways along the river banks, steel bridges crisscrossing the chasm, and boat rides down the rapids. *Admission charged.*

3. Burlington

Chamber of Commerce, 209 Battery St. On the campus of the **University of Vermont** is the **Robert Hull Fleming Museum,** which features 18th- and 19th-century American art, European paintings, and ethnographic collections. **Ethan Allen Park** offers views of the Adirondacks, Lake Champlain, and the Green Mountains. The patriot's nearby homestead, now preserved, is open to visitors. *Admission charged for some attractions.*

4. Shelburne

The 45 scenic acres of the **Shelburne Museum** encompass furnished 18th- and 19th-century homes. There's also a collection of American folk art, with dolls, decoys, quilts, rugs, and carvings. At **Shelburne Farms,** visitors can explore barns, a working dairy, formal gardens, and a 3-mile walking trail. At the nearby **Vermont Wildflower Farm,** pathways lead past flowers and woodlands. *Admission charged.*

5. Lake Champlain Maritime Museum

Basin Harbor Rd., Basin Harbor. The history of Lake Champlain is traced here with the aid of ancient rocks, artifacts from past Indian and colonial settlements, and ex-hibits on modern recreational and commercial activities. One noteworthy display is a replica of Benedict Arnold's gunboat, which was sunk in 1776. *Admission charged.*

6. Crown Point

Ruins of fortifications from both the French and Indian and Revolutionary wars are preserved at the **Crown Point State Historic Site,** where a visitor center displays archeological and historical exhibits. In the Ironville Historic District, self-guided tours at the **Penfield Homestead and Historical Museum** pass 19th-century buildings and the remains of iron works.

7. Middlebury

Chamber of Commerce, 2 Court St. Visitors to town can stroll past the lovely trees and old buildings of **Middlebury College.** The 1809 **Congregational Church** boasts an interior with impressive wooden columns, each made from a single tree. Other attractions include the 19th-century **Sheldon Museum,** filled with period furnishings and artifacts; the **Vermont State Craft Center at Frog Hollow;** and the **Morgan Horse Farm,** a breeding and training center for Vermont's official state animal. *Admission charged for some attractions.*

8. Ticonderoga

Chamber of Commerce, 146 Montcalm St. The historical gem of this resort area is the reconstructed **Fort Ticonderoga,** a strategic stronghold in the Revolutionary War. The fort was built by the French, taken by the British, then captured during the Revolution by Ethan Allen and the Green Mountain Boys before being recaptured by the British. A museum displays muskets, uniforms, and period memorabilia; nearby the **Ticonderoga Heritage Museum** examines the area's industrial history.

9. Hubbardton Battlefield and Museum

Monument Rd., East Hubbardton. The visitor center contains an interpretive exhibit on the only Revolutionary War battle fought on Vermont soil, and the hilltop location offers sweeping views of the Green and Taconic mountains. *Admission charged.*

10. New England Maple Museum

Rte. 7, Pittsford. A slide show, displays, and a self-guiding tour detail the history of maple syrup, beginning with the American Indians, who cooked the sap over an open fire. *Admission charged.*

11. Proctor

The **Vermont Marble Exhibit** displays various kinds of marble brought here from around the world, and visitors can watch skilled artisans as they transform the stone into sculpture. Another attraction in town is **Wilson Castle,** an extravagant mansion dating to the 19th century and filled with lavish furnishings from Europe and the Far East. *Admission charged.*

12. Woodstock

Chamber of Commerce, 18 Central St. This quaint village is known for its charming old homes, such as the 1807 **Dana House,** complete with authentic furnishings and exhibits on local history. The **Billings Farm and Museum** re-creates farm life as it was in the state's past, with reconstructed buildings and demonstrations of period activities. Nearby at the **Vermont Institute of Natural Science,** the **Raptor Center** displays 26 different species of birds of prey. *Admission charged.*

13. Joseph Smith Birthplace Memorial

Off Rte. 14, near South Royalton. Here a granite monument marks the birthplace of the founder of the Church of Jesus Christ of Latter-day Saints. A chapel and visitor center stand near his family's old farmhouse.

14. Justin Smith Morrill Homestead

Justin Smith Morrill Hwy., Strafford Village. This charming Gothic Revival cottage was built by the author of the Morrill Land-Grant College Act, which granted public lands to states to assist in the establishment of colleges. The house contains original furnishings as well as family memorabilia. *Admission charged.*

15. Lower Shaker Village

Thirteen buildings remain today of what was once a prosperous Shaker village from 1793 to 1923. Visitors can watch artisans demonstrate a variety of crafts and take a self-guiding walking tour that leads to a church, cemetery, barn, and museum. *Admission charged at museum.*

16. Lost River Reservation at Kinsman Notch

Rte. 112, North Woodstock. Walkways, stairs, and bridges attempt to track the Lost River as it darts through caverns and past granite boulders and other startling rock formations. A nature garden and museum are also popular. *Admission charged.*

17. St. Johnsbury

Chamber of Commerce, 30 Western Ave. In this quaint town are the **Fairbanks Museum and Planetarium,** offering mounted rare birds and animals, arts and antiques, and artifacts from local history; the Victorian **St. Johnsbury Athenaeum,** which houses 19th-century American paintings, many from the Hudson River School; and the **Maple Grove Maple Museum,** a tribute to maple sugaring. *Admission charged for some attractions.*

18. Rock of Ages Quarry

Main St., Graniteville. On the guided tour, guests can watch hulking derricks lift slabs of granite weighing up to 100 tons from one of the world's largest and deepest granite pits, which has been in operation for more than a century. At the **Craftsman Center,** artisans cut, polish, and transform stone into fine monuments, examples of which can be seen in nearby **Hope Cemetery.** *Fee charged for tour.*

19. Floating Bridge

Rte. 65, Brookfield. This span is supported by 380 drums filled with foam. It is the seventh floating bridge on Sunset Lake, the first of which was built in 1819.

20. Montpelier

The elegant **Vermont State House** features a gold-leaf dome. Changing exhibits at the **Vermont Historical Society Museum** relate some 200 years of state history. Works by 19th- and 20th-century American artists are on display at the **T.W. Wood Art Gallery.** In nearby Waterbury, visitors can tour **Ben & Jerry's** ice cream factory. *Admission charged for some attractions.*

21. Mount Mansfield

Rte. 108, Stowe. This 4,393-foot-high mountain — the shape of which is said to resemble the profile of a reclining man's face — is the state's highest and offers some of the East's finest skiing. A steep, winding road to the top offers magnificent vistas, as does a gondola ride to the "chin." *Admission charged.*

22. Old Round Church

Bridge St., Richmond. Constructed in 1813, this round structure actually has 16 sides. According to local lore, the church was built in its unique shape in order to keep the devil from lurking in corners. It has served at various times as a place of worship and as the town hall.

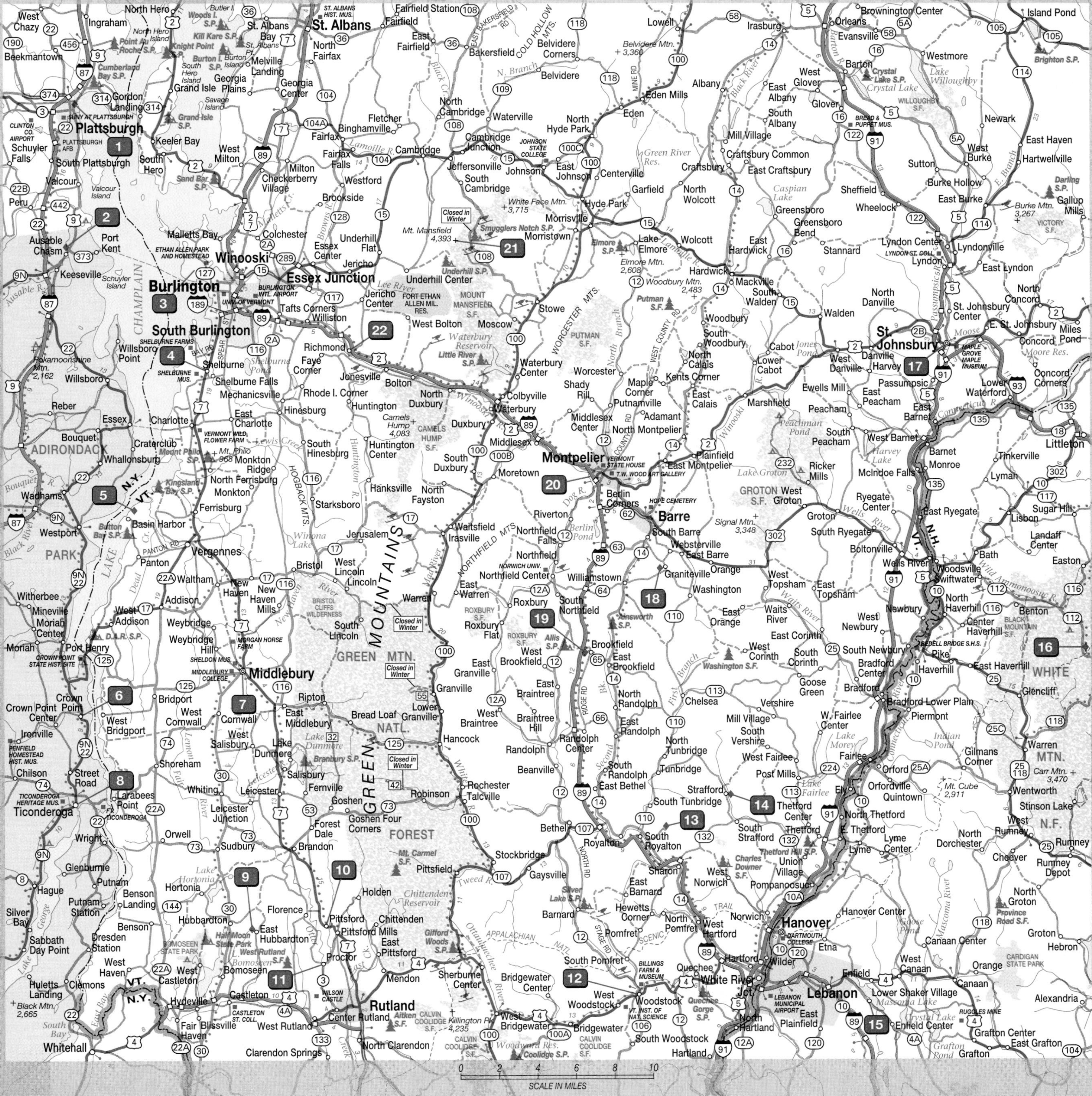

SCALE IN MILES

0 2 4 6 8 10

1. Guy Park State Historic Site

366 West Main St., Amsterdam. This Georgian mansion was once the home of Guy Johnson, a staunch loyalist who became superintendent of Indian Affairs. Johnson vacated the house when the Revolutionary War began. Today, the site holds the town chamber of commerce and has displays on the history of the Johnson family and the building of the Erie Canal.

2. Petrified Sea Gardens

Off Rte. 29, Saratoga Springs. These gardens hold the petrified remains of cabbage-like plants, potholes, grinding stones, glacial crevices, and fossils of prehistoric animals, including snails once dwelling in the sea that covered the Adirondack area some 500 million years ago. There are picnic areas, a walking trail, and a gift shop. *Admission charged.*

3. National Museum of Dance

South Broadway, Saratoga Springs. This museum traces the history and development of American professional dance. The Dance Hall of Fame honors a number of well-known performers. Brief videos of the inductees — a group that includes Fred Astaire and Martha Graham — are shown. When in session, dance rehearsals in an adjacent studio may be observed by visitors. *Admission charged.*

4. Casino and Congress Park

Broadway, Saratoga Springs. An elaborate Victorian casino, dating from 1870 (when gambling was still legal in New York), today houses the **Historical Society of Saratoga Springs Museum,** which details the area's history from its rural beginnings to its rise as a Victorian resort. Features include the local mineral springs, elegant hotels, and stories about the colorful personalities who came to try their luck. The park is also home to the **Walworth Memorial Museum,** which displays 19th-century furniture and decorative arts, and the **Ann Grey Art Gallery.** *Admission charged.*

5. National Museum of Racing and Hall of Fame

Union Ave. and Ludlow St., Saratoga Springs. The history of Thoroughbred racing in America is traced by paintings, sculptures, and memorabilia. Famous racehorses and their jockeys are honored in the Hall of Fame. Videotapes of well-known trainers explaining their techniques are shown. *Admission charged.*

6. Saratoga Spa State Park

Off Rtes. 9 and 50, Saratoga Springs. This park includes the **Performing Arts Center,** a 5,000-seat amphitheater that is the summer home of the Philadelphia Orchestra, the New York City Ballet, and the New York City Opera. Other attractions include the 500-seat indoor **Little Theater;** golf courses; tennis courts; swimming pools; walking and ski trails; picnic areas; and the Lincoln and Roosevelt baths, which offer mineral treatments and massages. *Admission charged.*

7. National Bottle Museum

76 Milton Ave., Ballston Spa. A collection of 18th- and 19th-century handmade glassworks are displayed in this museum. The site also maintains a research library, a reconstructed pharmacy with a variety of glass medicine containers, and glass-blowing equipment. *Admission charged.*

8. Saratoga National Historical Park

648 Rte. 32, near Bemis Heights. In the fall of 1777, a major battle of the American Revolution was fought in this peaceful countryside along the Hudson River. The result of the 2½-week-long series of encounters was a decisive victory for the Americans. A 9-mile drive — marked with signs describing the various battle scenes — winds through the park. The visitor center, where the drive begins, offers a brief film on the historic event. *Admission charged.*

9. Troy

Chamber of Commerce, 31 Second St. In the late 1600's Dutch farmers settled in the countryside along the eastern bank of the Hudson. The town of Troy, known as Vanderhayden until 1789, began to grow, developing in the 19th century into a manufacturing and steel-producing center. The **Hart-Cluett Mansion,** a town house built in 1827, contains period furnishings and decorative arts. In nearby **Oakwood Cemetery,** a tablet marks the grave of Samuel Wilson, who shipped beef marked "U.S." to the army and thus became known as the original Uncle Sam. *Donation encouraged at mansion.*

10. Ten Broeck Mansion

9 Ten Broeck Pl., Albany. Built in 1798, this brick Federal mansion was the home of General Abraham Ten Broeck, a commander in the Battle of Saratoga. The house contains fine examples of period furnishings and is the headquarters of the Albany County Historical Association. The landscape includes extensive lawns and several gardens. *Admission charged.*

Revolutionary War scenes are reenacted at Saratoga National Historical Park.

11. Albany Institute of History and Art

125 Washington Ave., Albany. Here, various aspects of the culture of the upper Hudson River Valley are examined by exhibits that include paintings by artists of the Hudson River School, early Dutch portraits, 18th- and 19th-century decorative arts and furniture, and a replica of a typical Dutch Colonial room. The McKinney Library is housed in the museum. Guided tours are available. *Donation encouraged.*

12. New York State Museum

Empire State Plaza, Albany. This museum depicts the cultural and natural histories of the state, from prehistory to the present. Visitors may view exhibits of murals, scientific displays, artifacts, and life-size dioramas, such as a reconstruction of a Mohawk Iroquois longhouse. The plaza, known for an observation deck on the 42nd floor of Corning Tower, is a concourse featuring modern sculpture and a group of government and business buildings.

13. Schuyler Mansion State Historic Site

32 Catherine St., Albany. Begun in 1761, this Georgian brick mansion was the residence of Philip Schuyler, who served as a general in the American Revolution and as a senator from New York in the first United States Congress. In 1780, Schuyler's daughter, Elizabeth, was married to Alexander Hamilton here. Visitors can tour the home, where beautiful furniture, English silver, glassware, and many other family belongings are on display.

14. Historic Cherry Hill

523½ South Pearl St., Albany. The gambrel-roofed farmhouse here, built in 1787 for Philip Van Rensselaer, remained in the family for almost 200 years. The last member to occupy the house, Emily Watkins Rankin, specified in her will that the home and the five generations' worth of furnishings within it become a museum. Tours of the mansion and its gardens are available. *Admission charged.*

15. Crailo State Historic Site

9½ Riverside Ave., Rensselaer. Located in the 1705 home of Hendrick Van Rensselaer, the museum here depicts the life and history of the Dutch settlers who came to the upper Hudson River Valley in the early 1600's. Through the years the house has undergone remodeling. In 1762, for example, a Georgian-style wing was added. In 1924 the building was given to New York State and, soon afterward, opened to visitors.

16. New York State Capitol

State St., Albany. This grand structure, which combines the Renaissance styles of France and Italy, was designed by five architects and constructed over a period of about 32 years in the late 19th century. The remarkable interior of the building includes three handsome stairways decorated by stone carvings. The Senate chamber, designed by Henry Hobson Richardson, is notable for its marble, onyx, mahogany, and stained-glass ornamentation.

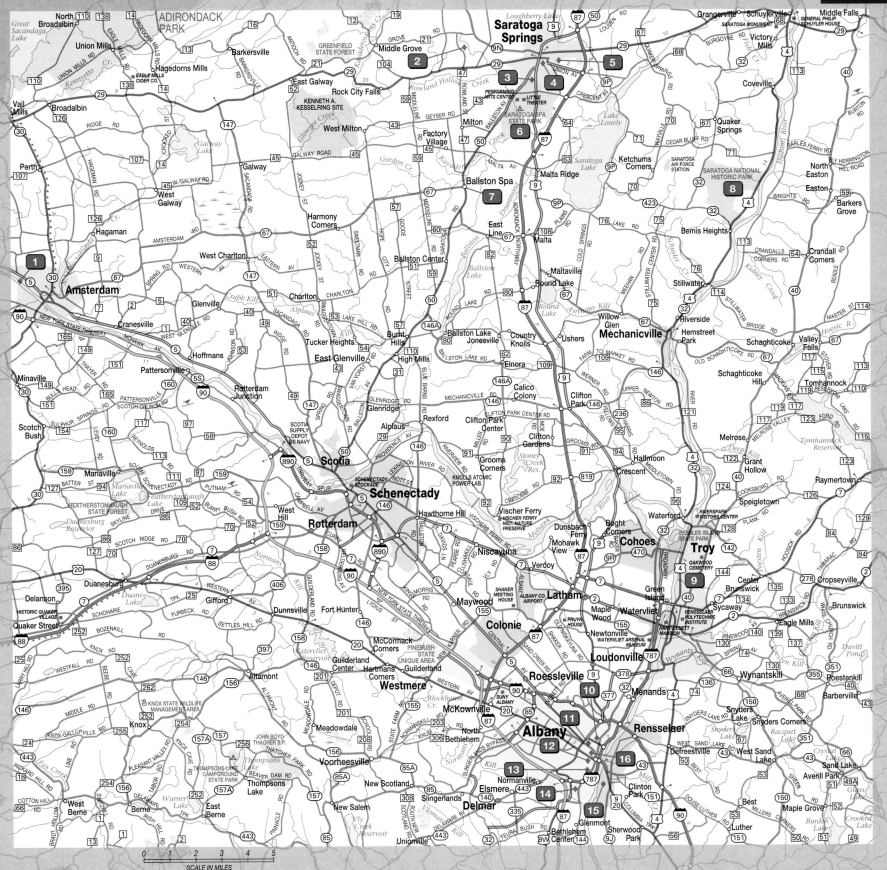

1. Ice Caves Mountain National Landmark

Nature trails and a scenic drive wind through this fascinating prehistoric landscape of ice caves, tunnels, narrow chasms, and steep cliffs. **Sam's Point** offers spectacular views. *Admission charged.*

2. New Paltz

Chamber of Commerce, 257 Main St. **Huguenot Street** — said to be the country's oldest to still have the original buildings intact — is lined by handsome stone homes. **Locust Lawn,** an 1814 Federal mansion in nearby Gardiner, displays the belongings of past residents. **Mohonk Mountain House,** a Victorian-era resort, offers fishing, hiking, boating, and horseback riding. *Admission charged.*

3. Kingston

Chamber of Commerce, 7 Albany Ave. Among the historic buildings in Kingston's Stockade District is the **Senate House State Historic Site,** a stone structure containing period furnishings and data on the forming of the state government. The nearby **Trolley Museum of New York** offers trolley car rides along the river. *Admission charged for some attractions.*

4. Rhinebeck

Chamber of Commerce, Mill St. The **Old Rhinebeck Aerodrome** holds a unique collection of antique aircraft, many of which take to the sky in summer air shows. The **Hudson River National Historic Landmark District,** a beautiful stretch along the Hudson, harbors regal country estates. The **Beekman Arms** has been open since 1766, making it the nation's oldest hotel to be continuously in operation.

5. Montgomery Place

River Rd., Annandale-on-Hudson. This 23-room Classical Revival mansion was built in 1805 by Janet Livingston Montgomery, widow of Gen. Richard Montgomery, a Revolutionary War hero. The home displays elaborate furnishings and artworks, while the estate encompasses gardens, hiking trails, waterfalls, and an orchard. **Bard College** is nearby. *Admission charged.*

6. Mills Mansion State Historic Site

Old Post Rd., Staatsburg. Originally built in 1832 in the Greek Revival style, the house was remodeled in 1895 as an elaborate 65-room mansion for Ogden Mills, a 20th-century political leader. Guided tours take visitors past marble fireplaces, tapestries, and other art objects. The estate also offers hiking, skiing, and summertime concerts.

7. Hyde Park

Tourism Promotion Agency, 532 Rte. 9. Built in the late 1820's, the **Home of Franklin D. Roosevelt** sits on a bluff overlooking the Hudson. The **Roosevelt Museum and Library** has family memorabilia. **Val-Kill** was built in the 1920's for Eleanor Roosevelt. Also with views of the Hudson is the **Vanderbilt Mansion,** an elaborate 1898 Beaux Arts residence. The prestigious **Culinary Institute of America** is nearby. *Admission charged for some attractions.*

8. Locust Grove

370 South Rd., Poughkeepsie. This 19th-century villa was the home of Samuel F.B. Morse, a pioneer of the telegraph. Exhibits include period furnishings and telegraphic equipment. Nearby is **Vassar College.** *Admission charged.*

9. Northeast Audubon Center

Rte. 4, Sharon. The home of Mrs. Clement R. Ford, who donated her 700-acre estate to this center, serves as a museum, where plant and animal specimens are exhibited. Nature classes, workshops, and guided field trips are available. *Admission charged.*

10. Kent

On a slope above the ruins of the Kent Iron Furnace, the **Sloane-Stanley Museum** features paintings as well as early-American hand tools. The nearby **Kent Falls State Park** is named for a stream that cascades over rocky cliffs and eventually joins the Housatonic River. *Admission charged.*

11. Beacon

The **Mount Gulian Historic Site** has an 18th-century fieldstone house used by Baron von Steuben as a headquarters during the Revolution. **Madam Brett's Homestead** is a 1709 Dutch Colonial house featuring family furnishings and gardens. *Admission charged.*

12. Washington's Headquarters State Historic Site

84 Liberty St., Newburgh. The general's headquarters at the end of the Revolutionary War was in the **Jonathan Hasbrouck House.** Exhibits in the adjacent museum depict the history of the Continental Army.

13. New Windsor Cantonment State Historic Site

Rte. 300, Vails Gate. In 1782 American forces made their last winter encampment here. Today, re-created military drills and other demonstrations are given at the site. The nearby **Knox's Headquarters State Historic Site,** in a 1754 Georgian house, displays period furnishings. The grounds include a wildflower sanctuary.

14. Storm King Art Center

Old Pleasant Hill Rd., Mountainville. More than 100 contemporary artists are represented at this museum complex, which includes a 400-acre outdoor sculpture park. *Admission charged.*

15. U.S. Military Academy

Rte. 218, West Point. Highlights of this historic institution include the **Cadet Chapel, Trophy Point,** and the **West Point Museum,** which contains one of the country's most extensive collections of firearms and military artifacts.

16. Boscobel

Rte. 9D, Garrison. Overlooking the Hudson River, this 1804 Federal residence features antique furnishings. In summer, concerts are held on the lawn. *Admission charged.*

17. Aldrich Museum of Contemporary Art

258 Main St., Ridgefield. Housed in a pre-Revolutionary building, this museum nonetheless displays works by contemporary artists. The grounds include a sculpture garden. *Admission charged.*

18. Katonah

The **John Jay Homestead State Historic Site,** once home to the first Chief Justice of the United States Supreme Court, includes period furnishings, memorabilia, gardens, and farm buildings. **Caramoor,** a Mediterranean villa built by Walter Tower Rosen, is the scene of an annual summer music festival. *Admission charged.*

19. Stamford

Convention and Visitors Bureau, 1 Landmark Sq. A 19th-century farm, nature trails, a country store, and a museum compose the **Stamford Museum and Nature Center.** The **Whitney Museum of American Art at Champion** offers changing exhibits, lectures, and concerts. *Admission charged at nature center.*

20. Greenwich

Chamber of Commerce, 2 Lafayette Ct. The 485-acre **Audubon Center** has nature trails and a visitor center, where the exhibits include a glass-enclosed beehive. The **Bruce Museum** displays local artworks and exhibits on science and culture. The 1690 **Putnam Cottage** maintains its original herb garden. The circa 1732 **Bush-Holley House** contains period furnishings and American Impressionist paintings. *Admission charged.*

21. Van Cortlandt Manor

Off Rte. 9, Croton-on-Hudson. Home of the Van Cortlandt family from the early 1700's to 1945, this 18th-century house contains family furnishings and memorabilia. A restored 18th-century inn, an open-hearth kitchen, and a brick-making kiln are located on the estate grounds. *Admission charged.*

22. Philipsburg Manor

Rte. 9 and Pocantico St., North Tarrytown. The 18th-century farm here includes a Dutch Colonial manor house, a Dutch barn, and a water-powered gristmill. Among the gravesites in the nearby **Sleepy Hollow Cemetery** are those of Washington Irving and Andrew Carnegie. *Admission charged.*

23. Tarrytown

Chamber of Commerce, 80 South Broadway. Among this town's many historic homes is **Sunnyside,** a charming stone cottage set on the banks of the Hudson River that was once home to author Washington Irving, and **Lyndhurst,** an 1838 Gothic Revival mansion. *Admission charged.*

24. Ringwood State Park

1304 Sloatsburg Rd., Ringwood. Located in the park, **Ringwood Manor** features 50 rooms and a valuable collection of antiques. On the estate are botanical gardens and **Skylands,** an imposing 44-room mansion. *Admission charged.*

25. Grey Towers

Old Owego Tpk., Milford. Guided tours are offered of this extravagant 1886 French château, which was once home to forester and politician Gifford Pinchot.

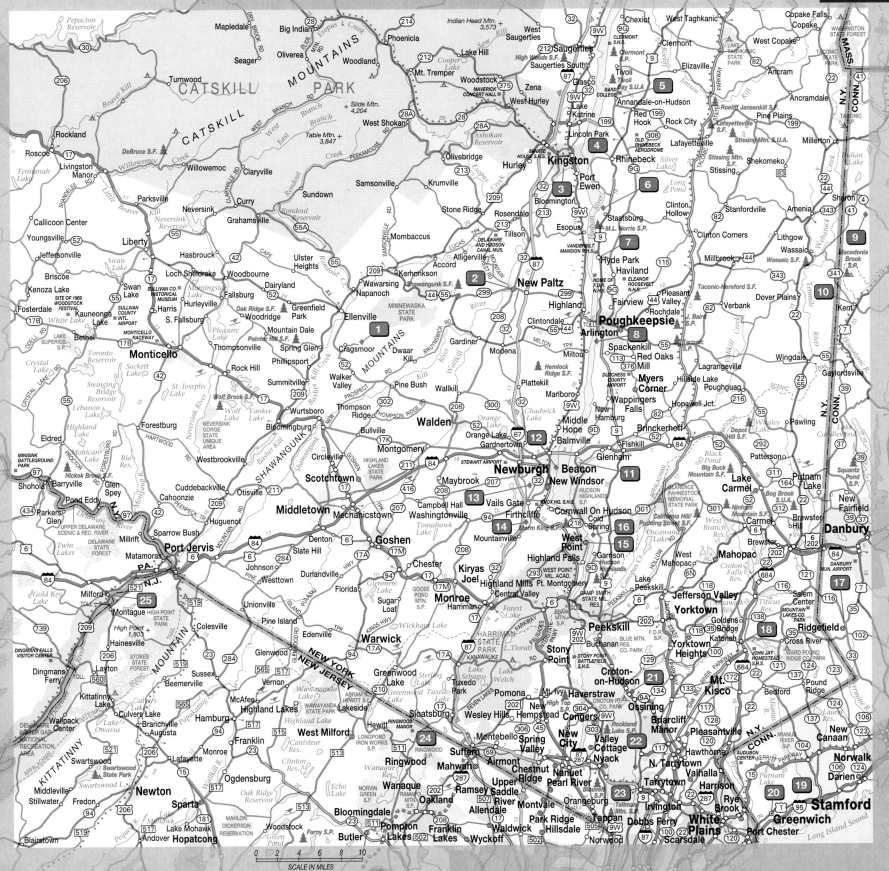

SCALE IN MILES
0 2 4 6 8 10

1. Bartholomew's Cobble and Colonel Ashley House

Cooper Hill Rd., Ashley Falls. This nature preserve is known for the various plants that grow about its rocky landscape. The 1735 Colonel Ashley House was the home of an early abolitionist. *Admission charged.*

2. Litchfield

The historic district here contains the **Tapping Reeve House and Law School.** Founded in 1774, it was the first in the United States to offer such a curriculum, training Aaron Burr and John C. Calhoun. Local history is detailed at the **Litchfield Historical Society Museum.** *Admission charged.*

3. Lock Museum of America

130 Main St., Terryville. Opened in 1972, this museum contains large collections of ornate hardware, keys, and locks — some dating to the 1500's. *Admission charged.*

4. Farmington

Built in 1720 in medieval style, the **Stanley-Whitman House** is furnished with authentic period pieces. The **Hill-Stead Museum,** a turn-of-the-century mansion, contains an outstanding collection of French Impressionist works. *Admission charged.*

5. American Clock and Watch Museum

100 Maple St., Bristol. This museum in the 1801 **Miles Lewis House** has a diverse collection of timepieces, memorabilia of clock makers, and a library. *Admission charged.*

6. New Britain Museum of American Art

56 Lexington St., New Britain. This museum displays an excellent collection of American artworks, from 1740 to the present.

7. Wethersfield

Three 17th-century homes once belonging to early patriots form the **Webb-Deane-Stevens Museum.** The town's history further unfolds at the **Ancient Burying Grounds.** Built about 1710 in medieval style, the **Buttolph-Williams House** contains colonial furnishings. At neighboring Rocky Hill, the **Dinosaur State Park** features tracks left by the ancient reptiles. *Admission charged.*

8. West Hartford

Chamber of Commerce, 948 Farmington Ave. In front of the town hall is a statue of Noah Webster, renowned lexicographer and author. The restored **Noah Webster House** displays memorabilia. The nearby **Science Museum of Connecticut** contains a planetarium and exhibits on science, nature, and technology. *Admission charged.*

9. Hartford

Convention and Visitors Bureau, 1 Civic Center Plaza. Highlights of this city include **Nook Farm,** with homes once occupied by Mark Twain and Harriet Beecher Stowe; **Wadsworth Atheneum,** America's oldest continuously operated public art museum; **Butler-McCook Homestead,** dating from 1782; **Raymond E. Baldwin Museum of Connecticut History,** focusing on the area's industrial development; and the Victorian-Gothic state capitol. *Admission charged for some attractions.*

10. Massacoh Plantation

800 Hopmeadow St., Simsbury. This site consists of several 17th-, 18th-, and 19th-century buildings, including a schoolhouse, a meetinghouse, and a tavern. Guided tours are available. *Admission charged.*

11. Old New-Gate Prison and Copper Mine

Newgate Rd., East Granby. The mine was opened in 1707 but failed as a commercial venture. In 1773, it was turned into a prison and held captured Tories during the American Revolution. *Admission charged.*

12. New England Air Museum

Bradley International Airport, Windsor Locks. This museum contains more than 80 aircraft, dating from 1909 to the present, along with a large assortment of aeronautical artifacts. *Admission charged.*

13. Windsor

Chamber of Commerce, 43 Poquonock Ave. The 1640 **Fyler House** displays period furnishings. The adjacent **Windsor Historical Society** features a research library and changing exhibits. The 1630 **First Church in Windsor** offers tours by appointment. *Admission charged for some attractions.*

14. Springfield

Convention and Visitors Bureau, 34 Boland Way. The **Springfield Library & Museums** has exhibits on local history, science, and art. The **Indian Motorcycle Museum** has motorcycles and early motorized vehicles. A collection of firearms is on view at the **Springfield Armory National Historic Site.** The **Storrowton Village Museum** has historical buildings. *Admission charged.*

15. Old Sturbridge Village

Off Rte. 20, Sturbridge. Some 40 authentic buildings brought to this site serve to re-create a typical 19th-century New England village. *Admission charged.*

16. Roseland Cottage

556 Rte. 169, Woodstock. This charming 1846 Gothic Revival mansion was the summer home of a New York publisher. The landscape has the original boxwood parterre. *Admission charged.*

17. Norwich

Chamber of Commerce, 35 Main St. Early patriots met at the **Leffingwell Inn.** The **Memorial Rose Garden** has nearly 2,000 rosebushes. An extensive collection of art is displayed at the **Slater Memorial Museum and Converse Gallery.** Artworks by several tribes are shown at the nearby **Tantaquidgeon Indian Museum.**

18. U.S.S. Nautilus Memorial/Submarine Force Library and Museum

Crystal Lake Rd., Groton. Visitors can explore the world's first nuclear-powered submarine. The adjacent library and museum detail the history of submersibles.

19. Mystic

Tourist Information Center, Bldg. 1D, Olde Mistick Village. The **Mystic Seaport Museum** contains some 40 buildings from the 19th century. The **Charles W. Morgan,** the last of the wooden whaling ships, is docked in the harbor. Nearby is the **Mystic Marinelife Aquarium,** home to more than 6,000 sea animals. *Admission charged.*

20. New London

Tourist Information Center, 27 Masonic St. This town's attractions include the **Lyman Allyn Museum,** known for its paintings by state artists; the 1678 **Joshua Hempstead House,** the city's oldest; the 1756 **Shaw Mansion,** where Washington stayed; the 1759 **Nathaniel Hempstead House;** the **United States Coast Guard Academy;** and **Monte Cristo Cottage,** the boyhood home of playwright Eugene O'Neill. *Admission charged for some attractions.*

21. Florence Griswold Museum

96 Lyme St., Old Lyme. In the early 1900's Florence Griswold established a celebrated art colony here. Today the museum exhibits paintings, sculptures, and antique furnishings. *Admission charged.*

22. Connecticut River Museum

Main St., Essex. Displays at this waterfront museum include ship models, navigational instruments, and a replica of the 1775 *Turtle* — considered to be America's first submarine. *Admission charged.*

23. Guilford

Chamber of Commerce, 741 Boston Post Rd. The 1774 **Thomas Griswold House** has local artifacts. New England's oldest stone house holds the **Henry Whitfield State Historical Museum.** *Admission charged.*

24. New Haven

Convention and Visitors Bureau, 195 Church St. Settled by Puritans in 1638, the town still maintains its original village green, a 16-acre square bordered by three churches, commercial buildings, and **Yale University.** Several prominent Americans, including Noah Webster and Eli Whitney, are buried in the **Grove Street Cemetery.** The **New Haven Colony Historical Society,** traces the city's history with exhibits of paintings, furniture, and memorabilia of local inventors. *Admission charged.*

25. Bridgeport

Convention and Visitors Commission, 303 State St. The **Barnum Museum** has displays that chronicle the growth of Bridgeport and the life of P.T. Barnum. Fine artworks, a planetarium, and hands-on science and art exhibits are contained in the **Discovery Museum.** The **Beardsley Zoological Gardens** cares for some 200 animals and offers pony rides, a children's zoo, and picnic areas. *Admission charged.*

26. Norwalk

Tourist Information Center, 297 West Ave. The 1868 **Lockwood-Mathews Mansion Museum** is a magnificent 60-room château. The **Maritime Center,** with an aquarium and a collection of nautical artifacts, examines the history of Long Island Sound. Cruises from Norwalk Harbor to Sheffield Island are available. *Admission charged.*

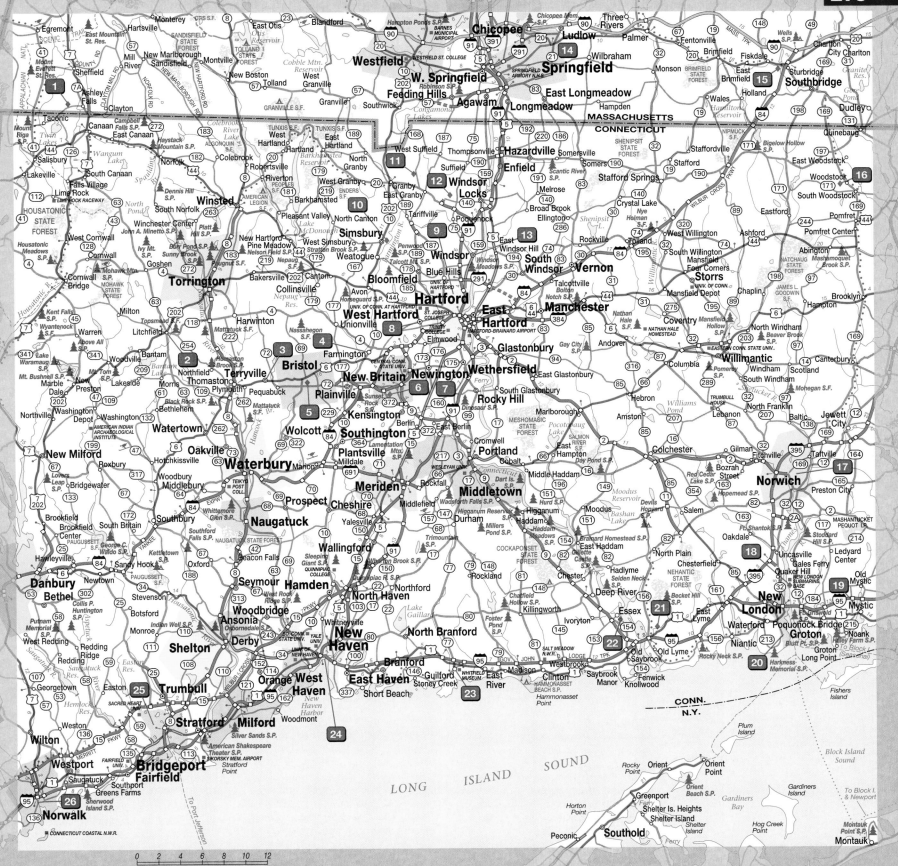

1. Block Island

Chamber of Commerce, Water St., Old Harbor. Once a hideout for smugglers and pirates, Block Island today is an inviting summer resort. Its 11 square miles encompass wide sandy beaches, towering bluffs with spectacular ocean views, five wildlife refuges, and hundreds of freshwater ponds that provide a habitat for migrating birds as well as good fishing opportunities. The island's only village, **Old Harbor** boasts charming inns, shops, restaurants, and art galleries. The **Block Island Historical Society** has exhibits on the island's seafaring and farming history. Travelers may contact the Chamber of Commerce for information on ferry service.

2. Concord

Chamber of Commerce, 244 North Main St. The capital of New Hampshire boasts the handsomely domed **State House,** claiming to be the oldest in continuous use in the country. The **New Hampshire Historical Society Museum** explores the state's culture with flags from the Revolution, early furniture, an old stagecoach, and examples of fine and decorative arts. **Pierce Manse,** the restored home of President Franklin Pierce, displays memorabilia and 19th-century family furnishings. The **Christa McAuliffe Planetarium** is a memorial to the country's first teacher in space, who died in the tragic explosion of the space shuttle *Challenger. Admission charged for some attractions.*

3. Canterbury Shaker Village

288 Shaker Rd., Canterbury. The fine workmanship and simplicity of design for which this religious group is known are evident throughout this community, which was one of the last with Shaker residents. Among the 23 historic buildings, six have examples of Shaker crafts, furniture, and inventions. *Admission charged.*

4. Daniel Webster Birthplace

Rte. 127, Franklin. This simple house constructed of brown shingles is a replica of the birthplace of Daniel Webster, one of the country's most distinguished statesmen and orators. The starkness of the interior — wide plank floors, a fireplace, and plain furnishings — reflects his beginnings as the son of a poor farmer. *Admission charged.*

5. Science Center of New Hampshire

Rte. 113, Holderness. Nature trails through this 200-acre wildlife sanctuary traverse meadows, forestland, and bridges, while bobcats, black bears, and other animals prowl in natural enclosures. Hands-on exhibits and a children's activity center are also offered. *Admission charged.*

6. Castle in the Clouds

Rte. 171, Moultonborough. This lavish 5,200-acre estate set high in the Ossipee Mountains is the realization of a multimillionaire's dream to surround himself with beauty. Guided tours of the mansion, which was completed in 1910 at a cost of more than $7 million, reveal hand-painted windows that depict some of the estate's breathtaking scenery. For a firsthand look, visitors can travel the hiking and horseback-riding trails that wind past waterfalls, ponds, and streams. *Admission charged.*

7. Kancamagus Highway

Passing Loon Mountain along the way, this 34-mile highway, one of New Hampshire's most popular roads for viewing the fall foliage, follows the Swift River. At **Sabbaday Falls,** a short walk from the highway, cascading water flows through two potholes.

8. Franconia

Chamber of Commerce, Rte. 118. The **Robert Frost Place,** a white clapboard farmhouse where the great poet lived for much of his adult life, has guided tours that include signed first editions of his books, a narrated slide show, and a nature trail dotted with plaques engraved with Frost's verses. **Franconia Notch State Park** offers recreational activities and mountain scenery, including the **Flume,** an 800-foot-long gorge and waterfall reached by stairs and boardwalks. The **Old Man of the Mountain,** a 40-foot-high head-shaped formation, looms 1,200 feet above Profile Lake. *Admission charged for some attractions.*

9. Mount Washington

Built in 1869, the **Cog Railway** still offers unique 3-mile rides in passenger cars

The Cog Railway on Mt. Washington

pushed by steam engines to the summit of Mt. Washington, home to an observatory and a weather station. Another way to climb the mountain is the **Auto Road,** with 8 miles of steep climbs and sharp turns. From turnouts along the way, there are spectacular views of the **Great Gulf Wilderness,** a heavily forested valley below. At nearby **Glen Ellis Falls,** water spirals some 70 feet down a rocky cleft. *Admission charged for some attractions.*

10. Dr. Moses Mason House

15 Broad St., Bethel. Once home to a prominent congressman, this restored 1813 home displays eight rooms furnished in period style. *Admission charged.*

11. Augusta

Chamber of Commerce, 1 University Dr. The capital of Maine, Augusta is dominated by the **Maine State House,** an imposing granite structure designed by Charles Bulfinch in 1832. The adjacent **Maine State Museum** examines the prehistoric cultures of the state's earliest inhabitants, as well as more recent commercial activities such as granite quarrying and shipbuilding. In the same area, the Colonial Revival **Blaine House** — dating to 1833 and the governor's residence since 1919 — offers midweek afternoon tours through some of its 26 rooms, including the Reception Room, the octagonal billiard room, and James Blaine's study. The **Fort Western Museum,** housed in a 17-room log building that is part of a 1754 fort, features 18th-century rooms with period furnishings. *Admission charged for some attractions.*

12. Redington Museum

64 Silver St., Waterville. In an elegant 1814 frame house, this museum focuses on Waterville's early history, with an exhibit on logging, Civil War memorabilia, and period rooms displaying Chippendale pieces and a Victorian dollhouse. On the grounds, a replica of a 19th-century apothecary shop has a stock of early patent remedies, a mirrored soda fountain, Tiffany glass, and mahogany cabinets. *Admission charged.*

13. Nordica Homestead Museum

Holley Rd., Farmington. This 1840 home was the birthplace of soprano Lillian Nordica. It contains costumes, jewelry, and other memorabilia from her opera career, which included leading roles at the Metropolitan Opera in the 1890's. *Admission charged.*

14. Wilhelm Reich Museum

Dodge Pond Rd., Rangeley. The life and work of natural scientist Wilhelm Reich are examined in his fieldstone observatory, built in the Bauhaus style. Guided tours offer a biographical slide show and visit Reich's study and library, where he developed his controversial theory on universal biological energy. A natural-history trail traverses the grounds. *Admission charged.*

15. The Stanley Museum

School St., Kingfield. Located in the heart of ski country, this museum has a collection of the famous Stanley Steamer cars, as well as paintings, photos, and handmade violins. *Donations encouraged.*

16. Blacksmith Shop Museum

98 Dawes Rd., Dover-Foxcroft. This restored mid-19th-century blacksmith shop underscores the vital role played by the village smithy. Among the displays are antique tools, early farm implements, household items, a cheese press, and an "ox lifter."

17. Burnham Tavern Museum

Main St., Machias. This tavern was the meeting place for the town's rebellious citizens who, armed only with small weapons and farm implements, managed to capture a British warship on June 12, 1775, in what was the first naval battle of the American Revolution. Today the historic site contains memorabilia from the period. *Admission charged.*

18. Roosevelt Campobello International Park

Campobello Island, New Brunswick. Campobello is the rugged island where Franklin D. Roosevelt spent his childhood summers and later returned with his own family. The 2,600-acre park, jointly administered by the United States and Canada, encompasses hiking trails through fragrant stands of pine, a freshwater lake, stunning ocean views, and Roosevelt's rambling 34-room home, part of which is open to the public.

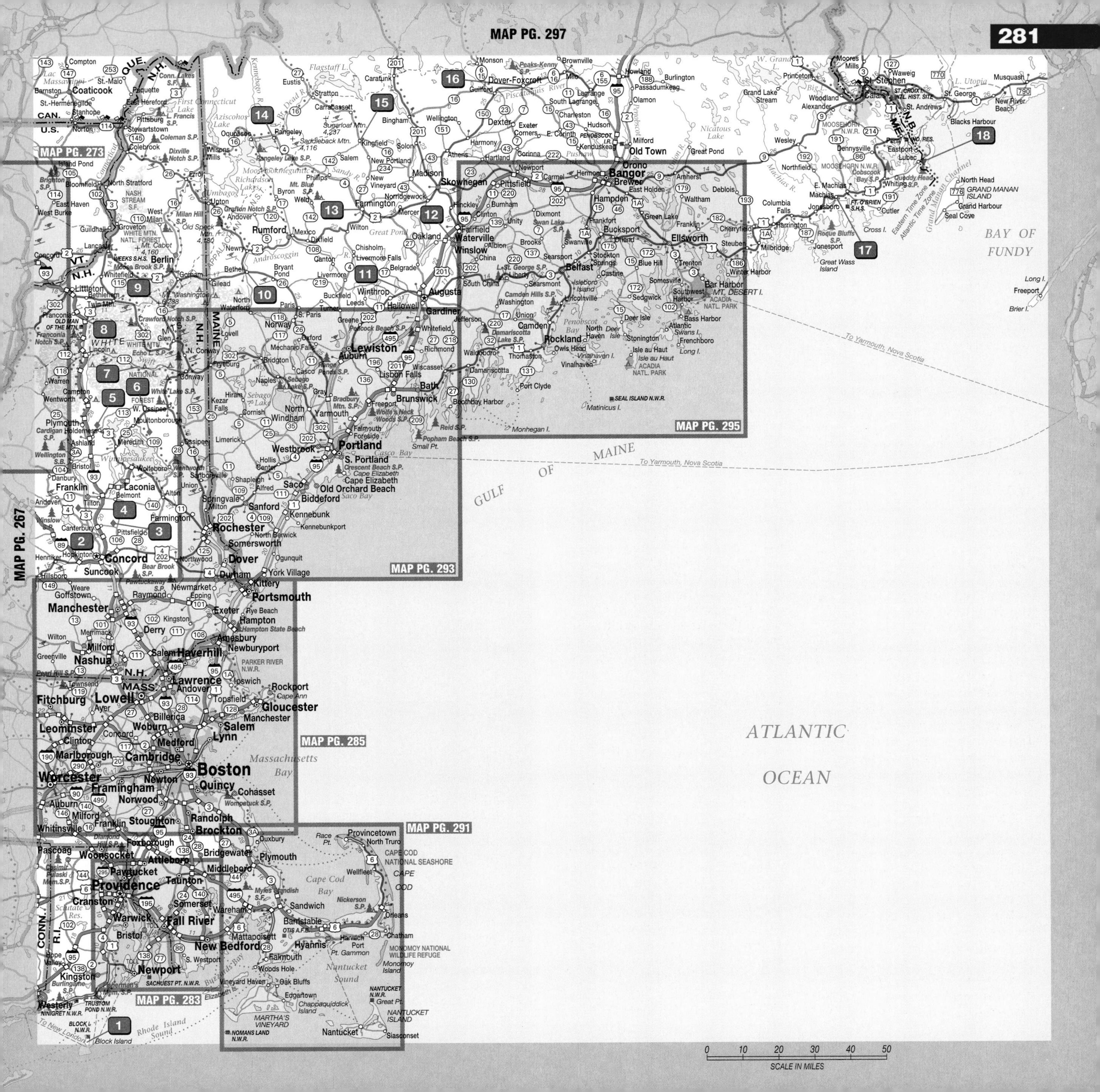

MAP PG. 273

MAP PG. 267

MAP PG. 293

MAP PG. 295

MAP PG. 285

MAP PG. 291

MAP PG. 283

BAY OF FUNDY

ATLANTIC OCEAN

GULF OF MAINE

To Yarmouth, Nova Scotia

Boston
Worcester
Providence
Manchester
Nashua
Lowell
Lawrence
Portland
Augusta
Bangor
Brewer
Old Town
Orono
Ellsworth
Bar Harbor
Rockland
Camden
Belfast
Waterville
Winslow
Fairfield
Skowhegan
Farmington
Rumford
Lewiston
Auburn
Bath
Brunswick
Portsmouth
Dover
Rochester
Concord
Laconia
Franklin
Berlin
Littleton
Plymouth
Fitchburg
Leominster
Cambridge
Framingham
Quincy
Brockton
Taunton
Fall River
New Bedford
Newport
Pawtucket
Cranston
Warwick
Woonsocket
Attleboro
Gloucester
Salem
Lynn
Haverhill
Newburyport
Exeter
Hampton
Derry
Plymouth
Provincetown
Hyannis
Barnstable
Chatham
Nantucket
Martha's Vineyard
Block Island

ACADIA NATL. PARK
MT. DESERT I.
CAPE COD NATIONAL SEASHORE
MONOMOY NATIONAL WILDLIFE REFUGE
Cape Cod Bay
Massachusetts Bay
Nantucket Sound
Rhode Island Sound

QUE.
N.H.
VT.
MAINE
MASS.
CONN.
R.I.
N.B.
ME.
CAN.
U.S.

SCALE IN MILES
0 10 20 30 40 50

1. Slater Mill Historic Site

67 Roosevelt Ave., Pawtucket. Built in 1793, Slater Mill was the country's first water-powered textile mill, introducing automated production to what had been a handicraft industry. Visitors can see hand-spinning and weaving demonstrations, an 8-ton waterwheel, mill worker's cottage, dam, and canal. *Admission charged.*

2. Rhode Island State House

82 Smith St., Providence. Completed in 1904 and topped by a gilded statue, this imposing building boasts the world's second-largest unsupported marble dome. On view inside are a full-length portrait of Washington by Gilbert Stuart and the original parchment charter granted by King Charles II in 1663.

3. First Baptist Church in America

75 North Main St., Providence. This architectural masterpiece is the home of a Baptist congregation established by Roger Williams in 1638. Designed by Joseph Brown and built in 1775, the lovingly preserved church features a 1792 Waterford crystal chandelier, Classical-style columns, and a soaring 185-foot steeple.

4. Providence Athenaeum

251 Benefit St., Providence. This Greek Revival structure is home to one of the country's oldest lending libraries, which was established in 1753. It was here that Edgar Allan Poe courted Sarah Helen Whitman, the inspiration for his poem *To Helen.* The library's rare books include original Audubon elephant folios. Benefit Street's **Mile of History** is a row of small, brightly colored homes, one of which was a residence of Walt Whitman.

5. John Brown House

52 Power St., Providence. Designed in 1786 by John Brown's brother, Joseph, this magnificent Georgian-style mansion was once visited by John Quincy Adams. Today the house is filled with antiques, fine paintings, 18th-century Chinese porcelains, silver, pewter, and glass. Another brother, Nicholas, was instrumental in locating a college in Providence, later renamed **Brown University.** *Admission charged at house.*

6. Museum of Art, Rhode Island School of Design

224 Benefit St., Providence. This intimate museum has changing exhibitions of textiles as well as permanent collections of fine Japanese prints, Paul Revere silver, 18th-century porcelain, Egyptian objects, and European paintings dating to the Middle Ages. **Pendleton House** is a replica of an early 19th-century house, complete with furnishings from that era. *Admission charged.*

7. East Greenwich

Chamber of Commerce, 127 Main St. In this yachting center on the Narragansett Bay, the **New England Wireless and Steam Museum** exhibits antique telegraph and radio equipment, a 1907 radio station, and steam engines. The **General James Mitchell Varnum House and Museum** is furnished as it would have been more than 200 years ago, when visitors included George Washington and Nathanael Greene. *Admission charged.*

8. Saunderstown

The 1750 **Gilbert Stuart Birthplace** was not only the early home of the celebrated portrait painter but also once a snuff mill. Today the house exhibits colonial furnishings and prints of Stuart's paintings, the most famous being of George Washington. The **Silas Casey Farm,** in operation since the 18th century, was the site of Revolutionary War activity. The farmhouse displays period furniture, paintings, and political and military documents from the 18th to the 20th centuries. *Admission charged.*

9. Hunter House

54 Washington St., Newport. This renowned example of Colonial architecture reflects the prosperous lifestyle of the city's 18th-century merchants. Newport's master craftsmen, Townsend and Goddard, made many of the furnishings, which are complemented by carved paneling, fine paintings, silver, and porcelain. *Admission charged.*

10. Hammersmith Farm

Ocean Dr., Newport. The childhood summer home of Jacqueline Bouvier Kennedy Onassis was the site of the reception following her wedding to John F. Kennedy, and later was used as a summer White House during the Kennedy administration. Built in 1887, the 28-room house today displays memorabilia. Visitors can stroll through the elaborate gardens designed by Frederick Law Olmsted. *Admission charged.*

11. The Breakers

Ochre Point Ave., Newport. Grand summer mansions, built by the very rich during the Gilded Age, are located mainly along Bellevue Avenue and Ocean Drive. The most magnificent is The Breakers, a 70-room Italian Renaissance home built for Cornelius Vanderbilt II in 1895. Its many wonders include a music room with a gold and silver coffered ceiling created in France, an ornate dining room with rose alabaster pillars, and a loggia with a mosaic ceiling. Combination tickets to see the homes are sold here and at the other mansions. *Admission charged.*

12. Trinity Church

Queen Anne Sq., Newport. This church has been in continuous use since 1726, when it ministered to the first Anglican parish in Rhode Island. Its architecture was inspired by the designs of Christopher Wren in London. The church features Tiffany windows, an extravagant pulpit, and an original brass chandelier.

Gardeners trim a giraffe at Green Animals.

13. Touro Synagogue

85 Touro St., Newport. This synagogue is the oldest in the country. It was built in 1763 by a congregation of Sephardic Jews who were exiled from Spain and Portugal. Considered an architectural masterpiece, the building has a simple Georgian-style exterior and an intricately detailed interior, with a dozen Ionic columns representing the 12 tribes of Israel.

14. Wanton-Lyman-Hazard House

17 Broadway, Newport. One of the oldest houses in Newport, this handsome structure was the site of the Stamp Act Riot of 1765. An outstanding example of early Colonial architecture, it was built in the 1690's and displays period furnishings and an 18th-century kitchen. *Admission charged.*

15. Green Animals

Cory's Ln., Portsmouth. Some of the country's finest examples of topiary — shrubs and trees pruned to resemble animal shapes or geometric designs — can be found in the gardens of this 7-acre summer home. There are flower beds and fruit trees, and the main house features Victorian toys. *Admission charged.*

16. Bristol

Some 33 acres of landscaped grounds at **Blithewold Mansion and Gardens** surround a 1908 mansion, where guided tours are offered. The **Haffenreffer Museum of Anthropology,** a 375-acre site, focuses on the Indian cultures of the world, especially those of North America. **Colt State Park** offers picnic sites, bicycle paths, and walks along Narragansett Bay. *Admission charged.*

17. Battleship Massachusetts

Off Rte. 195, Fall River. Twentieth-century naval sailing vessels, most of which can be toured, are anchored in this harbor. There are two PT boats from World War II, a destroyer that saw action in Korea, a World War II attack submarine, and a battleship that survived 35 encounters. Fall River is also the site of the Lizzie Borden house — now occupied by a business — where the infamous Borden reputedly murdered her father and stepmother with an ax. *Admission charged.*

18. New Bedford

Visitor Center, 72 North Second St. This city's 200-year history as a commercial whaling port is chronicled at the **New Bedford Whaling Museum,** one of the largest museums in the country devoted to the whaling era. Its collection includes scrimshaw, prints, logbooks, the skeleton of a humpback whale, and an imposing half-scale model of a fully rigged whaling ship. The 1832 **Seamen's Bethel** has a prow-shaped pulpit designed after Melville's description of a chapel in *Moby Dick.* The 1834 **Rotch-Jones-Duff House and Garden Museum** is a 28-room mansion containing fine furnishings. *Admission charged.*

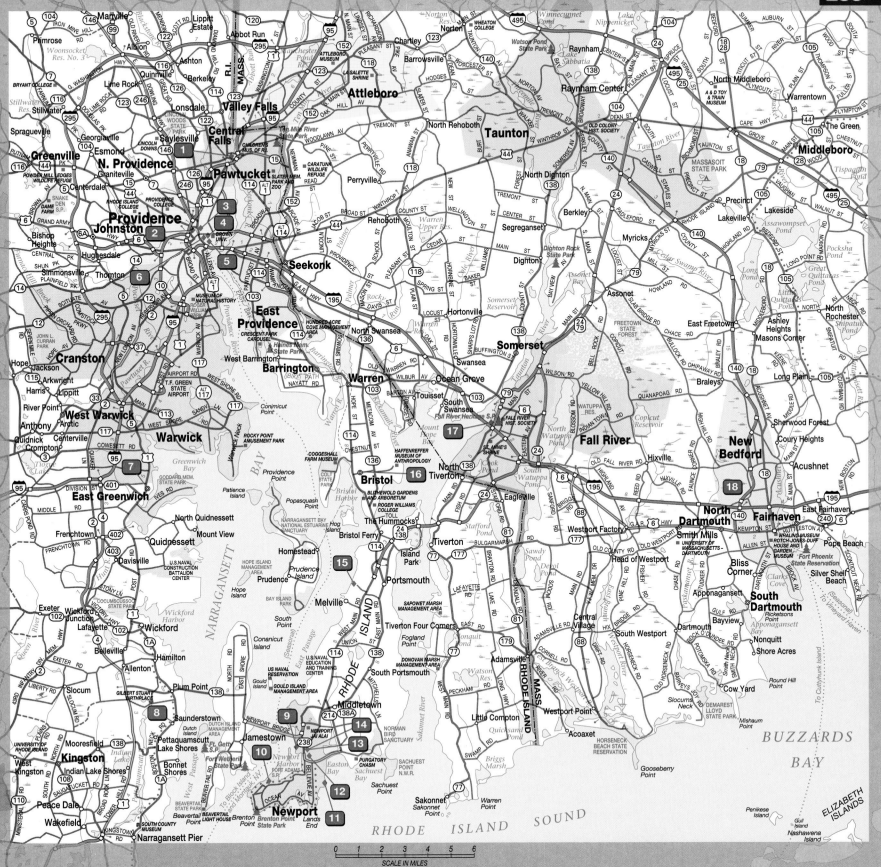

SCALE IN MILES

1. Portsmouth

Chamber of Commerce, 500 Market St. This city's historic homes clearly evoke Colonial times. Maps of the **Portsmouth Trail,** a walking tour, are offered at the chamber of commerce. The route passes six preserved structures dating from 1716 to 1807, such as the **John Paul Jones House,** where the famous naval commander stayed. **Strawbery Banke Museum** is a restoration of an early waterfront community, featuring some 42 buildings that date as far back as 1600. *Admission charged for some attractions.*

2. Fort Constitution

Off Rte. 1B, New Castle. Built on the site of an old British stronghold, this fort has exhibits that trace its history from 1632.

3. Amesbury

Chamber of Commerce, 41 Main St. The cozy **John Greenleaf Whittier Home** brims with mementos of the poet and abolitionist, who lived here for most of his life. The **Mary Baker Eddy Historic House,** where the founder of Christian Science briefly resided in 1868 and 1870, contains original furnishings. *Admission charged.*

4. Newburyport

Chamber of Commerce, 29 State St. An assortment of artifacts from the area's maritime history are on display at the **Custom House Maritime Museum.** The sprawling **Cushing House Museum** has exhibits of period furnishings, clocks, silver, china, and glassware. *Admission charged.*

5. Ipswich

Chamber of Commerce, 46 Newmarch St. Here the 1655 **John Whipple House** is a fine example of an early Puritan residence. Across the street, the **John Heard House,** built by a sea captain in 1795, has items from voyages to China. *Admission charged.*

6. Gloucester

Chamber of Commerce, 33 Commercial St. This old seaport is home to the 1786 **Sargent House Museum,** displaying period

furnishings and paintings by John Singer Sargent. **Beauport** is a mansion with a wealth of early decorative arts and furnishings. The **Hammond Castle Museum** includes such rarities as a Roman bath and an 8,200-pipe organ. The **Cape Ann Historical Museum** has commentaries on the area's fishing industry. *Admission charged.*

7. Marblehead

Chamber of Commerce, 62 Pleasant St. At this port, generals Lafayette and Washington were entertained in the 1768 **Jeremiah Lee Mansion. Abbot Hall** displays the original *Spirit of '76* painting. **Saint Michael's Church** has a bell recast by Paul Revere. *Admission charged at mansion.*

8. Salem

Chamber of Commerce, Old Town Hall, 32 Derby Sq. Suspected witches were once questioned in the **Witch House,** home of a judge. Visitors can tour the **Salem Maritime National Historic Site,** which preserves 9 acres of waterfront, or explore the area's mansions with the **Peabody & Essex Museum,** which depicts the history of the county and has a vast collection of marine art. Also in town is the **House of the Seven Gables,** which was immortalized in Nathaniel Hawthorne's novel. *Admission charged for some attractions.*

9. Rebecca Nurse Homestead

149 Pine St., Danvers. This was the home of Rebecca Nurse, executed for witchcraft after a bogus trial during the panic of 1692. Several restored rooms have 17th- and 18th-century furnishings. *Admission charged.*

10. Saugus Iron Works National Historic Site

244 Central St., Saugus. At this reconstructed 1600's ironworks — the first successful one in the country — waterwheels turn and the forge fire glows once more.

11. Copley Square

A Boston landmark, this busy square is home to **Trinity Church,** a handsome Romanesque building; the **Boston Public Library,** a Renaissance Revival structure displaying a large mural by John Singer Sargent; and the **John Hancock Tower,** where, on the 60th-floor observatory, multimedia exhibits and an expansive view of Boston are offered. The nearby **Prudential Center,** a complex of offices, shops, and restaurants, covers 32 acres of Back Bay. The Skywalk, on the 50th floor, is an obser-

vation deck. The **Institute of Contemporary Art** has paintings, sculpture, video art, and photos. The theater regularly schedules productions of performance art. *Admission charged for some attractions.*

12. Adams National Historic Site

135 Adams St., Quincy. This was the home of the Adams family for four generations, beginning with John Adams, the second U.S. president. Furnishings, documents, and porcelains are on display. Nearby are the houses where John Adams and his son, John Quincy, the sixth president, were born. *Admission charged.*

13. Museum of Fine Arts

465 Huntington Ave., Boston. This site's collection includes antique musical instruments and textiles, European art from the 11th to 20th centuries, and a large selection of Asian pieces. Nearby, the **Isabella Stewart Gardner Museum** contains a collection of priceless artworks, which date from antiquity to the beginning of the 20th century. *Admission charged.*

14. Brookline

Chamber of Commerce, 1330 Beacon St. The **John F. Kennedy National Historic Site** in this affluent Boston suburb was the birthplace and childhood home of the 35th president; the house is restored to its 1914 appearance. The **Frederick Law Olmsted National Historic Site** was the home of the father of American landscape architecture. Drawings, photos, and models from his many projects are on display. *Admission charged at Kennedy home.*

15. Babson College Map and Globe Museum

Forest St., Wellesley. The highlight here is the Great Relief Map, representing a detailed and accurate topographical view of the United States as seen from 700 miles above the earth. Outside the building is a 25-ton rotating globe mounted on a hollow shaft that represents the earth's axis.

16. Worcester

Convention and Visitors Bureau, 33 Waldo St. The **Worcester Art Museum** has displays covering a 5,000-year period, with works from America, Europe, and the Far East. The **Higgins Armory Museum** has a collection of medieval and Renaissance armor. Visitors to the **New England Science Center** can see exhibits on natural science, an observatory, and a planetarium.

The **American Antiquarian Society** maintains a research library specializing in American culture and history up to 1876. *Admission charged for some attractions.*

17. Concord

Chamber of Commerce, 2 Lexington Rd. Daniel Chester French's famous statue *Minute Man* is in **Minute Man National Historical Park,** which honors the battle that set the Revolution in motion. The **Concord Museum** boasts Ralph Waldo Emerson's study, furniture from Henry David Thoreau's Walden Pond retreat, and Revolutionary War relics. More history is found at both the **Old Manse,** where Nathaniel Hawthorne penned *Mosses From an Old Manse,* and the **Orchard House,** home of Louisa May Alcott. At the **Sleepy Hollow Cemetery,** the graves of such literary giants as Hawthorne, Thoreau, Alcott, and Emerson lie on Authors' Ridge. *Admission charged for some attractions.*

18. Lexington

Visitor Center, 1875 Massachusetts Ave. A monument on the **Battle Green** pays tribute to eight minutemen who died in the Battle of Lexington. The **Lexington Historical Society** offers tours of Revolutionary homes, and the **Museum of Our National Heritage** has exhibits on American history. *Admission charged for some attractions.*

19. Lowell

Convention and Visitors Bureau, 45 Palmer St. The **Boott Cotton Mills Museum** depicts the town's life in the 19th century. The **Whistler House Museum of Art,** birthplace of painter James Abbott McNeill Whistler, contains 19th- and 20th-century American works, while the **New England Quilt Museum** displays a delightful array of quilts and exhibits. *Admission charged.*

20. America's Stonehenge

Off Haverhill Rd., North Salem. These curiously arranged stones date as far back as 4,000 years. Scholars and visitors alike can only speculate as to who created the configuration and why. *Admission charged.*

21. Robert Frost Farm

Off Rte. 28, Derry. This restored farm was home to Robert Frost from 1900 to 1911. The clapboard house contains original family pieces, and the barn has displays on Frost's writings. Self-guiding nature trails lead through the countryside that so inspired the poet. *Admission charged.*

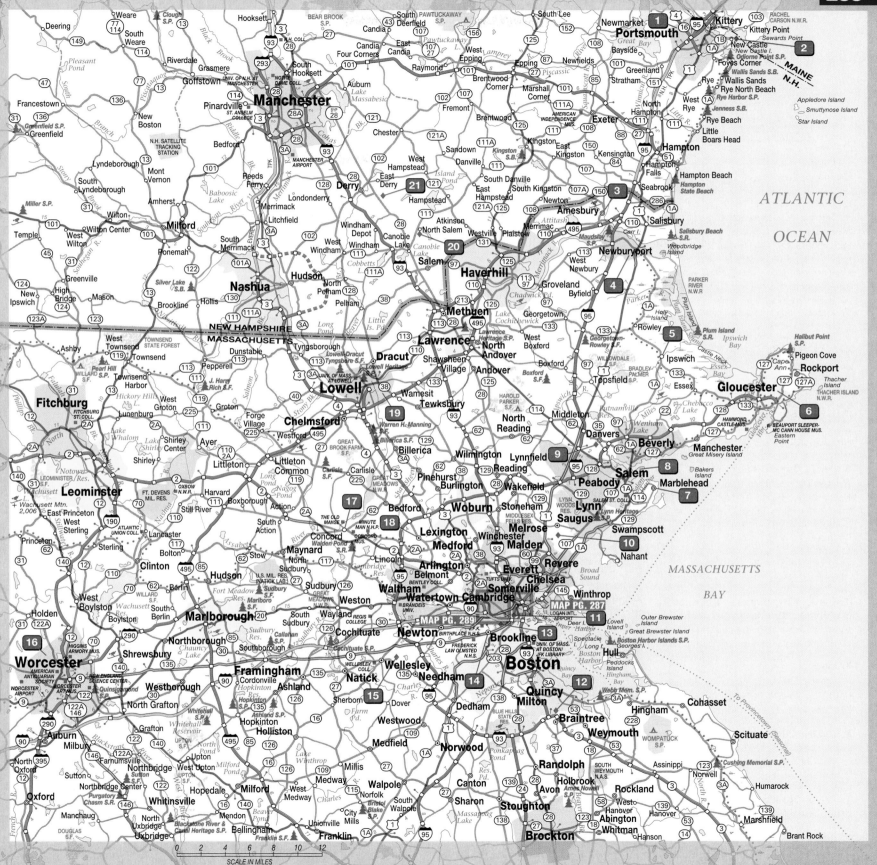

DOWNTOWN BOSTON

1. Bunker Hill Monument

Monument Sq., Charlestown. This 221-foot-high granite obelisk commemorates the famed battle. A 294-step-long spiral staircase leads to the top, which offers spectacular views of the Boston area. Dioramas in the adjacent visitor center describe the battle, and rangers give talks regularly.

2. Bunker Hill Pavilion

55 Constitution Rd., Charlestown. Within this modern pavilion adjacent to the U.S.S. *Constitution,* a multimedia show runs continuously during the day. A reenactment of the Battle of Bunker Hill, the presentation utilizes life-size figures and dramatic special effects to place the visitor in the midst of the battle. *Admission charged.*

3. U.S.S. Constitution

Charlestown Navy Yard, off Constitution Rd. Launched in 1797, this frigate is the oldest commissioned warship still afloat in the world. She gained her famous nickname, Old Ironsides, during a battle against a British ship in the War of 1812. The museum next door offers participatory exhibits and demonstrations of various crafts. *Admission charged at museum.*

4. Copp's Hill Burying Ground

Hull and Snowhill Sts. The Reverend Cotton Mather, an influential clergyman in colonial America, is among those buried in this cemetery, which dates to 1659. From the hill here, the British once aimed their cannons across the Charles River toward Charlestown and Bunker Hill.

5. Old North Church

193 Salem St. Officially named Christ Church but known to many as Old North, Boston's oldest church dates to 1723. On April 18, 1775, the sexton hung two lanterns from its steeple to signal that the British were launching their raid by sea. Services are held each Sunday, and box pews have plaques engraved with the names of the original owners.

6. Paul Revere House

19 North Sq. Built in 1680, making it one of the city's oldest, this house was Paul Revere's between 1770 and 1800. It was from here that the silversmith departed on his historic ride on April 18, 1775. Inside are various examples of Revere's work as well as exhibits of early Americana. *Admission charged.*

7. Quincy Market

Off Congress St. Composed of three structures, this complex has been a retail and wholesale meat and produce distribution center for more than 150 years. Gentrified in 1976, the buildings are now occupied by shops, bars, and restaurants. There's also a pedestrian mall with kiosks, food vendors, and street entertainers.

8. Faneuil Hall

Merchants Row. Just before the Revolution, heated debates took place in the upper hall of this site, also known as the Cradle of Liberty. Park rangers give talks every 30 minutes; there are also paintings on exhibit and a military museum. The downstairs area is a marketplace.

9. New England Aquarium

Central Wharf, off Atlantic Ave. Hundreds of species of sea animals are on view here, one of Boston's most popular attractions. Included in the exotic exhibits are a 3,200-gallon re-creation of an Amazon rain forest and a 187,000-gallon tank featuring sharks and huge sea turtles. There are also frolicsome sea lions on an adjacent barge. *Admission charged.*

10. The Computer Museum

300 Congress St. Quite interesting to the hands-on, high-tech crowd, this museum is filled with things futuristic, including a two-story computer, a virtual-reality exhibit, and a robot theater. *Admission charged.*

11. Boston Tea Party Ship and Museum

Congress St. Bridge. Aboard a replica of the Tea Party Ship, costumed tour guides reenact the famed rebellion of 1773. Visitors are even encouraged to participate by tossing tea. There are audiovisual presentations, and complimentary tea is served. *Admission charged.*

12. Old South Meeting House

310 Washington St. Perhaps the most venerated structure in the city, Old South was the scene of important town meetings during pre-Revolutionary times. In 1773, following a gathering here of some 5,000 patriots, the Boston Tea Party took place. The exhibits include walls and pews with audio recordings that simulate the arguments of Revolutionary orators. *Admission charged.*

13. Old State House

State and Washington Sts. The city's oldest public building, this served as the seat of government for the Royal Governors prior to the Revolution. Outside its walls, the Boston Massacre took place; from its balcony, the Declaration of Independence was first read to locals. Exhibits describe the area's history. *Admission charged.*

14. King's Chapel

Tremont and School Sts. In 1749 construction began on this granite structure, the nation's first Unitarian church. It was built on the site of an even older 17th-century Anglican church whose wooden altar — a gift from William and Mary in 1696 — was retained. The **King's Chapel Burying Ground** is the city's oldest cemetery. *Donation encouraged at church.*

15. Granary Burying Ground

Tremont St. Begun in 1660 on the site of an ancient granary, this cemetery is the final resting place of many illustrious Americans. Among its 1,600 graves are those of Paul Revere, John Hancock, Samuel Adams, and the martyrs of the Boston Massacre.

16. Park Street Church

Park and Tremont Sts. Built in 1809 from a design by the British architect Peter Banner, this church, with its 217-foot-high steeple and spire, resembles the London churches of Christopher Wren. During the War of 1812, gunpowder was stored in the basement, earning it the sobriquet Brimstone Corner. It was here in 1831 that the song *America* was sung for the first time.

17. State House

Park and Beacon Sts. One of America's finest early architects, Charles Bulfinch, designed this golden-domed Neoclassical building, located at the summit of the posh Beacon Hill residential area. It contains the House and Senate Chambers, the State Library, a Hall of Flags, and artworks.

18. African Meeting House

46 Joy St. Built by African-Americans in 1806, this meetinghouse is where the New England Anti-Slavery Society was founded. Then, for nearly a century, it was used as a religious, educational, and social center. Brochures and maps are available here for the **Black Heritage Trail,** a marked walking tour past 15 sites pertaining to African-Americans in 19th-century Boston. Further information is available at the **Museum of Afro-American History.**

19. The Freedom Trail

Maps of this walking tour are available at the Boston Common Information Kiosk, where the trail begins. The marked way

A popular pastime: Swan boat rides in Boston's Public Garden

Faneuil Hall is today a festive marketplace.

visits 16 sites that played a key role in the founding of the nation. *Admission charged for some attractions.*

20. Boston Common

In 1634 this 48-acre tract was a cow pasture. It is now a lavish green park containing the Boston Massacre Monument and the ancient Central Burying Ground.

21. Public Garden

One of the loveliest sites in Boston, this lush park is decorated with formal gardens, rare trees, and statuary. There's also a pond, where, in summer, the famed swan boats glide. *Fee charged for boat rides.*

22. Gibson House Museum

137 Beacon St. The museum is in a Victorian home that is typical of the Back Bay residences owned by uppercrust Bostonians in the mid-19th century. The original furnishings and fixtures still decorate the house. *Admission charged.*

23. Museum of Science

Science Park. Many hands-on exhibits are within reach in this superb science museum. Model displays range from a giant dinosaur to what is believed to be the world's largest magnifying glass; there are also exhibits using computers and live animals. Besides being home to the **Hayden Planetarium,** the museum also contains a children's discovery center and the Mugar Omni theater. *Admission charged.*

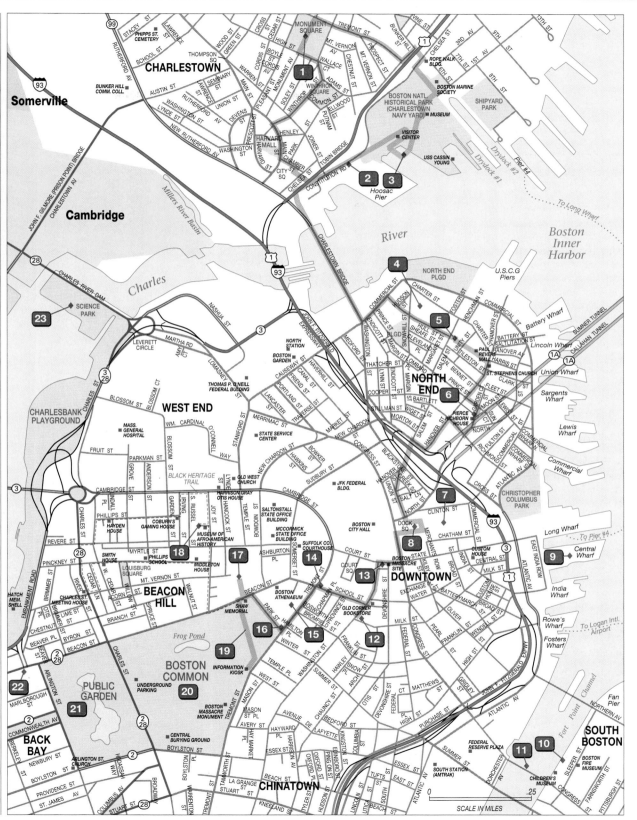

CAMBRIDGE

1. Brattle Street

Extending from Harvard Square to Watertown, this street contains a magnificent assortment of some of the finest 18th- to 20th-century private homes in Cambridge. During the Revolutionary War many of the residents here remained loyal to the British — a fact that led to the street being nicknamed Tory Row.

2. Longfellow National Historic Site

105 Brattle St. This lovely pre-Revolution mansion has been at different times home to a famous president and to a famous poet. George Washington lived here in 1775 and 1776. Henry Wadsworth Longfellow, author of the renowned *The Song of Hiawatha* and a professor at Harvard, was a resident from 1837 until his death in 1882. Today, visitors can see Longfellow's furnishings, including his desk and book collection. Down the street is **Blacksmith House,** the former home of the village smith, which has been converted into a bakery. *Admission charged at Longfellow site.*

3. Radcliffe College

Founded in 1879 with the purpose of providing women with a Harvard education, this college is now one of the country's foremost institutions in regard to its research programs on women, offering curricula at the undergraduate, graduate, and post-graduate levels. Radcliffe's undergraduates are now fully integrated Harvard students. The **Arthur and Elizabeth Schlesinger Library,** dedicated to the history of women in America, is one of the best in its field. The library boasts a superb culinary book collection, and its archives hold papers of Harriet Beecher Stowe, Susan B. Anthony, and Amelia Earhart, among others.

4. Cambridge Common

Just north of Harvard Square, this large park is rich in colonial history, having been established in 1630 by the city of Cambridge, before the founding of Harvard University. Local legend has it that George Washington stood under a tree here on July 3, 1775, and took command of the Continental Army, which was marching before him. Although the story is tenuous at best, one tree in the common is designated the Washington Elm. The park includes a baseball diamond and a playground, as well as a statue and model cannon that pay tribute to the park's history. Across from the common is the **Harvard Law School.**

5. Harvard Museums of Cultural and Natural History

26 Oxford St. Four spectacular museums housed in one building complement one another with their unique and impressive displays. The **Peabody Museum of Archaeology and Ethnology,** dating from 1866, is the oldest museum in the Western Hemisphere devoted to these two fields. It is especially well known for its exceptional anthropological displays of prehistoric and modern cultures from all over the world. One of the most famous exhibits at Harvard is the "Glass Flowers" display at the **Botanical Museum.** Created by two German artisans, the remarkable models represent 847 plant species. The **Mineralogical and Geological Museum,** considered one of the finest in the world, displays more than 50,000 specimens of gems, minerals, ores, and meteorites. The **Museum of Comparative Zoology** showcases a large variety of mounted animals and a collection of rare and unique fossils, such as a mastodon and the largest turtle shell ever discovered. *Admission charged.*

6. Arthur M. Sackler Museum

485 Broadway. This ultra-modern building provides an unexpected home for an impressive collection of antiquities. The focus is on Asian and Islamic art, with displays of Japanese woodblock prints, Chinese jade, rare Persian and Indian paintings, and Greek art. *Admission charged.*

7. Christ Church

Zero Garden St. Located in Harvard Square across from Harvard Yard, this simple church is the oldest in Cambridge to be continuously used. Besides serving the spiritual needs of its congregation, this church has taken part in secular affairs: Its organ pipes were melted down for bullets during the American Revolution. The **Old Burying Ground** is some 350 years old and contains the graves of soldiers killed in that war, as well as many early residents.

8. Harvard Square

Surrounding the Harvard campus is a busy commercial center catering to the academic and professional communities, where a colorful ambience is created by the many bookstores, cafes, boutiques, clothing stores, and stores selling Harvard mementos. A festival of musicians, magicians, and other street performers takes place here every Friday night during the summertime. Located in the heart of the square is the Harvard Cooperative Society, known as the Coop. Founded more than a century ago as a bookstore, it operates today as a large department store.

9. Harvard University

Founded in 1636 and named for a Puritan minister who left the college his library and half his estate, Harvard is the nation's oldest institute of higher education and the alma mater of six U.S. presidents. Several original buildings, designed in Colonial style, are in **Harvard Yard.** These include **Massachusetts Hall,** a dormitory dating from 1720, and **Holden Chapel,** built in 1744. In the center of the yard stands the white granite **University Hall,** designed by Charles Bulfinch in 1815, and the **John Harvard Statue,** by Daniel Chester French. There's also **Sever Hall,** one of H. H. Richardson's late-Victorian masterpieces. Nearby is **Widener Library** — a stone building fronted by 12 columns — which, along with the school's other holdings, composes the largest university library system in the country. A copy of the Gutenberg Bible and other rare books are on exhibit. Upperclassmen reside in the **Harvard Houses,** the majority of which are Gregorian-style buildings, located between Harvard Yard and the Charles River. Free student-led tours of the university campus originate from the information office as well as from Byerly Hall in Radcliffe Yard.

Members of the Harvard crew train on the Charles River.

The Longfellow National Historic Site was once home to the well-known American poet. Visitors can tour the elegant mansion, which contains many of his personal belongings.

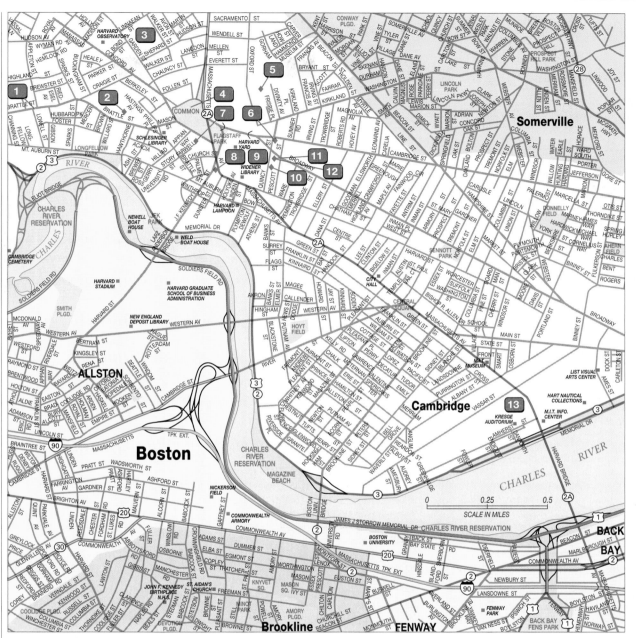

A dormitory at Harvard University

10. Carpenter Center for the Visual Arts

24 Quincy St. This museum has a cubist, machinelike exterior designed by the acclaimed French architect Le Corbusier. Inside are studios and exhibits of works by both professionals and students, with a particularly fine photograph collection.

11. Fogg Art Museum

32 Quincy St. Located just outside Harvard Yard, the Fogg is one of three museums that comprise the Harvard University Art Museums, which contain some of the most impressive and wide-ranging displays of art, as well as some of the best facilities for studying art, in the world. Established in 1891, the Fogg contains works representing all major periods and every corner of the world. Exhibits include French and Italian sculpture; contemporary photographs; fine drawings, prints, watercolors, and paintings by masters such as Rembrandt, van Gogh, and Picasso; and the largest Ingres collection outside of France. Special exhibitions are displayed around the museum's lovely Italian Renaissance–style courtyard.

12. Busch-Reisinger Museum

32 Quincy St. Entered through the Fogg, this museum is dedicated to central and northern European art. Of special note are the displays of Expressionist paintings — probably the best such collection in the country — with works by Beckmann, Klee, and Kandinsky. *Admission charged.*

13. Massachusetts Institute of Technology

Founded in 1861 and relocated to the banks of the Charles River in 1916, this university is one of the most esteemed engineering and science schools in the world. Divided into the East and West campuses, it is famous for its permanent collection of outdoor sculpture, with works by Calder and Picasso. A memorable part of the East campus is an 825-foot-long corridor, known as the infinite corridor, which connects the buildings. The **M.I.T. Museum** relates the history of the university by tracing its scientific and technological developments. Two other museums associated with the M.I.T. Museum are the **Hart Nautical Collections,** which follow the evolution of ship design by displaying models of both rigged merchant vessels and naval ships, and the **Margaret Hutchinson Compton Gallery,** where there are changing exhibits on the institute's many activities and programs. Also on the East campus is the **List Visual Arts Center,** which displays the work of contemporary artists, and the **Charles Hayden Memorial Library,** the university's largest. On the West campus is the cylindrical **M.I.T. Chapel,** an architectural marvel in which sunlight reflecting off a moat eventually appears in sparkling dots on the chapel's interior walls. The **Kresge Auditorium,** designed by Eero Saarinen, who also created the chapel, has a 3-point curved roof. Guided tours of the campus begin at the information center.

CAPE COD, NANTUCKET, & MARTHA'S VINEYARD

1. Duxbury
In 1653 John Alden, a Puritan settler who came to America on the *Mayflower,* built what is now known as the **John Alden House,** a veritable treasure trove of early Americana. The **King Caesar House,** a shipbuilder's mansion, contains period furnishings. *Admission charged.*

2. Plymouth
Chamber of Commerce, 91 Famoset St. After their long journey aboard the *Mayflower,* the Pilgrims landed on **Plymouth Rock,** which now lies beneath a Neoclassical monument at the beach off Water Street. The **Mayflower II,** a replica of the original ship, is at State Pier, where costumed performers reenact 17th-century shipboard life. Memorabilia can be seen in the **Pilgrim Hall Museum,** and life-size figures tell the colonists' story in the **Plymouth National Wax Museum.** **Cranberry World** has displays on this local crop. Other glimpses into the past can be enjoyed by simply walking or driving along the streets of town, which are lined with historic homes. *Admission charged for some attractions.*

3. Plimoth Plantation
Warren Ave., Plymouth. A superb reconstruction of the 1627 English settlement on these shores, this living-history museum has interpreters who dress, speak, and live as the Pilgrims did centuries ago. Also on the grounds is a re-created Wampanoag Indian settlement. *Admission charged.*

4. Aptucxet Trading Post Museum
24 Aptucxet Rd., Bourne. On the site of what may have been home to the first free-enterprise center on the continent, this replica of an early 17th-century complex includes relics, a runestone, old windmill, saltworks, and Grover Cleveland's private railroad station. *Admission charged.*

5. Sandwich
Cape Cod's oldest town is home to the 1848 **First Church of Christ,** whose spire is reminiscent of one designed by Christopher Wren, and to the **Sandwich Glass Museum,** which displays 19th-century glassware. The **Town Hall Square Historic District** includes the **Hoxie House,** a 1675 saltbox. Several architectural styles and a plethora of Americana are featured at the 76-acre **Heritage Plantation.** *Admission charged for some attractions.*

6. Barnstable
Information on Cape Cod can be found in the **Sturgis Library,** the nation's oldest such building, which dates back to 1644. Another historic local structure is the **West Parish Meetinghouse,** considered to be the oldest Congregational church in the nation. Historic documents and marine exhibits are on display at the **Trayser Memorial Museum.** In the summertime, **Sandy Neck Beach** is an excellent spot for swimming and sunbathing. *Admission charged for some attractions.*

7. Hyannis
Chamber of Commerce, 319 Barnstable Rd. With its scenic railroad, harbor tours, whale-watching excursions, and ferries departing for Nantucket and Martha's Vineyard, Hyannis is a major tourist hub. Photographs at the **John F. Kennedy Hyannis Museum** depict the time spent by the late president on the Cape, from 1934 to 1963. The 12-foot-high **JFK Memorial** overlooks the harbor in which he was fond of sailing. The **Craigville Beach,** southwest of town, is a good swimming beach. *Admission charged for some attractions.*

8. Monomoy National Wildlife Refuge
The headquarters for this wilderness area is located on Morris Island, which is accessible by car; the refuge itself, however, can be reached only by boat. The area offers splendid vistas and surf fishing, and shelters more than 200 species of birds. Tours are available by advance request. *Fee charged for tours.*

9. Chatham
One of the most stylish towns on the Cape, as well as a center for fishing, the town of Chatham boasts such sites as the **Old Atwood House,** with memorabilia and a collection of shells from around the world. The **Railroad Museum** has some 8,000 models on display, including a caboose from 1910. **Chatham Light** is occasionally opened to the public and affords expansive views. *Admission charged for some attractions.*

10. Brewster
In addition to a picturesque gristmill and historic homes that once belonged to sea captains, attractions in the Brewster area include the **New England Fire & History Museum,** whose exhibits feature early firefighting equipment and a restoration of an old apothecary. The **Cape Cod Museum of Natural History** offers various films, exhibits, and lovely nature trails. *Admission charged for some attractions.*

11. Wellfleet Bay Wildlife Sanctuary
This 1,000-acre preserve has winding trails past ponds, salt marshes, pinewoods, and moors. The visitor center provides a guidebook to the Goose Pond Trail; other facilities include a nature center and a picnic area. *Admission charged.*

12. Cape Cod National Seashore
Marconi Station serves as the headquarters of this 28,000-acre natural treasure, which encompasses dunes, cliffs, and forestland. Along the coastline are six swimming beaches, including **Orleans (Nauset) Beach,** considered to be one of the most spectacular on the Atlantic coast. There are hiking, biking, and bridle trails, along with picnic areas and campgrounds. Visitor centers are located at **Salt Pond** in Eastham and **Province Lands** in Provincetown. *Admission charged for some attractions.*

13. Truro
Chamber of Commerce, Rte. 6, North Truro. The rolling sand dunes of Truro were once explored by Myles Standish, a *Mayflower* passenger who took charge of the military defense of Plymouth colony. Today the town is popular with artists and writers, many of whom no doubt enjoy **Pilgrim Heights,** which has walking trails and exhibits on the area's early history.

14. Provincetown
Chamber of Commerce, 307 Commercial St. With its art galleries, picturesque wharf, beaches, and whale-watching cruises, Provincetown is a popular tourist destination. The **Pilgrim Monument and Provincetown Museum** pays tribute to the Pilgrims' landing, while the **Provincetown Heritage Museum** displays antique firefighting equipment and period rooms that are "peopled" with lifelike wax figures. *Admission charged for some attractions.*

15. Siasconset
Sconset, as it's called by many, features not only a beach but also an enchanting village of cottages, often festooned with roses in the spring and summer.

16. Windswept Cranberry Bog
Bicyclists and hikers alike can enjoy the trails through some 205 acres of bog, marsh, and woodlands located here. In the fall visitors have the opportunity to watch the cranberries being harvested.

17. Nantucket
Chamber of Commerce, 15 Main St. The pretty historic district here features a cobblestoned Main Street lined with lovely homes and shade trees. Furnishings of the affluent whaling period are displayed in the Greek Revival **Hadwen House,** while the simpler **Macy-Christian House** exhibits 18th- and 19th-century decors. One of the country's first women astronomers is remembered at the **Maria Mitchell Birthplace.** More of the town's history can be visited at the 1686 **Jethro Coffin House,** the oldest in Nantucket, and the **Thomas Macy Warehouse.** The **Whaling Museum** includes a whale skeleton, and next door the **Peter Foulger Museum/ Research Center** contains clocks, artworks, and exhibits on the China trade. *Admission charged.*

18. Falmouth
This quaint town, settled in 1660, is home to the **First Congregational Church,** the bell of which was cast by Paul Revere. Tours at the **Falmouth Historical Society Museum Complex** include the 1790 **Julia Wood House,** decorated with period furnishings, and the **Conant House,** which contains whaling artifacts and a room dedicated to Katharine Lee Bates, lyricist of *America the Beautiful.* Marked trails in the **Ashumet Holly and Wildlife Sanctuary** wind through a garden of holly. *Admission charged for some attractions.*

19. Woods Hole
This town is home to several research centers and is also a departure point for ferries to Martha's Vineyard and Nantucket. The **Marine Biological Laboratory,** established in 1888 as a research and education center, offers guided tours and a slide show in summer, for which reservations are re-

quired. Exhibits at the **National Marine Fisheries Service Aquarium** include a seal pool and a hands-on tank. Films at the **Woods Hole Oceanographic Institution Exhibit Center** explain how a submarine is used for both exploration and research and how remote-controlled vehicles are designed to locate shipwrecks.

20. Vineyard Haven

Chamber of Commerce, Beach Rd. Once an important port in the days of colonization, the town today goes by the name of its township, Tisbury. Old schoolbooks, exotica brought by whaling ships from foreign lands, and exhibits on scrimshaw and spinning wheels are on view at the **Old Schoolhouse Museum.** *Admission charged.*

21. Oak Bluffs

This delightful Victorian village evolved from a mid-19th-century Methodist meeting place. The annual Illumination Night festival has been held here since 1869. Visitors may ride the Flying Horse, the country's oldest operating carousel, which has been designated a National Historic Landmark.

22. Edgartown

Interesting architectural designs here include the houses along North Water Street, of which the 1672 **Vincent House** is said to be the oldest. There's also the **Old Whaling Church,** a fine example of the Greek Revival style. Scrimshaw, ship models, and whaling gear are among the exhibits in the **Vineyard Museum** of the Dukes County Historical Society. Nearby public beaches include **South Beach** and **Lighthouse Beach.** *Admission charged for some attractions.*

23. Joseph Sylvia State Beach

A 2-mile-long stretch of sand, gently lapping waters, and magnificent views make this a popular destination for vacationers.

24. Felix Neck Sanctuary

Information on this 350-acre sanctuary, part of the Massachusetts Audubon Society, is available at the visitor center. Nature lovers can roam the area's 6 miles of trails, which lead past woodlands, a turtle pond, and various waterfowl. *Admission charged.*

25. Gay Head Cliffs

These dramatic formations on the island's western end are composed of multicolored clay. The town of Gay Head offers shops selling American Indian crafts.

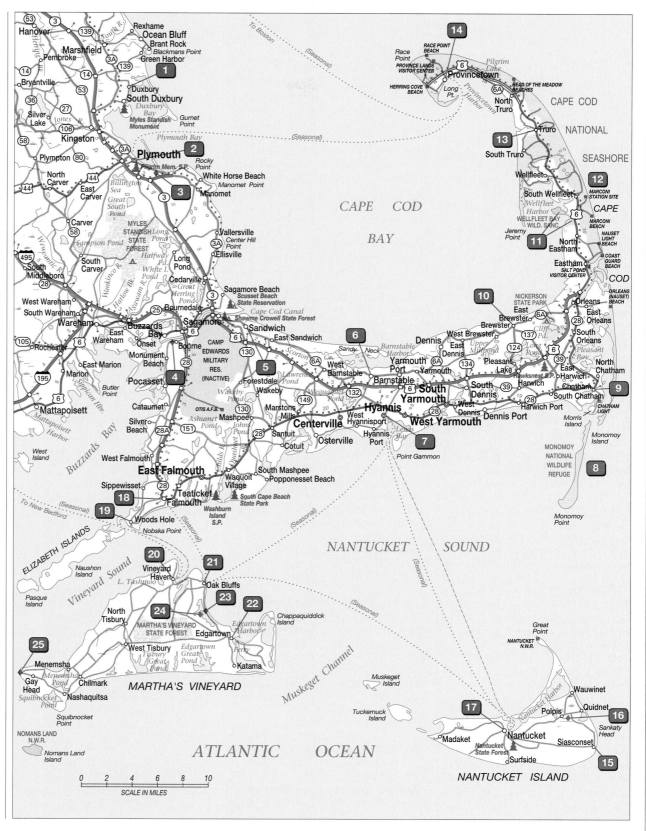

1. North Conway

Chamber of Commerce, Main St. Several local ski areas make this town a popular destination for winter-sports enthusiasts. From mid-April to December, the **Conway Scenic Railroad** offers rides affording striking views of Mt. Washington. To glimpse more natural wonders, visitors should travel the scenic road from **Echo Lake State Park** to **Cathedral Ledge.** *Admission charged for some attractions.*

2. Willowbrook

Elm St., Newfield. Nearly 40 structures are on display in this restored 19th-century village, including furnished homes and an early printing shop. Other exhibits include sleighs, an 1894 carousel, and an 1849 stagecoach. *Admission charged.*

3. Sebago

Home to beaches and nature trails, **Sebago Lake State Park** lies on the shores of the state's second-largest lake. Sebago and Long lakes are connected via the Songo Lock, and excursion boats ply the waters. There are several antiques stores in the area. The **Jones Museum of Glass and Ceramics** has more than 7,000 pieces. *Admission charged for some attractions.*

4. Sabbathday Lake Shaker Village

Established in 1782 and today the last active Shaker settlement in the country, this village exemplifies the simple lifestyle advocated by the sect. The museum here displays crafts and furnishings. *Admission charged at museum.*

5. Androscoggin Historical Society Library and Museum

2 Turner St., Auburn. Among the displays are exhibits on birds, tools, and military items pertaining to the area's history.

6. Freeport

As the home of L. L. Bean and many other outlet stores, this can be a great place to find bargains. Nearby is the **Desert of Maine,** where sand dunes extend for some 100 acres and reach as high as 80 feet. *Admission charged for some attractions.*

7. Brunswick

Chamber of Commerce, 59 Pleasant St. The campus of **Bowdoin College** features both the **Peary-MacMillan Arctic Museum,** where exhibits pertain to the two explorers, and the **Museum of Art,** with classical works and paintings by Winslow Homer. The **Skolfield-Whittier House** and the **Pejepscot Historical Society Museum** contain collections relating to regional history. The **Joshua L. Chamberlain Museum** displays Civil War mementos. *Admission charged for some attractions.*

8. Maine Maritime Museum

243 Washington St., Bath. Exhibits here explore the state's seafaring history. Nearby is an old shipyard where large wooden sailing vessels were built. *Admission charged.*

9. Wiscasset

Notable sights in this pretty little town include the **Nickels-Sortwell House,** a three-story Federal mansion, and the **Lincoln County Museum and Old Jail,** an 1809 structure housing early Americana. The Georgian-style **Castle Tucker** has a free-standing elliptical staircase. The **Musical Wonder House** displays antique music boxes, phonographs, and pianos. *Admission charged for some attractions.*

10. Boothbay Harbor

Chamber of Commerce, Rte. 27. The **Annual Windjammer Days Festival** is a popular attraction, as are excursion boats and fishing. The nearby **Boothbay Railway Village** re-creates an old village and features antique vehicles and rides aboard a steam train. *Admission charged at railway village.*

11. Fort Popham State Memorial

Rte. 209, Popham Beach. This site highlights an unfinished fortress in which staircases ascend brick-and-granite towers.

12. Eagle Island

Ferry rides to this small island, which is owned by the state of Maine, make for pleasant summertime day-trips. A house here was the former residence of the courageous North Pole explorer Adm. Robert E. Peary. *Admission charged.*

13. Portland

Convention and Visitors Bureau, 305 Commercial St. The **Wadsworth-Longfellow House** contains the poet's cradle, desk, and mementos. The opulent 1862 **Victoria Mansion** was built by a wealthy hotelier. The vast collection of the **Portland Museum of Art** includes works by European masters and 18th-century decorative and fine arts. The architecture and cobblestone streets of the **Old Port Exchange** evoke the city's seafaring days. The 1807 **Portland Observatory** offers fine views. *Admission charged for some attractions.*

14. Cape Elizabeth

The Portland Head Light, Maine's oldest lighthouse, still illuminates the darkness with a bright beacon. **Two Lights State Park** offers peaceful locales for strolls and picnics. **Crescent Beach State Park** has a sandy swimming beach. *Admission charged for some attractions.*

15. Old Orchard Beach

Chamber of Commerce, First St. Thousands come to frolic on this 7-mile strip of white sand, where area attractions include golf and deep-sea fishing. The **Palace Playland** offers several diversions, such as a 1906 carousel. The **Scarborough Marsh Nature Center** is located on the state's largest salt marsh. Francophiles can practice the language in this largely French-speaking area. *Admission charged for some attractions.*

16. Saco

An extensive collection of documents pertaining to Maine history can be viewed in the **Dyer Library.** The **York Institute Museum** includes Federal-era decorative arts and furnishings. The **Maine Aquarium** displays both local and tropical marine life. *Admission charged for some attractions.*

17. Biddeford

Chamber of Commerce, 170 Main St. Host of the annual La Kermesse Festival, a large Franco-American celebration, this town also boasts the isolated **Biddeford Pool,** with five beaches and a bird sanctuary. The **City Theatre,** with its horseshoe balcony and excellent acoustics, opened in 1896. *Admission charged for some attractions.*

18. Kennebunkport

This town is home to painters, writers, and, in the summer, former president George Bush. Walking tours of the historic district begin at the Greek Revival **Nott House.** The handsome **Captain Lord Mansion** is now an inn. Visitors to the **Seashore Trolley Museum** can learn about antique electric streetcars. The sights along **Ocean Avenue** provide a pleasant scenic drive. *Admission charged for some attractions.*

19. Kennebunk

Chamber of Commerce, Rtes. 9 and 35. A summer resort with fine beaches, this 17th-century ship-building town is filled with historic homes. A standout is the **Taylor-Barry House,** built in 1803 and containing period decor. The **Brick Store Museum** is a complex of 19th-century commercial buildings. There's also **William Lord's Brick Store,** with changing exhibits on decorative arts and displays of historical and maritime memorabilia. *Admission charged for some attractions.*

20. Wells

Chamber of Commerce, Rte. 1S. Aficionados of the great outdoors can visit this locale's 7 miles of beach and the **Rachel Carson National Wildlife Refuge.** The **Wells Auto Museum** displays vintage cars and more. *Admission charged at auto museum.*

21. Ogunquit

Chamber of Commerce, Main St. Strollers on **Marginal Way,** a lovely mile-long footpath atop rugged cliffs, are sometimes sprinkled by the spray of the crashing surf below. **Bald Head Cliff** looms 140 feet above the ocean and has a lookout with spectacular views. Works of 20th-century American artists are featured at the **Ogunquit Museum of American Art.** A fine, 3-mile beach extends toward New Hampshire.

22. York

Chamber of Commerce, Rte. 1. Tours are conducted of the seven 18th-century buildings that compose the Old York Historical Society. Visitors can also see picturesque **York Harbor** and the **Nubble Lighthouse,** one of the many such landmarks in the area. *Admission charged for some attractions.*

23. South Berwick

Founded in the 17th century, this town is home to the 1774 **Sarah Orne Jewett House,** a fine example of Coastal Georgian architecture, featuring an interior with elaborate woodwork. The 1785 **Hamilton House** is a Georgian mansion perched on a river bluff. *Admission charged.*

24. Woodman Institute

182-192 Central Ave., Dover. Focusing on natural history and early Americana, this institute maintains three display buildings, the oldest of which dates from 1675.

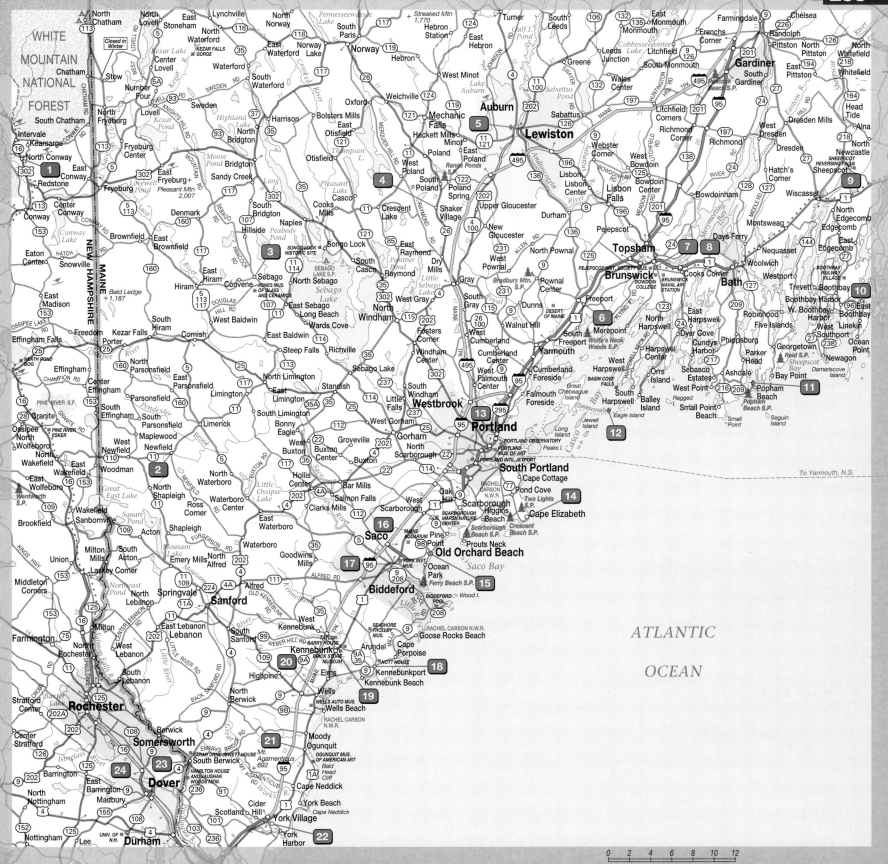

SCALE IN MILES
0 2 4 6 8 10 12

1. Bangor

Chamber of Commerce, 519 Main St. Many landmarks are located in this city, an important mercantile and cultural center. The **West Market Square** and **Broadway Historic districts** preserve commercial and residential structures from the 19th century. The **Thomas A. Hill House,** with a posh Victorian parlor in its restored first floor, is an 1834 Greek Revival building. The **Cole Land Transportation Museum** displays more than 200 vehicles, including a train and train station. *Admission charged for some attractions.*

2. Bucksport Mill Tour

River Rd., Bucksport. Champion International makes a lightweight coated paper that is used by many magazines. Summer tours of the mill are conducted by guides who explain the paper-making process, from raw materials to finished product.

3. Fort Knox

Rte. 174, Prospect. Named for Gen. Henry Knox, this massive fort was constructed out of granite from nearby Mt. Waldo. Although the walls are 40 feet thick, the fort never

At Pemaquid Point, a puffin holds its prey.

had to defend itself. Visitors in search of far-reaching views can climb the parapets. *Admission charged.*

4. Penobscot Marine Museum

Church St. and Rte. 1, Searsport. The extensive nautical history of the area is examined here. Seven buildings, including an 1860 captain's house, exhibit ship models, navigational instruments, and other seafaring memorabilia. *Admission charged.*

5. Belfast

Chamber of Commerce, 31 Front St. The **Belfast Museum** illuminates the past of this old port town, founded in 1770. The **Church Street Historic District** and the **Commercial Historic District** preserve both commercial and residential buildings from the 1800's. Pleasure boats depart from the Public Landing for cruises past the bay islands. *Admission charged for cruises.*

6. Castine

In 1779 Great Britain built **Fort George** here; the ruins can still be visited. The town also features many Federal and Greek Revival residences. The oldest, the 1763 **John Perkins House,** is part of the **Wilson Museum** complex, which also displays prehistoric, colonial, Indian, and Victorian items. When in port, the Maine Maritime Academy's training vessel, *State of Maine,* is open to the public. *Admission charged for some attractions.*

7. Blue Hill

This inviting town sits at the foot of its namesake. Two buildings reflect its early days. **Holt House** is a restored Federal-style home with stenciled wall decorations. **Parson Fisher House,** designed by the community's first minister, contains his handmade furniture, paintings, and woodcuts. Today Blue Hill is renowned for its wheel-thrown pottery, and two companies, Rackliffe Pottery and Rowantrees Pottery, conduct tours. *Admission charged at houses.*

8. Ellsworth

Chamber of Commerce, 163 High St. This historic town maintains several buildings from its early days. The Federal **Tisdale House,** built in 1817, now serves as a library. The **First Congregational Church** is an excellent example of Greek Revival architecture. The **Colonel John Black House,** a handsome structure dating from 1824, contains antiques; also located on the estate are a carriage house and gardens.

The **Stanwood Homestead,** a simple white-frame cottage, is on the grounds of the **Stanwood Wildlife Sanctuary and Birdsacre,** which maintains a rehabilitation center for injured birds. *Admission charged for some attractions.*

9. Schoodic Peninsula

A virtually pristine stretch of wilderness, this rugged peninsula is protected as part of **Acadia National Park.** Turnouts along a road running parallel to the rocky shoreline offer views of the pines and the sea beyond. At **Schoodic Point,** powerful waves crash against pink granite; **Schoodic Head,** the summit, provides a dramatic overview of the spectacular coast.

10. Deer Isle

On this lovely wooded island, **Caterpillar Hill** offers a splendid view across the bay. Visitors can tour the restored 1830 **Salome Sellers House,** which has a tool room containing antique farming and carpentry equipment, and also see contemporary craftworks in the making at the **Haystack Mountain School of Crafts.** Both rental and sightseeing boats are available for exploring the waters off Deer Isle's jagged shoreline. *Fee charged for boats.*

11. Camden Hills State Park

A road in this 5,600-acre park leads to the top of Mt. Battie, with captivating views of the coast and the town of Camden. The tollhouse at the base supplies information on the 20 miles of hiking trails, one of which takes hikers to the summit of lofty Mt. Megunticook. *Admission charged.*

12. Camden

Chamber of Commerce, Commercial St. This idyllic town lies where the mountains meet the sea. In contrast to the many luxurious 19th-century summer mansions here is the **Old Conway Homestead & Museum,** a restored 18th-century farmstead. The frame house holds antique furnishings, and the barn shelters old sleighs and carriages. Cruises aboard windjammers depart regularly from town. *Admission charged.*

13. Rockland

Chamber of Commerce, Public Landing. This fishing port is home to the **Shore Village Museum,** where prominent displays of lighthouse lenses and Civil War memorabilia are on view. The rugged Maine coast inspired Andrew Wyeth and others who are represented at the **Farnsworth Art**

Museum. The adjacent **Farnsworth Homestead** contains antique furniture. The **Owls Head Transportation Museum** offers ferry service to nearby islands and displays antique airplanes and other vehicles. *Admission charged for some attractions.*

14. Montpelier

Rte. 31, Thomaston. Gen. Henry Knox, secretary of war under George Washington, built an elegant Federal-style mansion here as his retirement home. Although the original house was destroyed in 1872, a detailed replica — complete with family furnishings and an opulent reception hall — now stands on the site. *Admission charged.*

15. Damariscotta

Chamber of Commerce, Main St. Now a shopping hub, this town was a prosperous ship-building community in the 19th century. Brick structures from that period still stand on Main Street, along with the 1754 **Chapman-Hall House,** one of the town's oldest buildings. New England's oldest Catholic Church in continuous use, **St. Patrick's,** is located across the Damariscotta River in Newcastle. The river has a peculiarity called the **Damariscotta Reversing Falls,** which sometimes flows up the rocks because of tidal forces. *Admission charged at house.*

16. Pemaquid Point

Sweeping views of the bay can be seen from the tip of this peninsula, where granite cliffs tower above the pounding surf. Located at this vantage point, the **Fishermen's Museum,** in the keeper's cottage of the **Pemaquid Point Lighthouse,** examines the state's fishing industry. In nearby Pemaquid Beach, artifacts excavated from a colonial settlement are displayed in the museum at the **Colonial Pemaquid State Historic Site.** The town is also the site of the reconstructed **Fort William Henry,** originally built in 1692. *Admission charged for some attractions.*

17. Monhegan Island

Known for its rugged beauty and delicious lobsters, this small island retains an unspoiled quality. With no automobiles allowed, visitors come here by boat to enjoy the quintessential Maine scenery — high headlands, rocky shores, and evergreen forests. There are many nature trails to choose from, and visitors can often observe harbor seals during half tide on the island's northern end. *Fee charged for boat.*

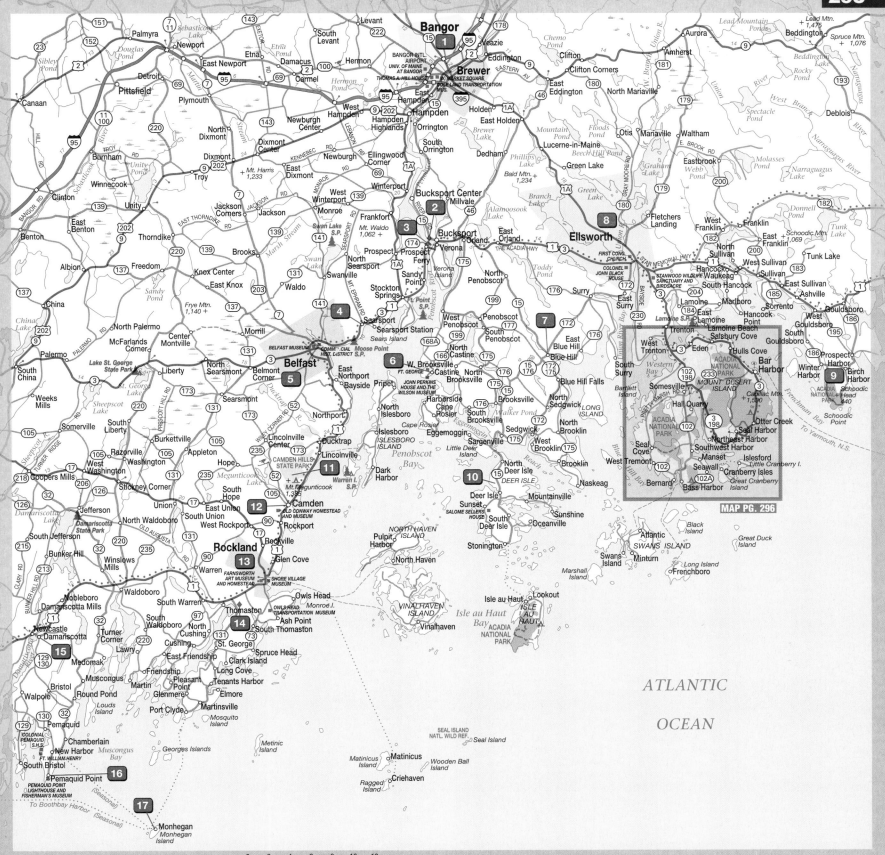

MAP PG. 296

ATLANTIC

OCEAN

0 2 4 6 8 10 12
SCALE IN MILES

ACADIA NATIONAL PARK

1. Somesville

Mt. Desert Island's oldest settlement, charming Somesville has manicured lawns and white clapboard houses. The **Mount Desert Island Historical Society Museum** traces the town's history through deeds, maps, and artifacts. Not far away, **Echo Lake** offers freshwater swimming,

and trails in the area climb mountains where eagles can sometimes be seen.

2. Hulls Cove Visitor Center

Off Rte. 3, Bar Harbor. As the starting point for scenic **Park Loop Road,** this center offers an introduction to the park, providing an orientation film and detailed maps of the many hiking, biking, and riding trails. Schedules for nature walks, hikes, and cruises are also available.

3. Bar Harbor

Chamber of Commerce, 93 Cottage St. Lavish 19th-century mansions and the 1932 Art Deco **Criterion Theatre** are but a few of the architectural treasures here. Visitors can browse through photos from the town's early days at the **Bar Harbor Historical Society Museum;** attend programs at the nearby **Jackson Laboratory,** a world-renowned facility for genetic research; or

examine the various life forms inhabiting the coast of Maine in the **Natural History Museum.** Ferries bound for Nova Scotia leave regularly from Bar Harbor. *Admission charged for some attractions.*

4. Robert Abbe Museum of Stone Age Antiquities

Sieur de Monts, Acadia National Park. Situated amid lush gardens, this private museum displays prehistoric artifacts from the Passamaquoddy and other Northeast Indian tribes. The adjacent nature center exhibits mounted wildlife, and the **Sieur de Monts Spring** provides refreshing water. *Admission charged.*

5. Cadillac Mountain

Park Loop Rd., Acadia National Park. This pink granite mountain is Acadia's highest point, rising 1,530 feet. A hike or drive up Summit Road leads to striking vistas. Several hiking trails lead from its apex.

6. Sand Beach

Park Loop Rd., Acadia National Park. This beach's pink sand, which is really crushed shells, strikes a marked contrast to the rocky shoreline. The water here is fairly cold, but hardy swimmers find it refreshing. The Shore Path on Ocean Drive provides a 2-mile course along the scenic coast. After following a fairly short trail, visitors can then climb a huge granite outcropping called the **Beehive.**

7. Thunder Hole

Park Loop Rd., Acadia National Park. This chasm, sliced into the granite by the force of the ocean, creates a thundering boom during heavy storms, when especially large waves surge in.

8. Baker Island

The 4½-hour cruise from Northeast Harbor to this spruce-covered island offers such exciting sights as ospreys and harbor seals. For transport to land, passengers must take a fishing dory offshore. There's also a geological wonder called the Dance Floor, which consists of immense chunks of pink granite that have separated from the shore's rock. *Fee charged for cruise.*

9. Islesford Historical Museum

Islesford, Little Cranberry Island. In order to depict the history of the Cranberry Isles, this museum presents artifacts, photographs, ship models, and documents. *Fee charged for ferry.*

10. Northeast Harbor

Chamber of Commerce, Sea St. Pleasure boats dot the waters here, and cruise boats head for the Cranberry Isles, where on **Great Cranberry,** the largest of the five, berries are harvested in the fall. **Somes Sound,** the only fjord on the East Coast, cuts through the center of Mt. Desert Island and can be viewed from a turnout off Sargent Drive. *Fee charged for cruise.*

11. Southwest Harbor

Chamber of Commerce, Main St. The ocean's role in this village is apparent everywhere. Lobster boats set out from its two wharves, and the **Mount Desert Oceanarium** features sea animals and fishing exhibits. A touch tank even lets visitors handle such sea inhabitants as sea cucumbers and horseshoe crabs. Some 200 wooden birds, all carved by a local resident, are on display in the **Wendell Gilley Museum.** *Admission charged.*

Admission charged for national park.

1. Québec

Tourism and Convention Bureau Information Center, 60 Rue d'Auteuil. Once an old Indian settlement, this region's colonial history began when Jacques Cartier visited in 1535. Samuel de Champlain arrived in 1608 and set up a trading post. Today **Cape Diamond,** a 350-foot-high promontory, divides this bi-level city into Upper Town, set on a cliff and protected by old stone walls, and, along the shore below, Lower Town, with its narrow roads and old homes. Among the many historic sites are the 1605 **Notre-Dame Basilica,** an elaborate cathedral; the **Assemblée Nationale,** an ornate government building; and the **Château Frontenac,** a baroque hotel.

2. Allagash Wilderness Waterway

Beginning at Telos Lake and stretching almost to Canada, this 92-mile waterway winds through dense forests, where many primitive campsites, accessible only by

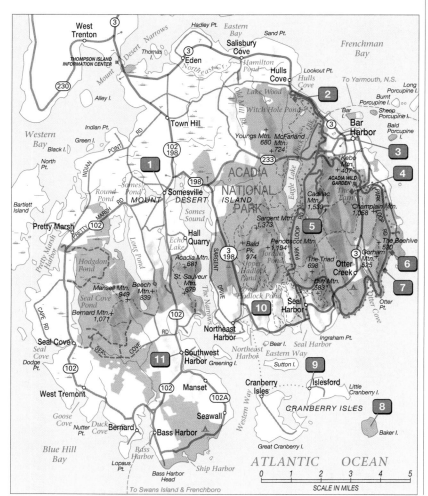

canoe, line the banks. Guides are available, but there are also put-in points for experienced canoeists. *Admission charged.*

3. Fort Kent Blockhouse Historic Site

East Main St., Fort Kent. In the 1800's, Great Britain, then in control of Canada, had a prolonged dispute with the United States over the Maine–Canada border, an area with valuable virgin forests. To protect its own interests, Maine built a fort out of cedar logs on this site — the blockhouse of which still stands, featuring a collection of antique hand tools inside.

4. Acadian Village

Off Rte. 1, Van Buren. This frontier village is composed of relocated and restored structures dating from the 18th and 19th centuries. It includes old shops, cabins, a general store, and a church. The buildings display period furnishings and tools. *Admission charged.*

5. New Sweden

Chamber of Commerce, 111 High St. As a testimonial to its heritage, this community is home to the **New Sweden Historical Society Museum,** which has a 19th-century log cabin containing possessions from the first Swedes who settled here. In the town's former general store and post office, the **Stockholm Museum** has photos and other items from the Scandinavian pioneers. The annual Midsommer Dagen celebrates the long midsummer days with a maypole, folk dancing, and other festivities.

6. Nylander Museum

393 Main St., Caribou. Olof Nylander, a Swedish-born naturalist, gathered rocks, fossils, shells, marine-life specimens, and Indian artifacts. This museum houses that extensive collection, along with displays of butterflies and mounted animals.

7. Houlton

Chamber of Commerce, 109 Main St. Old commercial buildings from the 1890's can be viewed in the **Market Square Historic District.** Set in a 1903 Colonial-style house, the **Southern Aroostook Historical and Art Museum** exhibits farming equipment, tools, and other regional artifacts.

8. Lumberman's Museum

Shin Pond Rd., Patten. Highlights at this museum include a barrel-making exhibit, replicas of early logging camps, and steam-powered log haulers. *Admission charged.*

9. Grindstone Falls

From a picnic area shaded by white pine trees, visitors can watch this small, lovely waterfall on the Penobscot River. Farther north, **Mud Brook** joins the river to form whitewater rapids — a real challenge for canoeists and kayakers.

10. Greenville

Chamber of Commerce, Main St. This town is a stopping-off point for sports enthusiasts headed to **Moosehead Lake,** which is some 35 miles long. The **Moosehead Marine Museum** offers cruises on the *Katahdin,* a refurbished 1914 steamer, and exhibits on the lake's steamship era. *Admission charged for some attractions.*

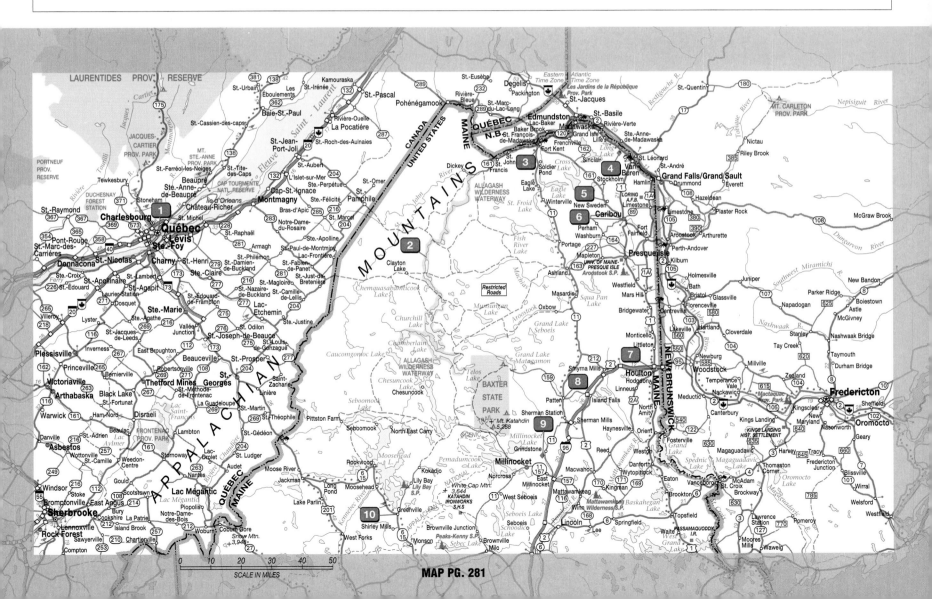

1. Serpent Mound State Memorial

385 Rte. 73, near Locust Grove. Ancient Indians built this well-known mound shaped like an uncoiling, open-mouthed serpent. An observation tower allows visitors to view the whole of this 1,348-foot-long snake, which is 20 feet wide and 5 feet high. *Admission charged.*

2. Hopewell Culture National Historical Park

16062 Rte. 104, Chillicothe. This area is home to a 2,000-year-old burial complex of the Hopewell Indians. It contains 23 mounds, which can be seen from a viewing platform and a self-guiding trail. Displays in the visitor center feature elaborate copper headdresses, effigy pipes carved as animal likenesses, exquisite artifacts, and trade goods. *Admission charged.*

3. Sherman House

137 East Main St., Lancaster. This was the birthplace of Gen. William Tecumseh Sherman and his brother, John, the author of the 1890 Sherman Antitrust Act. Displays include family memorabilia, Civil War artifacts, and the general's old field tent. On the grounds are herb and flower gardens. *Admission charged.*

4. Malabar Farm State Park

4050 Bromfield Rd., Lucas. This park contains the estate of Louis Bromfield, a Pulitzer Prize–winning author. It features hiking trails and self-guiding tours of barns and flower gardens. The 32-room mansion has antiques, a mirrored living room, floating double staircase, and a bedroom in which Humphrey Bogart and Lauren Bacall honeymooned. *Admission charged at house.*

5. National Road/ Zane Gray Museum

8850 East Pike St., near Norwich. Exhibits here examine the construction of the National Road, the nation's first federally funded thoroughfare. There are also manuscripts, first editions, and memorabilia of the writer Zane Gray. *Admission charged.*

6. Degenhart Paperweight and Glass Museum

65323 Highland Hills Rd., Cambridge. Works by John Degenhart and other regional glassmakers are displayed here. Included in the exhibition are variously designed paperweights and colorful glassworks — all of which reflect the changing tastes and styles from the 1840's to 1900. *Admission charged.*

7. Campus Martius Museum

601 Second St., Marietta. Here visitors will find part of a 1790 fort, the home and furnishings of a Revolutionary War general, George Washington's masonic apron, an extensive frontier rifle collection, and Hepplewhite and Chippendale furniture. The nearby **Ohio River Museum** displays 19th-century steamboats. *Admission charged.*

8. Blennerhassett Island Historical Park

Off Rte. 77, near Parkersburg. Visitors are transported by sternwheelers to this island, where Aaron Burr and Harman Blennerhassett engaged in military activities. The rebuilt **Blennerhassett Mansion** offers glimpses of early 1800's extravagance. *Admission charged at mansion.*

9. Charleston

Convention and Visitors Bureau, 200 Civic Center Dr. The Italian Renaissance **State Capitol** has a 180-foot-high golden dome. Nearby in the state museum at the **Cultural Center** are Civil War exhibits. The **Sunrise Museum,** housed in two mansions on 16 wooded acres, offers a planetarium, nature center, and more.

10. Exhibition Coal Mine

New River Park, Beckley. Tours here descend approximately 1,500 feet underground, where exhibits and guides demonstrate the techniques used by miners prior to mechanization. *Admission charged.*

11. New River Gorge Bridge

Rte. 19, near Fayetteville. This is the world's longest steel arch. It spans one of the world's oldest rivers, the New River, which is also one of the few that flow northward. **Canyon Rim Visitors Center** features exhibits and views of the river and bridge.

12. Pearl S. Buck Birthplace

Rte. 219, Hillsboro. Restored to its 1892 appearance, this onetime home of the highly acclaimed author of *The Good Earth* con-

tains original and period furniture, rare autographed books, and memorabilia relating to the cultures of China and America. *Admission charged.*

13. Cass Scenic Railroad State Park

Rte. 66W, Cass. Restored logging cars, pulled by original Shay steam locomotives, take visitors through 12 miles of Allegheny Mountain scenery to the summit of Bald Knob, the state's second-highest peak. Tours of the nearby **National Radio Astronomy Observatory** feature some of the world's largest radio telescopes. *Fee charged for train ride.*

14. Appomattox Court House National Historic Park

Rte. 24, Appomattox. This village is known as the site where Robert E. Lee surrendered to Ulysses S. Grant on April 9, 1865, ending the Civil War. The park offers living-history programs and contains 28 restored and reconstructed buildings, including the onetime headquarters of both generals. *Admission charged.*

15. Old Bedford Village

Rte. 220, Bedford. More than 40 reconstructed buildings dating from 1750 to 1850 as well as a working farm are included in this village. Costumed staff members reenact rural life in that era, with gunmaking, tinsmithing, leathermaking, and other craft demonstrations. Theater performances and special events are scheduled from May through December. *Admission charged.*

16. Allegheny Portage Railroad National Historic Site

Off Rte. 22, near Hollidaysburg. Here visitors can see how trains pulled canal boats over the mountains in the mid-1800's. Preserved structures include the **Lemon House Tavern,** the **Skew Arch Bridge,** and the 1834 **Staple Bend Tunnel.**

17. Altoona

Convention and Visitors Bureau, 1231 11th Ave. Points of interest in this city include the Greek Revival **Baker Mansion,** known for its hand-carved Belgian oak furniture; the **Railroaders Memorial Museum,** examining the roles and contributions of railroad workers; **Horseshoe Curve,** where trains negotiate a 2,375-foot-long bend; and **Fort Roberdeau,** a reconstructed fort from the Revolutionary War. *Admission charged for some attractions.*

18. Johnstown

Chamber of Commerce, 111 Market St. One of the nation's worst natural disasters was the flood that occurred here in 1889. The event is memorialized at the **Johnstown Flood National Memorial,** located near the faulty dam that released a 75-foot-high wall of water; at the **Johnstown Flood Museum,** housed in a former library of Andrew Carnegie; and at **Grandview Cemetery,** where 777 flood victims are buried. The **Johnstown Inclined Plane Railway** runs on a 71 percent grade, linking a suburb to the city some 500 feet below. *Admission charged for some attractions.*

19. Fort Ligonier

216 South Market St., Ligonier. Originally built in 1758, Ft. Ligonier was a stronghold of the English during the French and Indian War. Now reconstructed, it includes a museum exhibiting artifacts, period rooms, and decorative arts. Reenactments of battles are featured. *Admission charged.*

20. Fallingwater

Rte. 381, near Ohiopyle. Designed in 1936 by Frank Lloyd Wright, this dramatic home is cantilevered over a waterfall. Today Fallingwater is one of the most acclaimed examples of 20th-century architecture. *Admission charged.*

21. Fort Necessity National Battlefield

Rte. 2, Farmington. The battlefield surrounds a reconstruction of a 1754 fort built by troops under the command of George Washington. The battle fought here on July 3, 1754, was Washington's first military campaign and marked the start of the French and Indian War. Nearby **Mount Washington Tavern,** a restored 1800's inn, was once frequented by stagecoaches. *Admission charged.*

22. Wheeling

Convention and Visitors Bureau, 1233 Main St. Victorian architecture has made this city famous. **West Virginia Independence Hall** is a restored 1859 Renaissance Revival customs house, where delegates drafted the state constitution. The 1,500-acre **Oglebay Park** features restored **Waddington Gardens;** a children's zoo called **Good's Zoo,** with some 200 animals; and the **Mansion Museum,** which displays period rooms from the 1750's to the 1870's as well as Wheeling china and glass. *Admission charged for some attractions.*

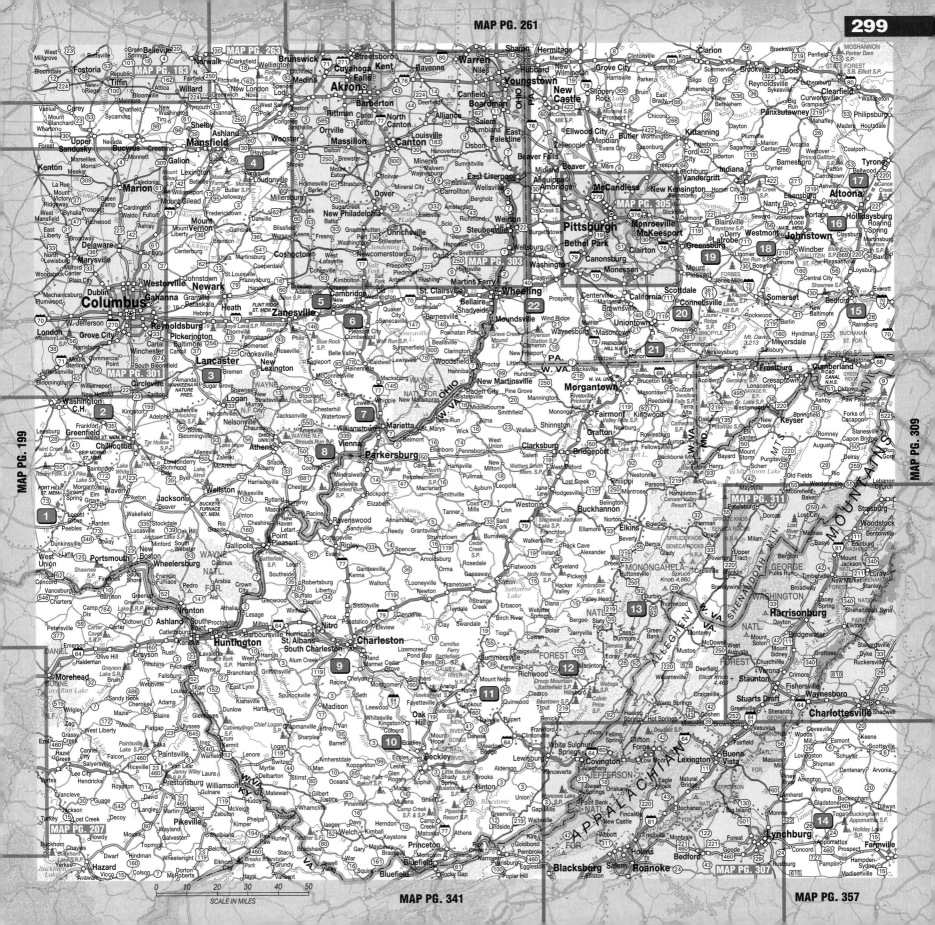

1. Lima

Collections at the **Allen County Museum** include American Indian artifacts, fossils, minerals, and vehicles — from a covered wagon to an electric car. Nearby, the Victorian **MacDonell House** displays period rooms and mounted animals. Across town, the **Lincoln Park Railroad Exhibit** features a Nickel Plate Railroad caboose and the last steam locomotive to be built in Lima. *Admission charged at house.*

2. Neil Armstrong Air and Space Museum

500 Apollo Dr., Wapakoneta. This museum honors the state's aviation pioneers, including Neil Armstrong, the first man on the moon; the Wright Brothers; and balloonist Thomas Kirby, among others. Exhibits feature a rocket engine, moon rock, and the *Gemini VIII* capsule in which Armstrong made the first orbital spacecraft docking. *Admission charged.*

3. Piqua Historical Area

9845 North Hardin Rd., Piqua. The **John Johnston Home,** a restored 1810 Dutch Colonial brick house, features period furnishings, a log barn, a springhouse, a cider house, and guides who perform a variety of craft demonstrations. There's also the **Historic Indian Museum,** which displays 18th- and 19th-century Indian artifacts and costumes. A mule-drawn canal boat takes visitors for more than a mile along a restored section of the Miami and Erie Canal. *Admission charged.*

4. Dayton

Convention and Visitors Bureau, Chamber Plaza, Fifth and Main Sts. The **Old Court House,** built from 1847 to 1850, is considered one of America's finest Greek Revival buildings. Inside, exhibits underscore county history and the Daytonians Orville and Wilbur Wright. The **Paul Laurence Dunbar State Memorial** contains the black poet's original furnishings, including his typewriter and a ceremonial sword presented to him by President Theodore Roosevelt.

The **Dayton Art Institute** houses important baroque and Asian collections, two medieval outdoor cloisters, and extensive contemporary American artworks. **Carillon Historical Park** depicts Miami Valley history from 1796 through 1939, with such displays as a Wright Brothers' 1905 Flyer, an early railway depot, an Erie Canal lock, and antique automobiles. The **U.S. Air Force Museum** exhibits more than 200 aircraft that chronicle the history of aviation. At **SunWatch Indian Village** the culture of the Fort Ancient Indians is interpreted by means of artifacts and reconstructions. **Carriage Hill Farm** features an original 1836 brick house on a working 1880's farm. The interactive exhibits and computerized planetarium shows at **Dayton Museum of Natural History** focus on the geology, biology, and anthropology of the Miami Valley. *Admission charged for some attractions.*

5. Miamisburg Mound

Mound Ave., Miamisburg. This is Ohio's largest conical burial mound, measuring 65 feet high and covering 1½ acres. Situated on a 100-foot bluff overlooking the Great Miami River, it was built by the Adena Indians between 800 B.C. and A.D. 1. Some 116 steps lead to a paved circle on top, with a spectacular view of the river valley.

6. Xenia

Chamber of Commerce, 334 West Market St. Local history is examined at the **Greene County Historical Museum,** located in a restored Victorian home next to the 1799 **Galloway Log House.** The **Carriage House Museum** contains antiques and historical county documents. Built in 1840 and listed on the National Register of Historic Places, **Eden Hall** features 32 rooms filled with antiques ranging from crystal chandeliers and cut-glass lamps to Chippendale, French, Empire, and Victorian furnishings. *Admission charged.*

7. The National Afro-American Museum and Cultural Center

1350 Brush Row Rd., Wilberforce. One of the nation's largest museums dedicated to African-American history and culture, the center offers permanent displays and changing exhibits. *Admission charged.*

8. Springfield

Convention and Visitors Bureau, 333 North Limestone St. The **Springfield Museum of Art** houses temporary exhibits and a small permanent collection of French and American artwork from the 19th and early 20th centuries. The nearby 4,030-acre **Buck Creek State Park** offers camping, hiking, snowmobiling, and water sports on a reservoir that has a half-mile-long sandy beach. *Admission charged at park.*

9. Bellefontaine

Convention and Tourist Bureau, 100 South Main St. Visitors to the area near the courthouse can see the nation's first concrete street. Guided tours are offered at both **Zane Caverns,** noted for its cave pearls, and **Ohio Caverns,** with vividly colored walls and pure white stalactites and stalagmites. **Piatt Castles,** built by two brothers, include a 30-room 1868 Norman French château with historic weapons and artifacts, and an 1881 Flemish-style castle featuring a collection of European and Asian art. *Admission charged for some attractions.*

10. Olentangy Indian Caverns

1779 Home Rd., south of Delaware. Once serving as a Wyandotte Indian shelter, this is Ohio's only three-level cavern. Visitors can descend 55–105 feet to see a variety of chambers with interesting subterranean formations. A museum features American Indian artifacts and geological displays. *Admission charged.*

11. Perkins Observatory

Rte. 23, south of Delaware. Operated by Ohio Wesleyan and Ohio State universities, this observatory has a lecture hall, library, and the state's second-largest reflecting telescope. It is open for a limited time on weekdays for tours, and several nights each month for telescope viewing. Advance tickets are required to use the telescope.

12. Westerville

Convention and Visitors Bureau, 5 West College Ave. **Hanby House,** the restored home of Benjamin Hanby, composer of *Darling Nelly Gray* and *Up On The Housetop,* contains his desk, piano, flute, and sheet music. At **Inniswood Metro Gardens,** paved paths lead through wonderfully landscaped grounds that include rose, herb, and rock gardens. The **Motorcycle Heritage Museum** chronicles the vehicle's history with changing exhibits. *Admission charged at house.*

13. Columbus

Convention and Visitors Bureau, 10 West Broad St. Attractions range from the small **Thurber House,** displaying drawings, books, and awards of writer-cartoonist James Thurber, to the **Ohio State Fair,** one of the largest in the nation. The 1861 **Statehouse** is considered a prime example of Greek Revival architecture. The **Ohio Historical Center,** with archaeological, historical, and natural history exhibits, may be America's finest pre-European history museum. It includes **Ohio Village,** a reconstructed 1800's rural community arranged around a town square, and **German Village,** a restored 19th-century settlement. The **Columbus Zoo** is noted for its gorillas and has one of America's largest collections of reptiles and amphibians. The **Columbus Museum of Art** is best known for its American and European paintings. **Ohio's Center of Science and Industry (COSI)** uses interactive displays, demonstrations, and a planetarium to examine science and technology. The **Franklin Conservatory** houses collections of orchids, cacti, bonsai, and carnivorous plants. Visitors to **Ohio State University** can tour both an arboretum and the **Wexner Center for the Visual Arts.** *Admission charged for some attractions.*

14. Mid-Ohio Historical Museum

700 Winchester Pike, Canal Winchester. Thousands of dolls — many of them rare antiques — comprise this museum's fascinating collection. Visitors will find them made of porcelain, papier mâché, and bisque. There are representations of famous personalities, such as Shirley Temple and the Beatles. Other exhibits include toys, model trains, and a miniature circus. *Admission charged.*

Dolls in the Mid-Ohio Historical Museum

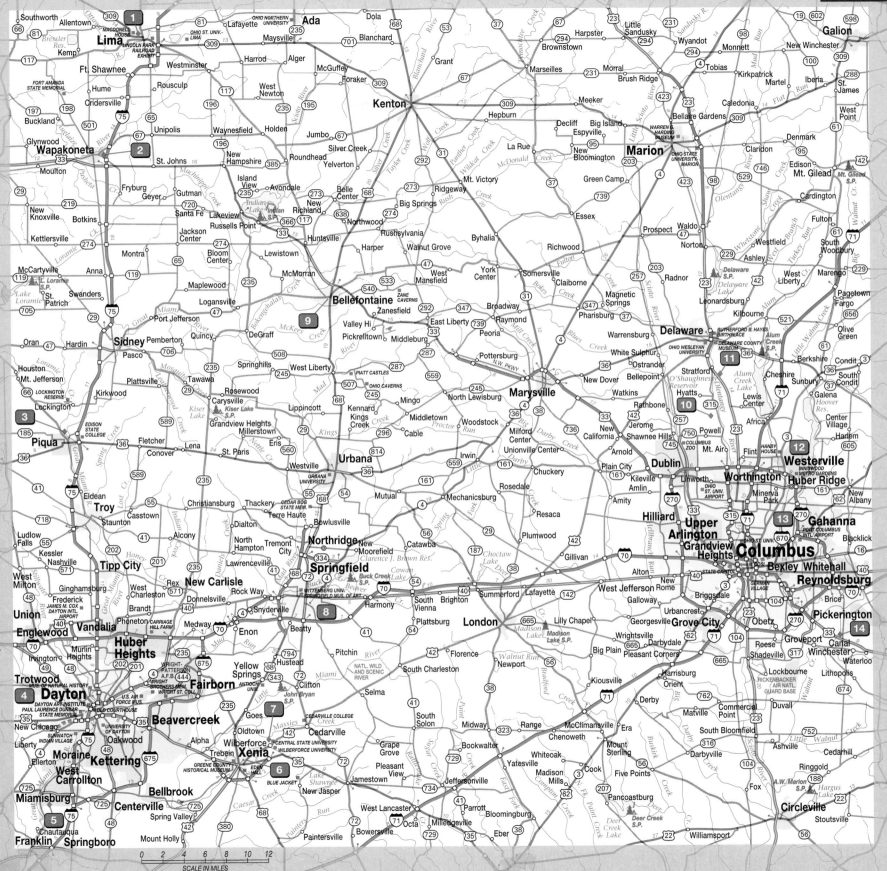

1. Wooster

Convention and Visitors Bureau, 237 South Walnut St. Housed in an 1815 residence, the **Wayne County Historical Society Museum** exhibits original furniture, porcelain, Indian artifacts, mounted animals, firearms, a Civil War–era log cabin, and an 1873 schoolhouse. The **Ohio Agricultural Research and Development Center** studies livestock, fruits, vegetables, and the conservation of energy and of the environment. The 2,500-acre site includes the picturesque Secrest Arboretum and the fragrant Garden of Roses of Legend and Romance. *Admission charged at museum.*

2. Amish Farm

4363 Rte. 39, Berlin. The unique lifestyle of Ohio's Amish is revealed on guided tours of this farm. Visitors can see animals in a barnyard, enjoy buggy rides, and pass through a farm home filled with antiques and furnished in both the Old and New Order Amish styles. *Admission charged.*

3. Roscoe Village

Whitewoman St., Coshocton. This restored 1830's canal town is a quaint living-history museum with small gardens, period shops, six exhibit buildings, costumed interpreters, craftspeople, and horse-drawn boat trips along the Ohio and Erie Canal. At the **Johnson-Humrickhouse Museum** exhibits range from pioneer artifacts, cornhusk dolls, firearms, and American Indian art to Oriental treasures and lace. *Admission charged for some attractions.*

4. Schoenbrunn Village State Memorial

Rte. 259, New Philadelphia. Founded as a Delaware Indian mission in 1772, this was Ohio's first Moravian settlement. Today the state memorial features 17 reconstructed log buildings, the 18th-century mission cemetery, cultivated fields, and a museum containing artifacts from the original village. Interpreters are on hand to explain the exhibits and to give crafts demonstrations. *Admission charged.*

5. Warther Museum

331 Karl Ave., Dover. On display here are the works of Ernest Warther, a master carver of a variety of materials — ivory, ebony, pearl, bone. There are also extensive arrowhead collections and 73,000 buttons, no two alike. Visitors strolling the **Swiss Gardens** can see Warther knives being handcrafted. *Admission charged.*

6. Zoar Village State Memorial

Off Rte. 77, Zoar. This tranquil village was built in 1817 by German separatists who came to America in search of religious freedom. Included among the restored buildings are a tin shop, general store, and bakery. Costumed guides conduct tours, and volunteers perform craft demonstrations. Eight museums exhibit artifacts and furniture. *Admission charged.*

7. Fort Laurens State Memorial and Museum

Off Rte. 77, Bolivar. This 82-acre site was once home to Ohio's only fort in the Revolutionary War, garrisoned during 1778–1779. The compound contains an outline of the stockade, a colorful museum, an interpretive center, and a monument marking the **Tomb of the Unknown Soldier of the Revolutionary War.** *Admission charged.*

8. Massillon

Chamber of Commerce, 137 Lincoln Way E. Built in the 1820's, **Spring Hill** was a stop on the Underground Railroad. The home contains original furnishings, a secret stairway, herb and flower gardens, smokehouse, and springhouse. Set in an 1835 home, the **Massillon Museum** contains historical and art exhibits, period decor, natural-science displays, and collections of quilts, coverlets, and glass. *Admission charged at Spring Hill.*

9. Canton

Convention and Visitors Bureau, 229 Wells Ave. NW. The **Pro Football Hall of Fame** chronicles the sport from 1892 to the present. Visitors to the complex's four buildings will find photographs, mementos from honorees, an action football movie every hour, and more. At the **Canton Classic Car Museum** more than 35 Franklins, Rolls-Royces, Pierce Arrows, and other antique automobiles are displayed amid period advertisements and relics. The **McKinley Museum of History, Science and Industry** examines some 200 years of the past and offers interactive science exhibits, a planetarium, and a large collection of memorabilia pertaining to President McKinley. The **McKinley National Memorial,** a 23-acre park in which the president and his family are entombed, is a National Historic Landmark. *Admission charged at museums.*

10. Hoover Historical Center

2225 Easton St. NW, North Canton. This center, the birthplace of the Hoover Company's founder, displays one of the world's most extensive collections of antique vacuum cleaners, as well as a tannery, a restored Victorian-era farmhouse, and herb gardens.

11. Akron

Convention and Visitors Bureau, Cascade Plaza. This city is an important industrial center primarily for major manufacturers of rubber. The fruits of such enterprise are apparent at the **Stan Hywet Hall and Gardens,** considered to be Ohio's largest private home. Built in 1912–15 by a cofounder of the Goodyear Tire and Rubber Company, the 65-room Tudor Revival mansion is set among some 70 acres of gardens. Displays include furniture, Chinese wall hangings, Flemish tapestries, and Persian rugs. The **Goodyear World of Rubber** depicts rubber's history by exhibiting plantation replicas, tire displays, and memorabilia of Charles Goodyear. Other attractions include the **Akron Zoological Park,** which contains close to 300 animals and a children's petting area. The 1837 **Perkins Mansion,** situated next door to the abolitionist John Brown's former home, has antique furnishings. The **Akron Art Museum** showcases international artworks and a sculpture garden. **Quaker Square,** an area of restaurants and shops, is located in the original, now-renovated Quaker Oats Company factory. **Blossom Music Center** is in an 800-acre woodland. The 1871 **Hower House** is a 28-room Victorian mansion with octagonal rooms and family furnishings. *Admission charged for some attractions.*

12. Hale Farm and Village

2686 Oak Hill Rd., Bath. Situated in the 33,000-acre **Cuyahoga Valley National Recreation Area,** this site re-creates rural life as it was in the mid-1800's, with a farmhouse, log schoolhouse, law office, barn, and Federal and Greek Revival buildings. There are also costumed guides on hand to perform traditional skills, such as blacksmithing, pottery making, and glass blowing. *Admission charged.*

13. National McKinley Birthplace Memorial

40 North Main St., Niles. William McKinley, the nation's 25th president, was born here in 1843. The Neoclassical Revival memorial, built in 1915, includes a museum with mementos, furniture, and military artifacts.

14. Youngstown

Convention and Visitors Bureau, 101 City Centre One. The attractions here include **Mill Creek Park,** where there are 6 acres of gardens, a gristmill, hiking trails, waterfalls, and three lakes. The **Butler Institute of American Art** has important antiques and paintings from the United States, including works by Remington, Homer, and Warhol. The **Arms Family Museum of Local History** specializes in the arts and crafts of the early 1900's, with paintings, books, and antiques. The **Youngstown Historical Center of Industry and Labor** chronicles the region's iron and steel industries. *Admission charged for some attractions.*

15. Museum of Ceramics

400 East Fifth St., East Liverpool. This museum contains life-size dioramas of the making of pottery at the turn of the century. Other exhibits are simple yellow wares, porcelains, bone china, and sophisticated Lotus ware. *Admission charged.*

16. Steubenville

Convention and Visitors Bureau, 630 Market St. The **Jefferson County Historical Association Museum,** in a Tudor-style mansion, has 14 rooms with articles from the last two centuries, such as Steubenville glass and model steamboats. **Jefferson County Courthouse** contains the first record of a county deed, signed by George Washington, and a statue of native Edwin Stanton, who was President Lincoln's secretary of war. *Admission charged at museum.*

17. Historic Bethany

Bethany College was chartered in 1840 by Alexander Campbell, cofounder of a large American religious movement, the Disciples of Christ. Self-guiding walking tours of the 300-acre campus pass the 1852 **Old Bethany Meeting House** and the Gothic Revival **Old Main,** styled after Scotland's University of Glasgow. Near the family cemetery, the **Campbell Mansion** showcases 18 rooms in which Campbell's furnishings are displayed, including a rosewood piano and silk wallpaper with scenes from the *Odyssey. Admission charged.*

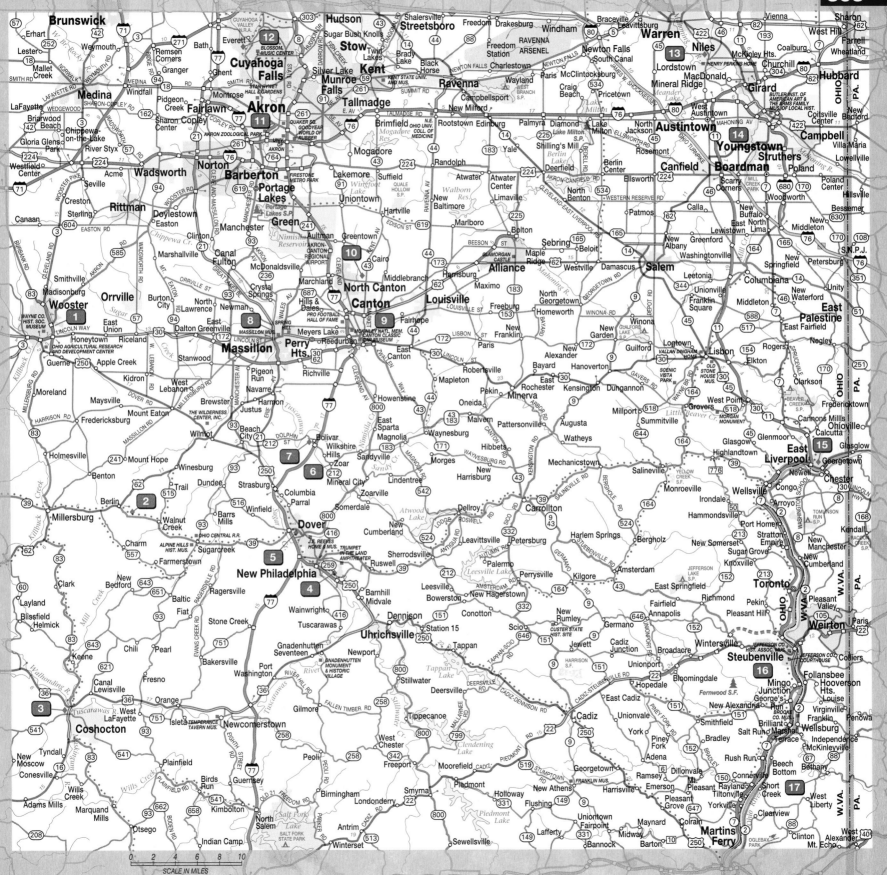

SCALE IN MILES

1. Old Economy Village

Church St., Ambridge. This village was founded in 1825 by the Harmony Society, a religious community of German craftsmen and farmers. The utopians, who practiced celibacy, disbanded in 1905 due to their dwindling population. Among the village's 15 original structures are a music hall and the 22-room **George Rapp House.** Visitors can also tour formal gardens and watch crafts demonstrations. *Admission charged.*

2. Hartwood

215 Saxonburg Blvd., Pittsburgh. This re-created English country estate features a mansion with American and British antiques. The 629-acre grounds have formal gardens and an elaborate farm-and-stable complex. Depending on the season, visitors can hike or cross-country ski. In summer, there are outdoor performances of theater, music, and dance. Tours and horse-drawn hayrides are available. *Admission charged.*

3. Pittsburgh Zoo

Located in Highland Park, this 75-acre zoo displays more than 6,000 animals in simulated natural habitats. Sharks swim in a 92,000-gallon tank, endangered primates inhabit a foggy tropical rain forest, giraffes and elephants roam an African savanna, and Siberian tigers prowl what appears to be an Asian forest. *Admission charged.*

4. Soldiers and Sailors Memorial Hall and Military History Museum

4141 Fifth Ave., Pittsburgh. This building displays memorabilia from the wars fought by the United States. There are photos, uniforms, weapons, sculptures, paintings, flags, and a collection of Civil War relics.

5. Rodef Shalom Biblical Botanical Garden

4905 Fifth Ave., Pittsburgh. Ancient Israel's flora is represented in this garden, where some 150 varieties of flowers and trees grow — each with a biblical name or reference. A stream represents the Jordan River.

6. Clayton

7227 Reynolds St., Pittsburgh. The mansion built on industrialist Henry Clay Frick's estate is considered an outstanding example of Victorian architecture. It contains original furnishings and family memorabilia that provide a real glimpse into the lives of the privileged during the Gilded Age. Visitors can tour the **Carriage Museum,** where vintage automobiles, carriages, and sleighs are displayed. The **Frick Art Museum** houses an important collection of 18th-century paintings as well as tapestries and bronzes. *Admission charged at mansion.*

7. The Carnegie

4400 Forbes Ave., Pittsburgh. This cultural complex was donated to the city by Andrew Carnegie, a steel magnate and philan-thropist. The **Carnegie Museum of Art** displays 19th-century American works, masterpieces by French Impressionists, and contemporary art. The **Carnegie Museum of Natural History** is famous for its collection of dinosaur skeletons, Egyptian artifacts, and rare minerals and gems. Often called an amusement park for the mind, the nearby **Carnegie Science Center** features exhibits that utilize robotics and lasers. There's also an Omnimax theater, as well as an observatory, planetarium, and World War II submarine. *Admission charged.*

8. Phipps Conservatory

Schenley Park, Pittsburgh. A gift from industrialist Henry Phipps, this conservatory contains plants and flowers from around the world. Thirteen display houses exhibit collections of orchids, tropical lilies, palms, roses, and cacti. The facility also maintains a Japanese garden, children's garden, and rock garden. *Admission charged.*

9. University of Pittsburgh

Established in 1787, this university is one of the oldest in America. The **Cathedral of Learning,** a 42-story Gothic stone tower, has more than 20 rooms that are designed to reflect the city's various ethnic influences. The nearby **Heinz Memorial Chapel** is a modern French Gothic structure with a marble altar, carved woodwork, and majestic stained-glass windows. The **Stephen Foster Memorial** displays musical instruments, photographs, and other artifacts that once belonged to the native composer. *Admission charged at cathedral.*

10. Mount Washington Inclines

Grandview Ave., Pittsburgh. In operation since the 1870's, these two cable railways offer rides to the top of Mt. Washington, where far-reaching views of the city can be seen. The **Duquesne Incline,** still using the original cars with cherry and maple interiors, climbs to the restaurant area of Grandview Avenue. The **Monongahela Incline** departs from West Carson Street across from Station Square and ascends to an observation deck. *Fee charged for ride.*

11. Point State Park

101 Commonwealth Pl., Pittsburgh. The park marks the place where the Allegheny and Monongahela rivers meet to form the Ohio River. Within its borders are the traces of five 18th-century forts, the veritable beginnings of Pittsburgh. The city's oldest structure, the **Fort Pitt Blockhouse** served as a lookout point for troops during the French and Indian War. Displaying artifacts and scale models of forts, the **Fort Pitt Museum** depicts the history of the fighting; other exhibits illustrate early life in the Ohio Valley. On Sundays in the summer, military drills are reenacted. *Admission charged at museum.*

12. Allegheny Observatory

Riverview Ave., Pittsburgh. Located in Riverview Park, this is one of the best-known observatories in the country; it boasts a 30-inch telescope. Would-be astronomers can tour the Greek Revival facility to learn about the stars and planets.

13. Pennsylvania Trolley Museum

1 Museum Rd., Washington. Devoted to trolley cars — a popular method of transportation during the first half of the 20th century — this museum features 1920's–1940's streetcars on which visitors can take a mile-long ride. In the car shop, craftsmen restore vintage trolleys, and in the museum some half-dozen fully operational cars are on display, including one example from the famous Desire line in New Orleans. *Admission charged.*

14. LeMoyne House

49 East Maiden St., Washington. This 1812 Greek Revival mansion was the home of antislavery leader Francis LeMoyne, who hid runaway slaves here on their journey north along the Underground Railroad. Outside, there's a 19th-century herb garden once used by Dr. LeMoyne to make medicines. *Admission charged.*

15. Bradford House

175 South Main St., Washington. Built in 1788, this striking stone house reflects the social prominence of its owner, a leader in the 1794 Whiskey Rebellion, which protested the high tax levied on alcoholic beverages. The interior boasts finely crafted woodwork, including a stately mahogany staircase. *Admission charged.*

16. Round Hill Exhibit Farm

651 Round Hill Rd., Elizabeth. Begun in 1790, Round Hill preserves the lifestyle of a typical family-run farm, few of which remain in this area. Attractions include an 1838 house, barns, orchard, herb garden, and cultivated fields. A variety of livestock — cattle, horses, pigs, sheep, and chickens — also evokes farm life. The adjoining park offers picnic sites and a duck pond.

A young visitor meets the chickens at the Round Hill Exhibit Farm.

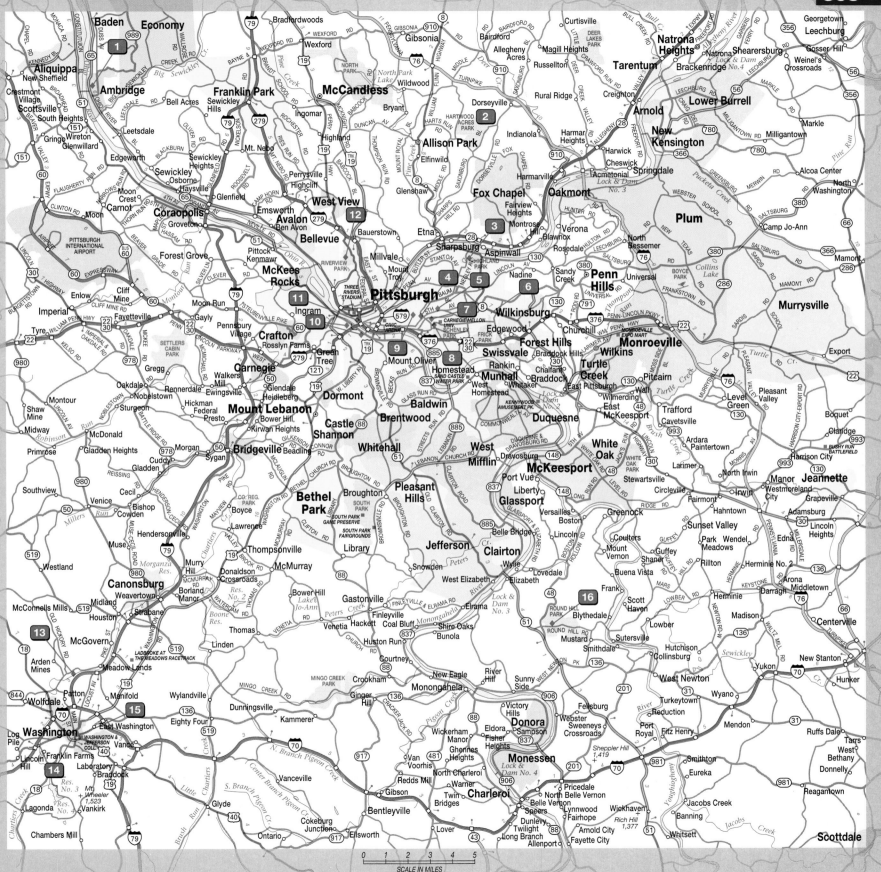

1. Covington

Chamber of Commerce, 241 West Main St. This town's curved, single-span, 100-foot-long covered **Humpback Bridge** was built in 1835. Its hand-hewn oak timbers are held together by pins of locust wood. **Fort Young** is a reconstruction based on a design by George Washington, who, at the age of only 23, was commanding the forces of the colony of Virginia.

2. Lee Memorial Chapel and Museum

The Victorian chapel on the campus of Washington and Lee University is the burial place of Robert E. Lee, who supervised its construction in 1867. Lee was president of the college between 1865 and 1870, and his office, also in the chapel, remains as he left it. A statue of the general is also on view. The museum exhibits items from Lee's family and memorabilia of George Washington.

3. Virginia Military Institute

Rte. 11, Lexington. Founded in 1839, this school is noted for the excellence of its academic and military programs. Before the Civil War, Stonewall Jackson taught artillery tactics and physics at the institute. The **Virginia Military Institute Museum** displays military artifacts, including the raincoat Jackson was wearing when he was shot in the arm at Chancellorsville. Also on the grounds is the **George C. Marshall Museum and Library,** a tribute to one of VMI's most accomplished graduates, who went on to serve as the army's chief of staff during World War II and to create the Marshall Plan, which earned him the 1953 Nobel Peace Prize.

4. Stonewall Jackson House

8 East Washington St., Lexington. Thomas "Stonewall" Jackson bought this simple, Federal-style town house in 1858. He lived in it for two years, then went to fight in the Civil War. Jackson rapidly rose to prominence as a great Confederate commander, but he was accidentally shot and killed by his own troops at the age of 39 in 1863. Dis-

playing many family and personal items, the house has been restored to its 1861 appearance. The nearby **Stonewall Jackson Memorial Cemetery** contains the man's grave; many of his fellow soldiers are also buried here. *Admission charged at house.*

5. Cyrus McCormick Wayside and Museum

Rte. 606, Steeles Tavern. Cyrus McCormick and his father, Robert, invented the grain reaper, which replaced the scythe for harvesting, thereby revolutionizing farming. McCormick later founded the International Harvester Company. Today the blacksmith's shop in which he built the first reaper contains a replica of the 1831 machine and models of other inventions.

6. Lynchburg

Visitor Center, 216 12th St. Today the home of several colleges, Lynchburg was a major hospital and supply center during the Civil War. **Point of Honor** is a Federal Piedmont mansion with twin semi-octagonal bays and a commanding view of the James River. Built by Dr. George Cabell, physician to Patrick Henry, the house features finely crafted woodwork, furniture, and decorative arts. The **Pest House Medical Museum** illustrates the medical practices of the late 1800's. *Admission charged at mansion.*

7. Poplar Forest

Rte. 661, southwest of Lynchburg. This Palladian-style house was designed by Thomas Jefferson as a retreat from his sometimes hectic life at Monticello. The eight-sided residence contains six rooms, of which all but one, the dining room, are also shaped as octagons or bisected octagons. Guided tours of the house are offered. *Admission charged.*

8. James River Visitor Center

At mile 63 on the Blue Ridge Parkway, this center illustrates the history of the James River and Kanawha Canal, which opened the mountains to the outside world in the mid-19th century. Visitors can take a walkway across a river to a restored canal lock; the site also offers a variety of hiking trails and fishing spots. The center itself is open from mid-May through October.

9. Natural Bridge of Virginia

Within this resort village is **Natural Bridge,** a monumental limestone arch over Cedar Creek. The span is 90 feet long, 215 feet high, and up to 150 feet wide. The re-

sult of millions of years of erosion, the formation joins two mountains and supports a part of Rte. 11. George Washington carved his initials in one wall when he surveyed here, and Thomas Jefferson bought the arch and 175 surrounding acres from King George III. A 45-minute light-and-sound show is presented each night beneath the span. At the entrance to the bridge, the **Natural Bridge Wax Museum** exhibits historical figures, and the tour of its factory reveals how the wax figures are made. *Admission charged.*

10. Peaks of Otter

From the summit of Sharp Top Mountain, accessible by a bus ride or steep hiking trail, there's a panorama of the Piedmont plateau, the Blue Ridge Mountains, and the Shenandoah Valley. Other hiking trails lead to the summit of Flat Top Mountain, the cascades on Fallingwater Creek, and the **Johnson Farm,** which has living-history demonstrations. The visitor center, at mile 86 of the Blue Ridge Parkway, has exhibits on regional history. *Fee charged for bus ride.*

11. Booker T. Washington National Monument

Rte. 122, southeast of Roanoke. The 1856 birthplace of the renowned educator and civil rights leader, this 223-acre plantation is a living-history museum that examines the lives of slaves. The one-room log cabin where Washington lived has been reconstructed, and 19th-century farming methods are demonstrated in summer. A self-guiding walking trail chronicles events in his life, which began in bondage. He would later found the Tuskegee Institute and advise three presidents. *Admission charged.*

12. Virginia Museum of Transportation

303 Norfolk Ave., Roanoke. Vintage steam, electric, and diesel locomotives bring railroad history to life in this museum. There are dozens of cars and engines, many built

in Roanoke, including a huge Nickel Plate locomotive. Visitors can also see classic automobiles, carriages, models of spacecraft, and a miniature traveling circus complete with a bandwagon drawn by 40 horses. *Admission charged.*

13. Center in the Square

1 Market Sq., Roanoke. This cultural center encompasses the **Mill Mountain Theatre** and three museums. The **Art Museum of Western Virginia** displays the works of Old Masters, 19th-century Americans, and Appalachian folk artists. The history of the region is highlighted at the **Roanoke Valley History Museum,** while the **Science Museum of Western Virginia** features interactive exhibits on natural history and a planetarium. *Admission charged for some attractions.*

14. Dixie Caverns

5753 West Main St., Salem. Estimated to be more than 100,000 years old, this cavern has several chambers containing unusual formations created by the constant dripping of mineral-laden water. Guided 45-minute tours lead uphill past shapes resembling the Leaning Tower of Pisa, a Portuguese warship, and a paratrooper. The dome-shaped Wedding Bell is popular with couples exchanging vows. *Admission charged.*

15. Smithfield Plantation House

Off Rte. 460, Blacksburg. Built in 1772 by Col. William Preston, this white clapboard plantation house remained in the family for nearly 200 years. The interior features a Chinese Chippendale staircase, a cupboard made on the plantation, and a striking mantelpiece in the drawing room. The basement contains the Michael-Schultz collection of Indian artifacts, which were unearthed in southwest Virginia and date to 7000 B.C. In the kitchen garden, vegetables, fruits, and herbs typical of late-18th-century gardens are grown. *Admission charged.*

Once used as a slave quarters, this small cabin at the Booker T. Washington National Monument was the early home of the educator and civil rights advocate. He went on to spark nationwide debate on the integration of African-Americans.

1. Winchester

Chamber of Commerce, 1360 South Pleasant Valley Rd. Winchester was an important site during the French and Indian Wars and the Civil War. **George Washington's Office Museum** is a small log and stone building that served as his office during the construction of Ft. Loudoun; today it displays military relics and a model fort. A limestone house built in 1754, **Abram's Delight Museum** is furnished in period style. **Stonewall Jackson's Headquarters Museum** preserves items from Jackson's winter encampment here in 1861–62. *Admission charged.*

2. Antietam National Battlefield

Rte. 65, near Sharpsburg. The Battle of Antietam was fought here on September 17, 1862. More than 23,000 soldiers were killed, wounded, or missing — making it the bloodiest single-day battle in the Civil War. About 4,000 Union soldiers are interred in the national cemetery. A visitor center has displays and a film. *Admission charged.*

3. Frederick

Visitor Center, 19 East Church St. The **Barbara Fritchie House and Museum** commemorates the indomitable woman, who, according to legend, waved a Union flag at Stonewall Jackson and his troops. **Trinity Chapel** has a stone tower dating to 1763. At the **Evangelical Reformed Church,** Stonewall Jackson reportedly slept through a pro-Union sermon before the battle of Antietam. With its 30-inch-thick walls and a vaulted food cellar, **Schifferstadt** is a fine example of German Colonial architecture. *Admission charged for some attractions.*

4. Leesburg

Visitors Bureau, Market Station. A mile-long drive leads to Morven Park, where an impressive 16-room mansion displays lush tapestries and furnishings. The north wing houses the **Museum of Hounds and Hunting.** On the grounds is the **Winmill Carriage Museum.** The **Oatlands Plantation** is a large estate, with a stately Greek Revival mansion and formal gardens displaying beautiful boxwood. Horse races and shows are held on the fields. *Admission charged for some attractions.*

5. Manassas National Battlefield Park

Visitor Center, off Rte. 234, Manassas. Two major Civil War battles were fought here: Waged in 1861, the First Manassas, known as Bull Run, earned Thomas Jonathan Jackson his nickname, Stonewall. Some 13 months later, Robert E. Lee's troops defeated Union forces on this same site. The visitor center has exhibits and audiovisual presentations, and both self-guiding walking and driving tours are available.

6. Fredericksburg and Spotsylvania National Military Park

Visitor Center, Lafayette Blvd. and Sunken Rd., Fredericksburg. This 7,500-acre park was witness to four Civil War battles. Self-guiding tours of the area include **Chatham Manor,** which was used as a Union field hospital, and **Fredericksburg National Cemetery.** Nearby are the **Stonewall Jackson Shrine,** where the general died, and **Old Salem Church,** a sanctuary for women and children during the fighting.

7. Fredericksburg

Visitor Center, 706 Caroline St. Historic sites here include the **Rising Sun Tavern,** a stagecoach stop in the 1700's; the **Mary Washington House,** bought by George Washington for his mother in 1772; and **Kenmore,** a Georgian manor built for Col. Fielding Lewis, who married Washington's sister. The **James Monroe Museum and Memorial Library** houses thousands of the fifth president's papers and artifacts, including the desk at which he wrote the Monroe Doctrine. *Admission charged.*

8. Stratford Hall Plantation

Off Rte. 214, Stratford. This superb Colonial mansion was home to four generations of the Lee family, including two brothers who signed the Declaration of Independence and the Confederate general, Robert E. Lee. *Admission charged.*

9. Historic St. Marys City

Rosecroft Rd., St. Marys City. On the site of Maryland's first capital, this 800-acre outdoor museum includes a reproduction of the 1676 State House, a replica of a 17th-century square-rigged ship, and an authentic Indian longhouse. *Admission charged.*

10. Chesapeake Bay Maritime Museum

Mill St. at Navy Point, St. Michaels. Life along the Chesapeake is illustrated by the exhibits that include a historic lighthouse, a dugout canoe, outlawed hunting boats, and carved decoys. *Admission charged.*

11. Historic Houses of Odessa

109 Main St., Odessa. Guided tours give visitors the opportunity to examine 18th- and 19th-century buildings. Built in 1774, the **Corbit-Sharp House** is a lovely mid-Georgian-style house that is furnished with many original pieces. Documents and various artifacts at the 1769 **Wilson-Warner House** trace its owner's fall into bankruptcy. An 1822 hotel and tavern, the **Brick Hotel** exhibits some 70 pieces of elaborately carved Belter furniture. *Admission charged.*

12. New Castle

This city was the first capital of Delaware. It features the **Old New Castle Court House,** which was once the capitol of colonial Delaware. The **Amstel House,** the residence of a former governor, is now a colonial museum. Dating to about 1800, the brick **Dutch House** is furnished in the Dutch Colonial style. The **George Read II House and Garden** is an elegant Federal-style house completed in 1804. *Admission charged for some attractions.*

13. Winterthur Museum, Garden and Library

Rte. 52, northwest of Wilmington. An extensive collection of decorative arts from 1640 to 1860 is housed at Winterthur; natural gardens surround the mansion. Nearby, on the site of the original Du Pont mills, is the **Hagley Museum and Library,** where a machine shop and a restored workers' community depict 19th-century life. **Eleutherian Mills,** built in 1803, is the Du Pont ancestral home. Also in the area is **Longwood Gardens;** once the estate of Pierre S. du Pont, it has a vast conservatory, formal gardens, fountains, lakes, and woodlands. *Admission charged.*

14. Dover

Visitor Center, 406 Federal St. The 1792 **State House** has been restored to its original appearance. Featuring archeological displays, the **Meeting House Galleries I and II** contain exhibits on state history and archaeology. The **Johnson Victrola Museum** has collections of Victor records as well as antique phonographs.

15. Trenton

Convention and Visitors Bureau, Willow and Lafayette Sts. The **New Jersey State Museum** has a planetarium and exhibits on the fine arts, natural and cultural histories, and archeology. The **Old Barracks Museum** is an outstanding example of a British Colonial barracks. *Admission charged for some attractions.*

16. Princeton University

Nassau Hall was the site of brief fighting in the Revolutionary War; it also served as the temporary home of the Continental Congress. The **University Chapel** houses a pulpit and lectern from mid-16th-century France. Sculptures by Picasso, Calder, and Moore dot the campus grounds.

17. Clinton Historical Museum

56 Main St., Clinton. The lives of area residents from 1810 to 1918 are portrayed here with an old schoolhouse, a general store, a tenant's house, a 19th-century gristmill, and a limestone quarry. *Admission charged.*

18. Bethlehem

Tourism Authority, 509 Main St. The oldest standing structure in the city, the 1741 **Moravian Museum** exhibits artifacts from early settlers. Moravian ingenuity shines in the **Historic Bethlehem 18th Century Industrial Area,** which includes a restored waterworks, a tannery, and a gristmill. *Admission charged.*

19. Morristown National Historical Park

Rte. 510, Morristown. This was the country's first national historical park. It contains log huts typical of those inhabited by the Continental Army, a house used as headquarters by George Washington, and a museum displaying 18th-century weapons, documents, and other artifacts. *Admission charged at headquarters.*

20. Morristown

Chamber of Commerce, 10 Park Ave. The **Morris Museum** displays artworks, costumes, and exhibits on the natural sciences. The **Macculloch Hall Historical Museum and Gardens** features period furnishings and a collection of political cartoons drawn by Thomas Nast. The first steamship to cross the Atlantic had its engine built in **Historic Speedwell.** The first telegraph was also perfected here. *Admission charged for some attractions.*

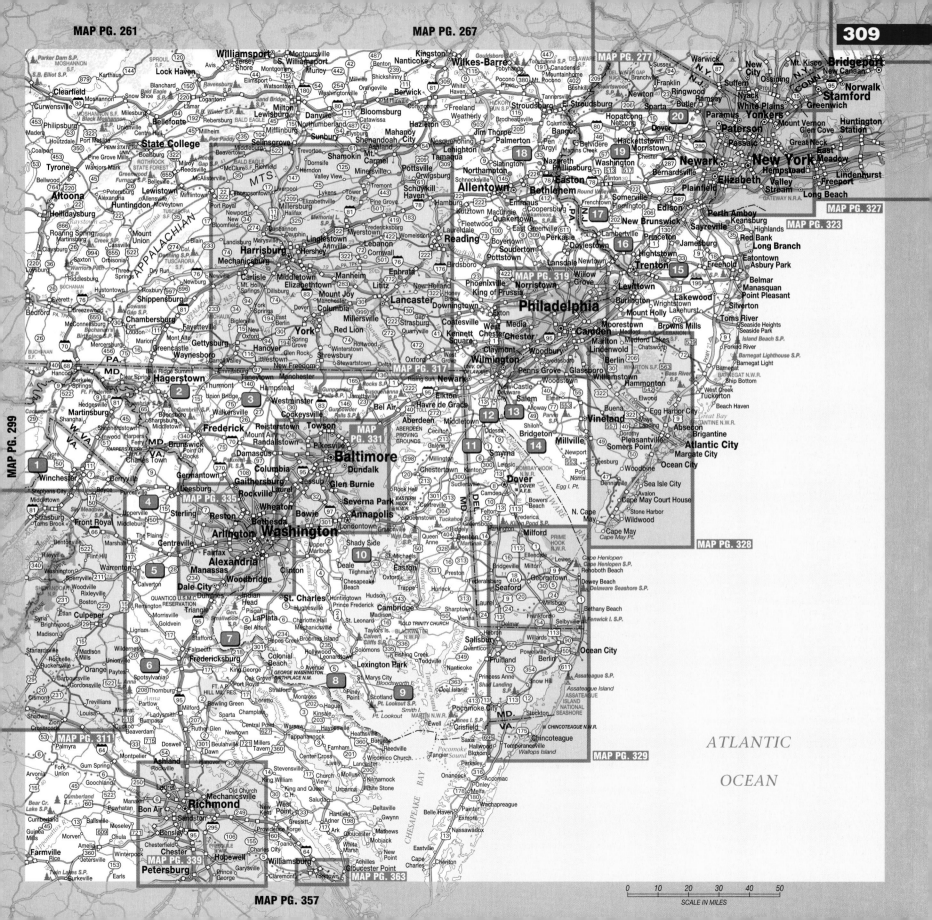

1. Smoke Hole Caverns

Rte. 59, near Petersburg. Among the remarkable formations here is a ribbon stalactite, said to be the world's longest. In the past, the cavern was used by Indians for smoking meat and by settlers for making moonshine. A wildlife museum and cabins are available. *Admission charged.*

2. Belle Grove

Rte. 727, Middletown. Partially designed by Thomas Jefferson, the mansion at this 100-acre estate is a museum and educational center. The grounds function as a working farm. This was Gen. Philip Sheridan's headquarters during the Battle of Cedar Creek in 1864. *Admission charged.*

3. Front Royal

Chamber of Commerce, 414 East Main St. Once a frontier outpost, this town is now the northern gateway to Shenandoah National Park. The **Warren Heritage Society Museum** has exhibits on Belle Boyd, a Confederate spy, and maintains the cottage where she lived. Front Royal's role in the Civil War is documented in the **Warren Rifles Confederate Museum.** *Admission charged.*

4. Skyline Caverns

Off Rte. 340, Front Royal. These caverns are known for unique flowerlike formations of calcite, called anthodites. Other highlights on the guided tour here include a 37-foot waterfall and a light-and-sound show. Picnic areas are available near the cave's entrance. *Admission charged.*

5. Dickey Ridge Visitor Center

Mile 4.6, Skyline Dr., Shenandoah National Park. A slide program is shown here, and maps are available to help visitors explore the scenic hiking trails, some of which lead past picturesque old homesteads. A nearly 100-mile-long section of the Appalachian Trail also runs through the park. Fox Hollow is a self-guiding hike that begins and ends at the center. *Admission charged.*

6. Culpeper

Chamber of Commerce, 133 West Davis St. The young George Washington's first job was to survey this town. In 1863 the largest cavalry encounter in the Civil War was fought nearby. Historical artifacts are on view in the **Museum of Culpeper History.** The **Dominion Wine Cellars** and **Prince Michel Vineyards** provide tours and tastings. *Admission charged for some attractions.*

7. Orange

Chamber of Commerce, 13323 James Madison Hwy. **Montpelier,** the home and burial place of James and Dolley Madison, was begun by Madison's father, enlarged twice by the fourth president, and, in 1844, auctioned off by his impoverished widow. Today the 55-room mansion, doubled in size by William du Pont in 1900, is a 2,700-acre estate that includes a steeplechase course. The **James Madison Museum** displays exhibits on his life, including his two terms as president. *Admission charged.*

8. Monticello

Off Rte. 53, near Charlottesville. In a letter, Thomas Jefferson once rhetorically asked, "Where has Nature spread so rich a mantle under the eye?" He then went on to enumerate the wonders he observed from his mountaintop home. He was to spend some 40 years designing and redesigning a mansion some believe to be the finest in America. Few things on the estate escaped his attention, from the layout of his beloved gardens, to the adding of subtle innovations, to the inscription on his grave marker. The mansion itself contains 43 rooms, of which 11 are open to the public. Nearby, the **Thomas Jefferson Visitors Center** displays some 200 related objects and artifacts. *Admission charged.*

9. Ash Lawn–Highland

Rte. 795, near Charlottesville. Between 1799 and 1826 this was the residence of James Monroe. Surrounded by boxwood gardens near which peacocks roam, the home contains French Empire furnishings, silver, and items from the White House. Guided tours are given, as are demonstrations of cooking, spinning, and weaving. *Admission charged.*

10. Michie Tavern

Rte. 53, Charlottesville. In the 1740's, Patrick Henry's father sold land to John Michie, and the house built upon it became a tavern. One of Virginia's oldest homesteads, it was moved to its present location during the

Thomas Jefferson's Monticello

1920's. There are also restored outbuildings and a wine museum. *Admission charged.*

11. University of Virginia

Thomas Jefferson thought highly of education and, with that in mind, undertook the creation of this university in Charlottesville, which began offering classes in 1825. He laid out the campus, designed the original buildings, selected the curriculum, recruited faculty, and then served as rector. The magnificent 1826 Rotunda is the meeting place for guided tours of the school.

12. Humpback Rocks Visitor Center

Mile 5.8, Blue Ridge Pkwy. At the southern terminus of the Skyline Drive, the 470-mile-long Blue Ridge Parkway begins, connecting Shenandoah National Park with Great Smoky Mountains National Park. Hundreds of scenic overlooks line the way, including Humpback Rocks, where the center has a reconstruction of a mountain farm, called **Pioneer Village.**

13. Staunton

Tourist Information Center, 1303 Richmond Ave. The nation's 28th president was born in the **Woodrow Wilson Birthplace,** an 1846 Greek Revival mansion containing many original furnishings, antiques, and memorabilia; even his 1920 Pierce-Arrow limousine is displayed in the carriage house. A short film about Wilson is shown in the reception center. At the **Museum of American Frontier Culture,** costumed interpreters work on re-created farmlands, demonstrating how the cultures of Northern Ireland, Germany, and England blended with that of Virginia. *Admission charged.*

14. Natural Chimneys Regional Park

Off Rte. 731, Mt. Solon. The park's exotic formations tower 120 feet. Other attractions include camping, swimming, picnicking, nature walks, biking trails, and a jousting tournament that has been held here in August ever since 1821. *Admission charged.*

15. Shenandoah Valley Heritage Museum

115 Bowman Rd., Dayton. Displaying photos, artifacts, and documents, this museum examines the Civil War. One exhibit reviews Stonewall Jackson's Valley Campaign of 1862.

16. New Market

Chamber of Commerce, Rte. 211. Visitors can tour underground realms at both the **Shenandoah Caverns** and the **Endless Caverns.** The **Tuttle & Spice General Store and Museum** displays early Americana, including antique toys and a doctor's office. The **New Market Battlefield Historical Park** commemorates a costly Confederate victory. *Admission charged.*

17. Luray Caverns

Rte. 211, Luray. These extensive chambers cover some 64 subterranean acres. Guided tours are available, in which visitors can see exotic stalactites, stalagmites, clear-water pools, and other intriguing formations. *Admission charged.*

18. Skyland

Mile 41.7, Skyline Dr., Shenandoah National Park. At an altitude of 3,680 feet, this is the highest point on the Skyline Drive. There are several nature and bridle trails, a nearby stable, campfire programs, and guided walks. The self-guiding Stony Man Nature Trail is a 1-hour round-trip wilderness hike. *Admission charged.*

19. Harry F. Byrd, Sr. Visitor Center

Mile 51, Skyline Dr., Shenandoah National Park. Information and maps are available here, as well as a film on the history of this region. **Big Meadows,** a natural clearing in the woods, offers campgrounds, trailer sites, picnic areas, and nature trails. Nearby, horseback riding is available. *Admission charged.*

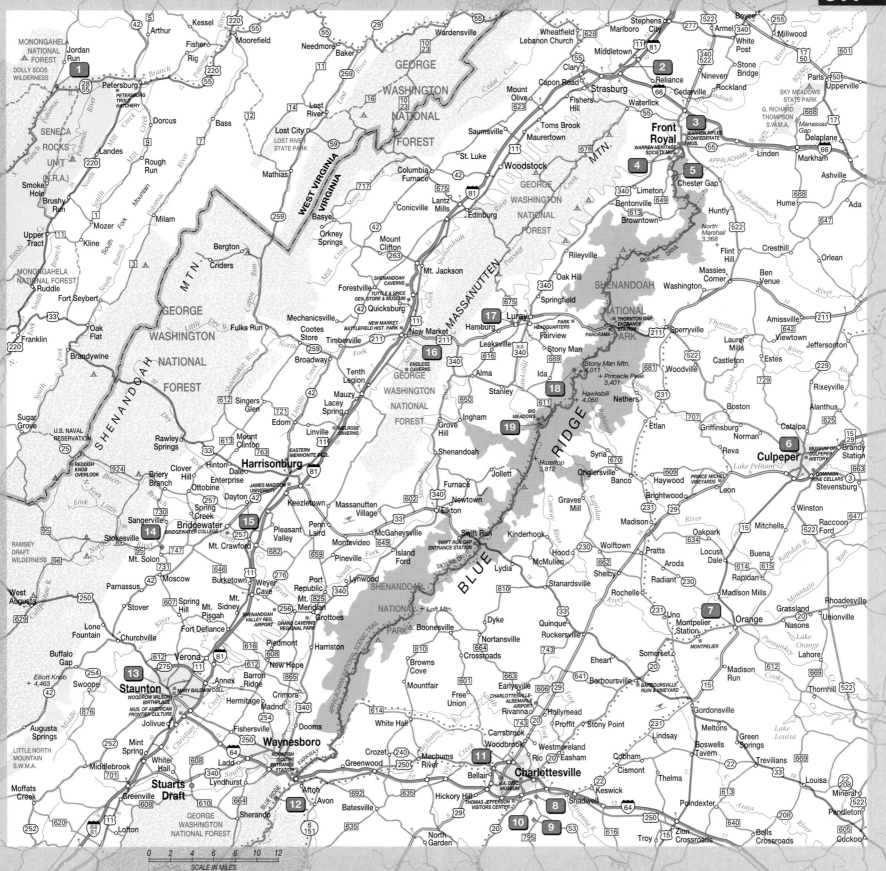

SCALE IN MILES
0   2   4   6   8   10   12

APPALACHIAN TRAIL
Mt. Katahdin, ME to Manchester, VT

In 1921, naturalist Benton MacKaye first proposed the idea of a footpath along the crest of the Appalachian Mountains. A few years later, he formed the Appalachian Trail Conference with others who shared his vision. Volunteers and workers began constructing new trails to connect existing trails and the Appalachian Trail became a reality: a continuous, marked footpath stretching some 2,140 miles through 14 states, from Maine to Georgia.

1. Baxter State Park

This park encompasses 5,267-foot-high **Mount Katahdin,** the highest point in the state, which serves as the trail's northern terminus. To reach its summit, visitors must make an arduous climb. An easier hike passes both Big and Little Niagara falls on the Nesowadnehunk Stream. Among the park's several campgrounds are those at Daicey Pond and Katahdin Stream. *Admission charged.*

2. Abol Bridge

Hikers to this area follow in the footsteps of Henry David Thoreau, who camped here in the 1840's. Today a campground and store are at the eastern end of the span, which can be reached from the Appalachian Trail or by car from Millinocket. *Toll charged for road.*

3. Gulf Hagas

This slate canyon forms a dramatic passageway for the Pleasant River. An offshoot of the Appalachian Trail, a circuit route passes along the rim of Gulf Hagas. The area can also be reached by the **Katahdin Iron Works** approach, a rough road off Rte. 11 that leads past a restored 19th-century iron-smelting works. *Admission charged.*

4. Rangeley

Chamber of Commerce, Main St. The 30-mile section of the Appalachian Trail near this town crosses seven high peaks — a scenic but often difficult hike. Beginning near Rangeley, another trail, a 5-mile day hike, ascends Saddleback Mountain. Lakes, ponds, and woodlands blanket this area, which offers a variety of accommodations. **Rangeley State Park** has camping facilities and a beach. *Admission charged at park.*

5. Mount Washington

After the trail enters the White Mountains from the north, it wends for nearly 13 miles to reach the top of 6,288-foot-high Mt. Washington, where the view is what P. T. Barnum once described as "the second-greatest show on earth." Relatively easier and quicker routes to the peak include the hairpin-turning **Auto Road** and the steam-powered **Cog Railway.** The mountain's treeless summit is home to the **Sherman Adams Summit Building,** which contains a glass-enclosed viewing area and a museum that has displays on history and nature. *Admission charged for some attractions.*

A bull moose in Baxter State Park

6. Crawford Notch State Park

A landslide stormed down a mountainside here in the 1820's, killing Samuel Willey and his family, but leaving their home untouched. Today the **Willey House Site** is located near parking for visitors. A trail leading to **Arethusa Falls** and the **Silver and Flume cascades** can be accessed from the park. *Admission charged at park.*

7. Franconia Notch State Park

This deep valley contains several natural phenomena, including the **Old Man of the Mountain,** a stone likeness of a human face; the **Basin,** a deep glacial pothole polished smooth by a waterfall; and the **Flume,** where a mountain stream flows down an 800-foot-long chasm. Just north of the visitor center at the Flume is a parking lot. From here, hikers can take the 1-mile Whitehouse Trail to the Appalachian Trail, which crosses Rte. 3 at the Whitehouse Bridge. Near the intersection is Lafayette Campground. The park also boasts an aerial tramway, which travels to the summit of Cannon Mountain. *Admission charged for some attractions.*

8. Hanover

Chamber of Commerce, 37 South Main St. This town is home to Dartmouth College, where, in summer, the Dartmouth Outing Club provides information to hikers, who can park in a college lot. Also on campus is a cottage where Daniel Webster once lived. Hanover's **League of New Hampshire Craftsmen** displays artwork by state residents. As it exits the southern part of town, the Appalachian Trail crosses easy terrain, except for two steep ascents.

9. Woodstock

Chamber of Commerce, 18 Central St. Visitors can take walking tours of this town's charming historic district. The attractions include the 1807 **Dana House,** home of the Woodstock Historical Society; the **Vermont Institute of Natural Science,** with more than 25 species of birds of prey; and the **Billings Farm & Museum,** encompassing both a modern and an 1890's farm. *Admission charged for some attractions.*

10. Gifford Woods State Park

Many migratory birds live among the sugar maples, alders, and other hardwood trees in this park. Anglers enjoy the fishing at Kent Pond, and Deer Leap offers extraordinary views. Many campsites are available. *Admission charged at park.*

11. Stratton Pond

A popular spot on the trail is Stratton Pond, a well-kept area with a campsite. As it leaves the pond, the trail climbs **Stratton Mountain,** where a fire tower affords a panoramic view. The 6-mile **Stratton Pond Trail,** starting at the Kelley Stand Road, offers an alternative way to explore the pond's habitats.

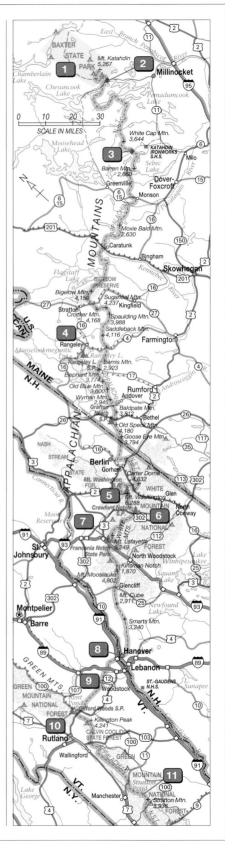

APPALACHIAN TRAIL
Manchester, VT to Harrisburg, PA

1. Mount Greylock

This is the highest point in Massachusetts, and the trail, as it passes through the dense forest here, becomes a virtual tunnel. The 11,000-acre **Mount Greylock State Reservation** has an extensive network of side trails. Other than driving, the fastest route to the mountain's top is the 3-mile **Cheshire Harbor Trail.** Interesting nearby towns include Williamstown, home of Williams College; North Adams, which boasts a restored railroad yard called **Western Gateway Heritage State Park;** and Pittsfield, containing **Arrowhead,** the house where Herman Melville wrote *Moby Dick. Admission charged at Arrowhead.*

2. Sages Ravine

The trail bisects this valley, graced with lovely trees and a fern-edged stream. Just to the north is the **Mount Everett State Reservation,** where the upper parking area has views of three states.

3. Salisbury

Chamber of Commerce, 24 Main St. The inns in this town often lodge Appalachian Trail travelers and the local school offers free showers. Most of the walks in the area are moderately difficult, but those to the summits of **Bear Mountain** and **Lion's Head** reward hardy hikers with excellent views. Nearby Sharon is home to the **Northeast Audubon Center,** a wildlife sanctuary with 11 miles of trails. *Admission charged at sanctuary.*

4. Kent

As it passes by this town, the trail follows the western side of the Housatonic River, an excellent area for bird-watching. The route is lined with woods and leads to **St. John's Ledges,** a series of craggy ridges that affords excellent views.

5. Pawling

Another interesting section along the trail is the somewhat swampy **Pawling Nature Preserve,** home to crumbling stone walls, abandoned orchards, and other vestiges of past farmers. Hikers can purchase supplies in town.

6. Clarence Fahnestock State Park

After it traverses a series of steep ascents, the Appalachian Trail becomes relatively level here. Passing through this park, a segment of the trail follows a narrow-gauge railroad bed. Fishing enthusiasts can try for trout, bass, and panfish in this region's many lakes and streams. There are also a number of campsites.

7. Bear Mountain and Harriman State Parks

The ancient mountains of these popular adjoining parks encompass many lakes and trails. The first official segment of the Appalachian Trail was completed here in 1923. Today, as it enters these parks from the north, the trail crosses the Hudson River via a spectacular suspension bridge. The **Trailside Museum & Zoo** marks the lowest elevation of the trail, which then climbs to the top of Bear Mountain. Cars can also reach the summit, with its sightseeing tower and picnic area.

8. Warwick

Chamber of Commerce, South St. and Railroad Ave. This historic town boasts many old homes, some of which date back more than 200 years and are open to visitors. Warwick and the nearby village of Greenwood Lake — on the opposite side of the trail — both provide lodging accommodations. The trail offers fine views as it passes above the lake itself.

9. High Point State Park

Set along the crest of Kittatinny Mountain, this wooded park offers a variety of outdoor activities. On the mountain named High Point, a stone monument marks New Jersey's highest elevation. The trail climbs to just below the marker, where an observation platform affords a panorama of three states. Leaving the park to the south, the trail moves into **Stokes State Forest,** which has many other footpaths, some intersecting the trail. *Admission charged.*

10. Delaware Water Gap National Recreation Area

The trail crosses the Delaware River at the Delaware Water Gap. The numerous activities in this recreation area include camping, boating, swimming, fishing, picnicking, and hiking. Still following Kittatinny Mountain, the trail, though rocky, remains relatively level. A 1½-mile, sometimes steep side trail leads to the beautiful **Buttermilk Falls.** On weekends in nearby **Peters Valley,** craftworkers allow visitors to tour their studios, which are housed in historic buildings. Campsites are available in **Worthington State Forest,** where the trail passes the glacial **Sunfish Pond.** A bit farther south, side trails climb to the summit of Mt. Tammany, which overlooks the gap and eastern Pennsylvania.

11. Hawk Mountain Sanctuary

Hawk Mt. Rd., near Eckville. Visitors from all over the world come to this sanctuary in autumn when migrating hawks, eagles, and other birds of prey congregate here. Two overlooks offer splendid year-round viewing. A short side trail, which can be accessed from the Appalachian Trail, leads to an escarpment with magnificent views. *Admission charged.*

The Appalachian Trail crosses the Hudson River via the Bear Mountain Bridge.

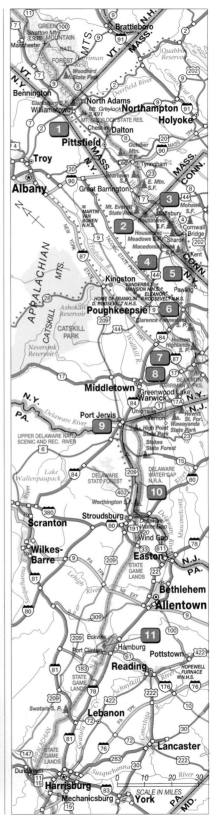

APPALACHIAN TRAIL
Harrisburg, PA to Blacksburg, VA

1. Cumberland Valley

The trail here winds past forest, farm pastures, and intriguing rock formations. An interesting site along the way is **Boiling Springs,** an iron-mining center in the 18th century and a summer resort in the 19th century. Structures from both eras have been preserved. They include a restored blast furnace, a 23-room mansion, and two brick-gabled churches. Trout fishing is popular at the town's spring-fed lake.

2. Pine Grove Furnace State Park

Trail hikers can stop here to swim, fish, boat, camp, bicycle, and even ski. The park preserves the ruins of an iron furnace, where cannonballs were made during the Revolutionary War. Evidence of the many ironworks from the period exists all along this part of the trail. There's also a museum on the region's past, explaining both its industry and its natural history.

3. Gathland State Park

The trail from Turners Gap to Crampton Gap is relatively easy. At the park earthworks and historical markers commemorate a Civil War battle that took place at Crampton Gap; there is also a memorial to war correspondents. Heading south, at the Potomac River, the trail joins the Chesapeake & Ohio Canal towpath, which offers hikers a chance to inspect both the waterway and surrounding wilderness. Camping is available throughout the **Chesapeake & Ohio Canal National Historical Park.** Nearby, the **Antietam National Battlefield** was the site during the Civil War of an extremely bloody battle. *Admission charged for some attractions.*

4. Harpers Ferry

Visitor Center, Rte. 340. Trail hikers cross the Potomac River into Harpers Ferry, home of the **Appalachian Trail Conference** headquarters. A walking tour of the **Harpers Ferry National Historical Park** includes **John Brown's Fort,** a brick structure once used by Brown and the other abolitionist raiders, and the **Master Armorer's House,** now a firearms-making museum. The trail leads through town to **Jefferson Rock,** an immense, balanced boulder offering a view considered "stupendous" by Thomas Jefferson.

5. Sky Meadows State Park

This large park encompasses a fishing pond, hiking and riding trails, viewing points, picnic areas, and hike-in camping facilities. In spring, the site blossoms with hundreds of trilliums. Mosby's Rangers, a Confederate force, once spent time in this area. One Confederate officer returned to buy **Mount Bleak House,** a late 1790's mansion that now holds the visitor center. *Admission charged.*

6. Shenandoah National Park

This magnificent park's 500 miles of trails include nearly 100 miles of the Appalachian Trail, which can be accessed from many of the parking overlooks on the **Skyline Drive.** White-tailed deer and other wildlife often appear along the trail, which is fairly smooth and easy for a mountain path. Side trails lead to a hemlock stand, known as Limberlost, and pass shimmering streams to the splendid Whiteoak Canyon. Following the crest of the Blue Ridge Mountains, the Skyline Drive is a wonderfully scenic alternative to walking. *Admission charged.*

7. George Washington National Forest

Some 65 miles of the Appalachian Trail traverse high mountain peaks and low valleys through a portion of this vast forest due south of Shenandoah National Park. Spanning four mountain ranges, the region contains several recreation areas, including **Sherando Lake,** where visitors can fish, camp, and swim. *Admission charged for some attractions.*

8. McAfee Knob

From the parking lot on Rte. 311, the trail ascends Catawba Mountain to McAfee Knob, an overhanging rock ledge. Although the climb is difficult in spots and takes at least two hours, the spectacular views of the Catawba and Roanoke valleys make it worthwhile. To the east, the **Blue Ridge Parkway** offers a splendid route through the mountains. Off the parkway, the city of Roanoke is home to the **Center in the Square,** which contains several museums. *Admission charged for some attractions.*

9. Dragon's Tooth

The trail in this section follows the crest of Cove Mountain to Dragon's Tooth, a monolithic rock offering excellent views. The trail also crosses Trout Creek Gorge and climbs Brush Mountain. On the way, it passes the **Audie Murphy Monument,** the site of a plane crash in which Murphy, America's most decorated soldier in World War II, was killed. An overlook behind the monument has fine views of the countryside.

Charming Harpers Ferry lies at the confluence of the Potomac and Shenandoah rivers.

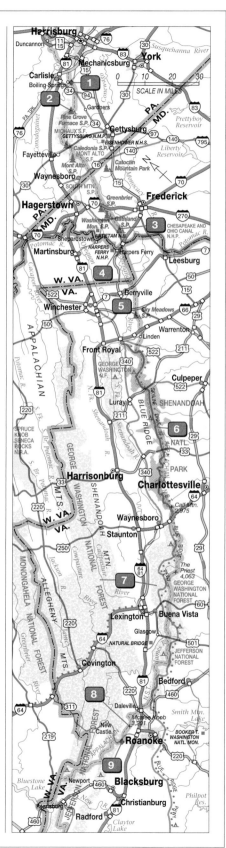

APPALACHIAN TRAIL
Blacksburg, VA to Springer Mtn., GA

1. Mount Rogers National Recreation Area

About 60 miles of the trail pass through this portion of the **Jefferson National Forest.** Intersecting footpaths lead to opportunities for swimming, horseback riding, picnicking, and fishing. Farther south, the trail runs through **Grayson Highlands State Park,** where mountain folklore and crafts can be seen in the visitor center and in reconstructed cabins. Both the **Beartree and Hurricane campgrounds** offer access to the trail. *Admission charged.*

2. Laurel Fork Gorge

Flowering shrubs, cascading waterfalls, wooded slopes, and sheer cliffs make this another highlight along the Appalachian Trail. This section includes the **Watauga Dam,** with dazzling views of Pond Mountain and Watauga Lake. Swimmers and water-skiers enjoy the waters, and campsites and cabins are available. Just west of Elizabethton, the **Sycamore Shoals State Historic Area** preserves colonial buildings.

3. Roan High Knob

A 600-acre rhododendron garden, blooming each June into a veritable sea of purple, lies on this mountain summit. It can be reached by both a highway and the trail. Situated at its base is **Roan Mountain State Park,** which has a swimming pool, playground, picnic areas, campsites, cabins, and opportunities to fish and cross-country ski.

4. Max Patch

Once used as a landing strip for biplanes, this mountaintop meadow encompasses 392 acres of grass and wildflowers. People come to the open area to walk, fly kites, camp, and gaze at extraordinary vistas of both the Black and the Great Smoky mountains. Surrounded by the **Pisgah National Forest,** the nearby town of **Hot Springs** features mineral baths, and the trail goes down the main street, where the locals have been known to welcome hikers to town.

5. Great Smoky Mountains National Park

The trail runs the length of this spectacular park, located in both Tennessee and North Carolina, where lofty peaks pierce the cloudy haze — hence the name *smoky.* At an elevation of 6,643 feet, **Clingmans Dome** is the highest point on the trail; its observation tower overlooks three states. Drivers can reach it via an approach off the scenic **Newfound Gap Road,** which crosses the park. At the road's north entrance are park headquarters and the **Sugarlands Visitor Center.** At its south entrance stands the **Oconaluftee Visitor Center,** with a restored 19th-century farmstead next door.

6. Fontana Dam

The trail crosses the Little Tennessee River at this dam, the highest one east of the Rockies. Hot showers are available, and trail shelters are nearby. On the other side, **Fontana Village,** first formed for dam workers, offers extensive facilities, including a lodge, drugstore, and laundry. This resort's recreational activities feature fishing, boating, and swimming in **Fontana Lake,** as well as horseback riding, biking, tennis, and golf. From here the trail becomes difficult, making steep ascents and descents over jagged ridges.

7. Wayah Bald

The trail threads through the **Nantahala National Forest** to the summit of Wayah Bald — a high, treeless area with an observation tower. The trail in this section climbs several peaks, with both rugged and relatively easy ascents. Water runs throughout the forest, so fishing, swimming, and white-water canoeing are available. The forest also contains a network of trails and a varied wildlife population.

8. Blood Mountain

Zigzagging along the pitched switchbacks of a designated wilderness area, a rugged 3-mile section of the trail here climbs to the top of Blood Mountain, where an overhanging boulder looks out on the smoky haze of the ancient mountains. The trail descends to **Slaughter Gap,** where a 2.7-mile trail leads to the **Lake Winfield Scott Recreation Area,** with swimming, fishing, and camping. These activities are also available in **Vogel State Park,** where **Lake Trahlyta** rests at the base of Blood Mountain. *Fee charged for parking.*

9. Springer Mountain

A bronze plaque at the summit of this peak marks the southern terminus of the Appalachian Trail. Campsites and a shelter are on hand to accommodate hikers. A road climbs the mountain, and a parking area is about a quarter mile from the trail. Below Springer Mountain lies **Amicalola Falls State Park,** named for its high, silvery cascades. Visitors to the park can hike, picnic, fish for trout, and camp out or stay in cabins or a lodge. *Admission charged at state park.*

The Appalachian Trail through the Great Smoky Mountains National Park; a native tree frog

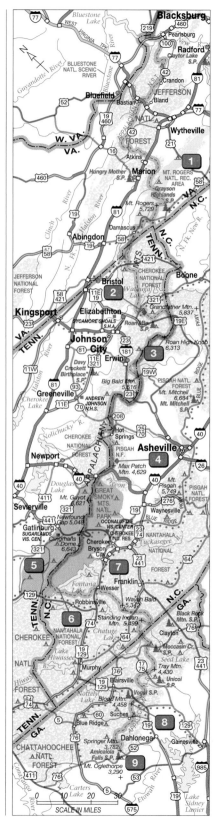

1. Tuscarora State Forest

The roads through this forest lead visitors to the Tuscarora Wild Area, equestrian and cross-country ski trails, creeks for fishing, splendid mountain vistas, giant hemlock trees, and sites for camping and picnicking.

2. Cumberland County Historical Society and Hamilton Library Association

21 North Pitt St., Carlisle. Early mechanical banks, an antique printing press, regional artwork, items from the Carlisle Indian School, and a large library containing extensive genealogical information are among this museum's eclectic collection.

3. Carlisle Barracks

Rte. 11, Carlisle. A museum here in a 1777 Hessian powder magazine has exhibits depicting the history of the complex, once home to the Carlisle Indian School, which was attended by Jim Thorpe, one of the nation's all-time greatest athletes.

4. Huntsdale Fish Cultural Station

195 Lebo Rd., Huntsdale. More than a million fish are produced here annually to stock the waters in many of the state's rivers and lakes. Laced with hiking trails, nearby **King's Gap Environmental Education and Training Center** is a natural forest preserve — home to deer, raccoons, wild turkeys, and other animals.

5. Shrine of St. Elizabeth Ann Seton

333 South Seton Ave., Emmitsburg. Mother Seton was the first American-born citizen to be canonized. This site includes a museum, a basilica, and the home in which she died.

6. Gettysburg

Travel Council, 35 Carlisle St. In the summer of 1863, Union and Confederate forces clashed here in a terrible, blood-soaked battle, today commemorated by the **Gettysburg National Military Park.** Exhibits in the visitor center and a circular painting in the **Cyclorama Center** portray the encounter. The museum in **Lee's Headquar-**ters contains both Union and Confederate memorabilia. More than 3,000 Civil War dead are buried in the **Gettysburg National Cemetery,** which Lincoln dedicated on November 19, 1863; the **Soldiers' National Monument** is near the site where he delivered his famous address. A walking tour of the town includes the **Lincoln Museum** in the Wills House, where Lincoln stayed. The **Eisenhower National Historic Site** preserves the 34th president's farmhouse. *Admission charged for some attractions.*

7. York

Convention and Visitors Bureau, 1 Market Way E. Exhibits at the **Historical Society of York County Museum** depict the area's history, while the **York County Colonial Court House** offers a multimedia presentation on the adoption of the Articles of Confederation by the Continental Congress. The **Bonham House** showcases a Federal-style dining room, a Victorian-era parlor, and Oriental artwork. Historic structures including the **General Gates House,** the **Golden Plough Tavern,** and the **Log House** richly evoke the early 18th century. *Admission charged.*

8. Watch and Clock Museum

514 Poplar St., Columbia. With an array of musical, chiming, and gonging clocks, this museum actually allows visitors to hear the passing of time. More than 8,000 items are on exhibit, from an early sundial to an atomic clock. *Admission charged.*

9. Lancaster

Convention and Visitors Bureau, 501 Greenfield Rd. This city is in the heart of Pennsylvania Dutch Country. The **1719 Hans Herr House** is the oldest surviving structure in the county and America's second-oldest Mennonite meetinghouse. The Federal-style **Wheatland** was once home to the nation's 15th president, James Buchanan. The **Heritage Center Museum of Lancaster County** displays works by local artists. The 1852 **Fulton Opera House** has been restored. The **Landis Valley Museum,** depicting early life in the region, includes a colonial farmhouse, Pennsylvania Dutch folk art, Conestoga wagons, and steam tractor engines. Guided tours of the **Amish Farm and House** provide an excellent glimpse into the lifestyle of this religious group. An 18th-century barn at **Rock Ford Plantation** displays antique folk arts and crafts. Other attractions include an interpretive center at the **Mennonite Infor-**mation Center and guided tours of the **Hebrew Tabernacle Reproduction.** Nearby **Bird-In-Hand** is a popular arts-and-crafts center, famed for its farmers' market. *Admission charged for some attractions.*

10. Strasburg

The **Railroad Museum of Pennsylvania** traces the history of the railroad from the earliest wood-burning engines to modern streamliners. Train buffs will love the **Toy Train Museum,** where they can activate models. The **Choo Choo Barn, Traintown, U.S.A.,** has a miniature layout of Lancaster County, complete with operating model trains and 130 animated scenes. All sorts of cars — rare, antique, classic, sports, high-performance — are at the **Gast Classic Motorcars Museum.** The **Strasburg Railroad,** with its historic steam engine and wooden cars, takes visitors through Pennsylvania Dutch country. *Admission charged for some attractions.*

11. Robert Fulton Birthplace

Rte. 222, south of Lancaster. One of the first to succeed in designing an operative steamboat, Fulton was born here in 1765. The restored house, which is open only on summer weekends, displays some of his personal items, including drawings and miniatures. *Admission charged.*

12. Ephrata Cloister

632 West Main St., Ephrata. The 11 buildings here stand in tribute to an 18th-century German religious order. The monastic sect was especially noted for creating excellent works of calligraphy as well as for its fine compositions of hymnal music. Examples of the sisters' beautiful hand-illuminated manuscripts are on display in the visitor center. *Admission charged.*

13. Conrad Weiser Memorial Park

Off Rte. 422, Womelsdorf. Visitors can tour a stone house that was once owned by an interpreter and peacemaker in the French and Indian Wars. *Fee charged for tours.*

14. Reading

The **Historical Society of Berks County** has a hands-on children's museum, a liberty bell dating from 1776, and a collection of regional exhibits such as a Conestoga wagon. Included among the attractions at the **Berks County Heritage Center** are the state's longest single-span covered bridge and an 18th-century wagon works. *Admission charged.*

15. Hawk Mountain Sanctuary

Hawk Mt. Rd., near Eckville. The visitor center here examines the behavior of the birds of prey for which the 2,200-acre refuge was created. Hiking trails lead to scenic lookouts, where eagles and hawks can be observed during their autumn migrations. *Admission charged.*

16. Roadside America

Roadside Dr., Shartlesville. Some 200 years of rural America's development are depicted here in a 6,000-square-foot exhibit of miniature villages that contain more than 300 buildings from the 19th and 20th centuries. *Admission charged.*

17. Cornwall Iron Furnace

Rexmont Rd. and Boyd St., Cornwall. In operation from 1742 to 1883, this is one of the world's best-preserved 19th-century iron-making facilities, at one time producing cannons and ammunition for the American Revolution. Tours and exhibits are available. *Admission charged.*

18. Indian Echo Caverns

368 Middletown Rd., Hummelstown. Rich with stalactite and stalagmite formations, the labyrinthine passageways and chambers here are silhouetted by glowing flowstone. *Admission charged.*

19. Hersheypark, Hershey's Gardens, and Chocolate World

Off Hersheypark Dr., Hershey. Tours of Chocolate World take visitors through a simulated factory. Hersheypark offers rides and entertainment, and Hershey's Gardens has 23 acres of flowers. *Admission charged.*

20. Harrisburg

Chamber of Commerce, 114 Walnut St. The **Capitol** here has a dome modeled after St. Peter's Basilica in Rome. In addition to its planetarium and its statuary hall, the **State Museum and Archives** showcases historical exhibits on the region and the nation. The **Midtown Historic District** is a neighborhood composed of turn-of-the-century town houses. The **John Harris, Jr. Mansion** was built in 1766 and named for the city's founder. **Riverfront Park** is considered one of the country's most scenic inland waterfronts. A recreation area, **City Island** offers numerous diversions as well as historical reconstructions. The **Museum of Scientific Discovery** has hands-on displays exploring science and technology. *Admission charged for some attractions.*

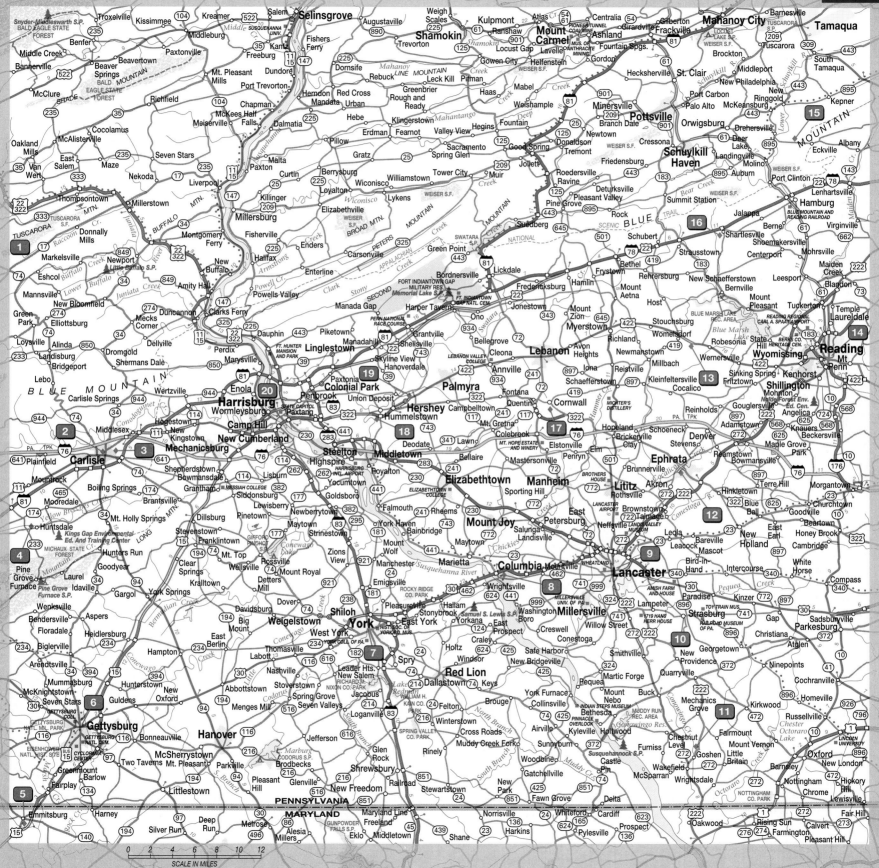

SCALE IN MILES

1. Mill Grove

1201 Pawlings Rd., Audubon. The **Audubon Wildlife Sanctuary** and its winding nature trails surround Mill Grove, home in the 1800's to naturalist John James Audubon. Displayed within the house are paintings, drawings, and examples of taxidermy.

2. Valley Forge National Historical Park

Rte. 23, King of Prussia. Besides displays of tools, weapons, and farm implements from the period, the visitor center here presents films on the bitter winter of 1777–78, when more than 2,000 of George Washington's men lost their lives. The park includes the **Isaac Potts House,** site of the general's headquarters. *Admission charged at house.*

3. Brandywine Battlefield Historical State Park

Rte. 1, Chadds Ford. Although the actual battle occurred nearby, reenactments of a British victory over the Americans in 1777 are held here each September. Exhibits in the visitor center depict the conflict. The park also contains the headquarters of Washington and Lafayette — the former's were reconstructed, the latter's restored. *Admission charged for some attractions.*

4. Wilmington

Convention and Visitors Bureau, 1300 Market St. The **Delaware Art Museum** has an outstanding collection of American paintings, pre-Raphaelite works by English artists, and a children's room with hands-on exhibits. The 102-room **Nemours Mansion,** built in 1910 by Alfred I. du Pont, contains priceless antiques and furnishings; the 300-acre estate features terraced French formal gardens. The **Rockwood Museum,** once the home of an English merchant in the mid-19th century, is arranged to portray the lifestyles of both the family and the servants. *Admission charged.*

5. Caleb Pusey House

15 Race St., Upland. This 1683 house was once visited by William Penn. Today it con-

tains period furnishings and is surrounded by a 17th-century herb garden, a restored 18th-century log house, and a 19th-century schoolhouse. Nearby **Chester,** founded in 1643, is the oldest English settlement in the state. Farther north is **Swarthmore College,** founded in 1864 and located on 339 wooded acres. *Admission charged at house.*

6. Media

Convention and Visitors Bureau, 200 East State St. The **Franklin Mint Museum** displays collectibles and works by Andrew Wyeth and Norman Rockwell. Within the borders of the **Ridley Creek State Park,** the 300-year-old **Colonial Pennsylvania Plantation** is a living-history museum depicting 18th-century farm life. *Admission charged at plantation.*

7. Morton Homestead

100 Lincoln Ave., Prospect Park. The great-grandfather of John Morton, a signer of the Declaration of Independence, built a house here in about 1655. The present log home, which has displays of colonial memorabilia and early Swedish furnishings, was reconstructed in 1937. *Admission charged.*

8. Nothnagle Home

406 Swedesboro Rd., Gibbstown. After reviewing historical records and examining the method of this log cabin's construction, some historians believe it to be the oldest in America — estimated to have been built about 1645. Its contents include the original fireplace and artifacts such as a butter churn and dough box.

9. Old Fort Mifflin

Fort Mifflin Rd., Philadelphia. In 1777, the British laid siege to this fort for 40 days. Guided tours are offered, and reenactments staged. *Admission charged.*

10. James and Ann Whitall House at Fort Mercer/Red Bank Battlefield

100 Hessian Ave., Red Bank. During the American Revolution, Ft. Mercer was built to ward off British attacks. In 1777, 400 patriots defeated some 1,200 British and Hessian soldiers, a victory that influenced the French decision to side with the Americans. Visitors can tour the battlefield and the 1748 fieldstone house, which contains a restored field hospital, a colonial kitchen, an herb garden, and exhibits pertaining to the battle and to the fort, which no longer exists.

11. Hunter-Lawrence-Jessup House

58 North Broad St., Woodbury. This was the boyhood home of Captain James Lawrence, a U.S. Navy hero who, after being mortally wounded in an encounter off the coast of Boston in the War of 1812, cried to his crew "Don't give up the ship!" Today the house is the headquarters of the Gloucester County Historical Society, whose museum showcases regional history, toys, costumes, books, period furnishings, and artifacts from both the Revolutionary and Civil wars.

12. Haddonfield

During the Revolution, members of the Continental Congress and the New Jersey Legislature convened in the public dining room of the 1750 **Indian King Tavern Museum.** Haddonfield Historical Society is headquartered in **Greenfield Hall,** which displays period furnishings, rare books and manuscripts, and other artifacts. The society also maintains the **Samuel Mickle House,** the town's oldest extant house.

13. Barclay Farmstead

209 Barclay Lane, Cherry Hill. The colonial origins of the property here date to 1684, when an early structure served as both a residence and a Quaker meetinghouse. Later, in the 1820's, a Federal-style farmhouse was erected, which can be toured today. There is a variety of American antiques, and the grounds encompass an 1830's blacksmith shop, a corn crib, and a pond with a footbridge. The nearby wooden **Scarborough Covered Bridge** was dedicated in 1959, ending a 93-year period during which no such bridge had been built in the state. *Admission charged at farmstead.*

14. Camden

Division of Public Information, 520 Market St. The **Camden County Historical Society** is composed of a museum displaying period furnishings, antiques, and exhibits on regional history; a 20,000-book library located in **Boyer Hall;** and **Pomona Hall,** a 1726 Georgian mansion with period furnishings. Among the 250 objects in the **Campbell Museum** are elaborate tureens and ladles used by royalty in the 18th and 19th centuries. The **Walt Whitman House,** the last residence of the poet from 1884 to 1892, contains original furnishings and memorabilia. The **Thomas H. Kean New Jersey State Aquarium** is a large facility with both indoor and outdoor exhibits, including a replica of an underwater research station,

an interactive display, and a 760,000-gallon tank. *Admission charged for some attractions.*

15. Gloria Dei (Old Swedes') Church

Christian St. and Delaware Ave., Philadelphia. Completed in 1700 by Lutherans from Sweden, this is probably the state's oldest church. Inside are models of the ships that brought the first Swedes to America.

16. Historic Bartram's Garden

54th St. and Lindbergh Blvd., Philadelphia. Begun in 1728 by John Bartram, this is considered to be America's oldest botanical garden. The house, barn, and cider mill here date from the 17th to 18th centuries. *Admission charged at buildings.*

17. Barnes Foundation

300 North Latch's Ln., Merion. The foundation boasts more than 1,000 artworks, including many by Renoir, Matisse, and Picasso. The surrounding 12-acre arboretum contains a number of rare trees and shrubs. *Admission charged.*

18. Stenton House

4601 North 18th St., Philadelphia. This Pennsylvania Colonial–style house, furnished with 18th-century antiques, was built in 1730 by James Logan, secretary to William Penn. At different times, both George Washington and General Howe stayed here. *Admission charged.*

19. Cliveden

6401 Germantown Ave., Philadelphia. This 18th-century Georgian house was the summer home of Benjamin Chew, Chief Justice of colonial Pennsylvania, and contains many original furnishings. *Admission charged.*

20. Hope Lodge

553 Bethlehem Pike, Fort Washington. The Hope Diamond was named for the family of Henry Hope, who, in 1784, bought this 1743 lodge for his son. After the Battle of Germantown in the Revolution, General Cochran used it as a headquarters. Today, visitors will find period furnishings and paintings. *Admission charged.*

21. Graeme Park

859 County Line Rd., Horsham. Dating from 1722, the Georgian-style stone home here was once the residence of a colonial governor of Pennsylvania. Much of the interior decoration was done by Thomas Graeme, who, in 1739, purchased the house as a summer residence. *Admission charged.*

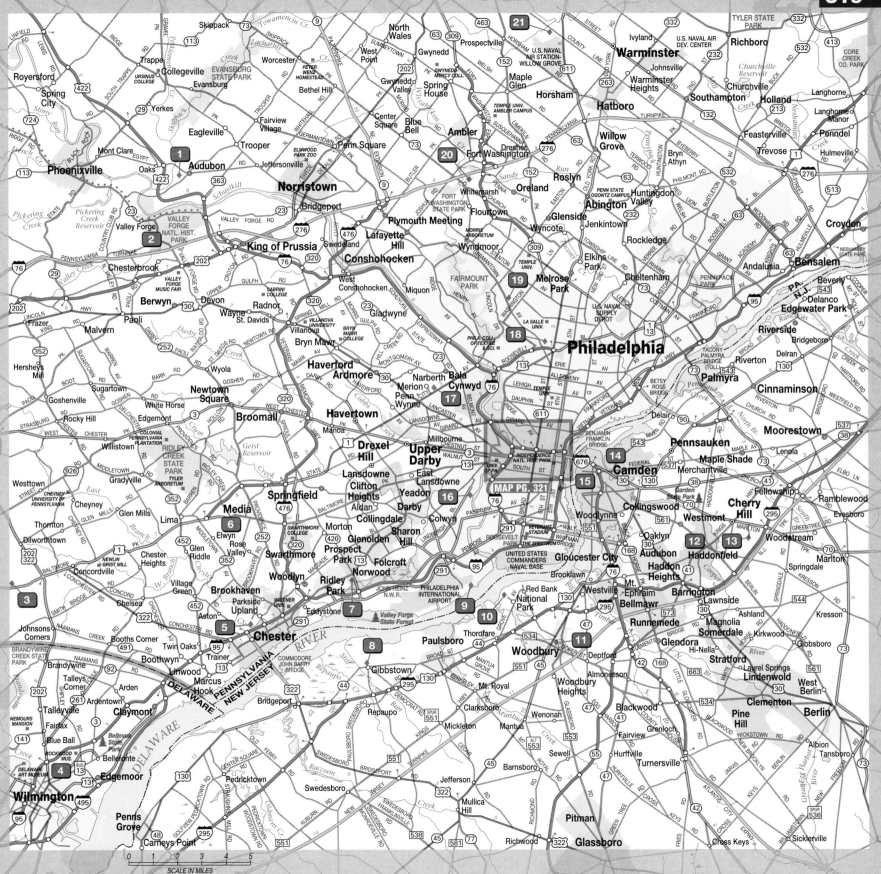

DOWNTOWN PHILADELPHIA

1. Fairmount Park

This area stretches along both sides of the Schuylkill River, offering some 9,000 acres of bridle paths, scenic drives, landscaped gardens, and jogging and biking trails. In 1876 the Centennial Exposition was held here. Today the park includes the **Philadelphia Museum of Art,** whose outstanding works range from ancient Chinese to modern art; the **Rodin Museum,** with its large collection of the famous artist's work; and the **Philadelphia Zoo,** America's first, which houses some 2,000 animals and birds. Several colonial mansions, some dating from the 18th century, have been preserved and are open to visitors. *Admission charged for some attractions.*

2. University of Pennsylvania

The university was founded in 1740 by Benjamin Franklin; in 1765 it established the

Historic homes line Elfreth's Alley.

nation's first medical school. The campus is home to the **Institute of Contemporary Art** and the **Museum of Archeology and Anthropology,** whose extensive display of artifacts — gleaned mostly on university expeditions — include ancient Egyptian and American Indian items. *Admission charged for some attractions.*

3. Rosenbach Museum and Library

2010 DeLancey Pl. Located in a handsome 19th-century town house near Rittenhouse Square, the museum contains a fine collection of paintings, prints, drawings, furniture, decorative arts, and rare books. Featured are Lewis Carroll's copy of *Alice in Wonderland,* James Joyce's manuscript of *Ulysses,* as well as manuscripts by Geoffrey Chaucer and Charles Dickens. *Admission charged.*

4. Civil War Library and Museum

1805 Pine St. This museum contains a large collection of arms, uniforms, and other artifacts of the war. Other features include the Lincoln Room, the Navy Room, and an armory. Memorabilia of generals Grant and Meade are also on display. The library has some 18,000 books and periodicals covering the historical eras that preceded and followed the Civil War, as well as the war itself. *Admission charged.*

5. The Franklin Institute Science Museum

20th St. and Benjamin Franklin Pkwy. This hands-on science museum has a wide range of exhibits, including a large walk-through heart, 101-foot-long steam locomotive, and planetarium shows. Also located here is the **Benjamin Franklin National Memorial,** which displays an impressive statue of the American statesmen and inventor. *Admission charged.*

6. Academy of Natural Sciences

1900 Benjamin Franklin Pkwy. Founded in 1812, this academy is America's oldest institution devoted to scientific research. Exhibits in the museum include Egyptian mummies, models of dinosaurs, gems, minerals, a hands-on children's area, and videos of animals. *Admission charged.*

7. Pennsylvania Academy of the Fine Arts

118 North Broad St. Housed in a restored Victorian structure known for its ornate interior, this academy was founded in 1805, leading many to classify it as the country's oldest art museum. The collection features

American artists, including Gilbert Stuart, Charles Willson Peale, Thomas Eakins, and Mary Cassatt. Guided tours are available. *Admission charged.*

8. The Balch Institute of Ethnic Studies

18 South Seventh St. Underscoring the lives of immigrants and the ethnic heritages of America, the museum and research library here present changing exhibits on household items, photographs, clothes, and other artifacts.

9. Afro-American Historical and Cultural Museum

Seventh and Arch Sts. African-American history and culture are examined here with displays of artifacts, historical documents, and artwork. Lectures, concerts, workshops, and other cultural events are offered. *Admission charged.*

10. Atwater Kent Museum-The History Museum of Philadelphia

15 South Seventh St. Named for a well-known radio pioneer, this museum is in an 1826 Greek Revival building. Featuring a variety of prints, paintings, toys, and other artifacts, this facility depicts the city's social and cultural history, covering a period of some 300 years.

11. Independence National Historical Park

Visitor Center, Third and Chestnut Sts. Appearing very much as it did in the 18th century, **Independence Hall** is this park's main attraction. Blemished by its famous crack, the **Liberty Bell** is displayed across the street in a glass pavilion. Other historic sites within the park include **Congress Hall,** where the legislature met when Philadelphia was the nation's capital, and **Carpenters' Hall,** site of the first Continental Congress.

12. Norman Rockwell Museum

601 Walnut St. This museum contains a replica of the American artist's studio and many of his works, including prints, paintings, drawings, sketches, and all of his famous *Saturday Evening Post* covers. There's also a film depicting his 60-year career. *Admission charged.*

13. Washington Square

Originally designed by William Penn, this square became a burial ground for hundreds of Revolutionary War soldiers and for the victims of a yellow fever epidemic. A

statue of George Washington overlooks the **Tomb of the Unknown Soldier of the American Revolution.** On the east side of the square, the **Athenaeum of Philadelphia** contains a research library as well as a fine collection of art.

14. Society Hill

This rise along the Delaware River was named for the Free Society of Traders, an English company that purchased several thousand acres from William Penn. Today the area is a fashionable residential district, where many charming early structures have been faithfully restored. They include the 1765 **Powel House,** an elegant Georgian town house; **A Man Full of Trouble Tavern Museum;** and the **Physick House,** a freestanding Federal-style town house that from 1815 to 1830 was the home of Philip Syng Physick, the father of American surgery. *Admission charged for some attractions.*

15. Penn's Landing

Marking the site where William Penn landed in 1682, this riverfront park features a sculpture garden and several historic vessels, including a tall ship. Festivals, special events, and summer concerts are scheduled. Due to relocate here in the spring of 1995, the **Philadelphia Maritime Museum** has interactive exhibits on Philadelphia's busy harbor. *Admission charged.*

16. Christ Church

Second St., between Market and Arch Sts. Built in the early 1700's in the Georgian style, this Episcopalian church has a wine-glass pulpit, the original chandelier, and a baptismal font from London. The pews of well-known early Americans, including George Washington, Betsy Ross, and John Adams, are marked by brass plaques. Buried in nearby **Christ Church Cemetery** are many soldiers from the American Revolution as well as several signers of the Declaration of Independence, including Benjamin Franklin.

17. Franklin Court

Market St., between Third and Fourth Sts. Part of Independence National Historical Park, this was once the site of Benjamin Franklin's home. It includes an underground museum, an exhibit on 18th-century printing, an operating post office, and a postal museum, the latter commemorating Franklin's appointment in 1775 as postmaster general.

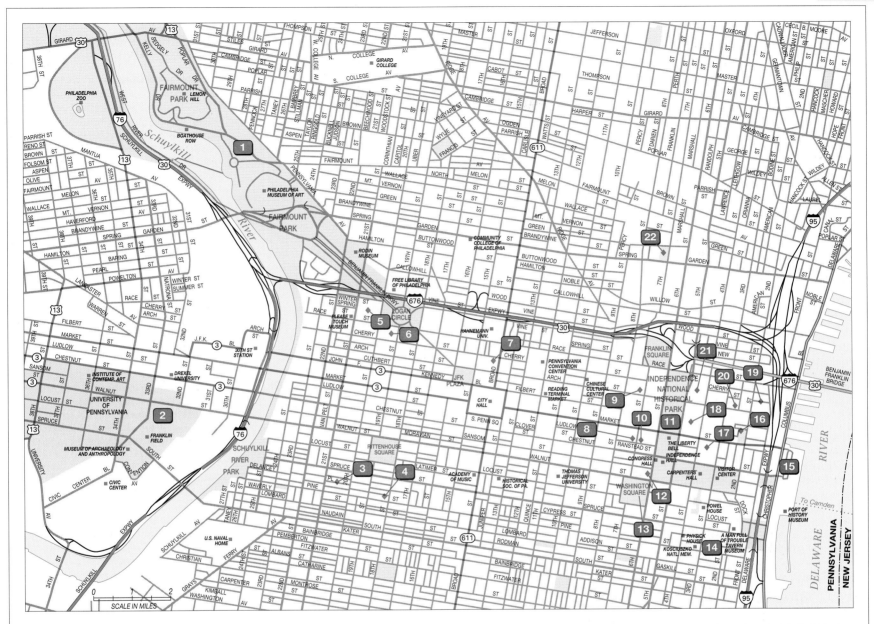

18. National Museum of American Jewish History

Independence Mall East, 55 North Fifth St. With paintings, documents, artifacts, and a video, this museum traces the history of Jewish people in the United States, from 1654 to the present. *Admission charged.*

19. Elfreth's Alley

Second St., between Race and Arch Sts. Picturesque 18th- and 19th-century houses line this 15-foot-wide passageway, the oldest continuously residential street in Philadelphia. The house at 126 is a museum with period furnishings, where displays depict

the lives of colonial artisans, many of whom lived on the street. *Admission charged.*

20. Betsy Ross House

239 Arch St. This 18th-century, 2½-story brick house is where Quaker Betsy Ross is said to have sewed the first United States flag. The home has been restored and furnished in period style. On display are several items that once belonged to the patriotic seamstress.

21. United States Mint

Fifth and Arch Sts. The largest in the world, this mint offers self-guiding tours

of the building. From a glass-enclosed gallery, visitors can observe the machines that produce coins.

22. Edgar Allan Poe National Historic Site

532 North Seventh and Spring Garden Sts. Guided tours are available of this three-story brick cottage, where the famous writer lived during the years 1842 and 1843. While in residence, Poe published several of his best-known, haunting stories, which included "The Black Cat," "The Gold Bug," and "The Tell-Tale Heart."

The Franklin Museum and Library

1. Paterson

Chamber of Commerce, 100 Hamilton Plaza. In 1791 Alexander Hamilton fashioned Paterson as the country's first planned industrial city. The **Great Falls S.U.M. Historic Landmark District** has some 50 buildings; the visitor center offers walking tours. Other highlights include the **Paterson Museum,** with exhibits on natural history, and the 1893 **Lambert Castle,** home of the **Passaic County Historical Society Museum.** *Fee charged for tours.*

2. Edison National Historic Site

Main and Lakeside Aves., West Orange. The several buildings here include the inventor's laboratories, his library, and a replica of the world's first motion picture studio. Nearby **Glenmont** was the family's elegant 23-room home. *Admission charged.*

3. Newark

Chamber of Commerce, 1 Newark Center. Founded in 1666, the city is today the largest in the state. The **Newark Museum** has paintings, decorative arts, and an outstanding Asian collection; it also contains a planetarium and a small zoo. The nearby **Catholic Cathedral of the Sacred Heart** is known for its stained-glass windows and handsome bronze doors. *Admission charged at planetarium.*

4. Snug Harbor Cultural Center

1000 Richmond Terrace, Staten Island. Once a home for retired sailors, this 80-acre parkland now offers outdoor concerts and festivals. Indoor events are held in Veteran's Hall, and changing exhibits in the **Newhouse Center for Contemporary Art.** The **Staten Island Botanical Gardens** and the **Children's Museum** are also on the grounds. Situated 2 miles from the center, the **Staten Island Ferry** connects with the southern tip of Manhattan. *Admission charged for some attractions.*

5. Historic Richmond Town

441 Clarke Ave., Staten Island. Dating from 1695, this was the island's first permanent settlement. It has been restored to depict local life from colonial times to the 19th century. There are some 27 historic buildings, including one of America's oldest elementary schoolhouses. Costumed guides demonstrate early crafts and trades.

6. Alice Austen House Museum and Garden

2 Hylan Blvd., Staten Island. Built about 1710, the charming cottage here was the long-time home of the well-known photographer. Now restored, it serves as a museum for her works.

7. Statue of Liberty National Monument

Perhaps the world's most famous statue, Lady Liberty has graced New York Harbor since 1886, when France presented her to America. Inside the monument, designed by Auguste Bartholdi, visitors can see exhibits pertaining to its recent restoration and enjoy spectacular views from observation areas. Nearby **Ellis Island,** America's main port of immigration from 1892 to 1924, has been restored as a museum honoring the millions who entered here. More than 400,000 names have been engraved on the American Immigrant Wall of Honor. Ferries depart from Battery Park to both sites. *Fee charged for ferry.*

8. The Brooklyn Museum

200 Eastern Pkwy., Brooklyn. Known for its outstanding collections of Egyptian and pre-Columbian art, this museum also features works by American artists, 27 period rooms, and the interior of a two-room 1675 Brooklyn house. *Admission charged.*

9. Brooklyn Botanic Garden

1000 Washington Ave., Brooklyn. This 52-acre site has many gardens — Japanese, fragrance, desert, and tropical among them. A pink wonderland from late April into May, the Cherry Walk and the Cherry Esplanade attract thousands of visitors.

10. New York's Aquarium for Wildlife Conservation

West Eighth St. and Surf Ave., Coney Island. Many kinds of marine life are displayed at the aquarium, in both indoor and outdoor tanks. The Sea Cliffs exhibit offers above- and below-water viewing of walruses, seals, penguins, and sea otters. In addition to its nearly 3-mile-long boardwalk, **Coney Island** is famed for its hot dogs and Astrolands Park's roller coaster. Nearby **Brighton Beach Avenue** has an abun-

dance of restaurants offering Russian cuisine. *Admission charged for some attractions.*

11. Jamaica Bay Wildlife Refuge

With views of the Manhattan skyline, this 9,155-acre salt marsh attracts thousands of migratory and nesting birds, including egrets, herons, hooded mergansers, ibises, hawks, and warblers. Seven miles of peaceful trails traverse the beautiful wilderness, offering visitors a year-round opportunity to readily escape the busy metropolis.

12. Flushing Meadows Corona Park

Grand Central Pkwy., Queens. The host of two World Fairs, this park contains bicycle paths, an ice-skating rink, carousel, marina, and the **Queens Zoo of North American Animals.** The complex includes **Shea Stadium,** home of the New York Mets; the **New York Hall of Science,** featuring hands-on scientific displays; and the **National Tennis Center.**

13. American Museum of the Moving Image

35th Ave. and 36th St., Astoria. Devoted to the history and technology of the film, video, and television industries, this museum has a theater, a screening room, and a large collection of movie memorabilia. *Admission charged.*

14. Harlem

With 125th Street as its unofficial main thoroughfare, this community has been the center of black American life and culture for the past century. Sights include **Strivers' Row,** a series of handsome town houses, and the Gothic-style **Abyssinian Baptist Church,** whose minister at one time was the Reverend Adam Clayton Powell, Jr., a powerful black congressman. Tours are offered of the **Apollo Theatre,** where popular artists perform. *Fee charged for tour.*

15. The Cathedral of St. John the Divine

112th St. and Amsterdam Ave., New York. This Episcopalian church, begun in 1892 and not yet completed, is the largest Gothic cathedral in the world. The main entry's great bronze doors depict biblical scenes and lead to the 600-foot-long nave; the apse is bordered by exceptionally beautiful small chapels. The grounds contain the Biblical Garden and the Peace Fountain. Nearby at Broadway and 116th Street is **Columbia University.** Founded in 1754, this Ivy League school has an entrance

of wrought-iron gates topped by gilded crowns, reminding passersby that the university was originally called King's College.

16. Riverside Church

122nd St. and Riverside Dr., New York. This modern Gothic church is known for its 400-foot tower, which houses the world's largest tuned carillon. Across the street in Riverside Park, the **General Grant National Memorial Monument** contains the sarcophagi of Ulysses S. Grant and his wife. *Admission charged at church.*

17. Fort Lee Historic Park

Hudson Terrace, Fort Lee. Situated on a cliff overlooking the Hudson, the fort was built to prevent the British from sailing up the river. Cannon batteries, soldiers' huts, and a firing step have been reconstructed. The visitor center contains historical exhibits. *Fee charged for parking.*

18. The Cloisters

Fort Tryon Park, New York. Located on a wooded hillside overlooking the Hudson River, this monasterylike stone building has a vast collection of medieval art. Included are tapestries, paintings, sculptures, sections of French cloisters, a 12th-century Romanesque Spanish chapel, and several medieval-style gardens. *Admission charged.*

19. The New York Botanical Garden

200th St. and Southern Blvd., Bronx. The Bronx River flows through this beautiful 250-acre area. Attractions include the Enid A. Haupt Conservatory, housing tropical and desert plants; formal plantings; herb gardens; a 40-acre uncut forest; a research library; and a herbarium containing more than 5 million plants. *Admission charged.*

20. International Wildlife Conservation Park/Bronx Zoo

185th St. and Southern Blvd., Bronx. Cable cars and a monorail offer visitors an overview of this park's many animals, almost 600 species, ranging from anacondas to zebras. The exceptional complex includes a rain forest, the World of Birds, and a children's zoo. *Admission charged.*

21. Old Westbury Gardens

71 Old Westbury Rd., Old Westbury. Here an 18th-century manor has inviting gardens and statuary, while the **Westbury House** features antique furnishings and major artworks, including paintings by Gainsborough and Sargent. *Admission charged.*

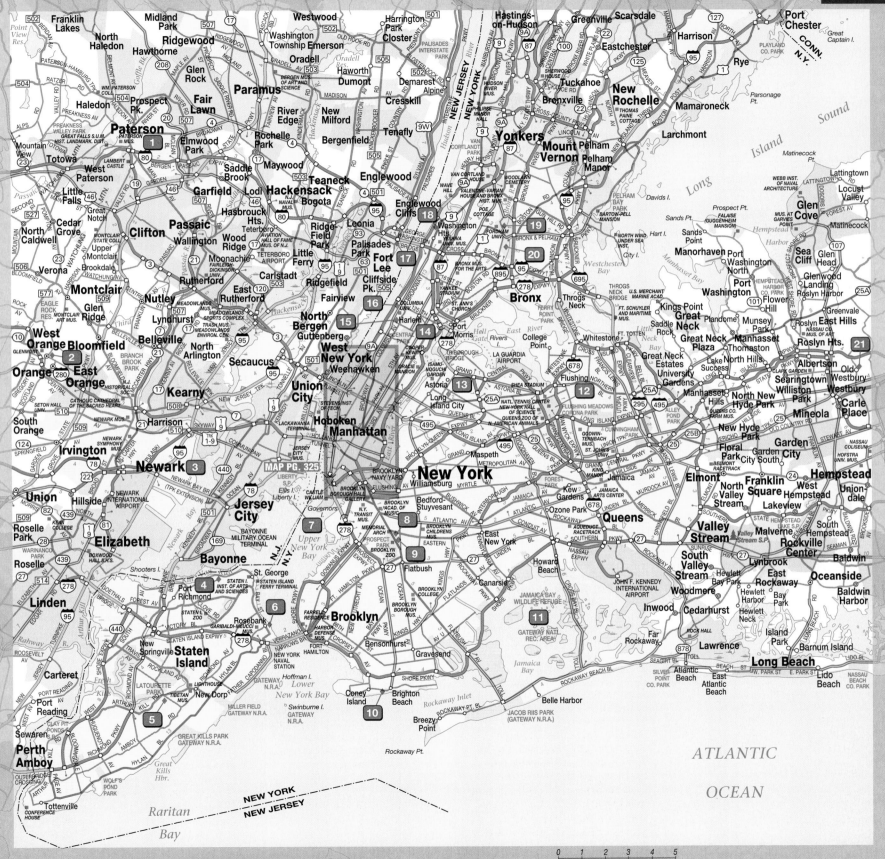

SCALE IN MILES
0 1 2 3 4 5

DOWNTOWN NEW YORK

1. Guggenheim Museum

1071 Fifth Ave. at 89th St. The main lobby of this striking building, designed by Frank Lloyd Wright, features a central rotunda with an ascending spiral walkway that leads past the artworks. The museum has been refurbished and now boasts a ten-story tower, which provides additional gallery space for this collection of 19th- and 20th-century works. *Admission charged.*

2. Metropolitan Museum of Art

1000 Fifth Ave. at 82nd St. With some 3 million objects, this is one of the world's greatest museums. Among its many highlights are paintings by the Old Masters, fine furniture, relics, African art, an Egyptian temple, Japanese paintings, vases and mosaics from antiquity, a gallery of 20th-century art, and a rooftop sculpture garden. *Admission charged.*

3. American Museum of Natural History

Central Park West and 79th St. This renowned museum has many extensive collections, featuring outstanding exhibits on early man, minerals, gems, and animals. Films, slide shows, and gallery talks are offered. The **Hayden Planetarium** has fascinating presentations on large wrap-around screens. *Admission charged.*

4. Whitney Museum of American Art

945 Madison Ave. at 75th St. Focusing on the 20th century, this museum has one of the country's largest collections of American paintings, sculptures, drawings, films, and videotapes. Alexander Calder's "Circus" is in the lobby. *Admission charged.*

5. The Frick Collection

1 East 70th St. at Fifth Ave. Built in 1914 for Henry Clay Frick, a wealthy steel baron, this elegant Neoclassical mansion was opened to the public in 1935 as a museum. It contains original furnishings and a fine art collection, including works by Rembrandt, Holbein, Titian, and El Greco. Children under 10 are not admitted. *Admission charged.*

6. Central Park

As Manhattan's playground, this beautifully landscaped park includes a model boat pond; a zoo with polar bears, sea lions, and monkeys; the **Wollman Ice Skating Rink;** the formal **Conservatory Garden; The Lake,** with a restaurant and row-boat rentals; and the **Dairy,** now a visitor center, which dates from the days when cows grazed here. Concerts are held on the **Great Lawn** during the summer.

7. Lincoln Center for the Performing Arts

Surrounding a wide plaza with a circular fountain, the center includes the **New York State Theater,** home of the New York City Opera; the **Metropolitan Opera House,** with brilliant Chagall paintings in its huge front windows; and **Avery Fisher Hall,** where the New York Philharmonic Orchestra plays. Other attractions include the **Vivian Beaumont Theater;** the **Mitzi Newhouse Theater,** with sculptures by Henry Moore standing in a great reflecting pool; and the adjacent **Guggenheim Bandshell** in Damrosch Park.

8. Intrepid Sea-Air-Space Museum

Pier 86, at West 46th St. and 12th Ave. This complex includes a World War II aircraft carrier, rockets, historic and contemporary aircraft, space vehicles, and a nuclear-missile submarine. Films are presented. *Admission charged.*

9. Carnegie Hall

154 West 57th St. at Seventh Ave. Throughout the last century, the world's greatest orchestras and soloists have performed in this 2,804-seat auditorium that is famed for its excellent acoustics. A small museum in the newly restored hall preserves photographs and memorabilia of the many musicians. Guided tours are available.

10. Times Square

Broadway and 42nd St. The theatrical center of New York — a colorful blend of theaters, movie houses, hotels, restaurants, and shops — is called the Great White Way for its thousands of brilliantly lighted signs. A TKTS booth at 47th Street offers half-price, same-day theater tickets.

11. Radio City Music Hall

Avenue of the Americas (Sixth Ave.) and 50th St. Built in 1932, this 6,000-seat theater is the home of the famed Rockettes. The Art Deco lobby has a sweeping stairway that rises to the balcony level. Theatrical extravaganzas, musicals, movies, and concerts are held here. Backstage tours are offered daily. *Fee charged for tours.*

12. Rockefeller Center

Toward the center of this 19-building complex, a promenade with gardens extends from Fifth Avenue to the Sunken Plaza, the scene of outdoor dining in summer and ice-skating in winter. The plaza is watched over by a soaring golden Prometheus. The buildings are connected by an underground concourse lined with shops. NBC Studios, a major tenant, offers guided tours of its TV studios. *Fee charged for tours.*

13. Museum of Modern Art

11 West 53rd St., between Fifth Ave. and Avenue of the Americas (Sixth Ave.). This renowned museum houses a number of art's most recent masterpieces, from the 1880's to the present. Painting, sculpture, drawing, photography, and design objects are displayed in five stories of gallery space. There's a sculpture garden, and films are shown. *Admission charged.*

14. The Museum of Television and Radio

25 West 52nd St., between Fifth Ave. and Avenue of the Americas (Sixth Ave.). Outlining broadcasting's history, the extensive displays here include radio programs, commercials, and television shows that can be viewed on individual screens.

15. St. Patrick's Cathedral

Fifth Ave. and 50th St. The Roman Catholic seat of the New York Archdiocese, this Gothic-style cathedral was begun in 1858, opening its doors in 1879. Its handsome twin spires rise to a height of 330 feet.

16. Grand Central Terminal

Park Ave. and 42nd St. Completed in 1913, this striking Beaux Arts building features a main concourse with a 12-story-high vaulted ceiling depicting the constellations of our solar system. A raised roadway carries Park Avenue around the terminal's upper level.

17. Chrysler Building

405 Lexington Ave. at 42nd St. With its eye-catching stainless-steel spire, this awesome skyscraper was the world's tallest building in 1930, only to be exceeded by the Empire State Building the next year. The Art Deco lobby is decorated with marble and ceiling murals.

18. United Nations

First Ave. and 45th St. Begun in 1949, this complex is marked at its entrance with flags from each of its member nations. It includes the 550-foot-tall Secretariat Building and the domed General Assembly, whose lobby holds a suspended golden ball that swings with the earth's rotation. Paths lead through the landscaped grounds, with statuary and fine views of the East River. Guided tours are available. *Admission charged.*

19. The New York Public Library

476 Fifth Ave. at 42nd St. This large and handsome 1911 Beaux Arts building is guarded at the entrance by two marble lions, which were named Patience and Fortitude by Mayor Fiorello La Guardia. It is known for its elegant double stairway, literary treasures, murals, paintings, changing exhibitions, rare books, and enormous main reading room. Free guided tours are available.

20. Empire State Building

350 Fifth Ave. at 34th St. Completed in 1931, this famed 102-story structure has an observation deck offering lofty views of the city and its surroundings. The **Guinness World of Records Exhibition,** located on the concourse level, depicts record-holding events with artifacts and life-size models. The top of the tower is lighted at night; the colors change according to seasons, holidays, and special events. *Admission charged.*

21. Greenwich Village

The narrow tree-lined streets, cobblestoned courtyards, patches of gardens, and 19th-century town houses have drawn artists, educators, and students to this area since the mid-1800's. Designed by Stanford White, the **Washington Arch** was erected in 1890 to honor George Washington's presidential inauguration. It stands in **Washington Square Park** at the southern end of Fifth Avenue. Surrounded by **New York University,** the park often provides entertainment by street performers; the Village area is the site of annual outdoor art shows. The vicinity nearby, including MacDougal and Bleeker streets, has a wide range of boutiques, coffeehouses, restaurants, bars, and clubs.

22. SoHo

Until the 1960's SoHo (short for South of Houston Street) was a wasteland of run-down factories and old warehouses. The handsome cast-iron architecture and spacious lofts caught the eyes of artists, however, and today it has become a fashionable, rejuvenated neighborhood. Thousands come to visit the many art galleries, boutiques, food shops, and restaurants. Located in a 1904 firehouse, the **New York City Fire Museum** contains firefighting equipment and tools ranging from colonial times to the present.

23. Chinatown

The sights, sounds, and aromas of the Orient greet visitors to this area. **Canal Street,** once a tree-lined waterway and promenade, is today a jumble of restaurants, food stores, jewelry stores, and sidewalk stalls selling fish and a great variety of vegetables. Narrow **Mott Street,** a business thoroughfare, is crammed with souvenir shops and pagoda-fronted eateries, ranging from fast-food cafes to fine restaurants.

24. World Trade Center

Known as the Twin Towers, this center's two skyscrapers are each 110 stories high. The observation area on the 107th floor of Tower 2 offers an incredibly sweeping view of the city, the harbor, and New Jersey. A pedestrian overpass connects the trade center with the **World Financial Center,** located in **Battery Park City.** The Winter Garden atrium, filled with high-reaching palm trees and bordered by shops and restaurants, looks out over the Hudson River and the handsome waterside esplanade. *Admission charged at observation area.*

25. Battery Park

Named for a string of cannons once lining the waterfront here in defense of the island, this park is the departure point for ferries to the Statue of Liberty and Ellis Island. Visitors can purchase ferry tickets in **Castle Clinton National Monument,** a fort from the War of 1812. Completed in 1907, the nearby **U.S. Custom House** is home to Federal courts and to the **National Museum of the American Indian.**

26. Fraunces Tavern

54 Pearl St. Built in 1719 and turned into a tavern in 1762, this colonial building was the site of George Washington's farewell address to his troops. The **Fraunces Tavern Museum** was opened in 1907 on the second floor of the brick structure; it contains period rooms, paintings, drawings, and other colonial artifacts. The ground-floor restaurant draws lively lunchtime crowds. *Admission charged at museum.*

27. Wall Street

Named for a wooden palisade that protected the Dutch colony of New Amsterdam from English invasion, this famous street is today known as the country's financial center. Attractions in the area include the **New York Stock Exchange,** the nation's largest stock market, and the historic **Trinity Church,** in whose graveyard Alexander Hamilton is buried. Nearby, visitors will find the **American Stock Exchange** and the **Federal Reserve Bank of New York.** Guided tours are offered at some buildings.

28. South Street Seaport

This restored area was an early-19th-century port; it includes an assortment of boutiques, art galleries, craft centers, food shops, and restaurants, many of which are housed in the **Fulton Market** and **Pier 17.** The **Seaport Museum** displays nautical memorabilia and, at dockside, historic ships. Walking tours and cruises of the harbor are available. *Admission charged for some attractions.*

29. Brooklyn Heights Historic District

Since the early 1800's, this neighborhood has been a fashionable residential area. Today it's a historic district containing more than 1,000 century-old homes. Sights include the **Plymouth Church of the Pilgrims,** where Henry Ward Beecher preached against slavery. The **Promenade,** a wide walkway above the river, offers spectacular views of the harbor, the Manhattan skyline, and the magnificent **Brooklyn Bridge,** which was completed in 1888.

30. Lower East Side

For almost 200 years, thousands of immigrants of all nationalities have settled in this downtown district. The history of these residents is recounted in the **Lower East Side Tenement Museum,** a preserved 19th-century tenement building containing diverse period furnishings; the museum also offers walking tours of the area. **The Bowery,** a major thoroughfare, served at various times in its past as an Indian trail and a path to Peter Stuyvesant's farm. *Admission charged at museum.*

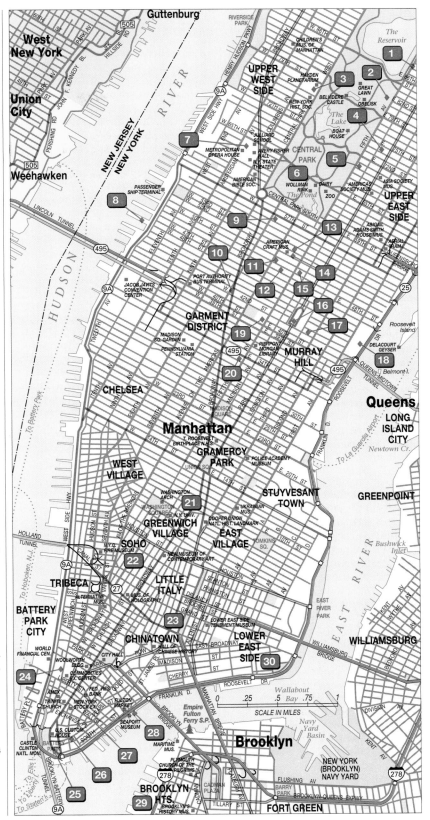

LONG ISLAND

1. Jones Beach State Park

Stretching 6½ miles off the southern shore of Long Island, Jones Beach is one of the most magnificent of all New York beaches. The surrounding 2,400-acre park offers a 1½-mile boardwalk, band shells, freshwater pools, golf courses, exercise trails, picnic areas, a fishing pier, and a concert theater. *Admission charged.*

2. Oyster Bay

Chamber of Commerce, Townsend Sq. This town's main attraction is **Sagamore Hill,** a 23-room Victorian mansion built in 1884 for Theodore Roosevelt. The **Planting Fields Arboretum** encompasses greenhouses and acres of beautifully landscaped gardens, plants, and lawns. Amid the arboretum's woods stands the 65-room **Coe Hall,** a 1920's Tudor Revival mansion. *Admission charged.*

3. Caumsett State Park

One of Long Island's best-preserved natural areas, this park boasts 1,500 acres of unspoiled meadows, cliffs, and woodlands. It offers hiking, cross-country skiing, surf fishing, and, by reservation, guided nature walks. *Admission charged.*

4. Cold Spring Harbor

Museums in this town reflect the area's seafaring past. The **Cold Spring Harbor Fish Hatchery and Aquarium** houses 50 species of fish in some 20 tanks; it also boasts one of the state's largest collections of native freshwater fish, turtles, and amphibians. Exhibits at the **Cold Spring Harbor Whaling Museum** relive the period from 1836 to 1862, when the town supported a fleet of 9 whaling vessels. Among the impressive displays visitors will find a fully rigged 30-foot-long whaling boat, a diorama, and a hands-on exhibit that features the bones of marine mammals. Displays in the **DNA Learning Center** examine the field of genetics. *Admission charged for some attractions.*

5. Heckscher Museum

2 Prime Ave., Huntington. The permanent collection here consists of sculpture, prints, drawings, and European and American paintings. There's a particularly strong collection of 19th-century landscapes. Also offered are changing exhibits that pertain to Long Island. *Admission charged.*

6. Walt Whitman Birthplace State Historic Site

246 Old Walt Whitman Rd., Huntington Station. In 1819 the acclaimed poet was born in this simple farmhouse. Tours of the site pass unique architecture, authentic 19th-century furnishings, and interesting Whitman memorabilia.

7. Old Bethpage Village Restoration

Round Swamp Rd., Old Bethpage. This re-created 19th-century Long Island farming community contains more than 55 historic structures. Among the restorations are an antiquated blacksmith shop, a general store, a church, craft shops, and residential homes. Visitors can watch village personnel practice various crafts. *Admission charged.*

8. Vanderbilt Museum

180 Little Neck Rd., Centerport. On the grounds of a 43-acre estate, this museum explores natural history, science, and art. One exhibition has more than 2,000 marine and wildlife specimens. The planetarium is one of the best equipped in the country. The estate's 24-room Spanish Revival mansion features exquisite fireplaces, original furnishings, and memorabilia from around the world. *Admission charged.*

9. The Museums at Stony Brook

1208 Rte. 25A, Stony Brook. This complex highlights 19th-century America. It includes a history museum exhibiting period clothing, textiles, toys, and decoys. The art museum contains 19th- and 20th-century artwork. Other attractions include a blacksmith shop, a restored 19th-century schoolhouse, and a carriage museum. Quaint historic houses overlook Stony Brook's harbor, and a pond flows into a 1751 gristmill. *Admission charged.*

10. Bayard Cutting Arboretum

Rte. 27A, Great River. Designed in 1886 by Frederick Law Olmsted, a creator of New York City's Central Park, this 690-acre park contains five nature walks and a magnificent variety of foliage. The Tudor-style **Cutting Residence,** a natural history museum, has displays of mounted birds and Indian artifacts. *Fee charged for parking.*

11. Sagtikos Manor

Montauk Hwy., West Bay Shore. Part of this 42-room mansion was built more than 300 years ago. During the Revolutionary War, it was used as headquarters for the British, and George Washington slept here in 1790. Impressive memorabilia, original colonial furniture, and Indian artifacts are on display. *Admission charged.*

12. Long Island Maritime Museum

86 West Ave., West Sayville. This interesting museum exhibits a variety of ship models, including South Bay sailboats, oyster vessels, and ice scooters. Also on display are paintings, artifacts, and an exhibit on the U.S. Life Saving Service — forerunner of the U.S. Coast Guard.

13. Fire Island

Home to a national seashore, this island stretches for 32 miles, paralleling Long Island's south shore. There are 17 beach communities. Two of the beaches, **Sailor's Haven** and **Watch Hill,** have self-guiding nature walks and naturalist programs; the latter also offers camping. On the island's western point, the 1,000-acre **Robert Moses State Park** features swimming, golf, picnic shelters, and bay fishing. The **Fire Island Lighthouse,** a 180-foot-high stone tower built in 1858, has a visitor center with exhibits on the area. Open to car traffic only on its eastern and western ends, the island can also be reached by ferry. *Fee charged for ferry.*

14. Brookhaven National Laboratory Science Museum

William Floyd Pkwy., Upton. One of the country's leading laboratories for scientific research, this teaching museum enthralls visitors with hands-on exhibits, historical memorabilia, a three-story decommissioned nuclear reactor, and audiovisual presentations on science and the lab's goals and accomplishments. The museum is open only on Sundays in July and August.

15. Splish Splash

2549 Splish Splash Dr., Riverhead. This 40-acre water park has a 1,300-foot-long river that visitors can ride down on an inner tube, a pool area with fountains and waterfalls, sea lion and tropical bird shows, and several unique water areas for children. *Admission charged.*

16. Cutchogue

The climate around this town is very good for growing grapes, so some dozen vineyards, many offering tours and tastings, dot the area. Two of the most popular are **Pindar** and **Hargrave.** Historic sites near the town's **Village Green** include the **Old House,** one of the best examples of English colonial architecture in the country; the 1700's **Wickham Farmhouse;** and the 1840 **Old Schoolhouse.** *Admission charged for some attractions.*

17. Southold Historical Society Museum Park

Main Rd., Southold. The first English settlement in New York state, this 1½-acre village complex has restored houses from the 1700's to the 1890's. Other buildings include a blacksmith shop, carriage house, and an 18th-century barn, complete with antique farm implements, quilts, and coverlets.

For nearly 200 years the Montauk Point Lighthouse has aided mariners.

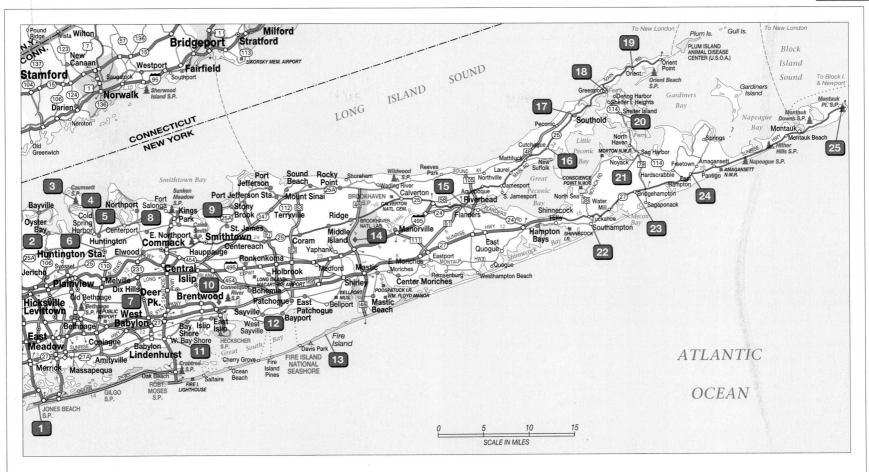

18. Greenport

Chamber of Commerce, Rte. 25. A historic fishing and whaling town, Greenport today has a picturesque harbor, quaint restaurants, and antique shops. The popular summer resort is home to the 1908 **Regina Maris,** one of the only two remaining barkentines left in the world. Ferries depart from the town to Shelter Island. *Admission charged.*

19. Orient

Located on Long Island's North Fork, this town was once an agricultural and seafaring center. The **Oysterponds Historical Society** consists of 18th- and 19th-century buildings, including an inn, a schoolhouse, a village house, and a barn that contains exquisite carriages. The many natural areas at the 357-acre **Orient Beach State Park** make it a favorite of nature lovers and bird-watchers. Ten miles of sand-and-pebble beach and a large shaded picnic area are the park's highlights. *Admission charged.*

20. Shelter Island

It is a short ferry ride from Long Island to this quiet haven of rolling green hills and white sandy beaches, where opportunities for fishing, boating, and hiking abound. The island's past is preserved at the historical society's **Havens House** and **Manhanset Chapel Museum,** which features exhibits and rooms with antique furnishings. *Admission charged for some attractions.*

21. Sag Harbor

Chamber of Commerce, Main St. Situated between Long Island's North and South forks, this historic town was once one of the largest whaling ports in the world. At the entrance to the **Sag Harbor Whaling Museum,** visitors pass through a whale's jawbone; inside are displays of whaling and fishing artifacts, logbooks, and scrimshaw. The **Custom House,** the 1790 home of the first customs official for the port of Sag Harbor, houses artifacts and restored furnishings. The **Morton National Wildlife Refuge** is a 187-acre area of woodland, salt marsh, and sandy beach. The refuge has trails, plus facilities for bird-watching, painting, and photography. *Admission charged for some attractions.*

22. Southampton

Chamber of Commerce, 76 Main St. A wealthy summer resort town, Southampton is known for its elaborate beachfront homes and white sandy beaches. Founded in 1898, the **Parrish Art Museum** houses more than 2,000 works and has a sculpture garden with rare trees. The re-created building at the **Southampton Historical Museum** display various artifacts, from antique toys to Indian and whaling memorabilia. *Admission charged for some attractions.*

23. Bridgehampton Historical Museum

Montauk Hwy., Bridgehampton. Located in the Greek Revival Corwith House, this museum is furnished in various historical periods, beginning with the late 1700's. On the grounds, displays include working antique engines, farm machines, and tools that were used to repair wagons.

24. East Hampton

Chamber of Commerce, 4 Main St. The greenery, windmills, public pond, and white sandy beaches lend to this charming town a quaint, colonial look. On Main Street, the **Guild Hall Museum** has three art galleries and a theater. Housed nearby in a 1680's saltbox, the **Home Sweet Home Museum** displays English ceramics, antique furniture, and an early 19th-century windmill. *Admission charged.*

25. Montauk Point State Park

Set on the easternmost tip of Long Island, this 724-acre park is a great place for outdoor activities including hiking, bicycling, and picnicking. Built in 1796, **Montauk Point Lighthouse** is the oldest in New York state. Visitors willing to climb to its top can see the automated beacon light, a foghorn, and fine views of the Atlantic Ocean. There are exhibits on maritime history and a video describing a construction project that is designed to halt erosion. *Admission charged.*

1. Wharton State Forest

Nestled among the pines and cedars in this part of the Pine Barrens is a restored 18th-century iron-making village called **Batsto**. The ironmaster's striking mansion, a general store, blacksmith shop, gristmill, and sawmill are on view. Swimmers and boaters flock to nearby Atsion Lake; hikers, to the 50-mile **Batona Trail**.

2. Edwin B. Forsythe Wildlife Refuge

A major stop for migrating birds along the Atlantic Flyway, this refuge has 34,000 acres — home to beaches, bays, wetlands, and woodlands. In addition to two nature trails, there is an 8-mile self-guiding auto tour. Observation towers offer views of bald eagles, ospreys, wood ducks, and more than 250 other species.

3. Atlantic City

Convention and Visitors Bureau, 2314 Pacific Ave. Glittering casino-hotels, beaches, ocean, and high-rolling adventure attract throngs of visitors from all over the world to this city, also known as the birthplace of saltwater taffy. Its famed 6-mile-long boardwalk features several amusement piers, shops, and food stores. Somewhat slower paced is **Gardner's Basin,** site of a historic maritime village.

4. Ocean City

Chamber of Commerce, 9th St. Causeway. No liquor is sold in this family resort, where the waves break near a pleasant boardwalk. Attractions include the **Ocean City Historical Museum,** which displays artifacts from *Sindia,* a four-masted bark that ran aground in 1901. Across town is the **Music Pier,** where concerts are held throughout the summer.

5. Sea Isle City

Visitors come here to enjoy the 5-mile stretch of sandy beach as well as the excellent fishing. Party boats make daily trips for bluefish and other catches. Crabbing in the bay is also popular.

6. Leaming's Run Gardens

Rte. 9, Swainton. Tranquil winding paths lead to 20 acres of gorgeous gardens, which bloom in the summer, attracting hundreds of hummingbirds in August. Also on the grounds is a re-created late-1600's South Jersey farm, which is open from May through October. *Admission charged.*

7. Cape May County Historical Museum and Genealogical Society

504 Rte. 9, Cape May Court House. Built before the Revolution, the building here has period rooms and an array of antiques. There are ship-building tools, whaling instruments, and artifacts from Indians and pioneers. *Admission charged.*

8. Stone Harbor

Some of New Jersey's prettiest beaches are found on Seven Mile Island, which contains Stone Harbor and nearby Avalon. The **Wetlands Institute** offers a hands-on museum, a trail through a salt marsh, and an observation tower overlooking 6,000 acres of coastal marshlands. **Stone Harbor Bird Sanctuary** is the summer home of some 6,000 birds, including several varieties of herons and egrets.

9. Wildwood

Chamber of Commerce, Schellenger Ave. at the Boardwalk. Wildwood, North Wildwood, and Wildwood Crest share a barrier island's 5-mile-long beach of fine white sand. The boardwalk has four amusement piers.

10. Cape May

Chamber of Commerce, 609 Lafayette St. Exquisite Victorian homes line the historic district here, said to be the nation's oldest seaside resort. Walking and trolley tours are offered of the elegant **Mainstay Inn** and the **Emlen Physick Estate.** Nearby, craftspeople demonstrate period trades at the 19th-century **Cold Spring Village.** *Admission charged for some attractions.*

11. Cape May Point

Bird-watchers may spot migratory songbirds, waterfowl, and seabirds at **Cape May Point State Park,** where the nature center displays Cape May diamonds — a semi-precious quartz found on the area's beaches. The oldest lighthouse still commissioned as a navigational aid, the 1859 **Cape May Lighthouse** offers fine views of the area. Nearby, the Cape May–Lewes ferry departs for Delaware. *Fee charged for ferry.*

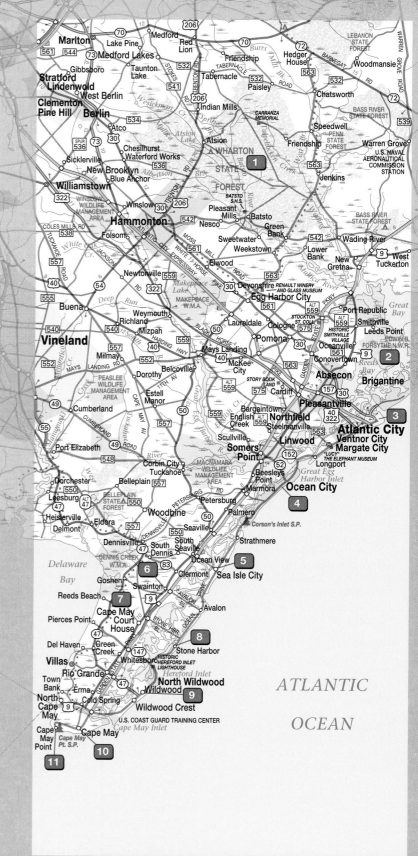

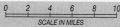

1. Lewes

Chamber of Commerce, 120 Kings Hwy.
Local artifacts dating from 1631 fill the
Zwaanendael Museum, which itself is a
replica of the town hall in Hoorn, the
Netherlands. The **Lewes Historical Society** preserves six 18th- and 19th-century
structures, including a country store, farmhouse, and blacksmith shop. Canada geese,
pintails, and black ducks can be seen at the
Prime Hook National Wildlife Refuge.
Admission charged at society.

2. Rehoboth Beach

Chamber of Commerce, 501 Rehoboth Ave.
Named for a biblical term meaning "room
enough," Rehoboth attracts many visitors
from the nation's capital, who come here —
and to **Dewey Beach** farther south — to
fish, sail, swim, and stroll the boardwalk.

3. Delaware Seashore State Park

This 7-mile stretch has both a calm bay and
a crashing ocean. Ospreys, piping plovers,
and an occasional bald eagle fly overhead.
Visitors come to swim, fish, surf, and boat.
Admission charged.

4. Fenwick Island

Chamber of Commerce, Rte. 1. This residential beach town and nearby **Bethany
Beach** are both known as quiet places for
family vacations. The boardwalk at Bethany
Beach has one of the area's best summertime arts-and-crafts shows, while Fenwick
Island features the 1859 **Fenwick Island
Lighthouse.** Surfing, fishing, swimming,
and sailing are popular activities at **Fenwick Island State Park.** *Fee charged for
parking at state park.*

5. Ocean City

*Convention and Visitors Bureau, 4001
Coastal Hwy.* Highlights include some 10
miles of beach, a 3-mile boardwalk, and two
full-scale amusement parks. Charter boats
take anglers deep-sea fishing, and the **Life
Saving Station Museum** describes shipwrecks, rescues, and indigenous marine
life. *Admission charged at museum.*

6. Assateague Island National Seashore

This national seashore is composed of
a pristine 37-mile-long barrier island,
Assateague, which is home to wild ponies
and a stopover for falcons. Endangered
piping plovers also come to nest in the area.
Naturalists guide canoe trips and nature
walks; they also give clamming and fishing
demonstrations. *Admission charged.*

7. Chincoteague

Chamber of Commerce, 6733 Maddox Blvd.
Every July, thousands of spectators watch
as wild Chincoteague ponies are rounded
up on Assateague Island. The animals are
then led across a channel to Chincoteague
and sold at auction. The **Chincoteague
National Wildlife Refuge** hosts more than
300 species of birds, many visible from the
3½-mile Wildlife Loop. Narrated cruises also
tour the refuge. *Admission charged.*

8. Furnace Town Historic Site

Off Rte. 12, near Snow Hill. This re-creation
of a 19th-century industrial village has a
broom house, blacksmith shop, smokehouse, church, company store, and period
gardens. On the grounds is the still-intact
Nassawango Iron Furnace, one of the
oldest of its kind. *Admission charged.*

9. Snow Hill

Tourism Office, 105 Pearl St. Summer cruises on the Pocomoke River recall the seafaring history of this charming port. The **Julia
A. Purnell Museum** displays farm tools,
spinning wheels, uniforms, and other artifacts. A historical walking tour includes
handsome century-old homes and the 1756
All Hallows Episcopal Church. *Admission
charged at museum.*

10. Salisbury

Chamber of Commerce, 300 East Main St.
The Newtown Historic District features a
number of Victorian homes as well as the
Poplar Hill Mansion, an early 1800's plantation home noted for its interior woodwork. On the campus of **Salisbury State
University,** the **Ward Museum of Wild-
fowl Art** features carvings of ducks, geese,
and songbirds. *Admission charged.*

11. Bethel

The entire town is listed on the National
Register of Historic Places. Its seafaring
heritage is evidenced by the 19th-century
homes that once belonged to captains and
marine carpenters.

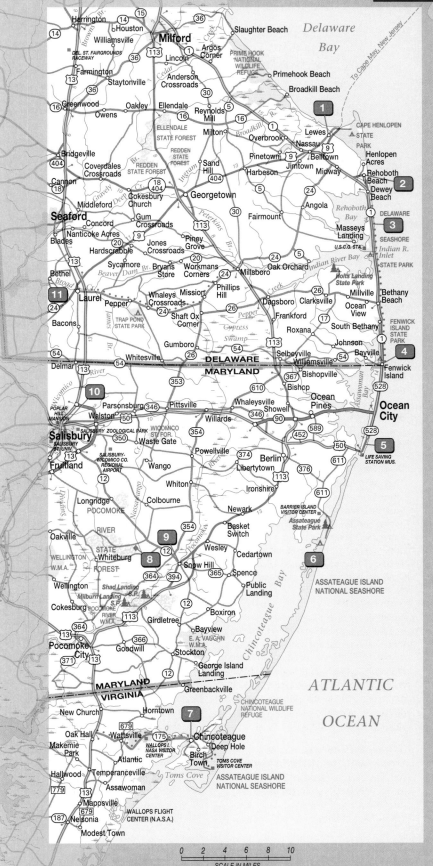

1. Edgewood Model Railroad

Bldg. E4310, Aberdeen Proving Ground, Edgewood. In a converted barracks, this scaled version of a railroad features some 1,500 feet of track leading through tunnels and over high bridges and mountain passes. Military personnel and civilian employees operate its rotary coal dumper and other special effects. Open only on Thursday evenings.

2. Hampton National Historic Site

535 Hampton Ln., Towson. Built from 1783 to 1790 for Captain Charles Ridgely, the three-story home is one of Maryland's largest late-Georgian-style mansions. It was once the center of a vast agricultural and industrial estate. The original furnishings reflect the elegance of the Ridgely family, who resided here until 1948. There are greenhouses, stables, slave quarters, farm buildings, and a reconstructed orangery.

3. Johns Hopkins University

This is one of the country's finest research universities, and visitors are welcome to tour the 126-acre campus. Nearby **Evergreen House** reveals how the wealthy lived in the early 1900's. It features Italianate architecture, Corinthian columns, and a formal garden. *Admission charged at house.*

4. Baltimore Zoo

Set in Druid Hill Park, this 200-acre zoo displays more than 1,200 exotic birds, mammals, and reptiles. They range from elephants and flamingos to African black-footed penguins and endangered white rhinos. At an 8-acre interactive children's zoo, youngsters can pass underground into a woodchuck's tunnel, jump on lily pads like a frog, and ride the Zoo Choo train. *Admission charged.*

5. Fort McHenry National Monument and Historic Shrine

East Fort Ave., Baltimore. Built in 1803, the fort was used in every American conflict through World War II. A 25-hour bombardment of the fort by the British during the War of 1812 provided the inspiration for Francis Scott Key to write "The Star-Spangled Banner." Historical exhibits are contained in the restored powder magazine, guardroom, officers quarters, and barracks. Presentations include performances by the Ft. McHenry Guard and reenactments of garrison life. *Admission charged.*

6. Ellicott City B & O Railroad Station Museum

2711 Maryland Ave., Ellicott City. The 1830 building that houses the museum is the nation's oldest terminus. Listed on the National Register of Historic Places, the site displays hundreds of railroad artifacts and scale model trains. In the restored 1885 freight house, a model railroad exhibit recreates the scenery and history of the original 13 miles of the Baltimore & Ohio (B & O) track between Baltimore and Ellicott's Mills. Other exhibits include an 1850's turntable and 1927 caboose, plus restored stationmaster's quarters, a ticket office, and an engine house. *Admission charged.*

7. Montpelier Mansion

Rte. 197 and Muirkirk Rd., Laurel. George and Martha Washington and Abigail Adams were once guests at this opulent home built in the 1770's. The National Historic Landmark features rooms with early 1800's furnishings and lovely boxwood gardens. A colonial herb garden, an 18th-century summerhouse, and the **Montpelier Cultural Arts Center** are also on the site. The center houses three galleries offering changing exhibits. Visitors can watch painters, sculptors, weavers, and jewelers create their wares. *Admission charged at mansion.*

8. College Park Airport Museum

6709 Corporal Frank Scott Dr., College Park. Once the place where Wilbur Wright trained the first military pilots, this is the world's oldest continually operating airport. Numerous aviation firsts occurred here, including the first civilian air-mail and controlled helicopter flights; the first test of an airplane machine gun, a bomb-dropping device, and radio-navigational aids; and the first mile-high flight. This National Register of Historic Places site displays photographs, early aviation memorabilia, and a 1919 U.S. Mail hangar.

9. NASA Goddard Space Flight Center Visitor Center

Soil Conservation Rd., Greenbelt. This facility was established in 1959 as the first major scientific laboratory devoted entirely to space exploration. It honors Dr. Robert Hutchings Goddard, the father of modern rocket propulsion. Visitors can observe some work areas, watch model rocket launches, and see satellites, capsules, and space research exhibits. Hands-on activities include steering gyro-chairs, piloting a maneuvering unit, and participating in star watches. Special events are held on the

Graduation day at the U.S. Naval Academy

second Saturday of each month; guided tours, presentations, and demonstrations are available for groups.

10. London Town Publik House and Gardens

839 Londontown Rd., Edgewater. The 1760 Georgian inn, restored and furnished in period style, depicts accommodations available to 18th-century travelers. Situated on the banks of the South River, the site also includes 8½ acres of woodland gardens, with native plants, a log tobacco barn dating to 1720, and a boat dock. Changing exhibits, as well as special programs and events, are presented here. *Admission charged.*

11. Saint John's College

Founded in 1696 as King William's School, this liberal arts college offers a curriculum based on the West's great books. Alumni include George Washington's nephews and Francis Scott Key. Changing exhibits are in **McDowell Hall,** begun in 1742 as a governor's mansion and used as a Civil War hospital. The 1722 **Carroll Barrister House** is the birthplace of the author of the Maryland Bill of Rights; its administration building can be toured by request. Revolutionaries rallied and Union troops camped under the school's 400-year-old **Liberty Tree.**

12. William Paca House and Garden

186 Prince George St., Annapolis. Built in 1763, this site was the estate of a former Maryland governor who also signed the Declaration of Independence. The 37-room red-brick mansion contains period furnishings. Among the estate's attractions are a restored 2-acre garden that features a Chinese Chippendale bridge, a domed summerhouse, a wilderness area with wildflowers, and formal parterres of holly, boxwood, and roses. *Admission charged.*

13. United States Naval Academy

Established in 1845, the academy occupies a beautiful 300-acre campus situated on the banks of the Severn River in Annapolis. It features buildings in a variety of architectural styles, in addition to numerous statues and memorials. The **Naval Academy Chapel,** its most prominent building, contains John Paul Jones's crypt, sword, and medals. A museum exhibits some 300 years of naval history, with battle flags, ship models, weapons, and items that once belonged to George Washington.

14. Hammond-Harwood House

19 Maryland Ave., Annapolis. Designed by William Buckland, perhaps the most prominent architect in Colonial America, this house is considered to be among the finest early homes in the nation. Built in 1774, it displays antique furnishings amid Buckland's exquisite moldings, cornices, and wood and plaster decoration. Located across the street, the **Chase-Lloyd House** exhibits more of the architect's exceptional ornamentation. *Admission charged.*

15. Maryland State House

State Circle, Annapolis. This is the oldest statehouse to be used continuously by a state government; once, it also housed the U.S. Congress. In 1783, Washington resigned his Continental Army commander's commission in the Old Senate Chamber, where Congress later ratified the Treaty of Paris, ending the American Revolution. Overlooking Annapolis from the highest hill, the building contains the country's largest wooden dome.

SCALE IN MILES
0 1 2 3 4 5

A carved lion in the Walters Art Gallery

DOWNTOWN BALTIMORE

1. Baltimore Museum of Art

Art Museum Dr. This Neoclassical building contains an outstanding exhibit of French Postimpressionist paintings, the largest collection of pieces by Matisse in the United States, works by other European masters, and a cast of Rodin's *The Thinker.* Additional displays include early Christian mosaics and one of the nation's most complete collections of prints and drawings. Also on view are items from Africa, the Americas, and Oceania. *Admission charged.*

The U.S.S. Constellation

2. The Great Blacks in Wax Museum

1601 East North Ave. African-American history is the focus of this museum. The more than 100 life-size wax figures here represent individuals who influenced events in ancient Africa, the Civil War, and the Harlem Renaissance, as well as in the crusade for civil rights. *Admission charged.*

3. Peabody Institute of Johns Hopkins University

Dating from 1857, this is one of the nation's oldest music conservatories. The 700-seat hall presents more than 60 concerts a year, some of which are free. The beautiful Peabody library features five tiers of wrought-iron balconies. A collection of research materials, also housed at the institute, is available to the public.

4. Washington Monument

Mt. Vernon Pl. This is the nation's oldest memorial to the first president. It is composed of a 164-foot-high Doric column that is topped with a 16-foot-high statue of George Washington. Inside the monument, visitors who climb a 228-step spiral staircase are rewarded with fine city views.

5. Walters Art Gallery

North Charles and Centre Sts. In an Italian Renaissance building, this world-famous museum contains more than 30,000 works, some as much as 5,000 years old. Exhibits include ancient, medieval, Baroque, and Byzantine art. An adjacent building houses the Asian collection. *Admission charged.*

6. Maryland Historical Society

201 West Monument St. The **Museum and Library of Maryland History** exhibits the original manuscript of Francis Scott Key's "The Star-Spangled Banner" as well as the world's largest collection of 19th-century American silver. The society also maintains a children's museum and another museum focusing on maritime history. The 1848 **Enoch Pratt House** contains period rooms. *Admission charged.*

7. Enoch Pratt Free Library

400 Cathedral St. This is one of the nation's largest public libraries. It contains an extensive collection of materials on the lives and works of writers Edgar Allan Poe and H. L. Mencken. Former homes of both authors are in the city, as is Poe's grave.

8. Lexington Market

Lexington and Eutaw Sts. Founded in 1782, this is one of the nation's oldest continuously operating markets. It features more than 140 vendors selling fresh meat, produce, seafood, baked goods, poultry, and other food from around the world.

9. B & O Railroad Museum

901 West Pratt St. The birthplace of the Baltimore & Ohio, the nation's oldest railroad line, this 12-acre facility dates to 1828. Visitors can see four 19th-century railway buildings, 120 locomotives and cars — including the most powerful steam locomotive ever built — and a variety of railroad models. On weekends a 2-mile round-trip ride on original tracks is offered. *Admission charged.*

10. Babe Ruth Museum

216 Emory St. Among the four adjoining row houses here are the baseball great's birthplace, which displays early 1900's furnishings, and a museum of memorabilia associated with Ruth and the Baltimore Orioles. Film clips and movies on baseball are also shown. *Admission charged.*

11. Charles Center

This 33-acre business area's several blocks contain parks, European-style plazas, restaurants, and an award-winning office building. The **Baltimore Center for the Performing Arts–Morris A. Mechanic Theatre** is in the nearby Hopkins Plaza. *Admission charged at theater.*

12. Basilica of the Assumption of the Blessed Virgin Mary

Mulberry and Cathedral Sts. This magnificent 1821 Neoclassical cathedral is the oldest in the nation. Designed by the architect of the Capitol, the church features six Corinthian columns, three large domes, a barrel vault, and stained-glass windows.

13. Eubie Blake National Museum and Cultural Center

409 North Charles St. The exhibits here interpret the career of the renowned composer of jazz and show tunes. Musicians, dancers, and actors perform; a gallery showcases local artists.

14. Peale Museum

225 Holliday St. Built in 1814 for American painter Rembrandt Peale, this museum is one of the nation's oldest. Its three floors of exhibit space contain mastodon bones, Victorian furnishings, 29 paintings from several generations of Peale family artists, and natural and man-made oddities. There are additional exhibits on early American museums and on the history of Baltimore. *Admission charged.*

15. Shot Tower

East Fayette and Front Sts. Some 1 million bricks compose this 234-foot-high tower that was built in 1828. Self-guiding presentations depict the shot-making process that took place here. Molten lead was dropped from the top, formed into balls in the air, and landed in water below. Other attractions include exhibits on antique guns and on the history of duck hunting, from colonial times to the present.

16. Jewish Heritage Center

11-27 Lloyd St. This site includes the historic 1845 **Lloyd Street Synagogue** and the 1876 **B'nai Israel Synagogue.** In addition to a collection of 150,000 documents, the center has exhibits on Jewish art and history. *Admission charged.*

17. Museum Row

Lombard St., between Front and Albemarle Sts. Baltimore's City Life Museums include the **H. L. Mencken House,** along with the Peale Museum. There are four additional attractions: The **1840 House** is a reconstructed wheelwright's row home, with costumed interpreters and hands-on activities. The **Carroll Mansion** is an elegant 1808 town house that was once owned by a signer of the Declaration of Independence. It contains Empire furnishings and paintings from the 1700's to the 1800's. The **Center for Urban Archaeology** has extensive displays of ceramics and glassware. The **Courtyard Exhibition Center** features changing exhibits on the history of the city. *Admission charged.*

18. Star-Spangled Banner House and 1812 Museum

844 East Pratt St. Home of the woman who sewed the flag that inspired Key to write the national anthem, this 1793 house contains period furnishings and Americana. The 1812 Museum displays relics, weapons, and memorabilia. *Admission charged.*

19. Holocaust Memorial

Gay St., between Water and Lombard Sts. Six rows of pear trees, each representing 1 million deaths, and a stark sculpture commemorate the 6 million Jewish victims killed by Nazis during World War II.

20. U.S. Custom House

40 Gay St. This 1907 structure features ornate Beaux Arts architecture, complete with three-story columns, a balustrade, and a 2,000-square-foot painted canvas that depicts sailing ships.

21. Harborplace

Light and Pratt Sts. These two glass-enclosed shopping malls have more than 100 specialty and gourmet shops, waterside restaurants, Parisian-style colonnades, and an outdoor amphitheater.

22. U.S.S. Constellation

Light and Pratt Sts. This is the U.S. Navy's first commissioned man-of-war. Launched in 1797, it is one of the nation's oldest warships to be continuously afloat, even after having seen action in Tripoli in 1802, against the British in 1813, and in the Civil War. *Admission charged.*

23. World Trade Center

401 East Pratt St. With 32 floors, this is one of the world's tallest pentagonal buildings. An observation deck on the 27th floor offers fine city views, as well as exhibits on Baltimore's harbor, culture, and economy. *Admission charged.*

24. National Aquarium in Baltimore

501 East Pratt St., on Pier 3. Thousands of aquatic animals are on view throughout this fascinating seven-level facility. One 335,000-gallon exhibit features more than 800 tropical fish. Also displayed are six species of sharks, a variety of whales, more than 50 rays, and one of the largest poison-dart frog collections in the world. Other exhibits include a South American rain forest complete with iguanas, parrots, and two-toed sloths; dolphin presentations; and hands-on activities for children. *Admission charged.*

25. The Maryland Science Center

601 Light St. Among the attractions children and adults might be captivated by here are science demonstrations, three floors of hands-on exhibits, a planetarium, and a five-story IMAX screen. *Admission charged.*

26. Baltimore Museum of Industry

1415 Key Hwy. Industries that flourished during Baltimore's early days are re-created here. The museum contains a print shop, a garment loft, and a late-1800's machine shop. Other attractions include participatory exhibits and a 1906 steam tugboat. *Admission charged.*

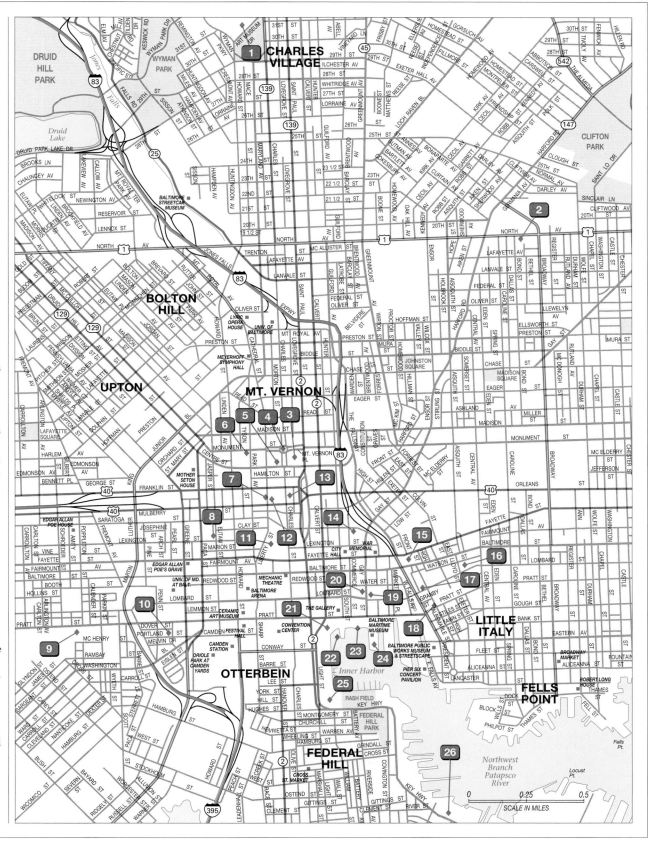

1. Chesapeake & Ohio Canal National Historical Park

11710 MacArthur Blvd., Potomac. This park encompasses the 184-mile-long canal. The offerings here include camping, picnicking, summer barge tours, canoeing, hiking, and bicycling. In an 1828 tavern, the main visitor center has exhibits and a lock model. *Admission charged at visitor center.*

2. Clara Barton National Historic Site

5801 Oxford Rd., Glen Echo. Built in 1891, this 35-room home of the founder of the American Red Cross was also its first head-quarters in the United States. The house is furnished in the style of the period when Barton was living here and contains some of her personal possessions.

3. National Museum of Health and Medicine

Walter Reed Army Medical Center, Washington, D.C. In order to interpret the history of medicine, this museum displays extensive collections of microscopes, diagnostic equipment, and surgical instruments. Other displays examine AIDS, drugs of abuse, and the assassinations of presidents Lincoln and Garfield. For children, the museum features five interactive exhibits that focus on the body's major organs.

4. Basilica of the National Shrine of the Immaculate Conception

Michigan Ave. and Fourth St. NE, Washington, D.C. Guided tours are available at this Byzantine-Romanesque shrine. The largest Roman Catholic church in the nation, it contains chapels, mosaics, sculpture, and stained glass. Nearby, the **Franciscan Monastery** displays Holy Land shrines and replicas of the catacombs in Rome.

5. The Phillips Collection

1600 21st St. NW, Washington, D.C. Billing itself as the first museum in America to be dedicated to modern art, the Phillips Collection features an excellent assortment of 19th- and 20th-century works by such American and European masters as Matisse, Goya, van Gogh, and O'Keeffe. In the nearby Anderson House, the **Society of the Cincinnati** has exhibits on the American Revolution and the decorative arts of Europe and Asia. *Admission charged at Phillips museum.*

6. Woodrow Wilson House

2340 S St. NW, Washington, D.C. The city's only presidential museum, this Georgian Revival town house was Wilson's residence from 1921 to 1924. The house contains original furnishings and gifts of state from the Paris Peace Conference. Located next door, the **Textile Museum** features a collection that is drawn from many cultures, including African, Asian, Near Eastern, and Native American. *Admission charged.*

7. National Zoological Park

3001 Connecticut Ave. NW, Washington, D.C. Ranked among the world's foremost zoos, this park exhibits some 5,000 animals representing some 500 species, including Komodo dragons and a famous giant panda. Also located within the complex is a re-created Amazonian rain forest, complete with many animals found in such a habitat. *Admission charged.*

8. Washington National Cathedral

Massachusetts and Wisconsin Aves. NW, Washington, D.C. After 83 years of construction, this Gothic cathedral was completed in 1990. Its attractions include flying buttresses, an herb cottage, and a bishop's flower garden, as well as the tombs of Woodrow Wilson and Helen Keller.

9. Dumbarton Oaks

1703 32nd St. NW, Georgetown. This former diplomat's estate contains an 1801 two-story brick mansion, renowned collections of Byzantine and pre-Columbian art, and 10 acres of formal gardens. In 1944 delegates from the Allied powers met here; the meeting led to the establishment of the United Nations. *Admission charged at gardens.*

10. Theodore Roosevelt Island

This 88-acre island has a 17-foot-high bronze statue honoring the conservation-minded president. The area is a refuge for a variety of native plants and has miles of nature trails. It's accessible by a pedestrian bridge from Virginia.

11. Arlington National Cemetery

Memorial Dr., Arlington. Home to the **Tomb of the Unknown Soldier,** this famous national cemetery contains the graves of John and Robert Kennedy, as well as more than 250,000 others. Built by George Washington's adopted son and once the residence of Robert E. Lee, the **Arlington House** displays original furnishings and is open to tours. *Fee charged for tour.*

12. The Pentagon

Off Rte. 395, Arlington. Encompassing some 29 acres, including 17½ miles of corridors and a 5-acre courtyard, this imposing structure serves as headquarters of the Department of Defense. A free 90-minute tour of the building— for which visitors are required to produce photo identification — features a hall that pays tribute to the recipients of the Congressional Medal of Honor.

13. Frederick Douglass National Historic Site

1411 W St. SE, Washington, D.C. The freed-man, statesman, and human-rights champion lived in this 21-room house from 1877 to 1895. Situated on a hilltop with fine views of the city, it contains original furnishings, a 2,000-volume library, and films documenting Douglass's civil rights activities.

14. Ramsay House Visitor Center

221 King St., Alexandria. As the home of the city's convention and visitor bureau, the early 1700's Ramsay House is the starting point for walking tours of Old Town. Among the historic sites visited are Christ Church, Gadsby's Tavern Museum, the Old Presbyterian Meeting House, and an apothecary. *Fee charged for tours.*

15. George Washington Masonic National Memorial

101 Callahan Dr., Alexandria. Modeled after an ancient lighthouse in Alexandria, Egypt, this 333-foot-high landmark contains Washington's belongings and original furnishings from the Alexandria–Washington Lodge No. 22, where he was a Worshipful Master. An observation deck offers spectacular views of the area.

16. Mount Vernon

Mt. Vernon Hwy., Mt. Vernon. This estate was home to George Washington from 1754 to 1799. Overlooking the Potomac River, the mansion contains the president's bed, chair, and sword, as well as Martha's porcelain tea service. Formal gardens, restored buildings, and Washington's tomb are on the grounds. *Admission charged.*

17. Woodlawn Plantation

9000 Richmond Hwy., Alexandria. This land was George Washington's wedding present to his foster daughter and nephew. Featuring period rooms and original furnishings, the 1805 Federal mansion here was designed by Dr. William Thornton, the Capitol's first architect. Formal gardens are on the grounds, as well as the **Pope-Leighey House,** designed by Frank Lloyd Wright. *Admission charged.*

18. Pohick Church

9301 Richmond Hwy., Lorton. This church's existence is largely owed to George Washington, who chose the site, supervised construction, and served as a vestryman for 23 years. It was built between 1769 and 1774. Today the restored interior displays the original stone baptismal font. During the Civil War, the church was gutted by Union troops; the exterior walls are marked with the initials of soldiers.

19. Gunston Hall

Off Rte. 95, Lorton. George Mason, author of the Virginia Declaration of Rights, which was used as a model by the framers of the Bill of Rights, built this elegant plantation house in 1755. The Georgian mansion has lovely interior wood carvings and views of the Potomac River. Outside there are formal boxwood gardens, a schoolhouse, and other buildings. *Admission charged.*

Situated on the banks of the Potomac River, Mount Vernon served for 45 years as the gracious residence of our nation's first president. Today visitors are welcome to tour the home and grounds.

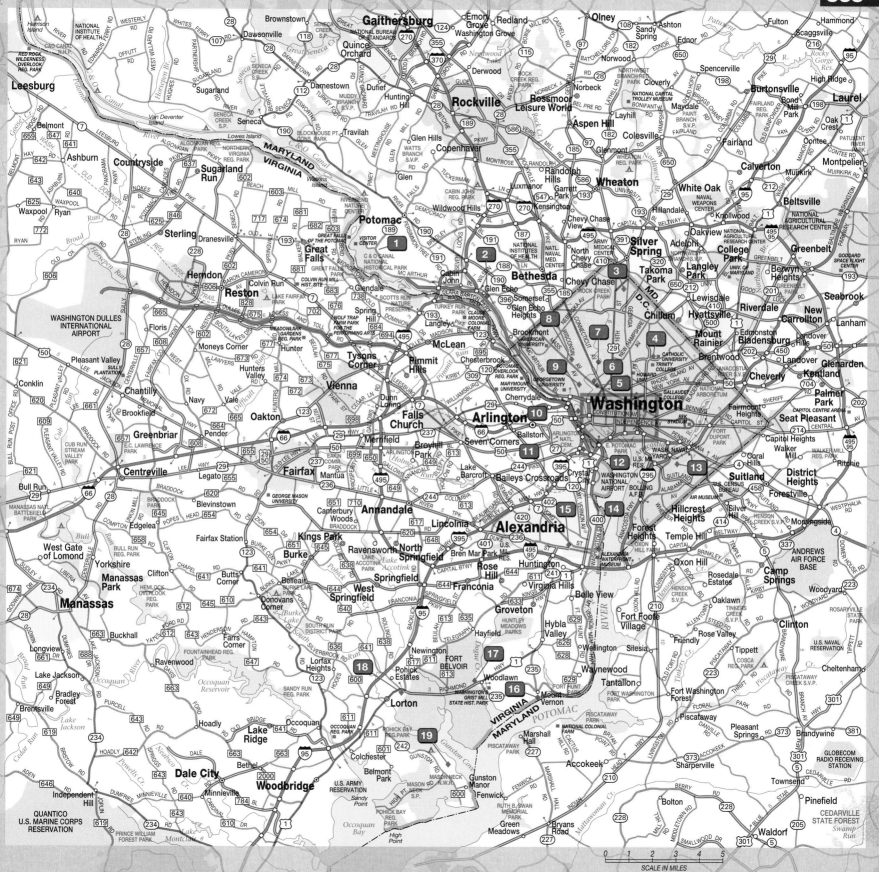

DOWNTOWN WASHINGTON, D.C.

1. Lincoln Memorial

West Potomac Park and 23rd St. NW. Dedicated in 1922, the 19-foot-high statue here by Daniel Chester French depicts a seated Abraham Lincoln who appears to be deep in thought about one of the difficult questions he was fated to decide. It is set within a columned temple, whose interior walls hold murals and engravings. Floodlights illuminate the monument at night, creating an especially dramatic scene. From the front of the memorial, visitors look out on the **Reflecting Pool,** the **Washington Monument,** and the **Capitol.** From the rear walkway there is a fine view of the **Arlington National Cemetery.**

2. Vietnam Veterans Memorial

Constitution Ave., between 21st and 22nd Sts. NW. This striking V-shaped monument is inscribed with the names of more than 58,000 dead or missing Vietnam veterans.

3. DAR Museum

1776 D St. NW. The rooms in this museum have been furnished to re-create the styles of specific periods and regions in early America. Together the displays contain more than 30,000 pieces of decorative and fine arts. There are also two galleries and a hands-on exhibit area for children.

4. U.S. Department of the Interior Museum

1849 C St. at 18th St. NW. On view are paintings, maps, models, surveying equipment, documents, and American Indian artwork. Other exhibits include fossils, a diorama of a mine explosion, and information on the Hoover Dam. Visitors must have photo identification.

5. B'nai B'rith Klutznick National Jewish Museum

1640 Rhode Island Ave. NW. Here Jewish ceremonial, decorative, and folk art exhibits

span some 20 centuries. Nearby, the **St. Matthew's Cathedral** displays a white marble altar with colored floral insets, plus beautifully crafted windows and mosaics.

6. National Geographic Society's Explorers Hall

1145 17th St., at M St. NW. This science center has exhibits on the many expeditions sponsored by the society. Amphitheater shows are given in **Earth Station One.** The **Geographica** is an interactive display on the earth, its geography, and the delicate balance among its inhabitants.

7. White House

1600 Pennsylvania Ave. NW. John Adams was the first president to occupy this famous residence, which opened in 1800. Tours are conducted Tuesday through Saturday mornings.

8. National Museum of Women in the Arts

1250 New York Ave. at 13th St. NW. Dedicated to women artists, this museum has some 1,600 items dating from the Renaissance to the present. The collection includes paintings, sculptures, and drawings.

9. Ford's Theatre

511 10th St. NW. In the basement of this restored theater, the **Lincoln Museum** depicts the assassination of the 16th president by John Wilkes Booth. Lincoln died in the Petersen house across the street.

10. National Portrait Gallery

Eighth and F Sts. NW. Displayed here are portraits, photographs, and lithographs of people who played a role in American history. Special collections include portraits of presidents by Gilbert Stuart.

11. National Museum of American Art

Eighth and G Sts. NW. Dating from the 1700's to the present, American sculpture, graphic arts, paintings, and prints are exhibited here. Highlights of the collection include the Lincoln Gallery and panoramas of the American West by Thomas Moran.

12. National Building Museum

401 F St., between Fourth and Fifth Sts. NW. Interpreting various aspects of building in America, this educational museum offers two permanent exhibits. The first traces construction in the Washington area over the past two centuries. The second displays

original drawings, photos, and other memorabilia on the 12 inaugural balls held in the museum's Great Hall. Ongoing temporary exhibits are also on view, featuring historical preservation, design, and crafts.

13. J. Edgar Hoover FBI Building

E St. between 9th and 10th Sts. NW. The popular tours of this building, which culminate with a firearms demonstration, cover exhibits on fingerprinting, espionage, crime, and those who are "most wanted."

14. The National Archives

Constitution Ave., between Seventh and Ninth Sts. NW. The original Declaration of Independence, the Bill of Rights, and a 13th-century Magna Carta are among the documents here. Genealogical information is cataloged; guided tours are available by appointment.

15. National Gallery of Art

Constitution Ave., between Fourth and Seventh Sts. NW. Andrew Mellon began this gallery by donating his private collection. Others followed suit, and the museum now has an outstanding collection of works by European and American painters.

16. The Capitol

Capitol Hill. Congress meets in the chambers of this landmark building, the cornerstone of which was placed by George Washington. Measuring 96 feet in diameter and 180 feet high, the building's Rotunda is decorated with murals, frescos, and a painted frieze depicting scenes from American history. North of the Rotunda is the Old Senate Chamber — in use until 1859 — where Henry Clay, Daniel Webster, and John C. Calhoun engaged in heated debates. Statuary Hall, built originally as the House chambers, contains an impressive collection of statues contributed by the states. Senators and representatives can provide their constituents with tickets to the visitors gallery.

17. The Supreme Court

1 First St. at Maryland Ave. NE. The country's highest court hears arguments for two weeks out of each month from October through April, then is in session from May through June on the first workday of every week. The courtroom is open to the public, and visitors may choose either a short or long tour. Lectures are held when the court is not in session. Exhibits and a film can be seen on the ground floor.

18. Folger Shakespeare Library

201 East Capitol St. SE. A 1623 folio is but one feature in this important collection of materials pertaining to William Shakespeare. The library offers an exhibition gallery, interactive videos, music performances, and lectures.

19. The Library of Congress

101 Independence Ave. SE. Housed in this library's three buildings are some 30 million books, including a Gutenberg Bible, and about 70 million additional items, such as maps, posters, manuscripts, and prints. The stacks are closed to the general public, but anyone age 18 or older with photo identification may use the library's collection by filling out a request form. Family roots can be traced in the Local History and Genealogy Reading Room, recordings of folk music and stories can be heard in the Performing Arts Reading Room, and classic films are shown in the Mary Pickford Theater.

20. Grant Monument

Eastern end of the Mall. Some 252 feet in width, the 1922 sculpture here portrays Ulysses S. Grant on horseback, with cavalry and artillery troops behind him.

21. National Air and Space Museum

601 Independence Ave. at Sixth St. SW. Among the aircraft displayed at this popular museum are the *Wright Flyer,* the *Spirit of St. Louis,* and an X-15. Exhibits on space include rockets, aerospace computers, capsules from the Mercury, Gemini, and Apollo missions, and a special moon rock display. There is also a five-story IMAX movie screen and a planetarium. *Fee charged for movie and planetarium.*

22. Hirshhorn Museum and Sculpture Garden

Independence Ave. and Eighth St. SW. This round, three-story museum focuses on painting and sculpture of the 20th century. The collection consists of some 20,000 works, featuring American, European, and Latin artists. The sculpture garden has pieces by Auguste Rodin and Henry Moore.

23. The Mall

Pierre L'Enfant's 1791 design for the capital city called for a grand avenue, but it was not until the turn of this century that his idea became reality. Today this stretch of greenery is bordered by some of the finest museums and art galleries in the nation.

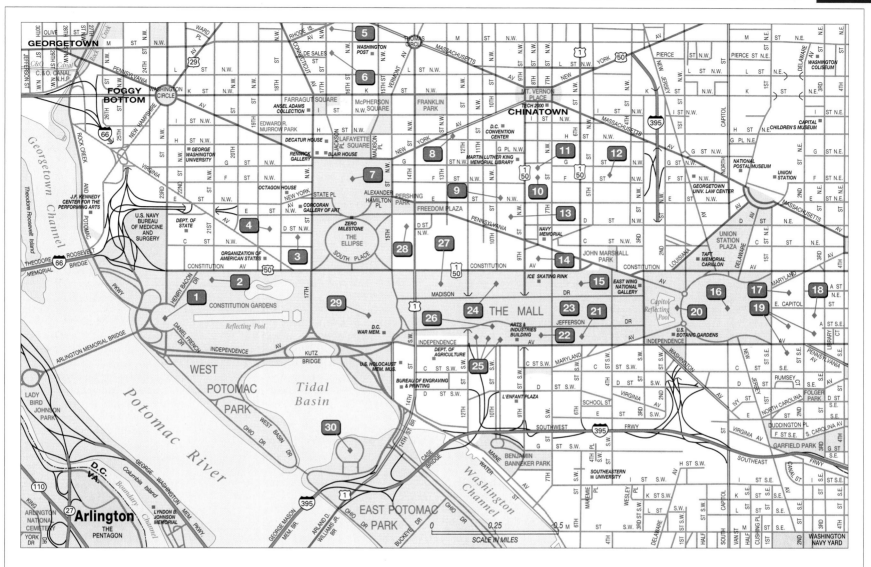

24. National Museum of Natural History

10th St. and Constitution Ave. NW. A division of the Smithsonian Institution, the museum contains displays of dinosaurs, ancient sea life, a living coral reef, and live insects. Other exhibits examine various facets of zoology, botany, geology, and the history of Western culture.

25. Arthur M. Sackler Gallery, Freer Gallery of Art, and National Museum of African Art

In the Sackler Gallery visitors may view Chinese jade and Persian manuscripts; the Freer Gallery has one of the world's finest collections of Asian art, as well as American works, such as paintings by James Abbott McNeill Whistler. The National Museum of African Art holds more than 6,000 objects, including jewelry, textiles, sculptures, and decorative arts. The **U.S. Holocaust Memorial Museum** is located nearby.

26. Smithsonian Institution Building

1000 Jefferson Dr. SW. The remarkable Smithsonian Institution, which today consists of 15 museums and the National Zoo, was made possible by James Smithson, a wealthy English scientist, who bequeathed his fortune to his nephew; the money eventually was left to the U.S. government to use "for the increase and diffusion of knowledge." In 1855 this building was completed after a design by James Renwick. Popularly known as the Castle, today it introduces visitors to the Smithsonian. Two films give an overview of the institution, staff members are on hand to answer questions, electronic wall maps help locate points of interest, and interactive programs give information on the city's attractions.

27. National Museum of American History

14th St. and Constitution Ave. NW. Under the auspices of the Smithsonian Institution, this museum examines the nation's cultural and technological developments. The flag that inspired "The Star-Spangled Banner," ship models, a Railroad Hall, and videos are among the exhibits.

28. The National Aquarium

14th St., between Pennsylvania and Constitution Aves. NW. This is the nation's oldest public aquarium, home to both freshwater and saltwater creatures — altogether some 1,700 examples. Attractions include a tank where visitors can touch the marine life. *Admission charged.*

29. Washington Monument

On the Mall, at 15th St. NW. Soaring some 555 feet, this tribute to the country's first president is the world's tallest masonry structure. An elevator ascends to the top.

30. Thomas Jefferson Memorial

South side of the Tidal Basin. An awe-inspiring sight, especially when hundreds of cherry blossoms are in bloom, this monument pays tribute to the nation's third president. Boats can be rented for paddling on the Tidal Basin. *Fee charged for boat rental.*

1. Meadow Farm Museum

3400 Mountain Rd., Richmond. With its farmhouse, outbuildings, and animals, this living-history museum depicts rural life in 1860. Other attractions include a flower-filled 150-acre park and a visitor center with exhibits. *Admission charged.*

2. Agecroft Hall

4305 Sulgrave Rd., Richmond. Built in England in the 15th century, this house was transplanted here in 1926. Inside are furnishings and artworks from the Tudor and early-Stuart periods. The adjacent **Virginia House,** also imported from England, displays an eclectic collection of 16th-through-20th-century furnishings; the grounds have formal gardens. *Admission charged.*

3. Virginia Museum of Fine Arts

2800 Grove Ave., Richmond. The exhibits here include Impressionist paintings, African masks, Fabergé eggs, and modern art. There are also works from India, Nepal, and Tibet. *Admission charged.*

4. Science Museum of Virginia

2500 West Broad St., Richmond. Omnimax films, planetarium shows, and more than 200 hands-on exhibits on various sciences are showcased here. *Admission charged.*

5. Maggie L. Walker National Historic Site

110½ East Leigh St., Richmond. The daughter of an ex-slave, Walker was the first American woman to become a bank president. In 1903, she established what is today the country's oldest surviving bank owned by African-Americans. Her 25-room Victorian town house has been restored and contains period furnishings.

6. John Marshall House

818 East Marshall St., Richmond. This is the restored home of the Supreme Court chief justice, who lived here from 1790 to 1835. It contains many original furnishings as well as memorabilia of Marshall's 34-year tenure on the Court, from 1801 to 1835. The

nearby **Valentine Museum,** once the home of sculptor Edward Valentine, whose studio is in the garden, traces the history of Richmond through displays of costumes, decorative arts, and architecture. Museum admission includes a tour of the 1812 John Wickham House. *Admission charged.*

7. The Museum and White House of the Confederacy

1201 East Clay St., Richmond. The opulent White House of the Confederacy was the home of Jefferson Davis during the Civil War; today it contains many original furnishings. The adjacent museum holds the country's largest collection of Confederate documents and memorabilia. To learn more about the war, visitors can explore the **Richmond National Battlefield Park,** encompassing 770 acres that are divided into 10 separate units. Among the areas are the sites of McClellan's 1862 Peninsula Campaign and Grant's 1864 attack. Information, exhibits, and maps of a self-guided auto tour are available in the Main Visitor Center. *Admission charged at museum.*

8. Edgar Allan Poe Museum

1914 East Main St., Richmond. The four houses here, including the 1730's Old Stone House, contain personal effects, manuscripts, and memorabilia of the author. At nearby **St. John's Episcopal Church,** Patrick Henry declared, "Give me liberty or give me death!" On Sundays from late May till early September reenactments are staged here of the Second Virginia Convention. *Admission charged.*

9. State Capitol

Capitol Square, between Ninth and Governor Sts., Richmond. Thomas Jefferson helped design this handsome structure, modeled after a Roman temple in France. Within its walls, Aaron Burr was tried for treason, Robert E. Lee was given command of the Confederate forces of Virginia, and the Confederate Congress met. The famous Houdon statue of George Washington stands in the rotunda. An equestrian statue of the first president and a monument to Stonewall Jackson are among the Capitol Square's statuary. News of Lee's retreat from Petersburg reached Jefferson Davis in the nearby **St. Paul's Episcopal Church,** which is notable for exquisite stained-glass windows, ceiling plasterwork, and a mosaic reproduction by Tiffany of Leonardo da Vinci's *The Last Supper.*

10. Maymont

1700 Hampton St., Richmond. Featured here are carriage and tram rides, an outdoor children's farm, a nature center, and an aviary. There are also Italian and Japanese gardens, as well as the 33-room Dooley Mansion, replete with 19th-century antiques. *Fee charged for rides.*

11. Trapezium House

224 North Market St., Petersburg. According to lore, the 19th-century owner of this house was influenced by his servant's belief that ghosts haunted right angles. So he constructed his home as a trapezium, a four-sided shape with no parallel lines. Now restored, it is furnished with period antiques. *Admission charged.*

12. Old Blandford Church and Cemetery

321 South Crater Rd., Petersburg. One of the country's first observances of Memorial Day was held in the cemetery next to the 18th-century brick church, which became a Confederate memorial in 1901. Its Tiffany stained-glass windows were contributed by the Confederate states. The cemetery holds the graves of 30,000 Confederate soldiers. *Admission charged.*

13. Petersburg National Battlefield

36 East Washington St., Petersburg. Robert E. Lee's army withstood a 10-month siege here before finally succumbing to Ulysses S. Grant's forces. During the blockade, Union soldiers tunneled beneath the Confederate lines, where they planted and detonated gunpowder. The explosion created much chaos as well as a gigantic crater. The hole can still be seen today, along with the tunnel entrance and miles of original entrenchments. Living-history demonstrations are reenacted during the summer. *Admission charged.*

14. Centre Hill Mansion

1 Centre Hill Court, Petersburg. This handsome 1823 mansion bears traces of several architectural styles. Among its antique furnishings is an 1886 Knabe Art grand piano. *Admission charged.*

15. Siege Museum

15 West Bank St., Petersburg. A film here describes Petersburg during the siege, and there are exhibits of weapons, uniforms, and household utensils. Nearby is the **Appomattox Iron Works,** a restored 19th-century industrial site. *Admission charged.*

16. City Point Unit, Petersburg National Battlefield

Cedar La. and Pecan Ave., Hopewell. While he was a lieutenant general in the Union Army in 1865, Ulysses S. Grant directed the siege of Petersburg from the lawn of Appomattox Manor, a house that has remained in the same family for more than three centuries. The home, with many original furnishings, and Grant's cabin have been restored.

17. Shirley Plantation

501 Shirley Plantation Rd., Charles City County. Dating from 1613, this is the oldest plantation in Virginia. A house here built about 1723 has belonged to the Hill-Carter family — a clan that includes Robert E. Lee's mother — for 10 generations. On display are family heirlooms and original furnishings. *Admission charged.*

18. Berkeley Plantation

12602 Harrison Landing Rd., Charles City County. This three-story brick house was built in 1726 by Benjamin Harrison IV. Among the family's illustrious members are a signer of the Declaration of Independence and two presidents, William Henry and Benjamin. "Taps" was composed here when Union Gen. George McClellan was headquartered on the plantation during the Civil War. *Admission charged.*

19. Westover

7000 Westover Rd., Charles City County. Only the extensive grounds of this fine 1730 Georgian home of William Byrd II, founder of Richmond, are open to the public. At nearby **Evelynton,** the home of Byrd's daughter, both the house and gardens are open daily. *Admission charged.*

20. Flowerdew Hundred Museum

1617 Flowerdew Hundred Rd., Hopewell. This 1,400-acre outdoor museum and archeological dig is on the site of a 17th-century plantation. Among the several thousand items displayed are Paleo-Indian artifacts, a commemorative 18th-century windmill, and a replica of a 19th-century kitchen. *Admission charged.*

21. Sherwood Forest Plantation

Rte. 5, Charles City County. This estate was the home of John Tyler, the nation's 10th president. Still owned by the family, the residence is the longest frame house in America. It also contains many original furnishings. *Admission charged.*

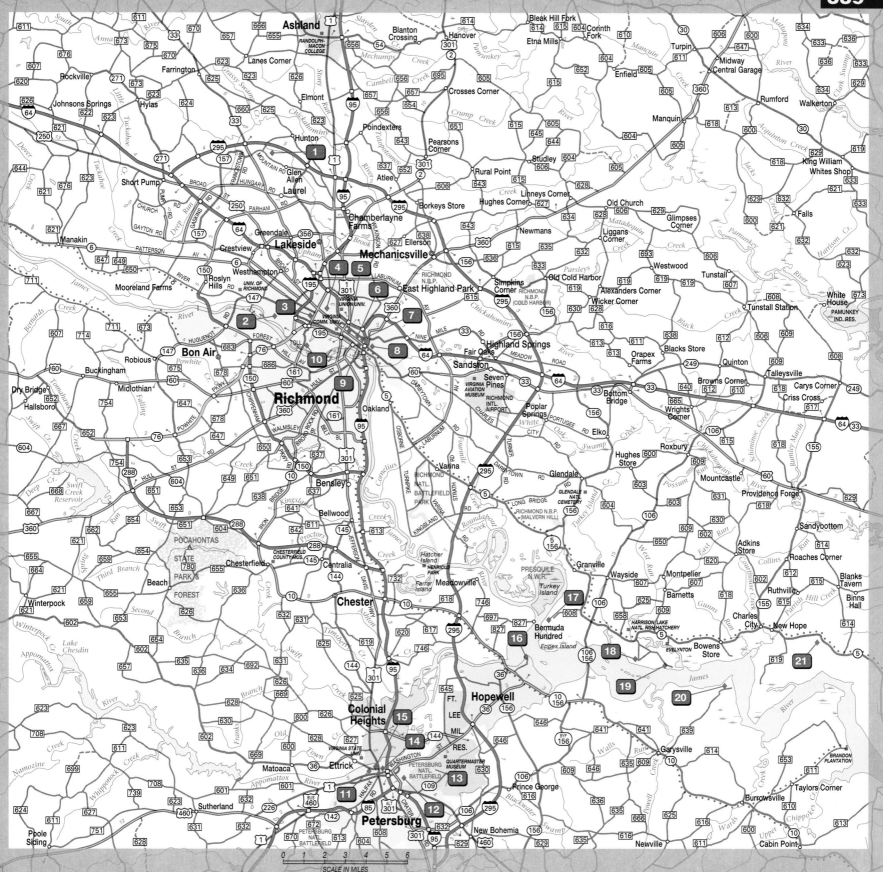

SCALE IN MILES

1. Abraham Lincoln Museum

Rte. 25E, Harrogate. This museum on the Lincoln Memorial University campus has more than 30,000 items pertaining to Lincoln and the Civil War. *Admission charged.*

2. Levi Jackson Wilderness Road State Park

Tribute is paid here to the more than 200,000 pioneers who traipsed the Wilderness Road. The **Mountain Life Museum** has primitive buildings and pioneer artifacts. One of the world's largest collections of millstones can be seen at **McHargue's Mill.** *Admission charged at museum.*

3. Cumberland Gap National Historical Park

This 20,000-acre park is laced with trails. Among the sights are the remnants of an abandoned settlement and the Pinnacle Overlook. Exhibits and a slide show in the park's visitor center examine the Indian Ancient Warriors Path, a trail that Daniel Boone followed, which led to its being renamed the Wilderness Road.

4. Southwest Virginia Museum Historical State Park

Wood Ave. and West First St., Big Stone Gap. This area's past comes alive in the park's museum, an 1888 house. The exhibits underscore 18th-century pioneer life as well as a coal-mining boom and include quilts, a whiskey still, and spinning and sewing machines. *Admission charged.*

5. Shot Tower Historical/New River Trail State Parks

Overlooking a bluff and rising about 70 feet, the 1807 tower was used to make shot for guns. From its platform, molten lead was dropped about 150 feet into kettles of water located some 75 feet down a shaft at the tower's base. The parks have picnic areas and trails for hiking, biking, and horseback riding. *Admission charged at tower.*

6. Blowing Rock

Chamber of Commerce, Main St. This resort area is named for a rocky cliff where, according to legend, an Indian brave was blown back into the arms of his beloved. The narrow-gauge train at **Tweetsie Railroad** carries passengers past thrills and an 1880's railroad town. **Mystery Hill** features hands-on science exhibits and a natural phenomenon in which water runs uphill. *Admission charged for some attractions.*

7. Grandfather Mountain

Blue Ridge Pkwy., Exit 305. At almost 6,000 feet, this is the highest peak in the Blue Ridge range. In addition to spectacular views, attractions include the Environmental Habitat, where bears, cougars, and eagles can be seen; a museum showing award-winning nature films; and hiking and picnic areas. *Admission charged.*

8. Emerald Village

Rte. 1100, west of Little Switzerland. The **North Carolina Mining Museum** traces the industry's history in the area. A trail leads through a mine, where mining paraphernalia is displayed. The village has several museums, and visitors can prospect for gems. *Admission charged.*

9. Andrew Johnson National Historic Site

College and Depot Sts., Greeneville. This site commemorates the one-time tailor who became Lincoln's vice president and then the nation's 17th president. It maintains Johnson's 1830's house, his 1850's homestead, and his grave. His tailor shop is a museum. *Admission charged at homestead.*

10. Highlands

Chamber of Commerce, Fourth and Oak Sts. Surrounded by the **Nantahala National Forest,** this resort area is in a rain forest environment some 4,000 feet above sea level. There are splendid vistas, especially at the 411-foot **Whitewater Falls,** the highest east of the Mississippi River. The **Highlands Biological Station and Botanical Gardens** has plant and wildlife exhibits. Nearby **Franklin** has mines and a museum.

11. Dahlonega

Welcome Center, Public Sq. The **Dahlonega Gold Museum State Historic Site** has exhibits and a film depicting the first major gold rush. At the **Consolidated Gold Mine,** visitors can see actual veins of gold; they may also pan for the mineral. The **Chattahoochee National Forest** offers swimming, camping, and picnic areas. *Admission charged for some attractions.*

12. Clemson

Chamber of Commerce, 103 Clemson St. **Clemson University** was founded here in 1889 by Thomas Clemson, son-in-law of John C. Calhoun. Situated on the campus are **Fort Hill,** a mansion displaying original furnishings of the Calhouns and Clemsons; the **South Carolina Botanical Garden,** lush with greenery; and the 1716 **Hanover House.** At the Oconee Nuclear Station in nearby Seneca, the **World of Energy Visitor Center** has hands-on exhibits on how energy is created as well as a 418-gallon tank filled with fish and turtles.

13. Pendleton Historic District

Visitor Center, 125 East Queen's St. The Pendleton historic district includes more than 50 structures from the 18th and 19th centuries, many of which border the village green. The Ashtabula and Woodburn mansions are open to visitors from April through October. *Admission charged.*

14. Toccoa

Chamber of Commerce, 901 East Currahee St. The Cherokee word that gives this town its name means "beautiful," certainly an apt term for the 186-feet-high **Toccoa Falls.** The **Traveler's Rest State Historic Site** has a restored stagecoach inn that was initially a private home. *Admission charged.*

15. Green Street Historical District

Chamber of Commerce, 230 E.E. Butler Pkwy., Gainesville. Handsome Victorian and Neoclassical homes line the wide street. Green Street Station is home to the **Georgia Mountain Museum,** containing artifacts from pioneer days to the 20th century.

16. Madison-Morgan Cultural Center

434 South Main St., Madison. A museum with 19th-century regional artifacts and galleries with changing historical and contemporary exhibits are housed in this former school, which was one of the first in the South to separate its students by grade level. *Admission charged.*

17. Athens

Welcome Center, 280 East Dougherty St. Home to the **University of Georgia,** Athens also boasts the **Georgia Museum of Art,** where the permanent collection features paintings by artists of the Hudson River School, and the **State Botanical Garden of Georgia,** offering a conservatory, gardens, and hiking trails. The **Taylor-**

Grady House has 18th- and 19th-century furnishings. Located in front of City Hall is a double-barreled cannon from the Civil War, said to be the only one of its kind. *Admission charged for some attractions.*

18. Washington

Chamber of Commerce, 104 East Liberty St. The **Callaway Plantation** is a working farm featuring 18th- and 19th-century structures that are furnished with antiques. The 1797 **Robert Toombs House Historic Site** was the home of a Georgia secessionist leader; it has been restored and contains personal effects and furnishings. The **Washington-Wilkes Historical Museum** exhibits Indian artifacts and memorabilia from the Civil War. *Admission charged for some attractions.*

19. A. H. Stephens State Historic Park

Rte. 22, Crawfordville. Liberty Hall, once home to the Confederacy's vice president, contains many of Stephens's possessions. A museum exhibits artifacts from the Civil War. *Admission charged.*

20. Congaree Swamp National Monument

200 Caroline Sims Rd., southeast of Columbia. Attractions at this old-growth, bottomland forest include a self-guiding canoe trail and 20 miles of walking trails. Some 85 species of trees, 170 species of birds, and a variety of fish are among nature's presentations here.

21. Edisto Gardens

Rte. 301, Orangeburg. Flowering trees and shrubs decorate this 110-acre city park, which nestles beside the Edisto River. Tennis courts and picnic facilities are among the attractions.

22. Swan Lake Iris Gardens

West Liberty St., Sumter. The 45-acre lake is home to graceful swans and water lilies. The surrounding landscape includes gardens, nature trails, and picnic areas.

23. Camden

Chamber of Commerce, 724 South Broad St. **Historic Camden** is a 92-acre complex on the site of the 1751 settlement here. Included within it are restored 18th- and 19th-century houses and a nature trail. Exhibits in the **Camden Archives and Museum** trace the city's history. Town founders are buried in the **Quaker Cemetery.** *Admission charged for some attractions.*

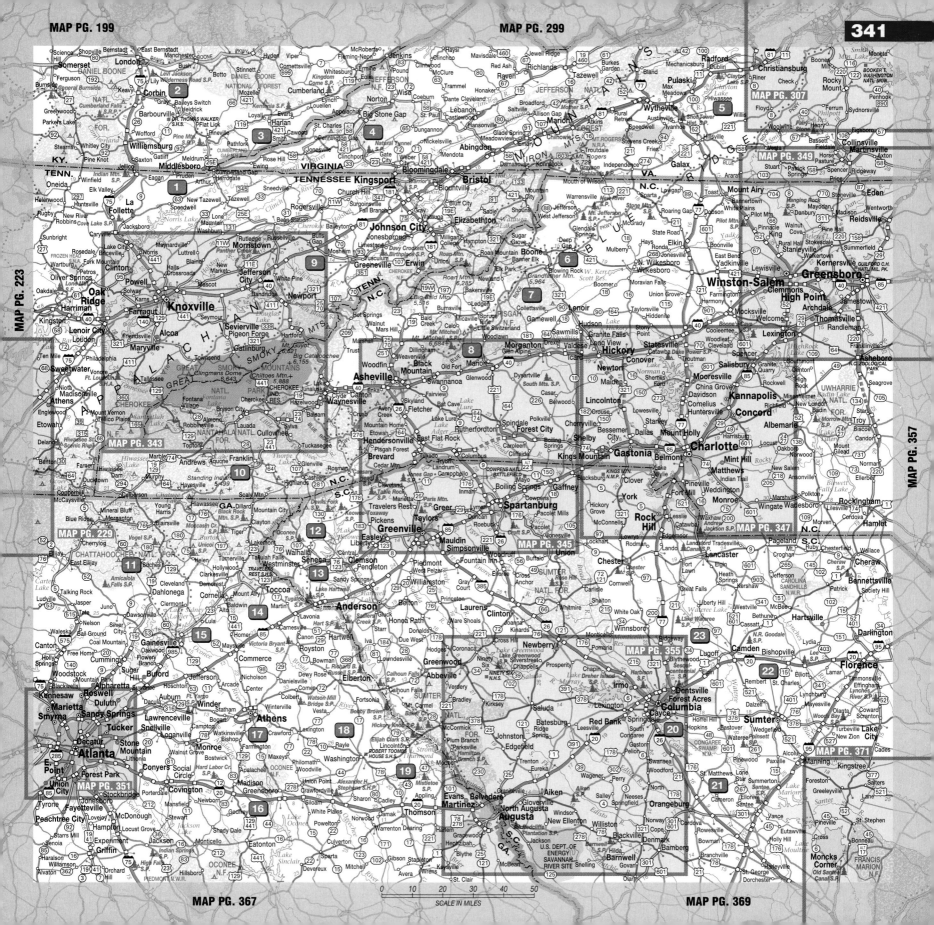

MAP PG. 307
MAP PG. 349
MAP PG. 223
MAP PG. 357
MAP PG. 343
MAP PG. 229
MAP PG. 345
MAP PG. 347
MAP PG. 355
MAP PG. 351
MAP PG. 371

SCALE IN MILES

1. Museum of Appalachia

Rte. 61, Norris. The 65-acre village here contains 35 buildings furnished with some 250,000 period artifacts. Structures include cabins, a log church, gristmill, underground dairy, iron jail, and a huge barn that exhibits collections of axes, baskets, bullet molds, and musical instruments. Demonstrations of pioneer skills and music are featured periodically. The Appalachian Hall of Fame contains items from the lives of famous mountain folk. *Admission charged.*

2. American Museum of Science and Energy

300 South Tulane Ave., Oak Ridge. More than 200 exhibits highlight this region's main endeavor, the research and development of energy. Operating until 1963, the nearby **Graphite Reactor,** the world's first full-scale nuclear reactor, is open to visitors.

3. General James White Fort

205 East Hill Ave., Knoxville. Within the fort is the 1786 home built by the founder of Knoxville. A restored smokehouse, blacksmith shop, and a museum are among the seven log buildings with pioneer furnishings and artifacts. *Admission charged.*

4. Governor William Blount Mansion

200 West Hill Ave., Knoxville. This restored 1700's frame house, which once belonged to a signer of the Constitution, contains period furnishings and memorabilia. A 1700's garden and Blount's office are also here. *Admission charged.*

5. Knoxville Museum of Art

410 10th St., Knoxville. In addition to its permanent collection, this museum displays traveling exhibitions of regional, national, and international works. Constructed of pink marble and glass, the building overlooks World's Fair Park. *Admission charged.*

6. Armstrong-Lockett House

2728 Kingston Pike, Knoxville. Known as Crescent Bend, the house was built in 1834 and is one of the oldest continuously occupied homes in Knoxville. It displays antique silver, decorative arts, and 1700's furniture. Terraced gardens with fountains extend to a riverbank. *Admission charged.*

7. Confederate Memorial Hall

3148 Kingston Pike SW, Knoxville. Once the headquarters of Confederate Gen. James Longstreet, the 15-room antebellum mansion here contains Civil War relics and an extensive collection of Southern literature. *Admission charged.*

8. Marble Springs/Home of Governor John Sevier

1220 West Governor John Sevier Hwy. An original cabin, a farmhouse, and other restored buildings that once belonged to John Sevier, Tennessee's first governor, display period furnishings. *Admission charged.*

9. Sam Houston Schoolhouse

Sam Houston Schoolhouse Rd., north of Maryville. On the National Register of Historic Sites, the park here includes a restoration of the log building where Houston taught in 1812. A visitor center displays various teaching tools and artifacts used by Houston. *Admission charged.*

10. Sevierville

Chamber of Commerce, 866 Winfield Dunn Pkwy. The **Smoky Mountain Deer Farm and Petting Zoo** exhibits wallabies, pygmy goats, miniature horses, zebras, and other animals. Visitors also can pet and feed some 140 deer. **Forbidden Caverns,** once an Indian shelter and later a moonshiner's hideout, contains a large onyx wall, natural chimneys, waterfalls, and a stream. *Admission charged.*

11. Pigeon Forge

Department of Tourism, 2450 Parkway. Visitors can take guided tours of the water-powered **Old Mill,** which has continuously ground flour since its construction in 1830. **Dollywood,** a seasonal entertainment park operated by Dolly Parton, features concerts, craft demonstrations, rides, and a museum devoted to her career. Potters at **Pigeon Forge Pottery** demonstrate shaping and glazing from March through December. *Admission charged for some attractions.*

12. Gatlinburg

Chamber of Commerce, 520 Parkway. Among the attractions in this popular mountain resort is the **American Historical Wax Museum,** where 75 life-size figures are displayed in 45 re-created scenes. **Christus Gardens** displays floral gardens, extensive collections of ancient coins and Bibles, as well as full-size dioramas that portray events from Jesus's life. The **Guinness World Records Museum** has exhibits detailing record-breaking accomplishments. The **Gatlinburg Aerial Tramway** and the **Gatlinburg Sky Lift** both offer fine views of the area. *Admission charged.*

Musicians at the Museum of Appalachia

13. Cades Cove Visitor Center

Off Laurel Creek Rd., near Townsend. This visitor center is on an 11-mile, one-way loop road that encircles a scenic and historic section of the park, where reminders of the early settlers' lifestyle are preserved. In addition to abundant wildlife, the region contains restored log cabins, barns, a gristmill, and campsites. Free ranger-led tours depart from the center during the peak tourist season.

14. Great Smoky Mountains National Park

Named for the deep blue haze that sometimes envelops its rolling mountains, this park covers some 517,000 acres across two states; it also contains the East's largest virgin forest, inhabited by an impressive variety of plants and animals. The lookout tower at Clingmans Dome affords a panoramic view of the many peaks. **Newfound Gap Road** is another great way to see the area, and audio tapes giving mile-by-mile information on history, points of interest, plants, and wildlife are available. More than 975 miles of horse and foot trails — including some 70 miles of the Appalachian Trail — meander through forests, past waterfalls, and into the high country. At the park's northern entrance, the **Sugarlands Visitor Center** provides details on the many attractions.

15. Oconaluftee Indian Village

Off Rte. 441, Cherokee. At this re-created 1750 Cherokee community, Native Americans wear tribal dress and demonstrate the making of basketry, beadwork, pottery, canoes, arrows, and blow guns. The **Cherokee Botanical Gardens** features indigenous plants and a preserved seven-sided council house. *Admission charged.*

16. Oconaluftee Visitor Center

Rte. 441, near Cherokee. At the park's southern entrance, the center provides visitors informational brochures. An adjacent **Pioneer Farmstead** presents 13 authentic structures, including a small farmhouse, a sorghum mill, a springhouse, and a barn. North of the center, cornmeal is ground and sold at the **Mingus Mill.**

17. Museum of the Cherokee Indian

Rte. 441 and Drama Rd., Cherokee. The tribe's culture, from prehistory to the present, is interpreted with audiovisual shows and with the area's most comprehensive collection of tribal crafts, clothing, household tools, and weapons. *Admission charged.*

18. Great Smoky Mountain Railway

1 Front St., Dillsboro. The railroad operates three tours, including a 4-hour round-trip excursion into 2,000-foot-deep and 8-mile-long Nantahala Gorge, which is known internationally for its whitewater rafting. Seating is offered in both open and closed cars. *Admission charged.*

19. Cullowhee

This town's nearby mountains and lakes provide opportunities for boating, fishing, and backpacking. Dedicated to the history of southern Appalachia, the **Mountain Heritage Center** exhibits hundreds of family heirlooms as part of an exhibit that chronicles the lives of the area's Scotch-Irish settlers. Nearby **Judaculla Rock** is a soapstone boulder covered with petroglyphs. According to Cherokee legend, the markings were created when a giant leapt from his mountaintop home.

20. Ghost Town in the Sky

890 Soco Rd., Maggie Valley. A chairlift and incline railway carry passengers 3,364 feet up a mountain to a theme park with separate western, mining, and mountaineer towns. There are 30 rides, saloon shows, staged gunfights, and country music shows. *Admission charged.*

1. Mount Mitchell State Park

Visitors can drive to the summit of Mt. Mitchell, which at 6,684 feet is the highest point east of the Mississippi River. The 1,677-acre park includes hiking trails, picnic areas, an observation tower, and museum. Camping is allowed from May to October.

2. Zebulon B. Vance Birthplace State Historic Site

911 Reems Creek Rd., Weaverville. Six log outbuildings, a reconstructed two-story log house, and a museum pay tribute to the lives of Zebulon Vance, North Carolina's governor during the Civil War, and his grandfather David Vance, who fought in the American Revolution.

3. Biltmore Homespun Shops

111 Grovewood Rd., Asheville. Mrs. George Vanderbilt established these shops to preserve the Old World skills of weaving, spinning, and dyeing. Ivy-covered buildings in the 11-acre park include the **Biltmore Industries Museum,** where exhibits consist of vintage machinery, handlooms, mountain crafts, woven cloth, and a film on manufacturing. There's also an antique automobile museum that displays cars built as early as 1905.

4. Thomas Wolfe Memorial State Historic Site

48 Spruce St., Asheville. The esteemed writer grew up in the 1880's residence here. Much of Wolfe's novel *Look Homeward, Angel* was set in the home, a boarding house operated by his mother, where today the displays include photos, clothing, and original furnishings. *Admission charged.*

5. Folk Art Center

Blue Ridge Pkwy., 7 miles east of Asheville. This 30,000-square-foot center has one of Appalachia's oldest craft shops and a comprehensive craft library. The culture and history of the region are interpreted through demonstrations and music programs. Contemporary crafts are also displayed. *Donations encouraged.*

6. Western North Carolina Nature Center

75 Gashes Creek Rd., Asheville. The world of nature is interpreted for children and adults here through programs, demonstrations, hands-on activities, and a menagerie. The complex includes a children's petting area, an aviary, and trails. *Admission charged.*

7. Biltmore Estate

Rte. 25, Asheville. Built in the 1890's as the private home of George Washington Vanderbilt, this is one of America's largest private residences. The 250-room French château has hand-carved limestone on the exterior; inside are hand-tooled Spanish leather walls in the breakfast room, 72-foot-high ceilings in the banquet hall, a bowling alley, Napoleon's chess table, and priceless antiques. The 8,000-acre estate features 75 acres of formal gardens, abloom from early spring to late autumn. Self-guiding tours take 3 to 4 hours and include restored barns, stables, a carriage house, and a winery. *Admission charged.*

8. Mount Pisgah

Named after the biblical mountain from which Moses saw the Promised Land, Mt. Pisgah was part of George Vanderbilt's estate. Trails crisscross the slopes, passing magnificent viewpoints, wildflower meadows, rocky outcroppings, a 137-site campground, and the 5,721-foot-high summit. Between June and October, educational programs are presented in an outdoor amphitheater. Facilities along the nearby Blue Ridge Parkway include picnic areas, an inn, and a restaurant.

9. Forest Discovery Center/ Cradle of Foresty in America National Historic Site

1 Pinchot Dr., 14 miles north of Brevard. The center is located at the Biltmore Forest School, where forest management was first practiced and taught by the conservation pioneers Gifford Pinchot and Dr. Carl Schenck. The history of forestry is traced through exhibits, puzzles, and demonstrations. The mile-long forest festival trail winds past logging locomotives, a portable sawmill, conifers, hardwoods, rhododendrons, and a trout pond. *Admission charged.*

10. Carl Sandburg Home National Historic Site

1928 Little River Rd., Flat Rock. The 247-acre estate here was the poet's home from 1945 to 1967. Originally the summer residence of the first Confederate treasurer, Christopher Gustavus Memminger, it includes the main residence, which was built in 1838; Sandburg's furnishings; a herd of Nubian, Toggenburg, and Sanaan goats; and the Swedish House, where the writer stored his magazines and research materials. *Admission charged.*

11. Chimney Rock Park

This park encompasses some 1,000 acres and includes picnic areas, playgrounds, an observation lounge, and a nature center. Visitors can reach the summit of Chimney Rock, a 315-foot-high monolith some 2,280 feet above sea level, by a trail and stairway or by an elevator that rises 26 stories within the mountain. Another trail leads to Hickory Nut Falls, twice as high as Niagara Falls. Other landmarks are Devil's Head and Moonshiner's Cave. *Admission charged.*

12. Cowpens National Battlefield

Visitor Center, 4001 Chesnee Hwy., northwest of Gaffney. This park memorializes the American patriots and British regulars who fought the Battle of Cowpens on January 17, 1781. American losses were comparatively few, while the more experienced British lost 75 percent of their troops. The original national battlefield site covered only an acre; today it has been increased to 845 acres and includes a restored 1830's cabin. Sites of heated action are marked by exhibits and audio stations along both a 1½-mile trail and a 3-mile auto tour. Interpretive exhibits in the visitor center include a lighted map that traces the armies' movements and a multi-image slide presentation. *Fee charged for slide show.*

13. Regional Museum of Spartanburg County

50l Otis Blvd., Spartanburg. Permanent exhibits here interpret the Battle of Cowpens and the founding of Spartanburg. Other displays include an extensive collection of dolls, quilts, maps, and photographs. Changing exhibits depict aspects of life in South Carolina's up-country.

14. Jammie Seay House

106 Darby Rd., Spartanburg. Built around 1790 for a Revolutionary War soldier who turned to yeoman farming, this hand-hewn log building covered with wood sheathing was owned by family members until 1974. Its chimney is constructed of a fieldstone common to Virginia but rarely found in upstate South Carolina.

15. Walnut Grove Plantation

1200 Ott's Shoal Rd., Roebuck. Built in 1765, the girlhood home of Revolutionary War heroine Kate Moore Barry is located on this plantation. The house is furnished with pre-1830 antiques, including utensils fashioned out of wrought iron, earthenware, and wood. The grounds encompass a kitchen, a barn, and the area's first school. Barry is said to have planted the walnut trees that give this site its name. *Admission charged.*

16. Bob Jones University Art Gallery and Biblical Museum

1700 Wade Hampton Blvd., Greenville. In addition to its displays of rare religious artwork, this museum has more than 400 paintings by European masters from the 1200's through the 1800's. Among the collection are works by the gifted artists Rembrandt, Van Dyck, Rubens, and Botticelli. Children under six are not permitted.

17. Greenville County Museum of Art

420 College St., Greenville. The exhibits here represent one of the nation's best collections of regional art. The permanent display of North American works from colonial to contemporary times features paintings by Thomas Sully and Jasper Johns. Changing exhibits include contemporary paintings, sculpture, and photography. Films, seminars, and lectures are also presented.

Garden statuary graces Biltmore.

1. Arts and Science Center of Catawba Valley

243 Third Ave. NW, Hickory. The 1920's Neoclassical building here is adorned with Corinthian columns, repeated arches, spiral staircases, and intricate Grecian designs. In addition to European, Oriental, and pre-Columbian art, the spacious galleries exhibit one of the southeast's finest collections of 20th-century American Impressionism. The science center includes antique toys, fossils, and interactive exhibits on physical science.

2. Catawba County Museum of History

21 North Main Ave., Newton. The galleries in this museum have exhibits on furniture, folk art, religion, and education. South of Newton on Rte. 321, another branch of the museum features a 1759 cabin, an 1800's blacksmith shop, a fire engine, and an agricultural display. The Bunker Hill covered bridge is in nearby Claremont. Just west of Catawba off Rte. 10, **Murray's Mill** is a turn-of-the-century gristmill; also harking back to the days of old is a country store. *Admission charged at mill.*

3. Statesville

Chamber of Commerce, 115 East Front St. Built during the French and Indian War, **Fort Dobbs State Historic Site** displays original artifacts and an excavated moat, cellar, magazine area, and well. Nearby is the grave of Peter Ney, who claimed to be one of Napoleon's aides. Although his boast has never been proved, his story has been the subject of many books.

4. Salisbury

Convention and Visitors Bureau, 215 Depot St. A trading, cultural, and judicial center since 1753, Salisbury is also known for having been resided in by both Daniel Boone and Andrew Jackson. Today the town boasts a large historic district, which includes the **Rowan Museum.** Built in 1815, it now interprets local history with period rooms, antique furniture, a 19th-

century garden, and various relics. The **Dr. Josephus Hall House,** an antebellum home once belonging to the surgeon of a Civil War prison located here, contains most of its original Victorian furnishings. *Admission charged.*

5. North Carolina Transportation Museum at Historic Spencer Shops

411 South Salisbury Ave., Spencer. The state's transportation history is interpreted at this former repair facility of the Southern Railway. The complex includes a 37-bay roundhouse and nine other buildings. Among the attractions are Conestoga wagons, vintage automobiles, steam locomotives, bicycles, and a dugout canoe. Steam and diesel trains tour the 57-acre site. *Fee charged for tours.*

6. Reed Gold Mine State Historic Site

9621 Reed Mine Rd., south of Concord. The nation's first documented gold discovery was on John Reed's farm in 1799; as a result, North Carolina was the country's leading producer of gold until the California rush. The site offers trails, demonstrations, exhibits, and guided tours of underground mines. It also contains an operating ore-crushing machine, called a stamp mill. For a fee, visitors can pan for gold between April and October.

7. Charlotte Museum of History and Hezekiah Alexander Homesite

3500 Shamrock Dr., Charlotte. The museum has exhibits on local and regional history. Built in 1774, the stone house here is the oldest in the county. Today it serves as a memorial to a Revolutionary leader and one of the writers of North Carolina's first constitution. Costumed guides conduct tours of the home, a spring house, a reconstructed hand-hewn log kitchen, and gardens. *Fee charged for tours.*

8. The Fourth Ward

501 North Graham St., Charlotte. The visitor center here offers a self-guiding tour of 18 historic sites in the ward, which contains excellent Victorian restorations. Among the attractions are the **Old Settlers' Cemetery,** dating to the 1700's; the **First Presbyterian Church,** an 1857 Gothic Revival structure featuring stained glass; the flamingo pink **Overcash House;** the **Spirit Square,** a cultural and performing

arts center housed in a Romanesque Revival church; and Fourth Ward park.

9. Discovery Place

301 North Tryon St., Charlotte. The hands-on exhibits in this educational complex explore science and technology. Visitors can take a simulated ride through space, handle sea life at a re-created tidal pool, and see a three-story-high rain forest — complete with exotic birds, large rock formations, and waterfalls. Designed especially for children, the **Charlotte Nature Museum and Planetarium** features a nature trail, a room with live animals, a physics playground, and a puppet theater. *Admission charged.*

10. Mint Museum of Art

2730 Randolph Rd., Charlotte. This Greek Revival building was the first branch of the U.S. Mint and, in the Civil War, served as a Confederate headquarters and hospital. It exhibits porcelain, pottery, American and European paintings, antique maps, pre-Columbian art, African artifacts, and gold coins minted here from as far back as 1835. *Admission charged.*

11. Wing Haven Gardens and Bird Sanctuary

248 Ridgewood Ave., Charlotte. In addition to wooded areas, this 3½-acre complex features a variety of gardens, including rose and herb. More than 140 species of birds have been sighted here. The peak periods of migration are in fall and spring; visitors can check the information boards, which list the birds most likely to be seen.

12. James K. Polk Memorial State Historic Site

Rte. 521, Pineville. This site has a main house and a separate kitchen that date back to the early 1800's. Although the buildings are not original to the Polk homestead, they are furnished in period style. The exhibits in a museum, guided tours, and a 25-minute movie examine the life and times of the nation's 11th president.

13. Museum of York County

4621 Mt. Gallant Rd., north of Rock Hill. This museum has a collection of mounted mammals from Africa as well as from North and South America. The site also offers art galleries, planetarium shows, nature trails, and picnic facilities. *Admission charged.*

14. Historic Brattonsville

1444 Brattonsville Rd., east of McConnells. Once owned by Col. William Bratton, a

commander of a Revolutionary militia, the restored plantation buildings here reflect the 1770's to 1850's lifestyle of the region. They include an 18th-century log house that was clapboarded in 1839, a homestead, a women's academy, and a family home. *Admission charged.*

15. Kings Mountain National Military Park

This site memorializes a 1780 Revolutionary War battle in which untrained and outnumbered patriot frontiersmen killed, wounded, or captured 1,104 Tory troops. Ultimately instrumental to success at Yorktown, it was the first major American victory in several confrontations. Self-guiding trails extend through the 3,950-acre battlefield, which contains several monuments. The visitor center offers a diorama and a film.

16. Schiele Museum of Natural History and Planetarium

1500 East Garrison Blvd., Gastonia. As well as offering movies and planetarium shows, this 16-acre complex has natural-history displays and a short nature trail that leads to a Catawba Indian village, where visitors can inspect re-created dwellings as well as native arts and crafts. A restored mid-1700's pioneer farm with living-history programs is also featured. *Admission charged for some attractions.*

17. Gaston County Museum of Art and History

131 West Main St., Dallas. Housed in the 1852 Hoffman Hotel, this museum contains the state's largest public collection of horse-drawn carriages and sleighs. The 1901 Dallas Depot and Caboose has a learning station with lectures and films. Changing exhibits include 20th-century American art, displays on the history of textiles, and local artifacts and documents.

18. Latta Plantation Park

5225 Sample Rd., 12 miles north of Charlotte. This 1,063-acre nature preserve on Mountain Island Lake abounds with recreational opportunities. Visitors can horseback ride, hike, canoe, bird-watch, and see horse shows. The park also has an Audubon sanctuary and a raptor center that treats injured birds of prey. Costumed guides conduct tours of **Latta Place,** a plantation house dating from the early 1800's, which includes replicas of a log house and an old-time kitchen. *Admission charged for some attractions.*

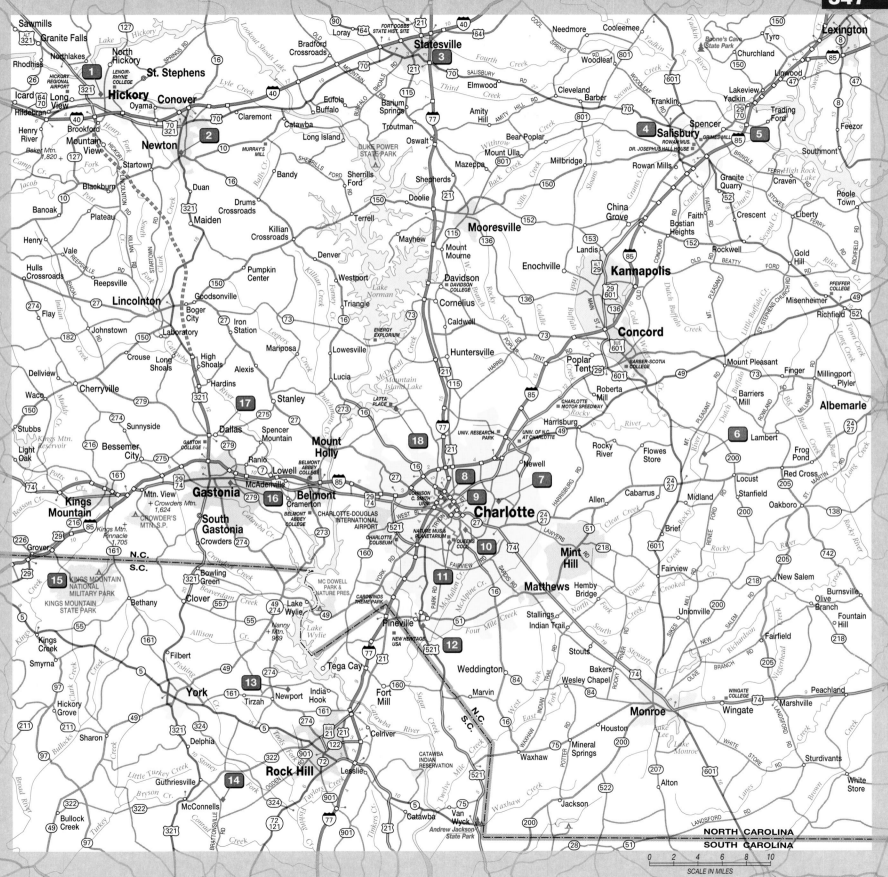

1. Danville Museum of Fine Arts and History

975 Main St., Danville. Housed in an 1857 Italian-style mansion that once briefly served as the last capitol of the Confederacy, this museum displays rooms used by President Jefferson Davis. Also featured are works by contemporary and earlier artists, 18th- and 19th-century decorative arts, and a historical collection that includes costumes, photos, and Civil War artifacts.

2. Virginia Museum of Natural History

1001 Douglas Ave., Martinsville. Situated among the rolling hills of the Blue Ridge Mountains, this museum has exhibits on science, history, and nature. Displays include animated replicas of reptiles that once inhabited the planet; actual tracks are also on view. Other attractions include a 9-foot model of a ground sloth and a fossilized whale skeleton. Visitors can operate a zoom video camera and see enlarged images on a 32-inch monitor.

3. Reynolds Homestead

Rte.1, Critz. Home of Hardin Reynolds, a successful businessman and father of the the founder of the R. J. Reynolds Tobacco Company, this 1843 farmhouse has been restored and contains many original furnishings and artifacts. The 717-acre estate includes several outbuildings, a family cemetery, a slave graveyard, several acres of landscaped grounds, and the Continuing Education Center — an art and science complex that offers lectures, crafts, and concerts. *Admission charged.*

4. Historic Bethabara Park

2147 Bethabara Rd., Winston-Salem. On the site of a 1753 Moravian settlement, this 80-acre park has a restored 18th-century garden and 6 miles of nature trails. Among the restored buildings are a 1788 church, a 1782 potter's house, and an 1803 brewer's house. A fort dating from the French and Indian War has been reconstructed. Guided tours and picnic grounds are available.

5. Reynolda House Museum of American Art

Reynolda Rd., Winston-Salem. Completed in 1917, this 100-room mansion was built by R. J. Reynolds, founder of the tobacco company that bears his name. Ranging from the mid-18th century to the present, the collection consists of sculptures and paintings, with works by Thomas Eakins, Mary Cassatt, Georgia O'Keeffe, and Frederick E. Church. The two-story living room, surrounded by a balcony, contains a 1917 Aeolian pipe organ. Early 20th-century toys and womens' clothes are also on display. The gardens here are especially lovely when the cherry blossoms bloom. *Admission charged.*

6. Southeastern Center for Contemporary Art

750 Marguerite Dr., Winston-Salem. In an existing Tudor-style mansion, this center was founded in 1956 to display works of contemporary artists and, with its series of annual awards, to promote excellence in the creative arts. Educational programs include gallery tours, lectures, and art classes. The landscaped grounds of the 32-acre estate are open to visitors. *Admission charged.*

7. Home Moravian Church

529 South Church St., Winston-Salem. The denomination's Southern headquarters, this 1800 church welcomes visitors to its services. The Easter Sunrise Service, the Christmas Eve Lovefeast, and the New Year's Eve Watchnight are especially popular. At nearby **God's Acre Cemetery,** some 4,000 graves are marked with simple headstones, most of them alike, as a symbol of the equalizing nature of death.

8. Old Salem

Visitor Center, Academy St. and Salem Rd., Winston-Salem. In 1766 Moravians founded the town of Salem. Today a restored neighborhood of some 90 original structures is again an active community, with several of the houses serving as private residences. Visitors are welcome at 12 of the buildings, including the 1768 **Fourth House,** the oldest of the structures, and the 1769 **Single Brothers House,** where teenage boys once lived in order to learn various trades. Also on the grounds is the **Museum of Early Southern Decorative Arts,** which displays 17th-century furnishings and decorative arts. Self-guided tours begin at the visitor center. *Admission charged.*

9. High Point

Convention and Visitors Bureau, 300 South Main St. So named because it was the highest point along an old railroad line, this town is one of the nation's leading manufacturers of furniture — a fact boldly depicted by the **Giant Bureau,** a building designed to resemble a huge chest of drawers. The **High Point Museum** includes the restored 1786 John Haley House, one of the oldest structures in the state; a blacksmith shop; and a weaving house.

10. Guilford Courthouse National Military Park

2332 New Garden Rd., Greensboro. One of the last battles of the Revolutionary War was fought here on March 15, 1781, when Cornwallis's forces encountered troops under the command of American Gen. Nathanael Greene. The British won the field, but the Continental Army inflicted many casualties. A 2½-mile-long driving tour takes visitors to several monuments, including the graves of two signers of the Declaration of Independence. The visitor center offers films and other displays.

11. Natural Science Center

4301 Lawndale Dr., Greensboro. In addition to its museum, zoo, and planetarium, this complex has an aquarium, exhibits on dinosaurs, and an exploration area for children age 7 and younger. A quarter-mile nature trail leads through a wooded area. *Admission charged.*

The North Carolina Zoological Park

12. Greensboro Historical Museum

130 Summit Ave., Greensboro. Located in a complex that includes an 1892 church, this museum features memorabilia of two famous natives, Dolley Madison and O. Henry. The reconstructed 19th-century village here includes a drugstore, doctor's office, and an antique fire engine. Other attractions are antique cars, a Conestoga wagon, a 19th-century bicycle, a depiction of a 1960 civil rights sit-in, and an exhibit on military history.

13. Charlotte Hawkins Brown Memorial State Historic Site

6136 Burlington Rd., Sedalia. In 1902 Charlotte Hawkins Brown, granddaughter of slaves, established the Palmer Memorial Institute, one of America's finest preparatory schools for African-Americans. The school was closed in 1971. Located on the old campus, the historic site was established to commemorate the outstanding achievements of the state's black educators. Guided tours are offered. The visitor center has exhibits and an educational video.

14. Alamance Battleground State Historic Site

Off Rte. 62, 6 miles south of Burlington. On May 16, 1771, the Regulators, a group of farmers who objected to the British government's taxes, marched against Governor Tryon's militia. Although the Regulators outnumbered the governor's forces, the farmers were soundly defeated, probably because they were so poorly trained. An audiovisual presentation is given at the visitor center. Picnic areas are available.

15. Asheboro

Chamber of Commerce, 317 East Dixie Dr. The Asheboro area has a long pottery-making tradition; collectors can visit nearby **Seagrove,** where descendants of 18th-century English potters still practice the craft. For auto-racing fans the **Richard Petty Museum,** north of town, features race cars, trophies, and other mementos of Petty's career. Off Rte. 64 some 6 miles south of Asheboro, the **North Carolina Zoological Park** has re-created natural habitats and walkways that lead to views of more than 32,000 plants and 800 exotic animals. Highlights include an aviary, home to some 150 beautifully colored birds; a pavilion, where some 200 animals from Africa are displayed; and simulations of North American regions, including an exhibit on the Sonora Desert. *Admission charged.*

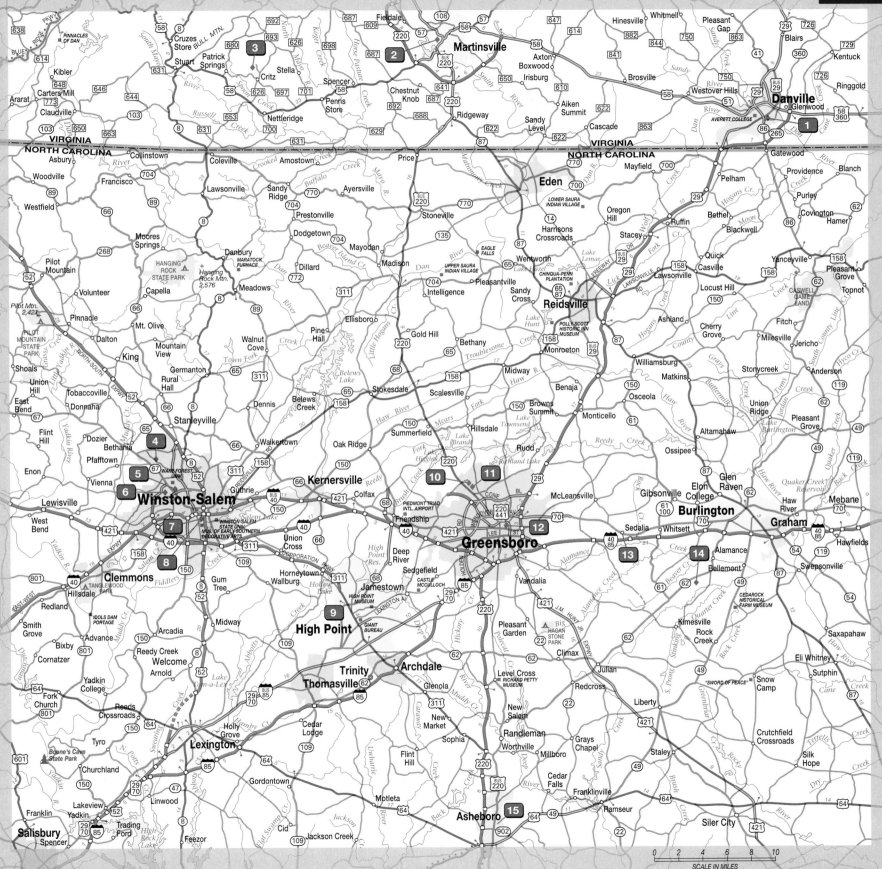

SCALE IN MILES
0 2 4 6 8 10

1. Roswell
Visitor Center, 617 Atlanta St. Period furnishings are displayed in **Bulloch Hall,** a Greek Revival house from the 1840's that was once home to Theodore Roosevelt's mother. On the banks of a river, the 100-acre **Chattahoochee Nature Center** features several trails through marshes and woodlands. There are also exhibits on local plants and wildlife. *Admission charged.*

2. Big Shanty Museum
2829 Cherokee St., Kennesaw. Housed in an old cotton gin, this museum displays a locomotive that was stolen during the Civil War by 21 Union raiders in an attempt to disrupt the Confederacy's supply route from Atlanta. Known as the General, the engine was abandoned some 86 miles to the north. Dioramas, memorabilia, and other exhibits document this and other Civil War events. *Admission charged.*

3. Kennesaw Mountain National Battlefield Park
Rte.41 and Stilesboro Rd., Marietta. In June 1864, a battle ensued here between Gen. Joseph E. Johnston's Confederate army and Union forces led by Gen. William T. Sher-

man that resulted in a short-lived Confederate victory, for the Union troops would soon lay siege to Atlanta. A self-guiding auto tour and several miles of hiking trails lead to the restored remains of earthworks, gun positions, and battle sites.

4. Marietta
Welcome Center, 4 Depot St. Maps are available of a walking tour through this town's historic district, which includes **Kennesaw House,** General Sherman's headquarters in 1864. **Marietta National Cemetery** contains the graves of American soldiers from every U.S. war, while some 3,000 Southern soldiers are buried in the **Confederate Cemetery. White Water Park** offers a myriad of watery rides. *Admission charged at park.*

5. Concord Bridge
Concord Rd., 3 miles west of Smyrna. Built in 1848, the original covered bridge was burned during the Civil War. This 133-foot-long reconstruction uses the same stone supports as the destroyed span. The historic district here also contains the **Concord Woolen Mill, Ruff's Mill,** and a miller's house, the last two from 1850.

6. Six Flags Over Georgia
7561 Six Flags Pkwy., Austell. Generating the thrills at this theme park are hair-raising roller coasters, a parachute drop, and water rides down falls and chutes. Many gentler attractions are included as well. *Admission charged.*

7. Wren's Nest
1050 Ralph David Abernathy Blvd. SW, Atlanta. Named for wrens that nested in its mailbox, this gabled Victorian house was the home of Joel Chandler Harris, a short-story writer who used authentic dialect and true-to-life characters to capture the African-American experience in the Old South. The house contains many of the original furnishings and mementos, including the author's typewriter, eyeglasses, and walking stick. *Admission charged.*

The boughs of a flowering dogwood tree frame the Confederate Memorial at Georgia's Stone Mountain Park. Inset, a dogwood blossom

8. Hammonds House Galleries
503 Peeples St. SW, Atlanta. Located in the restored 1857 Victorian home of Dr. Otis T. Hammonds, a noted physician and art patron, this museum contains works by African-American and Haitian artists, ranging from the mid-1800's to the present. Films, videos, and guided tours are available. *Admission charged.*

9. Georgia Governor's Mansion
391 West Paces Ferry Rd. NE, Atlanta. Eighteen acres of landscaped grounds and formal gardens surround this handsome Greek Revival residence built in 1968 for the state's governor. Beautifully furnished with antiques and Federal-period pieces, the building contains the Circular Hall, where adornments include an elaborate chandelier and a rare porcelain vase with a portrait of Benjamin Franklin on it.

10. Atlanta History Center
3101 Andrews Dr. NW, Buckhead. On a landscaped 32-acre estate, this center has a collection of artifacts from the Civil War and other periods important to Atlanta's history. There are also two restored homes. The 1840 **Tullie Smith House** is an example of Plantation-style architecture, and the **Swan House,** an elegant structure from the 1920's, displays maps, photographs, and manuscripts. *Admission charged.*

11. Emory University Museum of Art and Archaeology
Carlos Hall, Emory University Quadrangle, Atlanta. Housed in an elaborate Beaux Arts building, this museum's collection ranges from pre-Columbian and ancient Greek sculpture and pottery to an assortment of prints, drawings, and paintings from the 13th century to the present. *Donations encouraged.*

12. Fernbank Museum of Natural History
767 Clifton Rd. NE, Atlanta. This museum's main exhibit traces the state's natural history and the evolution of the earth with a large-screen video and life-size replicas of dinosaurs. A collection of seashells from around the world and a high-tech installation examining the laws of physics are other attractions. *Admission charged.*

13. Fernbank Science Center
156 Heaton Park Dr. NE, Atlanta. In addition to its sizable planetarium, this center features exhibits on spacecraft, indigenous

animals, and the state's geology. Nearby greenhouses are home to exotic plants and displays of annuals and perennials. The 65-acre Fernbank Forest has 2 miles of nature trails. *Admission charged at planetarium.*

14. Decatur
Convention and Visitors Bureau, 750 Commerce Dr. This city's restored 1898 courthouse contains the **DeKalb County Historical Society and Museum,** where the exhibits include artifacts and memorabilia relating to local and Civil War history. The **DeKalb Historic Complex** is composed of three early 1800's buildings — a simple farmhouse and two log cabins. Walking tours of the area are available. *Admission charged.*

15. Georgia's Stone Mountain Park
Rte. 78, Stone Mountain. Located on the north face of a granite-domed mountain, a 90-foot-high sculpture depicts Robert E. Lee, Jefferson Davis, and Stonewall Jackson, each on horseback. A cable car carries visitors to the summit for one-of-a-kind views. Memorial Hall has exhibits on the site's geology as well as on the history of the carving. The surrounding land portrays early Georgia with its antebellum plantation, a paddle-wheel riverboat that offers cruises on the lake, and an old-fashioned railroad. Other attractions include a swimming beach, golf course, nature trails, and a carillon. *Admission charged.*

16. Yellow River Game Ranch
Rte. 78, Lilburn. This wildlife center contains species native to the area. Gentle animals are free to roam, but others, such as mountain lions, bears, and buffalo, are caged. A half-mile walking trail traverses the grounds. *Admission charged.*

17. Panola Mountain State Conservation Park
Dominated by an unmarred 100-acre granite outcrop, this park is a preserve for native plants and animals. The interpretive center depicts the ecology of the region and offers guided nature and hiking trails. Picnic areas are provided. *Admission charged.*

18. Atlanta State Farmer's Market
16 Forest Pkwy., Forest Park. Said to be the largest in the Southeast, this 146-acre outdoor market offers fruits, vegetables, meats, eggs, preserves, pickles, plants, shrubs, seasonal specialties, and souvenirs.

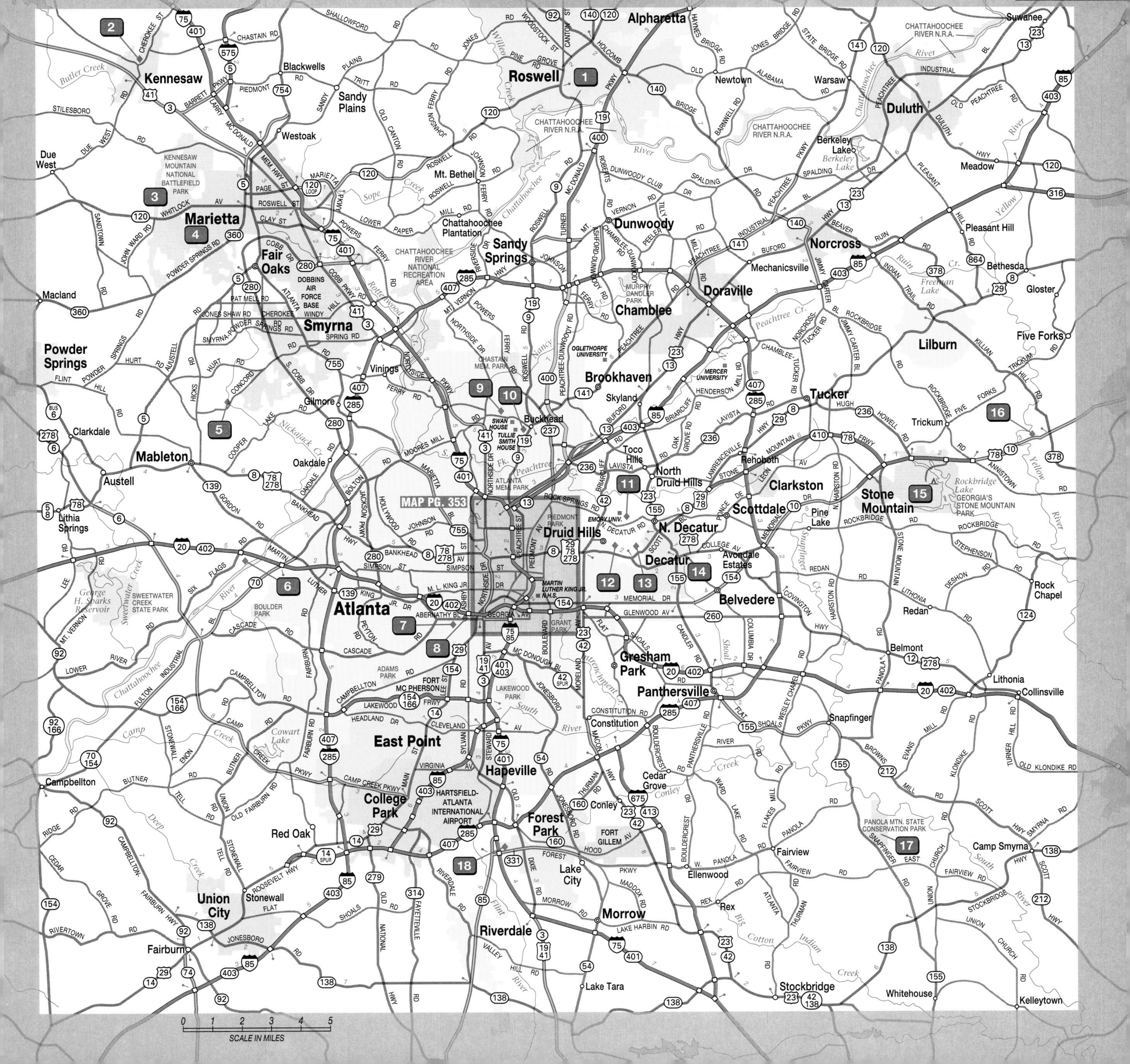

MAP PG. 353

Alpharetta
Suwanee
Roswell
Duluth
Kennesaw
Blackwells
Sandy Plains
Westoak
Newtown
Warsaw
Meadow
Due West
Mt. Bethel
Chattahoochee Plantation
Dunwoody
Berkeley Lake
Pleasant Hill
Marietta
Fair Oaks
Sandy Springs
Norcross
Bethesda
Gloster
Mechanicsville
Doraville
Chamblee
Five Forks
Lilburn
Smyrna
Powder Springs
Macland
Vinings
Brookhaven
Oglethorpe University
Mercer University
Tucker
Trickum
Clarkdale
Gilmore
Skyland
Buckhead
Swan House
Tulle Smith House
Toco Hills
North Druid Hills
Rehoboth
Clarkston
Stone Mountain
Mableton
Oakdale
Austell
Scottdale
Pine Lake
Lithia Springs
Atlanta Mem. Park
Druid Hills
Emory Univ.
N. Decatur
Decatur
Avondale Estates
Rock Chapel
Boulder Park
Belvedere
Redan
Belmont
Atlanta
Gresham Park
Lithonia
Collinsville
East Point
Panthersville
Snapfinger
Adams Park
Fort McPherson
Lakewood Park
Cedar Grove
Fairview
College Park
Hapeville
Forest Park
Fort Gillem
Conley
Ellenwood
Camp Smyrna
Red Oak
Hartsfield-Atlanta International Airport
Lake City
Union City
Stonewall
Morrow
Rex
Riverdale
Fairburn
Lake Tara
Stockbridge
Whitehouse
Kelleytown

Kennesaw Mountain National Battlefield Park
Dobbins Air Force Base
Chattahoochee River National Recreation Area
Chattahoochee River N.R.A.
Murphy Candler Park
Chastain Mem. Park
George H. Sparks Reservoir
Sweetwater Creek State Park
Cowart Lake
Camp Creek
Martin Luther King Jr. N.H.S.
Grant Park
Georgia's Stone Mountain Park
Rockbridge Lake
Panola Mtn. State Conservation Park

SCALE IN MILES
0 1 2 3 4 5

DOWNTOWN ATLANTA

1. Rhodes Hall

1516 Peachtree St. NW. Built in 1903, this mansion is the headquarters of the Georgia Trust for Historic Preservation, which offers tours of the first floor. Each of the elaborate rooms reflects a different theme, from American Indian to Louis XIV. Of particular interest are the nine stained-glass windows that portray the Confederacy's rise and fall. Several original furnishings are displayed. *Admission charged.*

2. Center for Puppetry Arts

1404 Spring St. NW. This museum is known for its extensive collection of puppets from around the world. There are performances, children's workshops, and guided tours. *Admission charged.*

3. The Margaret Mitchell House

Peachtree and 10th Sts. In the late 1920's, this Victorian residence was home to the author of *Gone With the Wind,* which she wrote in the ground-floor apartment.

4. Robert W. Woodruff Arts Center

1280 Peachtree St. NE. In an eye-catching modern building designed by Richard Meier, the **High Museum of Art** contains paintings and sculptures from Europe and America. Visitors can also see African masks and ceremonial figures. Other galleries have collections of decorative arts. The center is also the home of the Atlanta Symphony Orchestra, the **Alliance Theatre/Atlanta Children's Theater,** and the **Atlanta College of Art.** A branch downtown in the Georgia-Pacific Center has photos and folk art. *Admission charged.*

5. Atlanta Botanical Garden

1345 Piedmont Ave. Located within Piedmont Park, a recreational area with tennis courts, a swimming pool, and hiking trails, this botanical garden includes native carnivorous plants, a 15-acre hardwood forest, a fern glade, and a variety of gardens — herb, rose, and wildflower. A 16,000-square-foot conservatory maintains tropical, desert, and endangered plants. *Admission charged.*

6. Virginia-Highland District

A veritable town within the city, this area combines single homes with restaurants, craft galleries, bookshops, and other stores. Since the turn of the century it has grown into a bustling community.

7. Museum of the Jimmy Carter Library

Cleburne and North Highland Aves. The life of President Carter and various events of his administration are portrayed with docu-

ments, photographs, interactive videos, and artifacts. Exhibits include a copy of the Egyptian-Israeli peace treaty, gifts from heads of state, and a full-scale replica of the Oval Office. *Admission charged.*

8. Inman Park Neighborhood/ Little Five Points Business District

Dating from 1890, the neighborhood is Atlanta's oldest suburb. It contains an area of Victorian dwellings and the **Candler Mansion,** the magnificent residence of Asa G. Candler, a marketer behind much of the Coca-Cola Company's phenomenal success. Nearby **Little Five Points** is a popular commercial center with exotic boutiques, artists' shops, theaters, and restaurants.

9. Martin Luther King, Jr. National Historic Site

526 Auburn Ave. NE. An area of some 38 acres includes Dr. King's birthplace, a Victorian home containing original furnishings; the **Ebenezer Baptist Church,** where three generations of the King family preached; and the **King Center for Nonviolent Social Change,** the location of the civil rights leader's grave.

10. SciTrek, The Science and Technology Museum of Atlanta

395 Piedmont Ave. NE. This museum's four main halls contain displays on mathematics, electricity, light, color, and magnetics. Hands-on exhibits explore various scientific discoveries. *Admission charged.*

11. Fox Theatre

660 Peachtree St. NE. The ornate Art Deco movie palace that was completed here in 1929 has been restored as a concert hall. It is also used for performances of ballet, Broadway musicals, trade shows, and a summer film series. Tours are offered. *Admission charged.*

12. The Telephone Museum

675 West Peachtree St. NE. Open for a few hours around noontime during weekdays, this small museum displays old telephones and shows a film on the history of communications. A replica of an early-20th-century street exhibits insulators, tools, and other telephone artifacts from the era.

13. Peachtree Center

Peachtree St. and International Blvd. Designed by the acclaimed architect John Portman, this center is a 13-block complex containing office towers, luxury hotels, restaurants, and a variety of shops. Strolling

through the charming area, visitors pass fountains, plantings, and displays of art.

14. Herndon Home

587 University Place NW. This handsome columned house was built in 1910 for Alonzo Herndon, a freedman who went on to found the Atlanta Life Insurance Company. It contains family furnishings, memorabilia, antiques, glass, silver, and other decorative arts. Tours of the 15-room mansion are provided.

15. Georgia Dome

1 Georgia Dome Dr. This sports and entertainment stadium is said to have the world's largest cable-supported dome. It is home to Atlanta's football team, the Falcons, and will be the site of many events during the 1996 Summer Olympic Games. Guided tours are offered. *Admission charged.*

16. CNN Studio Tour

1 CNN Center, Marietta St. and Techwood Dr. The 45-minute tour of the Cable News Network's headquarters takes visitors to an observation area that looks onto the newsroom and studio, where writers, producers, and anchors are at work. The tour begins with a ride on one of the world's longest freestanding escalators, which rises nonstop to the 8th floor. *Admission charged.*

17. Federal Reserve Bank Monetary Museum

104 Marietta St. NW. Money is the subject here, and its history is traced from the very beginning to today's banking system. Exhibits include gold coins minted in Georgia and an assortment of rare and unusual coins.

18. The World of Coca-Cola

55 Martin Luther King, Jr. Dr. From 1886 to the present, the history of the famous soft drink is traced here. Exhibits include a collection of advertisements, a futuristic soda fountain, and a movie. *Admission charged.*

19. Atlanta History Center Downtown

140 Peachtree St. NW. Exhibits, tours, lectures, and audiovisual shows here examine local history and historic sites. It is also a state welcome center, providing visitor information.

20. Atlanta Heritage Row

55 Upper Alabama St. This site examines the city's history up to the present. Among

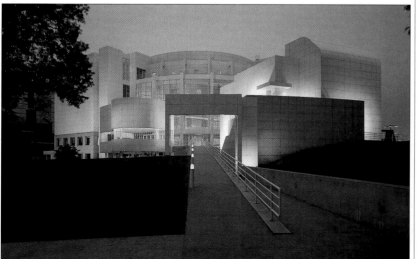

The High Museum of Art features an exterior as memorable as its treasures within.

the exhibits are historical photos, interactive displays, videos, and panoramas. *Admission charged.*

21. Underground Atlanta

The heart of the city in the mid-1800's occupied this six-block area, which has been restored as an entertainment and shopping center, offering boutiques, specialty shops, food marts, restaurants, and nightclubs. Peachtree Fountains Plaza, with a 10-story light tower, serves as a town square.

22. Georgia State Capitol

Off Washington St. Dedicated in 1889, this building is crowned by a golden dome topped by a statue representing Freedom. The capitol displays portraits and busts of statesmen and houses the **Georgia Museum of Science and Industry,** with exhibits on minerals and animals. Located nearby, the **Georgia Department of Archives** — unusual in that none of its windows are visible from the outside — is a repository of state documents.

23. Preservation District

The Sweet Auburn area is today a center of urban African-American culture. It includes the **APEX Museum,** which contains a welcome center, an art collection, exhibits on local history, and memorabilia of Auburn Avenue. Other important sites include the **Royal Peacock Club,** opened in 1930 as the Top Hat, where many black artists have performed; the 19th-century **Big Bethel African Methodist Episcopal Church;** and the *Atlanta Daily World,* the nation's first black-owned newspaper.

24. Historic Oakland Cemetery

248 Oakland Ave. SE. Many of Atlanta's prominent citizens, including writer Margaret Mitchell and golfer Bobby Jones, are buried here. Begun in 1850, the cemetery also contains the graves of Confederate soldiers and freed slaves. On weekdays, brochures and maps for self-guiding tours are available in the visitor center.

25. Grant Park

This beautiful park with miles of scenic trails contains **Zoo Atlanta,** where naturalistic habitats include a rain forest inhabited by primates, and an African plain populated with rhinos and gazelles. Also in the park, the **Atlanta Cyclorama** re-creates the Battle of Atlanta with narration and music, a diorama, and a dramatic 42-foot-high circular painting. *Admission charged.*

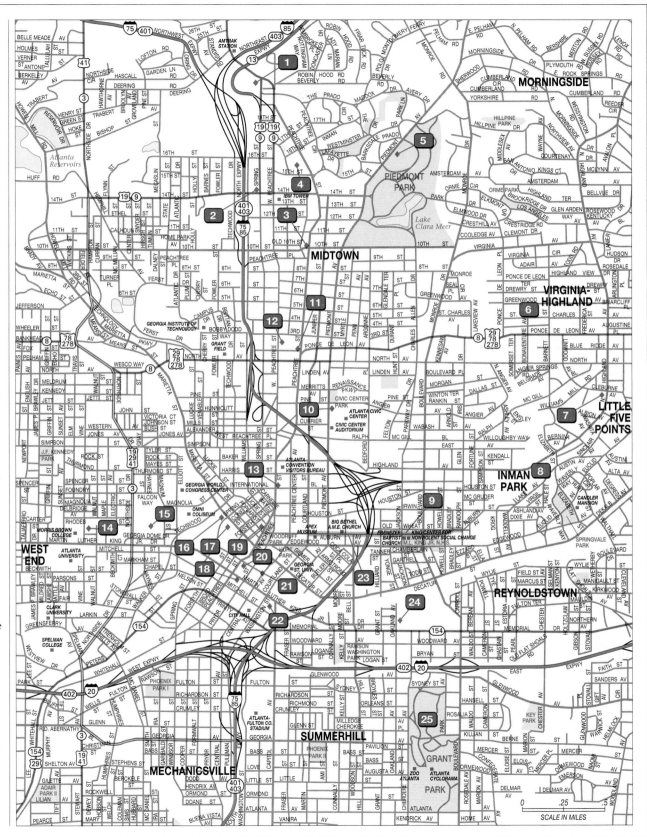

1. Park Seed Company Gardens

Rte. 254, Greenwood. This mail-order seed business offers self-guiding tours of its experimental gardens, floral displays, and greenhouses. The gardens are one of the main attractions of the South Carolina Festival of Flowers, held in late June.

2. Greenwood

Chamber of Commerce, 518 South Main St. Once a plantation known as Green Wood, the city today is a hub of highways and railroads. In addition to its art gallery and its exhibits on local history, **The Museum** displays Indian artifacts, African artwork and mounted animals, and a worldwide collection of cultural objects. Visitors to Greenwood can also gain entry to several sections of the 353,000-acre **Sumter National Forest,** where activities include hiking, canoeing, trout fishing, and hunting.

3. Ninety Six National Historic Site

Rte. 248, Ninety Six. The original town here was a Loyalist stronghold and an important military objective during the Revolutionary War. The British constructed Ft. Star to protect it, but in 1781 abandoned both the fort and the settlement. The present town of Ninety Six was constructed some 2 miles to the north, but the well-preserved remnants of the early fort can be visited.

4. Edgefield

This town's historic district preserves some 40 buildings and homes from the 19th century. Built in 1835, **Oakley Park** is of special interest for its chandeliers, furnishings, portraits, decorative arts, and carved mantels. Framed by trees that are more than 100 years old, **Magnolia Dale** is headquarters for the Edgefield County Historical Society. *Admission charged.*

5. J. Strom Thurmond Lake and Dam

Visitor Center, Rte. 221, Clarks Hill. One of the largest projects ever undertaken by the U.S. Army Corps of Engineers, the dam here on the Savannah River created the 70,000-acre lake. There are boat ramps, picnic sites, nature trails, and campgrounds.

6. U.S. Army Signal Corps Museum

Avenue of the States, Bldg. 36305, Ft. Gordon. Communications and military signal devices in this museum range from flags used in the Civil War to the sophisticated microwave equipment used in Vietnam. Visitors can examine a magneto, early keying mechanisms, and gear belonging to the 10th Armored Division.

7. Augusta

Convention and Visitors Bureau, 32 Eighth St. This historic city hosts the renowned Masters Golf Tournament in April. A walking or auto tour of the downtown area includes the Victorian houses in the **Olde Towne Historic District; St. Paul's Episcopal Church,** on the site where Augusta was founded; the **Augusta-Richmond County Museum,** with local artifacts from the Revolution through the Civil War; and **Meadow Garden,** the home of a signer of the Declaration of Independence. **Harris House** is an outstanding 18th-century home noted for its fine woodwork and vaulted breezeway. The **Springfield Baptist Church** is one of the oldest black congregations in the country. Buried at the **Signers' Monument** are two signers of the Declaration of Independence. The **Confederate Monument** is dominated by statues of famous Confederate generals. Markers designate several miles of the **Bartram Memorial Trail,** which follows the journeys of naturalist and artist William Bartram. *Admission charged for some attractions.*

8. Redcliffe Plantation State Park

181 Redcliffe Rd., Beech Island. The centerpiece of this 350-acre area is an antebellum plantation house built for South Carolina governor James Henry Hammond. Situated on a hill, the mansion contains family furnishings, artworks, and historic documents and books. *Admission charged at house.*

9. Aiken

Chamber of Commerce, 400 Laurens St. NW. This region is known for its Thoroughbred horses and polo matches. **Hopeland Gardens** offers a trail for the blind as well as a charming landscape of water-lily ponds, camellias, and live oaks. In a restored carriage house also on the property is the **Thoroughbred Racing Hall of Fame,** where displays include trophies, photos, and memorabilia. The **Aiken County His-** torical Museum has rooms that depict local life in the 18th and 19th centuries. The chamber of commerce has maps for a self-guiding tour in the town's historic area.

10. Barnwell

Chamber of Commerce, Rte. 278. Much of this town was burned by General Sherman's troops during the Civil War. One of the few buildings to survive was the historic **Circle Theatre.** Built in 1848 as a church, it eventually served as a courthouse and jail. The **Barnwell County Museum** displays local artifacts. *Admission charged at theater.*

11. Woodlands Plantation

Rte. 78, near Bamberg. This was the home of William Gilmore Simms, a prolific novelist and poet. The plantation was set alight by army stragglers during General Sherman's raid through Columbia in 1865. The home has been reconstructed.

Gardens at the Park Seed Company

12. Fort Jackson Museum

Ft. Jackson Blvd., Building 4442, Ft. Jackson. Named for President Andrew Jackson, the fort here was built in 1917; today it's the army's largest basic combat training post. On display in the museum are Japanese and German weapons from World War II, a barracks, uniforms of early American soldiers, and a replica of a training village.

13. Columbia

Convention and Visitors Bureau, 1201 Main St. With its enormous blue granite columns, the **State House** is considered by many to be one of the most beautiful state capitols.

The **South Carolina State Museum** presents exhibits on state history, archeology, fine arts, science, and technology. The 1846 **Trinity Cathedral** is an excellent example of English Gothic architecture. The Horseshoe, the University of South Carolina's original campus, is the site of **McKissick Museum,** where the collection includes antique European silver, gems, minerals, and Southern folk art. The **Columbia Museum of Art** displays the Kress collection of Renaissance, medieval, and baroque paintings as well as other works that emphasize the Southeast. The **Woodrow Wilson Boyhood Home** has family photographs and memorabilia; the **Hampton-Preston Mansion** reflects antebellum life with furnishings and decorative arts. Designed by the architect of the Washington Memorial, the **Robert Mills Historic House and Park** contains outstanding mantels and chandeliers. The **Mann-Simons Cottage,** home of a freed slave in 1850, now houses a museum on African-American culture. *Admission charged for some attractions.*

14. Riverbanks Zoo and Botanical Garden

500 Wildlife Pkwy., Columbia. The highly regarded zoo cares for some 2,000 animals in simulated natural habitats. There are Siberian tigers, bald eagles, and other endangered species. The Aquarium Reptile Complex has a 60,000-gallon tank with a coral reef. A cageless aviary shelters a variety of birds. Throughout the grounds, labels have been placed near many of the plants and trees. *Admission charged.*

15. Lexington County Museum

Rte. 378, Lexington. Having been faithfully outfitted and furnished, the 18 period buildings here re-create this region's past. Among the structures are a schoolhouse and a 1772 one-room log building. There's also a house built in 1774, where demonstrations of spinning and quilting are performed. On the grounds are beehives, rabbit hutches, an herb garden, cotton gin, and smokehouse. *Admission charged.*

16. Lake Murray

Off Rte. 6, near Columbia. This 41-mile-long lake was created in 1930 by the construction of a dam. Fishing for striped and largemouth bass, bream, and crappie is popular, as are swimming, boating, and waterskiing. Picnic sites and campgrounds dot the 520 miles of scenic shoreline.

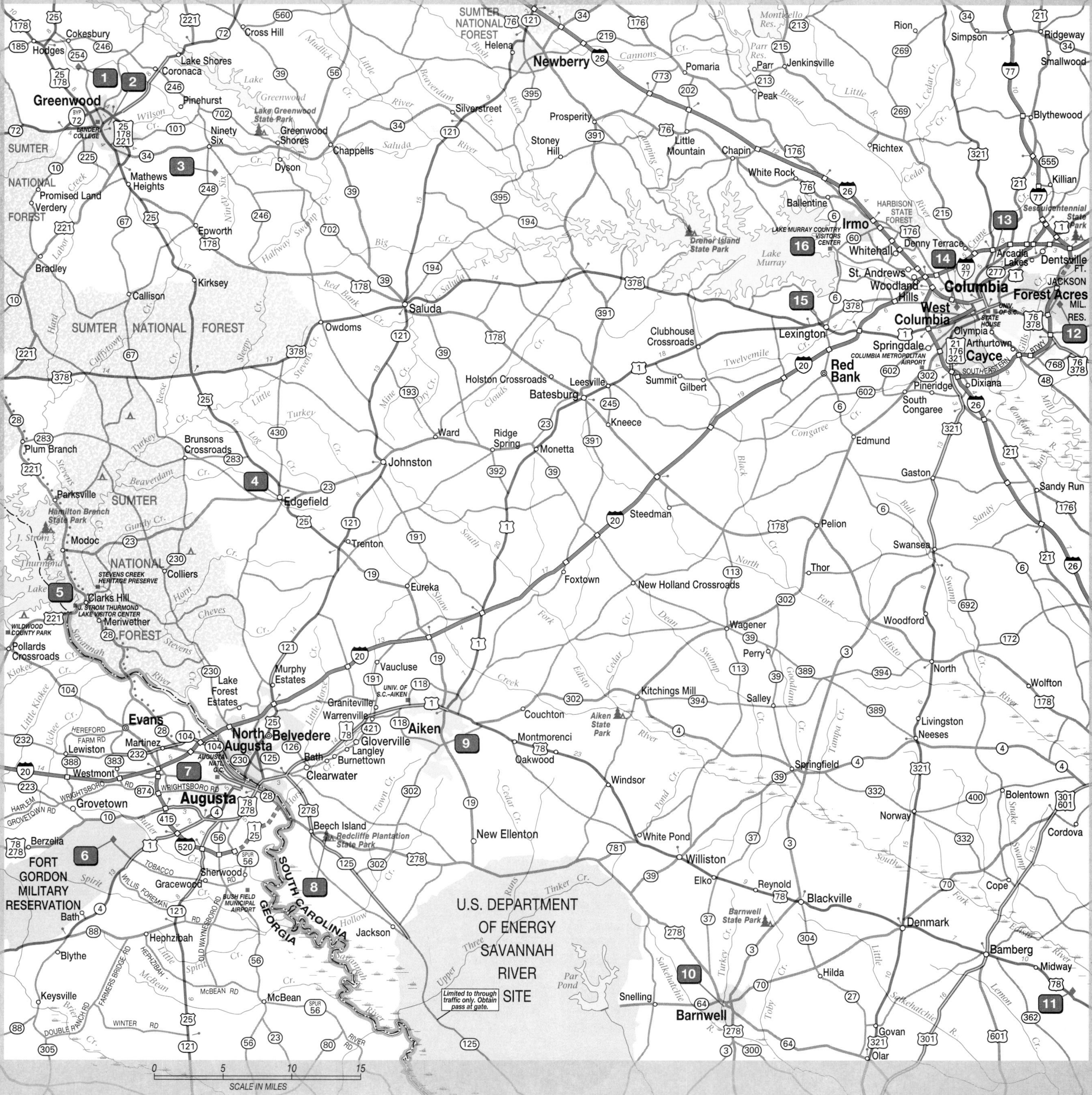

Greenwood
Cokesbury
Hodges
Cross Hill
Lake Shores
Coronaca
Pinehurst
Ninety Six
Greenwood Shores
Lake Greenwood State Park
Chappells
Dyson
Mathews Heights
Epworth
Kirksey
Bradley
Callison
Promised Land
Verdery
SUMTER NATIONAL FOREST
Saluda
Owdoms
Holston Crossroads
Batesburg
Leesville
Summit
Gilbert
Ward
Ridge Spring
Monetta
Kneece
Johnston
Brunsons Crossroads
Plum Branch
Parksville
Modoc
Colliers
Clarks Hill
Meriwether
Pollards Crossroads
Wildwood County Park
Hamilton Branch State Park
Stevens Creek Heritage Preserve
J. Strom Thurmond Lake Visitor Center
Edgefield
Trenton
Eureka
Foxtown
New Holland Crossroads
Steedman
Pelion
Evans
Martinez
Lewiston
Westmont
Grovetown
Berzelia
Harlem
FORT GORDON MILITARY RESERVATION
Bath
Blythe
Keysville
Hephzibah
Gracewood
Sherwood
North Augusta
Belvedere
Augusta
Martinez
Graniteville
Warrenville
Gloverville
Langley
Bath
Burnettown
Clearwater
Aiken
Couchton
Montmorenci
Oakwood
Windsor
Kitchings Mill
Salley
Wagener
Perry
Woodford
North
Livingston
Neeses
Springfield
Norway
Cope
Blackville
Denmark
Bamberg
Midway
Williston
Elko
Reynold
Snelling
Barnwell
Govan
Olar
Hilda
Cordova
Bolentown
Wolfton
Swansea
Sandy Run
Gaston
Edmund
South Congaree
Pineridge
Dixiana
Red Bank
Lexington
Springdale
West Columbia
Cayce
Columbia
Olympia
Arthurtown
Forest Acres
Dentsville
Arcadia Lakes
Woodland Hills
St. Andrews
Whitehall
Irmo
Ballentine
White Rock
Chapin
Little Mountain
Peak
Pomaria
Parr
Jenkinsville
Newberry
Silverstreet
Prosperity
Stoney Hill
Helena
Rion
Simpson
Ridgeway
Smallwood
Blythewood
Killian
Richtex
Denny Terrace
Lake Murray
Dreher Island State Park
Harbison State Forest
Sesquicentennial State Park
Lake Murray Country Visitors Center
U.S. DEPARTMENT OF ENERGY SAVANNAH RIVER SITE
Limited to through traffic only. Obtain pass at gate.
Beech Island
Redcliffe Plantation State Park
New Ellenton
White Pond
Jackson
McBean
Clarks Hill Lake
J. Strom Thurmond Lake
SOUTH CAROLINA
GEORGIA
Savannah River
Aiken State Park
Barnwell State Park
Bush Field Municipal Airport
Columbia Metropolitan Airport
UNIV. OF S.C.-AIKEN
UNIV. OF S.C.
STATE HOUSE
SUMTER NATIONAL FOREST
Stevens Creek National Forest
Lander College
Ninety Six

SCALE IN MILES
0   5   10   15

1. Surry

Smith's Fort Plantation is a restored mid-18th-century house named for the nearby **Smith's Fort,** an uncompleted fortification that Capt. John Smith wanted to build for the Jamestown Colony as a place of refuge in case of attack. A working farm since the 1600's, **Chippokes Plantation State Park** includes a museum, mansion, pool, fishing, hiking, and 6 acres of formal gardens. **Bacon's Castle** was used as a stronghold by a band of insurgents during Bacon's Rebellion in 1676. It features six chimneys, curved gables, and a staircase enclosed in a tower. *Admission charged for some attractions.*

2. Historic Halifax State Historic Site

Dobb and Saint David Sts., Halifax. This area was a busy commercial center that became a supply depot during the American Revolution. Guided and self-guiding tours of the town's many restored buildings include the 18th-century **Owens House,** the **Eagle Tavern,** and an early jail. Built atop the remains of a 1762 home, a museum features displays on archeology. The visitor center has artifacts and a film on the area.

3. Historic Hope Plantation

Rte. 308, Windsor. Guided tours of this Georgian plantation house, built by Gov. David Stone about 1800, include period furnishings and an 18th-century garden. The nearby **King-Bazemore House** is a Colonial-style plantation house with a gambrel roof, dormer windows, and an herb garden. *Admission charged.*

4. Tarboro

Chamber of Commerce, 112 West Church St. This town's history as an important tobacco and cotton market is preserved in its large historic district, which has beautifully maintained Colonial, Victorian, and antebellum homes. Built around 1808, the **Blount-Bridgers House** is a fine example of Federal-style architecture. The restored residence is furnished in period style and

contains the Hobson Pittman Memorial Gallery, which displays that artist's paintings and personal belongings.

5. New Bern

Convention and Visitors Bureau, 219 Pollock St. Founded in 1710 by Swiss and German immigrants, New Bern was a colonial capital, then later the state capital until 1794. Historic sites and exceptional examples of early 19th-century architecture can be seen on self-guiding tours; maps are available at the visitors bureau. The **Tryon Palace Historic Sites and Gardens** re-creates the splendor of one of the finest colonial buildings in the nation, the 1770 compound for Royal Governor William Tryon. The main building burned down in 1798, but it has been meticulously reconstructed and furnished with 18th-century antiques. There are costumed guides, demonstrations, and formal 18th-century English gardens on view. The **New Bern Firemen's Museum** displays firefighting equipment from the early 19th century, as well as maps, photographs, and other artifacts. *Admission charged for some attractions.*

6. Hammocks Beach State Park

Wilderness lovers are attracted to the pristine beauty of this largely undeveloped park, which, from June through August, can be reached by ferry. Attractions include swimming, surf fishing, and sand dunes up to 60 feet high. In June, giant loggerhead turtles come ashore during the night to nest above the tide line.

7. Moores Creek National Battlefield

200 Moores Creek Dr., Currie. Here, in February 1776, an army of patriots successfully ambushed 1,600 kilted Highlanders and Loyalists. Instilled with confidence a few months later, North Carolina voted for independence. The visitor center features an audiovisual presentation that outlines the events of the skirmish. The History Trail explores the battleground.

8. U.S.S. North Carolina Battleship Memorial

Off Rte. 17, near Wilmington. Considered the world's most lethal when she was commissioned in 1941, the battleship today is a tribute to the 10,000 North Carolinians who lost their lives in World War II. A self-guiding tour leads visitors through much of the ship, including the crew's quarters, the engine room, and the bridge. There's also a

museum with photographs and artifacts from World War II. *Admission charged.*

9. Historic Poplar Grove

10200 Rte. 17, near Wilmington. Living-history tours of this 19th-century peanut plantation include visits to a gracious Greek Revival manor house, a smokehouse, tenant house, and farm animals. There are demonstrations by craftspeople, and locally made wares can be purchased in a country store. *Admission charged.*

10. Wilmington

Convention and Visitors Bureau, 24 North Third St. The state's major seaport, Wilmington has a rich history. Local resistance to the Stamp Act took place here in 1765, and the city was later an important Confederate port. The convention and visitors bureau provides maps for the walking tour of **Historic Wilmington.** Built in 1858, **Thalian Hall** featured an opera house and city hall, both of which are still in use. Once the headquarters of British General Cornwallis, the restored **Burgwin-Wright House** has 18th-century furnishings and a garden. The 1852 **Zebulon Latimer House** is an ornate Italianate Revival–style residence that displays original Empire and Victorian furnishings. Various aspects of the region's history are examined at the **Cape Fear Museum,** where the displays include a model of the city's harbor as it appeared in 1863, artifacts from the Lower Cape Fear Indians, and old photographs. **St. John's Museum of Art** has a fine collection of works from the last three centuries. Highlights include prints by Mary Cassatt and a sculpture garden. *Admission charged for some attractions.*

11. Carolina Beach State Park

This 1,700-acre park is home to the rare Venus's-flytrap, which is only found within a 60-mile radius, as well as five additional species of insect-eating plants. Well-marked nature trails lead through the changing terrain, encompassing sand dunes, grasslands, and swamp. Songbirds, laughing gulls, and ospreys soar overhead, and the Cape Fear River offers excellent fishing and boating.

12. Fort Fisher State Historic Site

1610 Ft. Fisher Blvd., South Kure Beach. The ruins of fortifications, mounds, and a restored palisade are the only remnants of the massive earthworks erected here by Confederates to protect the entrance to

Cape Fear River. The museum displays old photographs as well as artifacts recovered from ships that were sunk while attempting to run the blockade. The nearby **North Carolina Aquarium at Fort Fisher** features more than 15 tanks that contain sea life commonly found in the Atlantic, including sharks, endangered sea turtles, and tropical specimens.

13. Orton Plantation Gardens

9149 Orton Rd. SE, Winnabow. Once a rice plantation, the gardens today have long stretches of ancient oaks that shade azaleas, magnolias, and flowering fruit trees. A variety of paths offer views of the area, which also contains the antebellum **Orton House.** The colorful gardens are open from March to November. *Admission charged.*

14. Florence

Chamber of Commerce, 610 West Palmetto St. The **Florence Air and Missile Museum Development Corporation** displays missiles, helicopters, rockets, and 22 combat aircraft. It contains a Titan I Missile, a Douglas Torpedo Dive Bomber used in World War II, and a Boeing 377 Transport plane. At the **Florence Museum of Art, Science, and History** visitors can see an eclectic collection that includes Hopi Indian pottery, Greek and Roman antiquities, African art, and artifacts from local history. *Admission charged at air and missile museum.*

15. Bennettsville

Chamber of Commerce, 300 West Main St. The highlight of the **Marlboro County Historical Museum** complex is the **Jennings-Brown House,** which served as headquarters for Union troops when they captured Bennettsville in 1865. Today the saltbox house is furnished with a variety of early-19th-century antiques. Nearby **Lake Wallace** attracts swimmers, boaters, water-skiers, and anglers. *Admission charged for some attractions.*

16. Pinehurst

Built in the 1890's as an exclusive resort village, the Pinehurst area today boasts more than 30 championship golf courses. The **PGA/World Golf Hall of Fame** has exhibits on its inductees, golf history, famous golfers, and tournaments. In nearby Southern Pines, the **Weymouth Woods Nature Preserve** has hiking trails through some 600 acres of pine forest and sand ridges. *Admission charged at hall of fame.*

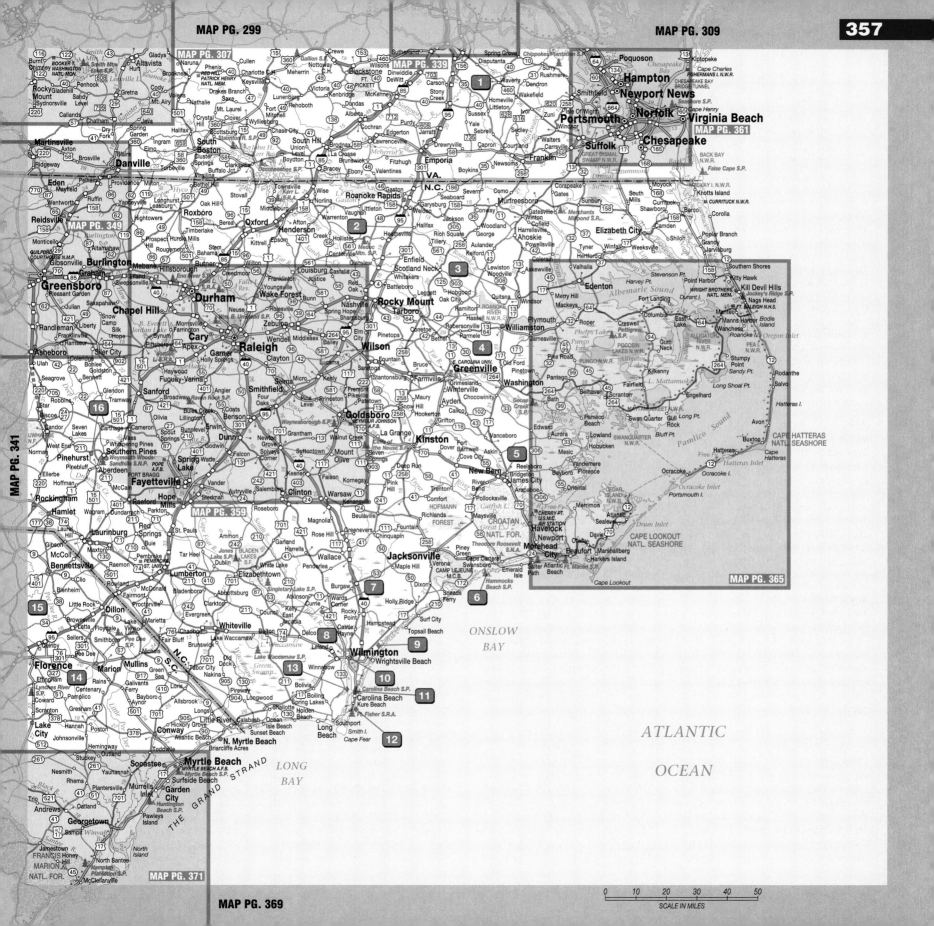

MAP PG. 307
MAP PG. 339
MAP PG. 361
MAP PG. 349
MAP PG. 341
MAP PG. 359
MAP PG. 365
MAP PG. 371

VA.
N.C.

ATLANTIC OCEAN

ONSLOW BAY

LONG BAY

THE GRAND STRAND

N.C.
S.C.

0 10 20 30 40 50
SCALE IN MILES

1. Stagville Preservation Center

Old Oxford Hwy., northeast of Durham. On the site of a once-prosperous plantation, the cluster of late-18th- and 19th-century buildings here evokes the lifestyles of both the wealthy planters and the hard-working slaves. Visitors can tour the Georgian-style residence of the owner, four slave houses, a barn, and a graveyard.

2. North Carolina Museum of Life and Science

433 Murray Ave., Durham. This 70-acre facility has participatory exhibits that examine tornadoes, physiology, geology, and aerospace. There are also displays on native animals. A train takes visitors through a wildlife sanctuary. *Admission charged.*

3. West Point on the Eno

5101 North Roxboro St., Durham. A reconstructed 1778 working gristmill, a restored 19th-century blacksmith's shop, a farmhouse, and a tobacco packhouse are the remnants of the West Point Mill community once located here. Other attractions at the 371-acre park include picnicking, hiking, canoeing, and rafting.

4. Duke Homestead State Historic Site

2828 Duke Homestead Rd., Durham. After the Civil War, Washington Duke and two of his sons turned this simple two-story farmhouse and the surrounding land into a cigarette empire. The homestead includes a tobacco packhouse, a curing barn, a reconstruction of the original log factory, and a later factory. The visitor center traces the history of tobacco.

5. Bennett Place State Historic Site

4409 Bennett Memorial Rd., Durham. History was made here in 1865 when Confederate General Johnston surrendered to Union General Sherman, ending the Civil War in the Carolinas, Florida, and Georgia. The visitor center has exhibits and an audiovisual presentation on the heavy toll the war exacted in North Carolina. Tours of a reconstructed homestead are offered.

6. Hillsborough

Chamber of Commerce, 150 East King St. With its displays of Indian artifacts, an antique loom, vintage firearms, and Civil War memorabilia, the **Orange County Historical Museum** examines the lives of early residents. It also provides maps for a self-guiding tour of the **Historic District**, home to more than 100 structures from the 18th and 19th centuries, including an 1845 courthouse and the residence of a signer of the Declaration of Independence.

7. Duke University

This outstanding university is divided into the West Campus, featuring Gothic-style architecture, and the East Campus, with mainly Georgian buildings. With its 210-foot bell tower, **Duke University Chapel** dominates the university. On the East Campus, the **Duke University Museum of Art** has excellent pre-Columbian and medieval collections. The **Duke University Libraries** are the largest of any school in the South, containing more than 4 million volumes and 7 million manuscripts. Color blazes throughout the **Sarah P. Duke Gardens**, where roses, chrysanthemums, flowering trees, and hundreds of rare and native plants grow.

8. University of North Carolina at Chapel Hill

Opened in 1795, this renowned school contains the first state university building in the country, **Old East.** The venerable **Davie Poplar,** which predates the school, was named for William Richardson Davie, the university's founder. A campus landmark, the **Old Well** was the school's original source of water. On display at the **Ackland Art Museum** are acclaimed collections of art, ranging from ancient Greek bronzes to abstract paintings. Ten bells that chime the hours ring out from the **Morehead-Patterson Memorial Bell Tower.** The **Coker Arboretum** covers five acres with various trees, seasonal displays of flowers, and native and exotic plants. The **Louis Round Wilson Library** is a repository of history. It includes a collection of George Bernard Shaw's works, the Southern Historical Collection, and a room devoted to Sir Walter Raleigh that contains 16th-century paneling and period furnishings. At the **Morehead Planetarium,** visitors can attend shows, walk through a model of the solar system, and see exhibits on both art and science. *Fee charged for planetarium shows.*

9. North Carolina Botanical Garden

Old Mason Farm Rd., Chapel Hill. A 2-mile interpretive trail through this nearly 600-acre property offers visitors a chance to view a native Piedmont woodland. Other highlights are carnivorous plants and a display of a southeastern habitat.

10. North Carolina Museum of Art

2110 Blue Ridge Rd., Raleigh. This cultural center has an excellent collection of European paintings from the 13th to the 19th centuries, including works by Botticelli, Rubens, Giotto, and Monet. Other major displays are African ritual masks, ancient Egyptian treasures, Judaica, pre-Columbian artifacts, oceanic art, and American works from the 18th to the 20th centuries.

11. Mordecai Historic Park

1 Mimosa St., Raleigh. Dating back to 1785, the Mordecai House was the center of a large plantation. Much about the lives of some five generations of the family can be gleaned from the home's many original furnishings. Other 18th- and 19th-century buildings, moved here to re-create an old-time village, include a post office, law office, kitchen, chapel, and the birthplace of President Andrew Johnson. *Admission charged.*

12. Historic Oakwood

A self-guiding walking tour of this well-preserved Victorian neighborhood in downtown Raleigh leads visitors past outstanding examples of Queen Anne, Greek Revival, Eastlake, and other styles of architecture. Brochures of the area are available at the visitor center located in the state government complex.

13. North Carolina State Government Complex

Visitor Center, 301 North Blount St., Raleigh. Little changed from its 1840's appearance, the Greek Revival **State Capitol** was the backdrop to many historic decisions until 1963, when political debates moved to the dramatically modern **State Legislative Building.** The nearby **North Carolina State Museum of Natural Sciences** displays the skeletons of whales, as well as living reptiles, amphibians, and fish. The **Executive Mansion** is an ornate structure of steep gables, verandas, and balconies. The interior displays 18th- and 19th-century furnishings, fine woodwork, and crystal chandeliers. In addition to hosting special events, the **North Carolina Museum of History** has exhibits on the state's heritage, including folk life and athletics.

14. Country Doctor Museum

515 Vance St., Bailey. The two 19th-century doctors' offices here display an intriguing collection of the instruments and medicines that were used from about 1800 to the early 1900's. Among the exhibits are Civil War surgeons' amputation kits, antique obstetrical equipment, an apothecary shop, and a garden of medicinal plants.

15. Bentonville Battleground

Off Rte. 701, 15 miles south of Smithfield. The battle fought here, in March 1865, was one of the last battles of the Civil War and the biggest land engagement in North Carolina. The **Harper House** is furnished as it was when it served as a field hospital during the 3-day-long combat. There are original Union field fortifications, a Confederate cemetery, plaques throughout the battlefield, and a visitor center with exhibits and an audiovisual program.

16. Fayetteville

Convention and Visitors Bureau, 515 Ramsey St. Brochures with self-guiding tours of this city's historic buildings are available at the visitors bureau. Sites along the way include the 1832 **Market House,** which has a square clock tower, and the **Sanford House,** the first federal bank in North Carolina. Originally constructed in 1816, the **First Presbyterian Church** was rebuilt after a great fire took place here 16 years later. It contains handwrought iron locks, finely carved woodwork, and crystal chandeliers that use whale oil. Built in 1789 but spared by the fire, **Cool Spring Tavern** housed the governor when the city was the state capital. A 1,500-year-old canoe and a steamboat are among the artifacts at the **Museum of the Cape Fear.** Other exhibits are on American Indians, pottery, and the Civil War.

17. Fort Bragg

This is one of the country's largest and most important military installations. The **82nd Airborne Division Museum** depicts the military unit's history with weapons, pictures, and artifacts from World War I to the Persian Gulf War. The **John F. Kennedy Special Warfare Museum** traces military operations from the French and Indian War to the present.

Miles • Efland • St. Mary's Rd • Cozart • Creedmore • Northside • Smith Cr. • Franklinton • Katesville • Louisburg • Stallings Crossroads • Castalia • Taylors Store • Hillardston • Salem

6 • **3** • **1** • 157 • 501 • 85 • 15 • 56 • 561 • 96 • 1 • Mapleville • 56 • Lancaster Crossroads • Mathews Crossroads • Dukes • Red Oak • 43

70 • Hillsborough • **5** • **2** • Weaver • Gorman • Grissom • Youngsville • Margaret • 581 • May's Crossroads • Edwards Crossroads • Corinth • Dortches • 95

Cheeks Crossroads • Buckhorn • 85 • **4** • Eno • 85 • 15 • Purnell • ALT 1 • Seven Paths • Justice • 39 • Harris Crossroads • Royal • Rolesville • Pearces • Pine Ridge • Gold Valley Crossroads • 64 • Nashville • Rocky Mount

Orange Grove • **7** • Blackwood • Oak Grove • Bilboa • Falls Lake • FALLS LAKE ST. REC. AREA • PURNELL RD • **Wake Forest** • Forestville • Walkers Crossroads • 98 • Barham • Riley • Sutton • Rocky Cross • Samaria • White Oak • Lamm's Crossroads • Sandy Cross • Langley Crossroads

Oaks • White Cross • 54 • **8** • **Durham** • 751 • Bethesda • 55 • 147 • Six Forks • Bayleaf • Falls • Hopkins • Pilot • 64 • Mount Pleasant • **14** • Frazier Crossroads • Taylors Crossroads • Joyners Crossroads • 97

Chapel Hill • **Carrboro** • Parkwood • Few • Lowes Grove • Leesville • Neuse • Wake Crossroads • 39 • Stanhope • Strickland Crossroads • Winstead Crossroads • Elm City • 58

Blands • **9** • Nelson • Genlee • RESEARCH TRIANGLE PARK • Clegg • Millbrook • New Hope • Lizard Lick • 97 • Zebulon • Earpsboro • Middlesex • ALT 264 • High Crossroads • Newhope • Dunn Crossroads • ROCKY MOUNT/WILSON AIRPORT

University Lake • 15 501 • Carpenter • Morrisville • RALEIGH DURHAM AIRPORT • WILLIAM B. UMSTEAD S.P. • **11** • 440 • **12** • Wilders Grove • Knightdale • Eagle Rock • Wendell • 231 • Bailey • Sims • 264 • Rosebud

Farrington • Green Level • Upchurch • WESTOVER • N.C. ST. UNIV. • **Raleigh** • NEW BERN • Milburnie • Emit • Connor • 581 • Stotts Crossroads • 95 • **Wilson**

Gum Springs • Bynum • JORDAN LAKE S.P. • **Cary** • MEREDITH COLL. • WADE AV • SHAW UNIV • 440 • **13** • Heflin • Buckhorn Crossroads • Filmore • 42 • BARTON COLL. • 301

64 • Griffins Crossroads • 751 • Wilsonville • Apex • 64 • Macedonia • **Garner** • 50 • Auburn • 70 • Archer Lodge • Jordan • Hares Crossroads • Rock Ridge • 264 • Evansdale

87 • Pittsboro • 902 • Friendship • New Hill • 1 • 55 • Sunset Lake • McCullers • Clayton • 42 • Flowers • Powhatan • Wilson's Mills • Beulahtown • Stancils Chapel • Buckhorn Crossroads • Lamms Crossroads • Dixie • 117

Bonsal • Holly Springs • Bass Lake • Macks Village • Drug Store • Shoeheel • Kirby's Crossing • Moores Crossroads • Lucama • Black Creek

Merry Oaks • Brickhaven • Corinth • Hollemans Crossroads • Wilbon • Willow Springs • Ogburn • Willow Springs • Edmondson • West Smithfield • Micro • Bagley • Kenly • Watson Crossroads • TOBACCO FARM LIFE MUS. • Fremont • Eureka

Cumnock • Osgood • Duncan • Fuquay-Varina • Kennebec • Johnson Crossroads • Selma • Pine Level • Aycock Crossing • Pinkney • 222

Northview • 421 • Colon • Cokesbury • Rawls • Chalybeate Springs • Angier • McGee's Crossroads • Coats Crossroads • Smithfield • Raines Crossroads • Nahunta • Pikeville • 117

Sanford • Broadway • Ryes • Cape Fear • CAMPBELL UNIVERSITY • Hardee Crossroads • Four Oaks • Brogden • Princeton • Belfast • Saulston • Patetown • Hood Swamp

Tramway • Seminole • Mamers • Lillington • Buies Creek • Coats • 27 • Benson • 95 • Blackman Crossroads • Strickland Crossroads • Bentonville • Rosewood • 111 • Langston • **Goldsboro** • New Hope

Cameron • Pineview • Buffalo Lakes • Harnette • Erwin • Turnington • Peacocks Crossroads • 40 • Grantham • Mar-Mac • SEYMOUR JOHNSON AFB • Elroy • 70

Johnsonville • Spout Springs • Anderson Creek • Bunnlevel • Averasboro • **Dunn** • Blackmans Mill • Brogden • Dudley • Lake Wackena

Lobelia • Lake Surf • 24 • Manchester • **Spring Lake** • Linden • WILLIAM C. LEE AIRBORNE MUSEUM • Goodwin • Timothy • Rosin • Newton Grove • Monks Crossroad • Suttontown • **Mount Olive** • Indian Springs

POPE AFB • Ft. Bragg • Carlos • Lane • Slocomb • Wade • Mingo • Spivey's Corner • McLamb Crossroads • Hobbton • Giddensville • MOUNT OLIVE COLLEGE • Calypso • CLIFFS OF THE NEUSE S.P.

FORT BRAGG • 82ND MUSEUM • JFK SPECIAL WARFARE MUSEUM • Beard • Eastover • Orange • Midway • Keener • Poplar Grove • Faison • Williams

MILITARY RESERVATION • **17** • Bonnie Doone • Shaws • Halls Store • Piney Green • Beamans Crossroads • McCullen • Hargrove Crossroads • Hatcher • Beautancus • Scotts Store

Cliffdale • **Fayetteville** • **16** • MARKET HOUSE • FIRST PRESBYTERIAN CHURCH • Rebel City • Kitty Fork • Bearskin • Bowdens • Friendship • Red Hill

Silver City • Wayside • Fenix • MUSEUM OF THE CAPE FEAR • COOL SPRING TAVERN • Vander • Stedman • Salemburg • Bonnetsville • Everton • Westbrook Crossroad

211 • Raeford • Rockfish • Pine Knoll • **Hope Mills** • FAYETTEVILLE REGIONAL AIRPORT • 210 • Autryville • Hayne • Concord • Moltonville • Turkey • **Clinton** • **Warsaw** • 903

SCALE IN MILES • 0 2 4 6 8 10

1. Smithfield

Chamber of Commerce, 132 Main St. In this town's historic district stand old storefronts, county buildings, and houses, including elaborate Victorian homes from the steamboat era. Among the points of interest are the 1752 **Smithfield Inn** and **St. Luke's Church,** built by English settlers.

2. Mariners' Museum

Rte. 60 and J. Clyde Morris Blvd., Newport News. Nautical history is the theme in this superb collection. Miniature models share the space with full-size craft, including a Venetian gondola, Norwegian rowboat, and Coast Guard cutter. Carved figureheads, marine paintings, and various kinds of gear are also exhibited. *Admission charged.*

3. Virginia Living Museum

524 J. Clyde Morris Blvd., Newport News. At this museum many of Virginia's animals live in simulated natural habitats. One exhibit allows visitors to observe the activities of owls and other nocturnal creatures. Other attractions include a planetarium, nature walk, and both indoor and outdoor aviaries. *Admission charged.*

4. War Memorial Museum of Virginia

9285 Warwick Blvd., Newport News. This museum outlines the nation's military history, starting with the Revolutionary War and continuing to the present. Posters, uniforms, weapons, insignia, vehicles, and other artifacts comprise the outstanding collection. *Admission charged.*

5. Newport News Waterfront

Tourist Information Center, 13560 Jefferson Ave. Here the Jamestown colonists are said to have received the news of Capt. Christopher Newport's return from England with reinforcements and supplies. Today large ships from around the world dock in the excellent harbor. Cruises take visitors past the Newport News Shipyard and the Norfolk Naval Base. The **Victory Arch** honors veterans of World War I.

6. Air Power Park

413 West Mercury Blvd., Hampton. Outside the information center here are jets, helicopters, rockets, and missiles. Specific examples include an F-100 Super Sabre and a Harrier, a jet that can hover.

7. Downtown Hampton

Visitor Center, 710 Settlers Landing Rd. Although many of its early structures were destroyed during the War of 1812 and the Civil War, Hampton is the oldest continuous community of English origin in America. **St. John's Church** was built in 1728. Another landmark is **Hampton University,** founded in 1868 as a school for freed slaves; today it has a museum with a collection of African art. On the waterfront is the restored 1920 **Hampton Carousel,** with hand-carved horses and chariots. The nearby **Virginia Air and Space Center** displays aircraft as well as artifacts from the nation's space program, including a moon rock and the Apollo 12 command module.

8. Fort Monroe

Off Rte. 64, Hampton. This stronghold is the country's largest stone fort. It contains the **Casemate Museum,** displaying the cell in which Jefferson Davis was confined. Also on the grounds is the **Chapel of the Centurion,** one of the region's first churches.

9. Buckroe Beach

Gentle surf, a bandstand, and a nearby fishing pier attract many visitors to this beach. The **Grandview Nature Preserve** offers excellent hiking and much wildlife.

10. Chesapeake Bay Bridge-Tunnel

This 17-mile roadway links Virginia Beach and the Eastern Shore. Four man-made islands are part of the route; one even has a restaurant and pier. *Toll charged.*

11. Old Cape Henry Lighthouse

Atlantic Ave., Fort Story. Built on a high dune in 1791, this sandstone structure was the nation's first lighthouse. It was replaced by the new **Cape Henry Lighthouse,** which has a powerful electric beam. Nearby, the **First Landing Cross** marks the spot where the first English settlers touched the New World's shores. Occupying much of Cape Henry, **Seashore State Park** has bald cypress stands and wildlife. *Admission charged for some attractions.*

12. Virginia Beach Oceanfront

Vacationers flock here in the summer to enjoy miles of public beach and the 40-block boardwalk. Popular activities include sailing, scuba diving, fishing, waterskiing, and swimming. The **Life-Saving Museum of Virginia** displays equipment used to save lives; it also has ship models and exhibits on shipwrecks. *Admission charged at museum.*

13. Virginia Marine Science Museum

717 General Booth Blvd., Virginia Beach. Hands-on exhibits, aquariums, and a boardwalk through a saltwater marsh allow visitors to explore the state's marine environment. One attraction simulates a dive to a shipwreck. *Admission charged.*

14. Adam Thoroughgood House

1636 Parrish Rd., Virginia Beach. Built in 1680, this small 45-by-22-foot four-room plantation house is one of the oldest brick houses in America. Its style, including chimneys on the sides, is that of a 17th-century English cottage. The garden, with its boxwood hedges, recalls the popular period designs of England. *Admission charged.*

With a wingspan of more than 19 feet, this hand-carved gilded eagle in the Mariners' Museum was the figurehead of a U.S. frigate from 1881 to 1921.

15. Norfolk Botanical Garden

Azalea Garden Rd., Norfolk. Small boats carry passengers along the canals that lace these seaside gardens. Visitors can also walk miles of paths to view azaleas, rhododendrons, camellias, roses, and other colorful plants. Special areas include a sunken garden and a fragrance garden for the blind. *Admission charged.*

16. Norfolk Naval Base

Rte. 564 and Hampton Blvd., Norfolk. At the world's largest naval installation, visitors can board designated ships and take a bus tour of the base. Boat cruises of the harbor are available, from which destroyers and submarines can be seen. *Fee charged for bus tours and cruises.*

17. The Hermitage Foundation Museum

7637 North Shore Rd., Norfolk. The expertly crafted Tudor-style house here has a fine collection of Eastern and Western art. Decorative works, such as Tiffany glass and Persian rugs, are displayed in the handsome rooms. Highlights include jade carvings and a marble Buddha. *Admission charged.*

18. Downtown Norfolk

Convention and Visitors Bureau, 236 East Plume St. This old port town celebrates the sea with a new center called **Nauticus,** where visitors can enjoy participatory exhibits as well as displays on shipbuilding, boating, marine life, and weather forecasting. Relocated at the center is the **Hampton Roads Naval Museum,** which underscores the area's naval history. **The Waterside** is a waterfront pavilion offering shops, restaurants, entertainment, and harbor cruises. Other Norfolk attractions include the **Douglas MacArthur Memorial,** which contains the military hero's tomb and memorabilia; the **Chrysler Museum,** featuring a renowned collection of art; and the **Moses Myers House,** an elegant 1792 Federal mansion. *Admission charged for some attractions.*

19. Portsmouth

Visitor Information Center, 6 Crawford Pkwy. Displaying paintings, models, maps, and other exhibits, the **Portsmouth Naval Shipyard Museum** traces naval history. The adjacent **Portsmouth Lightship Museum** was built in 1915; it was used to guide other vessels through dangerous waters. Visitors can take cruises of the busy harbor. They can also take a trolley to see **Olde Towne,** a historic district that preserves three centuries' worth of structures, including the 1762 **Trinity Church** and a grand Victorian home. *Admission charged for some attractions.*

20. Great Dismal Swamp National Wildlife Refuge

This tranquil landscape's forests and waterways provide a haven for birds, bears, deer, and numerous other animals. Picnic waysides and viewing areas line Rte. 17. An interpretive boardwalk trail begins near the entrance to Washington Ditch Road.

Hampton Roads Area Map

CHESAPEAKE BAY

Newport News · **Poquoson** · **Hampton** · **Norfolk** · **Portsmouth** · **Virginia Beach** · **Chesapeake** · **Suffolk**

Hampton Roads

James River · Warwick River · Nansemond River · Elizabeth River · Back River · Poquoson River · Intracoastal Waterway · Lynnhaven Roads · Broad Bay · Back Bay

Major places and landmarks:
- U.S. ARMY TRANSPORTATION MUSEUM
- FORT EUSTIS MILITARY RES.
- NEWPORT NEWS/WILLIAMSBURG INTL. AIRPORT
- CHRISTOPHER NEWPORT COLLEGE
- MARINERS MUS. PK.
- NASA RESEARCH CENTER
- LANGLEY A.F.B.
- HAMPTON ROADS COLISEUM
- HAMPTON UNIVERSITY
- FORT MONROE MILITARY RESERVATION
- Buckroe Beach · Grand View · Ocean View · Willoughby
- GRANDVIEW NATURAL PRESERVE
- PLUM TREE ISLAND N.W.R.
- Cape Charles · Kiptopeke
- EASTERN SHORE OF VIRGINIA N.W.R.
- FISHERMANS ISLAND · FISHERMANS ISLAND N.W.R.
- CHESAPEAKE BAY BRIDGE-TUNNEL
- MONITOR-MERRIMAC MEM. BRIDGE TUNNEL
- HAMPTON ROADS BRIDGE-TUNNEL
- U.S. ARMY CORPS. OF ENG. DISPOSAL AREA (CRANEY ISLAND)
- U.S. NAVAL SUPPLY CENTER
- OLD DOMINION UNIVERSITY
- NORFOLK NAVAL BASE
- NORFOLK NAVAL STATION
- NORFOLK INTERNATIONAL AIRPORT
- VIRGINIA WESLEYAN COLLEGE
- LITTLE CREEK U.S. NAVAL AMPHIBIOUS BASE
- FT. STORY MILITARY RES.
- SEASHORE STATE PARK
- LIFE SAVING MUSEUM OF VIRGINIA
- OCEANA N.A.S.
- CAMP PENDLETON · U.S. NAVAL AMPHIBIOUS BASE
- DAM NECK U.S. NAVAL FLEET TRAINING CENTER
- CHRYSLER MUSEUM
- MACARTHUR MEMORIAL
- NORFOLK STATE UNIV.
- PORTSMOUTH NAVAL SHIPYARD AND LIGHTSHIP MUSEUM
- U.S. NAVY SHIPYARD
- U.S. NAVAL AMMUNITION DEPOT
- U.S. NAVAL TRANSMITTER STATION
- ST. LUKE'S CHURCH
- HARBOR CRUISE AT WHARTON'S WHARF
- LYNNHAVEN HOUSE
- GREAT DISMAL SWAMP NATIONAL WILDLIFE REFUGE
- U.S. NAVAL RESERVATION (FENTRESS FIELD)
- BACK BAY N.W.R.
- Lake Tecumseh · Stumpy Lake · Western Branch Res.
- WESTERN BRANCH RES.
- NANSEMOND N.W.R.

Towns and localities:
Grafton · Tabb · Dare · Oriana · Denbigh · Lawson · Battery Park · Rescue · Smithfield · Carrollton · Bartlett · Benns Church · Longview · Chuckatuck · Oakland · Everets · Reids Ferry · Beamon · Wilroy · Kings Fork · Nansemond · Magnolia · Elephant Fork · Washington · Nurney · Saunders · Hobson · Belleville · Huntersville · Pughsville · Driver · Shoulders Hill · Sleepy Hole · Twin Pines · Churchland · West Norfolk · Bowers Hill · Chadswyck · Deep Creek · Millville · Grassfield · Oak Grove · Great Bridge · Butts · Essex Meadows · Portlock · Mears Corner · Fentress · Mount Pleasant · West Landing · Douglas Landing · Benefit · Hickory · Land of Promise · North Landing · Princess Anne · Pungo · Sigma · Nimmo · Mapleton · Kempsville · Oceana · London Bridge · Pleasant Ridge · Back Bay

Geographic points:
Mulberry Island · Jail Pt. · Blunt Pt. · Ragged Island · Marsh Pt. · Messick Pt. · Northend Pt. · Tanner Pt. · L. Tormentor · Pagan R. · Jones Cr. · Chuckatuck Cr. · Nansemond River · Crittenden Ct.

Highway markers include: I-64, US 17, US 58, US 60, US 13, US 460, US 258, US 168, US 460, and numerous state routes (134, 143, 171, 172, 173, 152, 306, 312, 351, 337, 564, 166, 165, 190, 194, 225, 247, 403, 407, 409, 410, 411, 414, 44, 279, 408, 149, 620, 621, 704, 665, 669, 644, 642, 634, 638, 688, 705, 674, 759, 604, 600, 601, 602, 603, 659, 626, 629, 191, 239, 135, 104, 141, 464, 264, 664, 278, 167, and others)

Reference grid markers (boxed numbers): 1 through 20

COLONIAL VIRGINIA

1. Jamestown Settlement

Rte. 31 and Colonial Pkwy. This site commemorates the first permanent English settlement in North America. The exhibits in the museum here give a historical overview of the undertaking. Other attractions include the **Susan Constant, Godspeed,** and **Discovery,** three full-scale replicas of ships that carried the colonists to America. Visitors can board one or more of the vessels, where a guide describes the overcrowded, four-month voyage from England. **James Fort** is a re-creation of the triangular fort in which the immigrants first lived. It contains wattle-and-daub structures that are indicative of Jamestown's earliest buildings. Just as the settlers did centuries ago, costumed interpreters cook meals, make repairs, and perform other chores. **Indian Village** re-creates the lifestyle of the Powhatan Indians. It includes dwellings and a ceremonial dance circle. Costumed interpreters perform daily tasks, such as making tools and pottery. *Admission charged.*

2. Jamestown–Colonial National Historical Park

Jamestown Island. This area was once part of the peninsula on which the British settlement was founded in 1607. The visitor center shows a film on Jamestown and displays 17th-century artifacts. Near the park's entrance, in a replica of an early factory, interpreters demonstrate glassblowing. Two roads pass through the island's pine forests and swamps. Among the remaining original structures are foundations and a church tower. *Admission charged.*

3. Busch Gardens

1 Busch Gardens Blvd., Williamsburg. This 360-acre park offers a unique experience, combining both past and present. Roller coasters, riverboats, and a miniature Le Mans racetrack share the grounds with re-creations of 17th-century villages. There's also live entertainment. *Admission charged.*

4. Carter's Grove

8797 Pocahontas Trail, near Williamsburg. This area is connected to Williamsburg by the Country Road, a scenic route past woods, marshes, and tidal creeks. The grove is home to a stately Georgian mansion completed in 1755. Lying between the house and a river is the site of an early 17th-century town, where reconstructed slave quarters contain interpretive displays. The **Winthrop Rockefeller Archaeology Museum** examines the town, one of the first English settlements in America. *Admission charged.*

5. Yorktown Victory Center

Old Rte. 238 and Colonial Pkwy., Yorktown. The center has exhibits, a film, and living-history shows on the Revolution. There are also reproductions of an army campsite and an 18th-century farm, each with costumed interpreters. *Admission charged.*

6. Grace Episcopal Church

Church St., Yorktown. Still in use, this church was constructed in 1697 of native marl — a compound of sand, clay, limestone, and seashells. During the Yorktown battle, the British stored their arms and ammunition here.

7. Nelson House

Main St., Yorktown. Built in the early 1700's, this elegant brick mansion was owned by Thomas Nelson, Jr., a signer of the Declaration of Independence.

8. Yorktown Victory Monument

Main St., Yorktown. A 95-foot-high granite column here recalls the victory of American and French allied forces. The 1881 cornerstone marks the 100th anniversary of the battle. Bronze plaques list the names of soldiers who died in the Revolution.

9. Yorktown Battlefield Visitor Center

Off Colonial Pkwy. George Washington defeated Cornwallis here in the Revolution's last major battle. The center offers displays, a movie, and self-guided auto tours.

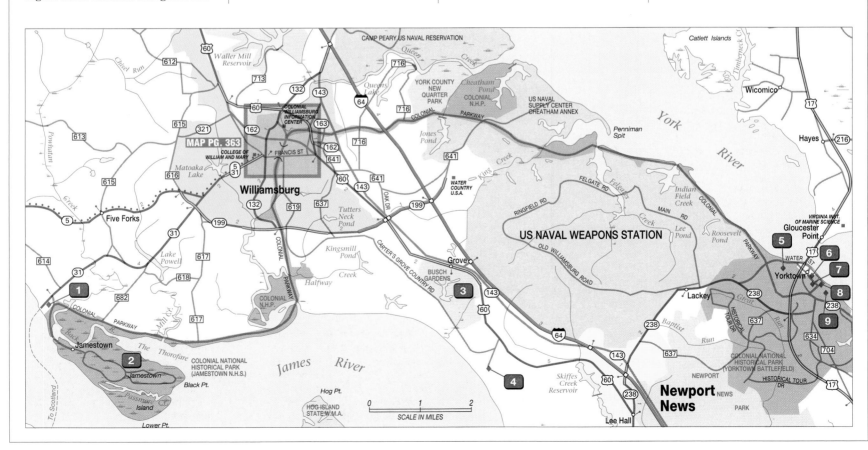

WILLIAMSBURG

1. Colonial Williamsburg Visitor Center

100 Visitor Center Dr. This site offers visitors the opportunity to come as close as possible to daily Colonial life. Complete with costumed craftspeople, the superbly restored 18th-century town includes hotels, houses, public buildings, restaurants, and shops. Even the landscaping is authentic to the period. The visitor center provides a parking area, shows an introductory movie, and sells tickets to exhibits and events. *Admission charged.*

2. Governor's Palace

End of Palace Green. Completed in 1720, the original palace served as the residence of both royal and commonwealth governors, including Patrick Henry and Thomas Jefferson. This reconstruction faithfully adheres to its 1768 appearance, when Governor Botetourt displayed muskets and swords as a sign of the king's power. The site has been extravagantly furnished with rare antiques. The grounds, which feature a formal garden and a carriage house, are also open to the public.

3. George Wythe House

Duke of Gloucester St.. This large brick residence is named for its onetime owner, a prominent lawyer and signer of the Declaration of Independence. The estate encompasses a poultry house, laundry, stable, and other outbuildings. Washington used the house as headquarters just before the Yorktown battle.

4. Bruton Parish Church

Duke of Gloucester St. Designed in the shape of a cross, this Episcopalian church has been in continuous use since its construction in 1715. The bell in the white wooden steeple rang out as the local liberty bell during the Revolutionary War; it still announces services.

5. James Geddy House and Foundry

Duke of Gloucester St. A family of artisans lived and worked here, crafting items in silver, gold, pewter, and brass. Demonstrations take place in the foundry. At a shop next door, visitors can purchase jewelry, cutlery, and other objects made in the 18th-century style. The Geddy house has features that were considered unusual for its time, such as a low-pitched roof without dormer windows and a doorway topped by a second-story balcony.

6. Peyton Randolph House

Nicholson St. A prominent colonial leader, Randolph eventually became the president of the First Continental Congress. His elegant white-frame home served as a political and social gathering place. Of particular note are the oak-paneled bedroom, the handsome library, and several pieces of the family's silver.

7. Raleigh Tavern

Duke of Gloucester St. The original building burned down in 1859, but a careful reconstruction of the tavern has been erected on the same site. In Colonial times, it was the scene of social gatherings as well as political rallies attended by such patriots as Washington and Jefferson. The tavern's Apollo Room hosted grand balls.

8. Public Gaol

Nicholson St. This jail was originally built in 1704, undergoing several additions until 1772. The site includes rooms for the jailer's family as well as the prisoners' cells. Chains, leg irons, and other artifacts indicate the severe treatment endured by inmates, who included debtors, pirates, and runaway slaves.

9. Capitol

Duke of Gloucester St. This H-shaped brick structure is a splendid re-creation of Virginia's stately original colonial capitol, where significant pre-Revolutionary political issues were debated.

10. Wetherburn's Tavern

Duke of Gloucester St. Not only is this the original tavern built by Henry Wetherburn in 1743, but its furnishings are also accurate reproductions, thanks to a detailed 1760 inventory and more than 2,000 artifacts later recovered at the site. Like the Raleigh Tavern, this hostelry served as more than an inn and restaurant; scientific

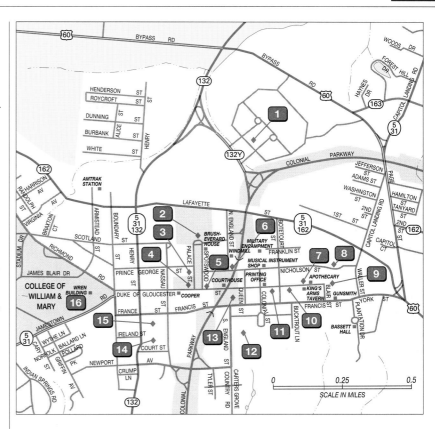

lectures, social events, and political meetings also took place here.

11. James Anderson Forge

Duke of Gloucester St. At the rear of the house here is the past owner's blacksmith shop, where arms were made for Virginia during the Revolutionary War. Today the forge is used to make hardware and fittings for local building projects.

12. Abby Aldrich Rockefeller Folk Art Center

South England St. This museum has an extraordinary collection of American folk art dating from the 18th to the 20th centuries. The collection, which has increased over the years to include some 2,000 items, features excellent examples of quilts, furniture, paintings, needlepoint, weather vanes, and toys. *Admission charged.*

13. Magazine and Guardhouse

Duke of Gloucester St. The magazine is an octagonal warehouse dating back to 1715 that used to store munitions for the Virginia colony and later for the Confederate army. The building today displays some of the early weapons. Originally constructed to protect the magazine, the guardhouse now contains a replica of a 1750 fire engine.

14. DeWitt Wallace Decorative Arts Gallery

Francis St. Funded by the founders of the *Reader's Digest,* this modern bi-level museum houses one of the world's finest collections of decorative arts. Dating from about 1600 to 1830, the English and American works include textiles, costumes, furniture, ceramics, paintings, prints, metals, and glass. *Admission charged.*

15. Public Hospital

Francis St. When the original hospital opened in 1773, it became the nation's first for the mentally ill. Among the exhibits featured in this reconstruction is a grim display of a cell with manacles attached to a wall.

16. College of William and Mary

This is the nation's second-oldest college, educating such distinguished alumni as Thomas Jefferson and James Monroe. Its walled-in campus contains the country's oldest academic structure, the U-shaped **Sir Christopher Wren Building,** based on the British architect's design.

CAPE LOOKOUT & CAPE HATTERAS

1. Historic Bath

Carteret St., Bath. Among the merchants, lawyers, and governors who lived here was a man named Edward Teach, better known as Blackbeard, Bath's most infamous resident. In 1718, after the king granted him a full pardon, the buccaneer settled here with his crew — though the high seas would in time lure the pirate back. Today North Carolina's oldest incorporated town includes the state's oldest church, **St. Thomas Church,** and several carefully restored 18th- and 19th-century homes.

2. Edenton

Chamber of Commerce, 116 East King St. Rich in pre-Revolutionary history, this town was the first capital of the province of North Carolina. Architectural treasures in the historic district include the **Cupola House,** a fine Jacobean dwelling; the Georgian-style **Barker House;** the **Iredell House; St. Paul's Episcopal Church,** one of the South's most notable churches from the colonial period; and the **Chowan County Courthouse.** Guided tours of the district depart from the **Historic Edenton Visitor Center.** *Admission charged.*

3. Somerset Place State Historic Site

Off Rte. 64, near Creswell. This was one of the state's most lucrative plantations, largely because a boatload of enslaved people was brought from Africa to dig a 6-mile canal, making the swampy land suitable for farming. Eventually, more than 350 persons toiled in the fields. Visitors can learn about the lives of the slaves from the owner's meticulously kept records. The main house was built in the 1830's and constructed of hand-hewn cypress. Nearby stands a kitchen, a dairy, an icehouse, and other clapboard structures.

4. Mattamuskeet National Wildlife Refuge

During winter near the shores of **Lake Mattamuskeet,** the state's largest natural lake, visitors can hear the whistles of swans and the honks of Canada geese. Bald eagles and a few golden eagles also inhabit the area. Come spring and summer, the 50,000-acre refuge is home to ospreys, herons, and egrets.

5. Nags Head Woods Preserve

701 West Ocean Acres Dr., Kill Devil Hills. Begun in 1978, this 1,100-acre preserve is one of the best remaining examples of a mid-Atlantic maritime forest, where towering hardwoods rise from the sand. A ridge of dunes prevents the salty ocean breezes from destroying the delicate habitats, whose forests and marshes are home to deer, woodpeckers, warblers, egrets, ospreys, otters, swans, and ducks.

6. Wright Brothers National Memorial

Rte. 158, Kill Devil Hills. A granite boulder pinpoints the spot where, on December 17, 1903, Orville Wright left the ground in the *Wright Flyer,* as brother Wilbur ran alongside. Markers show the length of that flight and three others. Nearby are reconstructions of the brothers' camp and hangar. A visitor center has a replica of the history-making plane that defied belief as well as gravity. *Admission charged.*

7. Jockey's Ridge State Park

A giant sand dune — probably the highest on the East coast — attracts many thrill-seeking hang gliders to this park. For those with more earthbound interests, this is also a great place for kite flying and hiking. There's also a museum of natural history, where visitors can discover how the dunes were made.

8. Cape Hatteras National Seashore

This 70-mile-long area contains pristine beaches, sand dunes, marshes, and maritime forest. It stretches from Ocracoke Inlet to Whalebone Junction, where an information station is located. **Coquina Beach,** one of the park's seven, offers swimming as well as a shipwreck site that visitors can explore. Distinguished by its horizontal black and white stripes, **Bodie Island Lighthouse** has two observation platforms and self-guiding nature trails.

9. Roanoke Island

The **Fort Raleigh National Historic Site** marks the location where Sir Walter Raleigh attempted to establish the first English settlement in the New World. Today it is called the Lost Colony, for all 116 inhabitants mysteriously disappeared. A reconstruction of a small earthen fort stands on what is thought to be the site of an original one built by the pioneers in 1585. In summer a musical drama, *The Lost Colony,* is performed here. Adjacent are the **Elizabethan Gardens,** planted in memory of the ill-fated settlers. The **Elizabeth II State Historic Site,** a re-creation of a 16th-century ship, was built to commemorate the colony's 400th anniversary. *Admission charged for some attractions.*

10. Oregon Inlet Fishing Center

Off Rte. 12, Cape Hatteras National Seashore. In this fisherman's paradise, anglers will find one of the largest fleets of sportfishing boats on the mid-Atlantic coast. In season, charter boats leave daily for inshore and offshore trips. Deep-sea catches include blue marlin, billfish, striped and channel bass, flounder, and bluefish. Twilight cruises are also available. *Admission charged.*

11. Pea Island National Wildlife Refuge

Bird lovers come here to see the tremendous number of snow geese that spend the winter on the 5,915-acre island, a major stop along the Atlantic Flyway. Peregrine falcons can often be spotted from the refuge's two observation platforms during the spring and fall. Egrets, herons, and ibises also nest here. The salt marshes and freshwater ponds are home to many other animals, from the elegant swan to the curious sea turtle.

12. Chicamacomico Lifesaving Station

Rte. 12, Rodanthe. Established in 1874 as one of the first lifesaving stations in North Carolina, this site was a participant in many daring rescues. It is now restored as a museum, where the exhibits trace the history of the station as well as a number of others that lined the Outer Banks. Early rescue drills are reenacted in the summer.

13. Cape Hatteras Lighthouse

Off Rte. 12, Buxton. Providing bird's-eye views of the churning Atlantic below, this is the tallest and perhaps best-known brick lighthouse in the country. Mariners still use it to guide them safely past Diamond Shoals, known as the Graveyard of the Atlantic. Exhibits on shipwrecks are displayed in the **Cape Hatteras Visitor Center.** Nearby is a landscape of tangled growth, the largest maritime forest on the Outer Banks.

14. Ocracoke Island

Although only a few can still be seen, thousands of wild ponies once roamed this secluded island. On Ocracoke Inlet in 1718 Blackbeard was killed by the British Navy, who, according to some reports, decapitated the pirate and put his head on their bowsprit, proving to all that the waters were safe again. The island's picturesque fishing village is home to the **Ocracoke Lighthouse,** built in 1823.

In pursuit of a catch, fishermen wade in a choppy sea at Cape Hatteras National Seashore.

15. Cape Lookout National Seashore

Reachable only by ferry and with no maintained roads, the narrow barrier islands that compose this seashore stretch 55 miles south from Ocracoke Inlet. The fishing is excellent, and shell seekers will find many delights. The 1859 lighthouse at **Cape Lookout** is still operational. Once an active port, the inlet at **Portsmouth Island** is now too shallow to accommodate large ships, but there's a quaint village with buildings from the 1800's, including a lifesaving complex. *Fee charged for ferry.*

16. Beaufort

Visitor Center, 128 Turner St. Costumed guides take visitors through the narrow streets lined with white frame dwellings at the **Beaufort Historic Site,** an old waterfront that has been restored. Constructed between 1732 and 1859, the buildings represent a wide variety of architectural styles. The tours include a jail, courthouse, apothecary, and doctor's office. With displays that include ship models, birds, fish, and fossils, the **North Carolina Maritime Museum** explores the natural history of the area's coastal regions. Narrated cruises of the harbor are available. *Admission charged.*

17. Fort Macon State Park

Built between 1826 and 1834, this fort is an excellent example of military architecture. Complete with gun emplacements, it once guarded the port of Beaufort. There was even an impressive moat that could be flooded with tidewaters from the sound. Yet for all its seeming impenetrability, the fort was captured by Union forces during the Civil War. The surrounding park offers picnic grounds and good swimming in protected waters. *Admission charged.*

18. North Carolina Aquarium at Pine Knoll Shores

Roosevelt Dr., Pine Knoll Shores. One of three aquariums on the North Carolina coast, this is a popular center for education and research on the state's coastal environments. It is located within the 265-acre **Theodore Roosevelt Natural Area,** donated to the state by the president's grandchildren, where the natural vegetation and important wildlife habitats remain undisturbed. As it winds through a dense forest of oaks, pines, and red cedars, a half-mile nature trail skirts the edge of a salt marsh, providing glimpses of birds and other wildlife.

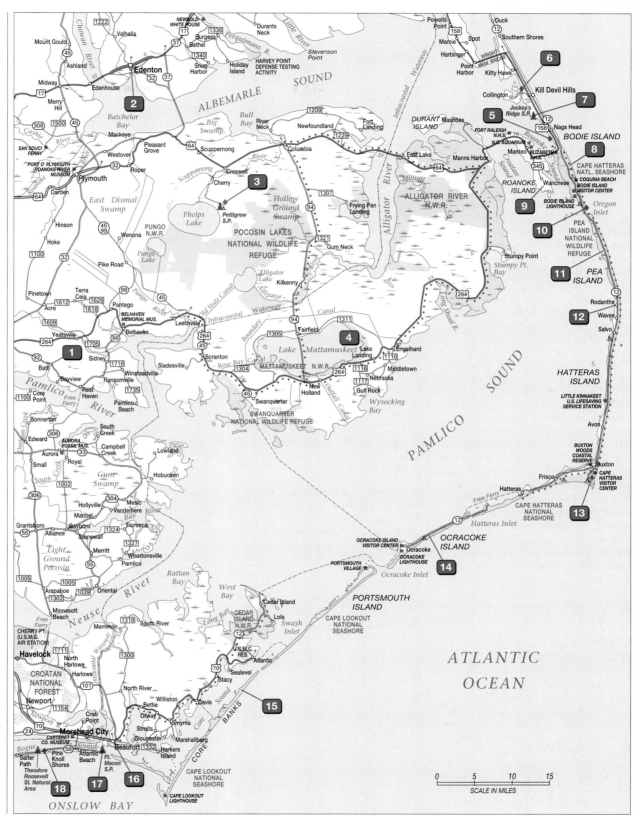

1. Selma

Chamber of Commerce, 513 Lauderdale St. Various sites relate this city's past from antebellum times to the 1960's civil rights movement. More than 1,200 buildings are in the **Old Town Historic District.** In a magnificently restored 1850's mansion, the **Sturvidant Hall Museum** displays period furnishings. One of the few antebellum riverfront business districts to survive the Civil War is located along five blocks of Water Avenue. Civil rights marches were organized at the **Brown Chapel A.M.E.,** and the **Edmund Pettus Bridge** was the site of violent clashes in 1965.

2. Montgomery

Chamber of Commerce, 401 Madison Ave. The refurbished **State Capitol,** dating from 1851, is opposite the **First White House of the Confederacy,** once the residence of Jefferson Davis and now a museum about the Confederacy. From 1954 to 1960 Dr. Martin Luther King, Jr., served as pastor of the **Dexter Avenue King Memorial Baptist Church.** Nearby is the **Civil Rights Memorial,** where the names of people who died in racial struggles are etched in granite. The **Montgomery Museum of Fine Arts** features a hands-on gallery for children and fine collections of 19th- and 20th-century American art. The Alabama Shakespeare Festival performs plays in the **State Theatre.** Visitors to **Old Alabama Town** can see more than 30 restored buildings. *Admission charged for some attractions.*

3. Jasmine Hill Gardens and Outdoor Museum

1500 Jasmine Hill Rd., Wetumpka. This 17-acre garden is decorated with Greek and Roman statuary and fountains. There's also a precise replica of the Olympian Temple of Hera. *Admission charged.*

4. Horseshoe Bend National Military Park

Rte. 49, near New Site. The deciding battle of the 1813–14 Creek Indian War was fought at this 2,040-acre park. The result contributed to Andrew Jackson's fame and increased settlement in Alabama. There are self-guiding tours, and a museum displays Indian artifacts and military weapons.

5. F.D.R.'s Little White House Historic Site

Rte. 85, Warm Springs. Built by President Roosevelt in 1932, this wood-paneled house is maintained as it was in 1945, the year the statesman died. A museum displays Roosevelt memorabilia. *Admission charged.*

6. Ocmulgee National Monument

1207 Emery Hwy., Macon. This area has been continuously occupied for some 12,000 years. Archaeologists speculate that the impressive mounds here were built between A.D. 900 and 1100 and used both as temples and for burials by an agrarian people. Displays include artifacts and a reconstructed earth lodge, complete with the original clay floor. *Admission charged.*

7. Andersonville National Historic Site

Rte. 49, Andersonville. This site commemorates a terribly brutal prisoner-of-war camp in the Civil War, where, amid unspeakable conditions, some 45,000 inmates lived and close to 13,000 perished. Visitors will find a visitor center, a museum, a cemetery, and remains of the old camp. *Admission charged.*

8. Georgia Agrirama

Off Rte. 75, Tifton. This living-history museum duplicates rural life in the South from 1870 to 1910. Some of the buildings, including a farmhouse, blacksmith shop, church, and gristmill, are staffed by costumed interpreters. *Admission charged.*

9. Albany

Chamber of Commerce, 225 West Broad Ave. The **Albany Museum of Art** has an exceptional collection of African art and changing exhibits of European and American works. Nearby Chehaw Park features the **Chehaw Wild Animal Park,** a 779-acre preserve, where African animals inhabit a simulated environment. *Admission charged.*

10. Jimmy Carter National Historic Site

100 Main St., Plains. A self-guiding tour begins at the depot, former president Carter's campaign headquarters and now a visitor center, and continues past sites that include his boyhood home, his old high school, and the church where he teaches Sunday school.

11. Lumpkin

Visitors Bureau, Cotton St. The impressive living-history village of **Westville** features more than 30 relocated and restored buildings from the 1830's. *Admission charged.*

12. Eufaula

Chamber of Commerce, 102 North Orange St. This town boasts many antebellum homes, including the 1830's **Sheppard Cottage.** A restored Neoclassical-style residence, the **Shorter Mansion** has displays of memorabilia and antique furnishings. *Admission charged at mansion.*

13. Columbus

Convention and Visitors Bureau, 801 Front St. **Fort Benning** is the largest infantry training center in America. Its **National Infantry Museum** depicts the changing role of the foot soldier from Revolutionary times, displaying artifacts, weapons, medals, and uniforms.

14. Tuskegee Institute National Historic Site

Old Montgomery Rd., Tuskegee. Many original buildings are located here on the campus of Tuskegee University, an industrial school for blacks founded by Booker T. Washington. Among the points of interest are **The Oaks,** which was once Washington's home, and the **George Washington Carver Museum,** displaying the horticulturalist's collections.

15. Pike Pioneer Museum

248 Rte. 231, Troy. This 10-building complex recalls rural life in the South at the turn of the century. Structures include a log cabin, country store, and tenant house. A museum contains more than 10,000 artifacts. *Admission charged.*

16. U.S. Army Aviation Museum

Bldg. 600, Fort Rucker. This museum traces the history of army aviation. Displays include both helicopters and planes used during World War II, the Korean War, and the Vietnam War.

17. Fort Walton Beach

Chamber of Commerce, 34 Miracle Strip Pkwy. Visitors can take guided tours of the vast **Eglin Air Force Base.** Among the attractions at the **Air Force Armament Museum** are 5,000 specimens of aerial armaments from World War I through the Persian Gulf War. The **Indian Temple Mound Museum** displays more than 4,000 Indian artifacts, some 10,000 years old. The **Gulfarium** features exhibits on the sea and shows with dolphins, whales, and sea lions. *Admission charged for some attractions.*

18. Panama City

Convention and Visitors Bureau, 415 Beckich Rd. This popular resort town offers fantastic beaches, fishing, hiking, camping, and boat trips to Shell Island.

19. St. Marks

Artifacts from the Civil War as well as from the Indian, Spanish, and British periods are displayed at the **San Marcos de Apalache State Historic Site.** Along the Gulf of Mexico, the **St. Marks National Wildlife Refuge** abounds with plants, waterfowl, and other animals. *Admission charged.*

20. Tallahassee

Convention and Visitors Bureau, 200 West College St. The present-day state capitol is across from the **Old Capitol,** now a museum displaying local artifacts. Modeled after an 1880's farm, the **Tallahassee Museum of History and Natural Science** includes a schoolhouse, church, and trails. Colorful flowers grace the **Alfred B. Maclay State Gardens.** The **Lake Jackson Mounds State Archaeological Site** contains the remains of the most significant ceremonial center in Florida between A.D. 1200 and 1500. The **San Luis Archaeological and Historic Site** displays artifacts from a 17th-century Apalachee village. *Admission charged for some attractions.*

21. Thomasville

Chamber of Commerce, 401 South Broad St. The five-building **Thomasville County Historical Society Museum** includes a log cabin, an 1800's bowling alley, and a museum. The uniquely shaped rooms at the restored **Lapham-Patterson House** contain original furnishings. The **Pebble Hill Plantation** has a lavish main house and extensive grounds. More than 2,000 flowers and plants grow in the **Rose Test Garden.** *Admission charged for some attractions.*

22. Stephen Foster State Folk Culture Center

Rte. 41, White Springs. Located on the Suwannee River, this center commemorates Stephen Foster, a writer of popular American songs, such as "Camptown Races" and "Oh, Susanna." Displays include dioramas, Foster's piano, and his original manuscripts. *Admission charged.*

1. Magnolia Springs State Park

During the Civil War a large prison camp was established among the pines, dogwoods, magnolias, and live oaks that grace this park. Today the area offers swimming, boating, fishing, camping, hiking, and rental cottages. A footbridge leads to the nearby **Bo Ginn National Fish Hatchery and Aquarium,** which raises fish for stocking the region's waters. The aquarium contains native species. *Admission charged at park.*

2. Walterboro

Chamber of Commerce, 109 Benson St. Dating from 1784 when some rice planters established a summer colony here, the town has retained much of its past. Self-guiding walking tours of the historic district include visits to old residences, churches, and slave cabins. **The Colleton Museum** displays local artifacts, artwork, photographs, and maps.

3. Beaufort

Chamber of Commerce, 1006 Bay St. Dating from 1710, Beaufort still features the quiet, picturesque atmosphere of its early days, when indigo and cotton brought great wealth to local planters. The highlights include the **Beaufort Arsenal Museum,** displaying Indian artifacts, decorative arts, and relics of the Revolutionary and Civil wars; the **John Mark Verdier House Museum,** a 1790 Federal mansion; the beautiful 1840 Greek Revival **George Parsons Elliott House; St. Helena's Episcopal Church,** built in 1724; the **Henry C. Chambers** waterfront park, home to a marina, picnic sites, and playground; and the **Beaufort National Cemetery,** where both Union and Confederate soldiers are buried. *Admission charged at houses.*

4. Penn Center Historic District

Martin Luther King Dr., St. Helena Island. The preserved buildings here were built in 1862 as a school for freed slaves. The collection at the **York Bailey Museum** depicts the history of Sea Island African-Americans. *Admission charged.*

5. Edisto Island

Once the site of lucrative plantations, the island today is a quiet vacation area. The **Edisto Beach State Park** offers rental cabins, camping, and swimming. Deep-sea fishing and charter boats are available at the island's marina. *Admission charged.*

6. Hunting Island State Park

Known for its stands of pine and palmetto trees, the park offers swimming, fishing, rental cabins, and campgrounds. The 140-foot lighthouse, no longer in use, affords fine views of the area. *Admission charged.*

7. Parris Island

Located at the Marine Corps Recruit Depot, the **Parris Island Museum** relates the history both of the marines and the area. The **Santa Elena Site** marks the site of a 16th-century French and Spanish settlement.

8. Jekyll Island

Welcome Center, 901 Jekyll Causeway. From 1886 until 1942, the island was an exclusive resort frequented by millionaires. Today tours are offered of the **Jekyll Island Historic District,** where a restored 19th-century clubhouse is now a hotel. Several elegant cottages can be visited, including the Rockefeller home. The island offers golf, tennis, biking, camping, swimming, and fishing. *Admission charged.*

9. Okefenokee Heritage Center

1460 North Augusta Ave., Waycross. This center is an outdoor museum that examines the history and culture of the area. Exhibits include a 1912 railroad depot, a steam locomotive, an 1840's farmhouse, horse-drawn carriages, early automobiles, and an old print shop. The adjacent **Southern Forest World** details the South's timber industry. *Admission charged.*

10. Okefenokee Swamp Park

Rte. 1, south of Waycross. Visitors here can tour some 1,200 acres of wilderness aboard flat-bottomed johnboats, which slip quietly through the mysterious junglelike terrain. A boardwalk leads through the swamp to an observation tower. The **Living Swamp Ecology Center** has exhibits on indigenous wildlife. *Admission charged.*

11. Olustee Battlefield State Historic Site

Rte. 90, east of Olustee. The largest Civil War battle in Florida occurred here on February 20, 1864. Beginning at the interpretive center, a self-guiding trail leads through the 270-acre battlefield. Artifacts from the encounter are displayed in a small museum, which, like the site, is open Thursday through Monday.

12. Gainesville

Convention and Visitors Bureau, 10 Southwest Second Ave. Highlights of this university town include the **Florida Museum of Natural History,** displaying Timucuan Indian artifacts and collections of indigenous flora and fauna; the **Fred Bear Museum,** with exhibits on archery and bow hunting; and the **Devil's Millhopper State Geological Site,** a 120-foot-deep sinkhole some 15,000 years old. *Admission charged for some attractions.*

13. Paynes Prairie State Preserve

Named for a Seminole chief, this wilderness preserve was once a large lake that drained suddenly a century ago, leaving behind several ponds. There are many birds and mammals here, including the reintroduced American bison. A 50-foot observation tower provides a panoramic view of the fascinating 20,000-acre area. Among the various activities permitted here are fishing, boating, and picnicking. *Admission charged.*

14. Ocala

Chamber of Commerce, 110 East Silver Springs Blvd. This city's historic district has homes built just before and during the turn of the century. Information on many of the area's Thoroughbred horse farms is available at the chamber of commerce. **The Appleton Museum of Art** displays a notable collection of African, European, pre-Columbian, and Latin American art and antiquities. *Admission charged.*

15. Silver Springs

5656 East Silver Springs Blvd. Jungle cruises through this 350-acre park glide on a river that is fed by the world's largest artesian spring. The semitropical landscape is inhabited by monkeys, alligators, and other exotic wildlife. Glass-bottom boats afford glimpses into the clear water of colorful marine animals and plants. The visitor center at the **Ocala National Forest,** a popular wildlife and recreation area, is located just east of the town of Silver Springs. *Admission charged at park.*

16. Ravine State Gardens

1600 Twigg St., Palatka. Guided tours are offered during the spring azalea festival.

The gardens also contain loblolly pines, dogwoods, magnolias, and sweet gums. Peregrine falcons rest here on their annual migrations. A loop drive and a fitness trail wind through the area, and picnic areas are provided. *Admission charged.*

17. Fort Matanzas National Monument

Rattlesnake Island, 14 miles south of St. Augustine. The fort here was built in 1742 to protect the southern approach to St. Augustine and guard the entrance to the Intracoastal Waterway. No enemies were able to conquer the stronghold, which has not been used since 1821. The surrounding 300-acre park has a beach and a small museum with videos on the fort's history.

18. Faver-Dykes State Park

Deer, foxes, alligators, otters, waterfowl, and migratory songbirds inhabit this park's 752 acres of marshes, pinelands, and hammocks. Bordering the region is Pellicer Creek, where visitors can boat, canoe, and fish. Camping, picnicking, and a boat ramp are available. Two nature trails loop through the area. *Admission charged.*

19. Marineland of Florida

9507 Ocean Shore Blvd., Marineland. Dolphins, sea lions, otters, flamingos, penguins, sharks, turtles, barracudas, and other marine life are featured at this seaside park. Other attractions include daily shows, a nature walk, marina, playground, and a small museum with shells from around the world. *Admission charged.*

20. Gamble Rogers Memorial State Recreation Area at Flagler Beach

A windswept landscape of sand dunes and scrub oaks between the Atlantic Ocean and the Intracoastal Waterway, this area is inhabited by fiddler crabs, sea turtles, and wading birds. The region offers excellent swimming, boating, camping, and picnicking. Guided walks along a nature trail are available seasonally. *Admission charged.*

21. Bulow Plantation Ruins State Historic Site

Off Old Kings Rd., 3 miles south of Rte. 100. This sugar plantation flourished in the early 1800's but was destroyed in 1836 by the Seminole Indians, who resented the intrusion of white planters. Ruins of the sugar mill have been preserved in the 109-acre park, where visitors will find picnic areas, a playground, canoe rentals, a nature trail, and fishing. *Admission charged.*

1. Myrtle Beach

Chamber of Commerce, 1301 North Kings Hwy. The **Grand Strand,** a 60-mile stretch of sandy beach from the North Carolina border to Georgetown, is home to many recreation areas, including Myrtle Beach. The **Myrtle Beach Pavilion Amusement Park** has a roller coaster, waterslides, and a miniature golf course. The **Ripley's Believe It Or Not! Museum** offers many unique displays. **The Carolina Opry** presents live music and comedy performances. *Admission charged for some attractions.*

2. Murrells Inlet

Deep-sea fishing cruises leave from this picturesque seaside village, known for its crabbing, its shrimping, and its many excellent seafood restaurants.

3. Brookgreen Gardens

Rte. 17, Murrells Inlet. The setting of some 500 sculptures from the 19th and 20th centuries, these landscaped gardens include 2,000 varieties of plants, a wildlife area, and nature trails. Surrounding a castlelike home situated on the other side of the highway, **Huntington Beach State Park** offers camping, surf fishing, picnicking, and nature trails. *Admission charged.*

4. Pawleys Island

This quiet summer resort of weathered cottages, oleanders, and oaks is well-known for its handwoven hammocks. Local artisans demonstrate their weaving skills at a boutique.

5. Bellefield Nature Center

Off Rte. 17, near Georgetown. At the entrance to Hobcaw Barony, a 17,500-acre wildlife refuge that was once the estate of the financier-statesman Bernard Baruch, this center has exhibits on ecology and natural history. Local marine animals, including sea anemones, are on view.

6. Georgetown

Chamber of Commerce, 102 Broad St. This region had important rice-producing farms in colonial times, and the town, established in 1729, became a hub of commerce. Housed in the 1842 Old Market Building, **The Rice Museum** tells the history of rice cultivation from 1700 to 1900. Still in use, the **Prince George Winyah Episcopal Church** was completed in 1755 and named for King George II. Built about 1769, the **Harold Kaminski House** once belonged to a rice planter; it displays 18th- and 19th-century antiques. *Admission charged.*

7. Hopsewee Plantation

Rte. 17, south of Georgetown. Amid large oak trees, the mansion here was the home of Thomas Lynch, delegate to the Continental Congress, and the birthplace of his son, Thomas Lynch, Jr., a signer of the Declaration of Independence. *Admission charged.*

A row of Victorian homes in Charleston

8. Hampton Plantation State Park

Located in McClellanville, these landscaped grounds with picnic areas are home to a handsome 18th-century plantation mansion that was the residence of Archibald Rutledge, a state poet laureate, until his death in 1973. A wildlife haven, the **Santee Coastal Reserve,** offers nature walks, hiking trails, canoeing, and 11 miles of beach. *Admission charged at park.*

9. Cape Romain National Wildlife Refuge

A string of barrier islands and salt marshes, the refuge protects many varieties of wildlife, including pelicans and wood storks. Departing from Moores Landing, a boat takes visitors to the otherwise inaccessible area. *Fee charged for boat.*

10. Francis Marion National Forest

Much of the 250,000-acre forest, named for a Revolutionary War general, was destroyed by hurricane Hugo, but outdoor enthusiasts can still enjoy miles of hiking and horseback trails. The **Buck Hall Recreation Area** offers camping, picnicking, and a boat ramp. The **Rembert C. Dennis Wildlife Center** raises deer, wild turkeys, and bass.

11. Cypress Gardens

3030 Cypress Gardens Rd., south of Moncks Corner. On boat rides and walkways visitors can traverse this watery, otherworldly landscape that was once a rice plantation. The unique gardens contain 163 acres of moss-draped cypress trees and lagoons. The banks of the swamps are lined with camellias and azaleas. *Admission charged.*

12. Old Dorchester State Park

Located here are an old fort and church tower, the remains of a 1697 town begun by a group of Congregationalists from Dorchester, Massachusetts. The area also features fine landscaping, nature trails, picnic areas, and fishing.

13. Middleton Place

Ashley River Rd., near Charleston. Much of the handsome 1741 mansion here was destroyed during the Civil War. The one surviving wing now displays period furnishing, paintings, and decorative arts. The beautifully restored gardens include formal plantings and twin lakes. At the stable are farm animals and demonstrations of early crafts. *Admission charged.*

14. Magnolia Plantation and Gardens

Rte. 61, near Charleston. Dating from 1685, the plantation features extensive plantings of magnolias, azaleas, and camellias. Other attractions include an 18th-century herb garden, a maze, cypress swamp, waterfowl refuge, nature and biking trails, and picnic areas. *Admission charged.*

15. Drayton Hall

3380 Ashley River Rd., near Charleston. This elegant mansion was built in 1742; it is one of the nation's finest examples of Georgian Palladian architecture. Left unscathed by the Civil War, the virtually unchanged hall features outstanding ceilings and hand-carved woodwork. *Admission charged.*

16. Charles Towne Landing-1670

1500 Old Towne Rd., Charleston. On the site of the state's first permanent English settlement, the landing features a reconstructed 1670 village, where visitors can see replicas of colonial homes and a 17th-century trading vessel. One attraction re-creates a typical forest of 1670, complete with animals native to the area in that era. Formal gardens, nature trails, picnic areas, and a playground are also here. *Admission charged.*

17. Downtown Charleston

Visitor Center, 375 Meeting St. Early buildings in this historic seaside city include the 1772 **Heyward-Washington House,** with its handsome furnishings; the 1808 **Nathaniel Russell House,** known for its free-flying stairway; and the 1803 **Joseph Manigault House.** Among the other highlights are **Cabbage Row; St. Michael's Episcopal Church,** the city's oldest; the **Old Exchange Building,** whose dungeon confined British soldiers during the Revolution; the 1840 Greek Revival **Congregation Beth Elohim;** and **Old City Market,** featuring locally made baskets. The **Charleston Museum** focuses on Southern decorative arts. The **Gibbes Museum of Art** has a collection that includes miniatures of both portraits and room interiors. *Admission charged for some attractions.*

18. Fort Sumter National Monument

Built on a man-made island in Charleston Harbor, the fort in 1861 was the site of the first shot fired in the Civil War. The battle that ensued resulted in the occupation of the fort by Confederate troops. Boat tours leave from the City Marina and Patriots Point. *Admission charged.*

19. Fort Moultrie

1213 Middle St., Sullivans Island. The 1776 fort that originally occupied this site was able to fend off the British during the Revolution. The restored stronghold here today was built in 1809 and controlled by the Confederates in the Civil War. A film tells the history of this strategic point.

20. Patriots Point Naval and Maritime Museum

40 Patriots Point Rd., Mt. Pleasant. The fascinating attractions here include an aircraft carrier, destroyer, submarine, nuclear ship, planes, and weapons. *Admission charged.*

21. Boone Hall Plantation

1235 Long Point Rd., Mt. Pleasant. Built in 1935, this columned mansion occupies an impressive landscape that features a long driveway bordered by oak trees, a painting of which was used as a backdrop in *Gone With the Wind.* The original slave quarters can also be visited. *Admission charged.*

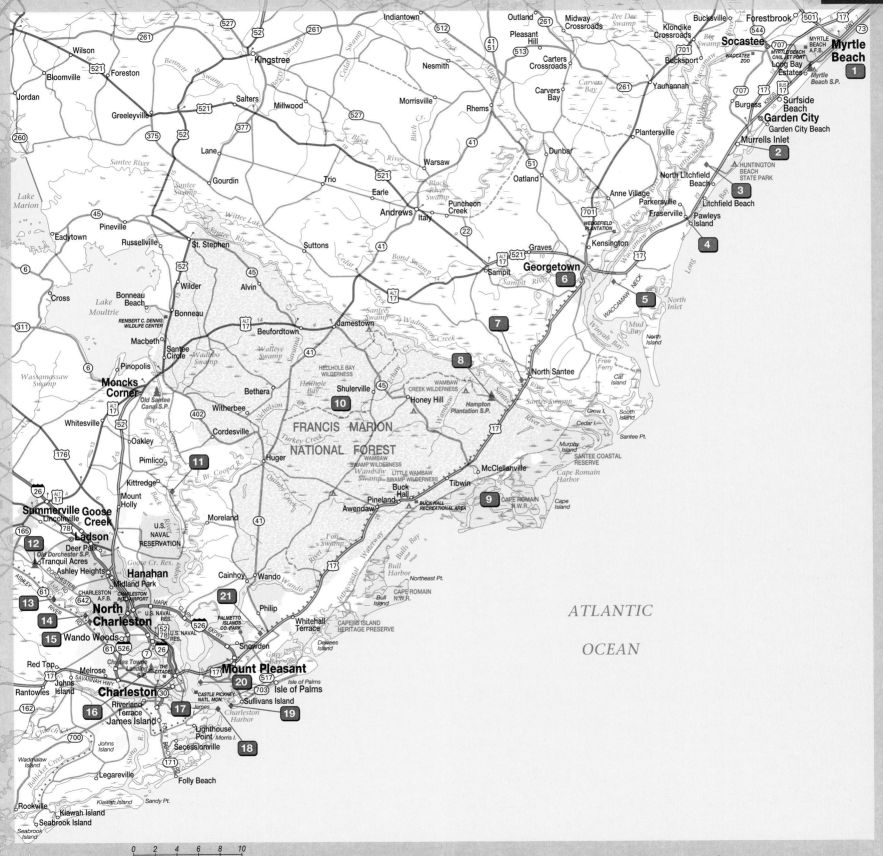

SCALE IN MILES
0 2 4 6 8 10

1. Pinckney Island National Wildlife Refuge

The 4,053 acres here contain various waterfowl and wildlife habitats, observable along the more than 14 miles of hiking and biking trails that traverse the refuge.

2. Hilton Head Island

Chamber of Commerce, 1 Chamber Dr. A 42-square-mile island, Hilton Head boasts a number of attractions, including posh resorts, public beaches, riding stables, world-famous golf courses, and tennis courts. Among the island's natural splendors are the **Newhall Audubon Preserve** and the **Sea Pines Forest Preserve.** The ruins of **Fort Mitchell** can be seen at **Hilton Head Plantation.** *Admission charged for some attractions.*

3. Tybee Island

The Atlantic meets spacious public beaches here, home also to marinas, recreation areas, and seafood restaurants. Other attractions include the **Tybee Museum** and **Tybee Lighthouse Historic Site.** The museum has exhibits on the island's history from the colonial period to the present; it also displays historic maps, gun collections, and hundreds of antique dolls. The lighthouse is the state's oldest and tallest. *Admission charged.*

4. Fort Pulaski National Monument

Eighteen years were required to complete the fort, which was begun in 1829. Named for a hero in the American Revolution, it is replete with moats and drawbridges. Robert E. Lee was assigned to the stronghold after graduating from West Point. In 1862 Union troops captured the strategic site after a 30-hour bombardment. *Admission charged.*

5. Old Fort Jackson

1 Fort Jackson Rd., 3 miles east of Savannah. Built by the federal government in the early 1800's, this is Georgia's oldest standing fort. It was garrisoned in the War of 1812 and in the Civil War, when the Con-federates used it to defend the Savannah River. Living-history demonstrations and battle reenactments are offered periodically. *Admission charged.*

6. Savannah National Wildlife Refuge

Covering some 25,000 acres, more than half of which is hardwood river-bottom swampland, this extensive refuge attracts whitetail deer, alligators, a variety of birds, and additional wildlife. Visitors can boat, canoe, fish, and hunt.

7. Savannah Historic District

Excellent tours visit many of some 1,100 buildings here that compose one of the country's largest urban historic districts. Within **City Hall** is a model of the S.S. *Savannah,* the first steam-powered vessel to cross the Atlantic Ocean; a tablet commemorates the *John Randolph,* the first commercially successful iron-sided steamboat launched in American waters. The **Savannah History Museum** depicts the city's history through multi-media exhibits. The colony's first congregation worshipped in **Christ Episcopal Church.** Period antiques fill the splendid 1819 **Telfair Mansion and Art Museum.** In 1825 the Marquis de Lafayette addressed the citizenry from a balcony at the **Owens-Thomas House.** The threatened demolition of the 1820 **Davenport House** launched Savannah's preservationist movement. The **Juliette Gordon Low Birthplace** was the childhood home of the founder of the Girl Scouts. After her marriage to William Low, she lived with him in the house his father built, the **Andrew Low House.** The colony's first burial ground was located in **Colonial Park.** A Gothic Revival synagogue, the **Temple Mickve Israel,** houses a Torah scroll brought here in 1733. Awash with scrimshaw, the **Ships of the Sea Maritime Museum** displays ship models and other nautical artifacts. A museum dedicated to African-American history and culture is housed in the **King-Tisdell Cottage,** a stop on the Negro Heritage Trail Tour. Along the centuries-old **River Street,** warehouses once used to store cotton have been refurbished to house museums, shops, and restaurants. *Admission charged for some attractions.*

8. Wormsloe State Historic Site

7601 Skidaway Rd., Savannah. In the early 18th century, Noble Jones, one of Georgia's original colonists, built a fortified house here after being awarded a royal grant. The property remained in the Jones family for two centuries, but today only vestiges indicate their lengthy presence. The visitor center has exhibits that outline the history of the state's founding. *Admission charged.*

9. Skidaway Island

Hiking on nature trails, camping, and fishing are among the attractions within the maritime forest at **Skidaway Island State Park.** The **University of Georgia Marine Extension Service** contains an outstanding aquarium. *Admission charged.*

10. Fort McAllister Historic Park

Off Rte. 144, Richmond Hill. An earthworks structure built in 1861 to protect Savannah from Union troops, Ft. McAllister was able to withstand repeated naval assaults. When General Sherman attacked by land, however, the fort succumbed, leading shortly afterward to the city's surrender. Today the park offers fishing, camping, picnicking, and splendid vistas. *Admission charged for some attractions.*

11. Hinesville

Chamber of Commerce, 500 East Rte. 84. The **Historic Downtown** is a restored commercial center with specialty shops. At **Fort Stewart,** the **Military Museum** displays weapons, uniforms, flags, and more from World War II to the Persian Gulf War.

12. Midway

Giant live oaks shade the renovated **Midway Church,** a clapboard structure built in 1792 by Puritans. Housed in a Colonial-style raised cottage, the **Midway Museum** displays historic documents and artifacts. *Admission charged.*

13. Fort Morris Historic Site

Rte. 38, east of Midway. The remains of 18th-century Ft. Morris and 19th-century Ft. Defiance can be seen here. A museum displays artifacts from the American Revolution and the Civil War. *Admission charged.*

14. Harris Neck National Wildlife Refuge

This small but lush refuge offers many recreational opportunities for botanists, photographers, and bird-watchers.

15. Sapelo Island

Tickets must be bought in advance from the chamber of commerce in Darien for the ferry that departs from Meridian to this island, once owned by R.J. Reynolds. Guided tours are conducted of the **Sapelo Island Research Reserve,** rich in both history and nature. *Admission charged.*

16. Darien

Chamber of Commerce, 105 Ft. King George Dr. Now a shrimping community, this town was established in 1736 by Scottish Highlanders who sided with the British in battles against the Indians, French, and Spanish. A reconstruction of an 18th-century stronghold is in the **Fort King George State Historic Site,** where a museum has exhibits on history. Hunting is permitted in the 25,000-acre **Altamaha Waterfowl Wildlife Management Area.** In the 1800's, **Butlers Island** contained one of the largest rice plantations on Georgia's coast. *Admission charged at museum.*

17. Hofwyl-Broadfield Plantation Site

Rte. 17, south of Darien. A variety of exhibits in the museum here depict 19th-century life on a coastal rice plantation. An array of period furnishings are on display in a frame house. *Admission charged.*

18. St. Simons Island

The island's **Neptune Park** offers a swimming pool, playground, picnic areas, beach access, and the 1872 **St. Simons Lighthouse.** Located next door, the **Museum of Coastal History** features exhibits on antebellum times, when plantations occupied the island. **Fort Frederica National Monument** commemorates an 18th-century fort whose walls once shielded an entire town. Today only the ruins remain, but a visitor center and wayside exhibits explain the site's past. Dating from 1884, the **Christ Episcopal Church** was built by ship carpenters. *Admission charged for some attractions.*

19. Brunswick

Tourist and Convention Bureau, 4 Glynn Ave. Founded in 1771, this city is known as the Gateway to the Golden Islands. **Old Town Brunswick** contains 36 historic buildings, many of them on Union Street. Landmarks include the majestic **Lanier Oak** and the 900-year-old **Lover's Oak.** The **Courthouse Square** is shaded by moss-draped oaks. Antique dolls are among the charming displays in the **Mary Miller Doll Museum.** *Admission charged at museum.*

1. Suwannee Canal Recreation Area

This is the eastern entrance to the **Okefenokee National Wildlife Refuge,** an area encompassing 396,000 acres of the Okefenokee Swamp — the largest and most primitive in the country. A driving tour, a boardwalk, and the 1920's **Chesser Island Homestead** are recreation area highlights. Small lakes offer good fishing, and the visitor center has exhibits. Guided tours of the swamp are available. *Admission charged.*

2. St. Marys

Founded in 1787, this town has a 20-block historic district, where tourists can see the **Toonerville Trolley,** a railcar that gained national fame when featured in a comic strip. Located in a lovely coastal setting, **Crooked River State Park** offers swimming, miniature golf, boating, fishing and camping. The nearby **McIntosh Sugar Mill Tabby Ruins** has some of the South's best-preserved structures of tabby, a material consisting of oyster shells, sand, and water. A ferry departs from St. Marys to Cumberland Island, where the **Cumberland Island National Seashore** offers wooded trails, pristine beaches, views of wild horses, backpacking, and camping. *Fee charged for ferry.*

3. Fort Clinch State Park

Visitors can tour the barracks, bakery, and blacksmith shop of this restored 1847 fort. An interpretive center traces the site's history, and rangers in Union uniforms perform some of the daily chores of soldiers. There are beaches, nature trails, and fishing, camping, and picnicking facilities in the park. *Admission charged.*

4. Fernandina Beach

The 50-block historic district in this centuries-old town includes numerous Victorian mansions and the 1878 **Palace Saloon,** decorated with a mural and fine antiques. The **Amelia Island Museum of History** has exhibits on local history, with artifacts and artwork from early settlers. *Admission charged at museum.*

5. Kingsley Plantation

Believed to have been built in 1798, this is the state's oldest plantation home. It is in an area of the **Timucuan Ecological and Historic Preserve,** where visitors can see the remains of old slave quarters.

6. Mayport Naval Station

One of the nation's largest naval ports, this station is home to some 30 ships, including an aircraft carrier. Tours of one of the ships are given on weekends. On the coast is the 450-acre **Hanna Park,** with hiking trails, picnic areas, campsites, and bike and boat rentals. *Admission charged.*

7. Jacksonville Beaches

Chamber of Commerce, 413 Pablo Ave., Jacksonville Beach. **Jacksonville Beach** is a resort community with hotels, galleries, antique shops, and a pier. Both **Atlantic Beach** and **Neptune Beach** are more residential. The **American Lighthouse Museum** displays ship models, photos, artifacts, and paintings. **Pablo Historical Park** has a restored 19th-century home and a museum that outlines the area's railroading past. *Donations encouraged at park.*

8. Fort Caroline National Memorial

12713 Fort Caroline Rd., Jacksonville. Built in the 1560's, the original fort was a part of the country's first French settlement. Tours are offered of a small replica of the old triangular structure. Other attractions include a museum and picnic grounds.

The Zorayda Castle in St. Augustine

9. Jacksonville Zoological Park

8605 Zoo Rd., off Heckscher Dr. Home to more than 700 mammals, birds, and reptiles, this zoo features an aviary, a wetlands area with a boardwalk, elephant shows, and miniature train rides. *Admission charged.*

10. Downtown Jacksonville

Convention and Visitors Bureau, 3 Independence Dr. The **Cummer Gallery of Art** displays more than 2,000 works amid formal gardens and pools. A marketplace on the banks of the St. Johns River, the **Jacksonville Landing** has a variety of shops, cafes, and restaurants. Directly across the river is **Riverwalk,** a 1.2-mile-long boardwalk with entertainments, shops, restaurants, and views of the city's skyline. The nearby **Museum of Science & History** has artifacts from Floridian Indians, various displays on history and science, hands-on exhibits, and a planetarium. *Admission charged for some attractions.*

11. Jacksonville Art Museum

4160 Boulevard Center Dr. Not only is this the city's oldest museum, but it also is one of the Southeast's finest. Displays include a permanent collection of pre-Columbian artifacts and traveling exhibits on contemporary painting, sculpture, and photography.

12. William Bartram Scenic Highway

Frequently passing alongside the St. Johns River, this route runs south from Julington Creek Bridge to the intersection of Rte. 207. There are spectacular views of untouched landscapes of oak, pine, and cypress. In the town of **Riverdale,** a park on the water's edge has camping, boating, and swimming.

13. Green Cove Springs

Poised on the banks of the St. Johns River, this city has 83 structures on the National Register of Historic Places. Since the 19th century, the mineral spring here has attracted visitors, including presidents Lincoln and Cleveland. The **Railroad Museum** displays a caboose, a depot, and a collection of rare lanterns. *Admission charged at museum.*

14. Gold Head Branch State Park

Hiking trails wend through this state park's more than 2,000 acres, where visitors can see an array of natural beauty, including a cascade through a fern-covered ravine. Other attractions are camping, fishing, swimming, and the remains of an old mill. *Admission charged.*

15. Fountain of Youth

155 Magnolia Ave., St. Augustine. The Spanish explorer Ponce de León is believed to have landed here in 1513. The area is also thought to be the site of the original colony of St. Augustine. The excavated grounds contain remnants of the settlement as well as an Indian burial ground. Located next door in an impressive 1890's Victorian structure, the **Old Jail** displays a collection of weapons. The oldest mission in America, the **Mission of Nombre de Dios** contains the nation's first shrine to the Virgin Mary.

16. St. Augustine Historic District

Visitor Information Center, 10 Castillo Dr. Built by the Spanish between 1672 and 1695, the **Castillo de San Marcos** is a massive stone fortress. A living-history complex, the **Spanish Quarter** consists of restored homes from the 1740's. The restored **Oldest Wooden Schoolhouse** is St. Augustine's first wooden structure. Other historic buildings include the authentically furnished **Oldest House** and the **Oldest Store Museum,** which boasts more than 100,000 items from the past, including a high-wheeled bicycle collection and steam-powered tractors. In what was once an elegant hotel, the **Lightner Museum** has one of the South's best displays of antiques and collectibles. A brightly colored replica of a wing of Spain's Alhambra Castle, the **Zorayda Castle** has exquisite treasures from around the world. The three floors at the **Ripley's Believe It Or Not! Museum** contain much that is incredible and bizarre. The **Government House Museum** traces the city's history with various artifacts and exhibits. Sightseeing trains take passengers on a 7-mile narrated tour of the area. *Admission charged for some attractions.*

17. Anastasia Island

Founded in 1893, the **St. Augustine Alligator Farm** is home to 22 species of crocodiles and alligators. There are also tropical birds and a variety of mammals. **Anastasia State Recreation Area** boasts a lovely beach, campsites, a picnic area, and nature trails. In summer it also features performances of *Cross and Sword,* the state's official play. The **Lighthouse Museum of St. Augustine** has a restored keeper's house and exhibits on maritime history. The town of **St. Augustine Beach** has miles of sparkling sand and dunes. *Admission charged for some attractions.*

1. Rainbow Springs State Park

At the headwaters of the Rainbow River is crystal-clear Rainbow Springs, offering boating, swimming, and superior scuba diving. Anglers can try for large bass, for which the river is also famous. Nature trails lead through the surrounding area.

2. Crystal River State Archaeological Site

3400 North Museum Point, near Crystal River. Contained here is a pre-Columbian Indian complex that dates from 200 B.C. to A.D. 1400. It contains ceremonial stones and a variety of mounds. More than 450 burial sites have been excavated, revealing that the Indians traded with tribes many miles north of the Ohio River. A museum in the visitor center displays artifacts, and several trails wind through the landscape. *Admission charged.*

3. Homosassa Springs

Chamber of Commerce, 3495 South Suncoast Blvd. The waters at the **Homosassa Springs State Wildlife Park** contain some 35 species of fish. There are river cruises and nature walks at the park, which is home to alligators, snakes, cougars, bobcats, manatees, and a black bear. Nearby, the **Yulee Sugar Mill Ruins State Historic Site** has the remains of an antebellum sugar mill. *Admission charged at park.*

4. Weeki Wachee Spring

6131 Commercial Way, Spring Hill. This park was built around a spring and takes as its theme the world of nature. It features underwater shows and river cruises past junglelike terrain. There are also performing parrots, vultures, owls, and hawks. Nearby on the Weeki Wachee River, **Buccaneer Bay** has sandy beaches, swimming, flume rides, and a children's play area. *Admission charged.*

5. Dade Battlefield State Historic Site

Rte. 301, near Bushnell. This area marks the site of a massacre that occurred in 1835, when Maj. Francis L. Dade and more than 100 soldiers were killed by Seminole Indians. Visitors will find reproductions of log breastworks, a museum, a nature trail, and picnic grounds. **Withlacoochee State Forest** is home to many kinds of wildlife, including alligators, black bears, and various birds. It offers campgrounds, picnic areas, swimming, fishing, and trails for both horseback riding and hiking. *Fee charged for parking at site.*

6. Pioneer Florida Museum

Pioneer Museum Rd., Dade City. This 10-acre complex includes a one-room schoolhouse, a turn-of-the-century railroad depot, a 1905 church, and an 1860's farmhouse that displays memorabilia and period furnishings. Dolls that are depictions of Florida's First Ladies in their inaugural gowns are also on display. Guided tours are available. *Admission charged.*

7. Florida's Cypress Gardens

2641 South Lake Summit Dr., near Winter Haven. Sheltered by towering cypresses, these famous botanical gardens offer a wide range of attractions, including some 8,000 varieties of plants, a butterfly conservatory, scenic cruises, rides for children, and amazing water-skiing shows. A 153-foot tower with a revolving platform provides an overview of the area. *Admission charged.*

8. Lake Wales

Chamber of Commerce, 340 West Central Ave. In addition to a 205-foot tower with a bell that chimes throughout the day, the **Bok Tower Gardens** has 128 acres of camellias, azaleas, magnolias, glades, pathways, a self-guiding nature trail, and picnic areas. Located in a stuccoed railroad station from 1928, the **Depot Museum** features memorabilia of early Lake Wales. At a nearby outdoor amphitheater, the *Black Hills Passion Play* is presented from mid-February through mid-April. *Admission charged for some attractions.*

9. Lake Kissimmee State Park

Bordering Kissimmee, Tiger, and Rosalie lakes, this 5,000-acre expanse is a superb habitat for wildlife, including bald eagles, sandhill cranes, ospreys, alligators, bobcats, and white-tailed deer. Thirteen miles of hiking trails meander through the marshes, live oak hammocks, and pine flatwoods. A marina, boat ramp, and several docks attract fishermen. An overview of Lake Kissimmee can be seen from an observation platform. The park is also home to a living-history area that re-creates an 1870's Florida frontier cow camp. Guided tours, primitive campsites, and picnic areas are available. *Admission charged.*

10. Prairie Lakes Unit of the Three Lakes Wildlife Management Area

With some 8,200 acres of forest, marsh, and grassland, this park is primarily concerned with protecting its wild species, especially the endangered ones. Visitors can picnic, camp, hunt, hike, and fish. The preserve contains three lakes — Marian, Kissimmee, and Jackson — all frequented by waterfowl.

11. Erna Nixon Park

1200 Evans Rd., West Melbourne. A trail in this 52-acre nature preserve passes through three ecosystems — a pine flatwoods, a wetland, and an oak hammock. Inhabiting the regions are many unusual plants and animals, including harmless indigo snakes and gopher tortoises. A picnic area is available. *Fee charged for parking.*

12. Melbourne

Chamber of Commerce, 1005 East Strawbridge Ave. Dating from 1880, historic downtown Melbourne contains galleries, cafes, antiques shops, and excellent examples of turn-of-the-century architecture. Other points of interest in the city include the **Brevard Art Center Museum;** the **Brevard Zoo;** the **Crane Creek Promenade,** an ideal spot for observing manatees; and the **Space Coast Science Center,** which offers hands-on exhibits for children. *Admission charged.*

13. Sebastian Inlet State Recreation Area

Located on a barrier island between the Atlantic Ocean and the Indian River, this 576-acre area offers opportunities for swimming, boating, camping, surfing, birding, and fishing. The **Indian River Lagoon** is home to hundreds of plant and animal species, including endangered manatees. Reservations are necessary for the guided walks given by park rangers in June and July to see the many turtles that come ashore during the night to lay eggs in the sand. The **McLarty Treasure Museum** displays artifacts recovered from the fleet of Spanish ships that sank off the coast here in 1715. *Admission charged.*

14. Turkey Creek Sanctuary

Wild olive trees, sand pines, palmettos, and several kinds of oak trees are found in this lovely sanctuary, where the abundant animal life includes raccoons, alligators, manatees, and many species of birds. An elevated boardwalk guides visitors through the 72-acre preserve.

15. Sebring

Chamber of Commerce, 309 South Circle. This town is perhaps best known for its automobile racetrack, which holds an annual 12-hour endurance contest. The **Highlands Hammock State Park,** with some 4,000 acres of semitropical jungle, cypress swamp, and pine flatwoods, is accessible by paved drives and well-marked hiking trails. Alligators, armadillos, Florida panthers, white-tailed deer, and many kinds of birds, including the anhinga and the bald eagle, are occasionally seen from a trackless tram that carries visitors through the park. Wild orchids are found throughout the area. A playground, bike rentals, nature trails, and areas for camping and picnicking are provided. *Admission charged.*

16. Lake Okeechobee

This lake's name means "big water" in the Seminole language, and indeed it is the second-largest freshwater lake located wholly within the country, covering some 750 square miles. The waters feed into the Everglades and are home to speckled perch, largemouth bass, and slapsided bluegill. There are fishing camps, marinas, boat rentals, and camping areas.

17. Pahokee Marina Campground

190 North Lake Ave., Pahokee. On the shores of Lake Okeechobee, this complex offers 86 camping sites with hookups, each one at lakeside. There are several boat ramps, swimming areas, a fishing pier, and facilities for both picnics and barbecues. *Fee charged for camping.*

18. Belle Glade

Chamber of Commerce, 540 South Main St. This city was destroyed by a hurricane in 1928, then rebuilt. Visitors can learn about the history of Belle Glade at the **Lawrence E. Will Museum,** whose collection contains a number of artifacts from the Seminoles and the Calusa Indians, an old but little-known tribe. Built on Lake Okeechobee's eastern shore, the **Herbert Hoover Dike** offers a spectacular view. Picnic grounds and parking areas are available.

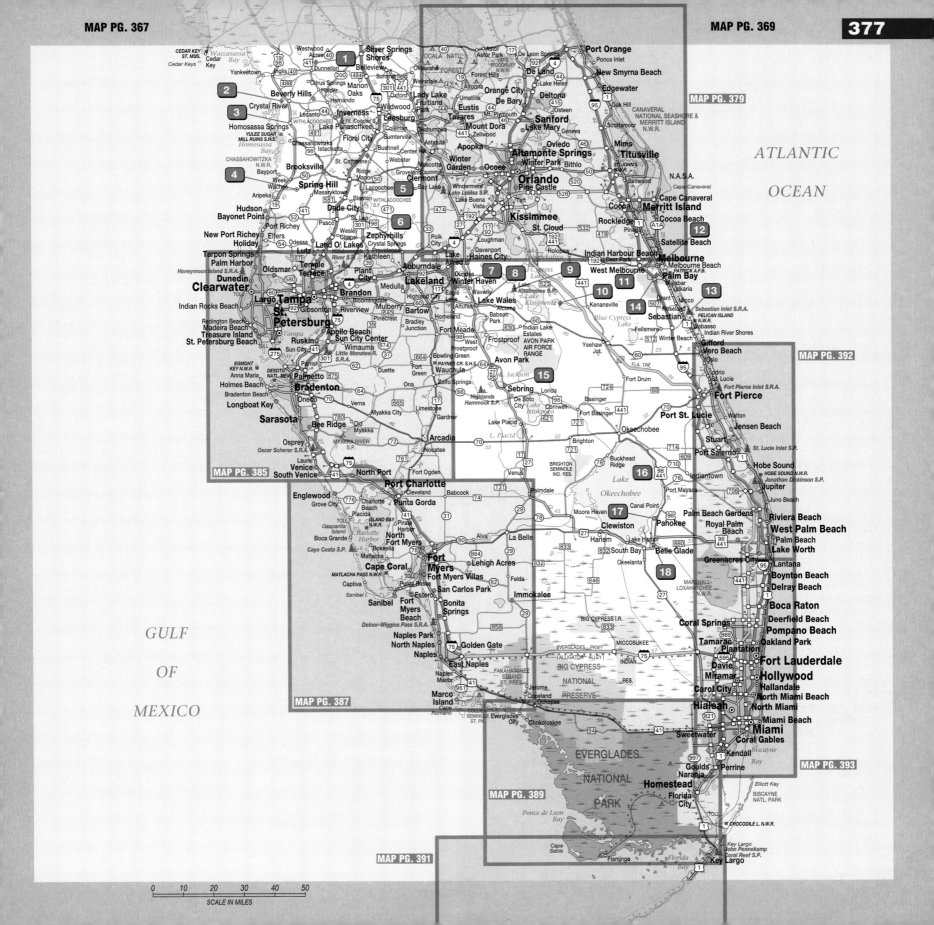

MAP PG. 379

MAP PG. 392

MAP PG. 385

MAP PG. 387

MAP PG. 389

MAP PG. 391

MAP PG. 393

ATLANTIC

OCEAN

GULF

OF

MEXICO

SCALE IN MILES
0 10 20 30 40 50

1. Tomoka State Park

This park was once an Indian village, then an indigo plantation — the ruins of which are still visible. The area's verdant woods and Tomoka River offer excellent camping, fishing, and boating. *Admission charged.*

2. Ormond Beach

Chamber of Commerce, 165 West Granada Blvd. Automobile races were held on the hard-packed sands here in the early 1900's, and the town still allows cars on one section of its large public beach. Featuring replicas of a Stanley Steamer and a Model T, the **Birthplace of Speed Museum** celebrates the automobile. **The Casements,** a cultural center in the former winter home of John D. Rockefeller, is located nearby. *Admission charged for some attractions.*

3. Daytona Beach

Destination Daytona, 126 East Orange Ave. This city is known for its busy beaches and its **Daytona International Speedway,** where bus tours are available. The **Halifax Historical Society and Museum** documents the early days of racing and other aspects of the area's history. The **Museum of Arts and Sciences** offers diverse attractions, including an outstanding collection of Cuban art and the skeleton of a giant ground sloth. *Admission charged.*

4. Ponce de León Inlet Lighthouse

4931 South Peninsula Dr., Ponce Inlet. Located in a restful area with boardwalks and dunes, this redbrick lighthouse is more than 100 years old. From the top are spectacular views, and three keepers' cottages have been preserved. Adjacent to the lighthouse grounds is a park with picnic areas. *Admission charged.*

5. New Smyrna Sugar Mill Ruins Historic Site

600 Mission Dr., New Smyrna. At this location a sugar plantation and mill were built in 1830. They were destroyed five years later during the Second Seminole War. Today only vestiges remain, such as old refining kettles, bits of machinery, and walls made of coquina — a mix of broken shell and coral. A nearby beach offers swimming.

6. Canaveral National Seashore

Swimming, beachcombing, shell collecting, crabbing, fishing, and boating are among the activities available on this area's 24-plus miles of golden sand. One attraction, **Turtle Mound,** is a 50-foot-high Indian construction that affords stunning views. At the southern end of the national seashore lies secluded **Playalinda Beach,** home to migratory birds and sea turtles.

7. Merritt Island National Wildlife Refuge

This scenic tidal area supports more than 300 kinds of birds, including the bald eagle, and some 500 species of other animals, many endangered. Hiking and auto trails allow visitors to catch glimpses of the wildlife. In the evening hours during June and July, sea turtles come ashore to nest and lay eggs — a fascinating spectacle that visitors can observe by making reservations for the ranger-led tours.

8. Kennedy Space Center/Spaceport USA

Rte. 405, near Titusville. In one of history's most dramatic moments, man left from here to explore the moon. Today visitors can tour much of the complex that helped make the epic journey possible. Spaceport USA, the visitor center, has spacecraft and space suits. There are bus tours to the launch complex and the **Cape Canaveral Air Force Station.** *Fee charged for tour.*

9. Titusville

Chamber of Commerce, 2000 South Washington Ave. Available to sightseers is a driving tour of this city's downtown historic district, which has buildings dating from 1895. Other attractions include the **U.S. Astronaut Hall of Fame,** with a focus on the Mercury, Gemini, and Apollo astronauts, and the **Valiant Air Command Museum,** displaying military aircraft. *Admission charged.*

10. Christmas

Each year thousands of people send their holiday mail here to be stamped with the Christmas postmark. In addition to displays of military and pioneer artifacts, **Fort Christmas Historical Park** has a replica of a 19th-century stronghold, complete with a magazine and blockhouses.

11. Cocoa

In addition to its quaint historic village, Cocoa has two important educational attractions. The **Brevard Museum of History and Natural Science** contains Indian artifacts, furniture, and clothing as well as other exhibits on Brevard County's past. Due to reopen in the spring of 1994, the **Astronaut Memorial Hall and Planetarium and Observatory** displays space memorabilia and offers various programs.

12. Cocoa Beach Pier

Shops, restaurants, nightclubs, and fishing areas fill this pier, which extends more than 800 feet into the ocean.

13. Reptile World Serpentarium

5705 East Bronson Memorial Highway, St. Cloud. Visitors can safely view cobras, giant pythons, and other snakes. Featured in outdoor enclosures are turtles, alligators, and iguanas. *Admission charged.*

14. Florida Citrus Tower

Rte. 27, Clermont. An elevator rises more than 200 feet to an observation deck overlooking hills, lakes, and citrus groves. Visitors can also take a tram that passes through a small grove containing 30 varieties of citrus fruits. *Admission charged.*

15. Dora Canal

Several companies offer cruises along this waterway, which flows under a canopy of moss-draped cypresses. At one end of the canal is Lake Dora; at the other, Lake Eustis. **Lakeshore Drive** provides a scenic route to the charming town of Mt. Dora, on a high bluff that overlooks Lake Dora.

16. Dr. Howard A. Kelly Park

400 East Kelly Park Rd., Apopka. The copious waters of Rock Springs form a swimming pool in this 200-acre park, where oak and palm trees shade trails, picnic areas, and campsites. *Admission charged.*

17. Wekiwa Springs State Park

Swamps, forests, and crystal-clear springs form this unusual park. Canoeing, hiking, and horseback riding are popular ways of seeing the diverse vegetation and wildlife. Visitors also enjoy swimming in the cool waters. *Admission charged.*

18. Sanford

Chamber of Commerce, 400 East First St. The ship *Grand Romance* departs from this town for cruises along the St. Johns River. Attractions at the **Central Florida Zoological Park** include birds, reptiles, mammals, and a children's zoo. In nearby **Big Tree Park** stands a natural wonder known as the Senator, a towering 130-foot-high bald cypress tree that is estimated to be more than 3,500 years old. *Admission charged for some attractions.*

19. Blue Spring State Park

Visitors come to this park to observe the manatees that migrate here in November and remain through March. Fishing, hiking, swimming, and camping are other popular activities. *Admission charged.*

20. De Land

Chamber of Commerce, 336 North Woodland Blvd. Oak trees line the streets of this town. The changing exhibits in the **De Land Museum of Art** often feature the work of local artists. On the stately campus of Stetson University is the **Gillespie Museum of Minerals,** home to an extraordinary collection of gems and minerals. *Admission charged at art museum.*

21. De Leon Springs State Recreation Area

Although these springs may not be the fabled fountain of youth, they are often found to be rejuvenating by swimmers. Other recreational opportunities include boating and fishing. The surrounding area has large oaks, a nature trail, and a restored old sugar mill that now houses a restaurant. *Admission charged.*

22. Pioneer Settlement for the Creative Arts

1776 Lightfoot Ln., Barberville. Preserved and re-created structures from the early 1900's pay tribute to Florida's settlers. Highlights include a railroad depot, a barn, a commissary, a blacksmith shop, and a caboose. There are also demonstrations of folk crafts, including quilting and candle dipping. *Admission charged.*

23. Ocala National Forest

Large stands of sand pine, hickory, palm, and other trees compose this landscape. Recreation areas include **Salt Springs,** which has a small information center; **Juniper Springs;** and **Alexander Springs,** the waters of which fill a pool 300 feet in diameter — a delight to swimmers and scuba divers. Visitor centers are located in Altoona and Silver Springs.

ATLANTIC

OCEAN

MAP PG. 383

MAP PG. 381

SCALE IN MILES

ORLANDO

1. Maitland Art Center
231 West Packwood Ave., Maitland. This center is a complex of stucco buildings, the walls of which are elaborately decorated with Mayan and Aztec murals and carvings. There are artists' studios and a gallery displaying contemporary American art.

2. Florida Audubon Society Center for Birds of Prey
1101 Audubon Way, Maitland. Injured eagles, hawks, vultures, and other birds of prey are treated, rehabilitated, and released by this facility. Permanently handicapped animals that cannot be returned to the wild remain in an educational aviary. Self-guiding and guided tours are available.

Just two of the many delicate Tiffany pieces on view at the Charles Hosmer Morse Museum of American Art

3. Park Avenue
Winter Park. Lined with specialty and upscale shops, this street is the city's answer to New York's Fifth Avenue. Park Avenue borders Central Park, where the Winter Park Sidewalk Art Festival is held each March. The **Scenic Boat Tour** on Lake Osceola is a relaxing way to see the sights. *Fee charged for boat tour.*

4. Charles Hosmer Morse Museum of American Art
133 East Welbourne Ave., Winter Park. This excellent collection contains more than 4,000 items created by Louis Comfort Tiffany. Museum displays include examples of his exquisite stained-glass windows, lamps, jewelry, and other decorative arts. *Admission charged.*

5. Rollins College
This lakeside college is home to the **Cornell Fine Arts Museum,** which displays European and American artwork, and the Gothic-style **Knowles Memorial Chapel.** The **Walk of Fame** consists of more than 500 stones that were collected from the birthplaces of well-known people.

6. Orlando Science Center
810 East Rollins St., Orlando. Hands-on exhibits and a planetarium are among the attractions at the center. Housed in the same building, the **Orange County Historical Museum** spotlights the region's past. The adjacent **Fire Station No. 3** displays the town's first steam pumper and other early firefighting equipment. *Admission charged.*

7. Orlando Museum of Art
2416 North Mills Ave., Orlando. In addition to its collection of African, pre-Columbian, and 19th- and 20th-century American art, this museum displays temporary exhibits from around the world. *Admission charged.*

8. Leu Botanical Gardens
1730 North Forest Ave., Orlando. Among the 56 acres here are camellias, azaleas, roses, an orchid conservatory, and a floral clock. The restored turn-of-the-century Leu home contains period furnishings. *Admission charged.*

9. Lake Eola Park
Rosalind Ave., Orlando. Paddleboats can be rented at the lake, and the surrounding park contains live oaks, a Japanese garden, and a children's playground.

Caretakers tend to a pair of manatees at Sea World of Florida.

10. Centroplex
600 West Amelia St., Orlando. This complex offers a variety of entertainments and sports events. The 70,000-seat **Citrus Bowl** hosts an annual college football bowl game on New Year's Day. **Tinker Field** is the home of a minor league baseball team. The **Bob Carr Performing Arts Centre** produces ballets, operas, symphonies, plays, and touring Broadway shows. The **Orlando Arena** is home to the Orlando Magic basketball team and also holds concerts by top-name entertainers. The **Ben White Raceway** is the winter training ground for trotters and pacers. *Admission charged.*

11. Church Street Station
129 West Church St., Orlando. Showcased at this entertainment complex are Dixieland bands and can-can dancers in **Rosie O'Grady's Good Time Emporium;** country and western music in the **Cheyenne Saloon and Opera House;** folk and bluegrass in **Apple Annie's Courtyard;** and dancing in **Phineas Phogg's Balloon Works.** *Admission charged.*

12. The Cartoon Museum
4300 South Semoran Blvd., Orlando. Of more interest to collectors and connoisseurs than to children, this unique museum contains some 2,500 pieces from 40 countries. Located on walls, in files, and on racks are cartoons, caricatures, comic strips and books, and mementos.

13. Mystery Fun House
5767 Major Blvd., Orlando. Attractions here include a shooting gallery, laser and video games, an Egyptian tomb, a miniature golf course, and a darkened maze with mirrors and undulating floors. *Admission charged.*

14. Turkey Lake Park
3401 South Hiawassee Rd., Orlando. Along with hiking and biking trails, the park has a sandy beach, a swimming pool, camping, and a farm with animals. *Admission charged.*

15. Universal Studios Florida
1000 Universal Studios Plaza, Orlando. Encompassing 794 acres, this is billed as the largest movie and television production studio outside of Hollywood. It's informative as well as fun, featuring rides and tours, with behind-the-scenes information on make-up, special effects, and more. Steven Spielberg is creative consultant for some of the attractions, and E.T. is on hand. Rides include encounters with Jaws and King Kong. Tourists can participate in scenes from Hitchcock thrillers, including *Psycho,* and act as executive producers for the television show *Murder, She Wrote.* Visitors can also make their own music videos at the MCA Recording Studio, which also airs audio and video productions. The television show *Nickelodeon* is based here and offers auditions for children. *Admission charged.*

16. Wet 'N Wild
6200 International Dr., Orlando. The many attractions here include water slides, wave pools, and whirlpools. *Admission charged.*

17. Mercado Mediterranean Village
8445 South International Dr., Orlando. Featuring Old World ambiance, this festive

marketplace with Spanish-style structures has restaurants, a dinner theater, murals, paintings, sculpture, and more than 60 specialty shops.

18. Sea World of Florida

7007 Sea World Dr., Orlando. One of the largest of its kind in the world, this marine park features dolphins, seals, penguins, otters, walruses, manatees, and sea lions. Attractions also include Shamu and Baby Shamu — both performing killer whales — and talented water-skiers. A 400-foot tower offers an overview of the area. *Admission charged.*

19. Gatorland

14501 South Orange Blossom Trail, Orlando. Thousands of alligators and crocodiles slither and sun here, and visitors can observe them along a train ride through the 52-acre park. There are other animals as well, including monkeys and snakes. *Admission charged.*

20. Xanadu

4800 Rte. 192, Kissimmee. There are self-guiding tours of this 15-room futuristic home, an energy-efficient passive solar structure. The many computerized features lend a high-tech look to the dome-shaped building. *Admission charged.*

21. Alligatorland Safari Zoo

4580 Rte. 192, Kissimmee. This 9-acre zoo contains some 500 animals, including lions, alligators, monkeys, birds, jaguars, and tigers. *Admission charged.*

22. Flying Tigers Warbird Air Museum

231 North Hoagland Blvd., Kissimmee. Focusing on the aviation of World War II, this restoration facility allows visitors the chance to observe mechanics at work on major reconstruction projects. The Warbird Weekend takes place each year in December, featuring air shows as well as displays of race boats, military vehicles, and an interesting variety of aircraft — from antiques to the experimental. *Admission charged.*

23. Moss Park

Moss Park Rd., Orlando. Nestled between two lakes and shaded by giant oaks, the 1,500 acres here compose Orange County's largest urban park. Nature walks, camping, picnicking, swimming, boating, fishing, and tennis are among the activities available. *Admission charged.*

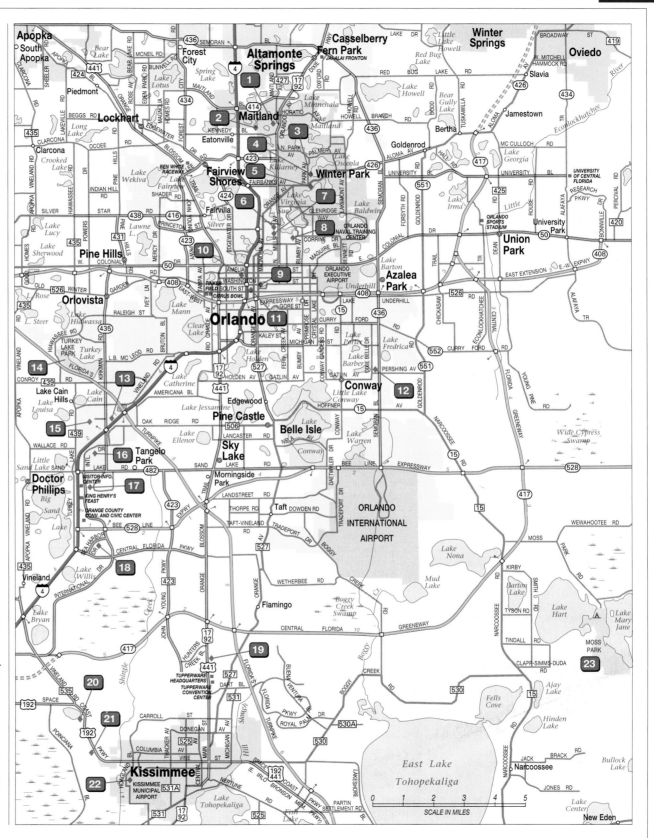

WALT DISNEY WORLD

1. Mickey's Starland

Built to celebrate the famed cartoon character, this area's attractions include a live show starring the bouncy mouse. Afterward, Mickey welcomes visitors to his dressing room in **Mickey's Hollywood Theater.** A wealth of memorabilia is on view in **Mickey's House,** and in its backyard tent Disney cartoons can be seen. Live farm animals can be petted at **Grandma Duck's Petting Farm,** which also has a playground for children.

2. Fantasyland

This part of Magic Kingdom Park will enchant children as they enter a world where storybook characters come to life. **Cinderella Castle** is the gateway, and the nearby Central Plaza is enlivened by parades and performances that showcase Mickey Mouse and company. **It's A Small World** is a boat ride featuring animated puppets who sing and are dressed in the native garb of many countries. The submarine ride in **20,000 Leagues Under the Sea** involves encounters with robots that resemble aquatic animals. At **Peter Pan's Flight,** small boats soar above replicas of London rooftops. **Magic Journeys** presents 3-D films, one an early cartoon and the other a story about joining the circus. The special effects create remarkable illusions that sometimes have the audience dodging what appear to be flying objects. **Cinderella's Golden Carousel** has finely crafted white horses. Visitors ride through spooky environs at both **Mr. Toad's Wild Ride** and **Snow White's Adventures.** Fairly tame carnival rides include **Dumbo the Flying Elephant** and the **Mad Tea Party.** The **Skyway to Tomorrowland** gondola offers a bird's-eye view of Fantasyland.

3. Frontierland

This section takes visitors to Disney's conception of the Old West. Based on animated scenes from the 1946 film *Song of the South,* **Splash Mountain** offers rides in hollow logs that carry eight passengers and reach a speed of 40 m.p.h. on the final descent into a pond filled with a brier patch. Complete with earthquakes and falling rocks, the **Big Thunder Mountain Railroad** is a roller coaster that takes riders past such images as a coal mine and ghost town. Rafts transport visitors to **Tom Sawyer Island,** where they can explore walking paths, caves, Aunt Polly's Landing, and Ft. Sam Clemens. Paddling in one of Davy Crockett's Explorer Canoes is another way to see the island. The **Frontierland Shootin' Gallery** offers participants a chance to take aim and shoot at tombstones. The **Country Bear Jamboree** features robotic bears that joke and make music. The **Diamond Horseshoe Jamboree** is a stage show that takes place in an old saloon.

4. Adventureland

Visitors to this realm of the Magic Kingdom journey to faraway and exotic lands. Complete with treasures and dungeons, the **Pirates of the Caribbean** features a boat ride past robotic swashbucklers. The **Swiss Family Treehouse** depicts the lives of the Robinsons, who according to the story were stranded on a lush tropical island. On the **Jungle Cruise** a canopied boat travels past cannibals, hippopotamuses, and elephants. Hundreds of chirping and talking robotic birds occupy a tropical setting in the **Enchanted Tiki Room.**

5. Liberty Square

Early America is revisited in this area. The **Hall of Presidents** presents more of Disney's realistic robots (Audio-Animatronics), in this case U.S. presidents, and a film on the nation's history. Featuring outstanding special effects, the **Haunted Mansion** offers buggy rides through a cemetery and other spooky places. Visitors can board the **Liberty Square Riverboat,** a re-creation of a 19th-century paddle wheeler.

6. Main Street U.S.A.

Here Disney creates a vision of small-town America during the turn of the century. Vintage vehicles depart from nostalgic **Town Square** for trips along a street lined with Victorian-style structures that contain retail shops and various attractions. The **Main Street Cinema** shows silent films. Diversions in the **Penny Arcade** range from old-fashioned player pianos to video games.

7. Tomorrowland

This land at Magic Kingdom Park was designed as a glimpse into the future. The top attraction is **Space Mountain,** within which a roller coaster sweeps through a dark realm with simulated meteors and stars. The **WEDway PeopleMover** affords an overview of Tomorrowland, including Space Mountain. **StarJets** features small rockets that wing up and down through the sky as they revolve around an axis. Drivers on the **Grand Prix Raceway** steer mini-race cars at about 7 m.p.h. In the **Carousel of Progress** revolving theater, robotic folk demonstrate technological developments in the American home. The **Dreamflight** ride traces the history of air travel. Shown on a wrap-around screen, the film **American Journeys** depicts the nation's vast and diverse landscape.

8. Discovery Island

This 12-acre zoological park offers visitors the chance to explore a tropical paradise that is home to 90 animal species, including scarlet ibises, lemurs, and miniature deer. Other highlights include one of the country's largest walk-through aviaries and a breeding ground for brown pelicans.

9. River Country

Located amid canyons and waterfalls, this area re-creates a country swimming hole, complete with rope swings. Visitors can seek thrills at the two flume slides or relax on a broad, sandy beach.

10. Future World

This imaginative exploration of science and technology is part of the **Epcot Center,** Walt Disney's vision of an Experimental Prototype Community of Tomorrow. Resembling a huge golf ball, the silvery geosphere contains the **Spaceship Earth,** a ride that traces the history of communications. The properties of energy are explored in the **Universe of Energy.** Located in the **Wonders of Life** exhibit, the Body Wars simulates a trip through a human body fighting a bacterial invasion; there are additional health-related exhibits and a film called *The Making of Me.* An imagined space colony can be seen on hemispherical screens in **Horizons,** and the **World of Motion** explores various aspects of transportation. Displays at the **Journey Into Imagination** focus on creative processes. **The Land** depicts experimental farming techniques that may one day help feed the world's increasing population. With a 5.7-million-gallon tank, the **Living Seas** is an aquarium holding some 8,000 animals; it also functions as a research facility. The attractions at **CommuniCore East** and **CommuniCore West** include exhibits on computers, energy, and communications.

11. World Showcase

Landmarks from 11 nations are represented by the separate pavilions at the Epcot Center. Each area contains retail shops, artwork, artifacts, ethnic foods, and entertainment. A major exhibit in **Mexico** is the River of Time, a boat ride that floats past scenes depicting the history and culture of the country. In **Norway,** the Maelstrom is a more adventurous boat ride, involving storms and other dangers. There's also a replica of Oslo's Akershus. Identified by its reduced-scale replica of the Temple of Heaven, **China** has a CircleVision film, *Wonders of China,* which shows much of the country's stunning beauty, including the Forbidden City, the Great Wall, and the Yangtze River. A *Biergarten* and oompah-pah bands are among the attractions in **Germany.** Visitors to **Italy** can see a re-creation of St. Mark's Square in Venice. There are also bridges, gondolas, a comedy troupe, and pasta-making demonstrations. A replica of Philadelphia's Independence Hall is the setting for the **American Adventure,** in which robotics of Mark Twain and Ben Franklin narrate a film depicting historical events. A pagoda rises in **Japan,** with a lovely landscape that features rock gardens. Exotic **Morocco** has bazaars, a reproduction of a minaret, and belly dancers. **France** showcases fine restaurants, perfume shops, and a replica of the Eiffel Tower. A typical London street, a thatched cottage, and retail shops with goods from all the British Isles are in the **United Kingdom.** Displays in **Canada** include a replica of one of the Rocky Mountains and a totem pole. A film, *O Canada,* is a picturesque travelogue. Each night, the **IllumiNations** show bathes the pavilions in the glow of colorful spotlights, lasers, and fireworks.

12. The Disney-MGM Studios

Featuring operating film and television studios, this theme park allows visitors a firsthand view of the entertainment industry as well as action-packed adventures. Recalling America's film capital in the 1930's and 40's, **Hollywood Boulevard** is lined with shops selling Disney wares. The boulevard, often frequented by Roger Rabbit and Kermit the Frog, offers visitors the chance to record their own music video. In the Chinese Theater, **The Great Movie Ride** takes visitors on a tour that passes re-creations of famous movies scenes. Participants will see robotic renditions of John Wayne, Gene Kelly, and other stars. In addition to visiting a backdrop for movies and television shows, part one of the **Backstage Studio Tour** passes **Catastrophe Canyon,** where fires, floods, and explosions erupt. The second part of the tour is a walk through the **Special Effects Workshop and Soundstages,** where ongoing productions are viewed. The **Honey, I Shrunk the Kids** playground is home to oversize exhibits. On the **Animation Tour,** visitors see an introductory film, then watch staff at work creating animated productions. The **Indiana Jones Epic Stunt Spectacular** has stuntmen who re-create scenes from the movie *Raiders of the Lost Ark.* After viewing a film at **The Monster Sound Show,** members of the audience are given the chance to be part of the action by creating their own sound effects. Visitors to **SuperStar Television** observe a re-created television set where volunteers are selected to act the roles and large screens display the action. Based on George Lucas's *Return of the Jedi,* **Star Tours** is a simulated, hair-raising space flight. Jim Henson's **Muppet Vision 3D** is an exciting show that combines a movie with robotics and actors. Available at the park's entrance, entertainment schedules list the time of daily performances by the Muppets, the Teenage Mutant Ninja Turtles, and others.

13. Typhoon Lagoon

This park's theme is water, and kids of all ages will find something here to entertain them. Youngsters can splash in shallow, bubbly pools, while more experienced swimmers can frolic in man-made waves or plunge down water slides. Leisurely paced trips on inner tubes take visitors down Castaway Creek, which passes a misty rain forest and a tropical village.

14. Pleasure Island

Three footbridges lead visitors to this enclave of clubs, restaurants, and shops. Geared toward adults, the nightlife here caters to a variety of musical tastes, including rock and roll, jazz, and country. The **Comedy Warehouse** features top-notch comedians, while special effects abound at the **Adventurers Club.**

Admission charged at Walt Disney World.

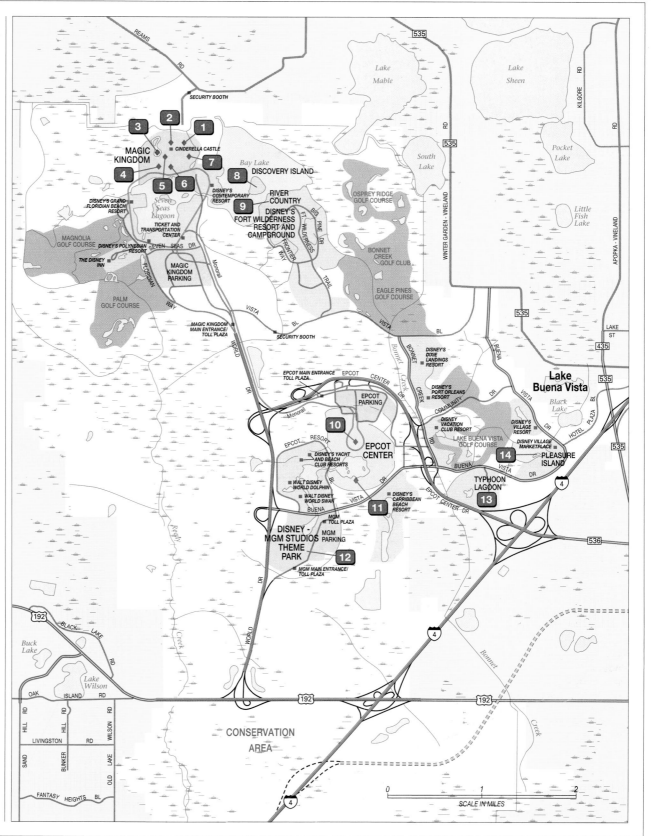

1. Florida Southern College

Frank Lloyd Wright designed many of the buildings here; in fact, the campus contains more structures by the architect than any other single site in the world. Constructed from native materials and predominantly low to the ground, the buildings exemplify Wright's organic approach. The Child of the Sun visitor center has tour maps. There are also guided tours. *Fee charged for guided tour.*

2. Museum of Science and Industry

4801 East Fowler Ave., Tampa. This large open-air facility contains hundreds of hands-on displays. Visitors can experience the high winds of a hurricane, take a simulated space flight, see shows in the Saunders Planetarium, and send a message by Morse code. They can also hike in Back Woods, a nature preserve. *Admission charged.*

3. Busch Gardens

3000 Busch Blvd., Tampa. This lively entertainment park is largely based on turn-of-the-century Africa. It features some 3,300 animals in its world-class zoo, which contains the Myombe Reserve, a spectacular natural habitat for gorillas and chimpanzees. There are many thrilling rides, including the Kumba, one of the Southeast's largest and longest roller coasters. Other attractions include games and live shows. *Admission charged.*

4. Lowry Park

7525 North Blvd., Tampa. The highlight of this park is the **Lowry Park Zoological Garden,** where the animals live in simulated natural habitats. Primates and birds share 24 acres with manatees, river otters, alligators, and other animals. Nearby is the **Lowry Amusement Park,** featuring rides as well as displays of well-known nursery-rhyme characters. *Admission charged.*

5. Ybor City

Chamber of Commerce, 1800 East Ninth Ave., Tampa. Cuban immigrants founded this city in the late 1800's as a cigar-manufacturing center. An old factory, **Ybor Square** operates today as a mall. Located in a former bakery, the **Ybor City State Museum** explains the community's history. *Admission charged at museum.*

6. Tampa Museum of Art

601 Doyle Carlton Dr., Tampa. This museum has an excellent collection of Greek and Roman artifacts as well as 20th-century American art. The galleries frequently display traveling exhibits from around the world. *Admission charged.*

7. Henry B. Plant Museum

401 West Kennedy Blvd., Tampa. Located in the south wing of what was once the extravagant Tampa Bay Hotel, this collection includes some of the resort's original furniture and art objects. With its minarets, cupolas, and domes, the building itself is a fantastic blend of Victorian, Spanish, and Moorish architectures. *Admission charged.*

8. Clearwater Marine Science Center Aquarium

249 Windward Passage, Clearwater. This organization conducts research and cares for stranded and injured sea turtles and marine mammals. Visitors can observe some of the recuperating animals as well as permanent residents, including a pair of dolphins. The Seaorama Room displays regional shells and replicas of fish native to the Gulf of Mexico. *Admission charged.*

9. Suncoast Seabird Sanctuary

18328 Gulf Blvd., Indian Shores. Visitors can observe and photograph the injured wild birds for which this nonprofit organization cares. More than 65 species live here, including the brown pelican.

10. Florida's Sunken Gardens

1825 Fourth St. N., St. Petersburg. There are more than 50,000 tropical plants and flowers in these spectacular gardens. An aviary is home to exotic and endangered birds, and a wax museum depicts biblical scenes. *Admission charged.*

11. Museum of Fine Arts

255 Beach Dr. NE, St. Petersburg. In addition to its outstanding French Impressionist paintings, this museum displays pre-Columbian, Asian, European, and American works. Nearby, the **Pier** offers entertainment of a different sort — rides, water sports, an aquarium, and an inverted-pyramid building that is home to shops and eateries. *Admission charged at museum.*

12. St. Petersburg Historical and Flight One Museum

335 Second Ave. NE, St. Petersburg. A walking tour of the city's downtown area starts at the site of the first commercial airline flight. A replica of the plane that made the trip is on view, along with other historical displays. *Admission charged.*

13. Salvador Dali Museum

1000 Third St. S., St. Petersburg. One of the world's largest collections of the Spanish surrealist's art is on view here. The works date from 1914 to 1970 and include oils, watercolors, drawings, and photographs. *Admission charged.*

14. DeSoto National Memorial

75th St. NW, Bradenton. This may be the place where Hernando de Soto and his conquistadores began the first European exploration of the Southeast. The visitor center has a film on the expedition, as well as artifacts from the era. Costumed interpreters re-create various activities of the Spanish soldiers, including the use of muskets and crossbows.

15. South Florida Museum and Bishop Planetarium

201 10th St. W., Bradenton. This museum has exhibits on the area's past, including replicas of de Soto's dwelling and an early doctor's office. It also provides a home for Snooty, the oldest manatee in captivity. The planetarium presents star and laser shows. *Admission charged.*

16. Gamble Plantation State Historic Site

Rte. 301, Ellenton. Before the Civil War, there was a sugar plantation here. Shortly after the war, Judah P. Benjamin, the Confederate secretary of state, hid in the fortresslike mansion, which is today restored and furnished in period style. *Admission charged.*

17. Manatee Village Historical Park

604 15th St. E., Bradenton. Preserved here are an 1860 courthouse, an 1887 church, a 1903 general store, a 1908 one-room schoolhouse, and a 1912 farmhouse. Located across the street, the **Old Manatee Cemetery** contains the graves of pioneers.

18. John and Mable Ringling Museum of Art

5401 Bay Shore Rd., Sarasota. The legacy of circus owner John Ringling, this museum displays works by such masters as Rubens and Rembrandt. Set on the beautifully landscaped grounds are a sculpture garden; Ca' d'Zan, Ringling's palatial mansion; the Asolo Theater; and the Circus Galleries. *Admission charged.*

19. Bellm's Cars and Music of Yesterday

5500 North Tamiami Trail, Sarasota. This museum presents an unusual coupling — antique cars and mechanical music-makers. More than 120 classic automobiles are on view, including a Pierce Arrow and an Auburn. Included among the 2,000 music machines are hurdy-gurdies, calliopes, and organs. Nostalgia lovers will also enjoy the old-time arcade. *Admission charged.*

20. Sarasota Jungle Gardens

3701 Bay Shore Rd., Sarasota. Flamingos and peacocks are free to roam these gardens, a 10-acre tropical jungle. Monkeys, leopards, and macaws are housed along foot trails leading past palm trees and exotic plants. Dioramas at the Gardens of Christ depict scenes from the life of Jesus. *Admission charged.*

21. Mote Marine Aquarium

1600 Thompson Pkwy., Sarasota. Rays, sea turtles, and other indigenous marine animals live here. An outdoor viewing tank allows visitors to see sharks both above and below the water's surface. There are also exhibits on marine research and plant life. *Admission charged.*

22. Marie Selby Botanical Gardens

811 South Palm Ave., Sarasota. Hibiscus, banyans, and bamboos grow in these lush gardens on the shores of a bay. The Tropical Display House contains a variety of plants, including bromeliads and orchids. A waterfall and lily pond adorn the grounds. The **Museum of Botany and the Arts** has changing exhibits of flowers, paintings, photos, and sculpture. *Admission charged.*

23. Resort and Spa at Warm Mineral Springs

San Servando Ave., Sarasota. The springs produce an astonishing 9 million gallons of 87° F water per day, creating a lake that covers more than 2 acres. Visitors can swim in the mineral-rich waters, take saunas, receive messages, and undergo hydrotherapy. There are picnic sites and a rotunda with murals that depict the exploits of Ponce de León. *Admission charged.*

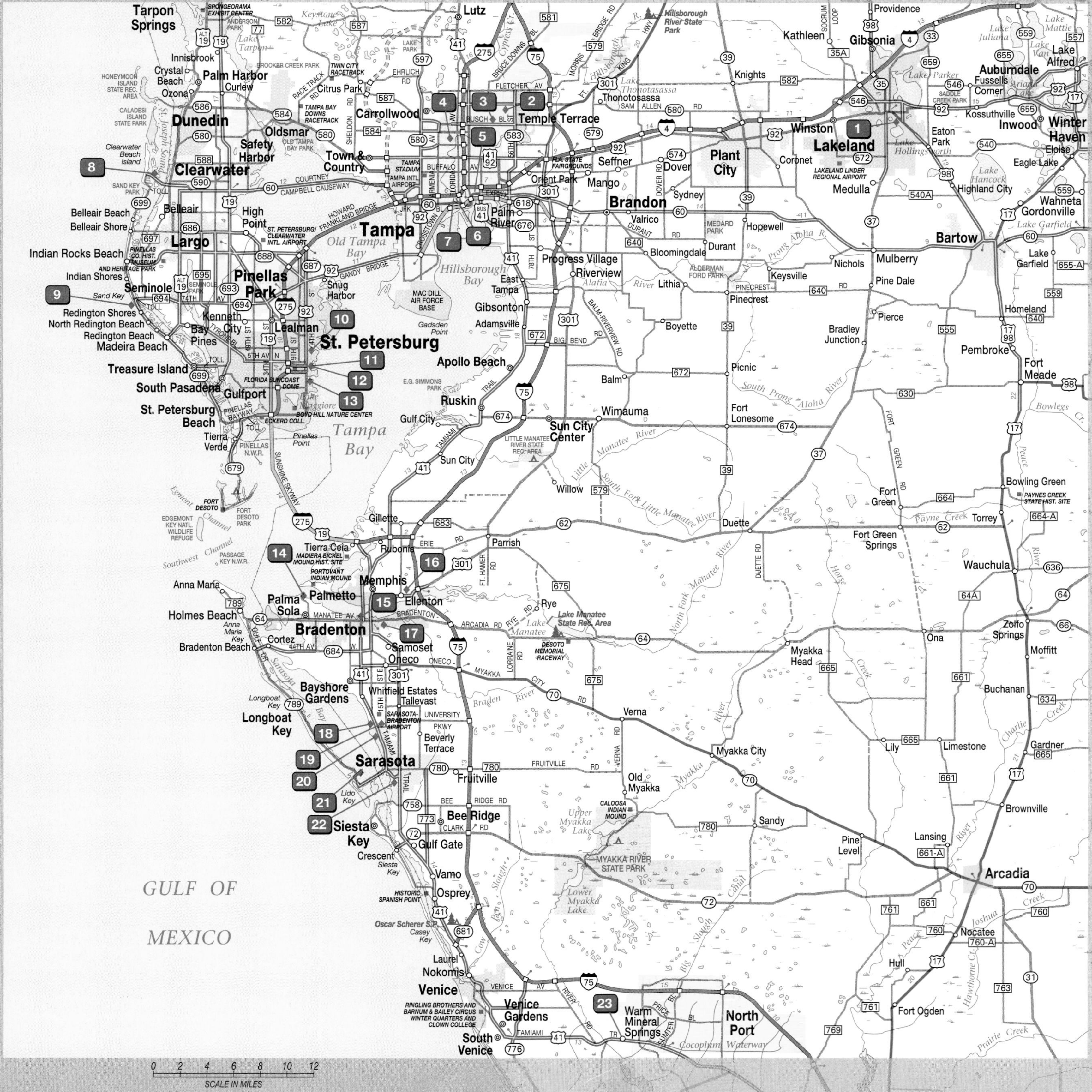

GULF OF MEXICO

Tarpon Springs
Innisbrook
Crystal Beach
Ozona
Palm Harbor
Curlew
Dunedin
Safety Harbor
Oldsmar
Clearwater
Belleair Beach
Belleair Shore
Belleair
High Point
Largo
Indian Rocks Beach
Indian Shores
Seminole
Redington Shores
North Redington Beach
Redington Beach
Madeira Beach
Treasure Island
South Pasadena
Gulfport
St. Petersburg Beach
Tierra Verde
Pinellas Park
Kenneth City
Bay Pines
Lealman
St. Petersburg
Town & Country
Carrollwood
Citrus Park
Lutz

SPONGEORAMA EXHIBIT CENTER
ANDERSON PARK
HONEYMOON ISLAND STATE REC. AREA
CALADESI ISLAND STATE PARK
CLEARWATER BEACH ISLAND
SAND KEY PARK
PINELLAS CO. HIST. MUSEUM AND HERITAGE PARK
BROOKER CREEK PARK
TWIN CITY RACETRACK
RACE TRACK RD
TAMPA BAY DOWNS RACETRACK
ST. PETERSBURG/CLEARWATER INTL. AIRPORT
TAMPA STADIUM
TAMPA INTL. AIRPORT

Keystone Lake
Lake Park
Lake Magdalene
Lake Carroll

Tampa
Old Tampa Bay
Snug Harbor
Hillsborough Bay
Gadsden Point
Port Tampa
MAC DILL AIR FORCE BASE
Apollo Beach
East Tampa
Adamsville
Gibsonton
Progress Village
Riverview
Ruskin
Gulf City
Sun City
Wimauma
Sun City Center
LITTLE MANATEE RIVER STATE REC. AREA

Temple Terrace
Seffner
Orient Park
Mango
Dover
Sydney
Valrico
Brandon
Bloomingdale
Durant
Hopewell
Balm
Picnic
Willow

Thonotasassa
Knights
Plant City
Coronet
Medulla

Lakeland
LAKELAND LINDER REGIONAL AIRPORT
Winston
Providence
Kathleen
Gibsonia
Auburndale
Inwood
Winter Haven
Fussells Corner
Kossuthville
Eaton Park
Eagle Lake
Highland City
Wahneta
Gordonville
Homeland
Pembroke
Fort Meade

Eloise
Lake Van
Lake Alfred
Lake Mattie
Lake Juliana
Lake Parker
Lake Hollingsworth
Lake Hancock
Lake Garfield

Bartow
Nichols
Mulberry
Pine Dale
Keysville
Lithia
Pinecrest
Bradley Junction
Pierce
Fort Lonesome
Fort Green
Fort Green Springs
Duette
Bowling Green
PAYNES CREEK STATE HIST. SITE
Torrey
Wauchula
Zolfo Springs
Moffitt
Buchanan
Brownville
Ona
Lily
Limestone
Gardner
Lansing
Pine Level
Nocatee
Huli
Fort Ogden
Arcadia

Myakka Head
Myakka City
Verna
Sandy
Old Myakka
MYAKKA RIVER STATE PARK
Upper Myakka Lake
Lower Myakka Lake
CALOOSA INDIAN MOUND

Palmetto
Palma Sola
Ellenton
Memphis
Rubonia
Tierra Ceia
Anna Maria
Holmes Beach
Bradenton Beach
Cortez
Bradenton
Samoset
Oneco
Whitfield Estates
Tallevast
Bayshore Gardens
Beverly Terrace
University
SARASOTA-BRADENTON AIRPORT
Longboat Key
Sarasota
Lido Key
Siesta Key
Bee Ridge
Gulf Gate
Crescent Beach
Vamo
Osprey
OSCAR SCHERER S.P.
Casey Key
Laurel
Nokomis
Venice
Venice Gardens
South Venice
Warm Mineral Springs
North Port

RINGLING BROTHERS AND BARNUM & BAILEY CIRCUS WINTER QUARTERS AND CLOWN COLLEGE
HISTORIC SPANISH POINT
DESOTO MEMORIAL RACEWAY
LAKE MANATEE STATE REC. AREA
Lake Manatee
Parrish
Gillette
Fruitville

FORT DESOTO PARK
EGMONT KEY NATL. WILDLIFE REFUGE
Tampa Bay
Pinellas Point
BOYD HILL NATURE CENTER
FLORIDA SUNCOAST DOME
ECKERD COLL.
E.G. SIMMONS PARK

Numbered markers: 1, 2, 3, 4, 5, 6, 7, 8, 9, 10, 11, 12, 13, 14, 15, 16, 17, 18, 19, 20, 21, 22, 23

SCALE IN MILES
0 2 4 6 8 10 12

1. Palmdale

This small town contains two special attractions. The **Cypress Knee Museum** exhibits hundreds of cypress knees — the protuberances sometimes found at the tree's base — which, with a little imagination, bear a likeness to dogs, bears, and other animals. The museum's founder has provided explanations to help visitors see the resemblance. Outside, a boardwalk passes through a cypress swamp. At **Gatorama** sightseers can observe some 3,000 alligators, crocodiles, and other indigenous animals. *Admission charged.*

2. Babcock Wilderness Adventures

8000 Rte. 31, Punta Gorda. A swamp buggy takes visitors here on a 90-minute tour of a working cattle ranch and the surrounding cypress swamp, which is home to bobcats, deer, alligators, bison, and other animals. Tour guides discuss various aspects of the state's history, natural phenomena, and the Babcock family — ranchers at this site since 1914. *Admission charged.*

3. Boca Grande

Chamber of Commerce, 5800 Gasparilla Rd. Long a winter haven for the well-to-do, Gasparilla Island's Boca Grande looks much as it has for more than a century. Huge banyan trees shade quiet residential streets lined with old wooden homes. **Gasparilla Island State Recreation Area** offers several wide, sandy beaches. A historic wooden lighthouse is located at **Boca Grande Lighthouse Beach,** where the fishing is good but the current is too strong for swimming. In spring **Boca Grande Pass** has some of the finest tarpon fishing in the world. *Admission charged for some attractions.*

4. Cayo Costa State Park

A relatively unspoiled barrier island, Cayo Costa Island can only be reached by boat, with ferries departing from Pine Island. Miles of pristine white beaches are dotted with seashells, and vegetation typical of temperate North America grows beside tropical plants. Bald eagles nest here, and white pelicans winter in the area. There are picnic sites, good fishing for tarpon and redfish, restrooms, showers, simple cabins, and primitive campsites.

5. Sanibel Island and Captiva Island

Chamber of Commerce, 1159 Causeway Rd. Connected to the mainland by a causeway, these resort islands are renowned for their exceptional beaches. A nature lover's paradise, the **J.N. "Ding" Darling National Wildlife Refuge** encompasses some 5,000 acres of wetlands — home to alligators, armadillos, and about 200 species of birds. There are trails for hiking, biking, and canoeing; a 5-mile wildlife drive; and an observation tower that offers bird-watchers a good vantage point. *Admission charged.*

6. Edison-Ford Winter Estates

2350 McGregor Blvd., Fort Myers. Guided tours of Thomas Edison's estate include the inventor's furnished house, a botanical garden consisting of some 6,000 species, and the laboratory and workshops where he researched domestic plant sources for rubber. Many of his inventions are displayed in a museum, along with his car and other memorabilia. The automaker Henry Ford, who was Edison's friend, wintered at the home next door. Visitors can tour his restored house, furnished in the style of the 1920's, and see antique cars. The grounds are planted with citrus trees and tropical plants. *Admission charged.*

7. Fort Myers Historical Museum

2300 Peck St., Fort Myers. Located in a restored railroad depot, this museum depicts the history of Ft. Myers and southwest Florida. There are shell tools made by Calusa Indians, a dugout canoe crafted by Seminoles, photographs of the 19th-century cattle industry, a glass collection, and the longest and last-built private Pullman railroad car. *Admission charged.*

8. Koreshan State Historic Site

Rte. 41 and Corkscrew Rd., Estero. In 1894 the Koreshan Unity utopian society was established on the banks of the Estero River. Members tended citrus groves and supplied services to the surrounding population. They also practiced communal ownership and celibacy, which eventually led to their decline. Today 12 of the original frame buildings are restored and open for guided and self-guiding tours. *Admission charged.*

9. Corkscrew Swamp Sanctuary

This National Audubon Society preserve features a 2-mile-long boardwalk through the nation's largest remaining subtropical stand of old-growth bald cypresses, some of which are 500 to 600 years old. Other landscapes here include pine flatwoods and wet prairie. A self-guiding tour booklet available at the visitor center describes the ecology of the swamp and lists the many bird species found in the area, which contains the country's largest nesting colony of endangered wood storks. *Admission charged.*

10. Everglades Wonder Gardens

Old Rte. 41, Bonita Springs. Wetlands are inhabited by a variety of species, and this attraction displays many such animals, including alligators, crocodiles, panthers, bald eagles, toy deer, and rattlesnakes. *Admission charged.*

11. Jungle Larry's Zoological Park at Caribbean Gardens

1590 Goodlette Rd., Naples. The 52 acres here are home to a variety of plants and animals. Walking through the junglelike environment, visitors can observe tigers, Indian leopards, chimpanzees, elephants, alligators, and exotic birds. Entertainment and education are combined in daily shows featuring a trainer-narrator and performing animals. *Admission charged.*

12. Collier Automotive Museum

2500 Horseshoe Dr., Naples. Some 75 gleaming antique and classic sports cars are displayed in this outstanding museum. The collection includes Gary Cooper's 1935 Duesenberg SSJ, a Ford GT-40 that won at Le Mans, a 1928 Hispano-Suiza, and the car that Bobby Unser drove to victory in the 1975 Indianapolis 500. *Admission charged.*

13. Collier County Museum

County Government Center, Rte. 41 and Airport Rd., Naples. The collection of regional artifacts here includes Calusa Indian shell tools and ornaments, some of which are 10,000 years old. Other exhibits are a Seminole Indian village, memorabilia of 19th-century cattle ranching, and a unique teaching garden. The Children's Discovery Cottage displays aspects of everyday life in turn-of-the-century Collier County.

14. Collier-Seminole State Park

This 6,423-acre preserve encompasses salt marshes, swamps, and pine flatwoods. Visitors can explore the area along two hiking trails and a 13-mile-long canoe trail. An observation platform offers the opportunity to spot the park's birds, including bald eagles, wood storks, and ospreys. A replica of an 1840's blockhouse used during the Seminole War contains photos of the area's plants and animals. A dredge from the 1920's is also displayed. *Admission charged.*

15. Fakahatchee Strand State Preserve

A strand is a regional term for a long, forested swamp in a shallow-water basin, and the Fakahatchee is the largest in the Big Cypress Swamp. About 20 miles long and up to 5 miles wide, it is home to giant ferns that can grow to 12 feet, rare palm trees, 45 kinds of orchids, and the only known habitat sustaining both bald cypresses and royal palms. A 2,000-foot-long boardwalk leads into the area. There are also 3-hour guided tours, and in winter, ranger-led canoe trips.

On Sanibel Island, Lion's Paw scallop shells are a collector's dream.

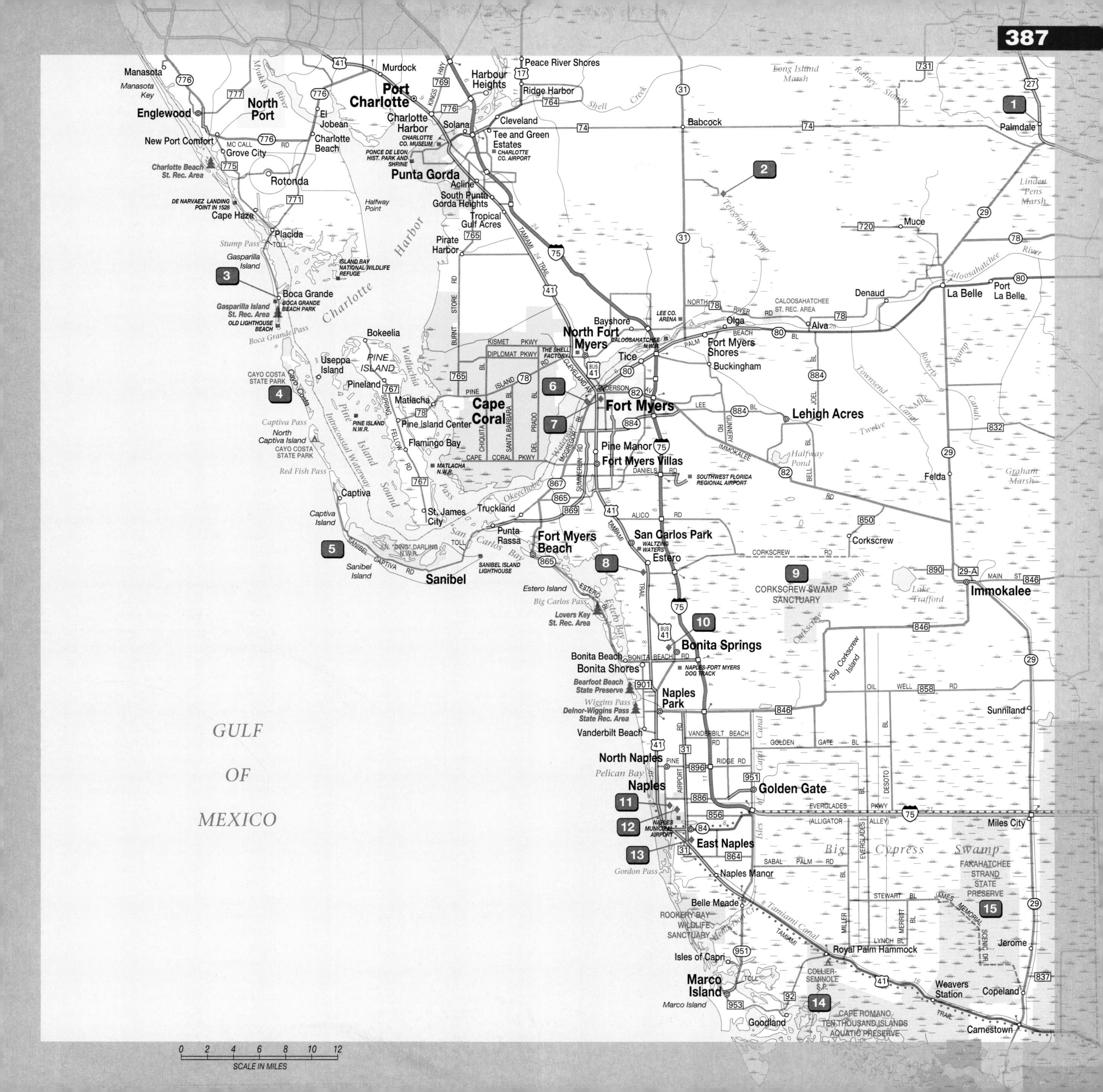

Manasota
Manasota Key
Murdock
Peace River Shores
Harbour Heights
Ridge Harbor
1

North Port
Englewood
El Jobean
Charlotte Beach
Port Charlotte
Charlotte Harbor
Solana
Cleveland
Babcock
Long Island Marsh
Kelney Slough

New Port Comfort
MC CALL RD
Grove City
Charlotte Beach
PONCE DE LEON HIST. PARK AND SHRINE
CHARLOTTE CO. MUSEUM
Tee and Green Estates
CHARLOTTE CO. AIRPORT
2

Charlotte Beach St. Rec. Area
DE NARVAEZ LANDING POINT IN 1528
Rotonda
Punta Gorda
South Punta Gorda Heights
Tropical Gulf Acres
Muce

Cape Haze
Placida
Halfway Point
Pirate Harbor
Linden Pens Marsh

Stump Pass
TOLL
Gasparilla Island
ISLAND BAY NATIONAL WILDLIFE REFUGE
Denaud
La Belle
Port La Belle

3
Boca Grande
BOCA GRANDE BEACH PARK
Bokeelia
Bayshore
North Fort Myers
LEE CO. ARENA
Olga
Alva
Caloosahatchee St. Rec. Area

Gasparilla Island St. Rec. Area
OLD LIGHTHOUSE BEACH
Useppa Island
PINE ISLAND
THE SHELL FACTORY
Tice
Fort Myers Shores
Buckingham

Boca Grande Pass
CAYO COSTA STATE PARK
Pineland
Matlacha
6
Fort Myers
Lehigh Acres

4
Pine Island Center
7
Cape Coral
Pine Manor
Felda

Captiva Pass
North Captiva Island
Flamingo Bay
Fort Myers Villas
SOUTHWEST FLORIDA REGIONAL AIRPORT
Halfway Pond
Graham Marsh

CAYO COSTA STATE PARK
MATLACHA N.W.R.
Daniels
San Carlos Park
Corkscrew

Red Fish Pass
St. James City
Truckland
Fort Myers Beach
WALTZING WATERS
Estero

Captiva
Captiva Island
Punta Rassa
5
8
9
CORKSCREW SWAMP SANCTUARY
Lake Trafford
Immokalee

N. "DING" DARLING N.W.R.
SANIBEL ISLAND LIGHTHOUSE
Estero Island
10
Big Corkscrew Island

Sanibel
Sanibel Island
Big Carlos Pass
Lovers Key St. Rec. Area
Bonita Springs

Bonita Beach
BONITA BEACH RD
NAPLES-FORT MYERS DOG TRACK

Bonita Shores
Bearfoot Beach State Preserve
Sunniland

Wiggins Pass
Delnor-Wiggins Pass State Rec. Area
Naples Park

Vanderbilt Beach
VANDERBILT BEACH RD
GULF
North Naples
Pelican Bay
RIDGE RD

OF
Naples
Golden Gate
EVERGLADES PKWY
Miles City

MEXICO
11
12
NAPLES MUNICIPAL AIRPORT
East Naples
(ALLIGATOR ALLEY)

13
Naples Manor
Big Cypress Swamp
FAKAHATCHEE STRAND STATE PRESERVE

Gordon Pass
Belle Meade
ROOKERY BAY WILDLIFE SANCTUARY
15

Isles of Capri
Royal Palm Hammock
Jerome

COLLIER-SEMINOLE S.P.
Weavers Station
Copeland

Marco Island
Marco Island
14
CAPE ROMANO TEN THOUSAND ISLANDS AQUATIC PRESERVE
Goodland
Carnestown

SCALE IN MILES
0 2 4 6 8 10 12

EVERGLADES NATIONAL PARK

1. Gulf Coast Visitor Center
One mile south of Everglades City, this ranger station is the starting point for boat tours of the area's waterways. It also offers canoe rentals, displays of native wildlife, and maps of the park.

2. Eden of the Everglades
Dupont Rd. and Rte. 29, Everglades City. Visitors can see this area aboard airboat rides or from nature trails that lead past reconstructed Indian dwellings. The Everglades Jungle Boat glides quietly through the intricate waterways of the Ten Thousand Islands region, where the indigenous plant and animal life can be easily observed. *Admission charged.*

3. E.J. Hamilton Observation Tower
Rte. 29, Everglades City. Reaching a height of 80 feet, this wooden tower offers a panorama that includes the Everglades and the Ten Thousand Islands. For a closer look, a boardwalk leads to a waterway, home to many birds. *Admission charged.*

4. Everglades City
The waterway area around Everglades City is called **Ten Thousand Islands,** where new islands are constantly being formed and others destroyed, making an accurate count of their number fairly impossible. Leaving from the Gulf Coast Ranger Station, **Sammy Hamilton Boat Tours** offers sightseeing trips of the area and the mangrove wilderness inhabited by alligators, egrets, herons, and sometimes rare American bald eagles. Complete with a visitor center, the **Western Water Gateway** has canoe rentals for a 99-mile inland trip to Flamingo. Boats leave from the **Park Docks** on Chokoloskee Causeway for scenic tours. The **Sandfly Island Nature Trail,** reached by boat, has exhibits on the history and wildlife of the area. *Admission charged for some attractions.*

5. Big Cypress National Preserve
Adjacent to Everglades National Park, this preserve encompasses the **Big Cypress Swamp,** which contains more than 2,400 square miles of prairie, marsh, cypress swamp, mangrove forest, hardwood hammock, and islands of slash pine. The visitor center has an audiovisual presentation on the region's ecology. It is also the starting point of a 23½-mile circuitous route into the vast swamp, affording glimpses of alligators, bobcats, and an occasional black bear or Florida panther.

6. Miccosukee Indian Village and Airboat Rides
This Indian outpost is inhabited by descendants of the Miccosukee tribe. The settlement has an Indian museum, traditional palm-thatched "chickee" houses, and raised buildings. Visitors can also watch alligator wrestling and demonstrations of basketry, doll making, and beadwork. Airboat rides through the Everglades feature a stop at an old Indian camp. *Admission charged.*

7. Shark Valley Visitor Center
From hiking and self-guiding bicycle trails that wind past limestone formations and a tropical hammock, visitors can see alligators, otters, the endangered wood stork, ibis, and many other varieties of birds. Also offered is a 15-mile narrated tram tour of the sawgrass wilderness, which features views of the many plants and animals and includes a stop at a 50-foot observation tower. Bicycles can be rented.

8. Chekika
Once inhabited by south Florida Indians, this tropical hardwood hammock is now a popular place to swim, fish, picnic, and camp. There are interpretive programs and ranger-guided nature tours through a junglelike grove.

9. Homestead
Visitor Information Center, 160 Rte. 1. This quiet farming community is a gateway to Everglades National Park, **Biscayne National Park,** and the Florida Keys. In the early 1900's a Latvian immigrant named Edward Leedskalnin dedicated 20 years of his life to constructing **Coral Castle,** an unusual building formed out of coral rock. He lifted blocks weighing between six and thirty tons out of the ground and, using only primitive tools, carved them into rooms, thrones, statues, a playground, and a 5,000-pound valentine heart. The **Preston B. Bird and Mary Heinlein Fruit and Spice Park** features 20 acres of exotic fruit, spice, and nut trees. Self-guiding tours explain how tropical fruits are grown, and visitors can sample the many treats, including canistel, tamarind, litchi, jackfruit, and mamey sapote. The Biscayne National Park's **Convoy Point Visitor Center** offers, by reservation, boat tours of the aquatic area, home to reefs and keys. It also has exhibits on the area's ecosystem. *Admission charged for some attractions.*

10. Main Visitor Center/ Park Headquarters
Rte. 9336, Homestead. Tracing a time period that begins with the area's Indian mounds, exhibits and a film underscore the history of the park and examine the evolution of its plant and animal life. Visitors seeking further information can stop by the bookstore or consult the naturalists who are on hand each day. A 38-mile road to Flamingo crosses six different ecosystems, including a dwarf cypress forest, the transition zone between sawgrass and mangrove forest, and ponds inhabited by flocks of wading birds. Featuring interpretive signs, boardwalks and trails lead along the main road.

11. Gumbo Limbo Trail
Leaving from the Royal Palm Visitor Center, this short, easy trail loops through a hardwood hammock. Although the area suffered some damage during Hurricane Andrew, there are royal palms and dense regions of gumbo limbo and wild coffee trees still standing. Gardens of ferns, orchids, and other air plants hang suspended from the tropical vegetation.

12. Anhinga Trail
During the winter, a walk along the elevated boardwalk across the sawgrass marsh of the Taylor Slough offers excellent opportunities for close looks at alligators, turtles, fish, anhingas, and many other wading birds. The trail originates at the Royal Palm Visitor Center.

13. Florida Pioneer Museum
826 North Krome Ave., Florida City. Located in a partially restored 1904 railroad building and a wooden caboose, this museum depicts the daily life of homesteaders. Displays include period furnishings, Indian artifacts, old photographs, and interpretive exhibits. *Admission charged.*

14. Pineland Trail
The pitted limestone bed that underlies all of south Florida is clearly visible along this half-mile trail. Although many of the trees in this region were destroyed by Hurricane Andrew, there are signs that identify the various types, including saw palmettos, short-leaf figs, and slash pines.

15. Rock Reef Pass
A limestone ridge above the water here is a good place to view the **Dwarf Cypress Forests,** an area of bald trees whose

Elevated boardwalks traverse Everglades National Park, home to species such as the streamlined anhinga, shown at right.

growth is stunted by a lack of surface soil and nutrients. Although the trees may look dead in winter, some are actually more than 100 years old. Visitors can also spot alligators and other wildlife.

16. Pa-hay-okee Overlook

A short walk along an elevated boardwalk leads to a high platform with a sweeping view of the grassy wilderness here. Beard grass, muhly grass, and sawgrass provide cover for vultures, red-shouldered hawks, pygmy rattlesnakes, and alligators.

17. Long Pine Key Trail

Seven miles of interconnecting trails cross an unusually diverse pine forest that harbors some 200 kinds of plants, including 30 plant types that are found only in this region. The pinelands are also home to white-tailed deer, raccoons, opossums, and the endangered Florida panther. The Long Pine Key area has camping, picnicking, and an environmental study area.

18. Mahogany Hammock

An elevated boardwalk winds through this junglelike forest, home to the largest mahogany tree in the country. Labels identify strangler figs, orchids, ferns, and other plants. Brightly colored liguus tree snails can be seen among the vegetation, as can the delicate webs made by golden orb weaver spiders.

19. Paurotis Pond

Rare paurotis palms and mangroves thrive here in brackish water, a transition zone between fresh and salt waters. A small picnic area is on the lakeshore.

20. Nine Mile Pond

In the dry winter months this area supports a variety of birds, including wood storks, herons, and egrets. The pond also offers a 5-mile canoe trail.

21. West Lake

Here an elevated boardwalk leads through a forest of red, white, black, and buttonwood mangroves that grow near a brackish lake. This forest, and others like it, take the brunt of a hurricane's force, protecting inland areas. In fact, damages wreaked by hurricanes in 1960 and 1965 are still apparent throughout the grove.

22. Coot Bay Pond and Mrazek Pond

These ponds offers excellent bird-watching, especially during late January and early

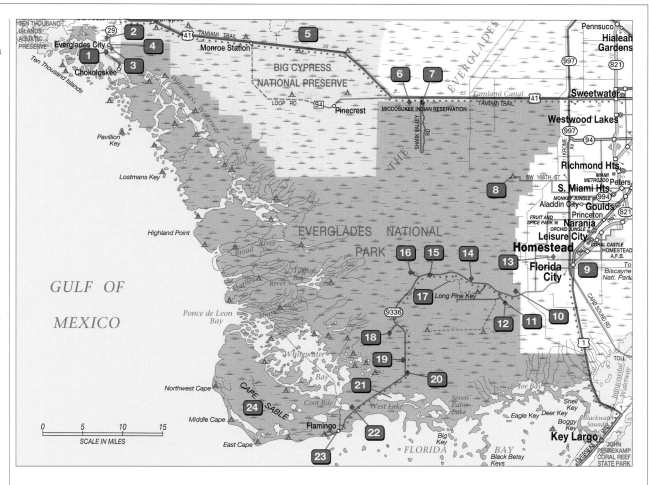

February. Coot Bay Pond is a haven for water birds, and Mrazek Pond attracts the rare roseate spoonbill. The banks of Eco Pond provide nesting sites for hundreds of ibis and egret. The best times for visitors to spot the birds are in the early morning and the late afternoon.

23. Flamingo

Located at the end of the road on Florida Bay, Flamingo is a base for excursions to the nearby bays, rivers, lakes, gulf waters, and tropical beaches. Canoes, skiffs, and houseboats can be rented at the marina, and sightseeing tours can be arranged, as can boat charters for some of the best sport-fishing on the Florida coast. Canoeists can choose from trails as short as three miles or as long as the 99-mile Wilderness Waterway, a well-marked backcountry route to Everglades City. Along the way visitors might spot manatees, sea turtles, and a variety of water birds. Bicycle rentals and hiking trails allow visitors to see the sights on land. There's also a tram tour through a

hardwood forest that harbors hundreds of bird species and nearly 100 types of butterflies. Other attractions include a visitor center, museum, daily interpretive programs, picnic grounds, and lodgings.

24. Cape Sable

This wild and remote spot at the southernmost tip of the U.S. mainland can be reached only by canoe or motorboat. Three pristine beaches offer a treasure trove of shells as well as excellent fishing for trout, shark, tarpon, and snapper. Loggerhead turtles, an endangered species, lay their eggs on a beach that is edged by prickly pear cactus, yucca, century plants, and other desertlike vegetation. Permits for overnight camping are available at the ranger stations.

Admission charged for national park.

As this baby alligator matures, the light bands on its back will eventually darken. An adult can reach a maximum length of about 19 feet, eating a diet consisting of small mammals, birds, and fish.

FLORIDA KEYS

1. Dry Tortugas National Park

Located 68 miles west of Key West, the Dry Tortugas are seven coral islets dominated by the sprawling remains of 19th-century **Fort Jefferson,** which once served as a prison, holding Dr. Samuel Mudd, who set the broken leg of President Lincoln's assassin. Today the islands provide a peaceful vantage point for viewing coral reefs and nesting seabirds. Other attractions include swimming, snorkeling, picnic sites, camping, and a visitor center. There is no fresh water on the islands, so visitors must plan their own provisions accordingly. The park can be reached by boat or air taxi from Miami and Key West.

2. National Key Deer Refuge

This is the only habitat of Key deer in the world. About 28 inches tall at the shoulder, the animals are making a slow comeback from near extinction. Visitors should be attentive to the park's guidelines, because many of the deer are killed by cars and by being fed. In the late afternoon, the deer might be seen at Blue Hole.

3. Looe Key National Marine Sanctuary

Reached by boat, Looe Key Reef has many beautiful coral formations, such as purple sea fans. The clear sea is also home to sponges, sea urchins, and colorful fish. The 1744 British frigate H.M.S. *Looe* and other shipwrecks lie here.

4. Bahia Honda State Park

Complete with a nature trail, this park has a lovely beach and rare West Indian plants, including sea lavender, Key spider lily, and silver palms. Boats take visitors to snorkel at offshore reefs. *Admission charged.*

5. Seven Mile Bridge

Opened to traffic in 1982, this impressive bridge connects Marathon and Little Duck Key. Divided into 266 spans, it is one of the world's longest segmental bridges.

6. The Museum of Natural History of the Florida Keys

Rte. 1, milepost 50, Marathon. Set in Crane Point Hammock, which contains an undisturbed area of thatch palms, this museum features pre-Columbian shell tools, artifacts from 17th-century shipwrecks, an underwater cave, and a lagoon with sharks and tropical fish. There is also an interpretive nature trail. The adjacent **Florida Keys Children's Museum** displays crabs, lobsters, and sea urchins. *Admission charged.*

7. Dolphin Research Center

Rte. 1, milepost 59, Grassy Key. The film

Blue Chromis, John Pennekamp State Park

Flipper originated here. Today this research facility cares for injured dolphins. Visitors can swim with healthy dolphins, but reservations must be made a month in advance. *Admission charged.*

8. Long Key State Recreation Area

Noted for its beachside campsites, this area also has fine swimming, fishing, and boating. The Golden Orb Trail leads to a boardwalk that passes through a swamp and a lagoon, where herons and other waterbirds flock in winter. Reservations are required for campsites. *Admission charged.*

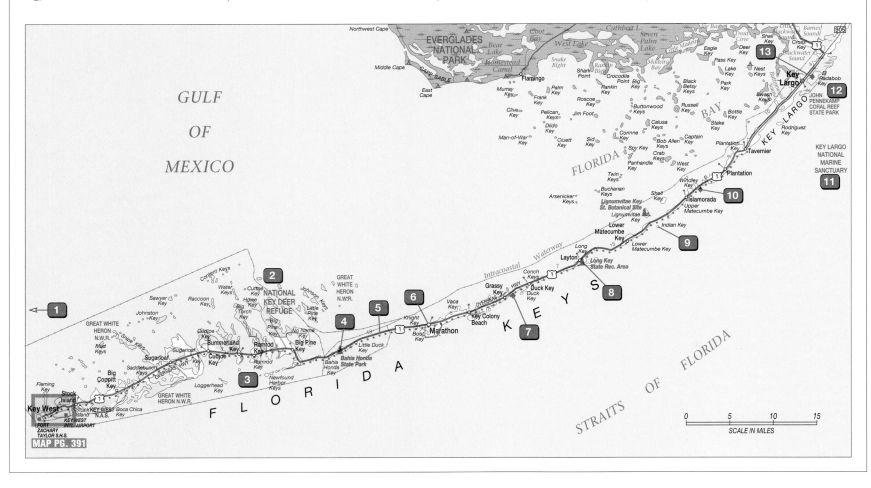

9. Indian Key

From docks in the Islamorada area, boats depart for three offshore state parks located on Indian Key. Surrounded by virgin hardwood forests traversed by nature trails, the **Lignumvitae Key State Botanical Site** contains a 1919 coral house. **San Pedro Underwater Archaeological Preserve** contains the wreck of a Spanish ship that sank in 1733. Divers and snorkelers can view the ship and a variety of marine life. **Indian Key State Historic Site** has the ruins of a shipwreckers' station.

10. Theater of the Sea

Rte. 1, milepost 84.5, Windley Key. Performing dolphins and sea lions are the stars at this marine park, which also features sharks, stingrays, and turtles. One attraction allows visitors to swim with dolphins. South of the park, **Hurricane Monument** commemorates the 423 workers on the Overseas Highway who died during a hurricane. *Admission charged at theater.*

11. Key Largo National Marine Sanctuary

Accessible only by boat, the more than 100 square miles of coral reefs here reach some 8 miles offshore and as deep as 300 feet. Divers and snorkelers can explore the habitats for fish, sea turtles, dolphins, sponges, and marine invertebrates. Other underwater attractions include the remains of Spanish galleons, a British warship, a torpedoed World War II freighter, and a submerged bronze statue of Christ.

12. John Pennekamp Coral Reef State Park

Brilliantly colored marine and plant life inhabit this underwater park, where divers come to see brain coral, sea fans, sea plume, and some 650 varieties of tropical fish. Visitors can swim, snorkel, fish, take scuba-diving lessons, and ride in glass-bottom boats. The visitor center offers an excellent aquarium. There's also a trail through a mangrove forest and a tropical hardwood hammock. *Admission charged.*

13. Key Largo Undersea Park

51 Shoreland Dr., Key Largo. Divers and snorkelers can visit a submerged museum, listen to underwater music, and observe a marine research lab. Jules' Undersea Lodge, an underwater hotel, accommodates six people. Nondivers can watch a multimedia show in a grotto. *Admission charged for some attractions.*

KEY WEST

1. Curry Mansion

511 Caroline St. This ornate 1899 mansion features fine 19th-century furnishings and the only widow's walk open to the public in Key West. *Admission charged.*

2. Conch Tour Train

1 Key Lime Square. The open-sided train takes sightseers on a 90-minute tour of the island. Included among the points of interest are the **Old Town Historic District;** the **Mel Fisher Maritime Heritage Society**

Museum, with treasures from two Spanish shipwrecks; and the **Wreckers' Museum,** believed to be the oldest home in Key West.

3. Key West Aquarium

1 Whitehead St. Tropical fish and other sea life inhabit this aquarium. One tank lets visitors handle live conch, starfish, sea urchins, and hermit crabs. There are guided tours and shark feedings. *Admission charged.*

4. Audubon House and Tropical Gardens

205 Whitehead St. Filled with antiques, this antebellum house also displays engravings by John James Audubon, who visited here in 1832. A walking tour leads through the surrounding gardens. *Admission charged.*

5. Fort Zachary Taylor State Historic Site

Southard St. at Truman Annex. The fort displays a wealth of Civil War weaponry and artifacts. Rangers conduct guided tours of the brick fortifications and parade grounds. *Admission charged.*

6. Key West Lighthouse Museum

938 Whitehead St. Built in 1847, the 92-foot lighthouse offers spectacular views of the island and sea. The restored keeper's quarters displays ship models, old photos, and artifacts. *Admission charged.*

7. Ernest Hemingway Home and Museum

907 Whitehead St. The famous writer composed many of his books in this house, which he bought in 1931. Now a museum, the home displays a variety of Hemingway's belongings. The lush garden was planted by the author. *Admission charged.*

8. East Martello Tower Gallery and Museum

3501 South Roosevelt Blvd. This former Civil War fort contains modern sculptures and carvings. Also on display are memorabilia from the U.S.S. *Maine,* destroyed in Havana Harbor in 1898; items from movies filmed in the Keys; and books by many of the authors who live in the area. The fort's tower has magnificent views. *Admission charged.*

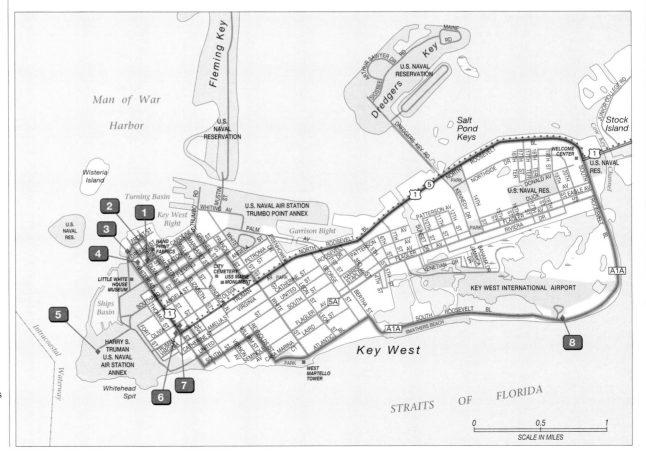

1. Harbor Branch Oceanographic Institution

5600 Rte. 1, north of Ft. Pierce. A center for the study of the marine environment, this institution along the Intracoastal Waterway covers 480 beautiful acres. The grounds are home to a diversity of plants and animals. Tours of the facility and exhibits on local sea life are available. *Admission charged.*

2. UDT-SEAL Museum

3300 A1A, Fort Pierce. Dioramas, photographs, and other exhibits chronicle the navy's Underwater Demolition Teams and Sea Air Land Teams since the 1944 invasion of Normandy. Weapons, equipment, and uniforms are also on display, and videos allow visitors an inside look at the unique training methods. *Admission charged.*

3. St. Lucie County Historical Museum

414 Seaway Dr., Fort Pierce. The area's history is examined with a variety of displays, including Seminole Indian artifacts, pioneer tools, items recovered from shipwrecks, photographs, a general store, and a replica of the town's early train station. *Admission charged.*

4. Elliott Museum

825 Northeast Ocean Blvd., Hutchinson Island. This eclectic museum was founded in 1961 by the son of inventor Sterling Elliott. The varied displays contain a charming array of Americana, including early shops, musical instruments, tools, toys, cut glass, automobiles, and bicycles. *Admission charged.*

5. Gilbert's Bar House of Refuge Museum

301 Southeast MacArthur Blvd., Hutchinson Island. This restored 1875 lifesaving station has exhibits on maritime history, including antique equipment, shipwreck artifacts, maps, and ships' logs. *Admission charged.*

6. Jonathan Dickinson State Park

In 1696 a group of Quakers led by Jonathan Dickinson was swept ashore near here. The party was captured by Native Americans, who eventually released the colonists. The park includes the scenic Loxahatchee River, pine flatwoods, and a 25-foot observation platform on Hobe Mountain. Accessed by boat, the **Trapper Nelson Interpretive Site** offers guided tours. *Admission charged.*

7. Loxahatchee Historical Museum

805 Rte. 1, Jupiter. There are exhibits here on Seminole Indians, shipwrecks, the steamboat era, pioneers, and the railroad. The nearby **Jupiter Lighthouse,** a 105-foot brick structure, is one of the oldest on the Atlantic coast. A museum at its base displays regional artifacts. Built about 1896, the **DuBois Pioneer Home** contains many original furnishings. *Admission charged for some attractions.*

8. Hibel Museum of Art

150 Royal Poinciana Plaza, Palm Beach. The work of American artist Edna Hibel is the focus of this museum, which contains her paintings, lithographs, porcelains, and drawings. Also on display are Oriental snuff bottles and European furnishings.

9. The Henry Morrison Flagler Museum

Whitehall Way, Palm Beach. This opulent 55-room mansion was built by a railroad developer. The museum displays period rooms, porcelain, silver, glass, artwork, and family memorabilia. On the grounds is a private railroad car. *Admission charged.*

10. Norton Gallery of Art

1451 South Olive Ave., West Palm Beach. In addition to its extensive collection of 19th- and 20th-century European and American paintings, this museum contains porcelain, jade, and sculpture. The nearby **Ann Norton Sculpture Gardens** feature works in granite and brick as well as some 300 species of palms. *Admission charged.*

11. South Florida Science Museum

4801 Dreher Trail N., West Palm Beach. Hands-on exhibits, an aquarium, and a planetarium examine the world of science. There are tropical plants and a discovery area for children. *Admission charged.*

12. Lion Country Safari

Rte. 80, Loxahatchee. More than 1,000 animals roam free in this 500-acre preserve. A 5-mile auto tour passes lions, elephants, rhinos, and other species. Safari World has a petting zoo, aviaries, and reptile habitats. *Admission charged.*

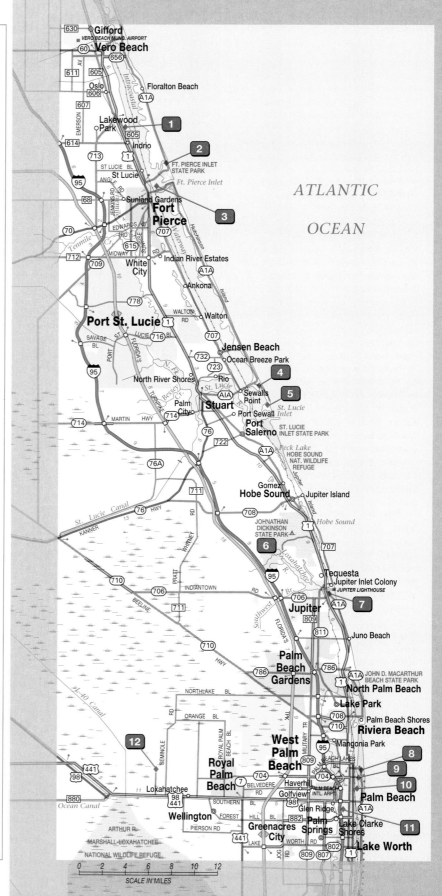

1. Arthur R. Marshall Loxahatchee National Wildlife Refuge

Located in the northernmost section of the Everglades, this unique ecosystem is inhabited by alligators, opossums, otters, wading birds, and a variety of endangered species. Visitors can fish, take a boardwalk stroll through a cypress swamp, and canoe. *Admission charged.*

2. Fort Lauderdale

Chamber of Commerce, 512 Northeast Third Ave. Many visitors are attracted to the sandy beaches here. The city is also home to the **Museum of Art,** which features 20th-century paintings and various artwork by American Indians. From the Seminole Indians to the present, the area's history is explored in the **Fort Lauderdale Historical Museum.** The **International Swimming Hall of Fame** honors the sport with exhibits of photos, medals, and related memorabilia; it also has two Olympic-size swimming pools. *Admission charged.*

3. Ancient Spanish Monastery

16711 West Dixie Hwy., North Miami Beach. Built in 1141 in Segovia, Spain, this former monastery is the oldest structure of European origin in America. Carefully reassembled here, the Romanesque-Gothic building has an Episcopal church and ancient artwork. *Admission charged.*

4. American Police Hall of Fame & Museum

3801 Biscayne Blvd., Miami. The intriguing and sometimes violent world of law enforcement is examined here. Firearms, lie detectors, and an electric chair are among the 11,000 items on view. At one exhibit visitors are called upon to solve a murder. A memorial honors officers killed in the line of duty since 1960. *Admission charged.*

5. Bass Museum of Art

2121 Park Ave., Miami Beach. European painting, sculpture and decorative arts from the 13th to the 20th centuries are the focus here. Highlights include Rubens' *The Holy Family* and two large tapestries. There are also changing exhibits. *Admission charged.*

6. Art Deco District

Pastels, portholes, and rounded corners prevail in this one-of-a-kind National Historic District in Miami Beach, featuring some 800 hotels, stores, restaurants, and homes in this distinctive style.

7. Historical Museum of Southern Florida

101 West Flagler St., Miami. Hands-on exhibits, dioramas, and photographs trace this region's human history from prehistoric to modern times. Displays of artifacts include ceramics, clothing, tools, and weapons. Other exhibits include maritime relics, a 1920's streetcar, and a rare edition of John James Audubon's *Birds of America.* *Admission charged.*

8. Miami Seaquarium

4400 Rickenbacker Causeway, Miami. Visitors can watch sea lion and dolphin shows, manatees, sharks, and a killer whale. There's an aquarium with a tropical reef, and the grounds contain 35 acres of colorful gardens. *Admission charged.*

9. Vizcaya

3251 South Miami Ave., Miami. Named for a Basque word meaning "elevated place," this villa, overlooking Biscayne Bay, has an outstanding collection of rare European furnishings and art objects. On the grounds is a classical garden with pools, fountains, and sculptures. The nearby **Museum of Science & Space Transit Planetarium** includes interactive displays, science demonstrations, a wildlife center, and an observatory. *Admission charged.*

10. Coral Gables

Chamber of Commerce, 50 Aragon Ave. Conceived of as the American Riviera, this city contains the **Fairchild Tropical Garden,** with 5,000 kinds of plants on 83 acres; the **Lowe Art Museum,** with excellent collections of primitive and fine arts; and the **Venetian Pool,** a pine-shaded paradise for swimmers. *Admission charged.*

11. Metrozoo

12400 Southwest 152nd St., Miami. This is one of the world's largest cageless zoos. Visitors can see Bengal tigers, rhinos, elephants, orangutans, and bears in simulated natural habitats. A monorail system affords panoramic views. *Admission charged.*

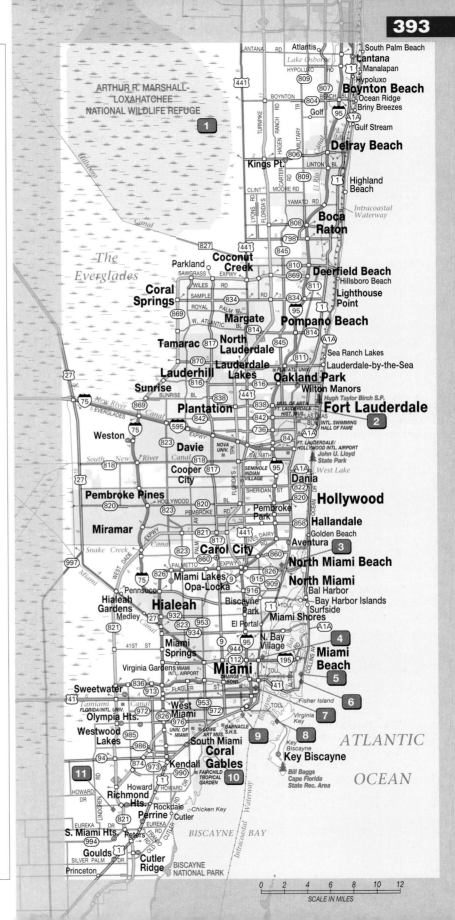

PUERTO RICO

1. Mayagüez

This city contains the **Mayagüez Zoo,** home to 500 animals, including Bengal tigers and an Andean condor. Gardens flourish at the **Tropical Agricultural Research Station.** *Admission charged at zoo.*

2. San Germán

This tranquil town still delights visitors with its Spanish Colonial charm. The island's oldest intact church, the 1606 **Porta Coeli,** is now a museum of religious art.

3. Phosphorescent Bay at La Parguera

On moonless nights, millions of phosphorescent microscopic plankton light up the sea like twinkling stars in a darkened sky. One-hour boat tours take visitors to observe the spectacle. Scuba diving, snorkeling, and swimming are also excellent here. *Fee charged for boat tour.*

4. Ponce

Tourist Information Center, Casa Armstrong-Poventud, Plaza Las Delicias. With marble-edged sidewalks, gas lamps, horse-drawn carriages, and lively street festivals, Puerto Rico's second largest city is replete with turn-of-the-century ambience. Located in a building designed by Edward Durell Stone, the **Ponce Museum of Art** features late-Renaissance, Baroque, and Puerto Rican work. Other sights include **Hacienda Buena Vista,** a coffee plantation dating from 1833, and the **Plaza Las Delicias,** with graceful fountains and colorful gardens.

5. Tibes Indian Ceremonial Park

Rte. 503, Ponce. The Antilles' oldest known burial site is in this park, home also to ball courts and dance grounds dating from 700 A.D. Indian artifacts are on view, and guided tours are available. *Admission charged.*

6. Caguana Indian Ceremonial Park

Rte. 111, west of Utuado. A 13-acre botanical garden with royal palm, guava, and ceiba trees, this area was used some 800 years ago by the Taino tribes for recreation and worship. The Indians played a game similar to soccer, and 10 rectangular courts remain. The park also features colorful petroglyphs, replicas of native huts, and a small museum with archaeological exhibits.

7. Río Camuy Cave Park

Rte. 129, north of Lares. A tram takes visitors to the entrance of this park. Footpaths lead past canyons, sinkholes, caverns, and one of the world's largest underground rivers. *Admission charged.*

8. Arecibo Observatory

Rte. 625, north of Lares. This observatory contains the world's largest radar-radio telescope, with a dish covering some 20 acres. The antenna detects emissions from galaxies, pulsars, quasars, and unknown sources at the fringes of the observable universe. Not surprisingly, the Search for Extraterrestrial Intelligence is based here.

9. Bacardi Distillery

Rte. 888, Cataño. This well-known rum manufacturer offers tours of its museum, bottling plant, and distillery, where 100,000 gallons can be processed each day. Samples of the finished product are available.

10. Museum of Contemporary Puerto Rican Art

Barat Building, Sacred Heart University, Santurce. Various cultures are represented by the 53 permanent works of painting and sculpture. The small museum also hosts traveling exhibitions.

11. University of Puerto Rico Botanical Garden

Rtes. 1 and 847, Río Piedras. More than 200 species of tropical and subtropical plants thrive in this setting. Walkways meander through dense vegetation to a lotus lagoon, bamboo promenade, and orchid garden.

12. Caribbean National Forest

The only tropical rain forest in the U.S. National Forest system, this lush area nestled in the Luquillo mountain range receives as much as 100 billion gallons of precipitation each year. Dozens of trails lead past lovely waterfalls, flowers, and trees. A rugged trail ascends 3,524-foot El Toro peak.

13. Las Cabezas de San Juan Nature Reserve

All of Puerto Rico's natural habitats, including mangrove swamp, coral reef, and dry forest, are contained here. Windswept promontories and a rocky beach offer

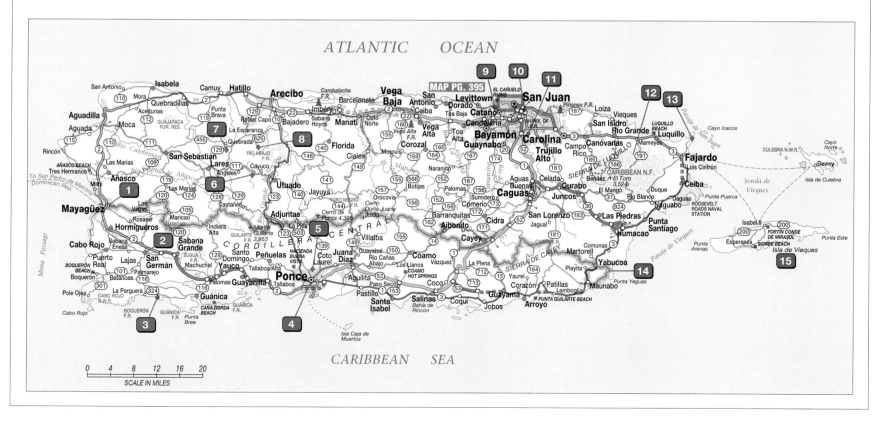

glimpses of ospreys, sea turtles, and manatees. The reserve is also home to one of
the island's oldest lighthouses, whose observation deck provides views of faraway
islands. Reservations are required for tours.
Admission charged.

14. Panoramic Route

This 165-mile network of roads connects
Yabucoa in the southeast with Mayagüez
on the west coast. Drivers see outstanding
views of seascapes, mountains, hamlets,
waterfalls, and forest. The entire route normally takes three days to drive, but some
segments make splendid day trips.

15. Vieques

Boasting 21 miles of pristine sandy beach,
this island is perhaps best known for the
phosphorescent **Mosquito Bay,** lit by the
glow from innumerable one-celled animals
called dinoflagellates.

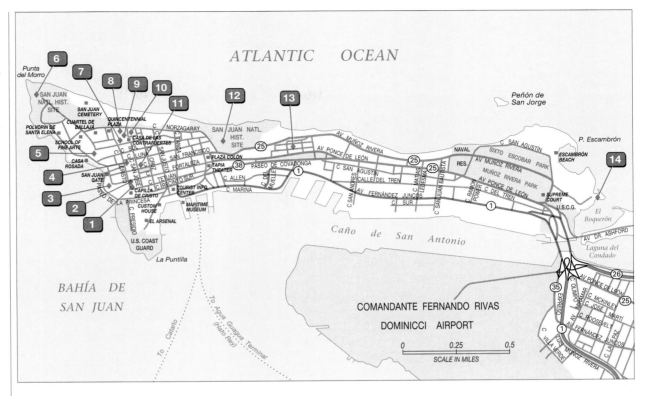

SAN JUAN

1. Casa del Libro

255 Calle Cristo. Of the 5,000 books in this
small museum dedicated to the art of printing and bookbinding, more than 200 date
back before the 16th century.

2. Puerto Rican Arts and Crafts Center

204 Calle Fortaleza. Offering a delightful
array of handicrafts made by more than 100
local artists, this is a browser's paradise.

3. La Fortaleza

Calle Fortaleza. Dating back to 1540, this
mansion has been home to some 170 governors, including the present one. Visitors on
guided tours can see its many interesting
features, such as medieval towers and
stained-glass galleries.

4. San Juan Cathedral

153 Calle Cristo. Begun in the 1500's, the
cathedral owes its current magnificence to
19th-century artists and artisans. A marble
tomb here contains the remains of explorer
Ponce de León. In the nearby **Plazuela de
la Rogativa** (plaza of the religious proces-
sion), a monument honors a bishop who,
along with his companions, frightened off
British troops during an attack.

5. Casa Blanca

1 Calle San Sebastián. Built in 1521 for
Ponce de León, the island's conqueror
and first governor, this residence was
inhabited by his descendants for some
250 years, making it one of the oldest
European-built homes in the western
hemisphere. Surrounded by luxuriant
gardens and elegant fountains, the "white
house" has authentic 16th- and 17th-
century furnishings. There are also two
museums here: the **Juan Ponce de León
Museum** and the **Taino Indian Ethno-
Historic Museum.** *Admission charged.*

6. San Felipe del Morro

Calle Norzagaray. Replete with dungeons
and turrets, this massive six-level fortress
was built by Spain between 1540 and 1783
to protect San Juan Harbor. Overlooking
the Atlantic from the highest spot in Old
San Juan, the nearby **Quincentennial
Plaza of America and Puerto Rico** was
built in honor of the 500th anniversary of
Columbus's discovery of the New World.

7. San José Church

Calle San Sebastián. In the center of the
San José Plaza stands this impressive 16th-
century Spanish Gothic structure. Built
under the direction of Dominican friars and
featuring a series of vaulted ceilings, it is
one of the oldest sites of Christian worship
in the western hemisphere.

8. Dominican Convent

98 Calle Norzagaray. Built by Dominican
friars in 1523, this beautifully restored structure contains an 18th-century altar and will
house the **Museum of Fine Arts,** a collection of 17th-century painting and sculpture.

9. The Pablo Casals Museum

101 Calle San Sebastián. This museum displays memorabilia of the renowned cellist,
who lived here for 16 years. There are
recordings, videotapes, manuscripts, photographs, and Casals's favorite cellos.

10. San Juan Museum of Art and History

Calle Norzagaray. Due to reopen in spring
1994, the museum has a fine collection of
Puerto Rican art and audiovisual presentations depicting the island's rich history.
Concerts take place in the courtyard.

11. City Hall

On the north side of the Plaza de Armas,
Old San Juan's original main square, is City
Hall. Styled after the city hall in Madrid —
with balconies, towers, and a courtyard — it
dates back to 1604. To the west lies **La In-
tendencia;** once home to the Spanish trea-
sury, it is now the state department.

12. San Cristóbal Fortress

Calle Norzagaray. Covering more than 27
acres, this striking 18th-century citadel
once guarded the city from land attacks.

13. Puerto Rico Capitol

Ponce de León Ave. This 1920's marble
building is the seat of the commonwealth's
legislature. A copy of Puerto Rico's constitution is on view, and a seaward observation
platform offers magnificent vistas. Guided
tours are available by appointment only.

14. Fort San Jerónimo

Puerta de Tierra. Built in the late 1700's on
the sea's edge, this small fort managed to
survive the British attack in 1797. Now
restored, it houses a military museum that
displays weapons, uniforms, and maps.

State Tourism Offices

Alabama Bureau of Tourism and Travel
401 Adams Ave.
Montgomery, AL 36103-4309
205-242-4169 or 800-252-2262

Alaska Division of Tourism
P.O. Box 110801
Juneau, AK 99811-0801
907-465-2010

Arizona Office of Tourism
1100 West Washington St.
Phoenix, AZ 85007
602-542-8687 or 800-842-8257

Arkansas Division of Tourism
1 Capitol Mall
Little Rock, AR 72201
501-682-7777 or 800-628-8725

California Office of Tourism
801 K St., Suite 1600
Sacramento, CA 95814
916-322-2881 or 800-862-2543

Colorado Tourism Board
1625 Broadway, Suite 1700
Denver, CO 80202
303-592-5510 or 800-265-6723

Connecticut Tourism Department
865 Brook St.
Rocky Hill, CT 06067-3405
203-258-4355 or 800-282-6863

Delaware Tourism Office
99 Kings Highway
Dover, DE 19903
800-441-8846

Florida Division of Tourism
107 West Gaines St.
Tallahassee, FL 32399-2000
904-922-0999

Georgia Department of Industry, Trade and Tourism
P.O. Box 1776
Atlanta, GA 30301-1776
404-656-3590 or 800-847-4842

Hawaii Visitors Bureau
2270 Kalakaua Ave., Suite 801
Honolulu, HI 96815
808-923-1811

Idaho Division of Tourism Development
700 West State St.
Boise, ID 83720-2700
208-334-2470 or 800-635-7820

Illinois Bureau of Tourism
100 West Randolph St., Suite 3-400
Chicago, IL 60601
312-814-4732 or 800-223-0121

Indiana Department of Commerce, Tourism, and Film Development
1 North Capitol, Suite 700
Indianapolis, IN 46204-2288
317-232-8860 or 800-289-6646

Iowa Division of Tourism
200 East Grand Ave.
Des Moines, IA 50309-3712
515-242-4705 or 800-345-4692

Kansas Travel and Tourism
700 S.W. Harrison St., Suite 1300
Topeka, KS 66603
913-296-2009 or 800-252-6727

Kentucky Department of Travel Development
500 Mero St., Suite 22
Frankfort, KY 40601-1968
502-564-4930 or 800-225-8747

Louisiana Office of Tourism
P.O. Box 94291
Baton Rouge, LA 70804-9291
504-342-8119 or 800-334-8626

Maine Office of Tourism
189 State St., Station 59
Augusta, ME 04333
207-289-5711 or 800-533-9595

Maryland Office of Tourism
217 East Redwood St., 9th floor
Baltimore, MD 21202
410-333-6611 or 800-543-1036

Massachusetts Office of Travel and Tourism
100 Cambridge St., 13th floor
Boston, MA 02202
617-727-3201 or 800-447-6277

Michigan Travel Bureau
P.O. Box 30226
Lansing, MI 48909
517-373-0670 or 800-543-2937

Minnesota Office of Tourism
121 Seventh Place East
St. Paul, MN 55101-2112
612-296-5029 or 800-657-3700

Mississippi Department of Economic and Community Development
P.O. Box 849
Jackson, MS 39205
601-359-3297 or 800-647-2290

Missouri Division of Tourism
P.O. Box 1055
Jefferson City, MO 65102
314-751-4133 or 800-877-1234

Montana Travel Promotion Office
1424 Ninth Ave.
Helena, MT 59620-0411
406-444-2654 or 800-541-1447

Nebraska Division of Travel and Tourism
P.O. Box 94666
Lincoln, NE 68509
402-471-3794 or 800-228-4307

Nevada Commission on Tourism
Capitol Complex
Carson City, NV 89710
702-687-4322 or 800-638-2328

New Hampshire Office of Tourism
172 Pembroke Rd., P.O. Box 856
Concord, NH 03301
603-271-2666 or 800-386-4664

New Jersey Division of Travel and Tourism
20 West State St., CN826
Trenton, NJ 08625
609-292-2470 or 800-537-7397

New Mexico Department of Tourism
491 Old Santa Fe Trail
Santa Fe, NM 87503
505-827-7400 or 800-545-2040

New York Division of Tourism
1 Commerce Plaza
Albany, NY 12245
518-473-0715 or 800-225-5697

North Carolina Travel and Tourism Division
430 North Salisbury St.
Raleigh, NC 27603
919-733-4171 or 800-847-4862

North Dakota Tourism
604 East Blvd.
Bismarck, ND 58505-0820
701-224-2525 or 800-437-2077

Ohio Office of Travel and Tourism
77 High St., P.O. Box 1001
Columbus, OH 43266-0101
614-466-8844 or 800-282-5393

Oklahoma Department of Tourism and Recreation
2401 North Lincoln Blvd.
505 Will Rogers Building
Oklahoma City, OK 73105-4492
405-521-3981 or 800-652-6552

Oregon Tourism Division
775 Summer St. NE
Salem, OR 97310
503-373-1270 or 800-547-7842

Pennsylvania Bureau of Travel
453 Forum Building
Harrisburg, PA 17120
717-787-5453 or 800-847-4872

Rhode Island Tourism Division
7 Jackson Walkway
Providence, RI 02903
401-277-2601 or 800-556-2484

South Carolina Division of Tourism
1205 Pendleton St., Suite 106
Columbia, SC 29201
803-734-0122 or 800-346-3634

South Dakota Department of Tourism
711 Wells Ave.
Pierre, SD 57501
605-773-3301 or 800-843-1930

Tennessee Tourist Development
P.O. Box 23170
Nashville, TN 37202
615-741-2158

Texas Department of Commerce, Tourism Division
P.O. Box 12728
Austin, TX 78711
512-462-9191 or 800-888-8839

Utah Travel Council
Council Hall, Capitol Hill
Salt Lake City, UT 84114
801-538-1030

Vermont Travel Division
134 State St.
Montpelier, VT 05602
802-828-3236 or 800-528-4554

Virginia Division of Tourism
1021 East Cary St.
Richmond, VA 23219
804-786-2051 or 800-847-4882

Washington Tourism Development Division
P.O. Box 42513, AX–13
Olympia, WA 98504-2513
206-753-5600 or 800-544-1800

West Virginia Tourism and Parks Division
2101 Washington St. East
Charleston, WV 25305
304-558-2286 or 800-225-5982

Wisconsin Division of Tourism Development
123 West Washington Ave.
P.O. Box 7970
Madison, WI 53707
608-266-2161 or 800-432-8747

Wyoming Travel Commission
I-25 at College Dr.
Cheyenne, WY 82002
307-777-7777 or 800-225-5996

Puerto Rico Tourism Co.
Old San Juan Station, P.O. Box 4435
San Juan, PR 00905
809-724-2800 or 800-223-6530

Major City Convention and Visitors Bureaus

Albany County Convention and Visitors Bureau
52 South Pearl St., 3rd Floor
Albany, NY 12207
518-434-1217 or 800-258-3582

Albuquerque Convention and Visitors Bureau
121 Tijeras Ave. NE
Albuquerque, NM 87125-6866
505-842-9918 or 800-284-2282

Atlanta Convention and Visitors Bureau
233 Peachtree St. NE, Suite 2000
Atlanta, GA 30303
404-521-6600

Austin Convention and Visitors Bureau
200 East Second St.
Austin, TX 78701
512-478-0098 or 800-888-8287

Baltimore Area Visitors Information Center
300 West Pratt St.
Baltimore, MD 21201
410-837-4636 or 800-282-6632

Baton Rouge Area Convention and Visitors Bureau
730 North Blvd.
Baton Rouge, LA 70802
504-383-1825 or 800-527-6843

Birmingham Convention and Visitors Bureau
1201 University Blvd.
Birmingham, AL 35203-1100
205-254-1654 or 800-962-6453

Boston Convention and Visitors Bureau
Prudential Tower, Suite 400
Boston, MA 02199
617-536-4100 or 800-888-5515

Buffalo Convention and Visitors Bureau
107 Delaware Ave.
Buffalo, NY 14202
716-852-0511 or 800-283-3256

Charlotte Convention and Visitors Bureau
122 East Stonewall St.
Charlotte, NC 28202-1838
704-334-2282 or 800-231-4636

Chattanooga Area Convention and Visitors Bureau
1001 Market St.
Chattanooga, TN 37402
615-756-8687 or 800-322-3344

Chicago Convention and Tourism Bureau
2301 South Lake Shore Dr.
Chicago, IL 60616
312-567-8500

Cincinnati Convention and Visitors Bureau
300 West Sixth St.
Cincinnati, OH
513-621-6994 or 800-344-3445

Cleveland Convention and Visitors Bureau
3100 Terminal Tower, Tower City Center
Cleveland, OH 44113
216-621-4110 or 800-321-1001

Dallas Convention and Visitors Bureau
1201 Elm St., Suite 2000
Dallas, TX 75270
214-746-6677

Denver Metro Convention and Visitors Bureau
225 West Colfax Ave.
Denver, CO 80202
303-892-1112

Des Moines Convention and Visitors Bureau
601 Locust St., Suite 222
Des Moines, IA 50309
515-286-4960 or 800-451-2625

Detroit Convention and Visitors Bureau
2 East Jefferson Ave.
Detroit, MI 48226
313-567-1170 or 800-338-7648

El Paso Convention and Visitors Bureau
1 Civic Center Plaza
El Paso, TX 79901
915-534-0600 or 800-351-6024

Fort Worth Convention and Visitors Bureau
415 Throckmorton St.
Fort Worth, TX 76102-7410
817-336-8791 or 800-433-5747

Galveston Convention and Visitors Bureau
2106 Seawall Blvd.
Galveston, TX 77550
409-763-4311

Houston Convention and Visitors Bureau
3300 Main St.
Houston, TX 77002
713-523-5050 or 800-231-7799

Indianapolis Convention and Visitors Association
1 Hoosier Dome, Suite 100
Indianapolis, IN 46225
317-639-4282 or 800-323-4639

Jacksonville and the Beaches Convention and Visitors Bureau
3 Independent Dr.
Jacksonville, FL 32202
904-798-9148 or 800-733-2668

Kansas City Convention and Visitors Bureau
1100 Main St., Suite 2550
Kansas City, MO 64105-2195
816-221-5242 or 800-767-7700

Key West Tourist Development Council
3406 North Roosevelt Blvd., Suite 201
Key West, FL 33040-4266
305-296-1552

Knoxville Convention and Visitors Bureau
810 Clinch Ave.
Knoxville, TN 37902
615-523-7263 or 800-727-8045

Las Vegas Convention and Visitors Authority
3150 Paradise Rd.
Las Vegas, NV 89109
702-892-0711

Lexington Convention and Visitors Bureau
430 West Vine St.
Lexington, KY 40507
606-233-1221

Little Rock Convention and Visitors Bureau
Markham St. and Broadway
Little Rock, AR 72201
501-376-4781

Los Angeles Visitor Information Center
685 South Figueroa St.
Los Angeles, CA 90017
213-689-8822

Louisville Visitors Information Center
400 South First St.
Louisville, KY 40202
502-584-2121

Madison Convention and Visitors Bureau
615 East Washington Ave.
Madison, WI 53703
608-255-2537 or 800-373-6376

Memphis Convention and Visitors Bureau
50 North Front St., Suite 450
Memphis, TN 38103
901-576-8181

Miami Convention and Visitors Bureau
701 Brickell Ave., Suite 2700
Miami, FL 33131
305-539-3000 or 800-933-8448

Milwaukee Convention and Visitors Bureau, Inc.
510 West Kilbourn Ave.
Milwaukee, WI 53203
414-273-3950 or 800-231-0903

Minneapolis Convention and Visitors Association
1219 Marquette Ave., Suite 300
Minneapolis, MN 55403
612-348-4313 or 900-860-0092

Nashville Convention and Visitors Bureau
161 Fourth Ave. North
Nashville, TN 37219
615-259-4760

New Orleans Tourist and Convention Commission
1520 Sugar Bowl Dr.
New Orleans, LA 70112
504-566-5011

New York Convention and Visitors Bureau
2 Columbus Circle
New York, NY 10019
212-484-1200

Newport County Convention and Visitors Bureau
23 America's Cup Ave.
Newport, RI 02840
401-849-8048 or 800-326-6030

Norfolk Convention and Visitors Bureau
236 East Plume St.
Norfolk, VA 23510
804-441-5266 or 800-368-3097

Oklahoma City Convention and Visitors Bureau
123 Park Ave.
Oklahoma City, OK 73102
405-278-8912 or 800-225-5652

Omaha Convention and Visitors Bureau
1819 Farnam St., Suite 1200
Omaha, NE 68183
402-444-4660 or 800-332-1819

Orlando Convention and Visitors Bureau
7208 Sand Lake Rd., Suite 300
Orlando, FL 32819
407-363-5800

Philadelphia Visitors Center
1625 JFK Blvd.
Philadelphia, PA 19102
215-636-1666

Major City Convention and Visitors Bureaus (continued)

**Phoenix Convention
and Visitors Bureau**
400 East Van Buren St., Suite 600
Phoenix, AZ 85004-2290
602-254-6500

**Pittsburgh Convention
and Visitors Bureau**
4 Gateway Center, Suite 514
Pittsburgh, PA 15222
412-281-7711 or 800-366-0093

**Providence Convention
and Visitors Bureau**
30 Exchange Terrace
Providence, RI 02903
410-274-1636

**Raleigh Convention
and Visitors Bureau**
225 Hillsborough St., Suite 400
Raleigh, NC 27603-1767
919-834-5900 or 800-849-8499

**Richmond Convention
and Visitors Bureau**
300 East Main St., Suite 100
Richmond, VA 23219
804-782-2777 or 800-365-7272

Rochester Visitors Association
126 Andrews St.
Rochester, NY 14604-1102
716-546-3070 or 800-677-7282

**St. Louis Convention
and Visitors Commission**
10 South Broadway
St. Louis, MO 63102
314-421-1023 or 800-325-7962

**St. Paul Convention
and Visitors Bureau**
55 East Fifth St.
St. Paul, MN 55101-1713
612-297-6985 or 800-627-6101

**St. Petersburg Convention
and Visitors Bureau**
1 Stadium Dr., Suite A
St. Petersburg, FL 33705
813-892-7892

**San Antonio Convention
and Visitors Bureau**
121 Alamo Plaza
San Antonio, TX 78298
512-270-8700 or 800-447-3372

**San Francisco Visitor
Information Center**
900 Market St.
San Francisco, CA 94102
415-391-2000

**Santa Fe Convention
and Visitors Bureau**
201 West Marcy St.
Santa Fe, NM 87501
505-984-6760 or 800-777-2489

**Savannah Area Convention
and Visitors Bureau**
222 West Oglethorpe Ave.
Savannah, GA 31401
912-944-0456

**Seattle-Kings County Convention
and Visitors Bureau**
520 Pike St., Suite 1300
Seattle, WA 98101
206-461-5800

**Syracuse Convention
and Visitors Bureau**
572 South Salina St.
Syracuse, NY 13202
315-470-1910 or 800-234-4797

**Tampa Convention
and Visitors Bureau**
111 Madison St., #1010
Tampa, FL 33602
813-223-1111

**Tucson Convention
and Visitors Bureau**
130 South Scott Ave.
Tucson, AZ 85701
602-624-1817 or 800-638-8350

**Washington D.C. Convention
and Visitors Association**
1212 New York Ave. NW, Suite 600
Washington, DC 20005-3992
202-789-7000

**Wichita Convention
and Visitors Bureau**
100 South Main St., Suite 100
Wichita, KS 67202
316-265-2800 or 800-288-9424

**Williamsburg Area Convention
and Visitors Bureau**
201 Penniman Rd.
Williamsburg, VA 23185
804-253-0192 or 800-368-6511

National Parks

Acadia National Park
P.O. Box 177
Bar Harbor, ME 04609
207-288-3338

Arches National Park
P.O. Box 907
Moab, UT 84532
801-259-8161

Badlands National Park
P.O. Box 6
Interior, SD 57750
605-433-5361

Big Bend National Park
Big Bend National Park, TX 79834
915-477-2251

Biscayne National Park
P.O. Box 1369
Homestead, FL 33090
305-247-7275

Bryce Canyon National Park
Bryce Canyon, UT 84717
801-834-5322

Canyonlands National Park
125 West 200 South
Moab, UT 84532
801-259-7164

Capitol Reef National Park
Torrey, UT 84775
801-425-3791

Carlsbad Caverns National Park
3225 National Parks Highway
Carlsbad, NM 88220
505-785-2232

Channel Islands National Park
1901 Spinnaker Dr.
Ventura, CA 93001
805-658-5700

Crater Lake National Park
P.O. Box 7
Crater Lake, OR 97604
503-594-2211

Denali National Park and Preserve
P.O. Box 9
McKinley Park, AK 99755
907-683-2294

Everglades National Park
P.O. Box 279
Homestead, FL 33030
305-242-7700

**Gates of the Arctic
National Park and Preserve**
P.O. Box 74680
Fairbanks, AK 99707
907-456-0281

**Glacier Bay National
Park and Preserve**
P.O. Box 140
Gustavus, AK 99826
907-697-2230

Glacier National Park
West Glacier, MT 59936
406-888-5441

Grand Canyon National Park
P.O. Box 129
Grand Canyon, AZ 86023
602-638-7888

Grand Teton National Park
P.O. Drawer 170
Moose, WY 83012
307-733-2880

Great Basin National Park
Baker, NV 89311
702-234-7331

Great Smoky Mountains National Park
Gatlinburg, TN 37738
615-436-1200

Guadalupe Mountains National Park
H.C. 60, Box 400
Salt Flat, TX 79847
915-828-3251

Haleakala National Park
P.O. Box 369
Makawao, HI 96768
808-572-7749

Hawaii Volcanoes National Park
Hawaii National Park, HI 96718
808-967-7311

Hot Springs National Park
P.O. Box 1860
Hot Springs, AR 71902
501-623-1433

Isle Royale National Park
87 North Ripley St.
Houghton, MI 49931
906-482-0984

Katmai National Park and Preserve
P.O. Box 7
King Salmon, AK 99613
907-246-3305

National Parks *(continued)*

Kenai Fjords National Park
P.O. Box 1727
Seward, AK 99664
907-224-3874

Kobuk Valley National Park
P.O. Box 1029
Kotzebue, AK 99752
907-442-3890

Lake Clark National Park and Preserve
4230 University Dr., Suite 311
Anchorage, AK 99508
907-781-2218

Lassen Volcanic National Park
Mineral, CA 96063
916-595-4444

Mammoth Cave National Park
Mammoth Cave, KY 42259
502-758-2328

Mesa Verde National Park
Mesa Verde National Park, CO 81321
303-529-4465

Mount Rainier National Park
Tahoma Woods, Star Route
Ashford, WA 98304
206-569-2211

North Cascades National Park
2105 Highway 20
Sedro Woolley, WA 98284
206-856-5700

Olympic National Park
600 East Park Ave.
Port Angeles, WA 98362
206-452-0330

Petrified Forest National Park
P.O. Box 2217
Petrified Forest, AZ 86028
602-524-6228

Redwood National Park
1111 Second St.
Crescent City, CA 95531
707-464-6101

Rocky Mountain National Park
Estes Park, CO 80517
303-586-2371

Sequoia-Kings Canyon National Parks
Three Rivers, CA 93271
209-565-3341

Shenandoah National Park
Route 4, Box 348
Luray, VA 22835
703-999-2243

Theodore Roosevelt National Park
P.O. Box 7
Medora, ND 58645
701-623-4466

Voyageurs National Park
HCR 9, Box 600
International Falls, MN 56649
218-283-9821

Wind Cave National Park
Hot Springs, SD 57747
605-745-4600

Wrangell-St. Elias National Park and Preserve
P.O. Box 29
Glennallen, AK 99588
907-822-5234

Yellowstone National Park
P.O. Box 168
Yellowstone National Park, WY 82190
307-344-7381

Yosemite National Park
P.O. Box 577
Yosemite National Park, CA 95389
209-372-0200

Zion National Park
Springdale, UT 84767-1099
801-772-3256

Appalachian National Scenic Trail
Appalachian Trail Conference
P.O. Box 807
Harpers Ferry, WV 25425
304-535-6331

Credits

MAPS: GeoSystems, an R.R. Donnelley & Sons Company, using U.S. Geographic Data Base. *LOCATOR MAPS:* David Lindroth. *MILEAGE CHART:* MicroColor, Inc.

1 *detail* Marc Muench. **2-3** Marc Muench. **6** *detail* Marc Muench. **14-15** Thomas Mangelsen/Images of Nature. **18** Joe Viesti/Viesti Associates, Inc. **20** Bruce Hands. **22** *top and bottom left* Pat O'Hara; *bottom right* John Marshall. **23** Tom and Pat Leeson. **24** *top* Pat O'Hara; *bottom* National Park Service, Harpers Ferry Center. **28** *top* John Marshall; *bottom left* Jeff Gnass; *right* Tim Christie. **30** *top and bottom left* Pat O'Hara; *bottom right* Tom and Pat Leeson. **31** Tom and Pat Leeson. **32** *top and bottom left* George Wuerthner; *bottom right* Tom and Pat Leeson. **33** Tom and Pat Leeson. **38** National Museum of American Art, Smithsonian Institution, gift of Mrs. Joseph Harrison, Jr./Art Resource, N.Y. **42** *top* Chuck Place; *bottom* Ray Atkeson/American Landscapes. **48** *top* Jeff Gnass; *bottom left* National Academy of Design, New York City; *bottom right* National Park Service. **49** Jeff Foott. **50** *top* Kathy L. Watkins/Images of Nature; *bottom* Jeff Gnass. **51** Alan D. Carey. **56** Alan and Sandy Carey. **62** Santi Visalli. **63** *top* Mark E. Gibson; *bottom* Santi Visalli. **66** *both* Chuck Place. **68** Chuck Place. **74** *top* Michael Philip Manheim/The Stock Solution; *bottom* Chuck Place. **76** Nicholas DeVore III/Photographers Aspen. **78** Denver Museum of Natural History. **84** Wayne Lynch/DRK Photo. **86** Jeff Foott/Bruce Coleman Inc. **88** *top* Courtesy The Bancroft Library; *left* Tom and Pat Leeson; *bottom* Tom Bean. **89** Pat O'Hara. **90** Tom and Pat Leeson. **91** Tom and Pat Leeson. **98** Riverside Municipal Museum, Riverside, California, photographed by Lorne L. Allmon. **100** Chuck Place. **104** *both* Chuck Place. **106** F. Damm/Leo de Wys, Inc. **108** Jerry Jacka. **114** Dorothy B. Jacobus. **116** *left* James Blank/Scenics of America; *right* Amanda Parsons/West Light. **117** Mark E. Gibson. **118** The Zoological Society of San Diego, photographed by Ron Garrison. **122** John Cancalosi/DRK Photo. **124** Orlando Padilla. **128** *both* Tom Bean. **130** Clark James Mischler. **134** Tom Bean. **136** *left* Jeff Gnass; *right* Douglas Peebles Photography. **138** Norbert Wu/Douglas Peebles Photography. **144-145** Santi Visalli. **148** Greg Ryan/Sally Beyer. **150** Daniel J. Cox. **156** Greg Ryan/Sally Beyer. **162** Purchased jointly by the Des Moines Art Center and The Minneapolis Institute of Arts with funds from Mrs. Howard H. Frank and the Edmundson Art Foundation, Inc., 1982.2. **166** Studebaker National Museum. **168** UPI/Bettmann. **174** *left* Gift of Dr. and Mrs. Edwin J. DeCosta and the Walter E. Heller Foundation, 1986.88, photograph courtesy of The Art Institute of Chicago; *right* Gift of the Graham Foundation for Advanced Studies in the Fine Arts, 1971.450, photographed by Robert Hashimoto, courtesy of The Art Institute of Chicago. **176** *left* Ron Goulet/Dembinsky Photo Associates; *right* Duff Stoltz. **182** Jonathan L. Stealey. **186** P. Michael Whye. **190** Old Cowtown Museum. **194** St. Louis Convention & Visitors Commission, photographed by Jack Zehrt. **196** Kathy Clay. **200** Courtesy of the Madame Walker Urban Life Center, Inc., Indianapolis. **206** William Strode Associates. **210** Myriad Botanical Gardens, photographed by Lynn Claytor Byers. **212** Woolaroc Museum, Bartlesville, Oklahoma. **220** Frank Driggs Collection. **224** *left* Paul Rezendes/Positive Images; *right* from the permanent collection of the Museum of the American Quilter's Society, Paducah, Kentucky. **228** Tennessee Aquarium, photographed by Richard T. Bryant. **232** Texas Ranger Hall of Fame & Museum, Waco, Texas, photographed by Gerard N. Schank. **238** David Muench. **244** Tom and Pat Leeson. **248** *top right* Bowie Lanford; *inset* Matt Bradley. **250** D. Donne Bryant Stock Photography. **252** C.C.Lockwood. **254** *left* D. Donne Bryant Stock Photography; *right* Mitchel L. Osborne. **258-259** Steve Dunwell/The Image Bank. **262** The Temple Museum of Religious Art, Cleveland, Ohio, photographed by Richard Kronenberg. **266** AP/Wide World Photos. **270** Nancie Battaglia. **274** Jim Kahnweiler/Positive Images. **280** Howard Millard. **282** Jerry Howard/Positive Images. **286** Patricia J. Bruno/Positive Images. **287** Joe Viesti/Viesti Associates, Inc. **288** *top* Jerry Howard/Positive Images; *bottom* Mike Malyszko/Stock, Boston. **289** Howard Millard. **294** Jacob Mosser III/Positive Images. **300** Mid-Ohio Historical Museum, Inc. **304** Jim Schafer. **306** Booker T. Washington National Monument/National Park Service. **310** Charles Shoffner. **312** Stephen G. Maka/Viesti Associates. **313** Ted Spiegel. **314** Jodi Cobb/Woodfin Camp & Associates. **315** *both* Adam Jones. **320** Robert Llewellyn. **321** Robert Llewellyn. **326** Santi Visalli/The Image Bank. **330** Steve Uzzell/Woodfin Camp & Associates. **332** *left* Ira Block/The Image Bank; *right* The Walters Art Gallery, Baltimore. **334** Mount Vernon Ladies' Association. **342** Museum of Appalachia, Norris, Tennessee. **344** Murray & Associates/Picturesque. **348** Murray & Associates/Picturesque. **350** *left* Andre Jenny/Stock South, Inc.; *inset* Peter Fownes/Stock South, Inc. **352** E. Alan McGee. **354** George W. Park Seed Company, Inc. **360** Courtesy of The Mariners' Museum, Newport News, Virginia, photographed by Ray Foster. **364** Leslie Bailey/Picturesque. **370** Steve Murray/Picturesque. **374** Ken Laffal. **380** *bottom left and bottom right, both,* from the collection of The Charles Hosmer Morse Museum of American Art, Winter Park, Florida; *top right* © Sea World of Florida. **386** J. Carmichael Jr./The Image Bank. **388** *left* Guido Rossi/The Image Bank; *inset* Tom and Pat Leeson. **389** Howard Millard. **390** Larry Lipsky/Bruce Coleman, Inc.

Index

The numbers of featured sites appear in brackets [ ].

The numbers of featured sites appear in brackets [ ].

The numbers of featured sites appear in brackets [ ].

The numbers of featured sites appear in brackets [ ].

The numbers of featured sites appear in brackets [ ].

The numbers of featured sites appear in brackets [ ].

The numbers of featured sites appear in brackets [ ].

I

The numbers of featured sites appear in brackets [ ].

The numbers of featured sites appear in brackets [ ].

The numbers of featured sites appear in brackets [ ].

The numbers of featured sites appear in brackets [ ].

O

The numbers of featured sites appear in brackets [ ].

The numbers of featured sites appear in brackets [ ].

The numbers of featured sites appear in brackets [ ].

The numbers of featured sites appear in brackets [ ].

The numbers of featured sites appear in brackets [ ].

The numbers of featured sites appear in brackets [ ].